Gene Thorp

Also by Rick Atkinson

*The Long Gray Line*

*Crusade*

*An Army at Dawn*

*In the Company of Soldiers*

# The Day of Battle

# The Day of Battle

*THE WAR IN SICILY AND ITALY,*

*1943–1944*

VOLUME TWO OF THE LIBERATION TRILOGY

## Rick Atkinson

Henry Holt and Company
New York

Henry Holt and Company, LLC
*Publishers since 1866*
175 Fifth Avenue
New York, New York 10010
www.henryholt.com

Henry Holt ® and 🛡® are registered trademarks of Henry Holt and Company, LLC.

Library of Congress Cataloguing-in-Publication Data

Atkinson, Rick.
 The day of battle : the war in Sicily and Italy, 1943–1944 / Rick Atkinson. — 1st ed.
  p. cm. — (The liberation trilogy ; v. 2)
 Includes bibliographical references and index.
 ISBN-13: 978-0-8050-6289-2
 ISBN-10: 0-8050-6289-0
 1. World War, 1939–1945—Campaigns—Italy.  2. Italy—History, Military—1914–1945.
I. Title.
 D763.I8A85  2007
 940.54'215—dc22
 2007007653

Henry Holt books are available for special promotions and premiums.
For details contact: Director, Special Markets.

First Edition 2007

Maps by Gene Thorp

Printed in the United States of America

1   3   5   7   9   10   8   6   4   2

*To John Sterling*

Muses, launch your song!
What kings were fired for war, what armies at their orders
thronged the plains? What heroes sprang into bloom,
what weapons blazed, even in those days long ago,
in Italy's life-giving land?

Virgil, The Aeneid

# CONTENTS

## PART TWO

## PART THREE

# MAPS

# MAP LEGEND

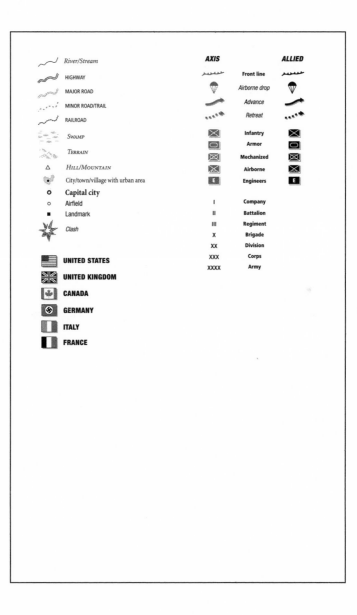

| | | AXIS | | ALLIED |
|---|---|---|---|---|
| | River/Stream | | Front line | |
| | HIGHWAY | | Airborne drop | |
| | MAJOR ROAD | | Advance | |
| | MINOR ROAD/TRAIL | | Retreat | |
| | RAILROAD | | | |
| | SWAMP | | Infantry | |
| | TERRAIN | | Armor | |
| △ | HILL/MOUNTAIN | | Mechanized | |
| | City/town/village with urban area | | Airborne | |
| ✪ | Capital city | E | Engineers | E |
| ○ | Airfield | | | |
| ■ | Landmark | I | Company | |
| | Clash | II | Battalion | |
| | | III | Regiment | |
| | | X | Brigade | |
| | | XX | Division | |
| | UNITED STATES | XXX | Corps | |
| | UNITED KINGDOM | XXXX | Army | |
| | CANADA | | | |
| | GERMANY | | | |
| | ITALY | | | |
| | FRANCE | | | |

# ALLIED CHAIN OF COMMAND

## Invasion of Sicily, July 1943

Commander-in-Chief: Eisenhower
Chief of Staff: Smith

Naval Forces: A. B. Cunningham          Air Forces: Tedder

15th Army Group: Alexander

| *Eighth Army (U.K.): Montgomery* | *Seventh Army (U.S.): Patton* |
|---|---|
| *XIII Corps: Dempsey* | *II Corps: Bradley* |
| 5th Div: Berney-Ficklin | 1st Div: Allen |
| 50th Div: Kirkman | 45th Div: Middleton |
| 1st Airborne Div: Hopkinson | |
| | *JOSS Force: Truscott* |
| *XXX Corps: Leese* | 3rd Div: Truscott |
| 51st Highland Div: Wimberly | |
| 1st Canadian Div: Simonds | *Reserve forces* |
| | 2nd Armored Div: Gaffey |
| *Reserve forces* | 82nd Airborne Div: Ridgway |
| 46th Div: Hawkesworth | 9th Div: Eddy |
| 78th Div: Evelegh | |

# ALLIED CHAIN OF COMMAND

## Operation diadem, Final Drive to Rome, May 1944

---

Supreme Allied Commander, Mediterranean: Wilson

Deputy: Devers

Naval Forces: J. Cunningham

Air Forces: Eaker

Allied Armies in Italy: Alexander

*Eighth Army: Leese*

*XIII Corps: Kirkman*

6th Armoured Div: Evelegh
4th Div: Ward
78th Div: Keightley
8th Indian Div: Russell
1st Canadian Armoured Bde: Murphy

*I Canadian Corps: Burns*

5th Canadian Armoured Div: Hoffmeister
1st Canadian Div: Vokes
25th Tank Bde: Tetley

*II Polish Corps: Anders*

3rd Carpathian Div: Duch
5th Kresowa Div: Sulik
2nd Polish Armoured Bde: Rakowski

*X Corps: McCreery*

2nd NZ Div: Freyberg
24th Guards Bde: Clive
2nd Para Bde: Pritchard
12th South African Bde: Palmer
Italian Motorized Bde Group

*Reserve forces*

6th South African Armoured Div: Poole
V Corps: Allfrey

*Fifth Army: Clark*

*II Corps: Keyes*

85th Div: Coulter
88th Div: Sloan

*VI Corps: Truscott*

1st Armored Div: Harmon
3rd Div: O'Daniel
34th Div: Ryder
45th Div: Eagles
1st UK Div: Hawkesworth
5th UK Div: Gregson-Ellis
1st SSF: Frederick

*French Expeditionary Corps: Juin*

1st Fr. Inf Div: Brosset
2nd Moroccan Inf Div: Dody
3rd Algerian Inf Div: Monsabert
4th Moroccan Mtn Div: Sevez
Fr. Goumiers: Guillaume

*Reserve forces*

IV U.S. Corps h.q.: Crittenberger
36th Div: Walker
Italian Bde Group

# The Day of Battle

# PROLOGUE

S HE could be heard long before she was seen on that foggy Tuesday
morning, May 11, 1943. Through the mist swaddling lower New York
Bay sounded a deep bass A, two octaves and two notes below middle C, not
so much blown as exhaled from the twin seven-foot whistles on the forward funnel, specially tuned to be audible ten miles away without discom-
fiting passengers at the promenade rail. Her peacetime paints—red, white,
and black—had vanished beneath coats of pewter gray, although only after
a spirited protest by camouflage experts who preferred a dappled pattern
of blues and greens, called the Western Approaches scheme, to better be-
fuddle enemy U-boats trying to fix her speed, bearing, and identity. Not
that anyone glimpsing the famous triple stacks, the thousand-foot hull, or
the familiar jut of her regal prow could doubt who she was. Gray paint had
also been slathered over her name, but she remained, in war as in peace, the
*Queen Mary.*

She slid past Ambrose Light at 8:30 A.M., precisely five days, twenty
hours, and fifty minutes after leaving Gourock, Scotland. Escorting U.S.
Navy destroyers peeled away to seaward. Like her antebellum colors, the
*Queen*'s prewar finery was long gone, stripped and stored in a New York
warehouse: the six miles of Wilton carpet, the two hundred cases of bone
china and crystal, the wine cabinets and humidors that had provided fourteen thousand bottles and five thousand cigars on a typical crossing in the
palmy days of peace. For this voyage, designated WW #21W, she had been
transformed into a prison ship. Carpenters had removed any belowdecks
fitting that could be used as a weapon, while installing alarm bells, locks,
sandbagged machine-gun redoubts, and coiled barbed wire around dining
and exercise areas. Now from deep in the hold came the drone of five thousand German prisoners, bagged in the North African campaign just ending
and held in Scottish cages before being tendered to the *Queen* in Gourock.
Three hundred British soldiers stood watch below; any guard inclined to
befriend the enemy was advised, "Remember their barbarities." In truth,
five days of violent zigzagging across the North Atlantic had rendered the
barbarians docile. This lot, bound for a constellation of camps in the

American Southwest, more than tripled the German POW population in the United States, which eventually would reach 272,000. To reduce heating bills, most camps sat south of 40 degrees north latitude; some commandants fed their prisoners bacon and eggs, encouraged camp pets and piano lessons, and permitted the Germans to order curtains from a Sears, Roebuck catalogue. That, too, encouraged docility.

But it was on the upper decks that the *Queen Mary*'s larger purpose on this voyage could be found. The secret passenger manifest listed the United Kingdom's most senior war chiefs, including commanders of the British Army, navy, and air force, bound for Washington, D.C., and TRIDENT, the code name for a two-week Anglo-American conference on war strategy. Officers crowded the rails as the ship glided through the Verrazano Narrows, peering into the fog in a vain effort to glimpse the Manhattan skyline seven miles north; they settled instead for dim views of Coney Island to starboard and Staten Island's Fort Wadsworth to port. Stewards and subalterns scurried about, sorting piles of luggage and tagging those bound for the White House with red slips bearing a large "W"—including two dozen bags belonging to a certain "Air Commodore Spencer." Secret documents were collected and filed in locked boxes stacked in the former children's playroom on the promenade deck, while classified wastepaper smoldered in an incinerator improvised from a bathtub in mezzanine suite number 105.

To mislead potential spies lurking in Scottish ports, great pains had been taken to obscure the details of this voyage. The ship's print shop in Gourock had engraved menus in Dutch to suggest that the mysterious traveler to New York was Wilhelmina, exiled queen of the Netherlands. Workmen also installed wheelchair ramps and handrails, and counterintelligence rumormongers in dockyard pubs let slip that the *Queen Mary* was being dispatched to pick up President Franklin D. Roosevelt for a secret visit to Britain. But all pretense ended shortly after nine A.M. The ship's great screws turned a final turn, the iron anchor sank with a rattle and a mighty splash, and Air Commodore Spencer strolled on deck, "looking well and fat and pink," and eager to get on with the war.

Like the *Queen Mary*, Winston S. Churchill was simply too obtrusive to disguise, "the largest human being of our time," as one contemporary concluded. There was the Havana cigar, of course, said to be long as a trombone and one of the eight he typically smoked in a day. The familiar moon face glowered beneath the furrowed pate he had taken to rubbing with a scented handkerchief. This morning, after leaving a £10 tip for the *Queen*'s service staff, he swapped the casual "siren suit" worn through much of the voyage for the uniform of the Royal Yacht Squadron. The effect had been likened to that of "a gangster clergyman who has gone on the stage." The previous night Churchill had celebrated both his imminent arrival in America and the third anniversary of his premiership with the sort of feast that recalled not only the *Queen*'s prewar luxury but the sun-never-sets Empire itself: croûte au pot à l'ancienne, petite sole meunière, pommes Windsor, and baba au rhum, all washed down with a magnum of Mumm's Cordon Rouge, 1926.

"We are all worms," Churchill once intoned, "but I do believe I am a glow-worm." Who could dispute it? For three years he had fought the good fight, at first alone and then with the mighty alliance he had helped construct. He had long warned minions that he was to be awakened at night only if Britain were invaded; that alarum never sounded. His mission in this war, he asserted, was "to pester, nag and bite"—a crusade that Roosevelt, who would receive thirteen hundred telegrams from Churchill during the war, knew all too well. "Temperamental like a film star and peevish like a spoilt child," the prime minister's army chief wrote of him; his wife, Clementine, added, "I don't argue with Winston. He shouts me down. So when I have anything important to say I write a note to him."

"In great things he is very great," said the South African statesman and field marshal Jan Smuts, "in small things not great." Certainly the small things engaged him, from decrying a shortage of playing cards for soldiers, to setting the grain ration for English poultry farmers, to reviewing all proposed code words for their martial resonance. (He sternly forbad WOEBETIDE, JAUNDICE, APÉRITIF, and BUNNYHUG.) Yet his greatness in great things obtained. It was perhaps best captured by an admirer's seven-word encomium: "There is no defeat in his heart."

Sea voyages always reinvigorated Churchill, and none more than WW #21W. The prime minister's traveling party privately dubbed him "Master," and he had worked them hard each day, from cipher clerks to field marshals, preparing studies and the memoranda known as "prayers" for the TRIDENT meetings set to start on Wednesday. Typists worked in shifts on a specially designed silent Remington, taking down dispatches and minutes he mumbled through billowing cigar smoke. (His diction was further impeded by his lifelong struggle with the letter "s.") He stamped especially urgent documents with the decree "action this day," then retired for another hand of bezique—played with multiple decks from which all cards below seven were removed—and another tot of brandy, or champagne, or his favorite whiskey, Johnnie Walker Red. He had insisted on mounting a machine gun in his lifeboat. If the *Queen* were torpedoed, he declared, "I won't be captured. The finest way to die is in the excitement of fighting the enemy. . . . You must come with me in the boat and see the fun." At times he seemed weighted with cares—"all hunched up and scowling at his plate"—and he rebuked those unblessed with his fluency by reading aloud from Fowler's *Modern English Usage* on the "wickedness of splitting infinitives and the use of 'very' instead of 'much.' " Yet more often he was in high spirits: discussing seamanship with the captain on the bridge, watching films like *The Big Shot* and *All Through the Night* in the lounge, or chuckling at stories swapped over supper in his cabin with his confederates. Particularly pleasing was a Radio Berlin report that placed him in the Middle East, supposedly attending a conference with Roosevelt. "Who in war," he asked, "will not have his laugh amid the skulls?"

Churchill had proposed inspiriting his American cousins by storming ashore in Manhattan's Battery Park, then promenading up Broadway. "One can always do what one wants if it takes people by surprise," he explained. "There is not time for plotters to develop their nefarious plans." Alas, the U.S. Secret Service disagreed, and instead three anonymous launches wallowed across the gray harbor toward the *Queen Mary* from Tompkinsville, on Staten Island. Waiting on the docks was Harry Hopkins, the president's closest counselor, with the *Ferdinand Magellan*, a seven-car presidential train pointed toward Washington.

As Churchill stepped into the lead launch, the *Queen*'s entire company stood at the rails and cheered him off, their huzzahs trailing him to shore, where he disembarked and tossed a farewell wave before clambering onto the waiting train. They also knew, as they stood baying into the fog, that there was no defeat in his heart.

Packed into the *Magellan* baggage car with the suitcases and document crates was a thick sheaf of maps that had covered the walls of a makeshift war room next to Churchill's cabin on the *Queen Mary*. Replicating the campaign maps in the subterranean Cabinet War Rooms beneath Great George Street in London, the sheets depicted—with pushpins and lengths of colored yarn—the battle lines on a dozen combat fronts around the globe on this Tuesday, the 1,349th day of the Second World War. The struggle that had begun in September 1939 was more than half over; yet if both commanders and commanded intuited that they were nearer the end than the beginning, they also sensed that less than half the butcher's bill had been paid in a bloodletting that ultimately would claim sixty million lives: one life every three seconds for six years. They also knew that if the Allied powers—led by the United States, Britain, and the Soviet Union—now possessed the strategic initiative, the Axis powers of Germany, Italy, and Japan still held the real estate, including six thousand miles of European coastline and the entire eastern littoral of Asia. This the maps made all too clear.

The exception to Axis territorial hegemony was Africa, a campaign now in its final hours. Seven months earlier, in November 1942, Anglo-American troops had landed in Morocco and Algeria, sweeping aside weak forces of the collaborationist Vichy French government, then wheeling east for a forced march into Tunisia through the wintry Atlas Mountains. There they joined cause with the British Eighth Army, which, after a hard-won victory at El Alamein in Egypt, had pushed west across the crown of Africa. A succession of battles lost and won against two German-Italian armies raged across Tunisia, a country the size of the state of Georgia; particularly galling was the drubbing at Kasserine Pass in February 1943, which had cost six thousand U.S. casualties and, in terms of yardage lost, would remain the worst American defeat of the war. Yet superior airpower, naval forces, artillery, and the combined weight of the Allied armies had trapped and crushed the Axis forces, which would formally surrender on Thursday, May 13. The booty included a quarter million Axis prisoners, among them the scruffy vanguard now queued up in the *Queen Mary*'s hold for delousing.

Victory in North Africa—exhilarating, unqualified victory—also gave the Allies control of the fine ports and airfields from Casablanca to Alexandria. It forestalled Axis threats to Middle Eastern oil fields, reopened the Suez Canal for the first time since 1941—saving two months' sailing time for convoys going out to India from Britain, since they no longer had to circumnavigate Africa—and exposed the wide southern flank of occupied Europe to further Allied attack. The triumph in North Africa also coincided with victory in the North Atlantic. Ferocious depredations by German submarine wolfpacks had abruptly declined, thanks to improved electronic surveillance and because cryptologists had cracked German naval radio codes, allowing Allied warplanes and ships to pinpoint and destroy the marauders. Germany would lose forty-seven U-boats in May, triple the number sunk in March, and more than 3,500 Allied merchant ships would cross the Atlantic in the summer of 1943 without a sinking; a year earlier, the Allies had lost a ship every eight hours. The German submariner casualty rate during the war, 75 percent, would exceed that of every other service arm in every other nation.

Elsewhere in this global war, the ebb and flow of battle was less decisive. In the Pacific, Japan had been driven from Guadalcanal and Papua; Japanese reinforcements had been badly whipped in the Bismarck Sea in February; and American forces on this very day, May 11, were landing on Attu in the Aleutians, a far-corner fight that would obliterate the Japanese garrison of 2,500 at a cost of more than a thousand U.S. lives. American fighter pilots on April 18, again thanks to a timely radio intercept, ambushed and killed Admiral Isokoru Yamamoto, architect of the sneak attack on Pearl Harbor. Yet Japan held firm in Burma, and still occupied ports, coastal cities, and much farmland in China, as well as Pacific islands from the Kuriles to the central Solomons. Tokyo had embraced a defensive strategy of attrition and stalemate in hopes of breaking the Allies' will and keeping the Soviet Union out of the Pacific war.

On the Eastern Front, the war retained the immensely sanguinary character that had prevailed since Adolf Hitler invaded the Soviet Union in June 1941. Here, too, the tide had turned against the Axis, which less than a year earlier had invested the suburbs of Leningrad and Stalingrad and stood but a few hours' drive from the Caspian Sea. The Germans had lost thirty divisions since January, most of them at Stalingrad or in Tunisia, a loss equivalent to one-eighth of Hitler's total order of battle; tank numbers had dropped in the past three months from 5,500 to 3,600. A Soviet counteroffensive recaptured Kursk, Rostov, and the entire eastern shore of the Sea of Azov. Joseph Goebbels, propaganda minister for the Third Reich, described the Führer's despair in his diary on May 9: "He is absolutely sick of the generals. . . . All generals lie, he says. All generals are disloyal. All generals are opposed to National Socialism."

And yet: the Red Army remained more than three hundred miles from Germany's eastern border, facing two-thirds of the Wehrmacht's combat strength. Hitler still commanded three hundred German divisions, plus ninety more from satellite armies. The pummeling of German industry and cities with vast bomber fleets showed promise but had had skimpy results so far, in part because much of America's airpower had been diverted from British bases to Africa. All of continental Europe, except for neutral Spain, Portugal, Switzerland, and Sweden, remained under the Axis boot, from the Bay of Biscay to the river Donetz, and from the North Cape to Sicily. Some 1.3 million forced laborers toiled in German factories, while another quarter million slaved on Atlantic Wall fortifications along the vulnerable west coast in France and the Low Countries; countless others deemed worthless or dangerous were herded into concentration or extermination camps, including a quarter million French, of whom only 35,000 would survive.

The next Anglo-American blow—after victory in North Africa—had been decided five months earlier, in Casablanca at the last big strategy conference. Operation HUSKY was summarized in twenty-one words by the Combined Chiefs of Staff, the amalgamation of American and British commanders who directed the war for Roosevelt and Churchill: "An attack against Sicily will be launched in 1943 with the target date as the period of the favorable July moon." The largest island in the Mediterranean lay only a hundred miles from Tunis, off the toe of the Italian boot, and its invasion would provide a postscript to the African campaign. American strategists had been leery of waging war in the Mediterranean since even before the November 1942 landings in northwest Africa; Roosevelt triggered that campaign by siding with Churchill and overruling his own generals, who argued that Allied power should instead be concentrated in Britain for a direct lunge across the English Channel toward Berlin. The American high command at Casablanca agreed to support HUSKY because the capture of Sicily would further safeguard Mediterranean shipping and perhaps divert Axis strength from the Soviet front; it would also provide air bases for bombing Italy and other targets in occupied Europe, and might cause weak-kneed Rome to abandon the war by abrogating its "Pact of Steel" with Berlin, formalized in May 1939.

Beyond Sicily, however, there was no plan, no grand strategy, no consensus on what to do with the immense Allied army now concentrating in the Mediterranean. For this reason, the TRIDENT conference had been convened in Washington. Churchill had harbored ambitions of a campaign on mainland Italy for nearly a year; in early April he petitioned Roosevelt to go beyond Sicily, which he decried as "a modest and even petty objective for our armies. . . . Great possibilities are open in this theatre." Knocking Italy from the war "would cause a chill of loneliness over the German people, and might be the beginning of their doom." Sensing Yankee reluctance, he had warned Harry Hopkins on May 2 of "serious divergences beneath the surface" of Allied comity; privately, he told King George VI of his determination to battle the "Pacific First" advocates in Washington, where many demanded a stronger American effort against Tokyo.

"We did not come here with closed minds or rigid plans," Churchill had dictated during the passage from Gourock in preparing his opening argument for the TRIDENT talks. His musings, pecked on that silent Remington across 10 Downing Street stationery, included "Objective 1: Get Italy out of the war" and "Never forget there are 185 German divisions against the Russians. . . . We are not at present in contact with *any*." And the heart of the matter: if Sicily fell "by the end of August, what should these [Anglo-American] troops do in the seven or eight months between this and a first possible BOLERO [the staging in Britain for a cross-Channel invasion of western Europe]? We cannot afford to have idle armies while the Russians are bearing such a disproportionate weight."

Beneath his brass lay a supplication. Forty-five months of war had stretched Britain as far as she would stretch. More than 12 percent of the

British population now served in the armed forces; with national mobilization nearly complete, severe manpower shortages loomed if the war dragged on, particularly if it required storming the glacis of Festung Europa across the Channel. British battle deaths already exceeded 100,000, with thousands more missing, 20,000 merchant mariners lost, and another 45,000 dead in the United Kingdom from German air raids.

Salvation lay here, in America. The green and feeble U.S. Army of just a few years earlier now exceeded 6 million, led by 1,000 generals, 7,000 colonels, and 343,000 lieutenants. The Army Air Forces since mid-1941 had grown 3,500 percent, the Army Corps of Engineers 4,000 percent. A Navy that counted eight aircraft carriers after Pearl Harbor would have fifty, large and small, by the end of 1943. More cargo vessels would be built this year in the United States—a Liberty ship now took just fifty days, from keel laying to launch—than existed in the entire British merchant fleet. Just today, perhaps as a subtle reminder to Churchill before his arrival, Roosevelt had publicly announced that "production of airplanes by the United States"—86,000 in 1943—"now exceeds that of all other nations combined." Of $48 billion in war supplies provided by the United States to its allies, two-thirds would go to Britain.

The first eighteen months of war for the United States had been characterized by inexperience, insufficiency, and, all too often, ineptitude. A long seasoning, still unfinished, was required, a sorting out: of strong from weak, effective from ineffective, and, as always, lucky from unlucky. That sorting and seasoning continued in combat units and among those who commanded them. The *New York Times*'s veteran military correspondent Hanson Baldwin, after a long trip through the war zone, had concluded on this Tuesday morning's front page that "the greatest American problem is leadership: the Army so far has failed to produce a fraction of the adequate officer leadership needed." As for the average GI, Baldwin added, he "is not mentally tough or sufficiently determined. Part of his heart is in it, but only part."

Yet at home, where the productive capacity of the American industrial base approached full mobilization, the process was more advanced. The country had heaved itself from the ways of peace to the ways of war, galvanized as never before and perhaps never again. A final automobile had emerged from American production lines on February 10, 1942; supplanting it in 1943 would be thirty thousand tanks—more than three per hour around the clock, and more in a year than Germany would build from 1939 to 1945. The Rudolph Wurlitzer Company now made compasses and deicers instead of pianos and accordions, International Silver turned out Browning Automatic Rifles rather than tableware, and various lipstick, typewriter, and hubcap manufacturers produced, respectively, cartridge cases, machine guns, and helmets. Similar conversions occurred throughout the economy, which this year would also make 6 million rifles, 98,000 bazookas, 648,000 trucks, 33 million sets of soldiers' cotton drawers, 61 million pairs of wool socks. And on, and on, and on.

So, too, had the war infiltrated every kitchen, every closet, every medicine cabinet. Sugar, tires, and gasoline had been rationed first, followed by nearly everything else, from shoes to coffee. "Use it up, wear it out, make it do, or do without" became a consumer mantra. Plastic buttons replaced brass; zinc pennies supplanted copper. To save fifty million tons of wool annually, the government outlawed vests, cuffs, patch pockets, and wide lapels; hemlines rose, pleated skirts vanished, and an edict requiring a 10 percent reduction in the cloth used for women's bathing suits led to the bikini. Regulation L-85, issued by the War Production Board, not only rationed natural fibers but also limited fabric colors to those approved by the Dyestuff Advisory Committee, including honor gold, valor red, and gallant blue.

German prisoners might order curtains from Sears, Roebuck but the catalogue no longer offered saxophones, copper kettles, or plows. A bobby pin shortage forced hairdressers to improvise with toothpicks, while paint-on hosiery replaced vanished silk with the likes of "Velva Leg Film Liquid Stockings." Nationwide, the speed limit was thirty-five miles per hour, known as "victory speed." A government campaign to salvage toothpaste tubes—sixty tubes contained enough tin to solder all the electrical connections in a B-17 bomber—resulted in 200 million collected in sixteen months. "Bury a Jap with scrap," posters urged, and elaborate charts informed Americans that 10 old pails held sufficient steel for a mortar, 10 old stoves equaled 1 scout car, and 252 lawn mowers would make an anti-aircraft gun.

But all those recycled mowers and toothpaste tubes, all the warships and planes and wool socks, would pay off only if they were flung into the proper battles, in the proper campaigns, guided by a proper, war-winning strategy. And such a strategy did not yet exist.

No place in America had been more transformed by war than Washington, which the *Ferdinand Magellan* entered from the northeast with a hypnotic *clack-clack-clacking* shortly after six P.M. "The once sleepy southern city of charm and grace on the Potomac has burgeoned into the frenzied capital of the world," fumed the *Washington Times-Herald*. "Lobbyists, propagandists, experts of every species, wealthy industrialists, social climbers, inventors, ladies of uneasy virtue and pickpockets infest the city."

To this panoply now were added a prime minister and his retinue of more than a hundred generals, admirals, clerks, bodyguard detectives, and Royal Marines. At 6:45 P.M., a convoy of limousines rolled from the White House grounds and turned south. Seven Secret Service agents sat in squad cars along the route, including an agent posted at the top of an inconspicuous ramp on Fourteenth Street, which sloped to a subterranean rail spur under the Bureau of Engraving and Printing. As the train lurched to a stop in a squeal of brakes, the limousines pulled onto the platform. Lifted from the lead vehicle and placed in a waiting wheelchair, Franklin Roosevelt scanned the *Magellan*'s rear passenger compartment. His gray pallor, the wattled neck, the bagged and hazy eyes, all the fretful symptoms of stress and age seemed to vanish at the sight of Churchill clumping forward in his improbable yacht squadron uniform. The president beamed, the prime minister beamed, and the conclave that would search for that war-winning strategy to save the world was under way.

But first the visitors must be settled, and this was no simple task. "If the war lasts much longer, Washington is going to bust right out of its pants," *Life* magazine had warned in January. Five months later, the busting was well advanced. The city's twelve thousand hotel rooms were always booked, forcing some visitors to find shelter as far away as Philadelphia. Houseboat colonies sprouted on the Potomac River, and sprawling hamlets of shabby temporary houses, known as demolishables, spread through the District of Columbia and its suburbs. There would be no houseboats or demolishables for the British delegation, of course: Churchill took a suite at the White House, and the rest of the delegation was shoehorned into the Statler Hotel, the Wardman Park, the British embassy, and various other hostels and private houses. Sixteen Royal Marines marched off to a U.S. Army barracks, sweating miserably in the clinging humidity that entitled British diplomats in Washington to "tropical post pay."

Churchill could sense that the country had indeed changed since his previous visit eleven months earlier, and so had its capital. The Pentagon, which in 1942 was still under construction across the river in Hell's Bottom, now stood complete as not only the world's largest office building, but also "the largest feeding operation under one roof in the world" (55,000 meals a day for 35 cents each). All those well-fed, poorly housed War Department bureaucrats were busier than ever. One wit proposed a new government motto—"Exhaustion is not enough"—and on Pennsylvania Avenue a makeshift information center for visiting contractors and businessmen was known as "the Madhouse." This month, the War Manpower Commission had announced plans to induct twelve thousand men into the military every day for the rest of the year, with childless married men called to the colors for the first time and those with children certain to be drafted soon. Perhaps not coincidentally, the FBI director, J. Edgar Hoover, disclosed that his agents had arrested more than five hundred draft dodgers in twenty cities, with warrants outstanding on three thousand others.

Among other signs of these frenzied times: thirty-five "rumor clinics" had been established across the country "to investigate malicious and meaningless rumors," which would be vetted by college professors—apparently immune to scuttlebutt—whose findings would be reported in local newspapers. There was such a crying need for lathe operators, machinists, and leather workers that some help-wanted ads even solicited "White or Colored"; a government press release urgently seeking skilled typists for the war effort contained forty-six errors on a single page. The Office of War Information reported that a recent plea for fine blond hair—used in weather instruments and optical equipment—had resulted in such a cascade of golden tresses that no further donations were needed.

Amid the mania and the melodrama, one notable addition had been made to the Washington landscape four weeks before Churchill's arrival. He could have seen it from his White House digs, looking past the fading azaleas and beyond the Washington Monument to a grove of cherry trees framing the Tidal Basin. There, the memorial to Thomas Jefferson had been dedicated, an elegant neoclassical temple sheltering a nineteen-foot statue of the third president—temporarily cast in plaster, because the War Production Board needed the bronze. Jefferson's manifesto, chiseled in marble, summarized perfectly the animating sentiment of the men who would begin meeting tomorrow in search of a path that could carry them to war's end: "I have sworn upon the altar of God eternal hostility against every form of tyranny over the mind of man."

They got to work at 2:30 P.M. on Wednesday, May 12, in Roosevelt's oval study, a snug hideaway above the Blue Room. Nautical paintings and etchings decorated the walls, and a bearskin covered the floor. The president sat in his armless wheelchair greeting Churchill and the ten other men—mostly from the Combined Chiefs—who joined that first session. Roosevelt's massive desk, positioned away from the windows by the Secret Service, held a blue lamp, four cloth toy donkeys, a stack of books, an inkpot, a medicine bottle, a small clock shaped like a ship's wheel, and a bronze bust of the First Lady, which had somehow escaped the scrap collectors.

Five months earlier, American strategists had left the Casablanca conference convinced they had been outfoxed by the British, who were better prepared and had been unified in their determination to continue the

Mediterranean strategy begun with the invasion of North Africa. To avoid another humiliation, the Yanks before TRIDENT had bombarded the British with position papers; they also drafted more than thirty studies on various war policies and doubled the size of the U.S. delegation. In searching for "a grand design by which to reach the heartland of Europe" in decisive battle, American planners scrutinized potential portals to the continent, from the Iberian Peninsula and southern France to Italy, Greece, and Turkey. Still, almost to a man they favored the most direct route across the English Channel.

The president's brain trust also worked hard to overcome what many considered the biggest obstacle to American strategic hegemony: Roosevelt himself, and his evident willingness to be swayed by Churchill's honeyed oratory. "The man from London . . . will have his way with our Chief, and the careful and deliberate plans of our staff will be overridden," the secretary of war, Henry Stimson, told his diary on May 10. "I feel very troubled about it." The U.S. Joint Chiefs had conferred with Roosevelt at the White House three days earlier and had wrung from him a vow to press the British for commitment to a cross-Channel invasion of Europe. Driving home the point, a Joint Chiefs memo reiterated the Pentagon's "antipathy to an invasion of the Italian mainland," while warning that the British "are traditionally expert at meeting the letter while avoiding the spirit of commitments." Roosevelt replied with a three-word scribble across the margin that echoed Churchill's minute on the *Queen Mary:* "No closed minds."

In this charged milieu, "the man from London" spoke. North Africa was done, Operation HUSKY in Sicily was near. "What should come next?" Churchill asked. The Allies had "the authority and prestige of victory" and must "grasp the fruits of our success." Following his typed notes, he laid out his arguments: Russia fighting 185 German divisions; Allies currently fighting none; Italy ripe for the plucking.

The prime minister had used the phrase "soft underbelly" in a cable to Roosevelt in November 1942, meaning the supposedly vulnerable southern flank of Axis Europe. Privately, to his military advisers this week, Churchill added, "We want them to agree to the exploitation of HUSKY and the attack on the underbelly taking priority." Now he pressed the point. "Need we invade the soil of Italy, or could we crush her by air attack? Would Germany defend Italy?" Answering himself, Churchill said it was imperative "to use our great armies to attack Italy" rather than leave them idle after Sicily. If Hitler rallied to defend his Fascist partner, Benito Mussolini, that many fewer German troops could fight the Russians. The prime minister did not believe a defeated Italy would present an economic burden to the Allies, nor did he even concede "that an occupation of Italy would be necessary."

There it was, the British strategy in a Mediterranean nutshell. Roosevelt replied immediately. Churchill's argument was vivid but unpersuasive. "Where do we go from Sicily?" the president asked, again echoing the prime minister. Some twenty-five Allied divisions—with roughly fifteen thousand men each—would muster in the Mediterranean by the end of Operation HUSKY and "these must be kept employed." But he had "always shrunk from the thought of putting large armies in Italy," a diversion that could "result in attrition for the United Nations and play into Germany's hands." Better to continue staging a mighty host in Britain. The subsequent invasion, a knockout punch aimed at the German homeland, "should be decided upon definitely as an operation for the spring of 1944." Finishing, the president smiled and gave the casual toss of the head that one admirer called his "cigarette-holder gesture."

This impasse persisted the next morning when the Combined Chiefs—the half dozen heads of the American and British armies, navies, and air forces—met without Roosevelt and Churchill in the Federal Reserve Building, a severe rectilinear edifice with a pillared portico facing Constitution Avenue. The scent of roses and fresh cut grass seeped past the rigid sentries into the wainscoted room used by the board of governors; here, the U.S. delegation presented an eleven-paragraph memo entitled "Global Strategy of the War." Point 3 held the crux: "It is the opinion of the United States chiefs of staff that a cross-Channel invasion of Europe is necessary to an early conclusion of the war with Germany."

A tall, austere man with sandy hair gone gray carried forward the American argument. General George C. Marshall, the Army chief of staff, knew his mind on this issue even as he fretted over the president's susceptibility to British blandishments. Marshall was a clean-desk man, famously convinced that "no one ever had an original idea after three o'clock in the afternoon," and he disdained orthodoxy, sycophants, and the telephone. To Churchill he was "the greatest Roman of them all"; a British general described him as "a little aloof, dignified, above the battle, unbuyable. . . . I never saw him show his feelings in any way." In fact, Marshall possessed a molten temper. He demanded that subordinates "expunge the bunk, complications, and ponderosities" from the nation's war effort, and his signature query, accompanied by the unblinking gaze of those ice-blue eyes, could terrify lieutenants and lieutenant generals alike: "Are you confident that you've thought this through?" Aside from horseback riding, gardening was his sole civil diversion; "the pride of his heart," according to his wife, remained the compost pile outside his Virginia home.

Invading Italy, Marshall said, "would establish a vacuum in the Mediterranean" that would suck troops and matériel away from a cross-Channel attack. Operations after Sicily "should be limited to the air offensive" or risk "a prolonged struggle" in the Mediterranean, which was "not acceptable to the United States."

Arguments spilled from those thirty War Department studies: eliminating Italy from the war could bring more burden than benefit, since precious Allied shipping would be needed to feed the Italian civilian population. Germany would recoup the twelve million tons of coal currently provided Rome each year, as well as the rolling stock now needed to supply Italy. The "soft underbelly" in general lacked sufficient ports to support the huge Allied armies needed to plunge into central Europe. American planners considered the British beguiled by "side-shows," "periphery-pecking," and "unremunerative scatterization." (That last must have disheartened every lover of the language regardless of strategic creed.) Privately, the Yanks suspected that Britain's fixation on the Mediterranean reflected both traditional imperial interests and fainthearted reluctance to again risk the horrific casualties incurred on the Western Front a generation earlier.

"Mediterranean operations," Marshall added, "are highly speculative as far as ending the war is concerned."

Listening attentively was General Sir Alan Brooke, chief of the Imperial General Staff, whose sharp-featured countenance did not betray his private assessment of Marshall: "a big man and a very great gentleman who inspired trust, but did not impress me by the ability of his brain." Brooke's brain was able enough, though he tended to dismiss as purblind those uncommitted to his own vision. At fifty-nine, with round shoulders and dark, pomaded hair, he could be petulant—"very liverish," in his phrase; this state was perhaps the handmaiden to exhaustion after four years of war with the Germans and, not infrequently, with Churchill. "When I thump the table and push my face towards him what does he do?" the prime minister said. "Thumps the table harder and glares back at me." Brooke calculated that each month battling Churchill "is a year off my life"; in a letter to a friend he added, "It is the night work after dinner till 1 a.m. with him that kills me." The ninth and youngest child of an expatriate Anglo-Irish baronet, Brooke had been born and raised in France, a history that bestowed on him both a native fluency and a lifelong dread of the nickname Froggie. He nurtured homely passions for birds and for wildlife photography, in which he was a pioneer. If Marshall had his compost pile, Brooke had Southeran's shop on Sackville Street, where he would sit transfixed in his red uniform braces, scrutinizing ornithological plates. On the *Queen Mary* he had put aside *Birds of the Ocean* long enough to note in his diary, with handwriting as vertical and jagged as the Irish coastline: "Running a war seems to consist in making plans and then ensuring that all those destined to carry [them] out don't quarrel with each other instead of the enemy."

Now he quarreled with Marshall, albeit without raising his voice. The eleven-paragraph U.S. strategic memo was answered with a thirty-one-paragraph British countersalvo. Point 5 encapsulated Britain's thesis: "The main task which lies before us this year in the European theatre is the elimination of Italy. If we could achieve this, it is our opinion that we should have gone a very long way towards defeating Germany."

Brooke pressed the point with staccato precision. Germany currently kept thirty-five divisions in France and the Low Countries, with another ten, available as reinforcements, in the Fatherland; attacking Italy would divert some of these German troops and weaken defenses against an eventual Allied cross-Channel attack, which might not be feasible until 1945 or 1946 anyway. If Italy collapsed, German soldiers would have to replace the forty-three Italian divisions occupying the Balkans and the seven others bivouacked in southern France. Without Italian allies, Berlin was unlikely to fight south of the Po Valley in northern Italy. "Our total commitment on the Italian mainland in the event of a collapse," a British staff memo estimated, "will not exceed nine divisions."

A stack of studies, bound in red leather folders, further advanced the British cause. "If Italy collapses, the Germans cannot hold Italy *and* the Balkans, and they will concentrate everything they can on the defence of the latter." The Mediterranean offered such enticing oppportunities that "we shall have every chance of breaking the Axis and of bringing the war with Germany to a successful conclusion in 1944."

But, Brooke warned his American colleagues, unless the fight was carried into Italy after the capture of Sicily, "no possibility of an attack into France would arise." Indeed, "to cease Mediterrranean operations on the conclusion of HUSKY would lengthen the war."

Momentary silence fell on the room as the session ended. The Allies were miles apart, still, and mutually suspicious. "Your people have no intention of ever crossing the Channel," one American planner had told his British counterpart. Admiral Ernest J. King, the irascible U.S. chief of naval operations, subsequently advised his fellow chiefs, "We ought to divert our forces to the Pacific."

At Marshall's suggestion they adjourned with a scraping of chairs and ambled next door to the Public Health Building. Lunch awaited them in the map room, where strategic thrust and parry momentarily yielded to small talk and the benign clink of cutlery. That night Brooke confided to his diary, "I am thoroughly depressed."

\* \* \*

Washington lacked the isolated tranquillity that had distinguished Casablanca five months earlier. Endless meetings, often three or more a day, were followed by endless social obligations, including four consecutive nights of black-tie affairs. For all its sophisticated war paint, the capital remained a provincially convivial place, eager to please and atwitter at hosting such distinguished battle captains.

Fans at a Washington Nationals baseball game applauded wildly at the appearance of a pair of genuine field marshals in the box seats. Bing Crosby and Kate Smith sang between innings as the visitors tried to divine the difference between home plate and a home run. At one dinner party, each arriving guest reached into a top hat—one for ladies, another for gentlemen—and drew a slip on which was printed the name of a famous lover in history. Table seating then was determined by uniting the paramours: Helen with Paris, Cleopatra with Antony, Chloe with Daphnis, Heloïse with Abelard. Also intimate, if less risqué, was a private showing at the White House of a new U.S. Army Signal Corps film, *The Battle of Britain;* doughty Royal Air Force pilots climbed into their cockpits, Spitfires tangled with Messerschmitts, mortally wounded planes heeled over in smoky spirals. Churchill sat transfixed by the spectacle, the flickering projector light reflecting off the tears that coursed down his plump cheeks. Only the Washington heat remained inhospitable, forcing some wilting Brits to desperate measures: the wife of the economist John Maynard Keynes was found perched, entirely nude, before the open door of a Westinghouse refrigerator in the Georgetown house where the couple was staying.

To escape both official Washington and social Washington, Marshall bundled the Combined Chiefs onto a pair of transport planes for a weekend in southeast Virginia. Landing at Langley Field, the men squeezed into eight waiting Army staff cars and motored up Route 17 for a tour of the Yorktown battlefield, where the British professed—amid guffaws—not to recall "the name of that chap who did so badly here" in 1781. Then it was on to Williamsburg, the meticulously restored former colonial capital.

If Washington had been atwitter, Williamsburg seethed with excitement at the visitation. Lawns had been trimmed, hedges clipped, honeysuckle cropped. At the Williamsburg Inn, linen and china emerged from wartime storage crates, and the silver was polished and repolished. Carpenters built a new table to seat thirteen diners and adjusted the floodlights to illuminate the dogwoods. Someone managed to circumvent government restrictions on Freon to procure the only two tanks of refrigerant south of Richmond: the inn would be pleasingly air-conditioned.

John D. Rockefeller, Jr., who had financed Williamsburg's resurrection, got wind of the visit and assigned various servants to oversee dinner preparations. Appalled to learn that inferior cream might be used to make the ice cream, Rockefeller ordered a fresh urn dispatched from his estate at Pocantico Hills in New York, along with select fruits and cheeses, while his private club in Manhattan prepared fresh terrapin à la Maryland, which required two days of simmering. Terrapin, cream, fruit, cheese, and a consignment of sherry all were tucked into the upper berth of a Pullman car at Penn Station by an overburdened butler, who staggered off the train in Richmond four hours later and continued with his bounty to Williamsburg by limousine.

Shortly before five P.M. on Saturday, May 15, the convoy of chiefs turned off Queen Street onto Duke of Gloucester Street before stopping at the old Capitol building, where they were greeted by a black doorman in colonial livery. Having admired the rubbed woodwork and the portrait of young George Washington, they strolled to the Raleigh Tavern for finger sandwiches and cinnamon toast in the Daphne Room, washed down with tea and highballs. Then it was on to the inn, where fires crackled in the twin lobby hearths—Freon be damned—and bourbon juleps were served in goblets made by a local silversmith. Dinner, at 8:15, included Rockefeller's menu, plus crabmeat cocktail, Virginia ham, beaten biscuits, and a 1929 Heidsieck Dry Monopole champagne. All agreed that the strawberry ice cream was divine.

After coffee and brandy, Marshall rousted the visitors for a midnight excursion to the colonial governor's palace, brilliantly lighted with hundreds of candles in each room and throughout the gardens. Admiral Sir Dudley Pound, the first sea lord, lost his way in the topiary maze and called for help from the other chiefs, who rushed to the rescue only to get lost themselves, with much boyish chortling.

Sunday morning, after breakfast on the terrace, the chiefs played croquet on the lawn or went swimming in borrowed trunks. Brooke, who was mulling whether to spend £1,500 for a forty-five-volume set of *Gould's Birds,* tromped off with his field glasses in search of catbirds and hairy woodpeckers. Before heading to the airfield for the return flight, the high command filed into Bruton Parish Church, where ushers escorted them to General Washington's pew. Parishioners jammed the sanctuary, clogging the twin transept aisles with folding chairs after the pews filled. Dudley Pound, who was suffering from an unsuspected brain tumor and had but a few months to live, had been asked to read the scripture. Stepping to the lectern, he thumbed to the sixth chapter of Matthew and sang out, "Consider the lilies of the field, how they grow; they toil not, neither do they spin." Pound finished in a strong voice:

Take therefore no thought for the morrow: for the morrow shall take thought for the things of itself. Sufficient unto the day is the evil thereof.

While the chiefs went south, Roosevelt and Churchill headed north. With Eleanor Roosevelt and Harry Hopkins also in the limousine, and a motorcycle escort clearing the road, the motorcade rolled up Massachusetts Avenue before angling out of the capital on Wisconsin Avenue toward the presidential retreat called Shangri-La—later renamed Camp David—in the Catoctin Mountains of central Maryland. Spying a billboard for Barbara Fritchie Candy, Roosevelt recited a couplet from John Greenleaf Whittier's ballad about the legendary Civil War heroine who defied passing rebel troops by waving the Stars and Stripes from her window.

"Shoot, if you must, this old gray head,
But spare your country's flag," she said.

To the president's amazement, Churchill then "gabbled the whole poem," all sixty lines—"She leaned far out on the window-sill , / And shook it forth with a royal will." Soon the Roosevelts and Hopkins were punctuating the prime minister's cadences with the refrain: "Shoot, if you must . . ."

For three days they unbent in the serene glades of Shangri-La, napping in the log cabins, angling for brook trout, discussing the hot tramp of Confederate troops through these hills toward Gettysburg eighty years earlier. Another guest, Roosevelt's daughter, Anna, wrote her husband on May 14 that Churchill "picks his teeth all through dinner and uses snuff liberally. The sneezes which follow the latter practically rock the foundations of the house. . . . I admired his snuff box and found it was one that had once belonged to Lord Nelson." Often the president sat by a window with his beloved stamp collection; when Churchill's pleas grew too insistent for more tanks or more planes, more this or more that, Roosevelt would cut him short by holding a stamp specimen to the light and murmuring, "Isn't this a beauty from Newfoundland?" On other occasions, to relieve the president from the "Winston hours," an aide would summon Roosevelt to an imaginary phone call.

They had much in common besides their ultimate responsibility for saving the world. They shared passions for secrecy, skulduggery, and military history. Roosevelt "loved the military side of events," one subordinate wrote, "and liked to hold them in his own hand," while Churchill seemed to fancy himself the reincarnation of his famous ancestor the Duke of Marlborough, the victor over the French at Blenheim in 1704. Despite his current resistance to Churchill's Italian gambit, the president had his own "diversionist tendencies" and harbored a fascination for the Mediterranean nearly as lurid as the prime minister's. Neither ever forgot, or tried to forget, the agony that war had brought to so many. (Marshall routinely sent Roosevelt brilliantly colored graphics detailing the latest combat casualty figures, "so that it would be quite clear.") Certainly the president's admiration and affection for Churchill ran deep. "Isn't he a wonderful old Tory to have on our side?" he once asked.

And yet: Churchill could draw near and no nearer. Convivial and charming, Roosevelt at his core remained opaque, mysterious, unknowable in what one aide called "his heavily forested interior." Trying to follow his thought process, Henry Stimson said, was "very much like chasing a vagrant beam of sunshine around an empty room." Seldom did he issue orders; rather, he intimated that he "wished to have things done." No politician ever was better at resolving problems by ignoring them; Roosevelt could elevate inaction to an art form. Yet on more than twenty occasions he rejected the advice of his military brain trust to follow his own instincts, as he had done in deciding to invade North Africa the previous November. "Not a tidy mind," one British observer noted, and the American chiefs could only agree. "The president," Eleanor once said, "never 'thinks'! He *decides*."

He reduced his own political philosophy to two nouns: democrat and Christian. A bit more nuanced were his inalienable Four Freedoms—of speech, of worship, from want, and from fear—which he had articulated in the State of the Union message of January 1941. Months earlier, he had begun to dream about the postwar world, and if he kept Churchill at arm's length it was partly because his vision did not include the restoration of colonial empires. Surely he had spoken from the heart in telling the prime minister, "It is fun to be in the same decade with you." Yet there was also cold conviction in Roosevelt's observation to his son Elliott: "Britain is on the decline."

America was ascendant, and Roosevelt had reason to hope that his countrymen possessed the stamina to remake a better world: a forthcoming Roper opinion poll, secretly slipped to the White House on Thursday, revealed that more than three-quarters of those surveyed agreed that the United States should play a larger global role after the war. Nearly as many believed that the country should "plan to help other nations get on their feet," and more than half concurred that Americans should "take an active part in some sort of an international organization with a court and police force strong enough to enforce its decisions." The president found it equally heartening that 70 percent approved of his war leadership and two-thirds favored him for reelection in 1944 if the world was still at war.

But if Britain was on the decline, so was Roosevelt personally, as he no doubt realized. Those who had seen him at Casablanca were dismayed at how frail he now looked, and all the pretty stamps in Newfoundland could not fully restore him. "Something at once attractive and pathetic in this man," a British diplomat wrote in his diary. "The great torso, the huge and splendid head, the magnificent frame, immobile, anchored to a sofa or a chair, carried from room to room." Roosevelt said little about his health, other than to grouse over a recurrent sinus condition. It was just another secret to keep.

Negotiations resumed at 10:30 A.M. on Monday. Camaraderie and good fun promptly popped like soap bubbles, and for three days the deadlock persisted as the military chiefs haggled. Brooke and his British colleagues renounced both imperial designs in the Mediterranean and any peripheral strategems; rather, they argued, an Italian campaign "in the spirit of the chase" would exploit a Sicilian victory, unhinge Rome, and unbalance Berlin. The Americans refused to concede, and declared that no U.S. ground or naval forces would be released for combat beyond Sicily. Marshall, whose beetling brows gave him a stern Old Testament look, reminded the chiefs "that in North Africa a relatively small German force" had fought an irksome rearguard campaign for six months; a German decision to fight in Italy "might make intended operations extremely difficult and time consuming."

Nearly three dozen aides and staff officers hovered behind the chiefs, rifling through documents or pulling out those red leather folders to prove this point or dispute that assertion. By 4:30 on Wednesday afternoon, Marshall had reached his limit. The chiefs were scheduled to meet Roosevelt and Churchill at the White House in two hours; to confess that the high command remained at loggerheads would likely mean ceding strategic planning to the president and prime minister, a prospect horrifying to every man in epaulets. Marshall proposed that the room be cleared except for the chiefs. The supernumeraries filed out; ninety minutes later, the door reopened, and on the mahogany table lay an agreement.

It was a curious compromise, because compromise it was. A cross-Channel attack would be launched—the target date was fifty weeks away: on May 1, 1944—"to secure a lodgement on the Continent from which further offensive operations can be carried out." To help assemble the twenty-nine divisions required for such an invasion, soon to be code-named OVERLORD, four American and three British divisions would be transferred from the Mediterranean after the Sicilian campaign to staging bases in Britain. As for the Med, the Allied commander-in-chief in North Africa, General Dwight D. Eisenhower, was instructed to plan whatever operations following the conquest of Sicily seemed "best calculated to eliminate Italy from the war and to contain the maximum number of German forces." The chiefs calculated that Eisenhower eventually would be left with twenty-seven divisions and 3,600 aircraft to continue his war against the soft underbelly, although a direct invasion of Italy was not specified.

The baby had been cut in half, a solution perhaps satisfying to the disputants but rarely auspicious for the baby. As the officers collected their papers and snapped shut their briefcases, a grumble of thunder rolled across Washington. Rain soon lashed the city from the west, breaking the heat.

TRIDENT had another week to run. If the central disagreement had been finessed, a dozen other issues required resolution, from shipping allocations to operations in the Pacific. The social round also continued without mercy. At a reception on the South Lawn of the White House, the Marine Band played Stephen Foster airs and "The Battle Hymn of the Republic" while guests sipped iced coffee and stared beyond the fence at tourists who stared back. During a British embassy luncheon on May 22, Churchill, fortified with whiskey, declared that he expected "England and the United States to run the world. . . . Why be apologetic about Anglo-Saxon superiority?" The bemused vice president, Henry A. Wallace, accused the prime minister of advocating "Anglo-Saxondom *über Alles.*" Churchill waved away the charge. "We Anglo-Saxons"—he pronounced it *schaxons*—"are the only ones who really know how to run the show." Poor Brooke left the luncheon to get a haircut and tumbled down fourteen stone steps; battered and bruised, he found consolation in the purchase of two rare bird books discovered in a local shop.

Rarely content and never quiescent, Churchill now threatened to overplay his hand. He kept Roosevelt up until 2:30 in the morning of Monday, May 24. (After TRIDENT, the exhausted president would flee to his Hyde Park estate and sleep ten hours for three consecutive nights.) Later that day the prime minister sought to repudiate the compromise reached by the chiefs, because it failed to specifically advocate an invasion of Italy. He also raised the notion of a continued attack into Yugoslavia and Greece. To Lord Moran, his personal physician, Churchill added, "Have you noticed that the president is a very tired man? His mind seems closed. He seems to have lost his wonderful elasticity. . . . I cannot let the matter rest where it is."

Harry Hopkins warned Churchill to do just that or risk an ugly rupture; even Roosevelt complained that the prime minister was acting like a "spoiled boy." Chastened, Churchill agreed instead to fly from Washington to Algiers to confer with Eisenhower, taking in tow both a scuffed-up Brooke and a grumpy Marshall, who likened himself to "a piece of baggage." Hopkins told Moran, "We have come to avoid controversy with Winston. We find he is too much for us." The physician agreed that Churchill "is so taken up with his own ideas that he is not interested in what other people think."

Still, the sweep of his rhetoric proved a tonic, as it had so many times before. At noon on a bright Wednesday, a joint session of Congress convened in the House of Representatives, joined by the British ambassador's son, a young subaltern who had lost both legs in North Africa and who was wheeled into the House gallery by his tall, stooped father. Churchill had spent nearly ten hours the previous day dictating speech drafts to his long-suffering typists, and he now stood at the podium, grasping the lapels of his dark suit, rolling his vowels and reminding free men everywhere that the road was long, but the cause was righteous. "War is full of mysteries and surprises. A false step, a wrong direction, an error in strategy, discord or lassitude among the Allies, might soon give the common enemy power to confront us," he said. "It is in the dragging-out of the war at enormous expense, until the democracies are tired or bored or split, that the main hopes of Germany and Japan must now reside."

After fifty minutes he finished, as he often finished, by taking flight:

> By singleness of purpose, by steadfastness of conduct, by tenacity and endurance—such as we have so far displayed—by this and only by this can we discharge our duty to the future of the world and to the destiny of man.

Roosevelt had remained at the White House to avoid crowding Churchill in the limelight. He listened to the speech on the radio he kept in the left drawer of his big desk. "Winston writes beautifully," the president told his secretary, "and he's a past master at catch phrases."

The conference sputtered to an end without the wistful sense of brotherhood that had characterized Casablanca. Mutual confidence remained a sometime thing; the ideal of an epoch when good men dared to trust one another was still imperfectly realized. They were tired of arguing, tired of shouldering the burdens they shouldered, tired of the whole catastrophe. They knew the hard time had come, and that it would require hard men.

For the Americans, the first leg of the century's most grueling race had come to an end, its emblem the Afrika Korps prisoners now trudging into camps in Kansas and Oklahoma. That leg, from Pearl Harbor through the capture of Tunisia, had required spunk and invention, unity and organizational acumen. Now the long middle leg of the race was about to begin, of uncertain duration, over an undetermined course, and few doubted that new virtues would be needed: endurance, impenitence, an obdurate will.

For the first time, the Allied high command had met with a clear sense that the war, at least in Europe, would be won—someday, somehow. "The mellow light of victory begins to play over the entire expanse of the world war," as Churchill would tell the House of Commons in June. During the conference, daily reports of U-boat sinkings affirmed that the tide in that particular struggle had turned, dramatically and irreversibly. The joint communiqué drafted for TRIDENT by Roosevelt and Churchill evinced a bluff optimism while proffering a few white lies, such as the assertion that "there has been a complete meeting of minds" about all theaters, including "the war in the Mediterranean."

Despite this glossing over, a plan now existed where there had been no plan. The British had succeeded in keeping the war centered in the Mediterranean, at least for a year, and in making the elimination of Italy from the Axis partnership an immediate goal. Churchill had again thwarted the American impulse to muscle up in the Pacific theater at the expense of the Atlantic (although, in the event, the U.S. war against Tokyo would be prosecuted almost as furiously as the European struggles). Assistance to China would continue, and Allied bomber fleets would grow ever larger, until they virtually blackened the skies over Germany and eventually Japan. The British had made extravagant claims—"over-egged the pudding," as one critic put it—to overcome Yankee skepticism by asserting that Germany was unlikely to fight hard for mainland Italy; that the long-term Allied commitment in Italy was likely to call for only nine divisions and to require no substantial occupation; and that a hard fight in the Mediterranean could end the war in 1944. All of these prophesies proved false.

The Americans had managed to put brakes on the Mediterranean campaign: seven divisions would decamp for Britain in the fall, and no additional reinforcements would be sent south. They also extracted a pledge that the Allies would invade western France by a specific date. The deal, Roosevelt told an aide, was "the best I could get at this time." Neither the president nor his warlords had answered the legitimate British questions about how, if the plug were pulled in the Mediterranean, German forces would be engaged during the many months until OVERLORD could be mounted in France; or how the Russians would be mollified if the Anglo-Americans took a powder for those many months; or whether it would not be prudent to draw Axis forces from the Atlantic Wall by making Berlin reinforce its southern flank.

The Allies had a plan where there had been no plan, but whether it was a good plan remained to be seen. Certainly it was vague. How Italy should be knocked out was left to the theater commander, General Eisenhower, and the concomitant goal of containing "the maximum number of German forces" implied a war of attrition and opportunism rather than a clear strategic objective.

The dispatch of Allied armies to North Africa and now to Sicily had created its own momentum, its own logic. In an effort to square the circle, a slightly cockeyed strategic scheme emerged that would guide the Anglo-Americans until the end of the war: a relentless pounding of Festung Europa from the air and from the southern flank, setting the stage for a cross-Channel invasion aimed at Berlin. Whether a meaningful Mediterranean campaign could be waged without endless entanglement, and whether the enemy reacted as Allied strategists hoped he would react also remained to be seen.

Perhaps the greatest achievement of the men meeting at TRIDENT was not the sketching of big arrows on a map but rather the affirmation of their humanity. This was their true common language: the shared values of decency and dignity, of tolerance and respect. Despite the petty bickering and intellectual fencing, a fraternity bound them on the basis of who they were, what they believed, and why they fought. It could be glimpsed, like one of Brooke's beautiful birds, in Churchill's gentle draping of a blanket on Roosevelt's shoulders; and in their grim determination to wage war without liking it.

At four P.M. on Tuesday, May 25, precisely two weeks after his arrival, Churchill strode down the narrow corridors of the West Wing to the Oval Office. His departure by flying boat from the Potomac off Gravelly Point was set for the next morning, his luggage was packed, his farewells were bid or soon would be bid. The code name for the morning flight had been repeatedly amended in the past forty-eight hours from WATSON to REDCAR to STUDENT, and the prime minister, evidently finding none of those words suitably warlike, had lobbied in vain to get it changed again, to NEPTUNE.

Roosevelt sat in the armless wheelchair. Sunshine flooded the Rose Garden outside the French doors. Bulletproof glass had been installed in the windows facing south, but the president had rejected several of the more hysterical security proposals, including machine guns on the terrace and air locks on the outer doors to thwart a poison gas attack. With Churchill at his side, he gave a nod and an aide opened the office door to admit a large gaggle of reporters for the 899th press conference of Roosevelt's presidency.

"We are awfully glad to have Mr. Churchill back here," he told the scribes after they had shuffled in. "Considering the size of our problems, these discussions have been done in practically record time." Roosevelt swiveled toward the prime minister. "I think that he will be willing to answer almost—with stress on the *almost*—any question."

"Mr. Prime Minister," a reporter said, "can you tell us generally about the plans for the future, probably beginning with Europe?"

"Our plans for the future," Churchill replied, "are to wage this war until unconditional surrender is procured from all those who have molested us, and this applies equally to Asia and to Europe."

Roosevelt beamed. "I think that word 'molestation' or 'molesting' is one of the best examples of your habitual understatement that I know."

The reporters tittered. "I am curious to know," another asked, "what you think is going on in Hitler's mind?" The titter turned to boisterous laughter.

"Appetite unbridled, ambition unmeasured—all the world!" the prime minister said. "There is no end of the appetite of this wicked man. I should say he repents now that he did not curb his passion before he brought such a portion of the world against him and his country."

"Do you care to say anything about Mussolini and Italy?"

Churchill scowled. "I think they are a softer proposition than Germany."

On it went, query and response, and the reporters were so beguiled that by the end they had interrupted with laughter twenty-one times.

The Allies had no intention of keeping Italian territory after the war, or of matching Axis barbarities, Churchill added. "We shall not stain our name by an inhuman act." As for the Italian people, they "have sinned—erred—by allowing themselves to be led by the nose by a very elaborate tyranny." But they "will have their life in the new Europe."

Churchill rose to his full five feet, seven inches. "We are the big animal now," he said, "shaking the life out of the smaller animal, and he must be given no rest, no chance to recover."

The door opened and the reporters reluctantly began to file out. Seizing the moment with unsuspected agility, the prime minister climbed up onto his chair, tottered unsteadily for a moment, then stood above the popping flashbulbs and the grinning president and the applauding scribes, flashing the V-for-victory sign with his stubby fingers, over and over again.

# Part One

# 1. Across the Middle Sea

*Forcing the World Back to Reason*

THE sun beat down on the stained white city, the July sun that hurt the eyes and turned the sea from wine-dark to silver. Soldiers crowded the shade beneath the vendors' awnings and hugged the lee of the alabaster buildings spilling down to the port. Sweat darkened their collars and cuffs, particularly those of the combat troops wearing heavy herringbone twill. Some had stripped off their neckties, but kept them folded and tucked in their belts for quick retrieval. The commanding general had been spotted along the wharves, and every man knew that George S. Patton, Jr., would levy a $25 fine on any GI not wearing his helmet or tie.

Algiers seethed with soldiers after eight months of Allied occupation: Yanks and Brits, Kiwis and Gurkhas, swabs and tars and merchant mariners who at night walked with their pistols drawn against the bandits infesting the port. Troops swaggered down the boulevards and through the souks, whistling at girls on the balconies or pawing through shop displays in search of a few final souvenirs. Sailors in denim shirts and white caps mingled with French Senegalese in red fezzes, and bearded *goums* with their braided pigtails and striped burnooses. German prisoners sang "Erika" as they marched in column under guard to the Liberty ships that would haul them to camps in the New World. British veterans in battle dress answered with a ribald ditty called "El Alamein"—"Tally-ho, tally-ho, and that was as far as the bastards did go"—while the Americans belted out "Dirty Gertie from Bizerte," which was said to have grown to two hundred verses, all of them salacious. "Sand in your shoes," they called to one another—the North African equivalent of "Good luck"—and with knowing looks they flashed their index fingers to signal "I," for "invasion."

Electric streetcars clattered past horsedrawn wine wagons, to be passed in turn by whizzing jeeps. Speeding by Army drivers had become so widespread that military policemen now impounded offenders' vehicles—although General Eisenhower had issued a blanket amnesty for staff cars "bearing the insignia of a general officer." Most Algerians walked or resorted to bicycles, pushcarts, and, one witness recorded, "every conceivable variety of buggy, phaeton, carryall, cart, sulky, and landau." Young Frenchmen strolled the avenues in their narrow-brimmed hats and frayed jackets. Arab boys scampered through the alleys in pantaloons made from stolen barracks bags, with two holes cut for their legs and the stenciled name and serial number of the former owner across the rump. Tatterdemalion beggars in veils wore robes tailored from old Army mattress covers, which also served as winding-sheets for the dead. The only women in Algiers wearing stockings were the hookers at the Hotel Aletti bar, reputed to be the richest wage-earners in the city despite the ban on prostitution issued by military authorities in May.

Above it all, at high noon on July 4, 1943, on the Rue Michelet in the city's most fashionable neighborhood, a French military band tooted its way through the unfamiliar strains of "The Star-Spangled Banner." Behind the woodwinds and the tubas rose the lime-washed Moorish arches and crenellated tile roof of the Hôtel St. Georges, headquarters for Allied forces in North Africa. Palm fronds stirred in the courtyard, and the scent of bougainvillea carried on the light breeze.

Vice Admiral Henry Kent Hewitt held his salute as the anthem dragged to a ragged finish. Eisenhower, also frozen in salute on Hewitt's right, had discouraged all national celebrations as a distraction from the momentous work at hand, but the British had insisted on honoring their American cousins with a short ceremony. The last strains faded and the gunfire began. Across the flat roofs of the lower city and the magnificent crescent of Algiers Bay, Hewitt saw a gray puff rise from H.M.S. *Maidstone,* then heard the first report. Puff followed puff, boom followed boom, echoing against the hills, as the *Maidstone* fired seaward across the breakwater.

Nineteen, twenty, twenty-one. Hewitt lowered his salute, but the bombardment continued, and from the corner of his eye the admiral could see Eisenhower with his right hand still glued to his peaked khaki cap. Unlike the U.S. Navy, with its maximum twenty-one-gun tribute, the Army on Independence Day fired forty-eight guns, one for each state, a protocol now observed by *Maidstone*'s crew. Hewitt resumed his salute until the shooting stopped, and made note of yet another difference between the sister services.

With the ceremony at an end, Hewitt hurried through the courtyard and across the lobby's mosaic floor to his office, down the corridor from Eisenhower's corner suite. Every nook of the St. Georges was jammed with staff officers and communications equipment. Eight months earlier, on the eve of the invasion of North Africa, Allied plans had called for a maximum of seven hundred officers to man the Allied Forces Headquarters, or AFHQ, a number then decried by one commander as "two or three times too many."

Now the figure approached four thousand, including nearly two hundred colonels and generals; brigades of aides, clerks, cooks, and assorted horse-holders brought the AFHQ total to twelve thousand. The military messages pouring in and out of Algiers via seven undersea cables were equivalent to two-thirds of the total War Department communications traffic. No message was more momentous than the secret order issued this morning: "Carry out Operation HUSKY."

Hewitt had never been busier, not even before Operation TORCH, the assault on North Africa. Then he had commanded the naval task force ferrying Patton's thirty thousand troops from Virginia to Morocco, a feat of such extraordinary success—not a man had been lost in the hazardous crossing—that Hewitt received his third star and command of the U.S. Navy's Eighth Fleet in the Mediterranean. After four months at home, he had arrived in Algiers on March 15, and every waking moment since had been devoted to scheming how to again deposit Patton and his legions onto a hostile shore.

He was a fighting admiral who did not look the part, notwithstanding the Navy Cross on his summer whites, awarded for heroism as a destroyer captain in World War I. Sea duty made Hewitt plump, or plumper, and in Algiers he tried to stay fit by riding at dawn with native spahi cavalrymen, whose equestrian lineage dated to the fourteenth-century Ottomans. Despite these efforts, his frame remained, as one observer acknowledged, "well-upholstered." At the age of fifty-six, the former altar boy and bell ringer from Hackensack, New Jersey, was still proud of his ability to ring out "Softly Now the Light of Day." He loved double acrostic puzzles and his Keuffel & Esser Log Log Trig slide rule, a device that had been developed at the Naval Academy in the 1930s when he chaired the mathematics department there. His virtues, inconspicuous only to the inattentive, included a keen memory, a willingness to make decisions, and the ability to get along with George Patton. *The Saturday Evening Post* described Hewitt as "the kind of man who keeps a dog but does his barking himself"; in fact, he rarely even growled. He was measured and reserved, a good if inelegant conversationalist, and a bit pompous. He liked parties, and in Algiers he organized a Navy dance combo called the Scuttlebutt Five. He also had established a soup kitchen for the poor with leavings from Navy galleys; he ate the first bowl himself. Two other attributes served his country well: he was lucky, and he had an exceptional sense of direction, which on a ship's bridge translated into a gift for navigation. Kent Hewitt always knew where he was.

He called for his staff car—among those privileged vehicles exempt from impoundment—and drove from the St. Georges through the twisting alleyways leading to the port. At every pier around the grand crescent of the bay, ships were moored two and three deep: freighters and frigates, tankers and transports, minesweepers and landing craft. Others rode at anchor beyond the harbor's submarine nets, protected by patrol planes and destroyers tacking along the coastline. The U.S. Navy had thirty-three camouflage combinations, from "painted false bow wave" to "graded system with splotches," and most seemed to be represented in the vivid Algiers anchorage. Stevedores swarmed across the decks; booms swung from dock to hold and back to dock again; gantry cranes hoisted pallet after pallet from the wharves onto the vessels. Precautions against fire were in force on every ship: wooden chairs, drapes, excess movie film, even bulkhead pictures had been removed; rags and blankets were ashore or well stowed; sailors—who upon departure would don long-sleeved undershirts as protection against flash burns—had chipped away all interior paint and stripped the linoleum from every mess deck.

Hewitt's flagship, the attack transport U.S.S. *Monrovia*, lay moored on the port side of berth 39, on the Mole de Passageurs in the harbor's Basin de Vieux. Scores of military policemen had boarded for added security, making her desperately overcrowded. Ten to twenty officers packed each cabin on many ships, with enlisted bunks stacked four high, and *Monrovia* was more jammed than most. With Hewitt's staff, Patton's staff, and her own crew, she now carried fourteen hundred men, more than double her normal company. She would also carry, in some of those cargo nets being manhandled into the hold, 200,000 rounds of high-explosive ammunition and 134 tons of gasoline.

The admiral climbed from his car and strode up the gangplank, greeted with a bosun's piping and a flurry of salutes. *Monrovia*'s passageways seemed dim and cheerless after the brilliant African light. In the crowded operations room below, staff officers pored over "Naval Operations Order HUSKY," a tome four inches thick. Twenty typists had needed seven full days to bang out the final draft, of which eight hundred copies were distributed to commanders across North Africa as a blueprint for the coming campaign.

Hewitt could remember his father, a burly mechanical engineer, chinning himself with a hundred-pound dumbbell balanced across his feet. Sometimes the HUSKY ops order felt like that dumbbell. Nothing was simple about the operation except the basic concept: in six days, on July 10, two armies—one American and one British—would land on the southeast coast of Sicily, reclaiming for the Allied cause the first significant acreage in Europe since the war began. An estimated 300,000 Axis troops defended the island, including a pair of capable German divisions, and many others lurked nearby on the Italian mainland.

More than three thousand Allied ships and boats, large and small, were gathering for the invasion from one end of the Mediterranean to the other—"the most gigantic fleet in the world's history," as Hewitt observed. About half would sail under his command from six ports in Algeria and Tunisia; the rest would sail with the British from Libya and Egypt, but for a Canadian division coming directly from Britain. Patton's Seventh Army would land eighty thousand troops in the assault; the British Eighth Army would land about the same, with more legions subsequently reinforcing both armies.

Under the elaborate nautical choreography required, several convoys had already begun steaming: the vast expedition would rendezvous at sea, near Malta, on July 9. A preliminary effort to capture the tiny fortified island of Pantelleria, sixty miles southwest of Sicily, had succeeded admirably: after a relentless three-week air bombardment, the stupefied garrison of eleven thousand Italian troops had surrendered on June 11, giving the Allies both a good airfield and the illusion that even the stoutest defenses could be reduced from the air.

A map of the Mediterranean stretched across a bulkhead in the operations room. Hewitt had become the U.S. Navy's foremost amphibious expert, with one invasion behind him and another under way; three more were to come before war's end. One inviolable rule in assaults from the open sea, he already recognized, was that the forces to be landed always exceeded the means to transport them, even with an armada as enormous as this one. From hard experience he also knew that two variables remained outside his control: the strength of the enemy defending the hostile shore and the caprice of the sea itself.

In HUSKY, not only did he have three times more soldiers to put ashore than in Operation TORCH, he also commanded a flotilla of vessels seeing combat for the first time: nine new variations of landing craft and five new types of landing ship, including the promising LST, an abbreviation for "landing ship, tank," but which sailors insisted meant "large slow target." Some captains and crews had never been to sea before, and little was known about the seaworthiness of the new vessels, or how best to beach them, or what draught they would draw under various loads, or even how many troops and vehicles could be packed inside.

Much had been learned from the ragged, chaotic preparations for TORCH. Much had also been forgotten, or misapplied, or misplaced. The turmoil in North Africa in recent weeks seemed hardly less convulsive than that at Hampton Roads eight months earlier. Seven different directives on how to label overseas cargo had been issued the previous year; the resulting confusion led to formation of the inevitable committee, which led to another directive called the Schenectady Plan, which led to color-coded labels lacquered onto shipping containers, which led to more confusion. Five weeks after issuing a secret alert called Preparations for Movement by Water, the Army discovered that units crucial to HUSKY had never received the order and thus had no plans for loading their troops, vehicles, and weapons onto the convoys. Seventh Army's initial load plans also neglected to make room for the Army Air Forces, whose kit equaled a third of the Army's total tonnage requirements. Every unit pleaded for more space; every unit claimed priority; every unit lamented the Navy's insensitivity.

Despite the risk of German air raids, port lights burned all night as vexed loadmasters received still more manifest changes that required unloading another freighter or repacking another LST. Transportation officers wrestled with small oversights—the Navy had shipped bread ovens but no bread pans—and big blunders, as when ordnance officers mistakenly sent poisonous mustard gas to the Mediterranean. By the time Patton's staff recognized that particular gaffe, on June 8, gas shells had been shipped with other artillery munitions; they now lay somewhere—no one knew precisely where—in the holds of one or more ships bound for Sicily.

Secrecy was paramount. Hewitt doubted that three thousand vessels could sneak up on Sicily, but HUSKY's success relied on surprise. All documents that disclosed the invasion destination were stamped with the classified code word BIGOT, and sentries at the HUSKY planning headquarters in Algiers determined whether visitors held appropriate security clearances by asking if they were "bigoted." ("I was frequently partisan," one puzzled naval officer replied, "but had never considered my mind closed.")

Soldiers and sailors, as usual, remained in the dark and subject to severe restrictions on their letters home. A satire of censorship regulations read to one ship's crew included rule number 4—"You cannot say where you were, where you are going, what you have been doing, or what you expect to do"—and rule number 8—"You cannot, you must not, be interesting." The men could, under rule number 2, "say you have been born, if you don't say where or why." And rule number 9 advised: "You can mention the fact that you would not mind seeing a girl."

One airman tried to comply with the restrictions by writing, "Three days ago we were at X. Now we are at Y." But the prevailing sentiment was best captured by a soldier who told his diary, "We know we are headed for trouble."

More than half a million American troops now occupied North Africa. They composed only a fraction of all those wearing U.S. uniforms worldwide, yet in identity and creed they were emblematic of that larger force. One Navy lieutenant listed the civilian occupations of the fifteen hundred soldiers and sailors on his Sicily-bound ship: "farm boys and college graduates . . . lawyers, brewery distributors, millworkers, tool designers, upholsterers, steel workers, aircraft mechanics, foresters, journalists, sheriffs, cooks and glass workers." One man even cited "horse mill fixer" as his trade.

Fewer than one in five were combat veterans from the four U.S. divisions that had fought extensively in Tunisia: the 1st, 9th, and 34th Infantry Divisions, and the 1st Armored Division, each of which was earmarked for Sicily or, later, for mainland Italy. "The front-line soldier I knew," wrote the correspondent Ernie Pyle, who trudged with them across Tunisia, "had lived for months like an animal, and was a veteran in the fierce world of death. Everything was abnormal and unstable in his life."

In the seven weeks since the Tunisian finale, those combat troops had tried to recuperate while preparing for another campaign. "The question of discipline has been very difficult," the 1st Armored Division commander warned George Marshall. "There is a certain lawlessness . . . and a certain amount of disregard for consequences when men are about to go back." In the 34th Division, "the men did not look well and seemed indifferent," a visiting major general noted on June 15. Among other indignities, a thousand men had no underwear and five thousand others had but a single pair. "They felt very sorry for themselves," he added. Thirteen hundred soldiers from the 34th had just been transferred to units headed straight for Sicily, leading to "incidents of self-maiming and desertion." A captain in the 1st Division wrote home, "Too much self-commiseration, that is something we all must guard against."

Even among the combat veterans, few considered themselves professional soldiers either by training or by temperament. Samuel Hynes, a fighter pilot who later became a university professor, described the prevalent "civilianness, the sense of the soldiering self as a kind of impostor." They were young, of course—twenty-six, on average—and they shared a sense that "our youth had at last reached the place to spend itself," in the words of a bomber pilot, John Muirhead.

They had been shoveled up in what Hynes called "our most democratic war, the only American war in which a universal draft really worked, [and] men from every social class went to fight." Even the country's most elite tabernacles had been dumped into a single egalitarian pot, the U.S. Army: of the 683 graduates from the Princeton University class of 1942, 84 percent were in uniform, and those serving as enlisted men included the valedictorian and salutatorian. Twenty-five classmates would die during the war, including nineteen killed in combat. "Everything in this world had stopped except war," Pyle wrote, "and we were all men of a new profession out in a strange night."

And what did they believe, these soldiers of the strange night? "Many men do not have a clear understanding of what they are fighting for," a morale survey concluded in the summer of 1943, "and they do not know their role in the war." Another survey showed that more than one-third had never heard of Roosevelt's Four Freedoms, and barely one in ten soldiers could name all four. In a secret letter to his commanders that July, Eisenhower lamented that "less than half the enlisted personnel questioned believed that they were more useful to the nation as soldiers than they would have been as war workers," and less than one-third felt "ready and anxious to get into the fighting." The winning entry in a "Why I'm Fighting" essay contest declared, in its entirety: "I was drafted."

Their pervasive "civilianness" made them wary of martial zeal. "We were not romantics filled with cape-and-sword twaddle," wrote John Mason Brown, a Navy Reserve lieutenant headed to Sicily. "The last war was too near for that." Military life inflamed their ironic sensibilities and their skepticism. A single crude acronym that captured the soldier's lowered expectations—SNAFU, for "situation normal, all fucked up"—had expanded into a vocabulary of GI cynicism: SUSFU (situation unchanged, still fucked up); SAFU (self-adjusting fuck-up); TARFU (things are really fucked up); FUMTU (fucked up more than usual); JANFU (joint Army-Navy fuck-up); JAAFU (joint Anglo-American fuck-up); FUAFUP (fucked up and fucked up proper); and FUBAR (fucked up beyond all recognition).

Yet they held personal convictions that were practical and profound. "We were prepared to make all sacrifices. There was nothing else for us to do," Lieutenant Brown explained. "The leaving of our families was part of our loving them." The combat artist George Biddle observed, "They want to win the war so they can get home, home, home, and never leave it." A soldier in the 88th Division added, "We have got to lick those bastards in order to get out of the Army."

The same surveys that worried Eisenhower revealed that the vast majority of troops held at least an inchoate belief that they were fighting to "guarantee democratic liberties to all peoples." A reporter sailing to Sicily with the 45th Division concluded, "Many of the men on this ship believe that the operation will determine whether this war will end in a stalemate or whether it will be fought to a clear-cut decision." And no one doubted that come the day of battle, they would fight to the death for the greatest cause: one another. "We did it because we could not bear the shame of being less than the man beside us," John Muirhead wrote. "We fought because he fought; we died because he died."

A later age would conflate them into a single, featureless demigod, possessed of mythical courage and fortitude, and animated by a determination to rebalance a wobbling world. Keith Douglas, a British officer who had fought in North Africa and would die at Normandy, described "a gentle obsolescent breed of heroes. . . . Unicorns, almost." Yet it does them no disservice to recall their profound diversity in provenance and in character, or their feet of clay, or the mortality that would make them compelling long after their passing.

Captain George H. Revelle, Jr., of the 3rd Infantry Division, in a letter to his wife written while bound for Sicily, acknowledged "the chiselers, slackers, people who believe we are suckers for the munitions makers, and all the intellectual hodgepodge looking at war cynically." In some measure, he wrote on July 7, he was "fighting for their right to be hypocrites."

But there was also a broader reason, suffused with a melancholy nobility. "We little people," Revelle told her, "must solve these catastrophes by mutual slaughter, and force the world back to reason."

Across the great southern rim of the Mediterranean they staged for battle, the farm boys and the city boys, the foresters and the steelworkers and at least one horse mill fixer. Much of the American effort centered in Oran, two hundred miles west of Algiers on the old Pirate Coast, where billboards above the great port now advertised Coca-Cola and Singer sewing machines. Two of the five U.S. Army divisions that would participate in the HUSKY assault mustered in Oran. The 2nd Armored Division had begun loading on June 21 after traveling five hundred miles by rail across the Atlas Mountains from bivouacs in Morocco, where locust swarms had dimmed the sun and training began at four A.M. to avoid the midday heat: temperatures could reach 140 degrees inside a tank. Only a hundred flatcars in all of North Africa were sufficiently sturdy to carry a thirty-two-ton M-4 Sherman, and the division's journey had taken a month; the erratic French colonial rail system so enraged one captain that he forced the engineer at gunpoint to keep moving.

Among HUSKY units, the 45th Infantry Division, comprising 21,000 soldiers in 19 ships, plus 46,000 tons of equipment—including 4 million maps—in 18 others, was unique in sailing directly from Hampton Roads to Sicily, with a one-week stop in Oran. Its embarkation in Virginia on June 8 had been beset by the usual SNAFUs, TARFUs, and JANFUs: a frantic, last-minute plea to the War Department for mine detectors; the diaspora of an engineer battalion across all nineteen troopships; and the stunned realization that the Army landing craft crewmen with whom the division had trained for weeks on the Chesapeake Bay had been abruptly ordered to the Pacific, to be replaced by Navy crews unfamiliar with both the 45th Division and the boats they were to man. Also, by the time the nineteenth ship slipped her lines, AWOLs had become so numerous that one regimental stockade was dubbed Company J, for jailbird. Still, the passage was pleasant enough: Red Cross girls passing out paper cups of iced tea; "Happy Hour" boxing matches on the weather deck; messboys dancing on the fantail as steward's mates beat time with their hands on the taffrail; afternoon naps in lifeboats swaying from their davits. One officer played classical music over his ship's public address system; when the contralto Marian Anderson sang "Ave Maria," a sailor remarked: "God, but isn't it good to hear a woman's voice again?"

The 45th was a National Guard division, among eighteen that had been federalized early in the war. Some Regular Army officers sneered that "NG" stood for "no good," and most of the Guard's senior officers had been purged by the War Department for age or incompetence. But the Pentagon considered the 45th—known as the Thunderbirds—"better prepared than any division that has left our control to date." They were westerners, with one regiment derived from Colorado mining camp militias like the Wolftown Guards and the Queen's Emerald Rifles. Two other regiments hailed from Oklahoma, and their ranks included nearly two thousand Indians from fifty-two tribes, including Cherokee, Apache, Kiowa, Comanche, and Navajo. On the night before the departure from Virginia, an artillery captain had organized a spirited war dance around a roaring council fire.

Now their week in Oran was up and the Thunderbirds shuffled back to the ships, at least a few emerging from the red-light district known as Chancre Alley. "I know I have a fighting outfit," said their commander, Major General Troy H. Middleton. "I can tell that from the provost marshal's report." Up the gangplanks they trudged; at the top each man received a life vest and a tiny bottle of brandy against seasickness. Finance officers brought aboard $2 million for the division payroll, drawn from the Bank of Oran; when a sack stuffed with ten thousand dimes burst and scattered coins across the deck, a quick-thinking officer called the troops to attention while paymasters crawled around the immobilized soldiers, scooping up coins.

Along with the money and the ninety tons of maps, stevedores had loaded two hundred Silver Stars, six thousand Purple Hearts, and four thousand other decorations for valor; in the coming months those medals proved but a down payment on the courage required of the 45th. As the ships began to warp away from the Oran piers on the afternoon of July 4, some soldiers pulled out bricks to use as whetstones: General Patton had inspected the division a few days earlier and declared their bayonets too dull for the harsh work ahead.

Three hundred and forty crow-flying miles east of Algiers, more U.S. legions prepared for battle in the treeless flats around Lake Bizerte, a shallow bay south of Tunisia's second-largest city. In early May, the retreating Germans had scuttled a dozen ships atop one another like jackstraws across the bay's narrow neck; Navy salvage divers for weeks trisected the sunken vessels with saws and acetylene torches, then dynamited the sandy bottom beneath the hulks to blow the wreckage *down* and reopen the channel.

Now Lake Bizerte presented "a solid forest of masts": LSTs and LSIs (landing ship, infantry) and LCTs (landing craft, tank) and the eleven other species of amphibious vessels. Ancient French hydroplanes and rusting scows, destroyed in the Tunisian campaign, lay half submerged along the shore, cluttering the waterway so that cumbersome landing craft routinely "ran into sunken ships, each other, on the rocks, and into anchored vessels," one witness reported. Popular doggerel held that "Poems are made by fools like me, / But only God can steer an LST." Luftwaffe raiders sometimes sneaked across the Sicilian Strait before dawn, waking the sleeping camps but rarely inflicting much damage. Alarms wailed, smoke generators churned out a thick gray blanket to hide the ships, and searchlight batteries impaled the planes on their beams as hundreds of antiaircraft guns threw up fountains of fire around the lake. Those on deck sheltered under the lifeboats from the spent fragments that fell like steel hail. On other occasions, German propaganda flights showered Tunisian villages with leaflets: "The day has come to fight against the Anglo-Americans and the Jews. . . . Bring up your children to hate them."

Here had gathered three of the Army's most celebrated units: the 1st and 3rd Infantry Divisions, and, farther south near Kairouan, the 82nd Airborne Division. In a scheme that would be replicated before Normandy, troops were assigned to areas coded by state and city: a regiment might bivouac in "Florida," with battalions at Miami, Daytona, and Jacksonville, or in "Texas," at Houston, Dallas, and Fort Worth.

None of the namesake camps were as pleasant as their originals. At first light the Arab vendors appeared, selling lemonade, or "wog wine," or haircuts, or ceramic "Roman" vases. By midmorning the heat was beastly, with Saharan winds "like a wall of fire" and tepid drinking water sprinkled with peppermint to make it palatable. Flies and mosquitoes infested the straddle-trench latrines and the mess tents where cooks made hash for tens of thousands on captured German field ranges. Commanders tried to occupy their men with morning hikes or full-contact volleyball. Anglers in the 19th Combat Engineers dropped half-pound blocks of TNT in Lake Bizerte, collecting enough belly-up fish in two hours to feed nearly two hundred men. Officers in the 82nd Airborne bought ten young bulls, a flock of sheep, and four thousand liters of beer for a preinvasion barbecue.

They were in an ugly mood, spoiling for a fight. Paratrooper marksmen "have practiced on some menacing looking Arabs," Colonel James M. Gavin, who commanded a regiment in the 82nd, wrote his daughter. "It makes [the Arabs] mad to get shot and we should stop it." Dummy tents and phony radio transmitters began to appear in Florida and Texas and Virginia and Kentucky, as the troops were trucked company by company to loading points around the lake. Herded by bellowing sergeants, they shuffled aboard the LSTs and LSIs and LCTs, every soldier's identity checked against a cumbersome passenger list; eight clerks assigned to each convoy kept twenty-three copies of the manifests, and a typical convoy—for reasons known only at echelons above reason—required more than six thousand pages of names.

Congestion and confusion remained the order of the day: truck drivers took wrong turns; sailors removed cargo from overloaded vessels only to have soldiers stow it back aboard; an ammunition dump caught fire, and flames jumped the firebreaks to consume two thousand tons of munitions in a spectacular series of explosions; novice boat crews fouled their anchors, and shouted curses carried across the water as they tried to free themselves with chains and hawsers and grappling hooks.

No wrong turn or fouled anchor could stop them, of course. Brute-force momentum—and ingenuity, and willfulness—had carried them this far and would carry them farther. One by one the vessels moved into the lake and assembled into color-coded convoys. Sweating soldiers settled belowdecks or found a patch of topside shade. Gazing north toward the open Mediterranean, they packed away their newly issued sulfa powder and battle dressings, wondering precisely where in this world they would need such things.

Still farther east the British made ready, from Benghazi to Haifa and Beirut. Eighth Army had fought across North Africa in various guises since 1940 and now resembled, one admirer wrote, "a vast gypsy camp on the move, or a tribal migration." Snatches of Arabic seeded the soldiers' palaver, notably *maleesh*, "no matter," and *bardin*, "in a little while." Many wore a mauve ointment on their arms and faces as treatment for septic desert sores caused by prolonged exposure to dust and sand. War weariness also afflicted them—no ointment could soothe three years of fighting. One soldier confessed to "some disintegration of corporate purpose," a state of affairs given voice by the drunken veterans who strode through their battalion encampments barking, "Fuck the bloody fuckers, we're doing no more fucking fighting."

But fight they would, *bardin*. One armada gathered in the northern Gulf of Suez, with regiments such as the Dorsets and Devons and Hampshires aboard, respectively, the former liners *Strathnaver, Keren,* and *Otranto*. White-coated Indian waiters served four-course dinners and the men sang nostalgic Edwardian airs—"*Daisy, Daisy, give me your answer, do!*"— before cashing in their sterling for invasion currency. The fleet squeezed through the Suez Canal in early July, past sunken wrecks and the open-air cinemas at Ismailiya. At Port Said, one regimental history recorded, "a great bathing parade was ordered and all the troops were taken ashore to march through the town" to the beach, which soon was covered for miles with naked Tommies. The troops gathered "round a huge desert campfire, consuming as much beer as possible," then marched back to their ships behind kilted pipers in white spats and full skirl.

On July 5, the invasion armada assembled in the Mediterranean roads off the Egyptian coast. Some efforts to boost morale simply annoyed the men, for example the incessant playing of "The Boogie Woogie Bugle Boy of Company B" over the loudspeakers of the ship carrying the 2nd Inniskillings. Padres offered eve-of-battle prayers, asking a "special intercession . . . for the recapture of Europe." Signalmen in khaki shorts wigwagged their flags at departing ships from the quays at Tripoli and Alexandria. Sergeants hectored the men to take their antimalaria pills, prompting one soldier in the 1st Royal Tank Regiment to conclude, "Like fat cattle who are pampered to the very doors of the slaughterhouse, it was important that if and when we died we should be in good health."

Many regretted leaving Africa, where they had been "sleeping under great ripe stars." Here Eighth Army had found as much glory as perhaps could be found in modern war. Here, too, they would leave thousands of comrades in African graves. "Yet we went with light hearts," the tanker added, "for somewhere at the end of all this we could go home."

The *Monrovia* singled up her lines shortly after ten A.M. on Tuesday, July 6, heaved in the starboard anchor, and with the help of two tugs edged from the Basin de Vieux to the twelve-fathom line outside the Algiers port. To Kent Hewitt's chagrin, as the French harbor pilot stepped over *Monrovia*'s side to return to shore, he yelled, "Have a good trip to Sicily!" Counterintelligence officers ordered the pilot and his tug crews arrested and held incommunicado until the landings had begun.

Despite elaborate security precautions, Hewitt remained uncertain whether HUSKY's secrets still held. Sealed maps of Sicily and other classified documents had been delivered throughout the fleet by armed couriers, to be stored before sailing under lock and key. Not until the last minute were Italian-speaking interpreters sent to their respective Army units. Yet breaches had occurred; there was loose talk on the wharves, while on some ships the premature distribution had occurred of "The Soldier's Guide to Sicily," which featured a large silhouette of the island on the cover. A British officer in Cairo had even sent his gabardine uniform to be dry-cleaned with a notebook containing the HUSKY battle plan left in the pocket; security agents raided the shop and found that the incriminating pages had been torn out and used as scratch paper to write customer invoices.

As Hewitt paced *Monrovia*'s flag bridge, listening to the commotion of eight hundred men practicing abandon-ship drills, he had a thousand other details to contemplate besides whether the Germans knew he was coming. The fleet included twenty LSTs carrying ten thousand gallons of water each. Was that enough? Seventeen hospital ships had been sent to North Africa, of which five now sailed toward Sicily. Was *that* enough? Six hundred miles of African coastline and the sea approaches to Malta had been swept for mines. Were they completely clean? What about enemy submarines? Hewitt had lost several ships and 140 men to U-boats after the landings in Morocco the previous November, and the memory still pained him.

As for the eighty thousand soldiers now in his custody, Hewitt could only take comfort in his favorite maxim: You do everything you can, then you hope for the best. Disagreements with the Army, which had begun a year earlier during the preparations for TORCH, had continued during the HUSKY planning. Some frictions were petty: Army and Navy supply officers had jacked up Algerian warehouse prices by bidding against each other, and the Army insisted on calling *Monrovia* a headquarters ship when any fool knew it was a *flagship*. Hewitt had been astonished, a few days earlier, to find sentries posted on Patton's orders outside *Monrovia*'s operations room, barring access to the admiral's own staff—*that* indignity had soon been corrected. More troubling had been Patton's months-long refusal to move his headquarters from Mostaganem, nearly two hundred miles from Algiers; the distance had made joint planning more difficult.

Still, Hewitt and Patton had found common ground and even mutual affection. The formality of TORCH, when they addressed each other as "Admiral" and "General," had yielded to a more intimate "Kent" and "Georgie." Patton was ecumenical enough to occasionally side with the Navy, as in one recent dispute when Army planners—contrary to Hewitt's advice—proposed to slip troops onto the Sicilian beaches in rubber boats. "Sit down!" Patton had finally snapped at his officers. "The Navy is responsible for getting you ashore and they can put you ashore in any damned thing they want." To celebrate their final evening on land, Hewitt on Monday night had invited Patton and several other generals to dinner at the admiral's quarters, a villa requisitioned from a Danish vintner. After several hours of convivial drinking Hewitt helped the generals to the staff cars that would take them to their ships; more sober than most, Patton on his way out the door studied the risqué wall frescoes of half-nude women and muttered, "Thank God I live in a camp."

At five P.M. *Monrovia* signaled anchors aweigh and moved into the swept channel, surrounded by warships and landing craft of every description. Panic briefly seized the fleet when radar showed an apparent swarm of hostile planes; the blips proved to be the ships' own barrage balloons, hoisted on tethers to discourage dive-bombers and strafing fighters. Semaphores blinked out Morse messages and the convoy began zigzagging, as previously agreed, at ten knots under sailing pattern number 35.

The white vision of Algiers fell behind. Hewitt studied the African mountains to starboard. Iron oxide in the scree was fired bloodred by the setting sun as it plunged into the purple sea. He had done everything he could, and now he would hope for the best.

Behind the bridge, in *Monrovia*'s spacious flag cabin, George Patton felt the ship's screws gnaw the sea as she picked up speed. The Navy had tried to make him feel like a wanted guest, greeting him with incessant piping when he came aboard and assigning two mess boys as his personal attendants. The cabin, opulent by warship standards, measured eighteen by fifteen feet, with a desk, bunk, table, and shower. Still, Patton harbored private reservations about both the sister service—"The Navy is our weak spot," he told his diary—and Kent Hewitt: "very affable and in his usual mental fog."

He was ready for battle and looked the part, immaculate in his whipcord breeches and tailored blouse, the famous pistols holstered and near at hand. He had lost weight in the last few months by running and swimming, and improved his fighting trim by cutting back on both liquor and tobacco. For six weeks Patton had commanded American forces in Tunisia, following the debacle at Kasserine Pass and the sacking of the II Corps commander; since resuming his preparations for HUSKY in mid-April, he had pondered the checkered performance of U.S. troops and their officers. In a memo to his commanders in June, Patton offered twenty-seven tactical adages, distilled from the campaign experiences in Africa and thirty-six years in uniform. Number 7: "Always fire low"; number 13: "In mountain warfare, capture the heights and work downhill"; number 22: "In case of doubt, attack"; and his personal maxim, number 18: "Never take counsel of your fears."

Yet fears possessed him—of failure, of flinching under fire. The sickly California infant had grown into a shy and sensitive boy, and then "a timid man by nature," one of his oldest friends had noted on June 26 after seeing Patton in Mostaganem. Flamboyance compensated for his inner doubts, and provided the mask he believed a confident commander should wear. "I don't like the whine of bullets any more than I ever did," Patton wrote on July 1, "but they attract me just the same." His superior officer in 1928 had concluded that Patton "would be invaluable in time of war but a disturbing element in time of peace." Now his time had come. Patton himself had predicted as a young man, "Someday I will make them all know me." That day had also come.

In recent weeks he had traveled from camp to camp, preaching violence and transcendent duty. "Battle is the most magnificent competition in which a human being can indulge. It brings out all that is best. It removes all that is base," he told the 45th Division. To their officers he added, "You have a sacred trust to your men and to your country, and you are the lowest thing that lives if you are false to this trust."

At a large outdoor amphitheater in Algiers, he strode onstage to "Ruffles and Flourishes," his tunic ablaze with decorations. "There is no better death than to die in battle for a noble and glorious cause," he told the troops. As for the Army's policy against fraternization, he added, "That's bullshit. An army that can't fuck can't fight." The soldiers "howled, stamped [their] feet and whistled with approval," one medic reported. Such profane performances, an observer said, were intended "to toughen them, to blood them with language." In a letter on June 19, Patton's aide wrote, "He is a great hate builder, and believe me, when the time comes, the Axis boys are going to be very sorry to meet him."

Some GIs were already sorry. Upon discovering a 45th Division soldier asleep in a foxhole during a landing exercise, Patton jabbed the man in the ribs with his own rifle and bellowed, "You son of a bitch. You get out of there." During another exercise near Oran, Patton yelled, "Captain, get these men off the beach and onto their objective."

"But, sir," the officer replied, "I am a chaplain."

"I don't give a damn if you are Jesus Christ himself," Patton snapped, "get these men the hell off the beach."

To a dilatory officer outside Bizerte, Patton shouted, "You son of a bitch. When I tell you to come I want you to run." "Sir," the soldier said, "I resent being called a son of a bitch. I think you owe me an apology." Patton apologized and drove off. Such apologies were rare. "Chew them out and they'll remember it," he said. But if chastened soldiers remembered, so did his superiors. In late May, during a profane tirade against a squad of 1st Division infantrymen at Arzew, all within earshot of Eisenhower and the visiting George Marshall, one general whispered, "That temper of his is going to finish him yet."

But the caricature of a raging martinet failed to capture Patton's nuances. Few officers had studied the art of war with greater care. If he had virtually memorized G.F.R. Henderson's biography of Stonewall Jackson, that it was to answer the inner interrogatory "What would Jackson do?" Patton had earned his pilot's license to better understand air attacks, and he had mastered enough navigation to sail to Hawaii for a better comprehension of movement on the open sea, which resembled the open desert.

He also was a loving if sometimes wayward husband, and as H-hour drew near his thoughts were with his wife, Beatrice, whom he had known since they were sixteen. In many ways she was more than his equal, the sort of woman to whom he could write in early May: "Read up on Cromwell and send me some ideas." Intelligent and wealthy, she was an accomplished sailor and a successful novelist who gulped down a raw egg from a shot glass for breakfast before riding to hounds. He had proposed marriage, in the summer of 1909, by riding his own horse up the stairs and onto the terrace of her house; when her father objected to such a suitor, she feigned a hunger strike, deepening her pallor with rice powder until he relented. Of Georgie she had later written in her journal, "What a man. He is very great—[has] all the flash, and drama, and personality, and everything to back it up."

"I have no premonitions and hope to live forever," Patton had written Bea just before *Monrovia* sailed. In fact, he had intimations of the immortality that only glory could bring a battle captain. It awaited him, he sensed, in Sicily. "I believe in my fate," he told his diary, "and, to fulfill it, this show must be a success."

Patton had designed the last cavalry saber adopted by the Army, a straight, double-edged weapon of thrust. The blade embodied the man. "If you charge hard enough at death," he claimed, "it will get out of your way." Shortly before boarding the *Monrovia*, he summoned his generals to a final conference. At the end, with tears streaming down his cheeks, he dismissed them with a slash of his swagger stick. "I never want to see you bastards again," he roared, "unless it's at your post on the shores of Sicily."

\* \* \*

From east and west the convoys converged, gaining mass and momentum: here was Hewitt's "most gigantic fleet." Red and green navigation lights gleamed from horizon to horizon, reflected in the phosphorescence churned in a thousand wakes. The bright pellets of "flying elephants"— barrage balloons—floated overhead, and twin-tail P-38 escorts flew higher still.

At last the troops learned their destination, and shipboard betting pools paid off the clairvoyant winners. "We are sailing to Sicily," the commander of the Oran convoy announced aboard U.S.S. *Ancon*. "We have bad news to deliver, but we are saving it this trip for Benito Mussolini." Men gathered on the weather deck to recite the Twenty-third Psalm. Seamen warned anxious landlubbers that jumping overboard during an air attack was pointless: the concussion from detonating bombs would rupture a swimmer's lungs and spleen at three hundred yards. Classicists tried to remember their Thucydides: few took comfort from his account of an Athenian expedition to Sicily twenty-five centuries earlier, in which the victors earned "the most brilliant of successes, the vanquished the most calamitous of defeats."

The *Monrovia* steamed past Bizerte harbor early on the morning of July 8. Now she zigzagged at 12½ knots, under sailing plan number 10, making for Cap Bon and the sea-lanes to Sicily. A squadron of British destroyers screened the seaward flank. Other ships sortied from the harbor to join the fleet threading the swept Tunisian War Channel. Atop Bizerte's battered custom house, an honor guard of American bluejackets and British tars stood at attention as the ships slid past. Sailors on the foredecks returned the salutes, then waved farewell. "Looking astern," one officer recorded, "there was another convoy even greater than ours, spread so far back it had the appearance of columns of marching ants, dots blurred by distance.

"It seemed," he added, "the whole world must be afloat."

## Calypso's Island

OVER the millennia, a great deal had happened on the tiny island the Allies now code-named FINANCE. St. Paul had been shipwrecked on the north coast of Malta in A.D. 60 while en route to stand trial in Rome for crimes against the state; he preached to the unconverted for three months, then continued on his fateful way. Successive waves of Vandals, Goths, Byzantines, Arabs, and Normans swept behind him, felling forests for farms and herds; the topsoil washed away to expose a parched, rocky knob, eight miles by eighteen. Some scholars believed that Malta was the place where the nymph Calypso had imprisoned wandering Odysseus as her love slave for seven years.

In 1530, Emperor Charles V garrisoned the island with the knights of Saint John of Jerusalem, a monastic order founded during the First Crusade and recently expelled from Rhodes by the Turks. After a siege, the Maltese knights spent years building complex battlements, with bastions and watchtowers and walls as much as thirty feet thick. Britain seized the fortress in 1800, taking also its fine harbor and the island's handsome capital, Valletta, built with ocher stone from local quarries. Most of the quarter million Maltese were illiterate peasants who scratched a living from the thin fields and pastures.

The first of 3,340 Axis air raids struck the island at dawn on June 11, 1940. During the next three years it became the most bombed place on earth, as the enemy tried to blast the British from their only harbor between Gibraltar and Alexandria and to neutralize the Maltese airfields, which expedited attacks on Axis supply convoys to North Africa. Some sixteen thousand tons of bombs fell on the island in attacks of exemplary viciousness: German pilots even heaved hand grenades from their cockpits. Valletta was reduced to ocher rubble, then to ocher powder. "Beauty was slain," wrote a Maltese poet, M. Mizzi, "and a great kingdom of terror was set up." More than beauty died: the number of casualties reached fifteen thousand. (Precise figures were elusive because it was common for families to conceal a fatality in order to keep drawing the victim's rations.) "Holy Mary," the Maltese prayed, "let the bombs fall in the sea or in the fields."

Those not killed or wounded simply suffered. Women prowled the wreckage after each raid in search of splintered furniture to burn as firewood. By July 1942, daily rations per person had been cut to four ounces of staples such as meat, fish, and cheese, and thirteen ounces of bread, often baked with sawdust filler. Newspapers printed articles on the virtues of "potato soup, potato puree, potato casserole." Public kitchens served "veal loaf," an odious confection of goat and horsemeat. The Maltese learned to live without soap, razor blades, toilet paper, shoelaces, or books. Contraceptives were fashioned from old inner tubes until people grew too exhausted for sex. To escape the bombs they used hand chisels to carve shelters from rock so obdurate that even experienced diggers rarely excavated more than eight inches a day. Maltese fishing boats called *dghajsa*s ferried food and kerosene from nearby islands, and on their return voyages carried off the dead for proper burial.

Thanks to the victory in North Africa, the first unopposed convoy since 1940 had reached the island on May 24, 1943. Food and other staples began to arrive, but Malta remained a gaunt, medieval wreck: sand flies swarmed in the ruins and white dust rose from every footfall. "Children, too thin and listless even to play in the bright sunshine, hung about the shabby, pitted streets," one visitor wrote. Valletta had not a single restaurant, and water flowed from the city's taps for only two hours in the morning and half an hour at night. Life in the British garrison was hardly easier, with beer rationed to a weekly pint, issued with "fifty inexpressibly foul Indian cigarettes." Axis bombers still pummeled the island; in the code used by Allied forces in early July, all BULLDOGS and UMPIRES (Americans and British) were advised to remain alert to POSTMAN TULIP AUCTION (German aircraft). Such jargon often drew the coded equivalent of a blank look: ICE-BERG (signal not understood).

For all its woes, FINANCE had the virtue of lying only fifty-five miles due south of HORRIFIED—Sicily—and on the late afternoon of July 8, the island's fortunes abruptly revived. "Everyone was on tiptoe with excitement," one British officer said, for at five P.M. General Eisenhower arrived to make Malta his headquarters.

Motorcyclists with numbers pinned to their backs guided the Allied commander's aircraft and escort planes to blast shelters along the runway. Eisenhower had left Algiers on July 6 to spend two days at his Tunisian command post before flying to Malta. To screen his movements, a dummy Allied Forces Headquarters in Oran began broadcasting simulated radio traffic; the staff cars sent to pick him up at the Valletta airfield bore no rank insignia on their bumpers. During the final approach to the island, Eisenhower had seen the feverish preparations for HUSKY along Dockyard Creek and French Creek at Grand Harbour, as well as the ambulance parking lot built on the jetties at St. Paul's Bay; Allied planners anticipated evacuating thirty thousand battle casualties from Sicily to North Africa, and Malta had been converted into a hospital port and medical way station. Eisenhower fingered the lucky coins—including a silver dollar, a French franc, and an English crown piece—that he always carried in a zippered purse when traveling.

The small convoy wound through ruined Valletta before climbing a hill outside town to the Verdala Palace, a square, moated castle with towers at each corner, built in 1586 as a summer home for the Maltese grand master. Escorted by his British hosts, Eisenhower wandered through the great hall and an immense banquet room, where biblical frescoes adorned the walls. Beneath the palace, hooks set into the walls of a dim oubliette still held rusting chains; the reporter John Gunther, who accompanied the commanding general, noted, "There are several rooms, dungeons, which the servants believe to be haunted, and which even today they will not enter." Climbing a spiral marble staircase—the risers were only two inches high so that Maltese priests could ride up the steps on mules shod with sandals—Eisenhower was shown to his bedroom, a magnificent chamber with a thirty-foot ceiling. A whitewashed back passage led to another dungeon. "I think it'll do," he said, with a flash of his now famous grin. "I'll have room enough."

Nine months earlier, Eisenhower had taken command in another British redoubt, at Gibraltar, on the eve of Operation TORCH, which he was chosen to command over 366 more senior U.S. officers. Since then, he had survived battlefield setbacks, political missteps, and his own inexperience to become the Allies' indispensable man. The "only man who could have made things work was Ike," Churchill's chief of staff, Lieutenant General Hastings Ismay, said after the war. "No one else."

Victory in North Africa had enhanced his stature and his self-confidence. Perhaps the lucky coins helped, but so too did hard work and a gift for square dealing. General Bernard L. Montgomery, who would command British forces in HUSKY, considered Eisenhower "the very incarnation of sincerity," with "the power of drawing the hearts of men towards him as a magnet attracts bits of metal." Another senior British general said, "He was utterly fair in his dealings, and I envied the clarity of his mind, and his power of accepting responsibility." He listened well, and spoke well. "I am bound to say," Churchill confided to a British colleague, "I have noticed that good generals do not usually have such good powers of expression as he has." Few could resist that infectious smile, and his physical vigor proved a tonic to others. "Always on the move," the reporter Drew Middleton noted. "Walking up and down, pacing patterns on the rug, his flat, harsh voice ejecting idea after idea like sparks flung from an emery wheel."

"I'm a born optimist," Eisenhower once said, "and I can't change that." He told his son, John, a cadet at West Point, that effective leadership could be learned by "studious reflection and practice. . . . You must be devoted to duty, sincere, fair, and cheerful." At times he could nitpick, grousing that "not one officer in fifty knows how to use the English language," and supposedly cashiering an aide for failing to master the distinction between "shall" and "will." Still, he remained humble and balanced despite having served seven years under a paragon of pretension, General Douglas MacArthur, whose refusal to ever acknowledge error and whose persistent references to himself in the third person baffled Eisenhower. Told that George Marshall proposed to nominate him for the Congressional Medal of Honor after TORCH, Eisenhower warned, "I would refuse to accept it." Just before leaving Algiers, he received a telegram from a publisher offering "at least $25,000" if he would allow any "nationally known writer" of his choosing to tell his story. "Too busy to be interested," Eisenhower replied.

His cosmology was simple. "You are fighting for the right to live as you please, providing you don't get in someone's hair," he told soldiers in Algiers on June 19. "We are fighting for liberty and the dignity of the human soul." He promised, if given the chance, to have Mussolini shot. "I'm not one who finds it difficult to hate my enemies." John Eisenhower, a shrewd observer of his father, noted that he pursued war with the same calculating intensity that made him an outstanding bridge and poker player, persuaded that "the Almighty would provide him with a decent set of cards. . . . He appeared not to share the metaphysical feeling that God owed him anything specific, such as good weather on a given day."

Yet as a field marshal he had built a spotty record in North Africa, and his aptitude remained unproven. "A coordinator rather than a commander," one British general wrote. Another asserted that "he was not a soldier, he was just a compromiser." Marshall believed he was so preoccupied with the politics of coalition warfare that "he had little or no opportunity to keep in touch with the troops." In truth, he lacked a great battle captain's endowments: to see the field both spatially and temporally; to intuit an opponent's intent; to subordinate all resistance to an iron will.

He was indeed a compromiser, a coordinator, but that was precisely what this war—this total, global war—required. Eisenhower had long recognized that in such an existential struggle the most robust coalition would likely prevail; he also intuited that centrifugal forces, from national pride to personal vainglory, threatened every alliance. He was a master of the sensible compromise, convinced that an Allied commander must lead by considering disparate national viewpoints "to solve problems through reasoning rather than by merely issuing commands." John Gunther had noted that "lots of Americans and British have an atavistic dislike of one another"; a senior British general warned General Brooke at the TRIDENT conference that "there is going to be grave risk of open quarrels unless someone can go round daily with a lubricating can." Eisenhower carried that can, and nearly everyone trusted him to apply it judiciously. His British political adviser, the future prime minister Harold Macmillan, considered Eisenhower "wholly uneducated in any normal sense of the word," yet "compared with the wooden heads and dessicated hearts of many British soldiers I see here, he is a jewel of broadmindedness and wisdom."

The long summer twilight lingered in the west when Eisenhower finished a pot of tea and emerged from Verdala Palace for the short ride to his command post. His stomach, he confided to an aide, felt like "a clenched fist." For two decades he had been plagued with intestinal ailments linked to stress, ever since the death of his elder son from scarlet fever in 1920.

Before the war he had been hospitalized repeatedly for enteritis and intestinal obstructions. (A disabling injury to his left knee in the 1912 West Point–Tufts football game had led to seven other hospitalizations.) A respiratory infection picked up at dank Gibraltar in November had never completely resolved, and Eisenhower's chain smoking—he was up to sixty or more Camels a day—was hardly salutary. Although he paid John $1.50 a week *not* to smoke at West Point, Eisenhower's habit had become so compulsive that he sometimes lit up in flight even when the crew of his B-17 Flying Fortress warned of gas fumes.

Cigarette in hand, he was escorted to the beetling walls above Grand Harbour. Landing craft and warships packed the port and inlets to the harbor's mouth at Fort St. Elmo. Tars scaled the superstructures on a pair of battleships—back at Malta for the first time in over two years—while Maltese waved from their precarious balconies above the docks; aboard H.M.S. *Nelson,* a band had been playing "Every Nice Girl Loves a Sailor." Eisenhower and his aides marched into the Lascaris Bastion, a tunnel complex originally dug by the Knights of Malta and now converted into a Royal Navy command post. Condensation glistened through whitewash on the limestone walls. Lascaris was bombproof, convenient, and wretched. Uniforms grew moldy in a day, and many staff officers suffered from lung afflictions or pappataci fever, passed by the biting sand flies. Portions of the citadel remained insufferably hot, while other chambers were so chilly that Eisenhower called for his overcoat. Even Admiral Andrew Browne Cunningham, the British naval commander in the Mediterranean who welcomed Eisenhower, conceded the place was "extremely smelly." Officers condemned to Lascaris fortified themselves at two o'clock each afternoon with gin and orange juice or banana cordials.

Eisenhower strode through Pinto Tunnel with Cunningham, past a gallery of sheds used by officers whose staff functions were denoted by cabalistic symbols scratched on their door placards. His own office measured fourteen by ten feet; the furnishings included a wicker chair and an oil stove burning next to a single table draped with a gray blanket. A rug tossed on the clay floor barely mitigated "a chill that had been gathering for four hundred years." Eisenhower found it hard to keep his cigarettes dry.

He shrugged off the discomfort and trailed Cunningham into a large war room with a forty-foot vaulted ceiling and enormous maps affixed to each wall. A twenty-by-thirteen-foot mosaic, compiled from five hundred photo reconnaissance missions, revealed all ten thousand square miles of Sicily. Gunther's jaw dropped at the cartographic display, and he marveled in his notebook at the "infinitude of detail, their extreme up-to-dateness, and the wonderful draftsmanship and lithography they represent. Have the Germans as good maps as these really super-maps, I wonder?"

Cunningham, his red-veined face florid above the white collar of his uniform, pointed out the colored lines that plotted the steaming Allied flotillas, from the Levant to the Pillars of Hercules. Collectively they represented 160,000 troops, 14,000 vehicles, and 1,800 guns aboard 3,000 vessels. Radio silence had been imposed across the fleets, the admiral added, so little was known about their progress except that three Canadian ships traveling from Scotland had been sunk by U-boats in the western Mediterranean; the Canadians had lost several dozen men, several dozen guns, five hundred trucks, and much of their communications gear. Under a relentless Allied air bombardment of Sicily—the detonations could be heard on Malta on quiet evenings—most surviving Axis planes had fled from the island to the Italian mainland. But precisely how alive the enemy was to the impending invasion was unknown. Cunningham cocked an eyebrow at the fancy maps, as if considering his favorite expression: "It's too velvet-arsed and Rolls-Royce for me." Son of an Edinburgh anatomy professor, Cunningham—who served as Eisenhower's chief naval deputy—had first come under fire in the Boer War, at age seventeen; now sixty, he remained fearless, pugnacious, and convinced that the optimum range in any fight was point-blank. Gunther noted that the underlids of his sailor's squint were "lined with bright red, like a bulldog's."

Eisenhower studied the central Mediterranean. Sicily, a triangular rock the size of Vermont, lay ninety miles north of Tunisia and only two miles off the toe of the Italian boot. Its eastern end was dominated by Mount Etna, an active volcano ten thousand feet high and twenty miles in diameter. "The coast is everywhere scalloped with wide, sweeping bights separated from each other by capes," an Allied terrain study noted. AFHQ planners had contemplated every inch of that three-hundred-mile coastline, scrutinizing thirty-two beaches as potential landing sites. Sicily had been overrun by even more successive invaders than Malta had endured: Greeks, Romans, Vandals, Ostrogoths, Byzantines, Saracens, Normans, Spaniards, Bourbons. And soon, the Anglo-Americans. "Sicily in all ages seems to have taught only catastrophe and violence," the American writer Henry Adams observed. "For a lesson in anarchy . . . Sicily stands alone and defies evolution."

An amphibious landing on a hostile shore, Eisenhower knew, was the hardest operation in warfare: wading ashore under fire, building a secure lodgement beyond the beach, then breaking free to the interior. In the long history of combat, the amphibious art had been mastered by no one. For every successful landing—such as the American assault at Vera Cruz in

1847—there was an equivalent catastrophe, like the British debacle at Gallipoli in 1915. For every failure—as of the Spanish Armada, or the Mongols in Japan—there was a military leader too daunted even to try, including Napoleon and Hitler, both of whom declined to cross the English Channel.

If amphibious warfare was inherently difficult, the Allies seemed determined to make it harder. The Combined Chiefs had ordered Eisenhower to begin planning HUSKY on January 23; initial schemes focused on seizing Sicilian ports and airfields, with the intent of putting ten divisions ashore within a week of the first assault. Yet he and his lieutenants remained distracted by the Tunisian campaign; their various headquarters were so far-flung—from Cairo to Rabat—that couriers shuttled more than two thousand miles every day, delivering documents, maps, and messages. The main planning cell occupied the unheated *école normale* outside Algiers, where officers typed with their gloves on.

Eisenhower in March and again in April warned that HUSKY would fail if the landing forces encountered "well-armed and fully organized German forces," which he defined as "more than two divisions." The British chiefs in London accused him of "grossly exaggerating" enemy strength, and Churchill sputtered with indignation at "these pusillanimous and defeatist doctrines. . . . What Stalin would think of this, when he has 185 German divisions on his front I cannot imagine." Duly chastened, Eisenhower forwarded a plan under which British troops invaded Sicily's southeast coast to seize the ports at Augusta and Syracuse, while the Americans landed in the west to take Palermo.

This drew unexpected fire from Eisenhower's flank. The Eighth Army commander, Bernard Montgomery, had resisted involvement in HUSKY planning while he was occupied with the Tunisian campaign: "Let's finish this show first," he snapped. When he eventually turned his attention to Sicily, Montgomery spread a large map of the island on the floor of his bedroom and mused aloud, "Well, now let's see how it would suit us for this battle to go?"

The existing plan suited him not at all, and he promptly shoved a spanner in the works. "It has no hope of success and should be completely recast," Montgomery declared. Falsely claiming that AFHQ planners had assumed that "opposition will be slight"—in fact, they presumed stiff resistance—Montgomery condemned all such "wooly thinking" and warned, "Never was there a greater error." By late April, he was in full throat, forecasting "a first-class military disaster. . . . I am prepared to carry the war into HORRIFIED with the Eighth Army but must do so in my own way." To his superiors, he proposed sliding Patton's Seventh Army under his command; to his diary he was even blunter: "I should run HUSKY."

Rather than divide the force, Montgomery argued, the attack should consolidate on the southeast coast, where American and British divisions could lend mutual support. With the invasion only two months away and the Combined Chiefs about to meet at the TRIDENT conference in Washington, Eisenhower convened another planning conference in Algiers on May 2. Over a lobster lunch—the lobsters cost AFHQ a thousand francs each—Montgomery pressed his point, then followed Eisenhower's chief of staff, Lieutenant General Walter B. "Beetle" Smith, into the men's latrine to continue the argument, first from an adjacent urinal and then with arrows sketched on a steamed mirror. "The Americans," a senior British staff officer, Lieutenant General Sir Charles Gairdner, told his diary, "are beginning to feel that the British Empire is being run by Monty."

A day later, Eisenhower broke the deadlock and accepted the Montgomery plan, shrugging off protests from Admiral Cunningham and others who preferred naval dispersion and the seizure of more airfields. Patton rebuffed Kent Hewitt's plea that he also contest the revised plan since American forces would no longer have the quick use of Palermo's port. "No, goddammit," Patton replied. "I've been in this Army thirty years and when my superior gives me an order I say, 'Yes, sir!' and then do my goddamnedest to carry it out."

To his diary, General Gairdner confessed, "I can't understand how democracies wage war."

HUSKY now called for seven divisions—four British and three American—landing abreast across a hundred-mile span of southeastern Sicily. The seaborne force would also be preceded by portions of two airborne divisions, a wrinkle that required attacking in the second quarter of the July moon when it would be light enough for paratroopers to see but dark enough to cloak the approaching armada. Thirteen Allied divisions ultimately would be committed to the invasion.

Of the 300,000 Axis troops defending Sicily, the bulk were in Italian units of doubtful pluck. One American intelligence officer described the two German divisions as "strictly hot mustard"; as for the Italians, "Stick them in the belly and sawdust will run out." Thanks to Ultra, the extraordinary British ability to intercept and decipher coded German radio traffic, Eisenhower knew a great deal about his enemy's strength and disposition. An Ultra team—those admitted to the great secret were said to be "bathed in the blood of the lamb"—was at his disposal on Malta, as well as in Algiers. Since first breaking a radio message encrypted with a German Enigma machine in 1940, Ultra cryptologists at Bletchley Park, north of London, had intercepted and broken thousands of messages to provide "a panoramic knowledge of the German forces." By mid-1944 nearly fifty separate Enigma codes would be deciphered, including a new German army code called Albatross that had just been broken on June 2, and others named Hyena, Seahorse, Woodpecker, and Puffin.

Eisenhower also knew that the Italian navy—the only substantial Axis naval force in the Mediterranean, with six battleships and eleven cruisers—lacked radar, fuel, and aircraft carriers. The Italian air force had lost 2,200 planes in the past eight months and had little sense of the Allies' whereabouts. "No one," an Italian admiral complained, "can play chess blindfolded." Not least, Eisenhower had a good sense of Italy's social disintegration under the pressures of war and Allied bombing: coal and food shortages, labor strikes, rail disruptions, even a profound lack of lightbulbs.

What Eisenhower did not know was how vigorously the Italians would fight for their homeland, or whether the Germans—who were believed capable of shipping an additional division of reinforcements to Sicily every three days—would fight to the death for an arid island a thousand miles from the Fatherland. Even Ultra could not see that deeply into the enemy's soul.

The Combined Chiefs had approved the detailed HUSKY plan on May 12. Yet a feeling lingered in Washington and London that the scheme lacked bravura and that the Allies were missing a chance to exploit their triumph in North Africa. For his troubles, Eisenhower received another rebuke. "Your planners and mine may be too conservative," George Marshall told him; they lacked the audacity that "won great victories for Nelson and Grant and Lee."

Marshall was right. HUSKY would be the largest amphibious operation of World War II—the seven divisions in the assault wave were two more than would land at Normandy eleven months later—but it lacked imaginative dash. Preoccupied with Tunisia, commanders lost sight of the larger objective: to seal the Strait of Messina, preventing Axis reinforcement of Sicily and forestalling an Axis escape to the Italian mainland. Amphibious doctrine stressed the capture of ports and airfields to the exclusion of the battle beyond the dunes, and the final HUSKY plan petered out twenty miles past the landing beaches.

A "terrible inflexibility" characterized all big amphibious enterprises, in Beetle Smith's phrase. Fitting the pieces together, getting from here to there, synchronizing the attack—these tasks absorbed enormous concentration and effort, leaving little time to consider the battle beyond the shingle. HUSKY also included the first sizable Allied airborne attack of the war. And Montgomery's revised plan meant that the Americans, lacking a port, would have to sustain a combat army over the beaches in ways never before attempted.

The die was cast, audacious or otherwise. In mid-June, Eisenhower gave reporters off-the-record details of the impending invasion in order to quell speculation about future operations. He asked them to keep the secret, and they did. "Don't *ever* do that to us again," one correspondent pleaded.

Feints and deceptions continued apace. An Anglo-American fleet of warships and cargo vessels steamed from Britain toward Norway to suggest a northern invasion. A British Mediterranean armada—four battleships, six cruisers, and eighteen destroyers—sailed toward Greece before reversing course in the dead of night to cover the sea-lanes near Malta. But in the clutter of prevarication could be found an occasional truth. Eight million leaflets fell on Sicily in early July. One message warned, "Germany will fight to the last Italian." Another contained a map showing the vulnerability of Italian cities to Allied bombers flying from North Africa. The caption read: "Mussolini asked for it."

A lustrous canopy of stars arched over Valletta as Eisenhower left the tunnel on the night of July 8. The briny scent of the midsummer Mediterranean was intoxicating after the Lascaris underworld. The blacked-out town gleamed in the blue starlight with a beauty denied the daylight ruins.

For all its size, the enormous bedchamber at Verdala Palace was furnished with the economy of a monastic cell: water pitcher, wash basin, soap dish, thunder mug, bathtub. Several small battle maps had been tacked up. Eisenhower at times lamented the countless details that required his attention— "folderol," he called it. "I used to read about commanders of armies and envied them what I supposed to be a great freedom in action and decision," he had written in a letter home on May 27. "What a notion! The demands made upon me that must be met make me a slave rather than a master."

Translators, for example. Two hundred Italian-speaking soldiers were to be sent to North Africa with the 45th Division and 82nd Airborne, but none had arrived with the 82nd. Where were they? Or prisoners: "We may have 200,000 prisoners of war from HUSKY," he had informed Marshall on June 28, but of the 8,000 guards required less than half that number could be combed from U.S. units. Did the Geneva Conventions permit using British or French guards in American camps? Or donkeys: an urgent plea to the War Department for pack saddles and bridles had drawn a query from Marshall: "How many hands high are these donkeys and what average weight?" On further investigation, Eisenhower told him, "Donkeys not now considered suitable. Limited number of native mules available, 14 to 16 hands high, average weight 850 pounds. . . . These mules accustomed to packs but very vicious."

And then there was AMGOT, the Allied Military Government of Occupied Territories, an organization preparing to establish postinvasion civil rule in Sicily. Wags claimed the acronym stood for "Aged Military Gentlemen on Tour," but Washington informed Eisenhower that AMGOT had an "ugly German sound" and also approximated a crude, explicit Turkish term for genitalia. "To change the name of AMGOT at this stage," the exasperated commander-in-chief told the War Department on June 1, "would cause great delay and confusion."

Not least, he worried about his wife. With John at West Point, Mamie lived alone in Washington. She suffered from a heart condition and was often bedridden. Her weight had dropped to 112 pounds, and she described herself as someone who "lived after sorts, read mystery thrillers through the night—and waited." Eisenhower wrote her frequently, by hand rather than employing his usual dictationist, with salutations of "my sweetheart" or "darling." Lately he had taken special pains to reassure her of his constancy, because lately she had asked pointedly about Kay Summersby.

The rumors had intensified. Kathleen Helen Summersby, born in County Cork, had served as Eisenhower's driver in London and then in North Africa before being put in charge of his correspondence; she was adept at forging his signature on letters as well as on autographed photos. A model and film studio extra before the war, she was beautiful, athletic, and lively, often serving as her boss's bridge partner or riding companion. Eisenhower, twenty years her senior, struck her "as a man who had had very little comforting in his life." She had needed comforting herself in the past month: on June 6, her fiancé, a young U.S. Army colonel, had been killed by a mine in Tunisia. Grief and strain shattered her emotionally, and Eisenhower offered to send her home to London. Instead, she asked to remain in Algiers. No convincing evidence would ever prove a carnal relationship between the two, but the gossips gossiped anyway, including some who should have known better.

"Just please remember that no matter how short my notes I love you—I could never be in love with anyone else," Eisenhower had written Mamie on June 11. "You never seem quite to comprehend how deeply I depend upon you and need you."

Translators and donkeys, Mamie and Kay, Germans and Italians. And now one more trouble had appeared on the horizon. It was fortunate that Eisenhower never counted on God for good weather, as his son had observed. Earlier in the evening the meteorologists in the Lascaris Bastion had issued a disheartening forecast: a storm was brewing in the west.

## *"The Horses of the Sun"*

THE convoys from Algeria and Tunisia hugged the African coast on July 8, joined by additional task forces from Sousse and Sfax. Ships stretched for sixty miles in a mile-wide corridor, strung on white wakes "like the buttons of an abacus." Smaller vessels made straight for Point X-Ray, the rendezvous east of Malta. To mislead German reconnaissance planes, the main fleet steamed close to Tripoli, then at eight P.M. wheeled north at thirteen knots.

Ships wallowed like treasure-laden galleons on the Spanish Main. The American convoys alone carried more than 100,000 tons of supplies: 5,000 tons of crated airplanes, 7,000 tons of coal, 19,000 tons of signal equipment. The expedition manifest was Homeric in scale and variety: 6.6 million rations, 27 miles of quarter-inch steel cable, rat traps, chewing gum, 162 tons of occupation scrip, and even 144,000 condoms, also known as "the soldier's friend." A ten-page glossary translated British terminology into proper American: "windscreen" to "windshield," "wing" to "fender," "regiment" to "battalion," "brigade" to "regiment."

Half the tonnage comprised munitions: the capture of Sicily was expected to take less than two months, but requisitions for ammunition and ordnance had overwhelmed the War Department without anyone knowing quite how to sort them out. Huge depots in Oran and Casablanca held a nine-month supply of munitions, triple the authorized stocks, because no one could say precisely what types of bullets and bombs had already been received: the inventory cards were kept by Algerian and Moroccan clerks who often spoke poor English.

The Army, one admiral concluded, invariably "doubled what they thought they needed, just in case." An emergency plea to Washington in June requested an extra 732 radios, plus 140,000 radio batteries. The Signal Corps complied, after a fashion, but for communications redundancy also shipped 5,000 carrier pigeons, a platoon of pigeoneers, and more than 7,000 VHF radio crystals. Intelligence units carried hydrographic charts; maps from the Library of Congress pinpointing Sicilian caverns; copies of the *Italian Touring Club Guide for Sicily;* coastal pilot studies; town plats; and shoreline silhouettes drawn with the help of a former New England rumrunner. Couriers from Washington and New York had brought several dozen heavy wooden crates, each stamped BIGOT HUSKY and containing plaster of paris relief models of the Sicilian topography. But a handsome map detailing Sicilian historical monuments and art treasures, printed in New York and temporarily mislaid in Algiers, never reached Allied troops:

a motorcycle courier belatedly hurrying it to the front would be captured in Sicily by the Germans.

Much had been learned through hard experience in Tunisia about caring for casualties, and the fleet was provisioned on the assumption that the assault force would suffer 15 percent wounded and sick in the first week. A chart distributed to medics helped assess what proportion of a man's body surface had been burned—4.5 percent if both hands were burned, 13.5 percent for both arms, and so forth; 500 cc of blood plasma would be administered for each 10 percent. For those beyond such ministrations, the convoys carried six tons of grave markers, as well as stamp pads to fingerprint the dead. A thirteen-page "graves registration directive" showed how to build a cemetery—"care should be taken so that graves are in line with one another, both laterally and longitudinally." A memo on the disposition of a dead soldier's effects advised, "Removal should be made of any article that would prove embarrassing to his family."

Not least important, because invading armies under international law bore responsibility for the welfare of civilians, were the vast stocks meant for the Sicilians: 14,000 tons of flour, evaporated milk, and sugar to feed half a million people for a month; 94 tons of soap; 750,000 cc of tetanus, typhus, and smallpox vaccines. Civil affairs authorities calculated that if Italy were to capitulate, the Allies would have another 19 million mouths to feed and bodies to warm south of Rome, requiring 38,000 tons of food and 160,000 tons of coal each month, a huge burden on Allied shipping. "Italy could not be expected to be self-supporting," one study concluded, "at any time during Allied occupancy."

Kent Hewitt spent the passage on the flag bridge or in his cabin, reading and working crossword puzzles. *Monrovia*'s operations room was small, stifling, and as overcrowded as the rest of the ship. To accommodate the extra staffs aboard, the signal bridge had been doubled in size, and the ship's carpenters had cobbled together three code rooms while expanding the radio rooms. But with radio silence imposed, Hewitt had nothing to say that could not be said by semaphore. He felt sanguine, convinced that his armada was giving battle against evil and that "God couldn't be very hard on a man or a country doing that."

When topside, Hewitt often trained his field glasses on the amphibious vessels, an eccentric fleet within the fleet. The 150-foot LCT carried five Sherman tanks and still drew barely three feet, earning the nickname "sea-going bedpan." (Vulnerable smaller landing craft were known generically as "ensign eliminators.") The bigger LSTs, originally designed by the British, had caught the fancy of U.S. military logisticians who had seen flatbottoms used to good effect by rumrunners along the Gulf of Mexico in the 1920s. Eleven hundred LSTs would be built during the war, mostly in river yards across the American Midwest. The square bow, with fourteen-foot hinged doors, made the vessel slow and ungainly, and the lack of a keel caused it to roll even in drydock—or so the sailors claimed. But each one could haul twenty tanks.

Hewitt knew that despite their shallow draft, the LSTs could be snagged on the sandbars protecting much of Sicily's south coast. The Army had proposed shoving tanks and vehicles overboard, dragging them with heavy chains through the runnel to shore, and then drying them on the beach. Navy engineers, aghast, countered with Project GOLDRUSH: a floating pontoon that could be towed or carried in sections on the LSTs, then bolted together to form an articulated bridge across the water gap from sandbar to beach. Tests in Narragansett Bay had proved the bridge could bear a Sherman tank. But as with so much of HUSKY, the scheme had yet to be tested in combat.

Among Hewitt's disagreements with the Army, none had been more heated than whether to soften the beach defenses with naval gunfire before the landings. To catch the enemy by surprise, Patton insisted that the guns not open up until the assault boats were fifteen minutes from shore. He wanted, one naval officer reported, "to take his chances on his own fighting." Hewitt considered surprise "illusory." He listed eleven reasons why the enemy would likely be alert, including the frequent Allied photo-reconnaissance flights over the island and the sad fact that of fourteen officers clandestinely dispatched from submarines to survey Sicilian beaches that spring, all fourteen had been lost, along with a number of enlisted scouts. Patton waved away Hewitt's arguments. The guns would remain silent.

In his own cabin, Patton read, paced, napped, and paced some more. "I have the usual shortness of breath I always have before a polo game," he noted in his diary on July 8, then added an epigram from Napoleon: "Attack and then look." He simply no longer worried about the enemy defenders. "Hell, they've been there for four years," he told one of Hewitt's officers. "They can't keep alert all the time. We're going to land and all of a sudden we'll be on their necks." In a letter to his brother-in-law he wrote, "The horses of the sun have always been celebrated. Whoop ho! for a kill in the open!"

In Field Order No. 1, Patton had advised his commanders, "Attack both by day and night to the limit of human endurance and then continue to attack." For the troops he composed a gassy exhortation that now was read from quarterdecks across the fleet:

When we land we will meet German and Italian soldiers whom it is our honor and privilege to attack and destroy. . . . The glory of American arms, the honor of our country, the future of the whole world rests in your individual hands. See to it that you are worthy of this great trust. God is with us. We shall win.

As he paced Patton brooded about his last meeting with Eisenhower, in Algiers on July 5. "You are a great leader," the commander-in-chief told him, "but a poor planner." Brood he might, but Patton had displayed a cavalier disdain for logistical niceties. To General Sir Harold Alexander, who would command all Allied ground forces on Sicily, he clicked his heels and said, "General, I don't plan—I only obey orders." To his civil affairs chief, who would be responsible for feeding and governing four million Sicilians, Patton asked simply, "Do you kill?" To Eisenhower himself he had once proposed the fatuous motto, "You name them, I'll shoot them." He was and would remain, as one old friend noted, "colorful, incorrigible, unexplainable."

In his slashing hand he scribbled Bea a letter, to be mailed only after the invasion had begun: "I doubt that I will be killed or even wounded, but one can never tell. It is all a question of destiny. . . . I love you."

Ernie Pyle was with them again, of course. He had shipped from Bizerte aboard the U.S.S. *Biscayne,* flagship for the nearly three hundred vessels carrying the 3rd Infantry Division. Each morning, as a favor to the skipper, he rose at three A.M. from his cot on the weather deck to edit the ship's mimeographed newspaper. Later he scratched away in pencil at his own copy for the Scripps-Howard papers, or read Joseph Conrad and marveled at the old sea dog's prose: "On fine days the sun strikes sparks upon the blue."

Pyle was forty-two now, but looked and felt "older and a little apart." He was drinking too much, and fretting about his alcoholic wife whom he had divorced, committed to a sanatorium, and then remarried. He quickly became a familiar figure on the *Biscayne,* a Mae West draped over his narrow shoulders, the fringe of hair like a graying halo around his triangular head. He rolled his own cigarettes and asked countless questions in a flat Hoosier twang. Pyle "only weighs about 100 pounds with a family Bible in his lap," another reporter noted; the artist George Biddle found him "ascetic, gentle, whimsical, shy. . . . His expression is fundamentally sad."

War made him sad. Pyle considered it "an unalleviated misfortune," and aspired to be the last combat correspondent. He had come to view soldiers—"the guys that wars can't be won without"—as "little boys again, lost in the dark." He was a bit lost himself, and it helped him to write—sometimes brilliantly—about other lost souls. "The years are dealing heavily with me," he wrote a friend on the eve of HUSKY. "No wine, no women, no song, no play—soon nothing will be left to me but my shovel and a slight case of athlete's foot." He wondered how anyone who survived war could "ever be cruel to anything, ever again."

His material—those guys that wars couldn't be won without—was all around him. War Department standards required that each berth on a transport have at least twenty-three inches of vertical clearance from other berths, with ventilation in the troop holds of thirty cubic feet of forced-draft fresh air per man per minute. Pyle knew better, and so did Private Paul W. Brown, sailing with the 1st Division. "No baths for over a week," Brown wrote in a letter home. "Dirty socks. Dirty underwear. Damned little ventilation. No portholes." Army inspectors also documented vermin in the food, pilferage, rampant black marketeering, filthy toilets, and a short-fall of vomit buckets. Little wonder that many soldiers already felt nostalgic for the tangerines and pomegranates of North Africa, to say nothing of "its vastness and its mystery."

They made do, with boxing and tug-of-war and, on one British ship, a mustache contest, judged after tea by a Royal Marine armed with a brush, a comb, and a magnifying glass. Officers gave lectures on Sicily, using mimeographed notes, which began, "Sicily has been conquered many times before and her history is largely one of successful invasions"; they also cautioned that the Sicilian murder rate was "seven times as high as that in other parts of Italy." Each man received "The Soldier's Guide to Sicily," which described the heat, filth, and disease in such detail that the 26th Infantry's regimental log concluded the island must be "a hellhole inhabited by folks who were too poor to leave or too ignorant to know that there were better places." Troops in the 45th Division practiced their Italian, producing, among other things, mangled conversational fantasies in which "*Bona sera, senorina*" was answered with "*Duo cento lira.*"

They packed and unpacked and repacked their kit, trying to get the gas mask and the first aid kit and the sand-fly headnet into the 2.524 cubic feet prescribed for an Army assault pack. Each rifleman was supposed to carry 82.02 pounds, allocated ounce by ounce, from 10.2 pounds for a loaded M-1 rifle and .2 pounds for a towel, to .01 pounds for a spoon and .5 pounds for a Bible with a metal cover. Some lightened their load by nibbling away at the four ounces of "D rations," which were supposed to be saved for emergencies. Most of the soldiers had been in uniform long enough to be immune to surprise and would not have raised an eyebrow at the fact that the chocolate bar in the D rations had been developed after two years of Army quartermaster testing with three hundred recipes and flavors, including soy flour, potato, tapioca, pulverized coffee, and even a splash of kerosene.

"It's interesting to see the officers and men," Brigadier General Theodore Roosevelt, Jr., son of the former president and assistant commander of the 1st Division, wrote to his wife. Eleanor. In a letter written aboard the U.S.S. *Barnett*, he added, "They're not young anymore. They're not the fresh, smooth-cheeked boys you saw at a dance more than two years ago. . . . They've got a hard-bitten look." A few hours later he wrote, "The sea is mill-pond still. . . . Everything is battened down, portholds closed, lights doused, no smoking on deck. It becomes roasting. It's worst of course for the men. There's a sort of dead hush over the ship now. No one is moving on deck."

On the night of July 8, Roosevelt wrote Eleanor again, in the precise, level hand that displayed just enough ornamentation to imply a poetic sensibility:

> We've had a grand life and I hope there'll be more. Should it chance that there's not, at least we can say that in our years together we've packed enough for ten ordinary lives. We've known triumph and defeat, joy and sorrow, all that goes to fill the pattern of human existence. . . . We have no reason to be other than thankful come what may.

Since leaving Algiers, Hewitt's chief aerologist had been sketching weather maps and taking the wind's pulse with his anemometer. Lieutenant Commander Richard C. Steere was a 1931 Naval Academy graduate who had fenced on the U.S. foil team that won the gold medal in the 1932 Olympics by beating a storied French squad. Steere loved fencing, which he considered a "complex puzzle"; he loved weather for the same reason, and had earned his master's degree in meteorology at MIT in 1940. During Operation TORCH, when a ferocious Atlantic storm flung waves eighteen feet high onto the Moroccan coast, Steere's accurate prediction that the tempest would abruptly subside had convinced Hewitt to proceed with the landings. Patton had nicknamed the aerologist "Commander Houdini."

Now his skills would be tested again. On *Monrovia's* bridge, Steere showed his calculations to Hewitt and Patton on Thursday afternoon, July 8. Normally few shores were more benign than those of southern Sicily in midsummer. But, as Eisenhower's forecasters on Malta had also recognized, a polar maritime air mass flowing across western Europe from the northwest was merging with a secondary cold front stretching from Sardinia across Italy to a low over Yugoslavia. That had tightened the pressure gradient in the central Mediterranean. High northwesterly winds and steep seas, Steere said, could be expected by Friday afternoon. The landings were scheduled for early Saturday.

Pressure gradients and barometric millibars interested Patton not at all. "How long will the storm last?" he demanded.

Summer blows in the Med typically were short-lived, Steere replied, and the fleet would be sheltered in Sicily's lee. "It will calm down," he added, "by D-day."

"It better," Patton said.

By noon on Friday, as the fleet drew near Malta, the wind had freshened from the west, turning the sea a forbidding hue and sculpting crests from the wavelets. Soon the halyards and the railings moaned, the nasty lop grew heavy with foam, and the bedpan LCIs—landing craft, infantry, denounced by one soldier as "flat-bottomed delight[s] of Satan"—began taking seas over solid. Barrage-balloon cables stretched on the horizontal as sailors in slickers tried to reel them in, cursing what was now widely decried as a "Mussolini wind." One by one the cables snapped, and soon two dozen balloons sailed up and east and out of sight. By late afternoon the wind reached a gale-force thirty knots—force 7 on the Beaufort scale—with green seas piled so high the smaller craft could no longer see one another and helmsmen struggled to avoid collisions. Gloomy, fearful soldiers clung to stanchions and ladders. "We could barely stand on deck," Ernie Pyle wrote aboard *Biscayne*, "and our far-spread convoy was a wallowing, convulsive thing."

Never had the amphibious vessels been tested in such seas. The LCTs, reduced to three knots, danced like corks on the spindrift. "Huge chunks of green water cascaded back over the flat open decks," one Navy lieutenant recorded. Many LCTs, he added, "had at least one engine out, so when they lost steerage way they had to fall off to leeward and come around 180 degrees to get back on course." The square-bowed LSTs lurched up from the sea, then dropped into the next wave with a thud and a heavy shudder. An Army engineer colonel reported that his LST rolled "47 degrees each way as I watched the roll indicator. . . . The LST would be rolling, rolling, and rolling, the roll pendulum swinging so that we expected her to turn right over." Destroyers weaved among the smaller craft, signaling orders to compensate for the wind by steering "nothing to the right of north all night," rather than the planned course of 020 degrees. Several of the GOLDRUSH pontoons broke loose from their tow ships; two tugs lumbered through the gale to fetch them back. Twenty-ton landing craft swung on their davits like charms on a watch chain; aboard the transport *Florence Nightingale*, one boat broke free and smacked against the bridge and fantail with each roll of the ship until it too was lassoed.

"You probably enjoy the slow rise and fall of the deck, or even its more violent heaving if you happen to be in a storm," advised a paperback book for soldiers titled *What to Do Aboard the Transport.* Even "the sickest land-lubber," the book added, soon "laughs at some other fellow with a green look about the gills."

No one was laughing. "All of us are miserable, anxious, jam-packed, over-loaded and wet," a soldier in the 26th Infantry wrote. "No place to be sick except on one another. There are no heroes, just misery." "First I am afraid that I shall die," a soldier in the 18th Infantry noted, "then afraid that I won't." Soldiers had been issued a chemical concoction called Motion Sickness Preventative, but most still resorted to the items officially labeled "Bags, Vomit for the Use of," or hung their heads over the side, "moaning softly as if it were a secret shame." A private first class wrote his girlfriend in Brooklyn that these were "the most miserable moments ever spent in my life."

Some tried for a semblance of stability. Aboard H.M.S. *Strathnaver,* a dinner of clear soup and lamb cutlets was served to Welsh soldiers, who belted out "Land of My Fathers." But most troops "swung in their hammocks, green and groaning," a Canadian soldier wrote. "Everything that was not lashed down had come adrift: kitbags, weapons boxes, steel crates of ammunition, mess tins, tin helmets." On *LST 386,* the only unfazed passengers had four hooves: thirty African donkeys had been boarded until Eisenhower found sturdier mules. "Ship rolled thirty degrees and pitched fifteen," a naval officer recorded. "Donkeys were unconcerned, and seemed to enjoy their hay splashed with salt water." A Ranger sergeant who found his miserably ill platoon hiding in a lifeboat reflected that at least their emptied stomachs would reduce the chance of peritonitis from gut wounds. "When I get off this boat," one corporal vowed, "I'm going to walk and walk and walk."

"Some thought of the Spanish Armada," another Canadian wrote, "and some asked the question, 'Is God on our side or not?'" Those classical scholars who had tried recalling their Thucydides now remembered that Aeolus, the mythical Greek custodian of the winds, supposedly lived on a floating island near Sicily; they swapped stories of seafarers who had fallen foul of Mediterranean weather, beginning with the Spartan king Menelaus, whose homebound fleet had been blown from Troy to Egypt, and St. Paul.

Others held more practical colloquies. "It's goddam foolish, I tell you," an officer on the *Barnett* declared. "What's the use of going ahead with the invasion when your boats aren't even going to reach shore?" An Army captain agreed. "It's not fear. No, goddamit! It's not fear. There's just no sense in risking the whole invasion in this sea." Aboard the *Samuel Chase,* Rear Admiral John L. Hall, whose charges included the 1st Division, considered signaling Hewitt to recommend a delay, then told his staff, "We're not going to be the first to yelp." The fleet beat on.

On *Monrovia,* Hewitt stared at the heaving sea and listened to the wind tear at the rigging. The whitecapped Mediterranean looked as if it were dusted in snow. He pondered whether to break radio silence and contact Admiral Cunningham on Malta to suggest a postponement. Some smaller craft had no radios, so spreading word of any delay through the fleet would take at least four hours. As he watched an LSI buck the waves, Hewitt observed that at least the wretched soldiers aboard would be "all the more willing to get ashore." Bad as this was, the Atlantic before TORCH had been worse.

Late on Friday afternoon, he summoned Commander Houdini to the bridge. Steere that morning had predicted winds of twenty-seven knots; they now had reached thirty-seven, with twelve-foot seas. Though nervous, the aerologist stuck to his forecast. The "whole wind structure" would ease after nightfall, he explained, even if strong winds persisted aloft. Steere had scribbled his H-hour forecast in longhand, like a racetrack tout posting odds: "Northwest winds 10–15 knots decreasing, with inshore breakers 3–4 feet or less."

Hewitt took the bet, nodding without a hint of emotion or even concern. They would continue toward Sicily unless ordered to the contrary.

"Always the vibration," a British soldier wrote in his diary, "the heaving and rolling, the dim blue lights below deck, and the masses of bodies, in bunks, or moving blindly to the lavatories awash with urine." Like many others, Captain Joseph T. Dawson of the 1st Division wrote a final letter to his family in Texas: "My heart is filled with unspeakable tenderness for you one and all. . . . We are trying to measure up. God grant that we may do our task."

By six P.M. the sea had grown so nasty, one naval commander observed, that "even the destroyers were taking it green." As daylight ebbed, the wind intensified. Officers of the deck throughout the fleet ordered smoking lamps extinguished. At 6:52 P.M., *Monrovia*'s log recorded the sighting of the tiny island of Gozo, nine miles off the starboard beam. Just beyond, through the gloom and flying spray, lookouts spied the sheer cliffs of Malta. The fleet beat on.

Seeking sanctuary from the folderol, Eisenhower had warned Marshall that during his stay on Malta "my communications with Washington and London will be almost nil . . . because of the need for reserving signal communications for operational matters." The gambit failed; Washington and

London showed no reluctance to pepper the commander-in-chief with advice and queries, including a message from Marshall on Friday afternoon asking, "Is the attack on or off?" Eisenhower studied the cable and muttered, "I wish I knew."

Wind and weather dominated the discussion in Admiral Cunningham's office as the hours ticked by. Chagrined meteorologists appeared to report yet another increase in the Beaufort scale, which then was translated for Eisenhower from knots to miles per hour. Cunningham drove to a nearby airfield to see conditions with his own scarlet-lidded eyes; he reported that "all the winds of heaven" were "roaring and howling around the control tower." In Grand Harbour, another flotilla of British landing craft cast off with a piper on the lead ship braced in the bow playing "The Road to the Isles." Cunningham described the vessels "literally burying themselves, with the spray flying over them in solid sheets, as they plunged out to sea." At six P.M. a bottle of gin appeared in the Lascaris Bastion and was soon drained.

Eisenhower reviewed his options, lighting one damp cigarette from another. Staff officers calculated that if the invasion were postponed, two to three weeks would be needed to remount it. No doubt by then the enemy would be alert, and perhaps was already: the fighter control room inside the bastion reported a German reconnaissance plane near the fleet at 4:30 P.M. and another at 7:30. Like Lieutenant Commander Steere, forecasters on Malta believed the storm would soon pass. So too did Cunningham, who had sailed these waters for the better part of a half century, and who once cited "recklessness and callousness" as the most vital qualities of a commander.

Eisenhower was usually quick to make a decision, and he made one now. "The operation will proceed as scheduled," he cabled Marshall, "in spite of an unfortunate westerly wind." Cunningham sent his own signal to the Admiralty in London: "Weather not favourable. But operation proceeding."

With "rather fearful hearts"—in Cunningham's phrase—they broke for dinner. Driving to Verdala Palace, Eisenhower eyed the spinning windmills above Valletta; the man who preached the importance of believing in luck now wondered aloud whether his had run out. "To be perfectly honest," another British sea dog, the lanky Admiral Lord Louis Mountbatten, told him over dinner, "it doesn't look too good."

After coffee, Cunningham rejoined them for a drive to Delimara Point, where an octagonal black-and-white-banded lighthouse crowned the island's southeast corner. Half a dozen searchlight beams pointed straight up as a signal to the waves of transport planes—some towing gliders, others full of paratroopers—that now began to appear overhead. Cunningham counted sixty-four aircraft, while Eisenhower, neck craned, rubbed his lucky coins and murmured a prayer for "safety and success." Had he watched more closely, he might have seen that many planes bucking the winds missed the vital turn at Delimara, continuing east rather than swinging due north.

Back in the Lascaris war room, the great wall maps charted the armadas as they inched toward Sicily: American convoys mostly west of Malta, the British mostly east. Cots and blankets had been dragged into an air-conditioned room nearby, but anxiety kept the men edgy and awake. Eisenhower prattled on about writing a book, perhaps an anthology that would profile two dozen public figures; he would "paint each one's character" and "tell some stories." Air Marshal Arthur Tedder, the senior air commander in the Mediterranean, reflected on the Punic Wars and previous invasions. "Fancy invading Italy from the south," Tedder said. "Even Hannibal had the sense to come in with his elephants over the Alps." Farther down the tunnel an officer shaving with an electric razor provoked a shrill protest that "some unmentionable noise" was making it "quite impossible for any signals to be picked up."

At ten P.M., Eisenhower scribbled a note to Mamie. "I'm again in a tunnel, as I was at the beginning of last November, waiting, as I was then, for news.

Men do almost anything to keep from going slightly mad. Walk, talk, try to work, smoke (all the time)—anything to push the minutes along. . . . Everything that we could think of to do has been done; the troops are fit; everybody is doing his best. The answer is in the lap of the gods.

## Death or Glory

PATTON woke to a loud crash against his cabin porthole. He lurched from the bed, fully uniformed, momentarily convinced that a bomb had struck *Monrovia*. Cocking an ear topside to the clank of tackle being loosened, he soon realized that a broken davit had let a landing craft slip from its pulley and smack against the ship's hull. One man had pitched overboard but soon was fished out. As the commotion subsided, two other sounds were conspicuous by their absence: the wind had died, and the flagship's engines had stopped. An odd, portentous hush settled over *Monrovia*.

Patton hitched up his whipcord breeches and straightened his blouse. He had dozed off after inviting the ship's chaplain in for a final prayer. Strange dreams had troubled his sleep, of a black kitten and then of many cats, spitting at him. "We may feel anxious," he scribbled in his diary, "but I trust the Italians are scared to death. . . . God has again helped me. I hope He keeps on."

He found Hewitt on the bridge. The quarter moon had set shortly after midnight, but stars threw down spears of light and the fleet stood in black silhouette against the gray horizon. Commander Steere had been right, again: the wind had ebbed to below ten knots; there was good visibility and a moderate swell. *Monrovia*'s radar had detected the Sicilian coast at 22,000 yards—thirteen miles. Then several destroyers knifed forward until they spotted blue lights, flashing seaward from a scattered school of British submarines. With doughty, rule-Britannia names like *Unruffled* and *Unseen* and *Unrivalled,* the subs had been lurking off the coast for two days to serve as beacons guiding the invasion convoys to their proper beaches. The skipper of the submarine H.M.S. *Seraph* later recalled, "As far as my night glasses could carry, I saw hundreds of ships following in orderly fashion, each keeping its appointed station." *Monrovia* and her sisters dropped anchor in fifty fathoms six miles from the coast, on station and on time. Hewitt also had been right, again.

He and Patton now raked the shore with their field glasses. Allied bombing earlier in the evening had set fire to the stubble in Sicilian wheat fields near the sea. Patton watched "a mass of flames" engulf a two-mile corridor directly inland. "All the beach seems to be burning," a soldier noted. Douglas Fairbanks, Jr., a matinee idol with more than sixty film credits who was serving as a Navy Reserve lieutenant on *Monrovia,* jotted in his diary, "Apparently the big ships have not yet been seen from the shore."

The HUSKY commanders intended to land the equivalent of 67 assault battalions—each with approximately 800 men—on 26 beaches along 105 miles of coastline. The British beaches chosen for General Montgomery's Eighth Army lay to the east, from Cape Passero on the island's southeast tip up through the Gulf of Noto almost to Syracuse. Hewitt's armada had split near Malta into three prongs, which would land the three assault divisions in Patton's Seventh Army along a forty-mile crescent on the Gulf of Gela. Farthest west, the 3rd Division now lay off Licata; farthest east, and closest to the British, the 45th Division lay off Scoglitti; in the center, with *Monrovia,* the 1st Division prepared to seize Gela. The objective for each division was the Yellow Line, a notional demarcation ten to thirty miles inland that would push enemy artillery beyond range of captured coastal airfields. Patton estimated it would take five days for his army to reach the Yellow Line. Beyond that he had no orders.

Since landing at Cadiz in 1625, the British over the centuries had embarked on some forty overseas military campaigns, with fortunes ranging from glorious to catastrophic. The Americans were somewhat newer at the expeditionary game, but Yanks and Tommies concurred that, as a British official history warranted, "invasions from the sea were professionally recognized to be all-or-nothing affairs." Death or glory was back in fashion.

Now those Yanks and Tommies made ready; so, too, the Canadians. "You will find the Mediterranean still choppy," a lieutenant advised over the *Ancon's* PA system, "but compared to what it was only a short time back, as quiet as if God had put his hand on it." Lights below burned blue or red to enhance night vision. Indonesian waiters in white coats struck little gongs to call British troops to an early breakfast; on *Strathnaver's* E-deck, the Dorsets shared mugs of tea and fancied they could smell Europe. GIs wrapped their dogtags in black friction tape to prevent rattling. Some prayed, or hurriedly scratched the letters they had meant to write earlier. "I could not, with a clear conscience, ask God to take me safely through this war," Randall Harris wrote his family in Pocahontas, Iowa, "but I can ask Him for strength and courage to do my job."

They had reached "the victim coast of Sicily," a soldier in the 45th Division told his father. A naval officer transporting the same unit described "wild Indians still playing poker and sharpening knives, betting on who'll get the first Italian." One officer on the *Biscayne's* weather deck later wrote, "The fellow standing next to me was breathing so hard I couldn't hear the anchor go down. Then I realized there wasn't anybody standing next to me."

Ted Roosevelt took time aboard the *Barnett* to finish his eleven-page letter to Eleanor: "The ship is dark, the men are going to their assembly stations. . . . Soon the boats will be lowered away. Then we'll be off."

"Land the landing force!" The order echoed down the chains of command east and west. "Aye-aye. Land the landing force." Soldiers in the British 50th Division shuffled single file, company by company, from the dim hold to the assembly deck on *Winchester Castle*. Sailors handed stiff tots of rum to the Dorsets on *Strathnaver* and pumped bilge oil over the side to calm the sea. "Do you hear there? Serial one! To your boat stations, move now," an amplified voice called on *Derbyshire*. "Serial two! Stand by." A soldier in the Canadian 1st Division, Farley Mowat, heard clattering steam winches lower the landing craft; on deck each man "gripped the web-belt of the man ahead. . . . The dim glow of blue-hooded flashlights gave a brief and charnel illumination."

No oil could settle the swell in the American sector, which was more exposed to the westerly wind. Helmsmen maneuvered their ships to form a lee, lowering boats first on the sheltered side, then coming about to shelter and lower the other side. Troughs swallowed the vessels anyway. "The rocking of the small landing craft was totally unlike anything we had experienced on the ship," wrote the journalist Jack Belden, who had shipped aboard the *Barnett*. "It pitched, rolled, swayed, bucked, jerked from side to side, spanked up and down." Confused coxswains, no less seasick then the soldiers, shouted to one another, "Are you the second wave?" Most craft lacked seats or thwarts, forcing troops to sit on metal decks awash in seawater and vomit. The rumble of landing-craft engines reminded one bosun's mate of "a basso coughing into his handkerchief at church."

"Seasickness and fear make an interesting combination," a medic observed. "They vie for dominance." Some boats were loaded at the rail and lowered by block and tackle; but many ships required that soldiers climb down braided nets, now slippery with sea spray and puke. Officers stood by to pry loose the fingers of those who froze on the ropes. "Oh, Jesus, oh, Jesus," a soldier moaned after slumping to the bottom of a bobbing boat. "How I wish I was back in Chicago." Many would have agreed with a 1st Division scout who declared, "We were not meant to be sailors." Aboard *Joseph T. Dickman* attempts were made to inspirit the troops by piping Glenn Miller's "American Patrol" over the PA system to the circling boats. "If casualties are high, it will not be a reflection on your leadership abilities," the Ranger commander, Lieutenant Colonel William O. Darby, told a young captain preparing to step over the side. "May God be with you."

On the extreme left of Hewitt's task force, four sailors and thirty-four soldiers from the 7th Infantry had just settled into boat number 2 on *LST 379* when the forward davit snapped, spilling the men into the sea or crushing them against the ship's hull. Half were saved, half perished. It was on the right flank, however, that the wind and lop were worst; aboard ships transporting the 45th Division, cleats snapped, painters parted, booms carried away. Nearly every mother ship lost at least one landing craft. The heavy roll on *Thomas Jefferson* caused a boat carrying rockets to break loose as sailors hoisted her overboard. "We really started to swing," reported the boat's ensign. "We started hitting both the kingposts, the boom itself, the blocks and falls, and anything else in the way. . . . I believed that we were going to be killed and expended without ever seeing action. Our barrage rockets were rolling all over the deck." On another wallowing ship, the steadying lines tore free on both a bulldozer and a lighter being lifted over the rail; soldiers cowered against the bulkheads as the equipment swung and crashed about, "knocking steel and fire from everything they struck."

Somehow the cockleshell flotillas took shape. Boat crews stood ready with mallets to hammer wooden plugs into any bullet holes. Minesweepers worked the approaches, but no one knew whether the shallows would be clear; coxswains were advised that if the boat in front blew up they should "steer through the water, rather than shy off, because the blown boat has made that water safe." Coxswains also received a list of nineteen radio code words, from COCA-COLA ("Stop") and BIG MICE ("Need assistance") to TOTEM POLE ("Resistance encountered") and SWEET CHARIOT ("Enemy tanks"). No advice was given on how to remember this vocabulary under fire, although all radio operators were ordered "to send or speak slowly, clearly, and distinctly."

By two A.M. the first waves had turned toward shore, using the burning wheat straw as a beacon or following compass headings. Gunboats with blue lights stood in toward shore, hailing the first waves: "Straight ahead. Look out for mines. Good luck." Now the Navy guns opened up, their concussive booms and smoke rings carrying on the wind. Shells glowed cherry red against the starlight. In graceful arcs they floated over the puttering boats before splattering in sprays of white and gold on the distant shore. Coxswains steered by the shells, but soldiers instinctively slumped in their vessels, peering over the gunwales.

Major General John P. Lucas, dispatched by Eisenhower as an observer of HUSKY, watched the spectacle from *Monrovia*'s bridge with Hewitt and Patton, then confided a small, filthy secret to his diary: "War, with all its terror and dirt and destruction, is at times the most beautiful phenomenon in the world."

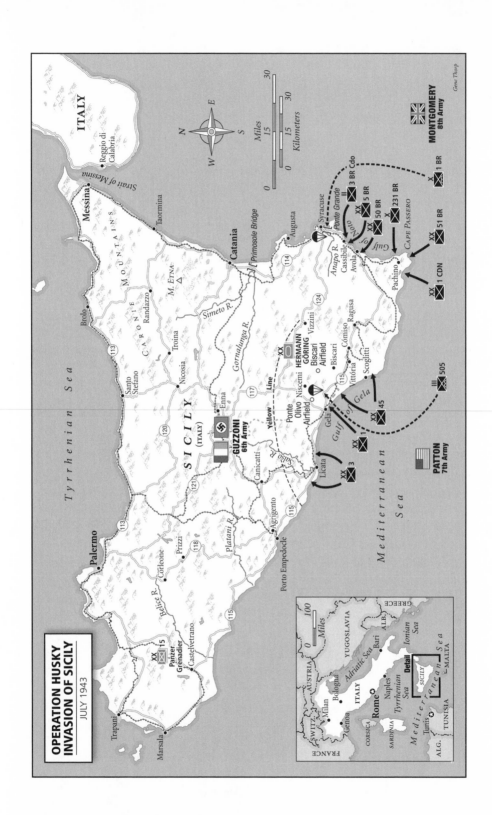

# OPERATION HUSKY
# INVASION OF SICILY
JULY 1943

ITALY

Reggio di Calabria

Strait of Messina

Messina

Taormina

CARONIE MOUNTAINS

Brolo

Randazzo

M. ETNA △

Troina

Nicosia

Santo Stefano

Simeto R.

Gornalunga R.

Catania

Primosole Bridge

114

Augusta

Syracuse
Ponte Grande

Cassibile

Avola

Anapo R.

Gulf of Noto

Vizzini

117

Enna

SICILY
(ITALY)

GUZZONI
6th Army

Ponte Olivo
Airfield

Niscemi

HERMANN
GÖRING

Biscari
Biscari
Airfield

Comiso

Ragusa

124

Yellow Line

Gela

Scoglitti

Vittória

115

Gulf of Gela

Pachino

CAPE PASSERO

3 BR Cdo

5 BR

50 BR

231 BR

1 BR

1 CDN

51 BR

45

505

MONTGOMERY
8th Army

PATTON
7th Army

Canicattì

Salso R.

Licata

3

Agrigento

Porto Empedocle

Platani R.

115

Prizzi

118

Corleone

Castelvetrano

Belice R.

120

121

Palermo

Trapani

Marsala

Panzer
Grenadier
15

Tyrrhenian Sea

Mediterranean Sea

N
E
S
W

Miles
0   15   30

Kilometers
0   15   30

Gene Thorp

FRANCE

SWITZ.
Milan
Genoa
ITALY
Bologna
Rome
Naples
Bari
CORSICA
SARDINIA
Tyrrhenian Sea
SICILY
Detail
MALTA
TUNISIA
ALG.
Tunis
TUNISIA
Mediterranean Sea
Ionian Sea
Adriatic Sea
YUGOSLAVIA
AUSTRIA
ALB.
GREECE

Miles
0   100

## 2. THE BURNING SHORE

### Land of the Cyclops

Few Sicilian towns claimed greater antiquity than Gela, where the center of the American assault was to fall. Founded on a limestone hillock by Greek colonists from Rhodes and Crete in 688 B.C., Gela had since endured the usual Mediterranean calamities, including betrayal, pillage, and, in 311 B.C., the butchery of five thousand citizens by a rival warlord. The ruins of sanctuaries and shrines dotted the modern town of 32,000, along with tombs ranging in vintage from Bronze Age to Hellenistic and Byzantine. The fecund "Geloan fields," as Virgil called them in *The Aeneid,* grew oleanders, palms, and Saracen olives. Aeschylus, the father of Attic drama, had spent his last years in Gela writing about fate, revenge, and love gone bad in the *Oresteia;* legend held that the playwright had been killed here when an eagle dropped a tortoise on his bald skull.

Patton planned a different sort of airborne attack by his invasion vanguard. On the night of July 9–10, more than three thousand paratroopers in four battalions were to parachute onto several vital road junctions outside Gela to forestall Axis counterattacks against the 1st Division landing beaches. Leading this assault was the dashing Colonel James Maurice Gavin, who at thirty-six was on his way to becoming the Army's youngest major general since the Civil War. Born in Brooklyn to Irish immigrants and orphaned as a child, Gavin had been raised hardscrabble by foster parents in the Pennsylvania coalfields. Leaving school after the eighth grade, he worked as a barber's helper, shoe clerk, and filling station manager before joining the Army at seventeen. He wangled an appointment to West Point, where his cadetship was undistinguished. As a young officer he washed out of flight school; a superior's evaluation as recently as 1941 concluded, "This officer does not seem peculiarly fitted to be a paratrooper." Ascetic and fearless, with a "magnetism for attractive women," Jim Gavin was in fact born to go to the sound of the guns. "He could jump higher, shout louder, spit farther, and fight harder than any man I ever saw," one subordinate said.

His 505th Parachute Infantry Regiment, part of the 82nd Airborne Division, had staged in central Tunisia. Gavin harbored private misgivings about the Sicilian mission—"many lives will be lost in a few hours," he wrote—and with good reason. The 82nd had received only roughly a third as much training time as some other U.S. divisions. The amateurish Allied parachute operations in North Africa had been marred by misfortune and miscalculation. No large-scale night combat jump had ever been attempted, and so many injuries had plagued the division in Tunisia—including fifty-three broken legs and ankles during a single daylight jump in early June—that training was curtailed. Much of the HUSKY planning had been done by officers who had no airborne expertise and whose notions were suffused with fantasy. Transport pilots had little experience at night navigation, but to avoid flying over trigger-happy gunners in the Allied fleets, the planes, staying low to evade Axis radar, would have to make three dogleg turns over open water in the dark. Airborne units had yet to figure out how to drop a load heavier than three hundred pounds, much less a howitzer or a jeep. An experimental "para-mule" broke three legs; after putting the creature out of its misery, paratroopers used the carcass for bayonet practice. Still, the ranks "generally agreed that training proficiency had reached the stage where the mission was 'in the bag,'" wrote one AAF officer, who later acknowledged "possible overoptimism."

At about the time that Hewitt's fleet neared Malta, Gavin and his men had clambered aboard 226 C-47 Dakotas near Kairouan. Faces blackened with burnt cork, each soldier wore a U.S. flag on the right sleeve and a white cloth knotted on the left as a nighttime recognition signal. Days earlier an 82nd Airborne platoon had circulated through the 1st Division to familiarize ground soldiers with the baggy trousers and loose smock worn by paratroopers. Parachutes occupied the C-47s' seats; the sixteen troopers in each stick sat on the fuselage floor, practicing the invasion challenge and password: GEORGE / MARSHALL. Dysentery tormented the regiment, and men struggled with their gear and Mae Wests to squat over honeypots placed around the aircraft bays. Medics distributed Benzedrine to the officers, morphine syrettes to everyone.

As the first planes began to taxi—churning up dust clouds so thick that some pilots had to take off by instrument—a weatherman appeared at Gavin's aircraft to affirm Commander Steere's prediction of lingering high winds aloft. "Colonel Gavin, is Colonel Gavin here? I was told to tell you that the wind is going to be thirty-five miles an hour, west to east," he said. "They thought you'd want to know." Fifteen was considered the maximum velocity for safe jumping. Another messenger staggered up with an enormous barracks bag stuffed with prisoner-of-war tags. "You're supposed to put one on every prisoner you capture," he told Gavin. An hour after take-off, a staff officer heaved the bag into the sea.

The slivered moon cast little light, and at five hundred feet salt spray on the cockpit windows further cut visibility. Men dozed in the blacked-out planes during the three-hour flight, unaware that the gale had quickly deranged the formations. Some pilots found the critical turn at Malta, where Eisenhower stood craning his neck. Most did not. Soon the central Mediterranean was swarming with lost aircraft as crews tried to dead reckon their way north.

Nearly all found Sicily, or at least some corner of it. Pilot Willis Mitchell spied Malta and turned accordingly, only to approach the drop zone north of Gela without thirty of the thirty-nine planes that were supposed to be behind him. Leveling off at eight hundred feet, Mitchell flipped on the green jump light. More than a hundred paratroopers from the bobtailed formation landed within two miles of the DZ, but badly scattered and hobbled with jump injuries. Others—aware only that they were somewhere over land—jumped from fifteen hundred feet at two hundred miles per hour, rather than from the preferred six hundred feet at one hundred miles per hour. Smoke and dust from earlier bombing obscured key landmarks and further befuddled the navigators. Some mistook Syracuse for Gela, fifty miles to the west. Machine-gun and antiaircraft fire ripped through the formations and the descending paratroopers, killing some before they hit the ground. Plane number 42-32922 collided with its flight leader above the beach; with his right elevator gone, the pilot, George Mertz, wobbled back out to sea and ditched five hundred yards off Scoglitti. "I hit the master switch to cut off both engines, and we glided in," Mertz recounted. "One paratrooper came crashing through to the cockpit. The airplane settled, slightly nose low." Crewmen and soldiers lashed their life rafts together and paddled ashore to hide in the dunes.

Jim Gavin's Dakota also tacked north after missing Malta, eventually crossing an unidentified coast on an unidentified landmass shortly after midnight. A red light flashed in the bay. "Stand up and hook up," Gavin ordered. Braced in the open doorway, he recognized nothing in the dark terrain below. A pearly stream of machine-gun tracers drifted up. The green light flashed, and Gavin leaped into the slipstream. After landing hard and slipping off his harness, he managed to round up five comrades. For hours they stumbled through the darkness, whispering "George!" and straining for "Marshall," until the distant grumble of naval gunfire just before dawn confirmed that they were at least on the proper island.

"No one knew where they were, including themselves," the tart General Lucas noted aboard *Monrovia*. Gavin eventually discerned that he was south of Vittoria, thirty miles from Gela. Although Troop Carrier Command claimed that 80 percent of the paratroopers had jumped onto the proper drop zones, even the Army Air Forces disputed that as "a prodigious overestimate." In fact, fewer than one in six had landed anywhere close to where they were supposed to land. Only one of Gavin's four battalions was intact, and it was twenty-five miles east of the correct DZ. More than 3,400 paratroopers were scattered across southeastern Sicily, as much as sixty-five miles off target. Some had jumped into the British sector, where—because no one had thought to impose identical passwords on the entire invasion force—they were greeted with gunfire. Eight planes were lost, none apparently to enemy fire, and the regiment's three-day casualty tally would reach 350, a literal decimation.

Certainly they wreaked havoc: slashing telephone wires, ambushing couriers, and causing the panicky Italians to inflate their numbers. They improvised, as paratroopers must. Captain Edwin M. Sayer, a company commander, mustered forty-five men to attack pillboxes near Niscemi with mortar, bazooka, and rifle-grenade fire; fifty enemy soldiers were captured, along with twenty machine guns and half a million rounds of ammunition. The operation, in Gavin's assessment, was "self-adjusting," a SAFU, as well as a TARFU and a JAAFU.

Still, only 425 paratroopers had landed in front of the 1st Division, and only 200 now occupied the vital high ground at Piano Lupo as a screen for the vulnerable units landing at Gela. The 82nd Airborne commander, Major General Matthew B. Ridgway, lamented the "miscarriage" that resulted from overweening ambition, deficient training, and bad luck. "At war's end," Ridgway later concluded, "we still could not have executed that first Sicily mission, as laid on, at night and under like conditions."

As paratroopers blundered hither and yon, the force they were intended to shield swept into the shallows off Gela. The 1st Division, bolstered by two Ranger battalions, closed on six beaches along a five-mile front shortly after three A.M. Their objective, beyond seizing the town, was the capture of Ponte Olivo airfield on Virgil's Geloan plain. Calamity struck quickly. Hardly had the strains of "American Patrol" faded when a Ranger lieutenant and sixteen of his men vaulted from their landing craft as it ground with a gritty jolt onto a sandbar; unaware of the runnel and deadweighted with those 82.02 pounds of kit, they sank to the bottom of the Mediterranean. Other men from the 1st Division dropped their life preservers into the forward hold as instructed by an LCI skipper, who assured them the water was only hip deep; scurrying down the dropped ramp they, too, sank and drowned.

The first Americans waded onto the beaches at 3:35 A.M. on Saturday, July 10, fifty minutes behind Patton's schedule. With a vicious *pop*, a mine tore open the chest of a Ranger company commander. "I could see his heart beating," said his first sergeant, Randall Harris. "He turned to me and said, 'I've had it, Harry,' then collapsed and died." Harris dashed forward only to have another mine shred his abdomen and legs; after flicking grenades into a line of pillboxes, he sprinkled sulfa powder on his protruding intestines, cinched his web belt to keep the innards in, and wandered down to the beach to find a medic. Harris would win a battlefield commission and the Distinguished Service Cross for gallantry.

If stunned by the Allied invasion, the defenders appeared unsurprised. With a great roar and a shower of masonry, Italian demolitionists blew up a long segment of the thousand-foot Gela pier. Italian gunners trained their fire on the 26th Infantry as the first wave closed to within a hundred yards of shore. "The water jumped and heaved" under the lashing bullets. Soldiers sheltered behind the LCT splinter plates and anchor winches, narrowing their shoulders and elbowing one another as rounds sang overhead or pinged off the hull. A barrage balloon torn free in the storm abruptly drifted overhead, weird and stately. "I've been wounded but there's so much blood I can't tell exactly where," one soldier muttered. As another boat dropped its ramp, a 16th Infantry rifleman felt a weight slump against his leg. "Somebody left his pack," he called out, then saw that the inert bundle was a sergeant who had been shot in the head.

Shouts and curses swept the beaches, swallowed by gunfire. A shower of Italian grenades landed around a 16th Infantry lieutenant, who escaped from the encounter with sixty-six small holes in his uniform shirt, a ruptured eardrum, and a pierced upper lip. Sappers chopped at the barbed wire with long-handled snips, and soldiers fell flat as trip flares bathed the shingle in magnesium brilliance. Searchlights swept the waterline, only to draw salvo after salvo from destroyers racing parallel to the shore like angry dogs along a fence. An Italian soldier "crept from a pillbox on all fours and ran down the hill, screaming and sobbing."

Dawn sluiced the eastern sky before five A.M., but daylight only enhanced the chaos. The heavy swell jammed several LST bow ramps, breaking ramp chains and flooding the tank decks. Seamen struggled against the current to assemble the cumbersome pontoon bridges, and a 16th Infantry battalion— stranded aboard several LCIs that had been snagged on sandbars thirty yards from shore—began to ferry men and weapons to the beach in rubber boats. Nothing in the arsenal of democracy now proved more providential than another new amphibian, a two-and-a-half-ton truck with flotation tanks and twin propellers. Built by General Motors and awkwardly called the DUKW—pronounced "duck"—it was difficult to load, slow in the water, and susceptible to brake damage from salt and sand. But it could carry a rifle platoon or a howitzer and its gun crew from ship to shore, and then make fifty miles per hour on roads. The War Department had been persuaded of the DUKW's merit the previous winter when a prototype rescued a foundering Coast Guard crew during a Cape Cod nor'easter. Eisenhower had been issued eleven hundred DUKWs for HUSKY; they scuttled through the Gela surf like a flotilla of horseshoe crabs.

Mines proved more galling than enemy guns. Rather than miles of good beach frontage, as intelligence reports had suggested, only a few hundred yards proved suitable, and exits through the dunes were sown with Teller mines planted a yard apart. DUKWs blew up, trucks blew up, five Navy bulldozers blew up. With no firefighting equipment at hand, they burned to the axles and blocked the beach exits. Many mine detectors remained buried in cargo holds; salt spray quickly shorted out those that made it to shore. "Everything on them goes bad," a signal officer complained. Drivers ignored the engineer tape laid to mark cleared lanes: more vehicles blew up. Some crews left their DUKWs at water's edge to collect souvenirs, or they were diverted by the Army for work elsewhere. Mines closed Yellow and Green Beaches in front of Gela, but boats diverted a bit south to Beach Red 2 found appalling congestion—"gasoline, ammunition, water, food, and assorted equipment were strewn about in a hopeless mass," Hewitt later wrote. Shellfire soon closed that beach, too.

"The beach was a scene of the greatest confusion," Lucas noted in his diary after an early-morning trip ashore. "Trucks bogged down in the sand. The surf filled with overturned boats and debris of all kinds." Beachmasters bellowed into the din to small effect; few had been armed with bullhorns. Troops loitered in the dunes, or traded potshots with flitting Italian gunmen. Some LSTs steamed away to anchorages offshore without unloading an ounce of cargo—much less tanks—and the Navy would inadvertently return to North Africa with much of the signal equipment for the Gela assault still crated in the holds. Shore parties searching for fuel and ammo instead found boxes packed with athletic equipment and clerical records.

Dawn also brought the first enemy air attacks. Sixteen miles offshore, the U.S.S. *Maddox* was screening troop transports from enemy submarines when, for reasons unclear, she wandered away from the main destroyer pack. German pilots had learned to hunt stragglers by tracking the ship wakes, then gliding out of the rising sun with their engines cut. An officer on the *Maddox*'s bridge realized he was under attack only when he heard the whistle of falling bombs. The first detonated twenty-five yards astern; a second hit beneath the propeller guard, detonating depth charges aligned on the aft deck.

Fire and steam boiled from the starboard main deck and the number 2 stack. The blast ripped open the aft deckhouse and catapulted a 5-inch gun over the side. *Maddox* settled by the stern, with power gone and the engine room annunciators dead. As she lost steering and headway, the ship listed slightly to port, then righted herself for an instant before cap-sizing to starboard and sinking to the perpendicular. She paused momen-tarily, as if for a last look around, her forward gun pointing vertically from the sea. Bulkheads collapsed with a groan. Then the powder magazine detonated.

"A great blob of light bleached and reddened the sky," reported a lieu-tenant, miles away aboard *Ancon*. "It was followed by a blast more sullen and deafening than any we have so far heard." More prosaically, a sailor on *Ancon*'s bridge added, "Look, they got one!" Two minutes after she was hit, *Maddox* vanished. In three hundred fathoms the ship sank, dragging down 212 men, their captain among them. A nearby tug rescued 74 sur-vivors.

Past the charred DUKWs and discarded mine detectors, two regiments from the 1st Division bulled through the dunes east of Gela. Succeeding waves followed the spoor of abandoned gas masks, blankets, life belts, snarled signal wire, and artillery shells packed in black cardboard clover-leafs. Gray stone houses with tile roofs stood beside the parched fields be-yond the beach. Wheat and barley sheaves lay on threshing floors in the side yards, where beanstalks had been stacked for winter fuel. Grapevines snaked between olive groves, and peach trees were heavy with fruit that hung "like red-and-yellow lamps." The tintinnabulation of sheep bells sounded above the *pock-pock-pock* of rifle fire.

Force X—two of Bill Darby's Ranger battalions—pushed into Gela town. Darby, a rugged thirty-two-year-old West Pointer from Arkansas, had proved his worth and that of his 1st Ranger Battalion in Algeria and Tunisia—they were the "best damned combat soldiers in Africa," according to Patton—and in consequence the force that spring had tripled in size. Posters recruited volunteers who had "no record of trial by court-martial" and who were "white; at least five feet, six inches in height; of normal weight; in excellent physical condition; and not over thirty-five years old." Recruiters also swaggered into Algerian bars, tendered a few insults, and signed up soldiers pugnacious enough to pick a fight. Already eclectic, the Rangers now included a jazz trumpeter, a professional gambler, steelwork-ers, a hotel detective, coal miners, a church deacon, and a recruit named

Sampson P. Oneskunk. El Darbo, as the men called him, would twice reject promotion to full colonel in order to stay with his Rangers. They returned his devotion with a jody call: "We'll fight an army on a dare, we'll follow Darby anywhere, Darby's Rangers . . . Fightin' Rangers."

The Fightin' Rangers now fought their way through Gela. Naval gunfire had shattered houses along the corniche and "ranged through the town, tearing roofs off or blowing in whole streets," a 1st Division soldier recorded. Blue-uniformed Italians from the Livorno Division made a stand at the cathedral. Gunfire echoed through the nave and up the winding tower steps, punctuated by the burst of grenades in the sacristy. Soon bloody bodies carpeted the altar and the front steps, where Sicilian women in black keened over their dead. Two other redoubts fell quickly: a naval battery on the northwest edge of town, which surrendered after thunderous salvos from the cruiser *Savannah,* and a barricaded schoolhouse from which fifty-two Italians surrendered after a brief firefight. A blue column of Livorno prisoners tramped toward the beach, where without evident dismay they wolfed down C rations and awaited the LST that would carry them away from the war.

More Italians counterattacked at 10:30. A column of thirty-two light Renault tanks with infantry pushed south from Niscemi, eight miles inland, only to be bushwacked by a hundred of Gavin's paratroopers and further discouraged by screaming salvos from the cruiser *Boise.* Twenty tanks managed to wheel onto Highway 115 toward Gela, but a smoking broadside from the 16th Infantry stopped the advance and sent the survivors fleeing north into the Sicilian interior.

On Highway 117, two dozen more tanks from Ponte Olivo airfield clanked toward town through 5-inch fire from the destroyer *Shubrick.* Several burning hulks soon littered the road, but ten Renaults reached Gela. Rangers scampered behind stone walls and along rooftops, firing bazookas, flinging grenades, and dropping blocks of TNT from the ramparts. With a .30-caliber machine gun mounted on his jeep, Darby hammered away as his driver darted through narrow alleys around the piazza. Seeing his slugs bounce like marbles off the armor plates, Darby raced to the beach, commandeered a 37mm antitank gun, split open a box of ammo with an ax, then hurried back into town. His second shot halted a Renault, and he flushed the surviving crew with a thermite grenade laid atop the hatch. "Soon the metal was red hot," the journalist Don Whitehead reported, "and the crew scrambled out screaming in surrender." As the remaining Italian tanks retreated, Italian infantrymen arrived in parade-ground formation west of Gela. Bracketed with mortar fire, they were cut to ribbons. Survivors "fled in disorder." Hewitt summoned the jut-jawed monitor

H.M.S. *Abercrombie* to harass other enemy forces sheltering in Niscemi; a shift of ballast cocked the ship's guns higher to obtain the requisite range, and 15-inch shells the width of tree trunks soon rained down.

By late morning, Gela, the town of Aeschylus and Saracen olives, had fallen. Darby pulled an American flag from his pack and tacked it to the front wall of the Fascist party headquarters. A sergeant from the Bronx strolled the streets, quoting Thomas Paine in Italian. An angry crone cursed from her balcony, but other townfolk—perhaps sensing the strategic direction of the young campaign—huzzahed the invaders with "*Viva, America.*" Civil affairs officers eventually counted thirteen hundred demolished houses, of Gela's fourteen thousand. They also counted 170 corpses. Geloans refused to touch the bodies, and prisoners were pressganged to haul the dead on donkey carts to the cemetery. By noon on July 10, U.S. patrols were four miles inland, well toward the Yellow Line objective. Still, the ranks felt unsettled: the assault, they agreed, had been too easy. The real enemy, those with panzers and coal-scuttle helmets, had not yet been met.

Fifteen miles west, it was easier still. The 3rd Infantry Division, bolstered by another Ranger battalion and tanks from the 2nd Armored Division, had appeared in the early morning off the coast at Licata, where the stink of sulfur, asphalt, and fish implied the local delicacies. As the flagship *Biscayne* dropped anchor just four miles off the town's breakwater, five searchlights from shore swept the sea, quickly fixing the vessel in their beams. "All five of them," wrote Ernie Pyle, who stood on deck, "pinioned us in their white shafts as we sat there." Then one by one the lights blinked out until a single beam still burned, lingering for a moment like the ghost light in a theater until it, too, was extinguished. "Not a shot had been fired."

No one was more relieved than the craggy officer standing near Pyle aboard *Biscayne*. He wore a russet leather jacket, cavalry breeches, high brown boots, a lacquered two-star helmet, and an expression that married a squint with a scowl. His front incisors were gapped and tobacco stained; one admirer wrote that his heavy-boned face had been "hewn directly out of hard rock. The large protruding eyes are the outstanding feature." Around his neck he had knotted a paratrooper's white silk escape map of Sicily, which soon would become his much-mimicked trademark. He had a blacksmith's hands, and the iron shoulders of a man with a four-goal polo handicap. His "rock-crusher voice" derived, so it was said, from swallowing carbolic acid as a child; for the past month he had been painting his vocal cords, inflamed from smoking, with silver nitrate. Many considered him the finest combat commander in the U.S. Army.

Major General Lucian K. Truscott, Jr., led the 3rd Division and was charged with protecting Seventh Army's far left flank. Now forty-eight, he was embarking on his second invasion, for he had also commanded Patton's left flank in Morocco. Born into a country doctor's family in Texas, Truscott for six years had taught in one- and two-room schoolhouses in Oklahoma and attended Cleveland Teachers Institute before enlisting in the cavalry. The schoolmaster never left him—"You use the passive voice too damn much," he once chided a subordinate—and he wrote long, searching critiques of subordinates' performances. Even in combat, he cherished cut flowers on his desk and enjoyed ontological inquiry: a staff meeting might begin with Truscott asking the division chaplain, "What is sin?" His kit bag included *War and Peace*, *Webster's High School Dictionary*, and perhaps a liquor bottle; some subordinates thought he drank too much. A stern disciplinarian, he had imposed fifty-year sentences on soldiers who maimed themselves in North Africa to avoid combat; lesser miscreants got "an application of corncob and turpentine," an aide said. Truscott had learned much in Morocco, about "the loneliness of the battlefield" and the need for physical vigor. Each 3rd Division battalion was required to master the "Truscott trot": marching five miles in the first hour and four miles an hour thereafter, for as long as necessary.

Nothing revealed more of him than his letters home to Sarah Randolph Truscott, which began, invariably, "Beloved Wife." Aboard *Biscayne* on July 7 he had written:

> Do you remember how you used to get after me for working so hard and how I answered that I had to be ready—prepare myself—for any responsibility that came to me? I am only sorry that my limitations were such that I could not accomplish more, because responsibilities are certainly falling on me. Your calm confidence in me is always with me and when doubt falls upon me—as it must on all—that thought soon restores that confidence. I can do only the best I can.

At Licata, his best was good enough. A few desultory Italian artillery shells greeted the invaders, who found the beaches unmined. Booby traps on the docks were still in their packing crates. Air attacks proved less intense here than elsewhere on the HUSKY front; only the star-crossed minesweeper U.S.S. *Sentinel* was lost. Hit four times by dive-bombers at five A.M., wrecked and abandoned, with sixty-one dead and wounded, she capsized and sank five hours later.

Infantrymen drowned or were gunned down without ever setting foot in Europe, but not many. *Biscayne*'s sisters poured shells into the town—

"scorched wadding came raining down on the deck," Pyle reported—and destroyers screened the landing craft with heavy smoke. Ten battalions made shore in an hour, with tanks. They soon captured two thousand Italian soldiers—some insisted on leading their pet goats into captivity—while many others bolted for the hills in what the Italian high command called "self-demobilization." Dry grass used to camouflage gun batteries caught fire, smoking out the gunners; others ran from German shepherds trained in Virginia to clear pillboxes and lunge for the throat. "Every time one of the poor Dagoes would wave a white flag over the edge, the tank gunner would shoot at it," an armor captain wrote his wife, "so I finally stopped him and ran them out with my pistol. . . . They were the most scared men I have ever seen."

Dawn revealed a U.S. flag flapping on a hill above Licata. Troops in olive drab scuttled through town, drawing only smiles from children who made "V for victory" signs with their upraised arms. At 9:18 A.M. the fleet signaled, "Hold all gunfire. Objective taken." Those seaworthy mules aboard *LST 386* flatly refused to cross the pontoon causeway to shore; exasperated sailors finally heaved them overboard and let them swim.

Truscott came ashore with greater dignity, by launch at noon. Fishing boats bobbed in the tiny harbor, their triangular lateen sails "white as sharks' teeth," one journalist wrote. Staff officers scurried about, settling a division command post in the Palazzo La Lumia and cleaning up a new bivouac. No amount of scrubbing could eradicate the reek of sulfur or the millennial grit. "Hell," a soldier complained within Pyle's earshot, "this is just as bad as Africa." Truscott recorded his impressions in another letter to Sarah. "I find this country interesting but distasteful to me," he wrote. "I certainly do not like the accumulated poverty and filth of the ages." *Responsibilities are falling on me,* he had told her. Licata was but the beginning.

Across the Gulf of Gela, the third and final prong of Seventh Army's invasion found the sea on Patton's right flank a more ferocious adversary than enemy soldiers. Twelve-foot swells and six-foot surf still bedeviled the convoys bearing the 45th Division to Scoglitti, where westerly winds chewed at the exposed bight. The destroyers *Knight* and *Tillman* laid down white-phosphorus naval shells for the first time in combat; the blinding flashes and dense smoke terrified Italian defenders in their pillboxes and gun batteries. Big cruiser shells followed on a flatter trajectory, three at a time, and fires soon danced along the shoreline.

The first assault wave hit the wrong beach, and from that point the invasion deteriorated. The eleventh-hour transfer to the Pacific of coxswains who had trained on the Chesapeake with the 45th now haunted the division. Their callow replacements, overmatched by rough surf, sandbars, and sporadic gunfire, veered this way and that along the coast, shouting across the water for directions to Blue Beach or Yellow Two. At Punta Braccetto, two boats in the second wave collided while sheering away from the rocks. Four sputtering GIs struggled to shore; thirty-eight others drowned, and 157th Infantry bandsmen pressed into service as gravediggers swapped their instruments for picks and shovels. Companies landed far from their designated beaches, and soon battalions and then finally an entire regiment—the 180th Infantry—had been scattered across a twelve-mile swatch of Sicilian shingle. "This," a regimental history conceded, "played havoc."

Dozens of landing craft broached or flooded—"a most deplorable picture throughout D-day," the official Army history observed—and soon two hundred boats stood stranded on beaches or offshore bars. The scattered vessels reminded one Navy lieutenant of "shoes in a dead man's closet." Landing and unloading operations were as inept as they had been in Morocco, where a sad standard for amphibious incompetence had been set eight months earlier. Among those coming ashore with the 180th Infantry was a puckish left-hander from New Mexico who had a knack for cartooning and whose impious characters Willie and Joe would soon become the unshaven, bleary-eyed icons of a million infantrymen. "My first practical lesson about war" came at Scoglitti, Sergeant Bill Mauldin later said. "Nobody really knows what he's doing."

"The beach was in total confusion," reported the senior Army engineer on the scene. "There had been no real planning. The beachmaster was not in control." Not least, pilferage of supplies and barracks bags by Army shore parties was common; their commanding colonel was subsequently court-martialed. Congestion grew so desperate that beaches Green 2 and Yellow 2 were closed below Scoglitti, and beaches Red, Green, and Yellow above the town would soon shut down, too. Later waves diverted to six new beaches where engineers blew exits through the dunes with bangalore torpedoes and laid steel-mesh matting for traction. As shore operations bogged down, the captains of some ships, fearing air attack, weighed anchor for North Africa without unloading. The 45th Division commander spent his first night on Sicily in a rude foxhole a mile inland, wrapped in a parachute. "To make it less comfortable," Major General Troy H. Middleton reported, "the friendly Navy shelled the area."

Still, as D-day drew to a close the Americans were ashore on their narrow littoral crescent. From Licata to Scoglitti more than fifty thousand U.S. troops and five thousand vehicles had landed, with more of each waiting offshore for first light on Sunday. Casualties had been modest, and the enemy seemed befuddled. Italian coastal-defense units had surrendered in such numbers that Sicilian women lined the sidewalks, jeering as their men shuffled into captivity. Yet neither the prisoner columns nor the stacks of enemy dead awaiting mass burial included many men wearing German field gray, and every GI on Sicily expected that soon the invaders would encounter a more formidable foe.

That left the British. Except for the saving grace of calmer seas, all the confusion that bedeviled the Americans in the Gulf of Gela also plagued the Eighth Army landings thirty-five miles away on the island's eastern flank. Commandos came ashore first, crossing the beach where some speculated that Odysseus, after leaving Calypso's island, would have made landfall in Sicily, "the land of the high and mighty Cyclops." The Canadian 1st Division anchored the army's left wing on a ten-thousand-yard front of the Pachino Peninsula, while the British 51st, 50th, and 5th Divisions beat for the beaches east and north.

"Some confusion and lack of control," the 50th Division acknowledged off Avola. "Many craft were temporarily lost and circled their parent ship more than once. . . . It was exceedingly dark. Most naval officers were uncertain as to their whereabouts." Transports unwittingly anchored twelve miles off the coast rather than the expected seven, confounding runs to the beach and putting shore parties beyond radio range. Some landings "were in no way carried out to plan," a British intelligence report noted. "Army officers had to take a hand in navigation, and had they not done so, many craft would have beached still further from the correct places." A Canadian captain was more direct. "Get on, you silly bastards!" he roared at his men. "Get on with it!"

Landing craft ground ashore in the early light. Voices sang out: "Down door!" Then: "Sicily, everybody out!" Fire from shore batteries proved modest, except of course for those it actually struck. "The water had become a sea of blood and limbs, remains of once grand fighting men who would never be identified," wrote Able Seaman K. G. Oakley, who saw a landing craft shattered in the 50th Division sector. From the surf Oakley pulled "a man whose arm was hanging on by a few bits of cloth and flesh. He cried, 'My arm! Look, it's hit me.' " Like tens of thousands of others on that Saturday morning, Oakley reflected, "So this is war."

Ashore they swarmed, scrambling through the dunes and across the coastal highway. A Scots regiment entered Cassibile skirling, in defiance of orders that bagpipes remain on the ships. A pungent smell briefly triggered gas alarms and fumbling for masks, until more sophisticated noses realized that the odor came from wild thyme churned by bombs. While some troops built makeshift jetties with stones salvaged from a beachfront vineyard, others darted between doorways, shouting the Eighth Army challenge—"Desert Rats!"—and listening for the proper parole: "Kill Italians." A Sicilian peasant charged from his house and fired an ancient shotgun at approaching Commandos, who killed him with return fire. "Sorry we had to shoot that farmer," a British soldier remarked. "He had the right spirit."

Eighth Army had prepared for up to ten thousand casualties during the first week of combat on Sicily; in the event, they would sustain only 1,517. But even those who escaped without so much as a sunburn shared a Royal Engineer corporal's view:

> We had learned our first lesson, mainly that fate, not the Germans or Italians, was our undiscriminating enemy. With the same callousness as Army orders, without fairness or judgement, "You and you—dead. The rest of you, on the truck."

More than a third of Eighth Army's casualties were sustained in one misadventure, code-named LADBROOKE, which was intended to complement Colonel Gavin's jump but which bore the signature traits of so many airborne operations in the Second World War: poor judgment, dauntless valor, and a nonchalant disregard for men's lives. LADBROOKE had a coherent purpose: 1,700 soldiers were to capture the Ponte Grande, a graceful highway bridge that arched above the river Anapo just south of Syracuse. After preventing demolition of the span, troops would push into the city, capture the docks, and give Eighth Army a vital port. Under General Montgomery's plan, the assault was to be made late Friday night by 144 gliders.

There was the rub: the only pilots available to fly the tow planes had little experience at night navigation and even less at towing a seven-ton glider full of infantrymen on the end of a 350-foot nylon rope. Skilled glider crews were also in short supply, as were the gliders themselves. So rudimentary was the art of combat gliding that jeeps had been tried—unsuccessfully—to tow gliders into the air that spring. Not least, the landing zones near the Ponte Grande appeared to be seamed with stone walls and stippled with rocks. Protests by subordinate officers proved unavailing. Once made, the daring plan could not be unmade; naysayers risked the appearance of timidity and the threat of removal from command. Again, senior officers with little airborne experience and unrealistic expectations held sway.

Several dozen Horsa gliders arrived in Tunisia in late June after a harrowing 1,400-mile tow from England. The wood-frame craft had "huge flaps, like barn doors." To supplement the Horsas, the Americans donated a fleet of smaller, metal-framed Wacos; each arrived in North Africa in five crates and required 250 man-hours to assemble. British airmen believed that every pilot needed at least 100 hours of flight training on the Waco for proficiency; in the event, they averaged less than 5 hours in the cockpit, including a single hour of night flying. Many had barely qualified for solo flights. Of 150 gliders used in training, more than half were destroyed, even though novices flew almost exclusively in daylight and a dead calm. Most of the tugs would be U.S. C-47 Dakotas, but not until mid-May were the tug pilots released from their duties flying freight in order to train with the gliders.

Pilots and passengers were doomed, of course. From six Tunisian airfields on that windswept Friday night, the gliders soared into the air, towed by 109 American Dakotas and 35 British Albemarles. Confronting "conditions for which we were completely unprepared," as the glider force commander conceded, they headed for Malta at five hundred feet, fighting the gale, as well as lingering turbulence from the day's thermal currents and the tow rope's nauseating tendency to act as a pendulum. Many inexperienced navigators quickly grew confused; some had the wrong charts or none at all. Strain on the tow ropes snapped the communication wires between many tugs and gliders. A Horsa's tow line parted north of Malta, and thirty men plummeted to their deaths; when a Waco's line also broke, fifteen more followed. One glider cast off from its tug and landed smartly, only to have a soldier pull up in a jeep and announce, "We are sorry to inform you that you are not in Sicily, but on the main airstrip at Malta." Another glider team, surprised to find Sicily so sandy, discovered that they had landed near Mareth, in southern Tunisia. Investigators later concluded: "Navigation generally was bad."

Ninety percent of the aircraft made the Sicilian landfall at Cape Passero, to be greeted moments later along the Gulf of Noto by flak, flares, searchlights, and dust clouds, which rattled the pilots and obscured their vision. "I guess that's Sicily," said one squinting captain. Formations disintegrated, and soon tugs and gliders were "milling in a blind swarm." Some tug pilots, shying from antiaircraft fire that seemed closer than it actually was, released their gliders too early. Plans called for all gliders to be cut free within two miles off the coast, but an optical illusion, magnified by the pilots' inexperience, made the shoreline appear to be directly below when the planes were thousands of yards out to sea. From altitudes of 2,000 to 4,000 feet, the scattered Horsas and Wacos cast off along a thirty-mile front and immediately found that gliding west into a thirty-knot wind was "unsound," as one account concluded.

"As we lost height it seemed as if a great wall of blackness was rising up to meet us," an officer wrote. For many, that blackness was the Mediterranean. A cry went up: "Prepare for ditching!" Dozens of gliders careered across the water like skipping stones. Some splintered and sank quickly; others would float for hours. Frantic passengers kicked at the fabric walls or hacked away with hatchets. "We went under almost instantly," Flight Officer Ruby H. Dees recalled. "When I reached the surface the rest of the fellows were hanging on the wreckage." An officer clinging to another fractured wing murmured to a British major, "All is not well, Bill." At least sixty gliders crashed into the sea, and ten more vanished—somewhere—with all hands lost. Men flailed and struggled and then struggled no more. In some instances Italian machine-gun fire raked survivors clinging to the flotsam.

Fifty-four gliders made land, often with equally fatal results. "Heavy tracer, left wing hit, flew over landing zone and landed sixteen miles southwest of Syracuse, hitting a six-foot wall," a survivor reported. "Left wing burning, also seventy-seven grenades ignited inside glider. Two pilots and twelve other ranks killed, seven wounded." Horsa number 132—among the dozen gliders that found the Ponte Grande—crashed into a canal bank four hundred yards from the bridge, killing all aboard but one. Another Horsa hit a treetop and flipped; a jeep was later found inside with the driver behind the wheel, dead.

Rather than five hundred or more British soldiers holding Ponte Grande, a mere platoon seized the bridge, ripping out demolition charges from the abutments. By Saturday dawn the force had grown to eighty-seven, with only two Bren machine guns among them, and little ammunition. Italian mortar fire and infantry counterattacks whittled the little band, killing troops on the span and in the muddy river below. By mid-afternoon the bridgehead was held by just fifteen unwounded Tommies, and Italian machine-gunners had closed to forty yards. At four P.M. the survivors surrendered. They were marched away toward Syracuse by "a pompous little man with a coil of hangman's rope around his shoulders," only to be promptly freed by a Northamptonshire patrol that had landed with the 5th Division. At the same time, Royal Scots Fusiliers bulled through from the south and easily recaptured the bridge.

The British high command would proclaim LADBROOKE a success because the Ponte Grande had been spared. But rarely has a victory been more pyrrhic. Casualties exceeded six hundred, of whom more than half drowned. Bodies would wash ashore on various Mediterranean beaches for weeks. If the courage of those flying to Sicily that night is unquestionable, the same cannot be said for the judgment of their superiors in concocting and approving such a witless plan. Anger and sorrow seeped through the ranks; British fury at American tow pilots grew so toxic that surviving Tommies who arrived back in Tunisia were confined to camp to forestall a fraternal bloodletting. A memo to George Marshall concluded, "The combat efficiency for night glider operations was practically zero." But the most trenchant summary of LADBROOKE appeared in a British Army assessment: "Alarm, confusion and dismay."

## The Loss of Irrecoverable Hours

I F much had gone wrong for the Allies during HUSKY's first twelve hours, almost nothing had gone right for the Axis defenders. Miscalculation and mischance, those handmaidens of military misfortune, dominated the initial response to the invasion and "irrecoverable hours were thus lost," as a German commander later acknowledged. The Anglo-Americans had a toehold, which soon became a foothold, and dislodging them from the island became more difficult with the arrival of every DUKW and LST. Among the alarums sounded that Saturday, in fact, was a report by an incredulous Italian officer of "amphibious contrivances" capable of beaching and then advancing inland "under their own power."

For weeks, Axis reconnaissance had deflected hints of invasion, including the presence of half a dozen hospital ships at Gibraltar on July 1—Italian pilots eventually counted sixteen in the Mediterranean—and the massing of landing craft and gliders in Tunisia. Yet Allied deception efforts for months had kept Axis intelligence off balance and befuddled. The British, for example, had created a fictional "Twelfth Army," supposedly based in Cairo, with the notional mission of invading the Balkans through Greece in the early summer of 1943. Particularly successful was Operation MINCEMEAT, which featured a corpse later celebrated as "the man who never was." A British submarine had dumped the body, dressed as a major of the Royal Marines, off the southern coast of Spain in late April. Manacled to the dead man's wrist was a briefcase containing forged documents; these, it was hoped, the Spanish authorities would share with the Germans. The Spanish duly obliged. Subsequent Ultra intercepts revealed that German intelligence, convinced that the "major" had drowned in a plane crash, considered the documents further evidence that the main Allied blow would fall on Sardinia and Greece rather than Sicily.

Six immobile and badly armed Italian coastal divisions now guarded the Sicilian shore, backed by four Italian infantry divisions positioned inland with two capable German units: the 15th Panzer Grenadier Division in western Sicily, and the Hermann Göring Panzer Division in the east. The first unequivocal alert had been issued on Sicily at 6:40 on Friday evening, July 9. Allied bombs had shattered the rudimentary Sicilian telephone system, so some units got the word but others did not. A few Italian commanders, presuming that no fool would attack in such foul weather, went to bed. Exhortations at one A.M. Saturday to defend "this most precious piece of Italian soil" fell on deaf or sleeping ears. British Spitfires, using signals intelligence to pinpoint the German Luftwaffe headquarters, shot up the San Domenico Palace—a grand hotel in Taormina, once favored by D. H. Lawrence—and unhinged the Axis air defenses just as invaders approached the island.

Little was expected from the Sicilian coastal divisions, and that expectation was fully met. Training had recently been reduced because of footwear shortages, and Italian coastal artillery was limited to the pea-shooter range of nine thousand yards, further impaired by morning glare that blinded defenders facing south and east. The Syracuse garrison commander was killed in the invasion's first minutes, and his skittish counterpart in Augusta spiked his guns without a fight. Italian foot soldiers surrendered by the thousands, or peeled off their uniforms and melted into the refugee hordes streaming inland.

The German response in those first irrecoverable hours, if less timid, was hardly impressive. Sicilian communications were so crude that the commander of the Hermann Göring Division first learned that he was under attack in a radio alert from Frascati, the German headquarters near Rome. Orders to subordinate commanders proved tardy or contradictory. The repositioning of one regiment was delayed when a courier carrying the movement orders died in a car wreck. Efforts to fling seventeen big Tiger tanks into the fight near Gela on Saturday were beset by mechanical breakdowns, poor leadership, naval gunfire, and the difficulty of picking a path through the olive groves. Fantasy prevailed over hard fact: Comando Supremo, the Italian high command in Rome, announced at noon on July 10 that the Gela and Licata landings were "almost cleaned up"; some Anglo-American troops were even said to have reembarked in their amphibious contrivances. A subsequent dispatch from Rome asserted that "the enemy is still actively landing but he is constantly in crisis."

Such fairy tales did not deceive the man who would ultimately direct the defense of Sicily. For now he remained at his Frascati headquarters, sifting through the fragmentary reports, rumors, and mendacities arriving from the island. But his tactical influence could already be felt on the young campaign, as well as his unquenchable optimism and a gift for battlefield improvisation. The Allies knew Field Marshal Albert Kesselring all too well. As the senior German commander in the Mediterranean—in effect, Eisenhower's counterpart—Kesselring had thwarted a quick Allied victory in Tunisia, fought the Anglo-Americans to a bloody draw for months, then dodged both capture and recrimination when Hitler's no-retreat decree consigned Axis forces in Africa to destruction. Ostensibly, he served under Italian authority, as a sop to the Pact of Steel signed in 1939, and to Mussolini's proprietary claim on the Mediterranean; in reality, he answered to Berlin and had few equals in any army. Kesselring was loyal to Hitler as "Germany's savior from chaos," and he had long found it "possible to ignore the less pleasing things" in the Nazi regime. Hitler repaid the loyalty with a field marshal's baton, which an aide carried in a zippered leather case.

Now fifty-seven, he had a face full of flashing teeth, which expressed both his Bavarian bonhomie and the nickname—"Smiling Albert"— coined by his soldiers. "Kesselring is a colossal optimist," Hitler had said on May 20, "and we must take care that this optimism does not blind him." An artilleryman who in midcareer had learned to fly and transferred to the Luftwaffe, he had a knack for the narrow escape, demonstrated most recently during an Allied bombing raid on Marsala in May that killed two staff officers; Kesselring fled the upper floor of a shattered building by rappeling down a rope to the street, badly skinning his palms.

For six months he had pondered how to defend southern Europe, and for six weeks he had believed that the next Allied blow would likely fall on Sicily. Kesselring's overarching strategic concept involved keeping the war as far from the Fatherland as possible for as long as possible; as an airman, he had a vivid understanding of what Allied possession of bomber bases in Italy would mean for Munich, Vienna, and Berlin. Unlike many German generals—including his rival, Erwin Rommel—he considered all of Italy defensible, *if* the Italians would fight. Kesselring believed they would, although his Italophilia was tempered with sardonic disdain. "The Italian is easily contented," Kesselring said. "He actually has only three fashionable passions—coffee, cigarettes, and women." As for the Italian man of arms, he was "not a soldier from within."

Kesselring in late spring had dismissed Sicilian defenses as "pretty sugar pastry," but reports on July 10 that entire Italian divisions were evaporating disheartened even the "colossal optimist." If Allied forces also landed in

Calabria, on the toe of the Italian boot, Sicily could become a "mouse-trap," with the result that another Axis army would be annihilated. To forestall this calamity, Kesselring realized, German forces on the island must strike before Allied troops consolidated their beachheads. The 15th Panzer Grenadier Division was too far west to attack quickly, because the field marshal, against Italian advice, had just shifted the grenadiers across 155 miles of bad roads to meet landings in western Sicily that now seemed unlikely. That left the Hermann Göring panzers to take the fight to the enemy. Badly mauled in Tunisia, the division had been hurriedly rebuilt and now mustered nine thousand combat troops with ninety Mk III and Mk IV tanks, in addition to the seventeen Mk VI Tigers.

From Frascati, Kesselring dictated an order to the division commander, General Paul Conrath: counterattack Gela at first light on Sunday, July 11, and drive the invaders into the sea. "Herr Feldmarschall," Conrath had told Kesselring, "immediate advance on the enemy is my strength!"

Brigadier General Ted Roosevelt had insisted on splashing ashore in Gela with the first assault wave from the U.S.S. *Barnett*. On Beach Green 2 before dawn on Saturday, he sent a heartening dispatch back to the ship— "The Romans are fleeing inland"—then spent the rest of the day helping the 1st Division make land behind him. As the sun rose and concussion waves from the naval guns shimmered across the sea, Roosevelt scuttled about on his stubby, puttee-wrapped legs with "the twinkling walk of a sandpiper on the beach." He wore no tie and often no helmet, and his rumpled uniform fit him like an olive-drab sack. The artist George Biddle described him in four adjectives: "bald, burnt, gnarled, and wrinkled." Despite congenitally weak vision, Roosevelt often disdained eyeglasses, and more than once he had given a tactical briefing with a map tacked upside down by practical jokers on the division staff. Occasionally he burst into verse—an admirer deemed him "one of the world's most fluent reciters"—and "in a rhythmic state of mind" he spouted passages of Kipling, *Pilgrim's Progress,* and the iambic pentameter of his favorite poet, Edwin Arlington Robinson. A bum knee and a rheumatic hip forced Roosevelt to carry a cane, which he wielded as if it were a rapier, slicing the air and pointing at exits through the dunes. Rarely did he speak at any volume lower than a bellow, and now in his foghorn voice he roared, again and again, "Get into the battle!"

"I will always be known as the son of Theodore Roosevelt," he had written in 1910, at the age of twenty-three, "and never as a person who means only himself." He spent the subsequent three decades proving himself wrong. Decorated for valor in the 1st Division during the Great War—he had been gassed at Cantigny and wounded at Soissons—young Ted then amassed both a fortune and a reputation independent of his father. A wealthy investment banker by age thirty, he lost the 1924 New York gubernatorial race to Al Smith by 100,000 votes, then pressed on in various public and private roles: as the governor of Puerto Rico and the Philippines; as the author of eight books; as a senior executive at American Express and Doubleday; as an early activist in the National Association for the Advancement of Colored People; and as an explorer and a hunter, whose trophies for the Field Museum in Chicago included the rare mountain sheep *Ovis poli* and a previously unknown deer subsequently named *Muntiacus rooseveltorum*. He was plainspoken—"I'm anti-bluff, anti-faker, anti-coward, that's all"—and unaffected. "Do fill your letters with the small beer of home, the things we knew in the kindly past," he had written his wife, Eleanor, on June 5. "Also gossip. I love gossip." A week later he wrote her a poem that began, "This dark, grim war has swallowed all / That I loved."

Perhaps not quite all, for certainly he loved the Big Red One, as the 1st Division styled itself. "Ted Roosevelt is perhaps the only man I've ever met who was born to combat," wrote the veteran war correspondent Quentin Reynolds, and soon after returning to active duty in 1941, Roosevelt became the division's assistant commander. "Whenever you write a message, remember you're writing it for a damned fool," he advised junior officers. "Keep it clear and simple." Troops adored his bluff pugnacity and considered him "an intellectual because he carries a considerable stock of books in his blanket roll," observed the journalist A. J. Liebling. A 26th Infantry medic recalled, "When he got up to leave, we willingly got up and saluted." In the Tunisian campaign, he again demonstrated extraordinary valor, winning the Distinguished Service Cross at the battle of El Guettar. Patton in his diary in late June deemed Roosevelt, now fifty-five, "weak on discipline and training but a fine battle leader. . . . There are too few."

That he was "weak on discipline" was hard to dispute, and in that deficiency lay controversy and consternation. When another general complained that Roosevelt and the 1st Division commander, Major General Terry Allen, "seem to think the United States Army consists of the 1st Division and eleven million replacements," Roosevelt quipped, "Well, doesn't it?" In Tunisia he told the troops, "Once we've licked the Boche, we'll go back to Oran and beat up every M.P. in town." The division's return to Algeria after the Tunisian campaign had indeed left a "trail of looted wineshops and outraged mayors." Some troops fired at Arab peasants from troop train boxcars "just to see them jump," admitted a 26th Infantry soldier, who added, "Too much vino, too cocky, and too much steam to blow off. . . . We just plain didn't give a damn for anyone or anything."

Toxic rumors that the 1st Division would be sent home from Africa—regimental bookies offered even money that they would be back in the States by August 1—simply fueled resentment when Patton instead requisitioned the Big Red One for his Sicilian spearhead. Grievances large and small accumulated: at being kept in filthy if durable wool combat uniforms when rear-echelon troops were switched to cooler khaki; at seeing men who had never heard a shot fired in anger sport the new brown-and-green African campaign ribbon; at service troops hoarding Camels and Lucky Strikes while sending inferior cigarettes to the frontline units. Patton's taunting helped not at all. "The yellow-bellies of the First Division don't need khakis," he told Terry Allen; most of the troops, Patton added, likely would be "killed trying to invade Sicily."

By late May, when the division bivouacked in a sere, shadeless camp outside Oran, not far from the TORCH invasion beaches of 1942, the troops agreed that the city should be liberated again. Swaggering eight abreast down Oran sidewalks, they shoved the khaki-clad into the gutters and ripped the campaign ribbons from khaki blouses. One group, slapping three months' pay on the bar of the Florida Club, told the barkeep, "Let us know when this is up." A division memo decried "excessive drunkenness" and the troops' "disheveled appearance"; brass knuckles and contraband German Lugers were confiscated, and a five P.M. curfew was imposed in the city's taverns. Still the "second battle of Oran" raged on, featuring "lively brawls in which sides were chosen by the cloth worn." An 18th Infantry soldier noted: "Truckloads of gun-toting GIs and cocky junior officers take over Oran . . . scaring civilians indoors and bringing M.P.s." Roosevelt inflamed the men by implying they need not salute officers outside the division, and an unconfirmed rumor put Terry Allen in the middle of an 18th Infantry scrap with MPs.

Higher authority was "bitched, buggered and bewildered," Roosevelt acknowledged. General Lucas told his diary on June 27, "The division has been babied too much. They have been told so often that they are the best in the world that so far as real discipline is concerned they have slipped." Eisenhower was furious, and ordered Allen's immediate superior, Lieutenant General Omar N. Bradley, to expel the 1st Division from Oran. For a prim sobersides like Bradley, the Oran rampage was yet another black mark in the ledger of black marks he had kept since Tunisia on the division and its commanders, whom he considered "freebooters." The 1st, Bradley sniffed, "was piratical at heart."

Now the hour for pirates and freebooters had come round. Just after dawn on Sunday, July 11, Roosevelt drove in his jeep, *Rough Rider,* from the division command post in a lemon grove beyond Beach Green 2 to the 26th

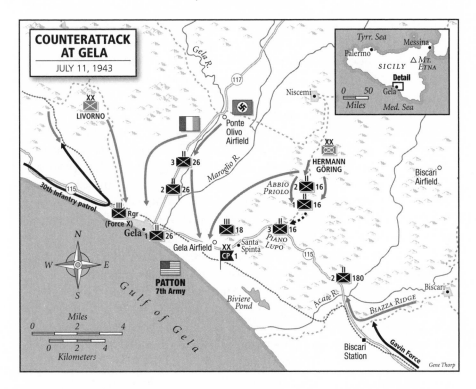

Infantry sector east of Gela. The mild Sabbath morning kissed the vineyards and orchards of the plain, which stretched north for eight miles to a crown of low hills beyond Ponte Olivo airfield. The division since first light had been making for those hills on a six-mile front: the 26th Infantry up Highway 117 on the left, and the 16th Infantry on the right up Highway 115 and the gravel road to Niscemi.

Roosevelt hopped out of the jeep and hurried to the regimental radios clustered beneath a camouflage net. Reports from the lead battalions were fragmented and unnerving: advancing U.S. infantrymen had smacked into advancing Axis tanks. German panzers were driving south from Ponte Olivo, southwest from Niscemi, and west from Biscari. Italian troops from the Livorno Division had massed farther west for an attack on Gela. At 6:40 A.M., at least a dozen German tanks swept past the pinned-down 3rd Battalion of the 26th Infantry on Highway 117, midway between Gela and Ponte Olivo. Swerving southeast across the wheat fields, the panzers were rolling toward the landing beaches.

Through his field glasses, Roosevelt squinted at the amber dust boiling on the northern horizon. A pair of Mk IV tanks with gray camouflage splotches bolted cross-country at top speed in an attempt to draw fire; to one officer they resembled "setters trying to flush quail." Other panzers worked the subtle folds and creases in the plain. Muzzle flashes stabbed the dust. Soon the morning air thickened with shouts and cackling machine guns and the scarlet gash of tank fire.

Shortly before seven A.M., Roosevelt rang the 1st Division command post on the field phone. "The 26th on our left has had a tank attack. Don't know how bad as yet," he told a staff officer. "Let me speak to General Allen." Upon hearing Allen's voice, Roosevelt wasted no time. "Terry, look. The situation is not very comfortable out here. The 3rd Battalion has been attacked by tanks and has been penetrated. The 2nd Battalion is in support, but that is not enough. No anti-tank protection. If we could get that company of medium tanks it sure would help."

Each battle report seemed more dire than the last. Panzers had infiltrated the rear of the 3rd Battalion, firing into foxholes and trenches. Low on bazooka and mortar rounds, the American rifle platoons leapfrogged south, pulling back three miles to the outskirts of Gela. "The 26th here is catching hell," Roosevelt told a division staff officer shortly after eight A.M. "What about a company of medium tanks? Not unloaded yet? Goddamn it, I'll come and pull those tanks out myself. We don't want them tomorrow." An hour later he told Allen, "Situation not so good."

Between phone calls he stumped about with his gamecock gait, brandishing his cane to rally the riflemen in their holes. "These guys can't hit me! They've been trying through two world wars. And if they can't hit an old grandfather like me, they surely can't hurt you," he barked. "Do you know who those bastards are? The Hermann Göring Division. We beat their asses in North Africa and we're going to do it again." Later he would tell Eleanor: "The old man still can fight."

In the lemon grove near Green 2, the 1st Division command post was identifiable only by a small sign—"Danger Forward"—and the radio antennas poking out from behind a stone wall. Here another old soldier also had his blood up. He was saddle-nosed and leathery, and deep pleats framed his brown eyes. Gray flecked the blue-black hair that bristled beneath his helmet rim, and he walked, one observer wrote, with "the slightly rolling gait of a man who has spent a great deal of time on horseback." Like Ted Roosevelt, he had been annealed in the Great War: a bullet through the face in the Argonne had perforated both cheeks and at times still caused him to emit a curious, leaky-tire hiss. Like Ted Roosevelt he also cherished the Big Red One, with that unconditional loyalty unique to comrades; their rivalry for the division's affections had contributed little to good order and discipline.

Yet neither order nor discipline had ever loomed large for Terry de la Mesa Allen. Before flunking out of West Point, he had amassed demerits for tardiness, bathing at midnight, yawning in class, yelling during a fire drill, and breaking ranks to pet a dog. As a young officer he "loved horses, women, dancing, and drinking," and as a major he graduated at the bottom of the staff college class in which a certain Major Eisenhower finished at the very top. Yet he knew how to fight and he knew how to lead, and the Army valued both enough to make Allen the first among his former West Point classmates to wear a general's stars. Now he wore a pair, the insignia of a major general.

"The soldier's greatest nightmare is to think he is being sent up to death foolishly," an aide later wrote. "Men didn't feel that way under Allen." A devout Roman Catholic, he regretted missing mass on this eventful Sunday morning, but he had privately prayed, as he always prayed before battle, for the souls of his men. As for generalship, he believed that "tactics are nine-tenths audacity," and his favorite military adages had a primitive simplicity: "Find 'em, fix 'em, and fight 'em," for example, and "You win or die." Allen's political philosophy was no more sophisticated. "It's crazy, this war," he said with a shrug. In June he advised his men, "Do your job. We don't want heroes—dead heroes. We're not out for glory. We're here to do a dirty, stinking job." At the same time he wrote his young wife, Mary Fran, "I feel sure that my luck will continue to hold in the future."

That luck had been sorely tested already this morning. "Couriers dashed in and out of the grove," wrote the reporter Don Whitehead. "Field telephones rang and men shouted into radios. Shells whined over." An agitated staff officer appeared and Allen said, "Don't tell me. I can guess. They've attacked from the east and west." The officer nodded. On the division's right flank, the 16th Infantry was even more deeply embattled than the 26th Infantry on the left. The 16th Regiment's 2nd Battalion held for two hours against forty panzers at Abbio Priolo on the Niscemi road before at least two companies broke, shoving past officers trying to stop them. "The men felt utterly frustrated because they had nothing with which to fight the tanks. Some of them were crying," a captain reported. By late morning, the survivors had dug in under scorching fire along a ridge at Piano Lupo, where their advance had begun at midnight. "Hell, let's not wait for them to attack us. Let's attack them first," a lieutenant said, then fell dead with a bullet in the head.

At 10:10 A.M., the 3rd Battalion reported thirty panzers northeast of the Gela-Niscemi road junction, before adding: "We are in heavy conflict with tanks." By now the regiment had lost six of nine antitank guns, and two battalion commanders had been badly wounded. Officers were reduced to sniping at observation slits with their .45-caliber pistols. The few artillery tubes ashore had begun firing furiously at nine A.M. with powder charge 5 for a range of 6,000 yards; by 10:30, as retreating riflemen streamed past, the gunners had cut their powder to charge 1 for targets less than a mile away. "Situation critical. We are being overrun by tanks," the 16th Infantry commander told Allen. "We have no idea what is going on to the east of us."

Allen climbed to the crest of a dune behind the command post, cheeks hissing, a map tucked under his arm. "The plain," an artilleryman later wrote, "was a mass of bursting shells, burning tanks and confusion." Behind Allen, the beach was hardly more orderly. Italian dive-bombers had struck the roadstead at dawn; since then, scarcely half an hour had passed without another Axis air attack. Of Allen's ten requests for air support missions on Saturday and Sunday, only one was met: Allied fighters—flying from North Africa and Pantelleria Island—were too busy protecting the fleet. Patton had ordered his floating reserve ashore early that morning, but the four 18th Infantry battalions landed with little more than they could carry. Some heavy weapons mistakenly landed in the 45th Division zone to the southeast, forcing the gun crews to plod for miles up the shingle; anti-tank guns for the 26th Infantry were lost when *LST 313* took an Axis bomb in the tank deck and burned to the keel. Two 1st Division signal trucks had also been destroyed, including one carrying thirty miles of phone wire, and a third, full of radio equipment, lay in seven feet of water. The Gela beaches remained so crowded that several dozen landing craft circled offshore or returned to their mother ships, unable to penetrate the broached vessels and supply crates heaped along the water's edge. Mortarmen borrowed fishing dinghies to row their ammunition ashore.

"I want tanks and I don't give a damn where they come from," Allen said. More than sixty M-4 Shermans would make land on July 11, but only a platoon—four tanks—made it beyond the dunes and into the battle on Sunday morning. Others were stopped by broken pontoons, congestion, and confusion, to say nothing of the complete dearth of functioning radios on armor vehicles ashore. Shermans crossing the beach found that the steel matting laid for traction snarled in their tracks and bogey wheels, requiring extensive pruning with large shears. Tanks that skirted the mats bogged down in the steep dunes, throwing one or both tracks.

Allen could hardly have dared to hope that comparable woes afflicted General Conrath at the Hermann Göring command post in Priolo, but they did. On the German left, grenadiers attacking from Biscari had blundered about in the dark, then lost their regimental commander, who left his post to explain himself to Conrath, only to be relieved and court-martialed. The leaderless troops panicked and pelted back toward Biscari before officers finally brought them to heel on the north bank of the Acate River. This "deficient inner cohesion," as a German staff officer put it, exposed the German left wing and forced the panzers to advance without enough infantry to chivvy the American riflemen from their knolls and gullies. Another German regimental commander was relieved for ineptitude, casualties mounted, the Tigers continued to break down—blocking roads and trails since they were too large to tow away—and Conrath had no inkling what the Italians were doing on his right. "The Italians practically are no longer cooperating," his operations officer complained. "They have not cooperated from the start." In fact, the Livorno Division had been ordered by the Italian high command to attack Gela "with utmost determination," though no one thought to tell the Germans. The Axis front by midday stretched on an eighteen-mile arc, without coordination or coherence. No matter: Comando Supremo in Rome announced that Gela had been recaptured and that the Americans were "returning to their ships."

From his sandy perch above the lemons and the panoramic chaos, Allen knew that to be untrue, but he also knew that it *could* be true if the tide did not turn soon. As he watched the panzers edge closer to the beach, a mob of 18th Infantry soldiers scampered back through the dunes. "They are carrying armloads of blankets, shovels, binoculars, and weapons in what seems like complete disorder," an 18th Infantry lieutenant reported. A staff officer asked Allen whether other troops should also retreat. "Hell, no," Allen replied. "We haven't begun to fight. They haven't overrrun our artillery yet."

Patton came ashore on Whiskey Knoll near Gela at 9:30 on Sunday morning, wading the last few yards from Hewitt's borrowed barge in thigh-deep water. Timing his own pulse, he was disgusted to find it slightly elevated. "You had better come now," he had called to a reporter on *Monrovia,* "or my men will have killed all the bastards." Slapping a leather swagger stick in his palm, he looked "beautiful and battle-fevered in boots and whipcords," the reporter noted. Binoculars and a camera hung from his neck, and in place of his trademark pair of pistols, a single Colt Peacemaker .45 hugged his hip. Crossing the beach, Patton studied a pair of minewrecked DUKWs as several German shells exploded in the water thirty yards from shore. "Get your asses off this beach," he yelled at loitering soldiers in his odd, high-pitched voice, "and go kill those Kraut bastards."

Aides stripped the waterproofing from his scout car and unfurled a three-star flag on the bumper. Patton intended to drive three miles east on Highway 115, now known as Adolf's Alley, to see Allen at Danger Forward, but the U.S. flag Darby had tacked onto the Fascist party headquarters in

Gela caught his eye and he swerved into town. Darby was off in the killing fields somewhere, but the rooftop offered Patton an Olympian view. Thirty hours into HUSKY, he had only a sketchy notion of how the invasion was progressing: the code rooms on *Monrovia* had been hopelessly swamped since H-hour, with many urgent messages from Seventh Army units backlogged for eight hours; more routine dispatches were backed up for two days. At least here, Patton could see for himself.

Dust and gray smoke smeared the landscape north and east of town. German tanks pushing past the 26th Infantry on the eastern edge of Highway 117 had crossed the shallow Gela River to menace Adolf's Alley and Allen's sanctuary. Italian tanks west of the highway had nosed within a mile of Gela. Patton shouted to a naval ensign with a walkie-talkie in the street below. "Hey, you with the radio! If you can connect with your goddam Navy, tell them for God's sake to drop some shell fire on the road." Minutes later thirty-eight shells from the cruiser *Boise* rushed over the rooftops. Explosions blossomed among the Italian tanks, and a syncopated thunder rolled across town. More blossoms opened, this time from white-phosphorus mortar shells falling among enemy infantrymen. The burning fragments, Patton noted, "seemed to make them quite crazy as they rushed out of the ravine, shrilling like dervishes with their hands over their heads." A Ranger captain added that "enemy troops could be seen staggering around as if thoroughly dazed. . . . There were human bodies hanging from trees." A column of prisoners snaked through the street below. "Make it double time," Patton barked at the military police escorts. "Kick 'em in the ass." Under Patton's glare, the prisoners stumbled into a ragged trot.

The Italian thrust stalled before noon, but now German artillery ranged the town. Two 88mm shells gouged the Fascist headquarters in a spray of steel shards and masonry, and a third holed the roof across the street. "No one was hurt except some civilians," Patton noted. "I have never heard so much screaming." The panic intensified with the appearance of two German warplanes. The heavy footfall of approaching bombs, Patton later wrote, caused the locals "to behave in a most foolish manner, running up and down the street. . . . It was necessary for us to use MPs and rifle butts to solace them."

If the Italians had been stopped, the Germans had not, and by midday Terry Allen's right wing faced obliteration. German infiltrators menaced the flank of the lemon grove, where the stink of cordite commingled with the citrus. Panzer fire had begun sweeping the beaches, causing casualties and consternation. German tanks near Santa Spina controlled Highway 115 and stood barely a mile from the waterline; landing craft had taken fire and enemy troops threatened the 26th Infantry supply dumps only seven hundred yards inland. Riflemen pried up slabs of dried mud to build pathetic adobe parapets. On the beach a naval officer "struck a heroic pose, shouting, 'To arms, to arms!' " Navy yeomen, electricians, and carpenters tittered even as they scrambled for their rifles. Men burned both personal and official papers, including maps, and a radar set was blown up for fear of capture.

Crouched in a trench at the aptly named Danger Forward, Allen—bleary-eyed and gray with fatigue—sifted through battle reports and pleaded for more firepower. Firepower arrived, and with it salvation. Four artillery battalions, with a dozen guns each, as well as the platoon of Sherman tanks and half a dozen cannon and antitank companies, finally trundled across the beach and into the dunes. "There's plenty of good hunting up there," the 1st Division artillery chief, Brigadier General Clift Andrus, told the arriving gunners. Smoking his pipe and polishing his spectacles, Andrus—a Cornell University civil engineer known to the troops as Mr. Chips—evinced the same sangfroid he had displayed at Kasserine Pass and El Guettar. Strolling from battery to battery, he pointed at targets with his walking stick and ordered the gunners to try ricochet fire, which had proved particularly lethal to enemy foot soldiers in Tunisia. Behind a battery of 155mm Long Toms, firing over open sights at the approaching panzers, a lieutenant reportedly drew his .45 and threatened to shoot any man who abandoned his gun.

Then, above the whine of artillery shells, came the locomotive shriek of *Boise*'s shells: fifteen 6-inch airbursts every six seconds, ripping up wheat fields and vineyards and Germans alike. She nearly sat on the beach, edging to within three thousand yards of the waterline as leadsmen took soundings in the chains; another cruiser, U.S.S. *Savannah,* joined the barrage, along with four destroyers that drew even closer at twelve hundred yards.

German tanks began to burn: first two, then six, then a dozen and more. U.S. infantrymen heard trapped crews screaming half a mile away, until the ammunition cooked off and the screaming stopped. "I was hit on the left side of the turret," an officer in a Tiger unit later recalled. "Fortunately it didn't penetrate, but rivets flew about our ears." A grenadier shot by a 16th Infantry rifleman tumbled beneath the tracks of tank; later, upon inspecting the body, the rifleman "took hold of his hair to pull his face around but he was melted right into the ground."

At two P.M., Conrath called off the attack. The panzers pulled back, slowly at first, then gathering speed when the naval shells thickened until they were rushing to the rear as if the landscape had somehow tipped northward. At four P.M. the Hermann Göring Division headquarters reported, "The counterattack against the hostile landings has failed." Terry

Allen urged his exhausted troops to "sock the hell out of those damned Heinies before they can get set to hit us again." As for the day's events, the twinkle returned to his red-rimmed eyes. "The situation could have been critical," he told Don Whitehead. "As it was, it was merely embarrassing."

Patton returned to the beach late in the day, still in full throat and still impeccable despite having been bombed, strafed, and shelled. During the afternoon he had tracked down Ted Roosevelt in Gela—rebuking him for failing to seize Ponte Olivo airfield already—and later he smoked a victory cigar while visiting Allen's command post. He ate his K ration lunch with a portly, white-haired brigadier general named William J. Donovan, a millionaire Wall Street lawyer whose résumé also included the Medal of Honor and three Purple Hearts in World War I and whose friend Franklin Roosevelt had appointed him director of the Office of Strategic Services. Donovan had come ashore from the *Samuel Chase* and spent the day shooting at Italians, "happy as a clam," a 1st Division captain reported. "You know, Bill," Patton said, "there are two things in life that I love to do—fucking and fighting." Donovan nodded. "Yes, George, and in that order, too."

Patton's cigar was fairly won. Two Axis divisions had been repulsed and were now skulking off into the Sicilian hinterland. "I had the bitter experience to watch scenes during these last days that are not worthy of a German soldier," Conrath fulminated in a July 12 field order that threatened summary executions for cowardice and rumor-mongering. On the Seventh Army left, Truscott's 3rd Division was pushing inland; on the right, paratrooper Gavin repulsed a sizable armor and infantry force at Biazza Ridge. As for casualties, Andrus counted 43 enemy tanks destroyed, including 6 by bazooka, a figure similar to a tally by the Hermann Göring Division. Conrath reported 630 men killed or wounded in the first three days of HUSKY; 10 of 17 Tigers had been knocked out. American casualties in the Sunday counterattack totaled 331. After two days of fighting, Seventh Army reported 175 dead, 665 wounded, and nearly 2,600 missing, most of whom were in fact lost. Nearly 9,000 prisoners had been bagged, almost exclusively Italians. Once again horse carts hauled dead civilians to a mass grave outside Gela.

Patton prowled the beach, waiting for his barge. Spying several soldiers digging foxholes amid stacks of five-hundred-pound bombs, he advised them that "if they wanted to save Graves Registration burials that was a fine thing to do, but otherwise they better dig somewhere else." At that moment German planes strafed the beach and the men plunged back into their lairs; Patton strutted and clucked until he had shamed them from the holes. By the time he regained *Monrovia,* the sun was sinking in the western Mediterranean and he was drenched with sea spray. "This is the first day in this camapign that I think I earned my pay," he told his diary. "I am well satisfied with my command today."

## *"Tonight Wear White Pajamas"*

KENT Hewitt had spent his Sunday fighting the naval war, a few thousand yards seaward of Patton's terrestrial battle. Pillars of black smoke and a faint clamor carrying from the beach implied the tumult ashore, but Hewitt had been far too busy to do more than cast an occasional glance inland.

His own losses were modest if worrisome: Axis air attacks kept intensifying as enemy pilots evaded Allied radar by sneaking through valleys notched across the coastal plain. The battleship H.M.S. *Nelson* had been attacked three times on July 10 but fourteen times today. A bomb detonated under the *Barnett*—Ted Roosevelt's ship—ripping a hole in hold number 1 and killing seven men. The hospital ship *Talamba,* illuminated and bedizened with huge red crosses, was sunk five miles offshore. "With a cracking, hissing sound her stern went under, her bows reared up and she began to slide under," a British lieutenant reported. "People were jumping off her sides." The loss of *LST 313* and twenty-two souls at Gela on Saturday had been equally grim. An Me-109 attacked out of the late afternoon sun so stealthily that not a defensive shot was fired until bombs were falling. Trucks loaded with mines and ammunition blew up, catapulting men from the main deck a hundred feet into the air; flaming axles and fenders rained across the beach. Fires raged, flash-burned men lay on the bow ramp reciting the Lord's Prayer, and all engines were stopped so that those who had leaped overboard might not be sucked into the propellers. *LST 313* settled on the bottom with a final, delphic distress call: "This goddamn thing isn't working."

At noon on Sunday, Hewitt boarded the minesweeper U.S.S. *Steady* and steamed west to inspect Truscott's landings. No sooner had the admiral arrived off Licata than ten dive-bombers hit the quays and beaches, straddling half a dozen LSTs with bombs and setting fire to another. By three P.M., when *Steady* came about to return to Gela, Hewitt had witnessed five more attacks.

Each successive raid vexed him more. Nearly five thousand Allied planes had been amassed for HUSKY, but Hewitt had little idea where they were or what they were doing. For months he and Patton had hectored the U.S.

Army Air Forces for what the admiral decried as an "almost complete lack of participation in battle planning" and for drafting an air plan "unrelated to the military attack plan and naval attack plan." Neither he nor Patton knew which Sicilian targets would be bombed, or "what, when, or where fighter cover would be provided."

Air Force commanders, wary of "parceling out" their aircraft or giving "personal control over the air units" to their Army and Navy brethren, countered that to neutralize Axis airpower they must concentrate Allied planes on targets—such as enemy airfields and supply lines—often invisible from the battlefront. Because the Navy insisted on deploying all aircraft carriers to the Pacific, not enough fighters were available in the Mediterranean to protect the beachheads during sixteen hours of daylight. Firing from Allied ships on friendly planes had become so promiscuous that air patrols originally planned for altitudes of five thousand feet had been forced up to ten thousand.

Considering that the Navy had been prepared to lose up to three hundred ships on July 9 and 10, actual sinkings by air attack through Saturday night—a dozen vessels—had been light indeed. That hardly appeased those under incessant bombardment on the beach and in the anchorage. Hewitt was angry, Patton was disgusted—"We can't get the goddamn Air Force to do a goddamn thing"—and a young soldier, when told of the impenetrable air umbrella ostensibly provided by Allied fighters, rolled his eyes to the heavens and said, "Only the good people can see them."

Back at the Gela roads aboard *Steady*, Hewitt was on the minesweeper's bridge when the Liberty ship S.S. *Rowan*—stuffed with ammunition and gasoline—caught a pair of bombs in the number 2 hold and another next to a gun tub. After twenty minutes of futile firefighting she was abandoned and an hour later, as Hewitt watched, blew up with a roar seen and heard halfway to Africa. One eyewitness described "a flat sheet of crimson fire in a frame of black smoke. . . . Pieces of the twisted metal and flaming wood hissed into the water as far as a mile distant." Broken in half, *Rowan* refused to sink despite 5-inch destroyer shells pumped point-blank below her waterline. She settled in just seven fathoms and would burn for two days as a beacon for enemy pilots. By twilight's last gleaming on Sunday, German planes sprinkled magnesium parachute flares to make the roadstead even brighter. They drifted like tiny suns over the fleet, reminding every swab and soldier—and admiral—of his vulnerability.

Just across Highway 115, a few hundred yards east of Terry Allen's command post, another major general stood on a makeshift landing strip and eyed the glowing night sky with trepidation. Matthew B. Ridgway was handsome, graceful, and charismatic. He was "hard as flint and full of intensity, almost grinding his teeth from intensity," in James Gavin's description, to the point that George Marshall had once counseled Ridgway to "cultivate the art of playing and loafing." Vaulting from major to brigadier general in eighteen months, Ridgway as a two-star now commanded the 82nd Airborne. Soldiers later dubbed him "Old Iron Tits" for his affectation of attaching a hand grenade and a first-aid kit to his chest harness. "There's a right way," they said, "a wrong way, and a Ridgway." He was "brave under fire to the point of being exhibitionistic," Gavin recalled, and so despised the Germans that in battle "he'd stand in the middle of the road and urinate. . . . Even with his penis he was defiant." God, he believed, would preserve him at least until the final defeat of the Third Reich.

He was less certain how the Almighty felt about the 82nd on this Sunday night. One of his regiments, under Gavin, was already scattered across half of Sicily, and another was now en route to the island. At 8:30 this morning, on orders personally issued by Patton, Ridgway had summoned the 504th Parachute Infantry Regiment from Tunisia with a coded radio message: "Tonight wear white pajamas." Twenty-three hundred men were to reinforce the Big Red One by jumping from 144 planes before midnight. Some planners had advocated a daylight drop, or, now that German troops had retreated, simply landing the C-47s near the beach to discharge the paratroopers. Yet, once again, plans had been made, orders had been issued, and a cruel inflexibility gripped both plans and orders. Patton before leaving *Monrovia* this morning had drafted a notification to his four divisions of the impending jump, adding, "It is essential that all subordinate units be cautioned not to fire on these friendly planes." Although Patton signed the order at 8:45 A.M., congestion in *Monrovia*'s signal room kept it from being coded and dispatched until 4:20 P.M. Ridgway this afternoon had traipsed among antiaircraft batteries along Green 2 asking whether the gunners knew that "aircraft bearing friendly parachute troops" would soon be overhead: five crews had in fact heard, while a sixth had not.

"There's always some son-of-a-bitch who never gets the word," a Navy axiom held. In this instance the word failed to reach thousands, at sea and on land. Smaller vessels in particular knew nothing of the jump. Hewitt—who was living on the same ship with Patton—later stated that he first learned the mission had been authorized at 5:47 P.M. on Sunday, too late to spread the warning and too late to protest. None of the three regiments in the 45th Division sector to the east, where the planes would first make landfall, received notification until after ten P.M.; signal officers struggled to decode the messages by moonlight.

Ridgway for six weeks had warned of fratricide, and in late June he advocated scrubbing the proposed jump because the Navy refused to guarantee safe passage for the transport planes over the fleet. A flight corridor had at last been grudgingly promised; but final aircraft routes had not been apportioned by the high command until July 5, and disseminating knowledge of those routes through the invasion forces took several days. After two days of Axis attacks, all troops around the Gulf of Gela were jumpy, and few were skilled at distinguishing friend from foe, especially at night. "Every plane that came over us was fired upon because we could not identify it," one corporal explained. A particularly vicious raid, the twenty-third of the day, hit the anchorage at 9:50 P.M., narrowly missing *Boise* and scattering ships to all points.

If Ridgway was anxious ashore, Patton aboard *Monrovia* was hard pressed to heed his own advice to eschew the counsel of his fears. His afternoon bravado melted away as he realized that he was sitting on a tinderbox. At eight P.M., he tried to abort the mission only to learn that the 504th was already airborne and beyond recall. In his cabin late that night, Patton confided to his diary, "Found we could not get contact by radio. Am terribly worried."

No one ever knew who fired the first shot. The lead C-47 arrived at 10:40 P.M. in the preternatural calm that drifted over the beachhead following the departure of the last enemy raiders of the evening. Amber belly lights flashed the prescribed recognition signal from a thousand feet up. Crossing the coastline thirty miles east of Gela, the planes banked left and the first stick of sixteen paratroopers leaped from the open door onto the airstrip where Ridgway stood craning his neck. Then the rapping of a single machine gun broke the tranquillity, and a stream of the red tracers used by U.S. forces floated up, and up, and up.

The contagion spread in an instant. Fountains of red fire erupted from the beaches and the anchorage. "I looked back," reported a captain in one of the lead planes, "and saw the whole coastline burst into flame." Pilots dove to the deck or swerved back to sea, flinging paratroopers to the floor and tangling their static lines. Men fingered their rosary beads or vomited into their helmets. Bullets ripped through wings and fuselages, and the bay floors grew slick with blood. "The tracers going by our plane were so thick that I think I could have read a newspaper," one lieutenant later reported.

Formations disintegrated. Some pilots flipped off their belly lights and tried to thread a path along the shore between fire from the ships and fire from the beach. Others fled for Africa, chased by tracers for thirty miles. Half a dozen planes were hit as paratroopers struggled to get out the door. "Planes tumbled out of the air like burning crosses," recalled a soldier in the 1st Battalion. "Others stopped like a bird shot in flight." A few pilots refused to drop their sticks, considering it tantamount to murder, although one crew chief told a 504th battalion commander, "It's a hell of a lot safer out there than it is in here." Nowhere was safe, of course. Men died in their planes, men died descending in their parachutes, and at least four were shot dead on the ground by comrades convinced they were Germans. Men also died for saying the wrong thing: the paratroopers had been given challenge and parole passwords—ULYSSES / GRANT—at odds with those in the 45th Division sector where the fire was heaviest: THINK / QUICKLY.

Those watching from the ground would be imprinted with a horror hardly matched through the rest of the war. "No! Stop, you bastards, stop!" the correspondent Jack Belden shrieked above the din. None stopped. Parachutes collapsed or failed to open, and men struck the earth with a sound like "large pumpkins being thrown down." Others with chutes aflame candlesticked into the sea. Ridgway stared at the carnage in tears, aghast. But it was a young sergeant, Ralph G. Martin, who gave voice to all: "I feel sick in body and soul."

Colonel Reuben H. Tucker, the thirty-two-year-old commander of the 504th, managed to jump onto the proper landing zone despite gunfire that killed his crew chief and put a thousand holes through his C-47. After rolling up his chute, Tucker stomped from tank to tank ordering the crews to stop shooting at his men with their .50-caliber machine guns. Too late. The final formation of two dozen planes was hit hardest, with half shot down. One pilot dropped his paratroopers, then took fire from eight ships as he banked back to sea; hit by more than thirty shells that left the cockpit instruments in his lap, he managed to ditch and escape in a rubber raft. The C-47 carrying Tucker's executive officer, Lieutenant Colonel Leslie G. Freeman, crashed five hundred yards from shore after being struck in the right engine by gunfire that also wounded three troopers. Marksmen on nearby ships sprayed the sinking wreckage with bullets. "Eleven more men were wounded or killed after we landed on the water," Freeman reported, including a lieutenant shot in the face after swimming to the beach.

At last the shooting ebbed, the guns fell silent, and an awful epiphany seeped across the beachhead and through the fleet, that men-at-arms had done what men-at-arms most fear doing: they had killed their own. Twenty-three planes had been destroyed, and another thirty-seven were badly damaged. Investigators put the casualties at 410, although the actual number long remained in dispute. That the mission had been a fiasco— among the worst friendly fire episodes in modern warfare—was beyond haggling. "The safest place for us tonight while over Sicily," one pilot said, "would have been over enemy territory." As late as July 16, Ridgway would report that he could account for only 3,900 of the 5,300 paratroopers who had left North Africa for Sicily on the ninth and eleventh.

Those who survived that Sunday night would never forget, even as they looked for ways to forgive. As he was carried away on a stretcher with a bullet in his shoulder, one paratrooper told an officer, "I was glad to see that our fellows could shoot so good."

Eisenhower arrived at the beachhead on Monday morning, July 12, ignorant of the previous night's fratricide. No one during his daylong visit thought to enlighten him. For the past two days on Malta he had been both giddy at HUSKY's apparent early success—"By golly," he exclaimed, "to think we've gone it again!"—and splenetic at the absence of hard news, particularly from Patton. He studied Cunningham's maps, rocked in a wicker chair in his Lascaris office, cadged dry cigarettes from reporters, and paced on the beach. "Ike had the fidgets," his naval aide, Commander Harry C. Butcher, wrote in his diary. "Lay on sand awhile, then got up and dug holes in the sand with a stick." To John Gunther he complained, "They treat me like a bird in a gilded cage." To see the battle for himself, he had boarded H.M.S. *Petard* in Valletta harbor and at two A.M. Monday set sail for Sicily at twenty-six knots.

The destroyer made landfall at Licata just as a lovely Mediterranean dawn tinted the distant hills with orange and gold. Columns of greasy smoke spiraled above the beach, but from two miles out the prevailing impression was "complete serenity," wrote a British officer aboard *Petard*. "More like a huge regatta than an operation of war." Shortly after six A.M., the destroyer's captain, dressed in a blue turtleneck and shabby white shorts, pointed to *Monrovia*, anchored five miles off Gela. Eisenhower crossed to the flagship in a bouncing launch to be greeted by the usual bosun's trill—"I never know what to do when they pipe me on," the commander-in-chief had muttered—as well as a smiling, saluting Kent Hewitt and a smiling, saluting George Patton.

Patton led the way to his cabin, where blue and red battle lines had been neatly drawn on a large map of Sicily. The Allies now had eighty thousand troops ashore, with seven thousand vehicles, three hundred tanks, and nine hundred guns spread on a hundred-mile arc across an island the size of Vermont. The British Eighth Army had captured Syracuse, and Augusta would fall soon. A tumultuous welcome from Sicilian civilians cooled when it became clear that the Tommies had little extra food to share. But instead of the anticipated ten thousand British casualties in the first week, there would be only fifteen hundred. General Montgomery had begun to wheel toward Catania, only twenty miles north of Augusta and the last sizable city before

Messina on the island's northeast tip. Brash as ever, Montgomery confidently predicted he would reach Catania as soon as Tuesday night.

As for his own Seventh Army, Patton pointed to Truscott's 3rd Division on the left—already across the Yellow Line and nearing Canicattì, fifteen miles inland—and Middleton's 45th Division on the right, a bit scattered but pressing toward the upland town of Vizzini. Comiso airfield had fallen Sunday afternoon, and 125 enemy planes had been captured, 20 of them still flyable. American troops had seized Ragusa, which technically stood in the Canadian sector, and amused themselves there by answering phone calls from anxious Italian garrisons further up-country. In the center, Patton reported, the Hermann Göring Division counterattack had forestalled Allen's 1st Division, but Ponte Olivo airfield would surely fall this morning. The enemy's distress was apparent in a message found banded to a homing pigeon, which on Sunday had landed on a U.S. minesweeper instead of flying to the Italian XII Corps headquarters. From an Italian coastal division, it read, "Heroic infantry and artillery still doing their duty after fifteen hours of fighting against tremendous odds. . . . Send more pigeons." A Royal Navy officer had advised: "Cross-examine in pigeon English, and release."

Hardly had the briefing ended than Eisenhower rounded on his army commander, and Patton's smile vanished. During the TORCH landings, Patton had earned a rebuke for failing to notify Eisenhower at Gibraltar of his progress in Morocco, and now he had repeated his sin. The high command in Washington and London wanted information, Eisenhower complained, and what was an ignorant commander-in-chief to tell them? How should he know whether Seventh Army needed help, particularly in the air? Harry Butcher, who witnessed the tongue-lashing, wrote, "When we left General Patton I thought he was angry. Ike had stepped on him hard. There was an air of tenseness."

Forty-five minutes after boarding *Monrovia,* Eisenhower climbed down to the barge for the return trip to *Petard.* "Patton stood at the edge of the rope ladder looking like a Roman emperor carved in brown stone," Gunther wrote. "He waved goodbye." Thirty minutes later, the *Monrovia* radio room decoded a message confirming that nearly two dozen "of our own troop transport planes [were] shot down last night." The report never caught up with Eisenhower. He spent the morning cruising the Sicilian shore, stuffing cotton in his ears during a brief exchange of salvos with a German shore battery, then riding a DUKW through hundreds of naked Canadian soldiers bathing in the creamy surf near Cape Passero. "I have come to welcome Canada to the Allied command," he declared, sweat beading on his broad forehead.

Eisenhower ended the day with a tumbler of gin, courtesy of the Royal Navy, and the conviction that HUSKY was unfolding rather well. "Provided everything goes satisfactorily," he privately informed reporters, "we should have Sicily in two weeks." Given limp Italian resistance, he had begun to believe that Allied forces should carry the fight to mainland Italy. Still, he was irked at Patton. Notwithstanding their twenty-year friendship, he told Butcher, he wished that Seventh Army for the rest of the Sicilian campaign could be commanded by his West Point classmate Omar Bradley, whom he considered "calm and matter-of-fact."

Only after returning to his dank command post in the Lascaris Bastion late Monday night did Eisenhower learn of the airborne calamity. His irritation at Patton now turned to fury. Face flushed, lips pursed, he dictated a scathing message to the army commander at 11:45 P.M., the syllables popping like whip cracks: "You particularly requested me to authorize this movement into your area. Consequently ample time was obviously available for complete and exact coordination of the movement among all forces involved." Such a catastrophe implied "inexcusable carelessness and negligence on the part of someone." Patton was to initiate an "exhaustive investigation with a view to fixing responsibility."

Investigations would go forth, sins of omission and commission would be duly documented, but no blame was ever formally assigned. Pentagon censorship kept the incident secret until many months after the Sicilian campaign ended. Hewitt angrily denied any culpability, as did everyone else involved. Eisenhower's air chief deemed the mission "not operationally sound," although the top AFHQ airborne adviser, fatuously determined to fashion a silk purse from the sow's ear, declared himself "well pleased with the entire operation" in Sicily.

Patton considered the 504th's misfortune "an unavoidable incident of combat." But as he moved into the marble-floored, bedbug-ridden Geloan villa that would become his first headquarters ashore, he felt the sting of Eisenhower's castigation. "If anyone is blameable, it must be myself, but personally I feel immune to censure," Patton wrote in his diary on July 13. "Perhaps Ike is looking for an excuse to relieve me. . . . If they want a goat, I am it."

## "The Dark World Is Not Far from Us"

THEY pressed inland on their hundred-mile front, past Sicilians shouting "Viva, Babe Ruth!" or "Hoorah, King George!" and waving homemade U.S. flags with too many stripes and too few stars. The July heat came on, and they knotted bandanas across their noses, marching invisible from the waist down because of the dust that beat up as if they were scuffing through flour. "After the first mile we were so worn out we barely had enough breath to bitch," a mortarman recalled, "but we managed." Salt stained their shirts, and their boots squished, and they denounced their steel helmets as "brain furnaces." They nibbled on grapes and green tomatoes and Benzedrine, or bartered one cigarette for eight oranges. By midday, the journalist Alan Moorehead wrote, "everything had turned into strident color—red rocks, green vineyards, a blaring cobalt blue in the sky." The troops were less vivid: sweat and dust blended to coat them with a gray paste. Occasional shells fell about, and they dove for a ditch or at least a dimple in the sun-hammered earth. "I put my face in the dirt," one soldier said, "and tried to dig deeper with my knees."

Jeeps returned from the front with dead soldiers trussed to the hood, threading a path through the columns heaving forward. "Right of way!" the drivers bellowed. "Right of way." The living moved aside, looking away as if they were Sicilians avoiding the evil eye. Many troops carried amulets, perhaps a St. Christopher medal or a smooth stone to rub whenever the tracers whizzed past. One soldier held a tiny carved wooden pig, murmuring as the shells thickened, "Pig, this one is not for us," or, "Pig, you know that the one that gets me, gets you." The novelist John Steinbeck, who had joined the press corps for the invasion, noted a belief that "the magic must not be called on too often. The virtue of the piece is not inexhaustible." This atavism, Steinbeck concluded, reflected a reasonable conviction in the ranks that "the dark world is not far from us."

They tramped through a land as exotic as North Africa, a land of village witches and exorcists, where the sick swallowed powdered amber or drank the dust of St. Rita's bones. Big-wheeled carts clattered on iron rims over the cobblestones; the scenes painted on their sides showed the martyrdom of Christ or cinema stars from the 1920s. Dray horses with blinkers "depicting the life and death of a saint, right and left respectively," clopped past women combing nits from their children's hair and old men pouring drinks from five-cornered canvas wine flasks splotched with purple stains.

Walls and public buildings were upholstered with Fascist slogans—"Few words, many deeds" or "Mussolini is always right"—which "after a while even ceased to be ridiculous," Moorehead wrote. A few had been freshly whitewashed, or overwritten with new scrawl, including "Finito, Benito." Military policemen hunted Fascist officials by scrutinizing the locals for store-bought shoes or unfrayed trousers; denunciation and betrayal soon became cottage industries. Blue butterflies and hoopoes and bee-eaters flew about, and the scent of honeysuckle and jasmine mingled with the stink of manure and human offal to produce the precise odor of poverty. "A carton of cigarettes would buy you a whole province here," an American officer reported, "and a suit of clothes would get you the whole island."

Dead enemy soldiers lay by the roads with their arms flung out as if making snow angels. They were hastily buried in graves marked "E.D."— enemy dead. Dead civilians lay about too, some next to painted carts flipped on their sides with disemboweled donkeys still in the traces to form a death tableau at a 90-degree angle from life. A grave-diggers' strike in some provinces complicated sanitation, as did a shortage of wood for coffins, which were necessarily reused. "Bury the dead and feed the living," a 1st Division civil affairs officer advised. That too was complicated. Food riots soon erupted, including one in Canicattì quelled by MPs who fired over the rioters' heads to no effect. "When they lowered their fire," an AMGOT report added, "the mob lay down in the streets and continued to scream." General Truscott ordered looters executed; when civilians stealing soap from a warehouse tried to flee, an officer "shot at some of the men in the crowd and the infantry rounded up others and shot them. Six men were killed." Also shot were seven alleged saboteurs accused of filching military signal wire.

Sometimes the living simply needed to be comforted. Seaman First Class Francis Carpenter, a former Broadway actor pressed into service as a beachhead scout because he had twice vacationed in Sicily, came upon eight terrified peasants hiding in a cornfield. Carpenter, whose credits included the 1938 revival by Orson Welles of *The Shoemaker's Holiday*, handed around his pack of cigarettes, then cleared his throat and sang "La donna è mobile," a winsome aria from *Rigoletto*.

No one was more eager to get inland than the lieutenant general who commanded most of the American troops now in Sicily. Omar Nelson Bradley, who as the II Corps commander ranked just under Patton, had battled adversity and affliction throughout his fifty years: the early death of his father; the extraction of his teeth after a skating accident; a near fatal bout of flu; the loss of a stillborn son. For the first thirty-six hours of the HUSKY invasion, Bradley's personal trials persisted. "Feeling worse than I have ever felt in my life," he had been confined to the U.S.S. *Ancon* after emergency surgery for hemorrhoids, known in the Army as cavalry tonsils. Still in agony, and seasick to boot, he eventually came ashore in his command car, cushioned on a life preserver and feeling slightly ridiculous. On Monday morning, July 12, he set up his headquarters in a sultry grove three miles north of Scoglitti.

Graying since his cadet days, Bradley wore an unadorned field jacket and "might have passed as an elderly rifleman" lugging his favorite 1903 Springfield rifle. Round, steel-frame GI spectacles magnified "his rural manner," wrote the historian Martin Blumenson, "and his hayseed expression gave him a homespun look." Nearly anonymous in Tunisia, although he had commanded U.S. forces during the triumphant coup de grâce, Bradley had recently been discovered by journalists and the public. They found his demeanor compelling—"as unruffled as an Ozark lake on a dead-calm day," *Life* gushed—and his personal story irresistible: the Missouri sodbuster boyhood without running water; the widowed mother, a seamstress, cooking game killed by young Omar—squirrels, quail, rabbit, and big green frogs; the .383 batting average and deadly throwing arm on the West Point baseball squad; the sharpshooter who could hit a pheasant on the fly with a .22 rifle and who eyed German planes overhead as if he were "shooting at the number 8 post at skeet." At Eisenhower's urging, Ernie Pyle would spend several days with Bradley in Sicily, writing a hagiographic six-part profile that forever sanctified him as the GI General. "He is so damn normal," Pyle wrote. "He has no idiosyncrasies, no superstitions, no hobbies."

Perhaps. But he also had depths beyond even Pyle's plumbing. "Underneath the mask was a cold and ruthless mind," Martin Blumenson concluded. He was "calculative"—the adjective appeared in his high school yearbook—and often intolerant. His distaste for the piratical Terry Allen, who considered Bradley "a phony Abraham Lincoln," had grown so toxic that he was looking for a chance to sack the 1st Division commander. He also was increasingly disaffected with Patton's flamboyance, his bullheaded tactics, and his penchant for issuing orders directly to the divisions, rather than through Bradley. "He's impetuous," Bradley later wrote. "I disliked the way he worked. . . . Thought him a rather shallow commander."

Among the most pressing problems facing II Corps was the floodtide of Italian prisoners: on Sicily, more enemy soldiers were captured in a week than were bagged by the U.S. Army in all of World War I. They came in skipping pairs from the villages, or in stolen trucks, or in long, chattering columns out of the hills, nervously glancing over their shoulders for muzzle flashes from disapproving Hermann Göring grenadiers. Wearing long-billed caps and the coarse-cloth uniforms the Germans called asbestos, they surrendered "in a mood of fiesta . . . their personal possessions slung about them, filling the air with laughter and song," as one soldier wrote. Some U.S. units were so overwhelmed that they posted signs in Italian—"No prisoners taken here"—or advised enemy troops to come back another day. "You can't work up a good hate against soldiers who are surrendering to you so fast you have to take them by appointment," Bill Mauldin observed.

Off they went in the LSTs, herded like livestock but singing as though caged in an aviary. An OSS officer who interrogated a captured Italian machine-gun crew reported that Axis officers had spread atrocity tales in a vain effort to halt the defections.

"When are you going to start?" one prisoner had asked.

"Start what?"

The prisoner cringed. "Cutting off our balls."

Told that they would not be harmed, the men sobbed in relief.

"A queer race these Italians," a lieutenant wrote his mother. "You'd think we were their deliverers instead of their captors."

Yet the dark world was not far removed. And now it intruded.

Operation HUSKY had exacted a particularly grievous toll from the 180th Infantry Regiment, the pride of Oklahoma and one of three National Guard infantry regiments in the 45th Division. During the 45th's brief interlude in Oran, en route from Norfolk to Sicily, Patton had lavished his attention on the unit, urging officers to "kill devastatingly," to be wary of white-flag ruses, and, if enemy soldiers surrendered only when nearly overrun, to "kill the sons of bitches." The 45th should be known as the "Killer Division," Patton told them, because "killers are immortal."

Despite these admonitions, not much had gone right for the killers in the 180th. On D-day the regimental commander, Colonel Forrest E. Cookson, was dumped by a confused coxswain on a 1st Division beach and failed to rejoin his men for thirty hours. Evincing "anxiety and indecision"—he tended to shake his head and mutter, "Not good"—Cookson seemed so overmatched that Patton had offered his command to Bill Darby, who opted to stay with his Rangers. With no suitable replacement in sight, Cookson kept his job for the moment but soon lost his most aggressive battalion commander, Lieutenant Colonel William H. Schaefer. A former West Point football player known as King Kong, Schaefer was "the ugliest looking man in the U.S. Army, maybe the Navy and Marines as well," one lieutenant said. He had repeatedly lectured his 1st Battalion officers against risking capture because "a captive can't fight." Several hours into the landings, Schaefer had been cornered by German grenadiers, who took him prisoner in a vineyard. "Dear General," he wrote the division commander, Troy Middleton, on a scrap of brown paper, "I'm sorry I got captured."

The 180th's chance for redemption came at remote, impoverished Biscari, which the regiment had attacked late Sunday afternoon, July 11. Hermann Göring troops fell back behind the high yellow walls of the town cemetery, sheltering among the cedars and marble tombs set into a hill. American mortar rounds rooted them out, brown smoke foaming over the mausoleums and machine-gun slugs chipping the seraphim. Again the Germans fell back, skulking north across the Acate River toward an airfield five miles north of Biscari town. In broken country the gunfight continued through Tuesday, July 13.

By early Wednesday morning, the airfield was at last in American hands. Bodies lay like bloody throw rugs on a runway gouged by more than two hundred bomb craters. The charred cruciforms of ruined warplanes smoldered near the hangars; enemy snipers had hidden in the cockpits, taking potshots until a platoon of Sherman tanks exterminated them, fuselage by fuselage. Flames crackled in the grain fields east and west of the airfield. Through the billowing smoke U.S. soldiers could be seen like wraiths in olive drab, dragging wounded comrades to safe ground or snatching first-aid kits and ammunition from abandoned packs.

Sniper fire still winked from the shadows along the packed-dirt Biscari road. Companies A and C of the 180th's 1st Battalion had landed five days earlier with nearly 200 men each and now counted 150 between them; the battalion casualties included King Kong's replacement, wounded, and the Company A commander, captured. "We had the killing spirit," one sergeant later observed. Another rifleman wrote his father that the summer dust "tasted like powdered blood," then added, "Now I know why soldiers get old quick."

By midmorning on Wednesday, the 1st Battalion had pushed through the smoke and dancing flames, flushing German and Italian laggards from caves along the thready Ficuzza River. Soon Company A had rounded up forty-six prisoners, among them three Germans. Frightened and exhausted, the captives sat naked but for their trousers on a parched slope above the Ficuzza, all shirts and shoes having been confiscated to discourage escape. A major separated nine prisoners for interrogation—the youngsters were considered most likely to talk—then turned both them and the other captives over to Sergeant Horace T. West with a small security detachment for removal to the rear.

West proved a poor choice. Born in Barron Fork, Oklahoma, he had joined the Army in 1929, then switched to the National Guard, training on weekends and working as a cook in his antebellum civilian life. Now thirty-three, he had two young children, earned $101 a month, and had gained a reputation, one superior said, as the "most thorough non-com I ever saw in the Army." But the past few days had badly frayed Sergeant West. "It was something sitting on me," he later said, "just to kill and destroy and watch them bleed to death."

In two shuffling columns, the prisoners marched four hundred yards down the road toward a stand of olive trees above the creek. West halted his charges—without being told, they executed a ragged left-face—and separated out the smaller group designated for interrogation. Turning to the company first sergeant, Haskell Brown, he asked to borrow his Thompson submachine gun "to shoot the sons of bitches." Brown handed him the weapon with an extra clip. "Turn around if you don't want to see," West advised, and opened fire.

They fell, writhing and jerking in the dust, then lurched to their knees, begging, only to be shot down again. Cries filled the morning—"No! No!"—amid the roar of the gun and the acrid smell of cordite. Three prisoners broke for the trees; two of them escaped. West stopped to reload, then walked among the men in their pooling blood and fired a single round into the hearts of those still moving. When he was done, he handed the weapon back to Brown. "This is orders," he said, then rousted the nine chosen for interrogation to their feet, wide-eyed and trembling, and marched them off to find the division G-2. Thirty-seven dead men lay beside the road, and their shadows shrank beneath the climbing sun as though something were being drawn up and out of them.

Five hours later, it happened again. As Sergeant West herded his surviving charges to the rear, German tanks and half-tracks counterattacked, recaptured the Biscari airfield, and drove the 180th across a ravine south of the runway. The brawling would continue throughout Wednesday afternoon until the enemy was again routed, this time for good. During the fight, Company C of the 1st Battalion swept down a deep gulch, taking a dozen casualties from machine-gun fire before white flags waved from an expansive bunker carved into the slope. At one P.M., three dozen Italians emerged, hands up, five of them wearing civilian clothes. Ammunition boxes, filthy bedding, and suitcases lay strewn about the bunker.

In command of Company C was Captain John Travers Compton. Now twenty-five, he had joined the Oklahoma Guard in 1934. Compton was married, had one child, earned $230 a month—minus a $6.60 deduction for government insurance—and had been consistently rated "excellent" or "superior" on performance evaluations. Standing on the hillside, bleary with fatigue, he ordered a lieutenant to assemble a firing squad and "have these snipers shot." The squad soon formed—several men volunteered— and Compton barked the commands even as the Italians pleaded for his mercy: "Ready. Aim. *Fire.*" Tommy-gun and Browning Automatic Rifle fire swept down the gulch, and another thirty-six men fell dead.

The next day, at 10:30 A.M., Lieutenant Colonel William E. King drove his jeep up the Biscari road toward the now secure airfield. It was said that

King had been temporarily blinded during World War I, and that the ordeal had propelled him into the ministry as a Baptist preacher. He now served God and country as the 45th Division chaplain, admired for his generosity and the brevity of his sermons. A dark mound near an olive grove caught his eye, and he stopped the jeep, mouth agape, to investigate.

"Most were lying face down, a few face up," King later recalled. "Everybody face up had one bullet hole just to the left of the spine in the region of the heart." A majority also had head wounds; singed hair and powder burns implied the fatal shots had come at close range. A few soldiers loitering nearby joined the chaplain, protesting that "they had come into the war to fight against that sort of thing," King said. "They felt ashamed of their countrymen." The chaplain hurried back to the division command post to report the fell vision.

Omar Bradley had already got wind of the massacre, and he drove to Gela to tell Patton that fifty to seventy prisoners had been murdered "in cold blood and also in ranks." Patton recorded his reaction in his diary:

> I told Bradley that it was probably an exaggeration, but in any case to tell the officer to certify that the dead men were snipers or had attempted to escape or something, as it would make a stink in the press and also would make the civilians mad. Anyhow, they are dead, so nothing can be done about it.

Two war correspondents who had seen the bodies also appeared at Patton's headquarters to protest these and other prisoner killings. Patton pledged to halt the atrocities, and the reporters apparently never printed a word. To George Marshall on July 18, Patton wrote that enemy troops had booby-trapped their dead and "have also resorted to sniping behind the lines"; such "nefarious actions" had caused "the death of quite a few additional Italians, but in my opinion these killings have been thoroughly justified."

Bradley disagreed and, Patton told his diary, "feels that we should try the two men responsible for the shooting of the prisoners." An investigation by the 45th Division inspector general found "no provocation on the part of the prisoners. . . . They had been slaughtered." Patton relented: "Try the bastards."

Captain Compton contracted malaria soon after the Biscari killings, and not until he had recuperated in late October would he be secretly court-martialed. The defense argued that Patton's pep talk in Oran had been tantamount to "an order to annihilate these snipers." "I ordered them shot because I thought it came directly under the general's instructions,"

Compton testified. "I took him at his word." The military prosecutor asked not a single question on cross-examination. Compton was acquited and returned to the 45th Division.

*Killers are immortal,* Patton had declared, but that too was wrong: Compton would be killed in action in Italy on November 8, 1943. A fellow officer in the 45th provided his epitaph: "Good riddance."

Sergeant West's case proved more convoluted. Like Compton, he was examined by psychiatrists and declared sane. He, too, claimed that Patton's rhetoric had incited him to mayhem, while conceding that he "may have used bad judgment." His conduct, he told the court-martial, "is something beyond my conception of human decency. Or something." The tribunal concurred and ruled that he had "with malice aforethought, willfully, deliberately, feloniously, unlawfully and with premeditation, killed 37 prisoners of war, none of whose names are known, each of them a human being."

West was sentenced to life in a New York penitentiary. Yet he never left the Mediterranean during the war, nor was he dishonorably discharged, and he continued to draw his $101 a month, plus various family allowances. Colonel Cookson, the 180th regimental commander, later said, "The whole tendency in the thing was to keep it as quiet as possible." A few weeks after West's conviction, Eisenhower reviewed the case. If West were sent to a federal prison in the United States, the Biscari story likely would become public; if he were kept confined in North Africa, perhaps the enemy would remain ignorant of the massacre. Eisenhower "feared reprisal to Allied prisoners and decided to give the man a chance," Harry Butcher wrote in his diary. "[West] will be kept in military confinement . . . for a period sufficient to determine whether he may be returned to duty."

That period amounted to a bit more than a year. West's family and a sympathetic congressman began pestering the War Department for news of "the most thorough non-com" in the U.S. Army. On November 23, 1944, he was granted clemency on grounds of temporary insanity and restored to active duty, though shorn of his sergeant's stripes. Classified top secret, the records of the courts-martial would remain locked in the secretary of the Army's safe for years after the war lest they "arouse a segment of our citizens who are so distant from combat that they do not understand the savagery that is war."

Those who knew of the killings tried to parse them in their own fashion. Brigadier General Raymond S. McLain, the 45th Division artillery commander, concluded that in Sicily "evil spirits seemed to come out and challenge us." Patton wrote Beatrice, "Some fair-haired boys are trying to say that I killed too many prisoners. The more I killed, the fewer men I lost, but they don't think of that." And a staff officer in the 45th wrote, "It was not easy to determine what forces turned normal men into thoughtless killers. But a world war is something different from our druthers."

*Nobody really knows what he's doing,* Bill Mauldin had written of his first week in combat with the 180th Infantry. Yet other primal lessons also could be gleaned, from Licata to Augusta. For war was not just a military campaign but also a parable. There were lessons of camaraderie and duty and inscrutable fate. There were lessons of honor and courage, of compassion and sacrifice. And then there was the saddest lesson, to be learned again and again in the coming weeks as they fought across Sicily, and in the coming months as they fought their way back toward a world at peace: that war is corrupting, that it corrodes the soul and tarnishes the spirit, that even the excellent and the superior can be defiled, and that no heart would remain unstained.

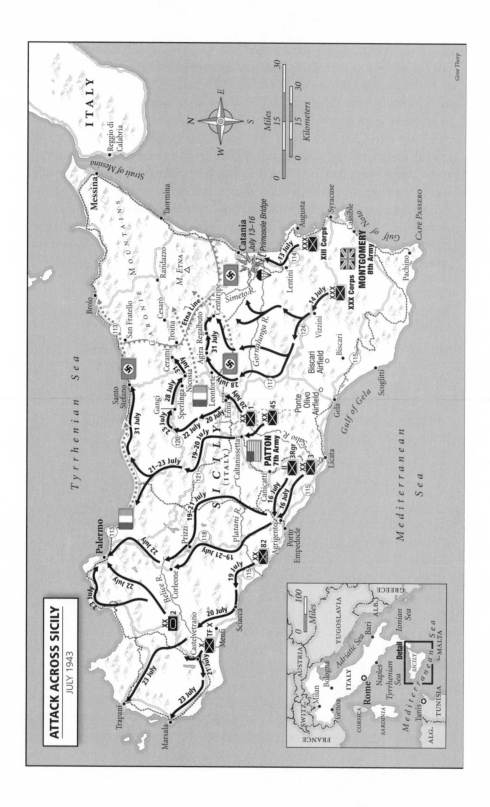

ATTACK ACROSS SICILY
JULY 1943

Gene Thorp

# 3. An Island Redoubt

## *"Into Battle with Stout Hearts"*

THE command car purred through the thronging soldiers, the big open car with three compasses salvaged from crashed Messerschmitts. Heedless of the raised dust, the troops pressed close, not just to snatch at the cigarette packs tossed from the backseat by their commanding general, but for a glimpse of the great man himself. At 147 pounds and just five foot seven even in his chukka boots, General Bernard Law Montgomery offered little to see: a black beret hid his thinning hair, and the khaki shirt—sleeves rolled to the elbows, tail tucked into his baggy shorts—was unadorned but for the Eighth Army flashes stitched to both shoulders. The Sicilian sun accented every cusp and serif in his narrow face, and made the luminous blue eyes even icier. Perhaps aware that he resembled "a rather unsuccessful drygoods shopkeeper," as a Canadian correspondent wrote, the general preferred sitting alone in back so "there won't be any doubt which one is me." As he flicked his Egyptian fly whisk, one observer thought him "tense as a mousetrap," but when the car stopped and he stood on the seat his raspy voice carried with the authority of a man accustomed to being heard. "I advise all of you to leave the Eyetie wine alone. Deadly stuff. Can make you blind, you know." He flicked the swish. "I will make good plans. I wouldn't be here today if I didn't make good plans," he said. "The campaign is going well. The German in Sicily is doomed. Absolutely doomed. He won't get away." Tossing out a few more packs of Lucky Strikes and handing lighters to his senior officers, Montgomery waved with both hands and gestured to the driver to move on in search of others to kindle. The men barked and bayed and doffed their soup bowl helmets. He knew they would.

If the campaign against the Axis was going well enough, a new front had opened between the British and the Americans; this battle had already hindered the struggle for Sicily and would impinge on Allied amity for the rest of the war. Montgomery was in the middle of the brouhaha, of course: on Tuesday, July 13, the Eighth Army commander had unilaterally ordered his troops to cut across Patton's front and into the American sector on Highway 124, a vital route that ran westward from Syracuse through Vizzini toward the central Sicilian crossroads town of Enna. Axis resistance had begun to clot south of Catania, so Montgomery chose to divide his army, with one corps butting north along the coast, and another looping west around Mount Etna via Highway 124.

Montgomery presented this maneuver as a fait accompli to General Harold R.L.G. Alexander, the senior ground commander for HUSKY and Eisenhower's British deputy, even though U.S. troops stood within half a mile of the highway and were much nearer to Enna than the British. Alexander accepted the impetuous deed without demur, and late Tuesday night he instructed Patton to get out of the way: "Operations for the immediate future will be Eighth Army to continue on two axes." Eisenhower declined to review the issue, much less intervene. Offering Eisenhower criticism of the British, General Lucas observed, "is like talking to a man about his wife."

Baleful consequences followed. Only two roads, hugging the island's east and north coasts, led to the ultimate prize of Messina, and the British now claimed both. Had the Yanks seized Enna by Friday, July 16, they might have severed the main escape route for Axis forces hurrying from western Sicily toward the bridgehead now forming on Mount Etna's flanks. Instead, Patton's army would be relegated to the role of flank guard for the British. The 45th Division began trudging back to the beach for a shift to the west, and Omar Bradley scrambled to regroup his corps engineer, medical, ordnance, quartermaster, and signal units. Montgomery now was driving on divergent axes toward objectives forty-five miles apart—coastal Catania and inland Enna—with half his army trundling into poor tank country beyond support of the Royal Navy. Any hope for a quick Allied triumph had vanished, as soon became evident to every man with a map.

The Americans were furious. "My God," Bradley told Patton, "you can't allow him to do that." But stung by Eisenhower's rebuke aboard *Monrovia* and reluctant to raise Cain after the paratrooper debacle, Patton remained docile, confining his anger to a slashing diary entry—"What fools we are"—and muttering private imprecations: "Tell Montgomery to stay out of my way or I'll drive those Krauts right up his ass." An enraged Bradley later declared the pilferage of Highway 124 "the most arrogant, egotistical, selfish and dangerous move in the whole of combined operations in World War II." The British move "tends to sell us down the river," Patton's deputy, Major General Geoffrey Keyes, wrote in his diary.

Beyond any tactical impact, the episode inflamed chauvinistic tensions in the British and American camps. "The feeling of discord lurking between the two countries . . . has increased rather than decreased," Harry Butcher had noted after the Tunisian victory. "It is disheartening and disconcerting." Alexander, for one, remained imprinted with the disagreeable image of fleeing U.S. troops during the Kasserine Pass rout six months earlier; like Montgomery and many British officers, he harbored a supercilious disdain for American fighting qualities. Yank resentment at that hauteur fueled the anglophobia afflicting the American high command. Patton already believed that Eisenhower was "a pro-British straw man" and that "allies must fight in separate theaters or they will hate each other more than they do the enemy." Now attitudes hardened, and mistrust threatened to mutate into enmity. "At great expense to ourselves we are saving the British empire," Lucas complained, "and they aren't even grateful." Another American general suggested celebrating each July 4 "as our only defeat of the British. We haven't had much luck since."

"What a headache, what a bore, what a bounder he must be to those on roughly the same level in the service," a BBC reporter wrote of Montgomery. "And at the same time what a great man he is as a leader of troops." That contradiction would define Montgomery through Sicily and beyond, confounding his admirers and infuriating his detractors. "A simple, forthright man who angered people needlessly," his biographer Alan Moorehead concluded. "At times a real spark of genius . . . but [he] was never on an even plane." Even the official British history of the Mediterranean war would acknowledge his "arrogance, bumptiousness, ungenerosity . . . [and] schoolboy humour." American disdain for Montgomery tended toward dismissive condemnation: "a son of a bitch," declared Beetle Smith, Eisenhower's chief of staff. His British colleagues, whose scorn at times ran even deeper, at least tried to parse his solipsism. "Small, alert, tense," said Lieutenant General Brian Horrocks, "rather like an intelligent terrier who might bite at any moment." Montgomery so irritated Andrew Cunningham—"he seems to think that all he has to do is say what is to be done and everyone will dance to the tune he is piping"—that the admiral would not allow the general's name to be uttered in his presence. "One must remember," another British commander said of Montgomery, "that he is not quite a gentleman."

That he had been raised in wild, remote Tasmania explained much to many. Son of a meek Anglican bishop and a harridan mother who conveyed her love with a cane, Montgomery emerged from childhood as "the bad boy of the family," who at Sandhurst severely burned a fellow cadet by setting fire to his shirttail. "I do not want to portray him as a lovable character," his older brother said, "because he isn't." Mentioned in dispatches six times on the Western Front, he carried from World War I the habits of

meticulous preparation, reliance on firepower, and a conception of his soldiers "not as warriors itching to get into action, which they were not, but as
a workforce doing an unpleasant but necessary job," in the words of the
historian Michael Howard. He also accumulated various tics and preju-
dices: a habit of repeating himself; the stilted use of cricket metaphors; an
antipathy to cats; a tendency to exaggerate his battlefield progress; "an obsession for always being right"; and the habit of telling his assembled officers, "There will now be an interval of two minutes for coughing. After that
there will be no coughing." No battle captain kept more regular hours. He
was awakened with a cup of tea by a manservant at 6:30 A.M. and bedtime
in his trailer—captured from an Italian field marshal in Tunisia—came
promptly at 9:30 P.M.

In Africa he had seen both glory, at El Alamein, and glory's ephemer-
ality, in the tedious slog through Tunisia. Montgomery much preferred
the former. Now the empire's most celebrated soldier, he received sacks of
fan mail, including at least nine marriage proposals, lucky charms ranging from coins to white heather, and execrable odes to his pluck. Profess-
ing to disdain such adulation, he had a talent for "backing into the
limelight," as one observer remarked. On leave in London after Tunis fell,
still wearing his beret and desert kit, he checked into Claridge's under the
thin pseudonym of "Colonel Lennox," then took repeated bows from his
box seat at a musical comedy as ecstatic theatergoers clapped and clapped
and clapped. "His love of publicity is a disease, like alcoholism or taking
drugs," said General Ismay, Churchill's chief of staff, "and it sends him
equally mad."

Success in snatching Highway 124 would encourage Montgomery to disregard both peers and superiors, especially the indulgent Alexander. "I do
not think Alex is sufficiently strong and rough with him," General Brooke
wrote of Montgomery in his diary, adding, "The Americans do not like him
and it will always be a difficult matter to have him fighting in close proximity to them." If audacious among allies, Montgomery became ever more
cautious with adversaries. "The scope of operations must be limited to
what is practicable," he advised John Gunther in Sicily. "The general must
refuse to be rushed." Still, his own men cherished his ability to convince
them "to believe in their task, to believe in themselves, and to believe in
their leader." Sailing about in the big command car, he stopped to ask a
Canadian unit, "Do you know why I never have defeats?"

> Well, I will tell you. My reputation as a great general means too much
> to me. . . . You can't be a great general and have defeats. . . . So you can
> be quite sure any time I commit you to battle you are bound to win.

In a printed broadside to Eighth Army he asserted that thanks to "the Lord Mighty in Battle," the enemy had been "hemmed in" on the northeast corner of Sicily. "Now let us get on with the job," Montgomery urged. "Into battle with stout hearts." To Brooke in London he later added, "All goes well here. . . . We have won the battle."

Neither assertion was true. On the third day of the invasion, Field Marshal Kesselring had arrived in Sicily from Frascati, and while wistfully abandoning hopes of flinging the Anglo-Americans into the sea, he soon began to reinforce the two German divisions on the island with two more, the 29th Panzer Grenadiers and the 1st Parachute Division. Thousands of Axis troops in western Sicily also hied east; Kesselring recognized that a stout bastion could be built around Etna's slopes, either to hold the Messina Peninsula indefinitely or at least to keep open the main escape route to mainland Italy. The task now was "to win time and defend," even though tension and misery gnawed at soldiers who feared being trapped on Sicily as so many comrades had been trapped in Tunisia. German attempts to commandeer Italian military vehicles led to internecine gunplay, with two Italians and seven Germans killed in one three-hour firefight. Still, Kesselring radiated his usual bonny optimism. As soldiers dug hasty fortifications along the Simeto River south of Catania, an elderly Italian nun dished out food and Holy Virgin medals.

Montgomery had expected the Catanian plain beyond Augusta to provide a flat alley for his armor, much as the desert had. Instead, he found "a hole-and-corner area, full of lurking places," in one soldier's description, with irrigation ditches and stone farmhouses perfect for concealing anti-tank weapons. "This is *not* tank country," a British officer lamented. Another Tommy complained that Sicily was "worse than the fuckin' desert in every fuckin' way."

Eighth Army's attempt to break through along the coast was first checked by yet another airborne fiasco, a mission patched together on short notice to seize the Primosole Bridge, seven miles south of Catania. Paratroopers and glider infantry on the night of July 13–14 ran into the now familiar hellfire from confused Allied ships, some of which mistook cargo racks on the aircraft bellies for torpedoes. Those managing to reach the coast met sheets of Axis antiaircraft fire. Fourteen planes were lost, a couple of dozen turned back to Tunisia without dropping, and 40 percent of the surviving planes suffered damage. By mischance, German paratroopers also jumped at the same time on adjacent drop zones. "One shouted for comrades and was answered in German," a paratrooper recalled. Of nearly two thousand men in the British parachute brigade, only two hundred reached the bridge, which they held with a few reinforcements for half a day until being driven off. By the time Tommies recaptured the bridge at dawn on Friday, July 16, the Germans had cobbled together a defensive belt just to the north that would halt Eighth Army for a fortnight. "It was yet another humiliating disaster for airborne forces," said Lieutenant Colonel John Frost, a much decorated battalion commander, "and almost enough to destroy even the most ardent believer's faith."

The XXX Corps, dispatched by Montgomery to the northwest on Highway 124, hardly fared better. Here hills were stacked on more hills in a Sicilian badlands, and hill fighting never suited Eighth Army: Montgomery "seemed to mislay his genius when he met a mountain," his biographer Ronald Lewin observed. The terrain's constricted visibility "makes for general untidiness," a British officer complained, and exposure to the July sun "is like being struck on the head." Every road and goat path was mined; soldiers perched like hood ornaments above the front bumpers of their creeping vehicles, scrutinizing the track for telltale disturbances. Artillery crashed and heaved, day and night. "We break the farmer's walls, trample his crops, steal his horses and carts, demand fruit and wine," a soldier wrote in his diary. "If he is unlucky he gets his home smashed by shells, his crops devoured by fire." Canadian troops howled with outrage upon finding their dead disinterred and robbed of their boots. Refugees desperate for meat could be seen wrapping dead dogs in butcher paper.

Pitched fighting persisted south of Catania along the Simeto River, where Hermann Göring troops and German paratroopers battled with backs-to-the-wall fury. "The enemy is tough. A real lot of sods," a British officer said. "When we kill them they have sneers on their faces." John Gunther described Tommies lying in "foxholes, sucking lemons. The earth is khaki-colored here, and they melt into it." All things white were hidden to avoid attracting Luftwaffe marauders; at the first hint of an air raid, shavers even toweled the lather from their faces. "Get down, Jock," a Scots officer called to an exposed soldier. "You'll get pipped."

Many were pipped anyway. Dead men shored the reedy banks of creeks and irrigation ditches, and a grisly sunken road dubbed Stink Alley was "paved with bodies." Medics jabbed the moribund with morphine and waited for them to die. "It would seem hard to tell the dead from the living," a regimental commander wrote. "I realized that you *could* tell them apart, because the flies walked on the faces of the dead." Close combat proved especially confusing in Sicilian vineyards, now in full leaf; enemy machine-gunners fired on fixed lines a few inches above the ground, raising welts of dust and wounding many in the feet and legs. At night in the moonlight, "shadows cast by the vines looked like moving men."

By Sunday morning, July 18, Montgomery conceded that his coastal thrust had sputtered into stalemate. Eighth Army casualties approached four thousand, including seven hundred dead. Efforts to burn the enemy out with RAF incendiaries failed when Sicilian flora proved disappointingly fire-resistant. Ordering a single division to hold the Simeto front, Montgomery shifted forces from his XIII Corps to the west in another effort to flank Axis defenses by further dividing his army. "I am pushing the offensive hard on the left, where the resistance is not so strong. The enemy is now hemmed in at the northeast corner," he wrote the 51st Highland Division commander on July 21. "I am sending you 50,000 cigarettes as a present to the division." Eisenhower, who had predicted the fall of Sicily by late July, began to grumble in Algiers. "Why doesn't Monty get going? What's the matter with him?" Gunther could have told him: "Both sides are tired, and whereas we are exposed in the plain, the Germans are high up, with good cover."

*The Germans are high up, with good cover.* Here in Sicily was revealed a ground truth that would obtain until the war's end twenty-two months hence: on no battlefield did topography dictate fate more than in vertical Italy. Officers pondered their 1-to-50,000 maps and realized that the compressed contour lines signified not only slope and steep ascent, but plunging fire and enemy omniscience. A *Gefreiter* with Zeiss binoculars and a field telephone could rain artillery on every living creature in sight.

For now the whitewashed houses and tile roofs of unattainable Catania shimmered in the midday haze, five miles to the north, down a road lined with fluttering poplars and hidden guns. Beyond the town loomed the pyramidal mass of Mount Etna, mysterious and indifferent.

## *"How I Love Wars"*

PATTON had been sulking outside Gela in a confiscated Fascist villa notable for its wardrobe of black shirts and a squawking menagerie of tropical birds in gilded cages. Fine tapestries covered the walls and the Seventh Army commander slept in a sturdy four-poster. "We can sit comfortably on our prats while Monty finishes the goddam war," a staff officer said bitterly. That was unlikely. On Saturday morning, July 17, Patton rose from his prat, grabbed a map, and flew to Tunisia, determined to get his army back into the battle.

He found General Alexander at his headquarters in the village of La Marsa, on the northern lip of the Gulf of Tunis. A chapel nearby consecrated the spot where Louis IX of France died of typhoid in 1270 while leading the Eighth Crusade. Across the blue bay loomed the jagged silhouette of Cap Bon, where the final fragments of the Axis armies had sought refuge before surrendering two months earlier. Alexander and staff officers of his 15th Army Group—the nomenclature reflected the sum of his subordinate Seventh and Eighth Armies—occupied tents in the white-walled garden and orangery of a villa deeded to Queen Victoria by the bey of Tunis. German commanders had used the manor house during their seven-month occupation; they absconded with the furniture but left untouched the English books, including a set of Benjamin Disraeli's novels. Senior British officers now messed in the dining room beneath a domed ceiling and arabesque traceries. "No fuss, no worry, no anxiety—and a great battle in progress," Harold Macmillan, the ranking British diplomat in North Africa, noted in his diary that weekend. "This is never referred to, except occasionally by some of the American officers on Gen. Alex's staff, but is understood to be going on satisfactorily."

Not in Patton's view. He unfolded his map and came to the point with a jabbing finger. "Have I got to stay here and protect the rear of Eighth Army?" he asked Alexander. "I want to get on with this and push out." The enemy was "back on his heels." Sixty thousand Italian troops remained in western Sicily, but Ultra two days earlier had revealed German plans to abandon half the island; demolitions were ordered for Trapani, the little port on Sicily's northwest coast where Aeneas' father had died. The best way to shield Montgomery's flank, Patton said, would be to sunder the island by driving Seventh Army north, toward Palermo. A gleam lit his gaze as he pointed to Sicily's largest city on the north coast, eighty miles from Gela. In his mind's eye, American tanks swept from the rolling hills and into Palermo's central piazza with a panache even Erwin Rommel had never achieved. "The glamour of capturing Palermo," Lucian Truscott later noted, "attracted Georgie Patton."

Harold Alexander studied the map, his head swiveling from Catania in the east through the still uncaptured inland crossroads at Enna to the Sicilian west. Except for a fascination with Kesselring—he devoured a biographical sketch compiled by Ultra intelligence analysts—Alexander's generalship lacked intellectual depth or even curiosity, relying more on his legendary sangfroid. "He's bone from the neck up," one British general insisted, and even Brooke conceded that he "had no ideas of his own." Yet Alexander possessed a sterling reputation, built at the cannon's mouth, and he looked the part: immaculate, unfazed, in command. His steep-peaked Guardsman's cap, high boots, and breeches "conveyed an air of Czarist Russia," one admirer said, and in fact he had once fought the Bolsheviks in Latvia as a volunteer in a unit of ethnic Germans. "He looked as though he had just had a steam bath, a massage, a good breakfast and a letter from home," wrote one journalist. "His well-shaped face, with its fine thin-nostriled nose, level eyes and well-trimmed mustache, was plainly pinkish under its tan." The "chestnut hair was sleekly brushed and parted high on the left side." Only a touch of gray at the temples, and the violet pouches beneath his eyes, hinted that Alexander was fifty-one and responsible for several hundred thousand souls.

It was said that he was "a born leader, not a made one." It was said that he "was an English country gentleman, almost uneducated, who never read a book." It was said that he could not write his name before the age of ten, but now spoke French, Italian, German, Russian, and Urdu. It was also said that he "might have been a greater commander if he had not been so nice a man and so deeply a gentleman." And it was said that he had gone over the top thirty times in the Great War before being wounded, and that, in hopes of sharing his good fortune, Irish Guardsmen liked to tread in his footsteps when crossing no-man's-land. Churchill's physician, Lord Moran, even said of him, "To be clever is not everything." Whatever Alexander's short-comings, Macmillan observed, "he has the great quality of seeing the point." Patton, unbeguiled, noted in his diary that Alexander "has an exceptionally small head. That may explain things."

Oblivious to the anguish that his July 13 order had caused the Americans, Alexander nevertheless sensed the tension in Patton's voice. He wondered, he later confessed, whether the impetuous American might simply strike off on his own, declaring, "The hell with this." True, he doubted that the Yanks could pull their weight. As he had written Brooke, even Eisenhower, Patton, and other U.S. commanders "are not professional soldiers, not as we understand that term." Yet Alexander saw no harm in allowing them to give it a go. With a nod of that solid-bone, beautifully coiffed, exceptionally small head, he turned Patton loose.

Off Patton's forces went at a gallop, west by north, an army unreined. In truth, many had slipped their fetters in advance of Alexander's approval. Patton on Friday had dispatched a huge reconnaissance force ten miles up the coast to Agrigento, "loveliest of mortal cities," in the opinion of the poet Pindar, where men once slept on ivory beds and interred their favorite horses in lavish tombs, and where the apricot-tinted Doric temples still had few equals outside Greece. Darby's Rangers assembled in an almond orchard a mile north of Agrigento's harbor, Porto Empedocle, then attacked with five companies in skirmish lines, followed by three battalions from Truscott's 3rd Infantry Division. Sweeping over strongpoints, they routed the defenders and took six thousand prisoners.

Unaware that Agrigento and the port had fallen, the light cruiser *Philadelphia* unlimbered her guns until frantic soldiers on the docks arranged oil barrels to spell YANK and U.S. ARMY for a spotter plane overhead. Sailors recased the guns, and several giddy Rangers, fortified with local cognac, emerged from a haberdashery wearing stovepipe hats and black wedding togs. Of greater value were three safes found in an Italian naval headquarters; after heaving them out of a second-story window, soldiers cracked them with farrier tools, crowbars, hand grenades, and rocks. Inside they found charts of enemy minefields, code books, and demolition plans for Palermo and Messina.

Axis troops not captured or killed drew back. "During the night of 17/18 July," Seventh Army's log recorded, "enemy withdrew from contact along the entire line." Truscott summoned his regimental commanders, ordered them to reach Palermo in five days or less, then hoisted a bottle of scotch for a toast: "To the American doughboy."

Off they went again at a gallop, again west by north. Among those American doughboys was the nineteen-year-old son of a Texas sharecropper who in the next two years would become the most celebrated soldier in the U.S. Army. A fifth-grade dropout, he had picked cotton, worked in a filling station, and fixed radios. Until enlisting, he had never been a hundred miles from the four-room shack in Hunt County that housed eleven children. The Army had issued him a uniform six inches too long in the sleeves and tried to make him a cook. In basic training, he balked at buying GI insurance because "I don't intend to get killed any way and it costs pretty high"; he still owed money for his mother's funeral. Bunkmates in the States had called him Baby—he weighed 112 pounds—but the nickname disappeared as he added muscle. This week he had been promoted, so he was now *Corporal* Audie Leon Murphy.

He had a slow, stooped gait, as if stalking prey. Audie Murphy's marksmanship derived from squirrel hunting, but he would learn to stalk Germans by the smell of their tobacco smoke. Hunt County had put a flinty edge on him. "There never was a peace time in my life, a time when things were good," he later said. "I can't remember ever being young in my life." When a chaplain tried to nudge him closer to God, Murphy replied, "You do the prayin' and I'll do the shootin'." As the 1st Battalion of the 15th Infantry Regiment plunged through the Sicilian interior, he did his first real shootin' while leading a patrol. Two Italian officers bolted from an observation post, and as they mounted a pair of white horses, Murphy dropped to a knee. "I fire twice," he recalled. "The men tumble from the horses, roll over and lie still." Many more would lie still before Murphy could return to Texas festooned with medals, but he had already shed any illusions. "Ten seconds after the first shot was fired at me by an enemy soldier," he said, "combat was no longer glamorous."

Unlike Tunisia, where hills were named by their height in meters, "here there was usually a small town on top with some Dago name that no one could pronounce," an artillery sergeant wrote. One by one they fell, often without a skirmish: Sciacca and Lercara Friddi and Castelvetrano. Cheering locals greeted them with figs, almonds, and sometimes a stiff-armed Fascist salute. "Kiss your hand! Kiss your hand!" obeisant peasants yelled with such fervor that an annoyed major banned the phrase. White bedsheets fluttered from every house in Prizzi, where Truscott bought a fine Italian saddle as a trophy for Patton. Italian troops from the Assietta and Aosta Divisions surrendered by the thousands, grousing at German betrayal. "One never seemed to be able to do enough to please them," an Italian POW explained.

Emulating Stonewall Jackson's foot cavalry, Truscott's infantry covered thirty miles or more a day in blistering heat and through dust said to be "composed of a mixture of chalk and cattle dung." "We are walking at the rate of 4.5 miles an hour," a private in the 15th Infantry told his diary. "Boy are my dogs barking now." The surging ranks reminded Truscott of "waves beating on an ocean beach." Alexander made a halfhearted effort from La Marsa to moderate the advance, but Seventh Army staff officers ignored his message. "Mount up and continue," Patton told his armor crews. "Don't stop except for gas." Omar Bradley conspicuously displayed in his II Corps headquarters a map of Sicily upon which the territory seized by U.S. troops was shaded in blue, sharply contrasting with the smaller, red-hued area held by the British.

From a roadcut in the ridge above Palermo, Truscott squinted through the midday haze at the ancient city on Thursday, July 22. Houses and apartment buildings spilled down the slope to the sea in a terra-cotta jumble redolent of blood oranges and smoke. Fires danced on the lowering hills as far as Monte Pellegrino, sparked by artillery or rearguard Italians burning munitions. Thousands of hungry refugees now camped in these highlands; judging by the desperate faces Truscott had seen while driving from his command post in Corleone, no cat in Palermo was safe from the carving knife.

Belisarius in A.D. 535 had captured the city from the Goths by hoisting archers to the mastheads of his fleet with ropes and pulleys so they could shoot over the harbor ramparts. Such tactics were hardly needed now. Palermo was defenseless, ripe for plucking. Comando Supremo a few hours earlier had ordered port demolitions to begin, and Truscott could hear the echo of explosions along the quays. Two infantry regiments stood poised above the city, but Patton forbade further advance until tanks arrived to spearhead the procession. "Everything was arranged so that Georgie could make a grandstand entry with tanks and what-not," Truscott wrote Sarah.

Hours passed. Italian envoys in shabby suits came and went under flags of truce, pleading for someone to accept the city's surrender. At six P.M., Seventh Army authorized reconnaissance patrols to enter the city and secure the docks. Truscott sent two battalions.

Into the city they clattered, into a cadaverous and ruined city, dismembered by months of Allied bombing. "Street after street of crumbled houses," one officer wrote in his diary.

> Whole blocks of shapeless rubble. Parlor, bedroom, and bath exposed . . . by the fantastic projectile that strips away the façade and leaves intact the hat on the bureau, the mirror on the wall, the carafe on the night table.

More than sixty churches had been damaged. At the National Library, "stacks full of rare books lay open like a sliced pomegranate." Drifts of rubble stood so deep near the waterfront that streets could no longer be recognized as streets, though a marble plaque still affixed to one battered house noted that Goethe had lived there in 1787. Forty-four ships had been sunk along masonry quays smashed to powder. The explosion of an ammunition freighter had raised a wave powerful enough to toss two other vessels onto the moles. Wreckage from hundreds of smaller craft cluttered the port. Salvage teams soon would find tons of unexploded land mines and other ordnance washed by tidal currents along the muddy harbor floor. In the Piazza Vigliena, a small army of bedraggled Italian soldiers stood in ranks, waiting to surrender. Priests in black soutanes genuflected and urchins on the Via Maqueda offered to sing Verdi arias for candy. American troops seized two large trucks, one full of new typewriters and the other full of sweet Sicilian nougat. In the coming days, they would find half a million tons of naval stores at Palermo, including crated matériel addressed to Herr Rommel in Alexandria, Egypt, his destination until Alamein had reversed his course.

Major General Geoff Keyes, Patton's deputy, arrived in Palermo's western outskirts at 7:15 P.M. He found an Italian general, Giuseppe Molinero, blotting his damp brow after fruitless hours of trying to capitulate. Searching for a translator, Keyes fastened on a Hungarian-born news photographer named Endre Friedmann, better known as Robert Capa. That Capa spoke no Italian hindered the negotiations—"Stop that jabbering, soldier!"

Keyes demanded at one point, "I want unconditional surrender and I want it immediately!"—but the gist soon emerged. "General Molinero says he is through and will fight no more." Sadly, the general lacked the power to surrender all forces in Palermo. Keyes bundled Molinero into his scout car; a white pillowcase requisitioned from a Sicilian housewife and tied to the radio antenna hung too limply, so an aide held a bedsheet lashed to a fishing pole as they drove to the Royal Palace on Via Vittorio Emanuele. Italian soldiers cheered and civilians tossed flowers and lemons. The proper general could not be found—Truscott's efficient men had arrested him earlier—so the weary Molinero agreed to exceed his authority. Palermo fell at last, formally and finally. Keyes checked into the Hotel Excelsior Palace, took a bath, and went to bed.

Patton woke him at ten P.M., flask in hand, giddy at his own flowers-and-lemons entry. "It is a great thrill to be driving into a captured city in the dark," he jotted in his diary. Patton moved into the king's apartment in the Royal Palace, dining on captured German champagne and K rations served on House of Savoy china. Built by Saracens and enlarged by the Normans in the twelfth century, the palace was a fit if dusty abode for a conquering hero. "All sorts of retainers live in holes about the place and all give the Fascist salute," Patton noted.

"The occupation of western Sicily must be considered as complete," Kesselring sourly advised Berlin on July 24. From the assault at Agrigento through the capture of the Trapani naval commander—who surrendered his sword and field glasses—American casualties totaled less than 300; some 2,300 Axis troops had been killed or wounded, and another 53,000 captured, nearly all of them Italian. Yet it was a slender triumph, strategically insignificant, and Patton's gaze soon swiveled east, where the real fight for Sicily must occur. Over highballs in the palace on July 26, he confided to Truscott that he would "certainly like to beat Montgomery into Messina."

Still, they savored the moment. "You will have guessed where I am and what I have been doing," Truscott wrote Sarah. "It has been a grand experience and we have opened lots of eyes." Patton summarized his sentiments in four words to Bea: "How I love wars."

## Snaring the Head Devil

A FTER months of procrastination and discord, the Allied high command had yet to agree on what to do with the million-man Anglo-American army in the Mediterranean once the campaign ended in Sicily.

At the TRIDENT conference in Washington, the Combined Chiefs—with the approval of Roosevelt and Churchill—had instructed Eisenhower to devise a plan "best calculated to eliminate Italy from the war and to contain the maximum number of German forces." The prime minister believed any such plan must include an invasion of mainland Italy. He hectored Eisenhower to that end, as he had hectored the president.

"No objective can compete with the capture of Rome," Churchill insisted. In a whirlwind visit to Algiers after TRIDENT, and in countless messages since, he had argued that if Berlin were uncoupled from its staunchest ally, German troops would be forced to supplant several dozen Italian divisions occupying the Balkans and southern France; that, in turn, would weaken Hitler's defenses in western Europe before the Allied cross-Channel attack, tentatively planned for the spring of 1944. If more Allied soldiers were needed for an Italian campaign, Churchill would strip British forces in the Middle East. If more ships were needed to transport and supply that invading army, he would snatch food from British tables by diverting cargo vessels. "It would be hard for me to ask the British people to cut their rations again, but I would gladly do so," he vowed. When Eisenhower balked at such blandishments, Churchill lamented that the Allied commander was "sicklied o'er with the pale cast of thought."

As the prime minister's rhetoric grew febrile, metaphors piled up. On July 13, urging bold action as far up the Italian boot as possible, Churchill declared, "Why should we crawl up the leg like a harvest-bug from the ankle upwards? Let us rather strike at the knee. . . . Tell the planners to throw their hat over the fence." He privately acknowledged that "the Americans consider we have led them up the garden path in the Mediterranean—but a beautiful path it has proved to be. They have picked peaches here, nectarines there. How grateful they should be!" ("Many of the Italian peaches," a U.S. Army commander later commented, "had gonorrhea.")

Eisenhower in May had leaned toward carrying the fight to the Italian mainland. But George Marshall's wariness, Churchill's chronic fixation on the Balkans, and the imminent return to England of seven British and American divisions, as agreed at TRIDENT, gave him pause. So too did contradictory assessments from his staff. An intelligence study in late June concluded that the Italian "population is war weary and apathetic, sees little hope of victory . . . and is becoming increasingly hostile to the growing German control." Bombing, amphibious landings, and a quick march toward Rome "might well cause a collapse in civilian will to resist"; if Italy collapsed, German forces "will withdraw and resistance met will be slight." Yet Eisenhower's intelligence chief warned on June 25 "that present indications are that Germany intends to reinforce Italy." Three days later, his operations chief cautioned that "the terrain through which we shall then have to force our way north is very mountainous and difficult in the extreme."

Success in Sicily tipped the scale. Having gained their first foothold in occupied Europe, sober men in Washington, London, and North Africa felt the euphoric impulse to roll the dice again. On July 17, shortly after Patton had left his meeting in Tunisia with Alexander, Eisenhower convened a conference of senior commanders at La Marsa. Without excessive deliberation, they agreed to advise the Combined Chiefs—Eisenhower called them the Charlie-Charlies—that "operations should be carried onto the mainland of Italy." Eisenhower sent the recommendation a day later, and at the same time canceled a proposed invasion of Sardinia. On July 20, the Charlie-Charlies consented, and another die had been cast.

Vital issues remained unsettled, and much dickering followed. Where in Italy should the invading host land? Capture of the great port at Naples was paramount, but Naples Bay had been heavily fortified with fifty big guns and lay just beyond range of Spitfires flying from Sicily. Air cover for the invasion fleet was considered indispensable. Memos flew back and forth across the Atlantic, and to and from North Africa, bearing accusations of conservatism, orthodoxy, and tactical tomfoolery. Absent was a searching inquiry into the strategic calculus: What if the Germans fought for every Italian hill and dale? How far up the boot should the Allied armies go? What benefit would the capture of Rome bring, besides big headlines? Was it possible to defeat Germany by fighting in Italy? Could Italy become a strategic cul-de-sac?

For now, analysis went begging. As to where the attack should fall, Eisenhower focused on a broad bay 30 miles southeast of Naples and precisely 178 miles from northeast Sicily: a Spitfire outfitted with an extra gas tank had a range of 180 miles, which permitted ten minutes' combat time before the pilot was forced to return to base for refueling. "If it is decided to undertake such operations," the AFHQ staff recommended on July 24, "the assault should be made in the Gulf of Salerno." Two days later the Charlie-Charlies concurred, authorizing an invasion at Salerno "at the earliest possible date" after the conquest of Sicily.

Churchill was delighted. "I am with you heart and soul," he cabled Marshall. But the prime minister had his eye on a bigger prize than Salerno or Naples. "Rome," he advised Eisenhower, "is the bull's-eye."

The man in the middle of that bull's-eye was a specter of the once mighty Duce, to whom even Hitler had displayed deference and affection. His ashy pallor and sunken cheeks made Benito A. A. Mussolini look older than his fifty-nine years and hardly the "head devil" that Roosevelt now called him. He still shaved his head, but more to hide his gray than in a display of Fascist virility. Because of his vain refusal to wear eyeglasses, Mussolini's speeches were prepared on a special typewriter with an enormous font. Duodenal ulcers—some claimed they were "of syphilitic origin"—had plagued him for nearly two decades, and his diet now consisted mostly of stewed fruit and three liters of milk a day. A German officer in Rome reported, "Often in conversation his face was wrenched with pain and he would grab his stomach." Once he had demonstrated vigor to photographers by scything wheat or by rubbing snow on his bare chest. Now, wary of assassins, he lolled about the Palazzo Venezia, in a back room with tinted windows and the signs of the zodiac painted on the ceiling. Sometimes he lolled with his mistress, Clara Petacci, the buxom, green-eyed daughter of the pope's physician, whose wardrobe was filled with negligees and goose-feather boas personally selected by Mussolini.

He had risen far since his modest boyhood as a blacksmith's son in the lower Po Valley, and he would fall even farther before his strutting hour on the stage ended. As a young vagabond he had been an avowed socialist, stalking the streets with brass knuckles in his pocket and reciting long passages from Dante. His politics devolved to ultranationalism and the Fasci di Combattimento, which he founded in Milan in 1919 and which was the precursor to the Fascist party he rode to power in 1922. By the late 1920s, he had extirpated Italian parliamentary government to become an absolute tyrant—*il Duce,* the Leader—cleverly accommodating both the Vatican and the popular monarchy of King Victor Emmanuel III. With an autodidact's quick mind and bombastic oratory, he raised national confidence, stabilized the lira, built a modern military, and boosted farm production by reclaiming vast tracts of swampland. The trains, famously, ran on time. His invasion of Ethiopia in 1935 helped destroy the League of Nations; he empowered Hitler by showing how easily Western democracies could be cowed and by condoning Germany's *Anschluss* with Austria. The Führer's gratitude led to the Pact of Steel in May 1939. "Believe, Obey, Fight," the Fascist motto advised, and hundreds of thousands of Italian women surrendered their wedding rings to be melted down for Mussolini's war effort. In Italian cinemas, moviegoers rose as one when the Duce strode across the screen in newsreels; he also required Italians to stand during radio broadcasts of armed forces communiqués, often delivered at one P.M. to ensure a captive audience in restaurants.

Lately the country was getting to its feet mostly for bad news. Italy's colonial adventures in Eritrea, Somaliland, Abyssinia, and North Africa had been ruinous. Without informing Berlin, Mussolini also had invaded Greece, only to require German help to stave off catastrophe. Rome declared war on supine France in 1940, but thirty-two Italian divisions failed to overwhelm three French divisions on the Alpine front. The Italian air force had been gutted in Libya; two-thirds of the Italian army fighting in Russia had been destroyed; 40 percent of Italian soldiers on Crete reportedly lacked boots; and three-quarters of the merchant fleet had been sunk in the lost-cause effort to resupply North Africa. Raw materials, from cotton to rubber, were now dispensed by the Germans, who even provided the fuel that allowed Italian warships to leave port. About 1.2 million Italian soldiers served on various foreign fronts, along with 800,000 in Italy; but few had the stomach to defend the homeland, much less fight a world war. A German high command assessment on June 30 concluded, "The kernel of the Italian army has been destroyed in Greece, Russia, and Africa. . . . The combat value of Italian units is slight."

Since December 1942, Mussolini had vainly urged Hitler to draw back from the Eastern Front, or even to forge a separate peace with Moscow. With combat casualties approaching 300,000, Italy found itself in the "ridiculous position of being unable either to make war or to make peace." On July 18, the Duce cabled Berlin: "The sacrifice of my country cannot have as its principal purpose that of delaying a direct attack on Germany." A day later, in a hastily organized meeting in Feltre, fifty miles from Venice, that sacrifice grew starker. At eleven A.M., Hitler launched into a gadding monologue in which he acknowledged being "of two minds" about how to defend Sicily, while insisting that HUSKY must become "a catastrophic defeat, a Stalingrad" for the Anglo-Americans. Thirty minutes later an Italian officer, said to be "white with emotion," interrupted to inform Mussolini in a stage whisper that a massive air raid had just ripped up Rome.

Months in the planning, this first attack on the capital targeted the Littorio rail yards, a sprawling hourglass-shaped network through which flowed most train traffic to Sicily and southern Italy. "It would be a tragedy if St. Peter's were destroyed," General Marshall had said in late June, "but a calamity if we failed to knock out the marshaling yards." More than five hundred bombers carrying one thousand tons of high explosives flew from bases in North Africa and Pantelleria. Roman Catholic aviators had been offered the option of skipping the mission; red stickers on navigation maps highlighted the Vatican and various historic sites with "Must Not Be Harmed" warnings. Even so, a Catholic chaplain stood on one runway and bellowed at departing B-26s, "Give them hell!"

Hell they got. As Pope Pius XII watched through binoculars and the Italian king peered through a telescope—"Look!" the monarch exclaimed. "Perfect formation!"—bombs tore up the Littorio yards, but also struck an adjacent working-class neighborhood. "It was the Americans," a mortally wounded boy screamed, "the sons of bitches." (A BBC broadcast the next day infuriated the Yanks by stressing that the raid had been exclusively American.) Estimates of the dead ranged from seven hundred to three thousand, with many more injured. A single thousand-pound bomb struck the Basilica of San Lorenzo, first built in the fourth century and considered among Rome's finest churches. The explosion destroyed the façade, damaged the twelfth-century frescoes, and left roof trusses, splintered beams, and bricks heaped in the nave. Priests strolled through the flaming streets, flicking holy water on the rubble.

At Feltre, Hitler rambled on for two hours to a stupefied Mussolini as courtiers scurried in and out with grim updates from Rome. At length the Duce took leave to return to his capital. "We are fighting for a common cause, Führer," he said.

A week later, on Sunday, July 25, Mussolini arrived at his enormous office in the Palazzo Venezia at eight A.M. He granted clemency to two condemned partisans and studied his daily compendium of telephone intercepts and informant reports. Over a lunch of broth and stewed fruit, he reassured his unsettled wife that "the people are with me," then changed from the gray-green uniform of the First Marshal of the Empire into a dark blue suit and fedora. The king had asked to see him.

Rarely had the Duce faced such challenges as now besieged him. For ten hours the previous day he had battled the Grand Council of Fascism, a phony parliament of his own creation whose members had last met in 1939. Mussolini's efforts to shrug off reverses in Sicily and elsewhere provoked reproachful glares. Dressed in black Saharan bush shirts, the councilmen had voted nineteen to seven, with one abstention, to ask the king to take command of the Italian armed forces. "When tomorrow I shall relate to him what has happened tonight, the king will say, 'The Grand Council is against you but the king will stand by you,'" Mussolini warned before stalking from the chamber. "Then what will happen to you all?"

Shortly before five P.M., the Duce's three-car convoy sped up the Via Salaria in northern Rome to the great eighteenth-century hunting estate at Villa Savoia. Here the king now lived in a handsome yellow palace set among pines and holm oaks. Mussolini climbed from his Alfa Romeo sedan and gestured to his bodyguards to wait outside the gate. He failed to notice several dozen carabinieri hiding behind hedges near the palace.

A millennium of royal inbreeding had disserved Victor Emmanuel III. Barely five feet tall, with malformed legs and a stunted intellect, he was said to be "taciturn and diffident," "as indifferent as marble under a flow of running water." Mussolini, his partner for more than two decades, privately called him "the little sardine." Now seventy-three, he preferred to talk of hunting ibex in the Alps, or how he once shot twenty-eight wood-cock on the estate of the king of Naples. But on this Sunday afternoon the discussion must necessarily turn to politics; Victor Emmanuel ushered the Duce into his corner study, where an aide stood with an ear pressed to the outer door.

After a few rambling sentences, interspersed with phrases in Piedmon-tese dialect, the king came to the point. Mussolini must resign. He would be replaced by Marshal Pietro Badoglio, a former chief of the armed forces. "Dear Duce, the situation is beyond remedy. At this moment you are the most hated man in Italy. You have not a single friend left, except for me," the king said, then shrugged. "I am sorry, but the solution could not be oth-erwise."

Even at five feet, seven inches, Mussolini towered over his monarch. "You are making an extremely serious decision. . . . The blow to army morale will be great." Before turning on his heel he added, "I am perfectly aware that the people hate me." In the entry foyer, the king shook Mus-solini's hand and shut the door, looking more shriveled than ever. "That," Queen Helena observed, "was not at all nice."

Mussolini strode across the courtyard toward his car only to be inter-cepted by a captain of the carabinieri. "Duce, I have been ordered by the king to protect your person." An ambulance backed up from the foot of the drive, its rear door yawning. The officer took Mussolini's arm. "You must get into this." Soon the vehicle careered down the Via Salaria and through the streets of central Rome. Across the Tiber they sped to a police barracks in Trastevere, where guards stood with bayonets fixed. Mussolini emerged to stand with arms akimbo, fists on his hips, staring at the slogan painted on a courtyard wall: "*Credere, Obbedire, Combattere.*"

A few minutes later, he was bundled back into the ambulance and driven to another barracks, in Via Legnano. Escorted to a small room, he refused dinner and complained of stomach pains. "My physical person interests me no longer," Mussolini told a physician summoned to examine him, "only my moral personality." At eleven P.M., he switched off the lamp but could still see a light burning in the adjacent room where a sentry kept watch. A nearby telephone rang and rang. No one answered.

A radio bulletin at eleven P.M. sent delirious Romans spilling through the blacked-out streets in their pajamas and nightgowns. "Citizens, wake up!" they yelled in the Via del Tritone. "Mussolini is finished!" Strangers embraced and danced in the cobblestone piazzi. Tricolors flapped from passing trucks, soldiers sang political songs not heard for twenty years, and a mob—"shouting all the invectives in the Roman vocabulary"—kicked and punched the darkened Palazzo Venezia as if the building itself had caused their misery. Torch beams played across the now vacant balcony where the declaiming peacock had struck so many poses. Bonfires crackled with furniture ransacked from the Fascist party headquarters. *"Viva l'Italia!"* they roared, and a few German soldiers, assuming that the war was over, joined the celebration.

"One did not see a single person in Rome wearing the Fascist badge," wrote Marshal Badoglio, who succeeded Mussolini as head of state. "Fascism fell, as was fitting, like a rotten pear." Even Mussolini's own newspaper on Monday morning replaced the usual front-page photograph of the Duce with one of Badoglio.

The new regime quickly assured Berlin that the Pact of Steel endured, and that Italy would prosecute the war against the Anglo-Americans with vigor. Few believed it. "The Duce will enter history as the last Roman, but behind his massive figure a gypsy people has gone to rot," Joseph Goebbels told his diary. "The only thing certain in this war is that Italy will lose it."

But in Rome a young woman spoke for a nation when she confided to her own diary on July 26: "Italy has had enough of heroes."

## *Fevers of an Unknown Origin*

PATTON had settled comfortably into Palermo's flat-roofed Royal Palace. Long tongues of scarlet carpet rolled through corridors lined with silk-upholstered chairs and gilt mirrors etched with the Savoy coat of arms. Half a dozen vaulted antechambers separated Patton's bedroom from the immense state dining room, and heroic oils of Hercules' labors decorated an assembly hall the size of a basketball court. During mass in the Palatine Chapel—the writer Guy de Maupasssant had likened walking through the chancel to entering a jewel—Patton knelt beneath the coffered wooden ceiling and prayed to Christ Pantocrator.

He asked for strength—"I know I have been marked to do great things," he wrote his brother-in-law—but his heart's desire was Messina, 147 tortuous miles to the east. The coup in Rome, while a pleasant surprise, had little impact on the Sicilian battlefield: no Germans had been deposed, and it was mostly Germans who blocked the roads to Messina. On July 23, having recognized that Eighth Army needed help, Alexander authorized the Americans to attack eastward on two roughly parallel roads: Highway 113, which hugged the north coast, and Highway 120, an inland route. Patton mailed Franklin Roosevelt a tattered Corps of Engineers map of Sicily, with a thick green line showing that Seventh Army occupied more than half the island "as of July 26." Above a tally of prisoners captured and guns seized, an arrow pointed to Messina with a blue crayon notation in Patton's jagged hand: "We hope!" In his reply the president proposed "that after the war I . . . make you the Marquis of Mt. Etna."

With victory in western Sicily, the fame Patton so ardently craved was finally his. Both *Time* and *Newsweek* had featured him on their covers this month. "Monty hardly figures at all in the papers," Bea told him on July 30. "Everyone wonders what he is doing and why he doesn't go ahead." Patton's army now exceeded 200,000 men, but true glory required audacity. "I have a sixth sense in war as I used to have in fencing," he told her. "Also I am willing to take chances." If taking chances cost lives, *c'est la guerre.* He advised Bradley, whose II Corps had met stiffening German resistance in central Sicily, that if he could reach Messina a single day earlier "by losing additional men," then he must "lose them." To Middleton, the 45th Division commander, he added on July 28, "This is a horse race, in which the prestige of the U.S. Army is at stake. We must take Messina before the British." When soldiers captured a fleet of Volkswagen staff cars, Patton offered to share them with Hewitt's officers if the Navy helped him reach Messina first.

Each morning his armored cavalcade bolted out of Palermo, trailing banners of dust across the Sicilian outback. On Highway 113 or Highway 120, Patton would hop from the command car with its radios and map boards, clasping his hands high like a prizefighter and urging his legions eastward. When enemy shells burst nearby he again timed his pulse, reproaching himself for the slightest upward tick. "You have killer eyes, just like I have," he told a wounded artillery captain in a hospital ward near Palermo. "Get back up to the front as soon as you can." At another ward, full of amputees, an orderly found him sobbing in the latrine. "It is hard to be an army commander and a hero at the same time," he told Bea.

Stress frayed him. Always irascible when his blood was up, he now seemed erratic and even abusive. Happening upon a narrow bridge where 2nd Armored Division tanks had been delayed by a peasant with a mule cart, Patton broke his swagger stick over the man's head, ordered an aide to shoot the mule, then had carcass and cart shoved into the creek bed below. When a gun crew took cover in a stand of trees during a German air attack, Patton reportedly charged them with his pistol drawn. "Get back on that gun, you yellow bastards," he roared. "And if you leave it again, I'll shoot you myself." When a company commander in the 16th Infantry who had refused medical evacuation despite badly infected leg boils was fined by Patton for removing his chafing leggings, the story quickly spread through the vexed ranks. "You son of a bitch," he yelled at one of Truscott's best battalion commanders, "why the goddam hell aren't you moving?" Unauthorized headgear particularly aggravated him. Men from the 12th Weather Squadron attempting to free the jammed bow door on an LST in Palermo harbor were nonplussed when Patton snatched the fatigue caps from their heads and flung them into the water. Spotting a 26th Infantry soldier wearing a watch cap beneath his helmet, Patton barked, "Take that goddam hat off and let my killers through."

At night he returned to his palace, to the Savoy china and the bloodred carpet, where he charmed staff officers at the long mess table with amusing tales of campaigns past. Then, abruptly drawing himself up, he said, "Let's talk about tomorrow." And after they had talked about tomorrow and drafted their battle plans, he would step onto the balcony behind the huge rosewood desk in his office. Below lay his fiefdom, the cruel city where for more than a century the Inquisition had its headquarters, where mafiosi had forced paupers to pay for the right to beg on the church steps, where for sport African immigrants had been doused in tubs of whitewash. Old men sat at green baize tables in the steamy night, playing cards and sipping ink-black wine.

"Wars are not won by apparent virtue," Patton observed, "else I would be in a hell of a fix."

Meticulous and even finicky in his warfighting, Patton was casual to the point of indifference about the more prosaic elements of running an army. Logistics snarled repeatedly in Sicily. In some sectors gunners ran desperately short of artillery shells, while mountains of small-arms ammunition accumulated. Lessons learned in North Africa were forgotten in Sicily, including the need for a disciplined air-raid warning system; at Palermo, a single gunshot caused a "wholesale exodus of dock workers" stampeding to shelters. Patton "never bothers his head about such things," John Lucas noted in his diary.

Nothing in Seventh Army was more SNAFUed, TARFUed, and FUMTUed than the vital issue of medical logistics. "It resembles a maniac driving a machine at high speed without pausing to oil or service the machine," a senior AFHQ surgeon reported. A combat force exceeding 200,000 had only 3,300 hospital beds, a number so inadequate that many minor cases were evacuated to North Africa for treatment and the 23,000 soldiers admitted for hospitalization during HUSKY tended to be stacked atop one another. Medics had only half as many ambulances as they needed; blankets and splints were scarce. Breakage and misplacement of medical supplies were enormous.

Sicily proved unforgiving. Many soldiers lost a pound per day to heat, dehydration, and intestinal miseries: Seventh Army appeared to be melting away. A chronic reluctance of cuts and bruises to heal was known simply as

"Sicilian disease." AFHQ adopted an elaborate code for the various afflictions for patients' general condition: "RNS" meant "recovery not satisfactory"; "SR," "sinking rapidly." Soldiers evacuated to the United States were "Z.I.'ed," for "Zone of Interior," and government-issue insurance policies provoked much sardonic banter. "I'll have to write the old lady tonight," said one soldier after a close call, "and tell her she missed out on that $10,000 again." Truscott's troops learned to ink their names and serial numbers on their leggings, which proved more durable in explosions than dogtags. The lucky extolled their good fortune. "Perhaps it will relieve you right at the start to know that I am still in one complete piece and *no* parts missing," a badly wounded soldier wrote his wife in late July.

The unlucky relied on the heroic efforts of doctors and nurses working in dreadful conditions. Surgeons operated by flashlight, with white sheets hung in the operatory for more reflected light. After watching surgeons lop off limbs for an hour, Frank Gervasi, a reporter for *Collier's* magazine, recalled Erasmus's astringent epigram "*Dulce bellum inexpertis*": Sweet is war to those who never experience it. "How am I doing, nurse?" a wounded eighteen-year-old in the 3rd Division asked. She kissed his forehead and replied, "You are doing just fine, soldier." He smiled faintly. "I was just checking up," he said, and then died. A physician described burn victims reduced to "cindery masses of burnt cloth and skin and hair." One charred soldier told him, "I guess I've lost my sunburn." For many, treatment consisted of a quarter-grain syrette of morphine and an "M" daubed on the forehead with iodine.

Now "M" took on another, more sinister connotation. In 1740, the writer Horace Walpole noted "a horrid thing called *mal'aria*" that afflicted Italy every summer. Before the war, the Rockefeller Foundation had published a sixteen-volume study on where the disease, which killed three million people each year, was most prevalent; Italy, infested with the mosquito *Anopheles maculipennis*—soon shortened to "Ann" in GI slang—had the highest malaria rates in the Mediterranean. Quinine had been used for centuries to suppress malaria's feverish symptoms, but U.S. supplies came almost exclusively from cinchona trees in the East Indies, now controlled by the Japanese. American scientists seeking a substitute examined fourteen thousand compounds, including dozens tested on jailhouse volunteers; the best replacement proved to be a substance originally synthesized by the German dye industry and given the trade name Atabrine.

Soldiers detested the stuff, which they dubbed "yellow gall." It tasted bitter, upset the stomach, turned the skin yellow, and was rumored to cause impotence and even sterility. Many soldiers stopped taking it, prophylactic discipline grew lax, and proper dosage levels were misunderstood. Moreover, some malaria control experts failed to reach Sicily until weeks after the invasion. Soldiers also grew careless about covering exposed skin in the evening. Protective netting was in short supply, and insect repellent proved ineffective: troops agreed "the mosquitoes in Sicily enjoyed it very much."

More than a thousand soldiers afflicted with malaria in North Africa on the eve of HUSKY had been left behind when the fleets sailed. On July 23, doctors detected the first case contracted in Sicily. By early August thousands of feverish, lethargic soldiers had been struck down. Ten thousand cases would sweep through Seventh Army, and nearly twelve thousand more in Eighth Army. (The swampy Catania Plain was particularly noxious.) All told, the 15th Army Group sustained more malaria casualties than battle wounds in Sicily. A medical historian concluded that "the disease record of the Seventh Army on Sicily was one of the worst compiled by any American field army during World War II." With soldiers also suffering from dengue, sandfly, and Malta fevers, distinguishing one malady from another became so difficult that many patients were diagnosed simply with "fever of unknown origin," soon known to soldiers as "fuo."

Among the ailing at a 45th Division clearing station was "a frail little fellow in Army fatigue coveralls, carrying a bedroll." Doctors originally diagnosed Ernie Pyle with malaria, then with dysentery, and finally settled on "battlefield fever," which ostensibly resulted from "too much dust, bad eating, not enough sleep, exhaustion, and the unconscious nerve tension that comes to everybody in a front-line area." Like so many others, Pyle had witnessed sights that gnawed at him, body and soul. Particularly grim was a field strewn with the bodies of two hundred Italian and German soldiers whose penises, swollen by rigor mortis, had "become hugely erect, some of them protruding through the buttons of their soiled trousers."

Nearly a week in a field hospital brought more awful visions. "Dying men were brought into our tent, men whose death rattle silenced the conversation and made all of us thoughtful," Pyle wrote. A trench outside a surgical tent was "filled with bloody shirt sleeves and pant legs the surgeons had snipped off wounded men." Pyle noted "how dirt and exhaustion reduce human faces to such a common denominator. Everybody they carried in looked alike." Among litter patients only "an extreme blond" seemed distinct, "like a flower in a row of weeds." Doctors covered the faces of the moribund with thin white gauze. Pyle would long remember one patient in particular:

> The dying man was left utterly alone, just lying there on his litter on the ground, lying in an aisle, because the tent was full. . . . The aloneness of that man as he went through the last minutes of his life was what tormented me.

\* \* \*

Under such circumstances Patton arrived at the 15th Evacuation Hospital, near Nicosia, for a visit shortly past noon on Tuesday, August 3. His morning had begun well, with a message from Eisenhower that Patton would receive the Distinguished Service Cross for his heroics at Gela during the July 11 counterattack. Driving on Highway 113 from Palermo before turning inland to Nicosia, Patton observed that "the smell of the dead along the road is very noticeable."

A different smell wafted from the hospital receiving tent, an odor of disinfectant and blood and oozing wounds. Green light filtered through the canvas, and the sound of labored breathing filled the ward as if the tent walls themselves suspired. General Lucas, who accompanied Patton while visiting from AFHQ, noted the "brave, hurt, bewildered boys" on their cots, including one who "had lost his right arm at the shoulder. He was still suffering from shock and was in tears. . . . A general has to develop a thick skin if he can, but it is sometimes hard to do."

On a stool midway through the ward slouched a private from the 26th Infantry, Charles H. Kuhl. A carpet layer from Indiana in civil life, Kuhl had been a soldier for eight months and in the 1st Division since early June. Examined at a battalion aid station the previous day, he received sodium amytal—a barbiturate to induce sleep—before being moved back to the 15th Evac, where an initial diagnosis concluded: "Psychoneurosis anxiety state—moderate severe. Soldier has been twice before in hospital within ten days. He can't take it at the front, evidently." A more discerning evaluation would reveal that Kuhl had malaria, chronic diarrhea, and a fever of 102.2 degrees.

Patton asked Kuhl where he was hurt. The soldier shrugged. He was "nervous" rather than wounded, Kuhl said. "I guess I can't take it," he added. To the astonishment of doctors and patients alike, Patton slapped the man across the face with his folded gloves. "You coward, you get out of this tent!" he shouted. "You can't stay in here with these brave, wounded Americans." Grabbing Kuhl by the collar, he dragged him to the tent entrance and shoved him out with a finishing kick from his cavalry boot. "Don't admit this sonuvabitch," he bellowed. "I don't want yellow-bellied bastards like him hiding their lousy cowardice around here, stinking up this place of honor." Alternately barking at the doctors and the quailing Kuhl, Patton said, "You send him back to his unit at once. You hear me, you gutless bastard? You're going back to the front."

His rage spent, Patton returned to his command car and drove off, already composing the message he would send his subordinates: "A very small number of soldiers are going to the hospital on the pretext that they are nervously incapable of combat. Such men are cowards, and bring discredit on the Army and disgrace to their comrades." Private Kuhl would be evacuated for treatment in North Africa; returning to the 26th Infantry, he landed at Normandy eleven months later and after the war worked in a South Bend factory before dying of a heart attack in 1971 at age fifty-five. Lucas, who saw "nothing serious" in the incident, soon returned to Algiers and neglected to mention it to Eisenhower. In his diary, Patton wrote of Private Kuhl, "I gave him the devil. . . . One sometimes slaps a baby to bring it to."

A week later, on August 10, a similar outburst would occur under nearly identical circumstances at the 93rd Evacuation Hospital, near Santo Stefano on the north coast. Private Paul G. Bennett, a gunner from South Carolina who had enlisted before Pearl Harbor, had been evacuated from the 17th Field Artillery despite pleading with medics to remain with his unit. Dehydrated, feverish, and unsettled by the severe wounding of a comrade, he appeared "confused, weak, and listless." At 1:30 P.M., during an impromptu visit to the receiving tent, Patton came upon the trembling Bennett, who tried to sit at attention on his cot. "It's my nerves," Bennett said. "I can hear the shells come over, but I can't hear them burst."

"What's this man talking about? What's wrong with him?" Patton demanded. The attending physician reached for a chart but before he could reply, Patton erupted. "Your nerves, hell. You are just a goddamned coward, you yellow son-of-a-bitch!" he shouted. "You ought to be lined up against a wall and shot. I ought to shoot you myself right now, goddam you." Tugging a pistol from his holster, he waved the gun in Bennett's face, then struck him with the flat of his hand. A nurse lunged toward Patton but was restrained by a doctor. "I want you to get that man out of here right away," Patton told the hospital commander, Colonel Donald E. Currier, who had been drawn to the tent by the commotion. Patton turned to leave but then whirled on Bennett again, smacking him with enough force to knock the soldier's helmet liner from his head. A few moments later, in an adjacent ward, Patton broke into sobs. "I can't help it. It breaks me down to see you brave boys." His voice rose nearly to a shriek. "It makes my blood boil to think of a yellow bastard being babied."

As he returned to his car, Patton told Currier, "I won't have these cowardly bastards hanging around our hospitals. We'll probably have to shoot them sometime anyway, or we'll raise a breed of morons." A reporter for the London *Daily Mail* who arrived at that moment heard Patton add, "There's no such thing as shellshock. It's an invention of the Jews." The fuming army commander drove to Omar Bradley's II Corps headquarters. "Sorry to be late, Bradley. I stopped off at a hospital on the way up. There were a couple of malingerers there." He had struck one, Patton added, "to put a little guts into them."

Few acts of corporal punishment would be more scrutinized, analyzed, and condemned than the two slapping incidents on Sicily in August 1943. If it seems likely that Patton suffered his own stress-induced breakdown, that makes his conduct no less "inexcusable and asinine," in Colonel Currier's words. He had brought shame on himself and on the Army he cherished, and for decades his name could hardly be uttered without conjuring not only his battlefield panache but also his reprehensible behavior, unworthy of an American.

For now, the occurrences in those two hot, malodorous tents remained hidden from public view, although whispers soon spread through the ranks. Private Bennett returned to the front after a week's rest and pastoral counseling. "Don't tell my wife!" he pleaded. Bradley took the initial report from the 93rd Evac and ordered, "Lock it up in my safe," a derelict act of misguided loyalty. No safe was likely to hold the secret for long.

As for Patton, he exhibited neither remorse nor introspection. After thrashing Private Bennett, he told both his staff and his diary, "I may have saved his soul, if he had one."

## A Great Grief

WHILE Patton fought his own demons, the battle for Sicily raged on, or rather up. "Christ!" a British officer exclaimed. "What a steep hill this is." That complaint encompassed the entire Sicilian badlands of washboard inclines, limestone pinnacles, and volcanic scarps. "Someday I hope we shall be able to fight downhill for a change," a captain in the 16th Infantry wrote his family on July 30. Cactus blanketed slopes seamed with ravines and razorback ridges. Highland grass fires—set with napalm flamethrowers to flush German infantry, on at least one occasion—tinted the sky red and perfumed the air with burning cork oaks.

Enemy demolitions made the bad terrain much worse. An estimated 160 bridge spans were blown up in the American sector alone, usually "the whole damned bridge, from abutment to abutment." Ernie Pyle noted that "the Germans were also more prodigal with mines than they had been in Tunisia." Iron ore in the volcanic soil around Mount Etna played hob with metal detectors, and German engineers displayed an ingenuity— placing Teller mines in road potholes, for instance, and covering them with asphalt—that grew ever more diabolical. True, Italian units fought with even less heart after Mussolini's overthrow. "Troops are tired and have lost faith," an Italian general advised Rome on July 31. But the forty thousand Germans now on the island showed no sign of flagging. The chatter of pneumatic drills and jackhammers could be heard in the hills along the Etna Line, an arc of fortified strongpoints stretching from San Fratello on the north coast around the volcano's southern flank to the Ionian Sea above Catania.

Allied air and naval superiority counted for little in the mountains. Rather, the mule became the upland equivalent of the indispensible DUKW. Troops scoured the countryside for forage, pack saddles, and scrawny Sicilian mounts; a single infantry battalion fighting a weeklong battle in the roadless outback might need several hundred mules to haul food, water, and ammunition. A British officer, praising the beasts' "sharp hearing [and] their sagacity over the choice of ground," grew weepy with admiration: "They shared men's dangers and hardships unsustained by ideals and hopes, and without even a sex life as compensation." Others remained wary: a U.S. Army manual advised that the mule is "restless and ugly," and "would probably want to know what he is to die for." Typical was a creature named Trouble, described by a 45th Division handler as "the orneriest piece of leather in Sicily." Bill Darby's personal mount, Rosebud, nipped him in the buttocks "every time I tried to mount him." (Ranger pranksters fed a handful of Benzedrine tablets to a fleabag named Whitey, who subsequently was renamed War Admiral.) Gifted mule skinners soon were more prized than sharpshooters. "The way to make a mule behave," one soldier urged, "is to bite his ears." A former veterinarian in the 45th Division organized his mule train with serial numbers and identifying brands, and even rewarded "outstanding performance" by promoting worthy animals to corporal or sergeant. Still, an insuperable language barrier confounded many soldiers. "The mules couldn't talk English," a 180th Infantry officer complained. "We actually had to rustle up some Italian mule interpreters so we could manage the beasts."

"Hills and then more hills, and dust, clouds of it," Ted Roosevelt wrote Eleanor in late July. "At the moment it's white and the men look like clowns at a circus." Kesselring continued to shove new units onto the island, Roosevelt added.

> They are fresh and we are worn. . . . The soldier who has climbed and hiked and fought days on end is completely done up. That's the case with some of our units now. . . . As Nicias said when the Athenians commenced their retreat on this same island [in 413 B.C.]: "Man does what he can and bears what he must."

With the British right flank still blocked at Catania, and Montgomery's main force crawling up the Etna foothills southwest of the volcano, the American advance toward Messina followed the two parallel axes ordered by Alexander. On Seventh Army's left, Truscott's 3rd Division on July 31 relieved the 45th Division along coastal Highway 113. Farther south, Terry Allen's 1st Division had taken Enna, which the Germans abandoned after Canadian forces threatened to outflank the town, and had advanced to Highway 120. There the division wheeled sharply to the east, capturing Gangi, Sperlinga, and Nicosia, where ax-wielding enemy troops vandalized shops and even churches before retreating. With a carbine across his lap, Roosevelt rode into Nicosia in *Rough Rider* to join his officers for wine and cheese in the mayor's office. A mortar fragment had chipped two of his teeth, but, wrote George Biddle, he "mumbled and rumbled to himself snatches of song and bits of poetry in French, in Latin and in English," while lamenting the lack of scholarship "in this hurried world."

Each town took a toll. The 1st Division had suffered nearly sixteen hundred casualties since HUSKY began three weeks earlier, about one soldier in ten. A 16th Infantry lieutenant who had lost most of his right elbow to a grenade walked all night until challenged by a sentry near an aid station; unable to recall the day's password, the lieutenant "simply started swearing like an American trooper until I was recognized and taken in." John Hersey, of *Time,* listened in Nicosia as a soldier whose shoulder had been shot away told a blinded comrade, "Let's go back there and get those bastards." The blind man hesitated. "Eyes," he said, "are very delicate things."

Wagging his cane as he stumped among the troops, Roosevelt noted "the sag of their clothes and their tired faces." Reports spread of nineteen men killed in a German white-flag ruse; anger and bloodlust spread, as well as an odd rumor that B-17s would bomb Etna's crater to bury the enemy in lava. Artillery boomed around the clock and muzzle flashes rippled like chain lightning along the gun lines. "Shelling these hills," Hersey wrote, "was like shaking lice out of old clothes." Every foot soldier approved of the lavish shooting. "I don't care if I'm paying taxes the rest of my life," one GI said, "just so they throw that stuff at them instead of throwing me at them."

Bread trucks brought up nine hundred loaves from a bakery near Gela each morning, then hauled bodies back to the makeshift cemetery at Ponte Olivo. At night the troops huddled close for warmth under blanket tents fashioned to hide their cigarette embers from enemy patrols. "Here we live and fight and die together in a bond of fellowship unequalled anywhere," Captain Joseph T. Dawson of the 16th Infantry wrote his family on July 31. But with camaraderie also came the solitude and self-doubt that haunted every battlefield. "I find myself jumping at any excuse that will keep me out of the danger zone," a quartermaster officer told his diary on July 27. "Hell, I'm disgusted with myself. If I knew how, I'd get myself transferred to a really dangerous job, just to see if I could take it."

*Man does what he can and bears what he must.* Patton believed an infantry division declined in efficiency after two weeks of sustained combat "due to the loss of riflemen and fatigue"; the 1st Division was entering its fourth week. "When this is over," one soldier mused, "I won't mind going back to Wisconsin and looking at cows the rest of my life." Like so many, Ted Roosevelt also drew comfort from thoughts of a different place. "Has the Boston ivy covered the front of the house? How are the yews?" he asked Eleanor. "Do put in fruit trees. The old trees are bound to die soon."

Sicilian towns "perched on hilltops like ragged caps stuck on the hoary heads of gray old men," wrote Don Whitehead, of the Associated Press. No ragged cap perched higher than Troina, fourteen miles northeast of Nicosia on Highway 120 and the highest town in Sicily. Here the 15th Panzer Grenadier Division had halted after the retreat from western Sicily that began three weeks earlier. Torrential rain on July 29 swelled streams and flooded roads, slowing the American pursuit. Grenadier regiments used the respite to dig strongpoints and lay mines in the high ground north and south of Troina, which became a linchpin in the Etna Line. Four artillery batteries occupied gullies east of town, and spotters in field gray climbed the twin spires of the Norman church above the piazza for a panoramic view of Mount Etna. For an armed defender, the westward vista was even more breathtaking: any attacker from that direction would be canalized into a treeless, three-mile stretch of Highway 120. Troina's twelve thousand citizens fled to the hills or barricaded themselves in their squat stone houses.

Five miles to the west, in the hilltop hamlet of Cerami on Saturday evening, July 31, Terry Allen followed that exposed stretch of highway with his field glasses until it vanished into the hazy, twin-spired redoubt on the next ridge. The sharp scents of eucalyptus and oleander wafted through the decrepit school that now served as a 1st Division command post. Fascist slogans covered classroom walls that shook from the concussive roar of the 155mm Long Tom battery nearby. Within goose eggs drawn on a tactical map, Allen scribbled the letter "E" wherever he thought the enemy had holed up. "This was about as stubborn as any resistance we've encountered so far," he had told reporters. "The fall of Nicosia"—he rendered the name as Nicodemus—"probably means that the Germans will have to retire to their next road net, at Troina."

With luck, Allen hoped, the enemy would counterattack before the attack began this evening, exposing himself to those Long Toms and other guns. But U.S. intelligence now believed the Germans would continue falling back through Troina toward Messina. "Germans are very tired, little ammo, many casualties, morale low," the 1st Division G-2 concluded on July 29. II Corps today had reported, "Indications are Troina lightly held"; refugees also claimed that few German soldiers occupied the town. Allen had planned to envelop Troina with two infantry regiments supported by 165 artillery tubes, but these heartening reports and the easy seizure of Cerami caused him to pare back the attack to a single regiment, the 39th Infantry, which had been loaned to him from the 9th Division several days earlier. Air reconnaissance could have revealed the true extent of German fortifications, but the latest film had been flown to North Africa for processing, and printed photos had not yet returned to Sicily. "You give your orders and the division will execute them," Allen told reporters. "The rest is chance." A soft hiss escaped from his perforated cheeks.

With his saddle-hardened gait, Allen strode to a secluded olive grove a hundred yards from the command post. "This war is really a very disagreeable job," he had written his wife, Mary Fran, two days before, "with long periods of tough going and the relaxation periods for the 1st Division are few and far between." Still, a break was in sight. Bradley planned to supplant the Big Red One with the rest of the 9th Division, which had recently arrived from North Africa. Tempting as it might be to let the newcomers carry the fight immediately, Allen would remind his officers of "our moral obligation to capture Troina before being relieved."

He sank to his knees beneath the gray-green boughs of an ancient olive. Asking God to spare the division "unnecessary casualties," he prayed that "tonight no man's life will be wasted." Upon rejoining his troops, a grizzled sergeant told him, "Hell, Terry, stop worrying. We'll take the goddam town for you."

As the long summer twilight faded in the west, three thousand soldiers from the 39th Infantry shuffled across the broken ground on either side of Highway 120 below Cerami. Their fatigue pockets bulged with toilet paper, K ration cans, and extra ammunition. Don Whitehead watched the columns snake toward Troina, jaggedly silhouetted on the horizon. "Every time I have watched troops plod into battle," he wrote, "I have choked back a desire to sob."

Coordinating the attack from an orchard command post was a thirty-five-year-old lieutenant colonel named John J. Toffey III. Sweat soaked his wool shirt, and tiny dust devils boiled beneath his boots as he paced between the map boards and radio transmitter. "Can you put mortar fire in the vicinity of 492-140?" Toffey asked, clutching the handset. "I want to get every goddamned weapon you've got and put them on 492-140. Do you understand? Okay. Get going."

He was a big man, six foot one and two hundred pounds, with such sporty good looks that he had once appeared in an amusing cover picture for *Collier's* magazine outfitted in a bathing suit and polo helmet while carrying a baseball glove, tennis racket, fishing rod, and golf clubs. His educational pedigree included Phillips Exeter Academy and Cornell. His father had fought with Pershing in Mexico and eventually retired as a major general in command of the New Jersey National Guard. His grandfather had earned the Medal of Honor for valor at Missionary Ridge in 1863. "It is very nice to read of a battle," John Toffey, Sr., had written, "but to be near to one is not so nice and I never want to be near one again." On April 14, 1865, while recuperating from battle wounds in Washington, D.C., he had attended the play at Ford's Theatre and witnessed Lincoln's murder. According to family lore, Toffey testified at the conspirators' trial—he had corraled a runaway horse possibly used in the crime—and watched them hang.

Young Jack Toffey, who had sold bottle caps in Ohio during the Depression, had proved worthy of his military lineage. Called to federal service from the National Guard in 1940, he landed with Truscott's force in Morocco during TORCH, then commanded a battalion through the Tunisian campaign until shot in the knee at Maknassy in late March. "Missed all bones," he wrote his wife, Helen. "Don't worry about a thing." After two months' recuperation, he limped back to duty as executive officer of the 39th Infantry, just in time for Sicily. Toffey's eventful fortnight on the island had already included a one-week stint commanding the regiment after his superior was injured in an air attack, and the capture of at least seven thousand prisoners.

Nine months at war had also aged him beyond his years. Both battle-wise and battle-weary, he was emblematic of the field-grade officers—major through colonel—who had learned much through hard combat and whose influence on a hundred European battlefields would be both decisive and disproportionate to their numbers in the U.S. Army. It was Toffey and his breed who would have to fix the tactical shortcomings the Army had revealed in Tunisia, such as the failure to seize high ground or to anticipate the German penchant for immediate counterattack; the defects in patrolling and map reading that got entire battalions ambushed or lost; and the inability to coordinate infantry, armor, and the other combat arms.

He now made war without illusions and certainly without pleasure. "War is as Sherman says and has no similarity with cinema or storybook versions," Toffey had written in North Africa. He tried simultaneously to care for his family, to care for his men, and to study the military art even as he practiced it: sending money orders and war bonds to Helen, who waited for him in Columbus with their two children; procuring thirteen hundred steaks for a holiday dinner in the unit mess; subscribing to *Infantry Journal*; reading *War and Peace*. "Every day is that much nearer the end," he wrote. "I still miss you terribly—a condition which will not improve." The wound in Tunisia sharpened his senses of irony and mortality. Three generations of Toffeys in uniform was enough, he told Helen; he hoped that John IV, age twelve, "will be a doctor or lawyer and stay the hell out of the army & if he does go in the army let him stay out of the infantry." To be near to a battle is not so nice, his grandfather had written, *and I never want to be near one again*. Jack Toffey understood that perfectly, though for now he had a job to do. "Been feeling a little rocky lately—but the knee is okay and feels better tonite," he wrote before Troina. "Short on sleep and tired but today was a good day for us."

The next six days, however, would be bad for all of them. The 39th Infantry's right wing edged to within a mile of Troina on Sunday, August 1. But lacerating mortar and machine-gun fire greeted the regimental left, and by midnight counterattacking grenadiers had shoved much of the regiment back to the high ground near Cerami, even whittling one battalion to three hundred men. "There is a hell of a lot of stuff there," a 1st Division officer warned. "We'll be moving right into the teeth of the enemy." Allen seemed to concur, and directed two additional regiments to loop north and south in a double envelopment. But then, perhaps hoping to avoid those "unnecessary casualties" he had prayed over, Allen rescinded his order and chose to let the 39th Infantry again try to take Troina alone.

The regiment's new commander—Jack Toffey's superior—was a wizened, dish-faced, Vermont-born legend, Colonel Harry A. "Paddy" Flint, whom Patton deemed the "bravest goddam soldier in the whole goddam Seventh Army." At fifty-five, Flint had survived innumerable polo injuries and, in 1940, an apparent stroke; as his men tried to winkle the Germans from their strongpoints, he stood on a prominent rock, stripped to the waist, with a black bandana knotted around his neck, rolling a Bull Durham cigarette with one hand and bellowing, "Hell's bells. Lookit them lousy Krauts. Couldn't shoot in the last war. Can't shoot in this one." Later in the battle, a young artillery commander, Lieutenant Colonel William C. Westmoreland, found Flint and Ted Roosevelt playing mumbletypeg with a jackknife. Advised that half of Westmoreland's ancient howitzers had broken recoil systems, "so you can expect half the firepower you've

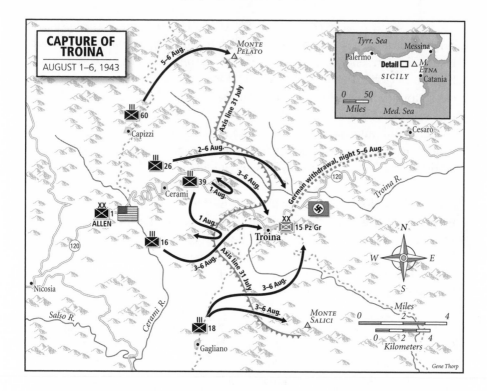

received before," Flint replied, "It don't make no difference. Just fire them twice as fast." Not to be outdone, Roosevelt upon being told that the division had fired a million dollars' worth of ammunition, ordered, "Spend another million."

Bravado would not win the day, or the next day, or the day after that. Allen finally recognized the need for a full-throated attack, ordering his 26th Infantry to loop north, the 18th Infantry to drive from the south, and the 16th Infantry to slice straight toward Troina with the weary 39th. "Troina's going to be tougher than we thought," he told Bradley by phone. "This will mean we can turn over to the 9th Division a tight zone. If it's all right with you, we can do this."

Hills were won and lost, won again and lost again. By now the Germans had dug in so deep that even the observers droning overhead could not spot the smokeless powder from their artillery and antitank guns. To break the stalemate, Allen ordered a renewed assault in the early minutes of August 3, with the attack weighted in the south. At daybreak, the 16th Infantry was pinned down by gashing German fire; when the enemy counterattacked with panzers and infantry, only deft shooting by Clift Andrus's division artillery kept the regiment from being overrun. By late afternoon, attackers and defenders had become so intermingled in the gullies southwest of Troina that American guns fell silent for fear of hitting friendly troops. When grenadiers infiltrated within a stone's throw, riflemen called out the day's challenge—"Chocolate"—and listened for the authorized parole: "Bon-bon."

Progress was no better in the north. Troops from the 26th Infantry fought with grenades, pistols, and rifle butts up and down a bitter knoll known as Hill 1035. The sharp *pops* of detonating mines were often followed by the howl that signified another severed foot or leg. Not until full dark, at eleven P.M., could the wounded be evacuated. Brush fires made the scorching days hotter still, and putrid German bodies polluted a creek trickling through a ravine. "Something is burning out front," a 16th Infantry battalion radioed. "We are running low on ammunition." Mule trains brought some supplies, but bundles dropped from aircraft fell mostly into enemy hands, and men chewed wheat straw to quell their hunger. Repeated air strikes by AAF planes beginning late Wednesday afternoon, August 4, cheered every GI except those bombed by mistake. A sergeant whose troops came under attack ordered his men to peel off their undershirts and spread them along a ditch embankment. "For some reason, the pilots were supposed to recognize the shirts as those of friendly troops," wrote Don Whitehead, who was among those stripping. "By the laundry mark, I suppose."

At dusk on Thursday, rifle companies throughout the 1st Division had been reduced by two-thirds, to sixty or seventy men; Company I of the 26th Infantry reported seventeen fit for combat. The commander of Company F in the same regiment lay with a radio a mile north of Troina as his unit was overrun, calling in barrages within fifty yards of his foxhole. "Perhaps," he wrote his father, "my luck won't hold up forever." Recovered from battlefield fever, Ernie Pyle showed up in Cerami to begin working on another bout. "Through our glasses the old city seemed to fly apart," he wrote after watching Troina bombarded. "Great clouds of dust and black smoke rose into the sky until the whole horizon was leaded and fogged." Dressed in his "usual collapsible style," Pyle was caught in an air attack without his helmet and covered his head with a shovel. He regretted "the terrible weariness that gradually comes over everybody. . . . You just get damned sick of it all."

Terry Allen was damned sick of Troina, and he meticulously planned a final assault for Friday, August 6, to outflank the town and obliterate any remaining Germans. Only when the first patrols crept into the outskirts after dawn did it become clear that the enemy had pulled back, fearful of encirclement. In launching two dozen counterattacks during the past week, the 15th Panzer Grenadier Division had lost more than sixteen hundred men. As the grenadiers scuttled down Highway 120 toward Cesarò and Randazzo, leaving the prints of their hobnailed boots in the dust, Kesselring also authorized Hermann Göring troops to pull out of Catania, on the coast. The Etna Line had snapped, to be replaced by a succession of defensive bulwarks across the Messina Peninsula.

"Town clear of enemy," a patrol reported shortly before ten A.M. Only misery remained. Troina was "found to be in a greatly destroyed condition," an Army after-action report noted. Reporters creeping into town were more explicit. They found "a town of horror, alive with weeping, hysterical men, women and children," wrote Herbert Matthews of *The New York Times;* he described a scene that would recur all the way to Bologna: on "torn streets, heaps of rubble that had been houses, grief, horror and pain." Dead soldiers, German and American, were "covered with a carpet of maggots that made it look as though the corpses were alive and twitching," a 16th Infantry officer reported. "You couldn't get the smell of the dead out of your hair, and all you could do with your clothes was burn them." A 26th Infantry captain, Donald V. Helgeson, stared at a charred German mortar crew. "This ain't very good for the troops' morale," Helgeson said. His first sergeant disagreed. "It's *great* for morale. They're German, aren't they?" A GI sliced the Wehrmacht belt buckle from a dead grenadier and declared that "*Gott mit Uns* changed sides."

Some 150 bodies lay in the streets and inside a feudal tower. A nauseating stench seeped from Troina's cellars. Broken water mains bubbled, and an unexploded bomb blocked a church aisle. At city hall, wounded civilians sprawled "naked on shutters or stretchers. Their skin was gray," George Biddle reported. An infant found in the ruins clutched his dead mother's hair so desperately that rescuers had to snip away a few locks. Whitehead pushed through a massive oak door leading into the fetid cathedral crypt. In the feeble light he found hundreds of refugees living in their own filth. "Men, women and children crouched like animals over their little hoards of food and piles of belongings," he wrote. A young girl told him in English, "We've been miserable but now everything is changed."

"Troina was the toughest battle Americans have fought since World War I," General Lucas concluded, "and there were very few in that war which were its equal." The 1st Division had suffered more than five hundred casualties, with scores more in the 39th Infantry. "Really could use a bit of an ocean voyage to your shores about now," Jack Toffey wrote Helen after the shooting stopped on August 6. He wondered, with that ironic sensibility that grew tauter with each battle, whether New York would choose to stage the city's postwar victory parade up Fifth Avenue, or *down*. But in a note to his young son, Toffey showed that hope still lined his heart: "The Krauts must now know they are licked and their days numbered. . . . Just pray me home & we'll be all set."

Two more casualties could now be added to the 1st Division tally. As gunfire ebbed at Troina, three telegrams arrived at the division headquarters. The first relieved Terry Allen as commanding general. The second relieved Ted Roosevelt as assistant commander. The third announced Allen's successor, Major General Clarence R. Huebner, a highly decorated Kansan who had commanded a regiment in World War I before the age of thirty. "Terry read the thing, said nothing for a while, and then burst into tears like a high-strung school girl," Clift Andrus recalled. "It came as a terrible shock."

Ever the ardent hunter, Omar Bradley had long held Allen in his sights before squeezing the trigger. He later claimed that "the hardest thing in war was to relieve people I knew," but Bradley seemed unruffled by the dismissal of Allen, whom he considered "temperamental, disdainful," and "too full of self-pity and pride." In a handwritten note to Eisenhower on July 25, Bradley described the 1st Division as "battle weary. I suspect that it is more Terry and Ted than it is the division as a whole." At Bradley's urging, Patton three days later formally requested the change in a message carried by Lucas to Algiers. In his diary, Patton described both men as "suffering from battle fatigue," a malady whose existence he himself denied.

Neither Bradley nor Patton ever offered a fuller explanation for the dismissals; at heart, the action reflected the corps commander's personal animus toward Allen. But prevarications soon followed. Patton and Bradley both claimed they were following a War Department policy of rotating senior commanders. Patton hinted that Allen would return home to command a corps. Bradley later claimed that he "personally took over the tactical planning" after Allen "flubbed badly" at Troina. But Allen's efficiency report for April 16 through August 5, 1943, written and signed by Bradley, asserted that "the division plans of attack" for Nicosia and Troina "were well planned, [well] executed and obtained decisive results." Bradley made no mention of the faulty intelligence from his headquarters, or of his own belief that the Germans would retreat through Troina to Cesarò, or of his endorsement of the initial single-regiment attack.

As the orders became public once Troina had fallen on August 6, anger and disbelief roiled the division. "Even shaggy old Regular Army sergeants weep unashamedly," an 18th Infantry soldier reported. By cruel coincidence,

Allen appeared on the August 9 cover of *Time;* the article detected in him "a special mark of war and history." In a note to Marshall, he thanked the chief for the chance to command the 1st Division for fifteen months; to Eisenhower, he conceded that he "may have appeared over solicitious, regarding the needs of the infantry." In truth he was exhausted, his denials notwithstanding: in a letter to his young son, he wrote not only the wrong date but the wrong month. "It is a wrench to leave the division," he told Mary Fran, "but such is the luck of the service." Later he would grow angry over rumors that he had suffered a breakdown, and he wondered if anti-Catholicism or his lack of a West Point commission played a role; back in Texas, he fled a welcome-home party in tears. But soon enough he bucked up, perhaps sensing that neither the Army nor the war was finished with him. As he prepared to leave the division near Troina, he sat for a sketch by George Biddle, a pen-and-ink that captured the boxer's nose, the ropy neck muscles, the wide-set eyes, and the sparse hair neatly combed across his crown; he even wore a slight smile. Glancing at his watch, Allen called to his driver, "Tell them to phone down to General Bradley that I'll be fifteen minutes late."

As for Ted Roosevelt, the blow left him "hurt, despondent and mentally in a black cloud," one officer said. In an open letter to the division he wrote, "I have been ordered away. It is a great grief to me." In a personal farewell to the 26th Infantry, which he had commanded in the Great War, "he broke down and wept. And the men kept silent." To Bradley he wrote, "Brad, we get along a helluva lot better with the Krauts up front than we do with your people back here in the rear." Beetle Smith told him that he was not qualified to command a division; instead, he would move to the newly created Fifth Army as a liaison to French forces. "Of course I was heartbroken," he told Eleanor, adding with a touch of self-pity, "Everyone loves me but our own high command." Perhaps trading on her name, she privately wangled an audience at the Pentagon with Marshall, who bluntly told her that Ted "still behaved like a regimental commander" and "did not grasp the full scope of the responsibilities and duties as a brigadier general in an infantry division."

But Roosevelt also sensed that a larger fate awaited him. Sharing a ride to Palermo with Robert Capa, he recited poetry with his usual fluency while his aide sang cowboy songs. Clues could be found in the dog-eared copy of *The Pilgrim's Progress* carried in his kit bag: "I do not repent me of all the trouble I have been at to arrive where I am. . . . My marks and scars I carry with me." To Eleanor he later wrote, "The longer I live the more I think of the quality of fortitude—men who fall, pick themselves up and stumble on, fall again, and are trying to get up when they die."

## *"In a Place Like This"*

RIDGE by ridge, road by road, town by town, the island fell to the advancing Allied armies. Montgomery's right wing, stalled for more than two weeks at Catania, finally lurched forward again, and Tommies sang, "We're Shoving Right Off." An Allied battlefront that had meandered for 170 miles inexorably contracted to 45 miles as 100,000 enemy soldiers retreated past Mount Etna into the long funnel of the Messina Peninsula. "I am enjoying this campaign," Montgomery wrote in his neat black script on August 4. "The Boche is getting very stretched and he cannot possibly stand up to my thrusts." Others were skeptical of Montgomery's claim to have cornered the Germans "in queer street." Air Marshal Sir Arthur Tedder, Eisenhower's air chief, wrote a colleague on August 7, "Napoleon insists on his usual frontal attack with no risks."

But although they were moving in fits and starts—nine thousand yards one day, three thousand the next—moving they were, despite mines, despite booby traps, despite snipers with telescopic sights hiding in baroque hillside tombs. The mayor of Catania surrendered his town with a theatrical affixing of signatures. Of 100,000 houses, only one in five was habitable. Germans had looted everything from beds to dinner forks, blowing up the Bank of Sicily and the Hotel Corona for good measure; British soldiers and hungry Sicilians picked through the leavings. Refugees fought over packets of British biscuits, while old women in black squatted in their doorways as if "they knew that all life was evil," wrote the reporter Christopher Buckley.

Often enough, the Allied air force solution for interdicting the retreating Germans was to obliterate Sicilian towns, which barely impeded Axis withdrawals but killed thousands of civilians and complicated the Anglo-American advance. Thirty unexploded bombs lay in the rubble at Adrano, on the southwest slope of Etna, a town so battered that combat engineers needed thirty-six hours to carve a single-lane path through the drifted wreckage. "Troops will refrain from shooting Italian carabinieri," advised signs posted by British officers. "They are entitled to carry rifles." Battalions leapfrogged one another through thistles and cornflowers, dodging the slap of enemy artillery. A local orchestra greeted Canadian troops in one town, alternately striking up "God Save the King" and "Deutschland über Alles." In Bronte, on Etna's northwest shoulder, welcoming civilians chanted "Lord Nelson! Lord Nelson!," and General Alexander added his name below Kesselring's in the visitors' book at an eleventh-century Norman castle that had once belonged to the British naval hero. Across the Catania plain and down the volcano's lower slopes, British graves dotted the landscape like small mastabas. Identity disks dangled from wooden crosses, and comrades manning the burial details scrubbed their hands with kerosene and collected the dead men's helmets for reissue.

Above them all loomed Etna, the mythical forge of Vulcan, scarred with charcoal furnaces and logging roads that were fenced with brush to corral the cattle. Refracted colors danced at sunset above the reeking crater: the air was tinted with sulfates and sublimated chlorides. By August 13, Tommies had nearly circumnavigated the cone, twenty-five miles in diameter. Still, a British colonel scrutinizing a map of territory occupied by the Seventh and Eighth Armies was said to have complained, "That bloody Patton. He has us surrounded."

Pleased as he would have been to surround Montgomery, Patton in fact was trying to encircle at least part of the retreating Axis army. The U.S. 9th Division, supplanting the 1st, bulled its way down Highway 120 from Troina to Randazzo, where only five houses in a town of fourteen thousand people remained livable. So many dead littered Randazzo—perhaps the most damaged place in Sicily—that "after a conference with the priest it was decided to burn the bodies in gasoline," an Army report noted. "I feel like crying lots of times," a soldier wrote his family, "but I don't think it would help me much in a place like this."

To exploit the flanking opportunities afforded by his command of the sea, Patton on August 10 ordered Bradley to mount an amphibious end run the following morning by landing a battalion twelve miles behind German lines, on Sicily's north coast. In seizing Monte Cipolla, which loomed above coastal Highway 113 near Brolo, U.S. troops could sever the escape route for the 29th Panzer Grenadier Division rear guard and give Truscott's 3rd Division a direct avenue to Messina, forty miles to the east. If bold, the plan was undermanned, as Allied amphibious operations so often were, and it led to another of the ugly confrontations that bedeviled Patton across Sicily.

Truscott, who was to provide a battalion from his 30th Infantry Regiment for the landing, requested a day's postponement to position artillery and infantry support closer to Brolo. Bradley agreed; he considered the operation "trivial" and even "foolhardy," and he resented Patton's meddling with the corps commander's tactical prerogatives simply to beat Montgomery into Messina. But the delay irked Patton: after several testy phone calls on Tuesday evening, August 10, he drove to the 3rd Division command post at 9:45 P.M., flushed with anger.

He found Truscott in an olive oil plant outside Terranova, pacing with a map in his hand. "What's the matter with you, Lucian?" Patton said. "Are you afraid to fight?"

"General," Truscott said, his carbolic growl in sharp contrast to Patton's shrill pitch, "you know that's ridiculous and insulting."

"General Truscott, if your conscience will not let you conduct this operation, I will relieve you and put someone in command who will."

"General, it is your privilege to reduce me whenever you want to."

"I don't want to," Patton said. "You are too old an athlete to believe it is possible to postpone a match."

"You are an old enough athlete to know that sometimes they are postponed."

"This one won't be," Patton said. "Remember Frederick the Great: *L'audace, toujours l'audace!* I know you will win."

Having pulled rank to settle the matter, Patton looped an arm around Truscott's shoulder. "Let's have a drink—of your liquor." Returning to Palermo and his bed in the Royal Palace, Patton confessed to his diary, "I may have been bull-headed."

It went badly. Lieutenant Colonel Lyle A. Bernard, a wiry thirty-three-year-old, arrived two miles off Brolo at one A.M. Wednesday with his understrength 2nd Battalion in nine vessels, protected by the cruiser *Philadelphia* and six destroyers. As an orange quarter moon set in the west, the men climbed into their DUKWs and landing craft. The strains of "Night and Day," played on a harmonica, carried across the water. "Why don't we do this more often?" someone quipped. Shortly before three A.M. the first wave scooted across the shingle and into a lemon grove. "Watch the fucking barbed wire!" a voice called. Two rifle companies held the coastal flats while two more scaled Monte Cipolla, clutching at tuft grass to avoid pitching backward. But five tanks and a battery of self-propelled howitzers found that the underpasses in a railroad embankment along Highway 113 were too narrow to squeeze through from the beach; before long, each tank was stuck in a ditch or immobilized from butting into stone orchard walls. Eight Germans had been captured in their sleep atop Cipolla, but soon enough the alarm sounded. Colored flares drifted overhead, and German tracers flailed the hill, the beach, and the sea. Don Whitehead, among several reporters with Colonel Bernard, noted the "sense of absolute confusion that falls over every amphibious landing."

Daybreak brought death, as German gunners began to see their targets. Fifteen soldiers died stringing phone wire uphill, along with thirteen of fifteen mules hauling ammunition. *Philadelphia* opened fire at 10:25 A.M., then steamed for Palermo with her escorts for fear of a Luftwaffe attack; an urgent plea from Truscott brought the cruiser back for another forty minutes of shooting before she sailed away again.

"Situation still critical," Bernard radioed Truscott from his hilltop command post. Grenadiers in coal-scuttle helmets crept through the purple shadows below. Puffing on his red pipe, Bernard told Whitehead, "We'll catch hell this afternoon." Panzer shells ignited grass fires that burned through the phone wire linking Bernard to his troops and to naval gunfire observers on the flats below. Water and ammo ran short, and men laid fir boughs across their slit trenches for shade from the molten sun. At four P.M., lusty cheers greeted seven U.S. attack planes as they roared over the hill; the cheering stopped when two bombs fell on Bernard's command post in a cauldron of flame and whizzing metal, killing or wounding nineteen. Other errant bombs hit the artillerymen below, wrecking the four remaining howitzers. Men swore, and wept, and swore some more. A wounded medic tried to amputate his own shattered arm with a pocketknife. German tank and machine-gun fire intensified. "Enemy counterattacking fiercely," Bernard radioed Truscott. "Do something."

At five P.M. *Philadelphia* again reappeared from the dreamy sea mist, firing a thousand shells in fifteen minutes and battling Focke-Wulf marauders before once more sailing for Palermo, this time for good. Bernard sent runners to summon survivors on the flats to join him in what he now called "our little old last stand circle." A few on the beach instead escaped by swimming westward. Dusk soon brightened the tracers. Wind tossed the olive boughs below, and bullets sang all about. Bernard pulled on his dead pipe. Men hacked at their foxholes with entrenching tools.

At dawn on Thursday, August 12, a sentry came running. The Germans had vanished, falling back to Cape Calavà, where they would blow a 150-foot mountainside section of Highway 113 into the sea, and then to Messina. "There are troops moving on the road with vehicles, sir," he told Bernard. From the west, soldiers of the 30th Infantry soon wheeled into view. Greasy smoke spiraled above the lemon grove. The morning air stank of cordite and sweat and burning fuel.

An open command car flying three-star pennants pulled up on the highway. Patton stood in the rear, his helmet gleaming in the sun. "The American soldier is the greatest soldier in the world," he proclaimed. He pointed to Monte Cipolla with his swagger stick. Men and mules lay like stepping stones up the blackened slope. *L'audace* had cost Bernard's battalion 177 casualties, to little effect. "Only American soldiers can climb mountains like those," Patton said. Listening near the road, Whitehead jotted in his diary, "The whole little tableau sickened me."

Field Marshal Kesselring had long realized that Sicily would be lost even as he insisted that his forces on the island could tie up a dozen Allied divisions for some time. Berlin wondered who was tying up whom. Mindful of Stalingrad and Tunis, the high command had insisted as early as July 15 that "our valuable human material must be saved." On July 26, Berlin ordered preparations made for the island's evacuation; the message was hand-carried to Kesselring in Frascati to avoid alerting the Italians. With Mussolini deposed, Hitler feared that the Badoglio regime would use the abandonment of Sicily as an excuse to renounce the Pact of Steel.

The defense of the Strait of Messina fell to an unorthodox colonel from Schleswig-Holstein named Ernst-Günther Baade. A devotee of Aristotle and Seneca who printed small volumes of verse for his friends, Baade favored a kilt rather than trousers, with a holstered Luger worn instead of a leather sporran. By August 10, he had made Messina perhaps the most heavily defended spot in Europe. Five hundred guns bristled on the Sicilian shore and on mainland Calabria, two miles across the strait. Engineers prepared a dozen camouflaged ferry sites on both sides of the water and assembled thirty-three barges, seventy-six motorboats, and a dozen Siebel ferries, big rafts with twin airplane engines mounted on pontoons and originally designed in 1940 for an invasion of England. Baade even cached food, brandy, and cigarettes for the rear guard.

Twelve thousand German supernumeraries and more than four thousand vehicles quietly left Sicily in early August; Kesselring calculated that five nights would be needed to evacuate the rest. With precise choreography, combat units fell back on five successive defensive lines, a retreat aided by the tapering shape of the Messina Peninsula. Vehicles that could not be evacuated were sabotaged by bashing fuel pumps and distributors with hammers and hatchets. "The hand grenade is especially effective," one directive advised. Enormous bonfires consumed surplus matériel, with German troops "yelling as they hurled it into the flames: crates, chairs, tents, camp beds, telephones, tools . . . all doused with petrol."

Italian commanders quickly got wind of the evacuation scheme and began their own measured withdrawals on August 3. Without informing Berlin or awaiting Hitler's approval, Kesselring authorized Operation LEHRGANG—"Curriculum"—to begin at six P.M. on Wednesday, August 11, just as Bernard's battalion was fighting for survival at Brolo. The Hermann Göring Division went first, under a flotilla commanded by the former skipper of the airship *Hindenburg;* hundreds of shivering malaria patients also huddled on the ferries for the thirty-minute ride across the strait at six knots. Oil lamps flickered on the makeshift piers. Overhead screens shielded the glare from Allied pilots, but every anxious *Gefreiter* stared upward and listened for the sound of the B-17 bombers that would blow them to kingdom come.

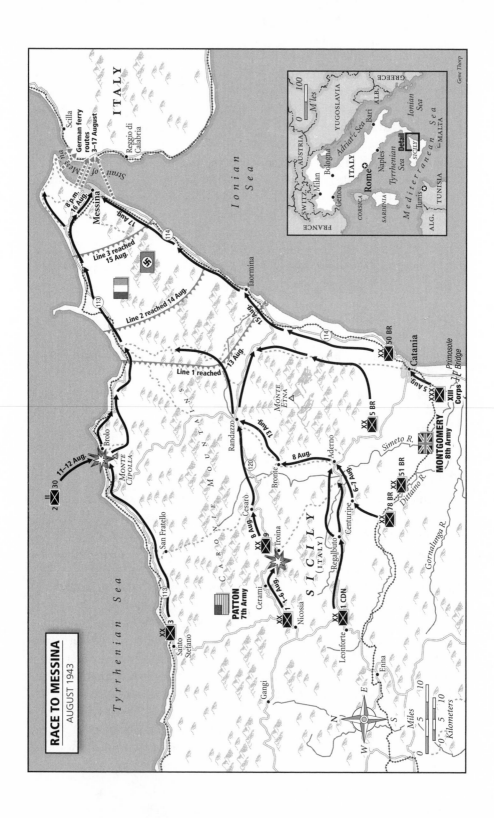

RACE TO MESSINA
AUGUST 1943

German ferry routes
3–17 August

Line 3 reached 15 Aug.
Line 2 reached 14 Aug.
Line 1 reached 13 Aug.

PATTON 7th Army

MONTGOMERY 8th Army

Gene Thorp

Tyrrhenian Sea

Ionian Sea

ITALY

Scilla
Messina
Strait of Messina
Reggio di Calabria

Taormina

Brolo
MONTE CIPOLLA
11–12 Aug.
2 30

Santo Stefano
3
San Fratello
113

Cerami
Nicosia
1 Aug.
1–6 Aug.
Troina

Cesarò
8 Aug.
9
120

Randazzo
13 Aug.
Bronte
8 Aug.
Aderno

MONTE ETNA

CARONIE MOUNTAINS
NEBRODI MOUNTAINS

SICILY (ITALY)

Gangi
Enna
Leonforte
1 CDN
Regalbuto
Centuripe
6–7 Aug.
78 BR
51 BR
Dittaino R.
Simeto R.
Gornalunga R.

5 BR
15 Aug.
114
50 BR
Catania
5 Aug.
XIII Corps
Primosole Bridge

Detail
SICILY

SWITZ.
FRANCE
AUSTRIA
YUGOSLAVIA
GREECE
ALB.
Milan
Genoa
Bologna
CORSICA
ITALY
Rome
Naples
SARDINIA
Tyrrhenian Sea
Bari
Adriatic Sea
Ionian Sea
Mediterranean Sea
TUNISIA
ALG.
Tunis
MALTA

Miles
0        100

N W E S

Miles
0    5    10
Kilometers
0   5   10

* * *

The B-17s never came. Allied commanders had had no coordinated plan for severing the Messina Strait when HUSKY began, nor did any such plan emerge as the campaign reached its climax. Inattention, even negligence, gave Kesselring something his legions never had in Tunisia: the chance for a clean getaway.

British radio eavesdroppers had picked up many clues as early as August 1, including ferry assignments for the four German divisions, and messages about stockpiles of fuel and barrage balloons. But AFHQ intelligence in Algiers on August 10 found "no adequate indications that the enemy intends an immediate evacuation," although General Alexander had noted signs of withdrawal preparations a full week earlier, in a cable to Admiral Cunningham and Air Marshal Tedder. "You have no doubt co-ordinated plans to meet this contingency," Alexander added. It was left to Montgomery to belabor the obvious: "The truth of the matter is that there is *no* plan." Not until ten P.M. on August 14, four days into the evacuation, did Alexander signal Tedder, "It now appears that [the] German evacuation has really started." Only a few hours earlier, AFHQ had again reported "no evidence of any large-scale withdrawal."

Allied pilots had reason to fear the "fire canopy" that Baade's guns could throw over the strait. But his antiaircraft guns, if plentiful, lacked range. The entire initial production run of the new German 88mm Flak 81, which could reach the rarefied altitude of 25,000 feet and higher where the B-17 Flying Fortresses flew, had been lost in Tunisia. Yet air commanders were reluctant to divert the Allied strategic bomber force, which included nearly a thousand planes, from deep targets in Naples, Bologna, and elsewhere. To be sure, swarms of smaller Wellingtons and Mitchells, Bostons and Baltimores, Warhawks and Kittyhawks raked the strait. Little sense of urgency obtained, however: of ten thousand sorties flown by bombers and fighter-bombers in the Mediterranean from late July to mid-August, only a quarter hit targets around Messina. B-17s attacked the strait three times before LEHRGANG began; yet, as the Axis evacuation intensified on August 13, the entire Flying Fortress fleet was again bombing Rome's rail yards.

Naval commanders had equal reason to shy from Baade's ferocious shore batteries and "the octopus-like arms of searchlights." Admiral Cunningham in Tunisia had famously decreed, "Sink, burn, and destroy. Let nothing pass"; here, he issued no such commandment. "There was no effective way of stopping them, either by sea or air," Cunningham said, and Hewitt agreed. Patrol boats and small craft staged nuisance attacks, but both British and American admirals declined to risk their big ships. "The two greatest sea powers in the world," the strategist J.F.C. Fuller wrote, "had ceased to be sea-minded."

Not once did the senior Allied commanders confer on how to thwart the escape. Increasingly preoccupied with the invasion of mainland Italy in September, they never urged Eisenhower to divert his strategic bombers and other resources for a supreme effort. Nor did he force the issue. On August 10, alarmed at signs of exhaustion, the commander-in-chief's doctors ordered him to bed. There he remained for three days, "as much as his nervous temperament will permit," Butcher noted. Perhaps sensing the missed opportunity, Eisenhower on Friday morning, August 13, "hopped in and out of bed, pranced around the room, and lectured me vigorously on what history would call 'his mistake,'" Butcher added—the failure to land HUSKY forces "on both sides of the Messina Strait, thus cutting off all Sicily."

"It is astonishing that the enemy has not made stronger attacks in the past days," the commander of the Messina flotilla, Captain Gustav von Liebenstein, told his war diary on August 15. The evacuation was so unmolested that crossings soon took place by day, exploiting "Anglo-Saxon habits" during the early morning, lunch hour, and tea time. The Italian port commander departed Messina on August 16 after setting time bombs to blow up his docks. Two hundred grenadiers held a crossroads four miles outside the city, then fell back to board the last launches; German engineers cooled a wine bottle by towing it in the sea, and drank a toast as they neared the Calabrian shore. An eight-man Italian patrol inadvertently left behind was plucked from the shore by a German rescue boat at 8:30 A.M. on Tuesday, August 17, just as Allied troops converged on Messina.

They were among 40,000 Germans and 70,000 Italians to escape. Another 13,500 casualties had been evacuated in the previous month. German troops also carried off ten thousand vehicles—more than they had brought to Sicily, thanks to unbridled pilferage—and forty-seven tanks. The Italian evacuees included a dozen mules. "The Boche have carried out a very skillful withdrawal, which has been largely according to their plan and not ours," a British major noted.

Kesselring declared the German units from Sicily "completely fit for battle and ready for service." That was hyperbole; since July 10, Axis forces had been badly battered, by the Allies and by malaria. But those escaping divisions—the 15th Panzer Grenadier, the 29th Panzer Grenadier, the 1st Parachute, and the Hermann Göring—would kill thousands of Allied soldiers in the coming months. "We shall now employ our strength elsewhere," Captain von Liebenstein wrote as he reached the mainland, "fully trusting in the final victory of the Fatherland."

\*    \*    \*

At ten A.M. on August 17, Patton arrived on the windswept heights west of Messina where Highway 113 began a serpentine descent into the city. Waiting on the shoulder, Truscott tossed a welcoming salute. As in Palermo, he had been ordered not to enter the town before his army commander, and Truscott earlier this morning had rejected the surrender proffered by a delegation of frock-coated civilians. A platoon from his 7th Infantry had reached central Messina at eight o'clock the evening before, swapping shots with stay-behind German snipers, until a Ranger battalion and other U.S. troops arrived with orders "to see that the British did not capture the city from us." By the time a colonel from Montgomery's 4th Armoured Brigade arrived, with bagpipes and a Scottish broadsword in the back of his jeep, the Yanks had staked their claim. Bradley was furious upon hearing that Patton had organized his own hero's entry even as some enemy troops remained on Sicily. "I'll be damned," he said. "Now George wants to stage a parade into Messina."

Patton had a fever of 103 from a lingering case of sandfly fever, and Bradley's sentiments concerned him not at all. The race to Messina was won; the campaign for Sicily was over. On a concrete wall above the highway the word "DUCE" was painted in white letters big enough to be seen from the Italian mainland. Hazy Calabria lay across the strait, whose waters were home to Scylla, twelve-footed, six-headed, barking like a puppy while she devoured half a dozen of Odysseus' oarsmen. German shells fired from the far shore spattered into Messina below or raised towering white spouts in the harbor. "What in hell are you standing around for?" Patton demanded.

Down they raced through the hairpin turns at breakneck speed, an armored car and Patton's command vehicle leading the cavalcade. "Doughboys were moving down the road towards the city," noted Lucas, who had arrived with Patton's entourage. "They were tired and incredibly dirty. Many could hardly walk." A shell slammed into the hillside above the highway, wounding a colonel and several others in the third car of the procession. Patton sped on.

Messina was a poor prize. Sixty percent of the city lay in ruins, the cathedral roof had collapsed, and German troops had booby-trapped door handles, light switches, and toilet cisterns. Enemy fire whittled the buildings still standing. Shells dislodged caskets from their wall niches in one cemetery, scattering skeletons among the Rangers who had bivouacked there. American artillery now answered, and a 155mm gun named Draftee fired the first Allied shell onto the Italian mainland. Millions would follow.

Although three-quarters of Messina's 200,000 citizens had fled the city, a throng lined the streets to greet Patton. Clapping solemnly, they tossed grapes and morning glories. At the city hall piazza, in a ragged ceremony expedited by howling shell fire, the mayor formally tendered Messina to the conquerors.

"By 10 A.M. this morning, August 17, 1943, the last German soldier was flung out of Sicily," Alexander cabled Churchill, "and the whole island is now in our hands."

A deflated Patton was more prosaic in his diary entry that Tuesday afternoon: "I feel let down."

He soon would feel worse. At noon on the same day, as the Messina ceremony concluded, Eisenhower in Algiers was rereading a detailed account of the slapping affair that had been sent directly to the AFHQ surgeon general by a medical officer in Sicily. Corroboration soon came from several incensed reporters who had quickly pieced together the story and alerted Harry Butcher and Beetle Smith. "There are at least fifty thousand American soldiers who would shoot Patton if they had the slightest chance," Quentin Reynolds of *Collier's* advised Butcher. Ushered into the commander-in-chief's office at the Hôtel St. Georges, Demaree Bess of the *Saturday Evening Post* told Eisenhower, "We're Americans first and correspondents second." But striking a subordinate was a court-martial offense. "Every mother would figure her son is next" to be slapped, Bess added. Sympathetic to Eisenhower's dilemma over how to handle his most aggressive field commander, the reporters agreed to kill the story "for the sake of the American effort." British hacks showed similar restraint; of the sixty Anglo-American reporters in Sicily and North Africa, not one wrote a word.

Eisenhower agonized through several sleepless nights. Patton was selfish, he declared while pacing in Butcher's bedroom one evening, and willing to spend lives "if by so doing he can gain greater fame." Still, he added, "in any army one-third of the soldiers are natural fighters and brave. Two-thirds inherently are cowards and skulkers. By making the two-thirds fear possible public upbraiding such as Patton gave during the campaign, the skulkers are forced to fight."

Such dubious arithmetic hardly excused reprehensible behavior, and Eisenhower's five-paragraph letter of censure, delivered to Patton by the AFHQ surgeon, was harsh:

> I must so seriously question your good judgment and self-discipline as to raise serious doubts in my mind as to your future usefulness. . . . No letter that I have been called upon to write in my military career has caused me the mental anguish of this one.

On Eisenhower's insistence, Patton was to apologize to the individuals he had offended; Lucas, who flew to Palermo on August 21 to hand Patton the Distinguished Service Cross won at Gela, also suggested that he publicly voice contrition for his "intemperate language." No other punishment was meted out, for now. A secret inspector general's report warned that the affair would likely leak and "result in embarrassment to the War Department." But Eisenhower chose not to tell Marshall; he offered only a vague allusion to the army commander's "habit of impulsive bawling out of subordinates." Patton, he added, "has qualities that we cannot afford to lose unless he ruins himself."

Patton groveled in his reply to Eisenhower, voicing "my chagrin and grief at having given you, a man to whom I owe everything and for whom I would gladly lay down my life, cause for displeasure with me." Privately, he vacillated between penitence and defiance. "I admit freely that my method was wrong," he told his diary. But to a friend he wrote, "If I had to do it over again, I would not make a single change." Using his private nickname for Eisenhower, he wrote Bea on August 22: "I seem to have made Divine Destiny a little mad, but that will pass."

As ordered, he apologized to Private Kuhl, who subsequently posited that Patton "was suffering a little battle fatigue himself." After a similar session with Private Bennett on August 21, Patton hosted a dinner in the royal palace for the entertainer Bob Hope and his troupe, who "sang and carried on until after midnight." When the singer Frances Langford finished crooning "Embraceable You," Patton cornered Hope and threw an arm around his neck. "You can do a lot for me," Patton said. "I want you to go on radio when you get back. I want the people to know that I love my men."

His oblique public confessions, delivered to five divisions over a week beginning on August 24, used a script of nineteen paragraphs, punctuated with much extemporaneous cussing. "I have been guilty on too many occasions, perhaps, of criticizing and of loud talking," he said, speaking from a makeshift stage. "I am sorry for this." Some units rejected even such a mild self-reproach. "No, General, no!" troops in Truscott's 60th Infantry shouted. Exuberantly tossing their helmets, they thundered "Georg-ie! Georg-ie!" with such passion that Patton could not make himself heard. "The hell with it," he said, then drove off in his command car, standing and saluting as tears streamed down his cheeks.

Others were less indulgent. Before noon on Friday, August 27, a day "hotter than the hinges of Hades," the entire 1st Division marched into a natural amphitheater along the Palma River. "Arms will not be carried," a division directive advised, and officers added, "There will be no booing." Massed regimental bands played martial airs as Patton's car pulled to the stage, siren wailing, through a sea of olive-drab wool. After speaking for twenty minutes, he concluded with an accolade—"Your fame shall never die"—then saluted the colors and sped away.

Fifteen thousand men sat in stony silence. "That has got to be the weirdest speech ever made by an American general," a 26th Infantry captain muttered. Patton "used so much profanity that it wasn't clear to me what he was talking about," one soldier said, while another complained, "That fucking fucker of a general swears too fucking much." Some wondered whether he was apologizing for sacking Allen and Roosevelt. Most did not care. They were silent "to express our rejection of his presence here," explained an artillery sergeant, who added, "We despise him."

Patton returned to the palace. His exile had begun, and he could only hope that it would end before the war did. "I shall be very glad to get out of this infernal island," he wrote a friend. "It is certainly the most desolate and dreary place that I have ever been in." To Beatrice he mused, "I have been a passenger floating on the river of destiny. At the moment I can't see around the next bend, but I guess it will be all right."

The thirty-eight-day campaign had ended, and another ten thousand square miles of Axis-held territory shifted to the Allied ledger. Patton deemed HUSKY "a damn near perfect example of how to wage war," and without doubt clear benefits obtained. Mussolini's downfall had been hastened. Mediterranean sea-lanes were further secured, along with southern supply lines to the Soviet Union and southern Asia via the Suez Canal. Allied air bases sprouted on Sicily as quickly as engineers could build them. German pressure had eased on the Russian front, where Hitler in July canceled a major offensive at Kursk after only a week, in part to divert forces to Italy and the Balkans.

American confidence, so badly battered at Kasserine Pass, was fully restored; four more Army divisions had become combat veterans, joining the four annealed in Tunisia. Cooperation between naval and ground forces had improved, and the many lessons learned, in mountain warfare and sniping tactics, in the arts of camouflage and combat loading, would be useful in Italy and beyond. The experience of launching a vast amphibious invasion against a hostile shore would be invaluable for the invasions yet to come, notably at Normandy. "We know we can do it again," said Brigadier General Ray McLain, artillery commander of the 45th Division, "because we have succeeded."

The butcher's bill was dear for both sides. American battle casualties totaled 8,800, including 2,237 killed in action, plus another 13,000 hospitalized for illness. The British battle tally of 12,800 included 2,721 killed. Axis dead and wounded approached 29,000—an Italian count found 4,300 German and 4,700 Italian graves on Sicily. But it was the 140,000 Axis soldiers captured, nearly all of them Italian, who severely tilted the final casualty totals.

For the Allies the campaign had been "a great success, but it was not complete," as a German admiral put it. Barely fifty thousand Germans had overcome Allied air and sea supremacy, and the virtual collapse of their Italian confederates, to hold off an onslaught by nearly half a million Anglo-Americans for five weeks. Kesselring considered much of the American effort misspent on seizing "uninteresting territory" in western Sicily; he detected an aversion to risk in Allied commanders, and now believed that he had a clear sense of his foes for future battles.

HUSKY also exposed lingering combat shortcomings and revealed a few new ones. Rugged terrain could annul the advantage of a highly mechanized but roadbound army. "Vertical envelopment," whether by parachute or glider, had yet to prove its value; in 666 troop carrier sorties flown over Sicily, the Allies lost 42 planes and had another 118 badly damaged, many from friendly fire. The meshing of infantry, armor, artillery, air, and other combat arms into an integrated battle force—the essence of modern combat—remained ragged; at times it was unclear whether Allied air and ground forces were even fighting the same campaign. Eisenhower claimed that the "international and interservice spirit" was now "so firmly established . . . that it was scarcely necessary any longer to treat it as a problem." This was sheer fantasy. Relations between flyboys and ground-pounders were almost as badly strained as those between Brits and Yanks. As the historian Douglas Porch later wrote, "Sicily demonstrated the many limitations of interservice and inter-Allied cooperation, ones that foreshadowed problems that the Allies would encounter in Italy."

If hundreds of combat leaders at all ranks proved their mettle under fire, others failed to measure up. The sorting out of the capable from the incapable continued, and Truscott's critique in relieving a regimental commander in August showed how ruthless that sifting could be: "You lack clear, calm judgment and mental stability under stress of battle, and you are unduly influenced by rumors and exaggerated reports."

But it was at higher echelons that leaders had yet to prove themselves entirely worthy of the led. Montgomery showed signs of being "a superb leader but a mediocre manager of armies in battle," as the historian Geoffrey Perret put it, "unable to tell a sufficiency from a superfluity." Patton had retired to the royal palace with his demons. Alexander had been conservative, unimaginative, and easily bamboozled by subordinates; his generalship in Sicily was "feeble from beginning to end," the British biographer Nigel

Hamilton concluded. As for Eisenhower, notwithstanding his growth since TORCH ten months before, all too often he still failed to grip the reins of his command, day by day and hour by hour. He had yet to become a great commander because he had yet to demonstrate the preeminent quality of a great captain: the ability to impose his will on the battlefield.

Still, they owned the island. Rome was closer; Berlin was closer. An enemy who a year earlier had been ascendant was now in retreat, everywhere. Half a million German soldiers lay dead, with as many more captured or missing. After Sicily, a Luftwaffe commander wrote, few could doubt "that a turning point had come and that we were on the road to final defeat."

The troops stood down. Many would soon decamp to prepare in Britain for OVERLORD, including Omar Bradley and the 1st, 9th, 2nd Armored, and, eventually, 82nd Airborne Divisions, as well as three British divisions. Others were consigned to the long Mediterranean campaigns ahead. Patton's sense of deflation was a common malady. "Have been in the dumps," Truscott wrote Sarah on August 25. "War would be OK if it was all fighting. It's these interims that give one the heebie-jeebies."

Perhaps the heebie-jeebies came from reflection, the rare chance to consider what they had been through and what they still faced. Audie Murphy, already describing himself as "a fugitive from the law of averages," wrote, "I have seen war as it actually is, and I do not like it." Paratrooper Jim Gavin lectured himself in his diary: "I have many more battles ahead of me. . . . Fight intensely, smartly, and tough. Take chances personally and in matters of decision." In a note to his daughter, he dreamed of taking a postwar pastorate, "with nothing to do but care for the flowers and meditate on the wickedness of the world."

Ernie Pyle found melancholy harder to shake than battlefield fever. "Yesterday is tomorrow," he wrote, "and Troina is Randazzo and when will we ever stop and, God, I'm so tired." Noting that "I couldn't find the Four Freedoms among the dead men," he wrote to his wife, Jerry, in New Mexico, "The war gets so complicated and confused in my mind; on especially sad days it's almost impossible to believe that anything is worth such mass slaughter and misery." Zealous MPs ticketed Pyle three times in one day for not wearing his helmet and leggings. A provost marshal commuted the $40 fines when Pyle agreed to recite ten times: "I'm a good soldier and will try to conduct myself as such by wearing my helmet and leggings at all times." After four hundred days overseas, he needed a long rest.

Several hundred thousand soldiers found at least a brief respite in the benign late-summer Mediterranean. Jack Toffey wrote Helen in mock complaint that he had "gotten fat and lazy and bored during the past 10 days since the battle ended here." His gimpy knee often stiffened; on August 31 he would turn thirty-six. Although much fighting remained, "we are certain now we can lick this guy," he told her, "and lick him we intend to"—but he permitted himself a postwar reverie, pondering whether "our new car should be a Buick, Oldsmobile, Cadillac, or what?" Someday, peace would return. "I'll get all cleaned up and never get disheveled again," he wrote. "What a dude I intend to be."

Battalions set up wineshops and charged ten cents for a canteen cup of "Dago red." "Migrant women" plied their trade in fleabag bordellos; some, for privacy, carried their own doors from room to room. The rates of venereal disease soared and the 82nd Airborne opened a medically certified brothel in Trapani under a supervising officer soon known as the Madam; Gavin noted in his diary, "Rates at 25 lire per piece." Troops stocked up on souvenirs, including overpriced hankies with "Sicilia" embroidered in the corner. At night they watched movies on bedsheet screens, visible from both sides, and sang new camp ditties, including "Luscious Lena from Messina" and "Filthy Fannie from Trapani." "I haven't seen a spigot since I left the United States," a 1st Division soldier commented. "It's a little thing, but it means a great deal." Snippets of Italian entered the soldier patois, including "*Prego*, Dago" and "*Grazie*, Nazi."

On Sunday morning, August 29, Eisenhower flew from Algiers to Catania, escorted on the final leg by four Spitfires. In the resort town of Taormina, he joined Montgomery for a sumptuous lunch. The table was set with linen, silver, and bone china in the dining room of an elegant Fascist villa from which the Eighth Army commander hiked down to the sea for a daily swim. Later in the afternoon, the two generals drove north to Messina and stood on the corniche, scrutinizing the Calabrian shore with their glasses. The spoor of the departed enemy littered the beach. On a sunny veranda nearby, a British artillery chief invited his guests to select targets on a map brought with their afternoon cocktails; pushpins marked the chosen aim points and a few minutes later, as the gin drained from their tumblers, a salvo of several hundred shells arched across the strait toward the Italian toe. "It was most spectacular," one guest exulted.

Soon the idyll would end. As Gavin subsequently wrote his daughter, "We in our hearts know of the hunger, heartaches, and graves yet ahead of us." Also scanning the Calabrian coast, the reporter Alan Moorehead mused:

> One was hardly prepared for its nearness. . . . When one looked across at that other shore, the mainland of Europe, the vineyards and village houses were utterly quiet and all the coast seemed to be gripped in a sense of dread at what inevitably was going to happen.

# Part Two

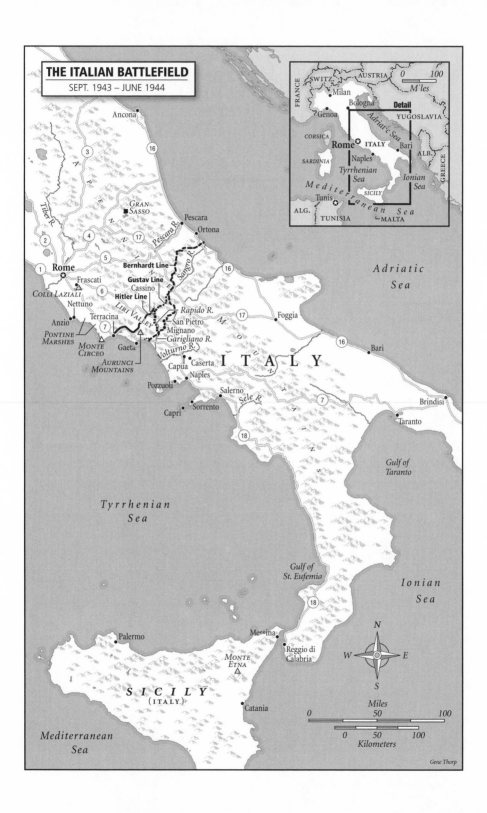

# THE ITALIAN BATTLEFIELD

SEPT. 1943 – JUNE 1944

Ancona

③

⑯

*GRAN SASSO*

Pescara

Pescara R.

Ortona

Tiber R.

②

④

⑰

Bernhardt Line

⑯

①

Rome

Frascati

Gustav Line

Sangro R.

*COLLI LAZIALI*

⑤

Cassino

Hitler Line

⑯

Nettuno

⑥

*Rapido R.*

*LIRI VALLEY*

San Pietro

⑰

Foggia

Anzio

Terracina

Mignano

*PONTINE MARSHES*

⑦

*Garigliano R.*

Gaeta

*Volturno R.*

*MONTE CIRCEO*

*AURUNCI MOUNTAINS*

Capua

Caserta

I T A L Y

Bari

Pozzuoli

Naples

Capri

Sorrento

Salerno

*Sele R.*

⑦

Brindisi

⑱

Taranto

*Tyrrhenian Sea*

*Adriatic Sea*

*Gulf of Taranto*

*Gulf of St. Eufemia*

⑱

*Ionian Sea*

Palermo

Messina

*MONTE ETNA*

Reggio di Calabria

N

W · E

S

*S I C I L Y*

(ITALY)

Catania

*Mediterranean Sea*

*Miles*

0        50        100

0    50    100

*Kilometers*

### Detail inset

FRANCE

SWITZ.

AUSTRIA

0    100

M'les

Milan

Bologna

Genoa

*Adriatic Sea*

YUGOSLAVIA

*CORSICA*

Rome

ITALY

Bari

*SARDINIA*

Naples

ALB.

*Tyrrhenian Sea*

*Ionian Sea*

GREECE

*M e d i t e r r a n e a n   S e a*

SICILY

Tunis

ALG.

TUNISIA

MALTA

Gene Thorp

# 4. SALERNO

## *"Risks Must Be Calculated"*

A gentle breeze barely riffled the sea, and a clement sun climbed through the early hours of Friday, September 3, 1943. Sicilian mongers peddled lemons and gladioli to British soldiers in battle kit queued up along the beaches. Three hundred DUKWs and other vessels swarmed between island and mainland "like so many gnats on a pond," a witness reported, and this first invasion of continental Europe—an all-British operation code-named BAYTOWN—had proved so placid that Tommies soon called it the Messina Strait Regatta. Only massed artillery broke the tranquillity: more than five hundred guns stood barking wheel-to-wheel on the slopes above Messina. Royal Navy ships, now steaming with impunity through the straits, added another hundred tubes to the cannonade. Rockets arced toward the Calabrian shore like "a kind of upward flowing yellow waterfall," wrote Alan Moorehead. "The noise was monstrous."

Just eight thousand Germans still occupied the entire foot of the Italian boot, and orders had long ago been issued to abandon Calabria—although again without notifying the Italians. Allied intelligence since August 30 had detected ample signs that Axis troops would retire northward rather than fight for the toe, but the ponderous invasion preparations continued, including a creeping barrage reminiscent of the Somme. British guns would fire 29,000 rounds on this Friday morning; the enemy in reply fired none.

General Montgomery sipped his morning tea in a seaside olive orchard and scanned the first reports from Eighth Army's vanguard, now poking through the battered streets of Reggio di Calabria on the opposite shore. German troops had melted into the hills. Montgomery lingered at a sound truck parked by the Messina beach to offer his thoughts to the BBC and to record a suitably lionhearted proclamation for Eighth Army. "I think that's all right, don't you?" he asked, listening to himself. "Good recording. Good recording." Then he called for his boat, "much as one would set out for a picnic on the Thames," and sang in his reedy voice, "Now, let's go to Italy."

To Italy he went, standing erect and khaki-clad in the DUKW's bow, his sharp chin lifted like a ship's figurehead. Several hundred cartons of cheap Woodbine cigarettes had been stacked along the hull. His batman would bring Montgomery's twittering aviary of parakeets and canaries, kept in cages outside his trailer; he hoped to find a pair of lovebirds for sale, although another feathered camp follower—a handsome peacock—had appeared at last night's dinner table on a platter, roasted and garnished. Several hundred yards from shore, the DUKW nuzzled up to a Royal Navy corvette. Scrambling aboard, Montgomery descended to the cramped wardroom, where he drank three cups of coffee and nibbled on cookies while telling reporters how he planned to wage war in Italy:

> You must never let the enemy choose the ground on which you fight. . . .
> He must be made to fight the battle according to your plan. Never his plan.
> Never. . . . You must never attack until you are absolutely ready.

Returning topside, he waved to the hooting troops packed to the gunwales in a passing landing craft. The Italians would likely fold "within six weeks," Montgomery predicted, but the Germans "will fight." As for this invasion, BAYTOWN, "it's a great satisfaction." His black-and-red pennant snapped from the corvette's mast.

In truth, he was peeved and disgruntled, and already had begun sulking in his trailer. Alexander had brushed aside his advice on how to fight the Italian campaign and Eighth Army was relegated to a supporting role; BAYTOWN had even shrunk to a mere four battalions until Montgomery's protests restored his invasion force to two divisions, the British 5th and the Canadian 1st. No effort had been made to coordinate Eighth Army with Fifth Army, now scheduled to land three hundred tortuous road miles north at Salerno in less than a week. To beach an army in the toe made little sense, even as a diversion; Montgomery thought it "daft." Alexander's instructions on whether to simply open the Messina Strait or to begin tramping up the length of Italy had been vague; when pressed to name an objective, he simply urged Montgomery to do what he could. Mounting BAYTOWN meant that AVALANCHE, the Salerno invasion, would be smaller and would comprise mostly inexperienced units and commanders. Eisenhower had prodded Montgomery to jump the strait sooner, but Eighth Army "wanted everything fully prepared" before moving. Again Eisenhower did not insist.

Strategic guidance was no more enlightened. Roosevelt and Churchill had convened another conference in mid-August, this time in Quebec. They reaffirmed the OVERLORD invasion of western Europe for the following spring, but the British still considered an extended campaign in Italy vital to that cross-Channel attack because it would siphon German reserves from the Atlantic Wall. The Americans disagreed, incessantly reciting Napoleon's maxim that Italy, like a boot, should be entered only from the top. Eight hundred miles long, it was the most vertebrate of countries, with a mountainous spine and bony ribs. No consensus existed on what to do if the Germans fought for the entire peninsula, or whether this was a worthwhile battleground if Italy quit the war.

A shout rose from the shingle just north of Reggio as the corvette drew close and troops ashore realized that Montgomery had come to join them. Clambering back into another DUKW, he rolled onto the continent at 10:30 A.M., goggles around his neck and beret cocked just so, tossing cigarettes with a grin. Hundreds of Italian soldiers also rushed to the beach "with hands upraised, shouting, laughing," eager to help unload enemy stores. Montgomery made straight for the local Fascist headquarters, where he purloined a sheaf of stationery on which he would scribble his correspondence for months. That evening he ate an early dinner and retired to bed with a novel. In a note to General Brooke in London before he drifted off, Montgomery wrote, "The only person who does not get tired is myself."

The next days passed with little sense of urgency. German demolitionists had wrecked bridges and road culverts, but active resistance was mounted only by a puma and a frightened monkey, both fugitives from the Reggio zoo. Fuel and ammunition dumps swelled in size. Eighth Army scouts pushed from the toe to the instep, at times conducting reconnaissance from the passenger carriages of local trains. Wild orchids and golden gorse grew in the uplands where for centuries Greek and Roman shipwrights had cut their timber. Women with scarlet petticoats beneath black skirts glided through the little villages, bundles of firewood balanced on their heads. The scent of crushed fennel sweetened the air, and nights grew chill as the soldiers tramped away from the Jasmine Coast and into the mountains. Canadian troops shivered in their khaki drill shorts, and some rifled through the abandoned uniform closets of the Blackshirt Legion for warmer garb.

Alexander advised London on September 6 that the Germans were resisting Eighth Army "more by demolition than by fire." In fact, as Brooke acknowledged the same day, "no Germans troops have been met so far." On the night of September 7, in a modest effort to flank the enemy, several battalions sailed from Messina with the intent of landing near Pizzo, on the Gulf of St. Eufemia, twenty-five miles northeast of the toe. "Everything went wrong," a Royal Hampshire account conceded. The wrong battalions landed on the wrong beaches in the wrong sequence. "Our exact whereabouts was not known to our naval friends," the Dorsetshires reported. "It was a pitch black night with no moon." Commando landing craft went astray; among the first Dorsets finally ashore was "an NCO with a bag of mail over his shoulder." A light drizzle of German mortar shells turned into a deluge, with "many casualties suffered by those in the craft or trying to land." The expedition accomplished little. A German war diary several days later noted that, in Calabria, "the enemy is not crowding after us."

Montgomery meanwhile made himself comfortable. He offered visiting journalists glasses of spiked lemonade and tours of the new shower and tub in his personal trailer, "happy as a youngster with a new electric train." The birds chirped in their cages. Was it true, he asked the reporter Quentin Reynolds, that fashionable girls in New York now wore Monty berets?

On Sunday, September 5, Eisenhower hosted a small bridge party at his seven-bedroom estate in Algiers, the Villa dar el Ouard: Villa of the Family. Often to relax he played Ping-Pong on the green table in his library, or sang old West Point songs at the grand piano in the music room. But cards remained his favorite pastime, and for this game he rounded up three skilled players: Harry Butcher, Lieutenant General Mark W. Clark, and the chief of staff for Clark's Fifth Army, Major General Alfred M. Gruenther. Tricks were taken, tricks were lost, and between hands there was little palaver. Clark seemed preoccupied and failed to count trump properly; he and Butcher lost the rubber to Eisenhower and the formidable Gruenther, who as a young lieutenant had supplemented his Army pay by refereeing professional bridge tournaments in New York.

Reluctantly, they threw in their cards. Summoning his limousine, Eisenhower bundled Clark and Gruenther in back and rode with them to the port, now alive with the usual embarkation frenzy of shouting stevedores and swinging booms. The commander-in-chief gripped Clark's hand— they had been close friends for three decades, since the academy—and wished him godspeed, then watched the two officers stride up the gangplank to join Kent Hewitt on his new flagship, the U.S.S. *Ancon*. Antennae wrapped her superstructure like a spider's web. Thirty staff officers of Fifth Army soon boarded, as well as a few commanders who had come to bid Clark good luck. Among the well-wishers was Truscott. "Hell, Lucian," Clark told him. "You don't have to worry about this operation. This will be a pursuit, not a battle."

Exhausted from the long weeks of preparing his army, Clark soon retired to his cabin, where the bunk barely accommodated his six-foot-three-inch frame. Before flicking off the light, he opened a small volume called

*The Daily Word.* "With Thee I am unafraid, for on Thee my mind is stayed," read the entry for September 5. "Though a thousand foes surround, safe in Thee I shall be found." Just in case, Clark had tucked several four-leaf clovers into his wallet.

"The best organizer, planner and trainer of troops that I have met," Eisenhower had written of Clark to Marshall two weeks earlier. "In preparing the minute details . . . he has no equal in our Army." It was precisely these attributes that had led Eisenhower to choose Clark for the immensely complex challenge of flinging an army onto a hostile shore, a task that would make him the senior American field commander in Italy. Long-limbed and angular, with a thick lower lip and prominent Adam's apple, Clark had dark eyes that constantly swept the terrain before him. To a British general, he evoked "a film star who excels in Westerns." When speaking, Clark often paused to purse or lick his lips; the ears flattened against his skull accentuated a long, aquiline nose that suggested a raptor's beak. "A fine face, full of bones," George Biddle observed. "An intelligent face and an expression of kindliness about the mouth."

He had been born into the Army and grew into a frail, skinny officer's son whose father let him attend "the college of your choice, providing it's West Point." As the youngest member of the entering class of 1917, Clark was promptly powdered, diapered, and put to bed early. Descended from immigrant Romanian Jews on his mother's side, he had himself baptized as an Episcopalian in the academy chapel. At age twenty-two, soon after graduation, he was commanding a battalion in the Vosges Mountains when German shrapnel tore through his shoulder and ended his war. Promoted twice during his first four months of service, he thereafter remained a captain for sixteen years, battling both national indifference to the Army and poor health: he suffered from a heart murmur, ulcers, a diseased gallbladder, and various infections. In 1923, he met the widow of a West Point classmate who had committed suicide two years earlier. Four years older than Clark and a graduate of Northwestern University, Maurine Doran, known as Renie, was petite, lighthearted, and his equal in intelligence and ambition; they married a year later.

Now forty-seven and known to his friends as Wayne, Clark had skipped the rank of colonel altogether and was among the youngest three-star generals in the Army's history. Still, he had last commanded troops in combat a quarter century earlier. If Biddle detected "kindliness about the mouth," he missed a few other traits. "He thought of himself as destined to do something unusual in this war," a Fifth Army staff officer said, "and so he carried himself with a dignity commensurate with that." An Anglophobe, he hid his disdain from both Eisenhower and the British; only within his inner circle would he rail against "these goddamned dumb British," or recite the Napoleonic maxim "Don't be an ally. Fight them."

He professed to "want my headquarters to be a happy one," but Clark was too short-tempered and aloof for easy felicity. One staff officer considered him "a goddamned study in arrogance," while another saw "conceit wrapped around him like a halo." Perhaps only in his correspondence with Renie did the sharp edges soften. He wrote of a yen to go fishing, of the rugs and silver dishes he was sending her, of his small needs from home, like vitamin pills and gold braid for his caps. From her apartment in Washington she cautioned him about flying too much, and complained of his infrequent letters, of difficulties with his mother, of how much she missed being kissed. She had sent him the clovers.

Clark's compulsive self-promotion already had drawn sharp rebukes from Marshall and Eisenhower, but he still instructed photographers to snap his "facially best" left side. The correspondent Eric Sevareid considered him fixated on "personal publicity without which warmaking is a dull job, devoid of glamour and recompense." Clark at times encouraged Renie to cooperate with the reporters in Washington who wrote profiles of him; at other times, he chastised her for extolling his virtues too vigorously. "From what I have told you about publicity," he wrote, "you should begin to put two and two together and see the picture." His public relations staff would grow to nearly fifty men, with each news release preferably carrying Clark's name three times on the first page and at least once per page thereafter. Reporters were encouraged to adopt the commanding general's preferred nomenclature: "Lieutenant General Mark W. Clark's Fifth Army."

That army would need his lucky clovers. Operation AVALANCHE was to land at Salerno, seize nearby Naples, and eventually establish air bases "in the Rome area, and if feasible, further north." As in HUSKY, preparations suffered from the diaspora of Allied planners across the ancient world. Instead of the three to five months needed to thoroughly plan a major amphibious expedition, Clark got forty-five days. Rehearsals were minimal and disheartening. Owing to the belated discovery of minefields in Salerno Bay, Hewitt would have to lower the landing craft nine to twelve miles from the beaches in order to avoid endangering his troop transports. Clark on August 24 also accelerated H-hour by thirty minutes, "upsetting all the detailed timings of convoys and assault waves." "Men of calm dispositions," one commander noted, "became quite irritable." Quartermasters struggled to overcome shortages of hospital beds, bakeries, laundry units, and—because planners had simply forgotten to requisition it—100-octane aviation fuel.

Only three assault divisions were available for AVALANCHE, so the operation would have less than half the heft of HUSKY. Clark had pleaded for at least four divisions, but, as usual, force size was determined by shipping capacity rather than battlefield needs. Even as Clark boarded *Ancon* it was unclear to Hewitt how many ships and landing craft he had in his fleet; some vessels still required refurbishing after duty in Sicily, and much shipping had been diverted to support Montgomery in BAYTOWN. Adding to Clark's burden, Eisenhower on September 3 told him he could no longer count on the 82nd Airborne Division in reserve, a blow that Clark likened to "cutting off my left arm."

Eisenhower had his own disappointments. Three times he asked Washington and London to temporarily double his heavy bomber force for AVALANCHE, and three times the Combined Chiefs refused to divert planes from the growing air campaign in Britain. A separate request—to ferry another infantry division to Salerno by borrowing ten LSTs bound for India through the Mediterranean—was rejected by the Charlie-Charlies in late August. Eisenhower advised his superiors that the invasion would proceed apace with "whatever forces we have at the moment," but that "risks must be calculated." To bolster fighter protection for Hewitt's ships, the Royal Navy had added a light fleet aircraft carrier—H.M.S. *Unicorn*—and four smaller escort carriers known as Woolworths. Allied air strength was roughly thrice that of the Axis, but most U.S. and British fighters would fly from distant Sicilian bases. Air planners estimated that they lacked about a third of the strength required to provide maximum protection for the invasion force, a shortfall Eisenhower found "rather disquieting." He told the Charlie-Charlies in early September that the Allied air forces could not, as they had done in Sicily, prevent the enemy from reinforcing the invasion beachhead with substantial reserves.

But would the Germans fight for Salerno? Ultra provided a detailed portrait of the sixteen German divisions now in Italy, including the four withdrawn from Sicily; those forces had grown steadily since Mussolini's overthrow in late July. ("Treachery alters everything," Hitler declared.) AFHQ intelligence still believed that, given limp Italian resistance, the German high command would fall back to a defensive line across northern Italy from Pisa to Rimini, blocking Allied occupation of the Po Valley, where three-quarters of Italy's industry was located. Yet "if and when the Germans realize that our assault is not in very great strength they may move to the sound of the guns," the Combined Chiefs were told at Quebec. An estimated 40,000 enemy troops would oppose the Salerno landings on D-day, but that number could grow to 100,000 within four days; the Germans may "attack us with up to six divisions some time during

September," while Clark would not have that many troops ashore until late fall. The key in amphibious landings was not the size of the landing force, but whether invaders could build up the beachhead faster than the defenders.

Salerno would be a poor place to fight outnumbered. As an invasion site it offered nearly perfect hydrography, with few sandbars, a negligible tide, a small port in a sheltered bay, and twenty-two miles of gorgeous beaches. "This is the finest strip of coast in the whole of Italy, perhaps anywhere in the Mediterranean," one British planner noted. But, he added, it had the misfortune of being "hemmed in by mountains." Mostly rugged limestone, those mountains encircled an alluvial plain traversed by a pair of modest rivers, the Sele and the Calore. A terrain study for AVALANCHE warned, "The mountainous terrain completely surrounding the Sele plain limits the depth of the initial bridgehead and exposes this bridgehead to observation, fire and attack from higher ground." Salerno's topography, a U.S. Navy planner added, was like "the inside of a cup."

Risks had been calculated. At 6:30 A.M. on September 6, *Ancon* cast off her lines and steamed from Algiers at twelve knots in a convoy of seventy ships that included three cruisers and fourteen destroyers. Sailors awake but not on duty watched an early showing on the boat deck of *Strange Cargo*, with Joan Crawford. Hewitt and Clark, fellow Freemasons who had known each other since they were both stationed near Puget Sound in the 1930s, chatted on the flag bridge and scrutinized an immense map of Salerno Bay. Belowdecks, a ten-by-twenty-foot map in the war room charted the position of every Allied ship between Gibraltar and Tripoli. In forty-eight hours, six hundred vessels sailing in sixteen convoys from six ports would converge on "an enchanted land," as Longfellow had called it, where "the blue Salernian bay with its sickle of white sand" awaited them.

What else awaited remained to be seen. A British commander had told Clark he had "high hopes of being in Naples the evening of D+2," or Saturday, September 11. "Boldness must be the order of the day," Eisenhower proclaimed. He was already planning to move his headquarters from Algiers to Naples in late September. "The time has come to discontinue nibbling at islands and hit the Germans where it hurts," he told reporters. "Our object is to trap and smash them."

Bravado was easier in Algiers than on the high seas steaming north. As Clark's gaze swiveled from horizon to horizon, he felt an unnerving fatalism. "I realized I might as well be on a raft, no control, no nothing," he later recalled. "If it wasn't going to work now, it wasn't going to work." The solitude of command—that "forlorn feeling," he called it—had set in. Surrounded by his army, with a great fleet fore and aft, he was alone.

## *Plots, Counterplots, and Cross-plots*

E VEN as the invaders bore down on Salerno, hope persisted that diplomacy might spare Italy from being dragged lengthwise by what Churchill called "the hot rake of war." Since Mussolini's arrest in late July, the Italian government had repeatedly sworn fealty to the Pact of Steel. Both the king and his new plenipotentiary, Marshal Badoglio, vowed to preserve the Axis. Rome decried—with huffy assertions of Italian honor— any notions of a separate peace. In truth, the Italians had been making diplomatic overtures to the Allies since early August—in Tangiers, Madrid, and Vatican City—in a surreptitious tangle of "plots, counter-plots and cross-plots," as diplomat Harold Macmillan put it.

Wary but intrigued, the Combined Chiefs had instructed Eisenhower to send two AFHQ officers to neutral Portugal for a clandestine rendezvous with an ostensible Badoglio emissary. On August 19, Beetle Smith and the AFHQ intelligence chief, Brigadier Kenneth W. D. Strong, flew via Gibraltar to Lisbon with forged papers in "an atmosphere of amateur theatricals," in Macmillan's phrase. Discomforted by chronic ulcers, Smith wore "an appalling Norfolk jacket which he had somehow purchased in Algiers and some grey flannel trousers which fitted him very ill"; only with difficulty was he persuaded to remove "a dubious hat with a feather in it," but he insisted on toting two pistols under his armpits, with another pair holstered on his hips. "I envisaged a desperate gunfight in the best Western manner," Strong confessed. The two envoys were chauffered around Lisbon in a rattletrap Buick by a young American diplomat named George F. Kennan.

Their Italian counterpart proved to be a short, swarthy character of Sicilian descent, with thinning hair, a hooked nose, and a loathing of the Germans matched only by his affection for political skulduggery. General Giuseppe Castellano had come to Lisbon to ask "how Italy could arrange to join the united nations in opposition to Germany"; as a token of good faith, he offered a stack of secret documents detailing the military dispositions of 400,000 Germans now in Italy. Castellano quickly discerned that the Allies were in no mood to forgive and forget. In an all-night session at the British ambassador's house, fueled by whiskey and soda, Smith made it clear that Italy's only choice was surrender or the ruination of total war. Paragraph by paragraph he read the proposed capitulation agreement aloud.

"We are not in a position to make terms," Castellano admitted. In contrast to the clumsy U.S. negotiations with Vichy French officials in North Africa a year earlier, Smith displayed admirable dexterity in mixing tact with resolve. Castellano slipped from the house at seven A.M., carrying an American radio and ciphers with which Rome could secretly contact AFHQ; his government was given until the end of August to accept the Allied terms. Smith, who privately began referring to Castellano as "my pet Wop," advised AFHQ, "The Italians expect bitter reprisals from the Germans, whom they both hate and fear."

If Rome was in no position to make terms, Eisenhower could hardly let an Italian surrender slip away. Admitting to feeling "very anxious," he told the Combined Chiefs on August 28 that the risks at Salerno "will be minimized to a large extent if we are able to secure Italian assistance." Alexander feared that without such assistance AVALANCHE "might fail," perhaps causing the fall of Churchill's government and "seriously compromising Britain's determination to remain in the war." Coded messages flew between Rome and Algiers with no real agreement on surrender terms. In a letter to Roosevelt, the diplomat Robert Murphy reported that the Italians seemed to be debating "whether we or the Germans will work the most damage and destruction in Italy."

The plots, counterplots, and cross-plots thickened. On September 1, an ambiguous radio signal from Badoglio declared, "The reply is affirmative." Castellano flew to Sicily a day later and was escorted to a private tent in the thirty-acre olive and almond orchard at Cassibile, south of Syracuse, where Alexander now kept his headquarters. In quizzing Castellano inside the tent, Macmillan and Murphy were distressed to learn that he still lacked authority from Rome to sign an armistice. Leaving the envoy to bake beneath the hot canvas, they rushed off to find Alexander in his trailer.

More amateur theatricals followed. Hearing a commotion through the nut trees, Castellano pushed back the tent flaps to find a British honor guard in parade order, smartly presenting arms as the commanding general's staff car roared up with flags flying. Alexander emerged in his finest dress uniform, "cut breeches, highly polished boots with gold spurs, and gold peaked cap." Medals and campaign ribbons spilled down his chest. "I have come to be introduced to General Castellano," he boomed. "I understand he has signed the instrument of surrender."

Macmillan stepped forward, his face a study in regret. "I am sorry to say, sir, but General Castellano has *not* signed the instrument, and says that he hasn't the authority from his government to sign such a document."

Alexander swiveled slowly. His icy gaze locked on the abject Castellano.

"Why, there must be some mistake!" Alexander said. "I have seen the telegram from Marshal Badoglio stating he was to sign the armistice agreement." Alexander's eyes widened, as if suddenly seeing the awful truth. "In that case, this man must be a spy. Arrest him!"

A dreadful fate would befall Italy as well as Castellano, Alexander intimated. Within twenty-four hours, Rome would be destroyed in reprisal for Italian recalcitrance. As the diplomats counseled moderation, Alexander seemed to reconsider. Perhaps, if Castellano telegrammed Rome, asking Badoglio to confirm his authority to sign the surrender, calamity might be avoided. That, Alexander said slowly, was "the only way out of this." Alexander turned on his heel, the guard again presented arms, and off he stalked, "booted, spurred, and bemedaled," a gold-capped avatar of imperial wrath.

The telegram was sent posthaste, and at four P.M. on September 3, explicit permission arrived from Rome. Seventy-five minutes later, beneath a gnarled olive tree on a scarred wooden camp table hastily upholstered with napkins, Castellano and Smith signed Italy's capitulation using a borrowed fountain pen. Eisenhower, who flew in for the occasion, looked on with Alexander. Someone produced a whiskey bottle and dirty glasses for a toast, and each witness plucked an olive sprig for a memento.

The surrender was to be jointly announced in Rome and Algiers on the eve of D-day. Castellano pressed to learn that precise date, but Smith in a low voice replied, "I can say only that the landing will take place within two weeks." Castellano soon advised his government that there was still a fortnight to prepare. "Today's event must be kept secret," Eisenhower cabled the Charlie-Charlies, "or our plans will be ruined."

Those plans grew more convoluted by the hour. Smith had rejected Italian demands that fifteen Allied divisions land north of Rome; had the Anglo-Americans possessed such a capability, he archly noted, they would not be treating with Castellano. But as an earnest of the Anglo-American commitment, the Allies would consider dropping the 82nd Airborne Division on Rome to help Italian forces secure their capital. With little consideration, Eisenhower and his lieutenants approved the scheme "to stiffen Italian formations"; the 82nd was thus plucked from Clark's reserves at Salerno. "They all thought the risk was worth taking," Murphy wrote Roosevelt, "even if the [division was] lost."

The scheme was cockamamie—"perfectly asinine," as Clark put it, and "tactically unsound," according to the AFHQ staff. In the course of the AV-ALANCHE planning, Major General Ridgway for more than a month had been ordered to prepare his 82nd for one ill-conceived mission after another, including a proposed amphibious landing north of Naples, although "not one individual in the entire division, officer or enlisted man, had ever had any experience or instruction in amphibious operations." Nothing, apparently, had been learned from the airborne disasters in Sicily. One 82nd Airborne officer, echoing Macmillan's phrase, lamented the "remarkable series of orders, counter-orders, plans, changes in plans, marches and counter-marches, missions and remissions, by air, water, and land."

GIANT II, as the drop on Rome was code-named, was the most "harebrained" notion yet, in Ridgway's estimation. The division would arrive piecemeal—because of an aircraft shortage, only two battalions could jump the first night—on a pair of airfields twenty miles northwest of Rome and nearly two hundred miles from the Salerno landings. Before leaving Cassibile, Castellano had rashly promised that Italian forces would silence all antiaircraft weapons; outline the runways with amber lights; block approach avenues to the drop zones; and provide vital matériel that included 355 trucks, 12 ambulances, 500 laborers, 50 interpreters, 100 miles of barbed wire, picks, shovels, switchboards, fuel, and rations.

The more Ridgway heard, the less he believed. The Italians, he warned Smith, "are deceiving us and have not the capability for doing what they are promising." Smith disagreed, insisting that inflamed Romans would assist the 82nd by dropping "kettles, bricks, [and] hot water on the Germans in the streets of Rome." Alexander was equally cavalier, crediting "full faith" to Italian guarantees. "Don't give this another thought, Ridgway," he added. "Contact will be made with your division in three days—five days at the most." But when Ridgway persisted, warning of the "sacrifice of my division," Alexander agreed to let him gauge Italian resolve by infiltrating a pair of American officers into downtown Rome.

As the sun sank into the Tyrrhenian Sea on Tuesday, September 7, the Italian corvette *Ibis* rounded the headland at Gaeta, a scruffy port midway between Naples and Rome where, Virgil recounted, Aeneas had buried his beloved nurse. As the helmsman eased through a minefield and into the harbor, two American officers on the corvette's lower bridge deranged their uniforms, tousled their hair, and splashed themselves with seawater. "Look disconsolate," an Italian admiral advised them. Dockworkers watched from the quay while bawling Italian tars prodded the men down the gangplank and into a naval staff car, apparent prisoners-of-war bound for an interrogation cell.

In truth they were the Italians' guests, having been plucked from a British patrol boat after a secret rendezvous north of Palermo early that morning. A handsome, graceful Missourian was the ranking officer of the pair. Brigadier General Maxwell D. Taylor had been first captain of his West Point class and now, at age forty-two, commanded the 82nd Airborne's artillery. A gifted linguist who had taught French and Spanish at the academy, Taylor evinced a diplomatic bearing that, together with his study of "Italian in Twenty Lessons," sufficiently qualified him for this secret mission. Beneath his Army field jacket he carried 70,000 lire—equivalent to $700—in a money belt borrowed from the photographer Robert Capa, who had won it in a poker game. Colonel William T. Gardiner, junior in rank but senior in age at fifty-one, wore his Army Air Forces dress uniform with ribbons earned in both this war and the last one. A former lawyer who was also fluent in French, Gardiner had served as the speaker of Maine's house of representatives and then, for four years, as governor. Both men knew intimate details of the Salerno invasion, set to begin in hours, and before leaving Sicily they had been advised: "If you get captured, put your forgetter to work."

Through Gaeta the staff car rolled, slowing to yield the right-of-way to military trucks packed with German soldiers in flanged helmets. On a remote road outside Gaeta, the vehicle lurched to a halt beside a waiting ambulance with frosted side windows. The Americans climbed in back with their luggage, including a radio in a fine leather case. North they sped, hugging the coast as far as Terracina, then veering inland at twilight on the ancient Via Appia, through the Latin countryside and the drained polders of the Pontine Marshes, past the walled vineyards and the roadside tombs and the stone highway markers that counted down the distance to Rome.

By 8:30 P.M., Taylor and Gardiner had been deposited at the Palazzo Caprara, a four-story mansion opposite the Italian war office at the intersection of Via Firenze and Via XX Settembre in central Rome. In a wainscoted suite on the palazzo's second floor, Italian waiters set a table with linen and silver, then served consommé, veal cutlets, and crêpes Suzette catered by the Grand Hotel. Italian staff officers came and went, shrugging off Taylor's requests to meet with the high command. "It appeared to me that they were attempting to stall," Gardiner later noted.

The excellent crêpes notwithstanding, Taylor's protests grew shrill; finally, at 9:30 P.M., the door swung open for the magisterial entrance of General Giacomo Carboni, commander of the four divisions responsible for Rome's outer defenses. In buffed boots and immaculate tunic, with pomaded hair and a thin sliver of a mustache, Carboni struck Taylor as "a professional dandy." Unfurling his map, he pointed to the German positions encircling the capital: 12,000 paratroopers bivouacked along the coast, from the south bank of the Tiber halfway to Anzio; another 24,000 men and 200 tanks in the 3rd Panzer Grenadier Division holding a crescent-shaped area to the north; still more forces around Frascati, to the southeast.

Italian garrisons had been virtually immobilized and disarmed, Carboni continued. The Germans had stopped supplying fuel and ammunition. Some artillery batteries had only twenty rounds per gun. The Italian air force needed another week to make arrangements for the 82nd Airborne's seizure of the two airfields; among other shortfalls, few trucks could be arranged to move the division. In a battle for Rome against the Germans, Carboni estimated, his forces would last just five hours. Some units had enough ammo to fight for only twenty minutes.

"If the Italians declare an armistice, the Germans will occupy Rome, and the Italians can do little to prevent it," he said. The arrival of U.S. paratroopers would simply "provoke the Germans to more drastic action." Carboni spread his manicured hands in a gesture of helplessness.

Clearly, Castellano's blithe assurances were shaky; so, it seemed, was the surrender signed at Cassibile four days earlier. Stunned and alarmed, Taylor and Gardiner demanded to be taken to see Marshal Badoglio. Carboni temporized. The marshal was an old man, fast asleep. Surely this could wait until morning. More demands, more demurrals, but at length the Americans found themselves speeding across Rome in Carboni's car to Badoglio's villa. A midnight air raid had already roused the household; servants with flashlights and officers in pajamas flitted across the veranda and through the lush garden. Carboni vanished across the foyer, leaving the Americans to pace the vast carpets, studying the statuary and the oil landscapes hung on the white marble walls.

Fifteen minutes later the marshal appeared, dressed in a charcoal-gray civilian suit and low brown shoes. Bald, aging, and cordial, he reminded Gardiner of "an old hound dog" as he invited the men to take chairs in his study. The conqueror of Ethiopia, Badoglio had resigned as chief of Italy's armed services in 1940 after the debacle in Greece. He passed his days playing cards and medicating himself with champagne from a wine cellar said to hold five thousand bottles. Only Mussolini's arrest and the king's summons had brought him from retirement. "I was a Fascist because the king was a Fascist," he later explained with a shrug. "I do what the king tells me."

Taylor asked in French whether Badoglio agreed with Carboni that "an immediate armistice and the reception of airborne troops" were impossible.

The marshal nodded. "Castellano did not know all the facts. Italian troops cannot possibly defend Rome." Stepping to a large map, he pointed to the "natural defenses across Italy" that aided the Germans. "Supposing, just for the sake of discussion, landings were made at Salerno," he continued with a knowing look. "There would be many, many difficulties."

"Are you more afraid of the Germans than you are of us?" Taylor asked. "If you fail to announce the armistice there will be nothing left for us to do but to bomb and destroy Rome ourselves."

Badoglio's voice thickened. "Why would you want to bomb the city of people who are trying to aid you?"

Would General Taylor return to Algiers and explain this predicament to General Eisenhower? he asked. General Taylor would not. But perhaps Marshal Badoglio should write a message describing his "change in attitude." Badoglio nodded, took up a pen, and drafted a single paragraph in Italian, which included the fatal phrase: "It is no longer possible to accept an immediate armistice." Taylor drafted his own concise message, dated September 8 at 0121 hours: "GIANT TWO is impossible." An aide took the cables to be encrypted and dispatched by radio.

Badoglio and Carboni stood, and snapped to attention with a sharp clicking of heels. "We returned the gesture," Gardiner recalled, "endeavoring to click our heels as loudly as the Italians. There was quite a contest." Badoglio spoke of honor, and of his half century as a soldier. He seemed near tears as the Americans left.

Disheartened and exhausted, Taylor and Gardiner returned to the Palazzo Caprara. They spoke in whispers for fear of eavesdropping microphones as Wednesday's sunrise brought Rome to life. Had the messages reached Algiers? There was no reply, and GIANT II was scheduled to begin in less than ten hours. At 8:20 A.M., Taylor sent another coded warning, stressing Italian rejection of the airborne mission. Pacing back and forth in what they now called "our hideout," the two men considered taking a stroll outside but could not find a civilian jacket big enough for the burly Gardiner.

At 11:35 A.M., Taylor radioed the two-word emergency code that urged cancellation of GIANT II: "Situation innocuous." From overhead came the drone of aircraft, followed by the distant grumble of bombs detonating to the southeast. At last a return message arrived from Algiers: "You will return to Allied headquarters." Grabbing the leather case, they again slipped into a waiting ambulance and sped to an airfield outside Rome, whence an Italian military trimotor spirited them to North Africa.

Eisenhower left Algiers early Wednesday morning to fly to his forward headquarters outside Tunis. The big white house at Amilcar, with its intricate mosaic floor and sun-washed terrace above the bright bay, hardly suggested a field camp; the only audible gunfire came from carbines plinking at targets tossed in the water beyond the dock. But moving to the forward command post on occasion gave desk-bound AFHQ—and its commander—at least the illusion of being on the march. With the landings at Salerno set to begin before dawn on Thursday, Eisenhower wanted to confer a final time with his top lieutenants in Tunisia. In a brief note to Mamie, he admitted to feeling "rather stretched out at the moment"; he was sleeping poorly, and the Mediterranean campaign had become so consuming, he told her, that he felt like "a creature of war."

So it was that when Badoglio's renunciation of the armistice was finally decoded at AFHQ headquarters at eight A.M.—seven hours after transmission—Eisenhower had gone. Smith forwarded the doleful message and Taylor's initial advisory to Amilcar, then fretted for three hours until also passing them to the Combined Chiefs with a request for advice. Marshall soon recommended publicly revealing the signed Cassibile agreement. "No consideration need be given the embarrassment it might cause the Italian government," he added. Churchill was visiting the White House and still in his wool nightshirt when Smith's cable arrived. "That's what you would expect from those Dagoes," he growled.

In the small schoolhouse outside Bizerte where Alexander kept his Tunisian headquarters, Eisenhower late Wednesday morning had just finished reviewing the AVALANCHE preparations when a staff officer handed him the dispatches from Smith, Badoglio, and Taylor. His face flushed until his cheeks were as pink as the message forms, one witness reported. The broad mouth tightened, the veins in his wide forehead thickened. Seizing a pencil he snapped it in half; seizing another he snapped it, too, and "expressed himself with great violence," a British officer noted. If angry at Smith's presumption in asking for help from Washington and London, he was enraged at the Italians. Badoglio was "an old man and inclined to temporize," especially with "the Germans pressing a revolver against his kidneys." Snapping off each syllable, he dictated a blistering reply to Badoglio: "If you or any part of your armed forces fail to cooperate as previously agreed I will publish to the world a full record of this affair. . . . I do not accept your message of this morning postponing the armistice." By the time he composed the twelfth and final sentence of his message, Eisenhower's voice had risen to a shout: "Failure now on your part to carry out the full obligations of the signed agreement will have the most serious consequences for your country."

"I always knew you had to give these yellow bastards a jab in the stomach before they would work," he added. To the Charlie-Charlies he dictated another message Wednesday afternoon: "We will not recognize any deviation from our original agreement."

Clearly a deviation was needed in the GIANT II plan. Some 150 C-47 transport planes were to begin lifting off at 5:45 P.M., carrying the first two thousand paratroopers over Rome. As Taylor's repeated warnings finally reached Tunisia, Alexander sent a postponement order to General Ridgway's command post at the Licata South airfield on Sicily. No acknowledgment came back. Eisenhower ordered Alexander's U.S. deputy, Brigadier General Lyman L. Lemnitzer, to personally carry the message to Licata. Still in his pinks-and-greens office uniform, Lemnitzer rushed to El Aouina airfield, commandeered a British Beaufighter, and by bracing against the fuselage struts managed to wedge himself behind the nonplussed pilot. After a harrowing takeoff, they reached Sicily in an hour but failed to find Licata until Lemnitzer, after spotting Mount Etna, ordered the pilot to turn around and follow the coastline south and west.

Sixty-two transports were already circling when Licata South appeared below, with more taking off each minute. Unable to land on the clogged runway, Lemnitzer grabbed a flare pistol and began firing from both sides of the cockpit as the Beaufighter skimmed the treetops. The takeoffs stopped, the Beaufighter landed, and Lemnitzer tore hell-for-leather to the small command post off the runway apron. There he found Ridgway, wearing his parachute and ready to climb into a C-47. The 82nd commander had whiled away the afternoon playing cribbage and strolling through the olive trees with a chaplain, "trying to reconcile myself" to the certain destruction of his command. "Didn't you get our message?" Lemnitzer asked over the engine roar. Ridgway's eyes widened. "What message?"

Jeeps raced about, herding paratroopers back to their bivouacs. Recall orders went out to those in the air. Exhausted and relieved, Ridgway stumbled into a tent where one of his officers sat trembling on a cot. Ridgway poured two drinks from a whiskey bottle, and as darkness fell and calm again enveloped Licata South, they sat slumped together, silent but for the sound of their weeping.

At 6:30 P.M. on September 8, Eisenhower's flat Kansas drawl announced over Radio Algiers: "The Italian government has surrendered its armed forces unconditionally. . . . All Italians who now act to help eject the German aggressors from Italian soil will have the assistance and support of the united nations." Ten minutes later, having heard no answering confirmation from Radio Rome, Eisenhower authorized the broadcast of Badoglio's proclamation, the text of which Castellano had provided at Cassibile: "The Italian forces will . . . cease all acts of hostility against the Anglo-American forces wherever they may be."

King Victor Emmanuel, Badoglio, and other Italian officials had assembled for a conference in the Quirinal Palace when a Reuters news bulletin at 6:45 P.M. informed them of Eisenhower's proclamation. After much anguished discussion, the king concluded that Italy could not change sides yet again. Badoglio hastened to the Radio Rome studio, and at 7:45 P.M. affirmed the capitulation.

For 1,184 days, Italy had fought shoulder-to-shoulder with Germany. Now she had cast her lot with her erstwhile foes, trusting in providence and an Allied shield for protection from Hitler's wrath. Neither would stay the hot rake. "Italy's treachery is official," Rommel wrote his wife. "We sure had them figured out right."

In the hours following Badoglio's announcement, jubilation and confusion radiated from Rome to the remotest hamlet of every Italian province. Citizens exulted at the presumed arrival of peace. But no intelligible orders had been issued to the Italian fleet or to the sixty army divisions of 1.7 million troops. Telephone queries from Italian garrisons in Greece, northern Italy, and elsewhere received incoherent replies or no reply at all. The frantic *ring-ring* of unheeded phones soon became the totemic sound of capitulation. The armistice caught fourteen of sixteen government ministers by surprise; one summoned a notary to witness his affidavit of utter ignorance.

No effort was made to stop six battalions of German paratroopers tramping into the capital from the south; their commander even paused to buy grapes at a farmer's market. Grenadiers closed on the city from the north. Rome's police chief estimated that six thousand German secret agents infested the capital, and within hours the only open escape route was on the Via Tiburtina to the east. It was on this poplar-lined avenue that the royal family fled by night in a green Fiat: the king—"pathetic, very old and rather gaga," according to a British diplomat—carrying a single shirt and two changes of underwear in a cheap fiberboard suitcase; the beefy queen, ingesting drops of uncertain provenance; and the middle-aged crown prince, Umberto, head in hands, muttering, "My God, what a figure we're cutting." Badoglio and a few courtiers fled with them in a seven-car convoy. Crossing the Apennines to the Adriatic port of Pescara, they scattered 50,000 lire among their carabinieri escorts, then boarded the submarine chaser *Baionetta* for passage to Brindisi, on the heel of the boot. In a suitable epitaph, a Free French newspaper observed, "The House of Savoy never finished a war on the same side it started, unless the war lasted long enough to change sides twice."

The biggest fish had escaped, but German troops snared thirty generals in Rome, as well as hundreds of Italian officials. A few firefights erupted, around the Caius Cestius pyramid and in Via Cavour and old Trastevere. Italian snipers near the railroad station crouched behind overturned carts to fire at Germans breezing into the Hotel Continentale. Swiss Guards at the Vatican swapped their pikes and halberds for rifles. Looting broke out near the Circus Maximus, as terrified Romans stockpiled cheese and bundled pasta, and buried their valuables in oilcloth parcels. "The Jews are in a panic and trying to leave the city," one witness reported. Italian envoys pleaded for a chance to negotiate Rome's fate.

Field Marshal Kesselring was disinclined to parley. He had narrowly escaped death at noon on September 8 in a decapitation attack on Frascati by 130 American B-17s; it was these planes and the subsequent detonation of four hundred tons of high explosives that Taylor and Gardiner heard from the Palazzo Caprara. The hour-long attack obliterated the bucolic vineyard town, including the charming restaurant with its panoramic view of St. Peter's where Kesselring had placed his command post. An estimated two thousand civilians and dozens of German staff officers died. Temporarily dispossessed of both his headquarters and his smile, Kesselring crawled from the rubble, convinced that the Italians had set him up. Even as he appealed to residual Fascist brotherhood, the field marshal threatened to blow up Rome's aqueducts and to raze the city. Among those trying to protect the capital, General Carboni mounted a brief, hapless defense; resistance soon sputtered and died. "It is finished, but there is no need to despair," Carboni told another officer. "I have saved what there is to be saved."

Kesselring, now viceroy of the Eternal City, shrewdly allowed Italian troops to leave the capital with marching bands and unfurled flags. There would be ample time to settle scores. Much had become clear to the Italophile who had so steadfastly clung to Rome's pledges of fidelity. He could see in retrospect that "every event was like a flash of sheet lightning, more foreshadowing than clearing the atmosphere." Suddenly Italy was just "a card missing from the pack." As for the Italians, Kesselring added, "I loved these people. Now I can only hate them."

## The Stillest Shoes the World Could Boast

UNMOLESTED and apparently undetected, Kent Hewitt's armada of 642 ships steamed north in a thousand-square-mile swatch of the Mediterranean, bound for HARPSICHORD, as the Gulf of Salerno was now code-named. If the sea remained calm, the sun was searing. Little ventilation penetrated the packed troop holds, and few were as lucky as those aboard the converted Polish liner *Sobieski*, which had a swimming pool. Food on most vessels during the three-day passage was dreadful. "Whenever I tore a bun open and found a worm, I would cover it with jam and butter and eat ahead," a mortarman wrote his family in Indiana. "I couldn't be watching out for those worms, as they had to look out for themselves." Troops in the three assault divisions—two British and one American— packed and repacked their kit, stuffing a week's supply of salt tablets and Atabrine pills in knotted condoms before scribbling just-in-case letters to be left with their battalion chaplains.

The usual muddles and nugacities followed the fleet. Four thousand combat soldiers had sailed without weapons, which were in short supply in North Africa (along with binoculars and wristwatches); they would disembark at Salerno as they had boarded: unarmed. Troops of the 36th Division wandered through the sweltering holds with cans of paint, heeding a recent War Department decree that the white-star insignia on all Army vehicles now be enclosed within a white circle. On one British ship, a loftman released his carrier pigeons for a bit of exercise only to see them wing toward Africa, never to return. The cargo manifest on a vessel loaded in Oran simply listed "400 cases military impedimenta." Hewitt was so incensed by loading infractions—bombs had been dumped into troop holds, for instance, and crates of shoes marked "Signal Equipment"—that he ordered a broad search for contraband. No little befuddlement resulted because the British Army and Royal Navy used different numbering systems for their LSTs. "Both numbers are painted on the hull of the ship and cause considerable confusion," the British X Corps noted. So many changes had disfigured the fleet's sailing formations that a senior Navy operations officer confessed to keeping himself "informed by hearsay" because he was "not sure who was where."

As always, soldiers found diversions to take their minds off the coming battle. British Commandos gambled away the hours with endless games of housey-housey, akin to bingo. Tommies in the 56th Division, concerned that their desert-bleached khaki would be too conspicuous on a mottled European battlefield, dyed the uniforms in cauldrons of boiling coffee; the treatment left them not only darker but also scented with espresso. Aboard the *Duchess of Bedford*, after listening to an intelligence officer lecture at length on Italian politics, one soldier told his diary, "We know nothing." Others studied the government-issue "Italian Phrase Book," which included not only the words for lobster, oysters, and butter, but five pages of handy medical language—*Arrestate il sangue!* "Stop the bleeding!"—as well as the hopeful *Voglio passare la notte*, "I want to spend the night," and the eternal *Il governo americano vi pagherà*, "The U.S. government will pay you."

Aboard Hewitt's flagship, the voyage evoked the dreamy days when *Ancon* had catered to well-heeled travelers on Caribbean runs from Panama to New York. White-jacketed mess stewards served thick steaks with apple pie and ice cream; the leather chairs and perpetual card games in the officers' lounge reminded one passenger of "the bridge room at the Yale Club." Clark sat for a few rubbers but again seemed distracted. "General Clark is feeling the strain of this period of waiting," his aide noted. "There is nothing that he himself can do now." To pass the hours he napped, did situps, and paced the weather deck to work up "a good sweat." Summoning reporters to his stateroom, Clark likened AVALANCHE to "spitting right into the lion's mouth."

Some 55,000 assault troops would invade Salerno, with a comparable number of reinforcements to follow. On Fifth Army's left, the British X Corps was to land two infantry divisions and pivot toward Naples; on the right, the U.S. VI Corps would initially land only the 36th Division, with part of the 45th Division afloat in reserve. "It's the most daring plan of the war," Clark said as a steward poured coffee into paper cups. "You can't play with fire without the risk of burning your fingers."

The 36th, entering combat for the first time, derived from the Texas National Guard. Both the officer cadre and enlisted ranks were dominated by Texans, from Carrizo Springs and Raymondville, Harlingen and Laredo, Houston and San Antonio. In stateside bars, 36th troops had been known to insist that all patrons stand and remove their caps whenever "Deep in the Heart of Texas" was sung. Since leaving Oran hardly an hour had passed on the division flagship, the *Samuel Chase,* without a rollicking chorus of "The Eyes of Texas." The division commander, Major General Fred L. Walker, was a Regular Army officer from Ohio, but he carried in his kit bag a Lone Star flag given him by Governor Coke Stevenson. When his men sang, Walker sang too.

How much did the Germans know? a reporter asked Clark. Would AVALANCHE catch them unawares? "We can't expect to achieve strategical surprise," Clark replied. "But we do hope to achieve a degree of tactical surprise." The British planned a fifteen-minute naval cannonade to soften defenses before the landings began. The 36th Division, on the contrary, had elected to forgo naval fire. General Walker believed the Germans were too dispersed for shelling to be effective—"I see no point to killing a lot of peaceful Italians and destroying their homes," he said. He also was wary of short rounds falling on his men, and he still hoped that "our landing may not be discovered until we are ashore." Hewitt had bitterly disagreed, waving his ten-page list of 275 targets with precise grid locations for machine-gun nests, bridges, and enemy observation posts. The admiral considered it "fantastic to assume that we could surprise them," but Clark had sided with Walker, in part on the assumption that only Italian troops would defend the beaches. The prodigious power of naval gunnery displayed in North Africa, Sicily, and the Pacific was spurned, foolishly.

At 6:30 P.M. on Wednesday, September 8, barely eight hours before the landings were to commence, Clark joined Hewitt in the admiral's cabin, where they heard Eisenhower's armistice announcement on Radio Algiers and Badoglio's subsequent affirmation. Many ships piped the broadcasts over their public address systems; officers with megaphones quickly spread the word to smaller craft.

Jubilation erupted across the fleet. On *Duchess of Bedford*, Eisenhower's final words were drowned out by the "dancing, kissing, backslapping and roaring of the troops." Aboard H.M.S. *Hilary*, they flung helmets in the air or banged them on the steel deck, yelling, "The Eyeties have jagged it in!" Those on the destroyer U.S.S. *Mayo* brayed, "The war is over!" The commotion "sounded like a ladies' pink tea," one Navy officer complained. "Yap, yap, yap." Chaplains offered prayers of deliverance, Grenadier Guards hoisted toasts to "the downfall of Italy," and a battalion piper was ordered to compose "The Scots Guards March Through Naples." British tars on a warship near Messina watched Italians light fireworks and dance in a floodlit church piazza. "Seldom in history," a Royal Navy officer observed, "can a people have celebrated so hilariously the complete defeat of their country."

Soldiers jettisoned bandoliers and grenades, stuffing their ammo pouches with extra cigarettes. A British officer regretted leaving his dinner jacket in Africa. "I never again expect to witness such scenes of sheer joy," Clark's aide wrote. "We would dock in Naples harbor unopposed, with an olive branch in one hand and an opera ticket in the other." Some lamented the lost opportunity for glory. A 36th Division artilleryman wrote his father, "Our chance to prove ourselves had vanished."

Hewitt noted with alarm that Fifth Army's "keen fighting edge" had been dulled. Officers prowled the decks, trying to talk sense to men now convinced that Salerno's beaches would be undefended. "Stop it, you bloody fools," a British captain bellowed, while on H.M.S. *Princess Astrid* a large sign advised, "Take your ammunition with you. You'll need it." Major General Ernest J. Dawley, commander of the U.S. VI Corps, warned soldiers on the U.S.S. *Funston* that they would "have to fight like horned Comanches if we mean to get ashore and stay there." The troops raised a cheer, then resumed their poker games on the fantail. "Expect a hostile shore," a 36th Division officer told his men. "Go in shooting."

The call to general quarters sixty miles from Salerno restored a modicum of sobriety. "The ship's company will man their stations," naval officers intoned. "Gunners, man your guns." Landlubbers aboard *Ancon* tried to parse the "plan of the day" for September 9: "The ship will be hove to for a while and then anchored, with the anchor at short stay ready to slip at a moment's notice, with a full steaming watch on and full steam at the throttles." Any residual hilarity dissolved at 8:15 P.M., when Luftwaffe planes attacked the fleet with flares, bombs, and torpedoes, though to little effect. As men blackened their hands and faces with burnt cork, a sergeant in the

143rd Infantry observed, "Imagination makes cowards of us all." John Steinbeck studied the pearly mists rising from the Mediterranean. "Each man, in this last night in the moonlight, looks strangely at the others and sees death there," he wrote.

Just before ten P.M., on the approach to HARPSICHORD, lookouts spied blue signal lights from the beacon submarine H.M.S. *Shakespeare* and the destroyer *Cole.* "Do you think we've been spotted by the enemy?" someone asked Hewitt on *Ancon*'s flag bridge. "If they haven't," replied the admiral, "they're blind." Off the port bow, a faint ruby glow radiated from Vesuvius. Capri appeared, as the official U.S. Navy history later reported, "swimming in a silver sea." The loamy scent of land drifted from the Sorrento Peninsula.

Twelve miles offshore, at the hundred-fathom line, captains ordered all engines stopped just before midnight. Water hissed along the hulls as the vessels lost weigh. Chains rattled. Anchors splashed. A bosun's whistle trilled. Each ship swung gently on its moorings. The night was bright and balmy, with barely a whisper of wind. "In peacetime," said an officer on *Hilary,* "honeymoon couples would pay hundreds of pounds for this." An eruption of tracer fire on the distant shore reminded Sergeant Newton H. Fulbright of "a red, beaded curtain rising in a theater." Someone murmured, "I think they know we're here."

Clark stood beside Hewitt, laved in soft red light on the flag bridge. Sailors tied manila lanyards to ten-gallon coffee urns and lowered them to the boat crews. "You'll be in total command by tonight," Hewitt said. Clark nodded. "I can't help thinking that casualties may be high. Pray God they won't."

Gold and crimson flares blossomed inshore, followed by the rumble of demolitions in Salerno harbor. Winches creaked: more boats eased into the water. An overburdened 36th Division soldier likened the creeping descent on the cargo nets to "crawling down a ten-story building on a mesh ladder with a file cabinet on your back." From below came the cough of landing craft. Brightened by moonset, their dim lights danced on the sea as the boat flotillas at last turned eastward and beat for the distant beaches, tugged by destiny.

A reporter scribbling in a notebook wrote of Clark: "tall, smiling, appearing unconcerned." The army commander composed a short dispatch for Alexander at two A.M.: "Arrived at transport area on schedule. Boats have been lowered and are in position. Sea is calm. Indications are that beaches will be reached on time."

In his diary he later jotted, "Hewitt and I on bridge. Helpless feeling. All out of my hands."

\*   \*   \*

"What's the weather like at Salerno," the poet Horace wrote a friend in 20 B.C., "and what sort of people shall I encounter there?" Since then the seaside Roman town had been occupied by Lombards in the ninth and tenth centuries, and Normans in the eleventh, among them one brutish knight known as the Weasel. By the twelfth century, Salerno's medical school was considered Europe's finest, lauded by Petrarch and St. Thomas Aquinas alike. Among the bones entombed in the local basilica were supposedly those of Matthew, the Roman tax collector turned apostle, who became the patron saint of bankers and bookies.

The latter-day town had grown to seventy thousand souls, with a handsome corniche fronting the Corso Garibaldi and tunny boats bobbing in the harbor. War had already come to Salerno: Allied bombing raids sent terrorized women rushing through the streets shrieking, "*Basta! Basta!*"— "Enough!" Soon the vegetable market and the gelateria and the tunny boats were wrecked, and messages chalked on charred walls listed both the resident dead and new addresses for the survivors. Many had dragged their bedding into the hills, as their ancestors had a millennium earlier in flight from predatory Saracens and the *mal aria*. South of Salerno, the coastal plain was watered by the Sele and Calore Rivers, which flowed parallel for seven miles before converging four miles from the sea. Tobacco, olives, and teardrop tomatoes grew in the fecund lowlands. But the most singular feature lay on the southern lip of the plain, at Paestum, a sixth-century-B.C. Greek colony famed in antiquity for its roses and violets, and still among the grandest complexes of Doric temples outside Athens. It was precisely here that the U.S. 36th Division planned to come ashore, while the British X Corps, comprising the 46th and 56th Divisions, landed twelve miles north, between the Sele's mouth and Salerno town. Darby's Rangers and British Commandos would also fall on the Sorrento Peninsula, seizing the mountain passes from Naples.

*What sort of people shall I encounter there?* On the morning of September 9, 1943, certainly many Germans. Neither Kesselring nor his lieutenants believed that Montgomery's landing in Calabria a week earlier presaged an Anglo-American march up the entire length of Italy; in recent days, Salerno had seemed an increasingly likely place for the Allies to force open a back door to Naples and Rome. German reconnaissance on September 6 detected assembling British aircraft carriers, and a German naval analysis warned that "a strike in the direction of the gulf of Salerno is not precluded." Another convoy was spotted north of Palermo a day later. A midafternoon alert on September 8 cited a "large naval force of more than 100 ships" approaching the southwest coast.

Following the capitulation announcement three hours later, Kesselring displayed the agility so characteristic of his generalship. With Hitler's authorization, at eight P.M. he invoked Operation ACHSE, a secret contingency plan drafted in August to disarm Italian forces and take over key fortifications. Confirmation that the Allied armada was closing on Salerno restored Kesselring's smile; at least he would not have to fight an invasion force near Rome while also subduing the capital. The invaders "must be completely annihilated and in addition thrown into the sea," he declared. "The British and Americans must realize that they are hopelessly lost against the concentrated German might."

That German might took the form of Tenth Army, created in mid-August and reinforced with retreating units from Sicily. Army command fell to a veteran of France, Yugoslavia, and Russia: General Heinrich von Vietinghoff, a capable Prussian infantryman with baggy eyes, graying temples, and a little Hitler mustache. Some 135,000 German troops now occupied southern Italy, and Kesselring channeled his resentment at Italy's betrayal—he called it "a spiritual burden for me"—into demands for swift vengeance. "No mercy must be shown the traitors," he cabled Vietinghoff. "Long live the Führer." As Allied soldiers danced on the decks of their ships Wednesday evening, Wehrmacht troops burst through the oak door of the office belonging to General Don Ferrante Gonzaga, commander of the Italian coastal division at Salerno. "Hand me your pistol, General," a German major demanded. Gonzaga stepped back from his desk, fumbling with the Beretta in his holster. "A Gonzaga never surrenders," he shouted. "*Viva Italia!*" A burst of Schmeisser fire to the head and chest cut him down. "He died as a great soldier," the major observed.

With Gonzaga's troops melting away or in German custody, defense of the Gulf of Salerno fell to the 16th Panzer Division. Claiming to be the first German unit on the Volga, the division subsequently crawled away from Stalingrad with only 4,000 survivors. Now rebuilt under General Rudolf Sieckenius, the 16th Panzer was perhaps the best equipped division in Italy, with 17,000 men, 104 functioning tanks, and 700 machine guns.

Sieckenius had split his forces into four battle groups, positioned about six miles apart down the length of the Sele plain. Communications were poor and Highway 18, the coastal road that would bring any German reinforcements, lay within range of Allied naval guns. Still, the defenders had fashioned eight strongpoints, from Salerno in the north to Paestum and Agropoli in the south, each a quarter mile wide and fitted with mines, automatic weapons, mortars, heavy guns, and an abatis of felled trees. As Fifth Army's landing craft swarmed across the bight, the Germans waited, alert and aggrieved, unburdened by delusion that the war might be over.

\* \* \*

On the far right of the Allied line, scout boats spaced half a mile apart flashed red, green, yellow, and blue lights at 3:10 A.M. to signify the four beaches upon which the approaching assault battalions of the 36th Division were to make land at Paestum. As the two-hour run from the transport anchorage neared an end, a soldier in a plywood Higgins boat finished the pocket novel he had been reading and "stood up to see what this war was all about."

For a moment—a long, queer moment—silence held sway except for the nattering boat engines. Down came the ramps with a clank and a splash, and the first riflemen scuttled nearly dryshod onto the shingle at precisely 3:30 A.M. Then a constellation of silver flares hissed overhead, bathing the beaches in cold brilliance, and the sawmill sound of a German machine gun broke the spell, followed by another and another and another. Mortars crumped, and from the high ground to the east and south came the shriek of 88mm shells, green fireballs that whizzed through the dunes at half a mile per second, trailing golden plumes of dust.

Bullets plumped the sea and slapped the boat ramps. "You can't dig foxholes in a boat," one sergeant observed with evident sorrow. To an artillery officer from Austin, the spattering shell fragments sounded like "spring rain on a taxi window going up Congress Avenue." A second wave landed eight minutes behind the first, and a third wave eight minutes after that; but fire discomposed the four subsequent waves as coxswains swerved left or right or back to sea without unloading. "Shells were *wopping* in all around us," a soldier in the third wave recalled. "We knew that when the ramp fell those red and yellow tracers would eat right into us." A landing craft hit nose-on by a tank shell "seemed to rise completely out of the water," one witness reported; a second shell caught the vessel's stern, spinning it around and flinging bodies over the splintered gunwales. A medic described swimming to another blazing boat forty yards from shore. "Some of the boys were on fire," he later wrote his wife:

> We could hear the bullets hitting the water all around us. . . . I climbed up in the boat. There were four in there, a major and three enlisted men. The fire was so hot by then my clothes started steaming. Went over to the major. He was burnt, bad. The major was dead. . . . I drug the three soldiers to the ramp.

On the beach, soldiers wriggled out of backpacks ignited by grazing tracers. "I'd rather been born a baby girl," one soldier muttered. Teller mines buried ten yards beyond the waterline exploded in geysers of sand

and shredded tires from the first jeeps ashore. The dunes were as hellish as the beach, raked with fire from a dense wood line just inland and from a fifty-foot stone turret built centuries earlier as a watchtower against Saracens. German gunners on Paestum's cyclopean walls poured plunging fire on every snapping twig, every rustle in the long grass. Panzers lurked in barns and sheds, firing point-blank on riflemen creeping past. "Great deal of confusion in landing," a surgeon told his diary. "Tough going. I see I am going to lose weight."

The first Luftwaffe planes arrived with the morning light shortly after four A.M., strafing and bombing, as the Navy's official history recorded, "on a scale never before or since equaled in a Mediterranean landing." An LST captain told his gun crews: "Steady now, steady, here they come. . . . Steady. *Fire away*, and good hunting." After the rejoicing that had met Italy's capitulation, an officer observed, many troops had "the feeling that someone had let them down." As the battle intensified, the reporter Don Whitehead overheard someone suggest, "Maybe it would be better for us to fight without an armistice."

By six A.M., two infantry regiments—the 141st and 142nd—had made land, with the 143rd soon to follow. But the foothold was tenuous. Each assault battalion carried two hundred smoke pots, big buckets of hexachlorethane that were ignited and dropped near the beaches to create a milky haze screening the landing craft. Offshore, destroyers darted through the anchorage and around the incoming LSTs, "trailing ribbons of white, choking smoke," as John Steinbeck noted. Ventilation fans sucked smoke into LST tank decks—"the sound of coughing is deafening," Steinbeck added—and some coxswains were forced to navigate through the miasma by compass heading.

Still, German observers on Monte Soprano and other high perches saw well enough to mass fires. DUKWs hauling artillery and antitank guns to Yellow and Blue Beaches sheered away under the sleeting fire; another sixty lay out of range off Green Beach, and 125 loitered near Red. Six LCTs attempting to land thirty tanks at 6:15 A.M. also hauled off rather than risk sinking. Three shells smashed into an LCT carrying part of the 191st Tank Battalion; the blasts shattered the pilothouse, killed seven men, and set fire to a Sherman tank, which was shoved into the sea only with enormous effort. LST officers scrambled from side to side of the bridge as German shells struck port, then starboard, then port again; *LST 336* alone took eighteen hits. Drumfire fell the length of the beachhead: a Royal Navy cruiser intercepted a dozen vessels headed for Salerno port and warned, "The harbor's under enemy fire. You'll be jolly well shot up if you go in there."

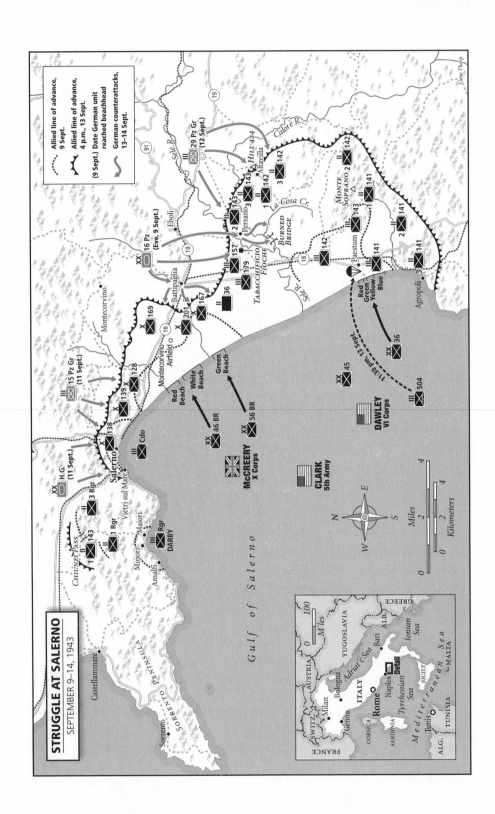

**STRUGGLE AT SALERNO**
SEPTEMBER 9–14, 1943

Allied line of advance, 9 Sept.

Allied line of advance, 4 p.m., 13 Sept.

(9 Sept.) Date German unit reached beachhead

German counterattacks, 13–14 Sept.

Gene Thorp

AVALANCHE planners had hoped the assault vanguard would be four thousand yards inland by daylight—to secure the beaches from mortar and machine-gun fire—and far enough by dusk on D-day to exterminate German artillery still capable of ranging the waterline. Instead, by midmorning the beachhead in a few spots hardly extended four hundred yards. A bulldozer crew trying to scrape an exit from the beach was incinerated by an 88mm shell. "They were completely black except for their teeth, which seemed whiter than living ones," a witness reported. On Blue Beach in the far south, a battalion was pinned to the dunes and would remain pinned for twenty hours; hundreds of men burrowed into the laurel brakes and ice plant, filching ammunition from the dead. There was more to filch after Mark IV panzers broke through the American line. "It was like fighting tanks barehanded," a lieutenant colonel in the 141st Infantry reported:

> I saw riflemen swarm over the top of moving German tanks trying to shoot through slits or throw grenades inside. Other tanks would machine gun them off. They ran over wounded men . . . and spun their treads.

An intelligence officer later found that medics had laid the dead "in a row, side by side, shoulder to shoulder, with extreme precision as if about to present arms." Their feet protruded from the covering blankets, "the stillest shoes the world could boast," one staff officer wrote. Other bodies were propped into sitting positions, "so it wouldn't look so bad to the troops coming in." A radioed query to the *Ancon*—among the few coherent messages to get through—gave Clark and Hewitt a sense of conditions ashore: "On what beach shall we put our dead?"

Salvation arrived shortly after nine A.M. Minesweepers finished clearing an inshore channel, allowing warships to press toward the beaches. Fire control parties, whose operations had been hampered for hours by balky radios, smoke, enemy aircraft, and utter confusion on the beach, now began sprinkling gunfire around the beachhead rim. By late morning, destroyers steamed within a hundred yards of shore, pumping 5-inch shells into the face of Monte Soprano. The cruiser U.S.S. *Savannah* soon opened on German tank concentrations with scores of 6-inch shells. Her sister *Philadelphia* flushed three dozen panzers detected by a spotter plane in a copse near Red Beach; salvo upon salvo fell on the tanks for nearly an hour, reportedly destroying half a dozen and scattering the rest. Eleven thousand tons of naval shells would be fired at Salerno, almost comparable in heft to the bombardments at Iwo Jima and Okinawa later in the war, but no barrage was more timely than the D-day shoot.

As German troops backed into the sheltering hills, two American regiments pushed east past Paestum's temples—"This place looks just like the cover of a Latin book," one soldier remarked—and north toward the Sele River. A third regiment, the 141st, remained trapped near Blue Beach by enfilading fire from high ground to the south. Forty-eight DUKWs finally made shore, each carrying a howitzer, a six-man gun crew, and twenty-one rounds.

Near a tobacco barn at Casa Vannula, three miles inland, guns from the 151st Field Artillery arrived at noon, just as a dozen panzers closed on the 36th Division command post; in what one major called "hip-shooting with howitzers," gunners demolished a stone wall for a better field of fire, cut their fuzes, then yanked the lanyards at two hundred yards' range. By 12:30 P.M., greasy smoke boiled from four burning tanks and the others had dispersed.

"It was thrilling," said Walker, the 36th Division commander, who had watched from the gun line. The shallow American beachhead was secure, for now.

A dozen miles to the north, the British also had won a lodgment on the hostile shore.

German air attacks had harassed the fleet even before the landing boats were lowered, and 88mm airbursts lacerated some of the approaching landing craft. Dive-bombers caught the U.S.S. *Nauset,* an ocean tug assisting the Royal Navy. Fire engulfed the boat deck, then scaled a ladder to the chart room before spiraling upward in fifty-foot orange flares behind the bridge. Powerless, rudderless, and listing, *Nauset* struck a mine, snapped in half, and sank in sixty-five fathoms, taking her captain and first mate. More than fifty other crewmen were killed or wounded.

But the preliminary naval bombardment eschewed by the Americans helped clear Red, White, and Green Beaches for the British. Hundreds of rockets flew from modified landing craft with a pyrotechnic *swish-swish-swish* that was "quite terrifying even when expected." The 46th Division, on the left, and the 56th Division, on the right, began wading ashore at 3:30 A.M. At the water's edge, a sailor escorting the Coldstream Guards stood waving a huge flag, urging, "This way to Naples, boys!" Among the "essential assault stores" first rolled from the landing craft ramps was a piano, soon followed by crated chickens, geese, and turkeys, all lashed to jeep hoods, as well as a sow for the officers' mess.

By day's end, X Corps would land about a third of its strength—23,000 soldiers, 80 tanks, and 325 guns—despite what one chronicler called "unutterable confusion" on some beaches as subsequent waves intermingled the two divisions. Besides the usual lost coxswains, confused soldiers, and fuming beachmasters, German gunfire soon intensified. *LST 375* caught nine 88mm rounds, with many near misses. *LST 357* suffered two dozen casualties. *LST 365* collided in-shore with *LST 430*, knocking her beam-on to the beach; enemy shells wounded *430*'s skipper in all four limbs, sprayed steel through the tank deck, set fire to an ammunition truck, and terrorized wounded soldiers as they hobbled aboard for evacuation from the shingle.

Beyond the beaches, the invasion unfolded with heady initial promise. Tommies rushed three miles inland to seize Montecorvino airfield, the preeminent D-day objective. Astonished Luftwaffe pilots pelted across the runway to their cockpits only to be shot down by tanks and self-propelled guns that blew apart three dozen parked planes. Yet the field remained within easy range of German guns, a misfortune discovered by an unwitting American air force colonel, John G. Ayling, who landed in a B-25 with a cargo of radio equipment. The aircraft had hardly taxied to a stop when 88mm shells riddled the fuselage, killing Ayling and his pilot, burning the plane to the spars, and, as it transpired, ending Allied hopes of using Montecorvino for the next eleven days.

For every heartening advance, the British front suffered a disheartening setback. The 5th Battalion of the Royal Hampshire Regiment had pushed six hundred yards inland down a narrow lane hemmed in with high stone walls when a German counterattack caught two companies and the battalion headquarters like sheep in a slaughterhouse chute. Three assault guns fired point-blank as the Hampshires clawed at slick stones soon made slicker with blood. Grenadiers in half-tracks rumbled through the lane, crushing the living and the dead alike; a Hampshire radio operator was found with working headphones on his ears and his legs flattened to the thickness of a table leaf. Forty Hampshires died and more than three hundred others were wounded or led away to German cages.

Past Montecorvino, Tommies in khaki drill hurried east toward the town of Battipaglia, soon known as Batty P, a squat, melancholy Fascist showcase straddling the key intersection of Highways 18 and 19, five miles inland. The 9th Battalion of the Royal Fusiliers capered forward by tractor, dray horse, barrow, and bicycle. Crossing dikes and tobacco fields, they entered Batty P shortly after midnight on Friday, September 10, exultant but isolated. German infiltrators in camouflage face paint soon crept through swales and irrigation ditches to flank the British salient. One wary Guardsman detected "a feeling of looseness, of porosity, where all should have been tightly sealed."

As another hot, luminous Mediterranean day dawned on Friday, German counterattacks added panic to that loose feeling. Fusiliers scoured westward past the Lombardy poplars and oleander, warning of Tiger tanks "like bloody great battleships." Some flung away their weapons, yelling, "Back to the beaches! We're overrun!" By Friday afternoon, a Guards officer wrote, "the small roads were full of frightened soldiers, many retiring pell-mell regardless of officers." Short, violent scraps flared across the beachhead, gunfights rather than battles. Outside Battipaglia at a three-acre complex encircled with an eight-foot spiked fence—labeled "Tabacchificio" on military maps, it was in fact a tomato canning plant—the 2nd Scots Guards made a valiant but bootless attempt to oust German squatters with grenade volleys and bursts of fire down darkened corridors. After reverses on the left flank, some Grenadiers clung to an overloaded truck, shouting in alarm. "They're coming! They're through!"

They were not coming, nor were they through. The line stiffened, shoving the Germans back to Batty P, and by early Saturday the British held roughly eight miles of beachfront that extended inland for two to four miles. British Commandos held a smaller, shallower adjacent plot at Salerno town, including the port. Every occupied inch was vulnerable to German guns—the "demented choirs of wailing shells," as Wilfred Owen had written on a different battlefield—and those without shovels soon dug with their hands. As one artillery major observed, "We've got them just where they want us."

Only on the extreme left of the Allied line could the invaders report unqualified success. Bill Darby's Rangers had captured the resort villages of Maiori, Minori, and Amalfi without opposition, then climbed a serpentine road through groves of thick-skinned lemons the size of a child's skull to seize the hogback crest of the Sorrento Peninsula. Five hours after crossing the black-sand beaches, Rangers held Chiunzi Pass, six miles inland and four thousand feet up.

"If ever there was an artilleryman's dream," Darby later said, "here it was." The windswept defile offered a panoramic view of Naples, Vesuvius's purple shoulders, and all German military traffic crawling south toward Salerno on Highway 18. "This is the place for fighting," said Robert Capa upon reaching Chiunzi. "It reminds me of Spain." Rangers nested like cliff swallows in the ridge face, then trimmed the chestnut branches for a better view and called for fire. "We have taken up a position in the enemy's rear," Darby radioed Clark on *Ancon*. "We'll stay here until hell freezes over if necessary."

Soon a battleship, two cruisers, and a plug-ugly, flat-bottomed British monitor crowded the Amalfi hollow, where Sirens once lured sailors onto rocks "white with the bones of many men." With their guns cocked like howitzers to clear the mountain crest, the ships unlimbered in a concussive mêlée of smoke rings and shrieking shells that soared above the pass like "a freight train with the caboose wobbling from side to side," one Ranger recalled. German infantry in long-billed caps furiously counterattacked Chiunzi, firing mortar barrages through holes chopped in farmhouse roofs below the pass and trying to flank the Ranger pinnacles by scaling higher pinnacles. The reporter Richard Tregaskis described "showers of white phosphorus rising like luminous fountains" from the saddles. Wounded Rangers sheltered in a stone roadside tavern at the top of the pass—now renamed Eighty-eight Junction—with mattresses wedged against the window; others filled a Catholic church in Maiori that had been converted to a hospital. OSS agents hired three hundred Italians—$1 a day for men, 75 cents for boys, plus two cans of C rations—to lug mortar shells and water up the switchback road, where poppies danced like candle flames. One officer forever remembered "that long line of men and boys in rags winding up Chiunzi Pass, each with his load."

Others forever remembered deep-chested Darby, ubiquitous and apparently sleepless, still a lieutenant colonel but leading a force that soon swelled in size to that usually commanded by a major general. Always washed and shaved, his uniform somehow always creased, he radioed orders using the call sign Snow White from a command post in the ramshackle, eight-room San Francisco Hotel. To various Bashfuls, Grumpys, and Dopeys he dictated map coordinates: "I want to give this a hell of a pasting. . . . I want to blast the crap out of this hill."

*Until hell freezes over,* Darby had vowed. Of all the commanders ashore in Fifth Army, only he could truthfully radio Clark, "We are sitting pretty." For the rest, American and British, in VI Corps and in X Corps, Naples still lay far to the north, and no man doubted that the beachhead had become a magnet for every *Gefreiter* in southern Italy with a machine pistol. At a cost of a thousand Anglo-American casualties, Fifth Army in two days had won a footing ashore; yet the struggle at Salerno would not be for the beach but for the beachhead.

"Corpses lay on the sand. The living ran for cover," wrote one soldier after slogging ashore near Salerno. "There was," he added, "an uneasy feeling of a hitch somewhere."

"In the land of theory . . . there is none of war's friction," the official British military history of Salerno observed.

> The troops are, as in fact they were not, perfect Tactical Men, uncannily skillful, impervious to fear, bewilderment, boredom, hunger, thirst, or tiredness. Commanders know what in fact they did not know. . . .

Lorries never collide, there is always a by-pass at the mined road-block, and the bridges are always wider than the flood. Shells fall always where they should fall.

Salerno did not lie in the land of theory. Frictions had accumulated since H-hour. Mistakes were made. Hitches occurred. Three miscalculations in particular would shape the battle, taking the Allied force from the benighted, braying optimism of invasion eve to the brink of obliteration five days later.

The first hitch involved command of the American force. With General Walker leading the 36th Division at Paestum, Clark intended to keep his VI Corps commander, Major General Dawley, out of the battle until September 11, the third day of AVALANCHE, when there would be enough troops ashore to warrant a corps headquarters. A decade older than Clark and also his senior in permanent rank, Mike Dawley was a stocky, cautious artilleryman from Wisconsin who had been described in his West Point yearbook as "a quiet lad that one seldom sees or hears of." A decorated protégé of George Marshall in the Great War, he had a small mouth, a pushbroom mustache, and a worried look. The brow would only become more furrowed. "Don't bite off more than you can chew," he had warned Clark during the Salerno planning, "and chew damn well."

Clark's plan to leave Dawley on the sidelines until D+2 lasted less than seven hours. With little information trickling out to *Ancon* from the beach, the army commander concluded that he needed another major general on the shingle to oversee the landings. Just after ten A.M. on September 9, Clark abruptly directed Dawley to "assume command of all American operations ashore." That order, however, was not decoded aboard the U.S.S. *Funston* until after three P.M., by which time Dawley had left his ship to explore the beachhead. A staff officer sent to find the corps commander returned empty-handed. Clark's message finally caught up with him at Paestum, and at nine P.M. Dawley departed to return to the *Funston* only to spend most of the night wandering the Mediterranean: German air attacks had scattered the anchorage, leaving no ship where it had been that afternoon. "Coxswain got lost, started for Naples, then Sardinia," Dawley told his diary. He finally reboarded *Funston* at four in the morning.

With his dispersed staff in disarray, Dawley returned to Paestum at eleven A.M., September 10, appearing at Walker's command post as an unwanted guest who now required radios, jeeps, and other support. Nominally in command of the battle since the previous morning, Dawley had actually commanded nothing. "Confusion and disorganization" beset VI Corps from the beginning, one staff colonel admitted. Dawley himself was exhausted and off balance. Another officer described him crouched in a ditch at Paestum watching howitzers battle panzers "pretty much as one would sit in the middle section of the stands at a tennis match and watch opponents bat the ball back and forth."

The second hitch had been foreseen by George Patton, who at Eisenhower's request reviewed the AVALANCHE plan on September 1. Patton noted that the Sele River had been chosen as the boundary between British forces in the north of the Salerno plain and Americans in the south. "Just as sure as God lives," Patton said, jabbing his finger at the map, "the Germans will attack down that river." As X Corps and VI Corps fought their separate fights on D-day, a seven-mile gap, bisected by the Sele, persisted between the two forces; neither could support the other. Clark recognized the rift, but not its vulnerability. "The gap," he had told Hewitt on Thursday night, "is not too serious."

On Friday morning, as Dawley struggled to take command, Clark also went ashore to inspect the beachhead. In the Paestum tobacco barn that served as the 36th Division command post, General Walker described the situation as being "well in hand." The gap between his force and the British persisted, but German troops seemed to be pulling back. The American beachhead had expanded, unloading proceeded apace, and another six-thousand-man regiment—the 179th Infantry, from the 45th Division—had splashed ashore. At one P.M., back aboard *Ancon,* Clark radioed Alexander: "Have just returned from personal reconnaissance of VI Corps sector. Situation there is good." To help unite his two corps, Clark ordered his last reserves, two battalions from the 157th Infantry, to make shore at the Sele. Yet the yawning gap remained, an ominous corridor to the sea between Batty P and the south bank of the river.

The third hitch derived from the failure to secure Montecorvino airfield. Consequences descended, like clattering dominoes. Instead of having more than twenty Allied fighter squadrons ashore in short order, Fifth Army was forced to depend on aircraft from distant Sicily and on little escort carriers like H.M.S. *Battler* and H.M.S. *Stalker,* which had intended to withdraw on September 10. Pilots grew fatigued and the number of accidents soared; more than forty carrier-based Seafires crashed, mostly during deck landings hampered by light winds, callow aviators, and flimsy undercarriages. (The accident rate later improved after mechanics sawed nine inches off each propeller blade, giving more clearance from the flight deck.) When a naval officer told *Ancon*'s crew over the public address system that "the operation in the bay of Salerno is going according to plan," a British pilot rescued at sea after bailing out heaved his shoe at the loudspeaker and barked, "Bloody nonsense."

Using flashlights for illumination and the stars as reference points, aviation engineers worked nights to build four emergency strips at Paestum and elsewhere on the littoral. But even such heroic "cow-pasture engineering"—filling ditches, felling trees, and chopping up rail fences for runway paving—produced only narrow, dusty, accident-plagued fields that were useless in wet weather. And although Allied air forces remained superior in quantity and quality, the Luftwaffe, which would fly 450 sorties against the beachhead on September 10 and 11, now displayed a pugnacity unseen in Sicily. Hewitt reduced his anxiety to four words in a message from *Ancon* on Saturday: "Air situation here critical."

A death struggle had begun, between Allied forces trying to mass enough combat strength to burst free of the Salerno plain and German forces trying to mass enough strength to fling the invaders into the sea. "I feel that AVALANCHE will be a matter of touch and go for the next few days," Eisenhower cabled the Combined Chiefs from Amilcar. "Our greatest asset now is confusion."

That was a thin reed. With Fifth Army's last reserves already committed, Alexander on September 10 urged Eighth Army to make haste from Calabria; Montgomery cheerfully agreed to "push on as soon as admin situation allows," while confiding to his diary that he intended to "act carefully." Despite modest opposition he issued no get-cracking orders and on September 11 declared a two-day rest for his 5th Division. The plodding march north resembled, in one description, "a holiday picnic."

On the other side of the hill, General Vietinghoff had his own worries in the German Tenth Army. Two-thirds of 16th Panzer Division's tanks had been knocked out in the first day of combat, leaving less than three dozen still in the fight. German scouts, wrapping their boots in rags to silence their footfalls, probed for seams in the Allied lines, but canals, stone walls, and those infernal naval guns hampered mobility. Allied bombers had pulverized most of the German airfields in southern Italy. And Kesselring's September 9 plea to divert two panzer divisions from Mantua, in northern Italy, to Salerno was denied by the Berlin high command, with profound consequences.

Hitches plagued Vietinghoff, too. His Tenth Army, only a few weeks old, had feeble quartermaster and signal units. Fuel worries persisted: a German tanker captain, fearing capture, had dumped his cargo into the sea; supply officers underestimated the extra stocks needed to move in mountainous terrain; and Frascati had provided the wrong locations for fuel depots in Calabria.

Still, reinforcements gathered in the shadowy glens east of Salerno, where confused villagers threw flowers at the passing panzers and shouted, "*Viva* English!" Vietinghoff estimated that by Monday, September 13, he would have five divisions ringing the beachhead, including Sicilian veterans like the Hermann Göring and 29th Panzer Grenadier. Company by company, regiment by regiment, they clanked into position with the precision of a clenching fist.

Within the Anglo-American beachhead, rumors flitted like small birds: that the British were in Naples; that the German garrison on Corsica had mutinied; that the Allies had landed in France; that Italian troops blocked the Brenner Pass; that the Germans were using poison gas. The savvy and the cynical soon credited only what their five senses confirmed. Few would dispute the 45th Division gunner who wrote in his diary, "From what we have seen, the surrender of Italy hasn't hindered the Germans too much."

Fresh dead joined the older dead. Walker reported that in the 36th Division alone 250 men had been killed in action by midday on September 10. Burial details next to Dawley's headquarters quickly hit water, and the shallow grave became a regular feature at Paestum. Soldiers dug a trench four feet deep and a hundred feet long, then straddled the trench line on planks to lower the dead with canvas straps. "The first body didn't have a mark on him, all his bones were broken and it was like lifting a bag of rags," recalled a 36th Division grave digger. Soon dead men lay "like railroad ties" until the trench was filled and another trench was dug. Wooden wedges served as grave markers, with the apex hammered into the ground; officers ordered a canvas screen erected around the Paestum cemetery to hide the forest of triangles growing there. "They've placed the graveyard, the latrines and the kitchen all in the same area for the convenience of the flies," an Army engineer wrote.

Stretcher bearers hurrying to the rear learned to walk off-step, John Steinbeck observed, "so that the burden will not be jounced too much." U.S. Army Medical Forms 52b, 52c, and 52d were tied to wounded soldiers with wire clasps; in the space labeled "place where injured," an overworked medic often just scribbled, as medics in Italy would so often scribble: "Hill." The evacuation hospital near Red Beach was so overcrowded that many patients lay "along the walls of the tents with their heads inside and their bodies outside." Surgeons operated by flashlight at night—much medical equipment had been lost in the landings—and sometimes both doctor and patient were concealed beneath blankets. German shells fell anyway, and a battalion medical history noted that "patients displayed unusual agility in jumping from operating tables into foxholes."

Not all. Richard Tregaskis watched a Catholic chaplain give extreme unction to a young soldier with a bullet in the throat; when the boy's eyes grew fixed and glassy, a doctor turned away, muttering, "Well, that's the way it is." Alan Moorehead wrote of Italian peasants mourning a child killed in the cross fire: "They cried over it with a nameless uncomprehending anguish, blaming no human agency, attributing everything to the implacable will of God. . . . This attunement to blind providence communicated itself to the soldiers." Again, not all. When a German shell killed a lieutenant sleeping in his slit trench at Chiunzi, a comrade concluded, "I don't think God has anything to do with this war."

Wishful thinking flocked with rumor. "Our forces have captured Salerno," the BBC declared, "and are advancing steadily inland." Just after midnight on Saturday, Fifth Army reported, "Combat efficiency all units excellent." At two A.M. Clark radioed Alexander, "Am satisfied in both corps sectors." Fifth Army was ready to march north toward Naples. As often occurred on even the fiercest battlefields, an odd lull briefly becalmed Salerno. "The worst is over," the 142nd Infantry commander told his Texans. "We are more than a match for all that can meet us."

## The Moan of Lost Souls

A s a gloriously warm and clear Saturday morning spread across the Gulf of Salerno on September 11, Kent Hewitt harbored no illusions that the worst was over. Four German bombs had landed off *Ancon*'s starboard bow the previous day, and four more had detonated a hundred yards astern just before five A.M. The ship's size and antennae made her conspicuous—"like a sore thumb," Hewitt complained—and radio intercepts revealed that German pilots were specifically hunting the flagship. Trenchant scuttlebutt could be heard about whether General Clark ever intended to "get off and get into the action" by moving his headquarters permanently ashore, allowing *Ancon* to return to Algiers.

Thirty "red alerts" had sounded in thirty-six hours, and frequent hailstorms of spent antiaircraft splinters forced sailors topside to flatten against the bulkheads. Even *Ancon*'s mess orderlies had joined the human chains passing ammunition to the gun turrets. Belowdecks, with safety hatches closed and ventilation fans turned off to avoid sucking in acrid smoke, the crew sweltered. At night, helmsmen tried to minimize the ship's silhouette by steering straight toward or away from the moon at twelve knots—slow enough to shrink her wake but fast enough to complicate any U-boat captain's torpedo trigonometry.

Three days into AVALANCHE, Hewitt's cares had doubled and redoubled. The beaches were now so congested that fuel, food, and ammo lay heaped in the shallows, drawing enemy fire and impeding further unloading. Army and Navy officers argued bitterly over who outranked whom and which service bore responsibility for clearing the shingle. Drivers could not find their vehicles, surgeons their scalpels, mortarmen their mortars. Sailors playing "cowboys and Indians" aboard one of *Ancon*'s barges had peppered floating crates, first with pistol fire, then with 20mm slugs. The scouring action of LST and other landing craft propellers had created formidable new sandbars and runnels 150 yards offshore.

Worst of all, Luftwaffe attacks had intensified almost hourly. Hewitt this morning had sent Admiral Cunningham an urgent plea for more air cover. Repeated alerts and shooting throughout the night rattled skippers and swabs alike. "All are jumpy and nervous and washed out now," one LCT commander told his diary. The cruiser *Philadelphia* reported that her crew was drinking a daily average of a gallon of coffee per man, and the ship's surgeon had begun distributing "nerve pills."

The demand for pills must have spiked at 9:35 A.M., when an enormous explosion fifteen feet to starboard caused a "very marked hogging, sagging, and whipping motion" from *Philadelphia*'s bow to her fantail. Nine minutes later, as Clark and Hewitt stood on *Ancon*'s flag bridge sorting through frantic reports of the mysterious blast, a slender, eleven-foot cylinder dropped from a Luftwaffe Do-217 bomber at eighteen thousand feet. Plummeting in a tight spiral and trailing smoke, the object resembled a stricken aircraft.

In fact, as Hewitt soon surmised, it was a secret German weapon: a guided bomb with four stubby wings, an armor-piercing delayed fuze, and a six-hundred-pound warhead. A radio receiver and movable fins permitted a German bomber pilot to steer with a joystick from his cockpit, tracking the falling bomb by the burning flare mounted on its tail. Four years in development, the FX-1400—soon known as the Fritz-X or Smoky Joe—had first appeared in combat in late August, sinking a British sloop in the Bay of Biscay; on September 9, two Fritz-Xs had sunk the Italian battleship *Roma* near Corsica as she sortied to join the British fleet at Malta. Allied intelligence would dispatch agents from Norway to Greece in an effort to capture one of the missiles, which an intelligence officer called "the holy grail." For now, as Hewitt knew, the only defense against the Fritz-X was to hope it missed, as the *Philadelphia* had been missed.

Closing at six hundred miles per hour with a "terrific screeching noise," the bomb appeared to Clark to be aimed straight for *Ancon*. Instead, it swooped over the flagship toward a cruiser five hundred yards to starboard.

The U.S.S. *Savannah* had been lying to while awaiting the morning's shore-bombardment assignment, but a red alert from *Ancon* caused her to ring for twenty knots and a hard left rudder. She had just leaned into her turn when calamity struck.

"It didn't fall like bombs do," an observer on *Ancon* later said. "It came down like a shell." At a 20-degree angle from true vertical, the Fritz-X hit just forward of *Savannah*'s bridge, punching a twenty-two-inch hole in the armored roof of turret number 3 and slicing through three more steel decks before detonating in the lower handling room, thirty-six feet down. No American vessel had ever before been struck by a guided missile, and no U.S. Navy warship in World War II would be struck by a larger bomb than the Fritz-X that caught *Savannah* at 9:44 A.M. Another witness concluded, "That hit wasn't natural."

A spurt of flame "flared like a sulphur match" from the turret. Quentin Reynolds on *Ancon* wrote, "The flame must have shot eighty feet into the air and then, as it receded, men who had been blown skyward fell with it, mingling with the flame and the orange smoke." Hewitt watched aghast as the explosion vented along the cruiser's port waterline: *Savannah* had been his flagship during North Atlantic convoy duty in 1941.

The blast vaporized bulkheads, buckled decks, and shattered watertight doors, killing every sailor in turret number 3, and ripping a thirty-foot hole in the ship's bottom. Flame licked through ventilation ducts, incinerating more men with flash burns; poisonous gases rolled up powder hoists and piping. Eight magazines were wrecked, and a design flaw caused ducts from the magazines to vent on the third deck rather than overboard, killing men in compartments that suffered little structural damage. Twenty-one sailors died in a gun room when visibility instantly dropped to six inches and toxic fumes overwhelmed them before they could escape through a rear hatch.

Not least, gunpowder lay scattered five inches deep. At Pearl Harbor twenty-one months earlier, a conventional bomb under similar circumstances had ignited a forward powder magazine and eviscerated the U.S.S. *Arizona* with a devastating explosion; *Roma* had died in like fashion on Thursday afternoon, broken in half with a loss of thirteen hundred lives. Only massive flooding preserved *Savannah* from the same fate: her powder had begun to burn but an abrupt tide of seawater through the side plates and lower hull quenched the fire just seconds before the magazines would have ignited.

Her rugged hull saved her, along with luck and heroic firefighting. Flooded for 152 feet of her length and listing 8 degrees to port, *Savannah* settled 12 feet in the bow until her forecastle was nearly awash. Frozen in a left turn, she crossed *Ancon*'s bow before gliding by the flagship's port side as if passing in review. Detonating 6-inch shells and burning balsa rafts on the weather deck complicated the rescue efforts of men playing hoses down gun muzzles and through the violated roof of turret number 3. The lucky died quickly, including one human torch who appeared on deck and leaped overboard—his body was never recovered—and a turret officer, naked and charred and entangled in phone wire, who passed within minutes. Others lingered for days. Among the unluckiest was Bosun's Mate John M. Wilhelm, who had been transferred from his minesweeper to *Savannah* the previous day for treatment of a broken ankle; he died with eight others in the sick bay, and would be buried at sea.

A deft shifting of fuel from bunker to bunker brought the cruiser to an even keel, and on Saturday evening *Savannah* retired with a destroyer escort for Malta. Across the Salerno anchorage, sailors braced the rails, saluting. At Valletta she would moor in Dockyard Creek, where rescuers hoisted bodies from the wrecked compartments below; wrapped in sheets or olive-drab blankets they covered the deck like toppled chess pieces. Four men trapped in a radio room emerged alive after sixty hours, but 206 others had perished.

*Savannah*'s fight was finished, at least for a year, but at Salerno the war continued. Hewitt desperately sought remedies against the glide bombs, pleading for more smoke generators from North Africa and toying with electronic countermeasures by having sailors flip on their electric razors and other appliances during an attack. The experiment was said "to improve morale without affecting the accuracy of the missiles." Fritz-X attacks in coming days would also cripple the battleship H.M.S. *Warspite* and the cruiser H.M.S. *Uganda,* among eighty-five Allied vessels hit by German bombs at Salerno. In a few months, effective jamming transmitters would emerge from Navy research laboratories, but for the moment every man afloat felt a dread vulnerability.

To the relief of *Ancon*'s crew, on Sunday morning, September 12, Mark Clark moved his Fifth Army headquarters from ship to beachhead. Clerks, drivers, and staff officers rode a Royal Navy landing vessel to shore, where a witness described "hundreds of soldiers streaming like ants to bring typewriters and filing cabinets up from the beach." Near Highway 18, in a pine grove southwest of the Sele-Calore confluence, a conspicuous pink-stucco palazzo with a lush garden was chosen for Clark's command post despite sporadic enemy artillery fire. The late-summer landscape blended the pastoral and the war-torn. Blue grasshoppers whirred among rioting zinnias, and water buffalo grazed in the plashy fens near the carcasses of goats killed in the cross fire. Naval shells had splintered gum trees and cratered the meadows, but a cat dozed on the windowsill of an empty peasant house where sweet peas and tomatoes and geraniums stretched toward the sun.

Clark immediately drove south to General Dawley's tobacco barn head-quarters, his long legs folded awkwardly into the jeep. Across his nose he knotted a bandana against the dust that soon powdered his uniform and whitened his eyebrows. At the Paestum cemetery, corpses lay in windrows awaiting interment—"lots of dead piling up outside the wall and beginning to get ripe," Dawley's aide had noted in his diary on Saturday. Inside the VI Corps command post, the rich fragrance of drying tobacco leaves in overhead flues masked the stink. Dawley tromped about in his cavalry boots, flicking a riding crop at the large map board covered with cabalistic red and blue symbols.

Twenty-eight thousand Americans were now ashore, with roughly twice that many British troops to the north. The Fifth Army beachhead stretched for forty miles, at an average depth of six miles. Nowhere was it deeper than eleven miles, and near Battipaglia the line had hardly advanced since the invasion began four days earlier. Montgomery's army still dawdled far to the south, and Clark could expect no significant reinforcements by sea until another infantry division and an armored division finished arriving in the fourth week of September.

The American right flank seemed secure, but the center worried Clark. This morning, German grenadiers had infiltrated a battalion of the 142nd Infantry in the hilltop village of Altavilla, then cut the unit to ribbons. Driven from Altavilla and the terraced heights to the east, the battalion was reduced by two-thirds, to 260 men. As described by a 36th Division soldier, Altavilla embodied another of those topographical truisms all too common in Italy: "a height of some sort with the enemy looking down at us." The battalion commander was captured, and among the other casualties was his intelligence officer, a former Southern Methodist University football star named John F. Sprague, who had played in the 1937 Rose Bowl. Bleeding from grenade fragments in his eyes and torso, Sprague told a comrade, "I'm a little hungry. Let's put on the pan and have some ham and eggs." Then: "I have a little headache. I wish I had an aspirin." With a flail of his arms and a final heave of his barrel chest, he died.

Of still greater concern to Clark was the American left flank. The Sele corridor, code-named BRYAN, was even more vulnerable after the loss of Altavilla. As one officer noted, the Sele had become not just a river but "a tribulation." In the V-shaped bottoms where the Calore flowed into the Sele from the northeast, the 179th Infantry for the past day had fought desperately against panzers spilling from the dells below Eboli. One artillery battalion was reduced to five rounds, to be "fired point blank in the final emergency," and as riflemen fixed bayonets and formed a 360-degree perimeter, gunners made contingency plans to spike their tubes and flee through the brush. On a commanding rise just north of the Sele, a tank battalion had been ambushed by 16th Panzer Division troops this morning at the Tabacchificio Fioche, a stronghold of five brick buildings with massive walls, red tile roofs, and small windows resembling gun ports; the tobacco factory would change hands several times through the afternoon, as tank rounds gnawed at the brick and machine-gun bullets scythed the Sele rushes. After seesaw fighting, American troops occupied the *tabacchificio,* digging in along the river and the dusty road to Eboli.

If German forces followed the Sele to the sea, Clark realized, they could turn the inner flanks of both X Corps in the north and VI Corps in the south. Was Dawley alive to the peril on his left? Clark wondered. The 45th and 36th Divisions were arrayed in a brittle cordon defense, and the 45th had just five infantry battalions in Italy. The enemy noose grew tighter by the hour, yet the corps had no reserves. Unmentioned was Clark's original decision to divide his army by landing on both sides of the Sele, rather than putting all forces north of the river and using it to shield his right flank. He ended the conference, folded himself back into the jeep, and drove to Red Beach, where he flagged down a patrol boat and roared off to the British sector in search of the X Corps commander, Lieutenant General Richard L. McCreery.

Here things were even worse. "Very heavy fighting today involving very great expenditure of ammunition," McCreery had informed Clark the previous night. On Saturday alone, the Germans had captured fifteen hundred Allied soldiers, mostly British; X Corps casualties at Salerno approached three thousand. A pious, blunt Anglo-Irish cavalryman—"tall, lean, and vague," as one Yank described him—McCreery limped from a Great War wound and tended when alarmed to lower his voice to a near whisper. He was whispering now. Hounded by panzers, the exhausted 56th Division was pulling back to a new line two miles west of Battipaglia, a town badly pulverized and reeking of seared flesh. Grenadier and Coldstream Guardsmen were only five thousand yards from the beaches; some battalion officers had burned their secret documents and maps as a precaution against capture. "Shells whined swiftly over us like lost souls. Moan, moan, moan, they wept," wrote a young Coldstream officer named Michael Howard. The Scots Guards official history later acknowledged "a general feeling in the air of another Dunkirk."

Shaken by the sight of the British dead stacked in the dunes, Clark at dusk raced the failing light back to Paestum. His first order was to abandon the pink palazzo, now within earshot of panzer fire; the army headquarters moved into a green calamity tent hastily erected in a thicket just a stone's throw north of the VI Corps barn. Under prodding, Dawley—who complained about "my paucity of reserves"—issued VI Corps Field Order No. 2 to shift his forces to the left. The 45th Division would sidestep north of the Sele, with two battalions on the far left of the American line stretching toward Batty P in an effort to seal the gap with the British; Walker's 36th Division now held everything south of the river on an exceptionally elongated thirty-five-mile front. In his pencil-written diary, Dawley scribbled: "Situation bad."

Grimy and dust-caked, Clark crawled into Al Gruenther's small trailer for a few hours' sleep. Flares limned the horizon to the east, bleaching out the rising moon. Muzzle flashes twinkled along the ridgelines, and the nag of artillery rolled down the hills, echoing and reechoing across the Sele tribulation. "Situation unfavorable in 10th Corps," Clark warned Alexander before dropping off to sleep. "It now appears I must await further buildup before resuming offensive." Two hours after receiving Clark's message, Alexander scratched a note to Eisenhower on a blank sheet of white typing paper: "The situation is not favorable, and everything must be done to help him."

September 13—"Black Monday," to those who outlived it—dawned "so quiet that the crowing of a cock cut the ears." Mist drifted in the flats, wet and eerie. Eight-foot tobacco fronds nodded on the morning airs. Somewhere a cow lowed, longing to be milked.

All tranquillity vanished at six A.M. Two battalions from the 36th Division struck Altavilla through the peach and apple trees in a futile lunge for the high ground behind the town, especially a cactus-infested knob known as Hill 424. Ferocious German counterattacks with twenty tanks eventually drove the Americans down the terraced slopes, firing over their shoulders. Off to a bad start, the morning only worsened when the 142nd Infantry's 1st Battalion, already reduced to 260 men, pushed through a ravine south of the village in a column of companies; artillery shells—some alleged they came from American guns—ripped the formation from front to back. By day's end, just sixty men were reported fit for duty. The 3rd Battalion of the 143rd Infantry, encircled and besieged by five counterattacks, would slip away only after nightfall, although Company K remained trapped in Altavilla for another twenty-four hours; fighting with desperate gallantry, three soldiers in the battalion earned Congressional Medals of Honor. Yet three battalions had been repulsed with heavy losses, and an uncharitable soldier in another division wondered "if the Texans were having any trouble getting the Germans to stand up and take off their hats when 'Deep in the Heart of Texas' was played."

Slapped around in the uplands at Altavilla, the Americans now faced mortal danger in the Sele flats. For only on Monday morning did General Vietinghoff confirm that a rift ran through the center of Fifth Army; German intelligence surmised that the two enemy corps had "independent and almost unconnected leadership." Vietinghoff, who had amassed six hundred tanks and self-propelled guns, now insisted that the Allies had "split themselves into two sections" to expedite evacuation of the beachhead. The arrival of more ships in the anchorage, as well as an intercepted radio message, seemed to confirm the enemy's intention of abandoning Salerno. A quick thrust down the Sele to the sea could thwart any escape; there would be no second Dunkirk.

Grenadiers sang "Lili Marlene" as they rolled into their assembly areas at midday. "The engines were started up again," a 16th Panzer Division history recorded. "Once more the dust rose in clouds above the hot, narrow roads."

Even in peacetime the five stout warehouses of the Tabacchificio Fioche offered scant shelter from the hard life of the Sele peasantry. Reclamation projects in the nineteenth century had converted malarial swampland—"altogether insalubrious," a visiting priest complained—into tenant farms growing tobacco for a state monopoly that by 1940 was producing nearly twenty billion cigarettes annually. Hundreds of women in homespun smocks labored under the *tabacchificio's* brick archways from dawn to dusk, typically for less than twenty lire a day, spearing leaves onto drying-rack spindles, or sorting them by grade into large wicker baskets. "*Andare al tabacco*"—"going to tobacco"—had become a euphemism for a hard life, often choked with tragedy.

Here the full fury of the German attack fell at 3:30 P.M. A spearhead of fifteen panzers clanked southwest down the Eboli road, followed by a shrieking battalion of grenadiers shooting colored flares and smoke grenades to simulate a bigger force. ("Fireworks created an appearance of large numbers," an American officer later observed.) Like a battering ram, the assault stove in first one flank and then the other of the 157th Infantry's 1st Battalion, part of Middleton's 45th Division. From the far bank, tank fire screamed through the Yank command post. The battalion soon broke, pelting west down the river for nearly two miles toward Highway 18 with a loss of more than five hundred men. A mortar company left unprotected near the *tabacchificio* continued to fire until German machine gunners closed to within two hundred yards, forcing the mortarmen to flee as well, their abandoned tubes unspiked.

The wolf was in the fold. "Tracers were going through my pack," a soldier later wrote his father. "My nose was all scratched trying to hug the ground." Across the river, a single battalion from the 36th Division—the 2nd of the 143rd Infantry—had been plopped after midnight between the Sele and the Calore, just beyond the hamlet of Persano. Germans from the *tabacchificio* looped behind the unit's left flank, while other panzers struck from the right and head-on, machine-gunning GIs in slit trenches along a dirt track. "For a description of the next five hours," one corporal later wrote in his diary, "I will reserve a space in my memory." A sergeant was reading the Twenty-third Psalm when grenadiers yanked him from his hole; he was surprised to see "*Gott mit Uns*" belt buckles, having been told that all Germans were atheists. Rifle companies, one witness said, "were swept aside like furrows from a plow." Of 842 men, 334 survived to fight another day; half the battalion was captured, including the commander. Some men dropped their weapons on the pretext that the barrels had become too hot to handle. Poor coordination between the 45th and 36th Divisions resulted in gunners from one firing into the backs of soldiers from the other. All afternoon panzers hunted GIs like game birds in the dense undergrowth. A major who escaped across the Calore summarized his report in five words: "It was hell up there."

And soon, back here. "Situation worse. Enemy closing. Heavy tank and artillery action," a 179th Infantry war diary recorded. "Aid station set up in haystack." The 191st Tank Battalion backed its Shermans into a semicircle to fire on three fronts; quartermasters dumped ammunition in a hedgerow, and tank crews took turns scuttling back one by one to rearm. Dead men lay on a gravel bar in the Calore as if sunning themselves. A young major in the 179th Infantry told his men, "Tonight you're not fighting for your country, you're fighting for your ass. Because they're behind us."

"Enemy on the run," the German vanguard reported. Only a charred, demolished bridge across the Calore, five miles from the beach, momentarily stalled Vietinghoff's drive to Paestum and the sea. Deep drainage ditches kept German tanks and armored carriers from veering off the narrow dirt road. Panzer commanders milled at the Burned Bridge, studying their maps.

Then, on the southwest bank of the Calore, hard by the junction with the Sele, two field artillery battalions from the 45th Division—the 158th and the 189th—shouldered two dozen guns into the brambles, and at 6:30 P.M. let fly volley after stabbing volley, point blank across the muddy stream. Drivers, bandsmen, and cooks crawled along the bank, and the crackle of rifle fire soon punctuated the roar of 105mm howitzers and the *pumpf* of white-phosphorus mortar shells springing from their tubes. Smoke billowed in the bottoms, swallowing the molten glare of flares floating on their tiny parachutes, and howitzer shells splintered trees on the far bank, clear-cutting the wood with steel and flame. Some guns fired nineteen rounds a minute, triple the howitzer's supposed maximum rate of fire, in a blur of yanked lanyards and ejected brass. Stripped to the waist and black with grit, soldiers staggered from dump to gun with a high-explosive shell on each shoulder, and sheets of flame bridged the Calore, hour after hour after hour.

Three miles down Highway 18, grim dispatches fluttered into the VI Corps tobacco barn: an enemy column a mile long was moving south from Eboli toward Persano to exploit the gash in the American line; several battalions had been ravaged if not obliterated; German shells had destroyed forty thousand gallons of fuel and thwarted efforts to reopen the Salerno port. The rude airstrips around Paestum were so dusty that pilots often took off and landed by instrument even in daylight. Runway construction work had been impaired this afternoon by the desertion of terrified Italian laborers. Also, a P-38 fighter had crashed into a water truck that was laying the dust, killing two engineers; a wrecking crew raced onto the field, cinched cables around the dead men's ankles, and dragged them off along with the other debris. "The work went on as if nothing much had happened," one officer noted. "A pretty hard-boiled business."

"Things not too hot for the home team today," General Dawley's aide wrote in his diary. Haggard and gray from lack of sleep, Dawley in his own diary entry assessed the afternoon with a single noun: "Disaster—." A Fifth Army messenger found him "resting on a cot, looking very bad." When the corps commander phoned Clark to warn of the enemy breakthrough at Persano, Clark asked, "What are you going to do about it? What can you do?" Dawley replied, "Nothing. I have no reserves. All I've got is a prayer."

Clark had spent the day in Gruenther's trailer hearing the same bleak reports. The beachhead, he concluded, had deteriorated from precarious to "extremely critical." Not until this morning had Alexander issued an unambiguous hurry-up order to Eighth Army, but Montgomery remained more than sixty miles away—despite annoying BBC broadcasts that portrayed him as heroically galloping to the rescue. Only the lightly armed 82nd Airborne Division in Sicily could provide quick reinforcement, and Clark this morning sent Ridgway a note so hastily scribbled that he omitted the final consonant from the 82nd commander's first name: "Dear

Mat . . . It is absolutely essential that one of your infantry regimental combat teams drop today within our defended beachhead."

At 7:30 P.M., as evening again enfolded the beachhead, Clark convened a
conference with Dawley, Walker, and Middleton in the hot, dim VI Corps
command post. To avoid drawing enemy fire, cigarettes were forbidden in
the capacious barn, and only a hooded flashlight illuminated the map
board. Staff officers drifted through the spectral gloom, and radios crackled in the corner. Clark recalled a staff college exercise at Fort Leavenworth
a decade earlier in which students prepared demolition orders to prevent
ammunition and other stocks from falling into enemy hands. "How the
hell would you do it?" Clark wondered. Set the stuff ablaze? "You just don't
go up with a match." Demolition preparations alone would shatter morale.
Staff college also had stressed the importance in amphibious invasions of
drafting an evacuation plan. Yet the 1941 Army field manual "Landing Operations on Hostile Shores" warned that reembarkations of forces under
fire "are exceedingly difficult and hazardous operations," which could require "the deliberate sacrifice of part of the forces ashore in order to extricate the bulk." Which forces should be sacrificed at Salerno?

Clark would subsequently deny seriously considering evacuation. "That
was never in our thoughts," he wrote his mother a month later. In fact, he
now revealed contingency plans still being cobbled together by the Fifth
Army staff. Under Operation SEALION, landing craft would shift British X
Corps troops to the VI Corps sector at Paestum; under Operation SEATRAIN,
the reverse would occur, with American troops ferried to join the British
near Salerno town. Under BRASS RAIL, Clark and his staff would leave the
beachhead for a "headquarters afloat" on H.M.S. *Hilary*. Gruenther was ordered to "take up with the Navy" the necessary arrangements. The plans
were strictly precautionary; George Meade had prepared a just-in-case retreat order for his Union army at Gettysburg.

Roused from his torpor, Dawley protested and announced his intention
to remain at Paestum, SEATRAIN or SEALION be damned. As the meeting
adjourned, others grumbled in discontent, or privately questioned Clark's
fortitude. "I don't want to tell you how to run your job, but give me support," Middleton told the army commander. Spitting in annoyance, he
added, "I want to stay here and fight." The time had come, Middleton advised his subordinates, "to do some hard fighting."

At nine P.M., 2,500 yards south of the Calore, a whistle blew in the Fifth
Army bivouac, summoning officers into the bright moonlight. In what the
reporter Lionel Shapiro described as a "level, lifeless voice," a colonel announced, "German tanks have broken through our lines. They are coming

down the Sele toward this camp. All officers will take a roll call of their men." Three quick pistol shots would signal the panzers' arrival.

Cooks, clerks, and orderlies loaded their rifles and fanned into a firing line. Slapping at mosquitoes, they hoarsely whispered the night's challenge—"Canadian"—and strained to hear the parole: "wheat." An officer arrived to find the Fifth Army headquarters "in the weeds no higher than your waist and crawling around on their hands and knees." Some men sidled down to the sea, determined, as one soldier explained, to wade "up to our necks and wait there until some ship comes along and picks us up." Clark ordered his staff to prepare for evacuation on ten minutes' notice: five landing craft bobbed offshore, waiting for a summons to Green Beach.

The waxing moon cast grotesque, unnerving shadows, and in a privet hedge outside the camp a soldier sang softly to himself:

> I'm a Yankee Doodle dandy,
> A Yankee Doodle, do or die . . .

General Vietinghoff had placed his headquarters in a tenth-century castle in Sant'Angelo dei Lombardi, an ancient mill town in the eastern hills, known for bell foundries and macaroni. From here the signs of Allied flight seemed unmistakable. "After a defensive battle lasting four days, enemy resistance is collapsing," the Tenth Army commander cabled Kesselring and the Berlin high command. "Tenth Army pursuing enemy on a wide front." Told by a subordinate that Allied resistance seemed to be stiffening, Vietinghoff insisted, "The fact that he is collapsing cannot be doubted if he voluntarily splits his force into two halves." As Black Monday drew to a close, the Tenth Army war diary recorded, "The battle of Salerno appears to be over."

## A Portal Won

FROM the rail of U.S.S. *Biscayne,* where Kent Hewitt had planted his flag after sending *Ancon* back to Africa, the distant beach on Tuesday, September 14, still radiated an illusory Mediterranean warmth. The dappled sea stretched to the shore in patches of turquoise and indigo. Beyond the golden ribbon of sand, the Sele plain spread in a silver-green haze. But there the arcadian vision abruptly ended in banks of gray and black smoke, and a pale penumbra of fire hinted at violent struggle and death ashore.

Hewitt bitterly opposed Clark's evacuation scheme, even as he made ready to carry it out. He spent Tuesday morning in *Biscayne*'s topside war room issuing orders and dictating messages. All unloading was halted on the southern beaches, and cargo ships prepared on half an hour's notice to steam beyond range of shore artillery. An awkward message to Cunningham in his Malta bastion reflected Hewitt's own exhaustion: "Depth of beachhead narrowing and ground forces now taking defensive. Fatigue existing. . . . Are heavier naval forces available?" Cunningham promptly dispatched the battleships *Valiant* and *Warspite,* both fire-breathing veterans of Jutland in 1916, and he sent three cruisers at flank speed to Tripoli, where they were to embark as many British combat troops as could cram the decks. "I will try to help you all I can," Cunningham signaled.

Hastily summoning his top lieutenants for an afternoon conference, Hewitt unveiled SEALION, SEATRAIN, and BRASS RAIL in the crowded war room. To a man they were horrified.

"If we withdraw we will lose our whole landing force," warned Rear Admiral Richard L. Conolly, who had landed Darby and his Rangers at Maiori. Amphibious crews lacked "the capability and training and experience to evacuate a force. We have never done this." The additional tonnage added to landing craft in the shallows would cause them to settle lower in the water and thus exceed the backing power of the vessels' engines. Fleet planners estimated that at most they could evacuate only half the load that had been landed at Salerno.

The senior British naval officer, Commodore G. N. Oliver, who arrived by barge from *Hilary* to find "intense gloom" suffusing the *Biscayne,* was equally adamant. To reembark "heavily engaged troops from a shallow beachhead" was impracticable and would "probably prove suicidal.

"It just cannot be done. Ships get deeper when being loaded, and it would be impossible to get them off the beaches," Oliver said. "If you shorten the beachhead, the Germans will be within kissing distance and able to shell us from both flanks." Enemy artillery would "rake the beaches," destroying mountains of matériel. An evacuation, the commodore added, was "simply not on." As for BRASS RAIL, he would happily take Clark and his staff aboard *Hilary.* But Fifth Army headquarters had grown to two thousand soldiers and five hundred vehicles, far beyond the flagship's capacity. The only recourse was "to stay and fight it out." Oliver all but spat the words. Heads nodded around the room.

Hewitt nodded, too. The logic was unimpeachable. But Clark was in command at Salerno; preparations for evacuation must proceed, as he requested. "Never mind, Commodore," Hewitt told Oliver. "You go and do it."

Yet the pack of fighting sea dogs had failed to sense a turning tide. Just as Fifth Army's plight had deteriorated from precarious to critical on Black

Monday, now it ebbed back to simply precarious. The plucky stand at the Burned Bridge had checked German momentum. Then, just before midnight, a fleet of C-47s had appeared overhead and an enormous letter "T"—with legs half a mile long, fashioned from pails of gasoline-soaked sand—abruptly burst into flame to mark the beachfront drop zone. Like "a cloud of monster snowflakes," as one witness reported, the 82nd Airborne's 504th Infantry sifted into the beachhead, on time, on target, and without a single instance of the friendly fire that had decimated the regiment in Sicily two months earlier. Thirteen hundred lightly armed paratroopers would hardly reverse Fifth Army's fortunes, but the boost to morale was incalculable: from their slit trenches and fluvial thickets, soldiers cheered themselves hoarse as they watched the snowflakes descend. "Men, it's open season on krautheads!" the 504th commander roared as his soldiers headed for the corrugated uplands. "You know what to do."

Perhaps to compensate for any fainthearted behavior on Monday evening, Clark on Tuesday was conspicuously daring, demonstrating the physical courage that in fact would characterize his generalship. Exposing himself to fire below the Calore, he helped position his battered battalions to suture the seam between VI Corps and X Corps. A German lunge south of the Tabacchificio Fioche at eight A.M. was met with a hot volley of flanking fire that left seven panzers burning in the mist. Early in the afternoon, 45th Division troops threw back two more attacks, and by late in the day two dozen German tanks had been destroyed. "In one case," an intelligence officer told his diary, "the trapped crew had been broiled in such a way that a puddle of fat had spread from under the tank."

South of the Sele the 36th Division shortened its line along La Cosa Creek, scattering mines and unspooling barbed wire from the Calore to Monte Soprano, and halting the German drive through Altavilla. To the north, the British still fought furiously from Vietri to Battipaglia, but McCreery showed studied nonchalance in his signal to Clark at five P.M. on Tuesday: "Nothing of interest to report during daylight."

Vietinghoff was loath to accept that he had not driven the Allies back to their ships. Yet frictions had accumulated in Tenth Army: a corps commander had been injured in a plane crash; many German troops suffered from heat exhaustion; and Allied artillery was profligate—U.S. gunners alone fired ten thousand shells on Tuesday, and howitzers sniped at individual German soldiers. Berlin's refusal to release the two tank divisions from Mantua had also hurt the cause in Salerno. Those reinforcements that did arrive often came in penny packets—a company here, a battalion there—and were committed to battle the same way, without providing a critical mass anywhere. Attacking downhill brought certain pleasures, but also exposed the attackers to blistering fire that unhinged German formations.

No fire blistered more than naval shelling, for which there was no antidote except to flee the littoral. "The heavy naval artillery barrages were especially unpleasant," a Hermann Göring Division commander confessed. Hewitt ordered every boat with a gun barrel into the fight, led by the big warships dubbed "the murderous queens." Steaming off the Sele's mouth, *Philadelphia* from nine P.M. Monday until four A.M. Tuesday fired nearly a thousand 6-inch shells at roads, intersections, and German troop concentrations, then yielded to the equally murderous U.S.S. *Boise.* Guns grew so hot that hydraulic rammers slowed, barrel paint blistered, and the canvas boots that kept seawater off the gun mounts charred. To clear their decks, sailors took fire axes to empty shell cases and heaved the splinters over the side. Soldiers ashore greeted new salvos with a baying war cry: "Adolf, count your children now!"

What naval shells missed, air force bombs hit. Several hundred bombers struck the Sele plain during daylight on Tuesday. That night, in an unusual tactical role, sixty B-17s battered road and rail targets around Eboli and Battipaglia; by late Wednesday, more than a thousand "heavy" sorties had been flown at Salerno. Over the next four days, the heavies would drop 760 tons of high explosives per square mile, annihilating intersections, rail yards, and villages. Smaller fighter-bombers grew pugnacious enough to strafe lone German motorcyclists, while flocks of Spitfires flew from Sicily every fifteen minutes and pilots in the tiny Piper L-4 Grasshopper spotter planes known as Maytag Messerschmitts took occasional potshots with their .45-caliber pistols.

By dusk on Tuesday, German commanders reported that movement during the day had become "almost impossible" without attracting Allied artillery, naval shells, bombs, mortar rounds, or tank fire—and sometimes all five. Having seen such firepower in Tunisia and again in Sicily, Kesselring now doubted that Tenth Army could mass enough combat strength to obliterate the beachhead. Still, the stakes made it worth one more try. Smiling Albert on Tuesday gave Vietinghoff his marching orders: make a final effort to throw Fifth Army into the sea, but be prepared to march north, perhaps as far as Rome.

The somber if sketchy reports from Salerno had so incensed Winston Churchill that he threatened to set things right by flying to the beachhead personally. Instead he sent his favorite *beau sabreur,* a man who had reputedly built sand castles under fire on Dunkirk beach and whose very name calmed tempests and stiffened spines. Harold Alexander—"General

Alex" to buck privates and brigadiers alike—arrived in the roadstead aboard the destroyer *Offa* before dawn on Wednesday, September 15, and clambered aboard the *Biscayne* to learn from Hewitt what all the fuss was about.

"*Quelle race!*" murmured a visiting French officer who watched Alexander at Salerno. What breeding, indeed. He was immaculate, as always, with his bloused britches, sleek mustache, and steep-peaked, red-banded cap, worn with an upward tilt of the head "that might be called supercilious if it were not so serene," John Gunther wrote. As always, he carried in his kit an Irish flag, which he intended to raise over Berlin. A talented draftsman who had been known to sketch a battlefield amid bursting shells, he evinced "a calm, gentle, friendly presence whose influence, like an oil slick, spread outward," according to a fellow Guardsman, the future military historian Michael Howard. He assumed that "nothing ever went right in battle," and thus was rarely surprised by confusion or calamity; in Alexander's cosmology, chaos at Salerno reflected the natural order. "Good chaps get killed and wounded, and it is a terrible thing," he once said of combat, though without great conviction. To him, war was simply "homicide on a scale which transformed it into a crusade and an art, dignified by its difficulties and risks." Churchill adored Alexander, according to the prime minister's physician, because he "redeemed what was brutal in war, touching the grim business lightly with his glove. In his hands it was still a game for people of quality."

No sooner had Hewitt laid out Clark's evacuation contingency than General Alex in a rare flash of temper cracked his bloused britches with a swagger stick and stepped to the front of *Biscayne*'s crowded war room. "Oh, no! We *can't* have anything like that," he said, bristling. "Never do, never do." All planning for SEATRAIN, SEALION, and BRASS RAIL would "cease immediately," lest panic infect the ranks. Alexander looked about as if seeking sand to build a castle. "There will be no evacuation," he said. "Now we'll proceed from there."

He and Hewitt found Clark awaiting them on the Paestum beach. Around a camp table in the Fifth Army headquarters thicket, an orderly served breakfast while *Philadelphia,* back on the Sele station, unlimbered at targets near Persano, rattling coffee cups and shivering the tent canvas with concussion ghosts. Alexander and Clark vanished for a private conversation in the army commander's little trailer; when they emerged, all evacuation schemes had been scrapped.

Clark accepted the bucking-up graciously, and managed to conceal his seething anger at Montgomery, who seemed impervious both to Alexander's exhortations and to the predicament of Fifth Army. This very day, the

Eighth Army commander had sent a message, both tactically and syntactically suspect, and with a misspelled salutation:

> My dear Clarke . . . It looks as if you may be having not too good a time, and I do hope that all will go well with you. . . . We are on the way to lend a hand.

In fact, Montgomery's 64,000 troops were still fifty miles from Paestum, patching demolished bridges and holding medals ceremonies. In nearly two weeks only eighty-five German prisoners had been captured; the rearguard 26th Panzer Division was suffering just ten combat casualties a day; and Montgomery's army on Monday reported a total of sixty-two British dead since arriving in Italy. Several squads of British reporters, chafing at the glacial pace, set off by road for Salerno with their public relations escorts, flinging wild hand gestures and demanding of cheerful Calabrian peasants, "*Dove tedeschi? Où* are the *Allemands?* Where the hell are the Germans?" This morning the first jeepload of hacks met American scouts south of Agropoli, having encountered nary an enemy soldier in two days. Not for another thirty-six hours would a British patrol make contact with the bridgehead, thirty-five miles south of Paestum, and no significant linkup would occur until September 19. Clark, whose casualty list had swelled to nearly seven thousand, swallowed his fury and replied to Montgomery, "It will be a pleasure to see you again at an early date. Here situation well in hand."

Of more immediate concern to Clark was General Dawley. "I would like you to go now and visit VI Corps headquarters and look over Dawley," Clark told Alexander. "I'm worried about him." Shortly before nine A.M., Alexander strolled into the big corps barn where Dawley stood before his map board like a condemned man on the scaffold. After little rest in nearly a week and no sleep at all for the past forty-eight hours, his voice cracked as he described, incoherently, both corps dispositions and his future plans. Asked to pinpoint Walker's 36th Division, he gestured vaguely with a trembling hand to a much larger sector around the Gulf of Salerno than even the doughty Texans could occupy.

"I do not want to interfere with your business," Alexander told Clark an hour later. "But I have some ten years' experience in this game of sizing up commanders. I can tell you definitely that you have a broken reed on your hands, and I suggest you replace him immediately."

"I know it, Alex," Clark replied. "I am up there every day." He asked Alexander upon returning to North Africa to tell Eisenhower what he had seen. With a hearty cheerio, Alexander sped off by patrol boat to the British sector, where McCreery had spread a checkered tablecloth on the beach, with picnic platters of sandwiches and crackers.

"Although I am not entirely happy about the situation," Alexander cabled Churchill after leaving Salerno, "I am happier than I was twenty-four hours ago."

As for Clark, perhaps inspirited despite himself, he wrote Renie, "No doubt you people are worried to death—far more so than I am. . . . I am not downhearted a bit." To Fifth Army he proclaimed on Wednesday night, "Our beachhead is secure. . . . We are here to stay."

He did not tell the Germans, however, and on Thursday morning, September 16, they struck again.

Hardly had the shrieking hordes begun to lunge seaward, however, than Allied cannonades smacked them down. An attempt by the 26th Panzer Division to thunder down Highway 18 from Battipaglia and join forces with the Hermann Görings in Salerno was "under bad auspices from the start," a German commander reported: fuel shortages in Calabria had delayed the division's arrival at Eboli by two days; Allied air attacks and naval gunfire raked the lumbering columns; scouts got lost in the dark; artillery observers failed to find the grenadier spearhead; and traffic bottlenecks near Batty P disrupted timetables. When two regiments finally attacked at midmorning, they covered less than two hundred yards before British tanks flayed them, with severe casualties. A regiment of German paratrooper reinforcements never penetrated the curtain of naval shells, and two Hermann Göring battalions reported being "put out of action in close-quarters fighting." The Allied weight of metal was now insuperable. Vietinghoff had shot his bolt.

This welcome news greeted Eisenhower when he arrived Friday afternoon in the Salerno anchorage aboard H.M.S. *Charybdis*. With Hewitt at his elbow, he clambered into a DUKW and headed to shore for his first look at the battlefield that had so vexed him for the past week. On Black Monday, with his usual impulse to take responsibility, Eisenhower had cabled Marshall that if the beachhead collapsed he intended to "announce that one of our landings had been repulsed due to my error in misjudging the strength of the enemy at that place." To Harry Butcher he added, "If things go wrong there is no one to blame except myself."

As recently as yesterday, Eisenhower had mused aloud during breakfast at Amilcar that if Salerno ended badly he "would probably be out" as commander-in-chief. Clark's now defunct BRASS RAIL plan caused particular anguish—a leader must "stay with his men to give them confidence," Eisenhower fumed—and he wondered whether he had erred in giving command of Fifth Army to Clark rather than to Patton, who at least "would prefer to die fighting." Alexander's report that he was "most favorably unimpressed by Dawley," and a message from Clark that Dawley "appears to go to pieces in the emergencies," made Eisenhower flush with anger at the Fifth Army commander. "Well, goddam," he snapped, "why in the hell doesn't he relieve Dawley?"

If Salerno plagued him, other things also gnawed, including the usual barrage of "most immediate" cables from Washington and London. "It is now 15 months since I saw you," he wrote Mamie. "My life is a mixture of politics and war. The latter is bad enough. . . . The former is straight and unadulterated venom." He had been thinking of their dead son, who would have turned twenty-six this month, but also of their living son, John, to whom he wrote at West Point as if lecturing himself: "Learn to live simply. . . . Do not be too free with advice. . . . Don't be afraid to do the dirty work yourself." Even his appearance on the cover of *Time* this week (the article included a backhanded compliment from a female admirer who called him "the handsomest bald man" she had ever met) caused him more chagrin than pleasure. "When this war is over," he wrote a friend, "I am going to find the deepest hole there is in the United States, crawl in and pull it in after me."

There was dirty work to be done at Salerno, but Eisenhower would leave it to others. Though fretful, he kept his temper during a conference in the VI Corps tobacco barn. But after traveling by jeep to a farmhouse command post occupied by the 36th Division, he listened distractedly for a few minutes, then whirled on Dawley. "For God's sake, Mike," he said. "How did you manage to get your troops so fucked up?" Dawley sputtered in reply. "I'll back you up, anything you do," Eisenhower privately told Clark. "I really think you better take him out of the picture." Later in the day, after Eisenhower had visited a gun battery and a field hospital, Dawley and Clark quarreled during a jeep ride back to Paestum, with Dawley deriding his younger superiors as "boy scouts" and "boys in short pants." Clark expelled him from the jeep, then drove off in anger.

The course was set. "I want you to go down and tell General Dawley that there will be an airplane in here for him at dawn," Clark subsequently told a staff officer. "Tell him to take it and go back to Algiers and they'll give him transport back to the States." The messenger found Dawley napping on a cot under mosquito netting. "I know what you're going to say," the corps commander said. "When do I leave?" He later added, with a shrug, "You can't fight city hall." In his diary, Dawley described the day in a single misspelled word: "Releived." After shaking hands with his staff he left Italy forever, playing gin rummy on the long trip home, for which he was authorized a fifty-five-pound baggage allowance and a $7 per diem. "It was just as well," he later said. "I couldn't work with Clark. He made decisions off the top of his head." Busted to his permanent rank of colonel, he would regain one star before the end of the war and eventually retire with both stars restored. "He is being promoted," Marshall ostensibly told a U.S. senator, "as a reward for keeping his mouth shut."

Even those who doubted Dawley's generalship fretted at the peremptory dismissal of senior commanders that had become commonplace in the U.S. Army. Of four American corps commanders to face the Germans thus far, two had been cashiered. "It makes a commander supercautious," James Gavin told his diary. "Lee would have been relieved in '61 if our present system were in effect." Major General Ernest N. Harmon, who was about to bring his 1st Armored Division to Italy, alluded to the oak leaf insignia of his own permanent rank when he wrote Clark in late September that Dawley's relief "has had a rather dampening effect on us general officers. . . . I will bring my lieutenant colonel's leaves along in my pocket, to have them ready."

As Eisenhower left, so did the Germans. Vietinghoff late on Thursday concluded that "complete success at Salerno could no longer be hoped for." Acknowledging Tenth Army's "grievous losses," Kesselring authorized a retreat, with the proviso that Vietinghoff hold the Volturno River, twenty miles north of Naples, until at least October 15. After a final mauling of two isolated American paratrooper battalions at Altavilla, the Germans stole away from the beachhead on Friday night, leaving a rear guard of 2,500 to discourage pursuit.

On Saturday morning, September 18, the long German convoy snaked up Highway 91 from Eboli. Ribbons of dust rose from the road, the spoor of an enemy retiring to fight another day. Northward they trudged with their plunder piled on trucks and dray carts: olive oil and salami, linen and silver. Under Tenth Army Order No. 3, roads were to "be destroyed most thoroughly," factories would be dynamited, and "all supplies and equipment that cannot be taken along must be destroyed." An "evacuation list" of items to be pillaged included rolling stock, machine tools, typewriters, cars, buses, the Alfa Romeo plant in Naples, ball bearings, lathes, saw blades, and measuring tools—"but not slide rules."

The scorching and salting of the earth had begun. Horses and mules were stolen or shot, and even surplus saddles and horseshoe nails were put to the torch. An estimated 92 percent of all sheep and cattle in southern Italy, and 86 percent of all poultry, were taken or slaughtered. "Rail rooters"—huge iron hooks pulled behind locomotives—snapped railroad ties like matchsticks. The echo of demolitions rolled from the mountains, and oily smoke smudged the northern skyline.

An unfinished letter found in the tunic of a dead German paratrooper foreshadowed the world ahead. "The Tommies will have to chew their way through us, inch by inch," the soldier had written, "and we will surely make hard chewing for them."

So ended the first great battle to liberate the continent of Europe.

Even in retreat, the Germans deemed the ten-day struggle at Salerno a victory. Kesselring told Berlin that he had captured three thousand Allied prisoners, inflicted at least ten thousand additional casualties, and left the invaders "incapable of attacking for a long time. . . . Above all, the value to us is the time won, which assists us in the building up of strength." General Sieckenius, the 16th Panzer Division commander, considered both the British and Americans to be inferior combat soldiers—devoid of "the offensive spirit," excessively dependent on artillery, and reluctant to close with the enemy. Hitler agreed. "No more invasions for them!" he said. "They are much too cowardly for that. They only managed the one at Salerno because the Italians gave their blessing."

Once again the Führer and his minions had misjudged their adversaries. Certainly Salerno was inelegant and brutal, a fitting overture for the Italian campaign that followed. Allied casualties totaled about 9,000—5,500 for the British and 3,500 for the Americans—of whom more than 1,200 were killed in action. Total German losses numbered roughly 3,500, of whom an estimated 630 had been killed, a modest butcher's bill for an army that in September alone would suffer 126,000 casualties in Russia.

Yet Salerno for the Allies was a blood chit, to be redeemed in the future. Much had been learned—some of it, sadly, for the second or third time— about combat loading, over-the-beach resupply, naval gunnery, and ground combat. No officer planning for Normandy nine months hence would ever forget that while land warfare offers "a road upon which you may retire, there is no road of retirement in amphibious operations," as one Navy commander put it. Eisenhower emerged from AVALANCHE convinced of the need "to turn the scales by turning every ship and every aircraft on the vital battle area"; he would also demand, when his hour at Normandy came round, absolute authority over air forces as well as those of the sea and land. But he had again neglected to make demands of Alexander, to insist on cohesion between V Corps and X Corps, and between Fifth Army and Eighth Army. Alexander's handling of Montgomery was said by his biographer Nigel Nicolson to resemble that of "an understanding husband in a difficult marriage." Eisenhower recognized what he called General Alex's "unsureness in dealing with certain of his subordinates," yet failed to intervene.

President Franklin D. Roosevelt with Prime Minister Winston S. Churchill at Shangri-La, the presidential retreat in Maryland's Catoctin Mountains, during an interlude in the TRIDENT conference, mid-May 1943 *(Franklin D. Roosevelt Presidential Library)*

The president and prime minister with their Combined Chiefs of Staff in a posed portrait at the White House on May 24, 1943, the last day of the TRIDENT conference. Standing from left to right: Field Marshal Sir John Dill, the senior British officer stationed in Washington; Lieutenant General Sir Hastings L. "Pug" Ismay, chief of staff to Churchill; Air Chief Marshal Sir Charles F. A. Portal, chief of the British air staff; General Sir Alan Brooke, chief of the Imperial General Staff; Admiral Sir Dudley Pound, the British First Sea Lord; Admiral William D. Leahy, Roosevelt's chief military adviser; General George C. Marshall, the U.S. Army chief of staff; Admiral Ernest J. King, the U.S. chief of naval operations; Lieutenant General Joseph T. McNarney, an Army Air Forces pilot who served as Marshall's deputy chief of staff. The senior AAF commander, General H. H. "Hap" Arnold, spent the conference in the hospital for treatment of a heart condition. *(Franklin D. Roosevelt Presidential Library)*

Unless otherwise noted, all photographs are from U.S. Army Signal Corps archives.

Allied troops boarding assault craft in a North African port, apparently Bizerte, Tunisia, en route to Sicily for Operation HUSKY in early July 1943

General Dwight D. Eisenhower (*left*) and General George C. Marshall during a meeting in Algiers in September 1943

Vice Admiral H. Kent Hewitt (*right*), who commanded American naval forces during the invasions of Morocco, Sicily, and Salerno, on the deck of his flagship with the war correspondent Quentin Reynolds
(*U.S. Navy, National Archives*)

Major General Terry de la Mesa Allen (*left*) commander of the 1st Infantry Division, studies a map with the man who became his nemesis, Lieutenant General Omar N. Bradley, commander of the U.S. II Corps. Censors have inked out a landmark between the two to avoid pinpointing their location in Sicily.

Brigadier General Theodore Roosevelt, Jr., assistant commander of the 1st Infantry Division during the invasion of Sicily, shown here with his jeep in January 1944. An admirer described him with four adjectives: "Bald, burnt, gnarled, and wrinkled."

Axis aircraft attack Allied invasion ships in the anchorage off Gela, Sicily, on July 11, 1943. After bombs struck the Liberty ship S.S. *Rowan* in this area on the same day, one witness described "a flat sheet of crimson fire in a frame of black smoke."

Dead and dying Italian soldiers lie in a road near Palermo in July 1943, after their truck inadvertently hit an Italian mine while being pursued by U.S. troops. Near a jeep in the background, medics dress the wounds of an American lieutenant.

Lieutenant General George S. Patton, Jr. (*right*), commander of the U.S. Seventh Army, at the Royal Palace in Palermo with his rival, General Bernard L. Montgomery (*center*), commander of the British Eighth Army, and Major General Geoffrey Keyes, Patton's deputy

Company A of the 16th Infantry Regiment, 1st Infantry Division, on July 28, 1943, moving toward Troina, the highest and perhaps most fiercely defended town in Sicily. "Troina was the toughest battle Americans have fought since World War I," one general concluded, "and there were very few in that war which were its equal."

Major General Matthew B. Ridgway (*left*), commander of the 82nd Airborne Division, with a Signal Corps camera-man in central Sicily, July 25, 1943. "Hard as flint and full of intensity, almost grinding his teeth from intensity," one subordinate said of Ridgway.

Field Marshal Albert Kesselring, the senior German commander in the Mediterranean, was a former artilleryman who had learned to fly and had transferred to the Luftwaffe. An exceptional tactician who believed that most of Italy could be defended, Kesselring argued for a strategic concept that involved keeping the war as far from the Fatherland as long as possible. (*U.S. Army Military History Institute*)

Riflemen from the 143rd Infantry Regiment, 36th Infantry Division, wade toward the beach at Paestum, south of Salerno, at the start of Operation AVALANCHE on September 9, 1943. The milky haze from artificial smoke was intended to blind German gunners on the high ground ringing the landing sites.

U.S. Navy sailors and Coast Guardsmen hug the shingle during a German air raid on the anchorage at Salerno. Debris from an exploding bomb can be seen in the background. The wire mesh laid across the beach was intended to improve traction for military vehicles.

RIGHT: Major General Ernest J. Dawley command-ed the U.S. VI Corps during the landings at Salerno in September 1943. A stocky, cautious artilleryman from Wisconsin who had been described in his West Point yearbook as "a quiet lad that one seldom sees or hears of," Dawley had warned his superiors before Salerno, "Don't bite off more than you can chew, and chew damn well."

LEFT: Lieutenant General Richard L. McCreery com-manded the British X Corps at Salerno, anchoring the Allied left flank. A pious, blunt Anglo-Irish cavalryman—"tall, lean, and vague," as one American described him—McCreery still limped from a World War I wound and tended when aggravated to lower his voice to a near-whisper.

BELOW: U.S. infantrymen push past the Temple of Neptune at Paestum, center of the American sector during the landings around Salerno Bay. Still among the grandest complexes of Doric temples outside Athens, Paestum had been a 6th-century B.C. Greek colony, famed in antiquity for roses and violets.

The Tabacchificio Fioche, known to American troops as the Tobacco Factory, just north of the Sele River at Salerno. A stronghold of five brick buildings with massive walls, red tile roofs, and small windows resembling gun ports, the complex changed hands repeatedly during the battle.

The cruiser U.S.S. *Savannah*, on fire and down in the bow on September 11, 1943, after a German radio-controlled bomb, known as a Fritz-X, punched through No. 3 turret and detonated belowdecks, killing more than two hundred sailors. No U.S. Navy warship in World War II would be struck by a larger bomb. One witness reported, "That hit wasn't natural."

Benito Mussolini on September 12, 1943, just before climbing into the cockpit of the Storch airplane that will carry him from the Gran Sasso ski resort where he had been imprisoned by Italian authorities following his arrest. On Hitler's orders, German paratroopers led by Captain Otto Skorzeny landed by glider on the mountaintop to free the Duce without firing a shot.

Naples and its famous bay, with Vesuvius in the background. Captured on October 1, 1943, the city for Allied soldiers soon became "the nearest symbol of every man's immediate aspirations," one British officer wrote, "a fairyland of silver and gold."

American infantrymen in an assault boat haul themselves across the Volturno River in mid-October 1943 during the first major river crossing in Europe by Allied troops. By moving quickly on a broad front, and by leaving the main roads to infiltrate around enemy strongpoints, Allied forces advanced thirty-five miles past Naples before rain and stiffening German resistance slowed the pace.

A wounded German prisoner awaits medical treatment along the bank of the Volturno on October 17, 1943.

A U.S. soldier north of the Volturno disables a mine, which has been discovered by the engineer holding his metal detector. "All roads lead to Rome," quipped General Harold Alexander, the commander-in-chief of Allied forces in Italy, "but all the roads are mined."

LEFT: Lieutenant Colonel John Toffey, Jr., as a battalion commander in the 3rd Infantry Division after the Volturno crossing. A combat commander since the invasion of North Africa, Toffey possessed "the bones and confirmation of a steeple-chaser rather than a racehorse," according to the combat artist George Biddle, who made this sketch on October 30, 1943. *(Courtesy of John J. Toffey IV and Michael Biddle)*

RIGHT: A Harvard-educated World War I veteran, George Biddle was a fine writer as well as a talented draftsman. Of the Italian campaign he wrote, "I wish the people at home, instead of thinking of their boys in terms of football stars, would think of them in terms of miners trapped underground or suffocating to death in a tenth-story fire."

Ships ablaze in Bari harbor after German bombers struck the Adriatic port in a surprise raid on December 2, 1943. Seventeen Allied ships were sunk in what was described as the "costliest sneak attack since Pearl Harbor." The explosion of a munitions ship secretly carrying mustard gas caused mass casualties among servicemen and Italian civilians.

British infantrymen in early December 1943 cling to the face of Monte Camino, described by one Tommy as a "steep solid rock leading God knows where." Stone breastworks offered little protection against German mortar fragments or the frigid cold. "A small earthquake added to the unpleasantness," a Scots Guard account noted.

Eisenhower (*left*) and Lieutenant General Mark W. Clark, commander of the U.S. Fifth Army, near the Mignano Gap in central Italy in December 1943. A few days later, Eisenhower would leave the Mediterranean to take command of OVERLORD, the invasion of France.

Italian women washing clothes in a village trough in central Italy as an Allied convoy crawls through mud that seemed to grow thicker and deeper by the day

Fifth Army engineers finish a bridge across a streambed in central Italy to replace the span destroyed by German demolitionists. In twenty months of fighting in Italy, the Allies would erect three thousand spans, with a combined length of fifty-five miles. This one took ten hours to build.

The view of Monte Sammucro from German positions on Monte Lungo. Highway 6 runs across the bottom of the photo, while a secondary road angles around Dead Man's Curve toward San Pietro, seen clinging to the lower slopes of the massif. The pinnacle of Sammucro, nearly four thousand feet high, was known as Hill 1205.

RIGHT: In covering the fighting at San Pietro, Ernie Pyle wrote about the death on Monte Sammucro of Captain Henry T. Waskow. "Beloved Captain," his most famous dispatch, was perhaps the finest expository passage of World War II. But Pyle told a friend, "I've lost the touch. This stuff stinks."

LEFT: "He was never young," a school classmate once said of Henry Waskow, "not in a crazy high school-kid way." To his family in Texas, Waskow wrote, "If I failed as a leader, and I pray God I didn't, it was not because I did not try."
(*Texas Military Forces Museum*)

In the mountains near Venafro, an Italian mule skinner (*right*) helps secure the body of a dead American soldier for removal to a temporary military cemetery. Blood stains can be seen on the stretcher.

U.S. troops from the 504th Airborne Infantry Regiment and 143rd Infantry climb through the rubble of San Pietro on December 17, 1943. A gunner described the village as "one large mound of desolation."

Christmas dinner 1943, on the hood of a jeep. The striped unit patch on the sleeve and helmet of the soldier on the right shows that he belongs to the 3rd Infantry Division; the other two men served in the 163rd Signal Company.

After a near-fatal bout of pneumonia, Winston Churchill rose from his sickbed in Tunisia for a Christmas lunch with Eisenhower (*left*) and Alexander (*center*). The prime minister, who is wearing his "siren suit" and Chinese dressing gown with blue-and-gold dragons, had begun pressing for a surprise Allied landing behind enemy lines at Anzio.

George Marshall had decreed that the "vital qualifications" for senior U.S. Army officers included "leadership, force, and vigor." Too often such traits were most conspicuous in their absence. Dawley's deficiencies made him an easy scapegoat, but he was hardly the only senior officer still struggling to meet the chief's high standard. Mark Clark was also in over his head at Salerno, as he showed in matters ranging from the confusion over H-hour to his approval of a plan that left a gaping hole between his corps. Salerno annealed Clark: he emerged stronger and wiser, if still so autocratic and aloof that soldiers now called him Marcus Aurelius Clarkus. "He is not so good as Bradley in winning, almost without effort, the complete confidence of everybody around him," Eisenhower wrote Marshall on September 20. "He is not the equal of Patton in refusing to see anything but victory in any situation that arises. But he is still carrying his full weight."

Others wondered. "Mark Clark really didn't have a true feel for what soldiers could and could not do, and how much power it took to accomplish a particular mission," James Gavin later wrote to Matthew Ridgway. Whether Clark had the mettle of a great field commander was yet to be discovered, a central subplot in the unfolding drama that was the war in Italy.

Still, the Allies were on the continent, never to be expelled again. An alert and skilled enemy, fighting on favorable terrain with the advantage of terrestrial rather than maritime lines of communication, had been cudgeled aside. A portal had been won, and through it poured men and matériel; from two divisions on September 3, the Allied host in Italy grew to thirteen by the end of the month, with captured airfields that would contribute to pummeling the Reich.

Precisely where they were going and what they would do when they arrived there remained in doubt. The avowed strategic purpose of the Italian campaign—to knock Italy from the war and to engage as many German divisions as possible—had been at least partly fulfilled. How to completely satisfy those war aims was as unclear in Salerno as it was in Washington, London, and Algiers. The strategic drift persisted.

That was neither the province nor the fault of those who had fought their way ashore. Perhaps only a battlefield before the battle is quieter than the same field after the shooting stops; the former is silent with anticipation, the latter with a pure absence of noise. Calm now settled over Salerno as the troops stood down, resting for the long march ahead.

Cooks bolstered their Army rations with Italian tomatoes, beans, and onions, while soldiers "made our acquaintance with vino, Alberti gin, 40-octane cognac, and grappa." Staff officers moved into the Fascist party headquarters in Salerno, slapping black paint across the gilt lettering of "*Credere, Obbedire, Combattere*" and other fatuous slogans. Civilians emerged from their hiding places to resume the interrupted harvest. Peasant women glided through vineyards with great baskets of blue and white grapes on their heads, or searched tomato vines for fruit overlooked by pillagers. An Italian farmer appeared at a command post with a note, in English, given him by retreating Germans: "The Americans will pay for the two pigs we took." George Biddle's artistic eye detected signs of life in the rubble: a man toting his framed legal diploma; a woman carrying an iron bedspring; an old man clutching a rabbit by the ears; another woman with a sack of potatoes and, on her head, a straw hamper holding a baby.

The living searched for the dead "by smelling them out," wrote one soldier assigned to a burial detail. "I covered my mouth and nose with a piece of parachute silk. . . . When I returned to the company no one would have anything to do with me because my clothes retained the smell of the dead and my own puke." Michael Howard described "the hunched, urgent diggers, the sprawling corpses with their dead eyes in a cold dawn light that drained all colour from the scene."

So many civilian bodies littered the mountain town of Avellino that they were doused with gasoline and burned in a pyre. Altavilla was even more horrible. The bloated corpses of civilians slaughtered in the cross fire, including many children, burst from their clothing. "The stinch was terrible," a military policeman reported. Entire platoons of 36th Division soldiers killed early in the battle lay in shallow revetments, their faces "black and hard like an eggplant."

Bulldozers now dug the trenches at Paestum, and proper grave markers replaced the crude wooden triangles. A visiting general complained that a Star of David among a row of Latin crosses "spoils the symmetry of the cemetery. Move it." A 36th Division chaplain refused. His boys held title to that ground.

# 5. Corpse of the Siren

## *"I Give You Naples"*

TOWARD Naples they pounded, long columns of jeeps and trucks and armored cars with German coal-scuttle helmets wired to the radiators as hood ornaments. British military policemen in red caps and white canvas gloves waved them north beneath the rocky loom of Vesuvius, through Nocera and Angri and Torre del Greco. Jubilant crowds strewed flowers beneath their wheels, and priests in threadbare cassocks crooked their fingers in benediction. Refugees trudged along the road shoulders, including boys "so dirty they didn't look human" and hatless, truant Italian soldiers, who carried their shoes to spare the leather and bathed their feet in hillside streams. Villagers who had been to the States shouted denunciations of Fascism in broken English spiced with recollected American profanities, or recited the brands of toothpaste and laxatives they had encountered in the land of opportunity. The reporter John Lardner found the Campanian countryside redolent "of bandits and light opera," while another American insisted that southern Italy "just stinks of the classics." After searching the ruins at Pompeii, a lieutenant from Indiana nodded toward the Roman amphitheater and observed, "They certainly make 'em to last."

A squadron from the King's Dragoon Guards was the first Allied unit to enter Naples, at 9:30 A.M. on Friday, October 1, 1943. Mark Clark followed a few hours later. Much discussion had been devoted to arranging a triumphal entrance, but in the event the procession had an air of hasty improvisation and slapdash stagecraft. On Highway 18 in the southern suburb of San Giovanni, Clark climbed into the open cockpit of an armored car with Ridgway, who clutched his Springfield rifle and squinted at the rooftops for snipers. Gavin led the convoy in a jeep, a city map spread across his lap, and a paratrooper battalion trailed behind in trucks. Laundry flapped from iron balconies and geraniums spilled from their windowsill pots, but every door and window remained shuttered in what Clark called "a city of ghosts." A team of OSS infiltrators warned that retreating

Germans had mined at least fifty buildings, and Italian bodies lay in the streets of a city "heavily scented with the sweet heliotrope odor of unburied dead," an OSS officer wrote. Now and then a gunshot echoed down the Corso Umberto, sharp as a single handclap: partisans were hunting Fascist collaborators. Clark surveyed the deserted Piazza Garibaldi, across from the central train station, and confessed to being "in a less happy mood than I had expected to be in."

He was in the wrong place. Thousands of joyful Neapolitans awaited their liberators barely a mile away, in the Piazza del Plebiscito, where conquering heroes traditionally appeared. As soldiers eventually tramped past the stately Palazzo Reale and into the semicircular plaza a great shout went up. "*Viva, viva!*" the throng screamed. "*Grazie! Viva!*" Weeping and genuflecting, they plucked at the uniforms of the passing troops or flung themselves down to kiss their boots. The pandemonium soon spread through the city. "Walls of shouting faces leaned out at us, and arms pelted us with grapes and chrysanthemums," wrote the reporter Richard Tregaskis, who likened the crowds to "ants swarming toward and over us."

"Naples has been taken by our troops," Clark radioed Alexander. "City quiet. No indications of disease or disorder." The delirious welcome buoyed Clark's spirits, and to Renie he wrote, "I give you Naples for your birthday. I love you. Wayne."

It proved an odd gift, neither quiet nor lacking in disease and disorder. Insurrection had flared in Naples on September 26, two weeks after Kesselring's troops occupied the city and began conscripting young men into labor battalions. A reign of German terror that featured public executions for minor infractions led first to gunplay by Italian snipers reportedly as young as nine, and then to pitched battles in the railroad station and Piazza Carlo III. Rebels manhandled streetcars to build barricades, and fought with shotguns, swords, ancient muskets, and roofing tiles. An estimated three hundred locals died in the brawling, and the OSS believed that Neapolitan fury had forced German troops to quit the city two days sooner than planned.

"There were still Germans fighting in spots," Gavin later told his diary, "but worse the Italians were fighting each other, accusing friends and foes alike of being Fascists or *tedeschi*." Teenagers in tin helmets roamed the streets, armed with kitchen knives, tire irons, and German Lugers; red Italian grenades dangled from their belts. Robert Capa photographed a schoolhouse converted into a morgue with twenty boys arrayed in twenty crude coffins shouldered by men in black fedoras; keening women blotted their eyes and held up photographs of their dead children. George Biddle took his sketchbook into the Ospedale degli Incurabili, where he found 150 dead civilians on stretchers and window shutters, slips of paper with their names and addresses tucked into their folded hands. There were no trucks to haul them to graveyards, nor was there water to wash their blood from the hospital floor. Families carrying clean shirts and white undergarments to dress the dead "wandered about the corridor in the semi-darkness, holding mufflers or handkerchefs over their faces," and peering at each body in dread of finding a familiar face.

Naples itself—"the most beautiful city in the universe," in Stendahl's judgment—had been mutilated. German vengeance at Italy's betrayal foreshadowed the spasmodic violence that European towns large and small could expect as the price of liberation. Half of the city's one million residents had remained through the German occupation, but none now had running water: Wehrmacht sappers had blown up the main aqueduct in seven places and drained municipal reservoirs. Dynamite dropped down manholes wrecked at least forty sewer lines. Explosives also demolished the long-distance telephone exchange, three-quarters of the city's bridges, and electrical generators and substations. Among the gutted industrial plants— about fifty in all—were a steelworks, an oil refinery, breweries, tanneries, and canneries; others were wired for demolition though they had been not fired. Saboteurs wrecked city trams, repair barns, and even street cleaners. A railroad tunnel into Naples was blocked by crashing two trains head-on. Coal stockpiles were ignited, and for weeks served as beacons for Luftwaffe bombers. The Germans had extorted ransom from Italian fishermen for their boats—a small skiff was worth one gold watch—and then burned the fleet anyway. Even the stairwells in barracks and apartment buildings were dynamited to make the upper floors inaccessible.

The opportunities for cultural atrocity were boundless in a city so rich in culture. A German battalion burst into the library of the Italian Royal Society, soaked the shelves with kerosene, and fired the place with grenades, shooting guards who resisted and keeping firemen at bay. The city archives and fifty thousand volumes at the University of Naples, where Thomas Aquinas once taught, got the same treatment, leaving the place "stinking of burned old leather and petrol." Another eighty thousand precious books and manuscripts stored in Nola were reduced to ashes, along with paintings, ceramics, and ivories.

Worse yet was the sabotage around the great port, which compounded grievous damage inflicted by months of Allied bombing. Half a mile inland, the city's commercial districts remained mostly intact, although looters had rifled the Singer Sewing Machine showroom and the Kodak shop on Via Roma. But along the esplanade—where the corpse of the beautiful

Siren Parthenope was said to have washed ashore after Odysseus spurned her "high, thrilling song"—all was shambles. Bombs had battered the Castel Nuovo, the National Library, and the Palazzo Reale, where every window was broken, the roof punctured, and the chapel demolished by a detonation beneath the ceiling beams. Grand hotels—the Excelsior, the Vesuvio, the Continental—had been gutted by bombs or by German vandals who torched the rooms and ignited the bedding in courtyard bonfires. An American port battalion stevedore, Paul W. Brown, described waterside buildings that had been

> sliced in half, leaving the remaining halves showing exposed rooms with furniture intact or half hanging out, pictures on a wall, a brass bed slanting down toward the street, bed linen still in place. From the open side of a third-story room the legs of a corpse dangled.

Not a single vessel remained afloat in the port, a drowned forest of charred booms, masts, and funnels. Thirty major wrecks could be seen, and ten times that number lay submerged. All tugs and harbor craft had been sunk; all grain elevators and warehouses demolished; all three hundred cranes sabotaged or toppled into the water. Vessels had been scuttled at fifty-eight of sixty-one berths, often one atop another. An Axis ship with seven thousand tons of ammunition had blown up at Pier F, wrecking four adjacent city blocks, and fires still smoldered on October 2. At Mole H, slips were blocked by a dozen rail cars and a pair of ninety-ton cranes shoved off the pier. Quayside buildings were dynamited so that their rubble tumbled like scree across the docks. To complicate salvage, German demolitionists had seeded the harbor with ammunition, oxygen tanks, and mines.

Only rats still inhabited the waterfront, and hungry urchins with knife-edge shoulder blades who reminded Paul Brown of "small, aged animals." Although U.S. Army engineers reported that the sabotage had been conducted "by a man who knew his business," a closer inspection revealed that the Germans "planned their demolitions for revenge, to wreck the economy of Naples, rather than to prevent Allied use of the port." As the Allies learned from each campaign, so did the Germans, and they would be less sentimental and more comprehensive when the time came to undo Marseilles and Cherbourg.

Still, the damage was monstrous. To sustain an army of half a million men—and Fifth Army would be half that size within weeks—required the monthly cargo equivalent of sixty-eight Liberty ships. Only Naples—sad, scuttled, big-shouldered Naples—could handle such commerce. There was nothing for it but to get to work, and to bring the Siren back from the dead.

\* \* \*

The capture of Naples gave Clark time to take stock of a campaign that grew bigger and dirtier by the day. Rommel's genteel *Krieg ohne Hass*—"war without hate"—was but a hazy memory from North Africa. The brutality of total war had long been felt on the Eastern Front, but as the Second World War entered its fifth year the stain spread throughout western Europe.

Contrary to Clark's hopes, the Italian army contributed little to the Allied cause after Rome's capitulation. Twenty-nine Italian divisions in the Balkans and five more in France mostly surrendered to the Germans, sometimes duped by forged orders and sometimes reduced by force. "Every bomb is chipping a little piece off my heart," the Italian garrison commander on Rhodes radioed during a Luftwaffe attack. Those defending Italia proper proved just as impotent.

Brave souls—and there were some—faced barbaric reprisals. On the rocky Greek island of Cephalonia, in the Ionian Sea, the 12,000-man Italian army garrison fought for five days at a cost of 1,250 combat deaths before surrendering on September 22. On orders from Berlin, more than 6,000 prisoners were promptly shot, including orderlies with Red Cross brassards, wounded men dragged to the wall from their hospital beds, and officers, executed in batches of eight and twelve. An Italian commander ripped off the Iron Cross given him by Hitler personally and flung it at his firing squad. The dead were ballasted on rafts and sunk at sea or burned in huge pyres that blackened the Ionian sky for a week; decades later, when the air grew heavy and clouds darkened before a storm, islanders would say, "The Italians are burning."

"The only Italian army that will not be treacherous is one that does not exist," said Field Marshal Wilhelm Keitel, the German chief of staff. Soon 600,000 Italian soldiers were en route to Germany in cattle cars, not as prisoners of war but as "military internees" to be used for slave labor in factories and mines. Ten thousand German railway workers poured into Italy to ensure that the trains still ran on time.

Three improbable escapes marked the early campaign in Italy. The first had occurred as Clark's forces came ashore at Salerno before dawn on September 9, when much of the Italian battle fleet fled La Spezia, in northern Italy, for Malta. A German radio intercept detected clandestine sailing preparations, but too late to prevent a sudden sortie for the open sea. The unfortunate battleship *Roma* would be sunk by the new radio-controlled glide bomb, and captains who, unable to flee La Spezia, scuttled their ships were summarily executed. But by September 21 five other battleships, eight cruisers, thirty-three destroyers, one hundred merchant ships, and many lesser tubs had found refuge in Allied waters, some flying surrender flags said to be "the size of a tennis court." German forces managed to impound hundreds of smaller naval and merchant vessels, part of a vast catalogue of booty seized in Italy: 1.3 million rifles, 38,000 machine guns, 10,000 artillery tubes, 67,000 horses and mules, 9,000 tons of tobacco, 13,000 tons of quinine, 551,000 overcoats, 2.5 million blankets, 3.3 million pairs of shoes, and, in Rome alone, 60,000 motor vehicles.

The second escape evoked unhappy memories of the Axis getaway from Messina a month earlier. Hitler on September 12 had ordered the evacuation of German forces on Corsica, including thousands who had crossed to the island from nearby Sardinia. As French troops stormed ashore at one end of Corsica, German soldiers decamped from the other end, crossing sixty miles of deep water to northern Italy in transport planes and a cockleshell fleet of ferries. Mostly unmolested by Allied naval or air forces, which pleaded a preoccupation with Salerno, more then thirty thousand enemy troops with their arms and vehicles reached safety by early October. Given the absence of Axis shore batteries or other defenses, the evacuation was "even more astonishing" than Messina had been, as the official U.S. Navy history later conceded. Surely it was every bit as disheartening.

The third escape was the most flamboyant. Since his arrest in late July, Benito Mussolini had been shuttled from cell to whitewashed cell in the islands off Italy's west coast, spending his days—including his sixtieth birthday—reading Ricciotti's *Life of Jesus* and underscoring the passages on betrayal and martyrdom. Hitler's search for his erstwhile ally included consultation with various occultists and astrologers, among them a certain "Master of the Sidereal Pendulum," as well as more conventional intelligence clairvoyants. In late August, the Duce was moved to the Hotel Albergo-Rifugio, a vacated ski resort atop the Gran Sasso peaks in the Apennines, accessible only by funicular and guarded by 250 carabinieri. To his daily regimen the prisoner added card games, strolls across the bleak heath, and endless carping about his ulcer. Gray stubble sprouted from his unshaved pate. When Mussolini vowed never to be taken alive, jailers removed all sharp objects, including his razor. "To redeem oneself," he told his diary, "one must suffer."

Soon enough his whereabouts leaked. Hitler entrusted the Duce's rescue to Captain Otto Skorzeny, a six-foot, three-inch Viennese commando whose badly scarred visage attested to the fourteen duels he had supposedly fought as a student. At one P.M. on September 12—just as conditions at Salerno turned grievous—Skorzeny packed 108 men into gliders and took off for the Gran Sasso, carving a hole in the canvas floor of his craft through which to watch for navigational landmarks. Mussolini was sitting at his open bedroom window, arms folded in his iconic pose, when gliders began skittering across the cobbled ground directly outside. Skorzeny bolted up a staircase three steps at a time, flung open the door to room 201, and announced, "Duce, the Führer has sent me to set you free." Off they went, wedged into a tiny Storch airplane and saluted by the carabinieri guards. After a giddy reunion with Hitler, Mussolini was installed in an Alpine town as the puppet head of a puppet regime called the Italian Social Republic. Even the Germans, rarely celebrated for ironic sensibilities, recognized the pathos. "The Führer now realizes that Italy never was a power, is no power today, and won't be a power in the future," Joseph Goebbels told his diary.

Whatever Mussolini's shortcomings as a world-historical figure, he had kept the Nazi reaper at bay by refusing to allow the deportation of Jews. That moratorium had now ended. On September 16 the first consignment of two dozen Jews was shipped from a town in northern Italy to Auschwitz. Among them was a six-year-old child, who was gassed upon arrival.

The liberation of Naples grew sanguinary again at 2:10 P.M. on Thursday, October 7, when the first German time bomb exploded in the southwest corner of the main post office on Via Monteoliveto. "The first two floors were blown completely away," a witness reported. "Chunks of steel and marble were thrown as far as 100 yards." The blast ripped apart an Army work detail and Neapolitans begging for food along a mess line. A soldier, Robert H. Welker, described the carnage in a letter home:

> From the huge smoke pall still hanging in the street staggered a sergeant in fatigues, bloody about the face, barely conscious. . . . The sergeant's head was rolling from side to side, and all he could mutter was, "What was it? What was it?"

The blast killed and wounded seventy people, half of them soldiers. Rescuers shimmied into the post office basement to dig for survivors, while medical details shoveled up heads and limbs. Welker's first sergeant called the unit roll that night, reading out names by flashlight. "I shout a word, and live," Welker wrote. "Another cannot give the word, and is accounted dead. . . . Here, now, was mortal danger for us all."

Three days later, on Sunday morning, Clark, Ridgway, and several thousand troops were attending a mass of thanksgiving in the Duomo beneath the vivid frescoes of Paradise when another muffled roar sent them hurrying to a nearby barracks. That blast, in the Corso Orientale, killed twenty-three combat engineers who had fought with Darby's Rangers at Chiunzi

Pass. The two generals helped extricate broken bodies—"sacks of burlap," in one paratrooper's description—as well as survivors. "Nice work, boys, thanks," said a soldier who was pulled from the rubble and hoisted to his feet before falling over, dead. "It makes us all the more determined to crush them completely," Clark wrote Renie that evening. A bomb squad "delousing" a different wing in the Prince of Piedmont Barracks later found nearly a ton of explosives in stacked boxes with a ticking German fuse set to detonate at seven A.M. on Tuesday, October 19.

Bombs would continue to explode for three weeks. Norman Lewis, a British intelligence officer in Fifth Army, described one demolished apartment building along Via Nazario Sauro in which survivors stood "as motionless as statues, and all coated in thick white dust. . . . A woman stood like Lot's wife turned to salt." Others, in fetal curls, reminded Lewis of "bodies overcome by the ash at Pompeii." Frantic sappers ultimately searched hundreds of buildings, disarming explosives in seventeen of them. An official "list of suspicious noises" grew to 150 entries. Maledictions on the German fiend grew proportionally fervent, although rarely was it mentioned that Allied planes were dropping thousands of bombs with delay fuses.

Fears that more hidden bombs would be triggered when electricity again surged through the repaired power grid led to a mass evacuation of western Naples in late October. Lewis watched "men carrying their old parents on their backs" and wounded soldiers being wheeled from hospitals. Any loud noise sent women and children stampeding in panic, "leaving trails of urine." Another British officer, Malcolm Muggeridge, described the evacuees as "a vast concourse gathered on the hills around the city, like a vision of the Last Day, when all the dead arise." The lights winked on without incident, and the citizenry shambled home.

Neapolitan life after liberation remained brutish for weeks. "There are 57 varieties of grief, but only about 7 of that number that some flour would not cure," an American officer told his superiors. "These people are hungry." All the tropical fish in the municipal aquarium were devoured, and the city's cat population was said to have thinned dramatically. Brackish watering holes and even broken sewer mains drew thousands of parched residents "with buckets, bottles, barrels, cauldrons, [and] coffee pots," George Biddle noted. Army engineers soon set up two dozen faucets but soldiers with bayonets were needed to quell the rioting.

Twenty-six thousand tons of wheat would be sent from North Africa and the Middle East, but even famine relief had to compete with war matériel for scarce shipping space. The port's ruin complicated the task, and a third of the food in the initial shipments was stolen. Prices spiraled, sometimes quadrupling overnight. A spectacular black market flourished. Frank Gervasi catalogued the apparently limitless cupboard of luxury goods available even as Neapolitans grew gaunt and the first cases of typhus appeared in October: "silver fox capes in furriers' windows . . . ladies' hats, shoes, gloves . . . Venetian lace . . . perfume by weight." Citizens joked bitterly that "when the Germans were here we ate once a day. Now the Americans have come we eat once a week."

Reconstruction had begun on Neapolitan roads and railways on October 2, and an engineer team entered the harbor from the sea at noon on the same day to take soundings. Bulldozers, minesweepers, and salvage ships soon resembled "an army of ants eating their way into the wreckage," in one admiral's description. Divers pumped compressed air into sunken wrecks to create buoyancy and tugs then dragged the hulks from the harbor with huge slings. Dynamite periodically scared off the Italian workforce, and only three berths were opened in the first weeks; but within three months Naples would claim more tonnage handled than New York harbor. Potable water began flowing on October 13; Italian submarines provided power for pumping stations, hospitals, and flour mills, and the sewers would be fixed by mid-December.

As thousands of Allied soldiers poured into Naples, street life rekindled in one of the world's most flamboyant cities. Garbagemen sang Rossini and hunchbacks sold lottery tickets, permitting each buyer a stroke of the hump for luck. A few restaurants reopened, though the veal Milanese often proved to be horsemeat and, as Norman Lewis observed, Italian patrons sat bundled in coats "made from our stolen blankets." Thievery, beggary, and harlotry flourished in a city that was desperately hungry. "It wasn't safe to go to town without a gun," a paratrooper recalled, and GIs joked that if you dropped even your voice an Italian pauper would pick it up. Thousands of Italian women turned to prostitution to avoid starvation. Little boys pimped for streetwalkers around the Piazza Garibaldi; troops who paid with Monopoly money, claiming it was occupation scrip, found the joke repaid with a strain of Neapolitan gonorrhea that proved resistant to sulfa. An airman told his diary on October 6: " 'Fik' can be had for chocolate."

Some soldiers behaved badly. Troops quartered in the zoological laboratories at the University of Naples smashed specimen cases, rifled the mineral collection, and used rare seashells as candle holders. GIs drove about in jeeps adorned with "stuffed toucans, parrots, eagles, and even ostriches" from the collections; the custodian of the Palazzo Reale complained that Allied troops were "carrying away anything that pleases them." Reuben Tucker, the commander of the 504th Parachute Infantry Regiment, ordered a bottle of champagne in a restaurant—for seventy-three cents—and toasted the capture of

Naples. "He drained his glass and smashed it on the table," a paratrooper reported. "The rest of us did likewise." To the proprietor, Tucker said, "That's the price you pay for collaborating with the Germans."

They were in fine fettle. High spirits infected all ranks after the grim struggle at Salerno. They now owned a major port and three hundred miles of Italian boot. On the same day that Naples fell, Montgomery's Eighth Army had captured the airdromes at Foggia, near the Adriatic, which would provide bases for the bombing of Austria, southern Germany, and the Danube basin.

Everywhere Allied forces were on the march. In the southwest Pacific, parallel thrusts in New Guinea and the Solomon Islands continued to pare away pieces of the Japanese empire; the first B-29 bombers were coming off U.S. assembly lines, doubling the range of existing planes and putting Japan's home islands at risk. British and American bomber fleets from England were already pummeling German cities, though at a frightful cost in aircrews. Hamburg had been incinerated in July with an estimated forty thousand German deaths, eight hundred died in Berlin in late August, and massive raids would batter Mannheim, Frankfurt, Hanover, and other targets across the Fatherland. On the Eastern Front, the Red Army in late September took Smolensk and crossed the Dnieper River, recapturing nearly half the territory seized by Germany since the summer of 1941. In the east, Hitler had already lost a half million dead and and two million wounded. Goebbels told his diary, "We are still retreating and retreating."

They were retreating in Italy, too. With Naples secure and the Allied vanguard approaching the Volturno River, Clark was keen to press the fight. "He always wants speed," Major General John Lucas, who had replaced Dawley as the VI Corps commander, observed in his diary. Clark, he added, "has ants in his pants."

Canadian soldiers proposed the slogan "Rome by Christmas," but they were pessimists. "Alexander and I both believe we will have Rome by [the end of] October," Eisenhower cabled Marshall on October 4. Alexander thought Florence might fall by December, and some zealous troops began studying German to prepare for occupation duty. Churchill posited that the enemy lacked "the strength to make a front"—Kesselring always looked weaker from Whitehall than from within artillery range—and the prime minister planned to visit the Eternal City before the month was out.

Even cautious Franklin Roosevelt, who had begun pushing for Allied forces to reach Berlin "as soon as the Russians," was swept along on the optimistic tide. To Stalin he wrote, "It looks as if American and British armies should be in Rome in another few weeks."

## *"Watch Where You Step and Have No Curiosity at All"*

ALL blithe predictions of a promenade to Rome would be challenged soon enough, but first the Allied legions faced a formidable obstacle twenty miles north of Naples. Here, at the wide Volturno, Fifth Army would make its inaugural crossing in Europe of a contested river, with six divisions abreast opposed by four from Vietinghoff's Tenth Army.

Lucian Truscott had kept most of his 3rd Division guns quiet for nearly a week to conceal his strength, but at one A.M. on Wednesday, October 13, gunners flipped back their camouflage nets and let fly a barrage that stamped and howled across the dells. Artillery rippled like chain lightning down the Volturno Valley, shaming the full moon that silvered the river. Flames soon guttered from the German-held hills and farmhouses north of the river. More guns barked downstream from the three British divisions joining the assault, and upstream where two other American divisions on Truscott's right—the 34th and 45th—anchored a forty-mile front.

From the third-floor window of an abandoned hilltop monastery, Truscott's gray eyes searched the river below. German sentries had shouted taunts in English from the far bank—"Sleep, swine. We kill you all before breakfast"—but now the roar of gunfire swallowed all insults. Blue and white machine-gun tracers swept like heated needles from enemy bunkers hidden in the orchards and stone quarries, and mortar bursts blossomed across the muddy fields on the south bank. American gunners flailed back with braids of crimson tracers, and riflemen popped away at the winking muzzles to the north. Here the Volturno was two hundred feet wide, swift but fordable, and Truscott's sector stretched laterally for seven miles in the center of the Allied line.

Drawing on a cigarette with his hands cupped to hide the ember, he watched two regiments in a line of trees below the monastery make ready by moonlight. Soldiers cinched life vests scavenged in an Italian torpedo factory and coiled cotton guide ropes over their shoulders. Others stacked rafts borrowed from the Navy and crude, canvas-bottom boats hammered together from scrap lumber and truck tarpaulins.

Garish signal flares—gold, green, red—drifted above the German lines. "Unfortunately I'm beginning to realize the truth that Ike spake when he described his loneliness to me," Truscott had written in a "beloved wife" letter to Sarah as the division approached the Volturno. "We are lonely." Never more than now, while watching men whom he had perhaps ordered to their deaths. He also told her:

I would love in the quiet of the evening to sit with you and tell you the thousand and one details of my life over here. . . . If and when I get back from this business I want to settle down somewhere . . . and spend a few years in peace and quiet.

At 1:55 A.M. the gun batteries began to mix white-phosphorus shells with the high explosives, training their tubes on the far bank. Silvery smoke soon boiled in a cloud three miles wide and five hundred feet high. With a shout and a clatter, the troops below hoisted their rafts and their homely boats. Surging across the fallow fields, they slid down the ten-foot embankment and splashed into the muddy Volturno.

It went well enough in the American sector, less well in the British. On the far left of the Allied line, three LCTs ferried a squadron of seventeen British tanks across the river's mouth to the north shore. But mines and boggy ground kept them immobile. British infantrymen struggled with a wider, unfordable stretch of river, as well as with German defenders—the 15th Panzer Grenadier and Hermann Göring Divisions, old adversaries from Sicily and Salerno—who found good cover in vineyards and behind the levees. Tommies lashed lumber to empty fuel cans and paddled across, or fashioned life belts from buoyant flax sheaves. Two brigades from the 46th Division secured a bridgehead near the coast, though by Thursday morning it was still only six hundred yards deep. On the 3rd Division's immediate left, ten assault boats from the British 56th Division were sunk midstream near Capua and not a single company made the far shore in what Truscott considered a botched, halfhearted effort. "Drowning wounded men were washed away by the current into the sea," Alan Moorehead wrote. "Everywhere machine-gunning and sniping was going on through the reeds."

With his left flank exposed and no American armor yet across, Truscott scrambled down to the flats at dawn. Milky smoke swirled like mist. GIs waded chest-deep through the water, holding their rifles overhead with one hand and clinging to a guide rope with the other. Worry etched Truscott's weathered face. Five battalions occupied the far shore, and American spearheads had reached Monte Caruso, four miles beyond the Volturno. But without armor they were vulnerable to counterattacking panzers. "Hurry!" he urged. "Hurry!"

Hissing fragments from a German shellburst pocked the river. "Get those damn tank destroyers and tanks across," Truscott ordered. A tank commander, puzzled by a sharp rapping on his hull, peered from the turret to see a two-star general wielding a shillelagh. "Goddamit, get up ahead and fire at some targets of opportunity," Truscott demanded. "Fire at anything shooting our men, but goddamit, do some good for yourselves." To an officer who complained of bridging difficulties, he responded with a growl. "What do you mean it can't be done? Have you tried it? Go out and do it."

They did. Below an oxbow loop, engineers hacked at the steep bank with picks and shovels. At eleven A.M. the first Sherman forded the river, muddy water streaming from the fenders as it clanked toward Highway 87. Fourteen more crossed close behind. A light bridge opened to traffic at 3:30 P.M.—eighty jeeps sped across in eight minutes—and heavier treadway bridges followed. Massed artillery discouraged German counterattackers; like a melting shadow, the enemy drew back. Clark shifted boundary lines to give one large bridge to the Tommies—the British in Fifth Army had only 3,500 engineers, compared with 15,000 for the Yanks—and soon the entire valley was in Allied hands. On the right flank, where the meandering river doubled back on itself and required some units to make three crossings, 34th Division soldiers asked whether every stream in Italy was named "Volturno," or whether it was simply the longest body of water in Europe.

"Like the earthworm, I seem to bore into what's in front and leave debris in the rear and am barely sensible of the passage of days and nights," Truscott wrote Sarah as the bridgehead expanded on October 14. "Days of the week? I hardly know there is a distinction between them." He added, "This business of killing Boche is an absorbing and all-consuming proposition."

Inelegant and exhausting though it was, the Volturno crossing would serve. By moving more quickly than expected on a broad front, and by leaving the main roads to infiltrate around enemy strongpoints, the Anglo-Americans had advanced thirty-five miles past Naples. Hills loomed ahead, as every corporal could see, and beyond those hills loomed higher hills. "This is not the place for masterminding," Eisenhower said with a shake of the head upon viewing the terrain. But beyond the higher hills, barely 130 road miles from the Volturno, lay Rome.

Italy would break their backs, their bones, and nearly their spirits. But first it would break their hearts, and that heartbreak began north of the Volturno, where the terrain steepened, the weather worsened, and the enemy stiffened. Allied casualties in Italy totaled eighteen thousand between September 3 and October 20—fifteen thousand in Fifth Army and three thousand in Eighth Army. Yet that was only a down payment on the campaign to come.

German demolitions had begun five miles from Salerno—"no bridge or culvert seems too small to escape their eye," an Army observer reported—and it soon became evident that Italy would be a battle of engineers: the speed of advance would be determined by bulldozers, if not by a nervous soldier on his hands and knees, prodding for mines with a bayonet. An AFHQ study estimated that one thousand bridges would be needed to reach the Po River in the north, a disheartening number given that for weeks the U.S. Army had only five prefabricated Bailey bridges in Italy. In the event, the Allies would erect three thousand spans in twenty months, with a combined length of fifty-five miles. Some were built and rebuilt, as autumn rains put the Italian rivers in spate. The fickle Volturno soon rose eighteen feet in ten hours, sweeping away every hard-won bridge but one. "The floods bring down quantities of debris, ranging from whole trees to bulls, the horns of which had a disastrous effect on the plywood sides of a pontoon," Fifth Army engineers reported.

Ingenuity became the order of the day, every day. When German sappers blew up stone houses to block narrow village streets, American sappers bulldozed "new tracks across the rubble heaps, often at the level of the second stories," Truscott noted. Engineers reportedly filled road craters with "broken bathtubs and statues and sinks and hairbrushes and fancy fedora hats." Bridge builders fashioned a pile driver from the barrel of an Italian 240mm gun, and the Allies built rolling mills, cement works, foundries, nail works, and enough sawmills to cut nine thousand tons of Volturno lumber a month. They used the timber to corduroy muddy roads, as armies had for centuries.

Yet no engineer could corduroy the weather. "It got darker, colder, wetter," a 45th Division soldier recalled. Autumn rains began on September 26, and soldiers soon realized why their Italian phrase books included *Piove in rovesci,* "It's raining torrents." Censorship rules forbade writing home about the weather—"One may write of mist," a wag proposed, "but not of rain"—though nothing precluded bivouac grousing. "No conversation, genteel or otherwise, can be carried on without mentioning the weather," a diarist in the 56th Evacuation Hospital noted in November. Campfires were banned after five P.M., so troops ate at four, bolting their supper before rain pooled in their mess kits, then went to bed at 7:30. Craps games lasted "until darkness obscures spots on the dice." Rain soon grayed the soldiers, making them one with the mud in which they slept and fought until they seemed no more than clay with eyes.

As Allied planners had misjudged the harsh North African winter, so they underestimated—perhaps less pardonably—the even harsher Italian climate: Rome shares a latitude with Chicago. "The desert war had made men forget the mud of Flanders," wrote the British general W.G.F. Jackson, but no veteran of Italy would ever forget Italian mud, which Bill Mauldin insisted lacked "an honest color like ordinary mud." A private from Michigan complained, "The trouble with this mud is that it's too thick to drink and too thin to plow." Even in summer, the roads of southern Italy were barely adequate; now the British and Americans would be canalized on the only northbound hard-surface roads—Highways 6, 7, 16, and 17—that could carry the prodigious traffic of armies. Foul weather constrained maneuver, obviated the advantages of motorization, and undermined air superiority by halving the number of Allied bombing sorties. Churchill cursed the "savage versatility" of Italy's climate, but GIs simply called it "German weather."

Mines made it much worse. "All roads lead to Rome," Alexander quipped, "but all the roads are mined." So were footpaths, lovers' lanes, alleys, goat trails, streambeds, shortcuts, and tracks, beaten and unbeaten. "I never had a moment that I didn't worry about mines and booby traps," a 7th Infantry officer said. Forty percent of Fifth Army battle casualties in early November came from mines. "Watch where you step," Clark's headquarters advised, "and have no curiosity at all."

North of the Volturno, "you could follow our battalions by the blood-stained leggings, the scattered equipment, and the bits of bodies where men had been blown up," the 168th Infantry reported. Big Teller mines could destroy a truck or cripple a tank, but German antipersonnel mines became particularly diabolical. "Castrators" or "nutcrackers" fired a bullet upward when an unwitting soldier stepped on the pressure plate. "Shoe" mines, built mostly of wood, proved nearly impossible to detect. Enemy sappers mined or booby-trapped doorknobs and desk drawers, grapevines and haystacks, apples on the tree and bodies on the ground, whether Italian or German, Tommy or Yank. At least two chaplains lost legs trying to bury the dead above the Volturno.

"A man's foot is usually blown loose at the ankle, leaving the mangled foot dangling on shredded tendons," an Army physician noted in his diary. "Additional puncture wounds of both legs and groin make the agony worse." A combat medic later wrote, "Even though you'd give them a shot or two of morphine, they would still scream." In a minefield, Bill Mauldin observed, "an old man thinks of his eyes and a young man grabs for his balls." The Army bought 100,000 of the SCR-625 mine detector—dubbed a "manhole cover on a stick"—but they proved useless in the rain and befuddled by the iron ore and shell fragments common in Italian soil. The device also required its operator to stand upright, often under fire, while listening for the telltale hum that signified danger. A secret program to train canine detectors—"M dogs"—failed when half the mines in field tests remained unsniffed.

\* \* \*

None of it—not the demolitions, nor the rain, nor the nasty Ms—would have thwarted the Allies' upcountry march even temporarily had the Germans adhered to their original plan of an expedient fighting withdrawal to fortifications in the northern Apennines. Then perhaps the prime minister could have enjoyed autumn Chianti in Rome, and Alexander might indeed have captured Florence by year's end.

Instead, as the Allies splashed across the Volturno, an intense debate raged in the German high command over whether to change strategies. Rommel, who still commanded nine divisions in northern Italy, had spent much of September recuperating from an appendectomy. "Domineering, obstinate, and defeatist," as one admirer described him, he was increasingly disaffected with his military superiors in Berlin and adamant that German forces must retreat to a line below the Po River valley, or risk being outflanked and encircled. He chalked that line in blue on his headquarters map.

Kesselring, commanding eight divisions in the south, argued otherwise. Italy remained a comparatively minor theater: 3 million Germans fought in 163 divisions on the Eastern Front, and 34 divisions occupied France and the Low Countries. But Italy was the one active battleground where the inexorable German retreat might be arrested. Abandoning Rome would be a psychological blow, Kesselring insisted. More important, in Allied possession the airfields around the capital would complement those already captured at Foggia, making Austrian aircraft factories, Romanian oil fields, and the Danube basin even more vulnerable to enemy bombers.

Smiling Albert had his own map, and his own chalked lines. The Italian Peninsula was narrowest south of Rome, just eighty-five miles from sea to sea. Across this neck of country so wild it was home to wolves and bears, the Germans could build three progressively stout fortified lines, to be named Barbara, Bernhardt, and Gustav. "The object is to create an impregnable system of positions in depth, and so to save German blood," Kesselring said. "Leaders of all ranks must never forget this high moral responsibility." The Gustav Line, anchored on the vertical massif at Monte Cassino, could become the most formidable defensive position in Europe, strong enough that "the British and Americans would break their teeth on it."

Even as Hitler vacillated he began shifting forces south, from northern Italy and elsewhere, in part to forestall an Allied leap into the Balkans. It was said that he was dictating the order appointing Rommel supreme commander in Italy when he changed his mind in favor of Kesselring. "Military leadership without optimism is not possible," the Führer later explained, adding, "Rommel is an extraordinarily brave and able commander. I don't regard him as a stayer."

Rommel shrugged. "I'll take it as it comes," he wrote his wife, Lucie, on October 26. Hitler in early November signed a formal order demanding "the end of withdrawals," thereby condemning a million men to the agonies of Cassino, Ortona, the Rapido River, and Anzio. Rommel would be sent west to oversee the Atlantic Wall coastal defenses, including those in Normandy, where he had won military glory in 1940. "The war is as good as lost," he told one comrade, "and hard times lie ahead."

Thanks to Ultra, the stiffening of German strategy had become all too evident to the Allied high command. Decrypted radio intercepts revealed both Hitler's growing reluctance to yield ground and the construction south of Rome of three fortified lines, which collectively would be known as the Winter Line. The Germans appeared ready to wage a protracted war of attrition, with a view to exhausting the Allies.

The optimism of early October vanished, supplanted by extravagant despair. After reviewing the latest intelligence, Alexander cabled London on October 21: "We are committed to a long and costly advance to Rome, a 'slogging match.'" The return of seven Allied divisions to Britain for OVERLORD left, for the moment, only eleven facing a German force that had swelled to twenty-three divisions and could grow "to the order of sixty." The Allied buildup had dwindled, too: where thirteen hundred vehicles had been arriving in Italy each day, now only two thousand came per week. The terrain was abominable, the weather filthy. (Twenty inches of rain would fall in the final three months of 1943.) Fifth Army was advancing less than a mile a day and had yet to hit the main German line. On the Adriatic, Eighth Army crept forward on a thirty-five-mile front into what Alexander called a "cul-de-sac of rather unimportant country."

In supposing that Hitler would abandon southern Italy after losing Naples, the Allies had once again underestimated German resolve—or capriciousness—in the Mediterranean. Eisenhower saw no alternative to bulling ahead. "It is essential for us to retain the initiative," he cabled the Combined Chiefs on October 25. Referring to the enemy, he added: "If we can keep him on his heels until early spring, then the more divisions he uses in a counteroffensive against us, the better it will be for OVERLORD."

Nor did the high command in Washington and London see a need to revise the rather vague strategic objectives in Italy: to engage as many German troops as possible and, although this goal remained more tacit than explicit, to liberate Rome. Churchill tried to sugar the pill by assuring Roosevelt on October 26, "The fact that the enemy have diverted such powerful forces to this theater vindicates our strategy."

The prospect of waging a bitter mountain campaign rather than wintering in lovely Rome pleased no one, although the official British history later doubted "whether anyone in high places fully understood what a winter campaign in Italy implied." Alexander translated the strategic objectives into a line on the map, roughly fifty miles above Rome and stretching northeast across the peninsula to the Adriatic, which he urged Clark and Montgomery to reach as soon as possible.

Alexander's despondency was aggravated by a bout of jaundice, and his ecru complexion compromised efforts to put on a determined public face. "We'll just have to punch, punch, punch, and keep Jerry on the run until we reach Rome," he told reporters. Privately, he saw "no reason why we should ever get to Rome."

Montgomery at least sensed what the Anglo-American legions were in for. He believed that Allied strategists needed to rediscover what W.G.F. Jackson called "ancient truths" about seasonal fighting in Europe. "I do not think we can conduct a winter campaign in this country," Montgomery wrote on October 31. "If I remember, Caesar used to go into winter quarters—a very sound thing to do!"

## The Mountainous Hinterland

LIEUTENANT Colonel Jack Toffey surely would have found sense in Montgomery's prescription had it reached his ear. "The road to Rome is a long one," Toffey wrote, "and in many respects like the road to hell—inclusive of the good intentions." Yet there would be no winter quarters, no sheltered wait for the roads to dry and the skies to clear, no Caesarian pause for a better day. Toffey commanded only one of a hundred Allied infantry battalions scattered from the Tyrrhenian Sea to the Adriatic, but he and his men were of a piece with the larger army group. What they endured, many endured. What they suffered, many suffered. As Toffey was emblematic of the young commanders who carried forward the battle experience of Morocco, Tunisia, and now Sicily, so his unit—the 2nd Battalion of the 15th Infantry Regiment, in Truscott's 3rd Division—typified others trying to chivvy the Germans out of the interlocking fortifications of the Winter Line.

Under a different star, Toffey would have been aboard a troopship bound for Britain with the rest of the 9th Division, with which he had served in Africa and Sicily. Instead, he was among two thousand veterans transferred to the 3rd Division for immediate duty in Italy. Though he still dreamed of the day when he would "never get disheveled again," he was pleased at the chance to serve once more under Truscott, whom he knew from Morocco, and proud to join both the 3rd Division—"the best in the

West," he called it—and the 15th Infantry, whose antebellum alumni included George Marshall and Dwight Eisenhower.

"Life is good," he wrote his wife, Helen, in Columbus. Having reached Italy during the final hours at Salerno, he felt that he was "really soldiering again." During the Volturno crossing "he was inexhaustible," reported George Biddle, who joined Toffey's men for a month of sketching and watercoloring. "He seemed to carry the whole battalion on his shoulders." Biddle admired Toffey's "keen, sharp mind and tough, salty American humor." The young colonel, who possessed "the bones and conformation of a steeple-chaser rather than a racehorse," was ubiquitous: urging his men forward, directing artillery fire, interrogating prisoners, evacuating the wounded and the dead.

For the last two weeks of October, they pushed north by northwest in Alexander's "slogging match," following a rugged corridor between the upper Volturno and Highway 6, known ever more sardonically as Victory Road. American maps often labeled the terrain here simply "mountainous hinterland." Through stone pines and flame-shaped cypresses they trudged, past farm cottages with chimneys poking like snorkels above the red tile roofs. Peasants keened over their dead, or rummaged through their ruined crofts to salvage a copper pot or a rag doll. "Nothing I can do for him," a medic told Toffey, pointing to a prostrate old man. "He is as dead as he will ever be." German corpses, most from the 3rd Panzer Grenadier Division, flattened the weeds; some had been carbonized by artillery fire, others were simply carrion. GIs pocketed their *Gott mit Uns* buckles and moved on.

Across the cobblestones of Liberi and Roccaromana and Pietravairano they plodded, past the townfolk dressed in mourning and the *bambini* diapered in newspapers. Mines detonated, gunfights erupted, and all too often Toffey stood over a dying boy, whispering, "The stretchers are coming up, kid. Hang on." Turning to a squad leader during one brawl he said, "I think we have the machine gun nest surrounded up there among the rocks. . . . Go get 'em—and don't bring 'em back."

At night they put the battalion command post in a fire-blackened cave or a farmhouse loft, sleeping on cold ground or corn shucks. Biddle sketched the tableau: battle maps spread across a camp table; flickering candle stubs flinging monstrous shadows on the whitewashed walls; empty cans of Spam or C ration peas tossed in a corner; a demijohn of rough red wine passed from hand to filthy hand. Cooks whipped up powdered eggs with powdered milk and powdered coffee; soldiers insisted that the Army would next issue powdered water. Sometimes the radio picked up Axis Sally, who closed her broadcasts by purring, "Easy, boys, there's danger ahead." Toffey slept with a field phone near his head, alert to calls for Paul Blue Six, his sign.

For a few weeks, Biddle—a Harvard-educated, World War I veteran whose brother was Roosevelt's attorney general—gave Toffey someone to talk to, a rare prize for a commander. Toffey told of being wounded in Tunisia, and of how so many recuperating officers had sought rear-echelon duties to avoid a return to combat. "If I had to do it again," he mused, "I wonder if I wouldn't look for a swivel chair?" He wondered aloud how to develop "the killing instincts. . . . Our boys aren't professionals, and you have to condition them to enjoy killing." He talked to Helen, too, in his letters, about how his knee grew "stiff and tired in the wet weather and rough country," and about how he "would like a rest, a bath, a home and my family." He fantasized about a stateside assignment. "At this point, Bragg would look good, and Dix or Lewis positively luxurious," he told her, ticking off Army posts.

He did not mention the close calls, as when a German shell detonated in a chestnut tree on October 21, wounding two staff officers ten yards from where he was reading an August issue of *Time*. Nor did he tell her of the shells that a day later chased him from a grassy ledge on Monte della Costa, where he had been puffing his pipe and writing her a letter. Nor of the deaths of two other battalion commanders in the 15th Infantry, including one crushed in his foxhole by the engine of a downed German fighter.

Then another wet, gray dawn arrived and they edged forward, and upward. One account likened the soldier's day in Italy to "climbing a ladder with an opponent stamping on his hands at every rung." They learned to shun skylines and to dull the glint of helmet rims and mess kits with mud. They listened for the mewing of cats, a favorite German signal. Barbasol shave cream was a good balm for sore feet, but nothing could compensate for the lack of overcoats, wool underwear, and shelter halves, which remained in barracks bags stranded in Palermo. Every man's shoulders instinctively hunched at the rush of artillery, but still they debated with theological intensity whether it was true that a man never heard the shell that hit him.

*Easy, boys, there's danger ahead.* On occasion Paul Blue Six lost his temper, as in late October when he berated staff officers for incaution. "I'm goddam sick and tired of seeing these picnic gatherings in the open," he barked. "I'm sick of telling you guys to wear your helmets and carry your arms." On October 28 he asked Biddle to sketch a sergeant who had been shot dead on Monte Caievola. Pulling back a blanket, Toffey nodded at the dead man's sunken face and said, "The people at home ought to see things like that." When artillery raked the battalion again, he rang the regimental headquarters. "This is Toffey. Get the meat wagon down here," he said. "There are two more killed and one wounded."

More often he was a sturdy, abiding presence, a steeplechaser. "Be alert and live," he told his soldiers, echoing the motto printed in *Stars and Stripes.* He urged new replacement officers to "get to know your own men, every man in your platoon," by name as well as by their strengths and weaknesses. "We need you, terribly," he continued. "You'll have less good personnel than you had at home. You'll find that your company has lost its top sergeant and that the best platoon sergeant is dead. But we need you and we've got a job to do." No officer was to sleep without checking perimeter security. Not a bandolier or canteen should be abandoned. "I wish you all luck," he told them. "We're glad to have you with us. Remember that if I can help you I'll do it."

Toffey's battalion punched through the Barbara Line, which was hardly more than a chain of outposts, but the Bernhardt Line proved obdurate. Two companies failed to oust the enemy from Monte Cesima, looming nearly four thousand feet above Highway 6. Under Truscott's orders, the entire battalion on November 4 looped through Presenzano to flank the mountain in a night climb through spectral chestnut groves. "We circle the meadows, keeping the shadow," Biddle wrote. Up and up they climbed, "the lips parted in that rictus which you see on the faces of distance runners." After ten hours they reached the stony crest to find the German observation post deserted. Toffey pointed among the ferns to a dead soldier with a bullet through his left temple. Here, he told Biddle, was another lost soul "to add to your collection."

From the summit Toffey squinted at the northern glacis of mountains that would bedevil the Allies for the next six months: Lungo and Trocchio, Sammucro and Cassino. "Hell," he said. "You can see all the way into Germany." More than half the battalion had become casualties since arriving in Italy. After watching the men of his division emerge from the high country on November 5, Lucian Truscott simply piled up adjectives: "Haggard, dirty, bedraggled, long-haired, unshaven, clothing in tatters, worn out boots."

"Just so many dead," Biddle wrote. Below Monte Cesima, in the valley town of Mignano, he watched in the rain as gloved soldiers heaved the pallid corpses of American and German soldiers into a truck trailer, the living "wrestling with the dead" until a full measure filled the bed. He added:

> I wish the people at home, instead of thinking of their boys in terms of football stars, would think of them in terms of miners trapped underground or suffocating to death in a tenth-story fire. I wish they would

think of them as cold, wet, hungry, homesick and frightened. I wish, when they think of them, they would be a little sick to their stomachs.

Toffey finally finished a letter to Helen he had started a fortnight earlier. "It at least assures you," he told her, "of my continued existence."

The panorama from Monte Cesima revealed the formidable tactical challenge confronting Fifth Army. The only viable overland passage to Rome followed Highway 6 through the narrow Mignano Gap, six miles long and dominated by mountains on either flank. Several hills also sat in the gap proper, like stoppers in a bottleneck, soaring a thousand feet or so above the valley floor. North of these impedimenta, the gap emptied onto the broad plain of the Rapido River Valley, across which a final mountain barrier—dominated by Monte Cassino—guarded the entrance to the Liri Valley, boulevard to Rome.

Mark Clark's plan called for his infantry divisions to force the Mignano Gap and then converge on the Liri Valley, where tanks could spearhead a run for the capital. On Fifth Army's far right, the 34th and 45th Divisions crept through the Apennine crags, using herds of goats to clear highland minefields. Vietinghoff accurately observed of his American adversary here: "Every step forward into the mountainous terrain merely increased his difficulties."

On the left flank, the British 56th Division tried to loop around the western lip of the Mignano Gap on November 5 by attacking Monte Camino, a "steep solid rock leading God knows where," as one rifleman put it. Expecting only German pickets, the 201st Guards Brigade instead found the Bernhardt Line: mines, machine guns, and mortar pits blasted from an exposed face dubbed Bare Arse Ridge. Heath fires lighted the scarps and cols, as Guardsmen clawed up a succession of summits only to find that they were false crests overshadowed by still higher ground.

Three panzer grenadier counterattacks on November 8 nearly flicked the British from the mountain. Tommies built stone breastworks against singing mortar fragments and a frigid east wind, stripping rations and ammo from the dead, and brewing tea with muddy water scooped from shell holes. Without blankets or winter battle dress, the wounded died from exposure; three forward Guards companies dwindled to a hundred men, combined. "A small earthquake added to the unpleasantness," a Scots Guard account noted. In the end, four British battalions could not overcome five entrenched German battalions; after a horrid week Clark approved a withdrawal from what was now called Murder Mountain. Dead men remained propped at their posts with helmets on and rifles ready, a rear guard faithful to the end and beyond. "Altogether," the Coldstream Guards history explained, "the difficulties were too great."

Too great as well for Truscott's 3rd Division in the Fifth Army center. A ten-day effort to seize Monte la Difensa, a geological appendage to Murder Mountain, proved just as futile. On the evening of November 5, corps commander Lucas phoned Truscott with orders from Clark to help the British by also attacking Monte Lungo, one of those isolated hill masses inside the gap. Protesting the lack of reconnaissance, air support, and artillery, Truscott asked to speak to Clark.

"Damn it," Lucas replied. "You know the position I'm in with him. That would only make it worse, and put me in a helluva hole. You have just got to do it."

"I still think it's wrong," Truscott said, then ordered his 30th Infantry forward. One battalion captured conical Monte Rotondo and another secured a modest foothold on Lungo: that far and no farther.

As the grim season wore on, the suffering grew epic. Audie Murphy noted that the "faces of the dead seem green and unearthly. This is bad for the morale, as it makes a man reflect upon what his own life may come to." Since arriving in Italy less than two months earlier, the 3rd Division had tallied 8,600 casualties. Losses included almost 400 officers—half of the division's second lieutenants among them—and nearly 4,000 privates. The three infantry regiments had lost 70 percent of their strength, an indicator of "how fragile an infantry division really is," Truscott told Beetle Smith.

To wife Sarah on November 10 he wrote, "You are in my thoughts a thousand times a day." He later added, "One day merges into another while time is measured only by the capture of the next ridge, the crossing of the next stream. I'm a bit grayer than when you saw me last, but otherwise unchanged in appearance." Even amid carnage Truscott tried to honor the beauty of this world by placing autumn flowers on his field desk every day. He also dispatched an aide to Naples to replenish the command post's liquor supply; the lieutenant returned with thirty-five bottles of cognac. "I only pray," Truscott told Sarah, "that I can live and measure up to what my lads seem to expect of me."

Ernie Pyle returned to the front in November after two months at home. Rested if not reinvigorated, he quickly sized up the Italian campaign. "The land and the weather were both against us," he wrote. "The country was shockingly beautiful, and just as shockingly hard to capture from the enemy." He listened to "shells chase each other through the sky across the mountains ahead, making a sound like cold wind blowing on a winter night." Pyle found "almost inconceivable misery," as well as a bemused fortitude. When gunners calculated that it cost $25,000 in artillery shells for each enemy soldier killed, one GI asked, "Why wouldn't it be better to just offer the Germans $25,000 to surrender?"

A diarist in the 56th Evacuation Hospital noted that even away from the front lines life was spare: "No shelves, no dresser, no hooks or nails on a wall. No bed table, no reading table, no cabinets. No floor except a muddy, wet one." Pyle described a soldier playing poker by candlelight who abruptly murmured, "War, my friends, is a silly business. War is the craziest thing I ever heard of."

Irony and dark humor—"the greatest of protections against crackup," in one soldier's estimation—grew ever sharper in the ranks. During a showing of *Casablanca* in a British camp, when Humphrey Bogart's gunshot victim crumpled to the ground, Tommies cried as one, "Stretcher bearer!" Spike Milligan, serving in the Royal Artillery, wrote his family, "The whole of this land we have arrived in is now top secret, in fact no one is allowed to know where it is. . . . However, the bloody Germans know where it is." On November 9, Milligan wrote, "Nothing much to report except World War 2. Is it still going on where you are?"

Burial details sent out at night to retrieve the dead were known as the Ghouls. When a mobile shower unit arrived at one artillery battery, a quartet of naked gunners stood singing in barbershop formation for an hour. "It's the loss of dirt," one explained. "It leaves you dizzy." A 36th Division soldier wrote his father that he now lived in "a remodeled pig shed. I say remodeled because there is no pig in it." Others occupied a heatless hovel they named Villa des Chilblains, and soldiers hooted at a mistyped headquarters order: "Latrines: all troops will ensure that faces are covered with soil after each person has deprecated." A platoon leader who learned that his battalion commander's radio call sign was "Big Six," speculated that to ring the division commander he should ask for "Big, Big, Big Six," and to reach Eisenhower he must request "Six to the Maximum Power."

Each man coped with calamity in his own fashion. Richard Tregaskis described a combat engineer sitting on a curb in Pietramelara in late October, nibbling the "cheese unit" from his C ration as a woman's shrieks carried from a ruined building nearby. "She's been yelling like that all day," the soldier said. "Sometimes I feel kinda sorry for these poor people." One night in mid-November, upon finding four dead 3rd Division soldiers in slit trenches, a sergeant said, "You can pray forever but those poor fellows are gone." Pretending to play his rifle like a bull fiddle, the sergeant sang "Heart of My Heart," while a comrade tipped his helmet forward like a vaudeville hoofer's bowler and danced a jig to cheer the dead.

"You can't believe men will do to each other the things they do," a forward observer wrote his sister. "I suppose I'm soft, but I've got to say, God forgive us all." A week later he was killed when a shell severed his jugular vein.

At 9:30 A.M. on Thursday, November 11, Clark drove through the hills below Naples to Avellino, where a new American cemetery was to be dedicated on the twenty-fifth anniversary of the armistice ending World War I. Sunlight glinted from hundreds of white crosses and stars of David, perfectly arrayed in a former potato field.

"Here we are, a quarter century later, with the same Allies as before, fighting the same mad dogs that were loose in 1918," Clark said, speaking without notes at the flagpole. "They gave their lives that the people at home could pursue the life which we have always wanted—a happy life—and that their children could go to the schools and churches they want, and follow the line of work they want. And we are fighting, first, to save our own land from devastation like this in Italy."

He drew himself to his full height, a ramrod in a peaked cap. "We must not think about going home. None of us is going home until it's over. . . . We've caught the torch that these men have flung us, and we'll carry it to Berlin and to the great victory—a complete victory—which the united nations deserve."

An honor guard fired thrice. Wadding from the blank cartridges fluttered across the graves. A bugler blew Taps, echoed by another, unseen bugler in a nearby arbor. "That was a good ceremony," Clark said. His jaw set, he climbed back into the jeep to return to the battlefield.

Imperfect as a commander and at times insufferable as a person, Clark knew what he was fighting for. Few men would love him, some would detest him, but most recognized in him a forceful field general who was willful enough, indomitable enough to wage the hard war that the Italian campaign had become. He believed, as he had told Alexander's chief of staff a week earlier, that "the war could be won in this theater"; he also believed that Fifth Army could seize Rome, "and intended to do so." In part this was vainglory: resentful of Montgomery, Clark wanted Eighth Army to steer clear of the Italian capital and the hosannahs its capture would merit. Yet it also reflected his single-minded grit, and a determination to keep faith. *He* had caught the torch tossed by his dead soldiers, and he would carry it as far as necessary.

Clark knew that the current battle had stalled. Since crossing the Volturno, Lucas's VI Corps had covered forty-five miles on Fifth Army's right flank and twenty-five miles in the center, at Mignano. McCreery's X

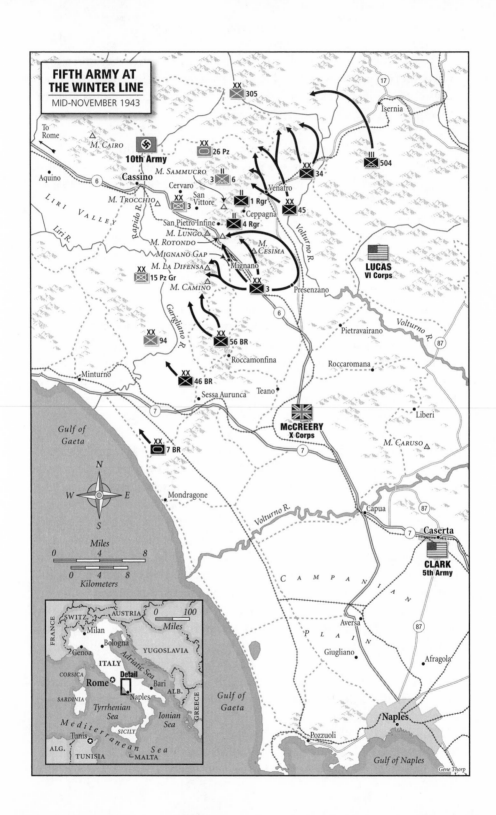

**FIFTH ARMY AT THE WINTER LINE**

MID-NOVEMBER 1943

To Rome

M. CAIRO △

🔴 **10th Army**

Aquino

Cassino

6

M. SAMMUCRO

Cervaro

San Vittore

M. TROCCHIO △

San Pietro Infine

M. LUNGO △

M. ROTONDO △

MIGNANO GAP

M. LA DIFENSA △

M. CAMINO △

LIRI VALLEY

Liri R.

Rapido R.

XX 305

Isernia

17

XX 📋 26 Pz

XX 3 🗡 6

II 🗡 1 Rgr

Venafro

Ceppagna

II 🗡 4 Rgr

XX 🗡 34

XX 🗡 45

III 🗡 504

M. CESIMA △

Mignano

XX 🗡 3

Presenzano

**LUCAS**
VI Corps

XX 🗡 15 Pz Gr

XX 🗡 94

XX 🗡 56 BR

Roccamonfina

Minturno

XX 🗡 46 BR

Sessa Aurunca

Teano

Pietravairano

Roccaromana

Volturno R.

6

87

Gulf of Gaeta

XX 📋 7 BR

Mondragone

N
W — E
S

*Miles*

0    4    8

0    4    8

*Kilometers*

Liberi

M. CARUSO △

**McCREERY**
X Corps

7

Volturno R.

Capua

87

7

**Caserta**

🇺🇸 **CLARK**
5th Army

C A M P A N I A N

Aversa

87

P L A I N

Giugliano

Afragola

**Naples**

Pozzuoli

*Gulf of Naples*

FRANCE
SWITZ.  AUSTRIA
Milan
Bologna   YUGOSLAVIA
Genoa
**ITALY**
CORSICA   Detail
**Rome** ✠
Bari
SARDINIA   Naples   ALB.
Tyrrhenian
Sea   Ionian
SICILY   Sea
M e d i t e r r a n e a n   S e a
Tunis
ALG.
TUNISIA   MALTA

0    100
*Miles*

Adriatic Sea

GREECE

Gulf of
Gaeta

Gene Thorp

Corps on the left had covered seventeen miles. That yardage had cost the army ten thousand casualties since mid-October, and the equivalent of two divisions since landing at Salerno, including more than three thousand dead. Although the Liri Valley was barely a dozen miles ahead, it might just as well have been on the moon. MPs posted warning signs across the front, including "Nothing But Jerry Beyond This Point" and "If You Go Any Further Take a Cross With You."

The British had disappointed Clark at the Volturno and in the attack on Monte Camino. "Why in the hell don't you get going?" he had asked McCreery. Privately, and unfairly, Clark believed that American units were "the only ones I really could depend upon to slug it out." In truth, although Fifth Army now numbered 244,000 men, Clark lacked enough reserves of any nationality to exploit a breakthrough even if he reached the Liri Valley.

Getting that far seemed doubtful in itself. Few of the troops now butting at the Bernhardt Line had mountain training. Most lacked "the born hillman's eye for the best way up, down, or across a mountain," as the official British history would conclude. Instead, "the major tactics of the Allies became, willy-nilly, a head-on battering" that also required enormous quantities of ammunition and the conversion of combat troops to porters and stretcher bearers. Will Lang of *Life* scribbled in his notebook: "Need one man carrying for every two men fighting."

Worse yet, the battered docks in Naples limited resupply efforts. Wool clothing scheduled to arrive in mid-October was delayed until mid-November after ammunition took shipping priority. Shortages of tires, batteries, and spare parts immobilized three of every ten trucks, further hampering quartermasters trying to move matériel from port to battlefront. As the frozen corpses on Camino could attest, the Allies were utterly unprepared for winter. Much of the cold-weather gear under development in the States would not reach Italy for another year. Heavy combat boots would not arrive until February. British units doubled the blanket allowance from two to four, requisitioned sheepskin coats from Syria, and increased the daily sugar ration by four ounces for those fighting at altititudes above two thousand feet.

Too little, too late. "Cold ground trauma" injuries soared in November, including the first thousand cases of trench foot among American troops. Clark was aghast to learn that the British had begun breaking up a division every two months to field replacements. "I wish so many things were not done on a shoestring," Lucas wrote. "This campaign was poorly planned in many respects. We should have at least twice as many troops."

True, the Germans were also in a bad way, and there was always comfort in the misery of one's adversary. Kesselring had stabilized the front by throwing two more divisions into the fight, but the first ten days of November cost him more than two thousand casualties. "Under heavy artillery fire," a German NCO wrote in his diary. "My morale is gone." A captured letter from a soldier on the Adriatic front lamented, "The lice are at me now and I haven't washed or shaved for a fortnight. . . . All I am doing is waiting for the war to end." Another letter, written by a German soldier in Poland to a comrade captured in Italy by the 3rd Division, included a grim confession: "We have already liquidated our 1,200 Jewish slaves. We sent them to another ghetto, beyond the borders of life."

Clark concluded that the time had come to pause. On Saturday, November 13, he met his senior commanders at the VI Corps command post and ticked off the battlefield realities: five of Fifth Army's seven divisions had been in the line almost constantly since Salerno; the British were stalled at Monte Camino; casualties and supply troubles kept mounting. The army would "hold to its present positions" for at least two weeks. Commanders would ensure "that the troops get all the rest possible." Planners would take the rest of the month to concoct a new scheme before the offensive resumed.

"We musn't kid ourselves," Truscott said, gesturing vaguely toward German lines to the north. "There's still a lot of fight left in the old son of a bitch."

But Lucas provided the apposite epitaph for the first Allied assault on the Winter Line. "The weather is cold as hell and the wind is blowing," he wrote in his diary. "Wars should be fought in better country than this."

## "The Entire World Was Burning"

A T 8:30 A.M. on Saturday, November 20, Six to the Maximum Power—otherwise known as Dwight D. Eisenhower—stood smoking a cigarette on the docks at Mers el-Kébir, the great French naval base six miles west of Oran. Snow crowned the majestic Atlas Mountains to the south and a chill breeze swept the dockyard, where sailors in peacoats and dungarees bustled about the piers and warehouses. A brilliant winter sun gleamed from the African heavens, and the Mediterranean sparkled like buffed lapis. In the sheltered anchorage, the newly arrived battleship U.S.S. *Iowa* swung on her chains after a transatlantic passage, and Eisenhower watched through field glasses as a whaleboat descended from her port davits. He had come to welcome the dreadnought's distinguished passengers, including a particular eminence code-named CARGO; in a few minutes, even Six to the Maximum Power would be substantially outranked.

He welcomed the diversion. Autumn at AFHQ had been an anxious season. Sanguine predictions of a promenade to Rome proved fanciful, and the Winter Line battle now teetered toward debacle. "We are very much disturbed . . . about the campaign in Italy," the British chiefs had cabled on November 4, even suggesting that a stalemate there might require postponement of OVERLORD. Tart messages from Marshall, faulting Eisenhower for not "cracking the whip" and for misusing Allied airpower, made him "burn the air" in frustration, Harry Butcher reported. His explications to Washington and London now had an occasional odor of martyrdom. By drawing the wrath of Kesselring's armies onto his own, he advised the Combined Chiefs, "it then makes little difference what happens to us if OVERLORD is a success." Fifth and Eighth Armies, segregated by the Apennines, continued to fight disjointed wars, but Eisenhower seemed powerless to contrive a better scheme. "I have sought in every possible way to avoid a mere slugging match along a wide front," he told Alexander on November 9. Since the TORCH invasions a year earlier, Allied casualties in the Mediterranean had eclipsed 100,000. In exhortations to his troops, who would have disagreed that "it makes little difference what happens to us," Eisenhower had been reduced to invoking prepositional deities: "The God of Justice fights on our side."

Politics and folderol beset him still: whether Capri should be an exclusive preserve of the Air Force ("contrary to my policies"); whether he disliked the photographer Margaret Bourke-White ("absolutely untrue"); why a professed man of faith would sometimes cuss ("Damn it, I *am* a religious man"); whether he would run for president ("I ain't and won't"). Some requests left him scratching his head, including an offer of £10,000 from a South African impresario "if you arrange for Mussolini's personal appearance on the stages of our Cape Town theaters. Three weeks' engagement." Beetle Smith proposed creating a special AFHQ staff "whose job would be solely to keep the home front frightened," since the Pentagon and Whitehall seemed more responsive when catastrophe threatened.

It all wore him down, although at age fifty-three he still radiated vigor. "He usually blew his top if anyone so much as intimated that he looked tired," Kay Summersby recalled. Most nettlesome in recent weeks was the rampant speculation over who would command OVERLORD, and suggestions that he and Marshall were rivals for the post. The topic made him "acutely uncomfortable," John Eisenhower later wrote. Eisenhower denounced the rumors as "false and malicious gossip," the quintessence of folderol.

The whaleboat drew close to the dock. Eisenhower picked out Marshall, King, Harry Hopkins, and General H. H. "Hap" Arnold, the Army Air

Forces chief, standing at the rail. A grinning, sea-tanned figure in a gray fedora gestured with his cigarette holder at the bright sunshine and yelled from his wheelchair, "Roosevelt weather!"

Handshakes and a blur of salutes greeted the president and his chiefs—"all the heavy maleness of the war," in Summersby's phrase. En route from Washington to strategy conferences in Cairo and Teheran, they planned to fly to Tunisia and spend the night before pressing on to Egypt. Secret Service agents lifted Roosevelt into an armored limousine, where he was joined by Eisenhower and two of the president's sons, Elliott and Frank, Jr., who were serving in the Mediterranean.

During the fifty-mile drive to La Sénia airfield, south of Oran, Roosevelt described with evident delight the near sinking of the *Iowa:* on Sunday afternoon, November 14, in fair weather and following seas off Bermuda, he had been on deck watching antiaircraft gunners take target practice at drifting weather balloons when the ship's bridge announced, "Torpedo! Torpedo on the starboard beam." A sailor bellowed, "This ain't no drill." Much excitement ensued: whistles; alarms; hoisted signal flags; a stampede to general quarters. Secret Service agents rushed about with drawn pistols. *Iowa* surged to flank speed and heeled sharply to port in evasion. "Take me over to the starboard rail," Roosevelt told his valet. "I want to watch the torpedo."

Streaking at forty-six knots, the torpedo hit *Iowa*'s turbulent wake several hundred feet astern and detonated with such violence that many aboard the battleship thought she had been struck. A mile away the culprit signaled apologies: the destroyer U.S.S. *William D. Porter,* part of *Iowa*'s escort, had accidentally fired tube number 3 during a simulated torpedo attack drill. Admiral King ordered the destroyer back to port with her entire company under arrest. "Tell me, Ernest," Hap Arnold had asked, "does this happen often in your Navy?" Hopkins speculated that the *Porter*'s skipper was "some damned Republican."

Roosevelt threw back his head in glee. The motorcade pulled onto the tarmac at La Sénia, where four C-54s waited to fly them to Tunis. There was much to discuss, including the imminent conferences with Churchill and Joseph Stalin, the looming campaign in western Europe, and the shape of the world after the Axis defeat. "The war, and the peace," Roosevelt said. "Can you wait, Ike?"

Eisenhower nodded. "Just about, sir."

The president had planned to fly to Cairo from Tunis at dawn on Sunday, but after a lively Saturday dinner overlooking the sea at La Marsa, he announced, over Secret Service objections, that he would linger an extra day to explore the Tunisian battlefields. On the Sabbath noon, Summersby pulled the Cadillac in front of Guest Villa Number 1. Roosevelt settled into the backseat with Eisenhower. A Secret Service agent carrying a machine gun in a large case climbed up front with Telek, the general's yapping terrier. Three truckloads of MPs, a radio car, and eight motorcycle outriders completed the convoy.

Past the bey's palace and the Roman aqueduct they drove, then turned southwest to follow the lush Medjerda River valley. Eisenhower narrated with fluency and passion: how British and American troops exactly a year earlier had pushed across the Tunisian outback and down this valley to Djedeïda, where they could even see the minarets of Tunis; how Kesselring's troops stiffened—*right here,* at Point 186—and drove the Allies back up the valley in pitched, heartbreaking winter battles at Tébourba and Medjez-el-Bab and Longstop Hill; how Rommel attacked in the south, lunging through Kasserine Pass and nearly reaching the vast supply depot at Tébessa; how the Allies gathered themselves in the spring to eventually encircle the Axis bridgehead at Tunis and Bizerte, where callow American troops redeemed themselves at Mateur and Hill 609, *right over there.*

They stopped for lunch in a eucalyptus brake on the north bank of the Medjerda. MPs formed a wide cordon, elbow to elbow, with their backs to the picnickers. Was it possible, Roosevelt wondered, that U.S. and German tanks had fought across the now lost battlefield at Zama, where Scipio Africanus smashed Hannibal to close the Second Punic War in 202 B.C.? Eisenhower could not say with certainty, but near the picnic grove once stood ancient Utica; here in 46 B.C., according to Plutarch, Cato the Younger revolted against Julius Caesar in defense of republican ideals, reading Plato's "On the Soul" as Caesar's troops closed in, then falling on his own sword to remain "the only free and undefeated man" in greater Rome. As the president finished his sandwich, Eisenhower wandered off to inspect a burnt-out tank. "Ike," Roosevelt said when he returned, "if, one year ago, you had offered to bet that on this day the president of the United States would be having his lunch on a Tunisian roadside, what odds could you have demanded?"

Late that night the presidential party lifted off for Cairo from El Aouina airfield in Tunis. Scant mention had been made of Italy. "Eisenhower showed no signs of worry about the success of the Italian operation . . . for which many of us did not think he had sufficient force," wrote Admiral William D. Leahy, chairman of the Joint Chiefs. Even less was said about the OVERLORD command, although, after several glasses of sherry, King asserted that Marshall would get the job and that Eisenhower would return to Washington as Army chief of staff. Roosevelt seemed to regard Eisenhower as a more formidable figure than the tentative young commander he had last met in Casablanca ten months earlier. But the president as usual remained cheerful and opaque, offering only the cryptic observation that "it is dangerous to monkey with a winning team."

A few days later, Eisenhower wrote Mamie, "The eternal pound, pound, pound seems a burden, but when it once ceases it is possible that many of us will be nigh unto nervous wrecks, and wholly unfit for normal life." As if adding a postscript to himself, he observed, "I know I'm a changed person. No one could be through what I've seen and not be different from what he was at the beginning."

Evidently no discussion at La Marsa had been devoted to a curious development in the Italian campaign, in which both Roosevelt and Eisenhower had a hand and which now played out in the Adriatic seaport of Bari.

Few cities in Italy had escaped war's havoc with greater panache than flat-roofed, white-walled Bari. Once an embarkation point for Crusaders headed east, it had been destroyed by William the Bad, restored by William the Good, and enhanced by the arrival of the bones of St. Nicholas—Father Christmas—which were stolen in Asia Minor by Bari seamen in the eleventh century. It was said that St. Francis's devotion to chastity had been tested in Bari by a comely temptress whose advances were repelled when the holy man heaved a brazier of hot coals at her. Horace called the town "fish-famous," and stalls of clams, sea urchins, cuttlefish, and oysters still lined the breakwater, where fisherman smacked dead octopuses on the rocks to tenderize them. Peddlers wheeled their barrows through Bari's serpentine alleys, selling amulets against the evil eye, while toothless pilgrims at the basilica sought Nicholas's intercession. *Netturbini* with handcarts swept the gutters of garbage heaved overnight from upper windows. Unlike that of Naples, Bari's "agile and ingenious criminal class consisted chiefly of small boys," wrote a British officer and novelist named Evelyn Waugh. Bari's newest landmark was the Bambino Sports Stadium, built by Mussolini as a reward for producing more male babies than any comparable city in Italy.

Liberating Tommies had been greeted with flowers and speeches, although a British major reported that by the time Montgomery arrived in an open jeep few of the city's quarter million souls "came to see him for by then the novelty had worn off." Shops still offered silk stockings for four shillings, and Allied soldiers, when not gawking at the sculpted fauns and nymphs at the opera house, prowled through a PX stocked with Palmolive soap and Hershey bars. The large port, enclosed by a mole of cyclopean blocks weighing 350 tons each, had been captured in good condition, and a thousand stevedores now labored around the clock.

They had much to unload. With Naples reviving slowly, Bari provided the main supply port for Eighth Army as well as for the Allied air forces now building four dozen fields at Foggia and elsewhere. To bring heavy bombers to Foggia required shipping comparable to that needed to move two Army divisions; keeping those planes flying would take a supply effort equal to the entire Eighth Army's. To floor a single all-weather airstrip against mud, for example, took five thousand tons of perforated steel planking. On December 1, the newly created Fifteenth Air Force opened its headquarters in Bari. The commander, a former professional bantamweight boxer who also held both a doctorate in aeronautical engineering and the Medal of Honor, Major General James H. Doolittle, moved into a plush first-floor office on the waterfront, in the former headquarters of the Italian air force.

Doolittle's job was to augment the bombing of strategic targets, such as German aircraft plants and oil facilities, now under way by British and American squadrons based in Britain. Doolittle had claimed that flying weather in Italy would be almost twice as good as that in the United Kingdom, a proposition sorely tested by the cancellation due to inclemency of roughly half his bombing missions in November. Still, Allied pilots now owned the Italian skies. German long-range bombers had flown only eight times in Italy since mid-October, including four attacks on Naples in November. Nearly three-quarters of all Luftwaffe fighters had retreated to Germany, and the Allied pummeling of enemy airfields had become so intense that the raids were known as Reich Party Days.

So cocky were Allied air commanders that on the afternoon of Thursday, December 2, Air Vice Marshal Arthur Coningham assured reporters, "I would regard it as a personal affront and insult if the Luftwaffe should attempt any significant action in this area."

As Coningham issued this challenge to the Fates, berth number 29 on the outer mole of Bari harbor was occupied by an ordinary Liberty ship, S.S. *John Harvey*. She had arrived four days earlier in a convoy of nine merchantmen, after an odyssey that began in Baltimore and included stops at Norfolk, Oran, and Augusta. Only her secret cargo was unusual: 1,350 tons of bombs filled with a toxin known to chemists as dichlorethyl sulfide and to Army chemical warfare specialists as HS, but more commonly called mustard gas. Several military port officials knew of *John Harvey's* lading, but other ships with medical supplies and conventional munitions took precedence, and she remained unloaded, nearly hull to hull with fourteen other vessels moored at the Molo Nuovo. German torpedo boats infested the Adriatic, and investigators later concluded that "the ship was at the time in as safe a place as could be found."

No Axis chemical stockpiles had been discovered in North Africa, and AFHQ believed that gas warfare by Germany "appears unlikely" except "at a critical moment of the war, when such a course might be expected to be decisive." But Eisenhower wondered whether that moment was approaching. Relying on Italian intelligence, he had warned Marshall in late August that Berlin had "threatened that if Italy turned against Germany gas would be used against the country and the most terrible vengeance would be exacted" as a lesson to other wobbly allies. Churchill also sounded the alarm in a note to Roosevelt. Fifth Army prisoner interrogations suggested intensified German preparations for chemical combat, and rumors circulated of a new, egregiously potent gas. "Many soldiers in the German army say, 'Adolf will turn to gas when there is no other way out,'" a Fifth Army memo noted in mid-October. Nineteen plants in Germany were suspected of making poisonous gases, with others scattered across occupied Europe.

Twenty-eight different gases had caused more than a million casualties in World War I, beginning with a German chlorine attack at Ypres in April 1915. Hitler himself had been temporarily blinded by British mustard; a liquid that emitted vapor at room temperature, mustard blistered exposed skin and attacked eyes and airways. No commander in 1943 could be cavalier about a manifest threat by Germany to use gas. Spurred by resurgent concerns in the Mediterranean, Roosevelt in August publicly warned Berlin of "full and swift retaliation in kind." Allied policy had long authorized large chemical depots near Oran and elsewhere; when mustard stocks were moved by convoy in Africa, MPs sat in the truck beds "in order to report any poison gas leaks, thus avoiding danger to the native population."

Now, to ensure a capacity for "swift retaliation," AFHQ and the War Department had secretly agreed to finish stockpiling a forty-five-day chemical reserve in the Mediterranean, including more than 200,000 gas bombs. (How the Germans would be deterred if the deterrent remained secret was never adequately explained.) With White House concurrence, a substantial cache would be stored in forward dumps at Foggia, beginning with the consignment that sat in *John Harvey*'s hold as the sun set on Thursday evening.

Several thousand Allied servicemen and Italian spectators sat in the oval Bambino Stadium near Bari's train station as a baseball scrimmage between two quartermaster squads entered the late innings under the lights. Moviegoers filled several theaters around town; the Porto Vecchio was showing *Sergeant York,* with Gary Cooper. In the British mess on the Molo

San Nicola, a female vocalist crooned to homesick officers sipping gin. Italian women drew water from corner fountains in the old city, or laid fresh pasta on wire tables to dry. Lights also burned atop port cranes and along the jetties: another convoy had arrived at 5:30 P.M., bringing to forty the number of ships in the harbor, and stevedores manned their winches and bale hooks. Merchant mariners finished supper or lay in their bunks, writing letters and reading. Sailors aboard the S.S. *Louis Hennepin* broke out a cribbage board. In his spacious waterfront office, Jimmy Doolittle leafed through reports from a recent bombing mission to Solingen; hearing airplanes overhead, he assumed they were more C-47s bringing additional men and matériel to Bari. It was 7:20 P.M.

The first two Luftwaffe raiders dumped cardboard boxes full of tiny foil strips. Known as Window to the Allies and Duppel to the Germans, the foil was intended to deflect and dissipate radar signals. The tactic confused Allied searchlight radars but was otherwise wasted: the main early-warning radar dish, on a theater roof in Via Victor Emmanuel, had been broken for days. British fighters, sent up on routine patrol at dusk, had already landed without incident. Ultra intercepts had revealed German reconnaissance interest in Bari, but no one guessed that Kesselring and his Luftwaffe subordinates had orchestrated a large raid on the harbor to slow both Eighth Army and the buildup at Foggia. "Risks such as were accepted in the port of Bari on this occasion must result in damage proportional to the risk taken," Eisenhower's air chief would tell him three weeks later. To avoid fratricide, a senior British officer had insisted that naval gunners not fire until fired upon.

That moment soon arrived. Guided by the harbor lights and their own hissing flares, twenty Ju-88 bombers roared in at barely 150 feet. A few tracer streams climbed toward the flares above the harbor, but gunners blinded by the glare were reduced to firing by earshot at the marauding planes. The first bombs fell near the Via Abate Gimma in central Bari. Explosions around the Hotel Corona killed civilians and Allied soldiers alike. A woman screamed, *"Non voglio morire!"*—I don't want to die—but many died. Near the Piazza Mercantile a house collapsed on a mother and her six sons. Baseball fans stampeded for the stadium exits. The door to Doolittle's office blew in and the windows disintegrated. Dusting himself off as bombs began to detonate in the flare-silvered harbor, Doolittle told another officer, "We're taking a pasting."

Much worse was to come. Bombs severed an oil pipeline on the petroleum quay. Burning fuel spewed across the harbor and down the moles, chasing stevedores into the sea. The *Joseph Wheeler* took a direct hit that blew open her starboard side and killed all forty-one crewmen. An explosion carried away half the *John Bascom*'s bridge, blowing shoes from sailors' feet and watches from their wrists. *Bascom*'s cargo of hospital equipment and gasoline ignited, burning away her stern lines so that she drifted into the *John L. Motley,* carrying five thousand tons of ammunition and already holed by a bomb through the number 5 hatch. Engulfed in flame, *Motley* smacked against a seawall and exploded, killing sixty-four of her sailors and catapulting shards of flaming metal over the docks. The blast caved in the burning *Bascom*'s port side—"The ship did not have a chance to survive," a crewman noted—and generated a wave that swept over the breakwater, tossing seamen who had climbed from the sea into the water again.

A bomb detonated belowdecks on the British freighter *Fort Athabaska,* killing all but ten of fifty-six crewmen. The Liberty ship *Samuel J. Tilden* caught a bomb in the engine room before being strafed by both a German plane and by errant antiaircraft fire from shore; a British torpedo boat soon sank the drifting freighter to prevent her from setting other vessels ablaze. Two bombs hit the Polish freighter *Lwów,* sweeping her decks with fire. Half an hour after the raid began, the last German raider emptied his bomb rack and headed north. "The whole harbor was aflame," the seaman Warren Bradenstein reported, "with burning on the surface of the water, and ships were on fire and exploding."

Among those burning vessels was the *John Harvey,* at berth number 29 with her secret cargo. Shortly after *Motley* blew up, *Harvey* detonated with even greater violence, killing her master and seventy-seven crewmen. A fountain of flame spurted a thousand feet into the night sky, showering the harbor with burning debris, including hatch covers, ruptured bomb casings, and a derrick, which punctured another ship's deck like a javelin. The blast ripped apart the freighter *Testbank,* killing seventy crewmen, and blew hatches from their frames aboard U.S.S. *Aroostook,* carrying nineteen thousand barrels of 100-octane aviation fuel. Windows shattered seven miles away, including those in Alexander's headquarters, and tiles tumbled from Bari roofs. A searing wind tore across the port—"I felt as if I were bursting and burning inside," recalled George Southern, a young officer standing on H.M.S. *Zetland*'s forecastle—followed by another tidal wave that rolled the length of the harbor, sweeping flotsam along the jetties and soaking men with seawater now contaminated by dichlorethyl sulfide. A sailor on H.M.S. *Vulcan* described "hundreds of chaps desperately swimming and floundering, screaming and shouting for help." To another sailor, "It seemed as if the entire world was burning."

Horrors filled the town. Civilians were crushed in a stampede to an air raid shelter; others drowned when ruptured pipes flooded another shelter after shattered masonry blocked the exits. A young girl pinned in the rubble next to her dead parents was freed only after a surgeon amputated her arm. Soldiers had been attending evening services in a Protestant church when bombs blew the chapel's front wall into the street, toppling the pulpit and splintering pews; gathering their wits, the men belted out, "If this be it, dear Lord, we will come to you singing." Dead merchant mariners and Italian port workers lay along the seawall or floated facedown in the scummy water. Screams carried across the harbor, mingled with pleas for help and the odd snatch of a hymn. Fire trapped sixty men on the east jetty until a plucky Norwegian lifeboat crew ferried them to safety at eleven P.M. Burning hulks glowed weirdly through the steam and smoke that cloaked the harbor. Explosions shook the Molo Nuovo through the night. Watching from the soot-stained waterfront, Will Lang of *Life* scribbled in his notebook, "Many little tongues of flame like forest fires . . . There goes Monty's ammunition."

Seventeen ships had been sunk, with eight others badly damaged. Not since Pearl Harbor had a sneak attack inflicted such damage on an Allied port. Medics darted along the quays, passing out morphine syrettes and cigarettes. Lang jotted down another observation: "There are a lot of men dying out there."

More deaths would follow, odd and inexplicable deaths. Perhaps the first clue came from a sailor who asked, "Since when would American ships carry garlic to Italy?" Others also noticed the odor, so characteristic of mustard gas. H.M.S. *Brindisi* took aboard dozens of oil-coated refugees and by early Friday morning inflamed eyes and vomiting were epidemic in the sickbay and on the quarterdeck. *Bistra* picked up thirty survivors and headed to Taranto; within hours the entire crew was nearly blind and only with great difficulty managed to moor the ship after she made port.

Casualties flooded military hospitals around Bari, including sailors still wearing their lifebelts but with both legs missing. "Ambulances screamed into hospital all night long," a nurse told her diary. Many with superficial injuries were wrapped in blankets and diverted to the Auxiliary Seaman's Home in their oily clothes. One chief surgeon admitted to being "considerably puzzled by the extremely shocked condition of the patients with negligible surgical injuries."

By dawn, the wards were full of men unable to open their eyes, "all in pain and requiring urgent treatment." Surgeons were mystified to also find themselves operating with streaming eyes. Many patients presented thready pulses, low blood pressure, and lethargy, yet plasma did little to revive them. "No treatment that we had to offer amounted to a darn," a doctor wrote.

The first skin blisters appeared Friday morning, "as big as balloons and heavy with fluid," in one nurse's description. Hundreds of patients were classified with "dermatitis N.Y.D."—not yet diagnosed.

A Royal Navy surgeon at the port on Thursday night reported rumors of poison gas, but in the chaos his account failed to reach hospital authorities. With *John Harvey* at the bottom of Bari harbor and the ship's company dead, few knew of her cargo. Those who did met at 2:15 P.M. on Friday in a conference of six British and American officers; they agreed that "in order to maintain secrecy, no general warning was to be given now." A ton of bleach would be dumped to disinfect the breakwater at berth number 29 and signs would be posted: "Danger—Fumes."

The first mustard death occurred eighteen hours after the attack, and others soon followed, each "as dramatic as it was unpredictable," according to an Army doctor dispatched from Algiers. "Individuals that appeared in rather good condition . . . within a matter of minutes would become moribund and die." The cellar of the 98th General Hospital became a morgue; hopeless cases were moved to the so-called Death Ward, including a doomed mariner who kept shouting, "Did you hear that bloody bang?" The passing of Seaman Phillip H. Stone was typical: admitted to the 98th General without visible injuries but drenched by oily seawater, he developed blisters a few hours later and by nine o'clock Saturday morning was unconscious, with "respirations gasping." At 3:30 P.M. he regained consciousness, asked for water, and "abruptly died." An autopsy revealed "dusky skin" and "epidermis easily dislodged," a badly swollen penis, black lips, and lungs with "a peculiar rubberlike consistency." Seaman Stone was eighteen.

By noon on Friday, physicians were reasonably certain that "dermatitis N.Y.D.," with symptoms ranging from bronzed skin to massive blisters, in fact resulted from exposure to mustard gas. Men who believed they were permanently blind eventually had their lids pried open until the "patient convinced himself that he could in fact see." But the damage was done. Simple measures that would have saved lives—stripping the exposed patients and bathing them—were not adopted until hundreds had spent hours inhaling toxic fumes from their own contaminated clothes.

More than 1,000 Allied servicemen were killed or went missing at Bari. Military hospitals documented at least 617 confirmed mustard casualties, including 83 Allied deaths, but investigators acknowledged "many others for whom no records can be traced." Comparable numbers of Italian civilians died; the precise figure remained uncertain, in part because Italian doctors never knew what they were facing. "With no treatment," one account later concluded, "the Italians suffered alone and died alone." Bodies bobbed to the surface of Bari harbor for days, many gnawed by crabs. Covered with a Union Jack and hauled away by truck, they were laid head to toe in trench graves.

News of the raid was heavily censored. "For purposes of secrecy all these cases have been diagnosed N.Y.D. dermatitis," an AFHQ memo noted on December 8. In Algiers, public acknowledgment of an enemy air attack at Bari manifested haiku-like brevity: "Damage was done. There were a number of casualties." *The Washington Post* in mid-December disclosed the "costliest sneak attack since Pearl Harbor," but no mention of gas was published. When reporters asked Henry L. Stimson, the secretary of war, whether Allied defenses at Bari had been lax, he snapped, "No! I will not comment on this thing." A British general on Eisenhower's staff wrote a colleague in London, "There is no one person who can be hanged in the affair."

Rumors spread that the Germans had used gas, but a chemical warfare expert sent to Bari from Algiers concluded in late December that the mustard aboard *John Harvey* was to blame, a finding affirmed in March 1944 by a secret investigative board appointed by Eisenhower. The commander-in-chief preferred prevarication: in his postwar memoir, he acknowledged shipping mustard to Bari but asserted that "the wind was offshore and the escaping gas caused no casualties." Churchill directed that British records be purged of mustard references, and all burns suffered on December 2 were to be attributed "to enemy action."

The extent of the catastrophe stayed hidden for years. Declassified in 1959, the episode remained obscure until 1967, when the U.S. Naval Institute published a scholarly article in its *Proceedings,* followed by a book on the subject in 1971 by Glenn B. Infield. British officers long denied knowledge of *Harvey*'s cargo, but *The Times* of London reported in 1986 that six hundred British seamen contaminated at Bari would receive backdated war pensions following an official admission that they had been gassed. Curiously, autopsies at Bari provided a vital breakthrough in modern chemotherapy when researchers recognized that mustard gas had attacked white blood cells and lymph tissue. Two pharmacists recruited by the U.S. government demonstrated shortly after the war, first in mice and then with human tumors, that a variant of the gas could treat cancers of the lymph glands, such as Hodgkin's disease.

In Bari, in December 1943, there was only misery. Thousands of refugees trudged from the city with bundles on their heads, tethered goats trotting behind. The port would remain closed for weeks, and not until February 1944 did full operations resume. The half-hour attack destroyed 38,000 tons of cargo, including vast medical stocks and 10,000 tons of steel planking needed for airfields.

Allied secrecy may have duped the public, but the enemy was not fooled. "I see you boys are getting gassed by your own poison gas," Axis Sally cooed. The Hermann Göring Division and other units intensified their chemical training. A memo from the high command warned: "The Allies could begin the gas war tomorrow."

# 6. WINTER

*The Archangel Michael, Here and Everywhere*

SINCE its founding in the eleventh century, San Pietro Infine had grown accustomed to calamity. Earthquakes, invaders, brigands, and the great migration to America in the 1880s had annealed the village; its fourteen hundred souls were hardy, fatalistic, and devout. Nestled amid wild figs and cactus on the southern flank of Monte Sammucro, overlooking the bucolic landscape soon to be known as Purple Heart Valley, San Pietro for centuries had eked out an existence from olives and *stramma,* a local hemp twisted into baskets and mats. In recent years obligatory Fascist slogans had been slathered on the walls along the steep cobblestoned paths—"Straight Ahead with Mussolini"—but life under the Duce was much as life had always been: Friday market in the Piazza San Nicola; women filling their water jugs from the sycamore-shaded *fontana;* prayers in the village church, where men and women came to God through separate doors beneath the carved inscription, "St. Michael Archangel always remember us, here and everywhere."

Then war came. One evening shortly after Italy's capitulation, a German patrol arrived to requisition all vehicles and firearms. Only four families in San Pietro possessed an automobile, but when one owner protested he was told, "Do you prefer we take your car or your son?" Soldiers dug trenches and strung barbed wire. Palazzo Brunetti, the most stylish house in town, became a command post. The smell of boiled pork and potatoes wafted from the windows, and men in coal-scuttle helmets stood with binoculars at the upper casements, watching Highway 6 where it snaked through the Mignano Gap between Monte Rotondo and Monte Lungo, barely a mile away.

On October 1, the day Naples fell, the Germans had requisitioned all donkeys and mules, and ordered every San Pietran male between fifteen and forty-five to muster in the little piazza above the *fontana.* Two hundred were press-ganged and forced to haul munitions or dig fortifications along the Bernhardt Line, which now angled past San Pietro and up

Monte Sammucro. Several hundred others fled into the mountains to shelter in caves or highland hamlets. One night in late October the village priest, Don Aristide Masia, a middle-aged man with wire-rimmed glasses and a downturned mouth, vanished from his sickbed. It was said that the Gestapo had taken him away, but the only trace ever found was Don Aristide's black cloak, snagged like a shadow in a tree branch below the town.

San Pietro's fate was sealed in mid-November. As Fifth Army butted at Monte Camino and Monte la Difensa a few miles away, Kesselring agreed to fall back from San Pietro to a better blocking position two miles up the valley. Hitler, ever more immersed in minute tactical decisions concerning battlefields a thousand miles away, agreed, then changed his mind several hours later. Tenth Army was "to hold and develop the line at San Pietro," an order Kesselring deemed "most unpleasant."

While Mark Clark paused to marshal his strength, Kesselring shifted units from the Adriatic until seven panzer grenadier battalions stiffened the Bernhardt Line across the Mignano Gap. The defense of San Pietro itself was given to a battalion from the 29th Panzer Grenadier Division, commanded by Captain Helmut Meitzel, at age twenty-three a veteran of Poland, France, Russia, and Salerno. Meitzel had been wounded five times, including severe injuries at Stalingrad that led to his evacuation on one of the last Luftwaffe planes to leave the besieged city. Antitank barrels and machine guns soon bristled from San Pietro and the terraced orchards to the east. Supply trucks barreling down Highway 6 ran a gauntlet of American artillery; a single motorcycle messenger was said to draw one hundred rounds as he raced through Dead Man's Curve on the approach track to San Pietro. Rain fell incessantly. Meitzel's grenadiers complained that their uniforms had become "sodden clumps of clay and filth."

For the San Pietrans, life grew more hideous by the day. Many had fled, but five hundred, mostly the old and the very young, took refuge in a warren of caves below the western lip of the village. With picks and even dinner forks they hacked at the soft tufa until the caves were connected. Each family had its own cramped cell, with a few crude shelves cut from the walls. German patrols sometimes swept through, searching for able-bodied men who slipped down from the mountains to visit their families, and who quickly hid in shallow trenches scooped from the cave floor and covered with planks. Stone baffles built in the cave openings shielded villagers from stray shell fire, but nothing repelled the lice, the cold, or the hunger. Stocks of flour and figs ran short. German sentries barred villagers from using the *fontana*—two girls who disobeyed were shot dead—and rainwater cisterns once used for livestock provided the only drinking water, even after soldiers heaved dead sheep into the wells. Villagers who died—and their numbers swelled as December arrived—were lugged outside the caves and laid in a dark glen soon known as the Valley of Death.

*St. Michael, always remember us.* On their knees they prayed, for strength and for deliverance. They prayed for the archangel to draw his flaming sword and lead the American host now gathering on the far side of the hill.

The temporal leader of Fifth Army, Mark W. Clark, had his own flaming sword and he was keen to thrust it through the Mignano Gap. The galling November repulses at Camino and La Difensa had sent Clark back to the map board for a new plan. His first impulse was to attack simultaneously across the front with three corps. Noting that none of the three would have adequate artillery or air support, Truscott argued that "a worse plan would be difficult to conceive."

Clark's revision, Operation RAINCOAT, had more nuance, although military imagination tended to impale itself on Italian pinnacles. Since first studying San Pietro through field glasses from a rocky den above Mignano on November 6, Clark had considered the village key to his northward advance. Five days later, he told subordinates that the "critical terrain in the operation [is] the hill mass running north of San Pietro": Monte Sammucro, nearly four thousand feet high, with rocky spurs radiating for several miles north and east. RAINCOAT called for an attack on the left by the British X Corps and the U.S. II Corps, which had just arrived in Italy under Major General Geoffrey Keyes, Patton's former deputy and now the successor to Omar Bradley. They would seize, respectively, Camino and La Difensa, the two windswept peaks that formed a single massif, six miles by four, on the west flank of the Mignano Gap. A subsequent lunge by VI Corps, including Walker's Texans in the 36th Division, which had relieved Truscott's 3rd Division, would grab San Pietro and Monte Sammucro on the gap's eastern flank.

The Allied force in Italy soon would reach fourteen divisions. Clark's intelligence estimated that 185,000 German troops in eleven divisions now defended southern Italy, with another twelve divisions in the north. The Allied strategy of tying up German forces appeared to be succeeding, albeit through a war of mutual attrition. Every hour's delay here gave enemy sappers another hour to strengthen their main defensive fortifications around Cassino, seven miles north. Yet Alexander worried at Clark's insouciance over the growing casualty lists in the Winter Line. Even the U.S. 34th Division, attacking as a diversion on Fifth Army's far right, was gaining barely three hundred yards a day at a cost of one casualty for every two yards.

"Oh, don't worry about the losses," Clark told Alexander. A stiff defense at San Pietro was unlikely, he added, and Sammucro even appeared to be clear of German troops. "I'll get through the Winter Line all right, and push the Germans out."

The attack began with the heaviest artillery barrage in Italy to date. More than nine hundred guns opened in the gathering gloom at 4:30 P.M. on Thursday, December 2. Flame reddened the clouds above Camino and La Difensa. Explosions blossomed across the upper slopes until the entire mountain appeared to be burning. Two hundred thousand shells would fall in the next two days, with some targets battered by eleven tons of steel a minute.

As the British once again trudged up Camino in what one soldier called "the blackness that only an Italian winter seems to have," several hundred infantrymen in ponchos began climbing the steep northeast face of La Difensa. Rain streamed from their helmets. In places nearly vertical they pulled themselves up hand over hand with manila climbing ropes. Recruited among American lumberjacks, Canadian prospectors, and assorted ruffians of both nationalities, the 1st Special Service Force had trained in Montana with emphasis on mountaineering, skiing, and kicks to the groin. The Forceman's credo, borrowed from the British *Handbook of Irregular Warfare*, held that "every soldier must be a potential gangster." In his backpack for the unit's first combat mission, the Force surgeon now carried five hundred codeine sulfate tablets, a hacksaw with a ten-inch blade, and a canvas bucket for amputated limbs.

Leading the gangsters up the precipice was a wiry, thirty-six-year-old American colonel named Robert T. Frederick, who had likened this ascent to the 1759 climb up the cliffs of French Quebec by the British general James Wolfe. The son of a San Francisco doctor, Frederick had joined the California National Guard at thirteen, sailed to Australia as a deckhand on a tramp steamer at fourteen, and graduated from West Point at twenty-one. "He was unusually fit," a classmate recalled. "Kind of like a cat." It was said that Frederick had made his first parachute jump after ten minutes' instruction, wearing bedroom slippers. In combat, he carried only his rifle, Nescafé, cigarettes, and a letter in Latin from the bishop of Helena, commending him as "altogether worthy of trust." Though sometimes dogmatic—he had purged the Force of most French Canadians on the supposition that "they lacked guts"—by war's end he would earn eight Purple Hearts and a reputation as one of the U.S. Army's greatest soldiers. "His casual indifference to enemy fire was hard to explain," a junior officer observed.

Their barked fingers blue from cold, the Forcemen had nearly reached the summit when the clatter of dislodged scree alerted the enemy just before dawn on December 3. Flares popped overhead, followed by the roar of machine guns and volleys of grenades and even thrown rocks. Through this fusillade the attackers heaved themselves over the final shaly lip, faces peppered with rock splinters from ricochets. By seven A.M. they had seized the crest of La Difensa, a shallow saucer the size of a football field, 3,100 feet above sea level.

A maddening wait for more ammunition delayed their westward push to link up with the British. German artillery raked reinforcements scaling La Difensa with such fury that they suffered 40 percent casualties without firing a shot. On the summit, Frederick and his men huddled under lacerating mortar fire. "A German was with me in my foxhole," recalled one lieutenant. "He didn't bum any cigarettes or anything, because he was dead." A direct hit killed a battalion commander—a former professor of history from New Brunswick—and a sergeant. "I looked back just in time to see them disappear," recalled one soldier. "It was just a red mist." A wounded private worked his way down the mountain praying aloud, "The Lord is my shepherd. He shepherds me hither, thither, and yon." Frederick passed word to supply officers below to send up whiskey, for fortitude, and condoms, to keep rain out of the rifle barrels.

Panzer grenadiers counterattacked in rain and hail, pushing the Forcemen back into their rocky saucer with machine-gun fire so ferocious it resembled "a huge shotgun blast." German snipers took a toll—a fatally wounded major plummeted over the cliff to the woods below—and officers soon smeared mud over their rank insignia to make themselves less conspicuous. Word spread that a captain had been shot in the face after an enemy white-flag ruse. "The Krauts fought like they didn't have any intention of losing the war," recalled one lieutenant. "We didn't take any prisoners. Fighting like that, you don't look for any." A soldier told to escort a captured German officer down the mountain soon reappeared. "The son of a bitch died of pneumonia," he said. After two days on La Difensa, Frederick's senior subordinate "couldn't quite speak properly" and displayed "extreme nervousness and indecision," according to several Forcemen. Emptying two clips from his .45-caliber pistol at a sniper no one else could see, he scrambled down the hill and earned the nickname Foxhole Willie.

By late Monday, December 6, Frederick's men had pushed west through a barren saddle to capture Hill 907, vital terrain below Monte Camino. In heavy pencil on a sequence of message blanks, Frederick scribbled dispatches to his command post far below, his cursive tidy and his punctuation proper even as he misdated the messages "November 6":

We have passed the crest of 907. We are receiving much machine gun and mortar fire from several directions. . . . Men are getting in bad shape. . . . I have stopped burying the dead. . . . German snipers are giving us hell and it is extremely difficult to catch them.

"I am OK," he added, "just uncomfortable and tired."

Early on Tuesday morning, a British patrol emerged from the fog to report that X Corps now controlled Camino after a five-day ordeal of attack and counterattack in which a hilltop monastery changed hands repeatedly. Parched Tommies had licked the mossy rocks for moisture; riflemen hauled up supplies on backs bent double by the incline and then hauled down casualties on stretchers whose eight bearers "slithered rather than walked," in Alan Moorehead's description. By noon on Wednesday, the last German defenders had slipped away through a valley to the west, firing a few defiant shots over their shoulders. The entire massif was at last in Allied hands, although "no one felt particularly triumphant," a Force historian wrote. Frederick scratched out a final message: "I expect to leave no wounded behind."

Survivors hobbled into the rear encampment to be greeted by a brass band playing jaunty airs. The Force had sustained 511 casualties, one-third of its combat strength, including 73 killed in action and more than 100 fatigue cases. The hospital admissions list ran to forty pages and the diagnoses summarized life on the Winter Line: gunshots, mortar fragment wounds, cerebral concussions, fractures and sprains, grenade lacerations, "amputation, right thumb, traumatic," contusions, "nervous exhaustion," jaundice, "severe diarrhea," powder burns, "hemorrhoids, extremely severe."

Of the last eighteen men treated, all but five had trench foot, including one soldier who studied the swollen, translucent appendages below his ankles and wrote, "They were almost like the feet of a dead man."

With his left flank secured, Clark could now throw a roundhouse right to capture Monte Sammucro and San Pietro. Darby's Rangers had skirmished with grenadiers on the flanks of the mountain since mid-November, usually in claustrophobic gunfights fought at close range across the talus. The 3rd Ranger Battalion had crept to the eastern fringe of San Pietro just before dawn on November 30; heavy fire pinned them down all day until they crawled away at nightfall with more than two dozen casualties. But two Ranger patrols in early December edged close to the village without drawing fire, fueling hopes that San Pietro and Sammucro had been abandoned. "I don't think there are any Krauts up there," declared Captain Rufus J. Cleghorn of the 143rd Infantry.

He soon learned otherwise. Cleghorn, a former Baylor University football player from Waco, Texas, impiously known as "Rufus the Loudmouth," led his Company A up Sammucro's east face on the evening of December 7. For five hours they climbed through swirling fog, the minesweeping detachment commanded by a lieutenant lugging a movie camera, a copy of Clausewitz's *On War,* and a fruitcake from home. As they neared the pinnacle, labeled Hill 1205 on Cleghorn's map, a sudden shout carried from above: *"Die kommen nach oben!"* Too late. The Americans swarmed over the crest in a brawl of muzzle flashes and pinging ricochets. By first light, 250 Yanks held the high ground. Flinging insults and grenades, Cleghorn and his band rolled boulders down the pitch at the field-gray shadows below. Grenadiers counterattacked, then counterattacked again, each time driven back until bodies lay like bloody stones across the slope. Private duels were fought in the fog, grenadier and rifleman darting among the rocks "like a couple of lizards." Surveying a squad of dead Germans he had just mowed down with his Browning Automatic Rifle, a soldier murmured, "This is fun. This is like what I dreamed about."

Two miles west and two thousand feet below, the attack on San Pietro proved less merry. Four battalions of long-range artillery shattered the village at five A.M. Wednesday, smashing the tailor shop and the post office and the Galilee porch of St. Michael's church with its separate doors for women and men. At 6:20 A.M., the 2nd Battalion of the 143rd Infantry crossed a shallow streambed from the southwest, "in magnificent skirmish lines just like the training manual ordered," reported one witness. With rebel yells and Texas whoops, the men clattered four hundred yards to the edge of the olive terraces. There the whine of Meitzel's machine guns stopped them as abruptly as a slammed door. Tracers lashed the ranks as the men dove for cover among the ancient olives, detonating mines and drawing mortar fire that boiled in orange clusters across the battlefield.

A sister battalion, the 3rd of the 143rd Infantry, surged into the fight, shaking out on either flank only to find the orchard terraces seeded with shoe mines and enemy pillboxes emplaced every twenty-five yards. "Ammo, damn it, we need ammo," someone yelled above the roar. Men with fingers shot off were hastily bandaged and shoved back into the fight. Enemy artillery opened from Monte Lungo, across Highway 6 to the west, where German observers had an unobstructed view of the American ranks. Still a quarter mile from San Pietro, the attack faltered and slid back in an olive-drab ebb tide. Levitating bodies lay snagged across the German barbed wire. By nightfall the attackers had retreated almost to where they had started. They tried again Thursday morning—the rebel yells a bit subdued

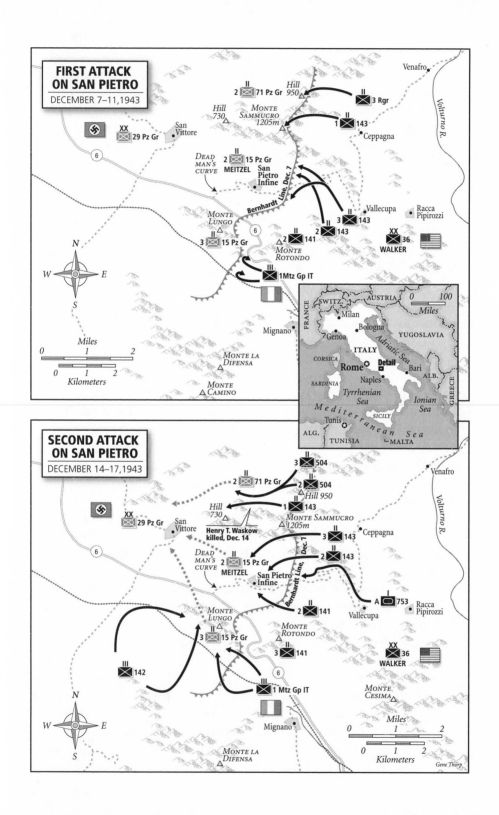

## FIRST ATTACK ON SAN PIETRO

DECEMBER 7–11, 1943

Venafro

Volturno R.

Hill 950

2 · 71 Pz Gr

II · 3 Rgr

Hill 730

MONTE SAMMUCRO 1205m

1 · 143

Ceppagna

San Vittore

XX · 29 Pz Gr

6

DEAD MAN'S CURVE

2 · 15 Pz Gr MEITZEL

San Pietro Infine

San Pietro Line, Dec. 7

Bernhardt Line

MONTE LUNGO

Vallecupa

Racca Pipirozzi

3 · 15 Pz Gr

6

3 · 143

143

2 · 141

MONTE ROTONDO

1 Mtz Gp IT

XX · 36 WALKER

N
W — E
S

Mignano

MONTE LA DIFENSA

MONTE CAMINO

Miles
0   1   2

Kilometers
0   1   2

SWITZ.  AUSTRIA
FRANCE
Milan
Bologna
Genoa
ITALY
CORSICA
Rome · Detail
SARDINIA
Naples
Tyrrhenian Sea
ALG.  Tunis
TUNISIA
MALTA

YUGOSLAVIA

Adriatic Sea

Bari
ALB.

Ionian Sea

GREECE

Mediterranean Sea

SICILY

0   100
Miles

## SECOND ATTACK ON SAN PIETRO

DECEMBER 14–17, 1943

3 · 504

2 · 71 Pz Gr

2 · 504

Hill 950

1 · 143

Venafro

Volturno R.

Hill 730

XX · 29 Pz Gr

San Vittore

Henry T. Waskow killed, Dec. 14

MONTE SAMMUCRO 1205m

Ceppagna

6

DEAD MAN'S CURVE

2 · 15 Pz Gr MEITZEL

San Pietro Line, Dec. 7

3 · 143

2 · 143

San Pietro Infine

A · 753

Racca Pipirozzi

Bernhardt Line

2 · 141

Vallecupa

MONTE LUNGO

3 · 15 Pz Gr

MONTE ROTONDO

3 · 141

XX · 36 WALKER

142

6

1 Mtz Gp IT

MONTE CESIMA

N
W — E
S

Mignano

MONTE LA DIFENSA

Miles
0   1   2

Kilometers
0   1   2

Gene Thorp

this time—and again Meitzel's grenadiers threw them back. In thirty-six hours losses in the two battalions exceeded 60 percent.

No assault on San Pietro was likely to succeed until German gunners were knocked from Monte Lungo. U.S. troops held the southern knob, but to seize the rest of the mile-long hogback the 1st Italian Motorized Group was chosen by General Keyes for Italy's first battle on the side of the Allied angels. With ROMA O MORTE chalked on their rail cars, sixteen hundred soldiers in Alpine uniforms and feathered caps arrived in Mignano. Uphill they marched in heavy mist, two chattering battalions abreast, shouting threats and vowing to punish their erstwhile Axis allies for deserting them in Africa and Russia. For a few glorious minutes the attack went well. Then machine-gun cross fire hit the Italians—"like corn cut by a scythe," in one account—and enraged grenadiers fell on the confused ranks with fists and clubs. Those who escaped downhill were said to be the fastest runners. Only massed U.S. artillery fire checked the German counterattack and prevented the Italians from being driven back to the Volturno. Losses at first were feared to exceed nine hundred, but stragglers reappeared and the final tally was pared to less than three hundred. "My troops," the Italian commander wrote Keyes, "are not in a condition to be able to accomplish the missions which you have assigned them."

Monte Lungo remained in German hands, and so too San Pietro. Only on Sammucro's icy parapets had the attack succeeded, and there Captain Cleghorn, with reinforcements from the 1st Battalion, held firm despite frenzied enemy efforts to dislodge him. Sardinian mule skinners plodded up the mountain from Ceppagna each night, following trails marked with white tape or toilet paper. They brought rations and phone wire, grenades and dry socks, sulfa and Sterno and a daily water ration of five gallons per squad. "*Brrrr*," the skinners told their little mules—the Italian equivalent of "Giddy-up"—urging the animals down the trail before daybreak, which was not difficult since the December nights were endless. Cooks and clerks wearing packboards also hauled up supplies, along with mail and a few improbable early Christmas gifts from home: one soldier shivering in a burrow was chagrined to receive a necktie. Seeing a small cairn of dead soldiers lying trailside near the crest, an officer wrote, "Splendid, husky young men. They seemed just barely dead."

A hundred yards or so down the back slope, grenadiers shivered in their own burrows, close enough that a GI could "feel the presence of the enemy through the pores of [his] skin," wrote Margaret Bourke-White. Once known as Huns or Jerries, now they were called Krauts or Teds—from the Italian *tedeschi*—or Blonds or Heinies or Graybacks. By any name, dead ones lay scattered about, green and grotesque, and every few hours another counterattack added more to the landscape. Sometimes the Germans' grenade volleys grew so intense, a U.S. soldier reported, that "we were holding our rifles so we could bat them off the way you bunt a baseball." American artillery swept the slopes with white phosphorus, silhouetting the attackers and spattering Krauts, Teds, and Blonds with incandescent flakes. A speck the size of a pinhead would burn clean through a man's leg unless plucked out with forceps or smothered with a mud poultice. Day and night, artillery reverberated against the low clouds, and the rumble echoed across the crags like querulous nagging. Men slept behind stone sangars with tracers whispering six inches overhead. "The fellow who stays out of sight the most is the one who lives the longest," an officer advised. Few needed to be told twice. "I may be prejudiced," a soldier told his buddy, "but I don't like this place."

Cleghorn's Company A had been reinforced by Company B, commanded by another Texan, a twenty-five-year-old captain named Henry T. Waskow. Raised in the cotton country south of Temple, one of eight children in a family of German Baptists strapped enough to sew their clothes from flour sacking, Waskow was fair, blue-eyed, short, and sober—"a sweet little oddball," in the estimate of a school chum. "He was never young," another classmate recalled, "not in a crazy high school–kid way." A teenage lay minister, Waskow took second prize in a statewide oratory contest, won the class presidency at Belton High School, and graduated with the highest grade-point average in twenty years. At Trinity College he joined the Texas Guard, in part for the dollar earned at each drill session, rising through the ranks on merit and zeal. At Salerno, Company B had fought with Darby at Chiunzi Pass.

"I guess I have always appeared as pretty much a queer cuss to all of you," Waskow had written in a "just-in-case" letter to his family as he shipped overseas. "If I seemed strange at times, it was because I had weighty responsibilities that preyed on my mind and wouldn't let me slack up to be human like I so wanted to be."

Now, after almost a week on Sammucro, the entire 1st Battalion was hardly bigger than a company, and Waskow's company no bigger than a platoon. Ammo stocks had dwindled again; the men threw grenade-sized rocks to keep the Germans dancing. At nightfall on Tuesday, December 14, the battalion crept forward beneath a bright moon and angled northwest along the massif toward Hill 730, a scabrous knoll almost directly behind San Pietro. The trail skirted a ravine with shadows so dense they seemed to swallow the moonbeams. "Wouldn't this be an awful spot to get killed and freeze on the mountain?" Waskow asked his company runner, Private Riley

Tidwell. The captain had a sudden craving for toast. "When we get back to the States," Waskow added, "I'm going to get me one of those smart-aleck toasters where you put the bread in and it pops up."

Those were among his last mortal thoughts. German sentries had spotted the column moving across the scree slope. Machine guns cackled, mortars crumped, and Henry Waskow pitched over without a sound, mortally wounded by a shell fragment that tore open his chest. He had never been young, and he would never be old.

Wearing his trademark knit cap and tatty field jacket, Ernie Pyle had arrived in Ceppagna, at the base of the Sammucro trail, earlier on Tuesday. Pyle's columns now appeared in two hundred daily newspapers, making him a national celebrity; Al Jolson joked that to soldiers he had become "Mr. God." But in this disfigured village, only two miles from San Pietro, Pyle could find near anonymity as just another unwashed Yank a long way from home. In a dilapidated cowshed near the olive orchard that served as a mule livery, he set his typewriter on a packing case and then poked about the battalion base camp. Engineers were corduroying the muddy paths to the gun batteries, filling ruts with logs, stones, and brush. Occasionally, a serenade—a barrage of every gun in the corps, fired at the same time at the same target—screamed over the hills toward San Pietro.

Late at night the pack mules returned from Sammucro with bodies trussed facedown across their wooden saddles, each corpse slithering "on the mule's back as if it were full of some inert liquid," as one corporal wrote. Sardinian muleteers feared the dead and trailed behind the trains.

Pyle stood outside the cowshed and watched as the first body was unlashed. "They slid him down from the mule, and stood him on his feet for a moment. In the half light he might have been merely a sick man standing there leaning on the others. Then they laid him on the ground in the shadow of the low stone wall beside the road."

Four other mules arrived. "This one is Captain Waskow," a man said. Pyle watched and said nothing. "You feel small in the presence of dead men, and you don't ask silly questions," he subsequently explained. A few days later, after returning to Fifth Army headquarters in Caserta, where he played gin rummy and drank to excess, Pyle would recall how the bodies lay uncovered in the shadows and how several of Waskow's men edged over to the dead captain to voice regret—"I sure am sorry, sir"— or to curse—"God damn it to hell anyway!" Riley Tidwell appeared and the company runner held his commander's hand, studying Waskow's waxy face.

Finally he put the hand down. He reached over and gently straightened the points of the captain's shirt collar, and then he sort of rearranged the tattered edges of the uniform around the wound, and then he got up and walked away down the road in the moonlight, all alone. The rest of us went back into the cowshed, leaving the five dead men lying in a line, end to end, in the shadow of the low stone wall.

Pyle had written his most famous dispatch, perhaps the finest expository passage of World War II. But still he felt small in the presence of dead men. "I've lost the touch," he told a friend. "This stuff stinks."

Mark Clark had proposed using tanks to capture San Pietro as early as December 9. He had pressed Eisenhower and Alexander in the fall to send the 1st Armored Division—Old Ironsides—to Italy, and he felt chagrined that the mountainous terrain afforded so few chances to unleash it. Fred Walker, the 36th Division commander, doubted that the gullies and six-foot olive terraces ringing San Pietro would accommodate tanks, a skepticism reinforced in an early foray when the lead Sherman threw a track and blocked the trail.

Walker planned to try again at midday, Wednesday, December 15. This time the attack would be filmed by a pair of Signal Corps cameramen perched on Monte Rotondo, part of a movie crew working for Captain John Huston. Assigned by the War Department to document "the triumphal entry of the American forces into Rome," Huston, who two years earlier had directed Humphrey Bogart in *The Maltese Falcon,* instead found himself trying to concoct a celluloid epic from the Army's frustrated assault on an anonymous village in southern Italy. At least his cinematography would be unimpeded by trees: after weeks of shelling, Rotondo reportedly "looked as if a large mower had been used on the side of the hill."

At eleven A.M. the mist lifted, the cameras rolled, and two platoons from the 753rd Tank Battalion clanked to a hairpin bend in the high road from Ceppagna. For fifteen minutes, Shermans and tank destroyers hammered San Pietro with 75mm shells. Then loaders with asbestos gloves shoveled the fuming brass from their turret floors, and at noon the attack by sixteen tanks trundled forward. It was doomed, of course. Only the lead Sherman made headway, churning through a terrace wall to shoot up several German machine-gun nests. The second tank struck a mine. The next three closed to within half a mile of the village only to burst into flames from German antitank fire. Three more hit mines. By midafternoon four surviving tanks were limping back toward Ceppagna with crews from the less fortunate Shermans clinging to the hulls like barnacles. Seven tanks had been destroyed, five others immobilized.

Walker's foot soldiers had no better luck. The 141st Infantry's 2nd Battalion launched another frontal assault across open ground at one A.M. on Thursday morning. "Dead and wounded marked the route of advance," a regimental account noted. A few intrepid souls grenaded and bayoneted their way into the lower village, scrambling through breaches in the wall by standing on one another's shoulders. Most were captured or killed by plunging fire; the 2nd Battalion fell back, now shorn to 130 men by "the stupidest assignment the battalion ever received," according to Major Milton Landry, the unit commander. A lieutenant disemboweled by grenade fragments repeated the name "Erika" through the small hours, then died at dawn. A second attack at six A.M. also failed, as did lunges on the right flank by two battalions of the 143rd Infantry. When a pinned-down soldier began waving his undershirt in surrender, a sergeant put his rifle muzzle to the man's temple and warned, "Put that damn rag away or I'll blow your head off."

Wisps of steam rose from shallow revetments in the rear where exhausted riflemen lay beneath their sodden blankets. Clark arrived at noon on Thursday, listening to the cacophony of mortars and machine pistols just ahead. Through field glasses he studied the charred tank hulks on the Ceppagna road. "What troops are in front of you?" he asked a lieutenant. "Sir," the officer replied, "Germans." Clark uttered a few words of encouragement, and drove off.

"The losses before the town have been heavy," Walker told his diary. "Many wounded had to be abandonded within enemy lines. . . . This is bad."

And then it ended. Monte Lungo had always held the key to San Pietro, and by dusk on Thursday two battalions from the 142nd Infantry had overrun the hogback from the west, threatening to encircle the village. Captain Meitzel's grenadiers launched a brief counterattack from San Pietro to cover the battalion's withdrawal. At midnight on Friday, December 17, a fountain of colored flares above the north slope of Sammucro signaled retreat. German troops fell back two miles to yet another hillside village, San Vittore, which they would hold for the next three weeks.

American riflemen creeping through the blue battle haze found San Pietro in ruins, "one large mound of desolation," in a gunner's description. The detritus of total war littered the rubble: cartridge belts, stained bandages, dead pigs, "a gray hand hanging limply from a sleeve." St. Michael's was reduced to a single upright wall, with a headless Christ hanging on His cross. The choir loft dangled above an altar now buried in masonry. The correspondent Homer Bigart also discovered a December 6 copy of the *Völkischer Beobachter* and, inexplicably, a baseball glove.

A few dozen wretched San Pietrans emerged from the ruins to huzzah their liberators. The dim, fetid caves below the village were "the nearest thing to a journey in Dante's *Inferno* that I was to know in the war," wrote J. Glenn Gray, an Army intelligence analyst. "Children were screaming, old men and women coughing or moaning, while others tried to prepare gruel over smoking coals." Some 140 San Pietrans were dead, one villager in ten. A baby's corpse lying in the mud was repeatedly run over by military vehicles before someone finally noticed and a medic buried the remains. Graves registration men arrived with their leather gloves to police the battlefield, folding the hands of dead GIs across their chests before lifting them into white burial sacks. As the soldier-poet Keith Douglas wrote, "About them clung that impenetrable silence . . . by which I think the dead compel our reverence."

Those who had fought for the past ten days supposedly "slept where their bedding fell from the truck." San Pietro had cost Fred Walker's 36th Division twelve hundred battle casualties, and two thousand nonbattle losses; the 143rd Infantry Regiment alone lost 80 percent of its strength. Engineers, tankers, Rangers, paratroopers, and the Italians who also fought for the village had hundreds more killed, missing, sick, and injured.

At an evacuation hospital near Mignano, patients lay listening to the shriek of artillery, calling out the guns by millimeter. A chaplain played "Ah! Sweet Mystery of Life" on his Victrola. Margaret Bourke-White spied "a small grim pile of amputated legs" covered with canvas outside a surgical tent. When one dying Texas boy asked for watermelon, a surgeon replied, "They're not in season, son." To Bourke-White he added, "They often ask for their favorite food when they're near death."

As the front lurched forward another mile or two, John Lucas advised his diary on December 18, "We find the country thick with dead as we advance. . . . I think the swine have taken a lacing." But, the VI Corps commander added, "Rome seems a long way off." A 36th Division soldier offered his own summary: "This is a heartbreaking business."

For John Huston, the battle for San Pietro went on. The director's footage of the star-crossed tank attack was dramatic but incomplete. Although he later claimed to have done most of his filming "during the actual battle," Huston in fact spent two months staging elaborate reenactments in olive orchards and on Monte Sammucro, using 36th Division troops. Casualty scenes were staged in a hospital, a dead German in a foxhole was actually a GI actor in a grenadier uniform, and sequences inside the ruined village were filmed at another town accidentally bombed by American planes. After draconian editing by George Marshall, who ordered the film cut from fifty minutes to half an hour, Huston added a brief introductory speech by Mark Clark and a soundtrack that included the Mormon Tabernacle Choir. *San Pietro* would be released nationwide in the spring of 1945 to rhapsodic reviews. *Time* called it "as good a war film as any that has been made."

The telegram announcing Henry Waskow's death would arrive at his Texas home on December 29, delayed by the War Department along with similar notifications until after Christmas. Henry's mother had been troubled with premonitions, and when the family appeared to break the news she blurted out, "I was right, wasn't I? Henry's gone." Pyle's column would appear on January 10, 1944, covering the entire front page of the *Washington Daily News*. Hollywood seized on the story and a year later released *The Story of G.I. Joe,* with Burgess Meredith as Pyle and Robert Mitchum as a "Captain Bill Walker," who dies on a mountainside in Italy.

But Waskow had the final word, a "last will and testament" mailed to his sister for safekeeping and made public more than fifteen years after his passing. "I would have liked to have lived," he told his parents in a ten-paragraph meditation. "But, since God has willed otherwise, do not grieve too much, dear ones, for life in the other world must be beautiful, and I have lived a life with that in mind all along. I was not afraid to die, you can be assured of that."

> I will have done my share to make this world a better place in which to live. Maybe when the lights go on again all over the world, free people can be happy and gay again. . . . If I failed as a leader, and I pray God I didn't, it was not because I did not try.

"I loved you," he added, "with all my heart."

## *"A Tank Too Big for the Village Square"*

L IFE in exile had its compensations for George Patton. As the viceroy of Sicily, he slept in a king's bedroom on three mattresses and dined on royal china. Every day he rode an Italian cavalry horse in the Palermo palace riding hall, serenaded by a mounted band and attended by 120 plumed, saber-wielding carabinieri. With a snub-nosed Colt revolver in his pants pocket ("for social purposes only," he said), Patton also took daily walks of precisely two miles, which a trailing driver measured on the jeep odometer. "I can now chin myself five and a half times and do it three times a day," he told his diary, impressive enough for a man who had turned fifty-eight on November 11.

On mild afternoons Patton sailed the Gulf of Palermo or swam at his beachhouse, where a young female attendant insisted on helping visitors disrobe. There was quail hunting with Sicilian guides at a beautiful lodge in the mountains. To brush up his French—just in case—he listened to language lessons on phonograph records. On cold winter nights he stirred the embers of a blazing fire while sipping wine and reading a biography of Wellington, later regaling his staff officers with stories of the Iron Duke. He flitted conspicuously about the Mediterranean; Marshall and Eisenhower hoped the enemy would assume he was preparing another invasion force. Sardinia intrigued him, but Cairo was "really a disgusting place. It looks, and the people act, exactly as they did in New York in 1928." He wrote verse, including a poem titled "God of Battles"—"Make strong our souls to conquer"—for which *Women's Home Companion* paid him $50. Visitors came and visitors went, including John Steinbeck and Marlene Dietrich, who thought Patton looked "like a tank too big for the village square." He even found time to reopen Palermo's opera house with a sold-out performance of *La Bohème*. Crowds packed the balconies and thronged the streets outside to listen by loudspeaker. As the house lights dimmed, a beam on the royal box revealed Patton holding an American flag, arm in arm with Palermo's mayor, who held an Italian tricolor. The audience cheered wildly, then wept from the overture through the final arias. For days, snatches of Puccini could be heard around the city from would-be Mimìs and Rodolfos.

Yet even a heartsick bohemian swain could not have been more miserable than Patton. A few months earlier he had commanded a quarter million men; now Seventh Army was reduced to a shell of five thousand, and in late November even his signal battalion was plucked away for service in Italy. "It almost looks like an attempt to strip the body before the spirit has flown," Patton wrote. John Lucas during a visit found him "very depressed," and a British general thought he looked "old and dessicated," chin-ups notwithstanding. His chief engineer strolled into Patton's office one day to find him "literally cutting out paper dolls" with a pair of scissors. On November 7 he had written Bea that in the 365 days since the TORCH landings, "I have been in battle seventy-two days." She replied with an eight-syllable telegram: "Atta boy. Love. Confidence. Pride."

Still, he had not heard a shot fired in anger since mid-August, except during occasional air raids. (German prisoners-of-war were issued wicker baskets and ordered to collect body parts from the rubble.) Gesturing vaguely toward the front, Patton told an old friend, "I want to go out up there where it is hot, with an enemy bullet in the middle of my forehead." When Jimmy Doolittle flew in for a chat, Patton threw his arms around the airman with tears streaming down his cheeks. "I didn't think anyone would ever call on a mean old son of a bitch like me," he said. As the 1st Division sailed from Syracuse for Britain, Patton waved farewell from a harbor barge, blowing kisses and yelling God-bless-yous. Still resentful at the treatment of Terry Allen and Ted Roosevelt, soldiers stood three deep at every rail and peered from every porthole, utterly silent. "It was awful," Clift Andrus reported.

"You need have no fear of being left in the backwater of the war," Eisenhower had told Patton, but that was before Patton slapped the two soldiers. For more than three months that secret had held, with at least sixty reporters in Algiers and Italy sitting on the story. But Sicily now felt like the ultimate backwater. Patton tramped around Gela and other Sicilian battlefields, reliving past glories while disparaging the commanders struggling on the Winter Line. "I wish something would happen to Clark," he told his diary. Montgomery was simply "the little fart." To Bea he wrote with his idiosyncratic spelling and grammar: "Send me some more pink medecin. This worry and inactivity has raised hell with my insides."

He took little interest in governing Sicily, which desperately needed a caring hand. Allied planners, drawing on irrelevant experiences from the U.S. Civil War and the occupation of the Rhineland after World War I, had assumed the Italian economy would "maintain itself at a minimum subsistence level," particularly in agrarian Sicily. That proved dead wrong. By early winter, to forestall famine and bread riots, Allied commissaries were forced to provide flour for three-quarters of the Sicilian population. At feeding centers, starving women feigned pregnancy with pillows stuffed beneath their skirts to claim an extra ration. Black marketeering drove up the price of salt a hundredfold, to 350 lire per kilo.

Shortages plagued the island, from coal and fertilizer to nails and lightbulbs. Typhoid appeared. Officers also reported "some recrudescence of Mafia activities," including occasional murders with the *lupara,* a sawed-off shotgun that was the traditional weapon of choice for revenge killings. Power outages were chronic, and courts handed down criminal sentences by matchlight. Occupation authorities jailed sixteen hundred "politically dangerous" Sicilians for months and scissored Fascist cant from school textbooks, but the locals still greeted Allied soldiers with absentminded Black Shirt salutes. The liberators soon grew weary of the liberated. "The Sicilian has been found by experience to be utterly untrustworthy," U.S. Army logisticians complained. "They adopt every possible ruse to cheat and generally outwit us." OSS agents agreed. "Lying, stealing, and general dishonesty . . . can be considered a prevalent folk characteristic."

Whatever mild curiosity Patton evinced in these local affairs vanished after the slapping story broke at home in late November. The Quaker muckraker Drew Pearson, apparently tipped off by an OSS source, broadcast a garbled but uncensored version of the incidents during his weekly radio show. Beetle Smith in Algiers made matters worse by disingenuously insisting that Patton had not been reprimanded, distinguishing between an official censure and Eisenhower's personal castigation in August.

Politicians and the press were in full throat overnight. "Army regulations specifically forbid this sort of thing," complained a former artilleryman from Missouri, Senator Harry S. Truman. Editorial opinion ranged from the condemnatory (the *Raleigh News and Observer:* "A man who cannot command himself lacks the supreme virtue") to the indulgent (the *Seattle Post-Intelligencer* held that "allowances must be made for the feelings of a high-spirited man under the stress of battle"). By mid-December, the White House and War Department had received fifteen hundred letters, pro and con, though a Gallup poll indicated that by a four-to-one margin Americans opposed sacking Patton.

"I am not so sure that my luck has held," Patton told Bea on December 4, adding, "The only thing to do is do nothing and make no excuses." In a conversation with Clark he contemplated retirement, then privately complained that the Fifth Army commander "treated me as an undertaker treats the family of the deceased." As usual his contrition was inconstant, a blend of contumacy, repentance, and irony. Of Drew Pearson he wrote, "I will live to see him die." He told Kay Summersby, "I always get in trouble with my goddam mouth. But if this sort of thing ever comes up, I'll do it again." When Lieutenant General Lesley J. McNair wrote that "in all frankness your temper has long threatened to undo you," Patton replied that in striking the soldiers "I was putting on an act." Perhaps his most reflective moment came in a note to a friend in December: "Very few of us fail to make mistakes. This does not excuse mistakes, but it at least puts us in good company."

Eisenhower had kept faith with his old friend, even as he recognized that personal foibles limited his utility in high command. While privately recommending Patton for another army command, he told Marshall, "I doubt that I would ever consider Patton for an army group or any higher position." In December, in the semiannual evaluations of his chief subordinates, Eisenhower rated Patton "superior" and ranked him fifth among the two dozen lieutenant generals he knew. Patton was "impulsive and flamboyant," Eisenhower added, and "should always serve under a strong but understanding commander."

Deliverance came from Franklin Roosevelt, a strong but understanding commander-in-chief. On Wednesday, December 8, en route to Washington after the conferences in Cairo and Teheran, the president landed at Malta for a quick inspection of the dockyard and then flew on to Sicily. Escorted by a dozen P-38 fighters, the aircraft touched down at two P.M. at Castelvetrano, fifty miles southwest of Palermo. Patton and Clark, who had flown in from the Winter Line, braced at attention at the foot of the ramp.

With the brim of his hat tipped up to catch a few final minutes of Mediterranean sun, Roosevelt took a jeep tour of the airfield before presenting the Distinguished Service Cross to Clark and several others for their heroics at Salerno. A receiving line formed, and as Patton shuffled past, a beaming Roosevelt grabbed his hand and held it for a long moment. According to Clark's later recollection, the president murmured, "General Patton, you will have an army command in the great Normandy operation."

He had been reprieved. In a secluded corner away from the president's entourage, Patton glanced about to be certain that he was alone and then burst into sobs. For a full minute he wept, tears of relief, of regret, of gratitude, and surely of defiance coursing down his cheeks. Wiping his eyes, he gathered himself and strutted back to the jeep to join the president for cocktails at the officers' club.

Official redemption would arrive several weeks later, in a message ordering him to the United Kingdom to take command of the new U.S. Third Army. His country needed him, and the forces of righteousness also required him. Had Patton known that he had but two years to live, he hardly would have cared. He had already heard the summons of the trumpet.

"My destiny is sure," he would tell his diary on Christmas Day, "and I am a fool and a coward ever to have doubted it."

## A Gangster's Battle

THE forces of righteousness also required Bernard Montgomery, but for the moment they required him in Italy, on the Adriatic front.

While Clark's Fifth Army struggled up the west coast, Eighth Army since invading Calabria had traced the ancient Crusaders' Coast for four hundred miles. Five divisions—Brits, Kiwis, Indians, and Canadians—armed with nearly seven hundred guns and two hundred tanks had pushed back four German divisions on a forty-mile front. With Fifth Army threatening Rome from the south, Montgomery intended to seize the seaside resort of Pescara, halfway up the boot, before swinging west on Highway 5 across the mountains through Avezzano to approach the capital from the east. Alexander hoped that if attacked on a broad front, from sea to sea, "the enemy would be sufficiently stretched to prevent him massing for the defense of Cassino."

That strategy still seemed plausible on November 20, when Eighth Army attacked the Sangro River, establishing a bridgehead on the far shore and nearly obliterating the German 65th Division, whose commander forfeited his right arm during an air attack. By early December, with thousands of Allied planes providing support and British tanks deftly maneuvering through snowdrifts, the Sangro defenses had been unhinged. New Zealand troops pushed into the crossroads town of Orsogna before panzers pushed them out again. "The Germans are, in fact, in the very condition in which we want them," Montgomery declared. "We will now hit them a colossal crack." He publicly announced, "The road to Rome is open."

Alas, no. The Bernhardt Line defenses extended nine miles deep north of the Sangro, in what Alexander came to call "ridge and furrow country." Montgomery discovered, as Clark had, that superior Allied air, artillery, and armor could be checked by poor weather, hellish terrain, and a stubborn *Feldwebel* with an antitank gun. A British analysis warned that for Sherman tank crews, "the average range of vision was about 50 yards, and the average range at which tanks were knocked out about 80 yards. . . . To hesitate spells death." In one especially trying stretch, German axes felled a half mile avenue of poplars, which had to be cleared from the road with bulldozers and chains at a rate of an hour per tree.

Drenching winter rains abruptly widened the Sangro from one hundred feet to four hundred and more, sweeping away so many bridges that an official history damned "this malignant river, rising to flood and fury." A half dozen ambulances returning to an aid station were halted so long by a washed-out bridge that the medics ran out of morphine. "I could hear the wounded men inside moaning dreadfully and shrieking," a Canadian officer wrote. Battle casualties, as well as sickness and injury, gnawed at Eighth Army; losses in the 78th Division would total ten thousand in the second half of 1943.

The Adriatic, in fact, was "an unprofitable sector" with "no real strategic objective," as an astute New Zealand brigadier, Howard K. Kippenberger, recognized. Montgomery lacked the combat power and reserves to reach Pescara, much less Avezzano or Rome. A giddy AFHQ intelligence summary on December 4 declared, "The enemy has lost the initiative. . . . The Winter Line has been breached and overrun in the Adriatic sector." Perhaps it seemed so in Algiers, but on the actual battlefield a strategy of maneuver had quickly devolved into a strategy of attrition and mutual bloodletting. An Eighth Army pause in early December let Kesselring's troops regroup; two more attacks on Orsona failed, leaving the New Zealanders stymied.

For those whose blood was let, the Winter Line in the east rivaled that in the west for vexation. In early December, a Canadian soldier described "a landscape that seemed almost lunar in its desolation," where "men lived and died in many unremembered ways." Each ridge seemed to conceal a constellation of enemy bunkers; every snow-dusted furrow might hold a mine, or a sniper all but invisible in a white snowsuit. In preparing for a patrol in the no-man's-land along the Winter Line, one soldier recounted how he "lay rigid, biting my hand and totally convinced beyond all doubt that waiting Germans were watching us. . . . I hated it; I hated the cold and the dark; above all I hated the loneliness."

"To preserve sanity," another Tommy told his diary, "the limits of imagination must stop at one's own miseries." Gun crews traded the heavy barrages known as "murder." As the season deepened and darkened, a Royal Fusilier observed that troops had revived a survival concept from the Great War known as "the better hole": the search for a burrow of relative security and comfort. His staccato summary of infantry life along the Sangro had universal merit: "Move forward. Stop. Dig in. Wait. What is happening? Who knows? Not us. Move on."

Montgomery kept his swank, at first. With his menagerie of canaries, lovebirds, hens, dogs, and the odd lamb or piglet, he waged war as he had with Eighth Army for sixteen months: from "Main 35," a compact and nomadic tactical camp of rickety trucks and caravans, well hidden by brush and camouflage netting, and calibrated to the commander's early-to-bed battle rhythm. To commemorate the first anniversary of El Alamein, Montgomery threw a party near Lucera, with staff officers assigned to provide wine, fresh meat, and a grand piano, which was somehow coaxed into an olive grove. Italian musicians, billed as the Lucera Swingers and featuring a pianist who claimed to have played New York, banged out "Lili Marlene" and "La Vie en Rose." For a few sweet hours, the greatest British victory since Waterloo seemed nearer than the muddy misery of central Italy.

Montgomery remained peremptory as ever, with subordinate and superior alike. A staff officer sent to fetch a brigadier told him, "The army commander wants to see you in exactly four minutes and thirty-five seconds. Thirty-four. Thirty-three . . ." When Alexander stood in a conference to explain his thoughts on shifting Eighth Army divisions to support Fifth Army, Montgomery impatiently snapped, "Sit down. I'll show you how to do it." He lamented what he saw as the lack of "a firm plan for waging the campaign. At present it is haphazard and go-as-you-please. . . . We each do what we like, when we like." A parody of Montgomery in conversation with God made the rounds, with the general advising the Almighty in a final heroic couplet:

> And after the war when I've nothing to do,
> I'll come up to heaven and run things for You.

Each night he prayed for fair skies, and each morning was peeved when his appeal went unheeded. "I *must* have fine weather," he insisted in November. "If it rains continuously, I am done." Rain fell continuously. When the Sangro spate washed out his bridges, he summoned a senior engineer, served a convivial cup of tea, then rounded on the poor fellow. "You are useless, quite useless," Montgomery charged. "I have a little geography book about Italy. It says it isn't unusual at this season for the rivers in Italy to rise even twenty feet in one night. Get out. You are fired." More to his liking was an Australian pilot, who was shot down, rescued, and brought to Montgomery's mess on the Sangro for lunch. When the army commander asked his opinion on "the greatest principle of war," the Aussie replied, "I should say it's: 'Stop frigging about.'"

But frigging about had become the order of the day in Italy. Whether any mortal commander could have flanked Rome across the Apennines in midwinter is problematic, but Montgomery's particular skills seemed ill matched to the task. He "had the unusual gift of persuasively combining very bold speech and very cautious action," as C.J.C. Molony would observe in the official British history of the Italian campaign. A methodical orthodoxy now defined his generalship, much as the beret and eccentric encampment expressed his persona. Again and again he chose limited objectives, which were attacked only after a painstaking accretion of men and matériel in such quantities that he could "scarcely fail, given time, to take that objective," as Molony wrote. Then the cycle began again, with the selection of another limited objective, and another slow buildup.

"He was in fact a very good First World War general, and he did not regard his troops as capable of any higher performance," concluded Michael Howard.

Years of calamity—in France, Norway, Crete, Singapore, and the Western Desert—had demonstrated the limits of this huge conscript army, including the capacity of staff officers and junior commanders to handle the immensely complex requirements of modern war. For Montgomery, simplicity was paramount, initiative to be discouraged. His battlefield was linear and sequential, meticulous and unimaginably violent.

This vision, which had made him Britain's most successful and celebrated field general, was unlikely to carry the day above the Sangro, and Montgomery knew it. In late November, even before Eighth Army stalled along the Bernhardt Line, his frustration boiled over in a private five-page screed, "Reflections on the Campaigns in Italy, 1943." He tattooed the cousins, of course: "The Americans do not understand how to fight the Germans. . . . They do not understand the great principles of surprise and concentration." But most of his fire fell on Alexander. "He has very little idea as to how to operate armies in the field. When he has a conference of commanders, which is very seldom, it is a lamentable spectacle. . . . No one gets any orders, and we all do what we like." He worried that "we may be led into further troubles in 1944 and will not finish off the war cleanly."

In short, Montgomery concluded, the war in Italy had become a detestable thing, "untidy and ad hoc."

Montgomery's last best hope to avoid a stalemate fell on the Canadian 1st Division, which in early December was ordered to force the narrow coastal plain in a final effort to at least reach Pescara and Highway 5, the lateral road to Rome.

Canada's hour had finally come. The country had entered the war in 1939 with fewer than five thousand professional soldiers and a callow militia of under fifty thousand. Within three years, the force grew to half a million, but Canadian troops had seen little action except for nine murderous hours in the French coastal town of Dieppe, where in August 1942 a raid gone awry left more than nine hundred Canadians dead and nearly two thousand captured. Canadian troops had fought with distinction in Sicily, but some feared that the war would end without a chance to avenge Dieppe or to prove the national mettle.

That chance would come fifteen miles south of Pescara, at Ortona, a port town built on its Adriatic promontory by Trojans fleeing their burning, high-walled city in the second millennium before Christ—or so it was said. Centuries of prosperity had ended in 1447, when Venetians fired Ortona's fleet and arsenal. Now a decrepit sandstone castle beetled over the harbor and a few scraggly palm trees ringed the Piazza Municipale. But the more beguiling local landmarks included a domed twelfth-century cathedral that held the bones of St. Thomas the Apostle, and an even older church founded by Mary Magdalene—or so it was said. Most of Ortona's ten thousand souls had fled to the mountains or toiled in German labor battalions; Wehrmacht sappers also blew holes in the harbor mole and sank two hundred boats to block the anchorage. The coastal road from the south, Highway 16, was easily severed by dropping a bridge below the town, leaving but a single approach road, which hugged a narrow ridge from the southwest. Still, the Germans were likely to fall back to more easily defended ridge-and-furrow country to the north—or so it was said.

The Canadian division commander, Major General Christopher Vokes, was a burly engineer who had been born in Ireland to a British officer and his wife but educated in Ontario, Quebec, and England. "A tough old bird, great boxer, tall, wide, and built like a bulldog, which also summed up his personality perfectly," said one aquaintance. Given to roaring through his red pushbroom mustache, Vokes at age thirty-nine was described as "a roughneck" by a Canadian reporter, who added, "I never knew a more profane man." Others considered him "a pompous bully" who imitated Montgomery by carrying a fly whisk and affecting a British accent. He preached a bracing stoicism, claiming that "a man's fate is written the day he is born and no amount of dodging can avoid it." The tactical corollary of this eschatology appeared to be the frontal assault, which Vokes ordered in sufficient numbers at Ortona to be known thereafter as the Butcher.

As commanded, the Canadians attacked across the Moro, a mustard-hued creek that emptied into the sea two miles south of Ortona. A lunge on the left flank gained sufficient surprise to find food abandoned on German mess tables. Other thrusts met stout resistance; when a Canadian gunner yelled that he was out of ammunition, his company commander yelled back, "Why, you stupid bastard, make military noises." So intense grew the shell fire that one corporal declared, "It was like a raving madhouse." Sweating artillerymen stripped to their bare chests, as blood trickled from their concussion-ruptured eardrums and gun barrels glowed a "translucent red." "The situation was undoubtedly confusing to the enemy as well as to ourselves," a staff officer wrote. But on December 9 the Moro line was breached, with 170 Germans killed in a single day. Montgomery sent Vokes "hearty congratulations."

The plaudit was premature. Beyond the Moro lay a ravine running northeast to southwest, and labeled Torrente Saraceni on Italian maps. Just south of the ridge road that offered the only access to Ortona, this gulch was more than three miles long, two hundred yards wide, and two hundred feet deep. Italian farmers had planted the bottoms with grain and olives; German sappers replanted with mines and booby traps. Troops from the 90th Panzer Grenadier Division, many of whom had escaped from Sardinia and Corsica in September, dug into the slopes and barricaded the stone farmhouses along the north lip. Vokes failed to sense how formidable was the barrier posed by the Gully—as Canadian troops called it—and beginning on Saturday, December 11, he flung a sequence of piece-meal attacks into the breach. Of eight assaults on the Torrente Saraceni, five

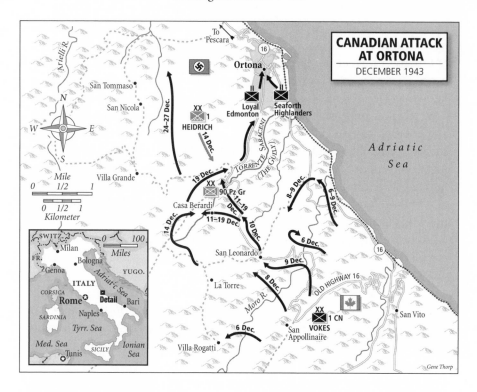

were made by single battalions, and only the last involved as many as three. When Montgomery dispatched a messenger to ask why the Canadians had stalled, Vokes snarled, "You tell Monty if he would get to hell up here and see the bloody mud he has stuck us in, he'd know damn well why we can't move faster."

For nine days the Gully held the Canadians in what infantry officer Farley Mowat called a "filthy limbo." A corporal with a notebook sketched the configuration of slit trenches around him, then listened to the shriek of an approaching shell and placed a pencil tick on the trench where he guessed it would land; he called the game "Dots and Spots." Horribly burned by white phosphorus, a sergeant cried to those rushing to help him, "Don't come near me, boys, don't let this stuff get on you." In agony he died, alone.

The limbo grew filthier on December 14, with the discovery of a German corpse wearing a round helmet and a Luftwaffe uniform—evidence that panzer grenadiers had been replaced by the 1st Parachute Division. Commanded by a corpulent, gray-eyed major general named Richard Heidrich, whose uncanny resemblance to Churchill extended to a fondness for enormous cigars, the paratroopers were "the best German troops in Italy," in Alexander's estimation. Their presence suggested to Allied intelligence that Kesselring intended to hold Ortona and not simply delay the Canadian advance.

On and on went the primordial struggle across this boggy rent in the earth. Heavy losses and exhaustion beset both sides of the Gully, now also known as Dead Man's Gulch for the bodies bricking the scorched heath. "You feel nothing," a Canadian soldier reported. "Only a weariness so great you couldn't sleep if they let you." Inexact maps led to errant Canadian shelling, including a barrage that straddled the Gully to hit friendly regiments on either side. So many shells puckered the landscape that one tanker was reminded of "a large porridge pot bubbling." An intrepid captain managed to capture Casa Berardi, a farm at the west end of the Gully, but Vokes lacked reserves to exploit the flank and instead launched another bootless frontal assault. "He frittered away everything, and everything was committed and he had no reserves, which is a terrible thing," the Canadians' chief engineer lamented.

A flanking attack from the west, code-named MORNING GLORY, finally unhinged the German line and by dusk on December 19 the Gully belonged to Canada. To plant the Maple Leaf flag had cost a thousand casualties. Two Canadian battalions were reduced to the size of companies, and one company was commanded by a corporal. The reporter Christopher Buckley entered a battered cottage to find "an old woman, her eyes closed, her face the colour of old parchment, moaning and keening to herself. . . . Stretched out on the floor lay the corpses of four young children."

A mile to the north, Ortona town still belonged to Germany. Any illusions that the enemy planned to quietly decamp should have been dispelled by a captured German paratrooper. Blinded by his wounds, he told his captors, "I wish I could see you. I'd kill every one of you."

*A man's fate is written the day he is born and no amount of dodging can avoid it.* Perhaps that also held true for towns, and if so Ortona had been doomed from the moment those fabled Trojans shipped their oars off the beckoning promontory. As the burning towers of Troy presaged Ortona's ashes, so did Ortona's fate offer auguries for a hundred towns to come. For here was fought the first large, pitched urban battle in the Mediterranean— not a skirmish against Italians as in Gela, or a village brawl as in San Pietro, but a room-to-room, house-to-house, block-to-block struggle that foretold iconic street fights with heavy weapons from Caen to Aachen, and from Nuremberg to Berlin.

Ortona had been spared razing because of a wan hope in Montgomery's headquarters that it would fall quickly to become an Allied port and winter hostel for weary troops. That fantasy vanished in a great roar at dawn on

Tuesday, December 21, when German demolitionists blew up a watchtower adjacent to the cathedral, leaving St. Thomas's dome "split in half like a butchered deer," in one witness's description. At the same hour, Canadian infantry and Sherman tanks rushed the town from the southwest, sirens wailing and every gun blazing. Machine-gun bullets chipped the cobblestones in a spray of orange sparks as riflemen crouched in the doorways and fired at every window. Just after noon Kesselring's chief of staff rang Tenth Army headquarters to report that Berlin assumed the town was lost. "The high command called me on the phone. Everybody was very sad about Ortona," he said. "Why?" a Tenth Army staff officer replied. "Ortona is still in our hands."

So it would remain for another week. Side streets proved too narrow for tanks, and German sappers blew up stone buildings to block the intersections and canalize Canadian attackers down the Corso Vittorio Emanuele. Antitank guns hidden in alleys shot the Shermans in the flank as they passed; others, tucked in the rubble, shot the tanks in the belly when they crawled over street barricades. Booby-trap trip wires seemed to stretch across every stairway and from every doorknob. Two Canadian regiments— the Loyal Edmontons on the left and the Seaforth Highlanders from British Columbia on the right—inched forward on a five-hundred-yard front in fighting described as "a gangster's battle" that raged "from cellar to loft, from one rubble pile to the next." Progress was "measured in a house or two gained every hour," wrote the historian Mark Zuehlke. No-man's-land was measured in the width of an alley, and sometimes the width of a bedroom wall. "For some unknown reason," a *New York Times* reporter noted, "the Germans are staging a miniature Stalingrad in hapless Ortona." Soldiers told one another, "Only three more shooting days till Christmas."

Rather than clear buildings conventionally, from the ground floor up, Canadian engineers perfected the art of "mouseholing" from one adjoining building to the next without setting foot in the street: a beehive explosive charge was placed on a chair next to a top-floor wall; after the blast blew a hole into the abutting building, infantrymen stormed through the dust, spraying all cupboards and bedsteads with "speculative fire" from tommy guns, then fought their way downstairs, floor by floor, grenading "any room which gave reason for suspicion." Sheets draped from designated windows indicated a cleared house, which then required a small garrison to prevent Heidrich's paratroopers from reinfesting it at night. Farley Mowat observed that his men soon developed an architectural "capacity to estimate the relative strength of a building at a single glance . . . the wall thickness, the firmness of the mortar, the number of rooms."

"The stench here is dreadful," one soldier wrote. "I can't understand why the Germans decay differently." Christopher Buckley spied a dead paratrooper with postcards spilling from his tunic, each featuring a photo of Hitler. An enemy sergeant, shot in the head and dying in a side street, told a Canadian in English, "We could beat you."

Not for want of effort did they fail. Two dozen Edmontons were buried alive when a booby-trapped building near St. Thomas's collapsed. Germans showered would-be rescuers with stick grenades; only four men were saved that day—a fifth, a corporal from Alberta, was pulled from the rubble three days later—and Canadian engineers retaliated by demolishing two buildings in which German voices were heard.

"We do not want to defend Ortona decisively," Kesselring complained to General Joachim Lemelsen, who had taken temporary command of Tenth Army after Vietinghoff fell ill. "But the English have made it appear as important as Rome."

"It costs so much in blood it cannot be justified," Lemelsen replied.

"No," Kesselring said, "but then you can do nothing when things develop in this manner."

And then, as such things do, the battle ended. Squeezed into the old quarter around the shell-torn castle, Heidrich's men waited until nightfall before slipping up the coastal road toward Pescara, leaving dead comrades spread-eagled on staircases and the grass-grown ramparts. "There is no town left," a German officer told his diary. "Only the ruins."

A new sign posted at the city limits disagreed: "This is Ortona, a West Canadian town." Tacking up that sign had cost General Vokes another 650 casualties; Canadian battle losses for the month of December would exceed 2,300, including 500 dead. "Everything before Ortona was a fairy tale," Vokes said. In one typical battalion, of forty-one officers who had landed on Sicily in July, only nine remained, and six of them had been wounded, according to the historian Daniel G. Dancocks. A Canadian psychiatrist who made his rounds from camp to camp on a motorcycle reported an alarming number of "gross hysterias with mutism [and] paralysis."

Alexander's plan had miscarried. In five weeks, Eighth Army had moved just fourteen miles, averaging less than thirty yards an hour. Pescara still lay ten miles to the north; Rome lay beyond the snowy Apennines, on the other side of the world. Montgomery recommended that the Adriatic campaign come to a halt, and Alexander agreed.

In Ortona, above the purple sea, a Seaforth piper played the threnodic "Skye Boat Song" in memory of those fallen. A Canadian combat artist who prowled the rubble with his sketch pad later summarized his aesthetic assessment: "The familiar world had disappeared."

## *Too Many Gone West*

A few minutes past sunrise on Saturday, December 11, a four-engine British York skidded to a stop on a bleak, deserted landing strip forty miles from Tunis. As crewmen tethered the propellers and chocked the wheels, a short, thick figure stumped down the metal stairway and sat heavily on a packing crate next to the runway. Removing his hat, Winston Churchill daubed the perspiration from his scowling gray face. A chill breeze teased his wispy hair, and sand swirled around the luggage now being unloaded from the aircraft belly, including the crated gifts he had recently received for his sixty-ninth birthday: a porcelain bowl from President Roosevelt; a silver drachma coin, minted in 300 B.C., from his daughter Sarah; a silver Isfahan cigar box; and, from the traveling press, a Persian astrakhan hat, which the prime minister had taken to wearing with his air commodore's uniform.

Nearly an hour passed. Churchill's physician, Lord Moran, entreated him to escape the wind and reboard the aircraft; the scowl simply deepened. The prime minister had planned to spend a single night with Eisenhower at Carthage before pressing on to inspect the battlefield in Italy with General Brooke, yet this diversion—Where was Eisenhower? Why had they landed *here*?—taxed both his patience and his strength. "I want to sleep for billions of years," he had recently told Moran. Churchill had logged more than 100,000 miles since the beginning of the war, but the last thousand, since leaving the strategy conferences in Teheran and Cairo, seemed especially cruel. In Egypt he had felt too exhausted to dry himself after a bath, and simply flopped sopping on the bed. "We are only specks of dust that have settled in the night on the map of the world," he told Moran.

At length the mystery was solved: through misunderstanding, the specks had settled on the wrong Tunisian strip. Baggage and shivering passengers were bundled back into the square-windowed York, and fifteen minutes later Churchill felt the grip of Eisenhower's hand at El Aouina field, where the worried general had been pacing for two hours. As he settled into the rear seat of Eisenhower's sedan, Churchill confessed, "I am afraid I shall have to stay with you longer than I had planned. I am completely at the end of my tether."

Ringed by sentries and antiaircraft guns, the La Marsa seaside cottage in December was a study in melancholy. Churchill collapsed in a chair, and was ordered to bed after Moran found that he had a fever of 101 degrees and a "shabby" pulse. "I feel much disturbed," the physician wrote. That evening, the lethargic prime minister complained of a sore throat. "It's pretty bad," he said. "Do you think it's anything?" At four o'clock on Sunday morning,

Brooke awakened to a dolorous voice in his room, crying, "Hullo, hullo, hullo." Bolting upright—"Who the hell is that?" he demanded—Brooke switched on a flashlight to find the prime minister in pajamas with his head bound in a brown bandage, wandering the room in search of Moran and complaining of a headache.

"My master is unwell," one of the prime minister's servants wrote home, "and future movements remain uncertain." Harold Macmillan found a portable X-ray machine in a Tunis hospital, and a pathologist arrived from Cairo, followed by a cardiologist and two nurses from Algiers. Chest film on Monday showed "a considerable opaque area at the base of the left lung," the telltale sign of pneumonia, and Moran prescribed sulfonamide antibiotics. The patient's pulse grew irregular and spurty, and the edge of his liver could be felt beneath his ribs. Churchill complained that his heart "feels to be bumping all over the place." The heart specialist administered digitalis.

More specialists were summoned, as well as the Churchill family and a Coldstream Guards battalion to protect the house. "He's very glad I've come," Clementine Churchill told Moran, "but in five minutes he'll forget I'm here." Randolph Churchill insisted on discussing French politics with his father. To daughter Sarah, the prime minister murmured, "If I die, don't worry—the war is won." Confessing to being "tired out—body, soul, and spirit," he flung out his arms and cried, "In what better place could I die than here, in the ruins of Carthage?" More heart fibrillations followed, and more digitalis. Moran, who found the patient "very breathless and anxious looking," feared that Winston Churchill had indeed come to the end of his mortal tether.

The preceding fortnight could have killed anyone, particularly a proud, aging Tory whose overarching war aim—to preserve the imperial construct of His Majesty's realm—now seemed jeopardized less by Britain's enemies than by her friends. The Allies had met in three distinct sessions: first in Cairo, where Churchill and Roosevelt were joined by the Chinese leader, Chiang Kai-shek; then in Teheran, where the Anglo-Americans met for four days with Stalin; then in Cairo again, in a conference exclusive to Yanks and Brits. The epicurean excess had taxed even Churchill's iron constitution. There were bottomless glasses of vodka and cognac with the Russians, of course, but the Cairo conferees also consumed 22,000 pounds of meat, 78,000 eggs, 4,600 pounds of sugar, and 1,500 cigars, as well as curried prawns, Turkish delight, and ice cream with chocolate sauce. Quartermasters reported an average daily consumption of 80 bottles of whisky, 34 of gin, 12 of brandy, 528 of beer, and 20,000 cigarettes.

If Egyptian and Persian excesses contributed to Churchill's physical malady, surely the diplomatic developments indisposed his soul and spirit. That Britain's senior role in the Grand Alliance was irrecoverable had never been more obvious than in the presence of the emerging superpowers personified by Roosevelt and Stalin. Even Churchill could see the tracings of a bipolar world that had no room for nineteenth-century empires. He and his small nation were overshadowed; no wonder he was sick at heart.

Much had been achieved in two weeks, but as usual all progress first required the spilling of fraternal blood. "Brooke got nasty and King got good and sore," one witness in Cairo, Lieutenant General Joseph W. Stilwell, wrote in his journal. "King almost climbed over the table at Brooke. God, he was mad. I wished he had socked him." When Churchill urged a British and American invasion of Rhodes—"muskets must flame," he thundered, grasping his lapels in both hands—Marshall replied, "Not one American soldier is going to die on that goddamned beach." Roosevelt archly presented U.S. and British manpower statistics showing the inexorable American preponderance: large as the American military overseas had grown, an even larger force still awaited deployment at home. "Our manpower is now fully mobilized for the war effort," Churchill told his advisers. "We cannot add to the total. On the contrary, it is already dwindling."

Perennial American suspicions that Churchill intended to sidetrack OVERLORD by subordinating the cross-Channel invasion to "peripheral and indecisive ventures in the Mediterranean" were again inflamed by British suggestions that a stalemate in Italy might require a postponement in France. The time had come, in Marshall's phrase, for the British to "fish or cut bait." Churchill had privately urged Brooke "to swing the strategy back to the Mediterranean at the expense of the Channel." An alert Henry Stimson, who as war secretary prayed every night for a cross-Channel attack, warned Roosevelt that the prime minister was prepared "to stick a knife in the back of OVERLORD." An ill-advised autumn campaign by the British in the Aegean—the debacle cost more than five thousand casualties and twenty-six ships—added to the distrust. The British had long justified the Mediterranean campaign as a vital antecedent to the death blow to be struck in northwest Europe; but, as Michael Howard observed, London now regarded "the Mediterranean theater not as subsidiary, but as an end in itself, the succcess of whose operations was its own justification." Major General John Kennedy, a British planner, later conceded, "Had we had our way, I think there can be little doubt that the invasion of France would not have been done in 1944."

They did not have their way. Stalin gruffly threw his support behind Roosevelt, insisting on both OVERLORD and a concomitant invasion of southern France. (It was said that Vyacheslav Molotov, the Soviet foreign minister, spoke only four words of English: "Yes," "No," and "Second front.") Moscow also agreed to join the war against Japan after Germany's defeat. Roosevelt left Teheran convinced that Stalin was "getatable"— susceptible to the president's charms. "The Russians are perfectly friendly," Roosevelt insisted. "They aren't trying to gobble up all the rest of Europe or the world."

Outnumbered and outmaneuvered, Churchill had little choice but to agree that OVERLORD, now scheduled for May 1944, would "have first claim on the resources ... of the Allies, worldwide." The strategic drift had ended. As the historian Mark A. Stoler later wrote, "After two full years of controversy and more than ninety days of meetings, the Allies had adopted a unified, coordinated strategy for the defeat of the Axis." Roosevelt capped the decision by selecting Eisenhower to command the western invasion, telling Marshall, "I could not sleep at night with you out of the country." Eisenhower, the president concluded, "is the best politician among the military men. He is a natural leader who can convince other men to follow him."

As for Italy, London and Washington agreed on the capture of Rome and a subsequent advance limited to the Pisa–Rimini latitude, two hundred miles above the capital. Churchill had at least won that concession.

Despite the frictions, the fortnight had also seen renewed brotherhood and mutual affection. "Large families are usually more closely united than small ones," Roosevelt proclaimed in a dinner toast. The president had roared with laughter when an Army band struck up a tune and Churchill danced with Pa Watson, the burly White House aide. Yet even before the second Cairo meeting adjourned, "things were changing," a British staff officer, Brigadier Ian Jacob, later recalled.

It was all too clear that "by the end of the war there would only be two great powers," Jacob said. "From that moment on, I would say, we were nothing so close as we had been." Though Roosevelt remained "extremely friendly," he seemed "to keep Churchill somewhat at arm's length."

The prime minister did not die amid the ruins of Carthage, of course. It would take more than curried prawns, Turkish delight, and Yankee estrangement to kill Winston Churchill. After six days the fever broke, although his pulse still raced to 130 on December 19; perhaps the acceleration came from the large cigar and the whiskey with soda he had consumed a couple of days earlier. Churchill became fixated on his own white blood-cell count, envisioning the battle against the pneumococci as a titanic clash of forces not unlike the world war itself. One visitor to La Marsa reported that "a lot of the fire had gone out of his eyes," but they seemed to rekindle at the discovery of some thirty-five-year-old brandy. Churchill spurned the efforts of Eisenhower's culinary staff to prepare meals suitable for an invalid; a Royal Navy cook was summoned to gratify his palate. When Sarah read aloud to her father from *Pride and Prejudice,* he interjected, "What calm lives they had, those people!"

"The Bible says you must do just what Moran orders," Roosevelt cabled from Washington, "but at this moment I cannot put my finger on the verse and chapter." Couriers came and went from the La Marsa cottage at all hours with war news, including landing craft tallies from the Indian Ocean and drydock status reports in the Mediterranean: Churchill had taken a keen interest in launching another amphibious landing to outflank the Winter Line. "The stagnation of the whole campaign on the Italian front is becoming scandalous," he cabled the British chiefs. When Beetle Smith and a gaggle of staff officers came to Churchill's bedroom, he peppered them with questions about available landing craft before snapping, "You don't seem to know much. You're no use."

Not until late Friday afternoon, December 24, did he rise from his sickbed. Wrapped in a padded-silk Chinese dressing gown with blue and gold embroidered dragons, he scuffed to the dining room in slippers stitched with his initials in gold thread across each foot. "Looking in his strange costume rather like a figure in a Russian ballet," as Macmillan put it, he joined Alexander and other senior British officers at the table for a discussion that lasted until midnight. When they broke, Christmas had come, and with it a consensus that an amphibious assault in Italy "must be carried out on a sufficient scale to ensure success." The most promising beaches lay southwest of Rome on the Tyrrhenian Sea, near a resort town called Anzio.

Churchill telegraphed the news to the British chiefs in London, then scribbled a note to Roosevelt in hope of the president's concurrence. "This," he wrote, "should decide the battle of Rome."

Christmas *had* come, and across the Mediterranean a million soldiers far from home opened gifts that, however impractical or improbable, made them long for home all the more: black silk socks, cologne, Life Savers, canned Spam, slivers of prewar soap, a volume of Lytton Strachey, polka-dot neckties, Cherry Blossom boot polish, straw house slippers, Brasso, louse powder, a carefully wrapped bottle of Coca-Cola, and crumbling loaves of "war cake," baked without benefit of sugar or shortening but larded with love.

Had he been home in Ohio, "I would be fussing with tree lights or a tree stand or doing my last second shopping or coming home from an office party," Lieutenant Colonel Jack Toffey wrote Helen on Christmas Eve. "As far as I am concerned it is time for me to see you all again." Sutlers shipped 170 tons of turkey to the troops, along with 90 tons of apples and 112 tons of Sicilian oranges. Combat units also received "morale crates" that implied a certain rear-echelon misapprehension of life on the Winter Line. Box no. 11, for example, included eighty phonograph records and a pair of tennis rackets, while box no. 21 contained 258 Ping-Pong balls and box no. 171 held wrestling mats, tennis nets, boxing gloves, makeup kits, and masquerade costumes.

In Naples, shoppers and boulevardiers swarmed along the Via Roma. Harbor restaurants offered decent black market meals for 140 lire, or $1.40. Soldiers polished their shoes for a dance at the enlisted club and wished one another "Merry Typhus!"—the disease had become epidemic. MPs prowled the streets, fining officers caught with their hands in their pockets; sergeants who had removed their chevrons at the front to confound snipers now risked $10 per stripe for not sewing them back on. The city evinced the "spurious brightness which you find whenever there is a rapid turnover of money," Christopher Buckley wrote. "There was a general atmosphere of jolliness."

Jolliness faded farther north. Mark Clark on Christmas Eve gave a carton of cigarettes to each man in his Fifth Army headquarters, which now occupied the enormous royal palace at Caserta. He then served eggnog to his staff officers during a round of caroling. After attending a concert by the Royal Artillery band, he mingled with revelers at the Red Cross club and went to midnight mass in the packed royal chapel. To his daughter, Ann, Clark wrote, "I am anxious to get this thing over and get back to see you and have a good old laughing contest."

In a Bari hospital, where mustard gas victims continued to die, a major walked the wards in a cotton beard and a St. Nick costume fashioned from two red hospital robes. Up the Adriatic coast, in Ortona, soldiers built plank tables in the candlelit church of Santa Maria di Constantinopoli, then laid the settings with white linen and silver scavenged from the ruins. Companies rotated through for Christmas dinner served by their officers in the British tradition, with soup, roast pork, pudding, and a bottle of beer apiece. A lieutenant with the wonderfully seasonal name of Wilf Gildersleeve played the pump organ while a battalion padre led the caroling. "Most of the men found it hard to take in," an officer said. Radio calls to units on the perimeter began with a few bars of "Silent Night," played by an adjutant strumming a mandolin near the microphone. General Vokes dined alone, and wept.

"The stars have crept low tonight / To comfort half-buried dreamers," wrote a mortarman-poet, Hans Juergensen. Sprigs of holly and mistletoe decorated various encampments, and C-ration foil festooned little pine trees. In Venafro, near the Mignano Gap, pealing bells competed with booming guns, and five priests tendered communion to filthy, bearded soldiers on their knees at the altar rail. "I prayed that there would be no more wars after this one," a private from Denver wrote his family.

Bells rang in Orsogna, too, but Kiwi troops heard them only at a distance since Germans still held the town. "I had not seen men so exhausted since Flanders. Their faces were grey," Brigadier Kippenberger wrote. An Italian woman living furtively in Orsogna wrote to her missing son about the "poor sad Christmas" in the battered town, then added plaintively, "And where are you?" On the other side of the hill, where German soldiers agonized over reports of carpet-bombed cities in the Fatherland, the 71st Panzer Grenadier Regiment order of the day declared: "Hatred and revenge overcome our hearts as we ponder the magnitude of our misfortune and the anguish which these attacks have brought to our German families."

"Usual targets of opportunity were engaged all through the day," an American field artillery battalion reported, "climaxed by a salvo of colored smoke for Xmas greeting." In one field hospital, surgeons operated by flashlight and fell flat whenever they heard the rush of approaching shells. When blood for transfusions ran short, nurses circulated among the gun crews and motorpool drivers, soliciting donations. A clerk in the 36th Division sorted Christmas packages and scribbled "KIA" on mail to be returned to the sender; at length, utterly spent, he sat at a typewriter and pecked out, "Now is the time for all good men to come to the aid of their country."

And in the 34th Division, Captain Leslie W. Bailey assembled his company and read aloud from the second chapter of the Gospel According to Saint Luke. "Glory to God in the highest," Bailey concluded, "and on earth peace and good will toward all men."

The bottom of the year brought the Allied camp more hope than despair, even if it delivered neither peace nor universal goodwill. "The war is won," Churchill had told his daughter, and War Department analysts now forecast Germany's defeat in October 1944. If too optimistic by eight months, optimism seemed warranted. *Life* magazine noted in a year-end editorial that American factories already planned to resume production of consumer goods on a modest scale in 1944, including bobby pins, baby buggies, hot water heaters, and two million irons. On all battlefronts, with the notable exceptions of Italy and Burma, Allied forces were advancing. In the Pacific, the outer perimeter of Japan's empire had been pierced in the

Gilbert and Marshall Islands, and the inner ring of the Carolines and Marianas would soon loom in American crosshairs. General Douglas MacArthur continued to angle toward the Philippines, which would provide a springboard to Formosa and the Chinese mainland. Allied domination of the seas, among the signal achievements of 1943, was further demonstrated on December 26 when the Royal Navy trapped and sank the German battleship *Scharnhorst* off northwest Norway. Nearly two thousand German sailors were lost. On the Eastern Front, 175 German divisions continued their epic retreat.

Italy was a different matter. "The campaign is heartbreakingly slow," John Lucas told his diary on December 26. "We haven't enough troops to go very fast and I am afraid we will get weaker instead of stronger as time goes on because I figure this is becoming a secondary theater." Fifth Army's strength of 200,000 had hardly grown since October, and in December alone the army tallied 23,000 hospital admissions. Battle casualties had whittled away more than 10 percent of U.S. combat power since Salerno; for the British, the figure was 18 percent. The German high command on December 31 noted with satisfaction that the Allied advance on Rome had been "equal to about six miles per month." Moreover, the Anglo-Americans were stuck not only in the Italian mud but also in the Mediterranean: more than twenty-five Allied divisions and five thousand combat planes remained in the theater "with no shipping available to move them elsewhere," the Army concluded. Except for the seven divisions already sent from Sicily, overburdened British ports could not handle additional transfers from the Mediterranean on top of the floodtide of Yanks now arriving from the States. Italy, as Martin Blumenson wrote in the official U.S. Army history, had become "a war of position, static warfare at its worst."

Dark thoughts intruded. "One rather wondered what we achieved," admitted Major General Freddie de Guingand, the Eighth Army chief of staff. "We began to think about Passchendaele." Farley Mowat told his family in Canada, "Things have changed so much since Sicily. Too many pals gone West. Too many things that go *wump* in the night."

Doubts about the battlefield leadership also intruded, among both high and low. Alan Moorehead decried "a plan that was distinctly conservative and lacking in imagination"; the Allied armies, he added, "had come into Europe with very muddled ideas of what we were going to find." Now when Alexander strolled into his war room to study the map in quiet reflection, some might wonder not what he was thinking but whether he was thinking at all. The manipulation of an army group "required weeks and months of forethought, not hours or days" as with smaller tactical units, his chief of staff later noted, and it was uncertain that Alexander possessed the capacity for such forethought. "He had the average brain of an average English gentleman. He lacked that little extra cubic centimeter which produces genius," said Lord Louis Mountbatten, commander of forces in Southeast Asia and hardly a towering intellect himself. The disjointed attacks by Fifth and Eighth Armies allowed German forces to shift back and forth across the peninsula to parry the blows in turn. Thanks to Ultra, Alexander was better informed about his adversaries than any general in modern history: "the Allies often knew almost as much about the enemy's formations as he did himself," a British intelligence history concluded. Yet the Allied brain trust seemed unable to overcome "the old methodical way" of war, as Kesselring put it.

Discontent clattered down the chain. Eisenhower privately wished that Patton rather than Clark commanded Fifth Army, although, given Patton's inattention to logistics and medical issues in Sicily, his mastery of the infinitely harder welfare issues in an Italian winter was hardly assured. Clark in turn groused about Lucas and threatened to sack Doc Ryder, commander of the 34th Division, while Lucas groused about Middleton of the 45th Division and Middleton groused about his own subordinates. "The battalion commander problem is serious. It is our weakest link," Middleton wrote in December. "My battalion executives are no good."

Fortunately for the Allied cause, the enemy had problems, too. Twenty-three German divisions were mired in Italy, with nearly 300,000 troops. Joseph Goebbels lamented that if the Wehrmacht had another fifteen or twenty division to throw into the Eastern Front "we would undoubtedly be in a position to repulse the Russians. Unfortunately we must put these fifteen or twenty divisions into combat in the Italian theater." Even Smiling Albert turned querulous. "For two months now," Kesselring complained, "I have not been able to exercise proper command because everything evaporates between my fingers."

War was never linear, and in the Mediterranean its road seemed especially meandering and desultory. "What will 1944 do to us?" Lucas asked his diary. Yet sometimes a soldier in a slit trench saw more clearly than the generals on their high perches. "You got the feeling that you were part of a vast war machine which could not be defeated and would never retreat," wrote P. Royle, a Royal Artillery lieutenant in the British 78th Division. "It had all been so different a year ago in Tunisia when we were very much on the defensive and at times hanging on for dear life."

For the Allies, things would continue to go *wump* in the night, and many more pals would go West. But the winter solstice had passed; each night grew shorter. Light would seep back into their lives, bringing renewed optimism as well as firm ground and fair skies.

\* \* \*

"A terrible year has ended," the monks in the Benedictine abbey atop Monte Cassino wrote in their log on December 31. "God forgive us our errors."

The old year slipped away, lamented by no one. A ferocious storm with gale winds howled through Italy, destroying forty spotter planes and uprooting acres of tentage. Undaunted, troops in the 36th Division commemorated New Year's Eve with a concoction of ethyl alcohol and grapefruit juice; the bitter weather made many nostalgic for a Texas blue norther. Soldiers across the front listened to German Radio Belgrade, which played "Lili Marlene" endlessly. "We'd pinched the enemy's song, pinched his girl in a way," said a British rifleman. Thousands wrote year-end letters to reassure their families. "We sleep plenty, eat plenty, and keep busy, so that's enough to keep a guy living," John S. Stradling, the seventh of eight children, told his mother. "And when the mail starts coming through, what else could a guy want besides a discharge?" In three weeks Stradling would be dead, killed by a mine.

Truscott's 3rd Division headquarters roasted a piglet, then threw an Auld Lang Syne party in an abandoned church. Officers danced with thirty nurses and Red Cross workers until midnight, when fireworks—machine-gun tracers, mortar shells, and Very lights—welcomed the new year. The festivities continued until dawn, ending with a champagne breakfast. "Thought I might as well let them get it out of their systems because it will be a long time before they have another fling," Truscott wrote Sarah. He added, "The road to Rome is one on which one does not make speed, at this season at any rate. After all, Hannibal spent 14 years on the road."

Out with the old year went two familiar faces from the Mediterranean theater. Escorted by Spitfires, Montgomery flew from Italy on December 31, having been ordered back to London to command an army group in OVER-LORD. He would be replaced in Italy by a protégé, General Oliver Leese, commander of the British XXX Corps. Before departing, Montgomery mounted the stage in the Vasto opera house to bid farewell to his assembled Eighth Army officers. He closed his half-hour address by telling them, "I do not know if you will miss me, but I will miss you more than I can say." Alan Moorehead reported, "There was a silence among the officers as he turned abruptly and began to walk off. Then a perfunctory, well-bred, parade ground cheer broke out."

"So there we are," Montgomery wrote in his journal, trying to assay the Italian campaign. "After a brilliant start, we rather fell off. And it could have been otherwise. . . . I have enjoyed the party myself and am full of beans." In northwest Europe he would start anew, if not quite afresh; for good and ill, he left the Mediterranean encumbered by a reputation. "No one who has not been in the Eighth Army can appreciate just what he meant to us," a British sapper wrote home. "He was a real human person."

Eisenhower also left on the thirty-first. At 11:30 A.M., he strode for the last time from the Hôtel St. Georges, where he had kept his headquarters through fourteen months of reversal and triumph. An hour later he lifted off from Maison Blanche airfield, bound for Washington via Morocco, the Azores, and Bermuda. Roosevelt a week earlier had announced Eisenhower's appointment as supreme commander of the Allied Expeditionary Force, and Marshall insisted that he come home for a brief rest before traveling to London. "Allow someone else to run the war for twenty minutes," Marshall urged. The new Mediterranean theater commander, Field Marshal Henry Maitland Wilson, known as Jumbo for his elephantine bearing, had hoped for three days' overlap with Eisenhower in Algiers; Wilson instead arrived from Cairo to find him long gone. Most of Eisenhower's inner circle would follow him to England, including Beetle Smith, Harry Butcher, and Kay Summersby.

Some believed his departure overdue. "He has lately been rather going to seed here," Harold Macmillan confided to his diary. After conferring with Eisenhower during his final visit to Italy, Lucas wrote, "Ike looked well but much older. The boyish look is gone and he has the guise of a man. I think he is. A job like his will either make or break anyone."

He left believing he had accomplished what had been asked of him. North Africa, Sicily, Sardinia, Corsica, and a large patch of mainland Italy had been liberated. "Fascism had been given its death blow," he wrote in his final assessment of the Italian campaign. "Elimination of Italy from the war had been accomplished." Some two dozen German divisions were tied down in Italy alone, and many more in the Balkans and Greece. The Mediterranean had become an Allied pond: more than a thousand ships crossed the sea in December, three times as many as in June. Even Stalin had conceded that fighting in Italy seemed to be easing some pressure on the Eastern Front.

Vigor, authenticity, and integrity remained Eisenhower's trademarks; he possessed a big brain and a big heart. He despised the enemy—hate had finally lodged in his bones—and cherished his polyglot alliance as the surest instrument of victory. From Algiers, he would take the template for an Allied headquarters and use it to build SHAEF—the Supreme Headquarters, Allied Expeditionary Force—and eventually NATO. He also would take with him sixty hard weeks of battle experience, in logistics, diplomacy, military governance, leadership, character, and mass slaughter.

He left with a nagging sense of loose ends, as well. "I am very disappointed to leave here before we could attempt one ambitious shot at

Rome," he told Marshall. Though he was uneasy at Churchill's advocacy of an amphibious landing near Rome, his prescience was imperfect. "Jerry is going to write off this southern front," he told reporters, "and I don't think he is going to defend it long." He vowed, wrongly, that there would be no frontal attacks against entrenched defenders. But he did not shy from the hardest of the hard truths he had absorbed: "Sometimes it just gets down to the dirty job of killing until one side or the other cracks."

Eisenhower's arrival in Washington would remain secret, allowing him a cocoon of privacy for perhaps the last time in his life. At 1:30 A.M. on January 2, after plucking the general's stars from his cap, he climbed the servants' stairs at the Wardman Park Hotel on Connecticut Avenue for his first reunion with Mamie in eighteen months. The White House sent a cooler of thick steaks and fifty Chesapeake oysters. Later he would visit John at West Point, and his mother in Kansas. "Why, it's Dwight!" Ida Eisenhower exclaimed. "Nothing seems real any more." To his family he appeared "heavier and definitely more authoritative," in John's words; when Mamie complained of his abrupt manner, he growled, "Hell, I'm going back to my theater where I can do what I want." Twice he absentmindedly called his wife Kay, and when the moment came to leave she told him, "Don't come back again till it's over, Ike. I can't stand losing you again."

He would go on to greater things, becoming perhaps the largest figure on the war's largest stage. But part of him would forever linger in the Mediterranean, where he had exchanged that boyish mien for the guise of a man. In a final message, dated January 1 and read to soldiers from Tunis to Ortona and from Palermo to San Pietro, he reduced his valedictory to fifteen words: "Until we meet again in the heart of the enemy's continental stronghold, I send Godspeed."

# Part Three

# 7. A River and a Rock

## Colonel Warden Makes a Plan

**M**ARRAKESH in midwinter remained a world apart, a world uninjured, a world where war was but a rumor. Snake charmers and professional storytellers thronged the teeming medina, along with tumblers, jugglers, henna *artistes,* monkey handlers, quacks, juice-squeezers, proselytizers, and dye merchants. An Army Air Forces officer described visiting a local sharif who "sat on his leather hassock fingering his white whiskers while his veiled wives brought in gorgeous five-hundred-year-old velvet robes, fists full of jade, emeralds, crystal and ambergris, and chests of gold and silver trinkets, all at very low prices." In addition to elegant minarets and rose-tinted ramparts, Marrakesh had 28,000 registered prostitutes, and U.S. authorities attempting to curb the harlotry complained that French law required either catching a strumpet in flagrante delicto or securing from her clients a signed "statement of intercourse." The skin trade flourished.

The Red City had been Winston Churchill's Shangri-La since 1936, and it was here that he chose to recuperate from the pneumonia that had laid him low at Carthage. It was also here that he intended to refine his brainstorm: the plan to toss two divisions onto the beach at Anzio and "decide the battle of Rome," as he had promised Roosevelt. Before leaving Tunisia, the prime minister donned his uniform in the La Marsa cottage—Clementine buckled the belt for him—and slowly shuffled past the drawn-up Coldstream Guard. Driving to El Aouina airfield, he led a spirited chorus of "When the Midnight Choo-Choo Leaves for Alabam'" before winging across Africa to Morocco on December 27 under the nom de guerre of Colonel Warden.

In Marrakesh he occupied La Saadia, a lush former olive plantation where he and Roosevelt had stayed for a night precisely a year earlier, after the Casablanca conference. Built in 1923, the stucco villa opened onto an orangery, with the distant, snow-crowned Atlas peaks framed by swaying palms. Bougainvillea vines climbed through the courtyard where lizards basked in the winter sun; the interior rooms featured shoulder-high Moorish wall mosaics and carved-wood ceilings. A huge staff flew in from London, among them half a dozen cipher clerks and enough naval officers for around-the-clock vigilance in the map room abutting Churchill's suite. Still weak, the prime minister loitered in bed until noon, then wallowed in a sunken bath filled with great gouts of hot water. For hours he listened to gramophone records of *The Pirates of Penzance* or played poker in a style described as "wildly rash but successful." At sunset, aides improvised a sedan chair and lugged him up the winding staircase of La Saadia's six-story observation tower—"it was certainly heavy going," one bearer reported. Here amid the fluttering moths he sipped his tea and listened to the muezzins' cry, as he had with Roosevelt. The mountains caught the dying carmine light, then stood as sentinels for the coming night. "This war," Churchill mused, "will be known in history as the Unnecessary War."

As his strength returned, he organized daily picnics in the Atlas foothills. The borrowed Cadillac roared through native villages, trailed by a retinue of servants, boon companions, and American MPs in open jeeps. Wearing a huge sombrero, Churchill flashed his V-for-victory at gaping Moroccan peasants, who soon began flashing it back. "We tear after him over the red plain in clouds of red dust," Moran reported. "Deck chairs and hampers are piled on top of the cars. . . . Arab children gather round like sparrows waiting for crumbs." Scrambling down a steep path to lunch beside a mountain brook, the prime minister found the return climb too arduous. "We took the white tablecloth, folded it like a rope and put it round his middle," Moran added. Two soldiers "tugged him up while two of us pushed from behind, and a third carried his cigar."

By early January, Churchill was again master of all he surveyed. "Can't I ever get any commanders who will fight?" he complained to one senior officer. "You don't care if we lose the war. You just want to draw your pay and eat your rations." Patting his staff officers on the shoulder, he had told them, "Be good boys and write me a nice plan." But when logisticians carefully documented the shortfall of landing craft needed to carry out his various amphibious schemes around the globe, he replied, "Magnificent, but negative as usual." In his air commodore's uniform, he mounted a reviewing stand to take the salutes of parading French colonial troops bound for Italy—"black as pitch, in reddish uniforms with red fezzes and bayonets on their rifles," one witness reported, "hopelessly out of step but obviously tough soldiers." The jubilant crowd huzzahed him with shouts of "*Vive, Churchill!*"

Finding that he could easily phone Algiers, he pestered AFHQ with calls despite warnings that the French had likely tapped the lines. "Undue discretion was never one of the P.M.'s faults," Macmillan wrote. In London, a peevish Brooke told his diary:

> Winston sitting in Marrakesh is now full of beans and trying to win the war from there. As a result a three-cornered flow of telegrams in all directions is gradually resulting in utter confusion. I wish to God he would come home and get under control.

Not likely. As Moran noted, "The P.M. has a bright idea. He is organizing an operation all on his own. . . . Twice the picnics have had to be sacrificed to stern duty." When Moran observed that Hitler seemed engrossed not only in grand strategy but also in the minute details of German war operations, the prime minister nodded. "Yes," he said with a smile. "That's just what I do."

Churchill's "bright idea" had been bandied about since shortly after the capture of Naples, when Fifth Army planners began studying the beaches southwest of Rome. Alexander in a dreamy reverie had envisioned five fresh divisions falling on the German flank. But when neither the troops nor the means to move them materialized, Clark proposed landing a single division, reinforced to 24,000 troops who would cling to the shingle for a week until relieved by their Fifth Army brethren arriving overland through the Gustav Line. The scheme in fact was code-named SHINGLE. Truscott's 3rd Division was to be given the honor of landing alone one hundred miles behind enemy lines. "You are going to destroy the best damned division in the United States Army," Truscott warned Clark. "For there will be no survivors." When stalemate froze the Winter Line, a chastened Clark recommended canceling the plan. On December 22, Alexander complied.

Churchill refused to capitulate. "It would be folly to allow the campaign in Italy to drag on," he said while still in his La Marsa sickbed. He wheedled and pleaded, bullied and petitioned. If Rome were not captured, the world would "regard our campaign as a failure," he insisted, because "whoever holds Rome holds the title deeds of Italy." Without Rome, the campaign would "peter out ingloriously," he wrote Clark. A jab in the flank could well compel Kesselring to withdraw his forces from central Italy, freeing Fifth and Eight Armies from their hyperborean fetters. Galvanized by the prime minister's elan, Clark replied, "I have felt for a long time that it was the decisive way to approach Rome."

The revival of Operation SHINGLE had gathered momentum on Christmas Day, when Churchill extracted from Alexander and other senior commanders pledges of support for a larger, two-division landing. With Eisenhower's departure, leadership in the Mediterranean devolved to the British; the malleable Field Marshal Wilson simply observed that it was "a good idea to go around them rather than be bogged down in the mountains." Eisenhower had tendered a few departing words of caution, noting that the enemy "hasn't been predictable so far, and there's no guarantee he's going to act the way you want him to now." If disquieted by SHINGLE, the departing commander-in-chief chose not to assert himself; the British formally recorded that he and his top lieutenants "signified their agreement with the prime minister's proposal." As Eisenhower left the theater, he concluded that Churchill had "practically taken tactical command in the Mediterranean."

"I have arrived in Italy, O Best of Emperors!" the Byzantine general Belisarius wrote to Justinian in A.D. 544 at the start of his campaign against the Ostrogoths. "In great want of men, of horses, of arms, and of money." For latter-day invaders, the want was mainly of ships. The Anglo-Americans from 1940 to 1945 would build 45,000 landing vessels of all types, but there would never be enough: every major American and British campaign in World War II began with an amphibious operation, and the global demand for shipping far outweighed the supply.

"Shipping [is] at the root of everything," Admiral King observed, and that prosaic truism obtained for Italy as it had for North Africa and would for Normandy. To land and sustain two divisions required 88 LSTs and 160 lesser landing craft; of the 105 LSTs currently in the Mediterranean, two-thirds were scheduled to return to England by January 15 for refitting in time for OVERLORD. First at La Marsa and then in Marrakesh, Churchill "produced set after set of calendar dates" to prove that delaying the departure of several dozen LSTs for a few weeks would not upset the sacrosanct Normandy timetable. To the prime minister's elated surprise, Roosevelt endorsed his efforts in a cable from Washington. "I thank God for this fine decision," Churchill replied. "Full steam ahead."

Operation SHINGLE now carried an inexorable momentum. "Clark and I are confident that we have a great chance of pulling off something big if given the means with which to do it," Alexander wrote Churchill on January 4. In truth, Clark felt ambivalent. Even two divisions landed behind German lines would be exposed "on a very long limb," he had confided to his diary on January 2; yet he felt that "a pistol was being held at [my] head" by the prime minister. He pressed without success for a three-division landing, and for restricting all assault troops to a single nationality to simplify logistics. "We are supposed to go up there, dump two divisions ashore . . . and wait for the rest of the Army to join up," Clark told his diary. Perhaps to buck himself up, he added, "I am convinced that we are going to do it, and that it is going to be a success."

To clinch the deal, Churchill proposed a conference in Marrakesh on Friday, January 7. Too busy to leave Italy, Clark sent several staff officers who arrived at the exquisite La Mamounia Hotel to find confusion beneath the Art Deco sconces and Moorish arabesques. Regardless of Fifth Army's request for enough shipping to provide fifteen hundred tons of supplies per day indefinitely, the Royal Navy planned to put the assault force ashore like castaways, with a week's provisions and no resupply. Alexander had consented to an American commander for SHINGLE, Major General John Lucas, while insisting on a multinational invasion because "heavy casualties might be expected" and should be shared, "lest undesirable reactions occur at home." Yet Alexander harbored several misapprehensions about Lucas, who had replaced Dawley as the U.S. VI Corps commander after Salerno. "Lucas, who is the best American corps commander, planned and carried out the Salerno landing, and consequently has experience of amphibious operations," Alexander had written Churchill and Brooke. None of that was true.

The conference convened at La Saadia at 6:30 P.M. on Friday evening. The throb of drums carried from the medina, and the perfume of honeysuckle drifted through the villa where Churchill sat in his living room amid nineteen officers. The prime minister quickly reviewed the history of SHINGLE: how the single-division plan had expired only to be resuscitated with a bigger, better plan that eventually would fling more than 100,000 Yanks and Tommies into the enemy rear; how at least eighty-four LSTs would remain in the Mediterranean until February 5, landing not only the U.S. 3rd and British 1st Divisions, but reinforcements from the U.S. 45th and 1st Armored Divisions; how Kesselring would be forced to thin his defenses near Cassino to confront this threat to his supply lines on Highways 6 and 7, allowing Fifth Army to sunder the German line; how the quick capture of Rome would give the Allies those "title deeds" to Italy.

Questions? There were a few. The AFHQ intelligence chief, Brigadier Kenneth Strong, wondered whether the landing force could "achieve a decisive success" in the face of certain German opposition. Strong also argued that the strength of the Gustav Line at Cassino was "seriously underestimated." Churchill had already heard Strong's qualms at La Saadia, and he was no more ready now than then to acknowledge what he called "the seamy side of the question." When the dour new Royal Navy commander in the Mediterranean, Admiral Sir John H. D. Cunningham, agreed that the landing "involves great risks," the prime minister snapped, "Of course there is risk. But without risk there is no honour, no glory, no adventure."

Cunningham fell silent. A Fifth Army colonel proposed postponing the landing by three days, until January 25, to permit a rehearsal he considered "absolutely necessary." Churchill scoffed. All troops were trained and needed no rehearsal, the prime minister said. A "single experienced officer or non-commissioned officer in each platoon" would give the force a sufficiently honed battle edge.

The conclave broke for supper, then reconvened for more discussion at the Mamounia without Churchill. Few cared to provoke the prime minister's caustic contempt with overt opposition to SHINGLE. "You take the most gallant sailor, the most intrepid airman, and the most audacious soldier, put them at a table together—what do you get? The sum total of their fears!" Churchill had recently complained. Hour by hour the officers edged closer to consensus. Minefields and shallow shore gradients had narrowed the landing site options to several beaches bracketing the resort towns of Anzio and Nettuno. Those beaches also had the virtue of *not* being overlooked by high ground, like those at Salerno; the Alban Hills—the southern portal to Rome—lay twenty miles inland. Initial photo reconnaissance showed Anzio to be heavily fortified, but analysts soon realized that the area had once been an Italian military training ground; most defenses now lay abandoned.

Could the Germans quickly reinforce the beachhead with troops from the north? This seemed unlikely, particularly given Allied air superiority. Would the beachhead force and Fifth Army be too far apart—at least sixty miles at the outset—to support each other? This was deemed "an unavoidable risk." Alexander's intelligence staff posited that German Tenth Army forces would "make an attempt to seal off the beachhead, and [would] thereby be maneuvered out of their strong defensive position at Cassino."

Field Marshal Wilson found the conversation so soporific that he went to bed. Beetle Smith, who remained the AFHQ chief of staff pending his departure for London, apologized for the commander-in-chief's early departure. "After all," Smith quipped, "he is getting old." Not until Saturday morning would Wilson learn that by 1:30 A.M. his minions had talked themselves into an invasion at Anzio. Skeptics remained, including Brigadier Strong and several logisticians, but a majority supported Churchill's daring gambit. Alexander voiced enthusiasm, but seemed to hedge his bets in a note to himself on Saturday: "Take no chances. Keep a reserve."

Bleary-eyed, they reassembled in the La Saadia villa at 9:30 A.M. Saturday. Churchill had prevailed through intimidation, endurance, and imaginative panache, wearing them down like water on stone. "It will astonish the world," the prime minister said of SHINGLE, "and it will certainly frighten

Kesselring." He remained contemptuous of logistical anxieties, telling Alexander, "I do hope, General, that when you have landed this great quantity of lorries and cannon you will find room for a few foot soldiers, if only to guard the lorries." As Harold Macmillan had recently noted, "Winston is getting more and more dogmatic . . . and rather repetitive."

SHINGLE was not a bad plan, and it embodied the military virtues of audacity and surprise. Yet enough pieces of it were bad to risk rotting the whole. The belief that Kesselring would ignore this spear in the ribs and withdraw to the north was simply wishful. "It was a bluff, to scare the Germans into pulling back," Alexander later admitted. No flinty-eyed assessment analyzed the likely strategic reaction of an enemy that did not scare easily. Once again, the Allies lacked the true measure of their adversaries.

Moreover, the SHINGLE force was sized not by the number of troops required to succeed, but by the number of divisions and ships available. "You need more men," General Middleton told AFHQ after examining the plan. "You can get ashore, but you can't get off the beachhead." A weak corps was being dispatched for a job that required an army. Respected voices that might have given the planners pause were unheard: Admiral Kent Hewitt had opposed SHINGLE in December, but was subsequently summoned back to Washington; Hewitt would not return to the Mediterranean until late January.

True, Allied air- and seapower caused perturbations in the German high command. "Where can the enemy land? Everywhere," Kesselring's chief of staff, General Siegfried Westphal, lamented in December. "When will he land? The enemy is not tied to any season." Yet if command of the seas gave Allied commanders the mobility to attack where they pleased—and the British had built an empire on that principle—Churchill continued to underestimate the ability of a motorized defender, using roads and rails on interior lines, to concentrate forces overland faster than they could be consolidated over a beach.

Another die had been cast, another lot of fates consigned. Churchill "had imposed his will on the generals and admirals against their better judgment," Samuel Eliot Morison concluded in the official U.S. Navy history of the Mediterranean. Alexander accepted SHINGLE "out of loyalty to his patrons," a British officer wrote. "It was an error of judgment to have done so." He also had failed to clarify precisely what his lieutenants were to do upon reaching shore; ambiguity rarely meliorated a flawed plan.

For now a buzz and bustle took hold, a sense of possibility and purpose. "Operation SHINGLE is on!" Clark told his diary on January 8 upon hearing the news. A chance to break the winter stalemate was at hand. Whatever ambivalence Clark harbored, surely the prime minister was correct: without risk there could be no honor, no glory, no adventure.

As for Churchill, he was the lion redux. Morocco had restored his health, his verve, his roar. Soon he would fly back to England, ending a two-month absence and keener than ever to obliterate Nazi despotism from the face of the earth. On January 8 he cabled Roosevelt:

> A unanimous agreement for action as proposed was reached by the responsible officers of both countries. . . . Everyone is in good heart and the resources seem sufficient. Every aspect was thrashed out in full detail.

The wariness of his lieutenants worried him not at all. Perhaps influenced by the lush ambiance of Marrakesh, Churchill turned to a horticultural metaphor. "They may say I lead them up the garden path," he said, "but at every stage of the garden they have found delectable fruit and wholesome vegetables."

## "Nothing Was Right Except the Courage"

At last, at long last, they had reached the end of Purple Heart Valley. On the chilly Sabbath morning of January 16, a footsore regiment from the U.S. 34th Division crept up the limestone flank of Monte Trocchio, four miles northeast of San Pietro Infine. Olive trees bearded the lower slopes and a few splintered cedars ringed the crest. So many American artillery shells had crashed across Trocchio before dawn—shells chalked in vengeance with the names of American soldiers killed or wounded in the recent fighting—that red-hot fragments "fell in gusts like a thunderstorm," wrote Margaret Bourke-White. Now the riflemen plodded upward, scrutinizing every lichen-covered rock for booby traps and straining for the telltale clap of exploding shoe mines. An occasional *pop!* carried across the slope, followed by an anguished shriek, but German troops had decamped. At noon the lead scouts wriggled onto the rocky summit to behold a panoramic view of the perdition behind and the perdition still ahead.

To the rear lay the Mignano Gap and a seven-mile stretch of sanguinary eminences: Camino and La Difensa, Rotondo and Lungo, Sammucro and the slag heap once known as San Pietro. To cross that seven-mile stretch and pierce the Bernhardt Line had taken the Fifth Army six weeks, at a cost of sixteen thousand casualties.

Ahead lay a pastoral river plain, three miles wide. Highway 6 bisected these alluvial flats from Monte Trocchio to Cassino—now the most fortified town in Italy—then swerved up the Liri Valley toward Rome, eighty miles distant, before vanishing in the midday haze. Behind Cassino loomed its beetling namesake, Monte Cassino, crowned with the gleaming white Benedictine abbey that for fifteen centuries had been among Christianity's most venerated shrines. A serpentine river threaded the alluvial flats from right to left past Cassino. The complex watercourse bore several names, but to American engineers—who had built intricate plaster relief models of this terrain, based on seventy thousand aerial photos—it was known as the Rapido. Several miles downstream, the Rapido swam into the Liri to become the Garigliano, which then flowed southwest for fifteen miles to the sea.

The Rapido-Garigliano floodplain and the steep uplands beyond it formed the western segment of the Gustav Line, the most ominous of Kesselring's fortified barriers below Rome. The line stretched for one hundred miles across the Apennines to the Adriatic north of Ortona, but nowhere was it stouter than around Cassino, gateway to the beckoning Liri Valley. Already in spate from January rains, the Rapido and other streams were enhanced by a German "flooding program" under which dikes were demolished and canals diverted to create shallow polders across the flats.

The highland glens above Cassino concealed more than four hundred German guns and rocket launchers. Field wire linked each battery to observers in field gray who nested in the high rocks like birds in a rookery, watching with supernal omniscience the movements of the living creatures below. For more than two months German engineers and press-ganged Italian laborers had blasted gun pits from the rock face, reinforcing the bunkers with telephone poles sawed into eight-foot lengths and roofing the structures with oak beams, more poles, and several feet of dirt. The defenses extended up to three thousand yards in depth. In Cassino town, fields of fire were cleared around the fortified rail station and Hotel Continental. Hitler provided even more defensive matériel than Kesselring demanded: more concrete, mines, and barbed wire; more antitank guns, engineers, and slave laborers; more three-ton armored turrets with charcoal burners to keep the gunners warm.

It was here that Kesselring hoped the Anglo-Americans would "break their teeth," and it was here that they intended to attack.

The impending landing at Anzio on January 22 lent urgency to Fifth Army's assault on the Gustav Line. On this southern front, Clark now counted seven divisions in his army, parceled into three corps across a thirty-five-mile front. Although the winter fighting had already left many units disorganized and bereft of reserves, Clark intended to press the attack immediately to divert German attention from the beachhead. "The momentum of our advance must be maintained at all costs," Alexander urged four days after leaving Marrakesh.

In Operations Instructions No. 34, confidently titled "The Battle for Rome," Alexander ordered Clark to force the enemy's retreat beyond Rome and to press on to Florence and Pisa. Intelligence analysts at 15th Army Group predicted that Kesselring would withdraw when confronted by the pincers of Fifth Army from the southeast and the SHINGLE force from the northwest. To speed the enemy's departure, all three corps would attack the Gustav Line. The two-division French Expeditionary Corps, or FEC, new to the theater and keen to redeem French honor, had surged forward on the far right of Clark's front on January 12 and was making a mile per day, mostly uphill, with grenades and bayonets. On the left, the British X Corps would attack across the Garigliano River beginning on January 17, with two divisions near the sea and another one eight miles upstream.

The heart of the assault would fall in the center. On January 20, the U.S. II Corps was to cross the Rapido River, just a mile from Monte Trocchio and three miles downstream from Cassino. With a bridgehead secured by the 36th Division—the same Texans who had fought at Salerno and San Pietro—tanks from Old Ironsides, the 1st Armored Division, would storm across two new-laid bridges, veer up the Liri Valley to Frosinone, and merge with the Anzio force for a grand entry into Rome.

Clark later denied paternity of this plan, fingering Alexander instead. Yet it bore a striking resemblance to a scheme concocted by the Fifth Army commander as early as mid-December. Like SHINGLE, it embodied audacity and tactical plausibility. The Rapido even at flood stage was hardly fifty feet wide, though steep-banked and deep. Here lay the most direct route into the Liri Valley, and thence to the beachhead and Rome.

But also like SHINGLE, the Rapido plan had defects. Possession of the heights at the mouth of the Liri Valley, particularly Monte Cassino, gave the Germans an unobstructed view of the river and the ability to mass fires on all approaches. Truscott, whose 3rd Division had briefly been considered for a Rapido assault before being consigned to SHINGLE, told Clark in December that the attack would fail unless those heights were captured or attacked with enough fury to divert German attention.

"As long as this condition existed, bridges over the river could not long exist and any of our troops that succeeded in crossing would be cut to pieces," Truscott's chief of staff, Colonel Don E. Carleton, later observed. But Clark seemed "convinced that by some act of divine providence the well-entrenched defenders at Cassino would fade away and his tanks would go storming up the Liri Valley."

\* \* \*

The prospect of being cut to pieces displeased Major General Fred Walker, and it preyed on him body and soul. Since shortly after Salerno and through the scalding fight at San Pietro, the 36th Division commander had eyed the Rapido on the big map in his command post, sensing that destiny was tugging him toward this obscure creek below Cassino. By early January he had persuaded himself that the Rapido resembled the Marne, where in July 1918, as a thirty-one-year-old battalion commander, he had earned the Distinguished Service Cross for repelling an attack across the river by ten thousand Germans. He had never forgotten the sodden enemy corpses lining the muddy banks and drifting on the current. "I do not see how we, or any other division, can possibly succeed in crossing the Rapido River," he confided to his diary on January 8. A week later he added, "This is going to be a tough job and I don't like it. There is nothing in our favor."

Square-jawed, with a heavy brow and a large nose that made him seem bigger than his actual five feet, ten inches and 173 pounds, Fred Walker once was described as an "amiable mastiff." Born in Ohio, he earned a degree in mine engineering from Ohio State and enlisted as a private in 1911. After fighting in the Punitive Expedition against Mexico in 1916, he won fame—and survived mustard burns—in France. Walker was curious, alert, and ironic, a chess player although not a good one, and an excellent dancer. He was the sort of man who jotted down unfamiliar words to memorize—"factitious," "chary," "pretentious," "abjure"—as well as quotes from Emerson and inspirational passages from Carl Van Doren's *Benjamin Franklin*. As an instructor at the Army War College in the 1930s, Walker had taught a young rising star named Mark Clark. Despite their nine-year age difference, the two became "very good friends," in Walker's estimation, and shortly before Pearl Harbor the ascendant Clark had persuaded Lieutenant General Lesley J. McNair, the Army Ground Forces chief, to give Walker command of the 36th Division.

The very good friends had since drifted apart. Perhaps envious of his former protégé, Walker had also begun doubting Clark's tactical acuity while the division was still training in North Africa. After Salerno and San Pietro, his disaffection blossomed. In a black, cloth-covered diary with red corners, he recorded his disdain in the neat cursive he had once used to scribble vocabulary words. "Our wasteful policy or method of taking one mountain mass after another gains no tactical advantage, locally," he wrote shortly before Christmas. "There is always another mountain mass beyond with the Germans dug in on it." The reserved Clark kept his distance, disinclined to heed advice from his old mentor yet admiring Walker's performance at Salerno. Clark suspected that Walker resented not receiving command of VI Corps after Dawley's relief at Salerno. Privately, he disapproved when

Walker chose one son as his operations officer and another son as his aide; soldiers grumbled that the division commander was keeping his kin out of harm's way.

At fifty-six, Fred Walker was now the oldest division commander in the field. Age and stress had taken a toll, which he carefully concealed. Since the summer of 1942, he had suffered from severe headaches and tachycardia. He wore heavy wool underwear to combat severe arthritis in the shoulder, hips, and knees. Easily fatigued, he had recurrent spells of "partial blindness and [an] inability to articulate properly." Several times a week he felt heart pain, or faint. A physician had diagnosed arteriosclerosis, and Walker privately complained of "impaired memory, lack of endurance, emotion tensions, [and] restlessness." As the third week of January unspooled, he caught a bad cold.

Walker also concealed his trepidation about the Rapido. In discussions with Clark and other senior officers, he told his diary on January 13, "I have mentioned the difficulties involved. They do not want to talk about them." He proposed attacking upriver, where the Rapido was fordable, but chose not to press his case forcefully. "They do not understand my problems and do not know what I am talking about," Walker wrote. Staff officers fed his anxiety. "General, it's going to be awfully hard for me to keep from sounding so pessimistic about this," his intelligence chief warned. The division engineer foresaw an attack that would "end in failure and result in the loss of a great many lives." On Monday, January 17, Walker wrote five anxious pages in his diary, including, "We have to cross the Rapido. But how? . . . We are undertaking the impossible, but I shall keep it to myself."

On Tuesday morning, Walker strode from his command post on the eastern face of Monte Rotondo and drove south through Mignano on Highway 6. The January sun sat low in the southern sky, "sickly, whitish and weak," as one lieutenant said, and even wool underwear hardly warmed Walker's bones. The usual odors of damp canvas and scorched coffee filled the II Corps headquarters tent, where staff officers drew on acetate maps with colored grease pencils. Walker was greeted by Major General Keyes, the corps commander, who was trim and impeccable in polished boots.

Walker reviewed his attack plan as crisply as if delivering a War College lecture. At eight P.M. on Thursday, the 141st Infantry Regiment would cross the Rapido in small boats at a single ferry site one mile upstream from the town of Sant'Angelo in Theodice; simultaneously, the 143rd Infantry intended to cross at two points downstream. In this sector, the Rapido meandered north to south, so the attack would flow east to west before securing Sant'Angelo and swinging north into the Liri Valley. In keeping with

Keyes's orders, "large, strong fighting patrols" had slipped across the river for the past two nights to "keep contact with the enemy" and assess German defenses.

Those were formidable, Walker said with a knowing look. German troops from the 15th Panzer Grenadier Division—escapees from Sicily who had also fought at Salerno and Monte Camino—were "very well organized, wired in, and in depth, supported by automatic weapons, small arms fire, [and] prepared defensive fires of artillery, mortars." Of seven boats launched the previous night by the 141st Infantry, five had been lost on a current clocked at four miles per hour. Scouts reported a double apron of barbed wire beyond the far bank and a broad mine belt nearly a mile long. As expected, German demolitionists had blown the bridge at Sant'Angelo three days earlier; the river had been dredged two years before, and spoil lined both banks to form steep gravel dikes. Mud remained "shoe mouth deep" despite recent dry weather. Six-man mine removal teams crawled about on their hands and knees each night, but German sappers sneaked over the river to reseed cleared approaches. Yesterday, a division surgeon reported "an epidemic . . . of traumatic amputations of one or both legs." As he finished sketching his plan, Walker again cocked an eyebrow.

Keyes listened intently. He was careful not to betray his own doubts, about the attack and about Walker. A frontal assault across the river was "unsound," Keyes had warned Clark; given German command of the high ground, the crossings would be made "in a fishbowl." Even back in Sicily, Keyes had drafted alternative plans for precisely this tactical conundrum. His favorite, dubbed Big Cassino, envisioned an assault across the Garigliano by both II Corps and the British X Corps, which then would scale the massif southwest of Cassino to outflank the fortified mouth of the Liri Valley. The scheme intrigued Clark. But Alexander and McCreery, the X Corps commander, considered it "a tactical monstrosity"; British troops had neither training nor equipment for mountain warfare. Clark sided with the British—he was increasingly beguiled by the image of American tanks roaring toward Rome—and Big Cassino slid into a drawer.

Keyes persisted. In late December, he proposed crossing the Rapido "a day or two" *after* the Anzio landings. "If the enemy withdraws forces now on our front to oppose VI Corps [at Anzio], there is a chance that this corps can make a real advance," he wrote. Clark demurred, insisting that the Rapido attack precede SHINGLE. On January 13, Keyes warned that the British 46th Division, which was to protect Walker's left flank, planned to cross the Garigliano with a modest, two-battalion assault. "The effort of the 46th Division should be made by the entire division," Keyes wrote, otherwise it risked a "gradualism" that could leave the Americans exposed. Clark again declined to intervene.

Geoff Keyes knew his business. He possessed, in the estimation of George Patton, "the best tactical mind of any officer I know." Son of a cavalry officer, Keyes grew up on horseback along the Mexican border. Two years ahead of Eisenhower at West Point, Keyes in one football game scored two touchdowns, kicked both conversions, and booted a forty-three-yard field goal to account for seventeen points; the academy's legendary Master of the Sword, Marty Maher, proclaimed him "the only man who could stop Jim Thorpe" on the gridiron. "If there is a man in the Corps who is more universally liked than he," the academy yearbook stated, "we have yet to find him."

Also a cavalryman, Keyes had attended the École Supérieure de Guerre in Paris and served as Patton's deputy during the invasions of Morocco and Sicily. "The impetuous, vitriolic, histronic Patton is considerably leavened by the calm, deliberate, circumspect Keyes," a War Department observer had reported to Washington from Palermo. Slender, pleasant, and tactful, Keyes was a devout Roman Catholic who attended mass each morning and eschewed profanity—"not even hell or damn," one comrade said. Eisenhower unfairly described him as "a man who has everything but a sense of humor"; in fact, he possessed a puckish streak. Behind Patton's endorsement, Keyes in September took command of II Corps after Omar Bradley's departure for England. "Don't be afraid to show pleasant reactions in your contact with your subordinates," Eisenhower told him. "Every commander is made, in the long run, by his subordinates. We are all intensely human, and war is a drama, not a game of chess."

Like so many American generals, Keyes distrusted the British, and his spare, bemused diary entries revealed an intense Anglophobia as the Rapido attack drew near. "God forbid we ever have to serve with or near the British again," he wrote on January 16. A day later he added, "Clark insists we are not being sold down the river but I am not convinced. Every move is a repetition of the slick maneuver of the British in planning HUSKY and the Sicilian campaign." On the day of Walker's visit, he wrote, "The British are going to contribute nothing as usual."

As the conference in the II Corps command post drew to a close, much remained unsaid, and in that silence sprouted mistrust and discord. Walker privately considered Keyes "too cavalry," with a "Boy Scout attitude" toward the grim infantry combat ahead. The notion of Sherman tanks storming up the Liri Valley was "visionary," Walker believed; the term was not a compliment. Sensing Walker's hostility, Keyes felt a reciprocal antipathy. He wondered whether the division commander was overmatched.

More important, both men remained mute about their shared disquiet. Can-do zeal required obedience and a bluff optimism. Walker finished his brief, then scooped up his maps and papers. He would prefer to attack elsewhere, he said. But in a final burst of bravado, and perhaps sensing that his rendezvous with the Rapido was ineluctable, he advised Keyes that he was "confident of success." The 36th Division, he added, would "be in Sant'Angelo on the morning of the 21st."

Only in his diary did Walker speak from the heart: "We have done everything that we can, but I do not now see how we can succeed."

Sant'Angelo was a drab farm village on a forty-foot bluff above the turquoise Rapido. The local *cantine* served Peroni beer and a *vino* renowned for potency. Pastel houses with iron balconies and red tile roofs crowded the narrow main street. Flying buttresses shored up the church of San Giovanni Battista, with its handsome campanile. Black-bordered death notices were pasted on a billboard beneath the narthex.

The notices had multiplied after the first bombs hit Sant'Angelo on September 10, killing a three-year-old girl and her parents. The Germans soon arrived from nearby Cassino, carrying large hooks with which to drag the haystacks in search both of contraband and of young men for their labor battalions. Electricity and running water became sporadic and then nonexistent. Mail delivery ended. Phones went dead. Farmers toiled at night, hitching oxen to their plows and listening for what the locals called the "she-wolf," the six-barreled Nebelwerfer mortar, which fired rounds that wailed in flight. As the Allied army drew closer, German sappers mined the local mill and demolished houses to fortify the town center, sparing the rectory, which had a deep cellar and became a command post.

Three hundred impressed Italians dug trenches and cleared brush on the Rapido flats for better fields of fire. German commanders now considered Sant'Angelo the "strongest point of the defensive line." The river's west bank was defended by two battalions from the 15th Panzer Grenadier Division, described by Allied intelligence as "the strongest single German division in the Italian theater," with a full roster and ample heavy weapons. Aggressive American patrolling kept them alert and edgy. "Extensive enemy movements observed opposite left wing of 15th Panzer Grenadier Division," the Tenth Army war diary recorded on January 17. "The enemy has crept up to the riverbank."

The Germans grew even edgier after the British attack began on the lower Garigliano at nine P.M. that night. The 5th and 56th Divisions surged across the river, a dozen miles downstream from Sant'Angelo. "The waiting is the worst part," the Royal Artillery signaler Spike Milligan had written as the assault began. "I oil my tommy gun. I don't know why, it's already oiled." To the surprise of Jerry and Tommy alike, by dawn on January 18 ten battalions occupied the far bank; German commanders had doubted the Allies would attack on a moonless night. "Moving off in trucks with our hearts in our mouths," a Scots Guards lieutenant told his diary. "Passing very ominous blood wagons coming back the other way. . . . I wonder if we look heroic filing away in the darkness."

They gained the far bank but not much more: the X Corps bridgehead barely extended three miles, and a ferocious German counterattack almost shoved the lead companies back into the river. The crossing sites would remain under German artillery fire for three months, and British soldiers complained that the alluvial plain resembled a "mine marsh." Still, they had made a promising start. "I am convinced that we are now facing the greatest crisis yet encountered," Kesselring advised Vietinghoff, his Tenth Army commander, shortly before ten A.M. on January 18. The Americans, he added, would now likely attack below Cassino in an attempt to storm the Liri Valley.

Not yet. On Wednesday night, January 19, British 46th Division soldiers, drawn from Yorkshire and the North Midlands, crept through the Garigliano mists four miles downstream from Sant'Angelo. This was "a bleak, disturbing place," a landscape of grays and blacks beneath scudding clouds. Assault troops cinched their Mae Wests, slung their rifles, and shoved the first boats into the dark water.

"Then nothing went right," the Royal Hampshires reported. Far upstream, German engineers had opened a set of sluice gates, raising the water level several feet and turning the Garigliano into a millrace. Boats bucked and spun on the current, then vanished in the fog as exhausted oarsmen slapped their way back to shore, a mile or more downstream. Again they tried, and then again. By early morning, despite only sporadic German opposition, a single company hugged the far bank. Gunfire riddled their vessels, and soon the isolated vanguard was besieged. A few survivors splashed back to safety beneath a smoke screen. At dawn on Thursday, enemy artillery sliced up the crossing site, and McCreery ordered the 46th Division to abandon further attempts.

A few hours later, the burly British division commander, Major General John Hawkesworth, known as Ginger to his friends, appeared at Fred Walker's command post in the lee of Monte Rotondo. Three old wounds from the Great War hobbled Hawkesworth, and he leaned on an ashplant stick. The attack had failed, he told Walker. The river had run higher than expected: a contumacious beast, really. No further attempt was possible. Walker's left flank would be exposed during the Rapido attack

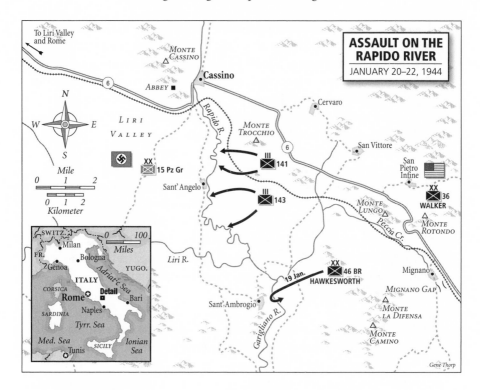

this evening. Hawkesworth was sorry, but there it was. Walker nodded and returned to his preparations. "The British are the world's greatest diplomats," he told his diary, "but you can't count on them for anything more than words."

Keyes and Clark were both alarmed. "Always the same story," Keyes wrote in his diary. "Too few, too little practical preparations. This is serious for us tonight." Clark attributed the aborted British crossing "to lack of strong aggressive leadership at the division level." Fifth Army engineers reported that Hawkesworth had failed to properly reconnoiter the river or the crossing site. In a memorandum dictated on Thursday, Clark added, "The failure of the attack of the 46th Division to reach its objective . . . was quite a blow. I was fearful that General Hawkesworth had a mental reservation." The army commander dispatched Gruenther to see McCreery, who warned that the Rapido attack "has little chance of success" and should be canceled. Unmentioned was McCreery's growing concern at Clark's apparent willingness to accept high casualties for dubious gains; the British commander now thought of Clark as "the Man of Destiny I somehow imagined he always wanted to be."

That surely was unfair, although not untrue. With Eisenhower gone from the theater, Clark now stood in the footlights at center stage as the most prominent American commander in the Mediterranean. Yet the Man of Destiny was hardly a free agent. Clark had been ordered by Alexander to attack quickly, and to eject the enemy from Rome; for all practical purposes, he also had been ordered by Churchill to plop two vulnerable divisions behind German lines the day after tomorrow. Were he to curtail the Rapido offensive, nearly fifty thousand men now embarking for SHINGLE would face the full fury of a German counterstrike in isolation.

Destiny held Clark in thrall, but not Clark alone. A great rolling tide of tragedy and fate and human folly swept them all along, like those fog-swaddled boats beating against the Garigliano current.

"It is essential that I make the attack, fully expecting heavy losses, in order to hold all the [German] troops on my front and draw more to it, thereby clearing the way for SHINGLE," Clark wrote on Thursday. "The attack is on."

Since the Salerno landings, nineteen weeks earlier, war had gutted the 36th Division. Rifle company losses in the 141st Infantry exceeded 60 percent. In one typical 143rd Infantry battalion, three-quarters of the officers had joined the unit in Italy. Texas drawls no longer dominated the division. "We were no longer a team," a captain complained. "Gone was the feeling that you knew you could rely on your people." Together the two assault regiments mustered about four thousand men; many units were under-strength, often by a third, and undertrained. New bazooka teams arrived at the front having never fired a bazooka. Training for a river assault was limited to paddling on the placid Volturno. A platoon leader in the 141st considered his soldiers "unprepared physically, mentally, and morally."

Several hundred replacements showed up on the eve of the Rapido attack to find that all troops had removed their unit insiginia to confound the enemy; sergeants spent hours trying to determine who belonged to whom. Many replacements never found their proper companies, and some would die without meeting their squad leaders or knowing a single comrade in their new platoons. "Can't expect these replacements to be good soldiers," an officer told the reporter Will Lang. "They ain't mad."

Walker continued to fret in private. "The mission should never have been assigned to any troops and, especially, when both flanks will be exposed when we get across," he scribbled on January 20. Clark phoned on Thursday afternoon to wish him luck. "He is worried over the fact that he made an unwise tactical decision," Walker concluded, then added:

If we get some breaks we may succeed. But they will have to be in the nature of miracles. . . . I will have little influence on the battle because everything is committed; I have no reserves.

And then it began. The last smudges of violet light faded in the west. Hundreds of soldiers rose from their burrows on Monte Trocchio and from behind the marsh hummocks on the Rapido flats. Fixing bayonets with an ominous metallic click, they looped extra bandoliers over their twill field jackets. Fog coiled from the riverbed and crept across the fields, swallowing the stars and a rising crescent moon. A company commander handed a cigar to each of his sergeants, as a talisman.

At 7:30 P.M., sixteen artillery battalions opened fire in gusts of white flame. Soldiers flinched as more than a thousand shells per minute shrieked overhead in a cannonade that ignited the mist and gouged the far bank with rounds calibrated to explode every six and a half yards. Crewmen flipped back the camouflage nets on fifty Sherman tanks, hidden four hundred yards from the river, and yellow tongues of flame soon licked from the muzzles to join the bombardment. Sixty fighter-bombers swooped down the river, and their tumbling silver pellets blossomed in fire and black smoke across Sant'Angelo, adding ruin to ruination. Four hundred white-phosphorus mortar shells traced the river line with topographic precision; the night was windless, and instead of billowing to form a low screen, the smoke spiraled vertically for 150 feet, framing the shore in fluted alabaster columns.

The attack was to fall across a three-mile front, centered on Sant'Angelo. On the right, the 141st Infantry tramped down a farm road toward an oxbow in the river, led by the 1st Battalion in a column of four companies. Wet fog grew as thick as cotton batting. Barely able to see their feet, soldiers bunched up to keep sight of the bobbing helmet ahead. Stragglers and shirkers melted away. When the column stalled, men dozed off and awoke to find that those in front had vanished. Units became jumbled, and sotto voce queries carried in the night, calling for 3rd Platoon or B Company.

Along the rail tracks south of Trocchio, boats had been readied in a hidden dump: rubber dinghies that carried two dozen men, of whom half would paddle, and M-2 plywood scows, weighing nearly a quarter ton each and capable of ferrying a dozen men with a two-man crew. German artillery that afternoon had already holed twenty rubber boats, and ugly gashes marred several M-2s. Wooden catwalks also lay scattered about the dump: laid across rubber rafts lashed together as pontoons, they would make footbridges. Two sturdy Bailey bridges, dubbed Harvard and Yale, would subsequently be erected for the two hundred tanks waiting behind Trocchio to storm the Liri Valley.

Hoisting the heavy boats, their rifles banging against the gunwales, the men staggered toward the river on a narrow, muddy road. Enemy artillery now answered the American barrage, and the shriek of westbound volleys was exceeded by the rush of eastbound German shells and that she-wolf howling of Nebelwerfer rounds, also known as screaming meemies, moaning minnies, and howling heinies. "It could damn near make your blood turn solid," one soldier confessed. Brown smoke foamed from mortar rounds tromping across the flats, and the maniacal cackle of machine guns carried from Sant'Angelo, including the dread MG-42, known in the Wehrmacht as "Hitler's bandsaw." Riflemen tossed away their cumbersome bandoliers, which soon lined the road like a trail of brass necklaces. A thousand smoke pots, ignited as a deception far south of Trocchio, drew more than five hundred German shells in two hours. U.S. artillery battalions received a frantic order to "check all shells for mustard gas as such shells had been issued by mistake" from an ammunition depot; no mustard was found or fired.

Little else went right. An engineer guiding Company B to the oxbow missed the path to the river by several hundred yards; as the troops and boats turned around for a reverse march, their clatter attracted a German volley that cut down thirty men, including the captain who had distributed his cigars. Paddles, rifles, and human limbs rained across the road. Survivors scattered for cover, but the cleared corridors through the minefields were no longer visible: minesweeping teams initially had marked the paths with white tape, but switched to a brown cord that was less conspicuous to German observers. Confused GIs pelted through the fog, triggering shoe mines and drawing more mortar fire as sergeants tried to hush the wounded. "It's pretty hard when you're dying to keep quiet," a platoon leader observed. Another befuddled guide also led Company A into a minefield. "We walked as men do in a cow pasture," said one man, "placing each foot carefully on a pre-selected spot."

Corpses and abandoned M-2s blocked the swept lanes to the river. Screaming Nebelwerfer rounds reminded an officer of "a streetcar coming down sideways with its brakes on." Exhausted men dragged the cumbersome rubber boats the last few hundred yards, tripping more mines. German flares silvered the water, and tracers sliced scarlet vectors through the fog, or bounced like flaming marbles off the Rapido. Those who managed to shoulder their vessels down the steep bank found that many had been holed and sank immediately; others capsized, dumping men and equipment into the icy river, or were swept away on the current.

Soldiers fell without ever firing a shot. "It was like fighting an octopus in a crooked sack," recalled Lieutenant William E. Everett, a platoon leader in Company C. Everett rebuked several men for shirking in a ditch, then realized they were dead. "I could hear paddles slapping and hitting together, and then the men yelling when their boat turned over," another lieutenant wrote. "It curdled your blood to hear those men drown." Sodden twill trousers and field jackets dragged the men under. "I had to let go of the young man and he drowned," a private later said of one comrade. "Eight of us drowned and four swam to the German side."

By nine P.M., an hour into the attack, fewer than one hundred men had reached the west bank. Many burrowed into the marsh, using their helmets to scrape a few inches of defilade and piling the spoil in parapets around their shallow trenches. Thirty-one thousand artillery rounds had not discouraged the fuming German guns at Sant'Angelo. Glowing shell fragments blew in orange swarms across the bottoms. "Close explosions leave one vibrating like a tuning fork," reported one soldier. At least four MG-42s stitched the oxbow crossing site with machine-gun fire. Of four footbridges to be laid across the Rapido, two were destroyed by artillery fire, and mines claimed a third. For hours engineers muscled the last span into the water, and by four A.M. on Friday the river had at last been bridged.

Dozing men on the east bank were awakened to scramble across the rickety catwalk, squad by squad, platoon by platoon. "The Germans opened fire with every automatic weapon they had," an officer said. "The slapping noise of the planks against the water would draw fire." Another officer confessed to feeling "like a Judas goat, leading the sheep to slaughter." By 6:30, as dawn leaked into the bottoms, about half of the 1st Battalion had reached the west bank. Shell fire damaged the bridge, dropping segments of the catwalk below the river surface. All radios had been ruined in the crossing; most artillery observers had been wounded or killed; and all phone lines back to the east bank were soon severed. So many litter carriers had fallen that few wounded could be evacuated across the river. "I don't know how many dead and wounded there were," a medic in Company A later recalled, "but there were plenty."

The 141st Infantry commander, Lieutenant Colonel Aaron A. Wyatt, Jr., had intended to send his 3rd Battalion on the heels of the 1st, but with the bridgehead barely two hundred yards deep he canceled the order. After a night of confusion, the new day simply brought more derangement, including contradictory orders that first instructed men on the west bank to hold fast, then advised them to pull back. A few scuttled across the submerged bridge or swam to safety, grabbing at tree roots to haul themselves onto the east bank. Most dug in to await reinforcements, or raised their arms in surrender. Engineers stretched a net across the Rapido, seining for bodies adrift on the current.

Downstream, on the division left, the attack proved no less gallant and no more successful. "When I saw my regimental commander standing with tears in his eyes as we moved up to start the crossing, I knew something was wrong," said the commander of Company L in the 143rd Infantry.

Two crossing sites had been selected for the 143rd, and at eight P.M. on Thursday night the point platoon at the upper site paddled across without drawing fire. Then German gunners leaped to life, riddling the boats and wrecking a footbridge in progress. Engineers scorched back to the boat dump, where the regimental commander, Colonel William H. Martin, found them cowering in foxholes. Rallied with threats and supplications, the men lugged more M-2s to the river, and by six A.M. Friday most of the 1st Battalion—the late Captain Henry Waskow's former unit—had reached the west bank.

Their stay was brief. Machine guns and panzers flailed the bridgehead with grazing fire, lashing the buttocks, backs, and legs of soldiers unable to hug the ground any tighter. Facing annihilation, Major David M. Frazior shortly after seven A.M. asked permission for his battalion to return to the east bank. Walker refused, but by the time his stand-fast order arrived, Frazior had abandoned the bridgehead with the remnants of his command.

Five hundred yards downstream, at the 3rd Battalion crossing site, no retreat was necessary since not a single soldier had reached the far shore. Plagued with bumbling engineers and skittish riflemen, companies had wandered in and out of minefields for hours. "The flashes seemed to turn the fog rising from the river into a reddish glow," one officer wrote. "The men were unable to identify even the path at their feet." At midnight the battalion commander reported that he had five boats remaining and still was unsure where to find the river; at five A.M. he was relieved of command, and his successor soon canceled the attack.

This bad news was scribbled on a message slip for General Keyes and entrusted to a carrier pigeon by a II Corps liaison officer near the Rapido. At 7:25 A.M., with a great flutter of wings, the bird was released and flew straight to a nearby tree, perhaps dispirited by the fog and gunplay. "I had to throw dirt at it to get it out," the officer reported. "When it flew to another tree, I just left it there."

Neither Keyes nor Walker needed a pigeon to tell him that the evening had not gone well. After sitting by the field phones in his command post all night, Walker advised his diary on January 21, "The attack last night was a failure." But now what? Crossing the river in daylight would be foolish, he believed. Time was needed to draft new orders, to position new boats, and to replace leaders who had been wounded or killed. At 8:30 A.M., Walker told the 141st and 143rd to resume the attack in just over twelve hours, at nine P.M.

Keyes had other ideas. At ten A.M. he strode into Walker's Monte Rotondo command post. A few minutes earlier, Clark had urged Keyes by phone to "bend every effort to get tanks and tank destroyers across promptly." Keyes concurred. Weren't there at least some troops from the 141st Infantry still on the west bank? he asked Walker. No effort should be spared to reinforce them, preferably before noon: the rising sun would blind German defenders. A II Corps staff officer with a clipboard sketched a crude map of the Rapido, with arrows pointing from east to west. Walker argued briefly, then agreed to set H-hour for two P.M.

"Anybody can draw lines on a map," he wrote after the corps commander drove away. "I felt like saying that battles are not won by wishing while ignoring the facts, but this was no place to court insubordination." Instead, Walker channeled his frustration into his diary: "The stupidity of some higher commanders seems to be profound."

Neither Keyes nor Walker was privy to the secret, but Fifth Army's attack had already fulfilled part of Clark's ambition. An Ultra intercept two nights earlier disclosed that Field Marshal Kesselring had ordered the 29th Panzer Grenadier Division near Rome—half of his reserve force—to reinforce Tenth Army on the Garigliano; another decrypt soon revealed that the other half, the 90th Panzer Grenadier Division, had also been ordered south, leaving the Anzio beaches virtually undefended. However ineffectual, the British X Corps attack had spooked the Germans. Kesselring believed that Tenth Army was hanging "by a slender thread."

This intelligence, available to Clark and Alexander but not to their subordinates, had little impact on the Rapido battle. Pressing the attack would further distract the enemy from SHINGLE, Clark believed. And if Walker could punch through at Sant'Angelo, unleashing his armored horde up the Liri Valley, so much the better.

Off they went, trudging like men sent to the scaffold. A soldier stumping down a sunken road toward the Rapido observed, "There was a dead man every ten yards, just like they were in formation." Close to the river, the formation thickened. Another soldier, carrying a rubber boat, later wrote, "It didn't seem what we were walking on was dirt and rocks. We soon found out it was dead GIs."

On the division left, the 143rd Infantry crossed more adroitly on Friday afternoon than it had on Thursday evening. Confusion delayed the attack for two hours, but at four P.M., beneath a vast, choking smoke bank, the 3rd Battalion began to paddle west. By 6:30 all rifle companies had found the far shore, and Colonel Martin ordered his 2nd Battalion to follow in train late that night. A quarter mile upstream, the 1st Battalion also crossed at dusk, although the laconic battalion commander, Major Frazior, radioed, "I had a couple of fingers shot off." Three battalions crowded a bridgehead only five hundred yards deep and six hundred yards wide. "When twilight turned to darkness," one soldier later wrote, "I was thinking this is my last old day on earth."

On the division right, delay begat delay in the 141st Infantry. Not least, engineers neglected to bring an air compressor to inflate fifty rubber boats, and Colonel Wyatt, the regimental commander, postponed the attack until nine P.M. without telling Walker. By two A.M. on Saturday, a pair of foot-bridges had been laid, and six rifle companies from two battalions soon crossed. They found no survivors from the previous night's combat. Engineers wondered whether the Germans had left the catwalks intact "to draw more of our troops over." Some soldiers balked at crossing the river, or deliberately tumbled into the water. Others displayed uncommon valor. Company E of the 2nd Battalion—the unit roster boasted mostly Spanish surnames, Trevino and Gonzalez, Rivera and Hernandez—advanced with bayonets fixed through sleeting fire from three sides. "Fire wholeheartedly, men, fire wholeheartedly!" cried their commander, Captain John L. Chapin, before a bullet killed him. Corraled by minefields and barbed wire, the 141st held twenty-five acres of bottomland that grew bloodier by the hour. "Well, I guess this is it," a major told a fellow officer. "May I shake hands?" Moments later a shard from a panzer shell tore open his chest. He dragged himself to safety across a submerged bridge, and medics saved him. "It was the only time," one witness said, "I ever saw a man's heart flopping around in his chest."

Artillery and Nebelwerfer drumfire methodically searched both bridgeheads, while machine guns opened on every sound, human and inhuman. GIs inched forward, feeling for trip wires and listening to German gun crews reload. "Get out of your holes, you yellow bellies!" an angry voice cried above the din, but to stand or even to kneel was to die. A sergeant in the 143rd Infantry described "one kid being hit by a machine gun—the bullets hitting him pushed his body along like a tin can." Another sergeant wounded in the same battalion later wrote, "I could hear my bones cracking every time I moved. My right leg was so mangled I couldn't get my boot off, on account of it was pointed to the rear." German surgeons would remove the boot for him, along with both legs.

A private sobbed as wounded comrades were dragged on shelter halves up the mud-slick east bank. Ambulances hauled them to a dressing station in a dank ravine behind Trocchio. Crowded tents "smelled like a slaughter-house," wrote the reporter Frank Gervasi. Outside a small cave in the hill-side, a crudely printed sign read: PIECES. Inside, stacked burlap bags held the limbs of dismembered boys. On average, soldiers wounded on the Rapido received "definitive treatment" nine hours and forty-one minutes after they were hit, a medical study later found: nearly six hours to reach an aid station, followed by another three hours to a clearing station, and an-other hour to an evacuation hospital. The dead were easier: they were buried fully clothed without further examination.

Certainly the doctors were busy enough with the living. Only five physi-cians manned the clearing station of the 111th Medical Battalion. They treated more than three hundred battle casualties on Friday, often strug-gling to mend the unmendable, and they would handle nearly as many on Saturday. A wounded sergeant undergoing surgery with only local anesthe-sia later reported, "The doctor stopped in the middle of the operation to smoke a cigarette and he gave me one too." Another sergeant from the same company told a medic, "Patch up these holes and give me a gun. I'm going to kill every son of a bitch in Germany."

Three hundred German artillery rounds danced across Monte Rotondo before dawn on Saturday, causing casualties and disorder in the 36th Divi-sion command post. Dire reports from the river made the morning worse: heavy losses, no troops yet on the bluff at Sant'Angelo, ammo shortages, bridges wrecked. "Nearly six battalions across but no bridges," Keyes wrote in his diary. "Something wrong." The corps commander had ordered two Bailey bridges built despite the Americans' shallow purchase on the west bank, but the effort—a six-hour task even under perfect conditions—had been undone by confusion among engineering units, rutted roads that kept trucks from reaching the Rapido, and incessant shooting. "Talking or coughing drew fire," an engineer with the 143rd Infantry reported. On Sat-urday morning a visiting general found the bridge builders "dug in and no work being done."

Smoke hardly helped. To screen the crossings, hundreds of smoke pots and mortar rounds had been laid along the Rapido. Some zealous mortar-men pumped out twenty-one shells per minute, a rate of fire so intense that many tubes burned out. By Saturday morning, visibility was only fifty yards, blinding the observation posts on Trocchio and concealing German snipers who lurked near the river. American artillerymen were forced to orient their fire by sound, a method rarely effective on a cacophonous battlefield. Chemical officers in both the 36th Division and II Corps complained about German smoke without realizing that the dirty banks were their own.

As the morning wore on, "a pathetic inertia seemed to take hold of American commanders," wrote Martin Blumenson, author of the official Army history of the Rapido operation. Exhaustion, guilt, regret, despondency—all gnawed at them. A II Corps major who had fought in Algeria and Tunisia reported, "The situation as I saw it needed no further explanation to me because I had seen the same indications at St. Cloud and at Kasserine Pass." Keyes remained pugnacious, if not prudent, and at ten A.M. on Saturday he ordered Walker to prepare his reserve regiment, the 142nd Infantry, to reinforce those six battalions on the west bank. Surely the Germans were "groggy" and could be overpowered by fresh troops, he told Walker.

But Clark in a phone call cautioned against throwing good money after bad. To Keyes's vexation, the 142nd also reported that it needed almost fifteen hours to get ready and could not attack until early Sunday. When further dispatches from the river suggested that the 141st Infantry had been "practically wiped out," Keyes rescinded his order. "You are not going to do it anyway," he told Walker. "You might as well call it off. It can't succeed as long as you feel that way about it." In his diary Keyes wrote, "Our failure due to 1) lack of means 2) poor division."

The finger-pointing began. Clark "seemed inclined to find fault with our decision to force the Rapido," Keyes wrote. The record, the corps commander added, would show that for months he had "pointed out [the] fallacy in going up the valley unless heights on either side were attacked! And each time I was overruled by [Fifth] Army." For his part, Walker was furious at Keyes's suggestion that he was disloyal and disobedient. "I have done everything possible to comply with his orders," he wrote. During a brief visit to the 760th Tank Battalion, parked a quarter mile from the river, Walker told a tank crewman: "I knew from the beginning that this would never work. Too many damned Germans over there."

Clark seemed to recognize that recriminations would be unseemly if not toxic. Joining Keyes and Walker at Monte Rotondo for lunch, he was affable and solicitous. "Tell me what happened up here," he said. Keyes replied that the attack had appeared worthwhile—risky but warranted. Clark interrupted. "It was as much my fault as yours," he said. But were the regimental commanders up to the task? How had the division staff performed?

As soon as Clark and Keyes drove off, Walker asked his assistant commander, Brigadier General William H. Wilbur, to write an affidavit documenting the conversation, including Clark's admission of culpability. "I fully expected Clark and Keyes to can me to cover their own stupidity . . . but they were not in a bad mood," Walker wrote. He taped Wilbur's memorandum into his diary, just in case.

While the generals dined and discoursed, the remnants of two regiments struggled to extract themselves from the Rapido kill sack. By midday on Sunday, every commander in the 141st Infantry except for a single captain was dead or wounded, along with all battalion staff officers. The 143rd Infantry was hardly in better shape. Orders to fall back filtered across the river. Major Milton J. Landry, commander of the 2nd Battalion, who was spending his thirtieth birthday at the Rapido oxbow, had survived three wounds, including a hip dislocation produced by a shell fragment the size of a dinner plate and a steel shard in the chest that was partly deflected by the Parker pen in his blouse pocket. Hobbling about with a pair of paddles for crutches, Landry went down again when machine-gun fire hit him in the legs, nicking an artery and severing a sciatic nerve. "Major," a medic told him, "I don't believe there are enough bandages this side of the Rapido to cover all the holes in you." Evacuated to the east bank, Landry heard another medic say, "You've got a boot on the end of something out here. I guess it's your leg."

Landry survived. So did a soldier who swam the river with one foot blown off. As dusk fell, a few dozen more struggled back, clinging to flotsam as bullets frothed the water. By early evening on Sunday, the division log estimated losses at 100 officers and 1,900 enlisted men. Gunfire dwindled to a mutter. From the darkness came an occasional plea for water or faint cries for a medic, but both sides had grown inured to supplication. Then, silence. "It was reported," the log noted at 8:30 P.M., "that American firing had ceased west of the river."

A rifleman from the 143rd Infantry who regained the east bank later reflected, "I had turned into an old man overnight. I know I was never the same person again."

The preliminary tally in the division log proved close to the mark. Official medical records listed 2,019 casualties, of whom 934 were wounded. Some counts were a bit lower, others higher; preposterously, Clark would accuse Walker of inflating his losses in a bid for sympathy. The Germans found 430 American bodies on the west bank, and took 770 prisoners; 15th Panzer Grenadier Division losses included 64 dead and 179 wounded. To the victors went a cocky insolence. A captured II Corps carrier pigeon returned on the fly with a banded message: *"Freuen wir uns auf Euren nächsten Besuch."* We look forward to your next visit.

By any reckoning, two U.S. infantry regiments had been gutted in one of the worst drubbings of the war; the losses were comparable to those suffered six months later at Omaha Beach, except that that storied assault succeeded. "I had 184 men," a company commander in the 143rd Infantry said. "Forty-eight hours later I had 17. If that's not mass murder, I don't know what is." Two scarecrow battalions of the 141st when merged under the command of a captain could barely muster two hundred riflemen. Engineers reported scavenging eight M-2 boats, 323 paddles, and 4,100 feet of half-inch manila rope "in a bad tangled mess." After pinning a Silver Star on a double amputee, Walker told his diary, "When I think of the foolish orders of the higher command which caused those broken bodies and deaths unnecessarily, it makes me feel like crying *halt*."

Clark soon summoned Walker for a conference at Mignano. The two men shook hands and then strolled down the road in the morning sun, the tall, bony army commander towering above his stocky former instructor. Clark worried about the division's morale. What could be done? Walker acknowledged a dejection after the "recent reverses and heavy losses of leaders." Yes, Clark agreed, but those reverses had reflected a dearth of capable officers in key positions. He intended to make wholesale changes by removing Brigadier General Wilbur, both of the regimental commanders who had fought at the Rapido, the division chief of staff, and Walker's two sons.

Stunned, Walker asked whether he also was to be sacked. "No, you are doing all right," Clark replied. "But you have surrounded yourself with officers whose abilities do not measure up." Walker doubted he would be spared. "This was a blow," he told his diary. "I am marked for relief from command of the division as soon as Clark can find an easy way to do it." When a new commander arrived to replace Colonel Martin in the 143rd Infantry, Walker told him, "Your predecessor has committed no sins of commission or omission as far as I'm concerned."

That was wrong. Every senior officer at the Rapido had committed sins; none emerged unstained. The Army's official history, rarely given to indictment, detected "a series of mishaps, a host of failures, a train of misfortune," including "a mounting confusion that led to near hysteria and panic." Clark soon found himself fighting a rearguard assault on his generalship. "If I am to be accused of something, thank God I am accused of attacking instead of retreating," he declared.

But bluff bellicosity would not serve, as even Clark sensed. In the last diary reference he would ever make to the Rapido, he wrote on January 23:

"Some blood had to be spilled on either the land or the SHINGLE front, and I greatly preferred that it be on the Rapido, where we were secure, rather than at Anzio with the sea at our back." Perhaps so. Some strategists linked the Rapido calamity with Normandy, and with the pinching need for landing craft that had dictated quick action in Italy. "The blame must rest with those who allowed the tyranny of OVERLORD to dominate the tactical as well as the strategic battlefield," wrote W.G.F. Jackson. Certainly Clark and Keyes had failed to enlighten Walker about how his attack at Sant'Angelo fit into larger strategic ambitions at Anzio and in western Europe.

At a cost of two thousand casualties, not even a toehold had been won at the Rapido. That also implied tactical malfeasance. "From a military standpoint, it was an impossible thing to attempt," Kesselring would observe after the war. German defenders were unaware that an entire U.S. division had attacked; despite Kesselring's shift of two reserve divisions from Rome to the Garigliano, no reserves had been diverted to Sant'Angelo, because none were needed. The Americans had failed to seize the high ground, failed to coordinate with the adjacent 46th Division, failed to use tank fire effectively, and failed to neutralize German artillery on the flanks.

"The attack was insufficiently planned and poorly timed," Kesselring added. "No general should leave his flanks exposed." Sergeant Billy Kirby of Gatesville, Texas, was no field marshal, but he concurred. "Anybody who had any experience knew this ain't the place to cross the river," Kirby said. A tank platoon leader expressed the prevalent disgruntlement. "It would be nice to be a private in the ranks," he said, "untainted by association with the leadership."

Those ranks were in a surly mood, "on the edge of mutiny," a lieutenant in the 141st Infantry reported. Some resented being used as "cannon fodder," as the departing Colonel Martin put it, and many shared his conviction that "a fine National Guard division was being destroyed on faulty orders from a West Point commander," presumably Clark. Unknown to Walker, a cabal of his Texas officers met secretly after the Rapido and resolved to request a congressional inquiry after the war.

That resolution would be revived in January 1946, when the 36th Division Association demanded an investigation into the "fiasco"; the Texans accused Clark of being "inefficient and inexperienced," and willing "to destroy the young manhood of this country." Both the Senate and the House of Representatives held hearings, which generated more heat than light. If the Texans blamed Clark, Clark blamed Walker. "Walker's mental attitude, that a defeat was inevitable, was a decisive factor," Clark would tell the Pentagon. The secretary of war determined that the Rapido attack "was a necessary one and that General Clark exercised sound judgment." The investigation ended, but the controversy endured for decades, a nasty, sup-purating wound.

For now, as accounts of the carnage spread across Italy, officers shook their heads and thanked their lucky stars to have been spared that particular agony. Brigadier Kippenberger, whose New Zealand troops were still recovering from their own ordeal in the Winter Line, studied the field reports and concluded, "Nothing was right except the courage."

Some hours after the final shots faded on the Rapido, a captured American private who had been released to serve as a courier stumbled into the 141st Infantry command post carrying a written message for *"den englischen Kommandeur."* The panzer grenadiers proposed a three-hour cease-fire to search for the living and retrieve the dead. GIs fashioned Red Cross flags from towels and iodine, and even before the appointed hour paddled across to both regimental bridgeheads.

They found a few survivors, including Private Arthur E. Stark, known as Sticks, who had carried a battalion switchboard across the river for the 143rd Infantry before being hit by shell fragments. For three days he had lain exposed to January weather. "Did you have a big Christmas? You should have seen mine," he had written his eleven-year-old sister, Carole, earlier that month. "The little boys and girls over here didn't have much Christmas." Sticks lingered for two days after his rescue, then passed over. Other cases ended better: a forward observer with half his face blown away appeared to be dead, but a medic noticed the lack of rigor mortis. Surgeons would reconstruct his visage from a photograph mailed by his family.

For three hours they gathered the dead, reaping what had been sown. Wehrmacht medics worked side by side with the Americans, making small talk and offering tactical critiques of the attack. German photographers wandered the battlefield, snapping pictures. An American reporter studied the looming rock face of Monte Cassino with its all-seeing white monastery. "Sooner or later," he said, "somebody's going to have to blow that place all to hell."

The short peace ended. Dusk rolled over the bottoms. The mists reconvened. A final clutch of medics emerged carrying a long pole with a white truce flag that caught the dying light. More than a hundred bodies had been retrieved. But hundreds more remained, and would remain for months, carrion for the ravenous dogs that roamed these fens. Here the dreamless dead would lie, leached to bone by the passing seasons, and waiting, as all the dead would wait, for doomsday's horn.

## *The Show Must Go On*

MUCH had happened through antiquity in the half-moon port once known as Puteoli. Just inland, at Lake Avernus, Aeneas reputedly entered the underworld, crossing the river Styx to find in the Fields of Mourning "those souls consumed by the harsh, wasting sickness, cruel love." On the Puteoli wharf, St. Paul had at last arrived in Italy aboard a grain packet after his shipwreck on Malta. The Roman amphitheater, third largest on the peninsula, featured sixty trapdoors that could be lifted as one to release wild beasts purchased from theatrical agents in Africa; it was said that the lions here refused to eat Saint Gennaro in A.D. 305, and authorities were forced to cut off his holy head. Modern Puteoli—renamed Pozzuoli—in January 1944 was home to a skinny nine-year-old girl called Stuzzicadenti by her schoolmates. After the war, skinny no more, the Toothpick would be better known as Sophia Loren.

Pozzuoli also was the temporary home for thousands of Allied soldiers. Here, ten miles northwest of Naples, the staging for SHINGLE neared completion even as the first sketchy reports arrived of fighting on the Rapido, fifty miles north. The Anzio assault force in VI Corps comprised two infantry divisions—the U.S. 3rd and the British 1st—plus paratroopers, American Rangers, and British Commandos, for a total of 47,000 men and 5,500 vehicles. Another 11,000 soldiers would follow immediately, including an armored brigade. The four-hundred-ship armada now loading in Pozzuoli and three other ports near Naples included four Liberty ships, eighty-four LSTs, eighty-four LSIs, and fifty LCTs. U.S. Navy and Royal Air Force meteorologists for days had studied their barometers and weather charts with the intensity of augurs scrutinizing entrails. Their forecast for H-hour on Saturday morning, January 22, was heartening: light airs, calm seas, haze, 55 degrees Fahrenheit.

A festive mood infused the docks. Along the Pozzuoli waterfront, LSTs had beached with bow doors yawning on the flat rocks used by fishermen to spread their nets. Columns of jeeps and overloaded trucks snaked through the crooked alleyways toward the ships. Italian vendors sang out from the street corners, offering fruit, wine, and—to the dismay of security officers—postcards of Anzio. Irish Guardsmen marched to their ships as a band played "Saint Patrick's Day"; their commander took his troops' salute while teetering on a statue pedestal. Supplies sufficient for fifteen days of combat were hoisted into the holds—and, upon discovery by vigilant quartermasters, some extraneous items were hoisted out, including a portable organ and several thousand hymnals.

Bum boats swarmed through the anchorage, peddling oranges to Royal Navy tars with shouts of "Good-a luck!" An airman wrote in his diary: "Native dagoes were fast to row alongside our boat and sell everything from nuts & apples to liquers." Troops awaiting embarkation in a nearby warehouse watched a feature film, which was repeatedly interrupted whenever more units were called to the gangways. Soldiers shrugged and gathered their gear, repeating a GI aphorism always uttered with irony if not contempt: "The show must go on."

Robert Capa arrived in Pozzuoli with his camera bag and $150 worth of black-market Spanish brandy. He joined Bill Darby, newly promoted to full colonel and now commanding three battalions that had been melded into the 6615th Ranger Force. "The boys were ordered to spread the rumor they were going home," Capa wrote. Hundreds of Italian girls swarmed to the docks

> to say goodbye, to remind their friends not to forget to send them the visas, and to collect the remaining C-rations. It was a grotesque scene: the soldiers sitting on the docks, having their shoes shined; holding in their left hand a box of rations; their right, the waist of their sweethearts.

Boarding the *Princess Beatrix,* the *Winchester Castle,* the *Royal Ulsterman,* and three LSTs, the Rangers slung their hammocks, filled their canteen cups with "Limey tar" from the coffee urns, and repaired to the weather decks for calisthenics. "They think it's gonna be all love and nickel beer," Darby said, "but I don't think it will be."

On the Naples waterfront, below broad-shouldered Vesuvius, the 3rd Division band crashed through a medley of marches as raw-boned infantrymen tromped past in a panoply of smart salutes and snapping guidons. "All that fanfare didn't seem quite right," a staff officer wrote. "The whole thing had a feeling of unreality about it." When the band struck up the division anthem in march time, soldiers burst into song:

> I'm just a dog-face soldier with a rifle on my shoulder
> And I eat a Kraut for breakfast every day.
> So feed me ammunition
> Keep me in the Third Division
> Your dog-face soldier boy's o-kay!

Aboard the U.S.S. *Biscayne,* a former seaplane tender now converted to a flagship, the roaring voices pleased Lucian Truscott, who stood on the fantail in his leather jacket and lacquered two-star helmet. GIs rarely sang as their fathers had in the Great War. "There was no inclination to lighten burdens with a song," as Truscott later put it. But the chorus now suggested resurgent spirits after the fraught Winter Line campaign. Many new men now filled the 3rd Division; since Sicily, the turnover of lieutenants had exceeded 100 percent. Truscott knew that esprit would be vital in the coming weeks. So, too, would robust health, and for the past month medicos had struggled to bring the division to fighting trim by treating ailments from trench foot to bronchitis to gonorrhea. To soothe his own chronically inflamed vocal chords, Truscott had scheduled three paintings of his throat with silver nitrate during the 120-mile voyage to Anzio.

The thump of drums from the dockside band carried into the crowded *Biscayne* deckhouse that served as the Army's floating command post. Another major general listened to the martial beat with both pride and irrepressible dread. "I have many misgivings but am also optimistic," John Porter Lucas had written in his diary after boarding the ship on Thursday afternoon. "I struggle to be calm and collected."

For Lucas, that struggle had just begun. The commander of VI Corps, and thus of SHINGLE, he hardly looked the part of the warrior chieftain. He was pudgy and gray, with a brushcut widow's peak, wire-rim spectacles, and a snowy mustache of the sort favored by French field generals in World War I. He puffed incessantly on a corncob pipe, and carried an iron-tipped cane given him by Omar Bradley. "Fifty-four years old today," Lucas had told his diary on January 14, "and I am afraid I feel every year of it." One Tommy thought he seemed "ten years older than Father Christmas." Lucas gave an Irish Guardsman the impression of "a pleasant, mild, elderly gentleman being helped out of layers of overcoats."

Born in West Virginia, he was commissioned as a cavalry officer at West Point in 1911, then rode into Mexico with Pershing's Punitive Expedition before being wounded in France, at Amiens. Lucas later commanded the 3rd Division at the time of Pearl Harbor and served as Eisenhower's deputy in North Africa. This was his third corps command, including a brief stint as Bradley's successor at II Corps before Marshall and Eisenhower picked him to replace Dawley at Salerno. Clark had privately preferred Matthew Ridgway, but accepted Lucas with a shrug.

Lucas drove a jeep named *Hoot,* quoted Kipling "by the yard," and had accumulated several nicknames, including Old Luke and Sugar Daddy; at Anzio he would acquire more, notably Foxy Grandpa. Although he considered the Germans "unutterable swine," one staff officer wrote that he "never seemed to want to hurt anybody—at times, almost including the enemy." A British general thought Lucas possessed "absolutely no presence"; a Grenadier Guards commander confessed that when Lucas visited his battalion billets above Naples Bay "our spirits sank as we watched this elderly figure puffing his way around the companies." An odd rumor circulated that he was suffering ill effects from a defective batch of yellow fever vaccine.

For Lucas's malady there was no inoculation. Empathy might ennoble a man, but it could debilitate a general. "I think too often of my men out in the mountains," he had written during the winter campaign. "I am far too tender-hearted ever to be a success at my chosen profession." A few days before boarding *Biscayne,* he added, "I must keep from thinking of the fact that my order will send these men into a desperate attack." Upon hearing that SHINGLE had been authorized, Lucas portrayed himself as "a lamb being led to slaughter"; accordingly, he revised his last will and testament. The sanguine assurance of his superiors baffled him. "By the time your troops land, the Germans will have already pulled back past Rome," Admiral John Cunningham, the British naval commander in the Mediterranean, had told him. Alexander claimed that the capture of Rome and subsequent hell-for-leather pursuit northward meant that "OVERLORD would be unnecessary."

Could Alexander and others, he wondered, have additional intelligence that spawned such confidence? AFHQ asserted that it was "very questionable whether the enemy proposed to continue the defensive battle south of Rome much after the middle of February." Fifth Army headquarters also claimed that enemy strength was "ebbing due to casualties, exhaustion, and possible lowering of morale." Four days after landing at Anzio, the SHINGLE force would face no more than 31,000 Germans, according to Fifth Army analysts, and nearly two more weeks would pass before the enemy would be able to move even two more divisions from northern Italy. The designated military governor of Rome had already requested $1,000 for an "entertainment fund" in the capital.

Lucas beheld a different vision. His VI Corps intelligence analysts believed the Germans would muster a dozen battalions and a hundred tanks at Anzio on D-day, which would grow to twenty-nine battalions within a week and to more than five divisions and 150 tanks by D+16. VI Corps also estimated that, "even under favorable conditions," reinforcement of the beachhead from the Cassino front "cannot be expected in under thirty days." Lucas confided to his diary, "This whole affair has a strong odor of Gallipoli"—the disastrous British amphibious invasion of Turkey in 1915.

An old friend shared his premonitions. George Patton flew from Palermo to bid Lucas farewell before returning to Britain for his new army command. "John, there is no one in the Army I hate to see killed as much as you, but you can't get out of this alive," Patton told him. "Of course you might be only badly wounded. No one ever blames a wounded general for anything." Patton advised reading the Bible. To Lucas's aide he added, "If things get too bad, shoot the old man in the back end."

Lucas's milquetoast demeanor obscured a keen tactical brain. He recognized, as did too few of his superiors, that the exalted ambitions for SHINGLE exceeded the means allocated to achieve them. Worse yet, those ambitions were muddled and contradictory, particularly with respect to the vital high ground northeast of Anzio, known as the Colli Laziali, or Alban Hills. Under Alexander's instructions to Clark on January 12, the SHINGLE force was "to cut the enemy's main communications in the Colli Laziali area southeast of Rome," and to threaten the German rear on the Cassino front. The two Allied forces were then to "join hands at the earliest possible moment," and hie through Rome "with the utmost possible speed."

Yet the Fifth Army order issued later the same day instructed Lucas to "seize and secure a beachhead at Anzio," then to "advance on Colli Laziali." Clark remained deliberately vague about whether VI Corps was to surmount the Alban Hills or simply amble toward them. Through painful experience, the Fifth Army commander now expected the Germans to fight hard, first for the beachhead, then for the approaches to Rome. Alexander might wish otherwise, but he was "a peanut and a feather duster," as Clark told his diary in an odd, impertinent blend of metaphors.

In a private message, Clark advised Lucas to first secure the beachhead and avoid jeopardizing his corps; if the enemy proved supine, then VI Corps could lunge for the hills to cut both Highways 6 and 7, the main supply routes from Rome to Kesselring's forces on the Garigliano and at Cassino.

"Don't stick your neck out, Johnny," Clark told Lucas. "I did at Salerno and got into trouble." He added, "You can forget this goddam Rome business."

Fantasy and wishful thinking suffused Alexander's SHINGLE plan; Clark added realism, flexibility, and insubordinate arrogance. Now confusion clattered down the chain of command. The XII Air Support Command, which would provide the invasion force with air cover, assumed that SHINGLE was intended to "advance and secure the high ground." The British 1st Division commander, Major General William R. C. Penney, also had the impression that his troops were to "advance north towards fulfillment of the corps mission to capture Colli Laziali." But Lucas's Field Order No. 19, dated January 15, lacked a detailed plan beyond the landings; Truscott's 3rd Division, for example, was told only to establish a beachhead and to prepare to move, on order, toward the hill town of Velletri. A baffled General Penney told his diary on January 20, "Corps at least talking of plans to break out of beachhead." Small wonder that Clark's deputy chief of staff, General Sir Charles Richardson, later observed, "Anzio was a complete nonsense from its inception."

One other issue added to Lucas's unease: the rehearsals for SHINGLE, on the beaches below Salerno, had been fiascoes. The British failed to disembark either brigade or division headquarters. The Americans, in an exercise code-named WEBFOOT, did worse. The Navy abruptly changed the landing beach, and only eleven of thirty-seven LSTs showed up. Rough weather and navigation errors on the night of January 17 kept the fleet fifteen miles offshore, and forty DUKWs making for land sank in the high seas, taking twenty-one howitzers, radio gear, and several men to the bottom. "I stood on the beach in an evil frame of mind and waited," Lucas reported. "Not a single unit landed on the proper beach, not a single unit landed in the proper order, not a single unit was less than an hour and a half late."

Truscott was so furious about the preparation for Anzio that he wrote Al Gruenther, "If this is to be a forlorn hope or a suicide sashay, then all I want to know is that fact." Before boarding *Biscayne*, Truscott—with Lucas's blessing—also sent Clark an account of WEBFOOT. The army commander was appalled at "the overwhelming mismanagement by the Navy." But he told Truscott, "Lucian, I've got your report here and it's bad. But you won't get another rehearsal. The date has been set at the very highest level. There is no possibility of delaying it even for a day. You have got to do it."

Italy for eons had been a land of omen and divination, of portents and martial prophecy. During earlier campaigns on the peninsula it was said that two moons had risen in the sky, that goats grew wool, that a wolf pulled a sentry's sword from its scabbard and ran off with it. It was said that scorching stones fell like rain, that blood flowed in the streams, that a hen turned into a cock and a cock into a hen, that a six-month-old baby in Rome shouted, "Victory!" It was said that soldiers' javelins in midflight had burst into flame.

Modern men had no use for bodings or superstition, of course. Still, it was a bit surprising that the SHINGLE force ignored the ancient sailors' injunction against sailing on a Friday, the day of Christ's crucifixion. But at 5:20 A.M. on Friday, January 21, the Anzio flotilla weighed anchor and made for the open sea after first feinting south. Some soldiers fingered their rosary beads or huddled with a chaplain. Others snoozed on deck or basked in the sun, scanning the distant shore for the Temple of Jupiter at Cumae, where an Allied radar team played a recording of "Carolina Moon." "Most talk is of home and regular G.I. stuff," an airman wrote in his diary. Steaming at a languid five knots, the convoys "look more like a review than an invasion armada," one British lieutenant wrote.

In his cabin aboard the crowded *Biscayne,* Lucas spread his bedroll and shoved his kit into a corner. Truscott, who had gone to have his throat painted, would sleep on the couch. "More training is certainly necessary," Lucas wrote in his diary, "but there is no time for it." He had resigned himself to his fate. "I will do what I am ordered to do, but these Battles of the Little Big Horn aren't much fun." The show must go on.

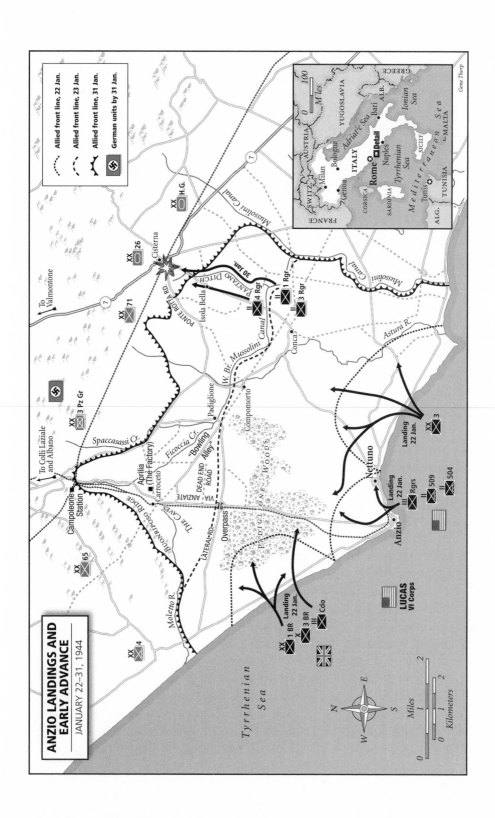

**ANZIO LANDINGS AND EARLY ADVANCE**

JANUARY 22–31, 1944

Allied front line, 22 Jan.
Allied front line, 23 Jan.
Allied front line, 31 Jan.
German units by 31 Jan.

Gene Thorp

# 8. PERDITION

### *"Something's Happening"*

ONLY the bakers were astir in the small hours of Saturday, January 22. The fragrance of fresh bread wafted through the dark streets from the wood ovens in Margherita Ricci's little shop, past the shuttered tobacco stall and the bronze statue of Neptune riding a huge fish. In Nettuno and adjacent Anzio—the woodlands of the Borghese villa separated the sister towns—bakery workers were among the few citizens still permitted in the coastal exclusion zone established by the Germans four months earlier. More than fifteen thousand exiles lived in shanties in the nearby Pontine Marshes or on the slopes of the Colli Laziali. Anyone caught within three miles of the coast risked a bullet to the nape, usually delivered against a wall in the Via Antonio Gramsci, where the condemned were told to turn their heads for a final glimpse of the sea before the fatal shot.

Dusted with flour and smelling of yeast, Orlando Castaldi shoved his flat wooden peel beneath a batch of rolls browning in the oven. Castaldi had been in Sicily during the Allied invasion six months earlier, eventually fleeing to Nettuno, where his brother and uncle worked in another bakery just two hundred yards north, in the Via Cavour. Brief but plucky resistance to the German occupation in September had been punished with executions, deportations, and the usual kidnapping of able-bodied men for labor battalions. Those consigned to the marshes had endured a bitter early winter, using ashes for soap and living on the loaves carted out from Ricci's each morning. Some chanced reprisals by sneaking into Rome to trade gold earrings or family linen for black-market pasta or a few liters of cooking oil. Allied bombing along the coast had gnawed the waterfront and forced the removal of the Madonna of Graces—an ornate wooden statue of Nettuno's patron—to a basilica in Rome for safekeeping.

Castaldi cocked his head, holding the paddle at high port like a halberd. Through the open window came a noise from the sea, a distant clamor. "Keep still a moment," he told two colleagues. "Something's happening." Clanking metal and the thrum of engines carried on the night. Castaldi recognized the sound, from Sicily. "I can hear them," he said. "I can hear them. The Americans are coming!" Grabbing his jacket, he yanked down the window blinds and sprinted through the door to alert his brother and uncle. As he rounded the corner into the Via Cavour, a brilliant light bleached the night sky and the ground trembled as if Neptune himself had impaled the earth with his trident.

The Americans were indeed coming, and so too the British. Three miles offshore the armada had dropped anchor at 12:04 A.M., four minutes late, in a dead calm and diaphanous haze. Scout boats puttered toward shore and at 1:50 A.M., just as young Castaldi darted into the street, a pair of British rocket boats opened fire with fifteen hundred 5-inch projectiles intended to cow coastal defenders and detonate beachfront mines. The five-minute bombardment "made a tremendous noise, achieved no good results, and was prejudicial to surprise," an intelligence officer reported. Only silence answered the barrage, and shortly after two A.M. the first infantrymen swarmed onto the beach, bent on adding injury to the rockets' insult.

Before the war, before the killings and the expulsions and those last sad looks at the sea, Anzio-Nettuno had been a thriving resort, just two hours from Rome by fast Fiat, with a fine harbor and garish bathhouses. In waterfront eateries known for their *zuppa di pesce,* patrons could watch the fireworks on feast days. Nettuno had grown a bit larger in modern times, but Anzio, ancient Antium, had greater notoriety. Nero and Caligula had both been born here—the former's fiddling during the conflagration of Rome was said to have occurred in Antium's theater—and the patrician rebel Coriolanus supposedly was slain here in 490 B.C. Silver-throated Cicero owned a villa in Antium; Trajan had enlarged the port; and various emperors bred elephants along the coast. Antium had worshipped the goddess Fortune as the town's protectress, but she proved inconstant. The harbor silted up during Rome's decline, and piracy eclipsed tourism. Through the centuries, the goddess alternately smiled and scowled capriciously.

Now her temper would be tested again. Anchoring the VI Corps' left flank, the British splashed ashore five miles up the coast on Red, Green, and Yellow Beaches. A few desultory rounds of German artillery plumped the shallows, but naval gunfire soon answered and the only resistance across the shingle came from mines and soft sand. Much bellowing with bullhorns accompanied the landings: a subsequent analysis advised that "no amount of shouting through loud-hailers will induce troops to advance through a minefield." British lorries, lacking four-wheel drive, tended to bog down in the narrow dune exits—"The waste of time was fantastic," a beach commander lamented—and tempers flared. When a landing craft coxswain scraped the hull of the flagship H.M.S. *Bulolo,* a naval officer roared, "Don't stand about like a half-plucked fowl. Cast off!"

Soon enough twelve-foot lanes were cleared through the mines and marked with luminous paint. Hundreds and then thousands of Tommies scuffed into the piney Padiglione Woods, searching in vain for an enemy to overrun. Three Germans were found sleeping in a cowshed amid plundered bottles of Italian perfume and nail polish. One surrendered in his underwear, though the other two escaped in an armored car. "It was all very gentlemanly, calm and dignified," the Irish Guards reported. Carrying a large black umbrella as he arrived in a DUKW, the Irish Guards commander "stepped ashore with the air of a missionary visiting a South Sea island and surprised to see no cannibals."

No cannibals appeared on the right flank either. Truscott's 3rd Division made land just south of Nettuno, while Darby and his Rangers beat for the white dome and terraces of the Paradiso, a casino overlooking Anzio harbor. Most troops came ashore wetted only to the knees, if not completely dryshod. A few spurts from a flamethrower encouraged shrieking surrenders in an antiaircraft battery; nineteen enemy soldiers emerged hands-up from a bunker that still sported a scraggly Christmas tree. Engineers found more than twenty tons of explosives stuffed in the docks and doorways, but winter weather had corroded the charges and a new German plan to blow up the mole had not yet been effected. Prisoners trickled in, including Wehrmacht rustlers captured while searching for cattle to feed their unit.

After watching through field glasses from the *Biscayne,* General Lucas advised his diary that he "could not believe my eyes when I stood on the bridge and saw no machine gun or other fire on the beach." At 3:05 A.M. he sent Clark a coded radio message: "Paris-Bordeaux-Turin-Tangiers-Bari-Albany," which meant "Weather clear, sea calm, little wind, our presence not discovered, landings in progress." Later in the morning Lucas signaled "No angels yet, cutie Claudette": No tanks ashore, but the attack was going well.

It continued to go well through the day. Truscott made for shore in a crash boat at 6:15 A.M., mute with laryngitis and so miserable from his inflamed throat that he lay down for a nap in a thicket near the beach. His men hardly needed him. All three regiments pushed the beachhead three miles inland, exchanging a few gunshots with backpedaling German scouts, and then blowing up bridges across the Mussolini Canal to seal the right flank against a panzer counterattack that never came.

By sunrise, at 7:30, Rangers occupied Anzio; paratroopers soon after reported that Nettuno also was secure. Local bakers, including the gleeful Orlando Castaldi, were ordered to bank their oven fires to prevent German gunners from aiming at the smoke. Soldiers liberated six women found chained to tethering rings in the Piazza Mazzini stable; they had been sentenced to death four days earlier while returning by train from Rome with black market food purchased in the Piazza Vittorio. The Americans gave them powdered milk, chocolate, and underwear, then sent them home.

DUKWs rolled through the streets like parade floats. Prisoners in long green field coats trudged to cages on the beach, "dusty, sweaty and noncommittal," as one witness put it. "Move on, superman," a GI jeered. Outside the former German command post, on a large sign that read KOMMANDANT, someone scribbled: RESIGNED. A few more shells fell along the waterfront and the Luftwaffe staged an ineffectual raid. "Maybe the war is over and we don't know it," said a lieutenant colonel. A GI added, "It ain't right, all right. But I like it." MPs tacked up road signs, and soon jeeps and trucks clotted the streets. An old woman stood at an intersection outside town, kissing the hand of every soldier tramping past. As one private reported, "She did not miss a man."

Success brought sightseers to the beachhead. At nine A.M., to the trill of a bosun's pipe, Alexander and Clark clambered aboard the *Biscayne* from a patrol boat that had whisked them north from the Volturno. Lucas summarized the news with a smile: resistance negligible, casualties light, most assault troops already ashore. Anzio's port was in such fine condition that at least a half dozen LSTs could berth simultaneously, and the first would unload this afternoon.

From *Biscayne* the boating party traveled by DUKW to the beach. Clark—immaculate in peaked cap, silk scarf, and creased trousers—inspected the 3rd Division and pronounced himself pleased. Poor Truscott croaked his thanks. Alexander—no less comely in red hat, fur-trimmed jacket, and riding breeches—motored among the British battalions in the turret of an armored car. To a Scots Guardsman he resembled "a chief umpire visiting the forward position and finding things to his satisfaction." General Alex, in fact, told a British colonel precisely that: "I am very satisfied." Reconvening on *Biscayne,* the two men complimented Lucas on his derring-do, then hopped back into the patrol boat and sped off toward Naples, leaving neither orders nor a sense of urgency in their wake. As one wit commented, "They came, they saw, they concurred."

Left alone to command his battle, Lucas decamped from *Biscayne* to Piazza del Mercato 16, a two-story villa in Nettuno with four bedrooms and an upstairs fireplace. Sycamores ringed the little square, framing the sculpture of Neptune straddling his fish. The previous occupant of number 16, the German commandant, had bolted so quickly—only to die on the beach in the early minutes of the invasion—that a sausage and half-empty brandy glass remained on the dining table.

The Allies had won what they least expected to win: complete surprise. By midnight on D-day, 27,000 Yanks, 9,000 Brits, and 3,000 vehicles would be ashore in a beachhead that was fifteen miles wide and two to four miles deep. Only thirteen Allied soldiers had died. As one paratrooper wrote, most soldiers found it "very hard to believe that a war was going on and that we were in the middle of it."

Lucas also found it hard to believe. From the north window of number 16, he could plainly see his prize. Fifteen miles distant, the Colli Laziali rose above the myrtles and umbrella pines, burnished by the setting sun that kissed the red tile rooftops before plunging into the Tyrrhenian Sea. White haze scarped the hills, which rose three thousand feet above the coastal plain in a volcanic massif nearly forty miles in circumference. Wind-tossed chestnut groves softened the tufa ridges, providing haunts for cuckoos and dryads and ancient enchantresses. Here too lay Castel Gandolfo, the pope's summer home, where in years past the pontiff could have been seen riding a white mule among the cypresses, trailed by cardinals robed in scarlet.

Dusk sifted over the beachhead. Lights winked on in up-country villages, and convoy headlights drifted in tiny chains across the hills like ships steaming on the far horizon. In his tidy, contained cursive, Lucas wrote, "We knew the lights meant supplies coming in for the use of our enemies, but they were out of range and nothing could be done about it."

Thirty-four miles from this window lay Rome, known in Allied codebooks as BOTANY. Two routes crossed the "hinterland," as the British called the landscape beyond the beachhead. One road angled northeast from Nettuno, across the Pontine Marshes to Cisterna, twelve miles distant, and then fifteen more miles to Valmontone, astride Highway 6 in the Liri Valley. The other road, known as the Via Anziate, ran due north for almost twenty miles from Anzio to intersect Highway 7, the twenty-three-century-old Appian Way, at Albano.

Both roads led to glory, and Lucas intended to follow both. The world seemed to believe that BOTANY was all but his. The Sunday edition of *The New York Times* reported the Allies "only sixteen miles from Rome." Radio broadcasts heard in the beachhead were even more optimistic. "Alexander's brave troops are pushing towards Rome," the BBC reported on Sunday, "and should reach it within forty-eight hours."

\*    \*    \*

Neither the *Times* nor the BBC had consulted Field Marshal Kesselring.

The first alarm had come from a German corporal, a railroad engineer sent to Anzio to buy timber. At four A.M. on Saturday, breathless and mud-spattered, he roared into Albano aboard a motorcycle, babbling about enemy ships as far as the eye could see. A major phoned the news to Rome, where panicked officers began to pack their bags and burn official papers. "The landing," a German naval log noted, "has come at a very bad time for us."

Certainly it was unexpected. Hardly a week earlier, Hitler's intelligence chief, Admiral Wilhelm F. Canaris, had told the Berlin high command, "There is not the slightest sign that a new landing will be undertaken in the near future." Kesselring's chief of staff, General Siegfried Westphal, subsequently advised senior commanders in Italy on January 15, "I consider a large-scale landing operation as being out of the question for the next four to six weeks." Thus reassured, Kesselring had dispatched his reserves—the 29th and 90th Panzer Grenadier Divisions—to confront the Garigliano threat on the southern front. Just three battalions and forty-one guns remained to guard a forty-mile coastal stretch from the mouth of the Tiber River to below Nettuno.

Few combat commanders were enjoying World War II more than Albert Kesselring. Having been bombed out of his Frascati headquarters in September, he now occupied a new command post in the Sabine Hills, twenty miles northeast of Rome on the western lip of Monte Soratte, which Lord Byron once described as "a huge wave about to break." The views of the upper Tiber Valley were breathtaking, and local wines proved equal to the Frascati whites. Kesselring often hosted dinner parties for visiting dignitaries and diplomats, indulging his vanity by swapping his blue Luftwaffe uniform for khaki regalia of his own design, and displaying his erudition as both a soldier-scholar and a convivial raconteur. Earlier in January he had been shot down yet again while piloting his little Storch. Managing to steer the plane into a pond, he arrived at a conference covered in green slime but smiling as usual with Bavarian bonhomie. Over the past fourteen months, in the invasions of North Africa, Sicily, and Salerno, he had demonstrated similar agility and panache, and it was the Allies' misfortune to face him again at Anzio.

The first report of the landings reached Monte Soratte at five A.M., an hour after the railway corporal's alarm. Kesselring instantly recognized the threat to Tenth Army's rear and to Rome, where he ordered roadblocks on all approach avenues. At six A.M. he told Berlin of the landings and received authorization for Operation RICHARD, one of five contingency plans drafted in case of Allied landings at various points on the Italian littoral. At

7:10 he ordered the forces in northern Italy designated for RICHARD to head south, on prearranged march routes with prearranged signage, fuel, and troops assigned to clear the snow-packed Apennine passes. At 8:30 he directed General Vietinghoff to transfer all spare troops from Tenth Army to the beachhead, along with the headquarters of I Parachute Corps. Within six hours, Kesselring had ordered all or parts of eleven divisions to converge around the Colli Laziali in what he would later term a "higgledy-piggledy jumble." By seven P.M., forces were moving not only from northern Italy, but from France, Germany, and the Balkans. Well-wishing Italians would toss flowers to Wehrmacht soldiers rolling toward the beachhead from Croatia. As John Lucas could see from the headlights streaming across the hills, the first reinforcements had arrived even before D-day turned to D+1.

They were just the beginning. Allied air strategists had asserted that the Italian rail system could be disrupted by aerial bombardment to prevent German forces from concentrating around Anzio; the Mediterranean Allied Air Forces now had more than seven thousand aircraft, compared with fewer than six hundred Luftwaffe planes in the entire theater. Yet carpet bombing of marshaling yards proved ineffective, to the pleasant surprise of German logisticians who nimbly rerouted trains around blocked lines and organized truck convoys on back roads. Most Italian rail workers remained at their posts, and within three days portions of eight German divisions would be at or near the beachhead, with five others en route.

They found terrain that favored the defender, as usual. From the Colli Laziali, as a Grenadier Guards history lamented, on "clear days it was possible to see the surf breaking on the shore, and almost every movement in the open country between. . . . The German gunners could mark the fall of every shell." Muzzle flashes betrayed the position of Allied guns, and the flat ground had few folds to conceal men or artillery. To organize the "higgledy-piggledy jumble," Kesselring ordered the commander of the Fourteenth Army, General Eberhard von Mackensen, to shift his headquarters south from Verona. A square-jawed, monocle-sporting cavalryman, with extensive combat experience in Poland, France, and eastern Europe, Mackensen also boasted good Prussian bloodlines: his father, a hussar whose political patrons included Kaiser Wilhelm II, had occupied Serbia and Romania as a field marshal in World War I.

Kesselring had expected the Allies to seize the Colli Laziali, but by Sunday evening he told Vietinghoff in a phone call that the danger of a flying column severing his supply lines on Highways 6 and 7 had passed. He guessed that VI Corps' strength included three infantry divisions and an armored division—in fact, it was less—which Kesselring considered "insufficient for an attack on a strategic objective" like the Alban Hills, given the need to also protect the exposed beachhead flanks.

Moreover, the Allies suffered from what Kesselring called a "Salerno complex." Only when overwhelming combat power had been amassed, he surmised, would the enemy venture far from the beaches and protective naval gunfire. Before that buildup gained momentum, Mackensen must strike across the entire Anzio front to throw the enemy into the sea. Hitler agreed, and advised, in his own inimitable idiom, "The battle must be waged with holy hatred."

"Please answer the following questions at once," Clark radioed Lucas on Monday, January 24. "How far have your patrols worked? What are your intentions for immediate operations? What is your estimate of enemy situation?" The Fifth Army commander had warned, "Don't stick your neck out," but now he confided to his diary, "Lucas must be aggressive. He must take some chances."

In reply, Lucas correctly surmised that the enemy "will attempt to contain our forces pending arrival of reinforcements with which to counterattack [the] beachhead." Few tanks had been included in SHINGLE's initial waves, because the Allies had expected a sharp infantry fight on the beaches. Yet the invasion to date had resembled a camping expedition. Guards Brigade officers slept in pajamas and played bridge, while their troops brewed tea, chain-smoked, and stamped their feet to keep warm: rime glazed the marsh grass at night, and thin panes of ice coated the puddles. Owl hoots carried through the quiet woods. Solders found it easy to dig in the sandy soil if they did not dig too deeply: slit trenches soon grew wet from the high water table. That hardly seemed to matter. An officer in the 56th Evacuation Hospital pointed to the northern horizon and proclaimed, "All those hills are ours, men! No need to dig foxholes." In the weeks to come, 56th Evac soldiers often greeted enemy barrages and air attacks with a sardonic cry: "All those hills are ours, men!"

As Allied patrols were discovering, the hinterland between the beach and those hills was a strange, haunted place. Fed by streams from the Colli Laziali, the Pontine Marshes for millennia had been a malarial dead zone. In 1928, a census of the entire plain found only 1,637 people and no permanent settlements; the area was said to be inhabited "only by a few web-toed, fever-ridden corkcutters" living in straw huts. The Italian Red Cross reported that during the warm months, four of every five travelers who spent a single night in the Pontine Marshes could expect to contract malaria. The English translations of local place-names suggested a certain obsession with mortality: Dead Woman, Land of Death, Pool of the Sepulcher, and—to honor the sullen ferryman of the dead—Charon.

Mussolini had reclaimed much of the land with an ambitious program known as the *bonifica integrale,* intended to transform the marshes into "smiling fields." Enormous pumps drained the bogs, aided by ten thousand miles of canals and irrigation ditches, and more than a million pine trees planted in windbreaks. Five model towns were built, plus eighteen satellite villages and hundreds of two-story stone farmhouses, usually painted bright blue. Thousands of Italians seeking work and shelter during the Depression had moved to these virgin lands, which Mussolini envisioned as "human nurseries" for breeding the "great rural warriors" of a new Roman empire.

War wrecked the dream. Kesselring and his engineers saw the marshes as a potential barrier against Allied armies from the south. With Mussolini's apparent consent after his rescue from Gran Sasso, German hydrographers studied "what measures could be taken to make this area rapidly and completely impassable by flooding." Demolitionists blew up pumping stations, blocked canals, and bulldozed dikes. Seawater flushed the fields. Eventually 100,000 acres of reclaimed farmland were submerged; in some places "only trees and houses were visible," a Kesselring staff officer reported. The stout farm buildings would make admirable pillboxes. Not least, German malariologists knew that come springtime the inundations would provide larval nurseries for *Anopheles labranchiae,* a Pontine mosquito proficient at breeding in brackish water. The scheme remains "the only known example of biological warfare in twentieth-century Europe," according to the Yale University historian Frank M. Snowden.

Into this landscape of "bog, bush, and water," as one soldier described it, the Allied force began to push. On the VI Corps left, British patrols edged up the Via Anziate, past Italian farmers who shouted from behind their plows, *"Niente tedeschi!"*—"No Germans"—even as occasional shell bursts sent their white longhorn cattle bucking across the fields. Italian women clapped and waved handkerchiefs from their croft doorways, leading a British captain to comment, "These peasants are really damned good people, aren't they?" Guardsmen with a squadron of tanks drove a panzer grenadier battalion out of Aprilia—one of those five model Fascist towns—and captured a hundred prisoners. By Tuesday, January 25, the British 1st Division was halfway to Albano and the Highway 7 intersection.

On the VI Corps right, the Yanks also extended the bridgehead despite Truscott's lingering indisposition. The commanding general's "throat is worse today and he goes to bed early, after remaining in command post all day," the 3rd Division chief of staff had noted on Sunday. Four companies cantered toward Cisterna on Monday, only to butt against unexpected resistance; a larger American force at dawn on Tuesday also found Hermann Göring Division troops with machine guns or antitank guns in nearly every farmhouse. Cisterna, through which Highway 7 also passed, remained three miles away.

Still, high spirits prevailed. A Ranger lieutenant rummaging through an abandoned villa emerged in a black stovepipe hat and a tuxedo; another Ranger dressed up as a butler to serve him lunch. Churchill cabled Alexander, "Am very glad you are pegging out claims rather than digging in beachhead."

Clark and Alexander came calling again shortly after noon on Tuesday. Now, on D+3, forty thousand American and sixteen thousand British troops occupied the beachhead, along with almost seven thousand vehicles. While warning Lucas to brace for an inevitable counterattack, Clark also urged him to finish seizing Campoleone on the left and Cisterna on the right. Alexander seemed delighted with VI Corps' progress. "What a splendid piece of work," he told Lucas. "This will really hurt the Germans."

"I must keep my feet on the ground and my forces in hand and do nothing foolish," the corps commander confided to his diary after his superiors left. "This is the most important thing I have ever tried to do, and I will not be stampeded."

Kesselring was an airman, and although the Luftwaffe could muster less than a tenth the strength of the Allies, it was from the air that the Germans initially struck back. The first costly raid came at twilight on Sunday, January 23, when an aerial torpedo demolished the bridge and forecastle of the destroyer H.M.S. *Janus*. She broke apart and capsized in twenty minutes, taking 159 men with her. Survivors clinging to the flotsam sang "Roll Out the Barrel."

More than one hundred bombers scorched the transport anchorage on Monday, again at twilight, killing fifty-three sailors aboard the destroyer U.S.S. *Plunkett*. But the most shocking attack came against the hospital ship *St. David*, which had sailed from Anzio at dusk after embarking wounded troops. With all lights burning and an enormous red cross displayed topside, she was ambushed twenty miles offshore at eight P.M. by Luftwaffe planes that sprinkled magnesium flares and then bombs. An explosion staggered the *St. David* and quenched the lights. Patients hobbled on deck or were carried by stretcher. "The ship is sinking," a voice cried. "Jump." Lieutenant Laura R. Hindman, a surgical nurse, leaped into a lifeboat only to hear shrieks from other castaways. Looking up, she saw

"the ship turning over and it seemed to be falling right on top of us."
Dumped into the sea, she later recalled:

> I was being dragged down by the ship's suction. I fought and tried to
> swim and moved about but came up only far enough to hit my head
> against something hard which appeared to be part of the ship. . . . I
> struggled frantically and thought I was trapped under the ship when
> suddenly my head bobbed up. I saw stars.

*St. David* sank five minutes after she was hit. Of 229 people aboard, 96
perished.

The strikes continued through the week, often with the guided bombs
previously seen at Salerno. Radio chatter by Luftwaffe pilots, who sometimes could be heard even while taxiing on runways near Rome, gave
beachhead eavesdroppers fair warning of impending attacks. Allied fighters
and antiaircraft gunners parried many raids, shooting down more than
two dozen bombers and scattering others. Still, the attacks so menaced the
fleet—particularly late in the day, when air cover was weakest—that all
cruisers and most destroyers were ordered to retire seaward each afternoon at four. The loss of minesweeper *YMS-30* with seventeen crewmen
was typical. "There was a terrific wall of flame," a witness reported, "then
the vessel disappeared."

Danger lurked below as well as above. Shortly after five A.M. on Wednesday, January 26, *LST 422* lay anchored twelve miles offshore, waiting for a
berth to open at Anzio harbor. Built in Baltimore but crewed by the Royal
Navy, she had carried seven hundred men from Naples; among them, two
companies of the 83rd Chemical Mortar Battalion were to rejoin Darby's
Rangers for extra firepower. Deteriorating weather had built twenty-foot
seas under a westerly gale that shoved the ship sideways, dragging her anchor yard by yard, until she tripped a German mine. The blast tore a fifty-
foot hole in the starboard hull, igniting diesel oil and barreled gasoline.
Flame licked through the ventilators. Within two minutes, the upper deck
and bridge were ablaze. Most mortarmen were asleep in the tank deck,
which simultaneously flooded and turned into a crematorium. Detonating
rockets and white-phosphorus rounds soared through an aft hatch, forcing
those topside to cower behind the gun mount shields. With power lost and
the ship engulfed, men tumbled into the frigid sea.

Ships churning to the rescue played searchlights across the heaving
waves. As *LCI 32* approached, she too struck a mine and was gone in three
minutes, taking thirty crewmen to the bottom. "Heavy seas and high winds
made it very difficult maneuvering ship alongside the unfortunates," the

war log of minesweeper *YMS-43* noted at seven A.M. "Using the boat hook was the best method, except many of the life belts tore under the strain. Survivors were drowning all around us."

At 8:45, with hail falling like grapeshot, the minesweeper's log recorded: "No more floating bodies visible." The mortar companies lost nearly 300 men, among 454 U.S. soldiers and 29 British tars who perished. *LST 422* broke in half and sank at 2:30 P.M. Recovered bodies were sewn into canvas bags weighted with antiaircraft shells and consigned to the sea. The drowned included Private Billy C. Rhoads of Albia, Iowa, whose brother years later said of the fatal news delivered by telegram to the family's front door, "It really was a grief which Mother never was able to be rid of."

As the air attacks intensified, so did German shelling. By midday on January 26, when sodden survivors from *LST 422* arrived in Anzio, the beachhead had assumed the shape of an irregular rectangle, seven miles deep and fifteen miles wide. Truscott's 3rd Division remained three miles from Cisterna, while Major General Penney's British 1st Division held Aprilia but stood more than a mile from the rail and road junction at Campoleone, and ten miles from Albano. Every square inch of the beachhead fell within range of German guns, and every square inch felt vulnerable. One shell hit a fragrance shop, perfuming the air with the odd scent of cordite and cologne. Another hit a British dump, firing ammunition as frantic Tommies dragged away leaking petrol cans. "Everyone was dashing around like demented beings," a Grenadier Guards corporal named E. P. Danger told his diary.

"The heavy shelling was beginning to shake us up a bit," Corporal Danger added. One of his American cousins agreed. "Anzio was a fishbowl," he wrote. "We were the fish."

*I will not be stampeded,* John Lucas had declared, and he would spend the rest of his life explaining that reluctance. Already skeptics had begun to wonder why the beachhead remained so compact, why the enemy had not been routed, why the campaign was not won. The senior Royal Air Force officer in the Mediterranean, Air Marshal Sir John Slessor, wrote a colleague in London five days after the landings:

> I have not the slightest doubt that if we had been Germans or Russians landing at Anzio, we should have had [Highway 6] two days ago and maybe Rome by now and the whole right of the enemy line opposite the Fifth Army would have crumpled.

Lucas also sensed that Alexander, despite his effusive praise during two visits to the beachhead, had grown uneasy, perhaps goaded by the impatient Churchill. As if seeking to persuade both himself and history, Lucas wrote in his diary:

> Apparently some of the higher levels think I have not advanced with maximum speed. I think more has been accomplished than anyone had a right to expect. This venture was always a desperate one and I could never see much chance for it to succeed, if success means driving the Germans north of Rome.

The excoriation of Old Luke had begun: for want of pluck, of audacity, of imagination. Long after the war ended, he would be pilloried as the modern incarnation of George B. McClellan, the timid Civil War general who was said to have "the slows." Even those who applauded Lucas's prudence regretted that he had not rushed to seize the road junctions at Campoleone and Cisterna, which would have complicated German encirclement of the beachhead. "Having gained surprise in the landing," the judicious official historian Martin Blumenson concluded, Lucas "proceeded to disregard the advantage it gave him."

Perhaps, although the Allied push to the north and northeast began within forty-eight hours of the landings. More than sixty years after the Allied perdition at Anzio, Lucas's caution seems sensible and even inevitable, given Clark's wooly instructions and Alexander's hail-fellow approbation. Those who most closely scrutinized the VI Corps predicament tended to concur that a pell-mell lunge for the Colli Laziali would have been reckless. Alexander's new chief of staff, the future field marshal John H. Harding, concluded that Lucas "probably saved the forces at Anzio from disaster." Clark came to a similar conclusion. Major General G.W.R. Templer, who would soon command a British division at Anzio and who detested Lucas, believed that if the corps had galloped north, "within a week or fortnight there wouldn't have been a single British soldier left in the bridgehead. They would all have been killed or wounded or prisoners." And George Marshall, who rarely condescended to adjudicate tactical squabbles, noted that "for every mile of advance there were seven or more miles to be added to the perimeter," which would have made the Allied flanks ever more vulnerable.

Five years after the war, Alexander conceded that "the actual course of events was probably the most advantageous in the end." His assessment echoed that of Field Marshal Wilson, Eisenhower's successor at AFHQ, who also concluded that to have pushed "to the Alban Hills with a half built-up force might have led to irreparable disaster." John Lucas might be found wanting as a battle captain, with transparent anxieties and an avuncular mien that failed to inspire men under duress. "He was absolutely full of inertia and couldn't make up his mind," General Templer later complained. "He had no qualities of any sort as a commander." But in staring through the north window of his villa on the Piazza del Mercato, Lucas found courage in convictions that would save his corps even at the price of his reputation. "Had I been able to rush to the high ground," he wrote in his diary as German artillery and air attacks intensified,

> . . . nothing would have been accomplished except to weaken my force by that amount because the troops being sent, being completely beyond supporting distance, would have been immediately destroyed. The only thing to do was what I did.

## Through the Looking Glass

O N a brisk January day in 1752, a column of soldiers more than half a mile long marched through a field outside the village of Caserta, twenty miles north of Naples, in a province famed in antiquity for "the beauty and gaiety of its women," as well as for the slave revolt led by the gladiator Spartacus in 73 B.C. With a quartet of cannons placed to denote four corners, the troops formed a rectangle that outlined the perimeter walls of a future royal palace inspired by Versailles. The building would require twenty years of toil by a regiment of stonemasons, reinforced by prison labor and galley slaves. The finished palace became a monument to Bourbon ostentation: twelve hundred rooms; four interlocking courtyards; a sweeping marble staircase grander than anything Louis XIV ever descended; a theater with forty boxes; a chapel trimmed in lapis lazuli; and interior furnishings said to cost six million ducats. Gold lined the queen's bathtub, and bas-relief figures on the wall had their eyes painted shut to prevent their peeking at the royal derrière; a hole-and-mirror contraption allowed the queen to watch townfolk passing on the street outside while she took her soak. The building's southern face alone was 830 feet long and 134 feet high, with 243 windows. In laying his cornerstone with a silver trowel on that January day, the Neapolitan monarch Charles III had selected a Latin invocation asking that the palace and grounds "remain forever Bourbon."

Alas, nearly two centuries later the Anglo-Americans were firmly ensconced. Captured on October 8, Caserta Palace now served as the headquarters for both Clark's Fifth Army and for Alexander's 15th Army Group, which claimed the fifth floor on January 20. Every map and stick of furniture, including a pair of General Alex's red plush chairs, had to be carried up 124 steps to what a British major described as "a muddling sort of maze through which one wandered." A staff school for Italian aviators had previously occupied the floor, which was cluttered with aircraft motors, wind tunnels, and even a bomber fuselage. "Everything," Harold Macmillan wrote in his diary, "was in disorder." A war room was built, with a sentry on the door and maps on the wall. Alexander messed at the palace kennel and slept in a bivouac two miles distant, so there was a great deal of chuffing up and down those 124 steps. Ultra intelligence agents worked in caravans near the palace, forever burning secrets in an elegant brick incinerator, surmounted by steep steps like a pagan temple.

Fifteen thousand Allied soldiers eventually worked at Caserta, which soon became a baroque parody of the Pentagon. The place was so cavernous that one resident claimed it was "the only house where I've had my hat blown off indoors." After studying a sheaf of palace blueprints, signal officers concluded that to thread wire through walls two feet thick was impossible; cable and phone lines therefore ran "in and out of windows and around the outside," giving the palace an appearance of being trussed if not hog-tied. One OSS officer thought Caserta resembled "a New England cotton mill," while another officer likened it to "Alcatraz without the bay." A brisk breeze caused hundreds of shutters to bang so that the headquarters "sounded like midnight in a madhouse."

The building had little heat, less sanitation, and "a 180-year accumulation of fleas." Staff officers sat at plywood-and-sawhorse desks, "alternately shivering and scratching fleabites." The British wanted the windows open, the Americans insisted they remain shut, and Alexander was forced to issue a Solomonic decree that "whoever arrived first at the office could have the windows as he liked for the day." A polyglot host streamed in and out of the palace: Tommies and GIs, RAF pilots and Red Cross girls, carabinieri in swallowtail coats and tricorne hats; Indians in turbans; Poles wearing British battle dress with red-and-white shoulder tabs; French colonials in fezzes and Uncle Sam's olive twill. Even an occasional Moroccan *goum* stumped past in the striped burnoose that GIs called a "Mother Hubbard wrapper."

The twelve hundred rooms had been converted into dormitories, dining halls, offices, bakeries, laundries, and a barbershop, where a comb-and-razor cut cost four cents. One spacious salon served as an indoor basketball court, and a three-room suite was devoted to an exhibit on venereal disease, with graphic color photographs intended to infuse soldiers with the fear of both God and loose women. Protective paper strips covered the huge palace mirrors, but nothing could keep GI fingerprints off the silk wall coverings and tapestries in the throne room and ministry chambers.

An errant bomb had bent the organ pipes in the palace chapel, and artillery rumbling sometimes carried from the Cassino front. But war seemed ever more removed for the "garritroopers" at Caserta, as Bill Mauldin called them—"too far forward to wear ties and too far back to git shot." An Army surgeon described the senior officers' mess as "a stuffy, swank private dining room full of elderly colonels dining on broiled steak and other luxuries." The tables were set with gold-trimmed palace porcelain and glassware etched with the royal crown. The chef had once worked at the Ritz in New York, but waiters were mostly "bomb-happy" GI convalescents. "It was said, rather unkindly, that if anyone dropped a plate they all dived for cover," one visitor reported.

Officers in the palace bar drank rum or cognac mixed with Coca-Cola; George Biddle found their faces "soft and puffy" compared with the frontline visages of Jack Toffey and his ilk. At parties, a female captain wrote, "Bill or Ralph or whoever had taken one got lit up on the very cheap wine and made less and less sense and got more and more amorous." Marathon poker games raged in the royal suite, including one in which Colonel Elliott Roosevelt, the president's son, allegedly lost $3,000; it was said that he eventually paid the debt with a sheaf of English five-pound notes "big as cabbage leaves." Twice weekly, the San Carlo Opera Company arrived from Naples to sing *Tosca* or *Madama Butterfly* in the palace theater. A box seat cost $1.25, and the cast was paid mostly in Army rations.

Caserta was a "looking glass world," one officer wrote. He added: "One doesn't hate on a full stomach and a hot bath." To preserve a semblance of Army life, some commanders insisted that their garritroopers at least camp outdoors. Bivouacs soon stretched for two miles through the palace gardens, evincing their own Wonderland qualities, with shower huts, softball diamonds, backgammon tables, and volleyball courts. Grenadier Guards practiced lugging their assault boats through the rose bushes before paddling furiously across the ornamental ponds, which hungry soldiers soon emptied of fish. Clark's floatplane landed among the lily pads on a reflecting pool a quarter mile long.

Just north of the palace, engineers built a colony for generals, known as Cascades. An elaborate fountain nearby depicted the goddess Diana and her handmaidens being surprised while bathing by the hunter Actaeon, who was consequently transformed into a stag and torn to pieces by his own hounds. Cascades included a lounge with a fireplace, a tennis court, a U-shaped dance hall, and a muddy, eel-infested pond that served as a swimming hole. The engineers who built the complex complained in their unit log: "The feeling of the men is that they came over here for the purpose of winning a war. The building of summer houses and swimming pools doesn't fall under this category."

Not least among Caserta's oddities, the 6681st Signal Pigeon Company maintained twenty-two lofts with eight thousand cooing birds, including a blue-check splashed cock named GI Joe who was credited with carrying a message that had forestalled bombardment of a town already captured by the British. Nightingales also filled Caserta's woods with music, leading one officer to write, "Everyone agrees that the nightingale's song is beautiful, but I have never seen it mentioned before that it is also extremely noisy." A British sergeant was blunter: "Wait till you've heard 'em every fucking night, the bloody sound they make will get in your bones."

Clark rarely missed a chance to flee Caserta's fleshpots for the front, and at 3:45 A.M. on Friday, January 28, he hopped in a staff car and sped down the grand driveway, past the silk mills and the rope factories, where hemp plants soaked in shallow pits to soften the fibers. Twenty-five miles due west, near the mouth of the Volturno, a wallowing launch ferried him downriver where a pair of seventy-eight-foot motor torpedo boats, *PT-201* and *PT-216*, bobbed at anchor. After snagging on a sandbar, the little launch shipped so much water that Clark was drenched to the skin by the time he climbed onto a stool behind *201*'s bridge. As the first gray hint of dawn tinted the eastern sky, the triple screws of the two patrol boats hurled them northwest across the indigo Tyrrhenian for the seventy-mile journey to Anzio. Neither boat crew took time to radio a sailing signal to the Allied fleet at the beachhead.

Alexander had prodded Clark to make this trip, wondering aloud on Thursday whether Lucas was sufficiently aggressive. Did the beachhead need "a thruster, like George Patton?" Alexander wondered. Certainly VI Corps should press forward to seize Campoleone and Cisterna. "Risks must be taken," Alexander added. Clark promised to deliver the message.

More than five months had passed since Clark had come ashore at Salerno, and the long season had aged him. During a visit to Caserta in early January, Patton had noted—with evident pleasure—symptoms of stress in the Fifth Army commander. "The left corner of Clark's mouth is slightly drawn down as if he had been paralyzed," he informed his diary. "He is quite jumpy." Clark on January 18 had asked Renie to send him some Kreml hair tonic. "I find that by massaging my hair using that it keeps from coming out, and for a while it was falling out quite badly." The crowding at the royal palace added more strains, and Clark planned to move his own forward command post to a hillside olive grove below Presenzano, ten miles from San Pietro. Alexander "and many lesser lights have moved into Caserta on top of my headquarters," Clark told his diary on January 23. "Never before in the history of warfare have so few been commanded by so many." As for the battle at Anzio, Alexander "apparently feels as though he is running that show. Not much I can do about it."

The solitude of high command oppressed him. "The more stars a man gets, the more lonesome he becomes," he told Renie. Comrades "used to come around in the evening, but they don't any more." He suggested that for companionship she send him Pal, the family cocker spaniel. A dutiful if indifferent letter writer, he at times vented his frustration at her. When she urged him to avoid personal risks, he answered, "You turn your lamb chops on the stove, and I'll run the Army." On January 11, after she told him that she had been too busy to accept a luncheon invitation from Eleanor Roosevelt, he replied, "I am distressed . . . I think you should take time to do those things."

As he soldiered on, so did she. Traveling for months on end, sometimes with Glenn Miller and other celebrities, Renie was credited with selling $25 million in war bonds. She also lectured widely about the virtues of both the American cause and her husband, whom she described as "working coolly [in] his tent virtually under enemy guns." To twelve hundred ladies at a Scottish Rite luncheon in Indianapolis, she pronounced him "an awfully good man, a rather religious man." Often she read from his letters, and even displayed the trousers, shrunk from immersion in Mediterranean brine, that Clark had temporarily lost during his celebrated secret mission to Algeria in October 1942. George Marshall had warned Clark about publicity mongering, which was so at odds with the selfless ethic embodied by the chief of staff. He also complained to Eisenhower that the army commander was "being victimized by his wife."

"It causes me some embarrassment," Eisenhower subsequently wrote Clark in late November, but "you are being unwittingly hurt by a particular type of publicity in the States. . . . G.C.M. has specifically noted that certain items so repeated have occasioned some merriment, possibly even sarcasm."

Clark was furious, rebuking Renie twice. If beguiled by public attention, he preferred to orchestrate it himself. "I do not want you to refer to me in any way in your talks," he wrote after reading Eisenhower's cable. "Positively no quotes from me, for some I have seen lately have been embarrassing. . . . Hate to write to you about this publicity business, for I feel your work is superior." A month later, after a magazine article cited his letters, he fairly sputtered while writing to her. "I deeply regret that. I have said so much about it and gotten no place that I do not know what to do," he complained. "For goodness sake let's see that no more of that stuff gets out."

Clark's virtues as a commander should have been evident enough without Renie's advocacy. He was disciplined, fearless, and, as one admiring colonel put it, "broad-gauged." He spent most waking hours among his troops, often in harm's way, with one long leg draped over the jeep's fender during what he called "ringside" visits. The enormous logistical and administrative complexities of running a big army fazed him not at all. He was attentive to requests from the front and to the perquisites due front-line troops returning to the rear for a rest. For esprit, he commissioned a Fifth Army song and distributed mimeographed lyrics so that puzzled theatergoers could belt out the anthem in the Caserta opera house. "I want my headquarters to be a happy one," he declared.

There was the rub. "The general was a difficult man to satisfy," recalled a former aide, Vernon A. Walters, who later rose to three-star rank and served as the U.S. ambassador to the United Nations. "I often lay in my sleeping bag at night reading by flashlight my letters of commendation and citations solely to reassure myself that I was not a complete damn fool." Disinclined to seek advice or admit error, Clark conveyed a hauteur made more pronounced by his height: he literally looked down on nearly everyone. "A very impatient man," a senior staff officer once said, and in Italy that was not necessarily a virtue. At times he berated his aides and castigated his staff, including the long-suffering Al Gruenther, whose pale skin, thin nose, and high forehead reminded one observer of "a rather Renaissance Florentine." Early each morning Clark called his corps commanders and then rebuked his staff for knowing less than he about overnight developments; Gruenther responded by dispatching officers to the front late at night so they could phone in reports before Clark awoke.

Already he had begun to think of Rome possessively. In late January, he told Field Marshal Wilson that Fifth Army had fought "a long and bloody battle up the Italian peninsula" and is "entitled to take Rome." He encouraged the reporter C. L. Sulzberger to remain close so "you can tell the world just how Mark Clark took Rome." Another correspondent, Eric Sevareid, concluded that for Clark the Italian campaign was foremost an opportunity for "personal publicity, without which warmaking is a dull job, devoid of glamour and recompense."

Surely that was too harsh. Like his thinning hair and drooping mouth, Clark's growing fixation on Rome was in part a manifestation of stress. The city's capture would not only fulfill a military and political objective but also affirm that this grievous campaign had been worthwhile. Since Salerno, battle casualties alone in Fifth Army exceeded 37,000. If one death was a tragedy and a million deaths a statistic, what would the twenty thousand dead required to take Rome amount to? In a confessional moment, Clark told Vernon Walters:

> Sometimes if I appear to be unreasonable, you must remember the burdens I bear are heavy. The time comes when I have to give orders that will result in the death of a large number of fine young men—and this is a responsibility that I cannot share with anybody. I must bear it by myself.

For two hours the torpedo boats bounded north at nearly forty knots, swinging wide of German shore batteries near Monte Circeo, where the enchantress Circe, daughter of the sun, had turned Odysseus's men into swine. Morning haze draped the sea and the throbbing engines drowned conversation. Clark perched on his stool, lost in thought. Lookouts scanned the waves ahead. "Sometimes," one Anzio veteran warned, "what looked like a piece of driftwood turns out to be a corpse."

At 8:40 A.M., twelve miles south of Anzio, the minesweeper U.S.S. *Sway* blinkered a challenge with its twelve-inch searchlight, asking the boats approaching out of the rising sun to identify themselves. Visibility was poor, air raids at the beachhead had just triggered an alert, and *Sway* several nights earlier had been attacked by German E-boats. Clark stood for a better view as *PT-201* blinkered back at a range of two thousand yards, then fired the day's recognition signal: green and yellow flares.

One minute after the initial challenge, *Sway* opened fire. Three-inch shells screamed across the sea. *PT-216* reversed course to port and sped away, but *201* stopped dead to acknowledge the shot across the bow. The next rounds splintered plywood and mahogany. A shell detonated against *201*'s deckhouse, shattering Clark's stool, and another blew through the tiny galley below. Fifty-caliber and 40mm rounds swarmed around the boat like hornets. "Machine gun bullets and heavier stuff tore the air overhead, making whistling sounds and swooshes," reported Frank Gervasi, the *Collier's* correspondent, who had come along for the ride. The initial salvo wounded five sailors, two of them mortally. Blood slicked the deck from an officer with a severed leg artery and a swab whose kneecap had been blown off. For a few moments, no one manned the helm, until an ensign took the wheel despite wounds to both legs. Clark seized the flare gun and fired more green and yellow flares, unaware that haze made the yellow pyrotechnics look red from *Sway*'s deck. The shooting continued.

"What shall we do?" Clark asked a wounded lieutenant.

"Don't know."

"Let's run for it."

Clark helped brace the helmsman as he opened the throttle and spun the wheel. The boat pirouetted and fled in a great flume of spray, chased by the minesweeper's shells. Half an hour later, *201* rendezvoused peacefully with H.M.S. *Acute,* transferring her wounded to the British warship. The skipper of *216* boarded *201* and guided her into Anzio harbor at noon, although not before another German raid on the port delayed Clark further. *Sway*'s crew was unrepentant. "The goddam light was bad and we couldn't read your goddam signals," one sailor told Gervasi. While averring that the incident was "a weight on the conscience of every officer and man aboard," *Sway*'s captain blamed the torpedo boats for their own misadventure. A Navy inquiry agreed, but Clark privately charged the minesweeper with "as flagrant an error of judgment . . . as I have ever seen."

If the morning had taken "a downward slant," in Clark's wry phrase, an afternoon in Lucas's command post hardly redeemed the day. Staff officers of VI Corps worked in a former Italian military barracks near Nettuno's Piazza del Mercato, but artillery fire and an unexploded bomb through the ceiling would soon drive the headquarters into the wine cellars under an *osteria* at Via Romana 9. For now, the sandbags around the barracks grew higher by the hour. Sailors steaming into Anzio harbor laid wagers on whether "this white apartment house or that pink villa would be standing on their return."

Wrapped in a belted Army trench coat and pulling on his corncob pipe, Lucas used a large map to show Clark his predicament. Heavy surf occasionally closed the landing beaches, and a sudden storm on Tuesday had marooned all Navy pontoons ashore before they could be hoisted from the water. Enemy raids often disrupted port operations and harassed the cargo fleet. Of greater concern was the imminent return to Britain of most LSTs; as few as a dozen would be left in the Medterranean after February 10, and at least seventy-two shiploads would be required in Anzio by mid-February. Daily matériel requirements had climbed from 1,500 tons a day to 2,300. Some LCIs sailing from Naples now carried a hundred tons of ammunition, triple the prudent load, and Navy brokers had begun identifying civilian schooners for use as cargo vessels.

As for the enemy, every day Lucas's G-2 identified more German units converging on the beachhead: the 29th Panzer Grenadier Division, then the Hermann Göring, then two armored divisions from southern France, then the 90th Panzer Grenadier. The day before, it had been estimated that four thousand German infantry and armor troops occupied Albano, including two paratrooper battalions and several hundred horse- and motorcycle-mounted troops. If the Allies were not already outnumbered, it was only a matter of time: by Sunday, an estimated 72,000 Germans would face 61,000 Anglo-Americans. The enemy appeared intent on shoving the beachhead into the sea, although that was uncertain. "We deal not with the true," as intelligence officers liked to say, "but with the likely."

Lucas sucked on his pipe stem. As he would soon write in a private note to Brigadier General Robert Frederick, whose 1st Special Service Force was heading to the beachhead, "Our enemies did not react exactly in the manner expected. Troops were rushed in."

None of this surprised Clark. Ultra intercepts had provided transparent detail of German movements under Operation RICHARD, including the shift of troops from fourteen divisions in France, Germany, northern Yugoslavia, and elsewhere. Even the German venereal disease hospital in Rome had been combed out. In many cases, however, only fragments of those enemy units had reached the beachhead. Clark told Lucas that the cumulative opposition "does not exceed three full divisions," with "indications that [Kesselring] is having difficulties reinforcing your front." All the more reason, Clark added, to seize Cisterna and Campoleone quickly.

Lucas agreed. In fact, Truscott today had drafted his order for an attack on Cisterna, to be led by infiltrating Rangers and two 3rd Division regiments, all bound for Highway 7. VI Corps Field Order No. 20 would coordinate a British lunge on the left with that American thrust on the right, both intended to "seize the high ground in the vicinity of Colli Laziali" and to "prepare to continue the advance on Rome." The attack was to begin the next day, Saturday, January 29.

Clark nodded. He hoped this would mollify Alexander, and whoever in London was lashing him on. With a few parting words of encouragment, he strode from the command post and climbed into a jeep for the short ride to the Villa Borghese; in a pine thicket behind the hundred-room seventeenth-century mansion, he planned to install another Fifth Army command post to keep a closer eye on the beachhead.

That prospect pleased Lucas no more than Alexander's hovering presence at Caserta pleased Clark. In his diary, the corps commander wrote:

> His gloomy attitude is certainly bad for me. He thinks I should have been aggressive on D-day and should have gotten tanks and things out to the front. . . . I have done what I was ordered to do, desperate though it was. I can win if I am let alone but don't know whether or not I can stand the strain of having so many people looking over my shoulder.

In a message to Clark on Saturday morning, Lucas affected a doughty determination. "Will go all out tomorrow," he signaled, "or at once, if conditions warrant." As Alexander had urged, risks must be taken.

The brightest news awaiting Clark at Anzio was not on the beachhead but a mile above it. On January 27 and 28, an obscure fighter unit, known formally as the 99th Fighter Squadron (Separate), made its first significant mark in combat with guns blazing, shooting down twelve German aircraft. Inspiriting as the action was for Lucas's corps, the contribution of a couple dozen black pilots—known collectively as the Tuskegee airmen, after the Alabama field where they had learned to fly—would resonate beyond the beachhead, beyond Italy, and beyond the war.

This moment had been a long time coming. Blacks had fought in every American war since the Revolution; of more than 200,000 to serve in Union uniforms during the Civil War, 33,000 had been killed. After the war, Congress created four black Army regiments, including two cavalry units later known to High Plains Indians as "buffalo soldiers" because of the supposed resemblance of the troopers' hair to a bison's coat.

More than one million blacks also served in uniform in World War I, but only fifty thousand saw combat. The white commander of one black unit denounced his troops as "hopelessly inferior, lazy, slothful. . . . If you need combat soldiers, and especially if you need them in a hurry, don't put your time upon Negroes." A lieutenant colonel quoted in a 1924 War Department study articulated the prevalent white bias: "The Negro race is thousands of years behind the Caucasian race in the higher psychic development." Between the world wars, military camps in the American south increasingly adopted local Jim Crow laws and customs; a War Department directive in 1936 appended the designation "colored" to any unit composed of nonwhite troops.

There were not many. When World War II began in September 1939, fewer than four thousand blacks served in the U.S. Army; more than two years later, the U.S. Navy had only six black sailors—excluding mess stewards—plus a couple of dozen others coming out of retirement. A seven-point White House policy issued in 1940 began with the premise that "Negro personnel in the Army will be proportionate to that in the general population (about 10 percent)" and ended with a bigot's pledge: "Racial segregation will be maintained." Few leadership opportunities existed. At the time of the Anzio landings, the U.S. Army had 633,000 officers, of whom only 4,500 were black. The U.S. Navy was worse, with 82,000 black enlisted sailors and no black officers; the Marine Corps, which had rejected all black enlistments until President Roosevelt intervened, would not commission its first black officer until several months after the war ended.

Another War Department decree of 1940 asserted that segregation "has proven satisfactory over a long period of years." A survey of white enlisted men in 1942 revealed "a strong prejudice against sharing recreation, theater, or post exchange facilities with Negroes"; of southern soldiers polled, only 4 percent favored equal PX privileges for their black comrades. White soldiers "have pronounced views with respect to the Negro," the adjutant general concluded. "The Army is not a sociological laboratory." Segregation created perverse redundancies—an Army memo in July 1943 noted that "the 93rd Division has three bands, and the 92nd Division has four bands"—but the status quo obtained. "Experiments within the Army in the solution of social problems are fraught with danger to efficiency, discipline, and morale," George Marshall warned.

The 1940 Draft Act banned racial discrimination, but only 250 blacks sat on the nation's 6,400 draft boards; most southern states forbade *any* African-American board members. White America's treatment of the hundreds of thousands of black volunteers and draftees ranged from unfortunate to despicable. The Mississippi congressional delegation asked the War Department to keep all black officers out of the state for the duration. Discrimination and segregation remained the rule in military barracks, churches, swimming pools, libraries, and service clubs. German and Italian prisoner trustees could use the post exchange at Fort Benning, Georgia; black U.S. Army soldiers could not. *Time* reported that "Negro troops being shipped through El Paso, Texas, were barred from the Harvey House restaurant at the depot and were given cold handouts. They could see German prisoners of war seated in the restaurant and fed hot food." A War Department pamphlet, "Command of Negro Troops," advised white officers in February 1944 that black soldiers preferred not to be called "boy, darky, nigger, aunty, mammy, nigress, and uncle." Churning resentment led to bloody confrontations between white and black troops, not only in the Deep South but also in Detroit, Los Angeles, New York, Arizona, and England. When a whites-only café in South Carolina refused service to sixteen black officers, they shouted, "Heil, Hitler!" Many blacks endorsed the "Double V" campaign proposed by a Pittsburgh newspaper: a righteous struggle for victory over both enemies abroad and racism at home.

Yet getting into the fight was itself a struggle. Among the prevalent stereotypes was a belief that blacks were too dumb, too lazy, or too apathetic to serve as combat troops. An Army study decried their "lack of education and mechanical skill," as well as "a venereal rate eight to ten times that of white troops, a tendency to abuse equipment, lack of interest in the war, and particularly among northern troops a concern for racial 'rights,' which often culminated in rioting." In the summer of 1943, only 17 percent of black soldiers were high school graduates, compared with 41 percent of whites. In Army tests that measured educational achievement rather than native intelligence, more than four in five blacks scored in the lowest two categories compared to fewer than one in three whites. General McNair, the chief of Army Ground Forces, declared that "a colored division is too great a concentration of Negroes to be effective."

Consequently, blacks were shunted into quartermaster companies for duty as truck drivers, bakers, launderers, laborers, and the like. By January 1944, 755,000 blacks wore Army uniforms—they made up 8.5 percent of the force—but only two in ten served in combat units compared to four in ten whites. Under pressure from black civic leaders and a crying need for fighters, three black Army divisions had been created: the 2nd Cavalry, which arrived in North Africa only to be disbanded to provide service troops; the 93rd Infantry, shipped to the Pacific; and the 92nd Infantry, which would arrive in Italy in late summer 1944 as the only African-American division to see combat in Europe.

Officered above the platoon level almost exclusively by whites, the 92nd would endure trials by fire that only partly involved the Germans. Training was halted for two months to teach the men to read, since illiteracy in the division exceeded 60 percent. A black veteran later described "an intangible, elusive undercurrent of resentment, bitterness, even despair and hopelessness among black officers and enlisted men in the division." That sentiment in some measure could be laid at the feet of the 92nd commander, Major General Edward M. Almond, an overbearing Virginian who would oppose integration of the armed forces until his dying day in 1975. "The white man . . . is willing to die for patriotic reasons. The Negro is not," Almond declared. "No white man wants to be accused of leaving the battle line. The Negro doesn't care. . . . People think that being from the south we don't like Negroes. Not at all. But we understand his capabilities. And we don't want to sit at the table with them." In a top secret report after the war, Almond asserted that black officers lacked "pride, aggressiveness, [and] a sense of responsibility." His chief of staff added, "Negro soldiers learn slowly and forget quickly."

Such obstacles and more faced the 99th Fighter Squadron. Before the war, only nine black Americans possessed commercial pilot certificates, and fewer than three hundred had private licenses. Training began at Tuskegee Army Air Field in July 1941; the first pilots received their wings the following spring, then waited a year before deploying to North Africa as the only black AAF unit in a combat zone. Commanding the squadron was Lieutenant Colonel Benjamin O. Davis, Jr., the thirty-year-old son of the Army's sole black general. Young Davis at West Point had endured four years of silence from classmates who refused to speak to him because of his race, reducing him to what he called "an invisible man." From that ordeal, and from the segregated toilets, theaters, and clubs at Tuskegee, Davis concluded that blacks "could best overcome racist attitudes through their achievements," including prowess in the cockpit.

Those achievements proved hard to come by. A week before the invasion of Sicily, a black lieutenant shot down an enemy plane over the Mediterranean. But for months thereafter the 99th was relegated to such routine duty that not a single Axis aircraft was encountered, much less destroyed. Accidents killed several pilots, and the squadron earned a hard-luck reputation. White superiors voiced doubts about "a lack of aggressive spirit," and accused the Tuskegee pilots of shortcomings in stamina, endurance, and cold-weather tolerance. "The negro type has not the proper reflexes to make a first-class fighter pilot," one general asserted. Hap Arnold, the AAF chief, suggested moving the 99th to a rear area, "thus releasing a white squadron for a forward combat area." Citing leaked classified information, *Time* reported in late September that "the top air command was not altogether satisfied with the 99th's performance."

Davis, who was promoted to command an all-black fighter group, returned to Washington to refute the criticisms before a War Department committee in October. Others rallied to the squadron's defense, including one accomplished white pilot who described the 99th as "a collection of born dive bombers." Lieutenant General Ira C. Eaker, the senior American airman in the Mediterranean, concluded that "90 percent of the trouble with Negro troops was the fault of the whites." The 99th moved closer to the action at an airfield outside Naples. Still, the squadron in six months had flown nearly 1,400 sorties on 225 missions without downing a single Luftwaffe plane.

Then came the morning of January 27. A patrol of sixteen P-40 Warhawks led by Lieutenant Clarence Jamison flew at five thousand feet over Peter Beach, several miles north of Anzio, just as fifteen FW-190s pulled out of an attack on the Allied anchorage. The Warhawks heeled over in a compact dive, each pilot firing short bursts from his half dozen .50-caliber machine guns. "I saw a Focke-Wulfe 190 and jumped directly on his tail," Lieutenant Willie Ashley, Jr., later reported. "I started firing at close range, so close that I could see the pilot." Flames spurted from the enemy fuselage, then from another and another. One Luftwaffe pilot dove to the treetops and fled toward Rome only to clip the earth in a flaming cartwheel. Bullets raked a fifth Focke-Wulfe from nose to tail until the plane fluttered in a momentary stall, then fell off on one flaming wing. "The whole show lasted less than five minutes," Major Spanky Roberts said. "It was a chasing battle, as the Germans were always on the move. We poured hell into them."

After refueling in Naples, the 99th returned to the beachhead, then in another snarling dogfight at 2:25 P.M. shot down three more enemy raiders, including one plane that was bushwacked while closing on a Warhawk's tail. On Friday morning, as Clark struggled to reach Nettuno on *PT-201*, the 99th slammed into another raiding party, shooting down four. In two days the squadron tallied twelve enemy planes destroyed, three probable kills, and four damaged. A single American pilot was killed.

It was a chasing battle, as Major Roberts had said, and it would remain a chasing battle. But nothing would ever be quite the same. One black soldier, fated to die in action in Italy a year later, wrote home: "Negroes are doing their bit here, their supreme bit, not for glory, not for honor, but for, I think, the generation that will come."

## *Jerryland*

O N Saturday afternoon, January 29, Lucian Truscott limped up the narrow staircase to the second floor of his new command post, an old stone monastery with a red tile roof in the medieval village of Conca, midway between Nettuno and Cisterna. Gum trees and sycamores gave the compound an arboreal tranquillity, dispelled by the proximate grumble of artillery. A squat tower resembling a blockhouse poked above the roofline; from the peak an American flag had briefly flown until German gunners began using it as an aiming stake. The 3rd Division war room filled the first floor with maps, jangling phones, and the anticipatory hum that always preceded a big offensive. Truscott had spread his bedroll in the tiled kitchen with no expectation of sleep.

He still spoke in a raspy whisper, although his morbid throat had improved along with his lacerated leg: on Monday afternoon, a falling 20mm antiaircraft round had detonated six inches from Truscott's left foot, peppering his cavalry boot, breeches, and ankle with steel fragments. After a surgeon tweezed out the shards, General Lucas insisted on handing him a Purple Heart. "It is truly superficial, but the doctors have my foot so strapped up that I hobble a bit when I walk," Truscott wrote Sarah a day later. As for the Anzio landings, he told her, no one at home should assume "that the war is about over. Far from it, believe me." He asked her to send his copy of *The Life and Morals of Jesus of Nazareth*, the rationalist edition of the New

Testament compiled by Thomas Jefferson beginning in 1804. The Jefferson Bible, as it was commonly called, seemed like good beachhead reading.

A window with casement shutters on the second floor gave Truscott a sweeping view across the Pontine Marshes. The west branch of the Mussolini Canal snaked through the farm fields a mile ahead. From Conca, the northbound road crossed the canal on a plank bridge and ran for three more miles to Isola Bella, a hamlet that marked the beachhead's outer boundary. Two miles farther on lay Highway 7 and Cisterna, known to St. Paul as Three Taverns. Here, while under arrest en route to Rome in the first century, the apostle "thanked God and took courage" after encountering a band of Roman Christians. Modern Cisterna lay at the confluence of five major roads and a rail line. Truscott on Wednesday had suggested seizing the town immediately, using his entire division along with British troops and a newly arrived regiment from the 45th Division. But Lucas preferred to wait until more tanks from the 1st Armored Division arrived to lend heft to the British effort on the left, which offered a more direct route to the Colli Laziali and Rome.

The delay hardly seemed imprudent. Prisoner interrogations and captured German diaries depicted a glum, disheartened enemy. "Spirits are not particularly high since 4½ years of war start to get on your nerves," a soldier in the Wehrmacht's 71st Division had written on January 26. Two days later, one of his comrades added, "The air roars and whistles. Shells explode all around us. Since January 21 I have not been able to take my boots off." This morning's 3rd Division intelligence report noted that "the enemy's attitude on our front is entirely defensive," with most forces hugging the hills five miles beyond Cisterna. Enemy "patrolling has not been aggressive. . . . There is evidence that [German] platoon and squad leadership has begun to deteriorate." Hermann Göring troops manned "our right flank and front," with a few other units fed "into the line piecemeal as they have arrived. . . . It does not now seem probable that the enemy will soon deliver a major counterattack involving units of division size." The VI Corps attack, originally planned for early this morning, January 29, had been postponed until the following morning because of an unfortunate incident in the British sector: on Friday, three jeeps carrying officers from the 5th Grenadier Guards had missed a turn on the road to Campoleone and blundered into a German ambush. Seven men were killed or captured, and with four Grenadier companies now stripped to only four officers, General Penney requested another day to organize his attack. Lucas agreed. Again, it hardly seemed to matter.

Truscott scanned the fenny landscape with his field glasses, unaware that the intelligence assessment was delusional or that the additional delay would carry baneful consequences. Kesselring had planned a massive counterattack for January 28, then chose a four-day postponement to bring more reinforcements through the Brenner Pass. Allied air attacks had temporarily snipped the rail lines across northern Italy, but because foul weather obscured rail targets for at least half of all heavy bombing sorties, Wehrmacht troops and supplies leaked through to the beachhead. On this very evening, the 26th Panzer Division would arrive in force from the Adriatic front, "a possibility that we had not seriously considered," Clark later confessed. Several thousand additional Germans shored up the thin Hermann Göring line at Cisterna, so that instead of encountering one division along a broad front on Sunday morning, Darby's Rangers and Truscott's infantry would find two. Eleven battalions defended Cisterna, roughly threefold the expected force. All told, German forces encircling the beachhead exceeded 71,000 men in 33 battalions, with 238 field guns. As General Penney noted in his diary, "The Germans don't let mistakes go unpunished and don't give second chances."

Birds sang in the marsh grass and a pale sun glinted off the brimming irrigation ditches. Here and there a soldier scurried from one soggy copse to another. Outside the Conca monastery, graceful sycamore branches nodded in the breeze. Truscott saw it all, and he saw nothing. He clumped down the stairs to finish his plan.

Darby's Rangers spent Saturday afternoon in a piney wood near Nettuno sharpening their blades, cleaning their rifles, and napping on pine-bough beds. A week on the beachhead had left them "solemn, tired, and quiet," one Ranger recalled. Few had shaved since sailing from Pozzuoli—a disgusted paratrooper wrote that they "looked like cutthroats [or] the sweepings of the bar rooms"—and company barbers stayed busy until the light failed. Each rifleman stuffed his pockets with grenades and coiled two extra bandoliers over his shoulders, removing the tracer rounds to avoid pinpointing a shooter's position at night. Bedrolls and barracks bags were stacked on a canvas ground cloth in the custody of the company cooks; souvenirs accumulated since Gela and Maiori were carefully tucked away: a German knife, a British Commando cap, a pumice fragment from Vesuvius. Mail arrived late Saturday, but with no time for mail call—a Ranger never carried personal letters into combat—the clerks promised to haul the sacks to Cisterna on Sunday morning. Teamsters from Nettuno also brought up extra ammunition. Shells rattled in the truck beds like dry bones.

Darby had been busy since dawn. After a war council with his three battalion commanders, at one P.M. he conferred with Truscott in the Conca monastery, then scouted the road to Isola Bella. His 4th Battalion, led by an eight-man minesweeping crew, would press down that road at two A.M. on Sunday, opening a path toward Cisterna for heavy weapons and supplies. The 1st and 3rd Battalions would creep up the Pantano *fosso*, a deep irrigation ditch that roughly paralleled the road from the Mussolini Canal to within a mile of Cisterna. Ranger infiltration had succeeded admirably in Tunisia, and Darby stressed "avoiding contact with the enemy" as long as possible through the terrain the Rangers now called Jerryland. Behind the Ranger spearhead, Truscott's 7th Infantry Regiment on the left and 15th Infantry on the right would advance on a seven-mile front, to cut Highway 7 north and south of Cisterna.

While careful to display only robust confidence to his men, Darby felt uncommon ambivalence about this evening's mission. The size of the attack heartened him, as did intelligence suggesting the road to Cisterna was lightly held, perhaps by a German infantry regiment protecting artillery and antitank batteries. An OSS agent—one of several anti-Fascists recruited in Naples and living in a Nettuno barracks equipped with a radio and a Ping-Pong table—had just returned from two days behind the lines to report seeing only four enemy battalions along the Conca–Cisterna corridor. The Rangers seemed indomitable. When Darby asked a young private first class if he was nervous, the soldier replied, "I'm not nervous, sir. I'm just shaking with patriotism." They were "the finest body of troops ever gathered together," Darby had told an OSS officer. "They don't surrender either. They fight for keeps."

Yet the expansion of the force from one battalion to three, and the loss of veteran Rangers since the TORCH landings fifteen months earlier, had led to deterioration in fighting skills, noise discipline, and fieldcraft. Too many men still bunched up when moving cross-country, or failed to freeze when a flare popped. How many knew to muffle a canteen with an old sock, or to suppress a cough with fingers pressed on the Adam's apple, or to dull a helmet's gleam with mud or wood smoke?

The Cisterna plan also nagged at Darby. Was it too risky, too bold? Would Truscott's infantry quickly reinforce the Ranger infiltrators? No Ranger reconnaissance had been possible past Isola Bella for fear of alerting the Germans. Aerial photos had seemed to show fields crisscrossed with hedgerows, which instead proved to be briar-choked irrigation ditches. The loss on Wednesday of two mortar companies aboard the ill-fated *LST 422* had been a blow, and this afternoon Darby realized that the ground was too boggy for other mortarmen to negotiate the Pantano Ditch; the heavy tubes instead would have to come up the road behind the 4th Battalion, along with the machine guns. Finally, a new fragment of intelligence had arrived an hour after sunset, at 6:35 P.M.: "The city may have considerable opposition."

By then the men had begun to filter out of their pine redoubt, singing "Pistol Packin' Mama" as they shambled under an overcast sky in columns of twos toward the line of departure, seven miles north. Usually the passwords chosen for an operation contained sounds difficult for German-speakers to pronounce: the "th" in "thistle" or the rolling "r" in "price." Tonight's challenge-and-parole was simple: "bitter/sweet." Upon reaching Cisterna—known by the unfortunate code-name EASY—the Rangers were to loft several red Very flares to signal their success.

The singing ceased. "Morale of men was excellent," the 1st Battalion log noted. The 3rd Battalion commander, Major Alvah H. Miller, had recently written a poem describing a walk through the Ranger bivouac late at night, listening to the sounds of his slumbering men: one laughs aloud, playing with the son he has never seen; another murmurs his wife's name, Marilyn; another whimpers under dreamy shell fire that unsettles his sleep.

At midnight, Darby met for a final time with his battalion commanders beside the Conca road. The officers stamped their feet against the biting cold as he reminded them to maintain radio silence for as long as possible.

Good luck, Darby told them. With his rolling gait, elbows cocked, he strode to an isolated farmhouse on the right side of the road where his command post had been set up. The commanders rejoined their waiting troops, blue and vague in the moonless night. Only their eyes glinted from faces daubed with burnt cork. Beyond the Mussolini Canal, four miles from Cisterna, the three battalions separated. The 4th veered left toward the road. The 1st and 3rd tramped single file across a fallow field. Soon the column descended into the Pantano Ditch, like a snake slithering into a hole. The officers took compass readings by matchlight, then pressed north.

At three A.M., near Isola Bella, barely half a mile up the Conca road, the 4th Battalion found trouble. A long burst from a German machine pistol tore open the night, and sheets of fire soon poured from several red farm buildings. One Ranger company was pinned down three hundred yards east of the road; fifteen minutes later a second company was immobilized. Enemy rifle pits had been dug every thirty feet and stiffened by machine-gun nests at hundred-yard intervals. Grazing fire swarmed a foot off the ground, killing a Ranger captain, among others. Mortar rounds stomped across a landscape that soon reeked of blown powder and turned earth. A crude roadblock built from two wrecked jeeps and an Italian truck halted the rest of the battalion, and for the rest of the night three hundred Rangers lay flat in their icy furrows, shooting at muzzle flashes fifty yards away. Worse yet, in the Anzio anchorage twelve miles distant a burning ammunition ship exploded at four A.M. in a white pillar of flame, casting long shadows across the Conca road and backlighting the Rangers for enemy snipers. From his farmhouse command post, Darby kept an ear cocked to the commotion two thousand yards north. "This was the first intimation," he later wrote, "that all was not well."

All was not well in the Pantano Ditch, either. Eight hundred helmets bobbed just below field level as the mile-long column meandered through the muddy scarp, often knee-deep in black water. "We could hear mortar and artillery barrages landing to our left flank," a Ranger later reported. "Someone whispered, 'The 4th must be having a bad time.' " Two miles from Cisterna, the 1st Battalion commander, Major Jack Dobson, realized that the 3rd Battalion had fallen behind. Ordering three companies to wait, Dobson pressed ahead with his other three. A runner dispatched to find the missing Rangers soon returned with inauspicious news: Alvah Miller, the 3rd Battalion poet-commander, had been blown to pieces by a point-blank panzer shell in a chance encounter at a German outpost. Avenging Rangers fired the tank with sticky grenades, but the column had been sundered.

Dobson's vanguard of 150 Rangers crept past a pair of Nebelwerfer batteries, near enough to hear German voices and to see whip antennas silhouetted against the sky. A mile from Cisterna, the ditch angled northwest to end in a culvert under the Conca road. German vehicles whizzed past in both directions, and a pair of self-propelled guns two hundred yards away fired at the beachhead with a monotonous thud. In hushed tones, Dobson tried to reach Darby by radio; the enemy force appeared much larger than expected, and with Miller dead perhaps it made sense to swing both battalions to the east, where the Mussolini Canal could shield their flank. After ten minutes, unable to raise the command post, Dobson cradled the handset. Without Darby's approval, he could not alter the plan.

Across the road the Rangers stole, melting into an olive orchard on the far side. A German sentry flopped beneath a silver bough, blood cascading from his slashed throat. Tendrils of gray light began to bleach the eastern sky. Dobson swerved north on a trail parallel to the Conca road, the Rangers now at a trot, racing the dawn. A shout carried, then another, then a gunshot. Dark figures wrapped in blankets rose from the earth, stumbling about as Dobson's men realized they had blundered into a German camp. Another sentry fell with his throat opened in a crimson crescent, screaming to wake the living and the dead alike. The mêlée spread across the bivouac—"chaos compounded," in one description—and the pulpy sound of plunging knives and bayonets could be heard between the grenade bursts and crackling rifles. "I emptied my M-1 so much and so fast that the wood [stock] was smoking," a Ranger later reported. The butt end of 1st Battalion scampered across the road toward the sound of the guns, followed by several companies from 3rd Battalion, including bazooka teams that shattered two tanks in a brilliant spray of orange flame.

Dawn, that harsh betrayer of predicaments, revealed this one. The Rangers occupied a triangular field half a mile across, bounded by the Conca road on the east, the Ponte Rotta road on the north, and a boggy skein of irrigation ditches to the west. Several hundred yards beyond the intersecting roads lay a rail embankment and the Cisterna train station. A ramshackle farmstead known as the Calcaprini house provided a command post for Dobson, who estimated that at least seven German machine guns now ranged his position from tree lines to the north and west.

Hardly had the Rangers begun to dig in than from the south came the creak of tank tracks. Certain that 4th Battalion had broken through with an armored spearhead, the men cheered lustily, until the underbrush parted to reveal the iron cross insignia of a Mk IV panzer.

"Then it opened up on us," Corporal Ben W. Mosier recalled. "After the first volley, you felt naked." Several self-propelled guns also clanked into view. Rangers swarmed forward. Shooting at vision slits, they leaped onto the hulls to lift the hatches and spray the crews with their tommy guns. Dobson shot a tank commander with his .45 pistol and flipped a white-phosphorus grenade into the turret. Milky smoke boiled from the vents; as he leaped from the tank, a bazooka round detonated against the bogie wheels, wounding him badly in the left hip.

From Highway 7 and the hills above Cisterna, German reinforcements boiled into the fight beneath an overcast sky that kept Allied warplanes at bay. Step by step the Rangers retreated until nine companies had squeezed into an exposed swatch three hundred yards across, just below the Ponte Rotta road; three others went to ground southeast of the main force. Wounded soldiers jammed a stone building near the Calcaprini house that had been converted to an aid station. As a German soldier crept toward the window with a grenade, medic Micky T. Romine shot him in the face with a .45. "I have shot that man a thousand times in my dreams," he later confessed. Panzer machine guns stitched the ditches and marsh brakes. "You could run about twenty yards and then hit the ground," Sergeant Thomas B. Fergen recalled. "If you waited longer, they got you." A Ranger severely wounded in the face asked Fergen to shoot him. "We're finished," he said, "and I don't want them to get me." Fergen shook his head. "Don't be crazy," he murmured.

Rangers held in reserve gave half their ammunition to comrades in the line, but by late morning precious little remained. German snipers fired from trees, houses, holes, and farm silos, each terrifying *pop!* punctuating the larger din. "The tracers were flying close enough to stop them with your hand," a Ranger said. A platoon leader shot in the chest sprayed blood with every breath; so many leaders had fallen that their inexperienced subordinates struggled to adjust artillery fires.

Shortly after noon someone cried, "Them bastards is giving up!" Three hundred yards to the south, a dozen captured Rangers from the 3rd Battalion walked with their hands high toward the Calcaprini house, trailed by a German paratrooper squad and a pair of armored personnel carriers. As the group approached, Rangers on the flanks opened fire, killing two guards. Other Germans bayoneted two American captives in the back. "Surrender," a voice called in accented English, "or we shall shoot the prisoners." More Rangers tossed aside their rifles and with hands raised joined the captives. When the ragged procession closed to within 150 yards of the command post, a Ranger "fired a shot into our column and killed one of our men," Captain Charles M. Shunstrom later recounted. "This one shot started everybody else firing, and the result was that two or three of our own men were killed in the column plus one or two German guards." The Germans scattered as grenadiers and armor crews "started to spray our column of prisoners with automatic fire." More Rangers surrendered, Shunstrom reported, and "even an attempt to stop them by shooting them failed."

Darby for several hours had labored under the sweet illusion that despite 4th Battalion's travails the infiltrators were "apparently okay," as he told Truscott's headquarters by phone. Shortly before five A.M., he added, "Things are going well." But by first light he was worried. At 6:15 he reported that the Ranger force "is having a hell of a time. There isn't any contact with my 1st and 3rd battalions." A reconnaissance troop barreling up the Conca road in jeeps hit "a solid sheet of machine gun fire and hand grenades"; of forty-three men, only one escaped capture or death.

News from Truscott's regiments was relentlessly grim. On Darby's flanks, the 7th Infantry and 15th Infantry were each to have infiltrated a battalion followed by tanks. The 1st Battalion of the 15th Infantry was pinned down immediately and by nightfall on January 30 had covered barely a mile. The 1st Battalion of the 7th Infantry fared even worse, struggling with barbed wire, steep ditches, German flares, and casualties that by sunset pared the unit from 800 men to 150. Sergeant Truman O. Olson, a machine gunner in B Company, fired more than three thousand rounds before being mortally wounded; he was among four 3rd Division soldiers awarded the Medal of Honor for valor at Cisterna, three of them posthumously.

At seven A.M., the first radio dispatch from Major Dobson—with word of Miller's death—told Darby that his entire command was at risk. An hour later, the news was even more dire, but the radio failed and not until early afternoon could signalers again raise the embattled Rangers at the Calcaprini house. A weepy 1st Battalion captain sounded so overwrought that Darby asked to speak to Sergeant Major Robert E. Ehalt, one of his original Rangers.

"Some of the fellows are giving up, Colonel." Ehalt spoke slowly, his voice steady. "We are awfully sorry. They can't help it, because we're running out of ammunition. But I ain't surrendering."

An eavesdropping stenographer at Conca jotted down Darby's frantic reply. "Shoot if they come any closer," he said. "Issue some orders but don't let the boys give up.... Who's walking in with their hands up? Don't let them do it! Get the officers to shoot.... Get the old men together and lam for it.... We're coming through.... Hang on to this radio until the last minute. How many men are still with you? Stick together."

Muffled gunfire crackled through the speaker. "They are coming into the building now," Ehalt said. "So long, Colonel. Maybe when it's all over I'll see you again."

"Use your head and do what is best," Darby said. "You're there and I'm here, unfortunately, and I can't help you. But whatever happens, God bless you.... God bless all of you."

Darby's voice thickened. "Ehalt, I leave everything in your hands," he said. "Tell the men I am with them to the end."

A moment later he phoned Truscott. "My old sergeant major stayed with the last ten men. It apparently was too much for them." Then, asking his staff to leave the room, Darby laid his head on his arms and sobbed. Sergeant Carlo Contrera, who had served as Darby's driver since North Africa, later observed, "He couldn't stand the thought of what was happening to them."

Truscott had stood watch on the second floor of his Conca monastery from two A.M. until first light on Sunday. To the north, German tracers flailed a landscape washed in cold flare light, and artillery flashes limned the horizon. "Situation is confused," noted the 3rd Division log. At dawn a fleet of Sherman tanks and tank destroyers lumbered up the Conca road.

"Smoke, dust, the tiny darting figures of men, a great cacophony," wrote another officer, watching through the upstairs casement.

Confusion and cacophony persisted all day. Teller mines halted the tanks just two hundred yards past the 4th Rangers at Isola Bella; eventually the German roadblock gave way, but an even stronger blocking position at Femina Morta—place of the dead woman—again thwarted the American drive. Darby's account of his conversation with Ehalt struck Truscott like a physical blow. "Whole show is folded," the division log recorded. "General very disturbed."

Litter bearers staggered back across the polders, "packing meat." Exhausted soldiers chewed malt and dextrose tablets, their eyelids "heavy as silver dollars," the mortarman Hans Juergensen wrote. Audie Murphy, now a sergeant and recently returned to the 3rd Division after a bout of malaria, described "jeeps drawing trailerloads of corpses. . . . Arms and legs bobble grotesquely over the sides of the vehicles." A German shell knocked Murphy senseless; upon regaining consciousness, he found the soldier next to him dead. "Living now becomes a matter of destiny, or pure luck," he wrote. "The medics are bloody as butchers. . . . I see one medic fall dead on a man whose wounds he was dressing. A scrap of metal severed his backbone."

For a renewed push on Monday, January 31, half a dozen generals crowded the Conca monastery, including Clark and Lucas. Lieutenant General Jacob L. Devers, visiting from Algiers, brought a bottle of Gilbey's gin for Truscott's throat, now "considerably worse" from too many cigarettes and too little sleep. Low clouds precluded air support, again, and the high command's hopes rested with Lieutenant Colonel Jack Toffey, whose 2nd Battalion of the 15th Infantry was to veer west of Isola Bella before driving north into Cisterna. Toffey had endured his own close calls at Anzio, escaping with a shredded field jacket and minor wounds when a mine demolished his jeep. "Generally decrepit but still in there punching okay," he wrote Helen on January 29. His men had deftly seized three bridges over the Mussolini Canal and destroyed four others. "Tired but sleepless; never loses aplomb or sense of humor," Will Lang jotted in his notebook after following Toffey across the beachhead. "Not a man to let a weapon sit around without using it."

"Toffey is rolling," a staff officer noted in the monastery at midday. Yet even with every weapon in the battalion blazing, the enemy entrenchment was too formidable. Toffey covered 2,500 yards, closing almost to the Calcaprini house before a German fusillade drove his troops to ground. On Toffey's left, riflemen from the 1st Battalion of the 7th Infantry crossed the rail tracks two miles northwest of Cisterna, a feat that would not be repeated for another four months; but by early Tuesday the battalion "barely existed as a fighting force," one captain reported. The enemy line buckled a bit, yielding a mile along a five-mile front, and more than two hundred German prisoners were seized around Femina Morta. Then the line stiffened. "All afternoon we throw ourselves against the enemy," Audie Murphy wrote. "If the suffering of men could do the job, the German lines would be split wide open. But not one real dent do we make."

The division was spent, and Truscott knew it. The final mile to Cisterna proved a mile too far. Some companies mustered fewer than two dozen men. Wary of a German counterattack, Truscott ordered his men to dig in and hold tight. He would give Toffey a Silver Star for "fearless leadership" in a lost cause.

As for the Rangers, the sanguinary weekend spilled into Monday. A mortar barrage hit the command post, killing Darby's intelligence officer and five enlisted men. Late in the day, his eyes red, haggard beyond his thirty-two years, Darby drove to the bivouac near the Mussolini Canal where hundreds of bedrolls and barracks bags stood piled on canvas ground cloths, neatly stenciled with the names and serial numbers of men who would never return to collect them.

Captured Rangers shuffled five abreast around Rome's Colosseum for the benefit of German photographers. Italian Fascists jeered and spat from their balconies as the column snaked off to temporary prison pens, including the grease pits in a Roman streetcar barn. A few escaped, but most would spend the duration in German camps like Stalag IIB, sharing huts with men captured a year earlier at Kasserine Pass. In mid-March, a thick stack of postcards would be mailed to wives and parents across America: "I am a prisoner in German captivity, but in perfect health."

The February 1 morning report for the 1st Ranger Battalion listed page after page of Rangers whose status was changed from "duty" to "MIA": Brown and Hendrickson, Hooks and Keough, Padilla and Perry and Hurtado and Buddenhagen. Of 767 men who had trekked up the Pantano Ditch with the 1st and 3rd Battalions, only 8 escaped the calamity at Cisterna. An estimated 250 to 300 were dead, and the others, including Sergeant Major Ehalt, had been captured. Moreover, the 4th Battalion suffered 50 percent casualties. Anglo-American losses on January 30 approached 1,500, more than double the D-day casualties at Salerno. German dead, wounded, and missing for the weekend exceeded 1,000. "The enemy has suffered heavily, but our own losses have been high," the Fourteenth Army log noted on January 31.

The hunt for scapegoats began promptly. Clark told his diary that he was "distressed" to discover that the lightly armed Rangers had been used to spearhead the 3rd Division attack at Cisterna, "a definite error in judgment." Clark blamed Truscott and contemplated relieving him until Lucas pointed out that as corps commander he had approved the plan, even though he was surprised to discover that Darby's infiltration tactic consisted of simply slogging up a ditch. The calamity remained secret for six weeks, when German newsreels of the captive Rangers and tales from the beachhead inspired febrile newspaper allusions to the Alamo and the Little Big Horn. An inquiry ordered by Clark made little headway—most witnesses were either dead or in German cages—and a VI Corps staff officer suggested that the massacre had been "contributed to by so many factors that it can be ascribed only to chance."

Today eclipsed yesterday, as it always did on the battlefield, and the high command turned to more pressing concerns. The beachhead on the VI Corps right had expanded roughly three miles in three days, while the British and the 1st Armored Division on the left had pushed a salient toward Campoleone four miles deep and two miles wide. Kesselring's counterpunch, postponed yet again because of the spoiling attack at Cisterna, had now been rescheduled for February 4, a fact gleaned by Clark a day in advance thanks to Ultra. In a radio message from Caserta, the army commander advised Lucas that orders to capture Cisterna were "rescinded. . . . You should now consolidate your beachhead and make suitable dispositions to meet an attack."

The war was far from over for Bill Darby, but it was finished for his 6615th Ranger Force. With three battalions all but obliterated, George Marshall disbanded the unit. In March, nearly two hundred surviving Ranger veterans from the original 1st Battalion would leave Naples for home to help train other units, including new Rangers bound for the cliffs at Normandy. Some 250 other survivors who had joined Darby more recently were transferred to Robert Frederick's 1st Special Service Force, now taking positions near the Mussolini Canal.

As his troops took up their entrenching tools and began to dig in, Lucas invited reporters to his upstairs suite at Piazza del Mercato 16 for a chat about battles past and future. Sitting in an armchair with his corncob before a blazing fire, speaking in a voice so low that those on the edge of the circle could barely hear him, the corps commander presented "the round face and the greying moustache of a kindly country solicitor," wrote Wynford Vaughan-Thomas, a BBC correspondent. In simply carving out a beachhead, VI Corps was already building toward six thousand casualties. "There was some suggestion that we should aim at getting to those hills,"

Lucas said, vaguely gesturing through the north window toward the Colli Laziali. He turned to his intelligence officer. "What's the name of them, Joe?"

But the enemy was strong, "far stronger than we had thought," Lucas continued. He paused, staring for a long moment into the hearth. Tiny flames danced across his spectacle lenses. "I'll tell you what, gentlemen," he said. "That German is a mighty tough fighter. Yes, a mighty tough fighter."

# 9. THE MURDER SPACE

## This World and the Next World at Strife

THE holy road up Monte Cassino made seven hairpin turns, each sharper than the one before. Hillside tombs and a Roman amphitheater stood below the first bend, along with remnants of Augustan prosperity from the ancient market town called Casinum. Wagon ruts still scored the paving stones, and the voluptuary Mark Antony was said by Cicero to have "indulged in his wild orgies" at a nearby villa. At the second turn, the Rocca Janula, the castle of a tenth-century abbot, stood above modern Cassino town "like a preacher above his congregation." Up and up the road climbed for six serpentine miles, through olive and scrub oak, on a track followed for centuries by pilgrims, poets, and armed encroachers. Each ascendant bend offered panoramas of the Rapido River and Mignano Gap to the south, and of the dreamy Liri Valley sweeping northwest toward Rome. The latter vista inspired one eleventh-century Italian versifier to scribble, "From here is the way to the apostolic city."

Rounding the last bend, fifteen hundred feet above the valley floor, the great abbey abruptly loomed on the pinnacle, trapezoidal and majestic, seven acres of Travertino stone with a façade twice as long as that of Buckingham Palace. On this acropolis, in an abandoned Roman tower, a wandering hermit named Benedict had arrived in A.D. 529. Born into a patrician family, the young cleric had fled licentious Rome, avoiding a poisoned chalice offered by rival monks and settling on this rocky knob with a desire only "to be agreeable to the Lord." Benedict's Rule gave form to Western monasticism by stressing piety, humility, and the gleaming "armor of obedience." Black-robed Benedictines not only spread the Gospel to flatland pagans, but also helped preserve Western culture through the crepuscular centuries ahead. It was said that Benedict died raising his arms to heaven in the spring of 547, entering paradise "on a bright street strewn with carpets." His bones and those of his twin sister, St. Scholastica, slept in a crypt hewn from his mountain eyrie. Over the span of fifteen centuries, the abbey had been demolished repeatedly—by Lombards, Saracens, earthquakes, and, in 1799, Napoleonic scoundrels—but it was always rebuilt in keeping with the motto *"Succisa Virescit"*: "Struck down, it comes to new life." After a visit to Monte Cassino, the poet Longfellow described the abbey as a place "where this world and the next world were at strife."

Never more than in February 1944. The town below had first been bombed on September 10, and within weeks more than a thousand refugees sheltered in the abbey with seventy monks. "To befoul the abbey," complained the abbot, Dom Gregorio Diamare, "was a poor way of showing gratitude." As the war drew nearer and wells ran dry, most civilians decamped for the hills or cities in the north. An Austrian lieutenant colonel, Julius Schlegel, who before the war had been an art historian and librarian, persuaded Diamarea to remove the abbey's art treasures for safekeeping. Throughout the late fall Wehrmacht trucks rolled up Highway 6 to the Castel Sant'Angelo in Rome, hauling treasures in packing cases cobbled together from wood found in an abandoned factory. The swag was breathtaking: Leonardo's *Leda;* vases and sculptures from ancient Pompeii; eighty thousand volumes and scrolls, including writings by Horace, Ovid, Virgil, and Seneca; oblong metal boxes containing manuscripts by Keats and Shelley; oils by Titian, Raphael, and Tintoretto; priestly vestments and sacramental vessels made by master goldsmiths; even the remains of Desiderius of Bertharius, murdered by Saracens in the eighth century. An immense thirteenth-century Sienese cross was "so large that it could only be carried diagonally across a lorry." The major bones of Benedict and Scholastica remained in their monastery crypt, but silk-clad reliquaries holding mortal fragments of the saints also went to Rome after a special blessing by the abbot. Two monks rode with every truck to keep the Germans honest; even so, fifteen crates went missing and later turned up in the Hermann Göring Division headquarters outside Berlin.

As the evacuation concluded, Monte Cassino on Hitler's orders became the linchpin of the Gustav Line. Kesselring in mid-December promised the Catholic hierarchy that no German soldier would enter the abbey, and an exclusion zone was traced around the building's outer walls. But day by day both the town and surrounding slopes became more heavily fortified. A Tenth Army order directed that *"allein das Gebäude auszusparen ist"*—only the building itself was to be spared—and Hitler in late December ordered that "the best reserves must stand on the mountain massif. In no circumstances may this be lost."

More observation posts and weapons pits pocked the south face. German engineers had acquired "every rock-drilling machine in the vicinity of greater Rome," a Wehrmacht officer reported. Sappers demolished abbey outbuildings and blew up selected houses in the town to improve fields of fire. More bunkers, pillboxes, and steel dugouts pocked the landscape; Italian laborers not forcibly press-ganged were offered tobacco bonuses to dig faster and deeper. Cassino schools had served as German field hospitals, full of groaning wounded from Sicily, then Salerno, then the Volturno, San Pietro, and a dozen other southern battlefields. But by late January rear-echelon units and civilians alike had fled the town, leaving only combat killers in their subterranean lairs, with orders to stand or die.

The first stray shell hit the abbey in mid-January. The monks went about their daily rituals, which began with matins before dawn. Seven more times during the day they assembled in the carved walnut choir stalls to recite the hours. The seventy-nine-year-old Abbot Diamare and his monks retreated to half a dozen rooms on two corridors of the lowest floor. German foragers confiscated fourteen cows and more than one hundred sheep, paying a pittance, and soon the remaining beasts, including goats, pigs, chickens, and donkeys, were given sanctuary in the abbey. An entry in the abbey log pleaded, "May God shorten these terrible days."

Hundreds of refugees sheltered against the outer walls, in farm buildings, and even in the rabbit warren. Artillery now rattled across the flanks of Monte Cassino, day and night, fraying nerves and killing innocents. A cannonade on the morning of Saturday, February 5, proved particularly unnerving. Forty terrified women rushed to the abbey's main gate, pleading for admission. Turned away by the reluctant monks, the women pounded on the oak door until their knuckles bled. "Insane with fear, they screamed, imploring asylum and even threatening to burn down the door," one account recorded.

The door swung open, the women rushed in. Soon dozens, then hundreds followed, until perhaps a thousand frightened people jammed the abbey. Fetid encampments sprung up in the porter's lodge and the post office, in the carpentry shop and the curia hall. Four hundred bivouacked on the abbey's grand staircase.

The monks chanted and prayed, seeking God's will in the liturgy of the hours. Day followed awful day, parsed by the rhythms of the divine office: matins, lauds, prime, terce, sext, none, vespers, compline. "Idleness is the enemy of the soul," Benedict had warned them. Beyond the stout walls, the artillery sang its canticles.

The failure of the frontal attack across the Rapido River had forced Mark Clark to look to his flanks in an effort to turn the Gustav Line. On the Fifth Army left, the British X Corps soon spent itself along the Garigliano, incurring four thousand casualties without substantive gains during the last two weeks of January. That left the "rain-sodden and dejected landscape" on the Fifth Army right. By driving west across a primordial outback of scarps and exposed saddles, Allied commanders hoped to outflank Monte Cassino and punch into the Liri Valley behind the abbey.

The French nearly won through. A force of mostly North African troops led by white officers had arrived in Italy, eighteen thousand strong and uniformed in U.S. Army twill. "Look for the fellow wearing the newest and best clothes, and he's sure to be French," one Yank grumbled. In bowing back the German line four miles in four days, the FEC—French Expeditionary Corps—had eviscerated a Wehrmacht mountain division. Under the command of a gallant Algerian, General Alphonse Pierre Juin, recognizable by both his Basque beret and his left-handed salute—his right arm had been maimed in 1915—the French renewed their attack on January 25. A day later, the 3rd Algerian Division occupied Monte Belvedere, five miles due north of Cassino and nearly as far inside the Gustav Line. French troops also briefly held Monte Abate above Belvedere, an escarpment so vital that Kesselring anticipated abandoning the entire Gustav Line if it fell.

"It is ordinary men who do the fighting," an officer in the 2nd Moroccan Division wrote, "and it is all on a human scale." Yet humanity was elusive in the Italian mountains. German barrages caused French troops to "scream out curses to the world in general," another officer reported. "That calmed them." An Algerian sergeant, whose skull was trepanned by shell fire, "ran screaming, tearing at his brains with his hands, and fell dead." A Tunisian lieutenant who had vowed to be first atop Point 862 also fell dead with a bullet in his forehead; three *tirailleurs* propped the body upright on a seat fashioned from a rifle stock and lugged him to the summit, "faithful to his oath."

Six German battalions, some reduced to a hundred men, counterattacked to plug the hole and recapture Abate. A French division log recorded: "Hill 700 has been taken by us four times. Hill 771 has been taken by us three times. Hill 915 has been taken by us and unsuccessfully counterattacked four times by the enemy." Parched colonials died while dashing to exposed mountain streams for a final sip of water; a note found on a dead French officer read, "Haven't eaten or drunk since we set out." Others survived by eating captured rations and firing captured munitions.

"The human mechanism has its limits," a French captain wrote in his diary shortly before a machine-gun bullet killed him. Juin reluctantly agreed. To Clark he wrote that his corps had dented the Gustav Line "at the cost of unbelievable efforts and great losses." One Algerian regiment alone had lost fourteen hundred men, including the commander. German losses amounted to a battalion each day, but Kesselring still held the high ground. To Juin's regret, the FEC "could do no more."

Now the thankless task fell to the Americans, specifically the 34th Infantry Division. Originally composed of Iowa and Minnesota National Guardsmen, the 34th in Tunisia had been much traduced before winning redemption at Hill 609 in the final days of the campaign; the division's newcomers included the 100th Infantry Battalion, fourteen hundred Japanese-American soldiers from Hawaii. Major General Charles W. Ryder, a fellow Kansan and West Point classmate of Eisenhower's, still led the division, as he had since TORCH. A tall man with big ears, full lips, and a sloping nose, "Doc" Ryder demonstrated a valor in the Great War—two Distinguished Service Crosses, a Silver Star, and a Purple Heart—that in this conflict was matched by his tactical acumen and level disposition.

As the French battered the Gustav Line on Ryder's right, the 34th attacked north of Cassino where the Rapido ran shallow enough to ford. For three days in late January, the riflemen struggled through plunging fire, minefields, and muddy sloughs. By midmorning on January 27, infantry troops and four Sherman tanks held two small bridgeheads across the river, while engineers corduroyed a road for armor reinforcements. Too late: by one P.M. all four Shermans were in flames, a jittery rifle company slid back down a hill it had just seized, and soon hundreds of soldiers were leaking to the rear in panic. Instead of five companies across the Rapido, Ryder had none.

The attack resumed farther north on January 29, only to stall while tank crews fired a thousand shells point-blank in an attempt to carve a ramp in the Rapido's steep far bank. A causeway hastily built with rocks proved more useful; some Shermans sank to their hulltops in mud, but nearly two dozen others gained the west bank. At five miles per hour the tanks crept forward in polar darkness, antipersonnel S-mines popping under their tracks like firecrackers. Each driver followed the faint glow from the tank exhaust pipe twenty yards ahead while a crewman in the turret repelled German boarders with bursts of tommy-gun fire. Riflemen followed in trail, finding shallow defilade against German artillery in the six-inch ruts cut by the tank tracks. Wraiths in field gray stole from their burrows and steel pillboxes—known to GIs as "crabs"—only to be shot down or captured; diehards were flushed with phosphorus. By Sunday evening, January 30, as the French drive sputtered, the Yanks held several key heights and the highland village of Cairo, three miles north of the abbey. "Believe we shall have Cassino by tomorrow night," General Keyes, the II Corps commander, told his diary on February 1. Clark cabled Alexander, "Present indications are that the Cassino heights will be captured very soon."

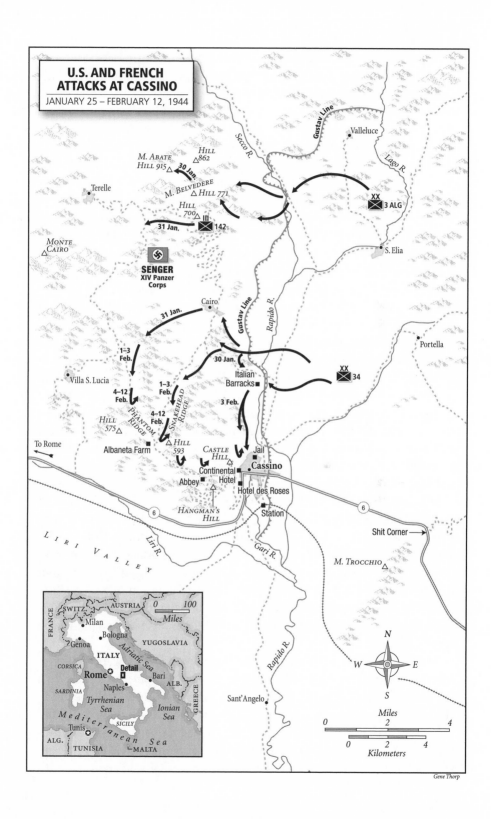

## U.S. AND FRENCH ATTACKS AT CASSINO

### JANUARY 25 – FEBRUARY 12, 1944

M. ABATE
HILL 915 △
HILL △ 862
30 Jan.

M. BELVEDERE
△ HILL 771

Terelle

HILL 700 △

31 Jan.    ⊠ 142

MONTE
CAIRO △

SENGER
XIV Panzer
Corps

Cairo
31 Jan.

1–3
Feb.

30 Jan.

Villa S. Lucia

1–3
Feb.

4–12
Feb.

Italian
Barracks

3 Feb.

HILL
575 △

4–12
Feb.

HILL
593 △

CASTLE
HILL △

Jail

Albaneta Farm

Continental
Hotel

Abbey

Cassino

Hotel des Roses

6

HANGMAN'S
HILL

Station

6

To Rome

Shit Corner →

M. TROCCHIO △

Secco R.

Gustav Line

Valleluce

Lago R.

XX
3 ALG

S. Elia

Portella

XX
34

Gustav Line

Rapido R.

L I R I   V A L L E Y

Liri R.

Gari R.

Rapido R.

Sant'Angelo

N
W    E
S

Miles
0        2        4

0        2        4
Kilometers

SWITZ.    AUSTRIA
FRANCE              0 ——— 100
Milan                    Miles
Bologna    YUGOSLAVIA
Genoa
ITALY        Adriatic Sea
CORSICA
Rome ✪    Detail
SARDINIA    Naples ● Bari    ALB.
Tyrrhenian    ● GREECE
Sea        Ionian
SICILY        Sea
ALG.    Tunis ✪
TUNISIA        MALTA    M e d i t e r r a n e a n   S e a

*Gene Thorp*

How pretty to think so. Kesselring had shifted the formidable 1st Parachute and 90th Panzer Grenadier Divisions from the Adriatic coast, increasing the Gustav Line defenses from four divisions to six by early February. The opposing armies, as Clark admitted in his diary, now resembled "two boxers in the ring, both about to collapse." By Thursday, February 3, Ryder's men had a toehold in the northern outskirts of Cassino town, clearing each house with grenade volleys and a sharp rush through the door. A day later a battalion from the 135th Infantry closed to within two hundred yards of the abbey; a patrol even brushed the building's eastern face and captured nineteen prisoners. Hills were won then lost, won then lost again, notably Point 593, known locally as Monte Calvario, a mile northeast of the abbey and the highest point on a critical saddle called Snakeshead Ridge. "Every day Cassino is reported taken, every night the rumor is disproved," a 34th Division ordnance officer told his diary.

Each yard, whether won or lost, pared away American strength. In a two-acre field diced by German artillery, survivors counted ninety bodies. Six new lieutenants arrived in the 2nd Battalion of the 135th Infantry; a day later just two remained standing. Medics jabbed morphine syrettes through olive-drab twill without taking time to roll up a sleeve; many kept their sulfa powder in salt shakers for easy dispensing. Snow dusted the dead, and the living woke in dank burrows to find their uniforms stiff with ice. By now few men still had their bedrolls; many had eaten nothing but iron rations and drunk only snowmelt for a week or more. A visiting New Zealand brigadier found the weatherbeaten 34th Division so hobbled by frozen feet that he considered the men incapable of launching another attack.

Still, they tried. In the first fortnight of February, three efforts were made to break through the final mile to the Liri Valley; each failed. On February 11 alone, fifteen hundred grenades could not dislodge German defenders from the cockpit of violence known as the Albaneta Farm, near Point 593; at the end of the day, two reinforcing battalions from the 36th Division mustered only 170 men together, one-tenth the authorized strength. Their regimental commander, who had survived the Rapido debacle three weeks earlier, was killed when a ricochet shell demolished his sandbagged command post.

A German corps commander believed the Americans were "within a bare 100 meters of success." Alexander and Clark had perhaps attacked on too broad a front, failing to exploit cracks in the Axis line with the requisite alacrity. Yet their men had given all they had to give. To eight thousand French casualties could be added ten thousand American; by mid-February, losses in the 34th Division's rifle companies totaled 65 percent. "Personally I'm glad we didn't take our objectives," a soldier in the 135th

Infantry wrote home, "else they would think us immortal and make us go on forever, despite fatigue, slaughter, almost annihilation." Allied field commanders looked to the heavens, averting their eyes from the carnage below. "Snow-clad Monte Cairo a beautiful pink," Keyes scribbled in his diary. "Full moon over the monastery."

Enemy flares also drifted above the abbey, hanging "as if suspended by invisible wires," one soldier wrote. A new mortar crew arrived at the front unaware that the building was a no-fire zone; a few rounds smacked the roof, provoking happy whoops from troops along the American line.

Early on February 14, the 4th Indian Division sidled forward to relieve the Americans. Scarecrow Yanks stumbled to the rear or were carried on stretchers, many unable to rise from their holes without help; the 34th Division alone used seven hundred litter bearers. Dead GIs lay stacked like sawed logs to await evacuation on mules that clopped uphill in long, steaming trains; the 34th Division also employed a thousand mules. "Thank God their mothers couldn't see the sadness and indignity of it all," a British officer wrote. A new arrival in the 141st Infantry, Lieutenant Harold Bond, found consolation in Shakespeare. "A man can die but once. We owe God a death," he recited, quoting Feeble in *Henry IV, Part 2.* "He that dies this year is quit for the next." Robert Capa, stumbling among slit trenches crammed with dead boys from the 34th Division, had murmured an invocation of his own: "I want to walk in the California sunshine and wear white shoes and white trousers."

As the Americans began to pull back a few miles to recuperate, a German courier bearing a white flag proposed a brief truce on February 14 to collect the dead near Cairo. Soon German soldiers fashioned litters from saplings and shelter halves; an American detail delivered 150 enemy corpses on bloodstained canvas stretchers and carried away an equal weight of comrades in olive drab. "There were bodies all over the hill and the odor was bad," a GI wrote in his diary. During a break the troops swapped cigarettes and family snapshots, chattering about Italian girls and favorite movie stars. An American officer asked *auf deutsch, "Wie geht's bei Hitler jetzt?"* Wrapped in a slate-blue overcoat, a redheaded sergeant from Hamburg shrugged. *"Gut, gut."* Rome was pleasant enough, the Germans advised, but the city "could not be compared with Berlin." From Monte Cassino came the rattle of musketry; the local cease-fire was scheduled to end at noon. *Auf wiedersehen,* they called to one another, trudging off with a last load of dead. *Goot bye.* A German soldier trotted forward for a final handshake. "It is such a tragedy, this life," he said.

Saddest of all were those who simply vanished, like Otto Henry Hanssen, known to the Army by serial number 37042492 but known to his family in

Monticello, Iowa, as Bud. The third of nine children, Hanssen had worked before the war as a farmhand for $10 a week. The pay was a bit better in the Army, and the job had heft: he had ascended to platoon sergeant in Company G of the 168th Infantry. A letter from the War Department reported Sergeant Hanssen missing after Germans ambushed his patrol near the abbey on February 4; the adjutant general expressed "heartfelt sympathy during the period of uncertainty." Almost a year later, a soldier who had lost a leg and had been captured in the same skirmish would write Hanssen's family after being medically repatriated from a German camp: "I'm very sorry that I have to tell you that I believe he was killed in action. . . . Us fellows when over there never thought of being killed." In April 1945, the government would declare that soldier 37042492 had died in combat—another comrade reported witnessing his death by gunfire—but his body was never found. Bud Hanssen was twenty-nine.

Ernie Pyle had joined Company E of the same battalion near Cassino. Two hundred men, mostly Iowans, had shipped overseas in the company two years before; only eight remained. Of those veterans, Pyle wrote:

> They had been at it so long they had become more soldier than civilian. Their life consisted wholly and solely of war. . . . They survived because the fates were kind to them, certainly—but also because they had become hard and immensely wise in animal-like ways of self-preservation.

Among the Company E old-timers was Sergeant Frank "Buck" Eversole, a twenty-eight-year-old former Iowa cowboy who had earned two Silver Stars and a Purple Heart, and who, like Hanssen, had risen to platoon sergeant. "I'm mighty sick of it all, but there ain't no use to complain," he told Pyle. Still, the losses frayed him. "I've got so I feel like it's me killin' 'em instead of a German. I've got so I feel like a murderer," Eversole said. "I hate to look at them when the new ones come in."

*I want to walk in the California sunshine and wear white shoes and white trousers.*

"They live and die so miserably and they do it with such determined acceptance that your admiration for them blinds you to the rest of the war," Pyle wrote in January. Few reporters were shrewder than Ernie Pyle, but his admiration may also have blinded him to frontline disaffection. After inspecting the Cassino front in early February at Alexander's request, Brigadier General Lyman L. Lemnitzer reported that morale was "becoming progressively worse," with troops "so disheartened as to be almost mutinous."

Certainly both life and death were miserable at Cassino, beginning at Shit Corner, where Highway 6 emerged from the shadow of Monte Trocchio. Every movement from that point north came under German observation; so many visiting officers from Naples and Caserta had blundered into the Cassino kill sack that British MPs posted a huge sign: "HALT! THIS IS THE FRONT LINE." Fifth Army replacements bound for that line later received an orientation booklet, which urged, "Don't be scared. . . . Remember that a lot of noise you hear is ours, and not dangerous." That soothing warrant was undercut by chapters titled "If You Get Hit" and "If a Buddy Gets Hit."

The lucky ones found shelter, perhaps a roofless ruin with a tarpaulin stretched overhead where they could cook supper over splintered sticks of furniture, nipping on the Canadian moonshine known as steam or cheap Italian cognac redolent of "perfume and gasoline." "We sit around quibbling and arguing like a bunch of old women about . . . whose turn it is to get water, who cooked up the last mess of eggs without cleaning the skillet, and who stood mail call last night," a sergeant from Indiana later wrote home. At night they might listen by wireless to Axis Sally, also known as the Berlin Bitch. "Who's sleeping with your wife tonight while you are over here fighting?" she purred before reciting, accurately, Fifth Army's daily passwords.

The unlucky crouched in damp sangars ringed with stone parapets or snow screens, so tormented by snipers that many hesitated to expose themselves even when authorized to strike for the rear. Royal Engineers in greatcoats and wool balaclavas kept the high passes open with wooden plows and rock salt, while skiers supplied the remoter outposts and evacuated the frostbitten. Infantrymen thawed their machine guns with matches and were advised to urinate, if necessary, on frozen rifles. An American tank officer, Lieutenant Colonel Henry E. Gardiner, catalogued his wardrobe in a February 7 diary entry: heavy underwear, "windproof slipover," wool shirt and trousers, sleeveless sweater, turtleneck gaiter, cotton socks, wool socks, one-piece coverall, combat jacket, tank boots, overshoes, wool cap, helmet, trench coat, and goggles. Winter clothing issued to frontline troops in January included kersey-lined trousers and 99,000 sets of what the quartermaster called "mittens, insert, trigger finger"; but "socks, arctic, wool" proved too thick for most GI boots, and parkas designed for Alaska were too bulky for riflemen scaling Italian mountains. An infantryman's lot, as one veteran observed, "is a life of extremes, either not enough or too much."

Rarely was the food excessive, in quantity or quality, although a porkchop dinner in mid-February provoked Colonel Gardiner to speculate that "the quartermaster must be running for reelection." More typical was a nurse's quip to her parents, "Our meat is dead but not edible." Some troops logged their deprivations. "I've had no fresh milk for nine months, no ice cream for ten months, no Coca-Cola for twelve months, no apple pie à la mode or lettuce-and-tomato sandwiches or chocolate malteds for over a year," one major complained. Lousy food contributed to the mutinous mood Lemnitzer observed. An engineer who referred to himself in the third person told his diary, "Sometimes it felt like he was fighting the whole fucking war by himself. Picks up his rifle, heads toward the line, swearing and burping peanut butter and jelly." Disaffected Tommies had their own cry from the heart: "What's the use of the food coming up if the tea's as cold as a corpse?"

As usual, frontline British troops paid more heed to personal hygiene than their Yankee cousins, who tended to be "disheveled, unshaven, unkempt," as a Royal Engineer officer noted. During lulls each Tommy was expected to whip out his razor, comb, and toothbrush so that "the outer man would be refurbished to the ultimate advantage and benefit of the inner." British tolerance for unorthodox battle dress also found free rein along the Gustav Line, where the finery included leather jerkins with extra sleeves cut from U.S. Army blankets, puttees made of empty sandbags and slathered with mud for insulation, soft-soled desert boots known as brothel creepers, and a sergeant major's hand muff sewn from a panther skin.

Artillery tormented everyone, aggravating the sense of isolation and life's caprice. Day and night the guns boomed, "regular as a scythe-stroke." One GI wrote, "There is something about heavy artillery that is inhuman and terribly frightening. You never know whether you are running away from it or into it. It is like the finger of God." Allied gunners fired 200,000 shells at Cassino in the first two weeks of February; the cannonade included new U.S. 240mm howitzers with a range of fourteen miles and a projectile weighing 360 pounds. A mortarman whose battalion had fired four thousand shells wrote his family, "That's sure a lot of war bonds." Cairo was said to be "the most heavily shelled pinpoint in Italy," but Cassino town, Shit Corner, Point 593, and other battered landmarks near the abbey vied for the title. An ambulance driver trying to sleep near an artillery battery told his diary in mid-February, "As the guns fire I feel as if someone is pounding the soles of my feet with a heavy board." Massed fires of sixty or more guns on a single target were known as serenades, bingos, stinkos, and stonks; open terrain exposed to complete artillery coverage was known as the murder space. White phosphorus particularly vexed the enemy: a captured German paratrooper document dated January 29 advised, "Extinguish burning clothing with wet blankets. . . . Scrape phosphorus particles from the body. Stretcher bearers must be issued olive oil. Wet earth gives some relief."

If less profligate, German artillery was just as vicious. GIs consigned to cramped immobility in their holes learned to relieve the overpressure from pounding shells by breathing hard with their mouths agape. A British gunner's diary for three consecutive days in January noted: "Digging and swearing"; then, "Digging and swearing"; then, "Digging finished. Swearing stops." Between barrages the carrion crows strutted and pecked, stiff-legged, unsentimental; when the rounds began to fall again, they rose in a flapping black gyre. "Keep your nut down," a veteran advised newly arriving troops. "Death-or-glory boys don't last."

Those who did last became hard and wise in the ways of war, as Pyle had seen. Cynicism sometimes helped. "Enlisted men expect everything to be fucked up," an American corporal explained. "It is a conceit founded on their experience from the day they are inducted." A British colonel concluded that most platoons under fire had a small number of "gutful men who go anywhere and do anything," plus a few who shirk and a majority "who will follow a short distance behind if they are well led." The "gutful men" who survived at Cassino needed cunning and luck as well as courage. "Use good judgment but use it fast," an Allied tactical study warned.

On few battlefields would soldiers endure harsher conditions or witness worse carnage. "Came across three dead GIs," a twenty-two-year-old American engineer told his diary. "They were killed by a shell concussion, skin on their face was burnt and rolled back, no eyelids or hair." Nearby, a German coal-scuttle helmet had "half a head still in it."

They found grace notes where they could: in the strains of Schubert's "Unfinished Symphony" picked up on the BBC; in a long letter from home, the pages radiant with what one officer called "bright beads of memory and of promise"; or in the apricot glow of another dawn, another dawn that they had lived to see, when the shelling had momentarily ceased and the world seemed new-made and uncorrupted.

A single rifle shot could break the spell. A 4th Indian Division signaler later wrote:

> The initial crack would be answered by a couple of shots which promoted a burst of Bren gunfire which bred a rapid stutter from the German light machine guns which started the mortars off, then the 25s and 88s and finally the mediums and heavies and the whole area would be dancing, booming and crashing.

And so the day began, much like the day before. In a letter to his family, Henry Gardiner summarized the Italian campaign in ten words: "He marched up the hill and he marched down again." But wherever they marched, or dug, or died, the abbey atop Monte Cassino seemed to loom over them. "You could never lose it," a British soldier reported; "it was always there looking at you." Another young British officer, Fred Majdalany, spoke for many: "That brooding monastery ate into our souls."

A new warlord arrived at Cassino in February, determined to burn and blast the enemy from the Gustav Line by whatever means necessary. As the Americans pulled back to regroup, the Kiwis, Indians, and Tommies moved in under the command of Lieutenant General Bernard C. Freyberg, a former dentist who had become one of the British empire's most celebrated soldier-generals. "The torch is now thrown to you," Al Gruenther told him in a telephone call from Caserta on February 11. Freyberg grunted. "We have had many torches thrown to us," he replied.

He was a great slab of a man, long known as Tiny. "I'm Freyberg the New Zealander," he would introduce himself, in a voice raspy as a gate hinge. "He seemed to be large all over, both broad and deep-chested at the same time," an admirer wrote. Freyberg's enormous head featured a prominent chin, a delicate nose, gray eyes, and, above the inverted parabola of his mouth, a tidy mustache for ornamentation. At age seventeen he had won the New Zealand long-distance swimming championship, and it was said that he could be mistaken for a porpoise in Wellington harbor. Decorations upholstered his massive chest, including a Victoria Cross from the Somme and four awards of the Distinguished Service Order, reflective of a reputation earned at the cannon's mouth in two wars. He believed that "a little shelling did everyone good"; one acquaintance thought "his great fearlessness owed something to a lack of imagination." From the Great War he had emerged with twenty-seven battle scars and gashes—"riddled like St. Sebastian," a friend said—and he would accumulate several more before this conflict ended. "You nearly always get two wounds for every bullet or splinter," he said with a shrug, "because mostly they go out as well as go in." One nurse insisted that he was made not of flesh but of india rubber. Between the wars physicians detected a "diastolic murmur," a diagnosis Freyberg challenged by demanding they climb Mount Snowdon together and reexamine him on the summit. "I love his lack of humour, his frank passion for fighting," a friend wrote of Freyberg in her diary. "There is a distinct grimness about him at all times."

Churchill in North Africa had anointed him "the salamander of the British empire" for his ability to thrive in fire, but Freyberg more resembled the hippogriff, that hybrid of eagle, lion, and horse. He was both sentimental—after digging the grave of his friend Rupert Brooke, he had lined it with flowering sage—and fond of aphorisms, including a line from another friend, J. M. Barrie, the author of *Peter Pan:* "God gave us memory so that we could have roses in December." Upon arriving in Naples he asked, "One used to be able to buy very fine gloves in Italy. Can you still get them?" His impulsiveness led one exasperated subordinate to tell another, "It will be your turn tomorrow to disobey orders."

Even his admirers acknowledged that Freyberg was at his most formidable when leading a division; temporary command of a corps in Africa seemed to overtax his powers, and he had reverted to command of the 2nd New Zealand Division after outflanking the Mareth Line in southern Tunisia. "Wouldn't it be nice if the general would think straight?" said his most talented Kiwi brigadier, Howard Kippenberger. "Or better still, if he wouldn't try to think at all?" Yet it was again as a corps commander that Freyberg arrived at Cassino, for Alexander in early February melded the 2nd New Zealand, the 4th Indian, and the British 78th Divisions into a new creation, the New Zealand Corps.

Described by one British observer as "clean and sprightly, rested and strong," the corps initially was called Spadger Force to confuse German intelligence; Freyberg remained "Spadger" in Allied councils long after the ruse ended. His Kiwis and Tommies were colorful enough, but few units could match the Indians for flamboyance. The Sikhs, Punjabis, Rajputs, Mahrattas, and Gurkhas, from Nepal, arriving in truck convoys resembled a traveling circus of cutthroats, laden, as one 4th Indian signaler wrote, with "all kind of excrescences such as crates of live chickens, fire buckets, water bags, bits of furniture and clothes drying in the wind."

At first Freyberg considered a wide flanking movement to breach the Gustav Line. But with a shortage of mules and limited experience in mountain warfare, he instead chose a more prosaic plan that followed in trace the failed American attack, targeting "the strongest point in a defensive line of remarkable strength," as the New Zealand official history later noted. To some subordinates, this scheme confirmed that Freyberg had "no brains and no imagination," in the phrase of the 4th Indian Division commander, Major General Francis Tuker. When two of his senior lieutenants proposed a conference on the tactical difficulties at Cassino, Freyberg refused to countenance "any soviet of division commanders."

Yet the longer Spadger studied the bleak silhouette of the ridgeline to the northwest, the more his eye was drawn to the white abbey. Was it possible to take the massif without seizing the building? Would German troops fail to occupy such an inviting observation post? How could Allied soldiers be asked to attack the hill without first eliminating that overbearing presence?

The 4th Indian Division had initially proposed bombing the abbey on February 4, as part of a scheme to reduce any German garrison "to helpless lunacy by sheer unending pounding for days and nights by air and artillery." Increasingly, Freyberg found that approach both prudent and inevitable. After a grim discussion about the challenge of storming the abbey's massive gate, he dispatched a subaltern to comb through Neapolitan bookstalls, where the young man found several studies on the history and structure of Monte Cassino. An 1879 volume contained architectural detail about how the abbey had been rebuilt as a citadel after the French despoliation in 1799, with loopholed, unscalable outer walls ten feet thick and nowhere less than fifteen feet high. A prewar Italian army staff college analysis deemed Monte Cassino impregnable.

Freyberg was convinced. In a memo to Clark and Alexander he wrote:

> No practicable means available within the capacity of field engineers can possibly cope with this place. It can be directly dealt with by applying blockbuster bombs from the air. . . . The fortress has been a thorn in our sides for many weeks.

Others disagreed. "Spadger still wants to flatten the monastery," Keyes told his diary. "I insist there is no evidence that it is holding up our attack and refuse to accede." Clark too demurred, although he sensed that Freyberg had General Alex's ear. Clark privately considered "Freyburg"—he consistently misspelled the New Zealander's name in his diary—"sort of a bull in a china closet."

Yet Clark was unsure how long he could resist pressure from above and below. Not least in his calculations was a growing bloodlust in Allied trenches. An antiaircraft gunner's letter home in mid-February perfectly expressed the prevailing sentiment. "I would level the Vatican itself with pleasure," the gunner wrote, "if there were Germans to be killed inside it."

## The Bitchhead

SIXTY miles away, the 92,000 Allied troops penned up at Anzio had been ordered to dig in, and dig in they did. The clank of picks and shovels sounded across the beachhead, and with each passing hour life became more subterranean. Soldiers near the Pontine Marshes found water weeping into their holes at eighteen inches, but those burrowing into the sandstone substrata around Nettuno excavated elaborate lairs lined with cardboard from ration cartons and furnished with plundered mirrors, commodes, and even candelabra. Some sheltered in huge empty wine barrels found in farmhouse vaults, the stink of stale *vino rosso* clinging to their uniforms. Catacombs and cellars also housed VI Corps offices—the sandstone seemed to telegraph every surface vibration and concussion—but engineers failed to find a tunnel rumored to have been built by Nero between Anzio and Rome. It all seemed vaguely familiar, as a 6th Gordons soldier noted in his diary:

> So back we go to World War I. Oozing thick mud. Tank hulks. The cold, God, the cold. Graves marked by a helmet, gashed with shrapnel. Shreds of barbed wire. Trees like broken fishbones.

An American medic in the 179th Infantry preferred to stress the positive. In a letter home he wrote, "My cost of living is very low."

Luftwaffe attacks made every man happy to have his hole. "We have found our religion," a soldier told his diary. "Jittery as can be. Five air raids tonight." Bombs punctured all fifteen ovens and damaged the dough mixer in the Army's beachhead bakery; eighty bakers in helmets sifted shrapnel from the flour, patched the holes, and soon turned out fourteen tons of bread a day. As on an island, everything at the beachhead arrived by sea. "Day and night, a thin black line of tiny boats moved constantly back and forth between shore and ships at anchor," wrote Ernie Pyle, who arrived for a visit in February. After German reconnaissance flights left each afternoon, skippers weighed anchor at last light to scramble the anchorage, steaming slowly to avoid raising telltale phosphorescent bow waves. Flares, tracers, and exploding shells illuminated Anzio harbor so garishly that one sailor claimed it was "brighter than Yankee Stadium." As they sailed back to Naples after another harrowing trip to the beachhead, LST crewmen sang, "Anzio, my Anzio, please don't take me back to Anzio."

Among the most exposed troops were those consigned to Hell's Half-Acre, the medical compound outside Nettuno and only six miles from frontline outposts. At 3:30 P.M. on February 7, a Luftwaffe bomber chased by a Spitfire jettisoned five antipersonnel bombs over the 95th Evacuation Hospital, where four hundred patients lay in ward tents. Newly wounded soldiers had just arrived by ambulance, and operating rooms were jammed when flame and steel swept the compound. "I went outside and saw several dead bodies in the parking area in front of the receiving tent," the hospital commander, Colonel Paul Sauer, reported. "One of the nurses in the first surgical tent was crying, 'I'm dying, I'm dying.' I went in to look at her and she was pulseless and white." Twenty-eight died, including three nurses, two doctors, and six patients; another sixty-four were wounded, and the blasts shredded twenty-nine ward tents. The German pilot was shot down and treated in the same hospital. Two days later, a shell fragment killed a VI Corps surgeon as he emerged from Lucas's command post in Nettuno.

"God, help us," a 1st Armored Division mess sergeant prayed after the hospital bombing. "You come yourself. Don't send Jesus. This is no place for children." By early February, General von Mackensen's Fourteenth Army had ringed the beachhead with 370 artillery tubes, putting every Allied soldier at risk—"like a dog on an iceberg," as a Fifth Army supply officer put it. Each German gun caliber sang a different tune, from the crying-cat noise of an 88mm to the railroad gun shells that were likened to "an outhouse going end-over-end with the door open and paper flapping." Shells killed bakers baking, cooks cooking, and clerks clerking. "Sometimes we heard them coming, and sometimes we didn't," Pyle wrote. "Sometimes we heard the shell whine after we heard it explode." One British officer described a near miss "as though someone had hurled a dining room table against my heart." All too often the fall of shot was followed with a cry, "Morphine, for God's sake, morphine." A company clerk confessed to a growing dislike for Italy: "Too much iron in the atmosphere here."

They did what they could. Deep holes grew deeper, including subterranean garages intended to reduce punctured tires and radiators. Every soldier learned the Anzio shuffle—also known as the Anzio amble or Anzio slouch—which required walking in a crouch, head hunched between the shoulders and helmet pulled low. Engineers clear-cut windbreaks along the Mussolini Canal to eliminate tree bursts, leaving the landscape as flat and shot-torn as Flanders. During one ferocious Nebelwerfer attack, a Scots Guardsman sang out, "The sons of the prophet were hardy and bold / And quite unaccustomed to fear," but an American tanker, lighting a new cigarette from the butt of another with trembling hands, philosophized, "You can't get used to bein' scared." Much discussion was devoted to the fabled "million-dollar wound," which would excuse a soldier from further combat. All agreed that it ought not be disfiguring and must not impair sexual function. "One ear could go, but not two," wrote Paul W. Brown, an enlisted medic who would become a professor of orthopedic surgery at Yale University Medical School. "Fingers and toes were deemed expendable, but no consensus was reached on how many." To channel anger and anxiety, riflemen zeroed their weapons by firing at the helmets of dead Teds—*tedeschi*—on a distant slope. A British company also organized a frontline shooting gallery for snipers, with targets sorted into "Large Teds," "Small Teds," "Crawling Teds," and "Bobbing Teds."

Each day new arrivals stepped onto the harbor jetty, where MPs barked, "Get moving, get moving!" They scurried past waterfront villas gnawed by shell fire—the masonry peeling "like sunburned skin," as the writer John Lardner put it—out to the "small, wet world" now known to its denizens as the Bitchhead. "You could see a squirt of white tracer and it seemed to float toward our lines. That was Jerry. Ours answered with bursts that had red tracer in them," a 3rd Division soldier recalled. Tommies veered to the left toward a sector called the Hatbox of Hell, where local landmarks were named for their shapes on a map or their ambiance: the Lobster Claw, Sheep Pen Farm, Piccadilly, Oh God Wadi. "I was alone in my lonely world," one British sergeant wrote. A British officer excessively steeped in the classics recalled his Virgil with each journey forward: *Facilis est descensus Averni*. Easy is the descent to Hell.

Yanks veered to the right, to a warren of trenches and hovels where young men wheezed like rheumy old men, scraping the muck from their uniforms with trench knives. Strange cries carried across no-man's-land, including a heartbreaking German voice: *"Otto, Otto! Ich sterbe, Otto!"* I'm dying, Otto. "Nerves became frayed," a lieutenant wrote. "The few abrasive personalities in the platoon seemed to become more abrasive." At a salvage dump outside Nettuno, quartermasters each day picked through truckloads of clothing and kit from soldiers killed or wounded—sorting heaps of shoes, goggles, forks, canteens, bloody leggings. "It was best not to look too closely at the great pile," advised Ernie Pyle. "Inanimate things can sometimes speak so forcefully."

Nearby, more trucks hauled the day's dead to a field sprouting white crosses and six-pointed stars. Grave diggers halted their poker game—the trestle-and-plywood table, in a bunker built from rail ties, could seat seven players—and hurried through their offices. Like the rest of the Bitchhead, the cemetery frequently came under fire, so burial services were short and often nocturnal. Grief was brief. The diggers tried to stay fifty holes ahead of demand, but keeping pace could be difficult when shells disinterred the dead, who required reburying.

Life went on, miserable and infinitely precious. "Remember," a gunner wrote in a note to himself, "it can never be as bad as it was at Anzio."

It got worse. Allied air attacks and the star-crossed American attack at Cisterna had disrupted Mackensen's timetable for reducing the beachhead, even as he massed 96,000 troops, nearly 100 tanks, and more than 200 heavy antitank and assault guns, plus all those artillery tubes. "Our grand strategy demands that the beachhead be wiped out promptly," Mackensen told his lieutenants, and they would begin by obliterating the exposed salient—four miles deep and two miles wide—held by the British 1st Division near Campoleone, on the VI Corps left.

The attack fell heaviest on the Irish Guards and 6th Gordons, positioned, respectively, on the left and right flanks of the salient. A thousand sheep, dragooned as minesweepers, led the German attack against the Irish Guards early on Friday morning, February 4. "Like a dirty, ragged wave, a huge flock surged over the crest of the Vallelata ridges and scampered crazily through No. 3 company," the battalion reported. Tanks and grenadiers followed the bleating vanguard through hard rain, threatening to trap the entire British 3rd Brigade by cinching the salient at its base. "The Germans are at the door," a British company commander radioed. Panzers demolished the rear walls of farmhouses, then drove inside to shoot through the front windows. Fire raked the Via Anziate. "I never saw so many people killed round me before in all my life," an Irish Guards corporal said later. Only valor and Allied artillery—VI Corps now massed 438 tubes, including 84 big guns on destroyers and cruisers—staved off annihilation. "You'd better get your boys out of it," Lucas advised Major General Penney, the 1st Division commander.

They retreated by the glare of burning hayricks. "All the shells in hell came down on us," a young soldier told the BBC. "Nothing but black smoke and what smelt like the stink of frying bodies." By Saturday morning nearly three miles was forfeit at a cost of fifteen hundred British casualties, including nine hundred captured; Mackensen's losses were also severe, with almost five hundred dead.

The attack resumed on Monday evening, February 7, and by midnight had spread through the badland gullies along the 24th Guards Brigade front. "Nothing heard of Number 1 company for forty-five minutes," a Grenadier Guards captain radioed. "Numbers 3 and 4 believed overrun. Ourselves surrounded, and there is a German on the ridge above me throwing grenades." By Tuesday enemy troops west of the Via Anziate held a key slope misnamed Buonriposo—place of good rest—and were hunting Tommies by looking for breath plumes in the frosty air. "It's very awkward," a Grenadier officer complained. "If we lie on our stomachs we are hit in the arse. If we lie on our backs we are hit in the balls." German infiltrators crept so close that British mortars fired almost vertically at targets only a hundred yards away. The sight of feral swine feeding on a dead comrade provoked an anguished sergeant to ask, "Is this what we are fighting for, to be eaten by pigs?"

Aided by a captured map that revealed British minefields, four German infantry regiments and Mk V Panther tanks swarmed toward the high ground at Carroceto, bagging another eight hundred prisoners on February 8.

A Scots Guards battalion held the Carroceto rail depot, with an observation post tucked into the stationmaster's apartment on the second floor; when two German platoons went to ground in a nearby ditch, the Scots propped a Vickers machine gun in the window, with bags of grain to steady the tripod, and slaughtered them. The enemy answered with a tank, which halted forty yards from the station and stitched each window and door with machine-gun fire at such close range that bullets chewed through brick; then the main gun opened, gouging great holes in the station walls until the staircase inside collapsed. "This was even more unpleasant," reported the Scots, who scrambled back three hundred yards to shelter behind a rail embankment.

More unpleasant yet was the loss by infiltration and frontal assault of Aprilia, the model Fascist town known as the Factory because a severe tower atop city hall gave the settlement an industrial aspect. By Wednesday evening, February 9, Wehrmacht troops held twenty buildings, including a police barracks, wine store, and theater; panzers refueled in the Piazza Roma, where a bronze St. Michael clutched a sword in one hand and a dragon's head in the other.

The salient was gone, the beachhead imperiled. Ominous noises drifted from the wadis and woodlands, the sounds of an enemy massing. "Where is the sea?" a captured German officer asked. "I just wanted to know, since you will all soon be in it."

On sleepless nights—and there were many now—John Lucas puffed his corncob and chatted with his watch officers about West Point, or Sherlock Holmes, or home sweet home. Rarely did he emerge from the VI Corps command post, now twenty feet beneath the Osteria dell'Artigliere, where engineers had punched through a wall to link two sets of cellars. Naked bulbs dangled above huge oak casks banded with iron hoops, and ramps for rolling barrels up to the Vicolo del Montano bracketed the steep steps to the sandbagged entrance. Staff officers hunched over plywood desks beneath the great stone arches, their brows furrowed as they pondered dispatches from the front. Jangling telephones echoed in the alcoves; even whispers carried to the dark corners of the crypt. A large wall map with grease pencil markings showed VI Corps positions in blue and the enemy in encroaching red. Clockwise around the semicircular perimeter the Allies stretched from U.S. 45th Division troops along the Moletta River, on the left; through British and U.S. 1st Armored Division regiments in the center; to American paratroopers, 3rd Division GIs, and 1st Special Service Forcemen on the right.

"The old Hun is getting ready to have a go at me," Lucas had advised his diary as the attack on the salient began. "He thinks he can drive me back into the ocean. Maybe so, but it will cost him money." The bravado dissolved as the salient melted away. "The situation changed so rapidly from offensive to defensive that I can't get my feet under me," he wrote. Although Allied air forces in the Mediterranean now exceeded twelve thousand planes—the largest air command in the world—clearly the effort to interdict German reinforcements had faltered: twenty-seven enemy battalions had already reached the beachhead from northern Italy, and an entire Wehrmacht division had traveled from southern France in just ten days. Lucas's own reinforcements failed to keep pace with his losses: of an average eight hundred Allied casualties each day—tantamount to a battalion— barely half were replaced. Lucas calculated that VI Corps was shrinking by nine thousand soldiers per month.

He blamed the cousins. "A terrible struggle all day trying to get the British to move," he told his diary on February 8. "I wish I had an American division in there." Blending the two nationalities produced a corps of "hermaphrodites." To Clark, a day later, he wrote, "My only present concern is the inability of one of my divisions to maintain its vigorous resistance." Clark had no doubt about *which* division; he derided General Penney—a meticulous, pious, high-strung engineer, who had been Alexander's chief signals officer in North Africa—as "a good telephone operator." When Clark confided that Lucas did not hold Penney in esteem, Alexander snapped, "Well, I do."

Lucas's disdain was fully reciprocated. "Complete gaff, no decision," Penney had told his diary after one rambling conference with Lucas. Later Penney added, "Quite infuriating delay and weakness . . . [Lucas] very vague and no corps order." Doubts about "Corncob Charlie," as the British now called him, had spread up the chain of command. "We'll lose the beachhead unless Lucas goes," Major General G.W.R. Templer, whose 56th Division was just arriving, warned Alexander. Even Whitehall was uneasy. "I trust you are satisfied with leaving Lucas in command at the bridgehead," Churchill cabled Alexander on February 10. "If not you should put someone there whom you trust." As each day ended without the ballyhooed sally into Rome, the prime minister grew ever more dour. The Allies now had eighteen thousand vehicles at the beachhead, he noted in a cable to Field Marshal Wilson in Algiers, adding, "We must have a great superiority in chauffeurs." No one bore greater responsibility for Anzio than Churchill, and he kept a pale eye peeled for possible scapegoats; a report from Washington that Marshall believed "Clark might be the man to go" intrigued him, but Lucas seemed the more likely candidate. "All this," the prime minister sighed, "has been a great disappointment to me."

As Mackensen tightened his grip on Aprilia and Carroceto, awaiting Hitler's personal authorization for his next move, the Allies struggled to regroup. At 5:30 A.M. on Thursday, February 10, Penney warned Lucas that the "situation cannot go on." His division had been halved. Some regiments were all but obliterated: more than three hundred North Staffords had been killed, wounded, or captured in eight hours, while the 5th Grenadier Guards had lost almost three-quarters of their eight hundred enlisted ranks, plus twenty-nine of thirty-five officers. In a tart note that afternoon, Penney asked Lucas for "the immediate corps plan, the corps plan for the future and the general programme, including the intentions of the higher command." In his diary, Lucas wrote, "Things get worse and worse."

He popped out of the command post long enough to brace the line with two reserve American infantry regiments from the 45th Division, the 179th and 180th. As usual, his plan lacked precision and nuance, having been drawn from a map rather than from careful reconnaissance. "Okay, Bill," he told the division commander, Major General William W. Eagles, "you give 'em the works. Go places." To Penney he wrote, "Reinforcements are on the way."

Too few, too late. A counterattack at dawn on Friday won a foothold in Aprilia's southeast corner, but poor coordination between U.S. rifle and tank companies hamstrung the assault. Grenadiers boiled from the Factory cellars, and panzers—followed by "deep ranks of gray-coated infantry"— drove the Yanks out on Saturday morning, February 12. A soldier in the 179th Infantry conceded, "The Germans just beat the holy hell out of us."

General Alex had long been celebrated for beachhead verve. His panache at Dunkirk was legendary, and his visitation during a dark hour at Salerno braced Yanks and Brits alike. Now he arrived, a deus ex machina, aboard a Royal Navy destroyer on Monday morning, February 14, wrapped in his fur-lined jacket and reading Schiller in German to hone his language skills. On this Valentine's Day, however, the old magic seemed elusive. After briefly touring the front, where American soldiers complained that his red hat drew fire, he repaired to a barren cell in the VI Corps headquarters just as air raid sirens began to wail across Nettuno. A covey of reporters, summoned to hear his assessment, filed in past wall posters that depicted wholesome American girls urging their soldier boys to "come home clean."

The campaign had not unfolded precisely as planned, Alexander acknowledged. "We wanted a breakthrough and a complete answer inside a week," he said. "But once you [have] stopped, it becomes a question of building up and slogging." No one should assume that the drive to Rome had stalled; any whiff of defeatism only helped the enemy. "I assure you the Germans opposite us are a very unhappy party," he said. "Don't compare this situation to Dunkirk or Salerno." Dispatches from the beachhead had been filled with "pessimistic rubbish." Ignoring the fact that all stories were censored at the beachhead and again in Naples, he worked himself into a fine pique. "Were any of you at Dunkirk? I was, and I know that there is never likely to be a Dunkirk here." Alexander was "very disappointed that you should put out such rot." Henceforth, access to the radios used to transmit news dispatches from the beachhead would be severely restricted— Churchill had urged just such a suppressive action—and reporters could expect even more vigorous censorship.

Lucas tried to intervene, noting that any defeatists had long since left. "I tried to stop the tirade and tell him he had the wrong people but he refused to listen," the corps commander jotted in his diary. Alexander tromped from the command post and soon sailed off on his destroyer, uncommonly overwrought and in need of a shave. The reporters trudged through cold rain to the decrepit waterfront villa they shared, perplexed and incensed; one hack consoled himself by picking out a tune from *La Traviata* on a battered upright piano.

Lucas was left alone to ponder the blue and red runes covering his wall map. Alexander seemed convinced that the enemy had been repulsed, but the map suggested otherwise. He also appeared indifferent to VI Corps' shortages of manpower and artillery ammunition. This time there had been no hail-fellow accolades from General Alex, no "splendid piece of work" encomium.

"I am afraid the top side is not completely satisifed with my work," Lucas wrote. "I can't help it. They are naturally disappointed that I failed to chase the Hun out of Italy."

General Mackensen, the Hun himself, hardly needed his monocle to appreciate the magnificent panorama of the beachhead he now intended to destroy. From his forward command post on the western lip of the Colli Laziali, in a farmhouse two miles southwest of mystical Lake Nemi, "not a flash of a gun or explosion of a shell from either side escapes him," a German visitor reported. With a telescope, between breaks in the Allied smoke screen that swaddled the waterfront, Mackensen could even make out the Liberty ships, LSTs, and zigzagging destroyers eighteen miles away.

But it was closer terrain that held the Fourteenth Army commander's interest as daylight faded on Tuesday, February 15. Three miles of open country stretched between Aprilia and the final Allied defensive line, like a moat around an inner keep. If German assault troops now massing around the Factory and Carroceto could cross that three-mile stretch to reach the scrub pines of the Padiglione Woods, they would almost surely be able to infiltrate the final four miles to the sea, splitting the beachhead in half much as Vietinghoff's forces had almost done down the Sele River corridor at Salerno. Here the counterattack would fling six divisions into the Via Anziate corridor; two more divisions would remain in reserve to exploit the cracked Allied line, along with two hundred Tigers, Panthers, and other tanks. A hard freeze tonight would give the panzers good footing, although the attack could not begin until first light on Wednesday because regiments just arriving were too unfamiliar with the ground to attack in darkness.

In truth, both Mackensen and Kesselring deplored this attack plan, which had been foisted on them by Hitler. The Führer, ever more entangled in tactical minutae half a continent away, had ordered a "concentrated, overwhelming, ruthless" assault on a narrow front, massing German armor and artillery. Excision of the beachhead "abscess," Hitler concluded, would compel the Anglo-Americans to delay their invasion of northwest Europe, which he expected in the spring or summer; he had turned a deaf ear to protests from his field commanders, who warned that a massed attack across open terrain offered lucrative targets to Allied gunners.

Still, great pains had been taken to ensure the success of FISCHFANG, Operation FISHING. So secret was the attack date that officers visiting from Berlin were forbidden to use the telephone. Luftwaffe strikes and artillery barrages would mask the clank of approaching panzers. Ammo shortages precluded a rolling barrage in front of the attack formations, but happily most streambeds ran perpendicular to the Allied line, providing sheltered approaches in the bottoms. Units imposed draconian measures to conserve fuel and vehicle wear: this week, the Hermann Görings had issued three bicycles to each platoon "to use for short errands."

Darkness cloaked the battlefield on this twenty-fifth night of the Anzio beachhead. Stars shone brilliantly without kindling the slightest hope of a better tomorrow in either camp. Shells arced back and forth as usual, then subsided after midnight for a few hours of uncommon tranquillity. To the BBC's Vaughan-Thomas, "It was as if the house lights were being lowered in the theatre."

At 6:30 on a cold, foggy Wednesday morning the curtain rose to the percussive roar of German artillery. For seventy-five minutes, shells fell in sheets on either side of the Via Anziate, the detonations melding "like the rolling of a drum," in one soldier's phrase. Birds tumbled from the trees, killed by concussion. Then from the swirl of smoke and mist came whistles and shouts and the thrum of panzer engines that reminded a GI of "so many coffee grinders." Gray-green waves of shouting, singing German

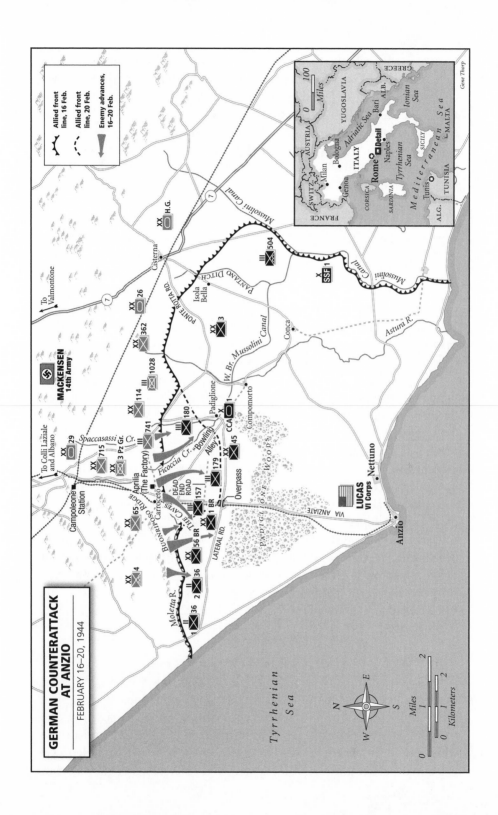

**GERMAN COUNTERATTACK AT ANZIO**

FEBRUARY 16–20, 1944

Allied front line, 16 Feb.

Allied front line, 20 Feb.

Enemy advances, 16–20 Feb.

MACKENSEN
14th Army

XX  H.G.

To Valmontone

Cisterna

7

XX  26

XX  362

III  1028

XX  114

III  504

X  SSF  1

PANTANO DITCH

Isola Bella

XX  3

Conca

W. Br. Mussolini Canal

Astura R.

Mussolini Canal

PONTE ROTTA RD.

To Colli Laziale
and Albano

Spaccasassi Cr.

XX  29

III  3 Pz. Gr.

XX  715

III  741

XX  180

Padiglione

X  CCA  1

Compomorto

Ficoccia Cr. "Bowling Alley"

XX  45

III  179

Campoleone
Station

BUONRIPOSO RIDGE

XX  65

Aprilia
(The Factory)

Carroceto

DEAD
END
ROAD

THE CAVES

XX  157

III  1 BR

Overpass

VIA ANZIATE

PADIGLIONE WOODS

XX  4

Moletta R.

XX  56 BR

LATERAL RD.

II  36  2

III  36  1

LUCAS
VI Corps

Nettuno

Anzio

Tyrrhenian
Sea

N
W   E
S

Miles
0        1        2

Kilometers
0        1        2

**Detail** inset map:

FRANCE

SWITZ.  AUSTRIA

Milan  Bologna  YUGOSLAVIA

Genoa  ITALY  Adriatic Sea

CORSICA  Rome ■ Detail  Bari

SARDINIA  Naples  GREECE

Tyrrhenian
Sea  Ionian
Sea

Mediterranean Sea  MALTA

ALG.  Tunis  SICILY

TUNISIA

Miles
0        100

Gene Thorp

infantrymen in ankle-length coats spilled down the road and across the fallow fields.

They were not unexpected. Aerial surveillance and captured prisoners had alerted VI Corps commanders to "a noticeable increase in enemy activity," and Ultra decrypts in the small hours Wednesday provided details on the "timing, direction and weight of assault." Still, few forward units had sufficiently girded themselves with mines, wire, sandbags, and tank obstacles. Compressed into a six-mile front, the German spearhead smashed into the 45th Division and, on the American left, the British 56th Division. Rifle battalions in the U.S. 157th and 179th Infantry Regiments—entrenched, respectively, left and right of the road below the Factory—buckled; only stalwart reserves and thawing mud slowed the enemy advance. Cries of "Medic!" swept the field, swallowed by the din. Panzer crews, intent on obliterating the second-story machine-gun nests that covered German infiltration routes, fired as many as ten rounds to kill a single soldier. A gunner on a tank destroyer with the 157th lashed himself to his .50-caliber machine gun with a leather strap, shooting until German fire killed him. "I watched the dust spurt out the back of his jacket as the bullets hit him," an officer reported. Company E in the same regiment was soon pared to fourteen riflemen. They, along with the rest of the encircled 2nd Battalion, would hold fast for a week in "a savage, brutish troglodyte existence" among the Caves, a sandstone badlands of vaulted tunnels east of the Via Anziate. Of nearly 1,000 men in the battalion, only 231 would survive their heroic stand in what one called "a bastard of a place."

Forward companies of Royal Fusiliers and the Oxford and Buckinghamshire Light Infantry disintegrated. So many enemy bullets swarmed across the landscape that a paratrooper reported "a strange chirping sound, like a flock of canaries." German artillery severed phone lines, punctured radios, and killed or wounded forward observers calling for counterfire, including a half dozen in the 179th Infantry alone. An urgent message to Nettuno reduced the plea to seven syllables: "Give us everything you've got."

Grim as the day had been, by dusk the German gains were limited to a mile or less here and there, at a cost of seventeen hundred casualties. "Enemy resistance was strong and determined," the Fourteenth Army log noted. The Infantry Lehr Regiment, stocked with ardent Nazis and touted by Hitler as a killer elite, had been smacked about below the Factory before skedaddling without permission. Another of the Führer's innovations—the Goliath, a small armored vehicle packed with 250 pounds of explosives and controlled remotely with a five-hundred-yard cable that unspooled from a drum—also failed abjectly. Of thirteen Goliaths sent into battle on Wednesday,

Allied artillery disemboweled three, and Wehrmacht handlers reeled in the other ten after they were thwarted by mud, ditches, and gunfire; derisive GIs dubbed them Doodlebugs. Scanning dispatches in his headquarters near Rome, Kesselring voiced dismay at the dwindling of German artillery ammunition stocks, and he pressed Mackensen to commit his reserves in the 26th Panzer and 29th Panzer Grenadier Divisions. Mackensen phoned his reply just before 6:30 P.M.: "The time has not yet come."

That time was coming, though, and Wednesday night brought it closer. Thousands of infiltrating German soldiers crept down streambeds and goat paths, bobbing helmets silhouetted against the skyline. At eight A.M. Thursday, after a softening raid by Luftwaffe bombers, sixty panzers and infantrymen from three divisions pressed along the Via Anziate and angled east, ripping the seam between the 157th and 179th Regiments. By noon, more air strikes and fourteen howling German battalions had driven a wedge two miles wide and a mile deep into the midriff of the 45th Division. The 179th commander, Colonel Malcolm R. Kammerer, ordered two battalions to fall back a thousand yards; fully exposed despite a milky smoke screen, the men were sliced to ribbons. Survivors stumbled back an extra thousand yards to a narrow farm lane known as Dead End Road. "Men on the verge of panic," one company commander reported.

"179th lost 1,000 men, mostly by surrender," Brigadier General Ray McLain, the division artillery chief, told his diary. "Poor leadership." Major General Eagles agreed and ordered Kammerer relieved. Staggering back alone after his squad had been destroyed, a sergeant squatted on his haunches and "for two hours tears rolled down his cheeks unchecked." A platoon leader bringing reinforcements from the Padiglione Woods ambled past a pile of dismembered corpses. "I wish to God I hadn't seen that," he muttered. A young soldier next to him cocked an ear to the raging battle ahead and asked, "Lieutenant, should I load my rifle now?"

Four hundred Allied gun tubes barked and barked throughout the day, spitting "murder concentrations" at German gun flashes. Smoking piles of spent brass littered the pits, and gunners stained black with powder shouted to uncomprehending mates long deaf from the relentless roar. Three dozen tanks joined the bombardment, along with four batteries of 90mm antiaircraft guns shouldered into the line to snipe at ground targets. Along the shingle, destroyers and two cruisers pressed "close enough for the Germans to count the rivets," according to a U.S. Navy account; their shells traced crimson parabolas into the enemy rear. Eight hundred planes dumped a thousand tons of explosives along the front line, the heaviest payload in a single day of close air support in the war thus far. A third of that weight fell from heavy bombers flying tactical missions, as they had at

Salerno. Bombs landed danger-close, some within four hundred yards of Allied lines. Nary a rifleman complained.

Another day faded with the beachhead intact, if shrunk by several square miles. Bodies lay stacked so high in front of the 157th Infantry that marksmen had trouble peering over them for fresh targets. Jeeps careering to the rear often carried half a dozen corpses. In the Nettuno crypt, staff officers parsed the fragmentary reports. "Don't leave the phone, son," a colonel shouted to a besieged lieutenant. "Let me know what is going on." No one really knew, of course; such was the way of desperate battles. Some things were best unknown: the Ox and Bucks battalion adjutant reported that when a machine gunner who had been killed by a sniper was found stiff with rigor mortis, still hunched in a sitting position, two men "were obliged to sit on the knees of the body in order to bring the Bren into action."

The crisis came on Friday, February 18. After parrying a weak midnight counterattack by three American battalions, field-gray wraiths flitted through pelting rain down the Moletta River ravines. Another German barrage fell before dawn, and cold, wet, heartsick GIs lay in their holes, defecating into helmets or C-ration cans and flinging the contents over the lip in the general direction of the enemy. Wounded soldiers still in the line smeared their bandages with mud to dull the white glint. *Now* the time had come to commit the reserves, Mackensen concluded, even if the Allied line had not yet fractured. Fresh battalions of panzer grenadiers, veterans of Sicily, Salerno, and the Winter Line, swept into battle, singing and shouting taunts, while predatory tanks roamed the fields, undaunted by the occasional shell that caused panzer hulls to peal like church bells. A sergeant in the 157th Infantry told his men, "Get as small as you can."

By noon the 179th Infantry had been eviscerated. Survivors retreated almost to the Flyover, a road overpass that marked the last defensive line before the Padiglione Woods. "Men trickled back in small groups, hysterical and crying," a company commander later recalled.

At two P.M., a reassuring, square-jawed figure sauntered into the regimental command post: Colonel Bill Darby had been sent by Lucas to take command. "Sir," a major said, "I guess you will relieve me for losing my battalion?" Darby smiled. "Cheer up, son," he replied. "I just lost three of them, but the war must go on." He pointed to the sparkle of muzzle flashes from a hundred artillery batteries to the rear. "Just look at that. That's the most beautiful sight in the world," Darby said. "No one can continue to attack through that."

He was right, although eight German divisions tried, carving a bulge from the Allied line almost three miles deep and four miles wide. Confusion swept the field; so, too, terror, valor, and profound sacrifice. Leaders fell, other leaders rose. A German shell burst in a tree above General Penney's trailer in a piney thicket. Peppered with shrapnel, his uniform in shreds, he crawled from the wreckage. "My face," Penney subsequently wrote his wife, "is not very attractive at the moment." General Templer took command of the 1st Division, as well as his own 56th.

In the midst of the crisis, Lucas was nonplussed to read in a message from Clark that Truscott had been appointed deputy VI Corps commander; the 3rd Division would go to Brigadier General John W. O'Daniel, a short and ebullient former Delaware National Guardsman known as Iron Mike for his foghorn voice. Truscott arrived in the command-post crypt, affecting insouciance but worried enough. If the beachhead fell, he suggested, "we'll fight our way back to Cassino." In his diary Lucas wrote, "I think this means my relief and that [Truscott] gets the corps. I hope I am not to be relieved. . . . I have done my best. I have carried out my orders and my conscience is clear."

For the moment, he had a battle to command. Shell by shell, bomb by bomb, bullet by chirping bullet, Allied firepower began to tell. Scudding clouds kept most planes grounded on Friday, but shortly before noon a Piper Grasshopper pilot spotted 2,500 Germans tramping south from Carroceto; in twelve minutes, VI Corps gunners unlimbered 224 tubes and chopped the formation to pieces. "Bits of Kraut all over the place," an Irish Guards sergeant reported. The same observation pilot massed fires on four additional targets in the next hour. The British 1st Loyals reported "clouds of exhausted, struggling field-grey figures." Wehrmacht officers shouted threats at men beyond threatening, and the clank of falling truck tailgates signaled the arrival of more fodder for the cannons. When artillery caught additional Germans on a lane from Carroceto, a forward observer radioed, "Please don't stop now. We are knocking them over like pins in a bowling alley. They keep on coming, marching right over their own dead." The road became better known as the Bowling Alley. A single British machine-gun company fired 32,000 rounds on Friday, and when the enemy attack axis swerved to the east the U.S. 180th Infantry held the right shoulder and threw them back. An American officer later described how some grenadiers "turned and ran up the slope with their tin mess kits shining on their back." With assault battalions pared to 150 men, German losses were likened to "the Light Brigade without the horses."

At 9:30 P.M. a lull settled over scarlet fields glazed with flare light. Tanks lurched forward from dumps in the Padiglione Woods, hauling water and rations to the parched and hungry. Men peered over their leaking sandbags at the scattered hummocks of olive drab and field gray that had once been men. General Mackensen had reached his high-water mark; this wrack of dead grenadiers and smoking wreckage marked the falling tide. The terrain proved "not suitable for tank employment as had been presumed," a staff officer wrote in the Fourteenth Army log, then added, "No decisive break-through."

Lucas sensed his shifting fortunes. At Truscott's urging, he ordered a counterattack for dawn on Saturday, February 19, the fourth day of a battle that had become an existential struggle between two exhausted armies. A preemptive German surge down the Via Anziate at four A.M. nearly spoiled his plan—Allied cooks, drivers, and Anzio dockworkers rushed forward to caulk the line. Sea mines dumped in the roadstead by Luftwaffe raiders kept British reinforcements from joining the counterattack as planned. But at 6:30 A.M., two rested American regiments—the 30th Infantry and 6th Armored Infantry—emerged from the Padiglione Woods with two dozen Sherman tanks and pivoted northwest up the Bowling Alley. Barrages of American artillery danced up and down the road ahead of the advancing troops.

Lucas had the right man in charge: Major General Ernest N. Harmon woke every morning spoiling for a fight. The Old Ironsides commander was barrel-shaped, with stubby legs, lungs like a blacksmith's bellows, and a cowcatcher jaw only slightly softened by a Clark Gable mustache. Raised in Vermont, Harmon had been Mark Clark's classmate at West Point, where he held the academy middleweight boxing title. Having ridden in the only U.S. horse cavalry unit to see combat in the Great War, he still wore breeches and knee-high boots. Admirers considered him a "poor man's George Patton": he lacked Patton's personal wealth, and his profanity, while just as intense, was marginally less inventive. "He was independent as a hog on ice," said Hamilton H. Howze, a subordinate who later rose to four-star rank. "But he loved to fight." Never reluctant to condemn "the stupidity of the high command," Harmon had castigated Lucas only a week earlier for the lack "of a well-established plan" to defend the beachhead. "The enemy has his troubles," Harmon told his men, "and is scared the same as you are."

Now he set out to make the German troubles worse. From foxholes lining the road, 45th Division soldiers cheered the passing platoons in their rain-slick ponchos. "Give 'em hell!" they cried. Harmon quickly won back a mile, but at 8:30 the attack stalled under galling panzer fire from the scrub-brush bottoms north of the Bowling Alley. For five hours engineers toiled to repair a blown bridge, as tank and machine-gun rounds sang all about. Harmon paced and snarled, cadging cigarettes from subordinates, until at 1:30 P.M. the attack resumed with a clattering drive into the German line. Stunned grenadiers threw up their hands or scorched to the rear. A dozen Shermans bulled north for a mile, crossed Spaccasassi Creek, and clanked toward the Factory until Harmon called them back at dusk to laager for the night.

Two hundred prisoners trotted with them; uncounted other Germans lay dead, shoring the red-stained creeks or corduroying the Bowling Alley. Initiative, that turncoat, had returned to the Allied camp. Asked by reporters in Nettuno to assess the enemy's intentions after the rout, the VI Corps intelligence chief replied, "We've made him worried."

Mackensen's troops poked and jabbed for two more days, but without conviction. Kesselring late on Saturday proposed suspending his counteroffensive, and Hitler agreed. "In the end, many hounds will kill even the swiftest hare," a German staff officer lamented. FISCHFANG had cost Fourteenth Army 5,400 casualties. "It has become very difficult to evacuate the wounded," the army log noted. "All ambulances, even the armored ones, have been lost, making it necessary to use assault guns and Tiger tanks." Some units existed only in name: the 65th Infantry Division on February 23 mustered 673 men.

If the hares had been hurt, so had the hounds. VI Corps casualties also exceeded 5,000. The 45th Division alone counted 400 killed in action since Wednesday. Their scrubs blood-caked, surgeons donned nurses' summer fatigues instead. In the month since the Anzio landings, 200,000 Axis and Allied troops combined had suffered 40,000 battle and nonbattle casualties, a double decimation that would impose at least a temporary stalemate at the beachhead.

One more casualty remained to be counted. "Message from Clark," John Lucas wrote on Tuesday, February 22. "He arrives today with eight generals. What the hell."

As Tommys and GIs fought their valiant fight, the delicate issue of what to do with their commander had obsessed the high command. Alexander, who privately told London that Lucas had "proved to be an old woman," complained that he lacked "the necessary drive and enthusiasm to get things done." A proposal by Brooke that a British general command VI Corps raised hackles in the Pentagon; Eisenhower, now in London, took a rare moment away from planning OVERLORD to send Marshall an eyes-only warning, then wrote Brooke, "It is absolutely impossible in an Allied force to shift command of any unit from one nationality to another during a period of crisis." Truscott would make an admirable corps commander, he added, although if necessary Patton could serve at the beachhead for a month.

Mortar crewmen drop another round down the tube near the Rapido River on January 24, 1944. Before the attack, the 36th Division commander, Major General Fred L. Walker, had scribbled in his diary, "We are undertaking the impossible, but I shall keep it to myself."

Two signalmen use a pig sty as a message center during the battle for the Rapido, January 23, 1944. A censor has marked through the sign indicating that the men belong to the 143rd Infantry Regiment of the 36th Division. Observed one sergeant, "Anybody who had any experience knew this ain't the place to cross the river."

Before leaving the Mediterreanean for Britain, Patton (*left*) in mid-January 1944 made a final trip to Italy to see his former deputy, Major General Geoffrey Keyes, now commanding the U.S. II Corps. "The impetuous, vitriolic, histrionic Patton is considerably leavened by the calm, deliberate, circumspect Keyes," a War Department observer had reported to Washington.

Anzio was the birthplace of two notorious Roman emperors, Nero and Caligula. Her sister city, Nettuno, can be seen down the coastline (*center right*), just beyond the dark patch of the Borghese estate; the seventeenth-century villa commandeered by Mark Clark as a Fifth Army command post is also visible in the center of the estate. Beyond the coast, the Pontine Marshes stretch to the distant hills.

Once described as an "amiable mastiff," Major General Fred L. Walker had been Mark Clark's instructor at the Army War College in the 1930s. As the Rapido attack turned into a debacle, Walker's disaffection increased. "The stupidity of some higher commanders seems to be profound," he wrote. (*Texas Military Forces Museum*)

LEFT: Lieutenant General Fridolin von Senger und Etterlin, commander of the XIV Panzer Corps at Cassino, had studied at Oxford University as a Rhodes Scholar before World War I. His high forehead, hooked beak, and sunken cheeks gave Senger the air of a homely ascetic; his long fingers and aesthete's mannerisms suggested a man "more French really than Prussian," as his daughter later claimed. (*U.S. Army Military History Institute*)

RIGHT: The senior U.S. air commander in the Mediterranean, Lieutenant General Ira C. Eaker, flying toward Anzio on April 15, 1944. "In the air in Italy," Eaker declared of the enemy, "the Hun is absolutely flat on his back."

BELOW: Tanks from the 1st Armored Division roll from an L.S.T. in Anzio harbor on April 27, 1944, among the reinforcements preparing to blast out of the beachhead after four months' confinement.

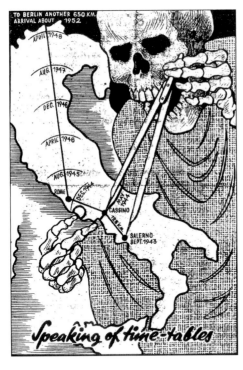

A German propoganda leaflet at Cassino, depicting the slow pace of the Allied advance in Italy *(Courtesy of Major R. C. Taylor)*

"Sprout after sprout of black smoke leapt from the earth and curled upward like some dark forest," one journalist wrote after watching the obliteration of Cassino town, by air and artillery bombardment, on March 15, 1944. Castle Hill can be seen through the smoke and dust in the upper right.

Artillery fire rakes Castle Hill above Cassino town on February 6, 1944. The famous Benedictine abbey looming on Monte Cassino would survive another nine days before Allied bombers pulverized the building.

RIGHT: Lieutenant General Oliver W. H. Leese (*left*), who succeeded Montgomery as commander of the British Eighth Army, was described by one American officer as "a big ungainly bruiser." In this photo, taken near Cassino on February 17, 1944, he stands next to the gallant Polish commander, General Wladyslaw Anders.

LEFT: A former dentist who had become one of the British empire's preeminent soldiers, Lieutenant General Bernard C. Freyberg commanded the New Zealand Corps at Cassino. An acquaintance suggested, "His great fearlessness owed something to a lack of imagination."

Fifth Army soldiers lined up outside the San Carlo opera house in Naples to see *This Is the Army*, a musical comedy by Irving Berlin.

U.S. Army military policemen toasting bread over molten lava from Vesuvius. The volcano's spectacular eruption, which began on March 18, 1944, would be the last of the twentieth century.

An Army chaplain baptizes a corporal in the ornate fountain at Caserta, the mammoth eighteenth-century palace where both Mark Clark and Harold Alexander kept headquarters among the twelve hundred rooms. A nearby reflecting pool was large enough to accommodate landings by Clark's pontoon airplane.

Actresss Marlene Dietrich, who frequently entertained Allied troops in the war zone, stands in a mess line while visiting the 47th Bombardment Group in this undated photograph. After meeting Patton in Sicily, Dietrich described him as "a tank too big for the village square." *(Courtesy of Russell H. Raine)*

Major General Lucian
K. Truscott, Jr., (*left*)
commander of the U.S.
VI Corps, and Lieutenant
General Ira Eaker, the
senior U.S. air commander
in the Mediterranean,
inspect sandbag-and–
wine barrel fortifications
around the Anzio airfield
on April 6, 1944.

American soldiers
march in step with
their shadows
toward Cassino
along Highway 6,
north of the
Mignano Gap.

Four pilots from the 99th Fighter Squadron on January 29, 1944, shortly after each had shot down a German plane over Anzio—among a dozen Luftwaffe aircraft bagged by the Tuskegee airmen in a two-day spree above the beachhead. From left: Lieutenant Willie Ashley, Jr., Lieutenant W. V. Eagleson, Captain C. B. Hall, and Captain L. R. Custis.

In Hell's Half Acre at Anzio, troops in early April 1944 dig in another hospital tent against German artillery and air attacks. In a single episode two months earlier, a Luftwaffe pilot jettisoned his bombs during a dogfight over the beachhead and the blasts killed twenty-eight people—including three nurses, two doctors, and six patients.

The Pontine Marshes for centuries had been a malarial dead zone until Mussolini transformed the region into "smiling fields" with enormous pumps. As the Allied armies neared Rome, German demolitionists flooded 100,000 acres of farmland to make the area both impassable and hospitable to malaria-carrying mosquitoes.

RIGHT: Colonel William O. Darby, seen here as a regimental commander in the 45th Division in April 1944, listened on the radio as much of the Ranger force he had built and led was destroyed at Cisterna a week after the Anzio landings.

LEFT: Major General John P. Lucas in his VI Corps office in Nettuno on February 10, 1944, shortly before the German counterattack that nearly shattered the Allied beachhead. Regarding the Anzio invasion, "Old Luke" told his diary, "This venture was always a desperate one."

RIGHT: Audie Murphy, a Texas sharecropper's son and fifth-grade dropout who became the most celebrated soldier in the U.S. Army, seen here as a lieutenant in 1945 with the Congressional Medal of Honor around his neck (*Texas Military Forces Museum*)

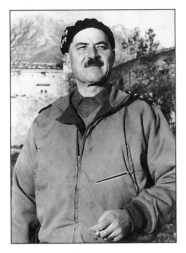

ABOVE: "Radiate confidence, and enjoy taking risks," advised General Alphonse Pierre Juin, commander of the French Expeditionary Corps, who believed that the formidable enemy defenses in the Gustav Line could be outflanked only by "invading the mountains."

BELOW: One of the twelve thousand *goumiers* in the French corps, irregular Berber tribesmen known for their agility and ruthlessness

Allied soldiers carry a dead comrade from the rubble of Monte Cassino, shortly after the abbey finally fell to Polish troops on May 18, 1944. Dead German defenders, including one stripped of his hobnail boots, lie along the trail.

Beneath the masonry shards atop Castle Hill, South African engineers clear Highway 6 through Cassino town on May 21, 1944.

Major General Keyes (*left*) with
Lieutenant General Clark and
Brigadier General Robert T.
Frederick (*right*), commander
of the 1$^{st}$ Special Service Force,
outside Rome in early June 1944

An Italian woman and a young girl cover dead GIs with cuttings from a rose bush
on June 4, 1944, the day Rome fell.

American infantrymen shelter behind the turret of a Sherman tank on June 5, 1944. Note the sniper's bullet hole beneath the "o" on the sign.

Jubiliant Romans throng the streets to greet Clark, the conquering general, on June 5, 1944, as his driver wanders through the city in search of the Capitoline. In the rear seat behind Clark are the Fifth Army chief of staff, Major General Alfred M. Gruenther (*left*), and Keyes, the II Corps commander.

GIs near Rome read of the Normandy invasion in *The Beachhead News.* "How do you like that?" Clark complained. "They didn't even let us have the newspaper headlines for the fall of Rome for one day."

An American column snakes through Rome's Piazza del Popolo before pressing north in pursuit of the retreating German armies.

From a window sill above a Roman street, Mark Clark watches his troops sweep across the capital in early June. "You ask the question, 'What after Italy?'" he wrote his wife. "Perhaps you can tell me." Clark would remain among the most controversial commanders of World War II, a man whose very name more than a half century later could cause brows to knit and lips to purse.

Clark still resisted sacking Lucas, arguing that he had "done all he could at Anzio." But with the battle in the balance, Alexander shrewdly recognized that the Fifth Army commander was "a man whose own ambition was key to his actions." Complaining that Lucas was "old physically and mentally," Alexander told Clark: "We may be pushed back into the sea. That would be very bad for both of us—and you would certainly be relieved of your command." Clark continued to balk at changing commanders in midbattle, but he had hedged his bet by agreeing to Truscott's appointment as deputy commander, privately telling him on February 18—without informing Lucas—that he would likely take over "in four or five days."

Now the moment had come. At midmorning on February 22, Clark and his entourage boarded two patrol boats in Naples. They arrived at the beachhead just as Anzio Annie, a German railway gun with shells the size of a refrigerator, raised several enormous geysers in the harbor. Clark toured the front, dodging desultory panzer fire, then at four P.M. repaired to his command post in the seventeenth-century Borghese Palace. Canadian miners from Gibraltar had carved out rooms beneath the mansion, linking the cellars to an abutting railroad tunnel, rigging lights and ventilators, and installing a rope-pulley elevator. They also converted an ancient Roman well into a septic tank instantly known as "Clark's Shitter." A sign on the tiled latrine read, FOR GENERAL OFFICERS ONLY.

At eight P.M., behind a closed door in Clark's subterranean office, Lucas took the news like a good soldier. Clark advised that "he could no longer resist the pressure," Lucas told his diary that night, adding wryly, "And I thought I was winning something of a victory." He would serve briefly as deputy Fifth Army commander at Caserta, swallowing his bitterness toward Clark and the British, then return home to command a training army in Texas. In a letter to his son, Lucas quoted Sir Walter Scott:

> One hour of life, crowded to the full with glorious action, and filled with noble risks, is worth whole years of those mean observances of paltry decorum, in which men steal through existence, like sluggish waters through a marsh, without either honor or observation.

Truscott was also summoned to the palace cellars. Despite persistent ailments—nasal polyps, abscessed tooth, raging throat—he had, in effect, served as the VI Corps shadow commander for the past five days; among other innovations, he authorized a gifted young artillery officer, Walter T. "Dutch" Kerwin, Jr., to coordinate every gun at the beachhead so as to better mass fires—setting a brigadier general at Kerwin's side to ensure that gunners heeded the twenty-six-year-old major. Yet in a voice reduced to a raspy whisper, Truscott now objected to Lucas's formal ouster as unwarranted and unfair. When Clark said he hoped to avoid wounding Lucas's pride, Truscott growled, "You can't relieve a corps commander and not hurt him." Clark waved away the protest. The decision had "already been made." Privately, he wondered whether Truscott "in the event of a reversal would prefer to be second in command."

The new corps commander returned to his Nettuno villa to have his throat painted yet again with silver nitrate. After a late supper, he sat by a crackling fire past midnight with a bottle of B&W scotch. "My one and only purpose is to serve my country," he wrote Sarah. "If this command offers a bigger opportunity, I must accept it even though I may feel my own inadequacy."

If Clark felt inadequate, he kept the sentiment to himself. A staff officer in the Borghese command post described him as "cool, level, taciturn." No one wore the mask of command better than Mark Clark. Yet the weight pressed. In his war diary he noted that as of this day Fifth Army had sustained 72,982 casualties since landing at Salerno, a man down every three minutes for more than six months. Now another had fallen, wounded in spirit if not in body. "Bringing Johnny back with me in the morning," he cabled Gruenther. "May send him direct to Sorrento for rest." To his daughter, Ann, Clark scribbled a note thanking her for a buoyant V-mail letter. "As you can well imagine, I don't have much to laugh about these days. I was pleased to hear you express confidence that you had in your dad. I hope that I will never disappoint you."

Only in a letter to Renie did his frustrations spill out. The officers and men at Anzio "have done all that could have been expected of them," he told her. The on-to-Rome carping of armchair generals in London and Washington infuriated him. "It is sheer nonsense for these people to criticize them for not having moved on to Rome. The troops would have been cut off," he wrote. "It is no use arguing. We will let history take care of that."

Prodded by Hitler, Kesselring and Mackensen would attack again on February 29, this time against the Allied right. The usual singing, shouting gray-green swarms advanced across the polders only to be flattened by 66,000 Allied artillery shells in a single day; German casualties topped 3,500, for no gain. When Alexander asked General O'Daniel how much ground his 3rd Division had lost to the counterattackers, Iron Mike replied, "Not a goddamned inch, sir."

Truscott pinned a Bill Mauldin cartoon over his desk, with one shabby GI telling another, "Th' hell this ain't th' most important hole in th' world.

I'm in it." His jaw jutting, Truscott told reporters, "We're going to have a tough time here for months to come. But, gentlemen, we're going to hold this beachhead come what may."

Still, February was sobering for the Allies. For the Americans it would be the bloodiest month in the Mediterranean to date, with nineteen hundred dead. There would be no quick, decisive success via the beachhead flank. Alexander believed the battles at Anzio and Cassino had revealed alarming Allied weakness and German strength. "He is quicker than we are," he wrote Clark, "quicker at re-grouping his forces, quicker at thinning out a defensive front to provide troops to close gaps at decisive points . . . quicker at reaching decisions on the battlefield. By comparison, our methods are often slow and cumbersome."

This was true enough, but it was not the whole truth. The greater revelation was of Allied strength and German weakness. "Without air support," a German staff officer complained, "all planning was an illusion." Lieutenant General Ira C. Eaker, the senior American airman in the Mediterranean, concurred. "In the air in Italy," Eaker wrote, "the Hun is absolutely flat on his back." If less prostrate, German artillery had proved another deficiency, particularly because of ammunition shortages. VI Corps fired 158,000 rounds during FISCHFANG, a ten-to-one advantage over German gunners. American artillery, singularly good since the Mexican War, kept getting better, aided by aerial spotting, the profusion of radios, nimble fire control, and those murderous queens offshore. Truscott soon demanded, and got, counterbattery fire in four minutes, less than half the time previously required. A single 105mm howitzer shooting every thirty seconds could, in one hour, seed 43,000 square yards with two tons of lethal steel fragments. Allied artillery inflicted three-quarters of all German battle casualties at Anzio.

The failure to exterminate the Allied beachhead carried sober implications beyond southern Italy, and even Kesselring's optimism dimmed. Not only were German forces overmatched in the air and outgunned on the ground, but "a perceptible weakening of the daredevil spirit" afflicted the ranks, he told a visiting general from Berlin in late February. This, he believed, was "the last year of the war." By the calculation of Kesselring's chief of staff, General Siegfried Westphal, more combat matériel had been brought to play in FISCHFANG than on any German battlefield since 1940, with the exception of Sevastopol, and the grim result revealed the "progressive exhaustion of the army after more than 4½ years of fighting," Westphal said. "The blanket had become too thin and too short."

Believing that the high command must hear that "a turning point had been reached in the war," Kesselring sent Westphal to deliver this revelation in a three-hour meeting with the Führer and his military brain trust at the Berchtesgaden retreat. "Hitler was very calm," Westphal reported, and he approved Fourteenth Army's shift to the defensive at Anzio. Field Marshal Wilhelm Keitel, the Wehrmacht chief, voiced surprise that Hitler had listened to "so many unpleasant things." Upon returning to Italy, Westphal told Kesselring that "the Führer appeared bowed down with care."

Such strategic nuances were beyond the ken of those consigned to the beachhead for the duration. German engineers trucked in forced-labor Italian carpenters from Rome—including movie set craftsmen from Cinecittà, the studio complex built by Mussolini—to fashion decoy panzers and gun tubes, as well as other military illusions in the Colli Laziali. In Allied camps, the departure of General Lucas stirred little sentiment beyond the hope, as one British gunner later put it, that his "successor would soon get us out of the mess we were in." Most licked their wounds, of body and soul, and steeled themselves for battles still ahead. "I'm a little tired," an Irish Guards sergeant confessed after emerging from the hellish Moletta gullies. "But then, I'm an old man now."

## *"Man Is Distinguished from the Beasts"*

A s FISCHFANG played out at Anzio, another crowded hour ticked away for Monte Cassino and the armies encircling the abbey. Freyberg the New Zealander had become ever more insistent on obliterating the building before launching an attack, and his bellicosity was soon to be inflamed by word that his only child, a young officer in the Grenadier Guards, had gone missing at Anzio. A Royal Artillery gunner said of the looming white edifice, "Somehow it was the thing that was holding up all our lives and keeping us away from home. It became identified in an obsessional way with all the things we detested."

Willy-nilly bombing of priceless cultural icons was discouraged by custom and forbidden by law. Months earlier the Combined Chiefs had reminded Eisenhower that "consistent with military necessity, the position of the church and of all religious institutions shall be respected and all efforts made to preserve the local archives, historical and classical monuments, and objects of art." Eisenhower in turn warned his lieutenants in late December that "military necessity" should not be abused as an expedient for military convenience. Alexander's headquarters in mid-January identified the Monte Cassino abbey and the papal estate at Castel Gandolfo as two preeminent "ecclesiastical centres which it is desired to preserve." An Allied pamphlet, titled "Preservation of Works of Art in Italy," included a section headed "Why Is Italy So Rich in Works of Art?" and the assertion that "man is distinguished from the beasts by his power to reason and to frame abstract hopes and ideas." Bomber-crew briefing packets included street maps, copied from Baedeker guidebooks, that highlighted historic buildings to avoid. Allied staff officers assigned to repair inadvertent damage were known as Venus Fixers.

Already the Venus Fixers had been busy. Bombs had damaged forty churches in Naples alone; the magnificent bronze doors on a cathedral north of the city were reduced to particles. Errant bombs hit Castel Gandolfo several times in early February, and one such misadventure killed seventeen nuns. But deliberate destruction of Monte Cassino would escalate this "war in a museum," as Kesselring called the Italian campaign, and within Allied war councils arguments for and against were marshaled with warm intensity.

The unit ordered to capture the massif, the 4th Indian Division, remained keenest to "drench" the hill with bombs. A dubious report from a captured German prisoner, who claimed that paratroopers had put a command post and an aid station within the abbey, led the 4th Indian on February 12 to publish an intelligence summary titled "Violation of Geneva Convention." Other imagined sightings included those by an Italian civilian who reported thirty machine guns, a 34th Division colonel who saw the flash of field glasses in an abbey window, and U.S. gunners who swore that hostile small-arms fire had streamed from the building. A British newspaper on February 11 printed the incendiary headline "Nazis Turn Monastery into Fort."

On February 14, two senior American generals, Ira Eaker and Jacob Devers, flew in an observation phase at fifteen hundred feet over Monte Cassino and reported seeing "Germans in the courtyard and also their antennas," as well as a machine-gun nest fifty yards from the abbey wall. Another American airman, Major General John K. Cannon, pledged, "If you let me use the whole of our bomber force against Cassino, we will whip it out like a dead tooth." An American artillery commander told *The New York Times,* "I have Catholic gunners in this battery and they've asked me for permission to fire on the monastery." Indeed, the wolf had risen in the heart. A U.S. air wing intelligence analysis declared on February 14, "This monastery has accounted for the lives of upwards of 2,000 boys. . . . This monastery *must* be destroyed and everyone in it, as there is no one in it but Germans."

Others passionately disagreed. The French commander, General Juin, pleaded with Clark to spare the building. General Keyes, also a devout Catholic, took his own plane above the abbey on the morning of February 14 and saw "no signs of activity." Bombing the building would be "an unnecessary outrage," he told his diary, particularly because II Corps intelligence detected as many as two thousand refugees now sheltering inside. Moreover, "a partially destroyed edifice is much better for defensive purposes than an untouched one." Keyes's irritation at Freyberg grew so intense that Clark rebuked him for "your somewhat belligerent attitude"; the men exchanged peace offerings, with Keyes sending a package of butter, catsup, and Nescafé, and Spadger reciprocating with New Zealand lambs' tongue, canned oysters, and honey. Still fuming, Keyes wrote, "Why we Americans have to kowtow to the British and by order of our American commanders is beyond me."

Freyberg was not to be denied, and with Clark at the beachhead he pressed Gruenther for a decision, even though he put the odds of capturing the massif after a bombardment at no better than "fifty-fifty." If Clark refused to destroy the building, Freyberg added darkly, he would "have to take the responsibility" for New Zealand Corps casualties. Alexander's new chief of staff, Lieutenant General John H. Harding, also pressured Gruenther. "General Alexander has made his position quite clear," Harding said in a phone call. "He regrets very much that the monastery should be destroyed, but he sees no other choice." General Alex "has faith in General Freyberg's judgment."

Clark had no such faith. "I now have five corps under my command, only two of which are American, all others of different nationalities," he wrote in his diary. "I think Napoleon was right when he came to the conclusion that it was better to fight allies than to be one of them." But he sensed that yet another die had been cast. In a phone call from Alexander, Clark made a last effort to forestall the attack. No clear evidence placed Germans in the abbey. "Previous efforts to bomb a building or a town to prevent its use by the Germans . . . always failed," he added. "It would be shameful to destroy the abbey and its treasure," not to mention any innocent civilians inside. "If the Germans are not in the monastery now, they certainly will be in the rubble after the bombing ends," Clark said.

Alexander conceded the points, then shrugged them off. "Bricks and mortar, no matter how venerable, cannot be allowed to weigh against human lives," he argued. Freyberg was "a very important cog in the commonwealth effort. I would be most reluctant to take responsibility for his failing and for his telling his people, 'I lost five thousand New Zealanders because they wouldn't let me use air as I wanted.'" Not least, Alexander felt scalding pressure from London. "What are you doing sitting down doing nothing?" the prime minister demanded in a preposterous cable. "Why don't you use your armour in a great scythe-like movement through the mountains?"

Clark capitulated. If Freyberg were American, he told Alexander, he would deny the request. But "due to the political daintiness" of the circumstances—Spadger in effect commanded a small national army—there was little choice but to procede with the plan now code-named Operation AVENGER. In a dictated memo, Clark condemned Alexander for "unduly interfering with Fifth Army activities," adding, "It is too bad unnecessarily to destroy one of the art treasures of the world."

The attack would be launched quickly, to exploit a narrow window of fair weather. Freyberg had proposed dropping a single token bomb as a warning to refugees hiding in the abbey. Instead, on Monday night, February 14, Allied gunners lobbed two dozen shells that burst three hundred feet above Monte Cassino, showering the abbey with leaflets. *"Amici italiani, ATTENZIONE!"* they read:

> Now that the battle has come close to your sacred walls we shall, despite our wish, have to direct our arms against the monastery. Abandon it at once. Put yourselves in a safe place. Our warning is urgent.

A pleasant morning sun peeped above the Abruzzi peaks on Tuesday, February 15, the harbinger of an Italian spring that surely must come soon. A battered, roofless Volkswagen sped downhill from a decrepit palazzo in Roccaseca, past the ruined castle where the saintly Thomas Aquinas had been born, then left onto Highway 6 in the Liri Valley. Beyond the village of Piedimonte, barely three miles northwest of the gleaming abbey ahead, the car turned onto a farm road and lurched to a stop. A tall, slender man wearing the high-collared tunic of a Wehrmacht lieutenant general climbed from the front seat, scanning the knifeblade ridges for enemies even as he admired the luminous vision crowning Monte Cassino.

For five months Fridolin von Senger und Etterlin had rambled across these hills, swinging his six-foot ashplant, his loping gait said to resemble a sailor's more than a soldier's, often chatting up peasants in his passable, lisping Italian. Since October he had commanded XIV Panzer Corps in Vietinghoff's Tenth Army, responsible first for defending part of the Bernhardt Line and now a fifty-mile stretch of the Gustav Line; no man contributed more to Allied miseries at San Pietro, the Rapido River, and Cassino than Senger. His high forehead, hooked beak, and sunken cheeks gave him the air of a homely ascetic, although his long fingers and aesthete's mannerisms suggested a man "more French really than Prussian," as his daughter later claimed. Descended from an ancient family of lesser princes that lost its estates in the Napoleonic Wars and its wealth in the Weimar inflation, Senger had studied at Oxford as a Rhodes scholar before finding his calling in the Great War; when his younger brother was killed at Cambrai in 1917, Senger dug for hours through a mass grave in no-man's-land, determined to give him a more dignified interment. "At last we got the body out, which had lain in the lowest of the three levels," he later wrote. "I took hold of my brother's legs and dragged him thus into my car. On the seat beside me sat my lifeless brother."

In this war he had helped capture Cherbourg, then commanded a panzer division near Stalingrad before serving as Kesselring's senior liaison to Italian forces in Sicily. Later, as commander of German troops on Corsica and Sardinia, Senger had refused Hitler's order to shoot turncoat Italian officers, an impertinence only pardoned after he successfully evacuated the entire German garrison. Since taking over the Cassino front he had scrupulously followed orders to keep his troops away from the abbey lest they anger the Vatican; when Abbot Diamare invited Senger to Christmas dinner and mass in the Monte Cassino crypt, he avoided looking out the windows rather than violate the abbey's neutrality by scanning Allied positions below. German observation posts were dug below the hill crest, where they were better camouflaged anyway.

"The rotten thing is to keep fighting and fighting and to know all along that we have lost this war," he told an aide, his brushy eyebrows dancing. Now, with his corps at times losing a battalion or more each day, "annihilation was only a matter of time." Kesselring's cheery attitude baffled him; after five months in the Italian mountains, Senger insisted that "optimism is the elixir of life for the weak." He bore the burden—and the stain of serving a National Socialist cause he despised—as best he could, sipping wine in his Roccasecca refuge while listening to evening concerts on his service radio, or sitting with comrades to again watch his favorite movie, *Der Weisse Traum*—The White Dream—about a lovesick Viennese theater manager. He read Aquinas and found cold comfort in the theologian's teaching that "no man can be held answerable for the misdeeds of those over whom he has no power." Upon learning of German atrocities in Poland, Senger wrote, "Oh the loneliness when one hears of such things on which one must be silent."

Now he heard something else. At 9:45 A.M., as he conferred with grenadier officers in a cylindrical concrete command post near Piedimonte, the drone of bomber engines drew Senger outside. He craned his long neck and shaded his eyes. Tiny cruciforms filled the blue sky three miles above Monte Cassino, their paths etched by milky contrails. Then swarms of bright pellets tumbled toward the abbey, as if heaven itself were throwing silver stones.

\*   \*   \*

An officer in the 4th Indian Division wrote in his battalion log, "Someone said, 'Flying Fortresses,' then followed the whistle, swish and blast as the first flights struck against the monastery." To a B-17 pilot peering down from his cockpit, "the mountain seemed to gust upward like a volcano." As the initial bombs struck the abbey roof, dust spurting from the windows reminded a 34th Division lieutenant of "smoke coming out of a man's ears."

They were the first of 250 bombers—B-17s, B-25s, B-26s—that by day's end would dump nearly six hundred tons of high explosives and incendiaries on Monte Cassino. Hundreds of artillery rounds joined the bombardment, including enormous shells from 240mm and 8-inch howitzers. In the Rapido Valley, a stand of poplar trees that had been sawed three-quarters through were now pushed over to give gunners a clear field of fire.

Soldiers on both sides of the hill watched spellbound as a caldron of smoke and flame boiled from the hilltop. "Scores of us—Yanks, British, Indians and Kiwis—line the ridge, looking at the destruction through glasses," an American ambulance driver noted in his diary. "Three lieutenants jump up and down with excitement every time a rack of bombs breaks over the hill." The sight was "gigantically stimulating . . . comparable to seeing the early Christians being eaten by lions," a Royal Artillery gunner wrote. "We all started cheering wildly and hugging each other. Here we are, cheering the destruction of one of the great monuments of Christendom." The reporter Martha Gellhorn found herself braying "like all the other fools," while her colleague Frank Gervasi heard someone murmur, "Beautiful precision." Maoris and Kiwis preparing to storm the Cassino rail station bellowed, "Shovel it on!" and "Give the fuckers hell!"

Hell they got. The leaflet barrage the previous evening had terrified the abbey's refugees—their numbers were estimated at between 800 and 2,500—but confused attempts to contact German troops about safe passage down Monte Cassino had failed. Some refugees suspected the monks of counterfeiting the warning leaflets as a ruse to clear the abbey of riffraff.

Abbot Diamare planned to evacuate the abbey in his own time, on Wednesday morning. His monks had been distracted by the death from fever of a young brother, whose corpse, dressed in a robe and laid in a coffin he himself had built from bed planks, was given to God in the little chapel of St. Anne. This morning they had observed the liturgy of the hours as usual in the abbey's deepest cells, and were on their knees before a painted Madonna, singing "Beseech Christ on Our Behalf," when the first stupendous shudder shook the building. Explosion followed explosion, the corridors filled with choking dust, smoke, and shattered masonry. The abbot offered absolution to each monk. They stuffed their ears with cotton wadding against the roar of the bombs and the screams of women and children overhead.

By two P.M. the abbey was a smoldering memory. Thirteen hundred bombs and another twelve hundred high-explosive incendiaries had smashed the cloisters, shearing off courtyard palms and decapitating the statue of St. Benedict. The grand staircase lay in ruins. Drifts of rubble fifteen feet high filled the basilica aisles, where frescoes, an ancient organ, and choir stalls carved by Neapolitan artisans were reduced to flinders. Protected in their subterranean vaults, the monks forced a passage upstairs through the wreckage to find scores of dead refugees—including many cut down by artillery fire as they fled outside—and those still alive "crazy with terror," in one monk's description. "Parents abandoned their shrieking children and fled to safety," according to a German account. "Sons fled, leaving their aged parents to their fate. One woman had both her feet blown off."

No mortal would ever know how many died. Estimates ranged from more than one hundred to more than four hundred; the official British history put the figure at "three or four hundred." After the war, 148 skulls would be found in the debris, with others no doubt pulverized. "Some of the bodies were found in small rooms in which they had suffocated, such as an old man who had tried to protect a child with his body," wrote Herbert Bloch, a Harvard classics scholar and author of *Monte Cassino in the Middle Ages*. The attitudes of the dead reminded archaeologists of Pompeii.

Alexander's headquarters asserted that two hundred Germans were seen fleeing the abbey ruins, a ludicrous claim. Shortly after noon, Senger tore himself away from the mesmerizing spectacle atop Monte Cassino to send Vietinghoff the message that damage was extensive and that "numerous civilian refugees are in the abbey." Under orders from Berlin, grenadiers searched the grounds soon after the bombing ceased; they found the abbey's outer walls battered but not breached at ground level. As Clark had foretold, Senger promptly ordered his troops to burrow into the rubble. Machine guns nested in the masonry, artillery observers perched on the broken ramparts, and a field kitchen opened in Benedict's cell.

Not until dawn on Thursday did Abbot Diamare lead the remnants of his flock out of the ruins. Forty monks and refugees emerged from the abbey's arched entryway, still intact with the inscription PAX carved in the stone lintel above the great oak door. A monk holding a large wooden crucifix led the procession down the serpentine road from one hairpin curve to another. A paralyzed boy rode on a monk's shoulders, and the old woman without feet was carried on a ladder until the burden grew too great and she was laid on the mountainside to die. Down they trudged, past yawning craters gouged in the roadbed and the rocky knob of Monte

Venere, now called Hangman's Hill because the wrecked funicular tower resembled a gibbet. Down, down the procession wound toward the seething valley, as the old abbot and his monks mumbled the rosary in contemplation of God's deepest mysteries, the joyful and the luminous, the glorious and the sorrowful.

The 4th Indian Division had expected Operation AVENGER to begin Wednesday afternoon, and only fifteen minutes before the bomber fleet appeared overhead on Tuesday morning did frontline troops learn that the attack had been accelerated to exploit the fair weather. Unable to retreat to better cover from their forward holes, two dozen Indian troops were injured in the bombardment, many by flying masonry. "They told the monks, and they told the enemy, but they didn't tell us," an enraged Royal Sussex commander said.

From that point, nothing was right except the courage, again. Hours passed without a follow-on assault. Freyberg's tactical incompetence in failing to couple the bombardment with a prompt attack by swarming infantrymen was aggravated by the loss of the 4th Indian's capable commander, Major General Tuker, whom malaria and rheumatoid arthritis had laid low. His replacement, Brigadier H. W. Dimoline, an artilleryman with little infantry experience, was "far out of his depth," another senior officer later complained. "There did not appear to be a glimmer of intelligent leadership anywhere from division up."

Not until Tuesday night did the attack begin, and then with but a single company sent to seize Point 593, that troublesome knuckle a mile behind the now ruined abbey. German machine guns and mortars killed or wounded half the men before they covered fifty yards. Another attack on Wednesday night by a full battalion collapsed when enemy defenders happened to fire three green flares, which by foul luck mimicked the Royal Sussex signal to withdraw. Early on Friday morning, February 18, Gurkhas assaulted the abbey directly, but booby traps, grenades, a dense thicket of throat-high thorns, and sleeting machine-gun fire drove them back. Dozens of dead Gurkhas would later be found with their legs trussed in tripwires.

In the town below, Maori riflemen at dawn on Friday routed grenadiers from the Cassino train station and roundhouse. But nine thousand Kiwi smoke shells fired to obscure those gains also hid German infiltrators, who counterattacked late in the afternoon to win back the lost rail yard. Supply columns trying to slip through the Rapido bottoms at night found the enemy on the frowning heights more omniscient than ever. "A star shell went up, followed by another," a 4th Indian signaler wrote. "As we had expected, Jerry had become suspicious and soon a string of flares lit the whole valley with an eerie blue light." Of two hundred mules clopping toward the front lines, twenty won through.

AVENGER petered out after nearly six hundred 4th Indian casualties and more than two hundred New Zealanders killed or wounded. Understrength, uncoordinated, and unimaginative, the attack "could not hold any surprise," Senger later wrote. "There was nothing new in it." Obliterating the abbey "brought no military advantage of any kind," the British official history concluded, and—as the U.S. Army's own history added—gained "nothing beyond destruction, indignation, sorrow, and regret."

Efforts to justify the bombing began even before the smoke had blown clear of Monte Cassino. Military authorities pressured the OSS, without success, for evidence that German troops had occupied the abbey. In a cable to London, Field Marshal Wilson wrote, "Suggest that we should confine our statement to the fact that military authorities on the spot have irrefutable evidence that the Cassino abbey was part of the main German defensive line." Long after the war, the U.S. Army claimed that no civilian bodies had been found in the abbey. Assuming that Rome would soon become a battleground, Allied propagandists began a campaign to blame Germany, in hopes of regaining the moral high ground and of pressuring Berlin to eschew scorched-earth tactics in the capital.

Yet Senger and Kesselring had already stolen a march. As Abbot Diamare worked his way down the hill on Thursday morning, a German staff car picked him up and drove him to the XIV Panzer Corps headquarters, where he spent the night. The next day, with movie cameras rolling and a German radio reporter present, Senger staged an interview.

"Everything was done on the part of the German armed forces," Senger said, "in order to give the opponent no military ground for attacking the monastery."

"General, I can only confirm this," the abbot said. "Until the moment of the destruction of the Monte Cassino abbey there was within the area of the abbey neither a German soldier, nor any German weapon, nor any German military installation."

Senger nodded. "It came to my attention much too late that leaflets which gave notice of the bombing were dropped over the area of the monastery."

"We simply did not believe that the English and Americans would attack the abbey," Diamare said. "We laid out white clothes in order to say to them, do nothing to us. . . . They have destroyed the monastery and killed hundreds of innocent people."

Senger leaned forward solicitiously. "Can I do anything more?"

"No, General. You have done everything."

Berlin overplayed its hand by pressing the abbot to sign a more venomous statement. He refused, but the damage was done; posters of the ruined monastery and Diamare's commentary appeared on Roman streets and in Vienna. A week after the bombing, the president of the Pontificia Accademia Romana di Archeologia condemned the destruction as "an everlasting shame to our age and to our civilization"—as if the Second World War were anything less. The British military strategist J.F.C. Fuller later denounced the bombing "not so much a piece of vandalism as an act of sheer tactical stupidity," confirmation that, "as in the years 1915–17, tactical imagination was petrified."

The ruined abbey—"that tomb of miscalculation," in one U.S. Army corporal's phrase—quickly came to symbolize the grinding war of attrition that the Italian campaign had become. Fifth Army's latest seven-mile advance had exhausted eight divisions and cost sixteen thousand casualties. Only "endless vistas of deadlock" seemed to loom ahead, as a New Zealand assessment put it. The search for scapegoats on the Cassino front also began: Marshall in a message to General Devers on February 18 suggested that Keyes and his division commanders "appear below [the] stern standard required. . . . Let nothing stand in the way of procuring leadership of the quality necessary."

Public opinion in the United States seemed largely indifferent to the destruction. Twenty-seven months of total war had severed sentimental attachments to the Monte Cassinos of this world. A Gallup poll taken shortly after the bombing found that if military leaders believed it necessary to bomb historic religious buildings and shrines in Europe, 74 percent of Americans would approve and only 19 percent disapprove. The wolf had risen in the heart at home, too.

Yet as shell fire and the odd bombing sortie continued to carve away Monte Cassino's crest, those entrenched in the Rapido flats could not help but feel that once again something had been lost in this dark epoch of loss. Even Major General Walker, whose 36th Division had been gutted on the Rapido in Cassino's shadow, felt unease. "Whenever I am offered a liqueur glass of benedictine," he wrote in his diary, "I shall recall with regret the needless destruction of the abbey." Of course the deeper regret extended beyond ecclesiastical landmarks. War was whittling it all away: civility and moderation, youth and innocence, mountains and men.

# Part Four

# 10. Four Horsemen

## *A Fairyland of Silver and Gold*

THE trolleys were running again in Naples, along with the stinking diesel buses and the trams that clacked uphill to the swank villas above the city. Few motor vehicles could be seen, except for jeeps and Army deuce-and-a-half trucks, but hundreds of dogcarts and rattletrap barouches pulled by swaybacked nags filled the boulevards. "The bay was as blue as ever, Vesuvius as black, and the pines as green," Fifth Army's OSS chief reported. Neapolitans in shabby clothes and shabbier shoes strolled the Via Francesco Caracciolo, "arm in arm, talking, laughing, crying, arguing, gesticulating," Frank Gervasi observed. Scavengers hunted cigar butts in the gutters, and slatterns with rented babies begged in the piazzi where quacks peddled their nostrums and shoeblacks, called *lustrini*, signaled their services by rapping on their wooden boxes. "Hubba, hubba," the urchins sang in mimicry of GIs. "Chicken-a shit, second-a lieutenant." In the public gardens, "storytellers have been drawn out by the sun to take up their positions," the British officer and writer Norman Lewis noted in late February. For a coin they "chanted recitations of the deeds of Charlemagne and the Paladins," using their hands to "build up their thoughts, like a potter at his wheel."

Naples over the centuries had lured the likes of Petrarch and Goethe, Rossini and Donizetti, Dickens and James Fenimore Cooper. While writing the *Aeneid*, Virgil was said to have driven the snakes from a city he adored, although two millennia later John Ruskin found it "the most loathsome nest of human caterpillars I was ever forced to stay in—a hell with all the devils imbecile in it." Now resurgent Naples drew hordes of Allied soldiers. Given that Cassino lay only fifty miles north and Anzio but ninety, the city conveyed "a complacency and lack of realism worse than that prevailing in New York City," the reporter Homer Bigart complained. But for many on leave from the front, Naples was "the nearest symbol of every man's immediate aspirations," wrote the British officer Fred Majdalany.

It was a fairyland of silver and gold and great happiness. . . . You could buy things in the shops; you could get drunk; you could have a woman; you could hear music.

Of course the war intruded at times. Each afternoon, a hospital train pulled into the Piazza Garibaldi station with broken boys from Cassino shelved in triple-tiered berths, the most grievous cases in the bottom bunks. Luftwaffe raiders still struck the port and anchorages, and "every ship opened up with its guns until there were a hundred necklaces of red tracer bullets over Naples bay," wrote Alan Moorehead. Just the rumor of an attack triggered orders to "make smoke," and within eight minutes a thousand soldiers manning fog-oil generators and smoke pots would lay a dense blanket along twenty miles of Neapolitan coast, thick enough that jeep drivers had to shine flashlights at the curb to follow the road. Despite the smoke and the swarming tracers, an occasional bomber got through, followed immediately by looters, who staggered from bombed-out buildings with "perhaps a door, a bedstead, a couple of kettles, a birdcage," wrote Margaret Bourke-White. After a raid in early spring, Norman Lewis watched as dead children were lifted from the rubble and laid out side by side with dolls "thrust into their arms to accompany them to the other world. Professional mourners . . . were running up and down the street tearing at their clothing and screaming horribly."

Yet for most soldiers Naples was a haven, a tabernacle of *la dolce vita* into which they poured for "I&I"—intercourse and intoxication—aboard trucks known as "passion wagons." Italian porters lugged their packs to the Volturno Enlisted Men's Hotel on Via Roma or to the city jail, which Fifth Army renovated as a rest center for twelve hundred men. "The Americans had control of the whole city," complained a British sapper, C. Richard Eke. "Everywhere were GIs and military police, the burly, truncheon-swinging Yanks." The Red Cross auditorium showed a new movie every day at four P.M., drawing big crowds despite frequent interruptions from power failures. A music hall on Via Constantinopoli sponsored dances several nights a week, and Irving Berlin's show *This Is the Army* drew packed houses; roars invariably greeted his rendition of "Oh, How I Hate to Get Up in the Morning." When a soldier spotted Humphrey Bogart in the Hotel Parca, he asked how he could purchase a pistol like the one the actor had used in *Sahara*, which "could fire sixteen shots without reloading." Bogart flicked away his cigarette and replied, "Hollywood is a wonderful place."

So, too, was Pompeii. Each morning at eight, a commuter train hauled hundreds of soldiers to the ruins, where guides offered tours of "The House of the Two Bachelors Who Were Never Married" and intimated that the city's awful fate resulted from "too many different positions." A 3rd Division soldier wrote home that "the old Romans certainly knew how to get the most out of life," but a diarist from the 56th Evacuation Hospital concluded that the lost city had been "built by a clever, wine-drinking, sensuous, evil-minded people."

Soldiers also jammed the reopened San Carlo opera house, despite the fleas in the padded seats and a lack of heat that kept everyone bundled up. From the balcony tiers they chattered like parrots, gawking at the depictions of Parnassus on the domed ceiling. Then the crimson curtain rose, the overture swelled, and the spell was cast. A private from Ohio slapped his knee during the second act of *La Bohème*. "That's good," he murmured, "that's real good." Soldiers spilled into the night humming arias, so many Carusos in olive drab.

New Neapolitan cabarets opened every week. The Orange Club above the Via Posillipo was said by Bourke-White to be "the most lively and popular night club on the European continent." Patrons on the circular terraces gazed at Vesuvius's ruby glow and the winking signal lights from warships in the bay below. Nurses danced the Jersey Bounce, and inebriated officers aimed champagne corks at the brooch on a singer's décolletage. No I&I to Naples was complete without a tour of Capri, where room and board could be had for a dollar a night, and the bars opened at nine A.M. The island struck Alan Moorehead as "a curious little nodule of lotus-eating," with "the slightly beaten air of a worn-out roué." Soldiers lounged on the rocks in straw hats and sandals, or rode to the Marina Piccola in carriages pulled by plumed horses. In hotel dining rooms, waiters served supper from silver chafing dishes to men who had not held a fork since leaving the United States. One visitor was happy simply to list the shades of the sea: turquoise, emerald, purple, peacock, violet.

"I could never forget," wrote Bourke-White, "that many of these boys would go back into the rain and mud and screaming dangers of the hills, never to return."

"The people are terribly poor and everything in the shops is shabby," an American nurse wrote home from Naples. "They all stand outside the mess hall and go through the 55-gallon drums into which we empty our mess kits." For most Neapolitans, there were no lotuses to eat, nor much of anything else. War had moved north, but famine, pestilence, and death tarried through the winter. Most of occupied Italy still relied on Allied food imports to stave off starvation. Ernie Pyle, described by Bill Mauldin as "a tiny wizened bundle of misery with two sharp eyes" who spent his I&I nights nipping brandy in an Air Force compound known as Villa Virtue, watched

Italian mobs on the docks battle for scraps tossed from LST decks by soldiers sailing to Anzio. "Every time a package of crackers went down from above," Pyle wrote, "humanity fought and stamped over it like a bunch of football players." A British lieutenant eating chops in a Pozzuoli café was astonished when "a ragged old woman dashed in and snatched the bones off my plate."

For two months, a particularly virulent strain of typhus raged unchecked, infecting more than two thousand Neapolitans of whom it killed one in four. Carts hauled away the dead at night, as in medieval times. Typhus, which had killed three million people in Russia and Poland during and after World War I, is spread by lice, and 90 percent of the civilian population in Naples reputedly harbored head lice. Each night "a disordered throng of miserable, frightened and soapless citizens" jammed the city's air raid shelters, which became disease incubators.

Army physicians had quarantined Naples on January 1; for weeks, soldiers on leave were diverted to Caserta. Mass delousing was planned for the entire population, which would be sprayed "on the hoof" at fifty "public powdering stations." Transport planes brought emergency supplies of a chemical first synthesized in 1874 but only recently recognized as a potent insecticide: DDT. A year earlier, the entire U.S. stockpile had amounted to a few ounces; now a chemical plant in Cincinnati was making seventy thousand pounds of DDT each month, and eventually sixty tons would be shipped to Italy. At one commandeered palazzo, MPs carrying sacks of the stuff stood by with spray guns. "People queued up in two lines many blocks long and marched slowly in and up the marble stairs," according to a witness. "The men were sprayed from head to foot. The women were shot down their bosoms and backs and were sprayed back and front." Other spray teams prowled caves and shelters, and soon the typhus epidemic ended. Like DDT itself, the spraying of more than a million Neapolitans remained a military secret for months. Only one Fifth Army soldier had been infected.

Venereal disease was another matter. "A victorious army found in Italy good-looking and amorous women, and cheap intoxicating vino in good supply," a British analysis concluded. As a result, "the damned army is all clapped up with slit-trench romances," a Fifth Army surgeon complained. Soldiers joked that Naples would be the world's largest bordello, if someone could roof it. "There's pox galore out here," a sergeant warned British soldiers arriving in the Piazza Dante. "One good screw and yer prick will swell up like a marrow and yer balls drop off." A crestfallen Tommy muttered, "Now why doesn't Thomas Cook put *that* in his brochures?"

With the average worker earning only sixty lire a day—sixty cents, less than the cost of a kilogram loaf of bread—thousands of desperate, destitute Neapolitan women turned to prostitution, which typically paid one to two thousand lire per night. On New Year's Day, after dubious studies and laboratory tests suggested that "60 percent of all women in Italy had some form of venereal disease," Neapolitan brothels had been placed off-limits; the skin trade simply moved into the streets and to nearby towns where "they have developed the most loyal and finest pimp system in the world," according to a provost marshal's report. Battalions of streetwalkers paraded down Via Roma, their tresses frosted in "DDT hairdos"; one soldier grew so weary of pimps plucking at his sleeve that he hung a sign around his neck: "NO." A strumpet on Capri who insisted on fixed-price services was known as "Madame Four-Dollars."

The "perfunctory jogging of the haunches," in Norman Lewis's phrase, brought dire results to Fifth Army. The VD rate exceeded one in ten for white soldiers—it was much higher for blacks—with the average gonorrhea infection in February requiring ten days' recuperation. "The Italian strain of gonococci proved to be 70 percent sulfa resistant," British doctors reported. Another new wonder drug, penicillin, was generally not available in Italy until mid-February, and then in such limited stocks that it commanded the same black market price as morphine. A secret debate raged over whether penicillin should be given to infected troops or reserved exclusively for those valorously wounded. Churchill himself directed that "it must be used to the best military advantage," and soon enough the drug would be administered to bedroom libertines and battlefield heroes alike.

Until then, Allied commanders struggled to curb their troops' lascivious impulses. GIRLS WHO TAKE BOARDERS PROVIDE SOCIAL DISORDERS, street signs warned. Twenty "personal ablution centers" operated around the clock in Naples, providing the postcoital GI with soap, water, an iodine solution, and a receipt for his trouble. Still, as battles raged at Cassino and Anzio, 15 percent of all American hospital beds in Italy were occupied by VD patients. Another five hundred beds in Naples were reserved for infected prostitutes, in clinics dubbed "whorespitals." At the Bagnoli racetrack outside Naples, the 23rd General Hospital filled hundreds of beds with diseased Lotharios, whose hospital tunics were stenciled with a large red "VD"; despite the barbed wire and sentries ringing the compound, an Army provost marshal reported that some patients were "jumping the wall and consorting with the prostitutes in the immediate neighborhood." An exasperated major who discovered a tryst under way in a Bagnoli cave flushed the miscreants with tear gas grenades.

Near Avellino, in the hills above Salerno, even sterner measures were taken. "The chaplains thought the whores from Naples had been using the straw huts up and down the valley," one infantryman reported, "so they set fire to all of them."

The Orange Club was pleasant enough, and the opera house and the Capri chafing dishes offered an interlude from the war. But above all else Naples was a port, and by late winter 1944 it was among the world's busiest. Here "that huge and gassy thing called the war effort"—John Steinbeck's words—took solid form as the broad-shouldered avatar of Allied logistical hegemony. To keep a single GI fighting for a month in Italy required more than half a ton of matériel. Can do. For every artillery shell fired at Anzio, for every bomb dropped or Sherman tank lost at Cassino, two more seemed to levitate from the holds of arriving cargo ships, winched out by gantry cranes and placed on rail cars, truck beds, or LSTs bound for the front.

By now the American war machine had become the "prodigy of organization" so admired by Churchill and so dreaded by German commanders. U.S. production totals in 1943 had included 86,000 planes, compared with barely 2,000 in 1939. Also: 45,000 tanks, 98,000 bazookas, a million miles of communications wire, 18,000 new ships and craft, 648,000 trucks, nearly 6 million rifles, 26,000 mortars, and 61 million pairs of wool socks. Each day, another 71 million rounds of small-arms ammo spilled from U.S. munitions plants. In 1944, more of almost everything would be made.

The nation's conversion from a commercial to a military economy was as complete as it ever would be. An auto industry that had made 3.5 million private cars in 1941 turned out 139 during the rest of the war while shifting to tanks, jeeps, and bombers. In artillery production alone, makers of soap, soft drinks, bedsprings, toys, and microscopes now built 60 species of big guns; they were among 2,400 prime contractors and 20,000 subcontractors in the artillery business, from a steam shovel company building gun carriages to an elevator firm fashioning recoil mechanisms.

In February 1944, the U.S. Army shipped 3 million tons of cargo overseas, parsed into 6 million separate supply items that included not only beans and bullets but mildew-resistant shoelaces and khaki-colored pipe cleaners. Enormous consignments throughout the war went to Allied armies under the Lend-Lease program, including 43,000 planes, 880,000 submachine guns, and enough cans of Spam that sardonic Russian soldiers called them "Second Fronts." Inevitably, largesse fueled resentment, "the constant irritation to have to live to a large extent on American bounty," as one British general acknowledged. Tommies could not help but bristle when the British Army's daily toilet paper allotment was 3 sheets per soldier compared to the U.S. Army ration of 22½.

The prodigy also was prodigal, nowhere more than in the Mediterranean. Pilferage and ineconomy meant that "as much as one ship out of every five is stolen or wasted," the U.S. Army's supply chief, General Brehon B. Somervell, calculated in a letter to senior commanders on March 23. From Algiers to Naples, "we are losing gasoline, oil, food, clothing and other items which nobody can see why anybody would steal," Major General Everett S. Hughes replied from AFHQ headquarters. A Fifth Army study estimated that two-thirds of the Naples economy "derives from transactions in stolen Allied supplies." Thieves punched holes in moving rail cars and tossed out the contents, or surreptitiously tapped fuel pipelines running to Foggia. Frank Gervasi reported that an entire trainload of sugar had vanished, along with the train itself; the sugar supposedly sold for 400 lire a kilo on the black market, while the engine and rail cars were traced to a steel mill scrapheap. Horse-drawn funeral hearses were found stuffed with stolen goods from the docks. Whispered offers—"Pork. Beef. Pork. Beef"—could be heard in Neapolitan alleys, and a civil affairs officer claimed that "even an uncrated German fighter plane could be bought on the black market."

A separate prison was built at the port, where a drumhead court-martial heard up to eighty cases a day. Still, despite the fifteen hundred American MPs on duty in the city, it was said that local thieves could "whip the gold out of your eyeteeth while you're yawning." Norman Lewis described stolen Allied kit arrayed on the Via Forcella, with a sign: IF YOU DON'T SEE THE OVERSEAS ARTICLE YOU'RE LOOKING FOR, JUST ASK US AND WE'LL GET IT.

It hardly mattered. "Total war" was largely a German concept, conceived by General Erich Ludendorff as an alternative to the grinding stalemate of World War I. But the Americans had made it their own, stamping it with a Yankee efficiency and management genius that outproduced the Axis fourfold in heavy guns, fivefold in bombers, and sevenfold in transport planes. U.S. tank production in 1943 alone exceeded Germany's during the entire six years of war. In the last eighteen months of World War II, Germany produced seventy thousand trucks; the Allies collectively turned out more than one million.

Even though Kesselring's divisions tended to get more men and matériel than other theaters, German forces in Italy had begun to feel a severe pinch as winter drew to an end. A dearth of fuel drums was followed by shortages of fuel itself; by summer, the allocation for Italy would be halved, and mechanics concocted ersatz fuel distilled from wine, the residue of grape presses, and even acetone salvaged from varnish factories. Tire shortages forced a reduction of truck speed limits from sixty to forty kilometers per hour, and led to experiments with wooden wheels. German motor pools contained three thousand different types of vehicles, a mélange that complicated spare parts supplies.

Wehrmacht quartermasters reported dwindling stocks of iodine, soap, insulin, plaster of Paris, X-ray film, insecticide, dentures, and glass eyes. Kesselring's total ration strength topped one million men, including the Luftwaffe and various support units, and the daily supply allocation was fixed at a lean one kilogram per man. Not least was the difficulty in also victualing 95,000 horses, which required 900 tons of fodder every day and 200 tons of horseshoes and nails each month. Shortages of trucks and of dray horses sometimes forced gun teams to harness oxen and even cows to pull their tubes. A scheme to produce German munitions in northern Italian plants collapsed when factory managers realized that virtually all raw materials would have to be shipped south from the Fatherland, from coal and brass to tungsten and molybdenum.

Allied quartermasters had their own woes, including shortages of 155mm ammunition, watches, and binoculars. The incessant shelling at Anzio also took a grievous toll in water cans and kitchen equipment, not to mention men. Three hundred varieties of ammo, from carbine cartridges to bunker-busters, required extravagant inventory controls: bimonthly ordnance requisitions, in sextuplicate, weighed sixty pounds each. Fifth Army's supply arm, known as the Peninsular Base Section, by early spring of 1944 employed 65,000 soldiers; like rear-echelon troops in every war, they provoked snarling resentment among frontline veterans—one account called them "the most hated folk in Italy, the Germans running a poor second." Yet it was only necessary to visit the shoe section in the VI Corps supply dump at Anzio to sense the miracle of Allied preponderance: on any given day, clerks could instantly lay hands on new combat footwear ranging in size from 4AA to 16EEE.

As the fifth year of carnage played out, more than ever the total war had become a struggle not between rival ideologies or opposing tacticians but between systems—the integration of political, economic, and military forces needed for sustained offensive power. Certainly courage, audacity, and sacrifice would be required to win through to Rome, and to prevail globally. But every pallet of bombs, shells, and 16EEE boots hoisted from a Liberty ship in Naples harbor amplified and complemented those battlefield virtues, ensuring that valor would never be practiced in vain.

## *The Weight of Metal*

O F Italy's 116,000 square miles, none tormented Fifth Army more than the 600-acre swatch occupied by Cassino town. Now overwatched by the gray stub of the ruined abbey, the town boasted four churches, four hotels, a botanical garden, and a jail. All 22,000 citizens had fled or died, ceding the cobbled streets to General von Senger and German paratroopers in their brimless helmets, who in late February replaced the panzer grenadiers previously holding this sector of the Gustav Line.

All approaches from the south in this "small, peculiar and unhealthy piece of Italy," wrote Martha Gellhorn, were marred by "sliced houses, the landslides of rubble, the torn roofs." Highway 6, now scorched and lifeless, ran "straight as a bar of steel" for three miles from Monte Trocchio into town before swerving up the Liri Valley. Riflemen traded potshots and gunners exchanged artillery barrages, but drear stalemate took hold, in an "endless vigil that is never a quiet one," as one Gurkha officer wrote. In his diary he added:

> Time seems to have stopped. It is as if we have been condemned to live forever in a cold, damp hell on earth, each of us obtaining but meagre shelter behind rocks or in holes in the ground.

Not far from here, in 217 B.C., Hannibal had found himself hemmed in by mountains and Roman troops. Lashing dry twigs to the horns of two thousand rustled cattle, his soldiers set fire to the faggots and drove the herd onto the heights above confused enemy sentinels who mistook the flaming beasts for an encircling army of men carrying torches. Fearful of being outflanked, the Romans fled, Hannibal escaped, and his Carthaginians went on to win one of the greatest victories in Western military history at Cannae a year later.

No such stratagem occurred to Alexander, Clark, or their lieutenants. The high command seemed in the grip of a plodding fatalism, as if no man "was master of his own destiny," wrote a British officer. "There was no firm conviction among the leaders that victory would result." Alexander was inclined to lie low until spring weather dried the ground and cleared the skies, as both his staff and General Juin urged. Yet, under pressure from London and Washington, he felt obliged to tie up as many German divisions as possible before the Normandy invasion; he also hoped to prevent Kesselring from massing for further blows at Anzio. The tail now wagged the dog: the Anzio landings had been launched to break the Gustav Line impasse at Cassino; now another attack at Cassino was deemed necessary to help the beachhead.

In meetings at Caserta in late February, Alexander decreed that come spring the Allied front would be reconfigured to concentrate more combat power around the maw of the Liri Valley. Fifth Army was to shift to the left, taking over a coastal sector with a force that was mostly American and French. Eighth Army would also shift left, leaving a small presence on the Adriatic, while assuming responsibility for the Cassino front with the British X and XIII Corps, as well as I Canadian Corps and the newly arrived II Polish Corps. Clark privately rejoiced at unshackling himself from the British. "Anything that will divest me of the terrific responsibilities that I have had in trying to command McCreery's [X Corps] and Freyberg's corps will be welcome by me," he told his diary on February 28.

Before that happy day arrived, however, Fifth Army was to make one final attempt to bull through at Cassino with Spadger Freyberg's Kiwis, Brits, and Indians. But how? For the past two months, beginning with the French thrust northeast of Cassino and the American debacle at the Rapido, Allied attackers had avoided a direct assault into the town. Minefields and inundations hemmed both sides of Highway 6, turning the roadbed into a narrow, exposed funnel for any battalion approaching from Monte Trocchio. Yet Freyberg saw no alternative to a head-on attack. Convinced that a wide flanking movement around Monte Cassino was impossible, he "put his faith in the weight of metal," as the Indian official history later observed.

As the abbey had been pulverized, so now the town. New Zealand intelligence analysts proposed dropping three 1,000-pound bombs for each of the estimated 1,000 German paratroopers believed to be sheltering in Cassino. Freyberg calculated that just half that payload—perhaps 750 tons, reinforced by 200,000 artillery shells—would allow Allied infantry and armor forces to "walk through" the town, which he asserted could be cleared by tanks in six to twelve hours after the bombardment.

The use of airpower to bludgeon a hole through the Gustav Line found favor with Hap Arnold, the Army Air Forces chief, whose cables from Washington had become increasingly shrill. Why were daily air sorties in Italy running at 1,500 or fewer when "you with the British have a total of approximately 5,000 airplanes?" he asked Ira Eaker on February 24. "Why not 3,000 [sorties] until the situation is more in our favor?" In a petulant letter a few days later, Arnold condemned "the lack of ingenuity in the air action," adding, "We are all very greatly disturbed here at the apparent bogging down of the Italian campaign." Was it not possible to "break up every stone in the town behind which a German soldier might be hiding?" Such an attack "could really make air history," he wrote. "The whole future of the air forces is closely knit into this whole problem." Behind Arnold's military advice lay a larger political calculus: Air Force success in breaking the impasse at Cassino would strengthen his campaign to make the service independent of the U.S. Army.

Lieutenant General Eaker yielded to no man in airpower enthusiasm. Born in Texas and raised in southeast Oklahoma, he had been commissioned as an infantry officer in 1917 before transferring immediately to the flying service. As chief pilot of *Question Mark* in 1929, Eaker demonstrated the potential of airborne refueling by remaining aloft over Los Angeles for six days; several years later he made the first transcontinental flight while navigating solely by instruments. Coauthor with Arnold of three books on what they fondly called "this flying game," Eaker personally had persuaded Churchill a year earlier to endorse the Combined Bomber Offensive, a round-the-clock pummeling of Axis strategic targets with U.S. heavy bombers by day and British bombers by night. "There is nothing that can be destroyed by gunfire that cannot be destroyed by bombs," he once proclaimed. Before taking over the Mediterranean air forces in January, he had commanded the U.S. Eighth Air Force in Britain, where appalling crew losses and irregular bomb accuracy failed to shake his belief that the Third Reich could be gutted from the air.

He was less certain about Cassino. Obliterating the abbey had simply given German defenders both the moral and topographical high ground. Contrary to Freyberg's sunny estimate, an Army Air Forces study warned that "due to cratering and debris, tanks would probably not be able to pass through the town for 48 hours after the bombing." To Arnold, Eaker wrote on March 6, "Do not set your heart on a great victory as a result of this operation. Personally, I do not feel it will throw the German out of his present position completely and entirely, or compel him to abandon the defensive role." Unless ground forces attacked promptly, "little useful purpose is served" by bombardment. "We shall go forward and capture Rome when the weather permits," Eaker added, "and not before."

Yet in the absence of a plausible alternative—the latter-day equivalent of flaming livestock—Freyberg's plan carried the day: after bombers flattened the town, the 2nd New Zealand Division with help from Indian troops and American tanks would occupy the ruins and forge a bridgehead across the Rapido, while Indian troops seized Monte Cassino and opened the Liri Valley for armored forces to trundle up Highway 6 toward Rome. The scheme was code-named Operation DICKENS in honor of Charles Dickens, who after visiting Monte Cassino abbey had written a lugubrious account of "the deep sounding of its bell . . . while nothing is seen but the grey mist, moving solemnly and slowly, like a funeral procession."

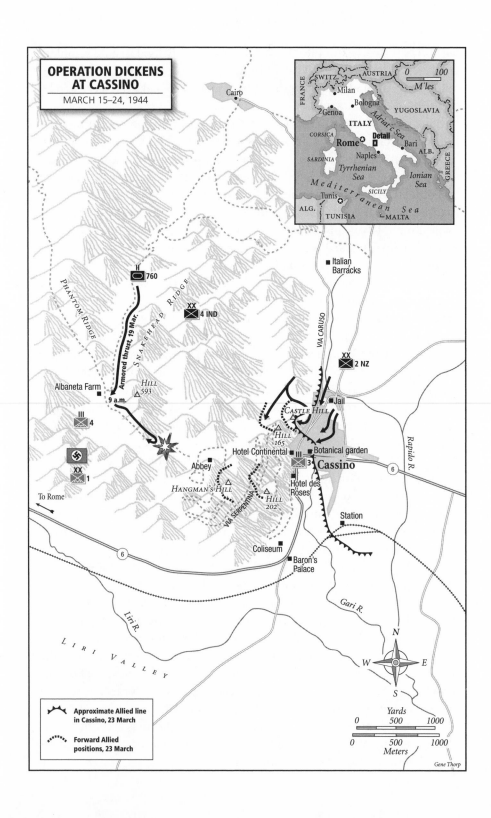

**OPERATION DICKENS
AT CASSINO**

MARCH 15–24, 1944

Cairo

SWITZ. AUSTRIA
FRANCE
Milan
Genoa **ITALY** Bologna YUGOSLAVIA
CORSICA Adriatic Sea
**Rome** Detail Bari
SARDINIA Naples ALB.
Tyrrhenian
Sea Ionian GREECE
Sea
Mediterranean Sea
Tunis SICILY
ALG.
TUNISIA MALTA

0    100
M'les

■ Italian
Barracks

VIA CARUSO

760

4 IND

2 NZ

PHANTOM RIDGE

SNAKEHEAD RIDGE

Albaneta Farm
*HILL*
△ 593

■ Jail

*CASTLE HILL*

III 4

XX 1

*HILL*
△ 165

Hotel Continental ■ Botanical garden
III 3 ■ **Cassino**

Abbey ■

*HANGMAN'S HILL* △

Hotel des
Roses

6

Rapido R.

VIA SERPENTINA

*HILL*
△ 202

To Rome

■ Station

■ Coliseum

Baron's
Palace

6

Gari R.

Liri R.

L I R I   V A L L E Y

N
W        E
S

Armored thrust, 19 Mar.

9 a.m.

Approximate Allied line
in Cassino, 23 March

Forward Allied
positions, 23 March

Yards
0    500    1000

0    500    1000
Meters

*Gene Thorp*

Freyberg insisted that the bombing coincide with three consecutive days of fair weather to dry the ground for attacking tanks. This demand fell on the Fifth Army meteorologist, Captain David M. Ludlum, a former high school history teacher who had earned his Ph.D. at Princeton and who was admired for his panache in wearing pajamas to bed during the darkest hours at Salerno. Perhaps to encourage a favorable forecast, the actual bombardment of Cassino town was named Operation LUDLUM.

Alas, the honor failed to inspire meteorological favor. Beginning in late February, rain fell day after dreary day. The eponymous captain studied his weather charts from dawn until midnight only to report yet again: more rain. A week passed, then another. In the hills behind Monte Cassino, Indian troops waited in their soggy holes, emerging only at night to briefly stretch their cramped muscles. Sickness or battle wounds claimed another Indian soldier every twenty minutes on average. Nebelwerfer fire raked the Allied positions, and by mid-March fifty-five German mortars had been counted around Cassino. With the entire New Zealand Corps keyed to attack on twenty-four hours' notice, "staleness, physical and psychological, was inevitable," as the official Kiwi history noted. Worse luck: on the afternoon of March 2, the able New Zealand division commander Howard Kippenberger climbed Monte Trocchio to survey the approaches along Highway 6 and tripped an undetected S-mine. The blast blew off one foot and mangled the other so badly that surgeons trimmed it away. In less than a month, Freyberg had lost his two best lieutenants, Tuker of the 4th Indian Division and now Kippenberger.

Never in his legendary career had he faced "so difficult an operation," Freyberg admitted in early March. The newly arriving commander of XIII Corps, Lieutenant General Sidney C. Kirkman, found Freyberg "very gloomy about the proposed attack" and furious at Clark, who, he complained, had "no ideas except to launch a succession of attacks regardless of casualties."

Unknown to Freyberg, Kirkman carried a note from the Eighth Army commander, General Leese, authorizing him to take command from Freyberg "if I saw fit." After several long conversations with the New Zealander, Kirkman chose to keep the warrant in his pocket, not least because Freyberg "would have been most annoyed and humiliated." But Operation DICKENS, he warned Leese on March 4, would likely gain little and cost much. The ground was too boggy for a sprightly advance and Allied reserves too meager to exploit any rupture in the Gustav Line.

The ground grew boggier: rain fell for a third week. Each evening, as twilight's gray tint faded to black in the west, the ravines and mountain roads leaped to life. Quartermasters hurried forward with supplies stacked in the beds of their grinding trucks, the cat's-eye blackout lights creeping up the muddy inclines until the track grew too steep or the enemy too bold. Swaying mule trains clopped behind the ridgelines, moving no quicker than a mile per hour despite whispered exhortations from the skinners; each animal could lug eighteen mortar rounds or an equivalent load, and a report from the front observed that "the mules are tranquil during shell fire, the Italian mule leaders are not." Only men could scale the steepest slopes, and panting bearers trudged toward the forward outposts with water cans and ammo belts lashed to their packboards, every ear cocked for the whine of a sniper's bullet or the telltale *pumpf!* of a mortar shell leaving its tube.

At dawn the landscape again grew still except for greasy smoke spiraling from one detonation or another. German ambulances rolled down Highway 6 with impunity until observers spied armed troops climbing from the rear; Kiwi artillery sent the next one fishtailing back up the Liri Valley. Careless enemy soldiers risked the frustrated wrath of the entire Fifth Army: a gunner on Monte Trocchio reported that when a solitary German strayed from his hole in Cassino town one morning "he was engaged by a holocaust of fire, including that of 8-inch howitzers."

At seven A.M. on Wednesday, March 15, Clark and Gruenther left the Fifth Army command post in Presenzano and drove by jeep past Monte Lungo to Freyberg's headquarters near San Pietro. Captain Ludlum had at last delivered good news. His Tuesday night forecast reported that a "frontal system over France yesterday morning has moved rapidly southeastward" to provide perfect bombing weather in Italy for the ides: sunshine, dead calm, a few thin clouds. The long-awaited warning order, drawn from cricket terms, was broadcast to all units: "Bradman will be batting tomorrow." Troops closest to Cassino crept back a thousand yards.

After a brief stop in the New Zealand encampment, Clark and Gruenther pressed ahead in a cavalcade that sped through Purple Heart Valley and past the rubble once known as San Pietro. Operation LUDLUM had attracted an eager crowd, including Devers, Eaker, Keyes, and Freyberg. Alexander appeared from Caserta in his own jeep with a gaggle of reporters in tow. Dressed in his fleece-lined jacket and red cap, he appeared as "calm, detached and attractive as usual," one admirer wrote; in a letter to his three children a few days earlier, Alexander had sketched a child in a nightshirt watching a hag with a pointed hat sail past on her broom. "So," the caption read, "there are witches after all!"

Before reaching Monte Trocchio, the convoy turned right to climb through San Vittore to the hill town of Cervaro. Clark followed a Kiwi officer into the decrepit stone house that would serve as his grandstand. After scanning the valley with his field glasses from a second-floor balcony, Clark climbed to the roof and straddled the ridgepole, his long legs dangling over the eaves. Three miles due west across the Rapido flats lay Cassino: the four churches, the four hotels, the botanical garden, the jail, all gleaming in the morning sun, all doomed.

He hardly cared. As of Tuesday, Fifth Army comprised 438,782 soldiers—205,000 Americans, 172,000 British, 49,000 French, 12,000 Italians—and to each of them Clark felt responsible for breaking the stalemate in Italy by whatever means necessary. The rain, the casualties, the internecine bickering, the impasse at Anzio, the brouhaha over the abbey—all had worn him down, even as the long winter made him harder, more obdurate. Every visit to a ward full of wounded boys left him "very depressed." When a sympathetic admiral wrote to remind Clark that "whom the Lord loveth he chasteneth," he replied, "Chastening already ample. Surely time has come to spare the rod." In early March he told Renie:

> I know you are upset about the Italian situation, and so am I, but there is nothing I can do about it except continue to do my duty. . . . You must look upon this Italian campaign as one little part of a world war where perhaps we do something the hard way in order to make successes in other places easier.

If broad-gauged and resolute, with what he described as "a keen and abiding interest in the little problems" of his men, he could also be pinched and querulous. To Geoff Keyes on Monday he had mused aloud about personally taking command at the Anzio beachhead. The feckless Lucas was gone, but Clark found Truscott "a difficult subordinate to handle. He makes demands, knowing full well that many of them can not be granted." Yet it was the British who annoyed him most. "I am convinced that Alexander is floundering in his effort to solve the tactical situation here," Clark told his war diary on March 8. Even Churchill seemed bent on provoking him from afar: an AFHQ staff officer reported that "all dispatches sent personally to the prime minister should spell 'theater' 't-h-e-a-t-r-e' and should not spell 'through' 't-h-r-u.'" When Churchill in early March ordered that troops at Anzio be known as the "Allied Bridgehead Force," Clark in a note to Alexander counterproposed "the Fifth Army Allied Bridgehead Force." He confessed in his diary to being "greatly annoyed," then added, "This is part of the steady effort by the British to increase their prestige."

For Clark, too, there were witches after all. Ever more convinced that others conspired to steal his thunder and deprive Fifth Army of battle honors fairly won, he struggled to keep his equilibrium against stress, exhaustion, pride, and insecurity. Only when he stood triumphant as an American proconsul in Rome would the world see that the sacrifices from Salerno to Cassino were justified. A gifted soldier, with a brain big enough and a spine stiff enough to wage the total war required in 1944, Mark Clark at times seemed to battle his own demons as bitterly as he fought the Germans.

A few days earlier he had mailed Renie a brooch set with red, white, and blue stones to form the Fifth Army insignia; it matched the three-star earrings she sometimes wore. "My problems get no less worrisome as the days go on," he confided in the accompanying note. "However, things will work out, and I am waiting for the day when I can lead my Fifth Army into victory."

At precisely 8:30 A.M., a faint sound overhead broke Clark's reverie. "Into the silence obtruded a drone, no louder than the buzz of a bee, but becoming louder by the second," wrote a British sapper. Heads swiveled, glasses glinted. Swarms of B-25 medium bombers appeared from the east at seven thousand feet, escorted by fighters. As the formation approached Cassino, the planes banked to the left. Bomb bays blinked open like a hundred dark eyes.

"The object of the attack," each flight crew had been told, "is to accomplish complete reduction of Cassino town." To terrorize German defenders, the lead squadrons were advised to "attach whistling devices"—known as screamers—"to as many bombs as practicable." The planes carried only thousand-pound blockbusters, with fuses set to detonate at basement depth: .1 seconds after impact in the nose and .025 seconds in the tail. Bombardiers had no aim points other than a quarter-mile radius around Cassino's heart. Medium bombers—the B-25 Mitchells and B-26 Marauders—were to strike the northern hemisphere, known as "A," while the heavies—the B-24 Liberators and B-17 Flying Fortresses—would hit the southern sector, "B." No Luftwaffe fighters appeared, and only a few flak blossoms blemished the cerulean sky.

The screamers screamed. Cassino abruptly vanished. "Sprout after sprout of black smoke leapt from the earth and curled upward like some dark forest," wrote Christopher Buckley. From Clark's ridgepole—it shuddered and swayed as each distant stick detonated—the first eight hundred bombs seemed to swallow the town in smoke and flame. "Target cabbaged real good," a crewman in the lead bomber reported. Soon after the first mediums flew off, Fortresses appeared, then more mediums, then more heavies, alternating between sector A and sector B.

"After a few minutes, I felt like shouting that's enough," wrote a Gurkha officer dug into a spur behind Monte Cassino. "But it went on and on until our ear drums were bursting and our senses were befuddled." Between bomb payloads, nearly nine hundred guns fired artillery concentrations code-named LENTIL, TROTSKY, and, improbably, GANDHI.

For more than three hours, the squadrons appeared at ten-to-twenty-minute intervals. Some bombs drifted into 4th Indian Division positions, provoking an adjutant's cry over the radio, "Stop those damn maniacs!" Even Freyberg was struck by the "terrible one-sidedness of the spectacle." But Buckley, who had been in Warsaw on September 1, 1939, wrote, "I remember from the evidence of my own eyes who was responsible for letting loose this terrible weapon."

At 12:12 P.M., as the last B-26 flew from sight, a lone P-38 swooped across Cassino, snapping reconnaissance photographs. They revealed buildings reduced to exoskeletons, a gray hive of door lintels and window frames, with the "peaks of broken buildings still standing, but the overall landscape only a misshapen pile of rubble." Cassino, the Army Air Forces reported, was "as flat as a stone city can be." The photos also showed that many craters already had begun to fill with groundwater.

Into the afternoon the artillery continued, six shells per second sweeping that piled rubble until nearly 200,000 rounds had fallen on the town and adjacent hills. Two New Zealand Corps divisions prepared to surge forward, the 2nd New Zealand through the town and the 4th Indian across Monte Cassino's flanks. Clark left his rooftop, strode half a mile down the road toward the town for a closer look, then circled back to other observation posts in Cervaro before once again dangling his legs over the eaves of his stone house. Alexander kept watch until two P.M. "Nothing," he declared, "could still be alive in the town." Eaker, keen to help Hap Arnold in the sacred quest for Air Force independence, publicly announced, "Today we fumigated Cassino and I am most hopeful when the smoke of today's battle clears we shall find more worthy occupants installed with little loss to our men."

He should have known better. Even before the bomb runs ended it was evident that more than a few payloads had fallen wide. At 10:15 A.M., several dozen Liberators plastered Venafro—eleven miles from Cassino. Six bombs hit the town and others splattered across an adjacent mountain. At 10:30, another Liberator group struck Venafro, followed by yet another at 11:25. Bombs battered General Juin's headquarters, killing fifteen French soldiers and wounding thirty others. More bombs hit the Eighth Army command post in a glade near Venafro, ripping open a mess hut and sending staff officers diving beneath their desks. "Ah," said General Leese upon returning to his headquarters, "I see our American friends have called." In an icy phone call to Clark, Leese said, "Tell me, as a matter of interest, is there anything we've done to offend you recently?"

Other bombs fell on the 4th Indian Division, the 3rd Algerian Division, a Moroccan military hospital, and a Polish bivouac. In a dozen incidents of imprecision during a two-hour period, nearly 100 Allied soldiers died and another 250 were wounded; in Venafro alone as many as 75 civilians were killed. Of 2,366 bombs dropped in LUDLUM, more than 300 were jettisoned or aimed at the wrong target. Less than half the total payload landed within a mile of central Cassino, while fewer than one bomb in ten struck inside the thousand-yard radius of sectors A and B.

Investigators found that flight leaders had flown no previous reconnaissance of the area. Some commanders treated LUDLUM too casually; heavy bomber crews, accustomed to hitting targets deep in enemy territory, often lacked the finesse required for a target tucked among friendly forces. Fifteenth Air Force also permitted bomber groups to select their own altitudes, and most flew too high despite the lack of enemy opposition. In the 459th Bomb Group, a malfunction in Liberator Dog 1-2 caused four bombs to drop prematurely; three other planes followed suit, despite orders to salvo their bombs only when the flight leader did. Similar violations in other groups "precipitated a contagious release throughout the entire attack unit." Through inexperience and "careless navigation," aircrews mistook Venafro, Isernia, Pozzilli, Montaquila, and Cervaro for Cassino. To make matters worse, the bombardier in a B-24H could not see the planes in front release their bombs and therefore relied on a bombs-away signal—usually a sharp kick in the back—from the navigator peering through a window. Clark and his fellow brass hats were fortunate not to fall in with the fratricidal dead.

Eaker and Devers favored prosecuting fourteen Air Force lieutenants, most of them bombardiers. Courts-martial proceedings began after an investigative report found "negligence, or at least poor judgment on the part of the accused"; yet the investigating officer, Brigadier General Joseph H. Atkinson, also recommended clemency for the airmen, whose average age was twenty-three. Charges subsequently were dropped against all but two lieutenants, who later went missing on subsequent missions.

"Let these young officers get on with the war," General Atkinson advised. "There is a lesson for all to learn from this very unfortunate incident."

Freyberg's intelligence had assumed that a thousand 1st Parachute Division soldiers occupied Cassino, but in fact only three hundred or so happened to be in the town when the first bomb fell. Thousands more held fortifications on Monte Cassino, Point 593, and neighboring slopes. Known as the Green Devils for the hue of their uniforms, the division's three regiments were considered the most formidable German troops in the Mediterranean. German paratroopers had fought ferociously against the New Zealanders on Crete in 1941, and against the Canadians at Ortona in December. After heavy losses in the winter campaign, replacements had nearly brought the division back to scratch under the portly, cigar-smoking Major General Richard Heidrich. Of Heidrich a 4th Indian Division assessment later concluded, "He was ruthless and not overnice."

Roughly half the paratroopers caught in Cassino on Wednesday morning outlived the day, and they described a maelstrom unlike anything experienced before or after. Explosions tossed men about like "scraps of paper," entombing them in cellars and tunnels. "We could no longer see each other," a German lieutenant recalled. "All we could do was to touch and feel the next man. The blackness of night enveloped us and on our tongues was the taste of burnt earth." To another lieutenant, "We were just like a submarine crew whose U-boat was being pursued by depth charges." Artillery fire proved especially devastating to German gun batteries, quickly destroying eighty-nine of ninety-four tubes in one regiment. The stench of decaying corpses soon seeped from Cassino's broken stones as it did from the abbey above; one sergeant thought the very dust tasted of bone. "The men clung to one another as if we were one lump of flesh," he said. "There was nothing we could do except weep and rage." A *Feldwebel* who was later captured told interrogators that the Allied bombardment was so unnerving that his men were forbidden to discuss it. "Speak about women, or anything else," he said, "but not about Cassino."

The town was "blown asunder and beaten into heaps of rubble," the official British history reported. Yet hundreds of bombs and thousands of shells failed to pound the town to powder, contrary to Allied expectations, nor were the surviving defenders "rendered comatose," as planned. A subsequent Air Force analysis found that although roofs and upper floors were obliterated, just south of the Hotel Continental "two rows of houses remain intact as to first floors and cellars," preserved by stout masonry arches and domed ceilings. The Continental's basement also survived, along with various "immensely solid" cellars, dugouts, caves, and a long tunnel from the Roman coliseum to Castle Hill. Munitions specialists later concluded that the .025-second tail fuses caused bombs to detonate just after punching through Cassino roofs; better to have set a slower fuse to penetrate deeper into the buildings, and to have followed them with incendiary bombs that would have ignited splintered floor timbers and smoked out any survivors.

Other paratroopers survived in steel, bell-shaped bunkers designed for two men but into which as many as six squeezed during the attack. "Bombs falling three to four yards from a pillbox lifted it out of its position without seriously harming the men inside," a prisoner later reported.

Under orders from Vietinghoff's Tenth Army, General von Senger told Heidrich to stand fast. The paratrooper commander eagerly agreed, convinced that he held an impregnable redoubt. Heidrich believed, he later said, that "Cassino was so ideally situated from a defensive standpoint that no frontal attack could have succeeded." Dust-caked paratroopers dug out of the rubble, stood to arms, then dug back in to prepare for the inevitable Allied assault. Sappers shored up the sagging ceilings in cellars around the Continental. The conversion of Cassino from crossroads market town to stand-or-die citadel was complete.

Still, Eaker continued to talk as if the Air Force had unlocked the gates of Rome. "The Germans would do well to bear in mind," he told reporters, "that what we have done to Fortress Cassino on the ides of March we will do to every other position they decide to hold."

Three hundred and fifty Allied tanks waited in the shadows to sweep through Cassino at one P.M. on Wednesday as a single New Zealand infantry battalion tramped south on Via Caruso along the Rapido River. Pushing into the smoke-draped town, the Kiwi riflemen found "a perplexing and dangerous shambles," with entire blocks reduced to "sprawling cairns of stone and brick." As scouts crept past the broken walls of the city jail, a spatter of picket fire broke the silence. Bullets nickered overhead and the cough of mortar tubes carried from Monte Cassino's lower slopes, along with the demented whine of a German machine gun.

The planned pace of one hundred yards' advance every ten minutes slowed to one hundred yards an hour. A squadron of Sherman tanks also trundled into Cassino, pitching up and down across the rubble "like a flotilla headed into a stormy sea," as the New Zealand official history described it. Crews dismounted with picks and shovels to clear the road for a few yards' advance only to find bomb craters so deep, so wide, and so plentiful that sappers would have to build bridges across them—some as long as seventy feet. After surveying the pocked landscape, now lashed with plunging fire from Monte Cassino's east face, Kiwi engineers calculated that they would need two days to bulldoze a path to the town center, even in peacetime.

Teeming rain fell at dusk, mocking Captain Ludlum's forecast and quickly turning the craters into moats. A second battalion followed the first into town; ordered to capture the rail station on Cassino's southern lip, the riflemen failed even to reach Highway 6 in the moonless labyrinth, "each soaked man . . . clinging miserably to the bayonet scabbard of the man in front," as Fred Majdalany recounted.

In the dying light, a single intrepid company had scaled the sheer hillside below the Rocca Janula, seizing the ancient bailey walls and the crumbling abbot's keep on Point 193, known as Castle Hill. It was the first good news of the day, and the last. Heidrich's paratroopers held several strongpoints on the rising ground of Cassino's southwest quarter, including the Hotel Continental, the Hotel des Roses, and a palazzo known as the Baron's Palace: each commanded views of Highway 6 in both directions. Hours passed before Kiwi reinforcements surged into the fight, and they amounted to a single rifle company; not for two days would as many as three battalions invest the town. By noon on Thursday, March 16, only nine tanks could be counted in Cassino, most of them immobilized by debris, craters, and galling fire. Rain and shell fire ruined radios and cut phone lines, leaving isolated companies to fight a dozen desperate, disconnected battles. Momentum stole away, and with it the chance to win through. The great armored fleet waited in the shadows, listening for a summoning trumpet that never sounded.

Several hundred feet above the town, the 4th Indian Division had its own miseries. Two companies of Rajputana Rifles reached Castle Hill with orders to seize the upper hairpins on the Via Serpentina. But artillery chopped two trailing companies to pieces, scattering the survivors and killing or wounding the battalion officers almost to a man. Another battalion, the 9th Gurkha Rifles, scuttled six hundred yards across the mountain face through gusts of mortar and machine-gun fire; one wounded captain commanded his company from a stretcher while clutching a pistol. By dawn on Thursday, March 16, the Gurkha vanguard held Hangman's Hill, a prominent shoulder only three hundred yards from the abbey walls.

However valiant, the feat proved a mixed blessing for Freyberg and his commanders. This isolated, eight-acre lodgment of five hundred Gurkhas on a steep brow of limestone became "a moral lien on the efforts of the corps," as the official Kiwi history acknowledged. Operation DICKENS quickly became as much about supporting the doughty, beleaguered Gurkhas as about breaking into the Liri Valley.

Beleaguered they were. "The fire was so heavy we could not lift our heads up," one survivor recalled. Riflemen built breastworks from stacked corpses and rummaged through the haversacks of dead comrades for crackers and grenades. Medics equipped with just scissors and pocket-knives amputated limbs in an open culvert. A courtyard well in a ruined farmhouse provided water, whose sharp flavor was found to derive from a dead mule at the bottom. Indian porters ordered to Hangman's Hill mutinied rather than cross half a mile of shell-swept no-man's-land; after the second day, resupply came only by air, in belly tanks dropped by A-36s from fifty feet, or by parachute. Gurkhas marked their position with colored smoke, which German paratroopers quickly mimicked to confuse the pilots. In 160 sorties, most bundles tumbled out of reach, including bags of blood for transfusions that floated onto the abbey to be seized by German surgeons.

Enough food and ammo fell within the perimeter to sustain the little redoubt on very short rations; a cask of rum helped comfort the wounded in their culvert. Yet unable to ascend or descend, tormented by mortar fire and creeping snipers, the Gurkhas remained marooned hour after hour, day after day. "Surely," a Gurkha officer, E. D. Smith, wrote in his diary, "it is pointless to keep on attacking the Monastery defences." He added, "God help us all."

An anxious Clark kept vigil at Presenzano, where the grumble of distant guns spilled down the valley like a drumroll. Hesitant to intrude on Freyberg's fight—meddling in a subordinate's tactical operation was considered bad form—Clark seethed at the plodding pace of the New Zealand attack.

"Freyberg's handling of the ensuing attack has been characterized by indecision and lack of aggressiveness," he told his diary on Friday. In visits to Spadger's command post, he urged that more infantry battalions be committed to battle. Freyberg and his staff resisted, convinced that three battalions in town and three more on the slopes sufficed; others must be held in reserve for a pursuit up the Liri Valley. Clark persisted, proposing that the British 78th Division attack the base of Monte Cassino while tanks struck from the north and more New Zealanders swept into town.

"I told Freyberg the tanks to be employed were American," Clark added in his diary entry on Friday. "He could lose them all and I would replace them within 24 hours." Freyberg replied that when casualties in the 2nd New Zealand Division reached a thousand he intended to abandon the attack unless success seemed imminent. By Saturday, Clark's exasperation was bitterly terse: "Freyberg is not aggressive; is ponderous and slow."

Whether additional firepower could have sundered the German line is problematic. Kiwi riflemen had captured Cassino's rail station and fought through the charred botanical gardens to within two hundred yards of the Hotel Continental. "Push on, you must go hard," Freyberg urged. But an attempt to capture the hotel "through the servants' entrance" by swarming downhill from the hairpin turn known as Point 202 ended badly: machine-gun slugs cut down the lead attackers and sent others scampering back up the slope. Freyberg finally threw a fourth battalion into the town late on Saturday, but paratroopers had reinforced their strongpoints as well as the battered houses below Castle Hill.

"Almost every building or stump of a building contained a sniper's or machine gunner's post," the New Zealand Corps noted. "The town was a place of unexpected encounters." Paratroopers reinfested structures already cleared; forty Maoris would share a house with the enemy for three days, occasionally shooting through the walls, and a dressing station was evacuated from one cellar so that Sherman tanks could blast an enemy machine-gun nest on an upper floor of the same building. Soldiers began referring to Cassino as "Little Stalingrad."

On Sunday, March 19, as the battle for the town stalemated, two death struggles on opposite faces of Monte Cassino decided the battle for the mountain. Just before dawn, three hundred paratroopers bounded down the slope from the abbey, green ghosts skidding on the scree and shooting from the hip. An outpost of Essex and Rajputana soldiers at Point 165 was said to have "disappeared in a smother of enemies"; moments later, howling Germans beat against the bailey walls from three sides on Castle Hill. Stick grenades twirled over the parapets into the inner courtyard, where 150 defenders fired their Brens and tommy guns through arrow loopholes. Scarlet, green, and orange tracers spattered off the walls, and German mortar rounds crashed among the tumbled stones in great sprays of red and silver.

An arcing signal flare after twenty minutes recalled the attackers, but as night thinned in the east they struck again, hammering the castle gate like insolent Saracens while Heidrich's gunners in the town below added more streams of fire. A sniper's bullet drilled the British commander through the brain—"We talked a bit and then he died," a fellow officer later reported—but once again the defenders, now reduced to barely sixty men, beat back the attack. In a third assault, at nine A.M., eight paratroopers drew close enough to detonate a demolition satchel beneath a buttress on the west wall; dust and smoke billowed through the bailey, and twenty-two Essex soldiers lay interred beneath the masonry. Yet every German who leaped into the breach was cut down with savage bursts of gunfire from the courtyard. Tommies ran the gauntlet from Via Caruso up to the castle keep, lugging sandbags stuffed with ammunition. Mortar barrels glowed like pokers in a hearth; after fifteen hundred rounds, several tubes lay bent and useless. By early afternoon the shooting had subsided to a sullen bicker and Castle Hill, unconquered, was paved with dead paratroopers; every Essex officer was dead or wounded. A captured German sergeant major offered congratulations and, lacking a sword, tendered his fur-lined gloves as a trophy. But the 4th Indian purchase on Monte Cassino's eastern slope was more precarious than ever.

Two thousand yards across the crest, below the mountain's west face, the second struggle also played out on the Sabbath morn. Over the past two weeks, sappers had built a rough road along Snakeshead Ridge, using bulldozers and a ton of explosives to chew through the limestone. With orders to "cause chaos and consternation in the ranks of the Hun"—not unlike Hannibal crossing the Alps with his elephants—an armored fleet moved south in two columns on the virgin road at six A.M.: sixteen Kiwi Shermans, eight Indian tanks, and sixteen light M-3 General Stuarts from the U.S. 760th Tank Battalion. By nine A.M., the road had narrowed to a corrugated lane as the procession turned toward the abbey at Albaneta Farm. Around Point 593, the weather-gnawed bodies of 34th Division soldiers killed six weeks earlier still lay wedged among the rocks, lost boys turned to bone and stone. Tankers could peer down into the Liri Valley on their right, then swivel left to see the abbey's fractured walls half a mile across the rift to the left known as Death Valley.

Then the noose cinched. A German lieutenant managed to lay three mines on the path, blowing the tracks off the lead Stuart. Immobile and angry, the Yank crewmen opened fire on an enemy mule train clopping toward the abbey, killing fifteen Germans and five animals with more than 80 tank shells and 2,500 coaxial machine-gun bullets. "I hated to shoot the mules as they looked like good ones," the tank commander later confessed. But the column was stuck, unable to maneuver on the narrow trail and insufficiently protected by lagging infantry. As more tanks came to grief, striking mines or brewing up from mortar fire, German snipers picked off crewmen squirming through their belly hatches. At 5:30 P.M. those tanks still capable of movement began to creep back up Snakeshead Ridge, turrets reversed, firing over their exhaust vents. Three Shermans and three Stuarts had been destroyed, and sixteen others damaged. As night descended on Sunday, flaming hulls stood like orange beacons along the futile path past Albaneta Farm.

General von Senger on several occasions had skirted the spiny ridge northwest of Point 593 as he stalked the battlefield with his walking stick. Using the abbey as a pole star, he traveled alone and on foot to be less conspicuous—an adjutant trailed several hundred yards behind the corps commander—and always in daylight, to see as much as possible. "No tree escaped damage, no piece of ground remained green," Senger noted. When shell fire drew near, he went to ground or zigged and zagged, aware of "the whistling of splinters, the smell of freshly thrown-up earth . . . smells from glowing iron and burnt powder." At times he imagined that he had been "carried back thirty years and was wandering across the battlefield at the Somme."

Little reliable information had seeped from Cassino during the first two days after the bombing. Senger knew that Heidrich often failed to report lost ground on the assumption that his paratroopers would soon reclaim it. At times it seemed the town must surely fall, rupturing the Gustav Line. "Things are not too splendid here," Tenth Army had advised Kesselring on Friday morning. Some battalions had been pared to platoon size: forty men. Machine gunners were even forced to fire sparingly lest the raised dust betray their nests. Senger hoped for more rain.

Yet the failed Allied tank foray on Sunday and the paratroopers' near seizure of Castle Hill gave renewed hope. Entrenched Germans held the abbey ruins with mortars, machine guns, and phones linked to a network of artillery observers; no one heeded the addled monk flitting through the ruined cloisters. Allied smoke was noxious—on Saturday alone 22,000 smoke rounds had been fired in an effort to blind the German observers—but the paratroopers simply donned their gas masks, which also mitigated the stench of decay. Falling smoke canisters caused "a number of unpleasant wounds," but Indian troops themselves complained that the smoke "screened nothing from nobody."

As for the town, Senger thought the initial Allied attacks lacked urgency. Enemy assault companies continued to butt against German strongpoints rather than skirting them to let follow-on forces mop up. The rubble canalized Allied armor, and German gunners, if overmatched, managed to mass fires with artillery, rockets, and even antiaircraft guns. Much had been learned from the catastrophes at Stalingrad and Ortona about urban warfare. Savage fighting remained, but there was a chance the town would hold. Perhaps the most heartening sign came from the irascible Heidrich, who despite Senger's offer to reinforce him with an entire panzer grenadier regiment balked at sharing the glory of defending Cassino with any forces not wearing paratrooper green.

General Freyberg also prowled the lowering hills—one morning, he stopped within mortar range of Monte Cassino to listen for nightingales—and he was reaching the same conclusion as his German adversary: the town would not fall. "Another lovely day—climatically," he told his diary on Monday, March 20, yet there was no climax, only more death and misery for niggling gains. Each day he parsed the casualty returns, his arithmetical scribbles covering the pages as the New Zealanders approached and then far surpassed his threshold of a thousand killed, wounded, and missing. "I think you and the Boche are both groggy," Clark told him, but Freyberg chose to press the fight despite private doubts. In a conference on Tuesday afternoon, March 21—the date St. Benedict died on Monte Cassino—he rallied Alexander, Clark, and Leese with hope of a breakthrough. "Surely the enemy is very hard pressed too," Churchill cabled Alexander.

No breakthrough obtained. "Unfortunately we are fighting the best soldiers in the world—what men!" Alexander wrote Brooke on Wednesday with perhaps excessive admiration. German troops still held the northwest and southwest corners of Cassino and enough of the beetling slope to isolate the Indian troops on Hangman's Hill and the Kiwis holding the lower hairpin at Point 202. On Thursday, eight days after the bombing, Freyberg asked to pull back. When Field Marshal Wilson urged him to soldier on, Freyberg replied with the single proper noun that froze the blood of any British general: "Passchendaele," the grisly Flemish battlefield of 1917.

Alexander concurred, as did Clark, who proposed keeping Kiwi casualty figures secret to avoid alarming the home front. "The NZ Division has shot its bolt, as well as the Indian Division," Clark told his diary, "but I wanted the recommendation to call off the attack to come from the British. . . . I hate to see the Cassino show flop. It has been a most difficult situation. . . . The New Zealanders and Indians have not fought well."

That calumny betrayed the valor of several hundred dead men, as well as several hundred still alive after eight days on bleak and wintry Hangman's Hill. The Gurkhas' daily rations had dwindled to one sardine and a single biscuit per man; weak with hunger, hectored by sniper fire from the abbey gardens, at dusk they nestled together like spoons and shivered until dawn. To evacuate the survivors without the risk that German eavesdroppers would intercept a radioed order, three officers below volunteered to carry the word uphill. Each in his tunic tucked a paper bag holding a carrier pigeon, respectively named St. George, St. Andrew, and St. David. Two of the officers reached Hangman's Hill, where they informed the Gurkhas of the withdrawal and released the birds to confirm that the message had been delivered. Despite what was described as "a considerable spot of shooing," St. George and St. Andrew flew just thirty yards before settling on a rock outcropping. There they remained "in full view of the enemy and preened themselves for about twenty minutes, watched by the anxious Gurkhas" before flying back to the brigade loft.

At 8:15 P.M. on Friday, March 24, some 259 Gurkhas crept down the slope, quiet as cats, between parallel walls of covering artillery. At Point 202 they picked up forty-five Kiwis and left their badly wounded with a keg of rum and a large red cross snipped from parachute silk. Swinging left down the Via Serpentina, the column slipped over the lip of Castle Hill at eleven P.M. Jeeps met them on the Rapido's far bank, ferrying the men to Portella for food and hot tea. "Never will I forget that nightmare of a march," a Gurkha officer wrote. "At times we had no alternative but to strike soldiers who just gave up interest in anything, including a desire to live."

By late Saturday, a swastika flag flew above Hangman's Hill. Heidrich's patrols counted 165 Gurkha corpses, now dusted in white. "There has been a heavy fall of snow," a German machine gunner jotted in his diary on March 25. "You would think we are in Russia."

The New Zealand Corps disbanded at noon on Sunday, March 26, having outlived its usefulness. In the past eleven days the corps had suffered 2,100 casualties, nearly twice as many as Senger's defenders. The 4th Indian Division in particular had been grievously injured at Cassino, with more than four thousand casualties since mid-February. Leaving behind what one British general called "that valley of evil memory," the Rajputs and Gurkhas limped to a quiet sector on the Adriatic to lick their wounds. Other divisions were to stand by for orders. "We are now to assume an attitude of 'very offensive defensive probing,'" Keyes advised his diary. "What in God's name is that?"

Operation DICKENS was the third Allied attempt in two months to break through at Cassino, and the third failure. Through the ranks spread "a persistent feeling that something, somewhere, had gone wrong," the official U.S. Army history later acknowledged. Most of the terrain won had been seized early by the Americans in their futile escalade in January; since then, little had been gained and many had been lost. In this most recent assault, as a Gurkha officer wrote, "The strongest defences in Europe were attacked by a single corps, consisting of two divisions, on a narrow front in the heart of winter without any attempt at diversionary operations." The New Zealand official history conceded that "the attack showed little of that tactical originality which is commonly called surprise."

Something *had* gone wrong. For Allied soldiers, each battle had become an attritive bloodletting on ground not of their choosing. No coherent master plan governed the offensives, but rather a succession of unsynchronized schemes that lacked the requisite heft: a division here, a division there, probing for soft spots. Limitations on the weight of metal had been revealed, first at the abbey, then in the town, which in addition to all those bombs absorbed almost 600,000 artillery shells. The Kiwi history concluded that

"Cassino was a battle of the First World War fought with the weapons of the Second," but at times it resembled a battle of the Second fought with weapons of the First.

Failure in combat usually implies inadequate leaders, and brilliant Allied generalship was conspicuously absent at Cassino. Freyberg and other Commonwealth commanders fretted at Clark's insouciance about casualties. Just so, but the strategy of "naked attrition"—as the British official history called it—belonged to Alexander. The British also still considered the tank a decisive arm, as if the Apennines were Alamein, rather than recognizing it for "what it was in Italy, a crawling monster which produced little except congestion, confusion and delay." Freyberg had six hundred tanks parked around Cassino, sixfold Senger's armored fleet, but he never could fling more than a tenth of them into the fight simultaneously. Other martial axioms had been forgotten or brushed aside at the Gustav Line: that command of the sea gave an open flank into the enemy's rear, often obviating the need for terrestrial frontal assault; that rubbly, cratered battlefields impeded mobility, as had been seen, in fact, at Passchendaele in July 1917; that the ancient requisite for an attacker to muster a three-to-one manpower advantage rarely was truer than in mountainous terrain, which devoured battalions. The New Zealand Corps never managed even a two-to-one ratio. General Tuker, sidelined in his sickbed, considered these accumulated miscalculations "military sins no less."

"Bombardment alone never had and never will drive a determined enemy from his position," Clark wrote, with the thin satisfaction of a man vindicated by calamity. Cassino had thrice proved "a terrible nut to crack," as Ernie Harmon observed in a sympathy note to Clark on March 28. If Heidrich was right, if direct assault was doomed to fail, then only a wide flanking maneuver through inaccessible terrain by a division or two of agile, well-provisioned troops would break the deadlock.

Juin, Keyes, and others had for months urged such a course, and Alexander now saw merit in their petition. To the prime minister he wrote, "A little later when snow goes off [the] mountains, the rivers drop, and the ground hardens, movement will be possible over terrain which at present is impassable." Churchill, whom one British strategist described as the "presiding deity throughout this soft underbelly campaign," replied sourly, "The war weighs very heavy on us all just now."

It weighed heavy on the far side of the mountain as well. Senger continued his lonely tramps over hill and dale, proud to still hold the superior high ground. Hangman's Hill, Point 593, the abbey itself—all remained in German hands. Yet Senger was too good a soldier for self-delusion. "All this," he wrote, "did not blind me to the fact that our successes were of a temporary nature."

## *Dragonflies in the Sun*

THE war weighed heaviest on the men actually fighting it, of course. Nine months of combat in Italy had annealed those whom it had not destroyed. The fiery crucibles from Sicily to Cassino left them hard and even hateful. "After you get whipped and humiliated a couple of times and you have seen your friends killed, then killing becomes a business and you get pretty good at it pretty fast," one Tommy explained. Plodding up the Italian boot, they left their peaceable civilian selves on the roadsides like shed skins. In a letter to his family in Indiana, a lieutenant who had once been a newspaper reporter described "a callousness to death, a bitter hatred of the Jerries, a burning desire to avenge what they have done to us. This supersedes fear for ourselves." Every payload dumped by a B-17 became a personal token of malice. "We get quite a kick out of the devastation wrought by our Fortresses," another soldier wrote home. "War is like that: you actually enjoy the knowledge that you are killing countless numbers of your enemies."

For soldiers in twenty or more Allied divisions, war by the early spring of 1944 seemed ever more primeval. "One goes on fighting, killing, simply because one has to," wrote Raleigh Trevelyan, a British lieutenant at Anzio. A 1st Special Service Force soldier from St. Louis told Eric Sevareid, "It's so easy to kill. It solves all your problems, and there are no questions asked. I think I'm getting the habit." Daily life in combat units resolved itself into noise, filth, isolation, confusion, fatigue, and mortality; everything else seemed extraneous. Soldiers distrusted the gung ho, the cocksure, and anyone less miserable than themselves. "We learned to live as perhaps once we were long ago, as simply as animals without hope for ourselves or pity for another," wrote John Muirhead, a B-17 crewman. The conceits of fate, destiny, and God comforted some, but believers and nonbelievers alike rubbed their crucifixes and lucky coins and St. Christopher medals with a suspicion, as Muirhead said, that "one is never saved for long."

They saw things that seared them forever: butchered friends, sobbing children, butchered children, sobbing friends. "Watched an amputation last night," an ambulance driver wrote in his diary. "A Tommy stretcher bearer had stood on a mine and he had to have both legs taken off. One above the knee and one below the knee." It made soft men hard and hard men harder.

A counterintelligence officer noted that combat veterans "are sometimes possessed by a fury that makes them capable of anything. . . . It is as if they are seized by a demon." Soldiers walking through a killing field sometimes stomped on the distended bellies of dead Germans to hear the flatulent noises the corpses made. "Slowly I am becoming insensitive to everything," wrote one soldier in his diary. "God in Heaven, help me to keep my humanity."

Many considered humanity an impediment to survival. A survey of infantry divisions in the Mediterranean later found that 62 percent believed hatred for the enemy could help them through tough times. "The more you hate, the better soldier you become," explained one command sergeant major. "Love is completely absent in the heart of a rifleman." Like lightning seeking a ground, the high-voltage animus surging through Allied combat regiments discharged on one conducting rod: the German. "He has no right to do this to me," the commander of the 132nd Field Artillery Battalion wrote his wife, "and I shall do something to him for it." From Anzio, a 3rd Infantry Division officer wrote, "They sure cause a lot of unnecessary suffering. I wouldn't mind participating in their complete elimination— like a rabid dog." Rancor at the beachhead grew intense enough that wounded German prisoners were isolated in a separate hospital ward for their own protection. "Those Krauts," a paratrooper in the 504th Parachute Infantry said, "I sure hate their guts."

Many atrocity stories circulated, particularly of German white-flag ruses. Some were true, all were believed. "There's no rules in this war," a 45th Division soldier said. "If they want to fight like that, it's okay with us." Because of a supposed German tendency to shoot surrendering Yanks, one soldier reported, the 6th Armored Infantry Regiment's unofficial slogan had become "Take No Prisoners." He added, "We now do the same thing, and we have plenty of Germans to do it to."

From the Tunisian campaign, four U.S. combat divisions had emerged full of killers. Italy created many more, American as well as British, Canadian, French, New Zealand, Indian, Polish, and others. Together they would form an avenging and victorious army, a terrible sword of righteousness. A VI Corps officer proposed that every soldier embody the "three R's—ruthless, relentless, remorseless." As the abbey and Cassino town had been pulverized, so would a thousand other strongholds. God could sift the guilty from the innocent. The war had come to that.

"This is a war for keeps," an Air Force captain wrote his mother from Italy. "We will not rest satisfied until starvation and butchery have been visited upon German soil. There can be no parleying with the Devil."

\* \* \*

Eager boys no longer scaled Rome's clock towers to watch for the Anglo-American legions pressing north from Anzio. For days after the SHINGLE landings in January, tens of thousands of Romans had kept vigil on their rooftops in the Eternal City. Allied flags flapped from balconies, and book-stores reported a run on English dictionaries. Jumpy German sentries one night fired on a sinister platoon of figures, which proved to be the stone saints lining the façade of the basilica of St. John Lateran.

Those heady hopes for imminent liberation had long faded. These days the nearest Allied troops flew four miles overhead in air armadas said to re-semble "dragonflies in the sun." Nervous Romans kept their weather eyes peeled for the clear skies of what came to be called *una giornata da B-17*, a B-17 day. The worst bombing of the capital since July occurred on March 14, when various rail yards were pummeled; civilian casualties proved par-ticularly grim among those queued up for water at street fountains. Graffiti on city walls now chided the liberators for dawdling. One mordant gibe proclaimed: "Allies, don't worry! We are coming to rescue you!"

Eight months of occupation had sharpened Roman cynicism. At first the German fist only lightly swiped the city. Wehrmacht looters plucked clean the palaces of the turncoat royal family, such as the Villa Savoia, where Mussolini had been arrested. "Everything went," one witness re-ported, "including the nails in the walls." But the cinemas soon reopened, and the royal opera house. Recruiting posters for German labor battalions showed a smiling Italian tradesman with a flower in his buttonhole, smok-ing a cigarette. "Do you want to work? Are you in need?" the caption asked. "Employment only within your country. You are assured good clothes, good food, good pay, and good fellowship." Fifty thousand Italians, volun-teers and otherwise, still toiled on fortifications along the country's west coast.

The shadows soon deepened. Berlin had always considered Mussolini to be weak-kneed on the Jewish question, and on September 24, 1943, with the Duce reduced to a pathetic puppet, the Reichsführer-SS, Heinrich Himm-ler, secretly ordered the Gestapo chief in Rome, Lieutenant Colonel Her-bert Kappler, to arrest all Jews in the city. The thirty-five-year-old Kappler, gray-eyed son of a Stuttgart chauffeur, had lived in Rome since 1939. He was described as "intolerant, cold, vengeful, unhappily married and with interests in Etruscan vases, roses, and photography"; when he grew an-noyed, the dueling scar on his cheek reddened. Two days later, Kappler gave Jewish community leaders thirty-six hours to deliver fifty kilograms of gold or face the deportation of two hundred men. On September 28, a con-voy of taxis and private cars pulled up to the Gestapo headquarters at Via Tasso 155 number with the ransom, which was laid on a scale pan amid much haggling over the last gram. Three weeks later, at dawn on Saturday, October 16, storm troopers swept through the Roman ghetto anyway, seizing twelve hundred Jews; sixteen of them survived the war. Most were promptly shipped to Auschwitz and gassed, including an infant born after the roundup. Mussolini on December 1 ordered the arrest of "all Jews living on the national territory." Italians showed admirable pluck in sheltering Jewish compatriots: nearly five thousand hid in Roman convents, monasteries, and the Vatican. More than forty thousand Jews in Italy would survive the war; nearly eight thousand perished.

Even for Romans not facing extermination, the occupation winter proved long and grim. Several hundred thousand refugees crowded the city, felling trees and chopping up park benches for firewood. Electricity supplies grew erratic: alternating neighborhoods went without power two nights each week. Tuberculosis and infant mortality spiked. Kesselring's retreat to the Gustav Line hampered efforts to feed the city, for much of Rome's granary lay in southern Italy; the destruction of supply trucks by Allied warplanes further complicated the task.

Prices doubled, and would redouble by early summer. Hungry livestock could graze on the new spring grass at the Villa Borghese, but the Romans had begun to starve. On downtown sidewalks women peddled their furs, scholars their books, children their shoes. The daily bread ration dwindled to the equivalent of two slices per person, from loaves made with ground chickpeas, maize flour, elm pith, and mulberry leaves. As spring arrived, so did bread riots; after one bakery was ransacked, SS troops dragged ten Italian women to a nearby bridge and shot them as they faced the Tiber.

Terror also doubled and redoubled. Blackshirts finding a film too tedious shot up the screen; another thug with a submachine gun leaped on stage at an opera and threatened to murder those who failed to stand for the Fascist anthem "Giovanezza." In the central telephone exchange, five hundred eavesdroppers reportedly listened in on local phone calls. Men were plucked from trams or rounded up in the Via Nazionale for labor battalions, with no mention made of good pay or good fellowship. A priest condemned for subversion blessed his firing squad as they shouldered their rifles.

Soon half of Rome was said to be hiding the other half. Interrogators in the Via Tasso extracted confessions by pushing pins through a suspect's penis or by stuffing his ears with cotton and lighting it; others had their shoes removed and their toes inserted between the cylindrical drum and base plate of a mimeograph machine. "They pulled out the hairs of my mustache, and by means of screws and a steel bar, they compressed my temples until I thought my eyes were going to burst out," a survivor said of his interrogation on the night of March 18. On the eve of his execution, one man scratched a message on his cell wall: "From my mother I ask forgiveness because in being faithful to myself I must be faithless to her love. . . . Long live Italy."

Allied planes flying from Brindisi dropped tons of supplies and scores of agents behind the lines. Intended to inspirit Italian insurgents and dishearten German troops, OSS "morale operations" ranged from the clever to the puerile. Scattered pamphlets listed the bombed streets in every German city. Leaflets instructed Wehrmacht soldiers on how to defect to Switzerland, and a "malingering booklet" prescribed methods to avoid combat by feigning various illnesses. *Scheisse*—shit—stickers mimicking the runic double "S" of the SS were designed to "be licked on the tongue and slapped on a wall in an instant." Small stencils could leave a painted message in seven seconds, including one in Italian that read, GERMANS OUT. Tiny rubber stamps, equipped with tiny ink pads, depicted a skull and crossbones over the word "Nazi." Project CORNFLAKES dropped 320 sacks of counterfeit mail along bombed Italian rail lines, as if the bags had been scattered from wrecked train cars; some envelopes—carefully franked with German postmarks—included forged subversive letters and copies of *Das Neue Deutschland,* the ostensible newspaper of an underground peace party. A "Father Schiller," who wrote a column advocating German capitulation, was in fact a pair of U.S. Army sergeants.

In Rome, the OSS by March 1944 had established a dozen observation posts on the main roads leading from the capital, with coded information about traffic radioed to the Anzio beachhead several times a day; one clandestine shortwave station operated in a boathouse belonging to the Italian Finance Ministry. An Italian operative in Kesselring's headquarters, an ardent royalist who served as a liaison with the Fascist command in Rome, also secretly provided the German order of battle and details about the FISCHFANG counterattack.

No OSS spy in Rome was more flamboyant than a twenty-four-year-old American named Peter Tompkins, who had lived in the city as a boy after his parents moved there to study art. Educated at English boarding schools—thanks in part to the patronage of his mother's alleged lover, George Bernard Shaw—and then at Harvard, Tompkins had worked as a foreign correspondent before joining the OSS. In late January, a Royal Navy patrol boat put him ashore near Rome carrying a Beretta pistol and papers that identified him as a Roman prince. Tompkins had expected to greet Fifth Army liberators in a few days; instead he waited week after week, jumping from safe house to safe house: a dressmaker's shop on the Via Condotti, a room in the Piazza Lovatelli.

Favoring a blue sharkskin suit with loose strands of Italian tobacco sprinkled in the pocket for verisimilitude, Tompkins collated the traffic reports, the order-of-battle lists, and other intelligence tidbits into daily radio bulletins to the beachhead. OSS operations in Rome, as in Italy at large, proved confused and often bootless, riven with rivalries and petty quarrels. Meaningful intelligence paled compared with that plucked from the airwaves by Ultra, of which Tompkins was ignorant.

Still, it was part of the good fight, requiring ingenuity, luck, and unspeakable courage. Tompkins kept moving, exchanging an identity card that identified him as Luigi Desideri, born in 1912, for one on which he was Roberto Berlingeri, born in 1914, or an employee in the War Ministry, or an archivist in the Corporations Ministry, or a corporal in the Italian African Police. Sprinkling bottled ammonia around his doorstep to discourage bloodhounds, he played cutthroat bridge, sipped brandy, and read Faulkner's *The Wild Palms* while waiting to transmit the next coded dispatch. "In a way it's a pleasant life," he told his diary in mid-March, "if it weren't for the nightmare of knowing that all the time you are hunted."

Nearly twenty highway watchers, most of whom earned $1 a day, were captured and shot; shot, too, was the spy in Kesselring's headquarters, after two months of torture that failed to break him. Yet German repression only steeled resistance. An estimated 25,000 Italian partisans were actively fighting in Italy in March 1944, and their number would triple in the next three months; later Alexander claimed they were "holding in check six German divisions." Some attacked bridges or looted supply trains; others encouraged civil disobedience, such as the strike by 800,000 Italians in early March that almost paralyzed industrial Milan. And still others plotted how to answer terror with terror, vengeance with vengeance, blood with more blood.

The clap of several hundred boots on cobblestones carried up the narrow Via Rasella at 3:40 P.M. on Thursday, March 23, another lovely *giornata da B-17*. As the 11th Company of the 3rd Battalion of the Bozen Police Regiment wheeled left into the street from the Via del Traforo, the men burst into song, an annoying martial ditty called "Hupf, Mein Mädel"—"Skip, My Lassie." "Singing at the top of our lungs," as one trooper later recalled, "chests pushed forward like a bunch of crowing roosters."

From the Piazza del Popolo they had marched three abreast, as they marched each afternoon, through central Rome: past the Spanish Steps and the house where Shelley lived and Keats died, skirting the royal gardens of the Quirinal as they angled back to the Interior Ministry compound in the Viminale barracks. Their accents identified them as men of the South

Tyrol; crow's-feet and graying temples beneath their helmets suggested that most were too old for combat regiments. Today they had taken the precaution of loading their rifles, but the capital seemed placid and benign in the afternoon sunshine.

They huffed uphill, past the barber and the photo shop and the laundry that took in German uniforms. Geraniums spilled from the sill pots of the five-story buildings and palmettos peered over the gutter lines. No one heeded the moonfaced Italian street sweeper smoking a pipe and cleaning the gutter near the head of the street, fifty yards or so from the intersection with the Via delle Quattro Fontane.

He was in fact a medical student named Rosario Bentivegna, known to his fellow partisans as Paolo. Earlier that afternoon he had eaten lunch in a little trattoria before changing into a sanitation department uniform, lacing his battered shoes with red string for authenticity. Then Bentivegna had muscled his ash cart—stolen from a city depot behind the Colosseum—through the streets before parking it against the curb at Via Rasella 156, a dilapidated palazzo where, coincidentally, Mussolini had lived in the 1920s. In the cart, beneath a thin stratum of rubbish, lay a powerful bomb: twenty-six pounds of TNT in a steel case stolen from the gas company, plus another thirteen pounds in loose bags and several iron pipes packed with explosives.

As the singing troops approached, Bentivegna lifted the cart lid and touched his pipe to a twenty-five-second fuse, carefully timed to detonate in the middle of the column. "There was a lot of ash and it took a while to ignite," he later reported. "Then I heard the sizzle." Removing his black-visored blue cap, Bentivegna laid it atop the cart as a signal, then wheeled around and hurried up the street before vanishing down a Roman alley; after tossing the uniform into a dark corner near the Church of St. Peter in Chains, he would spend the evening playing chess to calm his nerves.

The blast struck the column as if it had been "blown down by a great wind." Other partisans stepped from the shadows to lash the company with grenades and gunfire before melting away. Shards of broken window glass showered the street, along with smashed dishes, furniture, and dislodged stucco. Severed limbs and at least one head lay in the gutter; one victim was said to resemble "pulp with a coat over it." A few survivors staggered to their feet, firing wildly at the building façades.

Lieutenant Colonel Kappler was enjoying a late lunch at the Hotel Excelsior with Lieutenant General Kurt Mälzer, military commandant of Rome, when word arrived of the carnage in Via Rasella. Arriving on the scene, they found thirty-two men dead and sixty-eight wounded; ten Italian civilians had also died in the explosion, among them six children. Fascist troops sent as reinforcements ransacked shops and houses, and the crackle of rifle fire carried to the Trevi Fountain and the Palazzo Barberini. Mälzer paced about bellowing, "Revenge! Revenge!" and calculating how best to raze the entire block. On his orders, two hundred Italians from the neighborhood were arrested and marched off with their hands raised to the Viminale barracks. A sanitation crew—genuine this time—arrived to scrub the bloody cobblestones with water and salt.

Late that afternoon the Berlin high command phoned Kesselring's headquarters at Monte Soratte to report that Hitler, then brooding at his Wolfsschanze headquarters in the East Prussian woods, wanted "an entire quarter of Rome to be blown up, including any living soul dwelling therein." If that reprisal was not feasible, fifty Italians should be shot for each Bozen martyr. Kesselring, who found this crisis awaiting him upon returning to Monte Soratte from an inspection trip, wondered whether the Via Rasella ambush presaged the long-awaited Allied breakout from Anzio. After phoning Kappler for further details, Kesselring retired to bed at 8:30 P.M. and left the matter to his chief of staff, Siegfried Westphal.

Shortly after ten P.M., General Alfred Jodl, Hitler's military chief, phoned to denounce the *Schweinerei*—swinishness—in Rome. "I am giving you now a Führer order which is in front of me in this matter," Jodl told Westphal. "This is the final version." Westphal scribbled down the edict: "The Führer's order is that for every German soldier killed in this treacherous attack in Rome, ten Italian hostages will be shot." That ratio, previously announced as the appropriate riposte for "outrages," was intended to "achieve a deterrent effect," Jodl added. Westphal phoned Kesselring in his bedroom. "I agree," Kesselring said. "Pass on the order."

Kappler spent all night compiling the inevitable typed lists. By noon on March 24—another luminous spring day—the roster had grown to 320 names; when a wounded man succumbed to his injuries, Kappler added fifteen more on his own initiative. None of those listed had participated in the Via Rasella ambush. At two P.M. several canvas-covered trucks normally used to deliver meat arrived at Via Tasso 155; others pulled up at the Regina Coeli, a sprawling prison across the Tiber. Cries of "Murderers!" echoed through the cell blocks as prisoners were led away with their hands bound behind their backs, some hobbling because their toenails had been yanked out. The convoy from Via Tasso rolled past the sightless saints atop St. John Lateran and through the Aurelian wall at Porta San Sebastiano, where the Appian Way begins its journey south. Turning onto Via Ardeatina beyond the city, the trucks passed the Catacombs of St. Calixtus, then halted at a remote warren of tunnels left by miners quarrying volcanic tuff used to make concrete.

"I feel the flowers growing over me," John Keats had said on his Roman deathbed. At the Ardeatine Caves, sweet tuberoses perfumed the air. The first batch of five men tumbled off the tailgate. An SS officer, Captain Erich Priebke, checked their names from the fatal list. A German storm trooper prodded them into the cave, where candles guttered in the chill draft. Kneel, he ordered. They knelt. Five sharp cracks sounded, as evenly spaced as a tolling bell.

Five by five by five they staggered into the cave, each to receive a machine-pistol bullet in the brain before pitching forward into the volcanic dust. The pile grew: actors and architects, lawyers and mechanics, shopkeepers and physicians, an opera singer, a priest. An uncommon number worked in the wood trades—cabinetmakers, carpenters, joiners. The youngest was fourteen, the oldest seventy-five. Communists, atheists, Freemasons, freethinkers, Catholics, and seventy-five Jews. Ten had been seized near Via Rasella, propinquity their only crime. A few shouted "*Viva l'Italia!*"; others recited the rosary.

Five by five by five, each quintet now forced to clamber over the corpses of those who had come before. Kappler fetched a bottle of cognac to fortify his killers, but liquor only made them sloppy: some victims required up to four bullets before the writhing ceased.

By 8:30 P.M. the last of the 335 lay in a heap. Flashlight beams flitted across the cave mouth, then went dark. The trucks rumbled away into the night.

Relatives of the dead from the Bozen Regiment would be flown to Rome at the Reich's expense for a grand funeral. The procession snaked down the city's boulevards and across the piazzi, led by a military band playing somber dirges. No one sang "Hupf, Mein Mädel."

A brief public statement on March 25 announced, without elaboration, that severe reprisals had been exacted. Kappler ordered garbage to be heaped at the Ardeatine Caves, hoping to mask one stench with another. A few days later, German soldiers blew up the shafts.

But some odors could hardly be hidden. Frantic women crisscrossed Rome in search of their husbands, their fathers, their sons. Word quickly spread of a horror near the Via Appia. A parish priest stood at the cave mouth to offer absolution. Weeping pilgrims trudged to the site, now swarming with flies. Someone left a large laurel wreath with a note: "You will be avenged." Accounts of the atrocity soon reached Allied intelligence. "When Rome falls, please do utmost to assure adequate flow of colorful material on hunger, disease, misery under the Germans," a memo from an American propaganda office in London urged. "Also do anything you can to get correspondents to dig up facts on reported massacre of 320 Italian hostages by Germans in reprisal for bomb explosion about March 23."

Not for three months would the tomb be excavated and the dead—reduced to rag-clad skeletons—exhumed by forensic pathologists. Justice and vengeance would take much longer. But shortly after the killings, some Roman families received a curt note, *auf deutsch:* Your relative died on March 23, 1944. You may collect his belongings at the German security police offices at Via Tasso 155.

Into that malevolent place they walked, emerging with pathetic little bundles: a coat, a cap, perhaps a frayed pair of trousers. In the seam of a soiled shirt, one family found a hidden note. "I dream of the hills around Siena, and of my love whom I shall never see again," the doomed man had written. "I shall become one gaping wound—like the winds, nothing."

# 11. A Kettle of Grief

## Dead Country

FIFTH Army meteorologists for months had occupied the Royal Vesuvius Observatory on Savior's Hill, less than two miles from the crater's lip. For those eyeing the summit through the observatory's Palladian windows in the late winter of 1944, the fateful signs of vulcanic distress were difficult to ignore. Vesuvius always slept with one eye open, the locals warned; some three dozen eruptions had been documented since the cataclysm that destroyed Pompeii in A.D. 79. Beginning in early January, magma had seeped from the inner conelet like molten tears. "Flamboyant banners of light" played above the crater, according to one witness, and a smoke plume was "washed back and forth by the wind across the summit." Then the weeping subsided and, on March 13, the smoke stopped, ominously. Naples—already plagued with typhus, hunger, and war—grew ever more anxious. It was said that dogs barked with uncommon urgency.

The eruption began at 4:30 P.M. on Saturday, March 18. By midnight, orange cataracts of lava spilled down the slopes to the west and southwest, carrying trees and brush like burning boats. Huge dust clouds billowed above the summit, brilliantly illuminated by blue forks of static electricity that danced across the sky. Neapolitans watched from their rooftops, pinked by the distant glow, and reporters trudged up the cone until a guide shouted above the roar, "Gentlemen, no farther, please! The risk of life!" On Sunday evening, tongues of lava licked the first houses in San Sebastiano, which exploded in flame. Priests carried "plaster statues of their saints out of the church and placed them before the advancing river of fire," wrote Eric Sevareid. The ubiquitous Norman Lewis watched several hundred kneeling villagers plead for intervention from Saint Gennaro, the patron of Naples. "Holy banners and church images were held aloft, and acolytes swung censers and sprinkled holy water in the direction of the cinders." Young men formed a skirmish line and advanced "brandishing crosses within a few yards of the lava," Lewis wrote. "Voices somewhere in the rear had begun to sing a *Te Deum*." Peasants wept at the ruination of their fields.

Just after nine P.M. on Tuesday, March 21, soldiers in a cinema at the Torre del Greco garrison were watching the 1934 British musical *Sing as We Go* when a violent paroxysm shook the theater. Shouting men beat for the exits, even as, onscreen, Gracie Fields belted out, "Blues, where are you now?" Great fountains of lava boiled three thousand feet above Vesuvius before falling back in incandescent sheets. Near the crater, a cascade of falling tephrite stones the size of golf balls were followed by stones the size of softballs. A vast gray nimbus rose twenty thousand feet overhead before showering purple ash up to three feet deep across the coastal plain. As Pliny the Younger had written to the historian Tacitus in describing the A.D. 79 eruption: "I believed that I was perishing with the world and the world with me, which was a great consolation."

The world, then and now, survived, but for another week the Vesuvian apocalypse persisted. "Smoke of a thick oily character like a factory chimney in the north of England," wrote Harold Macmillan, still Churchill's envoy in the Mediterranean. "The smoke practically obscures the whole Bay of Naples." A Scots Guards account noted that "the streets became strangely quiet, as after a snow"—stranger still when, on March 26, snow showers fell on Naples. "We cannot help but admire this gesture of the gods," a BBC correspondent wrote. Soldiers trooped up the hairpin road toward the undamaged observatory to gawk at molten tributaries forty feet deep and to buy ashtrays a local entrepreneur made from cooling lava.

At last the pyrotechnics faded, ceasing altogether on March 29: the last eruption of the twentieth century. The damage had been done. Twenty-six deaths were reported, some from roofs collapsing under the weight of ash. Rail lines remained blocked for days while Italian crews manned shovels, snow plows, and bulldozers to free the tracks and switches. A heavy fall of soot, ash, and vitrified clinkers pummeled the Pompeii airfield, destroying more than eighty B-25 bombers parked there—"the only group," said one wag, "to lose its planes to enemy rocks."

Ash mixed with rain formed an abrasive mud that ruined brake drums and curtailed military transport because of a critical shortage of replacement brake linings in the theater. Pumice scoured the bearings in ship engines, forcing captains to flee seaward for safety. Across the fleet, from Salerno to Pozzuoli, bosuns mustered their swabs on the ashy weather decks and called out, "Sweepers, start your brooms!" A B-25 bombardier who had lost his plane to Vesuvius wrote home on April 1, "Never trust a volcano."

The world had not ended, and neither had the war. Along the Neapolitan docks, soldiers scuffed through drifted ash to the gangplank queues, where boys hawked an English-language newspaper with the headline "Anzio Worse Than Salerno." On average, five hundred men sailed each day to reinforce the so-called Beachhead Army, including those from the U.S. 34th Division, which after duty at Cassino had spent two months resting and rehabilitating before embarking for another maelstrom.

Wide-eyed they lined the rails as the ships slid into Anzio harbor—now known as Bomb Bay—utterly unconvinced by a memo from higher authority that declared, "The chances of being hit by a shell from a shore battery are negligible, being approximately 37,000 to 1 for every shell actually falling in the anchorage." Stevedores moved with feline agility, unloading fifty vehicles from an LST tank deck in four minutes or stacking three tons of cargo into a DUKW in six minutes, all the while straining for the whistle of artillery or the glint of an enemy plane. In twelve weeks the port and anchorage had sustained 277 Luftwaffe raids, one every seven hours. Radio-controlled Fritz X bombs had been largely neutralized by electronic jammers on destroyers and minesweepers, but torpedoes, aerial mines, machine-gun strafings, and conventional bombs—plus shells by the tens of thousands—continued to batter both roadstead and beachhead. The toll could be seen in the hundred or so casualties waiting dockside each day for the return convoy to Naples: wounded men on litters clutched their own X-rays in big brown envelopes, and those in casts wore medical descriptions of their injuries scribbled on the plaster. When German rounds began to fall, patients lashed to stretchers sometimes outscreamed the screaming shells. One commander greeted a new consignment of troops by telling them, "You're going to suffer. You came here to suffer."

A British officer arriving in March described Anzio as "a small town rapidly getting smaller." Beyond the barrage balloons along the seawall "there was hardly a building intact. Lonely walls leaned drunkenly against piles of rubble; roofs seemed to have gone out of fashion: and wires dangled everywhere." The captain of H.M.S. *Grenville* concurred that "the whole waterfront had a very moth eaten look about it." Upon making shore with reinforcements for the 1st Armored Division, tank commander Henry E. Gardiner told his diary, "Our first sight as we drove inland was a shockingly large United States cemetery."

Most of the cargo hoisted from the arriving ships was ammunition—150 truckloads every day—which was hauled to seven American dumps under constant attack. Bulldozers cut trenches and L-shaped bunkers to contain fires, several of which blazed each week. Firefighters at first had only shovels to battle the blazes, but now they used Sherman tanks with dozer blades and steel tracks. Still, the loss of ammunition to fire averaged more than sixty tons a day.

That the cost was not greater reflected ferocious antiaircraft defenses—a thousand guns made the beachhead among Europe's most fortified precincts—and an elaborate smoke screen that blinded enemy pilots and gunners. With each dawn, hissing smoke generators spaced half a mile apart spewed a light haze that stretched fifteen miles along the coast and four miles inland. Technicians with flatbed trucks stood by to move the generators like chess pieces should changes in wind direction, air temperature, or convection currents thin the miasma. At night, smudge pots and a different set of generators hid the port, although GIs swore the smoke simply attracted more fire.

Six Allied divisions—approaching 100,000 troops—now occupied eighty square miles, a plot slightly larger than the District of Columbia. Since the epic struggles of February, a sullen stalemate had obtained. Newcomers found that life in the Beachhead Army was not only subterranean but nocturnal, with a battle rhythm known as "Dracula days." Soldiers near the "dead country"—the no-man's-land between the opposing armies—often slept in their holes until four P.M., patrolled until three A.M., ate a hot meal before sunrise, then slipped underground until the next afternoon. Rumors "slide from hole to hole," wrote Audie Murphy, now a platoon sergeant in the 3rd Division. "We believe nothing, doubt nothing." At night the beachhead turned restless, with raids, patrols, harassing fire, and chandelier flares that stretched men's shadows grotesquely. Mines and shell fire grew so nerve-racking, wrote Robert Capa, that "every time I sat in my jeep I put my bedroll between my legs." Bill Mauldin noticed that during barrages, military policemen remained in their crossroads trenches and controlled traffic by "holding up a wooden hand to point directions."

The demand for sandbags and barbed wire along the thirty-two-mile perimeter had reached Flanders proportions. The "Anzio Ritz" was an underground cinema, given to grainy showings of Cary Grant in *Mr. Lucky*. On fine mornings, a British soldier wrote, men beyond sniper range sunned themselves on the lip of their holes "but with one ear cocked, like rabbits ready to pop back in again." Soldiers kept their helmets on so long that they wore bald spots in their scalps. "Men dreamed of steaks, milk, toilet seats, running water, and the exquisite problem of what color clothes to wear," a 179th Infantry account noted. Everyone grumbled at the static "Sitzkrieg" war. One physician compiled a beachhead glossary that included "anziopectoris"—a general indisposition—and "anziating," a distant look in the eyes. Beachhead denizens called themselves "Anzonians," and not without pride.

"The main thing you want is not to be alone," wrote Ernie Pyle, who had come to Nettuno for a few days and stayed for a month. With a dozen other reporters, he lived at Via Gramsci 35, a four-story waterfront villa that "trembled like a palsied old gentleman" whenever the guns barked. Plagued by anemia and intimations of mortality, Pyle wrote a friend, "Instead of growing stronger and hard as good veterans do, I've become weaker and more frightened. . . . I don't sleep well, and have half-awake hideous dreams about the war."

Those perturbations only intensified at seven A.M. on March 17 when a German five-hundred-pound bomb detonated thirty feet from the villa. Pyle had taken the top floor for better light, and the blast flung him to the floor, ripping doors and windows from their frames. Glass and broken brick sprayed the room. "The only wound I got was a tiny cut on my right cheek," Pyle reported, although he found himself combing his wispy hair with a handkerchief. He lingered at the beachhead for another week "to get my nerve back," then sailed for Naples. On April 5, he left Italy forever. "There's such a thing," he wrote, "as pressing your luck too far in one spot."

Lucian Truscott had also pressed his luck by moving to the spacious top floor of a three-story Nettuno house. The VI Corps headquarters remained in the cellars beneath the Osteria dell'Artigliere, but Truscott believed a commander must display conspicuous sangfroid. Engineers sandbagged the doorways of his billet and laid rail ties across the roof, just in case.

"I have almost become oblivious to the passage of time," Truscott wrote Sarah in mid-March. "One day is just another group of problems and each day seems to bring its own regardless of the situation." A week later he added, "I do not want to return until the job is done and I can return to an America on the way back to normal—and then I want *peace* in large doses!" Two years had passed since he left her for "the great adventure, and what an adventure it has been. . . . I can only do the best I can. It is your faith in me that has brought me this far on the road."

His throat still nagged him, along with a hacking cough, nasal polyps, and aching teeth. After an examination on March 31 the doctor recommended voice exercises and cigars rather than cigarettes. Truscott quit smoking for ten days, then resumed after complaining of weight gain. The "lack of voice really affects my efficiency," he told Sarah. Cognac, scotch, gin, and two ounces of rye before supper remained staples in the Truscott mess, but without evident impairment of the commander. He remained energetic, buoyant, and intensely absorbed in every detail of his beachhead domain.

"I can close my eyes and imagine Virginia's countryside now," he wrote in April as the weather warmed. "The redbud and dogwood must be beautiful, and the blue mountains and green trees. There may be something romantic about southern Italy, but personally I have not found it yet." On Easter Sunday, April 9, he slept eight hours straight for the first time since reaching Anzio; more typically he was awakened each night by emergencies small and large, trudging downstairs in bathrobe and slippers, gray hair tousled and face lined with fatigue, but ready to take command. In his rare free moments he studied French—like Patton, he suspected it might be useful—or listened to a German radio broadcast of Handel's *Messiah*.

But heartbreak was never further away than the next letter, such as one in early April from the mother of a nineteen-year-old corporal who had vanished during the FISCHFANG attack on February 16. "Please tell me if you think it could be possible he is a German prisoner, or tell me if the worst has happened, and there wasn't even his dog tag left from him," she wrote from Ohio. "I have dreamed of my baby son every night."

Truscott had ordered the beachhead evacuated of all twenty-two thousand civilians, and by early April every Anzonian except for 750 Italian laborers wore a military uniform. After treatment with DDT, families gathered at the church of St. Teresa to await passage to Naples. Some carried mattresses on their backs; others clung to cardboard suitcases or a wheel of cheese, scooping up a little sand as a token of remembrance. A few screeched in protest, hurling curses at the sky or gnawing their fists. "They hate Mussolini, the Germans, and I believe they hate us," Lieutenant Ivar H. Aas wrote his parents in Minneapolis. "I don't think they go for this liberation idea too well." Soldiers purchased livestock from departing farmers—$4 for a lamb, $20 for a pig. When a pregnant cow was mortally wounded by a shell fragment, an enterprising soldier performed a Cesarean delivery with an ax, delivering a calf, which he fed from his helmet.

"This beachhead is the craziest place I have ever seen," Lieutenant William J. Segan, a signal officer, wrote to his brother in New Jersey. "The boys have their own private horses, chickens, livestock, bicycles, and everything else that the civilians left." Near Borgo Sabatino, soldiers hitched mule to plow and planted fields of cabbage and potatoes. "I can't do a thing with those sons of bitches," a 1st Special Service Force officer complained. "They patrol all night and they farm all day." Other soldiers angled for eels in the Astura River, or hunted pheasant and rabbit with shotguns used to guard German prisoners. After finding that grenade fishing ruined the sashimi, Japanese-American troops in the 100th Battalion seined with mosquito netting and gathered watercress garnishes from the Mussolini Canal.

Troops played baseball on improvised diamonds, using folded T-shirts for bases and slit trenches for dugouts. Daredevil water-skiers slalomed across the Tyrrhenian Sea behind a DUKW. A private who called himself the Baron ambled around the beachhead in a tuxedo, performing magic shows with Chinese rings and a pet duck. Bike steeplechases, lizard races, sniper contests, and husbandry—including cattle-breeding experiments—kept the men busy while they waited for their fates to unfold. The Anzio Derby, organized by a former Baltimore handicapper now wearing sergeant's stripes, was run over a shell-pocked course laid out with tent pegs and engineer tape. As each steed clopped from the vineyard paddock, a bugler blew the call to the post. A quartermaster bay named Six-by-Six beat a half dozen other nags and a jackass named George, surmounted by a 240-pound jockey from Brooklyn; judges ruled that in future races all steeds must outweigh their riders. Pretty nurses awarded the purse, a two-pound box of chocolates.

More than thirty Anzonian newspapers covered such activities; the *Beachhead Bugle* also printed travel notes, including a roster of departing reporters that began: "The following rats deserted the sinking ship yesterday . . ." No sport aroused greater passion than beetle racing, in which insects—stabled in jam jars and daubed with racing colors—were dropped in the center of a six-foot circle; the first to reach the perimeter was declared the winner. Thousands of dollars were wagered on big sweepstakes, and it was said that shady bookmakers fixed one race by purchasing the favorite and stomping it to death.

Alcohol provided some consolation to losing bettors, as well as "catacomb courage" to the frightened and lonely. Distilleries built from fuel cans and tubing salvaged from aircraft wreckage produced "gasoline," a potent hooch flavored with pineapple juice. Bootleggers from the 133rd Infantry blended fifty pounds of fermented raisins and a dash of vanilla to make "Plastered in Paris," while others preferred fermented fig bars from Army rations. "The still blew up," a corporal wrote in his diary, "but they got some good liquor while it lasted." In April the first authorized beer arrived at the beachhead, roughly a pint per man each fortnight, brewed in Naples under specifications provided by Budweiser. To prevent pilferage, sutlers rolled the kegs ashore and stored them under guard behind barbed wire.

Lieutenant Colonel Jack Toffey's change-of-command party featured whiskey sours made from C-ration lemon powder and medicinal alcohol. Having led an infantry battalion in combat with little respite since TORCH in November 1942, Toffey in mid-March left his 2nd Battalion of the 15th Infantry to become executive officer—second in command—of the 7th Infantry, another 3rd Division regiment that also had bivouacked at the beachhead. Truscott personally ordered the change to give Toffey a bit of relief while allowing a larger unit to benefit from his battle expertise.

"There are days and other days in this game—some good—some bad," he wrote Helen in Columbus. "All in all it is a terrific strain on health, mind & body. . . . I am somewhat easier in the mind than I was and more confident of our ability to kick hell out of this damn Hun." He apologized for letters that are "dumb, dull and stupid—but perhaps I'm getting that way." To his old friend George Biddle he confessed, "Efficiency in general and combat efficiency in particular suffer when individuals remain too long and too constantly under the gun." In joining the 7th Infantry, he had come full circle: his father had served as the regimental adjutant at Fort Wayne, Michigan, when Jack was born in August 1907. After moving into a tiny subterranean trailer outside Nettuno, with light provided by a jeep battery and Helen's photo hung on the wall, Toffey wrote, "I have seen about enough of Italy and enough of war. . . . I live in a cave-like place which is damp and makes me stoop over. I'm full of kinks and aches as a result."

Only a few miles from the beetle races and volleyball tournaments, the dead country remained as dangerous and forbidding as any battle zone in Italy. "For four months no man dared stand upright by day," wrote the BBC reporter Wynford Vaughan-Thomas. Unable to bury the dead, soldiers in the foremost foxholes crawled out at night to sprinkle creosote on the ripening corpses; others swapped shouted insults with the enemy. "Roosevelt is a Jew" would be answered with "Hitler is a bastard." Tommies trapped rats in empty sandbags and slung them into German observation posts. Private First Class Robert W. Komer described watching no-man's-land through field glasses: "Here a few helmeted heads peeping cautiously from a foxhole, there a couple of tanks snuggled against the side of a shattered house. . . . A squad of infantrymen straggled by across the field toward their positions, an ambulance came tearing down the road, litter bearers picked their way carefully among the ditches and the holes."

No field glasses could reveal how badly the Germans at Anzio had been bruised and bled. From 133,000 men on March 9, the Fourteenth Army in the next six weeks would shrink, through battle losses and transfers to the Cassino front, by 43,000 men, 170 guns, and 125 tanks, while Allied strength steadily grew. Kesselring condemned the "lack of aggressiveness by both officers and men," and Berlin insisted that "we must continue the attack in the Nettuno sector in order to keep the initiative." General Mackensen replied angrily that "German divisions are battle weary," with some reduced to three thousand men or less. For every German shell fired, the Allies now answered with fifteen—"quantities hitherto hardly imaginable," complained one German commander, who also lamented the "enormous blast and gouge effect" of naval gunfire. Even Sherman tanks joined the barrages, their barrels elevated with logs stacked beneath the tracks. Crews slammed another shell into the breech and sang out, "Call the roll, Kesselring. Here we come."

To be sure, the biggest German guns remained terrifying. A pair of seventy-foot barrels, called Robert and Leopold by the Germans but known variously to the Allies as Anzio Annie or Whistling Pete, each fired a six-hundred-pound shell as far as thirty-eight miles. Near misses in the anchorage raised water spouts two hundred feet high; even duds ashore burrowed fifty feet into the earth. Mounted on rail flatcars, the guns after firing a half dozen shells withdrew into a tunnel two miles from Ciampino. Despite muzzle flashes brighter than any dragon's fire, Allied pilots and gunnery observers never pinpointed the battery. Perhaps the only saving grace was a shortage of shells: Robert and Leopold by the end of April would together throw just 523 rounds.

Yet it was the close fight, at distances from bayonet length to potshot range, that remained most sinister and most intimate. Toffey organized three "battle patrols" of fifty ruthless men each, ensured that they got regular hot meals and dry clothing, then sent them out to wreak havoc. Pulling a wicked blade from his leggings, one soldier slashed at the air. "My friends back home gave me this knife," he said. "I'm saving it to use on Hitler when I see him." Snipers, known in the 7th Infantry as "pickers-off," sprayed themselves with camouflage paint, shielding their eyes with scraps of cardboard, then lay motionless for hours in hopes of one clean shot.

"The march up is something that no one likes," a soldier told his diary on April 1. "If you stumble into each other, the procedure is to blast away for a short time and then take off in a hurry." Patrols navigated in the dark by using various corpses as landmarks—"just skeletons in clothes." Scouts sniffed the air for the telltale scents of tobacco and fresh-turned earth. Audie Murphy earned the first of his many valor decorations for leading a patrol near Cisterna to fire an immobilized panzer with a grenade through the hatch. Like most of his comrades, he distrusted bravado—"All the heroes I know are dead," he later said—but he had concluded that "audacity is a tactical weapon. Nine times out of ten it will throw the enemy off-balance and confuse him."

Propaganda tried to do the same. Leaflets covered the beachhead like Vesuvian ash. More than four billion Allied leaflets would be printed in the Mediterranean, the equivalent of four thousand truckloads; among the many variants dropped or fired at Anzio was *"Fünf Minuten Englisch,"* a glossary of handy phrases for Germans contemplating surrender, such as "Where is the hot water?" and "Some more coffee, please." German propagandists replied with their own paper barrages. The "Abe Levy" series showed a Jewish contractor at home molesting the girlfriend of a wounded soldier; another leaflet, aimed at British units, showed a scantily clad Englishwoman pulling on her stockings as a GI reknotted his tie. "What goes on at home whilst you are away?" the caption asked. "No woman can resist such handsome brutes." As one Tommy observed, "Jerry has become very cheeky."

Enemies who could not be talked from their works must be winkled out. Night after night, "house-blowing" patrols whittled away the beachhead skyline between the opposing armies: tanks, mortars, and 8-inch howitzers pulverized the upper floors of suspected strongpoints while riflemen screened by thick smoke splashed across the polders to exterminate any survivors. On the foreheads of dead Germans, Forcemen left calling card stickers with a spearhead insignia and a warning that *das dicke Ende kommt noch:* the worst is yet to come. Every haystack, every manure bin, every outdoor oven—anything that could hide an enemy soldier with a machine pistol—came under seething fire. "Houses 5 and 6 are in our possession," reported a battalion commander after suffering fifty-three casualties in one nameless skirmish. "Our front line is now 500 yards closer to Rome. We turn our faces grimly toward Houses 7, 8, 9."

In this "kettle of grief," as one Anzonian called it, death seemed not just capricious but cruel and willful: a random shell killed six men watching a movie; another killed eight more at supper; a bomb on a combat engineer bivouac killed twenty-one; two died when an artillery shell pierced their Piper Grasshopper a thousand feet up. A German mortar round through a barn roof left a corporal "holding his face together with his hand," a witness reported. A Forceman whose leg was blown off rode to the aid station atop a tank. "Hey, doc," he yelled to the battalion surgeon, "you got an extra foot around this place?"

All frayed, some broke. "Yesterday made 60 days of hell on this blessed beachhead," wrote a soldier in the 15th Infantry. "The fact that it cannot last forever seems to be the only thing that keeps us going." After weeks in the line, "foxhole-itis" made even pugnacious sergeants reluctant to leave their burrows. "All the boys who never prayed before now pray with devotion, and they cry when they are faced with death," a soldier in the 6th Armored Infantry reported. The Beachhead Army comprised "common ordinary men in whom the instinct of self-preservation is very strong," the 3rd Division headquarters advised new platoon leaders. By late March, an entire hospital ward was filled with what the Army labeled S.I.W.—self-inflicted wounds—usually a bullet to the heel or toe. One battalion commander in the 3rd Division kept a bottle of tranquilizers for officers who seemed especially jittery, and doctors formed the Anzio Beachhead Psychiatry Society to discuss intriguing "neuro-psychiatric" cases. "I saw him as they led him past my foxhole," a young soldier in the 179th Infantry wrote of one comrade, "a pathetic, shaking and stumbling figure."

All frayed, yet many also grew flinty and remorseless, as victorious armies must. "This war has become a very personal affair to lots of us here in the beachhead," one Forceman wrote. An American Indian in the 45th Division was said to have collected a sheaf of German scalps; comrades nauseated by the odor forced him to stop. In a letter to his family in New Haven, a soldier wrote in April that his friend Henry had shot a German climbing over a fence. The dead man lay on the wire "all day long. About once every hour Henry would shoot him again just for the hell of it." Nocturnal pleas for *Mutter* mingled with cries for Mama from those trapped and mewing in the dead country. "The wounded struggle so hard to tell us so much," said one GI. But a captured German paratrooper surmised that those "who simply refused to die and screamed and screamed were the ones who changed the soldiers' reactions from pity to hatred as the night progressed." When a pathetic voice repeatedly called in English, "My name is Müller. I am wounded," a GI heaved a grenade and muttered, "What's your name now, you sonofabitch?"

The days warmed, the season advanced. Crews in the 1st Armored Division painted their tanks a darker, vernal green. Reforestation teams in early April began camouflaging craters and defoliated patches for concealment along the beachhead perimeter. Malaria returned, but much had been learned from the Sicilian debacle. Aware that "mosquitoes alone could accomplish what the German counterattacks had failed to achieve," Truscott in April sent two thousand VI Corps soldiers to "anti-malaria training." The consumption of Atabrine tablets was enforced by watchful sergeants. "Dusting patrols" sprayed more than one hundred miles of streams and ditches with DDT and kerosene, while repairing pumps, dikes, and canal banks. Soldiers complained that if they spilled a cup of water someone either drained the puddle or sprayed it. Barely two thousand malaria cases would be reported in June among Fifth Army troops, a tiny fraction of the previous summer's epidemic.

The warming weather also brought hope to badly wounded boys whose cases would have been hopeless just a few months earlier. "We seem to be having phenomenal success with a new drug called penicillin," wrote Lawrence D. Collins, a physician in the 56th Evacuation Hospital. Gas gangrene had killed two of every three soldiers afflicted in Italy; now the rates plummeted. "We've snatched them right out of the grave," Dr. Collins told his diary. "We're pleased, the survivors are pleased." Less pleased were wounded German prisoners, "upon whom we're not allowed to use penicillin that is in short supply," Collins noted. "No one doubts that war is hell."

The new season stirred the dull roots. Lilacs and violets blossomed even in the dead country. A 45th Division soldier told his family in April that he had just eaten fresh eggs for the first time in five months. "Maybe," he surmised, "they are getting us fat for the kill." Maybe so. If Anzio remained "the largest self-supporting prisoner-of-war camp in the world," as Axis Sally insisted in her nightly broadcasts, every soldier at the beachhead sensed a change in the air.

The advancing season also sharpened their loneliness and made them long, as Truscott did, for those redbuds and dogwoods, for children's laughter and for baseball played with dugouts instead of slit trenches. To his son John and daughter Anne, now twelve and seven, Jack Toffey wrote, "Next to missing you all terribly I think that big league ball is the one great void in my life."

There was only one way home. The greening breast of the Colli Laziali loomed above the hazy coastal plain, beckoning and enchanted. The hours ticked toward a more fateful hour, inexorable if still unknown. Soon they would leave this pestilential plot, this woe, this kettle of grief. None would leave it unchanged. "Anzio," one officer wrote, "was the place where many of us ceased to be young."

## *"Put the Fear of God into Them"*

HIGH above the mud and the misery, far from the house-blowers and the pickers-off, one phase of the Allied war had long been won. The Mediterranean Allied Air Forces owned the skies with a swaggering hegemony comparable to Allied naval dominion of the high seas. Ira Eaker's legions now included 13,000 aircraft and 300,000 troops, although several thousand of those planes, notably in the RAF's Middle East squadrons, were "non-operational." The 8,000 or so that *could* fly had reduced the Luftwaffe to hit-and-run niggling. Barely 500 German planes now stole from bases in southern France and northern Italy. Antiaircraft defenses against Allied raids were also puny, given the crying need to defend the Fatherland and the Eastern Front; of 4,300 German flak batteries, only 260 were deployed in Italy, along with just 14 of 470 searchlight batteries.

By contrast, Hitler's robust defense of central Europe had made the Allied strategic bombardment of German cities and war industries a protracted death struggle at thirty thousand feet. The sanguinary vision of pummeling the Reich from two directions—with Fifteenth Air Force in Italy complementing Eighth Air Force and British Bomber Command in England—was only now showing unambiguous promise. Although a crewman flying from Italy listed in his diary all the countries he had bombed—Germany, France, Italy, Austria, Hungary, Bulgaria, Romania, Yugoslavia—the contributions from Fifteenth Air Force during the winter had been curtailed by impenetrable clouds crowning the Alps, unexpectedly nasty Italian weather, fighter escort shortages, and growing pains. As late as March 1944, Eaker was still describing the Fifteenth as "a pretty disorganized mob."

Losses in the fall of 1943 at deathtraps like Regensburg and Schweinfurt had been so appalling that the Allies temporarily lost air superiority over much of Germany. Still, by November the fate of forty-one German cities could be reduced by Bomber Command to a single sheet of paper, starting with Berlin: "480 acres of housing devastation and great industrial damage has already been caused so that Berlin is relatively as badly hit as London." Ruination elsewhere ranged from Hanover ("largely destroyed") to Frankfurt, Stuttgart, and Munich ("seriously damaged"). Entire regions were reduced to a fatal phrase: "the Saar—small coal and steel towns to be mopped up." A memo from Hap Arnold, also in November, compared the bomb damage at Coventry in central England (120 of 1,922 acres devastated) with that at Hamburg (6,220 of 8,382 acres) and Cologne (1,785 of 3,320 acres). And they had only begun. "Are we beasts? Are we taking this too far?" Churchill wondered aloud. Later the prime minister, who had ardently pressed for some of the most ruinous raids, would voice regret "that the human race ever learned to fly."

As the war's fifth winter ended, the Combined Bomber Offensive was well along in dropping more than a million tons of explosives on German targets, which would kill or wound over a million civilians and destroy almost four million dwellings. American commanders belatedly realized that despite the hundreds of .50-caliber machine guns bristling from B-17 Flying Fortress formations, long-range fighters were needed to escort the bombers deep into the Reich. That need had been answered with the swarming arrival in early 1944 of P-51 Mustangs, which by March had a range of 850 miles, well beyond Berlin; truculent P-51s dropping their wing tanks to meet oncoming Luftwaffe fighters were likened to "barroom brawlers stripping off their coats." American pilots were ordered "to pursue the Hun until he was destroyed. Put the fear of God into them."

In late February, a long-delayed bombing offensive code-named ARGU-MENT attacked almost two hundred industrial and military targets, from aircraft factories to rubber plants. Nearly 4,000 bombers from Britain and Italy struck for days on end in a relentless bashing soon known as Big Week. Eighth Air Force dropped almost as much bomb tonnage in six days as it had during its first year in combat. Allied losses were bitter: 226 bombers, 28 fighters, and 2,600 crewmen. Hopes of crippling Germany's aircraft industry fell short; more Luftwaffe planes rolled from German plants in 1944 than in any other year of the war, although at the expense of bomber production. Factories dispersed underground and into remote forests. Yet the blow was severe. The Luftwaffe in February lost more than one-third of its single-engine fighters and nearly one-fifth of its fighter pilots. The latter loss was especially grievous; the combat career of a new German pilot now lasted, on average, less than a month.

The weight of metal had begun to "un-gear the German war economy," in Eaker's phrase. Daylight bombing by the Yanks and night bombing by the Brits finally achieved the synergy that air theorists had promised for more than a year. With better weather, Allied heavy bombers in April dumped on average two tons of high explosives on German targets every minute of every day. The Luftwaffe would become almost as ineffectual in central Europe as it already was in the Mediterranean. German synthetic oil facilities, the Achilles' heel of Hitler's war machine, were now clearly within range and attacks began in earnest in mid-May.

Even so, the hard winter for airmen yielded to a hard spring. Allied air forces flying from England lost twenty bombers a day in March; another three thousand Eighth Air Force bombers were damaged that month. Morale problems could be seen in the decision of nearly ninety U.S. crews in March and April to fly to neutral countries, usually Sweden or Switzerland, to be interned for the duration. The Army Air Forces hardly helped their reputation for precision when they repeatedly bombed Switzerland. One pummeling, on April 1, left a hundred casualties in the town of Schaffhausen.

Losses remained dreadful from flak that was thicker than ever. Only one in four Eighth Air Force bomber crews flying in early 1944 could expect to complete the minimum quota of twenty-five missions required for reassignment to the United States; those not dead or missing would be undone by accidents, fatigue, or other misadventures. Bomber Command casualties were comparable to those of British infantrymen in World War I. Here was a pretty irony: airpower, which was supposed to preserve Allied ground forces from another Western Front abattoir, simply supplemented the butchery. A B-17 pilot described one harrowing mission:

When a plane blew up, we saw their parts all over the sky. We smashed into some of the pieces. One plane hit a body which tumbled out of a plane ahead. A crewman went out the front hatch of a plane and hit the tail assembly of his own plane. No chute. His body turned over and over like a bean bag tossed into the air. . . . A German pilot came out of his plane, drew his legs into a ball, his head down. Papers flew out of his pockets. He did a triple somesault through our formation. No chute.

"When I fly a mission, I'm scared," John Muirhead told a friend. "When I'm not flying, I'm bored. When they get killed, I'm glad it's not me." Crewmen sang a parody of the theme song from *Casablanca:* "You must remember this / The flak can't always miss / Somebody's gotta die." Accidents alone killed 13,000 U.S. airmen; by war's end, 140,000 Allied crewmen would be dead. "On my last four raids I have been hit three times," a flier in the 17th Bomb Group wrote home in late February. "The flak was so thick I couldn't see the planes in front of me, and that's no lie." Many fuselages were quilted with the aluminum patches used to repair bullet holes and flak perforations. A B-25 bombardier in a letter home described "the enlarged pupil, the quickened breath, the dry mouth. . . . It is a terrible responsibility not to hit a hospital."

Propeller turbulence, faulty electrical suits—temperatures in unheated bombers could reach −60 degrees Fahrenheit—and anoxia from defective oxygen masks all added to the risk. Enemy fighters modified their tactics to break through bomber defenses; Allied airmen were warned about Luftwaffe attack profiles dubbed the "Sisters' Act," the "Twin-Engine Tailpecker," and the "Hun in the Sun." A flight leader's momentary lapse could have catastrophic consequences. One squadron commander, a Hollywood actor named Jimmy Stewart, later said, "I didn't pray for myself. I just prayed that I wouldn't make a mistake."

In the Mediterranean the Air Force steadily increased mission quotas, especially for medium bombers, whose sorties tended to be shorter and less hazardous than the heavies, at least in theory. In February the "fixed tour" was abolished altogether in favor of "a variable one subject to local conditions." Airmen now wore T-shirts that read, "Fly 'til I die."

Among those affected by the ever spiraling quotas was a twenty-one-year-old bombardier from Brooklyn, whose B-25 bomber group moved to Corsica with new airplanes in April after being violently evicted from Vesuvius airfield by the volcano's eruption. Lieutenant Joseph Heller would fly sixty sorties over Italy and southern France, refracting his experiences through the story of an iconic B-25 bombardier named John Yossarian in the greatest novel to emerge from the war, *Catch-22.*

"They were trying to kill me, and I wanted to go home. That they were trying to kill all of us each time we went up was no consolation," Heller later wrote in a memoir. "They were trying to kill *me*. . . . I began crossing my fingers each time we took off and saying in silence a little prayer. It was my sneaky ritual."

Command of the Italian skies emboldened Allied airmen to aver that they could extend their dominion to the ground. An interdiction campaign that severed enemy logistical lines in central Italy would force "a German withdrawal made necessary by his inadequate supply," Eaker wrote Hap Arnold in early April. Starving Kesselring's armies of food, fuel, and ammunition might even make a "ground offensive unnecessary," opening the road to Rome while saving countless lives. The campaign would be code-named STRANGLE.

Extravagant claims for airpower's efficacy had been made before, at Messina, Salerno, and Anzio, and at Cassino, twice; Eaker had even promised Truscott that his pilots would silence Anzio Annie. STRANGLE was the boldest assertion yet "of the airmen's claim to be able to win the land battle for the soldiers," as W.G.F. Jackson wrote. Italy seemed an ideal laboratory for air interdiction, given the narrowness of the peninsula, the long supply lines from Germany, and the steep terrain, which canalized rail tracks through narrow defiles with many bridges and tunnels.

Much of the thinking about how best to hurt the Germans from on high had been entrusted to a South African–born anatomist and primate specialist named Solly Zuckerman, who had moved beyond studies such as *The Social Life of Monkeys and Apes* to consider the pernicious effect of bombs falling on human beings. A Churchill favorite whose friends before the war included Evelyn Waugh, Lillian Hellman, and the musical Gershwins, Zuckerman with his logarithms and probabilities had loomed large in AFHQ's bombardment planning since before the invasion of Sicily. In a report endorsed by the British Air Ministry in late 1943, he posited that the best way to "isolate the battlefield" in southern Italy was through the relentless bombardment of rail marshaling yards, especially those with big repair shops. Zuckerman's influence had led to a keen focus in the last several months on such rail center bottlenecks in central and northern Italy.

But Zuckerman had decamped to join Eisenhower in London, and at Caserta a backlash developed against his theology. Intelligence analysts noted that since the capture of Naples more than eight thousand tons of bombs had fallen on Italian marshaling yards "without critically weakening the enemy supply position." The Italian rail system under German control included at least four dozen major marshaling yards, and a hundred other centers with ten or more tracks; all were hard to cut and easy to either fix or circumvent. Kesselring's divisions on the Cassino, Anzio, and Adriatic fronts needed an estimated four thousand tons of supplies each day, hauled on fifteen trains that used less than a tenth of the Italian rail capacity. Germany also had so many locomotives—63,000 in all of Europe—that it "could have afforded to discard at the end of each haul the locomotives needed for the fifteen trains," according to Allied intelligence.

Eaker and his apostles, particularly Brigadier General Lauris Norstad, insisted that the campaign must also target bridges, defiles, and even open track across an "interdiction belt," forcing German logisticians to rely on inefficient, fuel-guzzling trucks, which also would be attacked. Fighter-bombers and medium bombers would be well suited to pinpoint attacks on viaduct spans and the like. With approval from the Combined Chiefs, Eaker on March 19 had laid out the campaign objectives in Bombing Directive No. 2: "to reduce the enemy's flow of supplies to a level which will make it impossible to maintain and operate his forces in central Italy."

STRANGLE began badly. On the early morning of March 22, an OSS team of fifteen uniformed American soldiers—mostly Italian-speakers from greater New York—paddled ashore northwest of La Spezia in three rubber boats with orders to blow up a tunnel on the main rail line from Genoa, which Eaker's planes could not reach. The mission was code-named GINNY. A pair of patrol boats that had ferried the men from Corsica returned to extract the team on two subsequent nights without success. Light signals from the beach flashed in the wrong color sequence, and aerial photos showed trains still traversing the tunnel. "Assumed lights were German trap," the OSS reported. "Mission assumed lost."

Lost it was. An Italian fisherman who spotted a dinghy cached in the rocks had alerted local Fascist authorities. German troops surrounded the Americans before they reached the tunnel and captured all fifteen men after a brief firefight. Under a Führer directive to exterminate all saboteurs, including those in uniform, the German corps commander, General Anton Dostler, ordered them executed. At sunrise on March 26, the men were marched to a glade near the village of Ameglia, hands lashed with wire behind their backs. On command, a firing squad cut them down; a German officer delivered the coup de grâce by pistol shot. An Ultra intercept from Kesselring's command post to Hitler reported that American "terror troops" in Italy had been "liquidated," but the precise fate of the GINNY team would not be known for another year. Justice, again, would take longer.

The bombing campaign proved more potent. Attacking planes swarmed across the interdiction belt, ultimately flying more than 50,000 sorties and dumping 26,000 tons of high explosives. By mid-April, twenty-seven bridges had been severed, despite spotty weather that grounded the medium bombers every other day. Some targets were pounded relentlessly, including the Florence–Rome line, which was hit at twenty-two points.

Stations, bridges, engine repair shops, and parked trains were all fair game. Fighter-bombers averaged one direct hit on a bridge span every nineteen sorties, a tenfold improvement in the accuracy of heavy bombers; they also shot up rail electrical conduits, a tactic that aggravated the shortage of German electricians. The number of cuts in Italian rail lines on any given day tripled to seventy-five. By mid-April, all tracks to Rome were blocked, and trains often halted in Florence so supplies could be unloaded and trucked south. Fuel drums necessarily replaced tanker cars, but drums ran short. Troop movements slowed, timetables unraveled; on occasion, enemy victualers were forced to choose between hauling food or hauling ammunition.

Kesselring in early April ordered supply columns to move only in darkness, which, as the days grew longer, made it impossible to complete a round-trip in a single night. Some expeditions from Florence to Perugia— barely two hundred miles round-trip—took nearly a week. Italian drivers proved "distressingly unreliable" under fire, despite the opening of a convoy school to improve night-driving skills. "The difficulties seemed to pile up," a German transportation officer later acknowledged.

Yet they did not pile up high enough. With that maddening blend of dexterity and purpose that so characterized German warmaking in Italy, the Wehrmacht simply made do. Traffic slowed but never stopped. Coastal lighters and dray carts supplemented a fleet of twelve thousand trucks. Several rail engineer companies arrived from France to mend tracks and bridges. For every boxcar destroyed, ten replaced it: the Germans owned two million in Europe. Extravagant camouflage, such as the threading of new bridge spans across the Po River through the wreckage of the old, made targets harder to find. Kesselring's ammunition and fuel stocks remained steady. "The supply situation," said General Walter Warlimont, Jodl's deputy in the Berlin high command, "could be viewed satisfactorily as a whole."

STRANGLE "achieved nothing more than nuisance value," the official U.S. Army history later concluded. That was unduly dismissive; the campaign complicated Kesselring's life and eroded his ability to resist a sustained ground offensive. Rail traffic in central Italy grew sclerotic. But even true-blue aviators voiced disappointment. Airpower "cannot absolutely isolate the battlefield from enemy supply or reinforcement," Eaker's British deputy, Air Marshal John C. Slessor, wrote in late spring. Nor could bombardment "by itself defeat a highly organized and disciplined army, even when that army is virtually without air support."

The most succinct appraisal came from General Norstad in a seven-word sentence that foreshadowed the terrestrial fight to the death now required of a million men along the Gustav Line.

"The enemy," Norstad said, "was *not* forced to withdraw."

## *"You Are All Brave. You Are All Gentlemen"*

SPRING crept up the Italian boot, gawdy and fecund. Green wheat emerged in April, as it had for millennia in war and in peace. Hawks wheeled on the thermals in the perfect blue sky, and flowers enameled the fields: buttercups, primroses, massed violets. The leggy poplars leafed out, along with wild quince and hawthorn. Rivers danced across the black rocks to the sea. Pink and white blossoms stippled the almond trees, the delicate scent mingling with the cruder whiff of charred villages.

Herders tended their white, sloe-eyed cattle and goats collared with clanking bells. Children with big mallets trailed the ox-team plows, breaking up dirt clods in the furrows. Wires were restrung in ruined vineyards to tease out new tendrils. "I have been in Italy so long I feel like a Dago, probably look like one too," a soldier in the 45th Division wrote home. "We speak about half Dago and about half English now, with a lot of Army slang thrown in." Shell craters floored Purple Heart Valley; after a rain shower they glistened in the sun like scattered coins. In a letter to a friend in California, a sergeant in the 141st Infantry described "a field of blood red poppies. . . . It makes one fill up inside and wish to cry." As for comrades gone west, he added, "There are so many of them sleeping under the sod, waiting for us, the living, to pick up and carry on the torch of liberty and freedom. . . . Life over here boils down to the simple essentials. No frills, decorations, or frivolities."

Only at Cassino did spring seem hesitant, as if repelled. Where acacia and olives should have silvered the hillsides, blackened stumps climbed the slopes toward the abbey, now dubbed Golgotha by a British padre. In the flats below, a patina of powdered stone whitened the drifted rubble with a spectral pallor. "If ever there was a dead town, this is it," the ambulance driver John G. Wright observed. "Shelled down to bedrock, for acres." Even with a telescope from the shaley brow of Monte Trocchio the town looked empty—"Ghost Village," some Tommies called it. The great trunk road of Highway 6 had been crimped to a goat path, littered with helmets and discarded bandoliers. Wayside graves dotted the landscape, usually in expedient clusters of three or four, but many corpses lay where they had fallen. "I realized I was smelling my own kind," the rifleman Alex Bowlby later wrote. "The unseen, unconsecrated dead assumed a most terrifying power."

Yet in Cassino the living were also unseen and surely unconsecrated. Fifteen hundred soldiers—half German, half British—inhabited the rubble. Neither STRANGLE nor any other Allied gambit had persuaded General von Senger's paratroopers to withdraw a single centimeter. They still held both the high ground and various Cassino strongpoints, including the Hotel Continental and the Hotel des Roses. Freyberg's Kiwis in early April had yielded to the 1st Guards Brigade, who occupied a wide crescent from the jail in the north to the rail station in the south.

Each evening Guardsmen porters smoked a last cigarette in the lee of Trocchio, then removed their wristwatches to avoid fatal glints in the moonlight and shouldered knotted sandbags stuffed with another day's provisions: food, ammo, mail, periscopes, rat poison, wire screening to thwart enemy grenades, quicklime to unstink the dead. Most wore gym shoes, or wrapped their boots in burlap sacking to muffle the footfall. The final stretch from Shit Corner into town—the Mad Mile—was navigated both by familiar landmarks, such as the dead American nurse unaccountably pinned beneath a bridge girder, and by "smell marks," like the ripe mule at one intersection. Sometimes an enemy gunner, Spandau Joe, opened fire on the crepuscular column, raking Highway 6 with bullets that caromed off the roadbed like sparks shed from a grindstone. The porters scuttled forward and dropped their loads, then hurried back to Trocchio to lay up until the next night. One Royal Artillery lieutenant who made frequent runs into Cassino found it "increasingly difficult to speak without a fairly serious stammer."

The Guards' command post occupied the crypt beneath a Catholic church, entered only on hands and knees through a hole scratched in the rubble. A decomposing German soldier lay near the entrance and those passing in or out would subsequently bow to him for luck, whispering, "Good evening, Hans." Shell fire and bombs had sliced open the burial vaults in the upper walls, scattering skeletons about the nave, and Tommies hung flypaper in a losing battle against insects. Pickets occupied three forward outposts, known as Jane, Helen, and Mary, in wrecked buildings barely a hundred yards from the German line. Sentries cradled their Bren guns beneath cockeyed wall prints of the Virgin, whose eyes remained fixed on heaven.

"There is no day, only two kinds of night—a yellow, smoky, choking night, and a black, meteor-ridden night," wrote one soldier consigned to a

Cassino cellar. Guardsmen plugged their nostrils with mosquito repellent against the stench, and took turns standing watch at their periscopes, like submariners. "We looked out upon a dead world," a Black Watch soldier reported. "Nothing stirred in the ruins. Even so, hidden eyes watched everything." They scribbled letters and sipped tea, saving a half inch in their morning mugs to shave. Endless hours were devoted to discussions about sex, politics, and life's absurdity, all to stave off what Fred Majdalany called "that deadly sameness which is the hardest thing of all to bear in war." German shells tumbled about; British gunners answered, targeting suspected strongholds code-named for film stars—Ginger Rogers, Fred Astaire. At dusk they crept out to relieve themselves, Majdalany recalled, ranks of buttocks "showing white in the semi-darkness like grotesque friezes."

Life across the rubble was no finer. German paratroopers in baggy smocks and chamber-pot helmets soaked bandages in cologne and tied them over their mouths and nostrils. Others wore bandages over their eyes, damaged from stone splinters. A German order dated April 16 warned, "Effective at once the word 'catastrophe' will be eliminated in all reports and orders, as well as from the conversational vocabulary." Half a dozen swastika banners adorned the rubble on April 20 to mark the Führer's fifty-fifth birthday, but if "catastrophe" was removed from the lips it was never far from the mind. German gunners fired leaflets that depicted Death holding a pair of calipers and measuring on an Italian map the scant 123 kilometers—76 miles—covered by the Anglo-Americans since landing at Salerno in September; the rest of the peninsula was marked with phase lines and projected dates, including a putative crossing of the Swiss border in April 1948, and then, "to Berlin, another 650 kilometers, arrival about 1952." If illustrative of Allied dawdling, the map also reminded each *Gefreiter* how far he was from home.

"Everything is in the hands of the fates, and many of the boys have met theirs already," a German machine gunner wrote in his diary. "I badly want to get home to my wife and son. I want to be able to enjoy something of the beauty of life again. Here we have nothing but terror and horror, death and damnation."

For all its inhumanity, a peculiar dignity obtained at Cassino for those condemned to share its squalor. Every Guardsman could appreciate the German voice that abruptly broke into the Coldstream radio network one evening to acknowledge, in English: "You are all brave. You are all gentlemen."

Shortly after seven A.M. on Monday, May 1, the entire Fifth Army staff, along with the army band, tiptoed through the olive grove beyond the carp ponds and marble statuary in the Caserta Palace gardens. Without a sound, they encircled the new caravan recently built for their commander in an ordnance depot. Slathered in green and brown camouflage paint, the trailer featured not only fluorescent lights and a flush toilet, but full-length mirrors and an extra-long bed.

Mark Clark was a meticulous creature of habit, so it was a bit odd when 7:30 A.M. passed without his usual ring for an orderly to bring his breakfast. Al Gruenther, who had organized this fête for Clark's forty-eighth birthday, impatiently glanced at his watch before finally ordering the air-raid siren sounded. As a shrill wail carried across the palace grounds, the bandsmen hoisted their instruments and struck up "There'll Be a Hot Time in the Old Town Tonight," followed by a new ditty, "The Fifth Army's Where My Heart Is," with music and lyrics by Irving Berlin.

The trailer door swung open and out stepped a smiling Clark—"His Highness," as Gruenther jokingly called him—clad in blue pajamas, bedroom slippers, trench coat, and cap. After the band crashed through a rousing rendition of "Over There," Clark thanked the assembled crowd, reminded them that there was "still much to be done in the war," and predicted that many in the Fifth Army would eventually "see action in the South Pacific." As he stepped back inside, the band took leave with "The Old Gray Mare." Later in the day, Clark flew to the beach below Castel Volturno for a swim in the frigid Tyrrhenian Sea. A birthday celebration that night featured two cakes, a hypnotist, comedians, and a "card manipulator." "He is a hard-boiled soldier, of course," Gruenther wrote after the party, "but he does get homesick every now and then."

Curiously, he had just been home. While Alexander rearranged his armies for the spring offensive now planned for mid-May, Clark had proposed returning to Washington for the first time in nearly two years. Marshall at first demurred, complaining that the visit "comes at a most inopportune moment," then relented. At three A.M. on April 11, wearing an unadorned olive-drab uniform and the green silk cravat that had become his trademark, Clark shambled down the plane ramp at Bolling Field, along the Potomac River. Renie, "as fluttery as a schoolgirl," was stunned at how haggard he appeared, "thin and tense and tired." A War Department colonel handed Clark a note from Marshall that contained no hint of welcome or praise, while stressing the need to keep the visit secret. A staff car took the Clarks past Arlington National Cemetery to Marshall's residence at Fort Myer for a few hours' sleep. "There was a strained sort of strangeness between us," Renie later wrote. "He might just as well have been in Italy for all the attention he was able to pay me."

Mrs. Clark had been promoting General Clark's career again, apparently without his knowledge, and the cool reception Marshall gave him may have reflected his annoyance. In a recent note to the chief of staff, Renie assured him, "Certainly Wayne is trying." She also enclosed a personal letter from her husband. "I never get things the easy way, my poor men have to do it the hard way," Clark had written her. He continued:

> You will never know, darling, the tense moments, and hours and days I have. . . . I go to the hospitals and see them and talk to every man in a big tent. . . . They lie there with their legs off and stomach and chest wounds and smile and never complain. . . . At times I need you to talk to—have no one I can go to and express my real feelings.

If Marshall was sympathetic, he kept the sentiment concealed. The chief returned the letter as Renie had requested, but not before making a copy. "You are aware," he warned in a frosty note addressed to "Remi" in early March, "of the necessity of guarding the confidential nature of letters which you receive from your husband."

The ten-day furlough flew past. A week after his arrival, with Marshall hovering over his shoulder at the Pentagon, Clark dictated a note to his mother, who also lived in the District of Columbia: "I know it will be somewhat of a shock to you to know that I am here in Washington. . . . It is absolutely imperative that you tell *no one* of my presence here." With Marshall's permission, she joined her son for a brief stay in a secluded cabin at the Greenbrier Hotel, a resort in West Virginia now converted to a rehabilitation hospital. Clark played golf and talked of retiring. When he whacked three consecutive drives into a lake, several German prisoners of war who were working as hotel groundskeepers chortled in glee. Clark stalked from the tee, grumbling, "I'm sorry I took those guys prisoner."

Before returning to Italy, Clark was whisked one evening from the basement garage of Renie's apartment building on Connecticut Avenue to the private entrance of a nineteenth-century town house at 1806 I Street in downtown Washington. Here in the Alibi Club, the well-heeled and well-connected of Washington's elite gathered to "cook oysters, lobsters and ducks to suit themselves, play poker, and put away a lethal sort of drink based on Medford rum," as Marshall's biographer wrote. To hear Clark's progress report on the war in Italy, Marshall had assembled a dozen powerful figures, including Vice President Henry A. Wallace and Speaker of the House Sam Rayburn. For more than an hour, while his auditors slurped oysters around the table and tossed the shells into a bowl, Clark in his deep, mellifluous voice described campaigns past and future: the desperate fight at Salerno, the march across the Volturno, the struggle at the Winter Line, the Anzio gamble, and now, soon, the great thrust that would carry Fifth

Army into Rome. None of these men, Clark concluded, had any inkling of what it was like to wage war in mountainous Italy.

The "long and bloody battle up the Italian peninsula," as Clark had called the ordeal in a note to Field Marshal Wilson, had only grown longer and bloodier. But the moment was approaching that would make it all worthwhile. Flying back to Italy, Clark carried both the family cocker spaniel, Pal, for companionship, and packages from Katherine Marshall, the chief's wife, for two sons from her first marriage who were now serving as young officers in Italy. The brief trip home, Clark wrote Renie from Caserta, "seems like a dream."

Under Alexander's reorganization of the Allied legions in Italy, Clark now commanded thirteen divisions—seven American, four French, and two British—a force quadruple the size of the army he had brought to Salerno nine months earlier. Even as he took pride in leading such a formidable host, the increased demands—and another fifty thousand Fifth Army casualties since mid-January—weighed heavily. Cool and remote, yet capable of conviviality and brilliance, Clark could also be picayune and mulish, protective of his prerogatives, and as the war went on he grew increasingly ready to take offense at slights real or imagined. The nickname Marcus Aurelius Clarkus never seemed to fade.

At times, Clark seemed to feud with every senior general in the Mediterranean. "He treats his corps commanders as he would a company commander—and of course with less consideration for us Americans," Geoff Keyes told his diary. Weary of Clark's carping, Truscott twice reminded him that he had the authority to sack the VI Corps commander "at any time"; in his diary, Clark decried Truscott's "whining attitude." An ancient grudge with his former West Point mathematics instructor, Lieutenant General Devers—now the senior American commander in the Mediterranean—grew so toxic that Devers refused to deal directly with Clark; he used Lyman Lemnitzer, Alexander's American deputy, as an intermediary. "They could not be together three minutes without being in a fight," Lemnitzer said later. Clark considered Devers "a dope" and informed him that he had "too many bosses already." To Field Marshal Wilson, Devers said of the Fifth Army commander, "He thinks he is God Almighty. He's a headache to me and I would relieve him if I could, but I can't."

Clark's frictions with the British had only intensified in the spring. He complained that the Royal Navy "acted in many high-handed ways" and was "in no way cooperating with me." On several occasions he grew so insolent with Alexander that Lemnitzer expected him to be fired, and warned

Clark accordingly. The British high command in the Mediterranean so resented Clark's "vexatious attitude" that in March there had been talk of requesting his relief; the insurrection collapsed after word of it leaked to the Pentagon, and for lack of support from Churchill.

"Many happy returns of the day," the prime minister had written in a birthday greeting to Clark. If still fond of the man he called "the American eagle," Churchill was not above using other wildlife metaphors to assail the stalemate at Anzio. "We hoped to land a wildcat that would tear out the bowels of the Boche," he told Eisenhower. "Instead, we have stranded a vast whale with its tail flopping about in the water." Churchill also fretted, as he told Wilson, about "a feeling of bitterness in Great Britain when the claim is stridently put forward, as it surely will be, that the Americans have taken Rome"; he urged that credit be "fairly shared." While refusing to countenance a coup in Caserta, Churchill mused aloud about having Alexander command the Beachhead Army while Wilson took over the Cassino front, a crackpot notion that caused poor Brooke to confide, "I feel like a man chained to the chariot of a lunatic."

The task of handling Clark fell to Alexander, who demonstrated both patience and the shrewd eye of a gifted draftsman. From his palette of adjectives, Alexander later captured the man with precise brushstrokes: "Temperamental, very sensitive, extremely ambitious, vain, learned a lot as the campaign went on." Although General Alex would have preferred to see Omar Bradley or Patton in command of Fifth Army—even if he suspected the latter was "too restless for slogging"—he rated Clark a fine commander. "Always cool in battle," he added. "Never saw him frightened."

Never frightened, perhaps, but often anxious. A thousand cares weighed him down. Air cover at the beachhead remained spotty, and Clark disrupted his birthday festivities at Caserta on May 1 for a snarling row with Alexander over the disproportionate fighter and bomber support given Eighth Army at the expense of the Fifth. Casualties had become so corrosive that each U.S. infantry division in Italy could expect to lose its entire allotment of 132 second lieutenants in less than three months of combat. Although basic training had expanded from thirteen to seventeen weeks, many enlisted replacements arrived with marginal military skills, and some were unable to read. The newest units to join Fifth Army—the 85th and 88th Infantry Divisions, both in Keyes's II Corps—were the first into combat of fifty-five U.S. divisions built mostly from draftees; their worth had yet to be proven. Four of six infantry regimental commanders in those two divisions had already been relieved, as Clark advised Marshall, "for a combination of age and physical reasons."

There was more: the two British divisions still at Anzio remained so weak that both Truscott and Clark believed they would contribute little to any renewed offensive. The British Army since Salerno had suffered 46,000 battle casualties, with thousands more sick, yet replacements had not kept up with losses. Moreover, as Gruenther also noted, "Many British troops have been fighting for four or five years, and are in some cases pretty tired."

Few British commanders disagreed. "Absenteeism and desertion are still problems," wrote General Penney, back in command of the British 1st Division at Anzio after recovering from his wounds. "Shooting in the early days would probably have been an effective prophylactic." On average, 10 British soldiers were convicted of desertion each day in the spring of 1944, and an estimated 30,000 "slinkers" were "on the trot" in Italy. "The whole matter is hushed up," another British division commander complained.

Nor was the phenomenon exclusively British. The U.S. Army would convict 21,000 deserters during World War II, many of them in the Mediterranean. Clark condemned the surge of self-inflicted wounds in Fifth Army and the "totally inadequate" prison sentences of five to ten years for U.S. soldiers convicted of "misbehavior before the enemy." A psychiatric analysis of 2,800 American troops convicted of desertion or going AWOL in the Mediterranean catalogued thirty-five reasons offered by the culprits, including "My nerves gave way" and "I was scared."

A twenty-two-year-old rifleman who deserted at Cassino after seven months in combat was typical. "I feel like my nervous system is burning up. My heart jumps," he said. "I get so scared I can hardly move." Those symptoms affected tens of thousands, and added to Clark's worries. "Combat exhaustion," a term coined in Tunisia to supplant the misnomer "shell shock," further eroded Allied fighting strength in Italy, as it did elsewhere: roughly one million U.S. soldiers would be hospitalized during the war for "neuro-psychiatric" symptoms, and half a million would be discharged from the service for "personality disturbances."

All troops were at risk, but none more than infantrymen, who accounted for 14 percent of the Army's overseas strength and sustained 70 percent of the casualties. A study of four infantry divisions in Italy found that a soldier typically no longer wondered "*whether* he will be hit, but *when* and how bad." The Army surgeon general concluded that "practically all men in rifle battalions who were not otherwise disabled ultimately became psychiatric casualties," typically after 200 to 240 cumulative days in combat. "There aren't any iron men," wrote Brigadier General William C. Menninger, a prominent psychiatrist. "The strongest personality, subjected to sufficient stress a sufficient length of time, is going to disintegrate."

Treatment by "narcosynthesis," often using sodium amytal or nembutal, healed some combat-exhausted soldiers with deep sleep. The 45th General Hospital in Naples, which would admit more than five thousand neuropsychiatric patients in 1944, also used extensive electric-shock therapy. But generally fewer than one "NP" patient in five returned to duty.

All of these issues impaired Fifth Army's ability to reach Rome, and it was Rome that increasingly obsessed Clark. In Washington, he had learned that OVERLORD was now scheduled for early June; to capture Rome and invade Normandy concurrently would provide a glorious double blow to Axis morale. Even if the Eternal City was of dubious military value, it offered a dramatic symbol, a rightful and prestigious prize after so many months of struggle.

But getting there quickly was paramount, before OVERLORD eclipsed the Italian campaign—and before the British could steal Fifth Army's thunder. Churchill's suspicion was well founded: Clark had no intention of sharing credit for capturing the capital. He had, in fact, begun to exhibit signs of paranoia about British designs.

"I know factually that there are interests brewing for the Eighth Army to take Rome," Clark confided to his war diary in early May, "and I might as well let Alexander know now that if he attempts anything of that kind he will have another all-out battle on his hands. Namely, with me."

## *"On the Eve of Great Things"*

A LEXANDER often quoted Lord Nelson's observation on the eve of Trafalgar that "only numbers can annihilate," and for weeks he had devoted his waking hours to amassing that annihilative amplitude without Kesselring's knowledge. The Allied host in Italy now exceeded half a million men in the equivalent of twenty-eight divisions, with huge advantages in artillery, armor, and aircraft. Under a battle plan drawn by Alexander's chief of staff, Lieutenant General A. F. "John" Harding, the Allies intended not only to drive the enemy north of Rome, but to exterminate so many Germans that Hitler would be forced to shore up his jeopardized southern flank even as OVERLORD swept into France from the west.

This grand offensive, code-named DIADEM and set to commence on May 11, required a three-to-one edge in infantrymen to knock the Germans from the Gustav Line at a familiar point of attack: the Cassino redoubt and adjacent heights looming above the Liri Valley. For this paramount honor, Alexander had chosen Eighth Army. "Between ourselves," he privately told Brooke, "Clark and his army HQ are not up to it, it's too big for them."

Fifth Army, including Juin's French Expeditionary Corps, would attack on the left through the Aurunci Mountains, advancing "on an axis generally parallel to that of Eighth Army." Once the Gustav Line was pierced, Truscott's VI Corps would burst from the beachhead, shouldering aside the German Fourteenth Army to help destroy the Tenth.

Alexander's final order, issued in early May, remained silent on which force would seize Rome and thus further inflamed Clark's suspicions. But for weeks the battle plan had clearly laid out a scheme in which Eighth Army bulled up Highway 6 before veering east of the capital toward either Florence or Ancona on the Adriatic, depending on whether the Combined Chiefs chose southern France or Austria as Alexander's ultimate destination. Fifth Army would follow the Tyrrhenian coastline to Viterbo and then Livorno.

There would be glory enough to go around. Still, sensing fraternal rivalries, AFHQ informed all reporters that "no invidious comparison [should] be made between Eighth and Fifth armies and the FEC; no exaggeration, no overcolorful narratives. . . . Speculation should be avoided."

Monochrome proved difficult, given the vivid legions assembled for DIADEM. On the Allied right, Eighth Army—having tramped from Cairo across two continents in the past nineteen months—now secretly sideslipped more than a quarter million men east to west over the Apennines. Their commander, Lieutenant General Oliver W. H. Leese, was as tall as Clark and much stouter, with a black mustache and twinkling brown eyes that could darken in sudden rage—"a big ungainly bruiser," in Keyes's tart description. Blooded at the Somme, with the scars to prove it, Leese was bluff and toothy, given to khaki plus-fours and a straw hat. He remained a Montgomery protégé at heart, fond of thunderous artillery barrages, cheap smokes tossed to the lads, and conferences with subordinates while he soaked in his tub. "Never frig about on a low level," he liked to advise. Leese later became an expert in horticultural succulents, such as cacti and begonias; now he settled for tending his tulips.

He compared this, his first big battle as an army commander, to "having a baby." Alexander thought him methodical to a fault. "Not the pusher Clark was," he said after the war. "Some army commanders have to be pushed with a little ginger, like Leese, who always needed a little prodding." A Canadian general at one point decried his "prancing about waving his hands like a whore in heat." Yet Leese's guffaws and ribald humor masked a shrewd cunning. "I think I can work with Clark," he wrote his wife. "He thinks I am a bloody fool. He will have a great awakening."

Leese's seven infantry and three armor divisions included a new contingent in the Allied panoply: 56,000 Poles, who had been assigned to take

Monte Cassino itself. They were led by General Władysław Anders, a slender, handsome cavalryman with "the ardour of a boy," in Macmillan's phrase, and the grit of a man intent on settling scores. Anders had fought both Germans and Russians in 1939; wounded three times and captured on crutches, he spent twenty months in Moscow's notorious Lubyanka prison and other dungeons, much of it in solitary confinement. After Hitler invaded Russia, he was released—reportedly wearing only a shirt and underpants—to eventually form a Polish corps against the common Nazi foe. His men were drawn from prison camps scattered as far away as Siberia; in an anabasis that took them through Iraq and Persia, they joined other Poles who had fled through Hungary and Romania to fight with valor in the Middle East under British patronage.

Anders's two divisions were understrength but as ardent as he: they drew lots to see which would have the privilege of liberating the abbey itself. "We never take prisoners," a Polish colonel told one Grenadier Guardsman. "It's such a nuisance having to feed them and, after all, they started it." None of the Poles would hang back on May 11, as Anders later said, "for we had no men to spare for reserves." For II Polish Corps, the way home led through the Gustav Line.

On the Allied left, wedged into a twelve-mile front from the Tyrrhenian Sea to the lip of the Rapido flats, Clark's army also included a contingent for whom DIADEM was a grudge match. "The eyes of suffering France are fixed upon you," Juin told his FEC. His corps had swelled to nearly 100,000 men, parceled among four divisions and three groups of *goumiers,* irregular Berber tribesmen known for agility and ruthlessness. After enduring eight thousand casualties in the winter fighting around Cassino, Juin had spent the spring retraining his forces in mountain warfare, with a stress on speed, stealth, and infiltration. Only by "invading the mountains," he believed, could the Allies widen their front and circumvent the constricted tank trap in the Liri Valley.

That meant scaling the Auruncis, a primeval upland three thousand to five thousand feet high forming a broad belt between the valley and the sea. Sculpted by defiles and pinnacles, the range was crowned by the Petrella Massif, a height peopled mostly by shepherds and charcoal makers, and deemed impassable by Germans and Anglo-Americans alike.

But not by Juin. Wrapped in a greatcoat, with his blue Basque beret pulled down around his ears, useless right arm dangling, and an unlit cigar clamped between his crooked teeth, he stumped through the shadows below the range, eyeing approaches and saddles. Photo reconnaissance showed two narrow trails winding over the massif—and little enemy fortification. With patience and persistence, in passionate French and fractured

English, he had persuaded first Keyes and then Clark to broaden and deepen the Fifth Army attack. "The Americans are not people one can hustle," he wrote a French colleague. "They like us a lot, but they are also imbued with their sense of omnipotence and with a touchiness that you could hardly imagine."

Rather than employ the FEC as a battering ram to punch a hole in German defenses, which would then be ploddingly exploited by Keyes's II Corps, Juin proposed attacking full-fury with both corps abreast: 170,000 men, 600 artillery tubes, 300 tanks. Given the tilt of the Italian boot, the attack would initially angle into the mountains from east to west. To provision a single corps in such terrain would be difficult; to supply two would be herculean. But Fifth Army could outflank German defenses and unhinge the Gustav Line. Once across the Auruncis, the Americans could sweep up the coast toward Anzio and Rome while the FEC veered into the Liri Valley from the southwest.

Clark's admiration for Juin had only deepened since their first encounter in Algiers during Operation TORCH. It was no accident that Fifth Army headquarters assigned him the radio call-sign Hannibal. Among other gallantries, the Frenchman had voluntarily surrendered one of his four stars in order not to outrank his army commander. "Radiate confidence," Juin advised, "and enjoy taking risks."

Audacious and improbable, the plan also offered Fifth Army a bigger role than the vague, subordinate mission outlined in Alexander's order. Clark still cherished one bit of arcana memorized by every West Point plebe: "A calculated risk is a known risk for the sake of a real gain. A risk for the sake of a risk is a fool's choice."

He knew the difference.

Half a million players scurried to find their places before the curtain rose. The landscape seethed with activity, concealed from German eyes by darkness or deception. On the far left, Italian laborers built dummy pillboxes at the mouth of the Garigliano under orders "not to camouflage too well." Farther upstream, twenty undetected French battalions squeezed into a swale barely four miles across; Juin's men donned British soup-bowl helmets to obscure the departure of McCreery's X Corps to the far side of Cassino. At night, engineers hacked trails into the Aurunci foothills with hand tools to minimize the noise, then scattered brushwood before dawn to hide their tracks.

Canadian signalers in April had gone off the air along the Adriatic; now they began broadcasting again near Salerno to persuade German eavesdroppers that an amphibious operation was being mounted. In truth, barely two hundred men operated sixty-one radios in a carefully scripted electronic deception. At Termoli, on the Adriatic, the 1st Palestinian Camouflage Company floated dummy landing craft in the harbor and spread garnished nets over two acres of jetties to inspire the imagination of any German reconnaissance pilot. To discourage collaborators, Allied leaflets resembling funeral announcements displayed the names and photos of those executed for espionage or sabotage.

Military traffic signs appeared in Polish, English, French, and Hindi. Engineers built new trails along the front, concealed with lime, straw, stones, and turf. Long screens made of chicken wire festooned with steel wool hid roads, bridges, and depots. Timber parties carefully thinned the olive groves to create fields of fire for artillery, sawing the trunks three-quarters through and bracing the trees upright until H-hour, when they would be tipped over. Anders's troops blackened their kit, donned seven thousand mottled sniper suits, and slapped six thousand gallons of camouflage paint on their vehicles.

Scouts in canvas shoes and dark pullovers swam the Rapido at night, creeping among fireflies blinking in the reeds. Indian sappers crawled along the banks, probing for mines left by the Yanks in January. Five hundred yards from the river, South African troops lay low in their sangars and foxholes during daylight, which now lasted from 4:30 in the morning until 9:30 at night.

Every tree along Highway 6 leading to Shit Corner concealed supplies. Dumps grew mountainous: Fifth Army alone stockpiled 11,000 tons of ammunition for the first two days of DIADEM, including 200,000 105mm shells. One hundred miles of six-inch fuel pipeline stretched from Naples to forward depots, and forty-three Italian sawmills turned forests into engineer lumber. Fifth Army artisans, working at their casting tables in twelve-hour shifts, made intricate models depicting every quarry, cliff, and monastery on the approaches to Rome. Map depots stocked millions of sheets on four different scales. To produce the five-color maps requested by Clark's headquarters, cartographers mixed ersatz inks from mercurochrome, tobacco juice, and Atabrine tablets, which turned paper as well as soldiers bright yellow.

Endless supply convoys crept forward at six miles an hour behind trucks outfitted with water sprayers to keep down telltale dust. Specially tuned jeeps crept to the forward dumps with their hoods wrapped in rubber pads to muffle any squeaks. And all night long the clop of hooves could be heard from the Garigliano to the Sangro. Fifth Army alone had mustered ten thousand mules and two thousand horses into pack trains. "No mules," Juin told anyone who would listen, "no maneuver."

\* \* \*

Truscott in early May returned to the beachhead, tanned and rejuvenated after a five-day furlough in Naples. "I think of you every day when I look at my garden," he wrote Sarah from Nettuno. "The roses are blooming in great profusion. You know how I love them." At his request, orderlies snipped bouquets for the hospital wards in Hell's Half-Acre. He reminded his wife that he had now served in uniform for twenty-seven years. "I suppose the passing years have taken their toll and left their marks. Strange to say I actually feel younger than I did at the time." In another note he added, "I hope that I have not become conceited or swell-headed, and I do not believe that I have. I have retained my sense of humor and am still able to laugh at myself."

At the beachhead, too, preparations for DIADEM took on a febrile intensity. More than one million tons of matériel would be stockpiled at Anzio to supply Fifth Army during the drive north. Engineers crushed stone from demolished houses for roadbeds and fashioned three hundred brush fascines for marshy ground. Phone lines toward the front were buried in trenches dug with a jeep-drawn plow. A stockade for five thousand prisoners sprang up near Conca.

Patrols reclaimed small swatches of dead country, and battalions took turns firing every weapon for a minute or two before dawn to discomfit the enemy. Truscott pestered Clark for "at least one additional infantry division," and soon he would receive Fred Walker's 36th Division. The entire 1st Armored Division also consolidated at the beachhead, giving Ernie Harmon 232 tanks and bringing the Anzio force to seven divisions. For weeks, a dozen or more Shermans had trundled forward each night to fire harassment rounds before retreating at first light; now each morning a few slipped into concealed forward laagers, joining a hidden armored spearhead gathering near the front. Some crews built extra ammunition racks with angle iron, cramming 250 shells inside and another 40 on the back deck, plus 16,000 machine-gun rounds. "It was crowded," a company commander said later, "but we went out shooting."

In a letter to his old friend Lesley J. McNair in Washington, Harmon reported that commanders at the beachhead wanted to be sure "that we have left no stone uncovered." Even so, Harmon confessed, "I am very tense." As for Truscott, he focused on the victory that must surely come. "We are on the eve of great things," he wrote Sarah. "I hope that this summer will carry us a long way toward the end of the war in Europe."

It was precisely this issue that General Alex intended to discuss when he ambled into the VI Corps cellars at Nettuno on Friday morning, May 5. When should the Beachhead Army break out, and in what direction? Pointing to a wall map with a thick forefinger, Truscott quickly described the four options developed by his staff. He and Clark favored a plan code-named TURTLE: Allied forces would knife up the Albano road toward the Factory, swerve northwest at Carroceto to turn the German right flank on the west side of the Colli Laziali, then follow Highway 7—the Appian Way—into Rome.

The quizzical tilt of Alexander's red-hatted head suggested that he had different ideas. For weeks he had eyed the stretch of Highway 6 that angled *east* of the Colli Laziali, and which gave Vietinghoff's Tenth Army both its main supply route to the Liri Valley and a line of retreat to Rome. Once the DIADEM attack lured German reserves to the Cassino front, the beachhead forces could thrust northeast to cut the highway at Valmontone, a cross-roads town fourteen miles beyond Cisterna. Truscott's staff officers had drawn precisely such a plan, code-named BUFFALO, as one of their four op-tions. Merging the Beachhead Army with the Cassino front might take a month, Alexander believed, but by seizing Valmontone VI Corps could trap Tenth Army in a decisive battle of annihilation. So certain was he of his course after talking to Truscott that Alexander issued an order of un-common clarity, dated May 5, directing Fifth Army "to cut Highway 6 in the Valmontone area, and thereby prevent the supply or withdrawal of troops from the German Tenth Army."

Clark had spent the morning in Caserta conferring with Juin, Keyes, and other lieutenants, followed by a lunch of cold cuts and beer. At two P.M. an aide handed him a coded radio message from Truscott, reporting that Alexander seemed intent on BUFFALO.

> Gen. Alex arrived this morning. When I informed him of the four plans on which I'm working, he stated that I was paying too much atten-tion to alternate plans. . . . I assume that you are fully cognizant of Gen. Alex's ideas on the subject, but I want you to know what he told me to-day. . . . You know that I am with you all the way. Truscott.

Clark was furious. "Alex trying to run my army," he told his diary. In a phone call across the Caserta compound to Lemnitzer, he railed at Alexan-der for "issuing instructions to my subordinate commanders" that contra-dicted Clark's desire to remain flexible by keeping several plans in play. Upon reaching General Alex himself, he complained of being offended and "thoroughly astounded." In a memo of the conversation, Clark quoted himself as insisting that "under no circumstances would I tolerate his di-rect dealings with my subordinates. . . . He assured me that he had no in-tention of rescinding my order."

Unappeased, Clark fumed. In a visit to Nettuno on Saturday, he told Truscott, "The capture of Rome is the only important objective." The British, he added, were hatching nefarious schemes to get there first. Moreover, BUFFALO was tactically dubious. Too many roads ran north from the Cassino front to trap Tenth Army by severing Highway 6. German forces, Clark believed, would simply detour onto other routes.

On Monday morning, May 8, he confronted Alexander directly in his Caserta command post. "I told him he had embarrassed me. He replied that he had no intention to do so," Clark recorded. Alexander "kept pulling on me the idea that we were to annihilate the entire German army. . . . I told him that I did not believe that we had too many chances to do that; that the Boche was too smart." Alexander asked whether the American had doubts about DIADEM. "I assured him," Clark wrote, "that the Fifth Army attack would be as aggressive as any plan or attack he had ever been in or read of." The tense session ended with Alexander solicitous but resolved: the Beachhead Army would strike for Valmontone, as ordered on May 5 and embodied in BUFFALO. "I am thoroughly disgusted with him and with his attitude," Clark confided to his diary.

At four P.M. on Tuesday, Clark met with thirty-one reporters at Caserta. Using a large map and a pointer, he was both calm and commanding in describing DIADEM in detail. Fifth Army now mustered 350,000 men, including the two new divisions under General Keyes. Each U.S. division had received an extra 750 men to accommodate expected casualties; the British divisions, Clark noted, "are not quite up to strength." Kesselring's force totaled 412,000 men in twenty-three divisions in Italy, including nine along the Cassino front in Tenth Army and five more at Anzio in Fourteenth Army. Clark kept to himself other particulars, which Ultra had revealed: Kesselring possessed 326 serviceable tanks, 616 antitank guns, and 180 assault guns—and that he rated only two of his divisions as "fit to take the offensive."

The animating principle behind the initial Allied attack scheduled for Thursday night was simple: "Everybody throws everything they have at the same time." At long last, "the total resources" of both Fifth and Eighth Armies would fall on the enemy simultaneously. The subsidiary attack out of the beachhead would depend on progress in cracking the Gustav Line. Clark expected a tortuous grind, with daily progress limited to two miles or less. In view of the German scorched-earth tactics in Naples, he assumed that Rome would be despoiled. In a veiled allusion to OVERLORD, he added, "The more Boche we can hold down here, the more we can kill, the more we will contribute to operations which will overshadow this one."

He made no mention of his quarrel with Alexander, or his assertion to Truscott that Rome "is the only important objective." Nor did he hint that he already had begun to consider disobeying orders.

"The attack I would like to make under proper conditions is right out toward Route 6, to cut it," Clark told the scribes. He gestured on the map toward Valmontone. "Rome is of political value and we hope to take it," he added, with studied nonchalance. "But our first mission is to kill as many Germans as we can."

General Alex would be pleased. The Americans had fallen into line.

Albert Kesselring knew nothing of the dispute within the Allied high command, but that condition was of a piece with his larger ignorance of enemy strength, deployment, and intentions. Axis troops—including Russian prisoner-of-war volunteers armed with antique Italian weapons—peered seaward on both coasts for the amphibious landing Kesselring was sure would fall. German intelligence analysts had identified nine of twenty-two Allied regimental command posts on the Fifth Army front, but could pinpoint none of them; nor could they identify or locate most Allied division headquarters. German gunners so consistently fired leaflets in the wrong language to the wrong troops—Urdu to the Kiwis, Arabic to the British, English to the French—that Clark's G-2 believed "it could be only a deliberate attempt to conceal his knowledge of our order of battle." In fact, Kesselring was blind.

A Moroccan deserter several weeks earlier had sworn that the Allied offensive would begin April 25. Senior Wehrmacht officers packed their kit and rose early, only to feel "rather sheepish" when the front remained quiet. "Whenever you are well-prepared," complained Major General Fritz Wentzell, the Tenth Army chief of staff, "nothing happens." Now the attack was predicted for May 20 or later. After telling his subordinates on May 10 that he did "not expect anything in the immediate future," Vietinghoff left for the Führer retreat in Bavaria to collect another medal. In late April, General von Senger also had taken a month's leave to receive a similar decoration and to attend a conference in Berchtesgaden, along with Ernst-Günther Baade, his most trusted division commander. Siegfried Westphal, Kesselring's exhausted chief of staff, had departed two weeks earlier on convalescent leave.

If Kesselring was blind and misinformed, he was not stupid. He assumed the Allied main attack would follow Highway 6, the only avenue where armor could deploy in mass. To strengthen defenses around Cassino, he rearranged his line, summoning LI Mountain Corps from the Adriatic and shifting Senger's XIV Panzer Corps across the Liri Valley.

With the Führer determined to fight for every Italian hilltop, engineers since December had built yet another bulwark across the peninsula: the Hitler Line, a fortified string of redoubts five to ten miles behind the Gustav Line. Some 77,000 German troops shored up the beachhead perimeter, and another 82,000 held the southern front, seventy miles away. The German strategy in Italy, Kesselring now declared, was "simply to make the enemy exhaust himself."

Still, he misread the omens: the bridging equipment unloaded near the Garigliano; the Allied patrols unspooling white tape; the oppressive silence. On Wednesday, May 10, Wentzell phoned Kesselring's headquarters with his daily report. "To my great pleasure, everything is quiet," he told a staff officer. "Only I do not know what is going on. Things are becoming ever more uncertain."

"I have told this to the field marshal," the officer replied. "He looks very intently towards the coast."

"In past times one heard at least once in a while that such-and-such division had left Africa. But now one hears nothing," Wentzell said. "I think it is not impossible that things are going on of which we have no idea."

Red Cross volunteers behind Monte Trocchio handed out sandbags filled with cigarettes, dates, and oranges to Allied troops tramping toward the Rapido staging areas. "It was like a goodbye gift," one soldier said. Mule hooves now were sheathed in sacking to quiet the clop, and conspicuously white animals had been culled from the trains. Every brake and copse along the front grew stiff with soldiers. Some thumbed through a GI's guide to Italian cities, which stressed Leonardo da Vinci's military inventions—"hand grenades, shrapnel, the parachute"—and assured them that Rome's Colosseum "wasn't wrecked by Long Toms. It got that way through the passage of time." A battalion surgeon recorded in his diary, "Blackjack for twenty dollars a card . . . I win over two hundred dollars and now worry where to carry all that money."

A Canadian soldier scrutinizing the blasted landscape near Cassino asked, "Who the hell would want to live here, let alone fight over it?" But Fred Majdalany concluded that "Cassino had become what in the earlier war Ypres was to the British, Verdun to the French. It was a cause in its own right, a cause to die for." Many had, more would. Polish troops swapped their boots for canvas slippers or wrapped their feet in rags before creeping toward Snakeshead Ridge behind the abbey. The scent of red clover mingled with ruder scents, and the Poles tried covering Indian corpses with blankets to contain the smell. "The place was alive with rats," a platoon leader in the 3rd Carpathian Division complained.

A dozen miles to the southwest, an officer in the 88th Division listened to the murmur of his men praying aloud. Between the lines, the blackened bodies of soldiers killed in earlier skirmishes reminded him of "irregular pieces of driftwood on a rocky beach." Jumpy Senegalese sentries fired at what appeared to be the glowing cigarettes of approaching strangers but proved to be fireflies, which they had never seen.

On the gun line in the rear, engineers blasted pits for a recently arrived 8-inch battery; each tube required thirteen cannoneers to manhandle the forty-five-foot staff used to swab the barrel after each round. Others stacked shells with new molybdenum fuzes capable of penetrating steel-reinforced concrete. Small holes were drilled in the casings to intensify the scream in flight.

From the beachhead to the Apennines, scribbling men struggled to find the right words in their letters home. "Busy days, nerve trying days," Jack Toffey wrote Helen. "One smokes too much—drinks too much if he can get it, and sleeps too little if he can get that." He burned most of Helen's letters to lighten his load. "This hurts me to do," he told her, "but space had become such a factor that I found it necessary to retain only yours of April and May." While certain that "the Kraut is going to catch hell from all sides at any time," Toffey confessed that "I am a bit war weary." He had resigned himself to fighting for the duration. "I'll be home when they build a bridge and we march over it," he told her. "How long Oh Lord—how long?"

Commanders evinced the requisite public élan while privately venting their anxieties. "If Alex is a military genius, I'm Greta Garbo," Keyes told his diary on May 10. "He is obsessed with the idea that the Germans are going to give up and run." A few hours later Alexander cabled Churchill: "Our objective is the destruction of the enemy south of Rome." As for the prime minister, a note of desperation had crept into the message he sent George Marshall. "We must throw our hearts into this battle for the sake of which so many American and British lives have already been sacrificed, and make it like OVERLORD—an all-out conquer or die."

H-hour was fixed for eleven P.M. on May 11, half an hour before moonrise. The day dawned gray and damp enough to lay the dust, then faired in the afternoon. A grizzled French spahi told a young American liaison officer, "I do not know where my son is tonight, and your father does not know where his son is. So tonight we will be father and son." The Frenchman had ten days to live. Shelling on both sides dwindled to a mutter at last light, then ceased entirely, yielding to what Alexander called "a strange, impressive silence." Stars threw down their silver spears. "New boys with fear and nerves and anxiety hidden under quick smiles," a Canadian chaplain wrote. "It is the hardest thing to watch without breaking into tears."

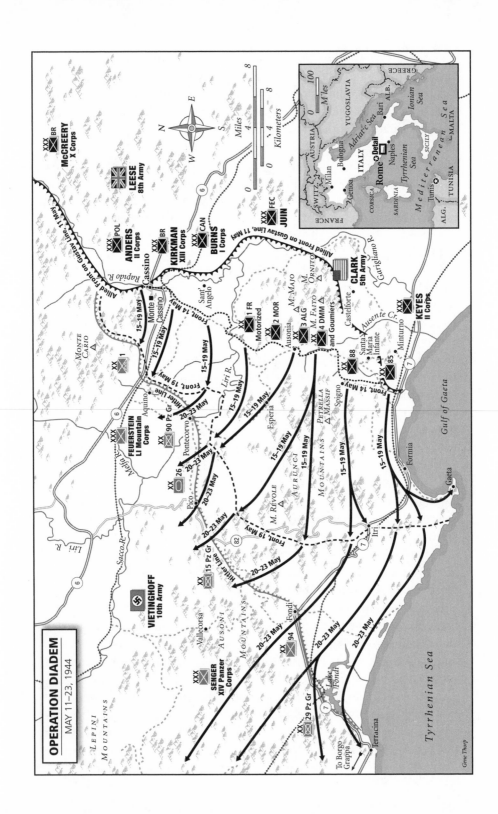

**OPERATION DIADEM**
MAY 11–23, 1944

McCREERY
X Corps

LEESE
8th Army

ANDERS
II Corps

KIRKMAN
XIII Corps

BURNS
I Corps

JUIN
FEC

CLARK
5th Army

KEYES
II Corps

Allied front on Gustav Line, 11 May

Allied Front on Gustav Line, 11 May

Monte Cassino

Cassino

Sant'
Angelo

MONTE
CARIO

Aquino

FEUERSTEIN
LI Mountain
Corps

90 Pz Gr

26

Pico

VIETINGHOFF
10th Army

15 Pz Gr

SENGER
XIV Panzer
Corps

29 Pz Gr

To Borgo
Grappa

Terracina

Lake
Fondi

Vallecorsa

Fondi

94

*AUSONI
MOUNTAINS*

*L E P I N I
M O U N T A I N S*

Liri R.

Sacco R.

Liri R.

1 FR
Motorized

2 MOR

3 ALG

4 DMM
and Goumiers

Ausonia

M. MAJO

M. FAITO

M. ORNITO

Castelforte

Santa
Maria
Infante

Minturno

88

85

Spigno

Esperia

M. REVOLE

PETRELLA
MASSIF

*A U R U N C I*

*M O U N T A I N S*

Itri

Formia

Gaeta

*Gulf of Gaeta*

*Tyrrhenian Sea*

Hitler Line

15–19 May
15–19 May
15–19 May
15–19 May
15–19 May
15–19 May
15–19 May
15–19 May
15–19 May
15–19 May
15–19 May

Front, 14 May
Front, 19 May
Front, 19 May
Front, 14 May

20–23 May
20–23 May
20–23 May
20–23 May
20–23 May
20–23 May
20–23 May
20–23 May
20–23 May

Pontecorvo

Ausente Cr.

Garigliano R.

N
E
W
S

Miles
0   4   8

Kilometers
0   4   8

*Detail*

Rome

FRANCE
SWITZ.
AUSTRIA
YUGOSLAVIA
GREECE
ALB.
ITALY
Milan
Genoa
Bologna
SARDINIA
CORSICA
Naples
Rome
Tyrrhenian
Sea
Adriatic Sea
Bari
Ionian
Sea
SICILY
Mediterranean Sea
MALTA
TUNISIA
ALG.
TUNIS

Miles
0        100

Gene Thorp

## 12. THE GREAT PRIZE

*Shaking Stars from the Heavens*

THE BBC pips had not finished signaling the top of the hour at eleven P.M. on Thursday, May 11, when gusts of white flame erupted in a thirty-mile crescent across the hills of central Italy. Light leaped from two thousand gun pits, laving the cannoneers as they danced bare-chested at their breechblocks, shoving home another shell, and another, and another. Ruby tongues licked from the muzzles, as drifting smoke rings lassoed the constellations and concussion ghosts chased one another through the night. "It seemed it must shake the very stars out of the heavens," a Black Watch soldier wrote.

Men peered from their trenches or crowded into farmhouse doorways to watch the spectacle, their faces reddened in the glow and their helmets jarred by the percussive shock. "Rome, then home!" they bellowed. Nightingales had sung in the silence before the cannonade; now they sang louder but to small effect. "The roar of the guns is so deafening that you can shout at the man next to you and still not be heard," a medical officer in the 88th Division wrote. "Sheets of flame spring behind every bush. The hills to our north are spattered with phosphorus bursts that illuminate the entire horizon." Above the abbey and Cassino town, scores of German flares added their own sibilant brilliance, tiny red and silver supernovas that stretched the shadows. "The sky," a Royal Hampshire account noted, "was full of noises."

Gunners draped wet rags over their sizzling barrels or poured cans of water down the muzzles, then reloaded. Fifth Army alone would fire 174,000 shells in the first twenty-four hours of DIADEM, requital for months of peninsular misery. "I felt as if a bridge of iron was being erected overhead, and wondered how it was that shells did not collide," a Polish corporal in the 3rd Carpathian Division reported. As the barrage continued, Alexander sent Churchill a prearranged confirmation that the offensive had begun: "Zip, repeat, zip."

*Rome, then home.* At midnight on the Allied right, the Eighth Army assault battalions shook out and surged forward through the vibrating air like wasps from an angry hive. Where the Americans and then the New Zealand Corps had attacked enemy strongpoints months before, Eighth Army would also attack but with twice the strength and more: two Polish divisions up Monte Cassino rather than just the 4th Indian, two British divisions across the Rapido—with two more to follow, and then the entire Canadian Corps—rather than just the U.S. 36th Division. Shell fire scythed the enemy redoubts. "We were confident," a British platoon commander said, "that no Germans could possibly outlive such a devastating bombardment."

The Poles found otherwise. "Soldiers! The moment for battle has arrived," General Anders told his men. "We have long awaited the moment for revenge and retribution over our hereditary enemy." Troops surged up Snakeshead Ridge toward Point 593, that scabrous knuckle, following trails marked with painted phosphorescent arrows. Within five hundred yards they were burrowing beneath the bodies of dead comrades, seeking cover from murderous machine-gun and mortar fire. By mischance, the hereditary enemy had chosen the night of May 11 to relieve defenders behind Monte Cassino with fresh troops: the hillside garrison was nearly double its normal strength. Nine German battalions opposed the Poles.

"Many of us had lost our exact bearings and there was a great deal of confusion," a Polish platoon leader reported. To keep secret the presence of the Polish corps at Cassino, Leese had refused to let Anders reconnoiter the terrain. Hand-to-hand fighting clattered across the slopes in what Anders called "a collection of small epics." The 5th Kresowa Division seized Phantom Ridge, a mile northwest of the abbey, but took a savage pounding on the exposed hogback. A 3rd Carpathian battalion captured Point 593 but an attack on nearby Point 569 collapsed after Polish artillery fire—hampered by a shortage of observation posts—lifted too quickly and riflemen were slaughtered in a saddle below the hill. When Polish sappers later balked at clearing a minefield, a Carpathian commander barked over the radio, "If they do not obey orders, shoot them." They obeyed: of twenty engineers in one minesweeping detail, eighteen would be killed or wounded. "You don't know how dreadful death can be," a dying Pole told his comrades. "Now I shall have to miss the rest of the battle."

At dawn, the rising sun fired the hilltops as if they had been dipped in copper. All morning and past the meridian the killing continued. German snipers used the light to lethal advantage, picking off Poles "like sitting birds." Anders had been given sixteen flamethrowers but little instruction in how to use them; most were ruined by German artillery and mortar fire, including two that burst into flame. "I was working on my knees. I was smeared all over with blood," a Polish surgeon reported. "A corporal came and stood among the wounded. . . . Through his torn tunic I saw a wound the size of two hands, the shoulder-bone bared." The corporal told him, "I shan't let you evacuate me until I've thrown all my grenades."

Yet even Polish valor could not win through. Hundreds of dead men sprawled among the poppies and wild irises. By four P.M. on Friday, May 12, all momentum had seeped away. With his assault battalions depleted by half, Anders ordered both divisions back to their starting lines. The attack, one Polish writer noted, "was really no more than a very costly reconnaissance."

A British officer who arrived at General Leese's command post late in the afternoon found him rambling through a field. As the officer began to deliver the bad news—attack repulsed, fearsome Polish losses—Leese held up a huge hand. "Let's pick some cornflowers," he said. They picked until their arms were laden with blue-headed stalks, then Leese said, "Right! Now tell me about the casualties."

Upon driving to the Polish II Corps headquarters, Leese found the usually elegant Anders slumped in his caravan, disheveled and in need of a shave. His eyes red, his face gray, the Polish commander turned and asked, "What do we do now?"

What, indeed? If Eighth Army's right wing had failed, the left wing was hardly capering toward Rome. Along the Rapido, the 8th Indian Division had been assigned to cross the river and capture Sant'Angelo, the dolorous village that had so bedeviled the 36th Division in January. As the barrage lifted early Friday morning, vapors from the river swallowed the rising moon. Khaki-drill columns wended through the fens, following white tape and hooded hurricane lanterns to the east bank. Vehicles crept forward, hauling boats or towing antitank guns. From upstream, a rude clanking carried on the night: a squad of 6th Lancers, crouching in defilade, banged angle iron against pieces of rail track as a deception to draw fire.

Fire they drew, but so did the rest of the bridgehead. Assault troops splashed and paddled across the Rapido only to trip both antipersonnel mines left five months earlier by the Yanks and smoke canisters emplaced by German gunners as aiming stakes. Within minutes smoke, mist, and cordite billowed through the bottoms "like a yellow London fog," in Leese's phrase. Visibility dropped to two feet.

Men stumped about in flame-stabbed confusion, pitching into ditches and walking in circles. British gunners fired Bofors tracers overhead to show the azimuth of liberation, but "in the mist the shells quickly dimmed and were lost to sight," a reporter observed. Royal Fusiliers reached the west bank above Sant'Angelo with few casualties, each soldier clinging to the bayonet scabbard of the man ahead. But now the ground between river and village was covered by a vermilion loom of enemy bullets, and stick grenades showered the bottoms from the Sant'Angelo bluffs. "Oh, God, don't let me die yet," Fusilier F. R. Beacham pleaded. "I promise that I will always be good if you let me live." Coming upon a mortally wounded comrade, Beacham lifted a water bottle to his lips. "Thanks a lot, mate," the man said, then passed over.

Twelve of sixteen Gurkha boats sank or floated away. The four surviving craft ferried men through the small hours, with much shouting above the din from bank to bank. Farther upstream, all forty boats manned by a brigade of the British 4th Infantry Division were soon gone. Drowned men drifted on the dark current that had drowned so many before.

By midday, no battalion in either the 8th Indian or the 4th Infantry had gained more than five hundred yards of an intended two thousand. Barely half of Leese's objectives had been secured on the left, none on the right. Snipers whittled away the British as they did the Poles. After a major in the Derbyshire Yeomanry fell dead with a bullet in the brain, a subordinate offered a terse elegy: "He was an autocratic man but a good leader, and we came to regret his death." A Fusilier who spent May 12 facedown in a ditch listening to the "sough and whiffle" of shells overhead later noted, "The day passed ever so slowly."

Yet the enemy had missed his main chance. The absence of Vietinghoff, Westphal, Senger, Baade, and others impaired German dexterity; so did 350 tons of Allied bombs that battered Kesselring's command post and demolished the Tenth Army headquarters near Avezzano, with "an unsteadying effect upon the occupants." Confusion, error, fear—the usual frictions—played hob on the far side of the hill, and the crushing counterattack that might have crippled DIADEM never took shape.

Three bridges, dubbed Cardiff, Oxford, and Plymouth, had been planned for the Rapido near Sant'Angelo. Cardiff was abandoned, but engineers carved ramps and filled ditches under scorching fire to throw a small span across at Oxford before nine A.M. on Friday. Two hours later and a thousand yards downstream, a pair of Sherman tanks muscled a one-hundred-foot Bailey bridge over the stream at Plymouth. Canadian tanks pelted for the far shore, "camouflaged with green boughs and looking like a harvest festival."

Upstream between Sant'Angelo and Cassino town, dead and dying engineers shored the riverbank. But by first light on Saturday, May 13, another span—Amazon—slid into place. A pipe major crossed, skirling, then fell mortally wounded. "Cries for help from the wounded . . . could be heard inside the tanks even though the crews were wearing headphones," according to a 6th Armoured Division account. The tanks bulled ahead, riflemen clinging to their hulls with one hand and shooting with the other. Every so often the smoke and marsh mist parted to allow glimpses of the abbey, floating toward heaven.

Gurkhas twice surged into Sant'Angelo on Friday, and twice machine gunners embedded in the rubble threw them back. Cairn by cairn, cellar by cellar, attackers rooted out defenders with grenades and curved kukri knives. A pair of Canadian tanks flanked the village, gunning down those who sought to slip away. By three P.M. Saturday, resistance had ended but for the odd sniper, at a cost of 170 Gurkha casualties. White dust floured the quick and the dead alike.

Putrefying corpses were soaked in gasoline and set ablaze, then shoved into a trench. Some captured Germans were found to have wounds dressed with paper: enemy medics had run short of bandages. "This is real war," a squadron commander in the 17th Battalion of the 21st Lancers scribbled in his notebook, "and makes Africa seem a picnic." A Royal Artillery gunner in the 78th Division studied the consequences of his fall of shot: splintered rifles, smashed field glasses, dead Germans. "This is the terrifying thing about war," he wrote. "When I saw what I had achieved, I had no regrets at all."

They pushed on, across the shot-torn fields, edging toward the mouth of the Liri Valley, where objectives had been code-named after famous Midlands hunts. A Canadian in the 48th Highlanders described being snagged by barbed wire with another soldier: "He was thrashing and fighting with the wire like a man gone insane. The bullets started socking into him, and he jerked and kicked with each new hit. Then he crumpled beside me. Nothing was very bad in the war after that."

Two secure bridgeheads merged to form a shallow purchase across the Rapido. Six more bridges opened, and thousands of smoke shells kept Monte Cassino swaddled in white. But unless the abbey and adjacent hills fell, German batteries threatened to flay anyone pushing up Highway 6 through the valley. "Flames of Jerry guns almost beautiful at dusk," a Guards officer observed. "Spitting crimson, amber and opal."

In four days Eighth Army would advance just four miles, at a cost of more than four thousand casualties—a man down every five feet. Still, Leese took satisfaction where he could, even as he pondered how to convert his fragile bridgehead into the battle of annihilation that Alexander coveted.

"Mark Clark has laid 4–1 against our crossing the Rapido," Leese wrote. "As they say at a private school, 'Sucks to him.'"

＊　＊　＊

Clark had troubles enough without British maledictions. Fifteen miles downstream from Cassino, on the far left of the Allied line, Geoffrey Keyes's II Corps—composed of the 85th and 88th Divisions—had used its foothold across the Garigliano to push forward from Minturno in DIA-DEM's early hours. Soldiers nervously worked their rifle bolts as they strode ahead, blankets and raincoats tied to their combat packs. Each man wore white adhesive strips or squares of white cloth on the back of his helmet and uniform sleeves to prevent fratricide; platoon leaders added extra white-tape chevrons to make themselves more recognizable to their men. Officers gobbled Benzedrine tablets. "Rome, Rome," a lieutenant in the 88th Division chanted, "who gets Rome?"

No one in II Corps, at least not yet. Sheaves of fire from the entrenched 94th Grenadier and 71st Infantry Divisions lashed the American ranks from the Gulf of Gaeta on the left to Ausente Creek on the right. Fifth Army intelligence had pinpointed 161 German machine-gun positions among some 600 along the front; that left more than 400 unaccounted for, until now. "The noise was all of a piece, an ocean of noise," one soldier recalled. Smoke and haze clotted so that no amount of identifying tape was visible much beyond arm's length. Red tracer vectors fired every few seconds pointed the way and demarcated unit boundaries—.50-caliber for companies, 40mm for battalions—but confusion still held sway. "What's going on, fella?" a soldier yelled to Eric Sevareid. "They never tell us nuthin'."

The rising sun dried their uniforms: GIs scuttling into the mountains looked to one soldier like "a serpentine column of steam." Sevareid described "bodies of men moving down narrow defiles or over steep inclines, going methodically from position to position between long halts."

Yet neither division moved far. The defiles grew narrower, the inclines steeper, the long halts longer. Most of all, the fire grew fiercer. An attack by the 351st Infantry against the hilltop village of Santa Maria Infante failed to take two critical hills known as the Tits. One company lost eighty-nine men; another fell for a German white-flag ruse, with fifty men captured. Among those killed in the day's fighting was Frederick Schiller Faust, a prolific writer known as the King of the Pulps, who, under the pen name Max Brand, had turned out nearly four hundred westerns, including *The Rangeland Avenger* and *Gunman's Reckoning*. Intent on writing a narrative about one platoon's odyssey to Rome, Faust died from German 88mm fire only three hours and six hundred yards into the journey. As Sevareid observed, "Those who live are incredibly alive, and the others are stupefyingly dead." By early Saturday morning, to Keyes's chagrin and Clark's dismay, the American attack had stalled.

That left Juin's FEC, which had pitched into the largest set-piece battle fought by the French army since 1940 with rousing choruses of the "Marseillaise" and "C'est nous les Africains." As thirty or more artillery rounds fell on every charted German battery with little enemy fire in return, three divisions abreast surged into the craggy Auruncis.

Plunging fire greeted them with the incivility of a slammed door. Moroccan infantrymen were pinned down in minefields beyond the Garigliano; those who breached the barbed wire and booby traps found flamethrowers and interlocking machine-gun fire waiting. Behind concrete German pillboxes stood more bunkers and blockhouses. French troops near Castelforte picked their way into a badlands teeming with snipers and mortarmen. Soon the landscape smelled of singed hair and burning flesh, human and mule. Counterattacking grenadiers slashed at the French flanks with such fury that FEC officers on Monte Faito called artillery onto their own positions to avoid being overrun.

By midmorning on Friday, May 12, Juin's legions were hardly beyond their starting lines. Ten assault battalions in the French center had achieved little penetration, and the FEC, like II Corps and the Poles, could claim few of its objectives. Fifth Army casualties approached sixteen hundred. Losses among French officers were particularly grievous, and it was said that German ferocity had triggered "considerable alarm in FEC headquarters." An officer with the Tunisians observed, "Due to the intense heat, the dead take on a waxy look. They're everywhere."

Juin went forward shortly before noon, beret tugged down to his ears, cigarette smoldering in its holder. First by jeep, then by hard climb, he scaled the flank of Monte Ornito on a path carpeted with dead mules, the odd mortar shell bursting nearby. Stretcher bearers passed him on the narrow trail, carrying three wounded battalion commanders to the rear. "This thing got off on the wrong foot," he announced at the 2nd Moroccan Infantry Division command post. "We must begin again."

Through much of the afternoon he scrambled up and back, watching, assessing. Upon returning to his headquarters at Sessa Aurunca he summoned his staff, rapped on a table, and said in his smoky voice, "It's gone wrong. But they are as tired as we are." Before defeating the Germans, the FEC must first "conquer the ground." Corps artillery would be redirected to support, preeminently, the 2nd Moroccan in a push through the center of the line toward Monte Majo, a three-thousand-foot limestone bastion that served as a gateway to the Petrella Massif. Infiltrators would first outflank enemy strongpoints on the right. Engineers could blow gaps in the barbed wire with bangalore torpedoes, and moonlight in the small hours on Saturday would suffice to lay a barrage just ahead of the attacking infantry. Juin also would fling his only reserve division into the fight. "We'll start again tomorrow morning after a full-scale artillery preparation," he said, "and it will go."

It went, spectacularly. A deft shift of artillery caught German counterattackers in the open at 5:30 A.M. on May 13, chopping them to pieces. Indifferent to enemy shells thudding nearby, Juin watched his Moroccans vanish into a ravine below Monte Faito, then emerge on the far slope, chanting *"La Allah ihl Allah"* as a column of prisoners in field gray streamed to the rear. Four hundred French and Fifth Army guns set the mountains ablaze. By midafternoon, Moroccan soldiers reported Monte Majo captured and a two-mile gap torn in the Gustav Line. The enemy 71st Division—mostly flatlanders from Lower Saxony who had considered the Auruncis impregnable—was cut in half, leaving both flanks open to exploitation. An intercepted German radio message advised, "Accelerate the general withdrawal."

By Sunday the French had advanced seven miles across a sixteen-mile front, unhinging German defenses beyond the Garigliano. *"En avant!"* Juin urged. FEC casualties exceeded two thousand, but nine hundred prisoners had been captured; many complained of shelling worse than in Russia. On Monte Majo's summit appeared an enormous tricolor, measuring twelve by twenty-five feet and visible from Cassino to the sea. "This," Juin said, "is warfare to which we are accustomed." The 71st Division commander's assessment was terser: "Most unpleasant."

The unpleasantries had only begun, for with the capture of Castelforte by Algerian troops on the French left, Juin was able to slip the leash from his Berber irregulars. The vanguard of twelve thousand *goumiers*—invariably shortened to *goums* by the Yanks—had passed through the north end of town on Friday night, many on horseback. Five hundred yards beyond the last house the column swung west off the road, following a narrow trail into the Aurunci wilds with orders to cut Highway 82 between Itri and Pico—nearly twenty miles in the German rear—and thus turn the enemy's right flank.

"Dark men, dark night," Montgomery had once said of the *goums*. "Very hard to see coming." Most wore sandals, wool socks, gloves with the trigger fingers snipped off, and striped djellabas; a beard, a soup-bowl helmet, and a foot-long knife at the belt completed the ensemble. "It was as if troops of the last century had been reincarnated and suddenly appeared at our side," said an American colonel in the adjacent 88th Division. Juin considered them "vigorous, reliable, [and] very abstemious"; another French general said they "lived only for brigandage and war." Some wore their booty, an Algerian officer observed: "dozens of wristwatches on their arms, collections of rings on their fingers, and strings of shoes and boots hanging on their backs." One unit kept a tiger as a mascot. Upon encountering their Anglo-American confreres they typically gestured for a cigarette, calling, "Smokie, smokie, Joe?"

It was said that in Sicily they took not only enemy ears as trophies but entire heads. It was said that *goums* creeping through the night would feel a sentry's bootlaces for the unique German loop before deciding whether to cut the man's throat. It was said that a *goum* had sold a GI a quart jar of fingers pickled in brandy. A U.S. military hospital treating French casualties handled so many *goums* with the same single names that doctors assigned numbers on their charts—Abdullah 4, Muhammed 6. "Their long hair is braided in pigtails. They sing, chatter, and howl," one physician wrote. "Many carry chickens under their arms." A nurse admired their skill in "cracking nuts with their teeth," but lamented the theft of hospital towels for turbans. "The Arab soldier is interested in just three things: women, horses, and guns," a French officer told an American colonel, who replied, "The American soldier is the same, except that he doesn't care anything about horses and guns."

Up and up they climbed with a Moroccan infantry regiment and Algerian artillery, splitting into three forces, each angling west and then north through nearly trackless terrain, including one vertical stretch that rose four hundred feet in less than a half mile. "The sky was a changeless blue, the heat implacable," a French officer reported:

> From a soil glistening with mica, the hard little hooves of the Arab horses struck up clouds of grasshoppers. Beside their horses and mules, the *goumiers* loped tirelessly onwards with long ambling stride, forage caps askew, an eternal rictus on the lips, ignoring the heat despite woolen *djellabas*.

By four P.M. on May 15, the lead scouts had scaled the forward heights of the Petrella Massif; by the next morning, they stood on the crest of Monte Revole, more than four thousand feet up and a dozen miles beyond the Garigliano. When an unwitting Wehrmacht battalion blundered into a nearby valley, *goumiers* encircled both flanks in a horseshoe ambush, then swept down the slopes "like falling boulders." German survivors later described "grinning savages with knives in their hands, obviously quite eager to begin the butchery."

Men and beasts had exhausted themselves and far outrun their supply lines. Just past noon on May 17, a fleet of U.S. bombers dropped forty tons of food and ammunition across the mountain peaks. The *goumiers* would spend a day recovering the crates and recuperating, then push on.

On the French left, the Americans also were on the move after punching through the stout but brittle enemy line that had thwarted II Corps for two days at a cost of three thousand casualties. With ample replacements in the wings, Keyes replenished his ranks and threw fresh troops against the depleted grenadiers on the same narrow front. Santa Maria Infante fell on May 14 after relentless pummeling by fighter-bombers and white-phosphorus shells. Soon the 85th Division was pressing along the Via Appia in the coastal flats with a dust-churning flotilla of men, trucks, mules, tanks, and tank destroyers. On the heights to their right, the 88th Division lunged through Spigno and onto the Petrella Massif, guided by local peasants along goat paths a few miles south of the FEC.

The enemy had been "rushed off his feet," in Juin's phrase. On the Fifth Army right, the nearly extinct 71st Division had suffered five thousand casualties, mostly from 150,000 artillery rounds; the division told Kesselring's headquarters that no more than a hundred riflemen were still fit to fight. Allied shells and aircraft battered the German rear, terrorizing horses hitched to gun carriages and supply wagons. After a gallant stand by one grenadier unit, Kesselring told Vietinghoff, "One could cry with admiration."

All this buoyed the Allied high command after so many miscarriages. Alexander bounded into Clark's command post to pronounce himself "very pleased" with the attack. Juin swanned about in his jeep, barking, "We've got them." The replenished *goumiers* would cut Highway 82 while the rest of the FEC converged on Pico in the German rear, within rifle range of the Liri.

Only Clark remained somber. He sent Juin two congratulatory bottles of whiskey, but the "delinquency" of II Corps irked him. The FEC had averaged about two miles a day since DIADEM began, compared with just over one for II Corps. The Americans also seemed unprepared for headlong pursuit, so much so that Clark threatened "disciplinary action" against all laggards. Keyes's troops overran surprised German artillery batteries at Spigno and then seized Itri on Highway 82. But traffic snarls at the narrow crossroads delayed the 88th Division's push toward Fondi, nine miles to the northwest and a linchpin of the Hitler Line.

"I am disappointed in the rigidity of II Corps plans," Clark told his diary with the reproachful tone of a man determined to disapprove. "They have not shown a flexibility of mind and an aggressive attitude." Keyes in turn wrote of Clark:

> Called me about 6 times. Each time finding fault, saying he was embarrassed and his face was red at the French and Goums doing so well and getting so many prisoners. . . . He acts like a 15-year-old kid. . . . A [shell] fragment tore a hole in the seat of my jeep. I wasn't in it.

Even as he lashed his commanders, and as much as he wanted to lead the liberation procession into Rome, Clark harbored tactical anxieties about his troops surging too far beyond the British. By May 18, the FEC would be six miles ahead of Eighth Army, putting the Allied front on a severe slant and exposing Fifth Army's right flank to counterattacks. Clark could only conclude, again, that Leese and the British were not pulling their weight. "I am disappointed," he wrote, "in the effort of the Eighth Army."

That same Eighth Army was about to claim the grandest prize on the Gustav Line. With British and Canadian troops inching past Cassino town to force the Liri Valley, Leese at seven A.M. on Wednesday, May 17, once again ordered Anders and his Poles into the breach. Once again the 5th Kresowa Division sortied against Phantom Ridge, a mile north of the abbey, while the 3rd Carpathian swarmed up Snakeshead Ridge, shooting at every silhouette suggestive of a paratrooper's chamber-pot helmet.

All through the night the fighting raged, with rifle butts and tank fire. Polish troops low on ammunition threw stones and sang their national anthem. German paratrooper units were reduced to "oddments," some battalions having fewer than one hundred men. "Impossible to get wounded away," a German major in the 3rd Parachute Regiment wrote in his diary. "Great number of dead on the slopes—stench—no water—no sleep for three nights—amputations being carried out at battle headquarters."

In danger of encirclement from the north and west, German defenders began slipping away—although only after Kesselring personally ordered the recalcitrant General Heidrich to fall back to the Hitler Line: the 1st Parachute Division had become as possessive of Cassino as a jealous husband of his bride. Across the hill in Cassino town, British loudspeakers blared, "To fight on is senseless. . . . Cassino is lost to Germany." From the Baron's Palace and the Continental Hotel, shadows darted up over Hangman's Hill. Fearful of vengeful Poles, a few surrendered by walking hands-high to the Crypt or up Highway 6, where the British 78th Division bagged eighty paratroopers creeping to the rear. By three A.M. on May 18, the town was empty of living Germans.

The struggle for the high ground behind the abbey ended with the dawn. At seven A.M., Point 593 finally fell for good. Two hours later a Polish lieutenant from the 12th Podolski Lancers led a six-man patrol up a slope carpeted with poppies and corpses, among them Poles and Germans wrapped in death embraces. Across the ruined parking lot the Lancers scuffed, past charred debris and a cracked church bell. A sergeant climbed on his comrades' shoulders to scale the broken wall, then helped hoist the rest inside. Fresco fragments and shards of marble statuary crunched beneath their boots. They found two German orderlies attending sixteen badly wounded paratroopers, including several lying in St. Benedict's candlelit crypt.

Just before ten A.M. the lancers' regimental pennant, fashioned from a Red Cross flag and a blue handkerchief, rose on a staff above Monte Cassino's western wall. A bugler played the "Hejnał Mariacki," a medieval military call once used to signal the opening of Kraków's gates. Then the red-and-white Polish flag rose against the midday sky. Anders's soldiers wept.

At 11:30 A.M. British signalers broadcast a single code word—WYE—to proclaim Cassino's fall. Leese arrived for tea in the Crypt, then toasted Anders with champagne. Polish casualties for the week exceeded 3,700, including 860 killed; 900 unburied German dead were counted. Alexander cabled Churchill: "Capture of Cassino means a great deal to me and both my armies."

For the first time in five months, men in the town stood erect during daylight. They discovered roses blooming near the jail and an undamaged statue of the Virgin in a stand of splintered trees; a panzer was found parked in the Continental lobby. Grenadier Guardsmen emerged from Jane, Helen, Mary, and other dank hovels, then marched from the town toward Shit Corner for a respite. Some 2,500 British and South African engineers stood ready to clear Highway 6 only to find the drifted rubble so dense that just a few hundred could get close to the roadbed; to bulldoze a one-mile stretch would take fifty-two hours.

In the abbey itself, further investigation brought further horrors: children killed in the February bombing; the bones of a nineteenth-century cardinal, robbed of his ring and pectoral cross, dumped in a garden tub; corpses tucked into large drawers used to store vestments. "The whole effect," one Venus Fixer reported, "is like that of a Mesopotamian tell." Polish, British, and Indian soldiers wandered about, scribbling graffiti and collecting souvenirs, including a carved angel's head yanked from a choir stall. Among German sketches found in the rubble was a portrait of Frau Göring and a river scene titled "On the Lovely Banks of the Rhine." A skillful cartoonist had also drawn a cigar-smoking Churchill standing on the Cassino plain while a German paratrooper straddled the abbey ruins. The caption read *"Denk'ste"*—"Think it over."

A solitary American fighter pilot flew low over the abbey and tossed a bouquet of roses from the cockpit. Gun flashes limned the northern horizon, a reminder that for most the war had moved on. "Don't expect normal letters from me because I won't be normal for some time," Lance Corporal Walter Robson of the Queen's Own Royal West Kent Regiment wrote his wife on May 18.

"We've been Stuka'd, mortared, shelled, machine-gunned, sniped, and although we've taken Cassino, the monastery, none of us feel any elation," Robson added. "The losses sadden and frighten us. . . . When, when, when is this insanity going to stop?"

General von Senger, freshly bemedaled, had returned from his month's leave on May 17 to find Vietinghoff, the bombed-out Tenth Army commander, squatting in his command post near Frosinone, thirty miles up the valley from Cassino. Senger also found the Gustav Line ruptured, his XIV Panzer Corps bisected, and German intelligence uncertain where on the Petrella Massif the French irregulars had gone. Vietinghoff pronounced the XIV Corps predicament "frightful." "For the first time in nine months the corps had been breached," Senger later wrote. Moreover, the Hitler Line had been assigned a new name to forestall embarrassment to the Führer in the event that it too failed: the Senger Line.

That line by any name must be held, particularly the seventeen-mile western stretch from Terracina on the Tyrrhenian coast to the hill town of Pico, where the Auruncis spilled into the Liri Valley. Here Fifth Army with its phantom *goumiers* now posed the greatest threat. "It was left to me," Senger added, "to prevent the annihilation of the corps."

The task was formidable. Longer days and better weather made the German rear ever more vulnerable to enemy aircraft, including the little spotter planes that adjusted Allied long-range artillery. "Constant, unremitting Allied fighter-bomber activity makes movement or troop deployment almost impossible," the Tenth Army war diary reported on May 18. So many horses had been killed that equipment had to be manhandled to the rear or abandoned. The fifty-nine German battalions on the southern front now averaged under 250 soldiers each; the 15th Panzer Grenadier Division, stalwarts of Troina and other southern battlegrounds, on May 20 reported only 405 men fit to fight.

Italian supply-truck drivers were now deserting en bloc despite mass executions for "cowardice in the face of the enemy"; round-trip convoys to northern Italy sometimes took up to three weeks. Artillery barrages severed phone lines, forcing German commanders to use radios, which were vulnerable to eavesdropping and to finicky reception in the mountains. "I demand a clear picture," Kesselring told Tenth Army in a peevish message, but there was no clear picture to be had: even Ultra cryptologists were baffled by the babel from German units.

In truth, Kesselring had been outgeneraled. Slow to recognize the Aurunci threat on his right, he also was slow to realize that another Allied amphibious landing was but a ruse, and slow to release his reserves. On May 14, Kesselring had dispatched the first of three strategic reserve divisions, the 26th Panzer, but the seventy-mile journey from the outskirts of Rome took so long that the unit's tanks could not fight cohesively until May 19, too late to caulk the Gustav Line. On that day, Kesselring also ordered Fourteenth Army to transfer the 29th Panzer Grenadier Division—defender of San Pietro six months earlier—from the Anzio beachhead to Tenth Army's right wing. Petulant delays by General von Mackensen, the Fourteenth Army commander, further damaged efforts to tighten the Hitler Line, as the Allies continued to call it. Mobile divisions such as the 15th and 90th Panzer Grenadiers were broken into penny packets, with battalions scattered about and eventually defeated in detail. The Führer was even forced to strip the equivalent of three divisions from Hungary, Croatia, and Denmark for defenses in Italy.

As for Kesselring, he was reduced to fulminating against impudent subordinates while urging his troops to resist "the enemy's major offensive against the cultural center of Europe." Few found such exhortations inspiriting. "You have no idea how hard this retreat is, or how terrible," a German reconnaissance commander wrote his wife after Cassino fell. "My heart bleeds when I look at my beautiful battalion. . . . See you soon, I hope, in better days."

Better days were difficult to see from either side of the firing line. A Canadian described DIADEM as a thousand individual battles erupting "like spontaneous fires exploding in a rag factory," and the rags continued to blaze. General Leese now had three corps with some twenty thousand vehicles crammed along a six-mile front in a narrow valley flanked by high hills and admirably suited to ambush and delay. Bucolic at a distance—one Canadian described an Italian village as "a vaporous fantasy on its beehive hill, topped by a grim, crenellated tower"—the Liri proved neither pastoral nor an easy avenue to Rome. Most trees had already been reduced to flinders by bombs and artillery shells. Retreating Germans fired the ricks and farmhouses, slaughtered the cattle, and murdered more than a few civilians. "German prisoners made to clear their own minefields," a Guards officer recorded. "Half a dozen blown to blazes."

A Kiwi tanker negotiating a hillside vineyard described "the Shermans pitching like destroyers in and out of the ditches that parallel every row, men sitting in front with heavy wire-cutters to hack a passage." Brick culverts under the side roads collapsed beneath the weight of thirty-ton tanks, and traffic jams soon rivaled those that had bedeviled Eighth Army at Alamein: one brigade trying to move toward the sound of the guns took eighteen hours to travel thirteen miles. A Canadian general complained that Highway 6 was "jammed by trucks nose to arse."

If the Hitler Line lacked natural impediments like the Rapido River and Monte Cassino, it boasted a fortification belt half a mile wide that had been under construction by a five-thousand-man labor force since December. The "medley of fieldworks" included mines, antitank ditches, double-apron barbed wire, and nearly three thousand firing positions. Panther tank turrets, sporting a high-velocity 75mm gun that was among the war's cruelest, had been mounted on brick plinths. An initial Eighth Army probe on May 19 ended with thirteen Canadian tanks in flames. Across the Auruncis, heavy fire also demolished five U.S. Shermans, including one named *Bonnie Gay* that burned so furiously that "the only trace of the crew were fillings of the teeth," a tank battalion history recorded.

"Head wounds are many and serious. Most occur in tank crews when tanks take a direct hit," wrote Klaus H. Huebner, a medical officer whose 88th Division battalion aid station occupied a village bakery. "On examination their skulls feel like shattered egg shells. . . . Our morgue in the backyard is soon full." In his diary Huebner added, "We are always on the bottom, and the Krauts always on top. The terrain is constantly in the enemy's favor."

There was nothing for it but to soldier on. Sergeants doled out rum rations in enamel cups after breakfast and sent their men off to commit mayhem. Or to have it committed upon them. A Tommy waiting at a field hospital to have both legs amputated murmured, "I couldn't run a race, but I've got plenty of fight left in me, and I'm going to live." He died after surgery. A British captain noted the "melancholy sight of a carpenter fashioning crosses for our dead." When an American tank commander was shot through the heart by a sniper suspected of sheltering among a clutch of surrendering Germans, a company commander ordered, "Do not take any more prisoners."

In fact, hordes were taken, by ferocious Poles and *goumiers* as well as by aroused Yanks. On average a thousand German prisoners marched into

Allied cages each day, and the pathetic condition of many heartened their captors. "The older men are a weird and wonderful collection," an interrogation report noted on May 22. "It would appear that the authorities had firmly closed their eyes to such things as a missing toe, lack of an eye, and other slight infirmities, not to mention age." Still, the days of underestimating German obduracy were long gone. "One of my aid men brings in a wounded German," the surgeon Huebner recorded. "He is smoking a cigarette. As he exhales, smoke pours out of the holes in his chest."

As the second week of the Allied offensive slid past, Alexander studied dispatches from the front with the intensity of a seer hunched over entrails. Each day he drove north from Caserta to see for himself, eyebrows and red hat floured with dust as he peered through field glasses into the middle distance. On the far left the U.S. II Corps on May 20 had captured Fondi, where Roman legions had stopped Hannibal during the First Punic War. Keyes's legions now threatened the port of Terracina at the southern lip of the Pontine Marshes. On the far right, Leese continued to batter the valley fortifications, dumping eight hundred artillery shells per minute on German strongpoints. In the center, French gunners caught exposed panzer grenadiers near Esperia, killing so many that bulldozers were needed to shovel away the carcasses; Senger complained that his battalions were "bleeding to death." After cutting Highway 82 the *goumiers* continued their uplands tramp, and Juin's legions on May 21 seized a foothold in the vital crossroads town of Pico, provoking ferocious German counterattacks with Tiger tanks.

From west to east the Hitler Line was crumbling. *We've got them,* Juin had exclaimed, and it seemed he might be right. Much fighting remained: the Germans—or, rather, ten thousand Italian laborers—had begun yet another string of fortifications below Rome, the Caesar Line. But Kesselring had been forced to transfer divisions from Anzio to check Allied momentum on the southern front. "The enemy has denuded the forces investing the beachhead of the bulk of their reserves," AFHQ intelligence reported on May 22. "The risk is so great as to be surprising."

Here was the chance Alexander had long awaited, a chance for redemption, for exculpation, for annihilation. Seven divisions in the Beachhead Army would fall on the enemy's flank, like a dagger in the ribs. The hour was ripe, at last.

## A Fifth Army Show

MARK Clark shifted his command post from Caserta to Anzio on Monday, May 22, arriving at noon in a little L-5 single-engine plane with a wingspan hardly bigger than his own. At ten P.M., after a late supper in the Borghese villa, he strode through the cellar command post to a conference room, led by a beefy colonel who barked, "'Ten-*shun!*" Several dozen correspondents, slouching on benches beneath the naked bulbs, came to their feet in various attitudes of resentment. "Sit down, gentlemen," Clark said. He cut the air with the flat of his hand.

For half an hour, unhurried and precise, he explained his attack plan in detail, occasionally pointing to the enormous map tacked like a pelt to the wall behind him. The artillery would open fire in less than eight hours, a thousand guns. General Truscott's VI Corps had grown to an army within Fifth Army: seven divisions plus Brigadier General Robert Frederick's 1st Special Service Force. The host included the U.S. 36th Infantry Division, which had secretly arrived by sea over the last four days as part of General Alex's plan "to dribble them in unseen." Clockwise around the beachhead perimeter, the attacking force included the British 5th and 1st Divisions on the left, then the U.S. 45th Infantry, the 1st Armored—with a regiment from the 34th Infantry—and the 3rd Infantry Divisions. The Forcemen protected the right flank, while the 36th and the bulk of the 34th remained in reserve. Opposing this juggernaut, Mackensen's Fourteenth Army comprised five and a half divisions.

Under Operation BUFFALO, "the main impetus of our attack" would be to seize Cisterna, Clark continued, no easy task since the town had been heavily fortified after the Rangers' disastrous assault in January. The spearhead would then stab northeast through Cori to cut Highway 6 at Valmontone, "with the ultimate objective of destroying as many Germans as possible." He intended to "bottle up the main body of the German army from the Cassino front," Clark said. The attack did not "have as its purpose to capture Rome," but he intended to keep "a flexible mind." After a glance at the map he seemed to correct himself. "We're going to take Rome," he said.

As the correspondents shuffled from the cellar, staff officers confided that the press could assure the public that General Clark was "in personal command." To drive home the point, Clark radioed Gruenther at Caserta. "There is no restriction placed on [disclosing] my whereabouts," he advised his chief of staff. "You tear anybody to pieces who attempts to change this." Moreover, Gruenther was to ensure that any communiqué announcing the attack "is properly worded and that it is a Fifth Army show. I do not want the first announcement of this to come out to the effect that Alexander's troops have attacked from the bridgehead."

If Clark had disclosed much of his plan, he also kept much to himself. Internecine bickering over the timing and direction of the attack had only intensified. Alexander remained adamant that once the Beachhead Army stood athwart Highway 6 at Valmontone, "fast, mobile patrols" could cut other German escape routes to the east. Clark just as vigorously insisted that trapping Tenth Army "couldn't be done"; he also noted that under BUFFALO the enemy would still occupy the Colli Laziali, with the usual high-ground advantages.

A face-to-face meeting at Caserta on May 20 had failed to resolve their differences. Alexander ordered the beachhead attack for the night of May 21, evidently on the misapprehension that the Hitler Line had been breached by Eighth Army at Aquino. When Clark protested, Alexander agreed to hang fire until the morning of the twenty-third; he also would simultaneously renew Leese's attack in the Liri Valley, while hoping to "conserve losses" in the battle-weary Eighth Army.

Clark suspected double-dealing. "I am convinced that Eighth Army will hold their attack and let the French carry the ball for them as they have done so far in this battle," he told his diary. "All their actions are always dictated by their desire to save manpower and let someone else do it."

Precisely what Clark intended may not have been evident even to him. Later he would acknowledge telling himself, "Hell, we shouldn't even be thinking about Rome. All we should be thinking about is killing Germans." Capturing the capital would be glorious to be sure, an honor "we felt that we more than deserved." Still, orders were orders, and Alexander's were explicit. Clark had radioed Truscott before leaving Caserta: "Operation BUFFALO will be launched at 0630 hours on May 23rd."

Yet he had also sent the corps commander a private message. As the attack unspooled, Truscott should be prepared to consider "an alternative plan," Clark wrote. "Regrouping would take place and [a] new attack launched northwest from Cisterna area." Rather than slashing east toward Valmontone, most of the Beachhead Army could swing west of the Colli Laziali on the shortest route to Rome, the "great prize." As Clark had told the reporters, a good commander should always keep a flexible mind.

Smoke generators fogged the front from the Tyrrhenian Sea to the Mussolini Canal. Third Division soldiers, who would carry the main attack against Cisterna, had marched forward from their wooded bivouacs, battalion by battalion tramping past a brass band that crashed through the division anthem as it had when they embarked for Anzio four months earlier:

> I'm just a dog-face soldier with a rifle on my shoulder
> And I eat a Kraut for breakfast every day.

Light rain had fallen earlier in the evening, but the skies cleared in the small hours. Stars twinkled through the artificial haze before a gray overcast louver again slid over the beachhead from the sea. Soldiers fumbled for a final time with their web gear; many carried lengths of parachute cord, said to make superior tourniquets. A nineteen-year-old sergeant in the 15th Infantry, after receiving no mail from home for six weeks, had been handed forty letters by the company clerk late Monday night; he tucked the envelopes into his combat pack, wondering if he would live long enough to open them. From the radio in a 1st Armored Division tank drifted the improbable strains of *Oklahoma!* As dawn's apricot glow brightened the eastern sky, an Old Ironsides lieutenant read aloud from Thucydides' history of the Peloponnesian War, then exclaimed, "There's nothing ever new in war!"

Expectation, anxiety, release—all fluttered across the front like bats looking to roost. Clark had snatched a few hours' rest on a metal cot; to escape the damp air of the Borghese cellar, he slept upstairs in a high-ceilinged salon with gilded chandeliers and enormous oils on the walls. After rising at four A.M. and wolfing down breakfast, he climbed into his jeep for the drive from Nettuno to the front. At 5:30, just as the sun started to peep over the horizon, he joined Truscott in a camouflaged observation post at Conca, where in January they had watched in misery as Darby's Rangers and the 3rd Division were impaled on Cisterna's defenses. Neither man said much, each lost in his thoughts.

With a thunderous roar the barrage opened precisely at 5:45 A.M.: howitzers, mortars, tanks—every tube with a powder charge. "They can hear this in Rome, maybe," one soldier shouted. Shock waves from the cannonade shimmered across the sky like heat rising off blacktop. Clouds of dust blanketed the battlefield, brilliantly lighted from within by bursting shells. Sixty fighter-bombers swept across the front, leaving charred, battered Cisterna more charred and more battered.

Then, at 6:30, the riflemen spilled over the top, no longer singing, fury in their eyes, and fear too, the deep roar of artillery now punctuated with the *pop! pop! pop!* of rifle fire and the keening of a thousand machine guns. On a five-mile front, three regiments abreast, the 3rd Division threw itself against four German battalions entrenched in platoon-sized redoubts around Cisterna, three to five hundred yards apart, each encrusted with mines, barbed wire, and automatic weapons. A half mile east of Isola Bella, hard by the Rangers' last-stand field, Company L from the 15th Infantry quickly lost 140 of 180 men. "The man in front of me was struck by a bullet," a sergeant in I Company wrote. "I rolled him over and saw his eyes were pulled up and set."

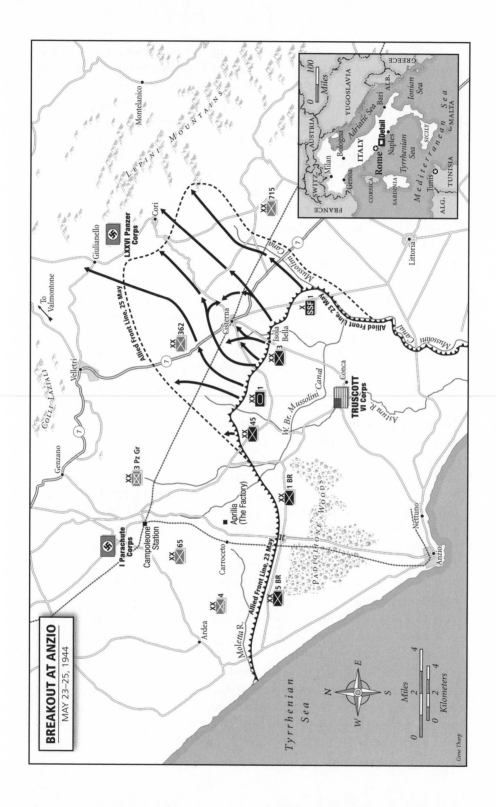

**BREAKOUT AT ANZIO**
MAY 23–25, 1944

Tyrrhenian Sea

Montelanico

L E P I N I  M o u n t a i n s

Cori

Giulianello

LXXVI Panzer Corps

XX 715

Allied Front Line, 25 May

XX 362

Velletri

To Valmontone

COLLI LAZIALI

Genzano

7

Cisterna

Isola Bella

X SSF 1

Allied Front Line, 23 May

Mussolini Canal

1

Littoria

Mussolini Canal

XX 3

XX 1

XX 45

W. Br. Mussolini Canal

Conca

Astura R.

**TRUSCOTT VI Corps**

3 Pz Gr XX

XX 65

Campoleone Station

Aprilia (The Factory)

XX 1 BR

P A D I G L I O N E  W O O D S

Nettuno

Carroceto

XX 4

Ardea

Moletta R.

Allied Front Line, 23 May

XX 5 BR

Anzio

I Parachute Corps

N
W E
S

Miles
0    2    4
Kilometers
0    2    4

Gene Thorp

**Inset map:**
FRANCE
SWITZ.
AUSTRIA
Milan
Genoa
Bologna
ITALY
CORSICA
SARDINIA
ALG.
TUNISIA
Tunis
ALG.
Rome ■Detail
Naples
Tyrrhenian Sea
Mediterranean Sea
MALTA
SICILY
Bari
Adriatic Sea
YUGOSLAVIA
ALB.
GREECE
Ionian Sea
Miles
0    100

Farther east, Company K of the 30th Infantry reported a dozen men left standing; German fire swept the fields like a sickle, leaving both the dead and the cut grass in windrows. On the right, Company E of the 15th fixed bayonets and in a shrieking charge swarmed through a woody grove, killing fifteen Germans and capturing eighty. Still, the line had hardly gained a quarter mile. "It is going too slow," Major General O'Daniel, the division commander, complained at eight A.M. "Throw everything you have at them." Jack Toffey and the 7th Infantry had been given the hardest nut to crack, in the center of the assault, but when a staff officer reported that two lead companies were pinned down, O'Daniel replied, "We have no such words in our vocabulary now."

Just past noon, five more Sherman tanks trundled into the fight, each towing an O'Daniel brainstorm: "battle sleds," fabricated in great secrecy from torpedo tubes sawed in half lengthwise, with steel runners welded to the bottom. Eight feet long, two feet wide, and just deep enough to carry a prostrate, nervous soldier, the sleds were joined end to end, six to a train, with each tank dragging two trains. Ditches and mines proved their undoing. Hardly had sixty sleds slid onto the stage than they could slide no farther; the riders spilled out, grateful to take their chances dismounted.

Yard by bloody yard, the advance drew nearer Cisterna. By day's end, beneath spattering rain, 3rd Division soldiers would close within six hundred yards of the town, and a mile nearer Rome than they had been at dawn. But none had severed Highway 7 or the parallel rail embankment, and casualties had been outlandish: one thousand killed, wounded, or missing, the division's most sanguinary day during World War II thus far, and among the costliest for any U.S. Army division on any day in the war. Damaged boys outnumbered the litter bearers available to carry them away. Seeing carnage all about, a young private lamented, "Must I be knocked off before I have had a woman?"

Truscott's flanks found hard fighting as well. On the right, Frederick's Forcemen scampered across Highway 7 below Cisterna only to retreat pell-mell under lashing fire from Tigers seemingly impervious to antitank rounds. "All hell has broken through up here," a staff officer radioed Truscott. "The Germans have unleashed everything." On the far left, British troops held their ground but no more in an attack designed mostly as a diversion. The 45th Division waded through thigh-high wheat, side-stepping skeletons in moldering field gray, until machine-gun cross fire sent the men to ground. German gunners traced the trails carved through the grain by low-crawling GIs, and the dull thud of bullets hitting home carried across the golden fields. A counterattack by more than a dozen

Tigers flayed one battalion caught in the open and chewed into another before artillery fire shooed them off.

By nightfall the 45th reported 458 casualties and aid stations were so taxed that wounded soldiers were forced to share cots. "The fellow in the bed next to me had been hit in the back with shrapnel and kept begging the doctors to let him die," one artilleryman later recalled. A captain who had stepped on a mine studied the stump where his foot had been and reflected, "That's the one that was always getting cold anyway."

The day's last best hope fell to the 1st Armored Division, attacking with 232 tanks on a three-mile front east of Cisterna. "Whether or not we can get our tanks through remains a question. I expect to lose heavily," Ernie Harmon had written a friend a week earlier. Those losses, he warned, could include one hundred tanks in the first half hour. Harmon's dark mood hardly brightened when his right wing—Combat Command B—blundered into a poorly marked American minefield sown during the winter's fighting. Thirty Shermans soon sat immobilized with fractured tracks and broken bogey wheels less than a quarter mile from the start line.

On the left, however, Combat Command A used another battlefield invention to excellent effect. Before dawn, tanks had shoved into no-man's-land a pair of four-hundred-foot "snakes"—four-inch pipe packed with several tons of explosives. While puzzled German pickets shook tin cans filled with rocks to sound the alarm, a burst of machine-gun fire detonated the pipes with "an appalling violence" that carved a smoldering channel twenty-five feet wide through the minefield. Two more snakes extended the corridor and Harmon's tanks poured into the gap like floodwaters through a ruptured dike. Riflemen from the 135th Infantry clung to the Sherman hulls then leaped clear to round up prisoners and slaughter the diehards.

By one P.M. U.S. tanks had crossed the cinder brow of the rail embankment, provoking a frantic flapping of white flags, and an infantry battalion held the high ground five hundred yards to the north. Combat Command B—which had eschewed the snakes for fear that a premature detonation would alert enemy defenders—belatedly blew its own gap and sallied within main gun range of Highway 7 before laagering for the night. Infantrymen slept on their arms behind sandbags hauled forward on the tanks.

The day had cost Harmon eighty-six tanks and tank destroyers, most of them crippled by American mines. He quickly made good the wastage from his reserves. Other losses were harder to fix. Fifth Army casualties for this Tuesday totaled almost two thousand, the highest single-day tally in the Italian campaign, with 334 killed in action: a life snuffed out every four minutes. By midnight the olive-drab crescent of men struggling to break free of the beachhead was dyed black with blood.

Yet across the front fifteen hundred enemy prisoners had been taken, and Cisterna was in danger of envelopment from the northeast. The German 362nd Division had lost half its combat strength, two regiments from the 715th Division were hurt almost as grievously, and the 94th Division—shifted to beachhead defense after a drubbing in the Auruncis—reported only two hundred fighters left. In a phone call at eight P.M. on Tuesday, Kesselring told Vietinghoff, "Things do not look good on Mackensen's front. Keep this to yourself."

In his own late-night dispatch to Clark, who had returned to the Borghese cellars, Truscott pared the news to ten words: "All attacks jumped off on schedule. Attack meeting moderate resistance."

By Wednesday afternoon, May 24, that resistance was crumbling. Harmon's tanks looped behind Cisterna from the east, fighting off the field-gray wraiths who popped from laurel thickets to shoot the passing Shermans in the rear grills. American artillery smashed German counterattacks on the flanks, but shells also fell on friendly infantrymen again and again. By nightfall O'Daniel and Harmon had nearly completed a double envelopment of Cisterna, bagging another 850 prisoners. Germans "scatter like frightened quail," wrote Audie Murphy. "As if we were shooting skeets, we pick them off." A mile-long stretch of Highway 7 had been cut north of town, along with three miles to the south, and a reconnaissance battalion rambled to within four miles of Velletri on the southern lip of the Colli Laziale. The VI Corps main force stood just thirteen miles from Highway 6. "I could get into Valmontone tonight if I was sure of my left," Harmon told Truscott.

Thursday morning was better yet. Charles Ryder's 34th Division widened the purchase on Highway 7 to five miles on the left, flushing more quail into the sights of homicidal fighter planes. "The carnage was extreme," one account noted; the kills included fifteen Tigers. Over one hundred .50-caliber machine guns poured scorching fire into Cisterna, now said to surpass even Cassino as the most devastated town in Italy. A battalion from the 7th Infantry had a foothold in Cisterna's southwest corner by first light, and two sister regiments, the 15th and 30th, closed to within shouting distance of each other northeast of town. The noose had been cinched.

Clark watched with pleasure as the blue grease-pencil lines on his battle map tracked the northeast surge of the Beachhead Army. In less than forty-eight hours, the front had shoved three to four miles in a salient seven miles wide. But it was the southern edge of the battlefield that held him rapt. Keyes's II Corps had covered almost sixty miles in two weeks; combat engineers had nearly finished carving a six-mile detour through the mountains around Terracina when scouts on Wednesday morning found the seaside town abandoned except for the stinking carcasses—mule and human, as usual—lining the curbs. More patrols nosed into the Pontine Marshes and reported heavy German demolitions, although shovel-wielding Italians filled the craters almost as quickly as they were blown.

The coastal road to the beachhead was open. Late Wednesday, in a tone that was peremptory to the point of imperial, Clark wrote Gruenther at Caserta:

> The joining up of my two Fifth Army forces will be one of the highlights of the Fifth Army's career. It is primarily a Fifth Army matter, and I want you to tell Gen. Alexander that I want authority given me immediately to issue a simple communiqué from here as soon as II Corps troops have moved overland.

If Alexander insisted on making the announcement himself, "you make damn sure that their communiqué is properly worded, making it a Fifth Army show." Clark even drafted proposed language that began: "Climaxing a spectacular advance of 60 miles . . ." Almost as an afterthought, he noted that Truscott's battle casualties approached 2,500. When Eric Sevareid wrote in his broadcast script that soon there would be "only one front in Italy," a press censor in Nettuno instead proposed, "There will be one *Fifth Army* front in Italy."

At 7:30 on Thursday morning, May 25, an engineer task force from the beachhead arrived outside Borgo Grappa, a coastal village beaten into rubble twenty miles north of Terracina. On a narrow bridge spanning an irrigation canal, Captain Benjamin Harrison Sousa of Honolulu, the engineer commander, spotted Lieutenant Francis X. Buckley of Philadelphia, a II Corps cavalryman.

"Where in hell do you think you're going?" Sousa demanded.

"Anzio," Buckley replied.

"Boy, you've made it."

The two men shook hands and sat down to share a box of candy from Buckley's pack.

Three hours later Clark roared up with a gaggle of two dozen correspondents piled one atop another in open jeeps. As faint battle sounds drifted south from Cisterna, gum-chewing soldiers removed their helmets and with much backslapping and exaggerated swapping of cigarettes reenacted the scene for movie cameras. In another message to Gruenther, Clark reported that the initial junction "took place this morning at 1010 hours on Anzio–Terracina road"—rewriting history by several hours.

After 125 days Anzio's isolation was over. The beachhead had dissolved. Clark wrote Renie:

> It may have sounded dramatic in the papers the way I rushed to witness the joining of the two forces, but it meant more to me than anything since our success at Salerno. The way some of the correspondents expressed it, it may have sounded as though I was looking for publicity. Did you get that impression? At any rate, I had to be there when the two forces joined up. It meant too much to me.

Soon enough the day would come when "I can return home to you and pick up our happy home life where we left it off. I think I will be ready to settle down." But before that day, Clark vowed, "We will capture Rome.... They can't stop us now."

Truscott drove toward his Conca command post at midday on Thursday after a tour of the battlefront. He felt, by his own description, "rather jubilant." His old 3rd Division was slashing through Cisterna, house by gutted house, toward a final German redoubt in the town hall, now known as the Castle. Other troops cantered toward Cori, six miles to the northeast on the western flank of the Lepini Mountains. More than 2,600 enemy prisoners had been caged.

The 1st Armored Division continued to bull north, although steep terrain, antitank guns, and a Panther counterattack near Velletri cost Harmon seventeen more tanks. Fighting was savage and confused. More American artillery fell on American soldiers, and at least ten incidents of fratricidal air attacks would be reported on this day. "Sniper shot off the lieutenant's elbow," Corporal Robert M. Marsh of the 81st Armored Reconnaissance Battalion advised his diary. After the miscreant was captured, Marsh added, "Lieutenant drew his .45 pistol with his left hand and shot the sniper through the heart." Germans who balked at surrendering were buried alive with tank dozers. Tankers found a huge wine barrel "standing on end with the top end bashed in," Marsh noted. "They drank lots of wine until they found a dead German in it."

At the point of the VI Corps spear, a four-battalion force led by Colonel Hamilton H. Howze sidled through olive orchards and deserted crofts into the handsome valley between the Colli Laziali on the west and the stony Lepinis to the east. Soon enough a dozen Sherman tanks would close to within half a mile of Highway 6. "I am in a soft spot," Howze reported. "For Pete's sake, let the whole 1st Amored Division come this way!" Truscott believed that sometime Friday his entire corps "would be astride the German line of withdrawal through Valmontone."

That agreeable vision dissolved the moment Truscott walked into his Conca war room. There, standing with five somber VI Corps colonels, was Clark's operations officer, Brigadier General Donald W. Brann. "The boss wants you to leave the 3rd Infantry Division and the Special Force to block Highway 6, and mount that assault you discussed with him to the northwest as fast as you can," Brann said.

Truscott was dumbfounded. While the Forcemen and O'Daniel's troops plowed ahead to Valmontone, most of the corps was to pivot 90 degrees to the left. That put them on the shortest path to Rome, west of the Colli Laziali, but the route angled into the most formidable segment of the Caesar Line, now manned by I Parachute Corps. Operation BUFFALO was succeeding. Why switch to the old Operation TURTLE?

"I discussed this with General Clark several days ago," Truscott said, "and I told him this was not to be done, in my opinion, unless there's a significant weakening on the left. I've seen no sign of such weakening. I need to talk to General Clark. Where is he?"

"He's not at the beachhead," Brann replied evenly. Clark had flown back to Caserta and could not be reached by phone or even radio. Truscott protested, his raspy voice thickening. This was "no time to change direction," he told Brann. Conditions were "not right." Untangling the current attack and swinging the 45th, 34th, 36th, and 1st Armored Divisions off in a new direction would take time. "A more complicated plan," Truscott warned, "would be difficult to conceive."

Then he fell silent. Later Truscott insisted that he had protested "in the most vigorous possible" terms, but believed that subordinate fealty required acquiescence. His staff now had responsibility for drafting the new attack plan, and any hint that he lacked confidence would evince "poor leadership." He considered Clark an able tactician, who was loyal to his lieutenants and ceded them autonomy even if he declined to offer public credit—no underling commanders were ever named in Fifth Army dispatches. A subordinate's duty demanded reciprocal fidelity; whatever misgivings Truscott had initially voiced about the new scheme, he soon professed full support. At four P.M. Brann radioed Clark—suddenly communicado again—and reported that the VI Corps commander was "entirely in accord." Two hours later Truscott phoned Brann at the Borghese villa. "I feel very strongly that we should do this thing," he said. "We should do it tomorrow."

Privately, however, the corps commander could not shake his qualms. When Clark flew back to Nettuno on Thursday night, a subdued Truscott laid out his doubts in the privacy of Clark's Borghese office. Dividing the corps was "a mistake" with Highway 6 so near; to the northwest, the Germans had "not thinned out their ranks on the line in front of the new main effort." Clark remained adamant, waving away Truscott's protests and insisting that German defenses had begun to thicken at Valmontone, thanks in part to reinforcements now arriving from northern Italy. Sure of his course, Clark seemed buoyant, as if a weight had been lifted from his shoulders. In a message to Gruenther, he depicted an enemy "in what may be a demoralized condition at the present time. You can assure General Alexander that this is an all-out attack. We are shooting the works!"

Glum yet resigned, Truscott drove back to Conca. Shortly before midnight, his division commanders filed into the command post, begrimed with war but convinced that the day was theirs. Cisterna finally had fallen late in the afternoon. In defiance of an order from Kesselring to "defend fanatically," Mackensen authorized the garrison to retreat: too late. After hours of street brawling around the Castle, a Sherman tank had blasted a seam into the inner courtyard. Riflemen stormed the keep, flipping grenades through cellar grates and flushing 250 dazed intransigents, gray with dust. The 3rd Battalion of the 7th Infantry had lost its commander, three company commanders, and 80 percent of its strength. Cisterna lay silent but for the crackle of flames and the crunch of armored tracks on masonry.

Truscott came to the point. "The fact that the enemy is withdrawing from the south and has brought reserves in from the north has led the army commander to believe that in the Valmontone gap the going will grow increasingly more difficult," he said. "The army commander feels that we have an opportunity to break this line very quickly by a drive through in *this* direction." Standing at a map, Truscott jabbed a tent-peg finger along the western rim of the Colli Laziali. "I might add that it is an idea in which I am heartily in accord."

None of his battle captains shared their leader's enthusiasm; even Truscott's chief of staff, Brigadier General Don E. Carleton, considered the move "a horrible mistake." Harmon and O'Daniel, whose divisions stood so near Highway 6, were especially waspish. "I realize perfectly the enormous problem that confronts us," Truscott said. Shifting artillery to the northwest and pulling Old Ironsides across the rear to the new front would require heroic efforts through the night. "I realize all of these troops are tired," he added. "There never has been a battle that wasn't won by tired troops."

Again he gestured at the map, as if laying hands on the new battlefield. "I propose to begin this with an artillery preparation of all the violence we can put into fifteen minutes, and then we shall strike just as we did three days ago," Truscott said. "I am confident—I am certain—that the Boche in that area is badly disorganized, has a hodge-podge of units, and if we can drive as hard tomorrow as we have done for the last three days, a great victory is in our grasp."

Truscott brought the conference to a close. Operations Instructions No. 24 from Fifth Army now called for "a new attack along the most direct route to Rome." The corps commander studied the skeptical faces of his subordinates, then added, "These are the orders."

Mark Clark would spend the rest of his long life defending an indefensible impertinence that for more than sixty years has remained among the most controversial episodes in World War II. Then and later he had plausible reason to doubt BUFFALO. "It was based on the false premise that if Route #6 were cut at Valmontone a German army would be annihilated," Clark told his diary on May 27. "This is ridiculous, for many roads lead to the north from Arce, Frosinone and in between."

True enough. Senger subsequently confirmed that his XIV Panzer Corps retreated on a road that branched from Highway 6 at Frosinone, well south of Valmontone, to snake through the Simbruini foothills. A parallel road also wound through Palestrina, and other tracks led to Highway 5, the lateral route from Rome to Pescara on the Adriatic.

Clark also feared that German artillery and panzers hidden in the Colli Laziali would "debouch from the mountains" to counterattack Truscott's left flank as he galloped toward Valmontone. From Ultra and field reports, he believed that Kesselring's last mobile reserve in Italy, the Hermann Göring Panzer Division, would soon congeal along Highway 6. These too were legitimate anxieties, although the staggering artillery, air, and armored firepower available to Truscott would surely punish any attack from Mackensen's battered legions. Fourteenth Army tallied 108,000 Allied shells on Thursday, then stopped counting. Allied air attacks on the same day destroyed 655 of Mackensen's vehicles. Moreover, only the Hermann Göring reconnaissance battalion would reach Valmontone by Friday, May 26. The rest of the division, forced to travel by day for 250 miles on exposed roads through a murderous gauntlet of Allied warplanes, would arrive piecemeal and in tatters.

Two final points must be conceded to Clark. No less an authority than George Marshall had urged the capture of Rome before OVERLORD, now less than two weeks away; with a second front opening in Normandy, the Italian theater would surely see a sharp decline in ammunition, supplies, troops, and public attention. Finally, Operations Instructions No. 24 attempted to sugar the pill for Alexander by keeping more than twenty thousand VI Corps troops pounding for Highway 6, and they soon would be reinforced by Keyes's II Corps.

Yet the harsh truth remains: with duplicity and in bad faith, Clark contravened a direct order from a superior officer. His assertion, to Keyes on May 28, that the British "are scheming to get into Rome the easiest way," was predicated on no substantive evidence. His "thirst for glory," as the official British history would later conclude, "spoiled the fulfilment of Alexander's plan in order to obtain for himself and his army the triumph of being the first to enter Rome."

Clark acknowledged as much in his postwar memoir:

> Not only did we intend to become the first army in fifteen centuries to seize Rome from the south, but we intended to see that the people back home knew that it was the Fifth Army that did the job and knew the price that had been paid for it.

This fixation, no doubt compounded by stress and exhaustion, marred his usually astute military judgment. He failed to see that Mackensen at Valmontone on May 26 would face at least three VI Corps divisions with only an eviscerated Wehrmacht division and at most a single Hermann Göring regiment. He failed to sense how badly the enemy had been hurt by Truscott, how strong the I Parachute Corps remained, or how the German high command's recommendation to Hitler of a partial withdrawal by both armies to the Caesar Line—a recommendation quickly known to Allied intelligence—offered a chance to whack Kesselring while he was on his heels. Clark also failed to recognize that with VI Corps forty miles ahead of Leese's plodding Eighth Army, the open terrain and ragged defenses up Highway 6 offered an expeditious path to Rome. And he failed to realize, as a U.S. Army study concluded, that he would have "been admirably situated to outflank the rest of the Fourteenth Army and to cut off the Tenth Army"—a conclusion also reached by General Wilhelm Schmalz, the Hermann Göring commander.

Juin warned Clark of "a terrible congestion of itineraries" as Eighth Army, II Corps, VI Corps, and the FEC converged on the Liri Valley and its northern extensions. Yet even his admirers suspected that one itinerary counted above all others: that of Marcus Aurelius Clarkus. His habitual antipathy toward the British surely was aggravated by the lackluster performance of the two beachhead divisions appended to Truscott's corps. "There is no attack left in them," Clark complained. But his actions went beyond battlefield frustration and petty xenophobia. He "appears never to have accepted Alexander as his real commander," wrote W.G.F. Jackson, an author of the official British history. Later, Clark claimed he had warned Alexander that he would order Fifth Army to "fire on the Eighth Army" should Leese attempt to muscle in on Rome. Shocking, if true; General Alex disputed the story.

Alexander had remained in the dark for almost twenty-four hours after Truscott was told to change direction. Not until 11:15 A.M. on Friday, May 26, did the Allied commander learn of Operations Instructions No. 24—fifteen minutes after the new attack had irrevocably begun, and forty-five minutes after Clark briefed reporters at Nettuno on his revised plan. As Clark had appointed Brann to break the news to Truscott, so he employed Gruenther to inform Alexander at Caserta. Strolling into Gruenther's office with Lemnitzer, Alexander lingered long enough to learn that the left wing of his army group had marched off to its own drummer. In a message to Clark at 12:20 P.M., Gruenther reported:

> Gen. Alexander agreed that the plan is a good one. He stated, "I am for any line of action which the army commander believes will offer a chance to continue his present success." About five minutes later he said, "I am sure that the army commander will continue to push toward Valmontone, won't he? I know that he appreciates the importance of gaining the high ground. . . . As soon as he captures that he will be absolutely safe."

Gruenther assured him that Clark would "execute a vigorous plan with all the push in the world." While Gruenther believed that Alexander had "no mental reservations," in fact his sentiments were mixed if well masked. Later he would confess to being "pretty upset"—Lemnitzer described him as "terribly disappointed"—even as he concluded that to impose his will would gain nothing. Although Churchill had recently insisted that "senior commanders should not 'urge' but 'order,' " such was not Alexander's way. His tolerance of impertinence, with Montgomery and then with Clark, simply encouraged more of what General Jackson labeled "prima donna" behavior.

The contretemps remained hidden from the American public until Italy had become a backwater theater of little interest. When Sevareid wrote that "there is a question whether the two aims"—capturing Rome quickly and annihilating Germans—"are compatible or mutually exclusive," Fifth Army censors scotched the line. Clark also remained niggardly in sharing public credit for his army's exploits; Marshall himself noted on May 26 that "this hurts Clark in this country." After Gruenther urged that Truscott's central role be publicly revealed, Clark told his diary, "I do not feel that his exploits have been sufficiently outstanding yet."

"I never violated his orders," Clark said of Alexander a quarter century after the war. "If he had wanted to do it differently he could have issued the order. To censure me for thinking only of the glory of capturing Rome is sheer nonsense." Perhaps so, although Alexander later claimed Clark had assured him that fierce enemy resistance led to the turn away from Valmontone—an exaggeration, at best.

Pride and solipsism had got the best of a good soldier. Perhaps Livy's observation of the Punic Wars still obtained: that the "power to command and readiness to obey are rare associates." But as Churchill wrote Alexander on May 28, "Glory of this battle, already great, will be measured not by the capture of Rome or the juncture with the beachhead, but by the number of German divisions cut off. . . . It is the cop that counts."

It was no small irony that even Clark's rivals wished him well for the sake of a greater good. "He is terrified that we might get to Rome first, which is the last thing we now want to do," wrote Leese, whose casualties in DIADEM were approaching fourteen thousand. "I only hope he can do it. It will save us a lot of trouble and lives."

The old gods deplored hubris, and they now seemed determined to punish Clark's army for his.

Beneath brilliant vernal sunshine on May 26, the right prong of the VI Corps attack—much reduced in combat heft—clattered on toward Valmontone. Led by three battalions under Hamilton Howze, who carried a red-leather copy of Clausewitz's *Principles of War* as "something to cling to," the column enjoyed a brief triumph. "There's infantry coming in through the wheat in our direction," a tank battalion commander radioed Howze. "Are they friendly infantry?"

"Hell, no!" Howze bellowed. "Shoot them up!" He dashed forward by jeep in time to see Sherman broadsides and machine-gun fire rip apart Hermann Göring grenadiers on a hillside three hundred yards away. Like drowning men the Germans thrashed and flailed in the shot-torn wheat until the field grew still.

The day soon darkened. Behind Howze, five confused P-40 Warhawks heeled over in a bombing and strafing run against the 3rd Division, which they mistook for retreating Germans. More than one hundred men were killed or wounded. Other planes bombed Cori, also in friendly hands. So many fratricidal air attacks occurred, despite copious yellow smoke intended to demarcate U.S. Army positions, that engineers were ordered to paint huge American flags on occupied rooftops along the front. What the pilots missed, gunners seemed to find. In Howze's armored infantry battalion, 160 green replacements had just plodded forward when U.S. 155mm rounds scourged the ranks for ten minutes with "ruinous effect." Terrified survivors leaked to the rear. When the shelling finally ceased, the battalion commander was dead and his unit had been chopped to half strength.

The Germans had their own troubles. "All daytime movement is paralyzed and the use of large repair crews has become impossible," Vietinghoff's Tenth Army war diary complained on May 26. The Hermann Göring Division, straggling south on three roads from Livorno under incessant attack, began arriving at Valmontone with only eleven of eighty Mk IV panzers and half the division artillery intact.

Somehow it was enough. Counterattacks against Howze's left flank, and enemy infiltration on Saturday night, May 27, prevented the 3rd Division from moving beyond Artena, a medieval village on a ridge three miles south of Valmontone. Howze watched trucks heaped with dead American soldiers jounce back toward Cisterna. A battalion in the 15th Infantry also reported two hundred men down with ptomaine poisoning from tainted C rations, further attenuating a force simply too weak to break through the makeshift German defense.

Reluctantly, Clark agreed to halt the drive toward Valmontone until II Corps could reinforce the attack. He would claim that American artillery had severed Highway 6, but that was wishful thinking: enemy traffic swept up and down the road all night, harried but undissuaded. Outside Artena, now thick with GIs licking their wounds, the BBC's Vaughan-Thomas watched a young mother run through a vineyard, clutching an infant. "You mustn't bring the war with you," she cried. "You must take your war away."

It was much too late for that, although the worst of the war had shifted westward where Truscott, as ordered, opened his new attack with a barrage by 228 guns at 10:30 A.M. on May 26. Half an hour later, the 45th, 34th, and 1st Armored Divisions surged forward, elbow to elbow to elbow. Infantry regiments covered a bit more than a mile by dusk, shuffling through the thigh-high grain past German graves with *"Unbek. Soldat"*—"Unknown Soldier"—scratched on the rude crosses. But Harmon lost eighteen tanks before pulling back to refit; by Saturday night, the attack remained two miles short of Campoleone Station, where VI Corps troops had fought and died in January. On Sunday at six P.M., the 34th Division commander, Major General Ryder, reported to Truscott in his Kansas drawl, "This thing is a little sticky up here."

Every yard proved costly. The I Parachute Corps improvised brilliantly, aided by poor tank country that bedeviled Harmon on the flanks of the Colli Laziali. Ravines and creekbeds ran perpendicular to Truscott's axis of advance, providing natural barriers. German gunners fired down the washes into the American flanks, and dense olive groves gave close cover to snipers

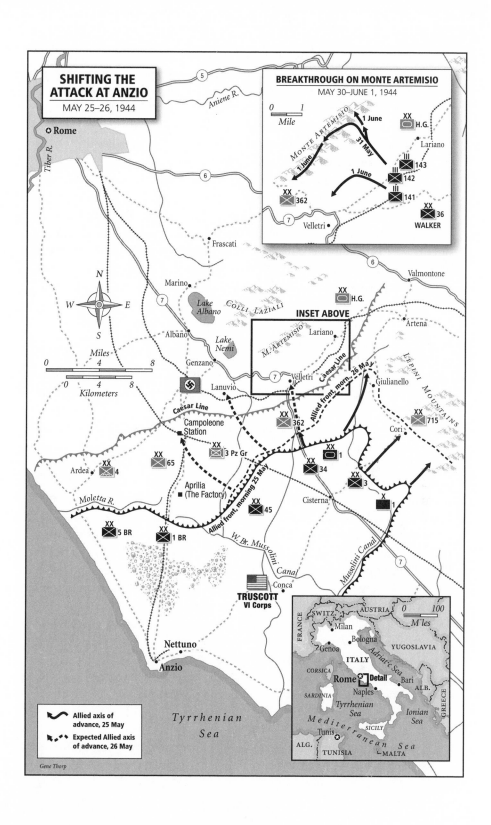

## SHIFTING THE ATTACK AT ANZIO
### MAY 25–26, 1944

⊕ Rome

Tiber R.

Aniene R.

5

6

### BREAKTHROUGH ON MONTE ARTEMISIO
#### MAY 30–JUNE 1, 1944

0 — 1
Mile

M O N T E   A R T E M I S I O

1 June

31 May

1 June

1 June

XX  H.G.

Lariano

III  143

III  142

III  141

XX  362

XX  36

WALKER

7  Velletri

Frascati

6

Valmontone

N

W      E

S

Marino

Lake Albano

COLLI LAZIALI

7

XX  H.G.

INSET ABOVE

Artena

Miles

0      4      8

0      4      8
Kilometers

Albano

Lake Nemi

Genzano

Lanuvio

M. ARTEMISIO

Lariano

7  Velletri

Caesar Line

Allied front, morn. 26 May

Giulianello

L E P I N I   M O U N T A I N S

Caesar Line

Campoleone Station

XX  362

XX  715

Cori

Ardea

XX  4

XX  65

XX  3 Pz Gr

Aprilia
■ (The Factory)

Allied front, morning 25 May

XX  1

XX  34

XX  3

Cisterna

X  1

XX  45

Moletta R.

W. Br. Mussolini

Mussolini Canal

7

XX  5 BR

XX  1 BR

Canal

Conca

🇺🇸
TRUSCOTT
VI Corps

Nettuno

Anzio

Tyrrhenian
Sea

**Detail inset:**

FRANCE   SWITZ.   AUSTRIA

0 — 100
M'les

Milan

ITALY

Bologna

YUGOSLAVIA

Genoa

Adriatic Sea

CORSICA

Rome ⊕ Detail

Bari

ALB.

SARDINIA

Naples

GREECE

Tyrrhenian Sea

Ionian Sea

M e d i t e r r a n e a n   S e a

SICILY

Tunis ⊕

ALG.

TUNISIA

MALTA

**Legend:**

Allied axis of advance, 25 May

Expected Allied axis of advance, 26 May

Gene Thorp

with the German bazookas called Panzerfausts. The Caesar Line, though rudimentary, boasted six-foot fire trenches, mortars, machine guns, and extravagant snarls of barbed wire. After months of wet feet and little exercise, U.S. riflemen now suffered such severe blisters that "blood could be seen seeping from some men's shoe seams," one soldier reported.

Before dawn on Monday, May 29, Truscott pushed Harmon's division up the Albano road with gunfire support from a French cruiser in the Tyrrhenian shallows. By midafternoon the tanks had bypassed German strongpoints and far outrun the infantry, exposing tanker and foot soldier alike to murderous fire from the rear and both flanks. "An 88-mm round blew up the Sherman in front of us and we could hear the screaming inside," a tank sergeant later recalled. "It was terrible to listen to men being burned to death and not being able to help." For negligible gains Harmon's losses would grow to sixty tanks. The 45th Division took such heavy casualties that a lieutenant commanded a battalion until he, too, was killed.

"The day's attack," a dispatch from Old Ironsides reported, "was costly and fruitless." Charred bodies hung from charred vehicles, "the grisly bric-a-brac of war." Among those killed: Lieutenant Allen T. Brown, a tank platoon leader, shot in the head by a sniper while standing in his turret hatch near Campoleone. As a twelve-year-old in 1930, young Brown had encouraged the marriage of his widowed mother, Katherine, once a prominent Shakespearian actress, to the widower George C. Marshall. Now it would fall to Marshall to tell his wife that her younger son was dead.

British troops on the left flank managed to cross the Moletta River, but on a twenty-five-mile front from Artena to the sea Truscott rued that his offensive had been "halted at every point." VI Corps intelligence now calculated that thirty German battalions held the Alban Hills and the Valmontone gap, a sharp increase from earlier estimates. Kesselring, fighting to save his armies rather than to keep Rome, had in truth been pummeled: in a report to Berlin he put his losses during DIADEM at 25,000 men or more already, along with 2,500 machine guns, 248 tanks, and nearly 300 guns. Many vehicles not blown apart were immobile for want of tires and spare parts.

Still, he held the high ground and he held the capital. A reproachful Clark phoned Truscott and his division commanders, then told reporters that "this attack does not have Rome as its primary objective." In his war diary, however, he yet again fretted that "the British have their eye on Rome, notwithstanding Alexander's constant assurance to me." To Renie he wrote:

> We are in as desperate a battle as Fifth Army has ever been in. If it were only the battle I had to worry about and not many other matters, it

would be easy, but I am harassed at every turn on every conceivable subject—political, personal and many others. . . . I pray for early results.

Perhaps the most plaintive cry came from Peter Tompkins, the OSS chief still awaiting deliverance in his Roman hideout. "I don't think I've ever been so depressed," Tompkins told his diary. "The offensive has bogged down."

## The Cuckoo's Song

I T had bogged in the south, too, despite a final shattering of the Hitler Line that cost the Canadian 1st Infantry Division nearly nine hundred casualties on May 23 alone. So intense was the carnage that a private from Calgary reflected, "I just don't know how I lived." A Canadian major, wounded four times, calmed his men by singing "Alouette" as bullets hummed counterpoint overhead. Survivors buried the dead, after gathering pay books and identity disks, and engineers mass-produced white wooden crosses. "Bodies keep coming in," an exhausted chaplain wrote on May 25. "I go to bed but not to sleep." Staggered by losses in his regiment, the commander of Princess Patricia's Canadian Light Infantry told another officer, "Those were fine boys. They are gone. I haven't anybody left. They are all gone."

Eighth Army had long "lacked the instinct to finish off a maimed foe," as one British historian later observed, beginning with the elusive Rommel at Alamein. Now Leese demonstrated the same incapacity. As Vietinghoff's Tenth Army staggered back up the Liri Valley and abutting hills, Leese insisted on further wedging two corps abreast—the I Canadian on the left, the British XIII on the right—into a narrow funnel that boasted a single decent road, Highway 6. He imprudently chose an armored vanguard to lead his host through poor tank country seamed with hedges, walls, sunken lanes, and creeks in spate. With fields high and untended, and trees and vineyards in full leaf, visibility often dropped to one hundred feet.

"After months of static warfare and monotony, we were thrusting northwards once more," an optimistic British diarist wrote. In truth, the pursuit turned into a ponderous stern chase, harassed at every turn by pernicious German rear guards. In six days after the Hitler Line ruptured, XIII Corps covered but eleven miles. Leese not only seemed determined to cram all 1,300 Eighth Army tanks into the valley but also, in set-piece fashion, he methodically built supply bases and trundled forward his artillery after every incremental gain. Radio failures, farm tracks made fluvial by spring rains, and fields fecund with mines added to the misery. Brute force again revealed its limits: nearly seven hundred Eighth Army guns dumped ninety-two tons of high explosives on Aquino simultaneously, pulverizing the hometown of Thomas Aquinas and the Roman satirist Juvenal. German defenders, apparently unimpressed, refused to decamp until out-flanked.

Worse yet, poor march discipline and shabby staff work led to monu-mental traffic congestion. "The road was hidden in dust as we edged into the northbound convoy and came to an immediate standstill," one ob-server reported. A British study cautioned that "the staff must not put more traffic on a road than the road will stand." Yet, by one authoritative tally, "inessential vehicles" accounted for more than half of Eighth Army's total, and roads were clogged with the sort of supernumeraries who in the Crimean War had been styled "Travelling Gentlemen." Units advanced, slowly; units withdrew, slowly; supply lorries lumbered up and back, very slowly. "Traffic criminals of every kind rejoiced," the British official history lamented. Inching Tommies sang, "I don't toil all day / Simply because I'm not made that way."

On May 28, just as Canadian engineers completed a 120-foot bridge across the Liri, the entire span broke apart and sank. The Sacco River valley beyond the Liri also proved inhospitable, with wooded ridges and a thou-sand ditches. On a sprightly day, touched by the spur, the army covered four miles, liberating another hilltop hamlet or two amid chortling vil-lagers who spilled into the streets. "You are welcome!" they yelled in re-hearsed English. "Kill all Germans!" Italian flags flapped from the rooftops and red-and-green Savoy bunting draped the balconies. Flowers were strewn, and local eminences presented the commanding officer with a rose and an egg.

Canadian troops would enter Frosinone on May 31, but the advance re-mained "muscle-bound"—in the sorrowful phrase of the official history, which concluded that Vietinghoff was "in very little danger from Eighth Army." Valmontone still lay twenty-five miles to the northwest. Without doubt, Clark's failure to provide an anvil on which to flatten Tenth Army was compounded by the feebleness of Leese's hammer.

The lurching convoys lurched on. Every soldier listened for the stutter of machine guns or the whip-crack of sniper bullets. A Canadian soldier de-scribed finding a German marksman who had been plinked by tank fire from his perch on an evergreen bough: "When we got to him he was sitting against a tree with a cigarette going. He had one leg off and he'd taken off his belt and made a tourniquet. His sniper's rifle had six notches in it." The dead were buried, the living moved on, again. "It's surprising how deep six feet is," a British rifleman noted. "It didn't take much to make the lot of us cry like children."

On Leese's left, Juin and his FEC made better progress, notwithstanding the French commander's distress at having his long right flank exposed by Eighth Army's dawdling. From Pico the French had swiftly scuttled northwest along the spine of the Lipini Mountains and through contiguous valleys. General Westphal, Kesselring's chief of staff, complained of "those damned French hanging around our necks."

Soon others damned them with equal vehemence. After contributing so much to Allied success in DIADEM, some colonial troops now disgraced themselves, their army, and France. Hundreds of atrocities—allegedly committed mostly by African soldiers—stained the Italian countryside in the last two weeks of May, including murders and gang rapes. "All day long our men observed them scouring the area for women," an American chaplain wrote Clark on May 29. "Our men are sick at heart, and are commenting that they would rather shoot the Moroccan Goums than the Germans. . . . They say we have lost that for which we fight if this is allowed to continue."

Another chaplain cited specifics: a fifteen-year-old girl raped by eighteen colonial soldiers; a twenty-seven-year-old raped by three soldiers; a twenty-eight-year-old raped by five. An American artillery battalion commander described an Italian woman shot in the right ankle and raped by four Moroccans while her daughter was shot in the left foot and also raped. In Ceccano, he added, "approximately 75 women ranging in age from 13 to 75 years had been raped; one woman claimed to have been raped 17 times on the night of the 29th and 11 times on the morning of the 30th." Another battalion commander described a three-year-old shot dead by French colonials after his mother resisted their advances. "A delegation of frenzied citizens and priests" begged GIs to post guards in Pisterzo to forestall further butchery, he reported. American soldiers "came in as crusaders to save Europe from such things," he added. "The occurrences are seriously affecting the morale and willingness to fight in my men." The U.S. commander of the 13th Field Artillery Brigade, attached to the FEC, advised Clark that all thirteen of his battalion commanders could testify to similar depravities.

Italian authorities tallied seven hundred crimes of "carnal violence" in Frosinone province alone. "All over the mountain," a woman in Esperia reported, "you could hear the screaming." Among many affidavits from victims was that of a sixteen-year-old girl in Lenola: "I was taken and violated four times by Moroccans. There was a 12-year-old girl with me . . . who suffered the same violation." Norman Lewis, the British intelligence officer and author, investigated various allegations and found "wholesale rape" in many villages. "In Lenola, which fell to the Allies on May 21, fifty women were raped, but—as there were not enough to go round—children and even old men were violated," Lewis wrote.

"At any hour of the day or night, men and women, old and young, are subject to acts of force of every type, which range from beatings to carnal violence, woundings to murder," an Italian general wrote Clark on May 25. "I beg your excellency . . . intervene for the honor of the Allied cause."

Vengeful Italians occasionally retaliated, Lewis noted. Near Cancello, five colonial soldiers were reportedly poisoned, then castrated, then beheaded. Some French officers responded with what an American officer described as "a 'so-what' shrug," or proposed that Italians were collecting the just deserts of making common cause with Hitler. J. Glenn Gray, a U.S. counterintelligence lieutenant with a doctorate from Columbia University, wrote that "the complaints have been taken to the French general in charge, who merely laughed and said, 'This is war.' "

General Juin was *not* laughing, although his initial crackdown lacked force. In a memorandum on May 24, Juin condemned "acts of brigandage," and warned that "however strong our feelings may be against a nation which treacherously betrayed France, we must maintain an attitude of dignity." As more accusatory reports flooded in, Clark dispatched Gruenther to FEC headquarters on May 27 and penned a sharp letter of rebuke to the French commander. Juin that day told his officers that the rapacious behavior had "excited indignation in Allied circles." He demanded "punishment without mercy." Fifteen colonial miscreants reportedly were executed—shot or hanged in village squares—and fifty-four others drew prison terms ranging from five years to life.

In an attempt to cool *goumier* concupiscence, Clark approved the transport of Berber women to Italy aboard Navy LSTs; to make them less conspicuous, some were said to wear men's uniforms. The Italian government, which kept meticulous records of Allied offenses against Italian civilians, documented more than five thousand alleged crimes by French colonials. "We suffered more during the 24 hours of contact with the Moroccans than in the eight months under the Germans," one Italian complained. They were "savages," a GI in the 88th Division concluded, and they "gave war and soldiers a bad name."

Lucian Truscott was in pain and poor humor at nine A.M. on Tuesday, May 30, when he arrived in the dilapidated dairy that served as the 36th Infantry Division headquarters in Torécchia Nuova, three miles north of Cisterna near the Via Appia. His enflamed throat tormented him again, and chest X-rays earlier that morning had revealed a cracked rib to complement the bruises he had sustained in a minor jeep accident. Every breath hurt.

Worse yet, the attacks by his 34th, 45th, and 1st Armored Divisions had again failed to sunder the Caesar Line along the western face of the Colli Laziali. That hurt too, but Truscott—goaded by Clark—had ordered another "day of slugging," with "hard assaults" by the three divisions, including four tank companies attacking abreast. If VI Corps could just reach the high ground beyond Lanuvio near Lake Albano, "the thing is cinch," Truscott promised. Still, he knew that Old Ironsides was nearly spent—Harmon calculated that the division had but one day's fight left in it—and other units were almost as frayed.

The usual camp smells of canvas and stale coffee mingled with a sharp bovine odor in the command post, where staff officers milled about in the abandoned barn stalls. Truscott hardly knew the 36th Division, which had arrived in Anzio just a week earlier, yet he was wary of his fellow Texans, whose travails at Salerno, San Pietro, and the Rapido had earned the unit a hard-luck reputation. Truscott had hoped to give the three infantry regiments an easy assignment to avoid "a crushing blow to their morale"; but four days of brutal combat quashed such sensibilities, and he had ordered the 36th to prepare today for an imminent attack into the line.

To the stocky officer at Truscott's elbow, squinting at the large map of the Colli Laziali, it all seemed too familiar: another frontal assault, not unlike the one he had been ordered to make at the Rapido. "You can't always trust the higher command," Major General Fred Walker had told his diary a few days earlier. "You have to watch them all the time to keep from being imposed upon." In his bunk late at night, Walker had been reading *Lee's Lieutenants,* the vivid group portrait of Civil War generals by Douglas Southall Freeman. When Walker studied the blue icons on the map showing VI Corps dispositions, he could only wonder: was this how Lee would have fought the battle?

In the five months since leaving hundreds of his soldiers to rot in the Rapido bottoms, Walker had struggled to keep his equilibrium. He had expected Clark to sack him, as so many other staff officers and subordinate commanders in the 36th had been sacked. "I am fed up with the whole damn mess," he told Geoff Keyes, who replied, "The fact that you are commanding a National Guard division means you have two strikes against you from the start." Yet here he was, still the Army's oldest division commander in the field; still concealing the headaches, tachycardia, and arthritis that plagued him; still doing his duty. The division had been pulled from the Cassino line in late February for several months of refitting and mountain training near Avellino. "Walker seems a new man—full of enthusiasm and optimism," Keyes wrote in late spring.

Now the new man was determined to find an alternative to bludgeoning an entrenched enemy who held the high ground. On the far right of the VI Corps line, two miles east of Velletri and Highway 7, patrols on Saturday had reported "an old shrubbery-covered cart path" up a steep ridge called Monte Artemisio. No enemy fieldworks or outposts could be seen. Walker scouted the area from a Piper Grasshopper on Sunday afternoon, then, late in the day, sat in a thicket below the heights, studying the terrain with the eye of the mining engineer he had once been.

"I didn't sleep much last night," Walker told his diary on Monday. "I worked out a plan in my head to take Velletri from the rear." Artemisio formed the southern rim of an ancient volcanic crater; rising three thousand feet behind Velletri, it extended four miles from southwest to northeast as the lower lip of the Colli Laziali. Ancient fingers of lava reached into the flats, now alight with the green fire of grapevines and young wheat. To the left, where Highway 7 swung west around lakes Nemi and Albano, Velletri clung to the lower slope like a lichen to a rock. "It looks to me," Walker wrote, "like this is the place to break through."

Truscott disagreed, brushing aside the notion as impractical when Walker on Sunday night first suggested he had found "a soft spot." But now in the malodorous dairy Walker restated his case with urgent conviction. Maps and his own reconnaissance showed that the faint ditch-and-washline up Artemisio's face was in fact an old logging road through the chestnut brakes. Aerial photos also revealed a two-mile gap between the left flank of I Parachute Corps and the right flank of LXXVI Panzer Corps. If two regiments crossed the Velletri–Valmontone road in the dead of night and followed the trace uphill, they could seize the heights above Highway 7 to outflank the Caesar Line and occupy the Colli Laziali. The Vatican stood just fifteen miles from Lake Albano.

"You may have something here," Truscott said. But a few thousand riflemen would not suffice, even on the high ground. Tanks and artillery would be needed to repel German counterattacks. Walker summoned his division engineer, Colonel Oran C. Stovall, a self-described "pick-and-shovel boy," who for three days had also been poring over maps and skulking through the woods. Stovall believed the soil across the Colli Laziali was volcanic and readily sculpted: bulldozers could widen the old scar into a military road, allowing armor and heavy weapons to "shoot up over Monte Artemisio and down the other side."

"I'll call you back within the hour," Truscott said, and rattled off to Conca in his jeep, his sore ribs momentarily forgotten. At eleven A.M., he phoned Walker. The VI Corps engineer adamantly opposed the scheme as harebrained, but Truscott was ready to gamble. He would also put an entire engineer regiment under Walker's command. Before ringing off he added in a low growl, "And you had better get through."

Walker summoned his own lieutenants to the dairy at three P.M. and laid out his plan. The 141st Infantry Regiment would attack Velletri to fix the German garrison while the 142nd and 143rd crept up Artemisio, engineers on their heels, after moving by truck to the woods below the Velletri–Valmontone road. The supply line would stretch for eight miles through rugged terrain, but the division's flinty experience in fighting at night in the high country on Monte Sammucro last December should serve it well.

"We are taking chances," Walker told his diary as his commanders pelted back to their units, "but we should succeed in a big way."

Across the Colli Laziali, Albert Kesselring was alive to his peril. In a visit to the front on Monday afternoon, the field marshal recognized that a gap persisted between the parachute and the panzer corps, and he ordered General Mackensen to suture it. Wilhelm Schmalz, the Hermann Göring commander, had also warned of "lively scouting" by American patrols east of Velletri. Schmalz sent his last reserve, an engineer platoon, into the wild uplands on Monte Artemisio. He repeatedly asked Mackensen's headquarters to compel the 362nd Infantry Division—now holding the western rim of the Colli Laziali—to send a detachment to literally shake hands with Schmalz's platoon, sealing the seam.

It never happened. The 362nd had lost half its fighting strength on May 23 alone, just as the Hermann Görings had lost two-thirds of their infantry in the past week; Fourteenth Army's functioning panzer fleet consisted of thirty-three tanks. The army was bleeding to death. Disorder and misapprehension carried the day: Mackensen, inattentive and resentful of Kesselring's meddling, believed that the porous boundary between the corps had been fused. Even if a few rifle companies slipped across Artemisio, surely no tank could scale that volcanic shoulder.

Cuckoos sang in the night woods. Just enough pale light seeped from the new moon for shadows to spread beneath the chestnuts. "Douse that cigarette," a voice snarled, "or I'll blow your head off." The offending glow proved to be the luminous face of a soldier's wristwatch.

For four hours on Tuesday evening, the assault regiments gathered in the forest, stacking bedrolls, filling canteens, fixing bayonets. Congested roads had delayed the truck convoys as one battalion after another slipped from the line along the Via Appia for the sixteen-mile loop back through Cisterna before swinging northeast past Cori to dismount east of Velletri. "I may not be able to write very often in the near future. Don't think anything of it, for it's just routine," a private in the 142nd Infantry scribbled in a note to his mother. "No news here, just the same old grind." Blued by starlight, sergeants padded through their platoons, vowing to court-martial any man who fired a shot without orders. Colonel George E. Lynch, the 142nd commander, confessed to feeling "breathless anticipation."

At eleven P.M., an hour late, the great column surged forward. A dog barked, another howled; a jackass brayed in the night. "We expected to meet the enemy in every shadow," a soldier later wrote. By 1:30 A.M. on Wednesday, May 31, scouts had scurried across the Valmontone road, darting past the wall tombs of a local cemetery and through grapevines that twined up leaning poles to form leafy cones. Artemisio loomed like a shadow cast against the sky, black and silent but for the cuckoos. Far to the left, distant machine-gun fire—"like corn popping in a deep kettle," Sevareid wrote—signaled the 141st Infantry's diversionary attack against Velletri. The soldiers were climbing now, up the thin, steep scratch of the logging trace, each man chuffing so that the column seemed to suspire like a dark, winded serpent.

At three A.M. the drone of a plane drew antiaircraft fire near Velletri. Then chandelier flares blossomed, drenching the mountain in silver light. The men fell flat as one, lying motionless for ten minutes, twenty. The flares winked out and they scrambled to their feet. The climb resumed.

The first gray wash of dawn, at 4:15, soon leached out the stars, but haze swaddled the slope to keep the men concealed. At 6:35, three German artillery observers were captured unawares, including one found bathing in a creek. Through the morning American soldiers spread across the ridgeline, shooing away Schmalz's engineer platoon with a spatter of rifle fire. The midday sun burned off the haze, revealing a panorama: Valmontone and Highway 6 seven miles to the east; Anzio, Nettuno, and the glittering sea twenty miles to the southwest; and directly below, Velletri and Highway 7. Tiny figures in field gray strolled about in the German rear, unaware that six thousand American soldiers were behind them.

Behind the column came the bulldozers, "roaring and rearing" along a strip of white engineering tape that demarcated the route, three dozers at first, and eventually fifteen, each adding another foot of width to the graded road. Blue sparks sprayed from the blades as they shoved rocks and saplings from the trail, slashing hairpins wide enough for a tank to turn without throwing a track. "Don't spare the horses," a captain told the lead dozer operator, Corporal John Bob Parks. Sappers blew over trees too big to bulldoze, or felled them with two-man timber saws. On the steepest grades, small dozers were hauled up with snatch block and cable, then slashed their way down while soldiers with shovels manicured the verges. "Up, up, up all the time," Parks later recalled, with the captain reminding him "again and again that I was holding up the whole damned Fifth Army. . . . I lost track of time and everything else except that damn white tracing tape that was always in front of me."

Through the night and the following day they toiled, scraping and grading, until a one-way boulevard led to Artemisio's crest. Behind them came the tanks, self-propelled guns, and artillery observers with optics and field phones, chortling at the vista from the high ground that was finally theirs. The 143rd Infantry reported so many observers flocking to the heights that they resembled "crows on a telephone line."

Kesselring learned that the enemy was in his rear when a German artillery officer on Artemisio reported GIs storming his command post. The field marshal had already lambasted Mackensen for neglecting to seal the corps boundary across the mountain. Yet the fog of war persisted even as the haze lifted. Mackensen discounted his jeopardy after a dispatch from the front at eleven A.M. on May 31 claimed that only eighty enemy soldiers had infiltrated; a subsequent report asserted they had been "mopped up completely." Reports to the contrary simply thickened the fog. The Fourteenth Army battle log on May 31 recorded that "the enemy managed to infiltrate two battalions," but Mackensen continued to estimate American strength on the mountain at no more than one and a half battalions.

Kesselring at nine P.M. on May 31 ordered Mackensen "at all costs" to extirpate the Allied salient on Artemisio, now five miles deep. Privately he feared the game was up: I Parachute Corps that same evening warned that the front was "ripe for collapse." Desperate for reinforcements, Mackensen summoned a police battalion from Rome to plug the gap; equally desperate and ineffectual, Kesselring ordered a Luftwaffe unit arriving in Livorno to hie for the front. The men were mounted on bicycles.

Ambushes and precise artillery now began to tear apart German convoys lumbering down Highway 7 from Rome. Bazooka teams struck a tank column pushing out of Velletri; the German commander flew from his turret "like a cork out of a champagne bottle." When enemy snipers in mottled camouflage signaled one another with cuckoo calls on Artemisio's flanks, GIs raked the woods with blistering fire, shooting up birds and Germans alike. After a captain with a tommy gun killed a gargantuan enemy soldier, his men lay beside the corpse as if comparing themselves to a sleeping Gulliver. "I only came up to his arm pit and I was six-two," one GI reported. "I measured him and removed his watch." Canteens taken from the dead were found to be filled with cognac.

By dawn on June 1, Velletri was surrounded and American scouts stood on the highest peaks in the Colli Laziali, staring down on Lake Nemi and at

Castel Gandolfo, on the far shore of Lake Albano; through the haze on the northern horizon floated the domes and spires of Rome. Only eleven 36th Division soldiers had been killed.

Outside Velletri, Walker paced beneath a rail trestle in a "state of perturbation," urging his men to smarten the pace. When a column of captured enemy soldiers shuffled past, he gave one his boot, then regretted the impulse. "Most unbecoming of a major general to kick a German prisoner," he wrote.

Through Thursday afternoon, tanks and infantrymen bulled through Velletri's rubble, battling diehards house to house and hand to hand. Those who tried to break the cordon by fleeing on foot or in trucks careering up Highway 7 drew sleeting fire that left the roadbed tiled with bodies. At dusk the final mutter of gunfire subsided, and the Allies owned another guttering town. Blood had risen in the gorge, and tankers drove across enemy corpses to hear the bones crack beneath their tracks. "It didn't bother me," a soldier wrote. As 250 dazed German prisoners emerged beneath white flags, Truscott drove up to find Walker again scrutinizing the landscape with his engineer's squint. "You can go in now, General," Walker said. "The town is yours."

General Schmalz reported that all phone communication within the Hermann Göring Division had ceased. He could no longer find his subordinate command posts; the reconnaissance battalion had a fighting strength of eighteen men; and his panzer grenadier regiment no longer existed. The front, he added, was "torn wide open."

A 36th Division artillery lieutenant offered his own assessment. "Getting little sleep these days," he wrote in his diary. "Going fine, victory is a wonderful thing."

## Expulsion of the Barbarians

CYPRESS trees stood sentinel along the northbound roads, tapered green flames that seemed to bend beneath the weight of the Allied advance. Near Highway 6, a child kicked the corpse of a Wehrmacht officer until a young woman shoved him aside and yanked off the dead man's boots. German caisson teams sprawled in the roadbed, butchered by Spitfires. "The horses had fallen in harness, with their heads high in the air, eyes opened and distended in terror," wrote J. Glenn Gray. "There were many of them, in columns, and the strafing bullet wounds were hardly visible." GIs scratched their initials on the gun carriages.

Outside Valmontone ranks of dead American soldiers lay within the garden walls of a Franciscan convent transformed into a mortuary. "Over each one of them we placed a blanket under which stuck out the shoes in the sun, giving the impression of being extremely large," an Italian witness later recalled. German snipers popped away across hill and dale. When a GI abruptly pitched over, a tanker yelled to a crouching rifleman, "Is he hurt bad?" The rifleman shook his head. "No, he ain't hurt. He's dead."

Clark took nothing for granted, even as the breakthrough on Monte Artemisio "caused all of us to turn handsprings." Ubiquitous and intense, aware of the imminent invasion at Normandy, he lashed the troops with unsparing urgency. Eleven of his divisions pounded north along five trunk roads that converged on Rome from the lower boot. Alexander on Friday, June 2, shifted the interarmy boundary north of Highway 6 to give Fifth Army—now 369,000 strong—a wider attack corridor. General Harding, Alexander's chief of staff, phoned Gruenther with effusive praise. "He stated it with such a sincere tone that I am certain he meant what he said," Gruenther told Clark. "For my part I am throwing my hat in the air and yelling, 'Hip, hip, hooray.'"

Clark's peaked cap remained on his head. "I'm disappointed in the 45th and 34th today. They've not gotten anyplace," he told Don Carleton in a call to VI Corps early Friday evening.

"They got a lot of prisoners and killed a lot of Germans," Carleton replied.

"But they haven't *gone* any place," Clark said. "I want to take ground."

With casualties climbing and Harmon's 1st Armored Division losing over two hundred tanks in eight days, Clark fretted that another delay likely meant waiting for Eighth Army "to get into the act." Indeed, Alexander on Friday night privately mused that if Clark failed to finish routing the enemy within forty-eight hours, "we shall have to stage a combined attack by both Fifth and Eighth armies when the latter gets up." Even Clark's mother urged alacrity. "Please take Rome soon," she wrote her son from Washington. "I'm all frazzled out."

He was trying, driven by dreams of glory undimmed and unshared. When Alexander's headquarters proposed a communiqué that would read, "Rome is now in Allied hands," Clark told Gruenther, "They carefully avoid the use of 'Fifth Army,' and say 'Allies.' You call Harding immediately. Tell him I don't agree to this paper." Churchill renewed his plea for shared Anglo-American honors. "I hope that British as well as Americans will enter the city simultaneously," the prime minister had written Alexander on Tuesday. But few Tommies could be found in the Fifth Army vanguard. When Alexander proposed that a Polish contingent join the spearhead into Rome as a tribute to their valor at Monte Cassino and in acknowledgment of their Roman Catholicism, Clark ignored the suggestion.

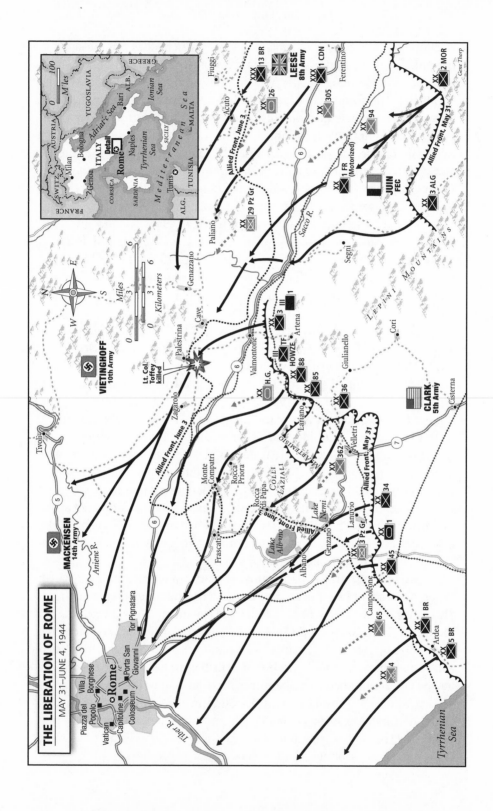

THE LIBERATION OF ROME

MAY 31–JUNE 4, 1944

"The attack today must be pushed to its limit," he told Truscott on Friday. Only to his diary did Clark confide, "This is a race against time, with my subordinates failing to realize how close the decision will be."

Valmontone was found abandoned on Friday, at last. "No contact with enemy anywhere along the front," the 3rd Division reported. A reconnaissance battalion crept up Highway 6, and by dawn on Saturday, June 3, Truscott's VI Corps and Keyes's II Corps were poised for a bragging-rights race into Rome from the south and southeast, respectively. Roving Italian barbers gave haircuts and shaves to unkempt soldiers keen to look groomed for the liberation.

Like Gruenther's tossed hat, the tonsorial primping was premature. German rearguard panzers lurked in the shadows to ambush the incautious. Fearful of a counterattack from the east that could sever the new Fifth Army supply route on Highway 6, Lieutenant Colonel Jack Toffey led two depleted 7th Infantry battalions into the rolling meadows below Palestrina, an ancient Etruscan town famous for its roses and said to have been founded by Ulysses. Early Saturday morning Toffey informed the regimental command post of a troublesome Tiger tank, "hull down in a road cut." Later in the day, as Palestrina's cyclopean walls hove into view, he reported seeing outriders from Juin's FEC on his flank.

That would be his last dispatch. At 2:14 P.M., a radio message to the regiment reported that Colonel Toffey had been wounded half a mile below Palestrina. After climbing to the second floor of a tile-roof farmhouse for a better view of German positions, Toffey was sitting on the floor with a radio between his knees when a tank round slammed into the upper story. At least one officer believed the shell came from a disoriented Sherman tank crew a few hundred feet behind the farmhouse; others insisted the round was German. Regardless, dust filled the dismembered room as Toffey lay sprawled against the front wall with a shell fragment in the back of his head. "His eyes were open but seeing nothing," an officer noted. At 2:40 P.M., a radio report to the command post announced his death. A lieutenant and three enlisted men had also been killed, and a tank battalion commander badly wounded.

Veiled with a blanket, Toffey's mortal remains were laid on a stretcher and driven by jeep to the rear. Since landing on the beaches of Morocco nineteen months earlier, he had fought as faithfully as any battle commander in the U.S. Army. Now his war was over, his hour spent. A short time later, Juin's troops relieved the 7th Infantry, which would not fight in Italy again. The 3rd Division history lamented the passing of "a mad, genial Irishman," among "the best-loved and most colorful characters in the division, if not our entire Army." One comrade wrote that "there will never be his like again," but that was incorrect: the country had produced enough of his ilk to finish the war Jack Toffey had helped win.

Upon learning of Toffey's death, Clark ordered Gruenther to draft a list of midlevel officers with long, sterling battle records who would be the generals in America's next war. "I am sending them home because they are too valuable to risk in further combat," Clark wrote.

For Toffey the gesture came too late. In a note to General McNair in Washington, a grieving Truscott called him "one of the finest officers I have ever known." But the most poignant epitaph came from a former comrade in the 15th Infantry: "Perhaps he was kept overseas a little longer than his odds allowed."

Even before the American thrust across Monte Artemisio, Albert Kesselring doubted whether the indefensible terrain below the Tiber River could be held much longer. Of 540 German antitank guns in Italy, 120 remained. On June 2, he advised Berlin that in three weeks his armies had suffered 38,000 casualties; among his divisions still fighting, only two were even 50 percent combat effective. Charred tanks and trucks fouled every road and cart path. The Subiaco Pass, through which much of Vietinghoff's Tenth Army would squeeze, resembled "a huge snake of burning vehicles."

Vietinghoff himself was a casualty: sick and spent, he handed command to his chief of staff and stumbled off to a hospital in northern Italy. A few hours later, Kesselring's own staff chief, Siegfried Westphal, collapsed from nervous exhaustion. Mackensen, too, was finished: Hitler approved Kesselring's demand that he be cashiered as Fourteenth Army commander for incompetence in defending the Colli Laziali, among other alleged failings.

Kesselring had earlier proposed a scorched-earth retreat that included the demolition of all Tiber River bridges, as well as power, rail, and industrial facilities around Rome. Hitler demurred. Roman bridges had "considerable historical and artistic merit"; moreover, the capital held little strategic value, and leaving it in ashes would merely enhance Allied political and propaganda gains. On June 3, less than two hours after Jack Toffey's death, the high command informed Kesselring: "Führer decision. There must not be a battle of Rome."

Rear guards would continue to harass the American horde in the Roman suburbs, buying time for the garrison to flee from what Berlin now declared to be an open city. Fourteenth and Tenth Army troops would hasten north, in small bands if necessary. A radio code word—ELEFANTE— warned that Allied forces were closing in on the capital.

The sound of gunfire from the Colli Laziali had been audible since May 29, and unease among the German occupiers in Rome now gave way to panic. Papers were burned, granaries fired; an ammunition dump in the Campo Verano cemetery was blown up, along with a barracks, a Fiat plant, a phone center. The white peacocks strutting about the German embassy garden had long been shot and roasted. The Hotel de la Ville in the Via Sistina, a pleasant redoubt known as "Brighter Berlin," emptied out. Near the Piazza Fiume, soldiers methodically looted a hardware shop, packing their booty into a covered truck. Officers living the high life on the Via Veneto pilfered the silverware and water goblets before decamping.

"Germans streaming through the city, pushing carts, trying to swipe cars, marching on foot," Peter Tompkins, the OSS operative, wrote in his diary. "The cafés were still open and doing big business." A six P.M. curfew was imposed, "but it isn't quite clear who is giving the orders." Tompkins filled his bathtub just before the city's water pipes ran dry. As Romans watched from behind shuttered windows, convoys streamed out of the city, vehicles three and four abreast on the Via Cassia, the Via Salaria, and abutting sidewalks. "Wild-eyed, unshaven, unkempt, on foot, in stolen cars, in horsedrawn vehicles, even in carts belonging to the street cleaning department," one witness reported. "Some of them dragged small ambulances with wounded in them." Fascist Blackshirts pleaded for rides or trotted north, furtively looking over their shoulders. Tompkins, the dutiful spy, recorded it all: Germans fleeing on bicycles, Germans hobbling on crutches, Germans on motorcycles with flat tires, Germans near the Piazza Venezia "trying to get away with cars that no longer have *any* tires, driving on the rims."

And in the Gestapo cells beneath Via Tasso 155, prisoners cocked an ear to the distant grumble of Allied guns. In hushed whispers, eyes agleam, they debated with urgent intensity the variables of ballistics and wind direction, trying to gauge just how far away their liberators might be.

Not far. Eleven months after the Allies first waded ashore in Sicily, the titanic battles between army groups that characterized the Italian campaign now subsided into niggling suburban gunfights between small bands of pursuers and pursued. Seventeen major bridges spanned the Tiber along an eight-mile stretch, linking eastern Rome not only to Vatican City and the capital's west bank but also to the highways vital to Fifth Army's pursuit up the peninsula to the northwest. Flying columns of tanks, engineers, and infantrymen began to coalesce with orders to thrust through the city and secure the crossings.

"Looks as if the Boche is pulling out, and [Truscott] wants you to get up there and seize the crossings over the Tiber as fast as you can," Carleton told Ernie Harmon early Saturday afternoon. "Make all the speed you can." A few hundred feet above Highway 6, Keyes from his observation plane dropped a penciled message to the armored task force led by Colonel Howze: "Get those tanks moving!" Howze put the spurs to his men, only to blunder into yet another chain of ambushes. "In a few minutes the lead tank would stop and burst into flames," Howze later wrote, forcing the cavalcade to idle until the enemy blockages could be outflanked and routed.

Such petty inconveniences hardly diminished the swelling euphoria. "The command post has gone to hell," Gruenther radioed Clark from Caserta at 4:15 P.M. on Saturday. "No one is doing any work here this afternoon. All semblance of discipline has broken down." According to II Corps intelligence reports, Germans were withdrawing "in such confusion and speed that their retreat has assumed proportions of a rout." Clark sternly reminded his lieutenants to keep killing. "Your orders are to destroy the enemy facing Fifth Army," he told the corps commanders shortly before five P.M. "Rome and the advance northward will come later."

Precisely who first crossed Rome's city limits early on Sunday, June 4, would be disputed for decades. Various units claimed the honor by filing affidavits and issuing proclamations and protests. An 88th Division reconnaissance troop and Frederick's 1st Special Service Force, which had been merged with Howze's task force, had the strongest claims, but Clark subsequently wrote that "it is impossible to determine with certainty the unit of the Fifth Army whose elements first entered the city." Patrols darted into the city only to be driven out by scalding gunfire. German paratroopers holding a strongpoint at Centocelle, just east of Rome, knocked out five American tanks before slipping away. On Highway 6 near Tor Pignatara, an antitank gun shattered two more Shermans, then vanished into a warren of alleys.

Traffic jams and friendly fire, orders and counterorders, flocking journalists and even a wedding party—the bride, dressed in gray and holding a rose bouquet, tiptoed around German corpses in the roadway—threatened to turn the liberation into opera buffa. Clark left Anzio in brilliant sunshine at 8:30 A.M. with a convoy of two armored cars and six jeeps packed with more journalists. Arriving at Centocelle, he hopped from his jeep in a flurry of salutes. When Clark asked why the drive had stalled, Frederick replied, "I'm holding off the artillery because of the civilians."

"I wouldn't hesitate to use it if you need to," Clark said. "We can't be held up here too long."

As he walked with Frederick and Keyes up a low hill for a better view, photographers asked the trio to pose beside a large blue and white road sign that read ROMA. Moments later a sniper's bullet blew through the metal face with a sharp bang. Clark, Keyes, and Frederick crawled down the hill and retreated two hundred yards to a thick-walled house. There would be no triumphant entry into the Eternal City this afternoon. Clark grumbled over delays in reaching the Tiber, then drove back to Anzio. Keyes in turn told subordinates he did not want "one little gun stopping us." He gobbled down a cold K ration and ordered another frontal assault up Highway 6 so "C could enter Rome," as he told his diary.

By late Sunday the rear guards had melted away but for snipers and a few stubborn strongpoints along the river. Some captured Germans proved to be boys dragooned into combat from a school for cooks and bakers; one prisoner was seized pushing a cart laden with looted chocolate bars. From the east and south, American troops streamed through the city's outer precincts. Howze dispatched platoons with instructions typed in Italian commanding any Roman stopped on the street to lead the patrols to specific Tiber bridges. A Forceman scuttling past the Colosseum muttered, "My God, they bombed that too!" An 88th Division soldier who peeked inside said, "I was not impressed by the interior: too small, too cluttered." Puzzled by the "S.P.Q.R."—"*Senatus Populusque Romanus*"—stamped on monuments and manhole covers, a GI speculated that it stood for "Society for the Prevention of Cruelty to Romans"; he was crestfallen to learn that "cruelty" was not spelled with a "q."

Howze at twilight led a tank company toward the central rail station to find boulevards empty and windows shuttered. Then a sash flew open, a voice shrieked "*Americano!,*" and Romans by the thousands swept into the streets despite the occasional *ping* from a sniper round. Delirious citizens flung themselves onto Howze's jeep and "kissed me until I threatened to shoot some of them," he reported. "Vino offered in glasses, in pitchers, in bottles, and even in kegs," the 88th Division noted. "Kisses were freely bestowed by both male and female citizens and suffered or enjoyed by the recipient accordingly." Signoras offered plates of spaghetti and bowls of hot shaving water. Italian men with ancient rifles and red sashes clapped their liberators on the back, then stalked off in search of Germans and Fascists. Communists and Blackshirts traded potshots, and the *pop* of pistol fire near the Colosseum signaled another summary execution. "It still won't be hard to be killed here," an American officer wrote in his diary on June 4.

Frederick set out for the Tiber shortly before ten P.M. with seven men and a radio car. Just west of the Piazza del Popolo he found the triple arches of the Ponte Regina Margherita intact in the moonlight, but a stay-behind German squad sprayed tracers across the dark river. A wild mêlée grew wilder when a confused battalion from the 88th Division blundered into the scrap and also fired on the Forcemen. Bullets struck Frederick in the knee and elbow; his driver was killed. With eight Purple Hearts by the end of the war, Bob Frederick would be described as "the most shot-at-and-hit general in American history."

From the Baths of Caracalla to the Quirinal, jubilation now grew full-throated—"a complete hysteria," as the 1st Armored Division reported. Romans in nightshirts and slippers poured into the streets, braying whatever scraps of English they could recall, including one old man who repeatedly shouted, "Weekend! Weekend!" At 1:30 A.M. on Monday, June 5, both the U.S. flag and a Union Jack were raised on staffs above the Piazza Venezia. A banner draped the Pantheon: WELCOME TO THE LIBERATORS. Shrieking crowds ransacked the flower stalls below the Spanish Steps to garland those liberators or to pelt them with roses and irises. Young men sporting hammer-and-sickle armbands marched up the Corso Umberto singing "Bandiera Rossa" and other socialist anthems. Romans stormed the Regina Coeli prison to fling open the cells. Others searched the yellow house at Via Tasso 155, where the walls and floors were flecked with blood. "Brothers," someone called into the cellar gloom, "come out."

Shortly before dawn, a column of nearly three hundred vehicles rolled through Porta San Giovanni carrying S-Force, a detachment of twelve hundred American and British counterintelligence and engineering specialists. As the convoy snaked down the Via delle Quattro Fontane, squads peeled away to secure telegraph offices, power plants, and pumping stations. Others rounded up Italian utility managers: Rome's power supply had been slashed to about 20 percent of the capital's needs, and repairs to damaged aqueducts were to begin within a day. An S-Force platoon poking through the German embassy found various photos of Hermann Göring, an Artie Shaw record on the phonograph, and a half ton of plastic explosives, which were later stuffed in weighted sacks and tossed into the Tiber. A half dozen safes upon cracking "revealed nothing of an unusual nature."

"Got across thirteen bridges. Occupied them on the far side last night," Harmon radioed Truscott at 6:30 A.M. "None destroyed. . . . I am the first boy on the Tiber."

"Go up to Genoa if you want to," Truscott replied.

Not yet. At seven A.M., Sergeant John Vita of Port Chester, New York, wandered through the fifteenth-century Palazzo Venezia to find himself in the Sala del Mappamondo. Mussolini's cavernous office, clad in marble, featured a desk the size of a yacht. Stepping onto the Duce's notorious balcony, Vita drew a crowd on the piazza below by tossing out rolls of Life Savers and declaiming, "Victory! Not for Mussolini, but for the Allies."

That Allied victory had cost them 44,000 casualties since DIADEM began on May 11: 18,000 Americans—among them more than 3,000 killed in action—along with 12,000 British, 9,600 French, and nearly 4,000 Poles.

German casualties were estimated at 52,000, including 5,800 dead. Americans losses in less than four weeks almost equaled those sustained during seven months of fighting in North Africa. Combat in the Mediterranean had achieved an industrial scale.

Columns of weary GIs shuffled through the city. Some carried small Italian tricolors. Others sported flowers in their helmet nets or rifle barrels. Eric Sevareid watched throngs of Italians sob with joy as they tossed blossoms at the tramping soldiers and cheered them to the echo. "I felt wonderfully good, generous, and important," he wrote. "I was a representative of strength, decency, and success."

A message to the Combined Chiefs in Washington and London formally announced, "The Allies are in Rome." How long it had taken to proclaim those five words; how much heartbreak had been required to make it so.

In classical Rome, a triumphant general returning from his latest conquest made for the Capitoline, the lowest but most sacred of the city's seven hills, where he sacrificed a snow-white bull in gratitude for Jove's beneficence. His face painted with vermilion, his head crowned with laurel, and his body cloaked in a purple toga, the victor rode to the hill in a chariot drawn by four white steeds. At the foot of the slope, the trailing column of prisoners fell out to be strangled or slain with an ax in the Mamertine Prison, where the apostle Peter also would be held in chains. It was here too that Brutus, bloody dagger in hand, harangued his fellow Romans after the murder of Julius Caesar, and here that Juno's geese were said to have gabbled in alarm when stealthy Gauls tried to scale the Capitoline ramparts. And it was amid the ruins atop the hill in October 1764 that the British historian Edward Gibbon—a plump man in "a bag-wig, a snuff-brown coat, knee breeches, and snowy ruffles," as the travel writer H. V. Morton later described him—claimed that "the idea of writing the decline and fall of the city first started to my mind."

Mark Clark had neither vermilion face paint nor a laurel wreath, but he possessed a sense of theater, and it was on the Capitoline that he bade his lieutenants appear for a rendezvous at ten A.M. on Monday, June 5. At 7:30 Clark flew from Nettuno by Piper Cub, landing in a wheat field outside the city where II Corps had been ordered to arrange an escort of clean tanks, trucks, and soldiers. Upon learning that it would take hours to wash the vehicles, Clark said, "Oh, the hell with that," and bolted with his retinue up Highway 6 through the Porta Maggiore.

Within minutes they were lost. Wandering across the blue-gray Tiber to St. Peter's Square, Clark flagged down a priest and asked, "Where is Capitoline Hill? My name is Clark." The cleric dragooned a boy on a bicycle to lead the convoy, bellowing "Clark! Clark!" to clear a path through the teeming streets. Arriving at the Via del Teatro Marcello at the foot of the Capitoline, Clark climbed the Cordonata ramp—designed by Michelangelo in 1536 to receive the Holy Roman Emperor Charles V—and crossed the elegant Campidoglio to find the peach-hued town hall locked. He pounded on the door, but when a caretaker finally peeked out, Clark chose to linger at the porch balustrade until Truscott, Keyes, and Juin arrived to join him. Opening a map and pointing with exaggerated pantomime toward Berlin, Clark turned to the reporters and photographers now gathered on the square.

"Well, gentlemen, I didn't really expect to have a press conference here—I just called a little meeting of my corps commanders to discuss the situation," he said slowly. "However, I'll be glad to answer your questions. This is a great day for the Fifth Army." A hundred flashbulbs popped as Clark delivered a brief victory oration—the equivalent of slaughtering a white bull—without mentioning Eighth Army or other contributors. His lieutenants flushed with discomfort, glancing self-consciously at a Movietone cameraman filming the scene. Truscott later voiced disgust at "this posturing."

Then it was off to a luncheon at the Hotel Excelsior, which engineers had searched for time bombs and booby traps. In starched black-and-white livery the hotel staff lined the lobby to greet the new occupiers, having said *arrivederci* to the Germans only a day before. Clark gave another short address from a second-floor balcony, then slipped into a suite for a private moment. Kneeling on the bedroom floor, he thanked God for victory and prayed for the souls of his men. A hand gently touched his shoulder. Clark turned to find Juin behind him. Beneath his brushy mustache, the Frenchman smiled and said, "I just did the same thing."

Along the Via Veneto, another happy throng gathered to huzzah their liberators. "We waded through crowds of cheering people," Keyes told his diary. "A couple of women nearly strangled Juin much to our amusement and his embarrassment. We had a fine lunch."

"You have made the American people very happy," Franklin Roosevelt cabled Clark. "It is a grand job well done." Similar plaudits hailed what Harold Macmillan called "the expulsion of the barbarians from the most famous of all cities." Even Stalin on June 5 cheered "the great victory of the Allied Anglo-American forces." Churchill cast a blind eye on fraternal frictions, notwithstanding reports that some British officers were turned away from Rome at gunpoint. "Relations are admirable between our armies in every rank there," he wrote Roosevelt in a sweet fib. "Certainly it is an absolute brotherhood."

Across the capital the celebration continued through Monday afternoon. The San Carlo restaurant offered GIs "the very finest cuts of horse meat." An Army doctor wrote home of "beautiful girls wearing lipstick, silk stockings, and, for a change, also shoes. Many people weep." At the Hotel Majestic, a porter greeted a *Life* magazine reporter with the Fascist salute, then apologized. "A habit of twenty years," he explained. One soldier awoke next to an Italian prostitute who wished him good morning *auf deutsch*. "Today I had my hair cut in Rome and drank gin and vermouth in the Excelsior," a British signaler wrote his family. "The Italians all said, 'We are so happy to see you at last. Why did it take you so long?' "

Exhausted soldiers wrapped themselves in blankets and dozed on the hoods of their half-tracks or in stone-dry fountains. "They slept on the street, on the sidewalks, on the Spanish Steps," the curator of the Keats-Shelley house reported. Some felt deflated. "We prowl through Rome like ghosts, finding no satisfaction in anything we see or do," wrote Audie Murphy. "I feel like a man reprieved from death; and there is no joy in me."

Yet others found redemption in the city they had unchained, a gleaming symbol of the civilized values for which they fought. "Every block is interesting, beautiful, enchanting," a 3rd Division officer wrote. "The very city fills the heart with reverence." At five P.M. on Monday, 100,000 Italians jammed St. Peter's Square. Bells pealed. Priests offered tours of the Vatican to GIs in exchange for American cigarettes. Pius XII appeared on his apartment balcony in brilliant white robes, then later met with reporters as flashbulbs exploded and photographers shouted, "Hold it, Pope. Attaboy!" The holy father advised Roman girls to "behave and dress properly and win the respect of the soldiers by your virtue." A papal secretary added with a shrug, "It's just another changing of the guard."

At six A.M. on Tuesday, June 6, an aide woke Mark Clark in his Excelsior suite with the news that German radio had announced the Allied invasion of Normandy. Clark rubbed the sleep from his eyes. "How do you like that?" he said. "They didn't even let us have the newspaper headlines for the fall of Rome for one day."

At the Albergo Città, a BBC correspondent burst into the Allied press headquarters. "Boys, we're on the back page now," he said. "They've landed in Normandy." Eric Sevareid later recalled that "every typewriter stopped. We looked at one another."

> Most of us sat back, pulled out cigarettes and dropped our half-written stories about Rome on the floor. We had in a trice become performers without an audience . . . a troupe of actors who, at the climax of their play, realize that the spectators have all fled out the door.

\* \* \*

On June 6, Alexander ordered the Fifth and Eighth Armies to make all possible speed for Pisa and Florence, respectively. Some 170 miles separated the Allied front from the next chain of German redoubts, the formidable Gothic Line, but many rivers and hills lay in between. "If only the country were more open," Alexander lamented, "we could make hay of the whole lot."

Howitzers barked wheel to wheel in the Villa Borghese gardens above the Via Veneto. Wreathed in smoke, the guns banged away at the retreating enemy north of the Tiber. Soldiers crowded around platoon radios with heads cocked and mouths agape, listening to the latest news from France and laying bets on when the war would end. "No one put down a date past Thanksgiving," a soldier in the 36th Division recalled. "I often wondered what happened to that money."

Weary sergeants ordered them to fall in and move out. "C'mon, man, c'mon," Ernie Harmon urged a Sherman commander. "There are places to go." A tanker in Old Ironsides told his diary: "Drove through Rome to the other side of Tiber River. People threw flowers at us. Stopped and had coffee." The 88th Division vanguard radioed General Keyes a two-word message: "Beyond Rome."

Olive-drab columns streamed across the river and past the cylindrical Castel Sant'Angelo, tomb of the warrior-emperor Hadrian. On the roof stood the bronze statue of St. Michael the Archangel, patron of soldiers, sheathing his sword. GIs smelling of Chianti and Chesterfields jammed the deuce-and-a-half trucks or straddled the towed artillery tubes, souvenir lithographs and Fascist postage stamps tucked into their packs.

Then up they climbed, along the dark ridge of the Janiculum, where the ancients once kept a shrine to two-faced Janus, the god of beginnings, and where augurs had studied their auspices. From the hillcrest on this cloudless day, Rome unfurled below in a tapestry of reds, browns, and yellows. Beyond the park where Cleopatra once lived in Caesar's villa stood the bell towers and the spires, the cupolas and the domes. On the southern horizon lay the faint blue smudge of the Colli Laziali.

*Why did it take you so long?* the Italians asked, and the answer could only be: *Because so many of us died to set you free.*

North they rolled, on the high ground beneath cypresses and umbrella pines, past Roman gardeners working the flower beds of gray marl and yellow sea sand. North they rolled, and the scent of roses lingered in their wake.

# EPILOGUE

MORE than three weeks passed before Jack Toffey's family learned of his death. "We see you captured Rome," his mother-in-law wrote him. George Biddle, also corresponding with a dead man, encouraged Toffey to "write one short word about the run into Rome. It left me restless and envious."

At the house on East Long Street in Columbus, Helen and the two children went about their days without knowing that their lives had changed forever. An early summer heat wave scorched central Ohio. Toffey's beloved Reds slipped to fourth place in the National League, but the minor league Columbus Red Birds climbed to second in the American Association. In an exhibition game featuring the pitching greats Dizzy Dean and Satchel Paige, Model Dairy of Columbus beat the Chicago American Giants, a Negro League club.

The news from Rome and Normandy electrified the city, which on the evening of June 6 observed a long minute of silence "in respect to the boys of the united nations now fighting to free an enslaved continent." Blood donors in Columbus set a new record by giving almost a thousand pints in one day, and absenteeism at local war plants plummeted. Three thousand inmates at the Ohio State Penitentiary held a prayer vigil, asking the Almighty to bless OVERLORD, and radio station WCOL broadcast twenty daily news reports to track "the beginning of a new world for all who cherish freedom."

Columbus organized a war bond parade on Sunday, June 11, and sailors in white caps marched down Broad Street past displays of jeeps, half-tracks, and a Navy Helldiver airplane that had been built in the local Curtiss-Wright factory. Rationing stamps were still required to buy sugar, shoes, gasoline, and liquor, but the nation suddenly had three billion surplus eggs and every family was urged to eat an extra dozen. Paley's Pants Shop on West Broad Street offered Father's Day slacks for as little as $4, while Roy's jewelry store advertised diamond rings from $65 to $225, including the 20 percent federal tax. Recalling the giddy rampage that followed the armistice announcement in November 1918, downtown merchants announced a victory plan that included locking their doors and boarding up windows when word arrived that World War II had ended.

The fatal telegram from the adjutant general came to East Long Street on Sunday morning, June 25. "The Secretary of War desires me to express his deep regret that your husband, Lieutenant Colonel John J. Toffey, Jr., was killed in action on 3 June in Italy. Letter follows." Helen received his posthumous Purple Heart, which was Toffey's third of the war, and a posthumous Silver Star, his second. Eventually a footlocker of personal effects arrived, including his pen-and-pencil set and a bloodstained glasses case.

As for Colonel Toffey himself, he would never get home. Instead he was buried among comrades in section J, row 4, grave 25, in the Nettuno cemetery, which had first opened two days after the Anzio landings. The muddy field, redeemed with bougainvillea and white oleander, soon became the Sicily-Rome American Cemetery, a seventy-seven-acre sanctuary where almost eight thousand military dead would be interred.

Here, on Memorial Day in 1945, just three weeks after the end of the war in Europe, a stocky, square-jawed figure would climb the bunting-draped speaker's platform and survey the dignitaries seated before him on folding chairs. Then Lucian Truscott, who had returned to Italy from France a few months earlier to succeed Mark Clark as the Fifth Army commander, turned his back on the living and instead faced the dead. "It was," wrote eyewitness Bill Mauldin, "the most moving gesture I ever saw." In his carbolic voice, Truscott spoke to Jack Toffey, to Henry Waskow, and to the thousands of others who lay beneath the ranks of Latin crosses and stars of David. As Mauldin later recalled:

> He apologized to the dead men for their presence here. He said everybody tells leaders it is not their fault that men get killed in war, but that every leader knows in his heart that this is not altogether true. He said he hoped anybody here through any mistake of his would forgive him, but he realized that was asking a hell of a lot under the circumstances. . . . He promised that if in the future he ran into anybody, especially old men, who thought death in battle was glorious, he would straighten them out.

The fall of Rome proved but a momentary interlude in a campaign that soon swept past the capital. Alexander's optimism was unbounded. "Morale is irresistibly high," he wrote Churchill. "Neither the Apennines nor even the Alps should prove a serious obstacle." The prime minister urged him on, cabling, "Your whole advance is splendid, and I hope the remains of what were once the German armies will be collected."

Late on June 7, a South African reconnaissance squadron found Kesselring's headquarters on Monte Soratte ablaze. The field marshal and his staff had fled, though a storeroom full of fine sherry and French wine was seized intact, along with German maps depicting escape routes to the Gothic Line.

Kesselring had tried to persuade himself that the Allied legions "might succumb to the demoralizing influence of a capital city." Yet for two weeks after Rome's capture the Fifth and Eighth Armies bounded up the peninsula, averaging eight miles a day. Then the retreating Germans stiffened under Kesselring's order to conduct demolitions "with sadistic imaginativeness." By June 17, the familiar pattern of blown bridges and antitank ambushes had slowed the pursuit to two miles a day, and vicious little firefights erupted across central Italy. When an artillery captain in the 36th Division was killed in mid-June, one of his lieutenants wrote, "Damned shame that after living through all the hell of Salerno, Altavilla & Cassino he should be killed in a skirmish that no one will ever hear of."

Alexander's blithe dismissal of the Apennines and the Alps suggested an enduring delusion about the road ahead, where the mountains grew steeper and enemy supply lines grew shorter. Moreover, profound strategic changes would redraw the Mediterranean campaign, leaving Italy a bloody backwater. The American high command in Washington, supported by Eisenhower in London, remained intent on a late-summer invasion of southern France to reinforce the Normandy landings. A British proposal to launch an amphibious landing in the northern Adriatic for an attack through the Balkans toward Austria and southern Germany drew skepticism if not scorn. General Charles de Gaulle also insisted that French forces in Italy participate in the liberation of France; no French soldier, De Gaulle warned, would fight beyond Siena.

On July 5, AFHQ ordered that "an overriding priority" be given in the Mediterranean to assembling ten divisions for the invasion near Marseilles, code-named ANVIL. Just as he had given up seven divisions after the fall of Sicily, Alexander now forfeited seven more, including Truscott's VI Corps and Juin's FEC, as well as substantial air support and many logistical units. By mid-August, Fifth Army would shrink by more than half, to 171,000 troops, even as the total American force in the Mediterranean peaked at 880,000 troops. Alexander deemed the denuding of his force "disastrous," and blamed Eisenhower for "halting the triumphant advance of my armies in Italy at a key moment." Clark, abruptly in harmony with General Alex, considered the move "one of the outstanding political mistakes of the war."

Their disappointment was understandable, yet the strategic judgment of Alexander and Clark remains suspect. Hitler had decided to rebuild Kesselring's army group with eight more divisions and to continue fighting for Italian real estate, while construction battalions turned the Gothic Line into a barrier as formidable as the Gustav Line had been. Although Allied intelligence revealed that four German divisions had retreated from Rome as "mere shells," and seven others were "drastically depleted," the Allied pursuit even before the decimation of Alexander's host was "neither strong nor quick," as a U.S. Army assessment concluded. Night continued to give the retreating Germans "a privileged sanctuary" since Allied air fleets had only a few dozen aircraft capable of night attacks. "The cloak of darkness saved the German armies from destruction," an Air Force study later concluded.

The stress in Fifth Army on capturing Rome led to a palpable deflation once the capital fell. Doctors in the 1st Special Service Force reported that men in the unit were "listless, perilously close to exhaustion, and infested with lice," a diagnosis valid for many other units as well. On July 4, the 1st Armored Division reported that barely half of Old Ironsides' tanks remained battleworthy and that the division in six weeks had lost thirty-eight company commanders.

If the past year had been among the most catastrophic in Italian history, with invasion, occupation, civil strife, and total war, the forthcoming year would hardly be less bitter. Partisan ambushes and assassinations increased, as did brutal reprisals: under Kesselring's orders, ten Italian deaths were exacted for every German killed. By early fall, an estimated 85,000 armed partisans roamed the mountains, with another 60,000 in Italian towns. Atrocities became commonplace.

Alexander in late August would shift Eighth Army back to the Adriatic in an effort to unhinge Kesselring's defenses. But autumn rains and heavy casualties halted the Allied drive toward the Po River, and even Churchill realized that "the Italian theater could no longer produce decisive results," in W.G.F. Jackson's words. As the days grew shorter, an American officer wrote, "I wished that I were dead if I had to stay in Italy another winter."

Alas, another miserable winter would pass, another wretched deadlock in which the campaign "sank to the level of a vast holding operation," as the official U.S. Army history put it. Alexander's armies grew increasingly polyglot, comprising troops from twenty-nine nations speaking a dozen languages, including Brazilians, Belgians, Cypriots, and Palestinian Jews— as well as two American forces, one white and one black. The Germans grew so feeble that eventually oxen would be harnessed to pull trucks, and any soldier on patrol who brought back a can of fuel received a thousand cigarettes. Yet not until April 1945 would the Gothic Line collapse, leading to capitulation twenty months after Allied soldiers had first made land at Reggio di Calabria.

Few who had been there at the beginning would be there to see the end. "Many men will never know if we win or lose," Lieutenant Will Stevens had written his mother. "But if anything does happen, I'll try to be good enough so I can meet you somewhere else and maybe we can have a cake together up where things are not rationed." He was killed on June 25, 1944. Such deaths forever haunted those who outlived the war. "I must pursue the shadows to some middle ground," wrote the pilot John Muirhead, "for I am strangely bound to all that happened to them."

The 608-day campaign to liberate Italy would cost 312,000 Allied casualties, equivalent to 40 percent of Allied losses in the decisive campaign for northwest Europe that began at Normandy. Among the three-quarters of a million American troops to serve in Italy, total battle casualties would reach 120,000, including 23,501 killed.

German casualties in Italy remain uncertain, as they were in North Africa. Alexander put German losses at 536,000, while the official U.S. Army history tallied 435,000, including 48,000 enemies killed and 214,000 missing, many of whom were never accounted for. Fifth Army alone reported 212,000 prisoners captured in the campaign. An OSS analysis of obituaries in seventy German daily newspapers found a steady increase in the number of seventeen- and eighteen-year-old war dead; moreover, by late summer 1944, nearly one in ten Germans killed in action was said to be over thirty-eight years old.

As the war moved north, Italian refugees returned home to find their towns obliterated and their fields sown with land mines. The Pontine Marshes again became malarial, and nine out of every ten acres around Anzio were no longer arable. The ten miles between Ortona and Orsogna held an estimated half million mines; those straggling home carried hepatitis, meningitis, and typhus. Ancient San Pietro was a ghost town, and a ghost town it remained, a shambles of plinths, splintered roof beams, and labyrinthine rubble. Only about forty San Pietrans returned to the old village; other survivors moved away or inhabited a new town that would be built down the slope, a bit closer to Highway 6. Some who outlived the war died violently from mines, or while trying to disarm live shells to sell the copper and brass for scrap.

Sant'Angelo refugees first returned in June 1944 to harvest wheat along the Rapido River. Mines quickly took a toll here too, and continued to take a toll for years: among the lost were Pietro Fargnoli, age six, and

Pietro Bove, age twelve, both born after the war, and both killed on February 27, 1959.

Malaria kept Cassino uninhabitable for two years. Eventually the Via Serpentina was rebuilt; so, too, the gleaming white abbey on the hill and the town itself, which within a few decades became prosperous and handsome, with a big Fiat plant nearby and a new *autostrada* that carried travelers from Naples to Rome in two hours.

Some scars were harder to heal. "The men that war does not kill it leaves completely transparent," one colonel observed after a night of heavy shelling. A soldier in the 36th Division later wrote, "I was scared for 23 months. I saw the best troops in the world cut down and replaced three or four times." Simply surviving exacted a price. As J. Glenn Gray told his diary, "My conscience seems to become little by little sooted." Or, as an old paratrooper from the 504th Parachute Infantry Regiment said almost sixty years after the war: "I hate the smell of anything dead. . . . It reminds me of Salerno."

Was the game worth the candle? Alexander thought so. "Any estimate of the value of the campaign must be expressed not in terms of the ground gained," he later wrote, "but in terms of its effect on the war as a whole." By his tally, when Rome fell six of Kesselring's nine "excellent mobile divisions had been severely mauled," and fifty-five German divisions "were tied down in the Mediterranean by the [Allied] threat, actual or potential." As the Combined Chiefs commanded, Italy had been knocked from the Axis coalition and hundreds of thousands of Hitler's troops had been "sucked into the vortex of defeat," in the glum phrase of a senior German general in Berlin. Churchill later wrote, "The principal task of our armies had been to draw off and contain the greatest possible number of Germans. This had been admirably fulfilled."

Yet the Allied strategy in Italy seemed designed not to win but to endure. "There is little doubt that Alexander fulfilled his strategic mission," General Jackson later observed, "[but] there is less certainty about the correctness of that mission." Two distinguished British military historians would voice similar skepticism. John Keegan saw the campaign as "a strategic diversion on the maritime flank of a continental enemy," while Michael Howard believed the Mediterranean strategy reflected Churchill's desire to divert American combat power from the Pacific. The British, Howard concluded, "never really knew where they were going in the Mediterranean."

Others would be even harsher. The Mediterranean was a "cul-de-sac," wrote the historian Corelli Barnett, "mere byplay in the conclusion of a war that had been won in mass battles on the Eastern and Western fronts."

(There were 22 German divisions in Italy on June 6, 1944; by comparison, 157 fought in the east on that day and almost 60 more in western Europe.) Another British eminence, J.F.C. Fuller, in 1948 would call Italy "tactically the most absurd and strategically the most senseless campaign of the whole war." B. H. Liddell Hart concluded that the Italian effort "subtracted very heavily" from Allied war resources, "a much larger subtraction from the total effort than the German had incurred by making a stand in Italy." And the American historian David M. Kennedy decried "a needlessly costly sideshow," a "grinding war of attrition whose costs were justified by no defensible military or political purpose."

Even Kesselring, ever cheeky for a man who had lost both the battle *and* the war, would observe in September 1945 that Anglo-American commanders "appeared bound to their fixed plans. Opportunities to strike at my flanks were overlooked or disregarded." Although "German divisions of the highest fighting quality . . . were tied down in Italy at a time when they were urgently needed in the French coastal areas," Kesselring later added, the Allies "utterly failed to seize their chances."

True enough, all of it, but perhaps not the whole truth. If "to advance is to conquer," in Frederick the Great's adage, then the Allies continued to conquer in the Mediterranean, albeit slowly. When Rome fell, only eleven German U-boats still operated in the entire Mediterranean, and no Allied merchantman would be sunk there for the rest of the war; controlling the middle sea proved vital in liberating Europe, and in guaranteeing another route for Lend-Lease matériel to Russia via Persia. The bomber offensive continued apace from Italian fields that crept ever closer to the Reich; a sustained and ultimately fatal campaign against German oil production facilities included six thousand Fifteenth Air Force sorties in the summer of 1944 that targeted vital refineries around Ploesti, Romania. As the historian Douglas Porch wrote, "One must not lose from view the Mediterranean's importance in breaking the offensive power of German arms, and forcing the Reich onto the defensive, after which any hope of victory eluded them."

Moreover, all criticism of the Italian strategy butts against an inconvenient riposte: if not Italy, where? "Events generate their own momentum, impose their own force, and exert their own influence on the will of man," wrote Martin Blumenson, who spent a professional lifetime pondering the Mediterranean campaign. "We went into Sicily and Italy because we had been in North Africa." No oceangoing fleet was available to move a half million men from the African littoral to England, or anywhere else; nor could British ports, rails, and other facilities, already overwhelmed by the American hordes staging for OVERLORD, have handled such a force.

Moscow would not have tolerated an idling of Allied armies during the ten months between the conquest of Sicily and the Normandy invasion—a ten-month respite the Germans badly needed. "The Italian campaign," wrote the naval historian Samuel Eliot Morison, "was fought because it had to be fought."

Historical tautology may be suspect, and opportunism lacks the panache of grand strategy. From beginning to end, Allied warmaking in the Mediterranean tended to be improvisational. The decision to continue pounding north after the capture of Rome remains especially difficult to justify. Yet the American commander-in-chief had grown comfortable with a campaign that in Italy more than in any other theater resembled the grinding inelegance of World War I. "Our war of attrition is doing its work," Franklin Roosevelt had said a week after the invasion of Sicily, and he never renounced that strategy.

Certainly lessons learned in Sicily and southern Italy paid dividends later in the war, notably the expertise gained in complex amphibious operations and in fighting as a large, multinational coalition. Kesselring went so far as to posit that without the Mediterranean experience, the invasion of France "would have undoubtedly become a failure." Many other lessons were prosaic but sterling, such as the realization that the truck hauling ammunition to the front was no less vital than the gun firing it.

For the U.S. Army, which would shoulder the heaviest burden in western Europe for the balance of the war, there was also the priceless conviction that American soldiers could slug it out with the best German troops, division by division, and prevail. A Japanese-American soldier in the 100th Battalion wrote from Italy, "I really belong to the great American Army here and feel that I am part and parcel of the forces that are fighting for the kind of America we always dreamed of back home."

On the day Rome fell, that great American Army numbered eight million soldiers, a fivefold increase since Pearl Harbor. It included twelve hundred generals and nearly 500,000 lieutenants. Half the Army had yet to deploy overseas, but the U.S. military already had demonstrated that it could wage global war in several far-flung theaters simultaneously, a notion that had "seemed outlandish in 1942," as the historian Eric Larrabee later wrote.

Of those eight million American soldiers in June 1944, about one in ten were in the Mediterranean. Most who were still in Italy, it may be surmised, would have endorsed a ditty circulating through the ranks:

> I'm glad that I came, and damned anxious to go,
> Give it back to the natives, I'm ready to blow.

\* \* \*

Some *would* blow. Kesselring continued to command German forces in Italy until October 1944, when he was badly injured in a collision between his staff car and a mobile gun. Hospitalized for months, he would eventually take command of the faltering Western Front in an hour when catastrophic defeat loomed ever closer for the Reich.

Some blew to other fronts. Charles Ryder left the 34th Division, which he had led since before the TORCH invasion, and would end the war as a corps commander in the Philippines, staging for an invasion of Japan. Fred Walker, awarded the Distinguished Service Cross for his heroics with the 36th Division on Monte Artemisio, was sent home soon after Rome's capture to become commandant of the Army's infantry school in Georgia. "I do not want to leave the division," he wrote, "but I will not be sorry to leave this theater and this army."

Others were fated to remain in Italy for the duration. General von Senger would fight to the end before his capture, struggling to preserve his humanity in the midst of relentless carnage. "You can never quite get over it," he reflected long after the war. The puppet dictator Mussolini lived near Lake Garda, where he read Tolstoy, played tennis—opponents still let him win—and pedaled about on his bicycle, trailed by a truckload of German soldiers. After moving his rump government to Milan in the spring of 1945, Mussolini would be captured by partisans while trying to escape to Switzerland, disguised in a German greatcoat and helmet; with his mistress, Clara Petacci, he was executed on April 28, 1945. The Duce's body, badly mangled and hoisted upside down in a gas station, would be stolen by neo-Fascists in 1946, recaptured three months later by Italian police, and hidden in a convent for eleven years before final interment in the Mussolini family crypt, where the faithful still sign their names in the guest book.

Alexander received a field marshal's baton for the capture of Rome, and a few months later succeeded Wilson as supreme commander in the Mediterranean, with responsibility for Italy, Greece, and the Balkans. "The limitations of his ability began to appear when the forces under his command became so huge that their manipulation required weeks and months of forethought, not hours or days," observed John Harding, his shrewd chief of staff. Elevated to the peerage as a viscount after the war, Alexander would serve for years as the governor-general of Canada.

Geoffrey Keyes continued to command II Corps, receiving his third star in April 1945, and eventually serving as the postwar Allied high commissioner for Austria. Bill Darby's life remained a compelling blend of the felicitous and the star-crossed: after a stint as a staff officer in the War

Department, he returned to Italy as assistant commander of the 10th Mountain Division, only to be killed near Lake Garda by a German artillery shell on April 30, 1945. Among the last casualties of the long campaign, Darby was posthumously promoted to brigadier general. He was thirty-four.

In an exchange of letters with Sarah after the fall of Rome, Lucian Truscott was astonished to find her unaware that he had commanded the Anzio beachhead. "I tried to tell you in every way I could," he wrote on June 15. "What in the world did you think I was doing?" He lamented being "far removed from the softening touch of woman and home," adding, "I'm a bit on edge. It is my belief that much hard fighting lies before us." He was right. Truscott would lead his VI Corps through southern France to the Vosges Mountains before succeeding Clark as the Fifth Army commander in December 1944. In postwar Germany he would serve as the military governor of Bavaria.

Clark also felt on edge. In letters to Renie he complained about her failure to send a congratulatory telegram after he captured Rome, then confessed that he was "badly in need of a rest. Never needed one more." An intestinal infection had caused him to lose weight until he was nearly skeletal, despite a bracing regimen of sulfa drugs. Worse yet, on June 10, he was nearly killed when his Piper Grasshopper collided a thousand feet up with a barrage balloon cable. "It wrapped around the wing and we couldn't get loose," Clark wrote. "Finally, in spiraling the third time, losing altitude rapidly, the cable became disengaged, although it tore the wing and ripped open the gas tank. . . . We miraculously got down into a cornfield . . . I never had a worse experience." On July 4 he wrote Renie, "You ask the question, 'What after Italy?' Perhaps you can tell me."

Italy would be with him for the rest of the war and beyond. He succeeded Alexander as commander of the army group and received his fourth star in March 1945 at age forty-eight, becoming by far the youngest of the thirteen U.S. officers to wear that rank during World War II. After the war Clark would precede Keyes as high commissioner in Austria before commanding United Nations forces in Korea and eventually serving as president of the Citadel, in Charleston, South Carolina.

The Rapido calamity continued to torment him, particularly when congressional investigators took up the cause of disaffected Texas veterans. To Renie he would write from Vienna in March 1946, "It is the most cruel and unfair attack ever made on an officer who worked so desperately, under such adverse conditions to make what I believed, and still do [believe] was a fine record." Lamenting Eisenhower's silence on the subject, and suspecting his former 36th Division commander of provoking the Texans, Clark added, "I believe Walker is the 'snake in the grass.' " To help commemorate that "fine record," he commissioned an immense history of Fifth Army, in nine volumes.

He would remain among the war's most controversial commanders, a man whose very name more than a half century later could cause brows to knit and lips to purse. If his admirers considered him "clairvoyant and energetic," in the phrase of General Juin, Mauldin spoke for many in the lower ranks in observing of Clark: "He had his limitations. But I think a lot of the criticism of him occurred because he was associated with a bad time."

Those who fought and suffered in Italy—that "tough old gut," as Ernie Pyle called it—were left to extract from the bad time what redemption they could. "Few of us can ever conjure up any truly fond memories of the Italian campaign," Pyle wrote in *Brave Men* in late 1944. "The enemy had been hard, and so had the elements. . . . There was little solace for those who had suffered, and none at all for those who had died, in trying to rationalize about why things had happened as they did."

He continued:

> I looked at it this way—if by having only a small army in Italy we had been able to build up more powerful forces in England, and if by sacrificing a few thousand lives that winter we would save a half million lives in Europe—if those things were true, then it was best as it was.
>
> I wasn't sure they were true. I only knew I had to look at it that way or else I couldn't bear to think of it at all.

Faith and imagination were required to elevate the Italian campaign, to see as the poet Richard Wilbur, a veteran of Cassino and Anzio, saw: "the dreamt land / Toward which all hungers leap, all pleasures pass." Even Pyle, who knew better than most that "war isn't romantic to the people in it," sensed the sublime in moments "of overpowering beauty, of the surge of a marching world, of the relentlessness of our fate."

George Biddle had found that in "misery, destruction, frustration, and death," certain annealed qualities seemed "to give war its justification, meaning, romance, and beauty. The qualities of valor, sacrifice, discipline, a sense of duty." Even Mauldin, that flinty-eyed skeptic, would concede, "I stopped regarding the war as a show to help my career. I felt a seriousness of purpose, and I felt it in my bones." A medic who had landed at Salerno later wrote his wife, "This is something that is born deep inside us, when we come to know *why* we are here, when we have learned how very important it was that we did leave you and all we love."

Somewhere north of Rome, Glenn Gray wrote in his diary: "I watched a full moon sail through a cloudy sky. . . . I felt again the aching beauty of this incomparable land. I remembered everything that I had ever been and was. It was painful and glorious."

Another day passed, and another night. The circling stars glided on their courses. The poets and the dreamers again struck their tents and shouldered their rifles to begin that long, last march.

# NOTES

The following abbreviations appear in the endnotes and bibliography.

**45th ID Mus**   45th Infantry Division Museum, Oklahoma City
**AAF**   Army Air Forces
***AAFinWWII***   W. F. Craven and J. L. Cate, eds., *The Army Air Forces in World War II*, vol. II unless otherwise noted
**AAR**   after action report
*AB*   *After the Battle*
**AD**   armored division
**admin**   administration
**AF**   air force
**AFHQ micro**   Allied Forces Headquarters microfilm, NARA RG 331
**AFHRA**   Air Force Historical Research Agency
**ag**   adjutant general
**AGF**   Army Ground Forces
**ALM**   Audie Leon Murphy papers, USMA Special Collections, West Point
**AR**   armored regiment
**AS**   Armored School
**ASEQ**   Army Service Experiences Questionnaire, MHI
**ASF**   Army Service Forces
**AU**   Air University
***Battle***   W.G.F. Jackson, *The Battle for Italy*
**bde**   brigade
**bn**   battalion
**CA**   working papers for *Cassino to the Alps*
***Calculated***   Mark W. Clark, *Calculated Risk*
**CARL**   Combined Arms Research Library, Fort Leavenworth, Kans.
**CBH**   Chester B. Hansen diary, MHI
**CCS**   Combined Chiefs of Staff
**CEOH**   U.S. Army Corps of Engineers, Office of History
**CGSC**   Command and General Staff School, U.S. Army
**Chandler**   Alfred Chandler, ed., *The Papers of Dwight David Eisenhower: The War Years*
**CINCLANT**   Commander-in-Chief, Atlantic Fleet
**CJB**   Clay and Joan Blair collection, MHI
*CM*   L. K. Truscott, Jr., *Command Missions*
**CMH**   U.S. Army Center of Military History, Fort McNair, Washington, D.C.
**co**   company
**Coakley**   Robert W. Coakley and Richard M. Leighton, *Global Logistics and Strategy, 1943–1945*
**Col U OHRO**   Columbia University Oral History Research Office

**corr**   correspondence
**CSI**   U.S. Army Combat Studies Institute, Fort Leavenworth, Kansas
**ct**   combat team
*CtoA*   Ernest F. Fisher, Jr., *Cassino to the Alps*
**DA**   Department of the Army
**Danchev**   Alex Danchev and Daniel Todman, eds., *War Diaries, 1939–1945: Field Marshal
    Lord Alanbrooke*
**DDE**   Dwight David Eisenhower
**DDE Lib**   Dwight D. Eisenhower Presidential Library
*Destruction*   I.S.O. Playfair and C.J.C. Molony, *The Mediterranean and the Middle East,*
    vol. IV
**diss**   dissertation
**div**   division
**DSC**   Distinguished Service Cross
**DTL**   Donovan Technical Library, now Donovan Research Library
**E**   entry
**EJD**   Ernest J. Dawley, including papers at Hoover Institution Archive
**ENH**   Ernest N. Harmon, including papers at U.S. Army Military History Institute
**ETO**   European Theater of Operations
**FA**   field artillery
*FAJ*   *Field Artillery Journal*
**FCP**   Forrest C. Pogue, including background material for *The Supreme Commander*
**FDR Lib**   Franklin D. Roosevelt Presidential Library
**FLW**   Fred L. Walker
**FMS**   Foreign Military Studies
**FOIA**   Freedom of Information Act
*FRUS*   *Foreign Relations of the United States: The Conferences at Washington and Quebec,*
    *1943*
**Ft. K**   Fort Knox, Ky.
**Ft. L**   Fort Leavenworth, Kans.
**Garland**   Albert N. Garland and Howard McGaw Smyth, *Sicily and the Surrender of Italy*
**GCM Lib**   George C. Marshall Library, Lexington, Va.
**GK**   Geoffrey Keyes, including diary, author's possession
*GS IV*   Michael Howard, *Grand Strategy,* vol. IV
*GS V*   John Ehrman, *Grand Strategy,* vol. V
**GSP**   George S. Patton, Jr., including papers at the Library of Congress
**Hansen**   draft of Omar Bradley's *A Soldier's Story,* C. B. Hansen, MHI
**HCB**   Harry C. Butcher, including papers
**HIA**   Hoover Institution Archives, Stanford University
**Hill/O'Neill**   "Report of Col. William H. Hill and Col. E. J. O'Neill on Conference Held
    in Marrakech, March 10, 1994, JPL papers, MHI, box 4, 1
**HKH**   Henry Kent Hewitt Papers
**Hq**   headquarters
**ID**   infantry division
*IJ*   *Infantry Journal*
**inf**   infantry
**intel**   intelligence
**Iowa GSM**   Iowa Gold Star Museum, Fort Dodge, Iowa
**IS**   Infantry School, Fort Benning, Ga.
**IWM**   Imperial War Museum, London
**JAG**   U.S. Army judge advocate general
**JCS**   Joint Chiefs of Staff

**JJT** John J. Toffey, IV, "A Game for the Young," author's possession
**JMG** James M. Gavin papers
**JPL** John P. Lucas, including diary, "From Algiers to Anzio," MHI
**LH** Basil Henry Liddell Hart
**LHC** Liddell Hart Centre for Military Archives, King's College, London
**lib** library
**LKT Jr.** Lucian K. Truscott, Jr.
**LOC MS Div** Library of Congress Manuscript Division
**MAAF** Mediterranean Allied Air Forces
**MBR** Matthew B. Ridgway
**MCC** Mina Curtiss Collection
**MEB** Magna E. Bauer
**Med** Mediterranean
**MHI** U.S. Army Military History Institute, Carlisle, Pa.
**micro** microfilm
**Molony V** C.J.C. Molony et al., *The Mediterranean and Middle East,* vol. V
**Molony VI** C.J.C. Molony, *The Mediterranean and Middle East,* vol. VI, part 1
**MP** military police
*MR* *Military Review*
**MRC FDM** McCormick Research Center, First Division Museum, Cantigny, Ill.
**msg** message
**mss** manuscript
**MTOUSA** Mediterranean Theater of Operations, United States Army
**MWC** Mark Wayne Clark, including papers at the Citadel, S.C., Archives and Museum
**N Af** North Africa
**n.d.** no date
**NARA** National Archives and Records Administration, College Park, Md.
**NATOUSA** North African Theater of Operations, United States Army
**NHC** Naval Historical Center, Washington, D.C.
**NSA** National Security Agency
*NWAf* George F. Howe, *Northwest Africa: Seizing the Initiative in the West*
**NWC Lib** National War College Library
*NYT* *New York Times*
**obit** obituary
**OCMH** Office of the Chief of Military History
**OCNO** Office of the Chief of Naval Operations
**OCS** Office of the Chief of Staff
**OH** oral history
**OPD** Operations Division, War Department
**OSS** Office of Strategic Services
**OW** Orlando Ward Papers
**Para** parachute
**pm** provost marshal
**PMR** Paul McD. Robinett papers
*PP* Martin Blumenson, *The Patton Papers, 1940–1945*
**PP-pres** Papers, Pre-presidential
*Proceedings* *U.S. Naval Institute Proceedings*
**Pyle** Ernie Pyle, *Brave Men*
**qm** quartermaster
**regt** regiment
**RG** record group
**RN** Royal Navy

**ROHA**   Rutgers University Oral History Archives of World War II
**s.p.**   self-published
**SC**   Signal Corps
**SEM**   Samuel Eliot Morison Office Files
**SM**   Sidney T. Matthews, including papers at MHI
**SMH**   Society for Military History
**SOOHP**   Senior Officer Oral History Program
**SOS**   Services of Supply
*SSA*   Samuel Eliot Morison, *Sicily-Salerno-Anzio,* vol. IX, *History of United States Naval Operations in World War II*
**SSI**   working papers for *Sicily and the Surrender of Italy,* National Archives
*SSt*   Omar N. Bradley, *A Soldier's Story*
*StoC*   Martin Blumenson, *Salerno to Cassino, USAWWII*
**td**   tank destroyer
**TdA**   Terry de la Mesa Allen, including papers
*Texas*   Fred L. Walker, *From Texas to Rome*
**Texas MFM**   Texas Military Forces Museum, Austin
*Three Years*   Harry C. Butcher, *My Three Years with Eisenhower*
**TR**   Theodore Roosevelt III Papers
**ts**   typescript
**UK NA**   National Archive, Kew, United Kingdom (formerly Public Record Office)
**USAF HRC**   U.S. Air Force Historical Research Center
**USAF**   U.S. Air Force
*USAWWII*   *United States Army in World War II*
**USMA Arch**   U.S. Military Academy Archives, West Point
**USMC**   U.S. Marine Corps
**USN**   U.S. Navy
**USNA**   U.S. Naval Academy, Annapolis, Md.
**USNAd**   "U.S. Naval Administration in World War II"
**USNI OHD**   U.S. Naval Institute, Oral History Department, Annapolis, Md.
**UTEP**   University of Texas at El Paso
**UT-K**   University of Tennessee, Knoxville, Center for the Study of War and Society
**VHP**   Veterans' History Project, National Folklife Center, Library of Congress
**WD**   War Department
*WP*   *Washington Post*
**WSC**   Winston S. Churchill
**WTF**   Western Task Force
**WWII**   World War II
**XO**   executive officer
**YU**   Yale University Library, Manuscripts and Archives

### EPIGRAPH

IX   Virgil, *The Aeneid,* trans. Robert Fagles (New York: Viking, 2006), book 7 lines 747–51.

### PROLOGUE

1   *She could be heard: NYT,* Cunard Line advertising supplement, Apr. 2004, ZM1; David Williams, *Liners in Battledress,* 114 (*Western Approaches*); Harold Larson, "Troop Transports in WWII," ts, March 1945, CMH, 4-13.1 AA12, 21–22.
1   *She slid:* corr, Lovetta Kramer, exec. dir, RMS *Queen Mary* Foundation and Archive, Long Beach, Calif., to author, Aug. 16, 2004; corr, Lorna Williams, Special Collections

and Archives, University of Liverpool, to author, Aug. 2004; William J. Duncan, *RMS Queen Mary: Queen of the Queens*, 78–79, 106 (*New York warehouse*); Steve Harding, *Gray Ghost*, 49 (*WW #21 W*); admin memo, Offices of the War Cabinet, May 3, 1943, UK NA, PREM 4/72/2 (*Scottish cages*); John Mason Brown, *To All Hands*, 203 ("*barbarities*"); Louis E. Keefer, *Italian Prisoners of War in America*, 35, 41; "Enemy POW Camps in the USA in World War II," CMH, Historical Resources Branch, Nov. 5, 1942, 2 (*272,000*); "Office of the Provost Marshal General: World War II, a Brief History," ts, 1946, CMH, 4-4 AA (*forty degrees*); Arnold P. Krammer, "German Prisoners of War in the United States," *Military Affairs*, Apr. 1976, 67+ (*piano lessons*); Gregory Kupsky, UT-K, paper, SMH, Bethesda, Md., May 21, 2004 (*Sears Roebuck*).

2  *But it was on the upper decks:* Danchev, 402 (*Officers crowded*); "Notes for Mr. Aubrey Morgan," May 13, 1943, UK NA, PREM 4/72/2 (*suite number 105*).

2  *To mislead potential spies:* Duncan, 117–18 (*Wilhelmina*); Winston S. Churchill, *The Hinge of Fate*, 783; Alexander S. Cochran, Jr., "Spectre of Defeat: Anglo-American Planning for the Invasion of Italy in 1943," Ph.D. diss, U of Kansas, 296 (*wheelchair ramps*); John Kennedy, *The Business of War*, 293 ("*well and fat and pink*").

2  *Like the* Queen Mary: Harold Evans, "Roy Jenkins' 'Churchill: His Finest Hour,' " *NYT Book Review*, Nov. 11, 2001, 1 ("*largest human being*"); Charles Richardson, *From Churchill's Secret Circle to the BBC*, 189 (*trombone*); Churchill Museum and Cabinet War Rooms, Whitehall, London (*one of the eight*); Arthur Bryant, *The Turn of the Tide*, 587 (*scented handkerchief*); admin memo, War Cabinet, May 3, 1943 (*ten-pound tip* and *Mumm's Cordon Rouge*); Paul Fussell, *Wartime*, 183 ("*gangster clergyman*").

3  "*We are all worms*": Churchill Museum; Martin Gilbert, *Winston Churchill's War Leadership*, 14 (*to be awakened*), 74 ("*pester, nag*"); Danchev, 451 ("*temperamental like a film star*"); Merle Miller, *Ike the Soldier*, 512 ("*He shouts me down*").

3  "*In great things*": Kennedy, 315; Winston S. Churchill, *Closing the Ring*, 658, 685, 660, 662 (*small things*); Martin Gilbert, *Winston Churchill's War Leadership*, 19 ("*There is no defeat*").

3  *Sea voyages always reinvigorated:* Richardson, 187 ("*Master*"); Gilbert, 10 (*silent Remington*); Churchill Museum (*Johnnie Walker*); W. Averell Harriman and Elie Abel, *Special Envoy to Churchill and Stalin*, 204–5 ("*I won't be captured*"), 207 ("*splitting infinitives*"); Lord Moran, *Churchill: Taken from the Diaries of Lord Moran*, 101 ("*all hunched up*"); W. H. Thompson, *I Was Churchill's Shadow*, 114–15 (*discussing seamanship*); admin memo, War Cabinet, May 3, 1943 (*watching films*); NYT, May 12, 1943, 24 (*Radio Berlin*); Churchill, *Closing the Ring*, 91 ("*Who in war*").

4  *Churchill had proposed:* Harriman and Abel, 202 ("*One can always*"); "Notes for Mr. Aubrey Morgan" (*entire company stood*).

4  *Packed into the* Magellan: Churchill Museum (*colored yarn*); Arthur Bryant, *The Turn of the Tide*, 595, 652 (*six thousand miles*).

5  *Victory in North Africa*: Ralph Bennett, "Ultra and Some Command Decisions," in Walter Laqueur, ed., *The Second World War*, 218 ("*cryptologists had cracked*"); GS IV, 450 (*forty-seven U-boats*); David M. Kennedy, *Freedom from Fear*, 590 (*more than 3,500* and *submariner casualty rate*); C.B.A. Behrens, *Merchant Shipping and the Demands of War*, 368 (*every eight hours*).

5  *Elsewhere in this global war:* Gerhard L. Weinberg, *A War at Arms*, 590, 632–33, 637.

6  *On the Eastern Front:* GS V, 2; Matthew Cooper, *The German Army*, 451–52 (*lost thirty divisions*), 448 ("*absolutely sick*"); Ray S. Cline, *Washington Command Post: The Operations Division*, 220 (*Soviet counteroffensive*).

6  *And yet: the Red Army remained:* GS V, 2; Martin Gilbert, *The Second World War*, 421 (*1.3 million forced laborers*).

6  *The next Anglo-American blow:* SSA, 10; David Hunt, *A Don at War*, 184 (*a postscript*); Maurice Matloff, *Strategic Planning for Coalition Warfare, 1943–1944*, 25–26.

7   *Beyond Sicily:* Anthony Eden, *The Reckoning: The Memoirs of Anthony Eden, Earl of Avon,* 390, 403; Warren F. Kimball, ed., *Churchill and Roosevelt: The Complete Correspondence,* vol. II, 184 (*"Great possibilities"*); Coakley, 63 (*"a chill of loneliness"*); Churchill to H. Hopkins, May 2, 1943, UK NA, PREM 3/443/2 (*"serious divergences"*); Churchill to George VI, Apr. 30, 1943, UK NA, PREM 3/443/2.

7   *"We did not come here":* UK NA, PREM 3/44/2.

7   *Beneath his brass:* Douglas Porch, *The Path to Victory,* 454; G. A. Shepperd, *The Italian Campaign, 1943–45,* 82; John Ellis, *World War II: A Statistical Survey,* 254 (*More than 12 percent*); Gilbert, *The Second World War,* 426 (*British battle deaths*); Martin Gilbert, *Winston S. Churchill,* vol. VII.

8   *Salvation lay here:* "Monthly Strength of the Army," May 31, 1943, CMH (*a thousand generals*); Forrest C. Pogue, *George C. Marshall: Organizer of Victory,* 280 (*aircraft carriers*); Alan Gropman, ed., *The Big L: American Logistics in World War II,* 1n, 73 (*just fifty days*), 89–93; Behrens, 366 (*British merchant fleet*); *NYT,* May 12, 1943, 1 (*"production of airplanes"*).

8   *"the greatest American problem":* *NYT,* May 11, 1943, 1.

8   *Yet at home:* Gropman, ed., 35, 54–55, 89–93, 367 (*full mobilization*); *NYT,* May 10, 1943 (*Wurlitzer*); *The Big Change-Over,* film, Office of Emergency Management, NARA, 208.211 (*lipstick*).

9   *So, too, had the war:* James Ward Lee et al., eds., *1941: Texas Goes to War,* 76–78 (*"Use it up"*); Fussell, 197–98 (*plastic buttons*); John Morton Blum, *V Was for Victory,* 95; Kennedy, *Freedom from Fear,* 645 (*the bikini*); Smithsonian Institution Museum of American History, exhibit, "The Price of Freedom: Americans at War" (*Regulation L-85*).

9   *German prisoners:* Lee et al., eds., 82–83 (*paint-on hosiery*); Fussell, 197 (*"victory speed"*); Dennis B. Worthen, "Pharmacists in World War II," *Journal of the American Pharmaceutical Association,* vol. 41, no. 3 (May–June 2001), 479+ (*toothpaste tubes*); *Salvage,* film, Office of War Information, 1942, NARA, 208.118 (*10 old pails*).

9   *No place in America:* Scott Hart, *Washington at War: 1941–1945,* 40 (*"frenzied capital"*).

10  *To this panoply:* memo, May 11, 1943, Secret Service records, file 103-1: President Roosevelt, 1943, box 5, FDR Lib. (*at 6:45 P.M.*); William D. Leahy, *I Was There,* 158 (*gray pallor*).

10  *But first the visitors:* David Brinkley, *Washington Goes to War,* epigraph (*"bust right out"*), 188, 232, 238; William H. Cartwright, Jr., "The Military District of Washington, 1942–1945," 1946, CMH, 8-2.4 AA, 190 (*twelve thousand hotel rooms*); "Notes for Mr. Aubrey Morgan" (*sixteen Royal Marines*); Hart, 108 (*"tropical post pay"*).

10  *Churchill could sense:* Cartwright, "The Military District of Washington, 1942–1945," 116–18 (*"largest feeding operation"*); Hart, 92, 135 (*"Madhouse"*); *NYT,* May 2, 1943, 3 (*twelve thousand men*); *Washington Evening Star,* May 15, 1943, 1 (*draft dodgers*).

11  *Among other signs:* *NYT,* May 2, 1943 (*"rumor clinics"*); *NYT,* May 9, 1943, 26 (*"White or Colored"*); Brinkley, 185 (*forty-six errors*); *NYT,* May 12, 1943 (*blond hair*).

11  *Amid the mania:* Hart, 178.

11  *They got to work:* William Seale, *The President's House,* vol. II, 918, 937–76; Danchev, 403 (*massive desk*).

11  *Five months earlier:* Matloff, 123; Cline, 219; Garland, 17 (*"grand design"*).

12  *The president's brain trust:* FRUS, 19 (*"The man from London"*); Coakley, 62 (*"No closed minds"*).

12  *"What should come next?":* FRUS, 25–26.

12  *The prime minister had used the phrase:* Cline, 218; GS IV, 145 (*"underbelly"*); FRUS, 25–26; Churchill, *The Hinge of Fate,* 794 (*"occupation of Italy"*). Churchill, in a conversation with Joseph Stalin in August 1942, also used the phrase "soft belly" while sketching a crocodile intended to represented Axis-occupied Europe. Churchill, *The Hinge of Fate,* 481.

13  *There it was, the British strategy:* FRUS, 30; Churchill, *The Hinge of Fate,* 794; John S. D. Eisenhower, *Allies: Pearl Harbor to D-Day,* 63 (*"cigarette-holder gesture"*).

13  *This impasse persisted:* Kenneth S. Davis, *Experience of War,* 393; *FRUS,* 223 ("*Global Strategy of the War*").

13  *A tall, austere man:* Eric Larrabee, *Commander in Chief,* 102–3 (*a clean-desk man*), 99, 112; OH, Gen. Lord Ismay, Oct. 18, 1960, FCP, transcript, tape 40, GCM Lib ("*a little aloof*"); OH, Andrew J. Goodpaster to author, Washington, D.C., Aug. 17, 2004 ("*Are you confident*"); author visit, Dodona Manor (Marshall home), Leesburg, Va., Apr. 1998. Churchill's "greatest Roman" accolade came in 1945.

13  *Invading Italy: FRUS,* 44–45.

14  *Arguments spilled:* Stephen E. Ambrose, *Eisenhower,* vol. I, 242; Garland, 17 (*twelve million tons*); Albert C. Wedemeyer, *Wedemeyer Reports!,* 134 (*lacked sufficient ports*); GS V, 115 ("*side-shows*"); Maurice Matloff, *Strategic Planning for Coalition Warfare, 1943–1944,* 74 ("*unremunerative scatterization*").

14  "*Mediterranean operations*": Wedemeyer, 218.

14  *Listening attentively:* Danchev, 247 ("*great gentleman*"), 448, xvi, xiv ("*Froggie*"), 400; Moran, 121 ("*a year off my life*"); Bryant, 685 ("*the night work*"); David Fraser, *Alanbrooke,* 341 (*Southeran's shop*); Kennedy, 290 (Birds of the Ocean).

15  *Now he quarreled: FRUS,* 225.

15  *Brooke pressed the point: FRUS,* 41–45, 269; Coakley, 64–65.

15  *A stack of studies:* Cochran, "Spectre of Defeat," 297 ("*If Italy collapses*"); Coakley, 64 ("*breaking the Axis*").

15  *But, Brooke warned: FRUS,* 43, 45.

15  *Momentary silence fell:* Wedemeyer, 211 ("*no intention*"); Coakley, 65 ("*divert our forces*").

15  *At Marshall's suggestion:* Danchev, 403.

16  *Washington lacked: GS* IV, 410 (*endless meetings*); "Notes for Mr. Aubrey Morgan" (*black-tie affairs*).

16  *Fans at a Washington Nationals:* "Memoirs of Sir John Dill, 1942–1944," Reginald Winn Collection, GCM Lib, 36; *FRUS,* 39 (*Helen with Paris*); corr, Anna Roosevelt Boettiger to John Boettiger, May 15, 1943, Boettiger Papers, box 5, FDR Lib (*Churchill sat transfixed*).

16  *To escape both official Washington:* Pogue, 202–3.

16  *If Washington had been atwitter:* Gerald Horton Bath, "A Report on the Visit of the British High Command to Colonial Williamsburg, May 15th and 16th, 1943," ts, n.d., Frank McCarthy Collection, box 27, folder 29, GCM Lib.

17  *Sunday morning:* ibid.; Danchev, 423 (Gould's Birds).

18  *While the chiefs went south:* memo, May 11, 1943, Secret Service records, file 103-1: President Roosevelt, 1943, box 5, FDR Lib; Robert Sherwood, *Roosevelt and Hopkins: An Intimate History,* 729 (*Whittier's ballad*); Moran, 101 ("*gabbled the whole poem*").

18  *For three days they unbent:* letter, Anna Roosevelt Boettiger to John Boettiger, May 14, 1943, Boettiger Papers, box 5, FDR Lib ("*picks his teeth*"); Jon Meacham, *Franklin and Winston,* 225, 234 ("*Isn't this a beauty*").

18  *They had much in common:* Larrabee, 13 ("*loved the military side*"); Maurice Matloff, "Mr. Roosevelt's Three Wars: FDR as War Leader," Harmon Lecture, No. 6, U.S. Air Force Academy, 1964, 6 ("*diversionist tendencies*"); Pogue, 316 (*combat casualty figures*); Meacham, 228 ("*a wonderful old Tory*").

19  *Churchill could draw near:* Larrabee, 644; OH, Stephen T. Early, June 9, 1947, MHI, OCMH, WWII, General Miscl ("*wished to have things done*"); Richard Overy, *Why the Allies Won,* 261 ("*Not a tidy mind*"); Larrabee, 644 ("*He* decides").

19  *He reduced his own political philosophy:* Overy, 260; Larrabee, 626 (*Four Freedoms*); Kimball, ed., vol. I, 337 ("*same decade*"); Elliott Roosevelt, *As He Saw It,* 130 ("*on the decline*").

19  *America was ascendant:* memo, Robert Sherwood to Harry Hopkins, May 13, 1943, H. L. Hopkins Papers, Sherwood Collection, book 7, TRIDENT, box 329, FDR Lib.

20  *But if Britain was on the decline:* Harold Macmillan, *War Diaries,* 316 ("*great torso*"); Roosevelt, 126 (*sinus condition*); Matloff, "Mr. Roosevelt's Three Wars," 4–5.

20  *Negotiations resumed:* GS IV, 419 (*"spirit of the chase"*); Garland, 21 (*refused to concede*); FRUS, 114 (*"extremely difficult"*).

20  *It was a curious compromise:* msg, WD to DDE, #278, May 26, 1943, CCS cables, OCMH, NARA RG 319, 270/19/6/3, box 243; GS IV, 432.

21  *The baby had been cut:* Danchev, 407.

21  TRIDENT *had another week:* diary, Henry A. Wallace, May 24, 1943, micro, FDR Lib (*"We Anglo-Saxons"*); Danchev (*fourteen stone steps*); Fraser, 346–47 (*two rare bird books*).

21  *Rarely content:* FRUS, May 23, 1943; Doris Kearns Goodwin, *No Ordinary Time,* 439 (*exhausted president*); Leahy, 162; Moran, 103–4 (*"a very tired man"*).

22  *Harry Hopkins warned:* Goodwin, 439 (*"spoiled boy"*); FRUS, 198 (*"piece of baggage"*); Moran, 111 (*"too much for us"*).

22  *Still, the sweep of his rhetoric:* Gerald Pawle, *The War and Colonel Warden,* 234; Gilbert, *Winston S. Churchill,* vol. VII, 409 (*"War is full of mysteries"*); *Times* (London), May 20, 1943, 4 (*"By singleness of purpose"*); Grace Tully, *F.D.R., My Boss,* 329 (*"catch phrases"*).

23  *For the first time:* Harriman and Abel, 211; Leahy, 165 (*"mellow light"*); FRUS, 377 (*"complete meeting of minds"*).

23  *"over-egged the pudding":* Brian Holden Reid, "The Italian Campaign, 1943–1945: A Reappraisal of Allied Generalship," *Journal of Strategic Studies,* vol. 13, no. 1 (March 1990), 128+.

23  *"the best I could get":* Leahy, 163.

24  *The dispatch of Allied armies:* Matloff, 76, 244.

24  *Perhaps the greatest achievement:* André Malraux ("Let victory belong to those who made war without liking it"), quoted by Jean-Paul Sartre, *Modern Times,* cited in Danchev, xxvi.

24  *At four P.M. on Tuesday:* PREM 4/72/3, UK NA.

24  *Roosevelt sat in the armless wheelchair:* Seale, 947, 976–77 (*bulletproof glass*); FRUS, 211–20 (*899th press conference*); *Times* (London), May 27, 1943, 1 (*"shaking the life"*).

## CHAPTER 1: ACROSS THE MIDDLE SEA
### *Forcing the World Back to Reason*

29  *The sun beat down:* corr, Heinz Seltmann to author, June 9, 2005 (*neckties*); memo, GSP, No. 57, June 17, 1943, NARA RG 338, II Corps, plans & policy file, box 146 (*$25 fine*).

29  *Algiers seethed:* Eric Sevareid, *Not So Wild a Dream,* 362 (*merchant mariners*); Paul W. Brown, *The Whorehouse of the World,* 134–35 (*"El Alamein"*); Benjamin A. Dickson, "G-2 Journal: Algiers to the Elbe," MHI, 76 (*"Sand in your shoes"*); Peter Schrijvers, *The Crash of Ruin,* 120 (*index fingers*).

29  *Electric streetcars:* memo, DDE to E. Hughes, July 23, 1943, PP-pres, DDE Lib, box 58 (*amnesty*); Malcolm S. McLean, "Adventures in Occupied Areas," ts, 1975, MHI, 31–32 (*"every conceivable"*); Sevareid, 361 (*young Frenchmen* and *Hotel Aletti*); F. Eugene Liggett, "No, Not Yet: Military Memoirs," ts, n.d., ASEQ, 158th FA, 45th Div., MHI (*pantaloons*); "History, Mediterranean Base Section, Sept. 1942–May 1944," CMH, 9-4 CA, 1944 (*ban on prostitution*).

30  *Above it all:* "History of Allied Forces Headquarters," CMH, 8-4 AD, vol. 2, Sept. 1945, sketch.

30  *Hewitt lowered his salute:* "U.S. Naval Operations in the Northwestern African-Mediterranean Theater," ts, n.d., HKH papers, box 3, NHC, 18.

30  *With the ceremony at an end:* "History of Allied Forces Headquarters," 243–46 (*approached four thousand*); "The Administrative History of the Eighth Fleet," ts, n.d., U.S. Naval History Division, #139, folder 3, 9–10 (*twelve thousand*); "Notes for Meeting with Colonel Warden," Jan. 14, 1944, NARA RG 331, AFHQ micro, R-225-B (*seven undersea cables*); S. W. Roskill, *The War at Sea, 1939–1945,* vol. III, part 1, 127 (*"Carry out"*).

31 *He was a fighting admiral:* OH, Floride Hewitt Taylor to author, Apr. 12, 2005, Newport, R.I.; L.S.B. Shapiro, *They Left the Back Door Open,* 118 (*"well-upholstered"*); OH, HKH, John T. Mason, 1961, Col U OHRO, 5–6 (*"Softly Now"*); "Keuffel & Esser correspondence," HKH, NHC, box 2; George Sessions Perry, "Why Don't They Write About Hewitt?," *Saturday Evening Post,* Dec. 16, 1944, 22+ (*"does his barking"*); OH, HKH, n.d., Julian Boit and James Riley, NHC, box 6, 1–2, 9 (*soup kitchen*).

31 *He called for his staff car:* Walter Karig, *Battle Report: The Atlantic War,* 233; David Williams, *Liners in Battledress,* 151–53 (*false bow wave*); Ivan H. "Cy" Peterman, "U.S.S. *Savannah,*" *Philadelphia Inquirer,* Sept. 1943, SEM, box 55, NHC; Pyle, 6–7 (*Precautions against fire*).

32 *Hewitt's flagship:* war log, U.S.S. *Monrovia,* NARA RG 38, OCNO, WWII war diaries, box 1233; Karig, 233 (*ten to twenty officers*); A. J. Redway, "Admiral Jerauld Wright: The Life and Recollections of the Supreme Allied Commander," ts, 1995, NHC, 295 (*fourteen hundred men*); action report, U.S.S. *Monrovia,* July 17, 1943, NARA RG 38, OCNO, WWII Action & Operational Reports, box 1231 (*200,000 rounds*).

32 *Twenty typists:* Alexander S. Cochran, "Chicken or Eggs? Operations TORCH and HUSKY and U.S. Army Amphibious Doctrine," paper, 14th Naval History Symposium, USNA, Sept. 1999.

32 *Hewitt could remember:* Perry, "Why Don't They Write About Hewitt?"; OH, Floride Hewitt Taylor to author, Apr. 12, 2005.

33 *More than three thousand:* No two lists agree on the total number of vessels in HUSKY; estimates generally range from 2,500 to 3,200. Roskill, 127; *SSA,* 28; HKH, AAR, "The Sicilian Campaign," n.d., 1; "The Administrative History of the Eighth Fleet," 20 (*"the most gigantic fleet"*).

33 *tiny fortified island of Pantelleria:* Edith C. Rodgers, "The Reduction of Pantelleria and Adjacent Islands," May 1947, AAF Historical Studies, No. 52, Air Historical Office, 40–45; "Allied Commander-in-Chief's Report, Pantelleria Operations, June 1943," 59–60; MEB, "The Fall of Pantelleria and the Pelagian Islands," Feb. 1959, NARA RG 319, E 145, OCMH, R-Series Manuscripts, 270/19/30-31/6-2, R-115, 24–32a; memo, "Lessons from Operations Against Pantelleria," July 12, 1943, AFHQ, "Survey and Analysis," Pantelleria, CMH, Geog Italy, 384.3; Solly Zuckerman, *From Apes to Warlords,* 185–95.

33 *A map of the Mediterranean:* Robert A. Hewitt, SOOHP, Earl D. Bevan, 1982, MHI, 126; Thaddeus V. Tuleja, "H. Kent Hewitt," in Stephen Howarth, ed., *Men of War,* 315 (*two variables*).

33 *nine new variations of landing craft:* S.W.C. Pack, *Operation Husky,* 44; Evelyn M. Cherpak, ed., *The Memoirs of Admiral H. Kent Hewitt,* 181 (*never been to sea*); "Notes on the Planning and Assault Phases of the Sicilian Campaign," Combined Operations HQ Bulletin No. Y/1, Oct. 1943, 4 (*little was known*).

33 *Much had been learned:* Harold Larson, "Handling Army Cargo in the Second World War," ts, 1945, CMH, 4-13.1 AA 19, 242, 250 (*Schenectady Plan*); H. H. Dunham, "U.S. Army Transportation and the Conquest of Sicily," Mongraph No. 13, March 1945, NARA RG 336, Chief of Transportation, ASF, Historical Program Files, box 141, 29 (*no plans for loading*); Walter B. Smith, "Mediterranean Operations," Oct. 13, 1943, ANSCOL, L-2-43, SM-67, NARA RG 334, NWC Lib, 4 (*neglected to make room*); HKH, AAR, "The Sicilian Campaign," n.d., 47 (*Every unit pleaded*).

34 *Despite the risk:* AAR, Amphibious Force Transport QM, U.S. Atlantic Fleet, Aug. 6, 1943, in Army Observers, Amphibious Forces, MHI, 1–2; William Reginald Wheeler, ed., *The Road to Victory: A History of Hampton Roads Port of Embarkation in World War II,* 99; "The Administrative History of the Eighth Fleet," 35 (*no bread pans*).

34 *gas shells:* Eventually the mustard would turn up in several Sicilian ammo dumps, including a stockpile fifty miles inland at Nicosia, three weeks into the campaign. "History of Ordnance Service in the Mediterranean Theater, Nov. 1942–Nov. 1945," CMH, 8-4 JA, 54.

34 *"I was frequently partisan"*: "The Reminiscences of George W. Bauernschmidt," 1969–70, USNI OHD, 160.

34 *A satire of censorship regulations*: John Mason Brown, *To All Hands*, 193–94.

34 *One airman tried to comply*: Fred Howard, *Whistle While You Wait*, 160; Steve Kluger, *Yank*, 101 (*"headed for trouble"*).

34 *More than half a million*: "Summary of Activities," analysis and control div., NATOUSA, June 1, 1944, CMH, 3; Brown, *To All Hands*, 7 (*civilian occupations*).

35 *"fierce world of death"*: Pyle, 2.

35 *In the seven weeks*: E. N. Harmon to GCM, Aug. 13, 1943, GCM Lib, corr, box 70 (*"question of discipline"*); JPL, 13–14 (*"felt very sorry"*); Bernard Stambler, "Campaign in Sicily," ts, n.d., vol. 2, CMH, 2-3.7 AA.L, 3 (*"self-maiming"*); corr, Joseph T. Dawson to family, May 22, 1943, 16th Inf, MRC-FDM (*"self-commiseration"*).

35 *"sense of the soldiering self"*: Samuel Hynes, *The Soldiers' Tale*, 151; *They were young*: "Age of Soldiers in Civil War, World War I and World War II," Legislative and Policy Precedent File, 183/122, NARA RG 407, 270/49/17/7, box 34; John Muirhead, *Those Who Fall*, 9 (*"our youth"*).

35 *"our most democratic war"*: Samuel Hynes, introduction, *Reporting World War II*, one-vol. abridgment, xx; *The Princeton Class of 1942 During World War II*; Lynn H. Nicholas, *The Rape of Europa*, 223 (*"men of a new profession"*).

36 *And what did they believe*: "Extract from Monthly Sanitary Report," Aug. 31, 1943, MWC, corr, Citadel, box 3; Eric Larrabee, *Commander in Chief*, 626 (*Four Freedoms*); Chandler, vol. II, 1276 (*"less than half"*); Margaret Bourke-White, *Purple Heart Valley*, 73 (*"I was drafted"*).

36 *Their pervasive "civilianness"*: Brown, *To All Hands*, 224; Donald McB. Curtis, *The Song of the Fighting First*, 132; Lawrence D. Collins, *The 56th Evac Hospital*, 90; Paul Dickson, *War Slang*, 113–23; *Three Years*, 389 (*A single crude acronym*).

36 *Yet they held*: Brown, *To All Hands*, 224; George Biddle, *Artist at War*, 123; John Sloan Brown, *Draftee Division*, 103 (*"lick those bastards"*).

36 *The same surveys*: Larrabee, 626.

36 "Many of the men": George Sessions Perry, "A Reporter at Large," *New Yorker*, July 24, 1943, 50+; Muirhead, 106–7 (*"could not bear the shame"*).

37 *"a gentle obsolescent breed"*: Samuel Hynes, *The Soldiers' Tale*, 143.

37 *"fighting for their right to be hypocrites"*: corr, George Henry Revelle, Jr., to Evelyn, July 7, 1943, author's possession.

37 *Across the great southern rim*: Paul A. Cundiff, *45th Infantry CP*, 6; Hamilton H. Howze, *A Cavalryman's Story*, 78–79; Hamilton H. Howze, "35 Years and Then Some," ts, n.d., Howze papers, box 10, MHI, VII, 1–2 (*locust swarms*); Charles F. Ryan et al., "2nd Armored Division in the Sicilian Campaign," May 1950, AS, Ft. K, 57 (*a hundred flatcars*); Donald E. Houston, *Hell on Wheels*, 148 (*engineer at gunpoint*).

37 *the 45th Infantry Division*: "History of Planning Division, Army Service Forces," vol. 1, n.d., CMH, 3-2.2 AA, 90–92; Joseph Bykofsky and Harold Larson, *The Transportation Corps: Operations Overseas*, 195; Cundiff, 19; Wheeler, 86 (*mine detectors*); Alfred M. Beck et al., *The Corps of Engineers: The War Against Germany*, 133 (*all nineteen troop-ships*); Leo J. Meyer, "Strategy and Logistical History: MTO," ts, n.d., CMH, 2-3.7 CC5, XIII-61 (*ordered to the Pacific*); Emajean Jordan Buechner, *Sparks*, 64 (*Company J*); Don Robinson, *News of the 45th*, 52 (*iced tea*); Brown, *To All Hands*, 27, 41, 228 (*"Happy Hour"*).

38 *The 45th was a National Guard division*: E. J. Kahn, Jr., "Education of an Army," *New Yorker*, vol. 20, no. 35, Oct. 14, 1944, 28+; Flint Whitlock, *The Rock of Anzio*, 18–19 (*"no good"*); Peter R. Mansoor, *The GI Offensive in Europe*, 102 (*"better prepared"*); unit history, Ben C. Garbowski, ASEQ, 157th Inf., MHI; Frank Farner, ed., *Thunderbird: 45th Infantry Division*, 15 (*Wolftown Guards*); Whitlock, 20–21; George A. Fisher, *The Story of the 180th Infantry Regiment* (*war dance*).

38  *Chancre Alley:* Loyd J. Biss, "Three Years, Four Months and Twenty-seven Days," ts, n.d., author's possession, 19; Fred Sheehan, *Anzio: Epic of Bravery,* 48 (*"provost marshal's report"*); Frank James Price, *Troy H. Middleton: A Biography,* 146 (*brandy*); Kenneth D. Williamson, "Tales of a Thunderbird," ts, n.d., 45th ID Mus, 73, 84, 87 (*scooping up dimes*).

38  *Along with the money:* DDE to CG, NATOUSA SOS, June 3, 1943, NARA RG 165, E 422, OPD Exec Files, box 16; OH, John E. Hull, 1974, SOOHP, James W. Wurman, MHI, 57 (*bayonets too dull*).

39  *Three hundred and forty crow-flying miles:* Quentin Reynolds, *The Curtain Rises,* 309–10; Cherpak, ed., 188–89.

39  *"solid forest of masts":* "Notes on PT History in Mediterranean: Letter from LCDR S. M. Barnes, commander of Motor Torpedo Squadron 15, to CDR Bulkley," n.d., SEM, NHC, box 54, 33; memo, Bert M. Rudd, "Landing Craft and Bases," AGF Observer, July 16, 1943, ANSCOL, NARA RG 334, NWC Lib, box 150, 1 (*"into anchored vessels"*); Edmund F. Ball, *Staff Officer with the Fifth Army,* 344 (*"Poems are made"*); Paul W. Pritchard, "Smoke Generator Operations in the Mediterranean and European Theaters of Operation," Chemical Corps, n.d., CMH, 4-7.1 FA 1; Pyle, 6 (*Luftwaffe raiders*); Anders Kjar Arnbal, *The Barrel-Land Dance Hall Rangers,* 100 (*steel hail*); Nigel Nicolson, *The Grenadier Guards in the War of 1939–1945,* vol. II, 347 (*"Bring up your children"*).

39  *"Florida":* OH, William Francis Powers, Aug. 1985, CEOH.

39  *None of the namesake camps:* Howard, 30, 103 (*"wog wine"*); AAR, 3/26th Inf, July 1–5, 1943, MRC FDM; Jean Gordon Peltier, *World War II Diary of Jean Gordon Peltier,* 91–92 (*peppermint*); AAR, "1st Embarkation Group, Eastern Base Section," Aug. 1943, CARL, N-2763, 39–48 (*German field ranges*); Maxwell D. Taylor, *Swords and Plowshares,* 48; Clifford W. Dorman, "Too Soon for Heroes," ts, n.d., author's possession, 57 (*TNT*); diary, July 7, 1943, JMG, MHI, box 10 (*ten young bulls*).

40  *They were in an ugly mood:* T. Michael Booth and Duncan Spencer, *Paratrooper: The Life of Gen. James M. Gavin,* 95; AAR, "1st Embarkation Group," 61 (*twenty-three copies*).

40  *Congestion and confusion:* AAR, "1st Embarkation Group," 51; Lida Mayo, *The Ordnance Department: On Beachhead and Battlefront,* 159 (*ammunition dump*); "Personal Diary of Langan W. Swent," July 7, 1943, HIA, box 1 (*novice boat crews*).

40  *Still farther east:* H. Essame, *Patton: A Study in Command,* 99 (*"gypsy camp"*); Alex Bowlby, *The Recollections of Rifleman Bowlby,* 12 (maleesh); P. Royle, ts, 1972, IWM 99/72/1, 82 (*desert sores*); Neil McCallum, *Journey with a Pistol,* 132 (*"bloody fuckers"*).

41  *"Daisy, daisy":* Christopher Buckley, *Road to Rome,* 11, 21; A. W. Valentine, *We Landed in Sicily and Italy: A Story of the Devons,* 9 (*"bathing parade"*); C. Richard Eke, "A Game of Soldiers," ts, n.d., IWM 92/1/1, 6 (*"desert campfire"*); Malcolm Munthe, *Sweet Is War,* 162 (*kilted pipers*).

41  *On July 5:* David Cole, *Rough Road to Rome,* 15; Robert Wallace, *The Italian Campaign,* 8 (*wigwagged*); Peter Roach, *The 8.15 to War,* 108, 110 (*"Like fat cattle"*).

41  *The* Monrovia *singled up:* war log, U.S.S. *Monrovia,* July 6, 1943, NARA RG 38, OCNO, WWII war diaries, box 1233; Karig, 234; H. Kent Hewitt, "Naval Aspects of the Sicilian Campaign," *Proceedings,* vol. 79, no. 7, July 1943, 705+ (*"Have a good trip"*).

42  *Despite elaborate security:* AAR, "1st Embarkation Group," 50; Oscar W. Koch, *G-2: Intelligence for Patton,* 35; David Hunt, *A Don at War,* 193 (*gabardine uniform*).

42  *As Hewitt paced:* Beck, 124; *The Sicilian Campaign,* 157 (*hospital ships*).

42  *As for the eighty thousand:* "The Administrative History of the Eighth Fleet," 27 (*warehouse prices*); corr, HKH to SEM, Sept. 18, 1953, SEM, NHC, box 51 (*headquarters ship*); OH, HKH, 1961, John T. Mason, Col U OHRO, 325; memo, "Command of Landing Arrangement HUSKY," GK to HKH, Apr. 12, 1943, HKH, NHC, box 1 (*Patton's refusal*); John T. Mason, Jr., *The Atlantic War Remembered,* 279 (*"Sit down!"*); Cherpak, ed., 183; OH, HKH, n.d., Julian Boit and James Riley, NHC, box 6, 2 (*To celebrate*).

43 *At five P.M.:* Hewitt, "Naval Aspects of the Sicilian Campaign," 705; war log, U.S.S. *Monrovia,* July 6, 1943, NARA RG 38, OCNO, WWII war diaries, box 1233 (*sailing pattern no. 35*).

43 *Behind the bridge:* corr, GSP to Bea, July 2, 1943, GSP, LOC MS Div, box 10; JPL, 34; diary, July 25, 1943, GSP, LOC, box 2, folder 15 ("*our weak spot*"); *PP,* 233 ("*mental fog*").

43 *He was ready: PP,* 260, 264, 270; memo, GSP, June 5, 1943, in Russell L. Moses, ASEQ, 179th Inf Regt., 45th ID, MHI (*tactical adages*).

44 "*a timid man*": JPL, 24–25; Martin Blumenson, *Patton: The Man Behind the Legend, 1885–1945,* 12–17; diary, July 1, 1943, GSP, LOC, box 3, folder 1 (*whine of bullets*); D. Clayton James, *A Time for Giants,* 225 ("*a disturbing element*"); Blumenson, *Patton: The Man Behind the Legend,* 77 ("*Someday I will*").

44 "*Battle is the most*": Harry H. Semmes, *Portrait of Patton,* 155; diary, June 27, 1943, GSP, LOC, box 2, folder 15 ("*a sacred trust*").

44 "*There is no better death*": Brown, *The Whorehouse of the World,* 131; Robert H. Patton, *The Pattons,* 264 ("*to blood them*"); Charles R. Codman, *Drive,* 99 ("*hate builder*").

44 "*You son of a bitch*": Albert C. Wedemeyer, SOOHP, Anthony S. Deskis, 1972–73, MHI; Wiley H. O'Mohundro, "From Mules to Missiles," ts, n.d., MHI, 47 ("*I am a chaplain*").

44 *To a dilatory officer:* John A. Heintges, SOOHP, Jack A. Pellicci, 1974, 156–59; *SSt,* 119 ("*That temper of his*").

45 "*What would Jackson*": Susan H. Godson, *Viking of Assault,* 65; Michael Carver, ed., *The War Lords,* 558 (*pilot's license*).

45 "*Read up on Cromwell*": Stanley P. Hirshson, *General Patton: A Soldier's Life,* 353); Ellen Birkett Morris, "The Woman Behind the Man," *The Patton Saber,* newsletter, Patton Museum Foundation, fall 2002, 1 (*rice powder*); R. H. Patton, *The Pattons,* 251 ("*What a man*").

45 "*I have no premonitions*": *PP,* 273; diary, May 7, 1943, GSP, LOC MS Div, box 2, folder 15 ("*my fate*").

45 *Patton had designed:* corr, Oscar W. Koch to James A. Norell, Dec. 15, 1960, NARA RG 319, OCMH, box 250; MWC, "General Patton," ts, n.d., Subject Files, MWC, Citadel, box 70, 4 ("*If you charge*"); Taylor, 49 ("*you bastards*").

46 *From east and west:* Perry, "A Reporter at Large," 50; Dickson, *War Slang,* 113–33.

46 *At last the troops learned:* Brown, *To All Hands,* 83–86; Peterman, "U.S.S. *Savannah*" (*anxious landlubbers*); Thucydides, *History of the Peloponnesian War,* trans. Rex Warner, 537.

46 *The Monrovia steamed past Bizerte:* war log, U.S.S. *Monrovia,* July 7–8, 1943, NARA RG 38, OCNO, WWII war diaries, box 1233; Bernard Stambler, "Campaign in Sicily," ts, n.d., vol. 2, CMH, 2-3.7 AA.L, 45; Pyle, 8; "Convoy to Gaeta," combat narrative #210, 1944, "WWII Histories and Historical Reports," OCNO, NHC ("*must be afloat*").

## Calypso's Island

46 *FINANCE:* "Geographical Code for Operation HUSKY," May 17, 1943, AFHQ G-2, NARA RG 319, OCMH, box 250; Karl Baedeker, *Southern Italy and Sicily,* 402 (*St. Paul*); Homer, *The Odyssey,* trans. Robert Fagles, 34, 78–80, 153–57.

47 *In 1530:* John Gunther, *D Day,* 155–57; Douglas Porch, *The Path to Victory,* 15–16 (*illiterate peasants*).

47 *The first of 3,340:* "Malta C.G.," *AB,* No. 10, 1975, 1+; Gunther, *D Day,* 85, 157–58; Charles A. Jellison, *Besieged: The World War II Ordeal of Malta, 1940–1942,* 166, 258, 178 ("*Beauty was slain*").

47 *Those not killed:* Jellison, 111, 133, 167, 174n, 221, 229; Gunther, *D Day,* 86 (*learned to live without*); Jack Belden, *Still Time to Die,* 197 (*contraceptives*).

47 *victory in North Africa:* Viscount Cunningham of Hyndhope, *A Sailor's Odyssey,* 532; James Leasor, *The Clock with Four Hands,* 255–56 (*"too thin and listless"*); Gunther, *D Day,* 43, 82 (*Indian cigarettes*); code, appendix 2, communication plan, MTOUSA SOS, NARA RG 492, 290/55/1-2/7-1, box 2738 (*BULLDOGS*).

48 *"Everyone was on tiptoe":* William Ernest Victor Abraham, "Time Off for War," ts, n.d., LHC, 69.

48 *Motorcyclists with numbers:* "Malta C.G.," 1+; Charles Cruickshank, *Deception in World War II,* 53–54 (*radio traffic*); F.A.E. Crew, *The Army Medical Services,* vol. III, 14–15 (*hospital port*); HCB, July 10, 1943, DDE Lib, A-559; Michael J. McKeough and Richard Lockridge, *Sgt. Mickey and General Ike,* 85 (*lucky coins*).

48 *"There are several rooms":* Gunther, *D Day,* 49–50; Kenneth S. Davis, *Soldier of Democracy,* 428 (*"it'll do"*).

49 *Nine months earlier:* David M. Kennedy, *Freedom from Fear,* 689; OH, Hastings L. Ismay, Dec. 17, 1946, FCP, MHI (*"No one else"*).

49 *"incarnation of sincerity":* Kennedy, *Freedom from Fear,* 690; Stephen E. Ambrose, *Eisenhower,* vol. 1, 273 (*"bits of metal"*); James, 95 (*"utterly fair"*); Merle Miller, *Ike the Soldier,* 514; John Kennedy, *The Business of War,* 289 (*"powers of expression"*); Drew Middleton, *Our Share of Night,* 308.

49 *"I'm a born optimist":* Richard Tregaskis, *Invasion Diary,* 54; Kennedy, *Freedom from Fear,* 689 (*"studious reflection"*); John Gunther, *Eisenhower: The Man and the Symbol,* 27 (*"one officer in fifty"*); OH, DDE, Aug. 29, 1976, D. Clayton James, DDE Lib, OH-501, 3–6 (*"I would refuse"*); Chandler, vol. 2, 1165 (*"at least $25,000"*).

50 *"You are fighting":* HCB, June 19, 1943, DDE Lib, A-491; Gunther, *Eisenhower,* 19 (*"hate my enemies"*); John S. D. Eisenhower, *Strictly Personal,* 67 (*"the Almighty"*).

50 *"A coordinator":* Brian Horrocks, *A Full Life,* 159; Brian Harpur, *The Impossible Victory,* 115 (*"a compromisor"*); JPL, May 24, 1943 (*"keep in touch"*).

50 *"solve problems through reasoning":* Carlo D'Este, *Eisenhower: A Soldier's Life,* 418; Gunther, *D Day,* 59; David Fraser, *Alanbrooke,* 347 (*"a grave risk"*); Harold Macmillan, *War Diaries,* 260.

50 *The long summer twilight: Three Years,* 343; Thomas W. Mattingly and Olive F. G. Marsh, "A Compilation of the General Health Status of Dwight D. Eisenhower," n.d., Mattingly Collection, DDE Lib, box 1, 19–22, 53 (*"disabling injury"*); Gunther, *Eisenhower,* 29 (*sixty or more Camels*); Chandler, vol. 2, 1344 (*he paid John*); HCB, June 29, 1943, DDE Lib, A-508c (*gas fumes*).

51 *Cigarette in hand:* Michael Simpson, *A Life of Admiral of the Fleet Andrew Cunningham,* 161 (*Tars scaled*); John Howson, ts, n.d., LHC, 302 (*"Every Nice Girl"*); Ernle Bradford, *Siege Malta, 1940–1943,* 86–87 (*limestone walls*); Cunningham, 547 (*"extremely smelly"*); McKeough and Lockridge, 87 (*banana cordials*).

51 *Eisenhower strode:* Gunther, *D Day,* 53, 61; Alden Hatch, *General Ike,* 173 (*four hundred years*); Gunther, *Eisenhower,* 23–24.

51 *He shrugged off:* Harry L. Coles, Jr., "Participation of the 9th and 12th Air Forces in the Sicilian Campaign," AAF Historical Studies, no. 37, n.d., CMH, 56; Gunther, *D Day,* 80.

52 *his red-veined face:* John Winton, *Cunningham,* 313; Daniel C. Dancocks, *The D-Day Dodgers: The Canadians in Italy, 1943–1945,* 27; George Kitching, *Mud and Green Fields,* 147, 151 (*three Canadian ships*); *Three Years,* 349 (*heard from Malta*); Martin Stephen, *The Fighting Admirals,* 65, 77, 83 (*"velvet-arsed"*); Simpson, 161; Gunther, *D Day,* 64 (*"like a bulldog's"*).

52 *"The coast is everywhere":* "Tactical Study of the Terrain—Sicily," AFHQ G-2, Feb. 1943, CMH, Geog Sicily 354, 1; Molony V, 13 (*thirty-two beaches*); L. V. Bertarelli, *Southern Italy,* 418; Ernest Samuels, ed., *The Education of Henry Adams* (Boston: Houghton Mifflin, 1973), 367.

52 *An amphibious landing:* Geoffrey Perret, *There's a War to Be Won,* 110.

53 *If amphibious warfare:* Garland, 54–58; Sidney L. Jackson, "Signal Communication in the Sicilian Campaign," July 1945, SC Historical Project E-3, CARL, N-9425.4, 6–7 (*couriers shuttled*); Arthur S. Nevins, "Looking Back," ts, n.d., A.S. Nevins papers, DDE Lib, box 1, 16 (*frigid officers*).

53 *Eisenhower in March:* "Allied Commander-in-Chief's Report on Sicilian Campaign 1943," 75; Meyer, "Strategy and Logistical History: MTO," XIII-14 (*"grossly exaggerating"*); GS IV, 368–69 (*"defeatist doctrines"*); Garland, 58.

53 *"Let's finish this":* OH, Francis de Guingand, March 31, 1947, G. A. Harrison, OCMH WWII, "Europe Interviews," MHI, 2; Abraham, "Time Off for War," 68 (*"how it would suit us"*).

53 *The existing plan:* Hunt, 189–90; Molony V, 22; Garland, 61 (*"wooly thinking"*); Stephen Brooks, ed., *Montgomery and the Eighth Army,* 191, 207, 217, 223, 226 (*"military disaster"*).

54 *Rather than divide:* diary, Lt. Gen. Sir Charles Gairdner, IWM 04/271/1, 39 (*a thousand francs*), 36 (*run by Monty*); Martin Blumenson, *Sicily: Whose Victory?,* 24; Carlo D'Este, *A Genius for War,* 493 (*men's latrine*).

54 *A day later:* Cunningham, 532–37; Garland, 62; *SSA,* 20n.

54 *"I can't understand":* diary, Lt. Gen. Sir Charles Gairdner, IWM 04/271/1, 37.

54 HUSKY *now called:* Richard Doherty, *A Noble Crusade,* 140; Garland, 88–91.

54 *"Stick them in the belly":* SSt, 114; George F. Howe, "American Signal Intelligence in Northwest Africa and Western Europe," U.S. Cryptologic History, series IV, vol. 1, NSA, NARA RG 57, SRH-391, 48–49; "Trip Reports Concerning Use of Ultra in the Mediterranean Theater, 1943–1944," NARA RG 457, SRH-031, 36; Ralph Bennett, *Ultra and Mediterranean Strategy,* 401–3; Peter Calvocoressi, *Top Secret Ultra* (*"panoramic knowledge"*); F. H. Hinsley et al., *British Intelligence in the Second World War,* vol. 3, part 1, 75, 483–86 (*Hyena*).

55 *Eisenhower also knew:* SSA, 35, 56; Jack Greene and Alessandro Massignani, *The Naval War in the Mediterranean, 1940–1943,* 313 (*"blindfolded"*); "I Reparto Riunione dal Duce del Giorno 3 Aprile 1943," Italian Collection, item 26, OCMH, SSI, NARA RG 319, 270/19/6/3, box 243 (*lightbulbs*).

55 *What Eisenhower did not know:* Battle, 35.

55 *The Combined Chiefs had approved:* Richard M. Leighton, "Planning for Sicily," *Proceedings,* July 1962, 90+; Garland, 67 (*"Your planners"*).

55 *Marshall was right:* Battle, 46; Garland, 89; "Outline Plan," Force 343, May 18, 1943, NARA RG 319, OCMH, 270/19/6/3, box 242; Cochran, "Chicken or Eggs?"; Alexander S. Cochran, "Constructing a Military Coalition from Materials at Hand: The Case of Allied Force Headquarters," paper, SMH conference, Apr. 16, 1999, 10–12 (*Amphibious doctrine*).

55 *A "terrible inflexibility":* Smith, "Mediterranean Operations," 1; Garland, 92–93.

56 *In mid-June, Eisenhower:* Three Years, 333; DDE, *Crusade in Europe,* 170; Davis, 425–26 (*"Don't ever do that"*).

56 *Feints and deceptions:* SSA, 167; memo, C. B. Hazeltine to McClure, July 14, 1943, AFHQ Psychological Warfare Branch, Carl A. Spaatz papers, LOC MS Div, box 13; *The Sicilian Campaign,* 8.

56 *Verdala Palace:* Three Years, 347–48, 353; DDE, *Letters to Mamie,* 125.

56 *Translators, for example:* DDE to GCM, May 7 and 11, June 22 and 28, 1943, NARA RG 165, E 422, OPD Exec Files, box 16.

57 *"Aged Military Gentlemen":* C.R.S. Harris, *Allied Administration of Italy, 1943–1945,* 82; Paul Dickson, *War Slang,* 118; http://www.sokrates-digital.de/produktkatalog/AQ493328 .php; DDE to AGWAR, June 1, 1943, NARA RG 165, E 422, OPD Exec Files, box 16. The abbreviation was shortened in August to AMG.

57 *he worried about his wife:* Ambrose, vol. 1, 244.

57 *Kathleen Helen Summersby:* Kay Summersby Morgan, *Past Forgetting,* 126, 136; finding aid, Barbara Wyden papers, DDE Lib; Miller, 516 (*Grief and strain*); Piers Brendon, *Ike: His Life & Times,* 125.

57 *Just please remember:* DDE, *Letters to Mamie,* 128.

### "The Horses of the Sun"

58 *The convoys from Algeria:* Karig, 235–36; *SSA,* 62–65; Tregaskis, 15 (*abacus*); war log, U.S.S. *Monrovia,* July 8–9, 1943, NARA RG 38, OCNO, WWII war diaries, box 1233 (*thirteen knots*).

58 *Ships wallowed:* Total tonnage included follow-on convoys. Memo, "Observations 'HUSKY'—Joss Task Force," July 10, 1943, MTOUSA, NARA RG 492, SOS, 290/55/1-2, 7-1, box 2736; msg, AFHQ to AGWAR, June 25, 1943, NARA RG 165, E 422, OPD Exec Files, box 16; Jackson, "Signal Communication in the Sicilian Campaign," 3; "Orders for Operation HUSKY," n.d., AFHQ, S.S.O. 17/3, CARL, N-14793A; msgs, DDE to AGWAR, May 28, 1943; AGWAR to AFHQ, June 10, 1943; and Office of Fiscal Director, WD, to DDE, June 17, 1943, all in NARA RG 165, E 422, OPD Exec Files, box 16 (*rat traps*); Robert W. Komer, "Civil Affairs and Military Government in the Mediterranean Theater," 1954, CMH, 2-3.7 AX, II-24 (*occupation scrip*); memo, "Medical Planning Instruction," Force 141, March 14, 1943, A. S. Nevins papers, MHI, box 1 (*condoms*); "British Abbreviations and Glossary," A. S. Nevins papers, MHI, box 1 (*glossary*).

58 *Half the tonnage:* Mayo, 154; "Logistical History of NATOUSA/MTOUSA," Nov. 1945, NARA RG 407, E 427, 95-AL1-4, box 203, 58.

58 *"what they thought they needed":* "Reminiscences of Walter C. W. Ansel," John T. Mason, Jr., 1970, USNI OHD, 148; AAR, 6681st Signal Pigeon Co., July 9, 1944, NARA RG 407, SG Co-6681-0.1, box 23228; msg, AGWAR to DDE, June 17, 1943, NARA RG 165, E 422, OPD Exec Files, box 16 (*pigeons*); Max Corvo, *The O.S.S. in Italy,* 61; "Reminiscences of Phil E. Bucklew," 1980, John T. Mason, Jr., USNI OHD, 44; memo, "Final Outline Plan, Force 343," June 8, 1943, NARA RG 338, II Corps historical section, box 148; "Beaches of Sicily," Strategic Engineering Study, No. 31, Nov. 1942, MHI (*rumrunner*); msgs, GCM to DDE, May 2 and 27, 1943, NARA RG 165, E 422, OPD Exec Files, box 16; Blanche D. Coll et al., *The Corps of Engineers: Troops and Equipment,* 455–56 (*wooden crates*); Nicholas, 222, 226, 234 (*motorcycle courier*).

59 *Much had been learned:* memo, HQ, I Armored Corps, annex 2, June 14, 1943, MTOUSA, NARA RG 492, SOS, 290/55/1-2, 7-1, box 2736; "Operating Instructions HUSKY," vol. IV, Force 343, FO No. 1, June 20, 1943, NARA RG 407, E 427, 95-AL1-3.17, box 201 (chart distributed to medics); memo, HQ, SOS NATOUSA, June 29, 1943, and "Graves Registration Directive," MTOUSA, NARA RG 492, SOS, 290/55/1-2, 7-1, box 2736; memo, "Disposition of Personal Effects," May 24, 1943, Harlan W. Hendrick, ASEQ, 1st ID, MHI.

59 *welfare of civilians:* "British Administrative History of the Italian Campaign," appendix, 1946, NARA RG 94, E 427, 95-USF2-5.0; Komer, "Civil Affairs," II-20 (*vast stocks*); "Post-HUSKY Operations, Military Government," NARA RG 319, OCMH, 270/19/6/3, box 242 (*nineteen million mouths*); "History of Planning Division, Army Service Forces," n.d., CMH, 3-2.2 AA, vol. 1, 92 ("*self-supporting*").

59 *Kent Hewitt spent the passage:* OH, HKH, 1961, John T. Mason, Col U OHRO, 314; HKH, AAR, "The Sicilian Campaign," n.d., 107; John H. Clagett, unpublished bio of HKH, ts, n.d., NHC, 392 ("*God couldn't be*").

59 *"sea-going bedpan":* "History of Amphibious Training Command, U.S. Atlantic Fleet," 1951, *USNAd,* #145 a–c, VIII, 24; Beck et al., 118; Perry, "A Reporter at Large," 50 ("*ensign-eliminators*"); author visit, *LST 325,* Alexandria, Va., May 28, 2005; Perret, 134

(*rumrunners*); Barry W. Fowle, ed., *Builders and Fighters*, 407; Kendall King, "LSTs: Marvelous at Fifty Plus," *Naval History*, 1992 (*river yards*); Pyle, 157 (*even in drydock*).

60  *Hewitt knew:* Beck et al., 124; Mason, 273–78 (*Sherman tank*).

60  *"take his chances":* "Reminiscences of Walter C. W. Ansel," 149; HKH, AAR, "The Sicilian Campaign," 44 (*"illusory"*); Hinsley, 86 (*fourteen had been lost*).

60  *In his own cabin:* PP, 275, 271 (*horses of the sun*); diary, GSP, July 8, 1943, LOC MS Div, box 3, folder 1 (*"Attack and then look"*); Mason, 284 (*"on their necks"*).

60  *Field Order No. 1:* HQ, Force 343 (7th Army), June 20, 1943, NARA RG 319, OCMH, SSI, box 242; "Seventh Army Report Summary," n.d., NARA RG 319, OCMH, 2-3.7 CC2 Sicily, box 250 (*"We shall win"*).

61  *"You are a great leader":* PP, 272; John North, ed., *The Alexander Memoirs, 1940–1945*, 45–46; Hirshson, 360 (*"Do you kill?"*); GSP to DDE, Feb. 20, 1942, DDE Lib, PP-pres, box 91 (*"You name them"*); memoir, Kenyon Joyce, ts, n.d., MHI, 345 (*"colorful"*).

61  *"a question of destiny":* GSP to Bea, July 5, 1943, LOC MS Div, Chrono File, box 10.

61  *Ernie Pyle was with them:* SSA, 66; Pyle, 12 (*"On fine days"*); Lee G. Miller, *The Story of Ernie Pyle*, 267 (*he rose at three A.M.*).

61  *"older and a little apart":* David Nichols, ed., *Ernie's War*, 18; Quentin Reynolds, *The Curtain Rises*, 256 (*"a family Bible"*); Miller, 261 (*"fundamentally sad"*).

62  *"lost in the dark":* Richard Collier, *Fighting Words*, 140, 144, 152; Miller (*"athlete's foot"*).

62  *thirty cubic feet:* Harold Larson, "Troop Transports in WWII," ts, March 1945, CMH, 4-13. AA12, 53; Brown, *The Whorehouse of the World*, 142; IG investigation, fall 1943, MTOUSA AG, NARA RG 492, 333.7, box 1432 (*Army inspectors*); Russell B. Capelle, *Casablanca to the Neckar*, 18 (*its mystery*).

62  *They made do:* Valentine, 10; George F. Hall papers, HIA, box 1 (*seven times as high*); AAR, 26th Inf Regt, "The Beginning of the End," n.d., MRC FDM (*hellhole*); Williamson, "Tales of a Thunderbird," 86 (*"bona sera"*).

62  *They packed and unpacked:* annex, Admin Order No. 1, June 14, 1943, Seventh Army, Walter J. Muller papers, HIA, box 2; chart, Wayne M. Harris, ASEQ, 157th Inf, MHI (*82.02 pounds*); Harold W. Thatcher, "The Development of Special Rations for the Army," 1944, Historical Section, QM General, MHI, 4-5 (*"D rations"*).

63  *"It's interesting to see":* corr, TR to Eleanor, July 7, 8, 1943, LOC MS Div, box 10.

63  *"Commander Houdini":* Graeme Zielinski, "Capt. Richard Steere, 92; Meteorologist for Patton," *WP*, March 22, 2001, B-6; "Navy Honors D.C. Officer, Weather Expert," *WP*, Dec. 7, 1943, B-9.

64  *Summer blows:* Charles C. Bates and John F. Fuller, *America's Weather Warriors*, 74.

64  *"flat-bottomed delight":* Collins, 200; Jack Belden, "As I Saw It," in Albert H. Smith, Jr., *The Sicily Campaign: Recollections of an Infantry Company Commander*, 143 (*"Mussolini wind"*); memo, Bert M. Rudd, "Landing Craft and Bases," AGF Observer, July 16, 1943, ANSCOL, NARA RG 334, NWC Lib, box 150, 6; Bill Mauldin, *The Brass Ring*, 143 (*two dozen balloons*); "Personal Diary of Langan W. Swent," July 9, 1943, HIA, box 1 (*helmsmen struggled*); Pyle, 13.

64  *Never had the amphibious vessels:* CM, 209; Karig, 255 (*"green water cascaded"*); Donald J. Hunt, "USS LST 313 and Battery A, 33rd Field Artillery," ts, 1997, MRC FDM, 46 (*heavy shudder*); William A. Carter, "Carter's War," ts, 1983, CEOH, box V-14, VII-3 (*"47 degrees"*); Mason, 279–82 (*"nothing to the right"*); James Phinney Baxter III, *Scientists Against Time*, 77 (*charms on a watch chain*); Karig, 237 (Florence Nightingale).

65  *"You probably enjoy":* What to Do Aboard the Transport, 244.

65  *"All of us are miserable":* Samuel David Spivey, *A Doughboy's Narrative*, 85; Franklyn A. Johnson, *One More Hill*, 81 (*"First I am afraid"*); John Ellis, *On the Front Lines*, 60 (*"Bags, Vomit"*); Ralph G. Martin, *The G.I. War, 1941–1945*, 67 (*"secret shame"*).

65 *"Land of My Fathers"*: Buckley, 24; Farley Mowat, *And No Birds Sang*, 46–50 (*"green and groaning"*); Francis A. Even, "The Tenth Engineers," ts, 1996, author's possession, 7 (*African donkeys*); memo, Bert M. Rudd, "Landing Craft and Bases," AGF Observer, July 16, 1943, ANSCOL, NARA RG 334, NWC Lib, box 150, 6 (*"Ship rolled thirty degrees"*); Martha Harris, ed., "The Harris Family in World War II," 23 (*peritonitis*); Steve Kluger, *Yank*, 105 (*"walk and walk"*).

65 *" 'Is God on our side' "*: Strome Galloway, *A Regiment at War*, 70.

65 *"It's goddam foolish"*: Jack Belden, "As I Saw It," in Smith, 144; "Reminiscences of Walter C. W. Ansel," 145 (*"first to yelp"*).

66 *On* Monrovia: *SSA*, 68; Garland, 109 (*at least four hours*); Hewitt, "Naval Aspects of the Sicilian Campaign," 705 (*"get ashore"*); OH, HKH, Jan. 23, 1951, Howard M. Smyth, SM, MHI.

66 *Late on Friday afternoon:* lecture, "Narrative by Rear Adm. Alan G. Kirk," Oct. 2, 1943, Pearl Harbor, NHC; Clagett, unpub bio of HKH, 392–98; Bates and Fuller, 74; Bernard Fergusson, *The Watery Maze*, 240–44.

66 *"Always the vibration"*: McCallum, 150; letter, John T. Dawson to family, July 9, 1943, MRC FDM.

66 *"taking it green"*: W. S. Chalmers, *Full Cycle*, 177; John F. Hummer, *An Infantryman's Journal*, 20 (*smoking lamps*); war log, U.S.S. *Monrovia*, NARA RG 38, OCNO, WWII war diaries, box 1233; "Account Written by Brig. Gen. McLain," ts, summer 1943, NARA RG 319, OCMH, 2-3.7 cc2, Sicily, "45th Div Landings," box 247, 1 (*sheer cliffs*).

66 *"my communications with Washington"*: Chandler, vol. 2, 1212; *Crusade in Europe*, 172 (*"I wish I knew"*).

67 *"all the winds of heaven"*: Winton, 316; McCallum, 146 (*"Road to the Isles"*); Cunningham, 550–51 (*"solid sheets"*); Francis de Guingand, *Operation Victory*, 289–90 (*gin*).

67 *Eisenhower reviewed:* Chandler, vol. II, 1247 (*"the operation will proceed"*), 1247n; F. M. Whitely to J. N. Kennedy, July 14, 1943, UK NA, WO 204/307 (*reconnaissance plane*); Stephen, 84 (*"recklessness"*); Roger Parkinson, *A Day's March Nearer Home*, 137 (*"not favourable"*).

67 *"To be perfectly honest"*: Three Years, 348–49; Alan Lloyd, *The Gliders*, 39 (*searchlight beams*); Garland, 109; John S. D. Eisenhower, *Allies*, 319 (*lucky coins*); Coles, "Participation of the Ninth and Twelfth Air Forces," 81 (*vital turn*).

68 *"tell some stories"*: Three Years, 350; Vincent Orange, *Tedder: Quietly in Command*, 225; Abraham, "Time Off for War," 70 (*razor*).

68 *"in the lap of the gods"*: Miller, 520; DDE, *Letters to Mamie*, 134–35.

*Death or Glory*

68 *Patton woke:* George S. Patton, *War as I Knew It*, 65; combat narrative, Mitchell Jamieson, "Invasion of Sicily," May 2, 1944, NHC, 4–5; diary, July 9, 1943, GSP, LOC MS Div, box 2, folder 15 (*pitched overboard*).

69 *"We may feel anxious"*: PP, 275–76.

69 *He found Hewitt:* Albert C. Wedemeyer, *Wedemeyer Reports!*, 224; HKH, "The Sicilian Campaign," n.d., NARA RG 319, OCMH, 270/19/6/3, box 242, 83 (*ten knots*); S. W. Roskill, *The War at Sea, 1939–1945*, 116 (Unruffled); N.L.A. Jewell, *Secret Mission Submarine*, 113 (*"I saw hundreds"*).

69 *"a mass of flames"*: Patton, 65; diary, Hobart Gay, July 9, 1943, USMA Lib, 98; Bernard Stambler, "Campaign in Sicily," ts, n.d., vol. 2, CMH, 2-3.7 AA.L (*"All the beach"*); Walter Karig, *Battle Report: The Atlantic War*, 238 (*"Apparently the big ships"*).

69 *The* HUSKY *commanders:* Molony V, 55; *SSA*, 72, 82 (*Yellow Line*).

70 *"all-or-nothing affairs"*: Molony V, 67.

70 *"You will find the Mediterranean"*: John Mason Brown, *To All Hands*, 116; S.W.C. Pack, *Operation Husky*, 139 (*Indonesian waiters*); Christopher Buckley, *Road to Rome*, 27, 31 (Strathnaver's E-deck); Flint Whitlock, *The Rock of Anzio*, 39 (*friction tape*); Martha Harris, ed., "The Harris Family in World War II," s.p., 1996, 20.

70 *"the victim coast"*: letter, Richard Pisciotta to father, May 18, 1944, 157th Inf, 45th ID, ASEQ, MHI; notes, Russell L. Nioses, ts, n.d., 179th Inf, 45th Div Museum (*"wild Indians"*); Lee G. Miller, *The Story of Ernie Pyle*, 268 (*"breathing so hard"*).

70 *"The ship is dark"*: TR to Eleanor, July 9, 1943, TR, LOC MS Div, box 10.

70 *"Land the landing force"*: Susan H. Godson, *Viking of Assault*, 70; "History of the 50th (Northumberland) Division During the Campaign in Sicily," ts, n.d., UK NA, CAB 106/473, 16–17 (Winchester Castle); *Three Assault Landings*, 1st Battalion, Dorsetshire Regiment, DTL, Ft. B, 10 (*tots of rum*); Farley Mowat, *The Regiment*, 56–57.

71 *"The rocking of the small landing craft"*: Jack Belden, "As I Saw It," in Albert H. Smith, Jr., *The Sicily Campaign: Recollections of an Infantry Company Commander*, 147–49; Bernard Nalty and Truman Strobridge, "The Lucky *Chase*," *Sea Classics*, date uncertain, 14+ (*"a basso coughing"*).

71 *"Seasickness and fear"*: Paul W. Brown, *The Whorehouse of the World*, 149; Malcolm S. McLean, "Adventures in Occupied Areas," ts, 1975, MHI, 75 (*pry loose the fingers*); Paul W. Brown, 164 (*"Oh, Jesus"*); George J. Koch, memoir, ts, n.d., 1st Reconnaissance Troop, 1st ID, ASEQ, MHI (*"not meant to be sailors"*); Robert W. Black, *Rangers in World War II*, 86 (*"American Patrol"*); James B. Lyle, "The Operations of Companies A and B, 1st Ranger Battalion, at Gela, Sicily," n.d., IS, 9 (*"God be with you"*).

71 *On the extreme left*: admin log, *LST-379*, July 10, 1943, and action report, "Landing at Torre de Gaffi, Sicily, *LST 379*," July 18, 1943; lecture, "Narrative by Rear Adm. Alan G. Kirk," Pearl Harbor, Oct. 2, 1943, NHC, 6 (*Cleats snapped*); *The Sicilian Campaign*, 38–39 (*"Our barrage rockets"*); George Sessions Perry, "A Reporter at Large," *New Yorker*, Aug. 14, 1943, 46+ (*"knocking steel and fire"*).

71 *Somehow the cockleshell*: "The Lucky *Chase*," 14+; OH, "The Reminiscences of Walter C. W. Ansel," 1970, John T. Mason, Jr., USNI OHD, 139 (*"steer through the water"*); Intelligence Notes No. 6, July 3, 1943, HQ, 1st ID (*Coca-Cola*).

71 *By two A.M.*: Jack Belden, "Battle of Sicily," *Time*, July 26, 1943, 27+; Donald J. Hunt, "USS *LST 313* and Battery A, 33rd Field Artillery," ts, 1997, MRC FDM, 33 (*Coxswains steered*); JPL, 42 (*"beautiful phenomenon"*).

## Chapter 2: The Burning Shore
### Land of the Cyclops

75 *Few Sicilian towns*: Robert D. Kaplan, *Mediterranean Winter*, 132; Karl Baedeker, *Southern Italy and Sicily*, 321; Pietro Griffo, *Gela*, 24, 49, 160, 211 (*bald skull*).

75 *Patton planned*: Edwin M. Sayer, "The Operations of Company A, 505th Parachute Infantry," Nov. 1947, IS, 6–7; Bradley Biggs, *Gavin*, 19–20; William B. Breuer, *Drop Zone Sicily*, 2 (*washed out of flight school*); Malcolm Muir, Jr., ed., *The Human Tradition in the World War II Era*, 178–84 (*"He could jump"*).

76 *His 505th Parachute Infantry*: Muir, 183; Matthew B. Ridgway, *Soldier*, 62 (*roughly one-third*); William T. Ryder, "Report on American Airborne Phase of Operation HUSKY," n.d., NARA RG 334, NWC Lib, box 44, 16; XO diary, 1st Bn, 505th Para Inf Regt, May 17–July 9 1943, NARA RG 407, 382-Inf-(505)-0.3.0, box 12459; MBR, SOOHP, John M. Blair, 1971–72, MHI, II-55 (*injuries*); Clay Blair, *Ridgway's Paratroopers*, 78 (*fifty-three broken legs*); John C. Warren, *Airborne Missions in the Mediterranean, 1942–1945*, 25, 28 (*without airborne expertise*); Ed Ruggero, *Combat Jump*, 110 (*"para-mule"*); Ryder, "Report on American Airborne Phase," n.d., NARA RG 334, NWC Lib, box 44, 17 (*"in the bag"*).

76  *white cloth knotted on the left:* Robert M. Piper, "The Operation of the 505th Parachute Infantry in the Airborne Landings on Sicily," 1948, IS, 13; Sayer, "The Operations of Company A, 505th Parachute Infantry," IS, 6 (*baggy trousers*), 8 (*Benzedrine*); Blair, 86–87 (*honeypots*).

76  *As the first planes:* Warren, 29, 33; James M. Gavin, *On to Berlin*, 19, 22 (*prisoner-of-war tags*).

77  *The slivered moon:* Garland, 117.

77  *Nearly all found Sicily:* Blair, 87; Breuer, 71 (*fifteen hundred feet*); Piper, "The Operation of the 505th Parachute Infantry," 20 (*before they hit the ground*); OH, George Mertz, Oct. 2000, Lewis E. Johnston, "The Troop Carrier D-Day Flights," CD-ROM, author's possession, 146–57.

77  *"Stand up":* Breuer, 57; Ruggero, 133–37 (*"George!"*); James M. Gavin, *Airborne Warfare*, 2.

77  *"No one knew":* Charles E. Smith, "The American Campaign in Sicily," ts, n.d., CMH, Geog Sicily 314.7, 10; Ryder, "Report on American Airborne Phase," 40; Warren, 33–36 (*"prodigious overestimate"*); Gavin, *On to Berlin*, 22 (*passwords*); Ridgway, 70; "Proceedings of Board of Officers Considering Airborne Operations," Aug. 1943, AFHQ, JPL, MHI, box 11; "Airborne Operations Conference," July 24, 1943, Algiers, MHI, D763.S5 A5 (*Eight planes*); David G. Fivecoat, "Against All Odds," thesis, May 6, 1993, USMA, 19–23 (*three-day casualty tally*).

78  *Certainly they wreaked havoc:* Sayer, "The Operations of Company A, 505th Parachute Infantry," 10–12; Jonathan M. Soffer, *General Matthew B. Ridgway: From Progressivism to Reaganism, 1895–1993*, 45 (*SAFU*).

78  *"At war's end":* corr, MBR to C. B. Hansen, April 5, 1949, CJB, box 48.

78  *As paratroopers blundered:* Garland, 99; Black, 87; James J. Altieri, *Darby's Rangers: An Illustrated Portrayal of the Original Rangers*, 50; Allen N. Towne, *Doctor Danger Forward*, 67.

79  *The first Americans:* Garland, 137; Harris, ed., 24–30 (*"I've had it, Harry"*).

79  *Italian gunners:* "History of the 26th Infantry in the Present Struggle," ts, n.d., MRC-FDM, 1991.25, box 445, 6; "Personal Diary of Langan W. Swent," July 10–11, 1943, HIA, box 1, copyright Stanford University; Jack Belden, "Battle of Sicily," 27+ (*"so much blood"*); John W. Baumgartner et al., *The 16th Infantry, 1798–1946*, 38 (*"Somebody left his pack"*).

79  *a 16th Infantry rifleman:* William T. Dillon, "Pearl Harbor to Normandy and Beyond," ts, n.d., 1/16th Inf, ASEQ, MHI, 5.

79  *Shouts and curses:* Stambler, "Campaign in Sicily," 2-3.7 AA.L; Belden, "Battle of Sicily," 27+ (*"screaming and sobbing"*).

79  *Dawn sluiced the eastern sky:* Neil McCallum, *Journey with a Pistol*, 150; *Building the Navy's Bases in World War II*, vol. II, 87; "Action Report, Commander Task Unit 86.222," July 31, 1943, NARA (*breaking ramp chains*); AAR, 3/16th Inf, Aug. 16, 1943, NARA RG 319, OCMH, 2-3.7 CC2, box 247; E. S. Van Deusen, "Trucks That Go Down to the Sea," *Army Ordnance*, vol. 25, Nov.–Dec. 1943, 555+; James Phinney Baxter III, *Scientists Against Time*, 243–50 (*DUKW*); Geoffrey Perret, *There's a War to Be Won*, 110–12; Linda Mayo, *The Ordnance Department: On Beachhead and Battlefront*, 163; Garland, 104; Henry F. Pringle, "Weapons Win Wars," ts, n.d., CMH, 2-3.7 AB.B, 150–52 (*Coast Guard crew*).

80  *Mines proved more galling:* OH, Samuel A. D. Hunter, naval intelligence, Advance Bases Group, March 7, 1944, NHC; AAR, HKH, "The Sicilian Campaign," 55–56; Alfred M. Beck et al., *The Corps of Engineers: The War Against Germany*, 130; R. L. Carmichael, Jr., "Report on Italian Campaign," June 15, 1944, #113, Observer Reports, NARA RG 337, AGF G-2, box 55, 8 (*"Everything on them goes bad"*); "Personal Diary of Langan W. Swent," July 12, 1943, HIA, box 1; *The Sicilian Campaign*, 83.

80  *"The beach was a scene"*: JPL, 43; "Action Report, Commander Task Unit 86.222," July 31, 1943, NARA (*Beachmasters bellowed*); Sidney L. Jackson, "Signal Communication in the Sicilian Campaign," July 1945, CARL, N-9425.4, 78; H. H. Dunham, "U.S. Army Transportation and the Conquest of Sicily," March 1945, Monograph No. 13, ASF, Historical Program Files, NARA RG 336, box 141, 68 (*athletic equipment*).

80  *Dawn also brought:* memo, D. L. Madeira, Aug. 7, 1943, Destroyer Squadron 17, in action report, U.S.S. *Maddox*, RG 38, OCNO, WWII Actions and Operational Reports, box 1219.

81  *"A great blob"*: John Mason Brown, 131.

81  *Past the charred DUKWs*: John P. Downing, "No Promotion," ts, n.d., MRC FDM, 1994.41.1, 218; author visit, Sept. 1996; SSA, 60–61; McCallum, 151–52 (*"red-and-yellow lamps"*).

81  *Force X:* David W. Hogan, *Raiders or Elite Infantry?*, 45; Jerome J. Haggerty, "A History of the Ranger Battalion in World War II," Ph.D. diss, 1982, Fordham University, MHI, 139–40 (*"no record of trial"*); Michael J. King, *William Orlando Darby*, 74; "The Rangers," *Life*, July 2, 1944, 59+; Thomas M. Johnson, "The Army's Fightingest Outfit Comes Home," St. Louis *Post-Dispatch*, Nov. 5, 1944, in *Reader's Digest*, Dec. 1944, 51+; James Altieri, *The Spearheaders*, 293, 247 (*"Fightin' Rangers"*).

82  *"tearing roofs off"*: "History of the 26th Infantry Regiment in the Present Struggle," ts, n.d., version provided author by Gen. Paul Gorman, 9; Altieri, *The Spearheaders*, 268–70; Black, 87; William O. Darby and William H. Baumer, *Darby's Rangers: We Led the Way*, 87–89 (*thunderous salvos*); AAR, 1st Ranger Bn, July 10–14, 1943, "Combat Reports," USMA micro., MP63-8, roll 1 (*fifty-two Italians*); SSA, 104.

82  *On Highway 117:* Garland, 152–53; diary, July 19, 1943, GSP, LOC MS Div, box 2, folder 15 (*thermite grenade*); John B. Romeiser, ed., *Combat Reporter*, 164 (*"metal was red hot"*); Altieri, *Darby's Rangers* (*"fled in disorder"*); SSA, 104.

83  *By late morning:* Robert Daumer, "Darby's Ranger," Darby interview with Jack Belden, www.grunts.net.; W. S. Allgood, "Once Upon a War," in "2004 Reunion Program Book," Fort Wayne, Indiana, Aug. 25–30, 2004, author's possession, 101; Ralph G. Martin, *The G.I. War, 1941–1945*, 71 (*Thomas Paine*); Romeiser, ed., 163; "Report on the First Phase of Amgot Occupation, Sicily and Region II," July–Aug. 1943, Frank J. McSherry papers, MHI, 18 (*170 corpses*).

83  *Fifteen miles west:* Max Corvo, *The O.S.S. in Italy, 1942–1945*, 69–75; Stambler, "Campaign in Sicily," 23; Pyle, 15.

83  *No one was more relieved:* George Biddle, *Artist at War*, 225; OH, James M. Wilson, Jr., former aide, with author, Apr. 23, 2004, Washington, D.C.; Will Lang, "Lucian King Truscott, Jr.," *Life*, Oct. 2, 1944, 97+ (*polo handicap*); corr, LKT Jr. to Sarah R. Truscott, Nov. 25, 1943, and Jan. 15, 1944, LKT Jr., GCM Lib, box 1, folder 6 (*silver nitrate*); Roger J. Spiller, ed., *Dictionary of American Military Biography*, 1110 (*finest combat commander*).

84  *Truscott for six years had taught:* Lang, "Lucian King Truscott, Jr.,"; Robert H. Berlin, *U.S. Army World War II Corps Commanders*; Hugh A. Scott, *The Blue and White Devils*, 66 (*"passive voice"*); aide's diaries, Sept. 12, 1943, LKT Jr., GCM Lib, box 18, folder 3 (*"What is sin?"*); OH, Robert T. Frederick, Jan. 7, 1949, SM, MHI (*drank too much*); CM, 206 (*fifty-year sentences*); OH, Wilson, with author (*turpentine*); memo, LKT Jr., to L. J. McNair, Dec. 27, 1943, Don E. Carleton papers, HIA, box 1 (*"Truscott trot"*).

84  *"Do you remember"*: corr, LKT Jr. to Sarah, July 7, 1943, LKT Jr., GCM Lib, box 1, folder 6.

84  *Booby traps on the docks:* Pyle, 20; John T. Mason, Jr., *The Atlantic War Remembered*, 285; Garland, 126–34; *The Sicilian Campaign*, 109; SSA, 86 (*U.S.S. Sentinel*).

84  *Infantrymen drowned:* Pyle, 17; CM, 213–14; MEB, mss, #R-127, in "Axis Tactical Operations in Sicily," ts, n.d., OCMH, #R-147, MHI (*"self-demobilization"*); memo, William W. Eagles, Jan. 17, 1951, SM, MHI (*German shepherds*); Norris H. Perkins, *North African Odyssey*, 82 (*"poor Dagoes"*).

85  *Dawn revealed:* Karig, 252.

85  *"white as sharks' teeth":* Richard Tregaskis, *Invasion Diary,* 23; Pyle, 22: corr, LKT Jr. to Sarah, July 25, 1943, LKT Jr., GCM Lib, box 1, folder 6.

85  *Across the Gulf of Gela:* lecture, "Narrative by Rear Adm. Alan G. Kirk," Oct. 2, 1943, Pearl Harbor, NHC, 6–7; Charles C. Bates and John F. Fuller, *America's Weather Warriors,* 75; Robert L. Clifford and William J. Maddocks, "Naval Gunfire Support of the Landings in Sicily," 1984, Monograph No. 5, MHI, 19 (*white phosphorus*); lecture, John F. Gallaher, U.S.S. *Laub,* "Naval Gunfire Support," Oct. 29, 1943, NARA RG 334, NWC Lib, box 170 (*cruiser shells*).

85  *The first assault wave:* SSA, 137; "Operations of II Corps in Sicily," Sept. 1, 1943, NARA RG 338, 333.5, box 134 (*eleventh-hour transfer*); Samuel Eliot Morison, *The Two-Ocean War,* 259 (*Punta Braccetto*); Emajean Jordan Buechner, *Sparks,* 66–67 (*grave diggers*); AAR, 180th Inf Regt, July 10–Aug. 16, 1943, 45th ID Mus (*"played havoc"*).

86  *Dozens of landing craft:* Garland, 161; John Mason Brown, 147 (*"dead man's closet"*); AAR, Amphibious Force Transport QM, U.S. Atlantic Fleet, Aug. 6, 1943, in "Report on Operation Husky," Army Observers, Amphibious Forces, MHI, 9; Claudia Levy, "Pulitzer-Winning WWII Cartoonist Bill Mauldin Dies," Jan 23, 2003, WP, B6; Bill Mauldin, *The Brass Ring,* 150 (*"Nobody really knows"*).

86  *"The beach was in total confusion":* William A. Carter, "Carter's War," ts, 1983, CEOH, box V-14, VII-7 and 13; SSA, 139, 140n (*court-martialed*); *The Sicilian Campaign,* 53; Garland, 161; lecture, "Narrative by Rear Adm. Alan G. Kirk," Pearl Harbor, Oct. 2, 1943, NHC, 9–12 (*bangalore torpedoes*); corr, Troy H. Middleton to James A. Norell, Nov. 29, 1960, NARA RG 319, OCMH, 2-3.7 CC2, box 250 (*"less comfortable"*).

86  *Still, as D-day drew to a close:* Precise numbers are elusive because the 45th Division figures are aggregated for three days. Garland, 161n; Clifford and Maddocks, "Naval Gunfire Support," 21.

87  *That left the British:* SSA, 152; Homer, *The Odyssey,* trans. Robert Fagles, 214; Ross Munro, "Landing Fairly Easy for Canadian Invaders," July 12, 1943, Toronto *Globe and Mail,* www.warmuseum.ca.

87  *"Some confusion":* "History of the 50th (Northumberland) Division During the Campaign in Sicily," ts, n.d., UK NA, CAB 106/473, 17–18, 23, 26; intel report, No. 6910, Dec. 11, 1943, CARL, N-6490 (*"in no way carried out"*); Daniel G. Dancocks, *The D-Day Dodgers,* 35 (*"you silly bastards"*).

87  *"Down door!":* C. R. Eke, "A Game of Soldiers," ts, n.d., IWM, 92/1/1, 14; K. G. Oakley, "Sicily, 1943," ts, n.d., IWM 96/22/1, 2–3; Field Marshal Lord Carver, *The Imperial War Museum Book of the War in Italy, 1943–1945,* 14–15.

87  *Ashore they swarmed:* Richard S. Malone, *A Portrait of War, 1939–1943;* Pack, 97 (*wild thyme*); Robin Neillands, *Eighth Army,* 220 (*makeshift jetties*); George Aris, *The Fifth British Division, 1939 to 1945,* 115 (*"Desert rats"*); John Durnford-Slater, *Commando,* 134, 136 (*"the right spirit"*).

88  *up to ten thousand casualties:* Molony V, 52; C. R. Eke, "A Game of Soldiers," ts, n.d., IWM, 92/1/1, 44 (*"We had learned"*).

88  *More than a third:* Alan Wood, *The Glider Soldiers,* 27; SSA, 160–61.

88  *There was the rub:* Warren, 23, 26; Wood, 27; George Chatterton, *The Wings of Pegasus,* 64, 67; Michael Hickey, *Out of the Sky: A History of Airborne Warfare,* 100.

89  *Several dozen Horsa gliders:* Hickey, 100; Blair, 76–77 (*at least one hundred hours*); Harry L. Coles, Jr., "Participation of the Ninth and Twelfth Air Forces in the Sicilian Campaign," 1945, AAF Historical Studies, No. 37, 85 (*barely qualified*); lecture, P. L. Williams, "Airborne Operations Against Sicily," Sept. 2, 1943, NARA RG 334, E 315, NWC Lib, ANSCOL, L-1-43, W-68, box 168, 3 (*more than half were destroyed*).

89  *Pilots and passengers were doomed:* Chatterton, 68; Lloyd, 39, 41 (*tow ropes snapped*); Tregaskis, 95; Hickey, 101 (*wrong charts*); Breuer, 41 (*thirty men plummeted*); Carlo

D'Este, *Bitter Victory,* 233, 233n (*"sorry to inform you"*); "Report of Allied Force Airborne Board," Oct. 13, 1943, AFHQ, NARA RG 407, E 427, 95-AL1 (A/B)-0.3.0 (*"generally was bad"*).

89  *Ninety percent of the aircraft:* Chatterton, 89; Lloyd, 41 (*"a blind swarm"*); "Interview with Brig. Gen. Ray A. Dunn," Oct. 14, 1943, MHI Lib, 4–5 (*"released their gliders"*); Richard Thruelsen and Elliott Arnold, *Mediterranean Sweep,* 111; "Tactical Employment in the U.S. Army of Transport Aircraft and Gliders in World War II," vol. 1, chapter 3, n.d., CARL, N-16464-H, 33; "Report on Airborne Operations, HUSKY," July 24, 1943, JPL, MHI, box 11; lecture, Williams, "Airborne Operations," 4–7 (*an optical illusion*); "Report of Allied Force Airborne Board" (*thirty-mile front*); Warren, 46 (*"unsound"*).

90  *"As we lost height":* Chatterton, 73; Thruelsen and Arnold, 111–15 (*"We went under"*); *By Air to Battle,* 57 (*"All is not well"*).

90  *Fifty-four gliders made land: By Air to Battle,* 57; Wood, 217 (*Horsa No. 132*); Chatterton, 94.

90  *Rather than five hundred or more:* Chatterton, 87–88; Hickey, 103.

90  *The British high command would proclaim:* Geoffrey Reagan, *Blue on Blue: A History of Friendly Fire,* 139; memo, HQ, Fifth Army Airborne Training Center to GCM, Aug. 15, 1943, NARA RG 165, E 419, WD GS, director of plans and ops, top secret gen'l corr, 312.4-319.1, 390/37/18/3, box 14 (*"practically zero"*); *By Air to Battle,* 59 (*"confusion and dismay"*).

### The Loss of Irrecoverable Hours

91  *If much had gone wrong:* Albert Kesselring, "The Campaign for Sicily: Concluding Considerations," n.d., in "Mittelmeerkrieg," part II, "Tunisien," FMS #T-3 P1, NARA RG 319, OCMH, box 245, 19; MEB, "Axis Tactical Operations in Sicily," ts, n.d., OCMH, #147, MHI (*"amphibious contrivances"*).

91  *hints of invasion:* "War Diary of German Naval Command in Italy," July 1, 1943, SEM, NHC, box 57; situation reports, *OB Süd,* July 1 and 7, 1943, NARA RG 319, OCMH, box 246; Michael Howard, *Strategic Deception in the Second World War,* 87–88 (*fictional "Twelfth Army"*).

91  *Operation MINCEMEAT:* Frank J. Stech, "Outguessed and One-Behind: The Real Story of *The Man Who Never Was,*" paper presented to conference, University of Wolverhampton, UK, July 2004; Ewen Montagu, *The Man Who Never Was,* 11, 73–74; "Mincemeat," in "Naval Deception," vol. III, ADM 223/794, 442–60, UK NA; monthly log, H.M.S. *Seraph,* UK NA, ADM 173/18038; Roger Morgan, "The Second World War's Best Kept Secret Revealed," *After the Battle,* no. 94, 1996, 31+; Ralph Bennett, *Ultra and the Mediterranean Strategy,* 227; "Historical Record of Deception in the War Against Germany and Italy," vol. 2, UK NA, CAB 154/101, 385–89.

92  *Six immobile and badly armed:* Garland, 110–11; Walter Fries, "Der Kampf Um Sizilien," ts, n.d., FMS #T-2, NARA RG 319, OCMH, box 245, 6–9; Eberhardt Rodt, "Studie über den Feldzug in Sizilien bei der 15. Pz Gren. Div, Mai–August 1943," n.d., FMS #C-077, NARA RG 319, OCMH, box 245, 15; *SSA,* 69–70 (*went to bed*); MEB, "Axis Tactical Operations in Sicily" (*"Italian soil"*); F. H. Hinsley et al., *British Intelligence in the Second World War,* vol. 3, part 1, 84 (*Spitfires*); Alice Leccese Powers, *Italy in Mind,* 302 (*D. H. Lawrence*).

92  *Little was expected:* MEB, "Axis Tactical Operations in Sicily: The Mission of General Guzzoni," May 1959, NARA RG 319, E 145, OCMH, 270/19/30-31/6-2, R-117, 38; Leo J. Meyer, "Strategy and Logistical History: MTO," n.d., CMH, 2-3.7 CC5, XIV-7 (*nine thousand yards*); Hellmut Bergengruen, "Kampf der Pz. Div. Hermann Goering auf Sizilien vom 10–14.7.1943," Dec. 1950, FMS, #C-087a, NARA RG 319, box 245, 13 (*morning glare*).

92  *The German response:* George F. Howe, "American Signal Intelligence in Northwest Africa and Western Europe," U.S. Cryptologic History, series IV, vol. 1, n.d., NARA RG

57, SRH-391, 52; Max Ulich, "Sicilian Campaign Special Problems and Their Solutions," March 1947, FMS, #D-004, MHI, 4 (*car wreck*); Bergengruen, "Kampf der Pz. Div. Hermann Goering," 14–16 (*olive groves*); "War Diary of German Naval Command in Italy," July 10, 1943 (*"cleaned up"*); war diary, German liaison staff, Italian 6th Army," July 10–11, 1943, in FMS, #C-095, MHI, 25–34 (*reembarked*); "Operazioni in Sicilia dal 9 al 19 luglio," Comando Supremo diary, July 11, 1943, 2100 hrs., NARA RG 319, OCMH, box 246 (*"constantly in crisis"*).

92  *Such fairy tales:* Kesselring, "The Campaign for Sicily," 19–22; Kenneth Macksey, *Kesselring: The Making of the Luftwaffe,* 206 (*"Germany's savior"*); Albrecht Kesselring, *The Memoirs of Field-Marshal Kesselring,* 27 (*"less pleasing things"*); Johannes Steinhof, *Messerschmitts over Sicily,* 27 (*leather case*).

93  *"Kesselring is a colossal optimist":* GS IV, 463; Paul Deichmann, "Italian Campaign," 1948, FMS, #T-1a, chapter 1, 29; Steinhof, 27 (*raid on Marsala*).

93  *For six months he had pondered:* Kesselring, *Memoirs,* 158; Garland, 46, 51; "Stellungnahme des verantwortlichen Oberbefehlshaber Süd zu den Betractungen des Oberst von Bonin," n.d., in Kesselring, "Mittelmeerkrieg," part II, "Tunisien," FMS #T-3 P1, NARA RG 319, OCMH, box 245, 3 (*strategic concept*); Kesselring, "Italy as a Military Ally," 1948, FMS, #C-015, MHI, 4–5, 9 (*"easily contented"*).

93  *"pretty sugar pastry":* Kesselring, "Mittelmeerkrieg," 69; Kesselring, "The Campaign for Sicily," 19–22; Kesselring, "German Strategy During the Italian Campaign," n.d., FMS, #B-270, MHI, 12, 29 (*"mousetrap"*); Frido von Senger und Etterlin, "Liaison Activities with Italian 6th Army," 1951, FMS, #C-095, MHI, 14–15; war diary, German liaison staff, Italian 6th Army, July 10–11, 1943, in FMS, #C-095, MHI, 25–34; Paul Conrath, "Der Kampf um Sizilien," Jan. 1951, FMS, #C-087c, NARA RG 319, box 245, 2–3 (*Göring panzers*); Bergengruen, "Kampf der Pz. Div. Hermann Goering," 4–9 (*nine thousand combat troops*); Garland, 171n.

94  *counterattack Gela at first light:* Garland, 163; Kesselring, "The Campaign for Sicily," 12–13 (*"immediate advance"*).

94  *"The Romans are fleeing":* "The Reminiscences of Walter C. W. Ansel," 146; Tregaskis, 29 (*"twinkling walk"*); Biddle, 71 (*"Bald, burnt"*); William A. Carter, "Carter's War," ts, 1983, CEOH, box V-14, VII-22 (*upside down*); John Lardner, "Up Front with Roosevelt," in Jack Stenbuck, ed., *Typewriter Battalion,* 127–28 (*"rhythmic state"*); Frederick T. McCue, ASEQ, n.d., Battery A, 171st FA Bn, 45th ID, MHI (*"Get into the battle!"*).

94  *"I will always be known":* H. Paul Jeffers, *In the Rough Rider's Shadow,* 152, 164, 174–75; Benjamin S. Persons, *Relieved of Command,* 66; Donald P. Darnell, "Brigadier General Theodore Roosevelt, Jr.," *World War II,* May 1998, 18+; Michael Pearlman, *To Make Democracy Safe for America,* 250 (*"anti-bluff"*); corr, TR to Eleanor, June 5 (*"small beer"*), June 12, 1943, TR, LOC MS Div, box 10.

95  *"born to combat":* Quentin Reynolds, *The Curtain Rises,* 214; corr, Robert A. Riesman [26th Inf Regt] to author, Sept. 10, 2002 (*"Keep it clear"*); A. J. Liebling, "Find 'Em, Fix 'Em, and Fight 'Em," *New Yorker,* part 2, May 1, 1943, 24+; author interview, Richard A. Williams, Jan. 25, 2003 (*"we willingly got up"*); diary, GSP, June 24, 1943, GSP, LOC MS Div, box 2, folder 15.

95  *"Well, doesn't it?":* Maxwell Hamilton, "Junior in Name Only," *Retired Officer,* June 1981, 28+; Omar N. Bradley, *A Soldier's Story,* 110–11 (*"beat up every M.P."*); Samuel David Spivey, *A Doughboy's Narrative,* s.p., 1995, 81–82 (*"Too much vino"*).

96  *Toxic rumors:* Jean Gordon Peltier, *World War II Diary of Jean Gordon Peltier,* 82; Benjamin A. Dickson, "G-2 Journal: Algiers to the Elbe," ts, n.d., MHI, 69 (*hoarding Camels*); "Terry Allen and the First Division in North Africa and Sicily," ts, n.d., TdA, box 5, MHI, 32 (*"yellow-bellies"*); Stanhope Brasfield Mason, "Reminiscences and Anecdotes of World War II," ts, 1988, MRC FDM, 150–51 (*"killed trying to invade"*).

96 *By late May, when the division bivouacked:* Willam E. Faust, ASEQ, divarty HHQ, 1st ID, MHI, 60; Donald McB. Curtis, *The Song of the Fighting First,* 103–4 (*"Let us know"*); memo, S. B. Mason, "Weapons," May 17, 1943, Stanhope Mason papers, MRC FDM (*brass knuckles*); memo, "Conference Notes, 24 May 1943," Mason papers, MRC FDM (*"disheveled appearance"*); "History, Mediterranean Base Section, Sept. 1942–May 1944," CMH, 8-4 CA 1944, 35 (*five P.M. curfew*); Dickson, "G-2 Journal," 69 (*"lively brawls"*); Franklyn A. Johnson, *One More Hill,* 76 (*"Truckloads"*); speech, Stanhope B. Mason, Apr. 24, 1976, 57th annual dinner of Officers of the First Division, NYC, in Smith, 194 (*"need not salute"*).

96 *"bitched, buggered and bewildered":* speech, Mason, Apr. 24, 1976; JPL, 24–25; Omar N. Bradley, *A Soldier's Story,* 110–11 (*Eisenhower was furious*), 118 (*"piratical"*); Benjamin S. Persons, *Relieved of Command,* 69; Robert John Rogers, "A Study of Leadership in the First Infantry Division During World War II," thesis, 1965, Ft. L, 118 (*"freebooters"*).

97 *vineyards and orchards of the Geloan plain:* author visit, Sept. 1996; Garland, 165.

97 *Through his field glasses:* Ladislas Farago, *Patton: Ordeal and Triumph,* 297; Jeffers, 225; "History of the 26th Infantry Regiment," 16–17 (*"trying to flush quail"*).

98 *Shortly before seven A.M.:* "History of the 26th Infantry Regiment," 18–19; H. R. Knickerbocker et al., *Danger Forward,* 105; Garland, 166–67; Farago, 297 (*"situation not so good"*); Robert W. Baumer, *Before Taps Sounded,* s.p., 2000, 174 (*"We beat their asses"*); corr, TR to Eleanor, July 17, 1943, TR, LOC MS Div, box 10.

98 *In the lemon grove:* Romeiser, ed., 162; "Terry Allen and the First Division in North Africa and Sicily," ts, n.d., TdA, box 5, MHI, 50 (*rolling gait*); Pearlman, 249–50.

99 *Before flunking out:* Gerald Astor, *Terrible Terry Allen,* 11–12; Thomas W. Dixon, "Terry Allen," *Army,* Apr. 1978, 57+ (*"loved horses"*); Liebling, "Find 'Em, Fix 'Em, and Fight 'Em," 221+.

99 *"The soldier's greatest nightmare":* obit, NYT, Sept. 13, 1969; Astor, 184 (*"win or die"*); "Allen and His Men," *Time,* Aug. 9, 1943, 30+ (*"It's crazy"*); Johnson, 77 (*"Do your job"*); corr, TdA to Mary Fran, June 6, 1943, TdA, MHI, box 2.

99 *"Couriers dashed":* Romeiser, ed., 166; "Addendum by Major Groves, 27 Oct. 1950," in OH, Bryce F. Denno and Melvin J. Groves, 16th Inf., Oct. 24, 1950, SM, MHI; Garland, 166–67; Smith, 21 (*"let's not wait"*).

99 *At 10:10 A.M., the 3rd Battalion:* Baumgartner et al., 41; Knickerbocker, 106; Peltier, 99; "Terry Allen and the First Division," ts, n.d., TdA, box 5, MHI, 37.

100 *Allen climbed to the crest:* Romeiser, ed., 166–67; Clift Andrus, notes on *A Soldier's Story,* ts, n.d., MRC FDM, 1988.32, box 215 (*"burning tanks and confusion"*); Garland, 160; memo, George A. Taylor, Dec. 26, 1950, SM, MHI; corr, John M. Brooks to author, Oct. 19, 2003; SSA, 109–12 (LST 313); Jackson, "Signal Communication in the Sicilian Campaign," 63; combat narrative, Curtis Shears, USNR, Apr. 3, 1944, NHC, 2; William S. Hutchinson, Jr., "Use of the 4.2-inch Chemical Mortar in the Invasion of Sicily," *MR,* Nov. 1943, 13+ (*fishing dinghies*).

100 *"I want tanks":* memo, TdA to OCMH, n.d., NARA RG 319, OCMH, box 250; AAR, 3/16th Inf, Aug. 16, 1943, NARA RG 319, OCMH, 2-3.7 CC2, box 247; Charles F. Ryan et al., "2nd Armored Division in the Sicilian Campaign," May 1950, AS, Ft. K, 24 (*large shears*).

101 *"deficient inner cohesion":* Bergengruen, "Der Kampf der Pz. Div. 'Hermann Goering,'" 14–19; Fridolin von Senger und Etterlin, "Die Abwehr der Achsenmächte auf Sizilien," *Allgemeine schweizerische Militär Zeitschrift,* Dec. 1950, 859–60 (*too mammoth to tow*); MEB, "Axis Tactical Operations in Sicily" (*"returning to their ships"*).

101 *"They are carrying armloads":* Johnson, 89; Romeiser, ed. (*"Hell, no"*).

101 *Patton came ashore:* Mason, 269; memo, GSP, July 11, 1943, GSP, LOC MS Div, box 11, folder 8; Dennis Showalter, *Patton and Rommel,* 315 (*timing his own pulse*); Jack Belden,

"Battle of Sicily," 27+ (*"beautiful and battle-fevered"*); Milton F. Perry and Barbara W. Parke, *Patton and His Pistols*, 62; Patton, 54; Paul W. Brown, 165 (*"Kraut bastards"*).

101 *Adolf's Alley:* D'Este, *Bitter Victory*, 317; Jackson, "Signal Communication in the Sicilian Campaign," 58–61 (*code rooms*).

102 *Dust and gray smoke:* SSA, 112; Carlo D'Este, *Patton: A Genius for War*, 507; corr, GSP to L. J. McNair, Aug. 2, 1943, GSP, LOC MS Div, box 11 (*"dervishes"*); James B. Lyle, "The Operations of Companies A and B, 1st Ranger Battlion, at Gela, Sicily," 1948, IS, 18–19 (*"hanging from trees"*); Blythe Foote Finke, *No Mission Too Difficult*, 130 (*"Kick 'em"*).

102 *"a most foolish manner":* note, GSP, ts, n.d., GSP, LOC MS Div, box 48, folder 20.

102 *If the Italians had been stopped:* TdA, "Commanding General's After Action Report," 1950, in Smith, 127; Garland, 170; MEB, "Axis Tactical Operations in Sicily"; Martin A. Shadday, "Operations of Company C, 41st Armored Infantry Regiment, 2nd AD, at Gela, Sicily," 1948, IS, 15 (*dried mud*); OH, Samuel A. D. Hunter, March 7, 1944, NHC, 8–9 (*"To arms"*); *The Sicilian Campaign*, 93; William H. Frazier, Jr., "The Operations of XII Air Support Command in the Invasion of Sicily," 1948, IS, 21 (*"Men burned"*).

103 *Firepower arrived:* DSC citation, Clift Andrus, NARA RG 338, ETO, Seventh Army awards, box 2; Thomas F. Lancer, "Goodbye Mr. Chips," in Albert H. Smith, Jr., ed., "Biographical Sketches, WWII," MRC FDM; bio file, Clift Andrus, n.d., MHI; Malcolm Marshall, ed., *Proud Americans*, 112 (*threatened to shoot any man*).

103 *Then, above the whine:* Clift Andrus, "Amphibious Landings—North Africa, Sicily, and Normandy," ts, n.d., MRC FDM, 26; Godson, 74.

103 *German tanks began to burn:* Patrick K. O'Donnell, *Beyond Valor*, 51; Franz Kurowski, *The History of the Fallschirmpanzerkorps Hermann Göring*, 159 (*"rivets flew about"*); William T. Dillon, 1/16th Inf, ASEQ, MHI, 6 (*"he was melted"*); Bergengruen, "Kampf der Pz. Div. Hermann Goering," 20–21 (*"counterattack against the hostile landings"*); TdA, "Commanding General's After Action Report," 127 (*"damned Heinies"*); Romeiser, ed., 167 (*"merely embarrassing"*).

104 *Patton returned to the beach:* PP, 279; D'Este, *Patton*, 507; Mark M. Boatner III, *The Biographical Dictionary of World War II*, 138 (*white-haired brigadier*); Patrick K. O'Donnell, *Operatives, Spies, and Saboteurs*, 45–50 (*"happy as a clam"*); Anthony Cave Brown, *The Last Hero*, 352 (*"fucking and fighting"*).

104 *"I had the bitter experience":* memo, Paul Conrath, July 12, 1943, AFHQ captured documents, NARA RG 407, E 47, 95 AL1-2.9, box 162; Andrus, "Amphibious Landings," 27; Kurowski, 157; MEB, "Axis Tactical Operations in Sicily" (*630 men killed*); Garland, 171n; Charles E. Smith, "The American Campaign in Sicily," ts, n.d., CMH, Geog Sicily 314.7, 17 (*American casualties*); report summary, Seventh Army, n.d., NARA RG 319, OCMH, 2-3.7 CC2 Sicily, box 250 (*nine thousand prisoners*); "Report of Activities," July 31, 1944, staff judge advocate, 1st ID, MRC FDM (*dead civilians*).

105 *"I am well satisfied":* memo, GSP, July 11, 1943, GSP, LOC MS Div, box 11, folder 8; PP, 279–80.

*"Tonight Wear White Pajamas"*

105 *His own losses were modest:* The Sicilian Campaign, 91–93 (*the* Barnett); Carver, 22; Roskill, 131 (Talamba); action reports, S. H. Alexander and Ralph C. Adams, LST 313, ts, n.d., in Donald J. Hunt, "USS LST 313 and Battery A, 33rd Field Artillery," ts, 1997, MRC FDM, 42; SSA, 108 (*flaming axles*); Knickerbocker et al., 103–4.

105 *Each successive raid:* AAFinWWII, 445; HKH, "The Sicilian Campaign," 17–18 (*"almost complete lack"*); "Notes on the Planning and Assault Phases of the Sicilian Campaign," UK Combined Operations HQ, Bulletin No. Y/1, Oct. 1943, CARL, 2–7.

106 *Air Force commanders:* AAFinWWII, 445 (*"parceling out"*); Coles, "Participation of the Ninth and Twelfth Air Forces," 177–78 (*"personal control"*); Garland, 106–7.

106 *Considering that the Navy had been prepared to lose:* "The Army Air Forces in Amphibious Landings in World War II," July 1953, CARL, N-16372.34, 32–46; corr, HKH to SEM, Feb. 9, 1953, SEM, NHC, box 51 (*"we can't get the goddamn Air Force"*); Ralph G. Martin, "Invasion of Sicily," Aug. 13, 1943, in Steve Kluger, *Yank,* 101+ (*"Only the good people"*).

106 *Back at the Gela roads:* action report, John McFadzean, gunnery officer, S.S. *Rowan,* Dec. 22, 1943, NHC, 17–18; Karig, 244–45 (*"a flat sheet of crimson fire"*); OH, Charles William Harwood, U.S.S. *Dickman,* Nov. 19, 1943, NHC; *The Sicilian Campaign,* 94.

107 *"hard as flint":* George C. Mitchell, *Matthew B. Ridgway: Soldier, Statesman, Scholar, Citizen,* 27, 35 (*"Even with his penis"*); Soffer, 22, 36 (*"cultivate the art"*); Blair, 111.

107 *"Tonight wear white pajamas":* "Report of Allied Force Airborne Board"; Garland, 175n; Warren, 22; Mason, "Reminiscences and Anecdotes," 171–73; AAR, 7th Army, G-3, n.d., NARA RG 319, OCMH, 2-3.7 CC2, box 250 (*"It is essential"*); Joseph M. Whitaker, "Report of Investigation Concerning Shooting Down of Airborne Troops, 11–12 July 1943," Sept. 21, 1943, GSP, LOC MS Div, box 49, folder 11 (Monrovia's *signal room*); memo, MBR, "Reported Loss of Transport Planes and Personnel," Aug. 2, 1943, CJB, box 48, 4–6 (*asking whether the gunners knew*).

107 *"There's always some son-of-a-bitch":* McLean, "Adventures in Occupied Areas," 36; Whitaker, "Report of Investigation"; Thomas B. Gage, 45th ID, in William O. Perry, "Report of Investigation," Aug. 14, 1943, 45th ID IG, NARA RG 338, AG 1943, 333.5, box 111 (*signal officers struggled*).

108 *Ridgway for six weeks had warned:* Garland, 175–77; Charles R. Shrader, "Amicicide: The Problem of Friendly Fire in Modern War," Dec. 1982, CSI, 70 (*"Every plane that came over"*); Warren, 40.

108 *"Am terribly worried":* PP, 280.

108 *The contagion spread:* Garland, 177; Willard E. Harrison, Co. A, 504th PIR, in Alvin B. Welsch, "Report of Investigation: Alleged Shooting Down of Friendly Troop Carrying Transport Planes," n.d., NARA RG 338, AG 1943, 333.5, box 111 (*"I looked back"*); Lee D. Carr, in Robert Miley, "But Never a Soldier," ts, 1987 (*Pilots dove*); Breuer, 143 (*rosary beads*); corr, John P. O'Malley to W. P. Yarborough, Jan. 20, 1980, CJB, "Chrono. File: Sicily," MHI, box 48 (*"read a newspaper"*).

108 *Formations disintegrated:* Whitaker, "Report of Investigation," 11; Welsch, "Report of Investigation" (*belly lights*); Garland, 178n; Ross S. Carter, *Those Devils in Baggy Pants,* 23 (*"bird shot in flight"*); Coles, "Participation of the Ninth and Twelfth Air Forces," 88 (*tantamount to murder*); OH, William P. Yarborough, 1975, J. R. Meese and H. P. Houser, SOOHP, MHI, 31–32; corr, W. P. Yarborough to Adam A. Komosa, Sept. 25, 1962, CMH, Geog Files, Sicily, 370.2; Adam Bernstein, "Lt. Gen. William Yarborough Dies," WP, Dec. 8, 2005, B5; "Report on Operation Husky," Army Observers, Amphibious Forces, U.S. Atlantic Fleet, 1943, MHI (*"at least four were shot"*); "Synopsis of Operations in Sicilian Campaign," n.d., 82nd Abn Div, NARA RG 319, OCMH, 2-3.7 CC2 Sicily, box 246; Adam A. Komosa, "Airborne Operation, 504th Parachute Infantry, Sicily," 1946, IS; "A Study of Operation Husky," June 28, 1947, Ground General School, DTL, Ft. B, 25 (*passwords*); Soffer, 48.

108 *"Stop, you bastards":* Romeiser, ed., 168; Samuel Hynes, *The Soldiers' Tale,* 153 (*"large pumpkins"*); Martin, 68–70 (*candlesticked*); Garland, 179; Breuer, 145.

108 *Colonel Reuben H. Tucker:* Welsch, "Report of Investigation"; Garland, 179, 181n; AAR, 52nd Troop Carrier Wing, July 12, 1943, JPL, MHI, box 11 (*half shot down*); John Mason Brown, 164 (*escape in a rubber raft*).

108 *At last the shooting ebbed:* "Tactical Employment in the U.S. Army of Transport Aircraft and Gliders," 39; "Airborne Operations Conference," St. Georges Hotel, Algiers, July 24, 1943, "Material on Operation HUSKY, 1943, Allied Forces," MHI, D763.S5 A5; memo,

MBR, "Casualties, Sicilian Campaign, CT 504," May 19, 1944, NARA RG 319, OCMH, 2-3.7 CC2 Sicily, box 246; Garland, 182; Blair, 102 (*only 3,900*).

110 *"I was glad to see"*: Maxwell D. Taylor, *Swords and Plowshares,* 50.

110 *"By golly"*: John Gunther, *D Day,* 61; *Three Years,* 357; John Gunther, *Eisenhower: The Man and the Symbol,* 154 (*"gilded cage"*).

110 *"More like a huge regatta"*: corr, J.F.M. Whiteley to J. N. Kennedy, July 14, 1943, UK NA, WO 204/307; Gunther, *D Day,* 67 (*"when they pipe me on"*).

110 *Patton led the way:* "Allied Commander-in-Chief's Report on Sicilian Campaign 1943," 92; Aris, 119 (*little extra food*); Richard Doherty, *A Noble Crusade,* 142 (*anticipated ten thousand*); Neillands, 223 (*Montgomery confidently predicted*).

111 *As for his own Seventh Army:* Garland, 189; ONB, "Operation of II Corps, U.S. Army in Sicily," n.d., CMH, Geog Files, Sicily, 370.2, 7; Howe, "American Signal Intelligence," 52 (*"Send more pigeons"*); Philip Vian, *Action This Day,* 105 (*"pigeon English"*).

111 *"Ike had stepped on him hard"*: *Three Years,* 360; JPL, 58.

111 *"Patton stood at the edge"*: Gunther, *D Day,* 70–71; HKH, "The Sicilian Campaign," timeline, 2–15 (Monrovia *radio room*); Gunther, *Eisenhower,* 156–57 (*"welcome Canada"*).

112 *"Provided everything goes"*: *Three Years,* 361, 363; diary, HCB, July 13, 1943, DDE Lib, A-578 (*"calm and matter-of-fact"*).

112 *"You particularly requested me"*: Chandler, vol. 2, 1255; DDE to GSP, July 12, 1943, GSP, LOC MS Div, box 49, folder 11 (*"inexcusable carelessness"*).

112 *Investigations would go forth:* memo, J. E. Hull to GCM, Aug. 2, 1943, "Report of Allied Force Airborne Board (Invasion of Sicily)," NARA RG 319, OCMH, box 250; OH, HKH, 1961, John T. Mason, Col U OHRO, 356; memo, Paul L. Williams to DDE, July 13, with notes by A. Tedder, Carl Spaatz papers, diary, LOC MS Div, box 13 (*"not operationally sound"*); F.A.M. Browning, NATOUSA conference, July 24, 1943, 82nd Airborne Div, "Synopsis of Operations in Sicilian Campaign," NARA RG 319, OCMH, 2-3.7 CC2 Sicily, box 246 (*"well-pleased"*).

112 *"unavoidable incident of combat"*: diary, July 13, 1943, GSP, LOC MS Div, box 2, folder 15; JPL, 58 (*bedbugs*).

### "The Dark World Is Not Far from Us"

112 *They pressed inland:* Smith, 28; Robert Capa, *Slightly Out of Focus,* 71 (*too many stripes*); Dancocks, 47 (*scuffing through flour*); Walter J. Eldredge, "First Shot in Anger," www.4point2.org (*"After the first mile"*); Farley Mowat, *The Regiment,* 64 (*"brain furnaces"*); Anders Kjar Arnbal, *The Barrel-Land Dance Hall Rangers,* 119 (*Benzedrine*); Gunther, *D Day,* 142; Alan Moorehead, *Eclipse,* 3; Charles R. Codman, *Drive,* 113; Walter Bernstein, *Keep Your Head Down,* 105 (*"face in the dirt"*).

113 *"Right of way!"*: Robert E. Coffin and Joan N. Coffin, "The Robert Edmonston Coffin–Joan Nelson Coffin Family Book," 84; John Steinbeck, *Once There Was a War,* 196–98.

113 *the dust of St. Rita's bones:* Norman Lewis, *In Sicily,* 157; Fred Howard, *Whistle While You Wait,* 71, 86 (*"life and death of a saint"*).

113 *"few words, many deeds"*: David Hunt, *A Don at War,* 201; Moorehead, 4; McCallum, 155; Howard, 86 (*"frayed trousers"*); Lewis, 33, 67 (*"bee-eaters"*); corr, anonymous U.S. Army civil affairs officer, Aug. 1, 1943, Malcolm S. McLean papers, MHI (*"carton of cigarettes"*).

114 *Dead enemy soldiers:* Mowat, *And No Birds Sang,* 66; annex, Administrative Order No. 1, June 14, 1943, Seventh Army, Walter J. Muller papers, HIA, box 2 (*"E.D."*); C.R.S. Harris, *Allied Administration of Italy, 1943–1945,* 37 (*grave-diggers' strike*); Harry L. Coles and Albert K. Weinberg, *Civil Affairs: Soldiers Become Governors,* 188, 483; "Report on the

First Phase of AMGOT Occupation, Sicily and Region II," 8 (*"the mob lay down"*); Jackson, "Signal Communication in the Sicilian Campaign," 82 (*"seven alleged saboteurs"*).

114 *"La donna è mobile"*: John M. Mecklin, "Former Actor Sings Aria," United Press, *New York World-Telegram,* Aug. 9, 1943; "statement made by Francis Carpenter," July 14, 1943, SEM, NHC, box 50, folder 22.

114 *No one was more eager:* Allan R. Milett, "Overrated and Underrated," *American Heritage,* vol. 51, no. 3 (May–June 2000); Omar N. Bradley and Clay Blair, *A General's Life,* 179 (*"Feeling worse"*); Paul L. Skogsberg, "A Slice of World War II," ts, n.d., 1st Recon Troop, 1st ID, ASEQ, MHI, 48 (*"cavalry tonsils"*); Hansen diary, July 10–11, 1943, Hansen, MHI (*seasick*); Bradley Commentaries, Hansen, MHI, box 1, 13-A, S-24 (*life preserver*); "Operations of II Corps in Sicily," Sept. 1, 1943, 6–7.

115 *"elderly rifleman"*: Robert H. Adelman and George Walton, *Rome Fell Today,* 55; Martin Blumenson, *The Battle of the Generals,* 31; Charles Christian Wertenbaker, "Omar Nelson Bradley," *Life,* June 5, 1944, 101+ (*"Ozark lake"*); OH, ONB, Aug. 14, 1969, George S. Pappas, ONB, MHI (*"big, green frogs"*); OH, ONB, n.d., Kitty Buhler, ONB, MHI, 170 (*"number 8 post"*); Bradley and Blair, 690n (*"so damn normal"*).

115 *"Underneath the mask"*: Blumenson, *The Battle of the Generals,* 31; OH, ONB, Buhler, 159–60; Bradley Commentaries, Hansen, 16-A, S-27 and S-29 (*"He's impetuous"*).

115 *Among the most pressing problems:* Just under fifty thousand enemy POWs were captured in World War I. Figure provided by MG William A. Stofft, USA (ret.), Meuse-Argonne staff ride, USAREUR, Sept. 2004; Steinhof, 74 (*"asbestos"*); Mowat, *And No Birds Sang,* 124; OH, Samuel A. D. Hunter, March 7, 1944, NHC, 22 (*"No prisoners taken here"*); Bill Mauldin, *Up Front,* 64.

116 *"When are you going to start?"*: P/W Interrogation Report, Aug. 15, 1943, in daily report, Psychological Warfare Branch, 7th Army HQ, Sept. 9, 1943, NARA RG 226, OSS History, E 99, 190/6/7/6, box 40; Peter Schrijvers, *The Crash of Ruin,* 120 (*"queer race"*).

116 *Operation* HUSKY *had exacted:* Martin Blumenson, *Patton: The Man Behind the Legend, 1885–1945,* 195 (*"kill devastatingly"*); Homer W. Jones, 7th Army JAG, Feb. 17, 1944, testimony, board of review, NATOUSA JAG, NARA RG 159, IG, 333.9, box 67; Albert C. Wedemeyer, *Wedemeyer Reports!,* 226; Paul A. Cundiff, *45th Infantry CP,* 91; George E. Martin, *Blow, Bugle, Blow,* 96; testimony, John T. Compton, Oct. 22, 1943, court-martial records, J. T. Compton, obtained under FOIA, JAG, Arlington, Va. (*"killers are immortal"*).

116 *Despite these admonitions:* "Report on Operation Husky," Army Observers, Amphibious Forces, MHI; Raymond S. McLain, "Account Written by Brig. Gen. McLain," ts, 1943, NARA RG 319, OCMH, "45th Div Landings," 2-3.7 cc2 Sicily, box 247, 7, 11 (*"Not good"*); Garland, 189–90; Troy H. Middleton, testimony, Feb. 19, 1944, board of review, NATOUSA JAG; Whitlock, 44 (*"ugliest looking man"*); Frank James Price, *Troy H. Middleton: A Biography,* 148; Martin, 93 (*"captive can't fight"*); AAR, 180th Inf Regt, July 10–Aug. 16, 1943, 45th ID Mus; Fisher, "The Story of the 180th Infantry Regiment," 70–71; D'Este, *Bitter Victory,* 286 (*"Dear General"*).

117 *By early Wednesday morning:* "History of the Aviation Engineers in the Mediterranean Theater of Operations," June 1946, AAF Engineer Command, MTO, CEOH, X-39 (*two hundred bomb craters*); "Operations of II Corps in Sicily," Sept. 1, 1943 (*"hidden in the cockpit"*); George A. Fisher, "The Story of the 180th Infantry Regiment," ts, 1945, 98–101 (*Flames crackled in the grain*).

117 *Sniper fire still winked:* Wallace Wing, Co. A, 1/180th Inf, July 16, 1943, statement, court-martial record, Horace T. West, obtained under FOIA, JAG, Arlington, Va. (*"killing spirit"*); corr, Richard Pisciotta to father, May 18, 1944, 3/157th Inf, ASEQ, MHI (*"soldiers get old"*).

117 *West proved a poor choice:* "Chronology of Case," Horace T. West, 7th Army JAG, NATOUSA JAG, NARA RG 159, IG, 333.9, box 67 (*"most thorough non-com"*); testimony,

H. T. West, Oct. 1943, court-martial records, obtained under FOIA; H. T. West, cited in board of review, NATOUSA JAG, NARA RG 159, IG, 333.9, box 67 (*"watch them bleed"*).

118 *In two shuffling columns:* testimony, Haskell Brown, Oct. 1943, court-martial records, H. T. West; memo, 45th Div IG to CG, "Report of Investigation of Shooting of Prisoners of War by Sgt. Horace T. West," Aug. 5, 1943 (*"Turn around"*).

118 *They fell:* board of review, NATOUSA JAG.

118 *Five hours later, it happened again:* "Operations of II Corps in Sicily," Sept. 1, 1943, 8.

118 *In command of Company C:* testimony, John Gazetti, Jim Hair, Raymond C. Marlow, Richard P. Blanks, court-martial records, J. T. Compton; James J. Weingartner, "Massacre at Biscari," *Historian*, vol. 52, no. 1, Nov. 1989, 24+.

119 *brevity of his sermons:* Cundiff, 49–50.

119 *"Most were lying face down"*: William King, testimony, n.d., board of review, West court-martial, NATOUSA JAG, NARA RG 159, IG, 333.9, box 67; William King, statement to investigators, July 16, 1943, West court-martial (*"They felt ashamed"*); Martin, 96.

119 *"I told Bradley"*: PP, 288.

119 *Two war correspondents:* "Talk with Alexander Clifford," Apr. 4, 1944, LH, 11/1944/29; letters, LH to Alexander Clifford, Nov. 8, 1948, and A. Clifford to LH, Nov. 17, 1948, LH, 1/175/28-29; corr, GSP to GCM, July 18, 1943, NARA RG 319, OCMH, 2-3.7 CC2 Sicily, box 250.

119 *"we should try the two men"*: PP, 316; IG report, Aug. 5, 1943, cited in West court-martial records; D'Este, *Patton*, 509 (*"Try the bastards"*).

119 *"an order to annihilate"*: Compton, testimony, court-martial records; Weingartner, "Massacre at Biscari," 24 (*"took him at his word"*).

120 *"Good riddance"*: Martin, 97.

120 *"The whole tendency in the thing"*: Forrest E. Cookson, testimony, Feb. 16, 1944, NATOUSA JAG, NARA RG 159, IG, 333.9, box 67; diary, HCB, July 13, 1943, DDE Lib, A-863 (*"feared reprisal"*).

120 *"the savagery that is war"*: "Memorandum for Gen. Brannon, 'Records of Trial,'" from "Lt. Col. W. H. Johnson, Jr., JAGC," May 26, 1950, and "Memorandum for Judge Patterson," from "Col. Stanley Grogan, GSC, acting director," Feb. 1, 1944, West court-martial records.

120 *"evil spirits seemed to come out"*: Roy P. Stewart, "Raymond S. McLain, America's Greatest Citizen Soldier," *Chronicles of Oklahoma*, vol. 59, no. 1 (spring 1981), 4+; Robert H. Patton, *The Pattons*, 265 (*"fair-haired boys"*); Cundiff, 92 (*"thoughtless killers"*).

### Chapter 3: An Island Redoubt
*"Into Battle with Stout Hearts"*

123 *The command car purred:* John Gunther, *D Day*, 111; Carlo D'Este, *Bitter Victory*, 93; L.S.B. Shapiro, *They Left the Back Door Open*, 42 (*dry-goods shopkeeper*), 68; Dick Malone, *Missing from the Record*, 45 (*"which one is me"*); Alan Moorehead, *Montgomery*, 36 (*"mousetrap"*); Farley Mowat, *And No Birds Sang*, 74 (*"Deadly stuff"*); Daniel G. Dancocks, *The D-Day Dodgers: The Canadians in Italy, 1943–1945*, 48 (*"good plans"*); J. K. Windeatt, "Very Ordinary Soldier," ts, 1989, IWM 90/20/1, 64 (*handing lighters*).

123 *If the campaign:* Garland, 206–7; Molony V, 93, 106.

124 *Montgomery presented this:* Stanley P. Hirshson, *General Patton: A Soldier's Life*, 372; Omar N. Bradley and Clay Blair, *A General's Story*, 188; AAR, Seventh Army G-3, n.d., NARA RG 319, OCMH, 2-3.7 CC2 Sicily, box 250 (*"on two axes"*); Alexander S. Cochran, "Constructing a Military Coalition from Materials at Hand," paper, SMH, Apr. 16, 1999, 12 (*Eisenhower declined*); JPL, 78.

124 *Baleful consequences followed:* Garland, 207; Molony V, 110–11; Benjamin A. Dickson, "G-2 Journal: Algiers to the Elbe," MHI, 84 (*Bradley scrambled*); Nigel Hamilton, *Master of the Battlefield*, 317 (*divergent axes*).

124 *"you can't allow him":* Bradley and Blair, 188–89; *PP*, 285 ("*What fools*"); Robert E. Coffin and Joan N. Coffin, "The Robert Edmonston Coffin–Joan Nelson Coffin Family Book," 80–81 ("*right up his ass*"); GK, July 13, 1943.

124 *"The feeling of discord":* Three Years, 321; *PP*, 243 ("*straw man*"); diary, Apr. 28, 1943, GSP, LOC MS Div, 166; JPL, 107; diary, Everett Hughes, June 22, 1943, David Irving Collection, micro 97276/5, MHI ("*our only defeat*").

125 *"What a headache":* Hamilton, 481; OH, Alan Moorehead, Jan. 21, 1947, FCP, MHI; Molony V, 512; OH, W. B. Smith, May 8, 1947, FCP, MHI; Brian Horrocks, *A Full Life*, 159; W.G.F. Jackson, *Alexander of Tunis as Military Commander*, 211 ("*dance to the tune*"); Brian Holden Reid, "The Italian Campaign, 1943–1945: A Reappraisal of Allied Generalship," *Journal of Strategic Studies*, vol. 13, no. 1 (March 1990), 128+ (*the general's name*); *PP*, 239 ("*not quite a gentleman*").

125 *Son of a meek Anglican:* T. A. Heatchcote, *The British Field Marshals, 1763–1997*, 213; John Keegan, ed., *Churchill's Generals*, 150 ("*bad boy*"); Moorehead, *Montgomery*, 29, 34 ("*I do not want to portray him*"); Michael Howard, "Leadership in the British Army in the Second World War," in G. D. Sheffield, *Leadership and Command*, 106 ("*not as warriors itching*"); Peter Roach, *The 8.15 to War*, 59 (*cricket metaphors*); Hamilton, 300 (*antipathy to cats*); T.E.B. Howarth, ed., *Monty at Close Quarters*, 36, 42 ("*always being right*"); Fred Majdalany, *Cassino: Portrait of a Battle*, 42 ("*no coughing*"); Richard S. Malone, *A Portrait of War, 1939–1943*, 175.

126 *In Africa:* Stephen Brooks, ed., *Montgomery and the Eighth Army*, 292, 381n (*white heather*); Moorehead, *Montgomery*, 157 (*odes*); Phillip Knightley, *The First Casualty*, 306 ("*backing into the limelight*"); John Kennedy, *The Business of War*, 291 ("*Colonel Lennox*"); Shapiro, 44 (*clapped and clapped*); Piers Brendon, *Ike: His Life and Times*, 117 ("*love of publicity*").

126 *"I do not think Alex":* Nigel Nicolson, *Alex: The Life of Field Marshal Earl Alexander of Tunis*, 197; Danchev, 417–18; Lt. Gen. Sir Frederick E. Morgan, "OVERLORD by the Under-Dog-in-Chief," ts, n.d., FCP, MHI; OH, Arthur Coningham, Feb. 14, 1947, FCP, MHI (*ever more cautious*); Gunther, 97; Michael Carver, ed., *The War Lords: Military Commanders of the Twentieth Century*, 501 ("*to believe in their task*"); Malone, *Missing from the Record*, 17–18 ("*Do you know why*").

127 *"Into battle with stout hearts":* "Personal Message from the Army Commander," July 1943, George F. Hall Papers, HIA, box 1; Brooks, ed., 255 ("*We have won*").

127 *Thousands of Axis troops in western Sicily:* Walter Fries, "Der Kampf Um Sizilien," FMS, #T-2, NARA RG 319, OCMH, box 245, 23; Fridolin von Senger und Etterlin, "Die Abwehr der Achsenmächte auf Sizilien," *Allgemeine schweizerische Militär Zeitschrift*, 116 Jahrang, Nr. 12, Dec. 1950, 861; Wilhelm Schmalz, "Der Kampf um Sizilien im Abschnitt der Brigade Schmalz," n.d., NARA RG 319, OCMH, box 245 ("*to win time*"); Martin Pöppel, *Heaven and Hell*, 126; Senger, "Liaison Activities with Italian 6th Army," 1951, FMS, #C-095, 56 (*internecine gunplay*); war diary, Comando Supremo, "Operazioni in Sicilia dal 9 al 19 luglio," NARA RG 319, OCMH, box 246 (*three-hour firefight*); Franz Kurowski, *The History of the Fallschirmpanzerkorps Hermann Göring*, 201 ("*Holy Virgin medals*").

127 *"a hole-and-corner area":* D'Este, 349; Christopher Buckley, *Road to Rome*, 71–72 ("*not tank country*"); Frank Gervasi, *The Violent Decade*, 469 ("*the fuckin' desert*").

127 *Eighth Army's attempt:* "Airborne Operations Conference," July 24, 1943, Algiers, "Material on Operation HUSKY, 1943, Allied Forces," MHI Lib; Garland, 218–19; John C. Warren, *Airborne Missions in the Mediterranean, 1942–1945*, 51; "Proceeding of Board of Officers Considering Airborne Operations," Aug. 1943, AFHQ, JPL, MHI, box 11;

*AAFinWWII,* 454; B. H. Liddell Hart, *The Other Side of the Hill,* 355 (*German paratroopers also jumped*); R. Priestly, "Volunteers," ts, n.d., IWM, 83/24/1, 6 (*"One shouted for comrades"*); T.B.H. Otway, *Airborne Forces,* 126–30; Michael Hickey, *Out of the Sky: A History of Airborne Warfare,* 104–5; John Frost, *A Drop Too Many,* 185.

128 *"seemed to mislay his genius"*: Carver, ed., 501; Gunther, 118, 141 (*"struck on the head"*); S.W.C. Pack, *Operation Husky,* 143; Neil McCallum, *Journey with a Pistol,* 153 (*"break the farmer's walls"*); Malone, *A Portrait of War,* 162 (*robbed of their boots*); Dancocks, 3 (*dead dogs*).

128 *"The enemy is tough"*: Gunther, 121–25.

128 *"paved with bodies"*: Field Marshal Lord Carver, *The Imperial War Museum Book of the War in Italy, 1943–1945,* 37, 46 (*"flies walked"*); "History of the 50th (Northumberland) Division During the Campaign in Sicily," ts, n.d., UK NA, CAB 106/473, 43–44 (*welts of dust*); Peter Stainforth, *Wings of Wind,* 167, 171 (*"moving men"*).

129 *By Sunday morning, July 18:* SSA, 179; Francis De Guingand, *Operation Victory,* 310 (*fire-resistant*); "History of the 50th (Northumberland) Division," 62; Hamilton, 317; Douglas N. Wimberly, "Scottish Soldier: The Memoirs of Major General Douglas Wimberly," vol. 2, 1979, IWM, PP/MCR/182, 178 (*50,000 cigarettes*); *Three Years,* 363, 372–73; Kay Summersby, *Eisenhower Was My Boss,* 113 (*"What's the matter"*); Gunther, 121 (*"Both sides are tired"*).

### *"How I Love Wars"*

129 *Patton had been sulking:* Charles R. Codman, *Drive,* 107–8; *SSt,* 140 (*"on our prats"*).

129 *He found General Alexander:* Harold Macmillan, *The Blast of War, 1939–1945,* 302; Harold Macmillan, *War Diaries,* 146–47, 154.

130 *"Have I got to stay here?"*: OH, Harold R.L.G. Alexander, Jan. 10–15, 1949, SM, NARA RG 319, OCMH, SSI, box 242; A. C. Wedemeyer, "Observer's Report," Aug. 24 1943, AGF File No.19.1, NARA RG 319, OCMH, 2-3.7 CC2, box 247, 18; Garland, 236–38; F. H. Hinsley et al., *British Intelligence in the Second World War,* 90–91 (*Ultra two days earlier*); OH, LKT and William W. Eagles, Apr. 19, 1951, SM, MHI (*"glamour of capturing Palermo"*).

130 *Alexander studied:* F. W. Winterbotham, *The Ultra Secret,* 105; Carlo D'Este, *Eisenhower,* 414 (*"bone from the neck up"*); Carver, 107 (*"no ideas"*); Gregory Blaxland, *Alexander's Generals,* 16 (*"Czarist Russia"*); Gervasi, 517 (*"just had a steam bath"*).

131 *"a born leader, not a made one"*: B. H. Liddell Hart, "Extracts," June 1946, LH 1/7/54; Hamilton, 473 (*"an English country gentleman"*); Frank L. Kluckhohn, " 'Attack, Attack Again' Is Alexander's Motto," *NYT Magazine,* Aug. 8, 1943, 20+ (*could not write his name*); Lord Moran, *Churchill: Taken from the Diaries of Lord Moran,* 187; Macmillan, *War Diaries,* 188 (*"seeing the point"*); *PP,* 267.

131 *Oblivious to the anguish:* Jackson, 221; OH, Alexander, SM (*"The hell with this"*); Alexander to Brooke, April 3, 1943, Alanbrooke Papers, LHC, 6/2/17 (*"not professional soldiers"*).

131 *Off Patton's forces went at a gallop:* letter, Oscar W. Koch to James A. Norell, Dec. 15, 1960, NARA RG 319, OCMH, box 250; Pietro Arancio, *Agrigento,* 14 (*"loveliest of mortal cities"*); *SSA,* 175; Robert D. Kaplan, *Mediterranean Winter,* 123; L.V. Bertarelli, *Southern Italy,* 459; Edward B. Kitchens, Jr., "The Operations of the 3rd Ranger Infantry Battalion in the Landings at Licata," 1949, IS, 18–24; Michael J. King, "Rangers: Selected Combat Operations in World War II," June 1985, CSI, 26–27; James J. Altieri, *Darby's Rangers: An Illustrated Portrayal of the Original Rangers,* 53; *CM,* 220–21 (*Darby's Rangers assembled*).

132 *Unaware that Agrigento:* William O. Darby and William H. Daumer, *Darby's Rangers: We Led the Way,* 99; Anders Kjar Arnbal, *The Barrel-Land Dance Hall Rangers,* 118 (*stovepipe hats*).

132 *three safes found in an Italian naval headquarters:* Some evidence suggests assistance from local mafiosi who had been contacted by U.S. Navy intelligence agents as part of a covert arrangement with Charles "Lucky" Luciano, the Sicilian-born New York crime boss then serving time in a New York prison. Rodney Campbell, *The Luciano Project,* 117, 126, 176–78; Patrick K. O'Donnell, *Operatives, Spies, and Saboteurs,* 50; Max Corvo, *The O.S.S. in Italy, 1942–1945,* 23.

132 *soldiers cracked them:* OH, Samuel A. D. Hunter, March 7, 1944, NHC, 15–18; *The Sicilian Campaign,* 131.

132 *"During the night of 17/18 July":* G-2 periodic report No. 9, July 19, 1943, Seventh Army, NARA RG 319, OCMH, 2-3.7 CC2 Sicily, box 247; *CM,* 224.

132 Corporal *Audie Leon Murphy:* Audie Murphy, *To Hell and Back,* 7–8; Harold B. Simpson, *Audie Murphy, American Soldier,* 18–20, 47.

132 *He had a slow, stooped gait:* corr, Albert Lewis Pyle to Carl Swickerath, Feb. 23, 1973, ALM, box 1, 2; Don Graham, *No Name on the Bullet,* 57, 60 (*tobacco smoke*), 39; Audie Murphy, "You Do the Prayin'," *Modern Screen,* Jan. 1956, 56+ (*"You do the prayin'"*); Murphy, *To Hell and Back,* 10; Simpson, 70; "Lieutenant Audie Murphy," *AB,* no. 3, 1973, 28+.

133 *"some Dago name":* William E. Faust, memoir, ts, n.d., ASEQ, 1st ID, MHI, 71; Franklyn A. Johnson, *One More Hill,* 105 (*Fascist salute*); John Hersey, "AMGOT at Work," *Life,* vol. 15, no. 8, Aug. 23, 1943, 25 (*"Kiss your hand!"*); aide's diaries, July 21, 1943, LKT Jr. papers, GCM Lib, box 18, folder 3 (*Italian saddle*); George Sessions Perry, "A Reporter at Large," *New Yorker,* Aug. 14, 1943, 46+ (*"One never seemed"*).

133 *Emulating Stonewall Jackson's foot cavalry:* AAR, HQ, 7th RCT, July 24, 1943; Leo J. Meyer, "Strategy and Logistical History: MTO," ts, n.d., CMH, 2-3.7 CC5, XIV–35 (*"chalk and cattle dung"*); Daniel R. Champagne, *Dogface Soldiers,* 29 (*"are my dogs barking"*); *CM,* 226; Garland, 246; Gordon A. Blaker, *Iron Knights,* 184 (*"Mount up"*); Edmund F. Ball, *Staff Officer with the Fifth Army,* 176–78 (*Bradley kept a map*).

133 *From a roadcut in the ridge:* corr, LKT Jr. to James A. Norell, Jan. 10, 1961, NARA RG 319, OCMH, box 250; Kaplan, 122; diary, July 23, 1943, GSP, LOC MS Div., box 3, folder 1; George Biddle, *Artist at War,* 66, 69 (*"no cat"*).

133 *Belisarius in* A.D. *535:* Charles Lee Lewis, "The Byzantine Invasion of North Africa, Sicily, and Italy," *Proceedings,* Nov. 1943, 1435+; msg, 1000 hrs, July 22, 1943, "Operazioni in Sicilia dal 9 al 19 luglio"; corr, LKT Jr. to Sarah, Aug. 25, 1943, LKT Jr., GCM, box 1, folder 6.

134 *Hours passed:* notes, William W. Eagles to OCMH, n.d., NARA RG 319, OCMH, box 250; *CM,* 227; Codman, 110 (*"Street after street"*).

134 *"stacks full of rare books":* Lynn H. Nicholas, *The Rape of Europa,* 225–26; Biddle, 67 (*Goethe*); Garland, 256; *SSA,* 188; lecture, W. A. Sullivan, Society of Military Engineers, Cincinnati, 1947, "Ship Salvage and Harbor Clearance," #445, WWII Histories and Historical Reports in the U.S. Naval History Division, NHC, 13 (*Salvage teams*); John T. Mason, Jr., *The Atlantic War Remembered,* 297–99, 307; Edward D. Churchill, *Surgeon to Soldiers,* 222 (*offered to sing Verdi*); OH, John A. Heintges, SOOHP, Jack A. Pellicci, 1974, MHI, 150–55 (*seized two large trucks*); Melvin F. Talbot, "The Logistics of the Eighth Fleet and U.S. Naval Forces, Northwest African Waters," ts, n.d., "The Administrative History of the Eighth Fleet," #139, U.S. Naval History Division, 37; memo, "Data for Logistical Planning," Seventh Army to CG, NATOUSA, Dec. 4, 1943, Walter J. Muller Papers, HIA, box 2.

134 *Major General Geoff Keyes:* AAR, HQ, Provisional Corps, July 15–Aug. 20, 1943, CMH, Geog Sicily, 370.2; Robert Capa, *Slightly Out of Focus,* 78; John B. Romeiser, ed., *Combat Reporter,* 179 (*bedsheet lashed to a fishing pole*); GK, July 22, 1943.

135 *"It is a great thrill":* PP, 297, 303, 305.

135 *"The occupation of western Sicily"*: situation report, OB Süd, July 24, 1943, NARA RG 319, OCMH, box 246; Garland, 255; AAR, HQ, Provisional Corps, July 15–Aug. 20, 1943, CMH, Geog Sicily, 370.2; *CM,* 228 (*"certainly like to beat Montgomery"*).

135 *"You will have guessed"*: *CM,* 227; *PP,* 300.

### Snaring the Head Devil

136 *"No objective can compete"*: *GS* IV, 498, 500, 505; John S. D. Eisenhower, *Allies,* 306 (*Churchill would strip British forces*); Winston S. Churchill, *The Hinge of Fate,* 826 (*"cut their rations again"*).

136 *"Why should we crawl"*: *GS* IV, 503; Kennedy, 295 (*"a beautiful path"*); Emajean Jordan Buechner, *Sparks,* 95 (*"gonorrhea"*).

136 *Eisenhower in May: StoC,* 15, 19; AFHQ G-2, "J.I.C. Algiers Estimates on Italian Morale," June 20, 1943, NARA RG 319, OCMH, from AFHQ micro, Job 10-A, reel 17C, box 242; Field Marshal the Viscount Alexander of Tunis, dispatch, "The Allied Armies in Italy," n.d., CMH, I-52 (*"might well cause a collapse"*); meeting notes, HQ Force 141, June 25, 1943, NARA RG 319, OCMH, from AFHQ micro, Job 26-A, reel 225B, box 242 (*"Germany intends to reinforce Italy"*); memo, AFHQ G-3, L. W. Rooks to W. B. Smith, June 28, 1943, NARA RG 319, OCMH, from AFHQ micro, Job 10-C, reel 138E, box 242 (*"very mountainous"*).

137 *Success in Sicily tipped:* Ed Cray, *General of the Army,* 406; *Three Years,* 460 (*Charlie-Charlies*); "Record of Meeting Held at La Marsa at 1430 Hrs, 17 July 1943," NARA RG 331, AFHQ micro, R-225-B (*"onto the mainland"*); Chandler, vol. 2, 1261; Garland, 260–61.

137 *Vital issues remained:* "Invasion of Italian Mainland: Summary of Operations Carried out by British Troops Under Command 5 U.S. Army," n.d., CMH, Geog Ital, 370.2, 30; *StoC,* 17–18; minutes, item 7, "post-HUSKY Operations," CCS, 103rd meeting, July 23, 1943; "Memorandum of the Representative of the British Chiefs of Staff," July 24, 1943, CCS 268/8; "Memorandum by the United States Chiefs of Staff," July 25, 1943, CCS 268/9; minutes, CCS, July 26, 1943: all in NARA RG 319, OCMH, SSI, box 243.

137 *For now, analysis:* "Notes on the Air Implication of an Assault on Italian Mainland, Naples Area," July 25, 1943, NARA RG 319, OCMH, from AFHQ micro, Job 10-A, reel 13C, box 242; David Hunt, *A Don at War,* 207–8; memo, "Appreciation of an Amphibious Assault Against the Naples Area," July 24, 1943, AFHQ G-3, NARA RG 319, OCMH, from AFHQ micro, Job 10-A, reel 13C, box 242 (*"If it is decided"*); minutes, CCS, July 26, 1943, NARA RG 319, OCMH, SSI, box 243 (*"earliest possible date"*).

137 *"I am with you"*: *GS* IV, 501, 503.

137 *"the head devil"*: Garland, 273; Peter Neville, *Mussolini,* 99 (*special typewriter*); Rudolf Böhmler, *Monte Cassino,* 3 ("of syphilitic origin"); Melton S. Davis, *Who Defends Rome?,* 64; Paul Deichmann, "Feldzug in Italien," ts, n.d., NARA RG 319, OCMH, box 250, 6 (*"grab his stomach"*); George Kent, "The Last Days of the Dictator Benito Mussolini," *Reader's Digest,* Oct. 1944, 13+; Peter Tompkins, *Italy Betrayed,* 19, 48 (*Zodiac symbols*); Gervasi, 91 (*"green-eyed daughter"*).

138 *He had risen far:* Denis Mack Smith, *Mussolini,* 5; Mark M. Boatner III, *Biographical Dictionary of World War II,* 384–85; Neville, 134 (*wedding rings*); Enno von Rintelen, "Psychological Warfare," n.d., FMS, #B-399, MHI, 4; Douglas Porch, *The Path to Victory,* 429.

138 *Lately the country was getting:* "Military Campaigns and Political Events in Italy, 1942–1943," Jan. 1946, Strategic Services Unit, WD, A-63366, CMH, Geog Files, Italy, 370.22, 16–17; Dharm Pal, *The Campaign in Italy, 1943–1945,* 3–4; Boatner, 385; Neville, 163 (*thirty-two Italian divisions*); R.J.B. Bosworth, *Mussolini's Italy,* 474 (*lacked boots*); Pietro

Badoglio, *Italy in the Second World War,* 48; Porch, 7; Rintelen, "The Italian Command," 3 (*Raw materials*); Garland, 32; "Vortragsnotiz: Die Lage in Italien," June 30, 1943, OKH, NARA RG 319, OCMH, box 243 (*"The kernel of the Italian army"*); Rintelen, "The Italian Command," 9.

139 *Since December 1942:* Vittorio Ambrosio, the Comando Supremo chief, claimed after the war that Mussolini never overtly favored a separate peace. "Ambrosio Project #46, Events in Italy, 1 Feb.–8 Sept. 1943," n.d., FMS, #P-058, NARA RG 319, OCMH, box 244; Howard McGaw Smyth, "The Command of the Italian Armed Forces in World War II," *Military Affairs,* vol. 15, no. 1 (spring 1951), 38+; casualty figures, *Il Momento,* Aug. 2, 1952, CMH, Geog Files, Italy, 704; Garland, 51 (*"ridiculous position"*), 242 (*"sacrifice of my country"*); "Memorandum of Conversation," Feltre, July 1943, *Department of State Bulletin,* vol. 15, no. 379, Oct. 6, 1946, NARA RG 319, OCMH, 2-3.7 CC2, Sicily, box 249, 607+; "Military Campaigns and Political Events in Italy, 1942–1943," 21 (*"white with emotion"*).

139 *Months in the planning:* Lewis H. Brereton, *The Brereton Diaries,* 194–95; minutes, item 9, "Bombing of Rome," CCS, 99th meeting, supplementary, June 25, 1943, NARA RG 319, OCMH, SSI, box 243 (*"It would be a tragedy"*); Quentin Reynolds, *The Curtain Rises,* 188 (*"Give them hell"*).

139 *"Perfect formation":* Robert Katz, *The Battle for Rome,* 17; Tompkins, 38–39; Alessandro Portelli, *The Order Has Been Carried Out,* 77–78 (*sons of bitches*); Vincent Orange, *Tedder,* 223 (*exclusively American*).

140 *Estimates of the dead:* casualty estimates in ascending order: Richard G. Davis, *Carl A. Spaatz and the Air War in Europe,* 261; Robert Katz, *The Battle for Rome,* 12; *SSA,* 186; Portelli, 77–78.

140 *Basilica of San Lorenzo:* "Report on the Bombing of the Basilica of San Lorenzo," Aug. 19, 1944, Allied Control Commission, Henry C. Newton Papers, MHI, box 4; Andrew Brookes, *Air War over Italy, 1943–1945,* 17; George F. Botjer, *Sideshow War,* 85–86 (*holy water*); "Military Campaigns and Political Events," 21 (*"a common cause"*).

140 *on Sunday, July 25:* F. W. Deakin, *The Brutal Friendship,* 458; Denis Mack Smith, *Mussolini,* 297 (*telephone intercepts*); Davis, 137, 141; "Military Campaigns and Political Events," 28–29; Tompkins, 61. One account contends that Mussolini when meeting the king still wore his marshal's uniform: Katz, 19, 21.

140 *Rarely had the Duce faced:* corr, Dino Grandi to Alexander Kirk, May 15, 1944; corr, Harold H. Tittman to A. Hull, Aug. 28, 1943; memo, Leonardo Vitetti, "Notes on the Fall of the Fascist Regime," n.d., all in NARA RG 319, OCMH, box 249.

140 *black Saharan bush shirts:* Tompkins, 60; Bosworth, 495; account, Dino Grandi, June 23, 1944; memo, Edward S. Crocker to C. Hull, "Overthrow of Mussolini," Feb. 7, 1944, both in NARA RG 319, OCMH, box 249.

140 *Shortly before five P.M.:* Deakin, 470; Katz, 21; Paul Deichmann, "Italian Campaign," 1948, FMS, #T-1a, chapter 1, 35.

140 *A millennium of royal inbreeding:* Boatner, 588; Tompkins, 22, 32 (*"taciturn and diffident"*); Neville, 175 (*"little sardine"*); Kenyon Joyce, "Italy," ts, n.d., Kenyon Joyce papers, MHI, 322 (*twenty-eight woodcock*); Katz, 21.

141 *After a few rambling sentences:* Deakin, 470; "Military Campaigns and Political Events," 28–29; Benito Mussolini, *My Rise and Fall,* 70–72.

141 *Even at five feet, seven inches:* Mussolini, 70–72; Tompkins, 62 (*"not at all nice"*).

141 *"Duce, I have been ordered":* Davis, 141–42; "Military Campaigns and Political Events," 28–29; Mussolini, 70–72, 77; Davis, 147 (*fists on his hips*).

141 *A radio bulletin at eleven P.M.:* Demaree Bess, "Power Politics Succeded in Italy," *Saturday Evening Post,* Oct. 30, 1943, 20+; Davis, 156 (*"Citizens, wake up!"*)

142 *"One did not see a single person"*: Badoglio, 46; Deakin, 475; Smith, 298 (*Mussolini's own newspaper*).

142 *"The Duce will enter history"*: Alan Bullock, *Hitler: A Study in Tyranny,* 710; Louis P. Lochner, ed., *The Goebbels Diaries, 1942–1943,* 437.

142 *"Italy has had enough"*: Iris Origo, *War in Val D'Orcia,* 47.

## Fevers of an Unknown Origin

142 *Patton had settled comfortably:* John P. Marquand, "Introduction," in Codman, xiv–xvi; *PP,* 303; JPL, 85 (*heroic oils*); Kaplan, 116 (*entering a jewel*); GSP to Beatrice, Aug. 2, 1943, GSP, LOC, MS Div, box 11 (*Christ Pantocrator*).

142 *"I know I have been marked"*: Fred Ayer, Jr., *Before the Colors Fade,* 139; Garland, 304; FDR to GSP, Aug. 4, 1943, GSP, LOC, MS Div, box 11 (*Marquis of Mount Etna*); Milton F. Perry and Barbara W. Parke, *Patton and His Pistols,* 66.

143 *The fame Patton so ardently craved:* Carlo D'Este, "The Slaps Heard Round the World," *MHQ,* vol. 8, no. 2 (winter 1996), 64+; Beatrice to GSP, July 30, 1943, GSP, LOC, MS Div., box 11 ("*Monty hardly figures*"); "Narrative of Operation HUSKY," n.d., Arthur S. Nevins papers, MHI, box 2 (*200,000*); GSP to Beatrice, Aug. 11, 1943, GSP, LOC, MS Div, box 11 ("*sixth sense*"); Hirshson, 392 ("*lose them*"); *PP,* 306 ("*horse race*"); "Reminiscences of Charles Wellborn, Jr.," 1971–72, John T. Mason, Jr., USNI OHD, 187 (*Volkswagen staff cars*).

143 *Each morning his armored cavalcade:* Dickson, "G-2 Journal," 90–91; Coffin, 91; Perry and Parke, 66; *PP,* 315–17 (*timed his pulse*); Jean Gordon Peltier, *World War II Diary of Jean Gordon Peltier,* 119 ("*killer eyes*"); Jack Pearl, *Blood-and-Guts Patton,* 102 (*sobbing in the latrine*); GSP to Beatrice, July 20, 1943, GSP, LOC, MS Div, box 11.

143 *broke his swagger stick:* Seymour Korman, Mutual Broadcasting reporter, quoted in IG report, NATOUSA, Sept 18, 1943, DDE Lib, PP-pres, box 91; *PP,* 296; Pearl, 100–101 ("*Get back on that gun*"); Clift Andrus, notes on *A Soldier's Story,* ts, n.d., MRC FDM, 1988.32, box 215 (*leg boils*); OH, Heintges, 1974, Pellicci, 159 ("*You son of a bitch*"); Charles C. Bates and John F. Fuller, *America's Weather Warriors,* 282n; Donald McB. Curtis, *The Song of the Fighting First,* 121 ("*let my killers through*").

144 *"Let's talk about tomorrow"*: Coffin, 91; Ladislas Farago, *Patton: Ordeal and Triumph,* 311; Codman, xiv–xvi; Norman Lewis, *In Sicily,* 1, 3, 39, 159 (*cruel city*).

144 *"Wars are not won"*: Robert H. Patton, *The Pattons,* 266.

144 *Meticulous and even finicky:* "Ordnance Operations in the MTO," Feb. 14, 1945, AGF, CMH, Geog Files, Med 353, 5-6; Lida Mayo, *The Ordnance Department: On Beachhead and Battlefront,* 167; Alfred M. Beck et al., *The Corps of Engineers: The War Against Germany,* 138; "Report of Visit to Sicily," Aug. 16–20, 1943, NARA RG 407, E427, 95-AL1-40-0.2, box 201; memo, "P.A.D. and civil defense in Sicily," Aug. 23, 1943, AFHQ, NARA RG 492, MTO, 290/54/25/6, 2191 (*exodus of dock workers*); JPL, 116.

144 *"It resembles a maniac"*: Churchill, *Surgeon to Soldiers,* 238; Charles M. Wiltse, *The Medical Department: Medical Service in the Mediterranean and Minor Theaters,* 165, 169 (*breakage*); "Field Operations of the Medical Department in the MTOUSA," Nov. 10, 1945, NARA RG 94, E427, 95-USF2-26-0, 196–97, 202 (*only half the necessary number*).

144 *Sicily proved unforgiving:* Albert H. Smith, Jr., *The Sicily Campaign: Recollections of an Infantry Company Commander,* 35; Russell B. Capelle, *Casablanca to the Neckar,* 22 ("*Sicilian disease*"); AFHQ circular #55, July 7, 1943, MTOUSA AG 444.1, box 1424 ("*RNS*"); Tregaskis, 239 ("*Z.I.'ed*"); *Reporting World War II,* vol. 1, 607 ("*she missed out*"); JPL, 64 (*ink their names*); Norris H. Perkins, *North African Odyssey,* 81 ("*one complete piece*").

145 *Surgeons operated by flashlight:* Theresa Archald, *G.I. Nightingale,* 165; Gervasi, 473; June Wandrey, *Bedpan Commando,* 55 (*"just checking up"*); J. A. Ross, *Memoirs of an Army Surgeon,* 148 (*"cindery masses"*); Dancocks, 90 (*morphine*).

145 *"horrid thing called* mal'aria*":* admin monologues, "Operations of British, Indian and Dominion Forces in Italy," part 5, UK NA, CAB 106/453, 4–5; Blanche D. Coll et al., *The Corps of Engineers: Troops and Equipment,* 456–57; James Phinney Baxter, *Scientists Against Time,* 301, 306–8, 316–17 (*Atabrine*); Paul Dickson, *War Slang,* 113+ (*"Ann"*); "Characteristics of Theater, Annex A," HKH, LOC MS Div, box 8, folder 8 (*highest malaria rates*).

145 *"yellow gall":* Albert E. Cowdrey, *Fighting for Life,* 63; John Ellis, *On the Front Lines,* 183–84; Wiltse, 173, 214; "Operations of British, Indian and Dominion Forces in Italy," part 5, UK NA, CAB 106/453, 4–5; "Report on Malaria in the Sicilian Campaign, 9 July to 10 Sept 1943," AFHQ surgeon, NARA RG 319, OCMH, box 250 (*some malaria control experts*); James Stevens Simmons, "The Prevention of Malaria in the U.S. Army," May 1944, Medical Historical Unit Collection, MHI, 2–4; A.A.C.W. Brown, "364 Days Service," ts, 1981, IWM 81/33/1, 10 (*"enjoyed it very much"*).

146 *More than a thousand soldiers:* "Report on Malaria in the Sicilian Campaign"; "Operations of British, Indian and Dominion Forces in Italy," 4–6 (*first case contracted in Sicily*); Wiltse, 173 (*ten thousand cases*); Ronald Lewin, *Montgomery as Military Commander,* 202 (*more malaria casualties*); Cowdrey, 132 (*"disease record of Seventh Army"*); "Characteristics of Theater," Annex A, HKH, LOC MS Div, box 8, folder 8 (*"fever of unknown origin"*); Hugh A. Scott, *The Blue and White Devils,* 57

146 *"a frail little fellow":* James Tobin, *Ernie Pyle's War,* 107–8; Pyle, 35–37.

147 *Under such circumstances Patton arrived:* memo, F. Y. Leaver, commander of 15th Evacuation Hospital, to Richard T. Arnest, II Corps surgeon, Aug. 4, 1943, DDE Lib, PP-pres, box 91; D'Este, "The Slaps Heard Round the World," 64 (*message from Eisenhower*); diary, Aug. 3, 1943, GSP, LOC MS Div, box 3, folder 2 (*"smell of the dead"*).

147 *Green light filtered:* James Wellard, *The Man in a Helmet,* 113; JPL, 100.

147 *On a stool midway through the ward:* report, Perrin H. Long to NATOUSA surgeon, Aug. 16, 1943, "Mistreatment of Patients in Receiving Tents of the 15th and 93rd Evacuation Hospitals," GSP, LOC MS Div, box 3, folder 2, appendix 125.

147 *Patton asked Kuhl:* ibid.; *PP,* 330–31; JPL, 103; Farago, 326–27 (*"gutless bastard"*).

147 *His rage spent:* Garland, 427; memoir, "Theodore L. Dobol, Command Sergeant Major," ts, 1976, MRC FDM, 1991.24, box 469, 18; OH, Linwood W. Billing, former commander, Co. L., 26th Inf, Jan. 2006, Andrew Woods, MRC FDM; Arthur L. Chaitt, ed., "Taps," *Bridgehead Sentinel,* vol. 30, no. 2 (summer 1971), MRC FDM, 25 (*dying of a heart attack*); JPL, 102.

148 *A week later, on August 10:* 93rd Evacuation Hospital movements, Donald E. Currier papers, MHI; report, Perrin H. Long to NATOUSA surgeon, Aug. 16, 1943, "Mistreatment of Patients," 331.

148 *"What's this man talking about?":* Bess, "Report of an Investigation," to DDE, Aug. 19, 1943, DDE Lib, PP-pres, box 91; memo, Donald E. Currier to Richard T. Arnest, II Corps surgeon, Aug. 12, 1943, Donald E. Currier Papers, MHI; Garland, 427–28; Henry J. Taylor, "The Patton Story: He Slapped, He Raged, He Sobbed in Anger," *Cincinnati Post,* Feb. 28, 1947, 26, from MRC FDM (*"makes my blood boil"*).

148 *As he returned to his car:* Bess to DDE, Aug. 19, 1943; Richard Collier, *Fighting Words,* 146 (*"no such thing as shellshock"*); SSt, 160 (*"couple of malingerers"*); Bradley Commentaries, CBH papers, MHI, box 1 (*"put a little guts"*).

149 *"inexcusable and asinine":* corr, Donald E. Currier to Fred Ayer, Jr., Aug. 14, 1964, Donald E. Currier papers, MHI.

149 *"Don't tell my wife"*: Kennedy, in *Reporting World War II,* vol. 1, 667–68; Bess to DDE, Aug. 19, 1943; *SSt,* 160 *("Lock it up in my safe");* corr, Paul Harkins to Garrison H. Davidson, n.d., in Garrison H. Davidson, "Grandpa Gar," ts, 1974, USMA Arch, 85; *PP,* 333 *("saved his soul").*

### A Great Grief

149 *"What a steep hill"*: Molony V, 154; letter, Joseph T. Dawson to family, July 30, 1943, MRC FDM *("fight downhill");* Brooks E. Kleber and Dale Birdsell, *The Chemical Warfare Service: Chemicals in Combat,* 593 *(flamethrowers);* Peltier, 105; William A. Carter, "Carter's War," ts, 1983, CEOH, box V-14, VII-28 *(cork oaks).*

149 *"the whole damned bridge"*: Pyle, 40–41; Beck, 141 *(metal detectors);* msg, 0030 hours, July 31, 1943, "Operazioni in Sicilia dal 9 al 19 luglio" *("Troops are tired");* Johannes Steinhof, *Messerschmitts over Sicily,* 237 *(pneumatic drills).*

150 *Allied air and naval superiority:* "Lessons from the Sicilian Campaign," AFHQ, training memo no. 50, Nov. 20, 1943, NARA RG 407, E 427, 95-AL1-0.4, 7; George H. Revelle, Jr., "Under Fifth Army a Division G-4 Operates," *MR,* vol. 25, no. 3 (June 1945), 49+; B. Smith, "Waltonia," ts, 1981, IWM, 76/254/1 *("without even a sex life"),* Michael Francis Parrino, "Introduction to Pack Transport and Pack Artillery," ts, n.d., CMH, 84–85 *("what he is to die for");* Elmer W. Norton, 1/157th Inf, ASEQ, MHI *(Trouble);* Darby and Daumer, 107 *(Rosebud);* C. W. Eineichner, "Assault on Messina," in "2004 Reunion Program Book," Fort Wayne, Ind., Aug. 25–30, 2004, author's possession, 69 *(War Admiral);* Ralph G. Martin, *The G.I. War, 1941–1945,* 114 *("bite the ears");* Guy Nelson, *Thunderbird,* 51 *("outstanding performance");* "Training Notes from the Sicilian Campaign," AFHQ G-3, Oct. 25, 1943, CMH, Geog Sicily 353, 18; letter, John M. Brooks [former 16th Inf officer] to author, Oct. 19, 2003, 7 *("mule interpreters").*

150 *"Hills and then more hills"*: corr, TR to Eleanor, July 23, 1943, TR, LOC MS Div, box 10.

151 *With the British right flank still blocked:* Garland, 320; Stanhope Brasfield Mason, "Reminiscences and Anecdotes of World War II," ts, 1988, MRC FDM, 1994.126, 181 *(ax-wielding enemy troops);* Kimball Richmond, 3/16th Inf, ASEQ, MHI *(wine and cheese);* corr, TR to Eleanor, Oct. 11, 1943, TR, LOC MS Div, box 10; Biddle, 82 *("mumbled and rumbled").*

151 *Each town took a toll:* "Battle Casualties," HQ, 1st ID, Aug. 1, 1943, MRC FDM; Jarvis Burns Moore, 2/16th Inf, ASEQ, MHI *("started swearing");* *Time,* Aug. 9, 1943, 30.

151 *Wagging his cane:* Biddle, 75; corr, Joseph T. Dawson to family, July 30, 1943, MRC FDM *(white-flag ruse);* William E. Faust, 1st ID artillery, ts, n.d., ASEQ, MHI, 73 *(bomb Etna's crater);* *Time,* Aug. 9, 1943, 30 *("shaking lice");* Martin, 76 *("paying taxes").*

151 *Bread trucks:* "Report of the Division Quartermaster—Sicilian Campaign," n.d., 1st ID, 11, and "Official Diary, 1st U.S. Infantry Div, Office of the Quartermaster," July 24, 1943 entry, both in Harlan W. Hendrick, 1st ID, ASEQ, MHI *("jumping at any excuse");* Tregaskis, 37, 47; corr, Joseph T. Dawson to family, July 31, 1943, MRC FDM.

152 *"loss of riflemen and fatigue"*: "Comments of General Patton," Aug. 27, 1943, Palermo, NARA RG 319, OCMH, 2-3.7 CC2 Sicily, box 250; V-mail, TR to Eleanor, July 22, 1943, TR, LOC MS Div, box 10.

152 *"like ragged caps"*: Romeiser, ed., *Combat Reporter* [mss], 212; MEB, "Axis Tactical Operations in Sicily," ts, n.d., OCMH, #R-144, MHI; author visit, Sept. 1996; Eberhardt Rodt, "Studie über den Feldzug in Sizilien bei der 15. Pz Gren. Div, Mai–August 1943," n.d., FMS, #C-077, NARA RG 319, OCMH, box 245, 20–21; Garland, 325–29.

152 *Five miles to the west:* Biddle, 76; *SSt,* 150 *(classroom walls);* Tregaskis, 51–52; Kenneth T. Downs, "Nothing Stopped the Timberwolves," *Saturday Evening Post,* Aug. 17, 1946, 20+ *("stubborn as any resistance").*

153 *the enemy would counterattack:* Andrus, notes on *A Soldier's Story;* Garland, 325 (*"lightly held"*); Steven E. Clay, *Blood and Sacrifice,* 176–77 (*pare back the attack*); OH, R. W. Porter, Feb. 8, 1961, Albert N. Garland, and Oscar W. Koch, Dec. 15, 1960, James A. Norell, both in NARA RG 319, OCMH, box 250 (*printed photos had not yet returned*); Biddle, 83 (*"You give your orders"*).

153 *"a very disagreeable job":* corr, TdA to Mary Fran, July 29, 1943, TdA papers, MHI, box 2; "Commanding General's After Action Report," in Smith, 125–35 (*"our moral obligation"*).

153 *He sank to his knees:* radio broadcast, Quentin Reynolds, June 8, 1944, TdA papers, box 7; Reynolds, *The Curtain Rises,* 216 (*"stop worrying"*).

153 *"Every time I have watched":* Romeiser, ed., 184.

153 *Coordinating the attack:* ibid., 182.

154 *He was a big man:* JJT, II-4, 9, 14–21.

154 *"It is very nice to read of a battle":* Another Medal of Honor was awarded for the same action near Chattanooga to Arthur MacArthur, Jr., father of Douglas MacArthur. "Medal of Honor citations," www.army.mil/cmh/; JJT, III-14-16.

154 *Young Jack Toffey:* JJT, VII-1, VIII-12; Will Lang, "Doughboy's Beachhead," *Time,* Feb. 7, 1944, 22; Robert W. Black, *Rangers in World War II,* 101 (*seven thousand prisoners*).

154 *Nine months at war:* JJT, V-17-20, 24–26; VI-2, 6; VIII-19.

155 *The next six days:* Garland, 336–37; "Commanding General's After Action Report," in Smith, 125–35; "Terry Allen and the First Division in North Africa and Sicily," n.d., TdA, MHI, 45 (*"hell of a lot of stuff"*).

155 *"bravest goddam soldier":* Codman, xviii; " 'Anything, Anytime, Anywhere Bar Nothing': Remembering 'Paddy' Flint," *Periodical: Journal of America's Military Past,* spring 1967, 52+; "Keeping Faith," ts, n.d., USMA Arch, 3–4 (*apparent stroke*); "Comments of General Patton," ts, Aug. 27, 1943, NARA RG 319, OCMH, 2-3.7 CC2 Sicily, box 250; *SSt,* 153; Henry Gerard Phillips, *The Making of a Professional,* 122; Harry A. Flint, DSC citation, NARA RG 338, ETO, 7th Army awards, box 2; OH, William C. Westmoreland, 1978, Duane G. Cameron and Raymond E. Funderburk, SOOHP, MHI, 104–5; "History of the 26th Infantry," 100 (*"spend another million"*).

156 *"Troina's going to be tougher":* SSt, 149; H. R. Knickerbocker, *Danger Forward,* 135.

156 *Hills were won and lost:* "History of the 26th Infantry," 95; Clay, 177 (*16th Infantry was pinned down*); Garland, 339; John W. Baumgartner et al., *The 16th Infantry, 1798–1946,* 58–59; Knickerbocker, 132–35 (chocolate).

157 *Progress was no better in the north:* "K Company History," 3/26th Inf, MRC FDM; "Company History," Co. I, 26th Inf, ts, n.d., MRC FDM (*Not until full dark*); Knickerbocker, 136–38 (*"Something is burning"*), 142–43; "History of the 26th Infantry," 99, 106, 109 (*wheat straw*); Romeiser, ed. (*"laundry mark"*), 189 ; Blythe Foote Finke, *No Mission Too Difficult!,* 150.

157 *At dusk on Thursday:* Garland, 344; James E. Kelly, ed., *The Wartime Letters of John and Vicki Kelly,* 54–56, 59, 70–71 (*"my luck won't hold up"*); Pyle, 55; Lee G. Miller, *The Story of Ernie Pyle,* 201, 273 (*"collapsible style"*); "History of the 26th Infantry," 106 (*"damned sick of it all"*).

157 *Terry Allen was damned sick:* SSt, 151; Rodt, "Studie über den Feldzug in Sizilien," 22, 27; MEB, Troina, "Axis Tactical Operations in Sicily," ts, n.d., OCMH, #R-144, MHI; Biddle, 86 (*hobnailed bootprints*); Martin Blumenson, *Sicily: Whose Victory?,* 124.

158 *"Town clear of enemy":* Baumgartner, 64; Clift Andrus, "Troina Addenda," *FAJ,* March 1944, 163+ (*"greatly destroyed"*); Collier, 147 (*"a town of horror"*); Finke, 163 (*"a carpet of maggots"*); corr, Donald V. Helgeson to author, Oct. 8, 2003; Peter Schrijvers, *The Crash of Ruin,* 85 ("Gott mit Uns").

158 *"naked on shutters or stretchers":* Biddle, 89–90; Romeiser, ed., 190 (*"We've been miserable"*).

158 *"Troina was the toughest"*: "Lessons from the Sicilian Campaign," Nov. 20, 1943, AFHQ, NARA RG 407, E 427, 95-AL1-0.4, 18; G-1 report, "Total Reported Battle Casualties for Period 1 August–20 August 1943, Inclusive, 1st Infantry Division," MRC FDM; JJT, VIII-22.

159 *Two more casualties:* Bryce F. Denno, "Allen and Huebner: Contrast in Command," *Army*, June 1984, 62+; Clift Andrus, notes on *A Soldier's Story.* For other accounts, see OH, Robert W. Porter, Feb. 8, 1961, Albert N. Garland, NARA RG 319, OCMH, box 250; OH, Robert W. Porter, 1981, John N. Sloan, SOOHP, MHI, 301–2.

159 *Ever the ardent hunter:* OH, James D. Ford, former USMA chief chaplain, March 21, 2000, to author, Washington, D.C. (*"hardest thing in war"*); *SSt,* 154–55 (*"temperamental"*); corr, ONB to DDE, July 25, 1943, DDE Lib, PP-pres, box 3; JPL, 90; diary, E. Hughes, July 28, 1943, micro 97276/5, David Irving collection, MHI; diary, GSP, July 29, 1943, GSP, LOC MS Div, box 2, folder 15.

159 *Neither Bradley nor Patton ever offered:* corr, TdA to E. C. Heid, Dec. 13, 1943, S.L.A. Marshall Military History Collection, UTEP; corr, TR to Eleanor, Aug. 17, 1943, TR, LOC MS Div, box 10; Bradley and Blair, 195 (*"flubbed badly"*); Albert H. Smith, Jr., "Allen and Huebner," ts, 1999, MRC FDM, 1999.124, box 392 (*"well-planned, executed"*); Bradley Commentaries, CBH, MHI, 14-B, S-27; Astor, 221, 228.

159 *As the orders became public:* memoir, William E. Faust, ts, n.d., 1st ID artillery, ASEQ, MHI, 76; OH, Porter, 1981, Sloan, 301–2; Johnson, 112 (*"sergeants weep"*); "Allen and His Men," *Time,* Aug. 9, 1943, 30+ (*By cruel coincidence*); corr, TdA to GCM, Aug. 13, 1943, and Sept. 15, 1943, GCM Lib, box 56; corr, TdA to DDE, Oct. 17, 1943, DDE Lib, PP-pres, box 4; corr, TdA to Mary Fran, Aug. 10, 1943, and TdA to Sonny, Aug. 7, 1943, both in TdA, MHI, box 2; corr, TdA to E. C. Heid, Dec. 13, 1943, Marshall Collection, UTEP; Astor, 226; e-mail, Consuelo Allen (granddaughter of Terry de la Mesa Allen) to author, Dec. 5, 2002 (*welcome-home party*); Biddle, 92.

160 *"mentally in a black cloud"*: speech, Stanhope B. Mason, Apr. 24, 1976, 57th annual dinner, Officers of the First Division, New York City, in Smith, 196; TR, msg to 1st Div, Aug. 6, 1943, TR, LOC MS Div, box 10 (*"a great grief"*); "History of the 26th Infantry," 97 (*"broke down and wept"*); *SSt,* 156; corr, TR to Eleanor, Aug. 17 and 24, 1943, TR, LOC MS Div, box 10; corr, Eleanor to GCM, Feb. 7, 1944, and GCM to Eleanor, Feb. 10, 1944, GCM Lib, corr, TR, box 83.

160 *Sharing a ride to Palermo:* Capa, 84; John Bunyan, *The Pilgrim's Progress,* in Molony V, 855; Eleanor Butler Roosevelt, *Day Before Yesterday,* 449 (*"the quality of fortitude"*).

*"In a Place Like This"*

161 *Ridge by ridge, road by road:* Tregaskis, 75–76; "Allied Commander-in-Chief's Report on Sicilian Campaign, 1943," 97 (*retreated past Mount Etna*); Carver, *Harding of Petherton,* 119 (*"I am enjoying"*); Lord Tedder, *With Prejudice,* 458.

161 *But although they were moving:* "History of the 50th (Northumberland) Division During the Campaign in Sicily," ts, n.d., UK NA, CAB 106/473, 67–69; Cyril Ray, *Algiers to Austria,* 67 (*snipers with telescopic sights*); Tregaskis, 65 (*mayor of Catania*); "Report on the First Phase of AMGOT Occupation, Sicily and Region II," July–Aug. 1943, Frank J. McSherry Papers, MHI, 24 (*only one in five*); Buckley, 111 (*"all life was evil"*) 123 (*Bank of Sicily*).

161 *Often enough, the Allied air force:* Geoffrey Perret, *Winged Victory,* 211; "Report on the First Phase of AMGOT Occupation," 24 (*"rubble at Adrano"*); Harry L. Coles, Jr., "Participation of the Ninth and Twelfth Air Forces in the Sicilian Campaign," 1945, AAF Historical Studies, No. 37, 148 (*"needed thirty-six hours"*); Shapiro, 51 (*"Troops will refrain from shooting"*), 101, 105 (*"God Save the King"*); Ray, 68–69; R. C. Taylor, "A Pocketfull [*sic*] of Time," ts, n.d., 52, and corr, to author, Aug. 11, 2003 (*"Lord Nelson!"*); Nicolson, 205; Buckley, 79; Tregaskis, 81–82 (*dead men's helmets*).

162 *Above them all loomed Etna:* Biddle, 110; Bertarell, 481 (*tinted with sulfates*); Kenneth S. Davis, *Soldier of Democracy,* 435–36 (*"bloody Patton"*).

162 *"decided to burn the bodies in gasoline":* "Report on the First Phase of AMGOT Occupation," 13, 27; "Report of William Russell Criss," corr to family, July 29, 1943, 45th ID Mus (*"I feel like crying"*).

162 *To exploit the flanking opportunities:* James L. Packman, "The Operations of the 2nd Battalion, 30th Infantry, in the Amphibious Attack on Brolo," 1949, IS, 2–7; Garland, 390–91.

162 *Truscott, who was to provide a battalion:* Hansen, "Research Draft," SSt, CBH, MHI, 10/24–25.

163 *"that's ridiculous and insulting":* CM, 234–35; PP, 319 (*"L'audace"*).

163 *It went badly:* Garland, 393–97; Jack Belden, *Still Time to Die,* 274 (*orange quarter moon*); Romeiser, ed., 196–200 (*"Night and Day"*); Betsy Wade, ed., *Forward Positions: The War Correspondence of Homer Bigart,* 24–25 (*captured in their sleep*); Max Ulrich, "29th Panzer Grenadier Division, Sicily," FMS, #D-112, MHI, 5.

163 *Daybreak brought death: The Sicilian Campaign,* 145.

164 *"Situation still critical":* Romeiser, ed., 200–206; Garland, 403; diary, Hobart Gay, Aug. 10–11, 1943, USMA Arch; Charles R. Schrader, "Amicicide: The Problem of Friendly Fire in Modern War," Dec. 1982, CSI, 34 (*errant bombs*); DSC citation, Martin Moritz, medical attachment, 2/30th Inf, Oct. 19, 1943, NARA RG 338, 7th Army awards (*tried to amputate*); Carlo D'Este, *World War II in the Mediterranean,* 73 (*"Do something"*).

164 *At five P.M. Philadelphia again: The Sicilian Campaign,* 146; Romeiser, ed., 205 (*"last stand circle"*); Donald V. Bennett, *Honor Untarnished* [galley], 145 (*swimming westward*); Belden, 284, 288.

164 *At dawn on Thursday, August 12:* Pyle, 45; Belden, 288; Romeiser, ed., 205 (*"troops moving on the road"*); Scott, 60 (*cordite and sweat*).

164 *An open command car:* Romeiser, ed., 206.

164 *Field Marshal Kesselring had long realized:* Garland, 368; Bogislaw von Bonin, "Considerations of the Italian Campaign, 1943–1944," Feb. 1947, SEM, NHC, box 57, file 108, 8 (*"valuable human material"*); MEB, "Axis Tactical Operations in Sicily," #R-145–46, MHI (*message was hand carried*); Walter Warlimont, *Inside Hitler's Headquarters, 1939–1945,* 374 (*Hitler feared*).

165 *A devotee of Aristotle:* Frido von Senger und Etterlin, *Neither Fear nor Hope,* 208–9; Corelli Barnett, ed., *Hitler's Generals,* 381; Alex Bowlby, *Countdown to Cassino,* 4n; Errnst-Günther Baade, "War Diary of Fortress Commandant, Messina Strait," July–Aug. 1943, SEM, NHC, box 52; Garland, 375–76 (*five hundred guns*); "The Choice of Sites for Ferry Points," appendix, "War Diary of Naval Officer-in-Charge, Sea Transport, Messina Strait," SEM, NHC, box 52; Friedrich von Ruge, "The Evacuation of Sicily," March 1948, SEM, NHC, box 50, 15 (*Siebel ferries*); Molony V, 166 (*cached food*).

165 *Twelve thousand German supernumeraries:* Molony, V, 166; Fries, "Der Kampf um Sizilien," 29–31 (*five successive defensive lines*); "Directions for the Systematic Destruction of Motor Vehicles," Feb. 1942, Supply Section, Reichminister of Aviation, Berlin, NARA RG 407, E, 47, AFHQ, 95-AL1-2.9, box 162; Steinhof, 242–43 (*"yelling as they hurled"*); Helmut Bergengruen, "Der Kamp der Panzerdivision 'Herman Goering' auf Sizilien," Nov. 25, 1947, NARA RG 319, OCMH, box 245.

165 *Italian commanders quickly got wind:* S. W. Roskill, *The War at Sea, 1939–1945,* 144; Kurowski, 178, 192, 201 (*"shivering malaria patients"*); Rodt, "Studie über den Feldzug in Sizilien," 31; "War Diary of Naval Officer-in-Charge" (*screens shielded the glare*); SSA, 210.

167 *The B-17s never came:* Garland, 379.

167 *"no adequate indications"*: Hinsley et al., 96–98; George F. Howe, "American Signal Intelligence in Northwest Africa and Western Europe," U.S. Cryptologic History, Series IV, vol. 1, NSA, NARA RG 57, SRH-391, 53; Ralph Bennett, *Ultra and the Mediterranean Strategy*, 234–35 (*"there is* no *plan"*); T. Milne, "The Sicilian Campaign," 1955, Air Ministry Historical Branch, UK NA, CAB 106/849, 80 (*"You have no doubt"*), 91 (*"no evidence"*).

167 *Allied pilots had reason to fear:* Garland, 376; Eduard Mark, *Aerial Interdiction in Three Wars*, 60, 72–73, 77; Edward B. Westermann, *Flak*, 293; Roskill, 147–49; *Battle*, 75; *AAFinWWII*, 472–73 (*swarms of smaller Wellingtons*); Vincent Orange, *Coningham*, 167 (*only a quarter hit targets*); Davis, *Carl A. Spaatz and the Air War in Europe*, 252 (*bombing Rome's rail yards*).

167 *"octopus-like arms"*: Dudley Pope, *Flag 4*, 126; Cunningham, 556 (*"no effective way of stopping them"*); Garland, 379; *SSA*, 214; Roskill, 149–50; J.F.C. Fuller, *The Second World War, 1939–45*, 265.

168 *Not once did the senior Allied commanders:* Pack, 166.

168 *doctors ordered him to bed:* Eisenhower's blood pressure of 142 over 90 on Aug. 15, 1943, indicated mild hypertension; his resting pulse of 80, weight of 172 pounds, and 33-inch waist indicated a reasonably fit 52-year-old man. Chandler, vol. 2, 1329n; Thomas W. Mattingly and Olive F. G. Marsh, "A Compilation of the General Health Status of Dwight D. Eisenhower," Mattingly collection, DDE Lib, box 1; *Three Years*, 386–87 (*"nervous temperament"*).

168 *"It is astonishing"*: "War Diary of Naval Officer-in-Charge"; *SSA*, 214–15 (*"Anglo-Saxon habits"*); MEB, "Axis Tactical Operations in Sicily," #R-145-146 (*time bombs*); Blumenson, *Sicily: Whose Victory?*, 146 (*Two hundred grenadiers*); Molony V, 182 (*cooled a wine bottle*).

168 *"The Boche have carried out"*: J. K. Windeatt, "Very Ordinary Soldier," ts, 1989, IWM, 90/20/1, 68.

168 *"completely fit for battle"*: "War Diary of Naval Officer-in-Charge" (*"employ our strength elsewhere"*).

169 *At ten A.M. on August 17:* CM, 243; Garland, 416–17; Nathan William White, *From Fedala to Berchtesgaden*, 40 (*swapping shots*); memo, William W. Eagles to OCMH, n.d., NARA RG 319, OCMH, box 250 (*"did not capture the city from us"*); Tregaskis, 86–88 (*bagpipes and a Scottish broadsword*); Hansen, "Research Draft," *SSt*, CBH papers, MHI, box 1, 16-A, S-27 (*"I'll be damned"*).

169 *Patton had a fever of 103:* corr, GSP to Arvin H. Brown, Sept. 12, 1943, GSP, LOC MS Div, box 27; John H. Rousch, ed., *World War II Reminiscences*, 64–65 (*"'DUCE' was painted"*); Tregaskis, 89 (*towering white spouts*); CM, 243 (*"What in hell"*).

169 *"They were tired and incredibly dirty"*: JPL, 122; corr, GSP to Beatrice, Aug. 18, 1943, GSP, LOC MS Div, box 11, folder 5 (*wounding a colonel*).

169 *Sixty percent of the city:* "Reports of the First Phase of AMGOT Occupation, Sicily and Region II," July–Aug. 1943, and "Reports of AMGOT Divisions," part 3, document B, both in Frank J. McSherry papers, MHI; "Attain by Surprise," ts, n.d., 30th Assault Unit history, LHC, 21 (*booby-trapped door handles*); Darby and Daumer, 109 (*scattered skeletons*); Don Whitehead, "Beachhead Don," John B. Romeiser, ed., 24 (*Draftee*); Mayo, 169.

170 *three-quarters of Messina's 200,000:* "Reports of the First Phase of AMGOT Occupation"; notes, William W. Eagles to OCMH, n.d., NARA RG 319, OCMH, box 250 (*mayor formally tendered*).

170 *"By 10 A.M. this morning"*: Jackson, 226; *PP*, 324–25 (*"I feel let down"*).

170 *He soon would feel worse: Three Years*, 390, 393; Quentin Reynolds, *By Quentin Reynolds*, 296–97 (*"We're Americans first"*); Garland, 429 (*"sake of the American effort"*).

170 *"he can gain greater fame"*: DDE diary, Aug. 1943, HCB papers, DDE Lib, A-678, 682.

170 *"I must so seriously question"*: corr, DDE to GSP, Aug. 17, 1943, Chandler, vol. 2, 1340.

171 *"intemperate language"*: JPL, 126–27; IG report, Sept. 18, 1943, NATOUSA, DDE Lib, PP-pres, box 91 (*"embarrassment to the War Department"*); Chandler, vol. 2, 1353.

171 *"my chagrin and grief"*: corr, GSP to DDE, Aug. 29, 1943, Donald E. Currier papers, MHI; *PP,* 333 (*"my method was wrong"*); letter, GSP to Walter P. Dillingham, Aug. 18, 1943, GSP, LOC MS Div, box 27 (*"would not make a single change"*); corr, GSP to Beatrice, Aug. 22, 1943, GSP, LOC MS Div, box 11.

171 *"suffering a little battle fatigue himself"*: *PP,* 334, 336; Bob Hope, *The Last Christmas Show,* 17 (*"I love my men"*); Codman, 114–15; "Frances Langford Dies," July 12, 2005, *WP,* B-6.

171 *"I am sorry for this"*: memo, "Gen. Patton's Address," n.d., GSP, LOC MS Div, box 48, folder 20; Edwin H. Randle, *Ernie Pyle Comes Ashore and Other Stories,* 134 (*"No, General, no!"*); OH, Theodore J. Conway, 1977, Robert F. Ensslin, SOOHP, MHI, III-2-4 (*"Georg-ie!"*).

171 *"hotter than the hinges of Hades"*: corr, John M. Brooks to author, Oct. 19, 2003, 7; memorandum, "Address by Lt. Gen. George S. Patton," Aug. 25, 1943, HQ, 1st ID, in "History of the 26th Infantry," 97 (*"Arms will not be carried"*); Gerald Astor, *Terrible Terry Allen,* 235 (*"no booing"*).

172 *"the weirdest speech ever made"*: corr, Donald V. Helgeson to author, July 25, 2003; Finke, 172 (*"fucking"*); memoir, William E. Faust, ts, n.d., 1st ID Division Artillery, ASEQ, MHI, 79–80 (*"our rejection of his presence"*).

172 *"I shall be very glad"*: corr, GSP to Walter F. Dillingham, Aug. 18, 1943, GSP, LOC MS Div, box 27; corr, GSP to Beatrice, Aug. 23, 1943, GSP, LOC MS Div, box 11.

172 *"damn near perfect example"*: *PP,* 328; *Battle,* 77–78; Gerhard L. Weinberg, *A World at Arms,* 595, 603 (*offensive at Kursk*); Porch, 445.

172 *American confidence:* Harry H. Semmes, *Portrait of Patton,* 174; "Training Notes from the Sicilian Campaign," n.d., AFHQ, NARA RG 331, micro box 21, R-320-A (*many lessons were learned*); Betty McLain Belvin, *Ray McLain and the National Guard,* 72.

172 *The butcher's bill:* Andrew J. Birtle, "Sicily," in *The U.S. Army Campaigns of World War II,* 1993, CMH 72-16, 25. As usual with World War II casualty statistics, no two estimates agree. See also: Garland, 417; Hanson Baldwin, *Battles Lost and Won,* 225; "Summary of Activities, MTO, 31 March 1945," NARA RG 94, 95-USF2-0.3, box 246; "British Battle Casualties in Sicily," Oct. 11, 1943, U.S. military attaché report, London, CMH, Geog Files, Sicily, 704.

172 *Axis dead and wounded:* Birtle, "Sicily," 25. See also: MEB, "Axis Tactical Operations in Sicily," #R-145-146; Blumenson, *Sicily: Whose Victory?,* 156; memo, HQ, SOS to CG, NATOUSA, June 25, 1944, NARA RG 492, MTOUSA, pm, records relating to prisoners, box 2246; "Allied Commander-in-Chief's Report on Sicilian Campaign 1943," 98; Volkmar Kühn, *German Paratroops in World War II,* 193.

173 *"a great success, but it was not complete"*: Ruge, "The Evacuation of Sicily," 53; *Battle,* 47; Baldwin, 235; Kesselring, "The Campaign for Sicily: Concluding Considerations of the Commander-in-Chief, South," n.d., FMS, MS #T-3 P1, 28–29; Kesselring, "Stellungnahme des verantwortlichen Oberbefehlshabers Süd zu den Betractungen des Oberst von Bonin," n.d., FMS, MS #T-3 P1, 3–4, both in NARA RG 319, OCMH, box 245.

173 *HUSKY also exposed:* Buckley, 147; "Proceedings of Board of Officers Considering Airborne Operations," Aug. 1943, AFHQ, JPL, MHI, box 11 (*Allies lost 42 planes*); Dwight D. Eisenhower, *Crusade in Europe,* 179 (*"interservice spirit"*); Porch, 449 (*"Sicily demonstrated"*).

173 *"You lack clear, calm judgment"*: memo, LKT Jr. to Charles R. Johnson, Aug. 23, 1943, LKT Jr., GCM Lib, box 11.

173 *"a superb leader but a mediocre manager"*: Geoffrey Perret, *There's a War to Be Won,* 185; Hamilton, 380 (*"feeble from beginning to end"*).

174 *Half a million German soldiers:* GS V, 2; Steinhof, 256 (*"a turning point had come"*).

174  *"Have been in the dumps"*: corr, LKT Jr. to Sarah, Aug. 25, 1943, LKT, GCM Lib, box 1, folder 6.

174  *"a fugitive from the law of averages"*: Roger J. Spiller, "The Price of Valor," *Military History Quarterly,* spring 1993, 100+; Graham, *No Name on the Bullet,* 45; diary, Aug. 10, 1943, JMG, MHI, box 10 (*"many more battles"*); Breuer, 195 (*"wickedness"*).

174  *"Yesterday is tomorrow"*: Pyle, 58; Miller, 275–77 (*"couldn't find the Four Freedoms"*); Tobin, 113 (*four hundred days overseas*).

174  *"gotten fat and lazy"*: JJT, VIII-27, IX-12 and 14.

175  *"Dago red"*: John P. Downing, "No Promotion," ts, n.d., MRC FDM, 1994.41.1, 238; Donald E. Houston, *Hell on Wheels,* 181 (*"Migrant women"*); Clay Blair, *Ridgway's Paratroopers,* 114 (*brothel in Trapani*); T. Michael Booth and Duncan Spencer, *Paratrooper: The Life of Gen. James M. Gavin,* 123; Johnson, 121–22 (*overpriced hankies*); Francis A. Even, "The Tenth Engineers," ts, 1996, author's possession, 15 (*bedsheet screens*); Jerry Countess, "Letters from the Battlefield," ts, n.d., author's possession (*"haven't seen a spigot"*); Robert H. Welker, "G.I. Jargon: Its Perils and Pitfalls," *Saturday Review of Literature,* Oct. 1944, 7+ ("prego, *Dago"*).

175  *On Sunday morning, August 29: Three Years,* 401; Hamilton, 375; film, United News No. 68, 1943, NARA RG 208, UN68 (*littered the beach*); De Guingand, 315.

175  *"We in our hearts know"*: Bradley Biggs, *Gavin;* Moorehead, *Eclipse,* 6, 12.

## CHAPTER 4: SALERNO
### *"Risks Must Be Calculated"*

179  *A gentle* breeze: Richard Lamb, *Montgomery in Europe, 1943–1945,* 36; Albert F. Simpson, "Air Phase of the Italian Campaign to 1 January 1944," June 1946, AAFRH-115, CMH, 92; Moorehead, *Montgomery,* 170 (*"gnats on a pond"*); Andrew Browne Cunningham, *A Sailor's Odyssey,* 559 (*Regatta*); George Aris, *The Fifth British Division, 1939–1945,* 138 (*five hundred guns*); Moorehead, *Eclipse,* 20.

179  *Just eight thousand Germans:* A. G. Steiger, "The Campaign in Southern Italy," Nov. 1947, Historical Section, Canadian Army HQ, report No. 18, 9n; De Guingand, 323; G. A. Shepperd, *The Italian Campaign, 1943–45,* 111; Ralph Bennett, *Ultra and the Mediterranean Strategy,* 241 (*detected ample signs*); Molony V, 239 (*29,000 rounds*).

179  *"I think that's all right"*: Frank Gervasi, *The Violent Decade,* 491–93; Moorehead, *Montgomery,* 170 (*"set out for a picnic"*).

180  *lovebirds:* Quentin Reynolds, *By Quentin Reynolds,* 303; Dick Malone, *Missing from the Record,* 53; Richard McMillan, *Twenty Angels over Rome,* 139; Gervasi, 491 (*roasted and garnished*); Moorehead, *Eclipse,* 22 (*"Never his plan"*).

180  *sulking in his trailer:* Vincent Orange, *Coningham,* 171; Nigel Hamilton, *Master of the Battlefield,* 406; Lamb, 32–33 (*Montgomery's protests*); Nigel Nicolson, *Alex: The Life of Field Marshal Earl Alexander of Tunis,* 216 (*coordinate Eighth Army with Fifth Army*); Charles Richardson, *Send for Freddie,* 135 (*"daft"*); OH, Francis De Guingand, March 31, 1947, G. A. Harrison, OCMH WWII Europe interviews, MHI (*do what he could*); De Guingand, 305; Vincent Orange, *Tedder,* 236 (*mostly inexperienced units*); OH, DDE, Feb. 16, 1949, Howard M. Smyth, SM, MHI (*"wanted everything"*); "Allied Commander-in-Chief's Report, Italian Campaign," MHI, 113.

180  *Strategic guidance:* Garland, 439–40; GS IV, 561–67, 570–71.

181  *Clambering back into the DUKW:* Moorehead, *Eclipse,* 23; Gervasi, 491 (*"shouting, laughing"*); StoC, 53; Lamb, 36–37; Stephen Brooks, ed., *Montgomery and the Eighth Army,* 278 (*"The only person"*).

181  *The next days passed:* Brooks, ed., 277; Moorehead, *Eclipse,* 31 (*passenger carriages*); H. V. Morton, *A Traveller in Southern Italy,* 314, 327, 337, 342, 360, 370 (*scarlet petticoats*); *From Pachino to Ortona: The Canadian Army at War,* 92.

181 *"no German troops have been met"*: Roger Parkinson, *A Day's March Nearer Home*, 179; David Scott Daniell, *The Royal Hampshire Regiment*, vol. 3, 130; *Three Assault Landings*, 1st Bn, Dorsetshire Regiment, DTL, Ft. B, 36–39 (*"bag of mail"*); war diary, Sept. 10, 1943, "Salerno Invasion," German naval command, Italy, NARA RG 334, NWC Lib, ANSCOL, ONI Z-28, box 649 (*"not crowding after us"*).

182 *Monty berets:* Reynolds, 304–5.

182 *On Sunday, September 5: Three Years*, 407; John S. D. Eisenhower, *Allies*, 363; diary, MWC, Aug. 28–29, 1943, MWC, Citadel, box 64 (*thirty Fifth Army staff officers*); corr, Don E. Carleton to Hal C. Pattison, Feb. 10, 1965, NARA RG 319, OCMH, 2-3.7 CC3 Salerno to Cassino, box 256 (*"a pursuit"*).

183 *"With Thee I am unafraid"*: *Calculated*, 182; MWC to Renie Clark, June 7, 1943, MWC, personal corr, Citadel (*clovers*).

183 *"The best organizer"*: Chandler, vol. 2, 1354, 1358; Des Hickey and Gus Smith, *Operation Avalanche*, 152 (*"a film star"*); George Biddle, *Artist at War*, 225.

183 *"college of your choice"*: OH, MWC, 1972, Forest S. Rittgers, Jr., SOOHP, MHI, 2; Martin Blumenson, *Mark Clark*, 11–16, 19–21, 28; obit, *Charleston Evening Post*, Oct. 5, 1966, in MWC, Citadel, Maureen Clark folder, box 70 (*petite, lighthearted*).

183 *"destined to do something unusual"*: OH, Robert J. Wood, 1973, William E. Narus, SOOHP, MHI, 3–30, 42–43; OH, MWC, Rittgers (*"Don't be an ally"*).

184 *"my headquarters to be a happy one"*: Charles S. D'Orsa, "The Trials and Tribulations of an Army G-4," *MR*, vol. 25, no. 4 (July 1945), 23+; Robert H. Adelman and George Walton, *Rome Fell Today*, ii (*"study in arrogance"*); William L. Allen, *Anzio: Edge of Disaster*, 48 (*"like a halo"*).

184 *"facially best"*: Charles F. Marshall, *A Ramble Through My War*, 94; Adelman and Walton, iii; Eric Sevareid, *Not So Wild a Dream*, 383; MWC to Renie Clark, May 15 and 16, 1943, MWC, personal corr, Citadel; Carlo D'Este, *Fatal Decision*, 58; OH, James M. Wilson, Jr., Apr. 23, 2004, with author, Washington, D.C.; Gervasi, 496.

184 *"if feasible, further north"*: *GS* IV, 580–81; *Battle*, 109; Bernard Fergusson, *The Watery Maze*, 252; Robert J. Wood, "The Landing at Salerno," lecture, Army-Navy Staff College, Dec. 1944–Jan. 1946, Robert J. Wood papers, MHI, 3; memo, EJD to L. J. McNair, "Notes on Operation AVALANCHE," Oct. 4, 1943, observer report #60, AGF G-2, NARA RG 337, box 52 (*forty-five days*); diary, MWC, Aug. 28–29, 1943, MWC, Citadel, box 64; Molony V, 264; *SSA*, 248 (*discover of minefields*); A. B. Cunningham, "Operations in Connection with the Landings in the Gulf of Salerno," Apr. 28, 1950, CMH, UH 0-1 CUN.2, 2175 ; S. W. Roskill, *The War at Sea, 1939–1945*, 159 (*advanced H-hour*); *StoC*, 40–41 (*"quite irritable"*); "History of the Peninsular Base Sction," 1944, CMH, 8-4 HA 1, 4; AAR, [U.K.] commander-in-chief, Mediterranean Station, March 8, 1945, CARL, N-11361 (*aviation fuel*).

185 *Only three assault divisions: Battle*, 107; H. H. Dunham, "U.S. Army Transportation and the Italian Campaign," Sept. 1945, monograph #17, NARA RG 336, ASF, chief of transportation, historical program files, box 142, 21; Wood, "The Landing at Salerno," 7; Charles S. D'Orsa, "The Trials and Tribulations of an Army G-4," *MR*, vol. 25, no. 4 (July 1945), 23+; Robert W. Coakley and Richard M.Leighton, *Global Logistics and Strategy, 1943–1945*, 192; *StoC*, 38–39; OH, MWC, Rittgers, 54–55; *Calculated*, 181 (*"my left arm"*).

185 *Three times he asked Washington:* msg, DDE to CCS, July 28 and Aug. 19, 1943, NARA RG 319, OCMH, 2-3.7 CC2 Sicily, box 247 (*"risks must be calculated"*); *AAFinWWII*, 495; Lord Tedder, *With Prejudice*, 457–58, 460; Cunningham, "Operations in Connection with the Landings in the Gulf of Salerno" (*"Woolworths"*); *StoC*, 52; Simpson, "Air Phase," 48, 90; "Allied Commander-in-Chief's Report, Italian Campaign," MHI, 112 (*"rather disquieting"*); E. McCabe, "The Plan for the Landing at Salerno," n.d., Cabinet Historical Section, UK NA, CAB 44/131, 30 (*could not prevent the enemy*).

185 *Ultra provided a detailed portrait:* F. H. Hinsley et al., *British Intelligence in the Second World War,* 106, 108; Walter Warlimont, *Inside Hitler's Headquarters, 1939–1945,* 349 (*"Treachery alters"*); minutes, AFHQ briefing to QUADRANT, Aug. 24, 1943, NARA RG 319, OCMH, box 244 (*"to the sound of the guns"*); Simpson, "Air Phase," 77; George F. Howe, "American Signal Intelligence in Northwest Africa and Western Europe," NSA, U.S. Cryptologic History, series IV, vol. 1, NARA RG 57, SRH-391, 63; "Operations Plan," HQ, Fifth Army, Aug. 26, 1943, NARA RG 492, MTOUSA, SOS, annex No. 1, G-2 plan, box 2735; OH, Viscount Mountbatten of Burma, Feb. 18, 1947, FCP, MHI (*whether invaders could build up*).

186 *Salerno would be a poor place:* "Observations in the European Theater Including Landing Operation at Salerno," Oct. 25, 1943, HQ, USMC, NARA RG 334, NWC Lib, ANSCOL, GB COB X-22, box 461, 3; "I.S.T.D.: 'C' Report on the West Coast," June 30, 1943, NARA RG 407, E47, 95-AL1-2.10, AFHQ, box 163; David Hunt, *A Don at War,* 211 (*"finest strip of coast"*); E. McCabe, "The Plan for the Landing at Salerno," 38; "Tactical Study of the Terrain: Naples and Vicinity," engineer appendix, AVALANCHE operational plan, NARA RG 331, AFHQ micro, box 118, R-123-D; "Engineer History, Fifth Army, Mediterranean Theater," vol. 3, appendix G, CMH, 9-2.5 AB, 19 (*"exposes this bridgehead"*); OH, "Reminiscences of George C. Dyer," 1969–1971, John T. Mason, Jr., USNI OHD, 330 (*"inside of a cup"*).

186 *Risks had been calculated:* L.S.B. Shapiro, *They Left the Back Door Open,* 117 (Strange Cargo); "Masonic Information," diaries, MWC, Citadel, box 61; John Clagett, "Admiral H. Kent Hewitt, U.S. Navy," *Naval War College Review,* summer 1975, 60+;. Simpson, "Air Phase," 107 (*sixteen convoys*); Henry Wadsworth Longfellow, "Amalfi."

186 *"high hopes of being in Naples"*: diary, MWC, Aug. 16, 1943, MWC, Citadel, box 64; "Allied Commander-in-Chief's Report, Italian Campaign," MHI, 112 (*"Boldness"*); minutes, AFHQ weekly executive planning section, Aug. 3, 1943, NARA RG 319, OCMH, 2-3.7 CC2 Sicily, box 247 (*planning to move*); Kenneth S. Davis, *Soldier of Democracy,* 448 (*"smash them"*).

186 *"might as well be on a raft"*: OH, MWC, Rittgers, MHI, 55.

*Plots, Counterplots, and Cross-plots*

187 *Even as the invaders bore down:* Moorehead, *Eclipse,* 77 (*"hot rake"*); Axis notes, Tarvis conference, ten A.M., Aug. 6, 1943, NARA RG 319, OCMH, box 244; msgs, "Former Naval Person to the President," No. 405, Aug. 5, 1943, and J. Hull to T. T. Handy, Aug. 15, 1943, NARA RG 319, OCMH, box 249; Harold Macmillan, *The Blast of War, 1939–1945,* 317 *"plots, counter-plots."*

187 *Wary but intrigued:* Macmillan, 313 (*"an appalling Norfolk jacket"*); Kenneth Strong, *Intelligence at the Top,* 145 (*"desperate gunfight"*); OH, George F. Kennan, Jan. 2, 1947, SM, MHI (*"rattletrap Buick"*).

187 *Their Italian counterpart:* Peter Tompkins, *Italy Betrayed,* 26; "Minutes of a conference held at the residence of H.M. Ambassador at Lisbon on August 18, 1943 [*sic*], at 10 p.m.," NARA RG 319, OCMH, box 244 (*"join the united nations"*); Garland, 459; minutes, Lisbon meeting, in msg, Aug. 21, 1943, AFHQ to WD, NARA RG 165, E 422, OPD exec files, 390/38/2/4-5, box 10.

187 *"We are not in a position"*: "Allied Commander-in-Chief's Report, Italian Campaign," 116; msg, W. B. Smith to Hastings Ismay, Sept. 12, 1943, W. B. Smith papers, DDE Lib, box 7 (*"my pet Wop"*); memo, W. B. Smith to Whitely, Rooks, Aug. 22, 1943, NARA RG 319, OCMH, box 244 (*"expect bitter reprisals"*).

188 *If Rome was in no position:* msg, DDE to CCS, Aug. 28, 1943, NARA RG 319, OCMH, box 244 (*"very anxious"*); corr, Robert Murphy to FDR, Sept. 8, 1943, NARA RG 319, OCMH, box 244.

188 *More amateur theatricals followed:* OH, Harold Alexander, Jan. 10–15, 1949, SM, CMH, Geog files, II-2; Harold Macmillan, *War Diaries,* 187; Macmillan, *The Blast of War,* 322.

189 *A dreadful fate would befall Italy:* Robert Murphy, *Diplomat Among Warriors,* 192–93; Strong, 157 (*"booted, spurred, and bemedaled"*).

189 *The telegram was sent:* "Story of the Signing of the Italian Armistice," Kenneth Strong to correspondents, in "Eisenhower Diary," HCB, DDE Lib, A-769-770; Garland, 482–84; Macmillan, *The Blast of War,* 323; Strong, 158 (*olive sprig*).

189 *"Today's event must be kept secret":* msg, DDE to CCS, Sept 3, 1943, NARA RG 165, E 422, OPD exec. files, 390/38/2/4-5, box 10.

189 *Those plans grew more convoluted:* Howard McGaw Smyth, "The Armistice at Cassible," *MR,* vol. 28, nos. 6 and 7 (Sept. and Oct. 1948), 13+; Pietro Badoglio, *Italy in the Second World War,* 70; msgs, DDE to Alexander, Sept. 1, 1943, FDR, Churchill to DDE, Sept. 2, 1943, both in NARA RG 319, OCMH, box 244 (*"stiffen Italian formations"*).

189 *"perfectly asinine":* OH, MWC, Rittgers, 54–57, 77; memo, AFHQ G-3 to W. B. Smith, Aug. 13, 1943, NARA RG 331, AFHQ micro, job 10A, R-13-C, in NARA RG 319, OCMH, box 244 (*"tactically unsound"*); R. P. Eaton, 82nd Airborne chief of staff, "Contact Imminent," ts, Dec. 26, 1943, Ralph P. Eaton Papers, MHI, 4; James M. Gavin, "Airborne Plans and Operations in the Mediterranean Theater," *IJ,* Aug. 1946, 22+ (*"not one individual"*); Clay Blair, *Ridgway's Paratroopers,* 126 (*"missions and remissions"*).

190 GIANT II: Blair, 132–33; Smyth, "The Armistice at Cassible," 13; Garland, 488–89.

190 *The more Ridgway heard:* corr, MBR to W. B. Smith, Dec. 5, 1955, and MBR to G. Castellano, Dec. 20, 1955, CJB, MHI, box 48, chrono file Italy; corr, MBR to Hal C. Pattison, Nov. 10, 1964, NARA RG 319, OCMH, 2-3.7 CC2 Sicily, box 251 (*"deceiving us"*); OH, W. B. Smith, May 13, 1947, Howard M. Smyth, SM, MHI (*"kettles, bricks"*); memo, MBR, "Development of Operation Giant," Sept. 9, 1943, CJB, MHI, box 48, chrono file Italy (*"full faith"*); Matthew B. Ridgway, *Soldier,* 81 (*"Contact will be made"*).

190 *As the sun sank:* AAR, Maxwell D. Taylor and W. T. Gardiner, "Mission to Rome," Sept 9, 1943, in Simpson, "Air Phase," 381–86; Richard Thruelsen and Elliott Arnold, "Secret Mission to Rome," *Harper's,* Oct. 1944, 462+; Maxwell D. Taylor, *Swords and Plowshares,* 55–57; Richard Tregaskis, *Invasion Diary,* 103–8; Melton S. Davis, *Who Defends Rome?,* 346–48.

190 *In truth they were Italians' guests:* Mark W. Boatner III, *The Biographical Dictionary of World War II,* 555 (*graceful Missourian*); John M. Taylor, *General Maxwell Taylor,* 65; Robert Capa, *Slightly Out of Focus,* 89 (*money belt*); Thruelsen and Arnold, 462 (*"If you get captured"*).

191 *By 8:30 P.M.:* AAR, Taylor and Gardiner, "Mission," 381–86; Thruelsen and Arnold, "Secret Mission to Rome," 462+; Taylor, 55–57; Tregaskis, 103–8; Davis, 346–48.

191 *The excellent crêpes:* Smyth, "The Armistice at Cassibile"; Taylor, 56–57 (*"professional dandy"*); Garland, 500; Volkmar Kühn, *German Paratroops in World War II,* 195.

191 *Italian garrisons had been virtually immobilized:* Garland, 495; Davis 353.

192 *He passed his days playing cards:* Douglas Porch, *The Path to Victory,* 465; Boatner, 23; Tompkins, 58–60 (*five thousand bottles*); Macmillan, *The Blast of War,* 330 (*"I was a Fascist"*).

192 *"Castellano did not know":* Davis, 353–55; Thruelsen and Arnold, "Secret Mission," 462 (*"Your bombers have blown up"*).

193 *"GIANT TWO is impossible":* AAR, Taylor and Gardiner, "Mission to Rome," in Simpson, "Air Phase," 381–86; Tregaskis, 107 (*"endeavoring to click our heels"*).

193 *"You will return to Allied headquarters":* Thruelsen and Arnold, "Secret Mission," 462; Taylor, 55–57.

193 *Eisenhower left Algiers:* Michael J. McKeough and Richard Lockridge, *Sgt. Mickey and General Ike,* 83–84; Kay Summersby, *Eisenhower Was My Boss,* 108 (*"illusion of being on*

*the march*"); OH, DDE, Feb. 16, 1949, Smyth (*"rather stretched out"*); Dwight D. Eisenhower, *Letters to Mamie,* 141, 147 (*"creature of war"*).

194 *Smith forwarded the doleful message:* Chandler, vol. 3, 1403n; msg, GCM to DDE or W. B. Smith, Sept. 8, 1943, NARA RG 165, E 422, OPD exec files, 390/38/2/4-5, box 10; "Unpublished Autobiography of General John E. Hull, USA (ret.)," ts, n.d., MHI (*"what you would expect"*).

194 *In the small schoolhouse:* OH, Lyman L. Lemnitzer, March 4, 1947, Howard M. Smyth, NARA RG 319, OCMH, CA, box 6; Peter Lyon, *Eisenhower: Portrait of the Hero,* 241 (*mouth tightened*); Stephen E. Ambrose, *Eisenhower,* vol. 1, 259–60 (*snapped it in half*); David Hunt, *A Don at War,* 224 (*"with great violence"*); OH, DDE, Feb. 16, 1949, Smyth (*"revolver against his kidneys"*); Chandler, vol. 3, 1402, 1403n (*"I do not accept"*).

194 *"I always knew":* OH, Arthur Coningham, Feb. 14, 1947, FCP, MHI; Chandler, vol. 3, 1404.

194 *Clearly a deviation was needed:* memo, MBR, "Development of Operation Giant," Sept. 9, 1943, CJB, MHI, box 48, chrono file Italy; L. James Binder, *Lemnitzer: A Soldier for His Time,* 113–14.

195 *Sixty-two transports:* OH, Lemnitzer, March 4, 1947, Smyth; Garland, 508–9;. Ridgway, 95 (*"trying to reconcile myself"*); Binder, 113–14 (*"What message?"*).

195 *Jeeps raced about:* Patrick K. O'Donnell, *Beyond Valor,* 66; Blair, 141 (*stumbled into a tent*).

195 *"The Italian government has surrendered":* msg, DDE, Sept. 8, 1943, NARA RG 165, E 422, OPD exec files, 390/38/2/4-5, box 10; Garland, 509–13.

195 *For 1,184 days:* Hugh Pond, *Salerno,* 10; David Irving, *The Trail of the Fox,* 305 (*"Italy's treachery is official"*).

196 *In the hours following Badoglio's announcement:* Garland, 513; "Memorandum Concerning the Events of September 8–9–10 in Rome," n.d., NARA RG 319, OCMH, box 249, 3 (*Telephone queries*); Robert Katz, *The Battle for Rome,* 32 (*fourteen of sixteen government ministers*); Howard McGaw Smyth, "The Command of the Italian Armed Forces in World War II," *Military Affairs,* spring 1951, 38+ (*summoned a notary*).

196 *No effort was made to stop six battalions:* Kühn, 196, 198; Badoglio, 81 (*only escape route*); Davis, 403, 407 (*green Fiat*); msg, F. N. Mason Macfarlane to DDE, Sept. 14, 1943, NARA RG 319, OCMH, box 244 (*"rather gaga"*); memoir, Kenyon Joyce, ts, n.d., Kenyon Joyce papers, MHI, 322; Katz, 32; "Military Campaigns and Political Events in Italy, 1942–1943," Jan. 1946, Strategic Services Unit, WD, A-63366, CMH, Geog Files, Italy, 370.22, 45 (*ingesting drops*); Tompkins, 271 (*"change sides twice"*).

196 *German troops snared thirty generals:* B. H. Liddell Hart, *The Other Side of the Hill,* 360; "Memorandum Concerning the Events of September 8–9–10 in Rome," n.d., NARA RG 319, OCMH, box 249, 3 (*firefights erupted*); John Patrick Carroll-Abbing, *But for the Grace of God,* 35 (*Italian snipers*); Jane Scrivener, *Inside Rome with the Germans,* 15–16 (*"The Jews are in a panic"*).

197 *Field Marshal Kesselring was disinclined to parley:* Simpson, "Air Phase," 102; Andrew Brookes, *Air War over Italy, 1943–1945,* 28; Albrecht Kesselring, *The Memoirs of Field-Marshal Kesselring,* 176; Hunt, 264; Count von Klinckowstroen, "Fighting Around Rome in September 1943," 1947, FMS, #T-1a, MHI, 5; Pond, *Salerno,* 7; Kesselring, "Commentary on MS #D-301," n.d., FMS, #D-313, MHI, 3; Garland, 526–27 (*threatened to blow up Rome's aqueducts*); "Translations, Campaign in Italy," NARA RG 319, OCMH, box 245 (*"It is finished"*).

197 *Kesselring, now viceroy:* Klinckowstroen, "Fighting Around Rome," 10–11; Albert Kesselring, "Special Report on the Events in Italy Between 25 July and 8 September 1943," n.d., FMS, #C-013, MHI, 5 (*"sheet lightning"*); Kesselring, *Memoirs,* 177 (*"card missing from the pack"*); Franz Kurowski, *Battleground Italy, 1943–1945,* 12 (*"I loved these people"*).

### The Stillest Shoes the World Could Boast

197 *Unmolested and apparently undetected:* StoC, 57; E. McCabe, "The Plan for the Landing at Salerno," 10–11 (HARPSICHORD); Warren P. Munsell, Jr., *The Story of a Regiment*, 21; Angelo Pesce, *Salerno 1943*, 99 (*"converted Polish liner"*); Howard H. Peckham and Shirley A. Snyder, eds., *Letters from Fighting Hoosiers*, vol. 2, 62 (*"Whenever I tore a bun"*); J. M. Huddleston, VI Corps surgeon, "Report for Colonel Carter," n.d., in Norman Lee Baldwin papers, HIA (*knotted condoms*).

198 *The usual muddles:* Mayo, *The Ordnance Department: On Beachhead and Battlefront*, 182 (*sailed without weapons*); *Texas*, 223 (*white-star insignia*); AAR, "Signal Reflections on the Planning and Execution of Avalanche," Oct. 13, 1943, 10th Corps, UK NA, CAB 106/395, 7 (*carrier pigeons*); "Observations in the European Theater," 2 (*"military impedimenta"*); Dunham, "United States Army Transportation and the Italian Campaign," 26–27; "The Administrative History of the Eighth Fleet," ts, n.d., U.S. Naval History Division, #139, NHC, folder 3, 34; John H. Clagett, unpublished biography, n.d., HKH, box 16, 436 (*Hewitt was so incensed*).

198 *endless games of housey-housey:* Hickey and Smith, 78; Eric Morris, *Salerno: A Military Fiasco*, 83 (*boiling coffee*); Norman Lewis, *Naples '44*, 11 (*"We know nothing"*); *Italian Phrase Book*, U.S. War Department, 1943.

198 *Aboard Hewitt's flagship:* http://www.nightscribe.com/Military/ww2/ancon_history _front.htm; Donald Downes, *The Scarlet Thread*, 140; Reynolds, 281 (*"in the lion's mouth"*), 300 (*"the Yale Club"*); diary, MWC, Sept. 7, 1943, MWC, Citadel, box 64 (*"feeling the strain"*).

199 *Some 55,000 assault troops:* Calculated, 185; Hickey and Smith, 52–53 (*"the most daring plan"*).

199 *The 36th, entering combat for the first time:* Lee Carraway Smith, *A River Swift and Deadly*, 5; Steven E. Clay, mss, 16th Infantry history [*Blood and Sacrifice*], MRC-FDM, 14 (*"Deep in the Heart of Texas"*); Hickey and Smith, 56 (*Lone Star flag*).

199 *"We can't expect to achieve":* Shapiro, 122; HKH, "Action Report of the Salerno Landings, Sept.–Oct. 1943," 1945, CMH, 130 (*fifteen-minute cannonade*), 142; FLW to MWC, "Conclusions Based on the Avalanche Operation," Oct. 11, 1943, CARL, N-6818, 1; *Texas*, 230–31 (*"may not be discovered"*) ; OH, FLW, May 15, 1953, John G. Westover, SM, MHI; StoC, 57; target list, operation plan 7-43, annex B, appendix 1, HKH, LOC MS Div, box 8, folder 8; Samuel Eliot Morison, *The Two-Ocean War*, 351 (*"fantastic to assume"*); Merrill L. Bartlett, ed., *Assault from the Sea*, 268; OH, MWC, 1972–73, Forest S. Rittgers, Jr., SOOHP, MHI, 53; lecture, Don Brann, ts, n.d., in Robert J. Wood papers, MHI, 4 (*Clark had sided with Walker*).

199 *Eisenhower's armistice announcement:* diary, MWC, Sept. 8, 1943, MWC, Citadel, box 64; *The Grenadier Guards, 1939–1945*, 27 (*officers with megaphones*).

200 *Jubilation erupted:* Downes, 3; Robert Wallace, *The Italian Campaign*, 53 (*"The Eyeties"*); Hickey and Smith, 42; Travis Beard, "Turning the Tide at Salerno," *Naval History*, Oct. 2003 (*"The war is over"*); John T. Mason, Jr., *The Atlantic War Remembered*, 328n (*"Yap, yap, yap"*); Pond, 16; *The Grenadier Guards, 1939–1945*, 27; Philip Vian, *Action This Day*, 117 (*"Seldom in history"*).

200 *Soldiers jettisoned bandoliers:* Wood, "The Landing at Salerno," 13; "Reminiscences of Phil H. Bucklew," 1980, John T. Mason, Jr., USNI OHD, 64; Pond, 18 (*dinner jacket*); StoC, 55 (*"sheer joy"*); corr, Armand G. Jones to father, n.d., 155th FA, Texas MFM, 3; Robert L. Wagner, *The Texas Army*, 4.

200 *"keen fighting edge":* HKH, "Action Report," 91; Downes, 3 (*"bloody fools"*); Pond, 68 (*"Take your ammunition"*); Newton H. Fulbright, "Altavilla: A Personal Record," ts, n.d., Texas MFM, 12 (*"horned Comanches"*); Clifford H. Peek, Jr., *Five Years, Five Countries, Five Campaigns*, 15 (*"Expect a hostile shore"*).

200 *"Gunners, man your guns"*: Shapiro, 122; Quentin Reynolds, *The Curtain Rises,* 287 (*"ship will be hove to"*); SSA, 252; Fulbright, "Altavilla," 2 (*"Imagination makes cowards"*); John Steinbeck, *New York Herald Tribune,* Oct. 3, 1943, in *Reporting World War II,* vol. 1, 636–37.

201 *Just before ten* P.M.: chronology, HKH, "Action Report," NHC; Shapiro, 18 (*"they're blind"*); AAR, H.M.S. *Brecon,* Sept. 22, 1943, in "Operation AVALANCHE—Report on Northern Assault," Oct. 16, 1943, CARL, N-6837 (*ruby glow*); SSA, 253 (*"silver sea"*).

201 *Twelve miles offshore:* Pond, 39; *Salerno: The American Operation from the Beaches to the Volturno,* 14; Anthony Kimmins, *Half-Time,* 204 (*"honeymoon couples"*); Fulbright, "Altavilla," 2.

201 *Clark stood beside Hewitt:* Reynolds, *The Curtain Rises,* 288; Hickey and Smith, 82 (*"You'll be in total command"*); Jack Maher, memoir, n.d., http://home.wi.rr.com//johnmaher (*"down a ten-story building"*).

201 *"tall, smiling, appearing unconcerned":* Reynolds, *The Curtain Rises,* 292–93; chronology, HKH, "Action Report," NHC (*"Arrived at transport area"*); diary, MWC, Sept. 9, 1943, MWC, Citadel, box 64.

202 *"What's the weather like":* SSA, 271; Karl Baedeker, *Southern Italy and Sicily,* 167; Robert M. Coates, *South of Rome,* 52; L. V. Bertarelli, *Southern Italy,* 316–17 (*Salerno's medical school*).

202 *The latter-day town had grown:* Pond, 40–41; Morton, 303, 396 (*predatory Saracens*); *Salerno,* 6.

202 *Neither Kesselring nor his lieutenants believed:* "Special Investigation and Interrogation Report: Operation Lightening" [*sic*], March 15, 1947, Military Intelligence Service, Austria, CMH, Geog Files 370.2, 7 and 13; intelligence summary, Sunset No. 91, Aug. 30, 1943, NARA RG 457, E 9026, NSA records, box 1; SSA, 261; war diary, Sept. 6, 1943, "Salerno Invasion," German naval command, box 649 (*"a strike in the direction"*); StoC, 67; Molony V, 274; Kurowski, 107 (*"large naval force"*).

203 *Following the capitulation announcement:* diary, Wehrmachtführungstab, OKW, Aug. 29, 1943, NARA RG 319, OCMH, box 245 (*invoked ACHSE*); SSA, 261 (*"completely annihilated"*).

203 *That German might took the form of Tenth Army:* StoC, 67, 69 (*"No mercy"*); A. Kesselring, testimony, war crimes trial, March 3, 1947, NARA RG 492, MTO, AG HQ, 000.5, box 816 (*"a spiritual burden"*); Hickey and Smith, 50; Pond, 9 (*"died as a great soldier"*).

203 *first German unit on the Volga:* Pond, 41; Rudolf Böhmler, *Monte Cassino,* 51 (*four thousand survivors*); MEB, "16th Panzer Division at Salerno," 1953, OCMH, R-series, NARA RG 319, E 145, R-36, 2–3 (*best-equipped division in Italy*).

203 *Sieckenius had split his forces:* "The German Defense at the Gulf of Salerno," Feb. 23, 1944, W.O.W.IR. #28, NHC, folder 33, 18–19, 23.

204 *On the far right of the Allied line:* StoC, 74; Harold G. Horning, "The Army Years," ts, n.d., part 2, 155th FA, Texas MFM, 36 (*"stood up to see"*).

204 *Bullets plumped the sea:* Belden, 292; Leo V. Bishop et al., eds., *The Fighting Forty-fifth,* 41 (*"You can't dig foxholes"*); corr, James E. Taylor, 131st FA Bn, to Walter H. Beck, March 2, 1944, Texas MFM, 2 (*"spring rain"*); AAR, "Historical Record, Headquarters, VI Corps, September 1943," JPL, MHI, box 12, 3; AAR, "Record of Events," 142nd Inf, Sept. 3–20, 1943, CARL, N-6818; Chester G. Starr, ed., *From Salerno to the Alps,* 17; "Field Operations of the Medical Department in the MTOUSA," Nov. 10, 1945, NARA RG 94, E 427, 95-USF2-26-0, 224 (*"Shells were wopping"*); Peek, 21 (*"seemed to rise completely"*); Glenn G. Clift, *A Letter from Salerno,* 6–7 (*"boys were on fire"*).

204 *On the beach, soldiers wriggled:* *Salerno,* 21; Peek, 22 (*"a baby girl"*); Wood, "The Landing at Salerno," 14; author visits, Oct. 1995, May 2004; Mayo, 178; diary, J. M. Huddleston, VI

Corps surgeon, Sept. 9, 1943, Norman Lee Baldwin papers, HIA ("*great deal of confusion*").

205 *The first Luftwaffe planes:* H. Kent Hewitt, "The Allied Navies at Salerno," *Proceedings,* Sept. 1953, 958+; *SSA,* 261; Bill Harr, *Combat Boots,* 40–41 ("*Steady, now, steady*"); Wood, "The Landing at Salerno," 13 ("*someone had let them down*"); Don Whitehead, "*Beachhead Don,*" 37.

205 *By six A.M. two infantry regiments:* "Amphibious Operations," Aug.–Dec. 1943, CINC, U.S. Fleet, CMH; Brooks E. Kleber and Dale Birdsell, *The Chemical Warfare Service: Chemicals in Combat,* 335 (*smoke pots*); Paul W. Pritchard, "Smoke Generator Operations in the Mediterranean and European Theaters of Operation," n.d., Office of the Chief of the Chemical Corps, CMH, 4-7.1 FA 1, 53; Norman Hussa, "Action at Salerno," *IJ,* vol. 53, no. 6 (Dec. 1943), 25+; John Steinbeck, *Once There Was a War,* 162; "COHQ Bulletin No. Y/25," Apr. 1944, CARL, N-6530.10; AAR, *LST 324* and *LST 363,* in "Operation AVALANCHE—Report on Northern Assault," Royal Navy, Oct. 16, 1943, CARL, N-6837 ("*Ventilation fans sucked smoke*"); "Amphibious Operations," Aug.–Dec. 1943, CINC, U.S. Fleet, CMH (*compass headings*).

205 *Still, German observers:* StoC, 80; Roskill, 175; AAR, 191st Tank Bn, n.d., AGF Board Reports, NARA RG 407, E 427, NATOUSA, 95-USF1-2.0; Bishop et al., eds., 41; memoir, Aidan Mark Sprot, ts, 1947, LHC, 72 (*LST officers scampered*); Walter Karig, *Battle Report: The Atlantic War,* 265, 268 ("*jolly well shot up*").

207 AVALANCHE *planners had hoped:* R. L. Connolly, "Operations of Landing Craft in the Mediterranean," Oct. 14, 1943, NARA RG 334, E 315, NWC Lib, ANSCOL, L-2-43, C-75, box 170; Downes, 14; *SSA,* 265 (*pinned to the dunes*); Mark W. Clark, "Salerno," *AB,* No. 95, 1997, 1+; Peek, ed., 20; Wagner, 11 ("*I saw riflemen swarm*").

207 *"in a row, side by side":* Norman Lewis, *Naples '44,* 12; Paul A. Cundiff, *45th Infantry CP,* 62 ("*the stillest shoes*"); Peckham and Snyder, eds., vol. 2, 63 ("*wouldn't look so bad*"); Reynolds, *The Curtain Rises,* 300 ("*On what beach*").

207 *Salvation arrived shortly after nine A.M.:* Richard J. Werner, 141st Inf Regt, in FLW to MWC, Oct. 11, 1943, CARL, N-6818, 1-2; *StoC,* 82; "Historical Tactical Study of Naval Gunfire at Salerno," 1948–49, Amphibious Warfare School, USMC, Quantico, Va., SEM, NHC, box 51, 25; "Amphibious Operations," Aug.–Dec. 1943, CINC, U.S. Fleet, CMH; Shapiro, 132 (*steamed within a hundred yards*); action report, U.S.S. *Philadelphia,* Sept. 25, 1943, NARA RG 38, OCNO, WWII Action and Operational Reports, box 1318; *SSA,* 280 (*Eleven thousand tons of naval shells*).

208 *"the cover of a Latin book":* Fred Howard, *Whistle While You Wait,* 167; memo, "Shore Party Organization for Amphibious Operations," AFHQ to WD, Dec. 17, 1943, NARA RG 407, E 427, 270/50/28/36; "Lessons from the Italian Campaign," March 10, 1944, NARA RG 407, E 427, NATOUSA, 95-USF1-04, box 250, 12.

208 *Near a tobacco barn at Casa Vannula:* journal, 36th ID chief of staff, Sept. 9, 1943, SM, MHI; *StoC,* 84; corr, James E. Taylor, 131st FA Bn, to Walter H. Beck, March 2, 1944, Texas MFM, 2 ("*hip-shooting*"); corr, Miles A. Cowles, 36th Div artillery CO, in *Texas,* 409 (*two hundred yards' range*); "Lessons from the Italian Campaign," March 10, 1944, HQ, NATOUSA, CMH, Italy 353, 12; FLW to MWC, Oct. 11, 1943, CARL, N-6818, chronology; *Texas,* 237 ("*It was thrilling*").

208 *Dive-bombers caught the U.S.S. Nauset:* http://www.ussorleck.org/Namesake.asp; *SSA,* 274.

208 *But the preliminary naval bombardment:* action report, LCA 403, Sept. 22, 1943, in "Operation AVALANCHE—Report on North Assault," RN, Oct. 16, 1943, CARL, N-6837; Phil H. Bucklew, "Skipping Salvos off Salerno," in Mason, 318; Pond, 59–61, 88 ("*This way to Naples*"), 91; Wallace, 58 (*a piano*).

208 *By day's end, X Corps would land:* Molony V, 286; Pond, 61 ("*unutterable confusion*"); E. McCabe, "The Plan for the Landing at Salerno," 190a (LST 357); AAR, HM LST 430,

Sept. 12, 1943, in "Operation AVALANCHE—Report on Northern Assault," Oct. 16, 1943, CARL, N-6837.

209 *Beyond the beaches, the invasion unfolded:* Molony V, 284; Simpson, "Air Phase," 339n; AAR, "Operation Avalanche," Apr. 21, 1945, Mediterranean Allied Tactical AF, CARL, N-11606, 17 (*88mm shells riddled the fuselage*).

209 *The 5th Battalion of the Royal Hampshire Regiment:* Daniell, 142; Morris, 108; Pond, 71; Molony V, 285.

209 *Past Montecorvino, Tommies in khaki:* Gervasi, 495; Molony V, 284, 290; *The Grenadier Guards, 1939–1945,* 28 (*"feeling of looseness"*).

210 *"bloody great battleships":* Hickey and Smith, 178; Pond, 111–12 (*"retiring pell-mell"*), 114; David Erskin, *The Scots Guards, 1919–1955,* 170n (*tomato canning plant*); Clark, "Salerno," 1.

210 *They were not coming:* "Invasion of Italian Mainland, Summary of Operations Carried Out by British Troops Under Command 5 U.S. Army," n.d., CMH, 370.2, 7–8; Wilfred Owen, "Anthem for Doomed Youth," *Oxford Book of War Poetry,* 188; Daniell, 141; Pond, 77 (*"We've got them"*).

210 *Only on the extreme left:* AAR, 1st Ranger Bn, Nov. 15, 1943, USMA micro, MP63-8, R-1; morning report, 1st Ranger Bn, HQ Co, Sept. 9, 1943, Robert W. Black papers, MHI, box 2, folder 8; *Salerno,* 19; William O. Darby and William H. Daumer, *Darby's Rangers: We Led the Way,* 113–16; James J. Altieri, *Darby's Rangers: An Illustrated Portrayal of the Original Rangers,* 57–58.

210 *"an artilleryman's dream":* Michael J. King, *William Orlando Darby: A Military Biography,* 115; author visit, Apr. 29, 2004; Tregaskis, 133–35 (*"reminds me of Spain"*); Anders Kjar Arnbal, *The Barrel-Land Dance Hall Rangers,* 155 (*"chestnut branches"*); Richard M. Burrage, "See Naples and Die!," ts, 1988, Texas MFM, 6 (*"until hell freezes"*).

210 *Soon a battleship:* Darby and Daumer, 117; Capa, 98 (*firing mortar barrages through holes*); Tregaskis, 135; Downes, 145 (*"men and boys in rags"*); memo, Donald Downes to W. Donovan, "OSS Activities in the Neapolitan Campaign, D-day to D-day plus 21," Oct. 19, 1943, NARA RG 226, E 99, OSS History Office, box 48; Virgil, *The Aeneid,* trans. Robert Fagles, 181 (*"white with the bones"*).

211 *Others forever remembered deep-chested Darby:* Wood, "The Landing at Salerno," 16–19; Downes, 142–49 (*"Snow White"*); Burrage, "See Naples and Die!," 15 (*San Francisco Hotel*); Tregaskis, 133 (*"hell of a pasting"*).

211 *"We are sitting pretty":* Shapiro, 133; Molony V, 286; Malcolm Munthe, *Sweet Is War,* 167 (*"Corpses lay on the sand"*).

211 *"In the land of theory":* Molony V, 325.

212 *The first hitch:* Edward J. O'Neill, "Memorandum to Commanding General, VI Corps," June 29, 1944, JPL, MHI, box 11; OH, MWC, May 10–21, 1948, SM, MHI; D. Clayton James, *A Time for Giants,* 140–41; *Howitzer,* USMA yearbook, 1910; Robert H. Berlin, *U.S. Army World War II Corps Commanders,* 17; Edmund F. Ball, *Staff Officer with the Fifth Army,* 186; 201 file, EJD, HIA, box 1; OH, GCM, July 25, 1949, SM, MHI (*decorated protégé*); corr, EJD to Hal C. Pattison, Dec. 15, 1964, NARA RG 319, OCMH, 2-3.7 CC3, Salerno to Cassino, box 255 (*"Don't bite off"*).

212 *Clark's plan to leave Dawley:* O'Neill, "Memorandum," June 29, 1944; "Historical Record, Headquarters, VI Corps," JPL, MHI, box 12; aide's diary, EJD, HIA, box 1; diary, EJD, Sept. 9, 1943, HIA, box 1 (*"Coxswain got lost"*).

212 *With his dispersed staff in disarray:* StoC, 87; CM, 253 (*required radios*); O'Neill, "Memorandum," June 29, 1944 (*"Confusion and disorganization"*); Ball, 197 (*"tennis match"*).

213 *"Just as sure as God lives":* PP, 344.

213 *a seven-mile gap:* Clark and others estimated the gap to be ten miles wide, but map positions show it was narrower. Wood, "The Landing at Salerno," 16; StoC, 90; Hickey and Smith, 139; *Calculated,* 192.

213 *"well in hand"*: diary, MWC, Sept. 10, 1943, MWC, Citadel, box 64 (*"Have just returned"*); speech, Robert B. Hutchins, "Personal Experiences of a Regimental Commander in Italy, 1944," in Russell L. Moses, ASEQ, 179th Inf, MHI, 4–7.

213 *To help unite his two corps:* Under pressure from AFHQ to return the transport ships to pick up more troops, Hewitt had in fact landed the 157th Infantry on the south bank of the Sele rather than the north, as Clark would have preferred. The admiral's presumption was more annoying to Clark than tactically significant. *Calculated,* 195; W.H.H. Morris, Jr., "Report on Observation Trip," n.d., DRL, IS, 9; *StoC,* 100–101.

213 *The third hitch derived:* Molony V, 273; Simpson, "Air Phase," 122; Roskill, 173; "History of the Aviation Engineers in the Mediterranean Theater of Operations," June 1946, AAF Engineer Command, MTO, CEOH, X-39; "Long Range Fighter Cover over Salerno Beaches," Oct. 1943, HW, NAAF, Monthly Operations Bulletin #6, NARA RG 334, E 315, NWC Lib, ANSCOL, box 132; "The Army Air Forces in Amphibious Landings in World War II," July 1953, USAF Historical Div, AU, CARL, N-16372.34, 62–64; Vian, 119 (*sawed nine inches*); Reynolds, *The Curtain Rises,* 305 (*"Bloody nonsense"*).

214 *Using flashlights for illumination:* D. E. Williams, "Air Operations—'AVALANCHE,'" Jan. 7, 1944, NARA RG 334, E 315, NWC Lib, ANSCOL, L-3-43, W-67, box 179, 4; Simpson, "Air Phase," 124–25, 135; Molony V, 299; *StoC,* 103 (*"Air situation here critical"*).

214 *"Our greatest asset now"*: Chandler, vol. 2, 1406.

214 *"as soon as admin situation"*: Brooks, ed., 284, 379n; Lamb, 39, 44, 47 (*"holiday picnic"*).

214 *On the other side of the hill:* Ralph S. Mavrogordato, "The Battle of Salerno," Dec. 1957, NARA RG 319, E 145, OCMH, R-series mss, R-88, 13; Moorehead, *Eclipse,* 43 (*boots in rags*); *StoC,* 86; Matthew Cooper, *The German Army,* 405; Liddell Hart, 363.

214 *Hitches plagued Vietinghoff:* Eduard Mark, *Aerial Interdiction in Three Wars,* 98; Mavrogordato, "The Battle of Salerno," 14–15, 36; Douglas Graf Bernstorff, "Operations of the 26th Panzer Division in Italy," 1948, FMS, #D-316, MHI, 1-7; *StoC,* 98.

215 *"Viva English!"*: Moorehead, *Eclipse,* 43; Molony V, 293 (*five divisions ringing*).

215 *Within the Anglo-American beachhead:* "Personal Diary of Langan W. Swent," Sept. 12, 1943, HIA, box 1; "World War II Diaries of Norman Maffei," 158th FA, 45th Div, ASEQ, MHI (*"surrender of Italy hasn't hindered"*).

215 *Fresh dead joined the older dead:* chronology, Sept. 10, 1943, 1500 hrs, HKH, "Action Report," CMH; James C. Ruddell et al., "Observers Notes on the Italian Campaign," Dec. 5, 1943, NARA RG 337, AGF, observer reports, 190/48/30-21/00, #59, box 52; LeRoy R. Houtson, "Dead Men by Mass Production," ts, n.d., Texas MFM, 2–4 (*"didn't have a mark"*); Clark, "Salerno," 1 (*Triangular wooden wedges*); Ball, 218; Hickey and Smith, 307 (*"They've placed the graveyard"*).

215 *Stretcher bearers hurrying to the rear:* Steinbeck, 158; medical forms from T. Nennniger, NARA, Modern Military Records; Tregaskis, 140; Charles M. Wiltse, *The Medical Department: Medical Service in the Mediterranean and Minor Theaters,* 228 (*"unusual agility"*), 231, 236; Edward D. Churchill, *Surgeon to Soldiers,* 257; J. M. Huddleston, VI Corps surgeon, "Report for Colonel Carter," 1943, Norman Lee Baldwin papers, HIA.

216 *"that's the way it is"*: Tregaskis, 139; Moorehead, *Eclipse,* 36; Burrage, "See Naples and Die!," 28 (*"I don't think God"*).

216 *"Our forces have captured"*: Pond, 129; report, Fifth Army, Sept. 11, 1943, 0045 hrs., Robert J. Wood papers, MHI (*"Combat efficiency"*); chronology, Sept. 11, 1943, 0208 hrs, HKH, "Action Report," CMH (*"Am satisfied"*); AAR, "Record of Events," 142nd Inf, July 10, 1943, 1200 hrs, CARL, N-6818; *StoC,* 97 (*"The worst is over"*), 101 (*ready to march north*); AAR, "Historical Record, Headquarters, VI Corps," 5–6 (*odd lull*).

### The Moan of Lost Souls

216 *Four German bombs had landed:* action report, *Ancon* commanding officer to CINC, U.S. Fleet, Oct. 15, 1943, MWC papers, Citadel, box 3, folder 1; OH, HKH, 1961, John T.

Mason, Col U OHRO, 347 ("*sore thumb*"); Howe, "American Signal Intelligence," 61; H. Kent Hewitt, "The Allied Navies at Salerno," *Proceedings,* Sept. 1953, 958+; OH, HKH, n.d., Julian Boit and James Riley, HKH papers, NHC, box 6, 5 ("*get into the action*").

216  *Thirty "red alerts":* Shapiro, 137 (*human chains*); Karig, 266; *Three Years,* 412 (*helmsmen tried to minimize*); OH, HKH, 1961, John T. Mason, Col U OHRO, 347 (*slow enough to shrink her wake*).

217  *Three days into* AVALANCHE: Dunham, "United States Army Transportation and Italian Campaign," 37; "The Administrative History of the Eighth Fleet," 36; George J. Horney, "Comments and Suggestions on the AVALANCHE Operation," n.d., NARA RG 407, E, 427, NATOUSA, 95-USF1-0.4, box 250.

217  *Drivers could not find their vehicles:* A chemical mortar battalion arriving at Paestum on Sept. 9 did not receive its mortars until Sept. 12. Kleber and Birdsell, 433; Reynolds, *The Curtain Rises,* 317 (*cowboys and Indians*); "Amphibious Operations, Aug.–Dec. 1943," CINC, U.S. Fleet, CMH; "COHQ Bulletin No. Y/25," Apr. 1944, CARL, N-6530.10.

217  *Hewitt this morning had sent Admiral Cunningham:* OH, HKH, 1961, John T. Mason, Col U OHRO, 373; *AAinWWII,* 525–26; "Personal Diary of Langan W. Swent," Sept. 12, 1943, HIA, box 1 ("*All are jumpy*"); newsletter, U.S.S. *Philadelphia,* Sept. 23, 1943, WWII Ship Files, NHC ("*nerve pills*").

217  *The demand for pills spiked:* Hewitt, "The Allied Navies at Salerno," 958+; chronology, HKH, "Action Report," NHC ("*hogging, sagging*").

217  *as Hewitt soon surmised:* msg, HKH to A. B. Cunningham, Sept. 12, 1943, 1547 hrs., chronology, HKH, "Action Report," CMH; http://www.vectorsite.net/twbomb3.html#m3; James P. Melanephy and John G. Robinson, *Surface Warfare,* vol. 6, no. 3 (March 1981), 2+; corr, D. H. Leathem to author, Jan. 20, 2003; James Phinney Baxter, *Scientists Against Time,* 194; William W. Downey, "Report on Simmons Project," n.d., OSS, NARA RG 226, E 99, OSS, 190/6/7/7, box 25, folder 6; memo, "Radio-Controlled Bombs Can be Jammed," March 10, 1945, SEM, NHC, box 47.

217  *"terrific screeching noise":* diary, MWC, Sept. 11, 1943, MWC, Citadel, box 64; *Calculated,* 196; Clark, "Salerno," 1; action report, R. W. Cary, U.S.S. *Savannah,* Oct. 1, 1943, NARA RG 38, OCNO, Action and Operational Reports, box 1413 (*hard left rudder*).

217  *"It didn't fall like bombs do":* Reynolds, *The Curtain Rises,* 328, 333 ("*wasn't natural*"); "U.S.S. *Savannah* (CL 42) Bomb Damage," War Damage Report No. 44, June 15, 1944, Bureau of Ships, Navy Dept., NARA RG 38, OCNO, WWII Action and Operational Reports, box 1413 (*twenty-two-inch hole*).

217  *"flared like a sulphur match":* Michael Stern, *Into the Jaws of Death,* 211; Reynolds, *The Curtain Rises,* 328; Hewitt, "The Allied Navies at Salerno," 958+; Evelyn M. Cherpak, ed., *The Memoirs of Admiral H. Kent Hewitt,* 121 (*his flagship*).

217  *The blast vaporized bulkheads:* Melanephy and Robinson, "*Savannah* at Salerno," 2; action report, George J. Pinto to CINC, U.S. Fleet, July 19, 1943; action report, R. W. Cary, U.S.S. *Savannah,* Oct. 1, 1943; war damage report, U.S.S. *Savannah,* Oct. 14, 1943; "U.S.S. *Savannah* (CL 42) Bomb Damage," War Damage Report No. 44, June 15, 1944, Bureau of Ships, Navy Dept., all in NARA RG 38, OCNO, WWII Action and Operational Reports, box 1413.

217  *At Pearl Harbor:* Jack Greene and Alessandro Massignani, *The Naval War in the Mediterranean, 1940–1943,* 305.

217  *Her rugged hull saved her:* Reynolds, *The Curtain Rises,* 328; war log, U.S.S. *Savannah,* Sept. 14, 1943, NARA RG 38, OCNO, WWII War Diaries, box 1425 (*Among the unluckiest*).

219  *A deft shifting of fuel:* SSA, 283–84; Beard, "Turning the Tide at Salerno," 34+ (*sailors braced the rails*); war damage report, U.S.S. *Savannah,* Oct. 14, 1943. Other accounts put the death tally at just under two hundred.

219  *Hewitt desperately sought remedies:* lecture, Richard L. Conolly, "The Landing at Salerno in World War II," May 14, 1957, Naval Historical Foundation, 8; Hewitt, "The Allied

Navies at Salerno," 958; Aileen Clayton, *The Enemy Is Listening,* 281; Pond, 127 (*electric razors*); memo, "Radio-Controlled Bombs Can be Jammed" (*"improve morale"*); StoC, 106–7 (*Fritz-X attacks in coming days*).

219 *To the relief of Ancon's crew:* Shapiro, 140; Lewis, 14 (*"streaming like ants"*), 19; diary, EJD, Sept. 12, 1943, HIA, box 1; StoC, 112; Morris, 240; Alfred M. Beck et al., *The Corps of Engineers: The War Against Germany,* 163; Downes, 16; Pond, 174.

220 *Clark immediately drove south: Calculated,* 197; aide's diary, EJD, HIA, box 1.

220 *Twenty-eight thousand Americans:* AAR, "Historical Record," 7–8; *Salerno,* 50; Molony V, 304; DDE, "Allied Commander-in-Chief's Report, Italian Campaign," 112.

220 *The American right flank seemed secure:* AAR, "Record of Events," 142nd Inf, Sept. 3–20, 1943, CARL, N-6818; StoC, 108–9; Wagner, 19 (*"a height of some sort"*); J. Tuck Brown, "Love, War, Etc.," ts, Jan. 1995, 132nd FA, 36th ID, ASEQ, MHI, 22–24 (*"I'm a little hungry"*); http://www.smu.edu/cul memorial/fellen.htm. Brown's eyewitness account contradicts the version of Sprague's death in Morris, 233.

220 *"a tribulation":* Thruelsen and Arnold, 179; *Salerno,* 43–47; Munsell, 26 (*"fired point blank"*); John Embry, "My Most Interesting Experience," ts, n.d., 160th FA Bn, 45th ID Mus, 117, 125 (*plans to spike their tubes*); AAR, 191st Tank Bn, n.d., AGF board reports, NARA RG 407, E 427, 95-USF1-2.0 (*tobacco factory would change hands*).

221 *If German forces followed the Sele:* Mark W. Clark, "Salerno," 1; Molony V, 302–3; diary, MWC, Sept. 12, 1943, MWC, Citadel, box 64 (*drove to Red Beach*).

221 *"Very heavy fighting":* chronology, Sept. 11, 1943, 2025 hrs, HKH, "Action Report," CMH; StoC, 107 (*fifteen hundred Allied soldiers*); Porch, 492 (*Anglo-Irish cavalryman*); OH, JPL, May 24, 1948, SM, MHI (*"tall, lean, and vague"*); Charles Richardson, *Flashback,* 160 (*near-whisper*); Pond, 156–59, 172 (*"another Dunkirk"*); Nigel Nicolson, *The Grenadier Guards in the War of 1939–1945,* vol. 2, 362–64; Michael Howard and John Sparrow, *The Coldstream Guards, 1920–1946,* 153–54; Michael Howard, *Captain Professor,* 73 (*"lost souls"*).

221 *Shaken by the sight of the British war dead:* Hamilton, 416; Hickey and Smith, 183; diary, EJD, Sept. 12, 1943, HIA, box 1; "Historical Record, Headquarters, VI Corps, September 1943—The Operation AVALANCHE," n.d., JPL, MHI, box 12, 7 (*Field Ordeor No. 2*); StoC, 109.

222 *Grimy and dust-caked:* diary, MWC, Sept. 12, 1943, MWC, Citadel, box 64 (*"I must await further buildup"*); corr, H. Alexander to DDE, Sept. 13, 1943, DDE Lib, PP-pres, box 3 (*"everything must be done"*).

222 *"the crowing of a cock cut the ears":* Shapiro, 145.

222 *All tranquillity vanished at six A.M.:* AAR, "Historical Record," 8; journal, Sept. 13, 1943, 36th ID, chief of staff, SM, MHI; *Salerno,* 61; AAR, "Record of Events," 142nd Inf, Sept. 3–20, 1943, CARL, N-6818. The U.S. Army official history states that the shelling came from German artillery. StoC, 113, 125.

222 *The 3rd Battalion of the 143rd Infantry:* StoC, 113–14; AAR, "Operation AVALANCHE," 143rd Inf, Oct. 2, 1943, CARL, N-6818; memo, Fifth Army IG to MWC, Sept. 19, 1943, MWC, Citadel, box 2, folder 3 (*repulsed with heavy losses*); Steven E. Clay, *Blood and Sacrifice,* 179 (*"getting the Germans to stand up"*).

223 *now faced mortal danger:* Mavrogordato, "The Battle of Salerno," 23 (*"split themselves into two sections"*); "Special Investigation and Interrogation Report: Operation Lightening," 29 (*"unconnected leadership"*); SSA, 285–87; Pond, 171 (*"dust rose in clouds"*), 177 (*"Lili Marlene"*).

223 *the five stout warehouses:* Rosella Baretta, *Tabacco, tabaccari, e tabacchine nel Salento: Vicende, storiche, economiche, e sociali,* 6; *Guide d'Italia,* 126; Ascanio Marchini, *Il Tabacco,* 10, 21.

223 *Here the full fury of the German attack:* Morris, "Report on Observation Trip," 7–8; *Salerno,* 63; W.H.H. Morris, Jr., "Salerno," *MR,* vol. 13, no. 12 (March 1944), 5+ (*"Fireworks*

*created an appearance*"); "Operation of the 45th Infantry Division in Italy," Sept. 10–30, 1943, 45th ID Mus; memo, I. C. Avery to MWC, investigation, actions of Co. B, 2nd Chemical Bn, Sept. 20, 1943, MWC, Citadel, corr, box 2 (*abandoned tubes unspiked*); *Salerno*, 65.

224 "*Tracers were going through my pack*": corr, Richard Pisciotta to father, May 18, 1944, 157th Inf, 45th Div, ASEQ, MHI; OH, FLW, May 15, 1953, John G. Westover, SM, MHI; journal, Sept. 13, 1943, 36th ID, chief of staff, SM, MHI; AAR, "Operation AVALANCHE," 143rd Inf, Oct. 2, 1943, CARL, N-6818; Eddie Douglas Adkins, "A P.O.W. Diary," ts, 1960, Texas MFM ("*I will reserve a space*"); Grady G. Tice, "POWs Never Forget War," *Commerce Journal*, March 4, 2001, Texas MFM (*Germans were atheists*); Shapiro, 152 ("*like furrows from a plow*"); FLW to MWC, Oct. 11, 1943, CARL, N-6818; Bruce L. Barger, *The Texas 36th Division*, 137; Morris, "Salerno," 5+ (*fired into the backs*); Wagner, 27 ("*It was hell up there*"), 34.

224 "*Situation worse*": diary, 1st and 3rd Bn aid station, 179th Inf, Sept. 12–13, 1943, 45th ID Mus; AAR, 191st Tank Bn, n.d., AGF board reports, NARA RG 407, E 427, NATOUSA, 95-USF1-2.0 (*tank crew took turns*); AAR, Van W. Pyland, 636th Tank Destroyer Bn, n.d., in *Texas*, 413 (*Dead men lay on a gravel bar*); Flint Whitlock, *The Rock of Anzio*, 87 ("*fighting for your ass*").

224 "*Enemy on the run*": F. Jones, "The Campaign in Italy: The Landing at Salerno," n.d., Cabinet Historical Section, UK NA, CAB 44 132, 133; *SSA*, 287.

224 *Then on the southwest bank: Calculated*, 201; *Salerno*, 65–66 (*Drivers, bandsmen*); "Operational History of Chemical Battalions and the 4.2-inch Mortar in World War II," part 1, 1947, CMH, 4-7.1 FB2, 56; Kleber and Birdsell, 433; Bishop et al., eds., 47; "World War II Diaries of Norman Maffei," Sept. 14, 1943, 158th FA, 45th Div, ASEQ, MHI; Betty McLain Belvin, *Ray McLain and the National Guard*, 74 (*nineteen rounds a minute*). The two artillery battalions fired 3,600 rounds in four hours.

225 *Three miles down Highway 18:* AAR, "Historical Record," 8–9 (*terrified Italian workers*); "Invasion of Italian Mainland, Summary Operations Carried Out by British Troops," 18 (*forty thousand gallons*); Simpson, "Air Phase," 135 (*landed by instrument*); Ball, 205 ("*The work went on*").

225 "*Things not too hot*": aide's diary, Sept. 13, 1943, EJD, HIA, box 1; corr, John W. O'Daniel to Hal C. Pattison, Sept. 3, 1964, NARA RG 319, OCMH, 2-3.7 CC3, Salerno to Cassino, box 256; diary, EJD, Sept. 13, 1943, HIA, box 1 ("*Disaster*"); *Calculated*, 200. Clark told an interviewer in 1972 that this exchange took place face-to-face. OH, MWC, Rittgers, MHI.

225 "*extremely critical*": diary, MWC, Sept. 13, 1943, MWC, Citadel, box 64; "Invasion of Italian Mainland, Summary Operations Carried Out by British Troops," 9; Nigel Nicolson, *Alex: The Life of Field Marshal Earl Alexander of Tunis*, 217; msg, MWC to MBR, Sept. 13, 1943, MWC, Citadel, corr, box 2.

226 *radios crackled in the corner: CM*, 255; Adleman and Walton, 71 ("*How the hell would you*"); FM 31-5, "Landing Operations on Hostile Shores," WD, June 1941, MHI, 99 ("*deliberate sacrifice*").

226 *Clark would subsequently deny:* corr, MWC to Hal C. Pattison, Sept. 17, 1964, NARA RG 319, OCMH, 2-3.7 CC3, Salerno to Cassino, box 255; MWC to mother, Oct. 6, 1943, MWC, Citadel, corr, box 3; msg, U.S.S. *Biscayne*, Sept. 14, 1943, 1609 hrs, MWC, Citadel, subject files, msgs, box 63 (*SEALION*); *StoC*, 117 ("*headquarters afloat*"); Shelby Foote, *The Civil War*, vol. 2, 494 (*George Meade*).

226 *Roused from his torpor:* corr, E. J. Dawley to Hal C. Pattison, Dec. 15, 1964, and Troy H. Middleton to Hal C. Pattison, Sept. 8, 1964 (*questioned Clark's fortitude*), both in NARA RG 319, OCMH, 2-3.7 CC3, Salerno to Cassino, box 255; *StoC*, 117; OH, Francis Reichmann, 45th Div G-2, Apr. 21, 1950, SM, box IIA1, 2 ("*give me support*"); Frank James Price, *Troy H. Middleton: A Biography*, 165 ("*some hard fighting*").

226 "*German tanks have broken through*": Shapiro, 148–49, 152; OH, William P. Yarborough, 1975, J. R. Meese and H. P. Houser, SOOHP, MHI, 39–40 ("*crawling around on their*

*hands*"); Ball, 214 ("*up to our necks*"); "Personal Diary of Langan W. Swent," Sept. 20, 1943, Hoover Institution Archives, box 1 (*summons to Green Beach*).

227 "I'm a Yankee Doodle": Shapiro, 150.

227 "*After a defensive battle lasting four days*": Mavrogordato, "The Battle of Salerno," 25–26.

### A Portal Won

227 *Hewitt bitterly opposed:* Mason, 327; chronology, Sept. 14, 1943, HKH, "Action Report," CMH ("*Depth of beachhead narrowing*"); F. Jones, "The Campaign in Italy: The Landing at Salerno," n.d., Cabinet Historical Studies, UK NA, CAB 44 132, 136–37; A. B. Cunningham, "Operations in Connection with the Landings in the Gulf of Salerno," Apr. 28, 1950, *London Gazette*, CMH, UH 0-1, CUN.2, 2173 ("*I will try to help*").

228 "*If we withdraw*": Mason, 318, 327; OH, "Reminiscences of George C. Dyer" ("*settle lower in the water*").

228 "*intense gloom*": StoC, 124; Roskill, 179; Pond, 192–93 ("*prove suicidal*").

228 "*It just cannot be done*": Pond, 192–93 ("*go and do it*"); Hickey and Smith, 249 ("*simply not on*"); Cunningham, 569 ("*stay and fight it out*").

229 *an enormous letter "T"*: MBR, "Description of Operation from Planning Phase to Execution," n.d., CJB, MHI, Chrono File Italy, box 48; John C. Warren, *Airborne Missions in the Mediterranean, 1942–1945*, 62; AAR, H.M.S. *Delhi*, Oct. 5, 1943, in "Operation AVALANCH—Report on Northern Assault," Royal Navy, Oct. 16, 1943, CARL, N-6837 ("*monster snowflakes*"); Patrick D. Mulcahy, "Airborne Activities in the Avalanche Operation," n.d., AFHQ, Arthur Nevins papers, MHI, box 2; James M. Gavin, *Airborne Warfare*, 28–29; StoC, 127; Pond, 190; Ross S. Carter, *Those Devils in Baggy Pants*, 36 ("*open season*").

229 *Perhaps to compensate:* Clark was awarded the Distinguished Service Cross for his heroics on this day.

229 *two dozen German tanks had been destroyed:* StoC, 129; Lewis, 21 ("*puddle of fat*").

229 *South of the Sele:* FLW to MWC, Oct. 11, 1943, CARL, N-6818; StoC, 129 ("*Nothing of interest*"); Mavrogordato, "The Battle of Salerno," 27; "Translation of Taped Conversation with General Hermann Balck, 12 January 1979," Battelle Columbus Laboratories, Ohio, USAWC Lib, 14 (*Frictions had accumulated*); Kurowski, 59–60 (*heat exhaustion*); *Salerno*, 73 (*ten thousand shells*); Pond, 224 (*howitzers sniped*).

229 *Berlin's refusal to release the two tank divisions:* Kesselring believed the two extra divisions could have been decisive; some historians argue they would not have arrived in time to significantly influence the battle. Kesselring, *Memoirs*, 183n; *Battle*, 119; AAR, 36th ID, "Conclusions on Avalanche," n.d., NARA RG 334, NWC Lib, ANSCOL, box 35; Friedrich Wentzell, "The Italian Campaign from August 1943 to February 1945," Dec. 1945, CMH, Ital 370.2, 5 (*penny packets*); Hamilton, "Italy, Sept.–Dec. 1943," n.d., Cabinet Historical Section, UK NA, CAB 101/124, 18 (*exposed the attackers*).

230 "*The heavy naval artillery*": Kurowski, 125; Clagett, unpublished HKH bio, 478–79 (*Hewitt ordered*); Molony V, 327 ("*murderous queens*"); "Historical Tactical Study of Naval Gunfire at Salerno," 43 (*U.S.S. Boise*); Beard, "Turning the Tide at Salerno," 34+ (*fire axes*); Peek, 24 ("*count your children*").

230 *What naval shells missed: Salerno*, 74; AAR, "Historical Record," 10 (*B-17s battered*); "The Employment of Strategic Bombers in a Tactical Role, 1941–1951," 1953, USAF Historical Div., no. 88, 53–54 (*more than a thousand "heavy" sorties*); AAFinWWII, 530–31, 535 (*760 tons*); Pond, 224; Hardy D. Cannon, *Box Seat over Hell*, 65–66 (*took occasional potshots*).

230 "*almost impossible*": "Special Investigation and Interrogation Report: Operation Lightening," 28; Mavrogordato, "The Battle of Salerno," 27 (*a final effort*).

230 *The somber if sketchy reports from Salerno:* Lord Ismay, *The Memoirs of General Lord Ismay*, 320; D'Este, *Eisenhower*, 319 (*sand castles*); Molony V, 319.

231 "Quelle race!": W.G.F. Jackson, *Alexander of Tunis as Military Commander*, 215, 282 (*"Nothing every went right"*); Nicolson, *Alex*, 37, 199 (*"so serene"*), 238 (*"transformed it into a crusade"*); Gunther, 99 (*Irish flag*); Michael Howard, "Leadership in the British Army in the Second World War," in G. D. Sheffield, *Leadership and Command*, 109; OH, Michael Howard, May 2003, with author, Washington, D.C.; Binder, 107 (*"Good chaps get killed"*); Moran, 186 (*"redeemed what was brutal"*).

231 *No sooner had Hewitt laid out:* Binder, 116; corr, HKH to SEM, Jan. 8, 1954, SEM, NHC, box 51; OH, HKH, 1961, John T. Mason, Col U OHRO, 344–45 (*"Never do"*); Nicolson, *Alex*, 222 (*"cease immediately"*); Mason, 327 (*"no evacuation"*).

231 *He and Hewitt found Clark:* Hewitt, "The Allied Navies at Salerno," 958+; Hickey and Smith, 257 (*unlimbered at targets*); corr, HKH to SEM, Jan. 8, 1954 (*vanished for a private conversation*).

232 *My dear Clarke:* B. L. Montgomery to MWC, Sept. 15, 1943, MWC, Citadel, corr, box 2.

232 *Montgomery's 64,000 troops:* Molony V, 252; *StoC*, 138.

232 *holding medals ceremonies:* Such a ceremony was held on September 13; a day later, an inspection ceremony was held of the entire 1st Canadian Division, which had no contact with the enemy from September 8 to 16. *From Pachino to Ortona:* The Canadian Army at War, CARL, N-14352, 96; Steiger, "The Campaign in Southern Italy," 15.

232 *In nearly two weeks only eighty-five:* Patrick Howarth, *My God, Soldiers*, 137; Mavrogordato, "The Battle of Salerno," 46 (*ten combat casualties a day*); "Narrative: Operations Against Italy," Sept. 15, 1943, Arthur S. Nevins papers, MHI (*sixty-two British dead*); John Lardner, "The Mayor of Futani," in *The New Yorker Book of War Pieces*, 268; Christopher Buckley, *Road to Rome*, 174–85; *StoC*, 142 (*British patrol make contact*); diary, MWC, Sept. 15, 1943, MWC, Citadel, box 64 (*swelled to nearly seven thousand*); MWC to B. L. Montgomery, Sept. 16, 1943, MWC, Citadel, corr, box 2.

232 *"I would like you to go now"*: Morris, 283; Alan Williamson, "Dawley Was Shafted," ts, n.d., Texas MFM, 8–10 (*no sleep at all*); Binder, 117 (*voice cracked*); OH, Lyman Lemnitzer, Jan. 16, 1948, SM, MHI (*gestured vaguely with a trembling hand*).

232 *"I do not want to interfere"*: diary, MWC, Sept. 20, 1943, MWC, Citadel, box 64.

232 *"I know it, Alex"*: OH, MWC, Rittgers, 60–63; Morris, photo, 175 (*checkered tablecloth*).

233 *"Although I am not entirely happy"*: Nicolson, *Alex*, 220.

233 *"No doubt you people are worried"*: MWC to Renie, Sept. 15–16, 1943, MWC, Citadel, personal corr; diary, MWC, Sept. 16, 1943, MWC, Citadel, box 64.

233 *Hardly had the shrieking hordes:* Douglas Graf Bernstorff, "Operations of the 26th Panzer Division in Italy," 1948, FMS, #D-316, MHI, 7–8; J. Hamilton, "Italy, Sept.–Dec. 1943," n.d., Cabinet Historical Section, UK NA, CAB 101/124, 18–19 (*never penetrated the curtain*); Franz Kurowski, *The History of the Fallschirmpanzerkorps Hermann Göring*, 210 (*"put out of action"*).

233 *This welcome news greeted Eisenhower:* memo, "Major Lee," aide-de-camp, Eisenhower Diary, HCB, DDE Lib, A-783-786; msg, DDE to GCM, Sept. 13, 1943, NARA RG 165, E 422, OPD exec files, 390/38/2/4-5, box 13; Chandler, vol. 3, 1418 (*"If things go wrong"*).

233 *"would probably be out"*: Three Years, 420; Butcher entries, Sept. 15–16, 1943, Eisenhower Diary, HCB, DDE Lib, A-756, A-773-74, A-779 (*"prefer to die fighting"*); Chandler, vol. 3, 1428 (*"unimpressed by Dawley"*); msg, MWC to DDE, Sept. 16, 1943, DDE Lib, PP-pres, box 23 (*"appears to go to pieces"*); OH, Lemnitzer, Jan. 16, 1948 (*"why in the hell"*).

234 *If Salerno plagued him:* Harold Macmillan, *War Diaries*, 195; Eisenhower, *Letters to Mamie*, 148; Chandler, vol. 3, 1442–43, 1473 (*"deepest hole"*); D'Este, *Eisenhower*, 443 (*"handsomest bald man"*).

234 *"For God's sake, Mike"*: Williamson, "Dawley Was Shafted," 8–10. A sanitized version quotes Eisenhower as saying, "How'd you ever get the troops into such a mess?" *Texas*, 257.

234 *"I really think you better take him out"*: OH, MWC, Rittgers, 64; OH, FLW, May 15, 1953, John G. Westover, SM, MHI; *Texas,* 258 (*Dawley and Clark quarreled*).

234 *"I want you to go down"*: OH, R. J. Wood, 1973, Narus, 22–28; Williamson, "Dawley Was Shafted," 8–10 (*"I couldn't work with Clark"*), 12 (*"for keeping his mouth shut"*); diary, EJD, Sept. 20, 1943, HIA, box 1 (*"Relieved"*); aide's diary; corr, DDE to E. J. Dawley, Sept. 23, 1943, EJD papers, HIA, box 1 (*$7 per diem*).

235 *Of four American corps commanders:* Lloyd R. Fredendall and Dawley had been fired; Patton and Bradley were the other two. Geoffrey Keyes in Sicily had briefly commanded a temporary "provisional corps."

235 *"It makes a commander supercautious"*: diary, Oct. 29 and 30, 1943, JMG, MHI, box 10; corr, ENH to MWC, Sept. 29, 1943, ENH, MHI, box 3.

235 *"complete success at Salerno"*: war diary, Sept. 16, 1943, "Salerno Invasion," German naval command, box 649; Kesselring, *Memoirs,* 186–87 (*authorized a retreat*).

235 *plunder piled on trucks:* Pond, 259; Steiger, "The Campaign in Southern Italy," 17 (*"destroyed most thoroughly"*); "Exploitation of Italy for the Further Conduct of the War," Tenth Army, Sept. 22, 1943, in Steiger, appendix G (*"evacuation list"*).

235 *The scorching and salting:* "Fifth Army Medical History," ts, n.d., NARA RG 112, MTO surgeon general, 390/17/8/2-3, box 6, 138; AAR, "Historical Record,"13; Macmillan, *War Diaries,* 354 (*92 percent of all sheep*); Clifford W. Dorman, "Too Soon for Heroes," ts, n.d., 19th Combat Engineers, author's possession, 67 ("Rail rooters").

236 *"The Tommies will have to chew"*: Farley Mowat, *And No Birds Sang,* 155.

236 *"incapable of attacking"*: war diary, Sept. 18, 1943, "Salerno Invasion," German naval command, box 649, 71; Mavrogordato, "The Battle of Salerno," 36a (*"offensive spirit"*); Ronald Lewin, *Ultra Goes to War,* 340 (*"No more invasions"*).

236 *Allied casualties totaled:* StoC, 144; Molony V, 325. As always, precise casualty figures are difficult to tease from the record; some accounts tally higher numbers, but usually draw from a greater time period. The U.S. Navy official history, for example, reports 13,614 Allied casualites, but includes Navy figures through the end of 1943. *SSA,* 313.

236 *Total German losses:* StoC, 144; Molony V, 325, 382 (*126,000 casualties in Russia*); D'Este, *World War II in the Mediterranean,* 110 (*630 were killed*).

236 *"a road upon which you may retire"*: lecture, R.W.D. Woods, USN, Sept. 14, 1943, NARA RG 334, E 315, NWC Lib, ANSCOL; corr, J.F.M. Whiteley to J. N. Kennedy, Sept. 22, 1943, NARA RG 319, OCMH, 2-3.7 CC2 Sicily, box 247 (*"turn the scales"*); OH, Andrew J. Goodpaster, Aug. 17, 2004, with author, Washington, D.C. (*absolute authority*); Nicolson, *Alex,* 163; DDE, "Memorandum for Personal File," June 11, 1943, Eisenhower diary, HCB, DDE Lib, A-472 (*"certain of his subordinates"*).

237 *"leadership, force, and vigor"*: Berlin, 15; Blumenson, *Mark Clark,* 282 (*Marcus Aurelius Clarkus*); msg, DDE to GCM, Sept. 20, 1943, NARA RG 165, E 422, OPD exec files, 390/38/2/4-5, box 13.

237 *"Mark Clark really didn't have"*: Blair, 157.

237 *from two divisions on September 3:* chart, growth of Allied force in Italy, n.d., SM, box 2.

237 *"made our acquaintance with vino"*: Wagner, 58; Paschal E. Kerwin, *Big Men of the Little Navy,* 58 (*Fascist party headquarters*); Harr, 47, 55 (*"Americans will pay"*); Biddle, 145.

238 *"I covered my mouth"*: O'Donnell, 168; Howard, *Captain Professor,* 73.

238 *So many civilian bodies:* Peckham and Snyder, eds., 66; Earl Mansee, 36th MP Co., n.d., Texas MFM website, 36th ID Assoc., www.kwanah.com/36Division/pstoc.htm (*"stinch was terrible"*); Whitlock, 90 (*"like an eggplant"*).

238 *A visiting general complained:* Herbert E. MacCombie, "Chaplains of the Thirty-sixth Division," ts, n.d., Texas MFM, 25.

## CHAPTER 5: CORPSE OF THE SIREN
### *"I Give You Naples"*

239 *British military policemen in red caps:* George Biddle, *Artist at War,* 142; Malcolm Munthe, *Sweet Is War,* 175 (*crooked their fingers*); Frank Gervasi, *The Violent Decade,* 499 (*"didn't look human"*); J. A. Ross, *Memoirs of an Army Surgeon,* 171; *Texas,* 267; John Lardner, "The Mayor of Futani," in *The New Yorker Book of War Pieces,* 266 (*recited the brands*), 269; John Steinbeck, *Once There Was a War,* 164 (*"stinks of the classics"*); Richard Tregaskis, *Invasion Diary,* 148 (*"make 'em to last"*).

239 *A squadron from the King's Dragoon Guards:* Molony V, 343; Matthew B. Ridgway, *Soldier,* 88; Leon Weckstein, *Through My Eyes; Calculated,* 214 (*"city of ghosts"*); AAR, Donald Downes to W. Donovan, OSS activities in Neapolitan campaign, Oct. 19, 1943, NARA RG 226, E 99, OSS history office, box 48; AAR, secret intelligence in Italy, n.d., NARA RG 226, E 99, OSS history office, box 39; Malcolm S. McLean, "Adventures in Occupied Areas," ts, 1975, MHI, 92 (*Italian bodies*); Donald Downes, *The Scarlet Thread,* 158 (*"sweet heliotrope odor"*); MWC, "Salerno," *AB,* no. 95, 1997, 1+ (*"less happy mood"*).

240 *He was in the wrong place:* James M. Gavin, *On to Berlin,* 73; Tregaskis, 149–52.

240 *"Naples has been taken":* msgs, MWC to H. Alexander, Oct. 1, 1943, and MWC to Renie, Oct. 5, 1943, diary, MWC, Citadel, box 64.

240 *It proved an odd gift:* George F. Botjer, *Sideshow War,* 61 (*conscripting young men*); Peter Tompkins, *Italy Betrayed,* 260 (*reign of German terror*); memo, John T. Whitaker, Psychological Warfare Branch, to MWC, "Attitude of People of Naples," Oct. 3, 1943, MWC, Citadel, corr, box 3; Robert Wallace, *The Italian Campaign,* 78 (*as young as nine*).

240 *An estimated three hundred locals:* Botjer, 61. Allied counterintelligence put the number at 227. "Counter Intelligence Corps, Information Bulletin No. 4," n.d., "Theater Com-Z Activities, ASF, 1944–1945," CARL, N-5990; AAR, Downes to Donovan, Oct. 19, 1943 (*two days sooner*).

240 *"There were still Germans":* diary, Oct. 19, 1943, JMG, MHI, box 10; Downes, 158 (*red Italian grenades*); Robert Capa, *Slightly Out of Focus,* 102–3; Biddle, 152–57; George Biddle, *George Biddle's War Drawings,* 49.

241 *"the most beautiful city":* *Naples with Pompeii and the Amalfi Coast,* 35; C.R.S. Harris, *Allied Administration of Italy, 1943–1945,* 85 (*blew up the main aqueduct*); msg, Fifth Army to AFHQ, Naples damage estimate, Oct. 13, 1943, MWC, Citadel, box 63 (*forty sewer lines*); *Building the Navy's Bases in World War II,* vol. 2, 88; "German Demolition Policy in Occupied Russia and Italy," June 15, 1944, Ministry of Economic Warfare Intelligence Weekly, NARA RG 334, NWC Lib, ANSCOL, box 467; Alfred M. Beck et al., *The Corps of Engineers: The War Against Germany,* 168; Leo J. Meyer, "Strategy and Logistical History: MTO," ts, n.d., CMH, 2-3.7 CC5, XIX-11 (*crashing two trains*); "Engineer History, Fifth Army, Mediterranean Theater," n.d., MHI, 69 (*Coal stockpiles*); "History of the First Special Service Force," n.d., Robert T. Frederick papers, HIA, box 1, 52–53 (*Even the stairwells*).

241 *The opportunities for cultural atrocity:* Tompkins, 276; *SSA,* 311 (*city archives*); memo, Mason Hammond and F.H.J. Maxse to F. J. McSherry, Nov. 5, 1943, "Report of AMGOT Divisions, up to Nov. 1, 1943," part 3, Frank J. McSherry papers, MHI; Downes, 159n; Lynn H. Nicholas, *The Rape of Europa,* 232 (*stored in Nola*).

241 *Worse yet was the sabotage around the great port:* U.S. Army engineers estimated that half the damage was from Allied bombs, half from German demolitionists. Beck, 167.

241 *Half a mile inland:* Tregaskis, 158; H. V. Morton, *A Traveller in Southern Italy,* 230; Homer, *The Odyssey,* trans. Robert Fagles, book 12, line 199 (*"high, thrilling song"*); memo, Paul Gardner, damage to cultural facilities, Naples, Oct. 27, 1943, and draft report, MTOUSA IG, Dec. 20, 1943, both in NARA RG 492, MTOUSA, IG, 333.5, box 2014; Gervasi, 499 (*Grand hotels*); Paul W. Brown, *The Whorehouse of the World,* 216.

242 *Not a single vessel:* Meyer, "Strategy and Logistical History," xix–10; Joseph S. Gorlinski, "Naples: Case History in Invasion," *Military Engineer,* vol. 36, no. 222 (Apr. 1944), 109+; *Battle,* 124; Beck, 168 *(fifty-eight of sixty-one berths);* "Rehabilitation of the Port of Naples," May 1944, NARA RG 336, ASF, Historical Program Files, chief of transportation, 190/33/30/00, box 559, 4–6 *(Pier F);* "Logistical History of NATOUSA/MTOUSA," Nov. 1945, NARA RG 407, E 427, AFHQ, 95-AL1-4, box 203, 104 *(pair of ninety-ton cranes);* HKH, "Action Report of the Salerno Landings, Sept.–Oct. 1943," 1945, CMH, 156–57 *(seeded the harbor).*

242 *"small, aged animals":* Brown, 219; *SSA,* 311; lecture, W. A. Sullivan, "Ship Salvage and Harbor Clearance," 1947, Society of Military Engineers, Cincinnati, in "World War II Histories and Historical Reports," #445, NHC, 16 *("demolitions for revenge");* Meyer, "Strategy and Logistical History," XIX–13 *(Marseilles and Cherbourg).*

242 *equivalent of sixty-eight Liberty ships:* HKH, "Action Report of the Salerno Landings, Sept.–Oct. 1943," 1945, CMH, 156–57; Gorlinski, "Naples," 109+.

243 *Twenty-nine Italian divisions:* StoC, 7; F. W. Deakin, *The Brutal Friendship,* 530; Tompkins, 229 *(forged orders);* David Hunt, *A Don at War,* 221 *("Each bomb is chipping").*

243 *island of Cephalonia:* E. F. Fisher, "Memo for the Record," March 28, 1973, from *Kriegstagebuch des Oberkommandos der Wehrmacht,* Band III, zweiter Halbband, 1118–133, NARA RG 319, OCMH, CA, box 006; Richard Lamb, *War in Italy, 1943–1945,* 132–33; R.J.B. Bosworth, *Mussolini's Italy,* 504; Alex Bowlby, *Countdown to Cassino,* 7n; Lamb, 132–33 *(sunk at sea);* Melton S. Davis, *Who Defends Rome?,* 466 *("Italians are burning").*

243 *"The only Italian army":* Lamb, 87, 88–89, 104; Michael Burleigh, *The Third Reich,* 741–42 *("military internees");* Karl Theodor Koerner, "Rail Transportation Problems in Italy," Apr. 1947, FMS, #D-010, MHI, 8.

243 *A German radio intercept:* Albert Praun, "German Radio Intelligence," March 1950, FMS, #P-038, CMH, 68; John Winton, *Cunningham,* 329; Hunt, 230–31 *("size of a tennis court");* Jack Greene and Alessandro Massignani, *The Naval War in the Mediterranean,* 307; *Nazi Conspiracy and Aggression,* vol. 7, NARA RG 319, OCMH, box 248, 931 *(catalogue of booty);* "Under the German Yoke," ts, n.d., U.S. Army Corps of Engineers, Historical Division, X-39, 1 *(60,000 motor vehicles).*

244 *The second escape:* S. W. Roskill, *The War at Sea, 1939–1945,* 188; *SSA,* 304–8 *("even more astonishing").*

244 *The third escape:* "Military Campaigns and Political Events in Italy, 1942–1943," Jan. 1946, WD, Strategic Services Unit, A-63366, CMH, Geog Files, Italy, 370.22, 34–35; Elizabeth Wiskemann, *The Rome-Berlin Axis,* 311; Otto Skorzeny, *Skorzeny's Secret Missions,* 57–58; Gerald Pawle, *The War and Colonel Warden,* 249–60; "The Rescue of Mussolini," *AB,* no. 22, 1978, 12+ *(vacated ski resort);* Bruton F. Hood, "The Gran Sasso Raid," *MR,* Feb. 1959, 55+; Denis Mack Smith, *Mussolini,* 300 *(endless carping);* Benito Mussolini, *My Rise and Fall,* 137 *(removed all sharp objects);* Peter Neville, *Mussolini,* 177 *("one must suffer").*

244 *Soon enough his whereabouts leaked:* O. Skorzeny and K. Radl, "The Rescue of Mussolini," n.d., intelligence translation no. H-7563, DA, 72–93; John Toland, *Adolf Hitler,* 754 *(badly scarred visage);* "Military Campaigns," 47 *(gliders began skittering);* Skorzeny, 98–99 *("the Führer has sent me");* "How Strong Is the Enemy Today?" 1944, OSS film, NARA RG 111, M2997 *(Storch airplane);* StoC, 539; Louis P. Lochner, ed., *The Goebbels Diaries,* 468–69.

245 *two dozen Jews:* Martin Gilbert, *The Second World War,* 462.

245 *The first German time bomb:* Clark, "Salerno," 1; "History of the Peninsular Base Section," 1944, CMH, 8-4 HA 1, vol. 2 *("The first two floors");* Robert H. Welker, *A Different Drummer,* 208–9.

245 *The blast killed and wounded:* Clay Blair, *Ridgway's Paratroopers,* 164; Welker, 212–14.

245 *Three days later, on Sunday morning:* "Engineer History, Fifth Army," 35; Blair, 164; *Calculated,* 218; OH, Louis Bednar, 82nd Airborne Div, Sept. 17, 2002, VHP *("sacks of*

*burlap*"); Ross S. Carter, *Those Devils in Baggy Pants,* 55 (*"Nice work, boys"*); MWC to Renie, Oct. 10, 1943, MWC, Citadel; memo, "Security of Material Bombs Explosion in Naples," n.d., 158th Bomb Disposal, NARA RG 331, AFHQ micro, R 367-F, box 216 (*Prince of Piedmont barracks*).

246 *"bodies overcome by the ash"*: Norman Lewis, *Naples '44,* 40; "History of the Peninsular Base Section," vol. 2; "Engineers in the Italian Campaign, 1943–1945," n.d., UK, MHI Lib, 21; Harry L. Coles, "The Army Air Forces in Amphibious Landings in World War II," 1953, USAF Historical Division, no. 96, 34 (*"suspicious noises"*).

246 *Fears that more hidden bombs:* memo, J. G. Barney to PWB, Fifth Army, Nov. 3, 1943, C. D. Jackson papers, DDE Lib, box 1; Margaret Bourke-White, *Purple Heart Valley,* 29; Lewis, 43; Malcolm Muggeridge, *The Infernal Grove,* 229.

246 *"There are 57 varieties of grief"*: Harry L. Coles and Albert K. Weinberg, *Civil Affairs: Soldiers Become Governors,* 316; Lewis, 31, 61; "History of the Peninsular Base Section," vol. 2; Biddle, 160; Robert L. Wagner, *The Texas Army,* 58; William J. Diamond, "Water Is Life," *Military Engineer,* Aug. 1947, 330+; Sullivan, "Ship Salvage and Harbor Clearance," 19.

246 *Twenty-six thousand tons:* Harris, 88; George C. S. Benson and Maurice Neufeld, "American Military Government in Italy," in Carl J. Friedrich, ed., *American Experiences in Military Government in World War II,* 137–40; Gervasi, 501; Lewis, 84 (*bitter jest*).

247 *Reconstruction had begun:* "History of the Peninsular Base Section," vol. 2; Gorlinski, "Naples: Case History in Invasion," 109; Viscount Cunningham of Hyndhope, *A Sailor's Odyssey,* 572 (*"army of ants"*); Lida Mayo, *The Ordnance Department: On Beachhead and Battlefront,* 187; H. H. Dunham, "U.S. Army Transportation and the Italian Campaign," ts, Sept. 1945, mono #17, NARA RG 336, ASF, historical program files, chief of transportation, box 142, 60 (*only three berths*); booklet, 6th Port Bn, Walter J. Muller papers, HIA, box 2 (*more tonnage handled*); McLean, "Adventures in Occupied Areas," 92.

247 *Garbagemen sang:* OH, Frank Schultz, Apr. 2002, March 2006, with author, Washington, D.C.; Lewis, 51–52 (*hunchbacks*); Carter, 53 (*"wasn't safe to go to town"*); Warren P. Munsell, Jr., *The Story of a Regiment,* 40n (*dropped your voice*); Mina Curtiss, ed., *Letters Home,* 93; Anders Kjar Arnbal, *The Barrel-Land Dance Hall Rangers,* 164 (*Monopoly money*); "Second Orientation Conference at Fifth Army Headquarters," Nov. 15, 1943, AGF observer report, #77, NARA RG 337, E 15A, box 53 (*resistant to sulfa*); John F. Hummer, *An Infantryman's Journal,* 37, 44; diary, William Russell Hinckley, Oct. 6, 1943, author's possession (*" 'Fik' can be had"*).

247 *Some soldiers behaved badly:* memo, Paul Gardner to W. W. Pence, Nov. 19, 1943, NARA RG 492, MTOUSA IG, box 2014; Nicholas, 233 (*"stuffed toucans"*); memos, Palazzo Reale custodian, Nov. 26, Dec. 5, 1943, in draft report, IG investigation, Dec. 20, 1943, NARA RG 492, MTOUSA IG, box 2014; T. Moffatt Burriss, *Strike and Hold,* 57, 61 (*"He drained his glass"*).

248 *Airdromes at Foggia:* Mary H. Williams, ed., *Chronology, 1941–1945, USAWWII,* 138.

248 *Everywhere, Allied forces:* Gerhard L. Weinberg, *A World at Arms,* 616–17, 636, 643; Gilbert, 455, 462–64 (*"We are still retreating"*).

248 *"He always wants speed"*: JPL, 165, 167.

248 *"Rome by Christmas"*: Strome Galloway, *A Regiment at War,* 103; Chandler, vol. 3, 1485; Russell B. Capelle, *Casablanca to the Neckar,* 21 (*studying German*); Ralph Bennett, *Ultra and the Mediterranean Strategy,* 252 (*"strength to make a front"*); Gilbert, 455 (*"as soon as the Russians"*); Robert Sherwood, *Roosevelt and Hopkins,* 764 (*"should be in Rome"*).

*"Watch Where You Step and Have No Curiosity at All"*

249 *inaugural crossing in Europe: From the Volturno to the Winter Line,* 53.

249 *"Sleep, swine"*: Audie Murphy, *To Hell and Back,* 31; John A. Elterich, "Patrol Actions Prior to and During the Operation of the 2nd Battalion, 7th Infantry Regiment," 1948, IS, 11; Tregaskis, 169–72.

249 *rafts borrowed from the Navy:* OH, Robert Petherick, n.d., CMH, Geog, Italy, 370.24; Orrin A. Tracy, "The Operations of the 7th Infantry, Volturno River Crossing," 1946, IS, 14, 19; Barry W. Fowle, ed., *Builders and Fighters,* 425–27; *CM,* 268–69.

249 *"Unfortunately I'm beginning to realize":* LKT Jr. to Sarah, Sept. 1, 30, 1943, LKT Jr., GCM Lib, box 1, folder 6; *StoC,* 197–98 (*1:55 A.M.*); "Lessons from the Italian Campaign," March 10, 1944, HQ, NATOUSA, CMH, Geog Italy, 353, 41 (*three miles wide*).

250 *British infantrymen struggled:* Chester G. Starr, ed. *From Salerno to the Alps,* 45–46; memoir, Aidan Mark Sprot, ts, 1947, LHC, 93; "Invasion of Italian Mainland, Summary of Operations Carried Out by British Troops Under Command 5 U.S. Army," n.d., CMH, 370.2, 15–16 (*six hundred yards deep*); *CM,* 271; Moorehead, *Eclipse,* 62.

250 *With his left flank exposed:* aide's diaries, Oct. 13, 1943, LKT Jr., GCM Lib, box 18, folder 3; AAR, "Report on Crossing of the River Volturno," 36th Engineer Regt, Nov. 5, 1943, JPL, MHI, box 11; Will Lang, "Lucian King Truscott, Jr.," *Life,* Oct. 2, 1944, 96+ (*"Have you tried it?"*).

251 *At eleven A.M. the first Sherman: From the Volturno to the Winter Line,* 31; Beck et al., 176; AAR, H. K. Koberstein, 10th Engineer Bn, "Engineer Phase on the Crossing of the Volturno River," Nov. 3, 1943 (*eighty jeeps*); "Invasion of Italian Mainland, Summary of Operations Carried Out by British Troops," 36 (*only 3,500 engineers* [as of early November]); Leslie W. Bailey, *Through Hell and High Water,* 131; Edmund F. Ball, *Staff Officer with the Fifth Army,* 232.

251 *"Like the earthworm":* LKT Jr. to Sarah, Oct. 14 and 22, 1943, LKT Jr., GCM Lib, box 1, folder 6.

251 *Anglo-Americans had advanced thirty-five miles:* Albert Kesselring et al., "German Version of the History of the Italian Campaign," CARL, N-16671.1-3, 36; Kenneth S. Davis, *Soldier of Democracy,* 450 (*"masterminding"*).

251 *Italy would break their backs:* "Narrative: Operations Against Italy," Oct. 20, 1943, Arthur S. Nevins papers, MHI.

251 *German demolitions had begun:* "Engineer History, Fifth Army," 7, 10 (*"only five prefabricated"*), 77 (*"whole trees to bulls"*); "Second Orientation Conference at Fifth Army Headquarters" (*"no bridge or culvert"*); diary, MWC, Nov. 1, 1943, Citadel, box 64 (*one thousand bridges*); Fowle, ed., 191 (*three thousand spans*); Beck, 178 (*eighteen feet in ten hours*).

252 *"new tracks across the rubble":* CM, 263; Ralph G. Martin, *The G.I. War, 1941–1945,* 105 (*"broken bathtubs"*); "Engineers in the Italian Campaign, 1943–1945," 23 (*rolling mills*); Beck et al., 175 (*They used timber*).

252 *"It got darker":* Don Robinson, *News of the 45th,* 149; Frank Henius, *Italian Sentence Book for the Soldier,* 1943 (*raining torrents*); Ronald Blythe, ed., *Private Words,* 4 (*"one may write of mist"*); Lawrence D. Collins, *The 56th Evac Hospital,* 94 (*"spots on the dice"*), 121; memoir, Henry E. Gardiner, ts, n.d., USMA Arch, 181 (*pooled in their messkits*).

252 *"The desert war":* Battle, 122; Peter Schrijvers, *The Crash of Ruin,* 247 (*"honest color"*); Martin, 105 (*"too thick to drink"*); Albert F. Simpson, "Air Phase of the Italian Campaign to 1 January 1944," June 1946, AAFRH, #115, CMH, 351n (*undermined air superiority*); John North, ed., *The Alexander Memoirs, 1940–1945,* 117 (*"savage versatility"*); Don Woerpel, *A Hostile Sky,* 140 (*"German weather"*).

253 *Mines made it much worse:* OH, Andrew J. Goodpaster, Aug. 17, 2004, with author, Washington, D.C.; *From Pachino to Ortona,* Canadian Army at War, CARL, N-14352, 104 (*"All roads"*); "German Tactics in Italy, No. 1, Salerno to Anzio," May 28, 1944, AFHQ, G-2, CMH, Geog files, 11–12; John H. Roush, ed., *World War II Reminiscences,* 60–61 (*"I never had a moment"*); "Second Orientation Conference at Fifth Army Headquarters" (*"Watch where you step"*).

253 *"you could follow our battalions":* report, AGF Board, Dec. 5, 1943, NARA RG 407, E 427, NATOUSA, 95-USF1-2.0; Frank Gervasi, "Battle at Cassino," *Collier's,* March 18, 1944, 20+;

Gerald Linderman, *The World Within War,* 117 (*"nutcracker"*); Charles F. Marshall, *A Ramble Through My War,* 19; Beck et al., 181; G-2 Periodic No. 28, II Corps, Aug. 9, 1943, Benjamin A. Dickson papers, MHI, box 4; report, AGF Board, Dec. 5, 1943, NARA RG 407, E 427, NATOUSA, 95-USF1-2.0 (*two chaplains lost legs*).

253 *"A man's foot":* Klaus H. Huebner, *A Combat Doctor's Diary,* 73; OH, Richard A. Williams, Jan. 25, 2003, with author (*"they would still scream"*); Bill Mauldin, *The Brass Ring,* 200; James Phinney Baxter III, *Scientists Against Time,* 101–2; Fowle, ed., 164–68; Beck et al., 183; Erna Risch and Chester L. Kieffer, *The Quartermaster Corps: Organization, Supply, and Services,* vol. 2, 331 (*"M dogs"*).

254 *expedient fighting withdrawal:* Kent Roberts Greenfield, ed., *Command Decisions,* 235.

254 *an intense debate raged:* Walter Warlimont, *Inside Hitler's Headquarters, 1939–1945,* 385–86; David Irving, *The Trail of the Fox,* 309–10 (*"Domineering, obstinate"*).

254 *Italy remained a comparatively minor theater:* Molony V, 381–82; Rudolf Böhmler, *Monte Cassino,* 67–68 (*more vulnerable to enemy bombers*).

254 *The Italian peninsula was narrowest:* H. Alexander, "The Allied Armies in Italy," CMH, II-7; brochure, "Ciociaria: A Land to Experience," n.d., Regione Lazio, 33 (*wolves and bears*); memo, A. Kesselring, Nov. 1, 1943, A. G. Steiger, "The Campaign in Southern Italy," Nov. 1947, Canadian Army hq, Ottawa, appendix L (*"impregnable system"*); Wallace, 101 (*"break their teeth"*).

254 *changed his mind in favor of Kesselring:* Böhmler, 71; Basil Liddell Hart, ed., *The Rommel Papers,* 445–47; Kenneth Macksey, *Kesselring: The Making of the Luftwaffe,* 186 (*"leadership without optimism"*); Thomas R. Brooks, *The War North of Rome,* 28 (*"extraordinarily brave"*).

255 *"I'll take it as it comes":* Liddell Hart, ed., 447; Greenfield, ed., 242 (*"end of withdrawals"*); Irving, 311–14 (*"hard times lie ahead"*).

255 *Thanks to Ultra:* Ralph Bennett, *Ultra and the Mediterranean Strategy,* 251–53; F. H. Hinsley et al., *British Intelligence in the Second World War,* 173–74.

255 *"We are committed":* "Review of Battle Situation in Italy, 21 October 1943," in H. Alexander, "The Allied Armies in Italy," CMH, II-50, II-13 (*"cul-de-sac"*); GS V, 69 (*only eleven facing a German force*); Molony V, 474n (*Twenty inches of rain*); StoC, 219–20 (*less than a mile a day*). The German force in Italy soon reached twenty-five divisions.

255 *"essential for us to retain the initiative":* Chandler, vol. 3, 1529.

255 *Nor did the high command:* StoC, 185–87; Winston S. Churchill, *Closing the Ring,* 247 (*"vindicates our strategy"*).

255 *The prospect of waging:* Molony V, 473; StoC, 187 (*line on a map*).

256 *Alexander's despondency:* W.G.F. Jackson, *Alexander of Tunis as Military Commander,* 248; Gervasi, 518 (*"punch, punch, punch"*); Lord Tedder, *With Prejudice,* 488 (*"ever get to Rome"*).

256 *"ancient truths":* Jackson, 253; corr, B. L. Montgomery to A. F. Harding, Oct. 31, 1943, Bernard L. Montgomery collections, IWM, ancillary collections 14, file 3.

### The Mountainous Hinterland

256 *"The road to Rome is a long one":* JJT, XIII, 12.

256 *among two thousand veterans transferred:* memo, LKT Jr. to MWC and CG, NATOUSA, Dec. 17, 1943, NARA RG 407, E 427, NATOUSA, 95-USF1-2.0.

257 *"Life is good":* JJT, X-1, 5; Biddle, 169, 172.

257 *Victory Road:* Gervasi, 513; "Lessons from the Italian Campaign," March 10, 1944, NARA RG 407, E 427, 95-USF1-04, box 250, 10 (*"mountainous hinterland"*); Alice Leccese Powers, *Italy in Mind,* 64 (*chimneys poking like snorkels*); McLean, "Adventures in Occupied Areas," 65 (*Peasants keened*); Biddle, 187, 204 (*"Nothing I can do"*).

257 *Across the cobblestones:* StoC, 210, 218; Lewis, 161; Marshall, 20 (*diapered in newspapers*); *George Biddle's War Drawings,* 2 (*"The stretchers are coming"*).

257  *Biddle sketched the tableau:* Biddle, *Artist at War,* 166–67, 204, 219; Brown, 337 (*powdered water*); Lloyd M. Wells, *From Anzio to the Alps,* 35 ("*Easy, boys*").

258  *For a few weeks, Biddle:* George Biddle, "Report from the Italian Front," *Life,* vol. 16, no. 1 (Jan. 3, 1944), 13+; *George Biddle's War Drawings,* 2 ("*a swivel chair*"); Biddle, *Artist at War,* 176 ("*killing instincts*").

258  "*Bragg would look good*": JJT, X-6, 17; Biddle, *Artist at War,* 194–95; *George Biddle's War Drawings,* 3; corr, LKT Jr. to DDE, Nov. 24, 1943, LKT Jr., GCM Lib, box 11, folder 11 (*two other battalion commanders*).

258  "*climbing a ladder*": Richard Doherty, *A Noble Crusade,* 169; "Lessons from the Italian Campaign," March 1944, HQ, NATOUSA, DTL, Ft. B, 113 (*dull the glint*), 48 (*mewing cats*); Arnball, 161 (*Barbasol*); *CM,* 276 (*lack of overcoats*); Bourke-White, 142 (*debated with theological intensity*).

258  "*I'm goddam sick and tired*": Biddle, *Artist at War,* 197, 207, 212–13.

259  "*Be alert and live*": ibid., 228–30 ("*lips parted in that rictus*"), 216–20 ("*all the way into Germany*"); Biddle, "Report from the Italian Front," 13+; *CM,* 283 ("*haggard, dirty*").

259  "*Just so many dead*": Biddle, *Artist at War,* 233 ("*wrestling with the dead*"), 177 ("*I wish the people at home*"); JJT, X-22 ("*my continued existence*").

260  *The panorama from Monte Cesima: Fifth Army at the Winter Line,* 8.

260  "*Every step forward*": *StoC,* 231–32.

260  "*a steep, solid rock*": Bowlby, 58; *The Grenadier Guards, 1939–1945,* 31 (*only German pickets*).

260  *Three panzer grenadier counterattacks:* Michael Howard and John Sparrow, *The Coldstream Guards, 1920–1946,* 167, 170 (*stripping rations*); David Erskin, *The Scots Guards, 1919–1955,* 186; Molony V, 453.

261  *Too great as well for Truscott's 3rd Division: CM,* 284.

261  "*faces of the dead*": Murphy, 50; memo, LKT Jr. to MWC and CG, NATOUSA, Dec. 17, 1943, NARA RG 407, E 427, NATOUSA, 95-USF1-2.0 (*8,600 casualties*); "Statistical Survey for the Italian Campaign, Sept. 17–Nov. 19, 1943," 3rd ID, CARL, N-12185, (*four hundred officers*); Peter R. Mansoor, *The GI Offensive in Europe,* 116 (*70 percent of their strength*); corr, LKT Jr., to W. B. Smith, Dec. 1, 1943, LKT Jr., GCM Lib, box 11, folder 11.

261  "*You are in my thoughts*": LKT Jr., to Sarah, Nov. 10 and 25, Dec. 5, 1943, LKT Jr., GCM Lib, box 1, folder 6; aide's diaries, Nov. 10, 1943, LKT Jr., GCM Lib, box 18, folder 3 (*thirty-five bottles of cognac*).

261  "*The land and the weather*": Pyle, 68, 73, 78, 97; Collins, 127–28 ("*No shelves*").

262  "*protections against crackup*": McLean, "Adventures in Occupied Areas," 68; Spike Milligan, *Mussolini: His Part in My Downfall,* 37, 105, 185 ("*Stretcher bearer!*").

262  *the Ghouls:* Munsell, 37; Milligan, 186 ("*loss of dirt*"); Lee G. Miller, *The Story of Ernie Pyle,* 294 ("*pig shed*"); McLean, "Adventures in Occupied Areas," 67 (*Villa des Chilblains*); Farley Mowat, *The Regiment,* 179 ("*Latrines*"); Wells, 61 ("*Big Six*").

262  "*She's been yelling like that*": Tregaskis, 181; George Kerrigan, "A Night at the Opera," ts, n.d., Co. A, 142nd Inf, Texas MFM ("*You can pray forever*").

263  "*You can't believe*": *The Princeton Class of 1942 During World War II,* 278.

263  *At 9:30 A.M. on Thursday, November 11:* diary, MWC, Nov. 11, 1943, Citadel, box 64; Tregaskis, 193.

263  "*war could be won in this theater*": diary, MWC, Nov. 4, 1943, Citadel, box 64.

264  *ten thousand casualties since mid-October:* Starr, ed., 77; "Second Orientation Conference at Fifth Army Headquarters" ("*equivalent of two divisions*"); diary, MWC, Nov. 23, 1943, Citadel, box 64 (*more than three thousand dead*); *StoC,* 226; Christopher Buckley, *Road to Rome,* 119 ("*Nothing But Jerry*").

264  *The British had disappointed Clark:* diary, MWC, Nov. 5, 1943, Citadel, box 64; OH, Robert J. Wood, March 4 and 15, 1948, SM, MHI ("*Why in the hell*"); corr, MWC to John Meade, Sept. 22, 1955, SM, MHI ("*only ones*"); Starr, ed., 53, 60.

264 *Few of the troops butting at the Bernhardt Line:* Just as the only U.S. armor division to fight in the desert was the only one to receive no desert training, so the 34th and 36th Divisions had little mountain training. "Lessons Learned in the Battle from the Garigliano to North of Rome," July 15, 1944, Fifth Army, training memo #12, DTL, Ft. B, 8.

265 *"head-on battering":* Molony V, 389; Will Lang, notebook, n.d., USMA Arch.

265 *Wool clothing scheduled to arrive:* OH, Ralph Tate, Fifth Army G-4, Jan. 19, 1949, NARA RG 319, OCMH, CA, box 005; "History of Planning Division, Army Service Forces," n.d., CMH, 3-2.2 AA, vol. 1, 93 (*"Shortages of tires"*); Charles S. D'Orsa, "The Trials and Tribulations of an Army G-4," *MR,* vol. 25, no. 4 (July 1945), 23+; "The ASF in World War II," ts, n.d., CMH, 3-1.1A AA, vol. 4, 27 (*cold-weather gear under development*); memo, N. P. Morrow to L. J. McNair, Jan. 28, 1944, AGF Board, NARA RG 407, E 427, 270/50/29 (*heavy combat boots*); Diana Butler, "The British Soldier in Italy, Sept. 1943–June 1944," ts, n.d., Cabinet Office, Historical Section, UK NA, CAB 101/224, 1, 5 (*daily sugar ration*).

265 *"Cold ground trauma":* Bowlby, 174; diary, MWC, Nov. 16, 1943, Citadel, box 64 (*Clark was aghast*); JPL, 237–39.

265 *Kesselring had stabilized the front:* Böhmler, 89; Bowlby, 73 (*two thousand casualties*); StoC, 214 (*"My morale"*); G. R. Stevens, *Fourth Indian Division,* 272 (*"The lice are at me"*); memo, 3rd ID G-2 to VI Corps, Oct. 7, 1943, captured documents, NARA RG 407, 206-2.9 (*"beyond the borders"*).

266 *Clark concluded that the time had come:* StoC, 251; diary, MWC, Nov. 13, 1943, Citadel, box 64 (*"hold to its present positions"*); Tregaskis, 195 (*"mustn't kid ourselves"*); JPL, 195 (*"in better country"*).

### *"The Entire World Was Burning"*

266 *U.S.S. Iowa swung on her chains:* "Log of the President's Trip to Africa and the Middle East," Stephen T. Early papers, FDR Lib, box 37; Elliott Roosevelt, *As He Saw It,* 133; Chandler, vol. 3, 1590 (CARGO).

267 *Autumn at AFHQ:* OH, Lyman Lemnitzer, Jan. 16, 1948, SM, MHI; msg, UK chiefs of staff to Joint Staff Mission, Nov. 4, 1943, NARA RG 165, E 422, OPD executive files, 390/38/2/4-5, box 18 (*"We are very much disturbed"*); Coakley, 231 (*might require postponement*); *Three Years,* 424; Eisenhower Diary, HCB, DDE Lib, A-884 (*eclipsed 100,000*), A-869; Chandler, vol. 3, 1529 (*"little difference what happens to us"*), 1555 (*"a mere slugging match"*).

267 *"The God of Justice":* Chandler, vol. 3, 1553.

267 *Politics and folderol:* Ibid., 1504, 1535, 1611; *Three Years,* 423–24 (*"keep the home front frightened"*), 438.

267 *"He usually blew his top":* Merle Miller, *Ike the Soldier,* 565; Dwight D. Eisenhower, *Letters to Mamie,* 151 (*"acutely uncomfortable"*); Dwight D. Eisenhower, *Crusade in Europe,* 209 (*"malicious gossip"*).

268 *"Roosevelt weather!":* Roosevelt, 133.

268 *"heavy maleness of the war":* Kay Summersby, *Eisenhower Was My Boss,* 86; Doris Kearns Goodwin, *No Ordinary Time,* 473 (*"president's sons"*).

268 *near sinking of the Iowa:* Charles F. Pick, Jr., "Torpedo on the Starboard Beam," *Proceedings,* Aug. 1970, 90+; war diary, U.S.S. *Iowa,* Nov. 1943, NARA RG 38; war diary, U.S.S. *William D. Porter,* Nov. 1943, NARA RG 38; deck log, U.S.S. *Iowa,* Nov. 1943, NARA RG 24; deck log, U.S.S. *William D. Porter,* Nov. 1943, NARA RG 24.

268 *"Tell me, Ernest":* Ernest J. King and Walter Muir Whitehill, *Fleet Admiral King,* 500–501; Sherwood, 768; William D. Leahy, *I Was There,* 196; Forrest C. Pogue, *George C. Marshall: Organizer of Victory,* 301.

268 *"damned Republican":* H. H. Arnold, *Global Mission,* 455. *Porter* would be sunk in a kamikaze attack in June 1945.

268 *"The war, and the peace":* Roosevelt, 133.

268 *The president had planned:* Eisenhower, *Crusade,* 196; Summersby, 93–94.

269 *They stopped for lunch:* "Log of the President's Trip to Africa and the Middle East"; Piers Brendon, *Ike: His Life and Times,* 124; Robert D. Kaplan, *Mediterranean Winter,* 81; (http://penelope.uchicago.edu/Thayer/E/Roman/Texts/Plutarch/Lives/Cato_Minor*.html (*Cato the Younger*); Eisenhower, *Crusade,* 209 ("*you had offered to bet*").

269 "*Eisenhower showed no signs*": Leahy, 198; Eisenhower Diary, HCB, DDE Lib, A-907; *Three Years,* 446; Roosevelt, 137 (*a more formidable figure*); Eisenhower, *Crusade,* 197 ("*dangerous to monkey*").

270 "*The eternal pound, pound, pound*": Eisenhower, *Letters to Mamie,* 157–58.

270 *The Adriatic seaport of Bari:* L. V. Bertarelli, *Southern Italy,* 385; Karl Baedeker, *Southern Italy and Sicily,* 209 (*St. Nicholas*); Morton, 99–100 (*smacked dead octopuses*), 110–12 (*comely temptress*); Evelyn Waugh, *The End of the Battle,* 219; Karel Margry, "Mustard Disaster at Bari," *AB,* no. 79 (1993), 34+ (*Bambino Sports Stadium*).

270 "*the novelty had worn off*": I. G. Greenlees, "Memoirs of an Anglo-Italian," ts, n.d., IWM, 89/1/1, 174, 179; Buckley, 216 (*silk stockings*); John Muirhead, *Those Who Fall,* 31–32 (*Palmolive soap*); "Engineers in the Italian Campaign, 1943–1945," 20, 79 (*350 tons each*); George Southern, *Poisonous Inferno,* 26 (*a thousand stevedores*).

271 *They had much to unload:* Simpson, "Air Phase," 251; *StoC,* 239; Andrew Brookes, *Air War over Italy, 1943–1945,* 38 (*five thousand tons*); *AAFinWWII,* 564–67; James H. Doolittle, *I Could Never Be So Lucky Again,* 367–68; Mark M. Boatner III, *The Biographical Dictionary of World War II,* 139.

271 *Doolittle's job:* Simpson, "Air Phase," 226, 365n; Brookes, 21, 38, 46; Vincent Orange, *Coningham,* 175.

271 "*I would regard it as a personal affront*": Orange, 175.

271 *As Coningham issued this challenge:* "Manifest of *John Harvey,*" in "Report on the Circumstances in Which Gas Casualties Were Incurred at Bari," March 14, 1944, NARA RG 492, MTO, chemical warfare section, 350.01, box 1747; minutes, board of officers, June 28, 1944, "adequacy of protective measures at Bari," NARA RG 331, AFHQ micro, 290/24/28/3, box 187, R-87 ("*as safe a place*").

272 *No Axis chemical stockpiles:* Brooks E. Kleber and Dale Birdsell, *The Chemical Warfare Service: Chemicals in Combat,* 108, 122; "Planning Instruction No. 9," March 23, 1943, "Operating Instructions Husky," NARA RG 407, E 427, 95-AL1-3.17, box 201; memo, DDE, "Chemical Warfare Policy," Apr. 21, 1943, NARA RG 492, MTO, 321.011, box 1744; memo, eyes only, DDE to GCM, Aug. 21, 1943, NARA RG 319, OCMH, 270/19/6/3, box 244; memo, J. Devers to DDE, n.d., NARA RG 319, OCMH, 2-3.7 CC2 Sicily, box 247; memo, "Former Naval Person to the President," No. 405, Aug. 5, 1943, NARA RG 319, OCMH 2-3.7 CC2 Sicily, box 249; POW reports, NARA RG 492, MTO, chemical warfare section, 350.09 (*interrogations of prisoners*); C. Reining, "IPW Report No. 9," Nov. 8, 1943, Fifth Army HQ, NARA RG 492, MTO, chemical warfare section, 350.09 (*new, egregiously potent gas*); G-2 report No. 35, Oct. 11, 1943, Fifth Army HQ, NARA RG 492, MTO, chemical warfare section, 350.052, "CW Intel Miscl" ("*Adolf will turn to gas*"); "Enemy Capabilities for Chemical Warfare," Military Intelligence Service, WD, NARA RG 334, NWC Lib, box 602 (*Nineteen plants in Germany*).

272 *Twenty-eight different gases:* Kleber and Birdsell, 3–5, 122; James W. Hammond, Jr., *Poison Gas: The Myth Versus Reality,* 16–17 (*Hitler himself*), 36; Glenn B. Infield, *Disaster at Bari,* 14–16 ("*swift retaliation*"); "Observations in the European Theater Including Landing Operation at Salerno," Oct. 25, 1943, HQ, USMC, NARA RG 334, NWC Lib, MC OR, box 556 (*depots near Oran*); Owen C. Bolstad, *Dear Folks,* 177 ("*report any poison gas leaks*"). Later investigations found little German appetite for another chemical war against Allied forces.

272 *more than 200,000 gas bombs:* "Implementation of Theater Plans for Gas Warfare," Aug. 18, 1043, WD; also, memos and draft memos dated Aug. 30, Sept. 7, 1943, Jan. 12, Feb. 14,

March 11, July 15, 1944; memo, "Report by Assistant Chief of U.S. Chemical Warfare Service," Oct. 27, 1943, all in NARA RG 492, MTO, chemical warfare section, 381, box 1706; Margry, "Mustard Disaster at Bari," 34.

272 *How the Germans would be deterred:* Kenyon Joyce, "Italy," ts, n.d., Kenyon Joyce papers, MHI, 332; "Report on the Circumstances," etc.; Infield, 14–16 (*forward dumps at Foggia*).

272 *Several thousand Allied servicemen:* Margry, "Mustard Disaster at Bari," 34; Infield, 93, 118; Southern, 61 (Sergeant York), 130; H. V. Morton, *A Traveller in Southern Italy,* 99 (*Italian women drew water*); Gerald Reminick, *Nightmare in Bari,* 95 (*cribbage board*).

273 *The first two Luftwaffe raiders:* C. L. Grant, "AAF Air Defense Activities in the Mediterranean," n.d., USAF Historical Study, No. 66, 107–8; Edward B. Westermann, *Flak,* 21; "Report on the Operation of Radar in Operation AVALANCHE," Dec. 31, 1943, AFHRA, 626.430-1; http://www.rafmuseum.org.uk/milestones-of-flight/british_military/1943_4.html; Southern, 130–34 (*confused Allied searchlight radar*); Arnold, 475; Infield, 31; Hinsley et al., 184 (*German reconnaissance interest*); Eric Niderost, "Bari: The Second Pearl Harbor," *World War II Magazine,* http://historynet.com/wwii/blluftwaffeadriatic/index1.html; memo, air commander-in-chief to AFHQ, Dec. 23, 1943, "Report on Adequacy of Protective Measures at Bari," NARA RG 331, AFHQ micro, R-87, box 197 (*"Risks such as were accepted"*); Justin F. Gleichauf, *Unsung Sailors: The Naval Armed Guard in World War II,* 295–96 (*insisted that naval gunners not fire*).

273 *That moment soon arrived:* action report, Murdoch Walker, *Lyman Abbott,* to CNO, March 10, 1944, NARA RG 38, OCNO, Naval Transportation Service, Armed Guard files, 370/12/31/4, box 437 (*firing by earshot*); Infield, 93 (*"We're taking a pasting"*), 117, 122.

273 *Bombs severed an oil pipeline:* "Report on the Circumstances," etc.; "History of the Naval Armed Guard Afloat," n.d., *U.S. Naval Administration in World War II,* NHC, Command File, World War II, 166–68 (Joseph Wheeler); Infield, 55–56, 66, 141–42; msg, Alfred Bergman to supervisor, U.S. Merchant Marine Cadet Corps, "SS *John Bascom,* loss of," Feb. 23, 1944, SEM, NHC, box 58; Southern, 7; diary, L. Stevenson, IWM, P100.

274 *The Liberty ship* Samuel J. Tilden: msg, Robert Donnelly to supervisor, U.S. Merchant Marine Cadet Corps, "SS *Samuel J. Tilden*—loss of," Feb. 2, 1944, SEM, NHC, box 58; "History of the Naval Armed Guard Afloat," 166–68; Southern, 36 (*"harbor was aflame"*).

274 *Among those burning vessels was the* John Harvey: Southern, 49, 53, 62–66; minutes, investigative board, Bari raid, June 28, 1944, NARA RG 331, AFHQ micro, R-87, box 197 (*Windows shattered seven miles away*); Gregory Blaxland, *Alexander's Generals,* 13; Walter Karig, *Battle Report: The Atlantic War,* 277 (*"the entire world was burning"*).

274 *Civilians were crushed:* Margry, "Mustard Disaster at Bari," 34; Southern, 124 (*"young girl pinned"*), 44–45 (*"If this be it"*); Infield, 62–63; Will Lang, notebook #9, "Bari raid," USMA Arch.

275 *Seventeen ships had been sunk:* "Report on Adequacy of Protective Measures at Bari"; Karig, 277.

275 *"Since when do American ships":* Infield, 86; "Report on the Circumstances," etc. (*H.M.S.* Brindisi); D. M. Saunders, "The Bari Incident," *Proceedings,* vol. 93, no. 9, Sept. 1967, 35+ (Bistra *picked up thirty survivors*).

275 *"Ambulances screamed into hospital":* Southern, 52, 91; Stewart F. Alexander, "Final Report of Bari Mustard Casualties," June 20, 1944, AFHRA, office of the surgeon, NARA RG 492, 704, box 1757 (*"considerably puzzled"*).

275 *"all in pain":* memo, H. Gluck, "ophthalmic casualties resulting from air raid on Bari," 98th General Hospital, Dec. 14, 1943, NARA RG 331, AFHQ micro, 290/24/27/2–4, R 235-D; corr, Stewart F. Alexander to William D. Fleming, Dec. 26, 1943, NARA RG 112, MTO surgeon general, 390/17/8/2-3, 319.1, box 6 (*"No treatment"*); Reminick, 115 (*"big as balloons"*); "Report on the Circumstances," etc. (*"dermatitis N.Y.D."*).

276 *A Royal Navy surgeon:* "Notes on Meeting Held at HQ 2 District, at 1415 Hours," in "Report on the Circumstances," etc.

276 *The first mustard death:* appendix G, "Medical Report," in "Report on the Circumstances," etc.; Southern, 89 ("*that bloody bang*"); Alexander, "Final Report" (*Seaman Phillip H. Stone*).

276 *By noon on Friday:* memo, "Casualties, Air Raid, Bari," Dec. 8, 1943, NARA RG 331, AFHQ micro, 290/24/27/2-4, R 235-D; Gluck, "ophthalmic casualties" (*lids forcibly pried open*); Saunders, "The Bari Incident," 35 (*hundreds had inhaled*).

276 *More than a thousand Allied servicemen:* memo, "Toxic Gas Burns Sustained in the Bari Harbor Catastrophe," Dec. 27, 1943, NATOUSA, office of the surgeon, NARA RG 112, MTO surgeon general, 390/17/8/2-3, 319.1, box 6.

276 *A comparable number of Italian civilians:* No precise casualty figures were ever compiled. Margry, "Mustard Disaster at Bari," 34; Infield, 177; Alexander, "Final Report" (*at least 617 confirmed mustard casualties*); Southern, 48, 125–26, 145 ("*head to toe in trench graves*").

277 "*For purposes of secrecy*": memo, "Casualties, Air Raid, Bari"; George S. Bergh and Reuben F. Erickson, eds., "A History of the Twenty-sixth General Hospital," 132 ("*Damage was done*"); Infield, 208 ("*I will not comment*"); corr, J.F.M. Whitely to J. N. Kennedy, Dec. 21, 1943, UK NA, WO 204/307.

277 "*the wind was offshore*": Eisenhower, *Crusade*, 204; Infield, 207 ("*enemy action*").

277 *Declassified in 1959:* Saunders, "The Bari Incident"; Orange, 176; Reminick, 169; L. S. Goodman et al., "Nitrogen Mustard Therapy," *Journal of the American Medical Association*, Sept. 21, 1946, 126+; John H. Lienhard, "Engines of Our Ingenuity," no. 1190, "Mustard Gas," University of Houston, http://www.uh.edu/engines/epi1190.htm; Rebecca Holland, "Mustard Gas," Bristol University, htttp://www.chm.bris.ac.uk/motm/mustard/mustard.htm; http://en.wikipedia.org/wiki/History_of-_cancer_chemotherapy#The_first_efforts_.281940.E2.80.931950.29.

277 *Thousands of refugees trudged:* Bergh and Erickson, eds., "A History of the Twenty-sixth General Hospital," 132; Infield, 235; *AAFinWWII*, 587 (*38,000 tons of cargo*).

278 "*I see you boys are getting gassed*": Infield, 207; Franz Kurowski, *The History of the Fallschirmpanzerkorps Hermann Göring*, 213–17.

## CHAPTER 6: WINTER

### *The Archangel Michael, Here and Everywhere*

279 *Since its founding:* Maurizio Zambardi, *San Pietro Infine*, 7, 11, 15, 17; author visits, Sept. 1995, May 2004; OH, Maurizio Zambardi, May 5, 2004, with author.

279 *a German patrol arrived:* Maurizio Zambardi, *Memorie di Guerra*, 22–30, 33, 42; Alex Bowlby, *Countdown to Cassino*, 83.

280 *San Pietro's fate was* sealed: A. G. Steiger, "The Campaign in Southern Italy," Nov. 1947, Canadian Army headquarters, historical section, No. 18, 41.

280 *While Mark Clark paused:* Bowlby, 51–52, 78, 84–85; Franz Kurowski, *Battleground Italy, 1943–1945*, 68–69 (*sodden clumps*).

280 *For the San Pietrans:* Zambardi, *Memorie di Guerra*, 34–39, 54–55; OH, Zambardi, May 5, 2004; Bowlby, 83–84.

281 "*a worse plan*": *CM*, 286.

281 "*critical terrain in the operation*": diary, MWC, Nov. 6, 11, 1943, Citadel, box 64; *Fifth Army at the Winter Line*, 17 (RAINCOAT *called for an attack*).

281 *Clark's intelligence estimated:* German figures indicated that Tenth Army had 142,000 troops in twelve divisions on Dec. 1, 1943. *StoC*, 246–47, 269 (*barely three hundred yards*).

281 "*Oh, don't worry*": OH, H. Alexander, Jan. 10–15, 1949, SM, CMH, II-3; *StoC*, 265, 270.

282 *More than nine hundred guns:* "Lessons from the Italian Campaign," March 1944, HQ, NATOUSA, DTL, Ft. B, 100; Robert H. Adleman and George Walton, *The Devil's Brigade,* 123–24; *Fifth Army at the Winter Line,* 23; Molony V, 517 (*eleven tons of steel*).

282 *"only an Italian winter":* Vincent M. Lockhart, ts, n.d., 36th ID Assoc, Texas MFM, www.kwanah.com/36Division/pstoc.htm; Geoffrey Perret, *There's a War to Be Won,* 179 (*American lumberjacks*); Charles F. Marshall, *A Ramble Through My War,* 88 ("*potential gangster*"); "Special List of Clothing and Equipment," Sept. 24, 1943, Robert D. Burhans papers, HIA, box 3 (*codeine sulfate*).

282 *Leading the gangsters:* OH, Paul D. Adams, 1975, Irving Monclova and Marlin Lang, SOOHP, MHI (*French Quebec*); mss notes, n.d., Robert T. Frederick papers, HIA, box 8 (*Son of a San Francisco doctor*); obit, Robert T. Frederick, *Assembly,* spring 1972, 106 (*sailed to Australia*); Perret, 179 (*bedroom slippers*); corr, Oct. 20, 1943, Robert T. Frederick papers, HIA, box 1 ("*worthy of trust*"); OH, Robert T. Frederick, Jan. 7, 1949, SM, MHI ("*lacked guts*"); OH, D. M. "Pat" O'Neill, n.d., Robert H. Adleman papers, HIA, box 10 ("*casual indifference*").

282 *Their barked fingers blue:* Adleman and Walton, 129; Bowlby, 113 (*thrown rocks*); Joseph A. Springer, *Black Devil Brigade,* 86 (*rock splinters*); Robert D. Burhans, *The First Special Service Force,* 107 (*shallow saucer*).

283 *A maddening wait:* Burhans, 107, 112; Springer, 100–102 ("*German was with me*"), 95 ("*red mist*"); Adleman and Walton, 138–44.

283 *Panzer grenadiers counterattacked: Fifth Army at the Winter Line,* 24; Springer 88–90, 109–10 ("*huge shotgun*"); Adleman and Walton, 138; Robert Wallace, *The Italian Campaign,* 108–9 (*white flag ruse*); affidavits, 2nd Regt investigation, Robert D. Burhans papers, box 19 ("*Foxhole Willie*").

284 *"We have passed the crest":* msgs, R. T. Frederick, Dec. 5–6, 1943, Robert D. Burhans papers, HIA, box 21.

284 *Early on Tuesday morning:* Burhans, 120; *StoC,* 263; Molony V, 517–18 (*hilltop monastery*); Bowlby, 120–21 (*mossy rocks*); Moorehead, *Eclipse,* 64; Burhans, 120; msg, Frederick, Dec. 7, 1943, 1630 hrs, Robert D. Burhans papers, HIA, box 21.

284 *Survivors hobbled:* Burhans, 120; surgeon's report, Dec. 2–9, 1943, Robert D. Burhans papers, HIA, box 19.

284 *"feet of a dead man":* Springer, 118.

284 *With his left flank secured:* James J. Altieri, *Darby's Rangers: An Illustrated Portrayal of the Original Rangers,* 65; *StoC,* 274; Frederick L. Young, "The First Casualty on Monte Sammucro," ts, 1991, Texas MFM, 62 ("*Krauts up there*").

285 *He soon learned otherwise:* Robert L. Wagner, *The Texas Army,* 74, 77 ("*couple of lizards*"); Homer Bigart, "San Pietro a Village of the Dead," *New York Herald Tribune,* Dec. 20, 1943, in *Reporting World War II,* vol. 1, 738–45; Don Whitehead, "Beachhead Don," 83 ("*Rufus the Loudmouth*"); Young, "The First Casualty on Monte Sammucro," 67, 72, 81 ("*Die kommen*"); Richard Tregaskis, *Invasion Diary,* 235 ("*This is fun*").

285 *Two miles west:* Bowlby, 141; Jack Clover, ts, n.d., HQ Co., 2/143rd Inf, 36th ID Assoc, Texas MFM, www.kwanah.com/36Division/pstoc.htm ("*skirmish lines*").

285 *pillboxes emplaced every twenty-five yards:* "The Battle for San Pietro," *AB,* no. 18, 1977, 1+; Bowlby, 142–45 (*fingers shot off*).

287 *Roma o morte:* author visit, Monte Lungo, May 5, 2004; photos, Italian memorial and museum, Monte Lungo; Wagner, 72 (*Alpine uniforms*); R. K. Doughty, "The Pink House," ts, n.d., 141st Inf, Texas MFM; *StoC,* 276; Wallace, 109; *Calculated,* 240–44 (*vowing to punish*); Bowlby, 146 ("*corn cut by a scythe*"); corr, Don E. Carleton to Hal C. Pattison, Feb. 10, 1965, NARA RG 319, OCMH, 2-3.7 CC3, Salerno to Cassino, box 256 (*fastest runners*); *CM,* 291; Thomas E. Hannum, "The 30 Years of Army Experience," ts, n.d., 91st Armored FA Bn, ASEQ, MHI, 58; corr, Vincenzo Dapino to GK, Dec. 23, 1943, MWC, corr, Citadel, box 3 ("*not in a condition*").

287 *trails marked with white tape: Reporting World War II,* vol. 2, 8–9; John F. O'Malley, "The Operations of Company I, 143rd Infantry, South of Rome," 1946, IS; Ernie Pyle, "One Demolished Town After Another," Dec. 28, 1943, *Reporting World War II,* vol. 1, 733–34; Pyle, 100 ("Brrrr"); Betsy Wade, ed., *Forward Positions: The War Correspondence of Homer Bigart,* 34 *(wearing packboards)*; Wagner, 77 *(necktie)*; Lance Bertelsen, "Texans at San Pietro," *Discovery Magazine,* University of Texas, vol. 14, no. 2 (1997), http://ftp.cc .utexas.edu/opa/pubs/discovery/disc1997v14n2/disc-sanpietro. html *("husky young men")*.

287 *"feel the presence of the enemy"*: Margaret Bourke-White, *Purple Heart Valley,* 42, 147–48 *("lives the longest")*; Pyle, 166; Paul Dickson, *War Slang,* 113+; T. Moffatt Burriss, *Strike and Hold,* 65 *(bunt a baseball)*; *Fifth Army at the Winter Line,* 51–52 *(white phosphorus)*; memo, "Phosphorus Burns," consulting surgeon, AAI, Nov. 8, 1944, NARA RG 331, AFHQ micro, R-235-D; memoir, Edward R. Feagins, ts, n.d., 143rd Inf, Texas MFM, 31; Ross S. Carter, *Those Devils in Baggy Pants,* 74, 81 *("don't like this place")*.

288 *Raised in the cotton country:* Michael S. Sweeney, "Appointment at Hill 1205: Ernie Pyle and Capt. Henry T. Waskow," 1995, http://www.kwanah.com/txmilmus/36division/ archives/waskow/sect1.htm; Michael L. Lanning, "Goodbye to Captain Waskow," *VFW Magazine,* May 1981, 19+; Berneta Peeples, "Requiem," *Belton* (Tex.) *Journal,* Dec. 16, 1993, reprint of 1953 article; Bob Tutt, "Young Officer Was Father Figure," *Houston Chronicle,* Feb. 6, 1994, 28A.

288 *"I guess I have always appeared"*: Henry T. Waskow, "Last Will and Testament," *Temple* (Tex.) *Daily Telegram,* reprinted, Texas MFM.

288 *after almost a week on Sammucro:* StoC, 280; Young, "The First Casualty on Monte Sammucro," 102; *Fifth Army at the Winter Line,* 51–52; Peeples, "Requiem" *("an awful spot")*.

289 *Wearing his trademark knit cap:* James Tobin, *Ernie Pyle's War,* 133; Lee G. Miller, *An Ernie Pyle Album,* 90 *("Mr. God")*; memoir, James R. Pritchard, 68th Armored FA bn, ts, n.d, ASEQ, MHI, 10 *(filling ruts with logs)*.

289 *"some inert liquid"*: Douglas Allanbrook, *See Naples,* 123; Pyle, 107 *("They slid him")*.

289 *after returning to Fifth Army headquarters:* Sweeney, "Appointment at Hill 1205."

289 *Riley Tidwell appeared*: ibid.; OH, Riley Tidwell, March 28, 1994, Jane Purtle, Cherokee County Historical Commission, Texas MFM.

290 *"Finally he put the hand down"*: Pyle, 107; Lee G. Miller, *The Story of Ernie Pyle,* 297 *("I've lost the touch")*.

290 *Mark Clark had proposed using tanks:* StoC, 277–79.

290 *This time the attack would be filmed:* Marco Pellegrinelli, *La Battaglia di S. Pietro di John Huston,* 7–10; Bertelsen, "Texans at San Pietro" *("triumphant entry")*; Ray Wells, "Battalion Commander," *Fighting 36th Historical Quarterly,* spring 1992 *("a large mower")*.

290 *loaders with asbestos gloves:* John E. Krebs, *To Rome and Beyond,* 37; "Lessons from the Italian Campaign," March 10, 1944, NARA RG 407, E 427, 95-USF1-04, box 250, 116; "The Battle for San Pietro," 1.

291 *The 141st Infantry's 2nd Battalion: Fifth Army at the Winter Line,* 62; Clifford H. Peek, Jr., *Five Years, Five Countries, Five Campaigns,* 31–32 *("Dead and wounded")*; Wagner, 84; Bowlby, 166, 171 *("stupidest assignment")*; AAR, 141st Inf, Jan. 11, 1944, Aaron W. Wyatt, Jr., ASEQ, MHI *(second attack at six A.M.)*; corr, Thomas A. Higbie, July 15, 2003, to author *("put that damn rag away")*.

291 *Wisps of steam rose:* Richard Manton, n.d., 2/141st Inf, 36th ID Assoc, Texas MFM, www.kwanah.com/36Division/pstoc.htm; *Calculated,* 248; diary, MWC, Dec. 16, 1943, Citadel, box 64, 287 *("What troops")*; *Texas,* 287 *("The losses before the town")*.

291 *And then it ended:* StoC, 285; *Fifth Army at the Winter Line,* 67; "The Battle for San Pietro," 1.

291 *"mound of desolation"*: Tom Roe, *Anzio Beachhead,* 37; Homer Bigart, "San Pietro a Village of the Dead," *New York Herald Tribune,* Dec. 20, 1943, in *Reporting World War II,* vol. 1, 738–45 *("gray hand hanging limply")*.

292 *"journey in Dante's* Inferno": J. Glenn Gray, *The Warriors,* 59–60; Zambardi, *Memorie di Guerra,* 13 (*140 San Pietrans*). The U.S. Army official history estimated that three hundred San Pietrans died. *StoC,* 285.

292 *A baby's corpse:* Daniel J. Petruzzi, *My War Against the Land of My Ancestors,* 147; "The Battle of San Pietro," Combat Report No. 2, 1945, NARA RG 111, film, CR 002 (*folding the hands of dead GIs*); Samuel Hynes, *The Soldiers' Tale,* 3 ("*impenetrable silence*").

292 *"where their bedding fell":* Wagner, 89–90; *StoC,* 285n.

292 *"Ah! Sweet Mystery":* Bourke-White, 118, 126–29, 131.

292 *"We find the country thick":* JPL, 271; *StoC,* 286 ("*a long way off*"); Bruce L. Barger, *The Texas 36th Division,* 144 ("*heartbreaking business*").

292 *For John Huston:* Peter Maslowski, *Armed with Cameras,* 75, 88–93; Bertelsen, "Texans at San Pietro"; *A Pictorial History of the 36th "Texas" Infantry Division,* no pagination ("*as good a war film*").

293 *"I was right, wasn't I?":* Lanning, "Goodbye to Captain Waskow," 19; Sweeney, "Appointment at Hill 1205"; Miller, *An Ernie Pyle Album,* 92 (*Pyle's column*).

## *"A Tank Too Big for the Village Square"*

293 *Life in exile:* Piers Brendon, *Ike: His Life and Times,* 115 (*three mattresses*); memoir, "Italy," ts, n.d., Kenyon Joyce papers, MHI, 347 ("*social purposes*"); corr, GSP to Arvin Harrington Brown, Oct. 22, 1943, GSP, LOC MS Div, box 27; *PP,* 362; diary, Sept. 9, 1943, GSP, LOC MS Div, box 3, folder 3.

294 *On mild afternoons:* JPL, 147–48; *The Princeton Class of 1942 During World War II,* 123 (*quail hunting*); *PP,* 367, 391 (*language lessons*); Ladislas Farago, *Patton: Ordeal and Triumph,* 364; Charles R. Codman, *Drive,* 135 (*Wellington*); George S. Patton, *War As I Knew It,* 74 ("*a disgusting place*"); Robert H. Patton, *The Pattons,* 232 ("*too big for the village square*"), 262; Robert E. Coffin and Joan N. Coffin, "The Robert Edmonstron Coffin–Joan Nelson Coffin Family Book," 96 (La Bohème).

294 *Seventh Army was reduced to a shell:* PP, 371; msg, W. B. Smith to GSP, Nov. 25, 1943, Walter Bedell Smith papers, DDE Lib, box 27 (*signal battalion*); diary, Dec. 2, 1943, GSP, LOC MS Div, box 3, folder 4 ("*strip the body*"); JPL, 147–48; Stanley P. Hirshson, *General Patton: A Soldier's Life,* 416 ("*dessicated*"); OH, Garrison H. Davidson, Nov. 1980, John T. Greenwood, CEOH, 231 ("*paper dolls*"); corr, GSP to Beatrice, Nov. 7, 1943, Beatrice to GSP, Nov. 1943, GSP, LOC MS Div, box 17, folder 20.

294 *issued wicker baskets:* Ivan Dmitri, *Flight to Everywhere,* 191; "Italy," Kenyon Joyce papers, 355 ("*middle of my forehead*"); James H. Doolittle, *I Could Never Be So Lucky Again,* 363; Clift Andrus, notes on *A Soldier's Story,* ts, n.d., MRC-FDM, 1988.32, box 215.

295 *"You need have no fear":* Martin Blumenson, *Patton: The Man Behind the Legend, 1885–1945,* 213, 215 ("*pink medecin*"); Kenneth S. Davis, *Soldier of Democracy,* 439 ("*at least sixty reporters*"); *PP,* 359, 361.

295 *He took little interest:* Carl J. Friedrich, ed., *American Experiences in Military Government in World War II,* 120; Robert W. Komer, "Civil Affairs and Military Government in the Mediterranean Theater," 1954, CMH, 2-3.7 AX, VI, 3–6 ("*subsistence level*"); *PP,* 371; Dmitri, 192 (*feigned pregnancy*); Malcolm S. McLean, "Adventures in Occupied Areas," ts, 1975, MHI, 56 (*Black marketeering*).

295 *Shortages plagued the island:* "History of the Island Base Section, Sicily," n.d., CMH, 8-4 FA, 14, 18 ("*every possible ruse*"); "Monthly Report for August 1943 on the Administration of Sicily," n.d., AMGOT, 15th Army Group, to H. Alexander, Frank J. McSherry papers, MHI ("*Mafia activities*"); "Reports of AMGOT Divisions, up to Nov. 1, 1943," part 3, n.d., Frank J. McSherry papers, MHI (*jailed sixteen hundred*); Norman Lewis, *In Sicily,* 56 (*revenge killings*); diary, Carleton Washburne, Oct. 22, 1943, Mina Curtiss collection, YU (*scissored Fascist cant*); John Hersey in *Reporting World War II,* vol. 1, 621; report, W. A. Eddy to W. L. Langer, Aug. 29, 1943, NARA RG 226, E 99, OSS history office, box 39.

296 *The Quaker muckraker:* Dennis Showalter, *Patton and Rommel,* 321; Donald Coe, "Army Releases Patton Story After Denial," Nov. 23, 1943, *Boston Traveler,* 1; Richard Collier, *Fighting Words,* 147; msg, DDE to AGWAR, NARA RG 165, E 422, OPD executive files, Nov. 27, 1943, box 14; Chandler, vol. 3, 1606 (*Smith in Algiers made matters worse*).

296 *Army regulations:* reprinted, *Army and Navy Journal,* Dec. 4, 1973, 394, Orlando Ward papers, MHI; *PP,* 377 (*fifteen hundred letters*); Hirshson, 427 (*Gallup poll*).

296 *"I am not so sure":* corr, GSP to Beatrice, Dec. 4 & 9, 1943, GSP, LOC MS Div, box 17; *Calculated,* 257; Hirshson, 433 (*"family of the deceased"*); diary, Dec. 25, 1943, GSP, LOC MS Div, box 3, folder 4 (*"live to see him die"*); Kay Summersby, *Eisenhower Was My Boss,* 81 (*"always get in trouble"*); corr, L. J. McNair to GSP, Nov. 27, 1943, and GSP to L. J. McNair, Dec. 29, 1943, NARA RG 165, E 418, director of plans and operations, box 1229; corr, GSP to D. S. Miller, Sr., Dec. 27, 1943, GSP, LOC MS Div, box 44, folder 1 (*"Very few of us"*).

296 *"I doubt that I would ever":* msg, DDE to GCM, Sept. 20, 1943, NARA RG 165, E 422, OPD exec files, box 13; *PP,* 393; D. Clayton James and Anne Sharp Wells, *A Time for Giants,* 230 (*"should always serve"*).

297 *Deliverance came:* "Log of the President's Trip to Africa and the Middle East," Stephen T. Early Papers, FDR Lib, box 37.

297 *"General Patton, you will have an army":* Mark W. Clark, "General Patton," ts, n.d., subject file, MWC, Citadel, biography folder, box 70, 3; Michael F. Reilly, *Reilly of the White House,* 188.

297 *burst into sobs:* Reilly, 188; William D. Leahy, *I Was There,* 215–16.

297 *"My destiny is sure":* PP, 391.

## A Gangster's Battle

297 *Eighth Army since invading Calabria:* Molony V, 481, 482n, 483n; *Battle,* 146; Richard Doherty, *A Noble Crusade,* 173; msg, DDE to CCS, Nov. 4, 1943, SM, MHI, box 2; *Fifth Army at the Winter Line,* 7; Field Marshal the Viscount Alexander of Tunis, "The Allied Armies in Italy," n.d., CMH, II-21 (*"sufficiently stretched"*).

298 *That strategy still seemed plausible:* Molony V, 493, 496; *StoC,* 258–59; B. H. Liddell Hart, *The Other Side of the Hill,* 343 (*"We will now hit them"*); Richard Lamb, *Montgomery in Europe 1943–45,* 56 (*"The road to Rome"*).

298 *The Bernhardt Line defenses:* Doherty, 171; Thomas R. Brooks, *The War North of Rome, June 1944–May 1945,* 4 (*"ridge and furrow country"*); "Current Reports from Overseas," March 11, 1944, War Office, CARL, N-148495 (*"average range of vision"*); Field Marshal Lord Carver, *The Imperial War Museum Book of the War in Italy, 1943–1945,* 98–99 (*avenue of poplars*).

298 *Drenching winter rains:* Doherty, 174; *Battle,* 148; Molony V, 488; Dharm Pal, *The Campaign in Italy, 1943–1945,* 35 (*"malignant river"*); Richard S. Malone, *A Portrait of War 1939–1943,* 201 (*"could hear the wounded men"*); *StoC,* 259 (*losses in the 78th Division*).

298 *"an unprofitable sector":* OH, Howard Kippenberger, Feb. 4 and 12, 1947, SM, MHI; weekly intelligence summary, no. 67, Dec. 4, 1943, AFHQ, G-2, NARA RG 407, E 427, 95-AL1-2.6 (*"lost the initiative"*); Michael Pearson Cessford, "Hard in the Attack: The Canadian Army in Sicily and Italy, July 1943–June 1944," Sept. 1996, Ph.D. diss, Carleton University, Ottawa, 215 (*strategy of attrition*); Molony V, 495–97.

299 *"almost lunar in its desolation":* Farley Mowat, *The Regiment,* 137, 146; Doherty, 191 (*"lay rigid"*).

299 *"To preserve sanity":* diary, O. Carpenter, Nov. 11, 1943, IWM, 79/38/1; John Gunther, *D Day,* 134 (*"murder"*); Gilbert Allnutt, "A Fusilier Remembers Italy," ts, 1979, IWM, 80/46/1, 18, 23 (*"Move forward"*).

299 *Montgomery kept his swank:* Gunther, 129; Malone, 193–95.

299 *"The army commander wants to see you":* L.S.B. Shapiro, *They Left the Back Door Open,* 44; OH, Francis de Guingand, March 31, 1947, G. A. Harrison, "OCMH WWII Europe

Interviews," MHI ("*Sit down*"); Stephen Brooks, ed., *Montgomery and the Eighth Army*, 313 ("*go-as-you-please*"); J. B. Tomlinson, "Under the Banner of the Battleaxe," ts, n.d., IWM, 90/29/1, 108 ("*And after the war*").

300 "*I must have fine weather*": Nigel Hamilton, *Master of the Battlefield*, 449; Dick Malone, *Missing from the Record*, 53 ("*You are useless*"); Andrew Brookes, *Air War over Italy, 1943–1945*, 38 (" '*Stop frigging*' "); Molony V, 511 ("*the unusual gift*").

300 "*a very good First World War general*": Richard H. Kohn, ed., "The Scholarship on World War II," *Journal of Military History*, vol. 55, no. 3 (July 1991), 365+.

301 "*untidy and ad hoc*": B. L. Montgomery, "Reflections on the Campaign in Italy, 1943," Nov. 24, 1943, ts, IWM, micro, reel 4, BLM 48, 1–4.

301 *Canada's hour had finally come round*: Mark Zuehlke, *Ortona*, 3; Martin Gilbert, *The Second World War*, 353–54; *From Pachino to Ortona*, CARL, N-14352; Arthur Bryant, *The Turn of the Tide*, 596 (*feared that the war would end*).

301 *a decrepit sandstone castle*: Combat Report No. 1, "Liberation of Rome," 1944, Signal Corps film, NARA RG 111, CR001; Zuehlke, *Ortona*, 31–32, 37–39; Karl Baedeker, *Southern Italy and Sicily*, 190 (*local landmarks*); Daniel G. Dancocks, *The D-Day Dodgers: The Canadians in Italy, 1943–1945*, 173–76 (*ten thousand souls*); Steiger, "The Campaign in Southern Italy," 30 (*holes in the harbor mole*); "Canadian Street Fighting in Ortona," June 15, 1944, Military Reports from the United Nations, No. 19, NARA RG 334, NWC Lib, box 184 (*easily severed*).

302 *The Canadian division commander*: http://www.junobeach.org/e/3/can-pep-can-vokes-ep.htm; Zuehlke, *Ortona*, 14 ("*pompous bully*"), 18; Dancocks, 69 ("*roughneck*"), 191 (*the Butcher*); Mark Zuehlke, *The Liri Valley*, 166 ("*a man's fate is written*"); Molony V, 504.

302 *A lunge on the left flank*: Dancocks, 156, 159 ("*raving madhouse*"); Mowat, 151 ("*stupid bastard*"); Zuehlke, *Ortona*, 124 ("*translucent red*"), 156, 160; *From Pachino to Ortona*, 133–34 ("*confusing to the enemy*"); war diary, Loyal Edmonton Regiment, Dec. 9, 1943, http://www.lermuseum.org/ler/cof/sacrifice/wwii/textwindow/wardiary1.html; "Victoria Cross Is Awarded Major Paul Triquet, Montreal, for Heroic Action in Italy," March 6, 1944, Hamilton (Canada) *Spectator*, www.warmuseum.ca.

302 *Beyond the Moro lay a ravine*: Cessford, "Hard in the Attack," 264; Zuehlke, *Ortona*, 48; Molony V, 504 ("*Of eight assaults*"); Dancocks, 171 ("*You tell Monty*").

303 "*filthy limbo*": Mowat, 161–65.

303 *replaced by the 1st Parachute Division*: *From Pachino to Ortona*, 139; Alexander, "The Allied Armies in Italy," II-29 ("*best German troops*"); Zuehlke, *Ortona*, 161, 201.

304 *Heavy losses and exhaustion*: Christopher Buckley, *Road to Rome*, 256; Cessford, "Hard in the Attack," 233 ("*You feel nothing*"); G.W.L. Nicholson, *The Canadians in Italy, 1943–1945*, vol. 2, 317 (*Errant maps*); Dancocks, 171 ("*He frittered away everything*"), 173; Zuehlke, *Ortona*, 212–14, 219 ("*porridge pot*"); Molony V, 503–5.

304 MORNING GLORY: Cessford, "Hard in the Attack," 233, 241; Dancocks, 240; Buckley, 256.

304 "*I wish I could see you*": Cessford, "Hard in the Attack," 233.

304 *first large, pitched urban battle*: Molony V, 507.

304 *Ortona had been spared razing*: ibid., 509; "Canadian Street Fighting in Ortona"; Nicholson, 323; Zuehlke, *Ortona*, 247; Dancocks, 186 ("*butchered deer*"); Steiger, "The Campaign in Southern Italy," 63 ("*Everybody was very sad*").

305 *Side streets proved too narrow*: Battle, 151–53; "Canadian Street Fighting in Ortona" (*shot the tanks in the belly*); Molony V, 507; Doherty, 184–85; *The Tiger Triumphs*, 28–29 ("*gangster's battle*"); Zuehlke, *Ortona*, 278, 289; Nicholson, 328 ("*miniature Stalingrad*"); Dancocks, 181 ("*three more shooting days*").

305 *Rather than clear buildings conventionally*: "Street Fighting," intelligence report, 5778-44, May 29, 1944, British GHQ, Cairo, CMH, Geog Files, Italy, 370.2, 6–7; "Beehives," appendix B, "Ortona," HQ, 1st Canadian Div, Feb. 16, 1944, C. W. Allfrey papers, LHC, 4/8; Mowat, 163.

306 *"The stench here"*: Dancocks, 1, 179 (*"We could beat you"*); Buckley, 260.

306 *Two dozen Edmontons were buried:* war diary, Loyal Edmonton Regiment, Dec. 27, 1943, http://www.lermuseum.org/ler/cof/sacrifice/wwii/textwindow/wardiary1.html.

306 *"We do not want to defend"*: Steiger, "The Campaign in Southern Italy," 65.

306 *"There is no town left"*: Zuehlke, *Ortona,* 348.

306 *"This is Ortona"*: Dancocks, 186, 189; *From Pachino to Ortona* (*"a fairy tale"*).

306 *Alexander's plan had miscarried:* Molony V, 509; Dancocks, 186 (*"The familiar world"*).

*Too Many Gone West*

307 *Removing his hat:* Lord Moran, *Churchill: Taken from the Diaries of Lord Moran,* 159; W. H. Thompson, *I Was Churchill's Shadow,* 124, 126 (*for his sixty-ninth birthday*).

307 *"I want to sleep"*: Roy Jenkins, *Churchill,* 719; WSC, *Closing the Ring,* 420 (*flopped sopping*); Richard Overy, *Why the Allies Won,* 268 (*"specks of dust"*).

307 *At length the mystery:* Jerrard Tickell, *Ascalon,* 14–15, 62–64; *Three Years,* 457 (*"had been pacing"*); Churchill, 457 (*"end of my tether"*).

307 *Ringed by sentries:* Gerald Pawle, *The War and Colonel Warden,* 277–80; Harold Macmillan, *War Diaries,* 326–27; Moran, 159; Roger Parkinson, *A Day's March Nearer Home,* 234 (*"much disturbed"*); Martin Gilbert, *Winston S. Churchill,* vol. 7, 604 (*"It's pretty bad"*); Danchev, 497 (*"Hullo, hullo"*).

308 *"My master is unwell"*: Gilbert, 606, 608 (*"bumping all over"*); Danchev, 497 (*pathologist arrived*); Moran, 161.

308 *"He's very glad I've come"*: Moran, 161–62; Gilbert, 606 (*"war is won"*); Thompson, 129–30 (*"In what better place"*); Macmillan, 326–27 (*"very breathless"*).

308 *The preceding fortnight:* Richard M. Leighton, "OVERLORD Versus the Mediterranean at the Cairo-Tehran Conferences (1943)," Kent Roberts Greenfield, ed., *Command Decisions,* 189–91; James Leasor, *The Clock with Four Hands,* 263 (*22,000 pounds of meat*); Macmillan, 320 (*curried prawns*); Molony V, 584 (*80 bottles*).

309 *That Britain's senior role:* Keith Eubank, *Summit at Teheran,* 486–88.

309 *"Brooke got nasty"*: Forrest C. Pogue, *George C. Marshall: Organizer of Victory,* 305, 307; Maurice Matloff, *Strategic Planning for Coalition Warfare, 1943–1944,* 352, 353n ; Greenfield, ed., 183–85.

309 *"peripheral and indecisive"*: Greenfield, ed., 182, 188–89; Leahy, 201; Ray S. Cline, *Washington Command Post,* 227 (*"fish or cut bait"*); Arthur Bryant, *Triumph in the West,* 35 ( *"swing the strategy"*); Mark A. Stoler, *George C. Marshall: Soldier-Statesman of the American Century,* 103 (*prayed every night*); Pogue, 294 (*"stick a knife"*); Douglas Porch, *The Path to Victory,* 474; S. W. Roskill, *The White Ensign,* 330; S. W. Roskill, *The War at Sea, 1939–1945,* 203–5; Michael Howard, *The Mediterranean Strategy in the Second World War,* 46, 70–71; John Kennedy, *The Business of War,* 301–5.

310 *Stalin gruffly threw his support:* Kent Roberts Greenfield, *American Strategy in World War II: A Reconsideration,* 34; David M. Kennedy, *Freedom from Fear,* 575 (*four words of English*); Greenfield, ed., 197; Robert Sherwood, *Roosevelt and Hopkins,* 799 (*"getatable"*); Maurice Matloff, "Mr. Roosevelt's Three Wars: FDR as War Leader," 1964, Harmon Memorial Lectures in Military History, no. 6, USAF Academy, 14 (*"perfectly friendly"*).

310 *"first claim on the resources"*: Greenfield, 40; Richard M. Leighton, "Overlord Revisited," *American Historical Review,* July 1963, 919+; Stoler, 107; Sherwood, 803 (*"could not sleep"*); Carlo D'Este, *Eisenhower: A Soldier's Life,* 467 (*"best politician"*).

310 *As for Italy:* Greenfield, ed., 191.

310 *"Large families"*: Doris Kearns Goodwin, *No Ordinary Time,* 475; OH, Ian Jacob, Verne Newton collection, "transcripts," FDR Lib (*"at arm's length"*).

310 *The prime minister did not die:* Danchev, 502; Jenkins, 727 (*whisky with soda*); Moran, 164 (*white blood cell count*); Vincent Orange, *Tedder,* 244 (*"fire had gone out"*); Pawle, 275 (*Royal Navy cook*); Churchill, 425 (*"What calm lives"*).

311 *"The Bible says"*: Gilbert, 609; Leasor, 271; WSC, *Closing the Ring*, 429 (*"becoming scan-dalous"*); Pawle, 277–80 (*"don't seem to know much"*).

311 *"Looking in his strange costume"*: Macmillan, 338; Pawle, 277–80; Gilbert, 620 (*"must be carried out"*); Warren F. Kimball, ed., *Churchill & Roosevelt: The Complete Correspondence*, vol. 2, 633 (*"should decide the battle"*).

311 *Christmas had come*: Pyle, 86; Tom Roe, *Anzio Beachhead*, 23; Glendower O. Haedge, "Memoirs of World War II," ts, n.d., Texas MFM; John F. Hummer, *An Infantryman's Journal*, 42; John Guest, *Broken Images*, 158.

312 *Had he been home*: JJT, XI-10; "History of the Peninsular Base Section," 1944, 5 vols., CMH, 8-4 HA 1 (*"morale crates"*).

312 *"Merry Typhus!"*: Spike Milligan, *Mussolini: His Part in My Downfall*, 212; Alton D. Brashear, *From Lee to Bari*, 168, 171 (*$10 per stripe*); Buckley, 252–53.

312 *Mark Clark on Christmas eve*: diary, MWC, Dec. 24, 1943, Citadel, box 64; MWC to Ann Clark, Dec. 23, 1943, Citadel, personal corr.

312 *In a Bari hospital*: George S. Bergh and Reuben F. Erickson, eds., "A History of the Twenty-sixth General Hospital," 133; S. W. Thomson, *Canadian Military History*, fall 1993, 24+; John Ellis, *On the Front Lines*, 279; Zuehlke, *Ortona*, 320–22; Strome Galloway, *A Regiment at War*, 118 (*strumming a mandolin*); Dancocks, 191 (*Vokes dined alone*).

313 *"The stars have crept low"*: Hans Juergensen, *Beachheads and Mountains*, 2; G. R. Stevens, *Fourth Indian Division*, 270; Edmund F. Ball, *Staff Officer with the Fifth Army*, 263; Ralph G. Martin, *The G.I. War*, 115 (*"no more wars"*).

313 *"I had not seen men so exhausted"*: Howard Kippenberger, *Infantry Brigadier*, 344–47; Donna Martha Budani, "Women, War, and Text: Orsognese Women's Experience in a Sector of the Italian Front in World War II," 1997, Ph.D. diss, American University, 119 (*"poor sad Christmas"*); order of the day, Dec. 25, 1943, 71st Panzer Grenadier Regt, "Intelligence Notes, No. 47," AFHQ, Feb. 22, 1944, NARA RG 407, E 47, 95-AL1-2.18.

313 *"Usual targets of opportunity"*: James R. Pritchard, ts, n.d., 68th Armored FA Bn, ASEQ, MHI, 12; censorship morale reports, Nov. 1943–June 1944, NARA RG 492, MTO adjutant general, 311.7 (*operated by flashlight*); Julian "Duney" Philips, "War Is Not All Bad," ts, n.d., 143rd Inf, Texas MFM, 2 (*"Now is the time"*); Leslie W. Bailey, *Through Hell and High Water*, 157.

313 *The bottom of the year*: "1944," *Life*, Jan. 3, 1944, 20; Greenfield, ed., 183; Kennedy, *Freedom from Fear*, 610; http://www.history.navy.mil/photos/sh-fornv/germany/gersh-s/scharn2.htm (Scharnhorst); John Ellis, *Brute Force*, table 35 (*175 German divisions*).

314 *"The campaign is heartbreakingly slow"*: JPL, 278; "Fifth Army Medical History," n.d., NARA RG 112, MTO surgeon general, 319.1, box 6, 183 (*strength of 200,000*); *Fifth Army at the Winter Line*, 87–88; Brashear, 168; "Summary of Activities," June 1, 1944, NA-TOUSA, CMH, 20 (*Battle casualties had whittled away*); MEB, "Shifting of German Units Before and During Nettuno Landing," Jan. 1956, NARA RG 319, E 145, OCMH, R-75, 36 (*six miles per month*); Coakley, 181 (*"no shipping available"*); Richard M. Leighton, "Overlord Revisited," *American Historical Review*, July 1963, 919+ ; Porch, 460 (*British ports could not handle*); StoC, ix (*"static warfare"*).

314 *"One rather wondered"*: Francis De Guingand, *Operation Victory*, 333; Farley Mowat, *And No Birds Sang*, 333.

314 *"a plan that was distinctly conservative"*: Moorehead, *Eclipse*, 60; Nigel Nicolson, *Alex: The Life of Field Marshal Earl Alexander of Tunis*, 238 (*"weeks and months of fore-thought"*), 239 (*"average brain"*); Mark M. Boatner III, *The Biographical Dictionary of World War II*, 379; "The German Operation at Anzio," Apr. 1946, German Military Document Section, Military Intelligence Div., WD, MHI, JPL, box 9 (*allowed German forces to shift*); Ronald Lewin, *Ultra Goes to War*, 343 (*better informed about his adversaries*); F. H. Hinsley et al., *British Intelligence in the Second World War*, 182, 507 (*"the Allies*

*often knew as much*"); J. Hamilton, "Italy, Sept.–Dec. 1943," n.d., Cabinet Historical Section, UK NA, CAB 101/124, 42 (*"old methodical way"*).

315 *Eisenhower privately wished:* Eisenhower Diary, HCB, DDE Lib, A-756, A-773-74, A-779; diary, MWC, Dec. 10, 1943, Citadel, box 64 (*groused about Lucas*); memo, Oct. 11, 1943, JPL, MHI, box 12 (*groused about Middleton*); Robert R. Palmer et al., *The Procurement and Training of Ground Combat Troops,* 467 (*"The battalion commander problem"*).

315 *Twenty-three German divisions: Battle,* 166–67; MEB, "Shifting of German Units," R-75 (*nearly 300,000*); Louis P. Lochner, ed., *The Goebbels Diaries, 1942–1943,* 435; Steiger, "The Campaign in Southern Italy," 59–60 (*"For two months now"*).

315 *"What will 1944 do":* JPL, 283; memoir, P. Royle, ts, 1972, IWM, 99/72/1 (*"You got the feeling"*).

316 *"A terrible year has ended":* David Hapgood and David Richardson, *Monte Cassino,* 95.

316 *A ferocious storm with gale winds:* N. P. Morrow, "Field Artillery in Italy," Feb. 2, 1944, HQ, NARA RG 334, NWC Lib, ANSCOL, AGF OR M83, box 148; Wagner, 90; Bowlby, 13 (*"pinched the enemy's song"*); Harriet Stradling, ed., *Johnny,* 251.

316 *Truscott's 3rd Division:* aide's diaries, Dec. 31, 1943, LKT Jr., GCM Lib, box 18, folder 3; LKT Jr. to Sarah, Jan. 2 and 5, 1944, LKT Jr., GCM Lib, GCM Lib, box 1, folder 6.

316 *"I do not know if you will miss me":* De Guingand, 337, appendix A; Moorehead, *Montgomery,* 175

316 *"So there we are":* B. L. Montgomery, "Reflections on the Campaign in Italy, 1943," ts, addendum, Dec. 26, 1943, IWM, BLM 48, micro, reel 4; T.E.B. Howarth, ed., *Monty at Close Quarters,* 44n (*"He was a real human"*).

317 *Eisenhower also left on the thirty-first:* Chandler, vol. 5, 14; Michael J. McKeough and Richard Lockridge, *Sgt. Mickey and General Ike,* 98; Dwight D. Eisenhower, *Crusade in Europe,* 217 (*"Allow someone else to run the war"*); OH, Henry Maitland Wilson, Apr. 3, 1947, Howard M. Smyth, SM, MHI (*hoped for three days' overlap*). Eisenhower asserted that he "exhaustively reviewed" the military situation with Wilson during Christmas dinner at La Marsa. Eisenhower, *Crusade,* 214.

317 *"rather going to seed":* Macmillan, 321; JPL, 273.

317 *He left believing he had accomplished:* Kenneth Strong, *Intelligence at the Top,* 169; DDE, "Allied Commander-in-Chief's Report, Italian Campaign," n.d., 155 (*"Elimination of Italy"*); Roskill, *The War at Sea,* 210 (*more than a thousand ships*); Anthony Eden, *The Reckoning,* 479 (*Even Stalin had conceded*).

317 *From Algiers, he would take:* Alexander S. Cochran, "Constructing a Military Coalition from Materials at Hand," Apr. 16, 1999, paper, SMH conference.

317 *"I am very disappointed":* Chandler, vol. 3, 1631, 1646n (*uneasy at Churchill's advocacy*); "Press Conference of General Eisenhower, 1430 hours, 23 Dec 1943, AFHQ Advance, Italy," MWC, Citadel, box 3 (*"Jerry is going to write off"*).

318 *The White House sent a cooler: Three Years,* 467; Dwight D. Eisenhower, *Letters to Mamie,* 161; Davis, 456 (*"Nothing seems real"*); John S. D. Eisenhower, *General Ike,* 100 (*"heavier"*); John S. D. Eisenhower, *Strictly Personal,* 51 (*"Hell, I'm going back"*); Stephen E. Ambrose, *Eisenhower: Soldier, General of the Army, President-Elect, 1890–1952,* vol. 1, 278, 280 (*absentmindedly called his wife "Kay"*).

318 *"Until we meet again":* Chandler, vol. 3, 1650.

## CHAPTER 7: A RIVER AND A ROCK

### *Colonel Warden Makes a Plan*

321 *Marrakesh in midwinter:* Seth Sherwood, "In an Ancient Desert, a Modern Oasis Beckons," *NYT,* Jan. 23, 2005; John Colville, *The Fringes of Power,* 463; http://whc.unesco.org/pg.cfm?cid=31&id_site=331; http://www.mincom.gov.ma/english/reg_cit/cities/marrakes/

marrakes.html; James Parton, *"Air Force Spoken Here,"* 229 (*"sat on his leather hassock"*); "Marrakech Air Base," n.d., in "Observations in A.B.S," NARA RG 492, MTO, pm gen'l. corr, 333 (*"statement of intercourse"*).

321 *The Red City:* Roy Jenkins, *Churchill,* 727; Lord Moran, *Churchill: Taken from the Diaries of Lord Moran,* 167; Martin Gilbert, *Winston S. Churchill,* vol. 7, 626; Gerald Pawle, *The War and Colonel Warden,* 280 (*"When the Midnight Choo-Choo"*); Duff Cooper, *Old Men Forget,* 318 (*"Colonel Warden"*).

321 *In Marrakesh he occupied La Saadia:* Lisa Lovitt-Smith, *Moroccan Interiors,* 78 (*wall mosaics*); Colville, 457–59 (*"wildly rash"*); Cooper, 318; Gilbert, 634 (Pirates of Penzance); W. H. Thompson, *I Was Churchill's Shadow,* 133 (*"certainly heavy going"*).

322 *The borrowed Cadillac roared:* Pawle, 288; Cooper, 318; Thompson, 133 (*V-for-victory*); Moran, 167–70.

322 *"Can't I ever get any commanders":* OH, C.A.P. Portal, Feb. 7, 1949, FCP, MHI; OH, C. E. Lambe, Feb. 26, 1947, FCP, MHI (*"negative as usual"*); Gilbert, 650; Cooper, 319.

322 *"Undue discretion":* Harold Macmillan, *The Blast of War, 1939–1945,* 370; Harold Macmillan, *War Diaries,* 347; Danchev, 510; Moran, 170.

323 *Churchill's "bright idea":* diary, Oct. 21, 1943, MWC, Citadel, box 64; OH, Lyman Lemnitzer, Jan. 16, 1948, SM, MHI; Martin Blumenson, "General Lucas at Anzio (1944)," Kent Roberts Greenfield, ed., *Command Decisions,* 245–50; diary, Dec. 18, 1943, MWC, Citadel, box 64; *CM,* 292 (*"destroy the best damned division"*); *SSA,* 324; *GS* V, 209.

323 *"It would be folly":* "Record of conference held by the prime minister at Tunis," Dec. 25, 1943, H. Alexander papers, UK NA, WO 214/13; H. M. Wilson, "Report by the Supreme Allied Commander Mediterranean," n.d., NARA RG 319, OCMH, historical background files, American Forces in Action, Anzio, box 119, 7–8 (*"regard our campaign"*); *SSA,* 325 (*"whoever holds Rome"*); *Calculated,* 260 (*"peter out"*); *StoC,* 352 (*"the decisive way"*).

324 *"a good idea to go around":* *StoC,* 352; Robert H. Adleman and George Walton, *Rome Fell Today,* 116 (*"hasn't been predictable"*); Greenfield, ed., 250; "Record of conference held by the prime minister at Tunis" (*"signified their agreement"*); *Three Years,* 465 (*"taken tactical command"*).

324 *"I have arrived in Italy":* Christopher Lee Lewis, "The Byzantine Invasion of North Africa, Sicily, and Italy," *Proceedings,* Nov. 1943, 1435+; John Ellis, *Brute Force,* 321 (*45,000 landing vessels*); Alan Gropman, ed., *The Big "L,"* 349 (*every major Allied campaign*).

324 *"Shipping [is] at the root":* Richard M. Leighton and Robert W. Coahley, *Global Logistics and Strategy, 1940–1943,* 697; H. M. Wilson, "Report by the Supreme Allied Commander Mediterranean," 1946, part 1, 7 (*sustain two divisions*); *GS* V, 210; James Leasor, *The Clock with Four Hands,* 273 (*"set after set"*); msg, WSC to FDR, Dec. 28, 1943, Warren F. Kimball, ed., *Churchill & Roosevelt: The Complete Correspondence,* vol. 2, 638.

324 *"Clark and I are confident":* msg, H. Alexander to Col. Warden, Jan. 4, 1944, NARA RG 331, AFHQ micro, R-369-F, box 216; OH, MWC, 1972, Forrest S. Rittgers, Jr., SOOHP, MHI, 86-88 (*three-division landing*); diary, MWC, Jan. 2 and 4, 1944, Citadel, box 65.

325 *Regardless of Fifth Army's request:* Hill/O'Neill, 1; diary, MWC, Dec. 27, 1943, Citadel, box 64; msg, WSC to H. Alexander, Dec. 26, 1943, UK NA, WO 214/13; msg, H. Alexander to WSC and A. Brooke, Dec. 1943, UK NA, WO 214/13 (*"the best American corps commander"*). Some accounts assert that Clark was not invited to the conference. Lloyd Clark, *Anzio,* 73.

325 *The conference convened at La Saadia:* Pawle, 285; Hill/O'Neill, 1; *StoC,* 303, 353; *Anzio Beachhead,* 5; *GS* V, 218.

325 *"the seamy side of the question":* Kenneth Strong, *Intelligence at the Top,* 171; OH, Kenneth W. D. Strong, Oct. 30, 1947, SM, MHI; Michael Carver, *Harding of Peterton, Field-Marshal,* 123 (*"Of course there is risk"*); Hill/O'Neill, 2.

326 *The conclave broke for supper:* Hill/O'Neill, 3; Macmillan, *War Diaries* 295 (*"sum total of their fears"*); H. Alexander, "The Allied Armies in Italy," n.d., CMH, II-25.

326 *Could the Germans quickly reinforce:* Nigel Nicolson, *Alex: The Life of Field Marshal Earl Alexander of Tunis*, 228; memo, I. Jacob to Hollis, record of Christmas conference, n.d., NARA RG 331, AFHQ micro, R-369-F, box 216; Greenfield, ed., 250 (*"unavoidable risk"*); *Calculated*, 284 (*"seal off the beachhead"*).

326 *"he is getting old":* Eisenhower Diary, Jan. 20, 1944, HCB, DDE Lib, A-995; "Hill/O'Neill," 3 (*"Not until Saturday morning"*); Nicolson, 228–30 (*"Keep a reserve"*).

326 *Bleary-eyed, they reassembled:* Hill/O'Neill, 3; JPL, Jan. 10, 1943, 295 (*"astonish the world"*); Pawle, 285 (*"I do hope, General"*); Macmillan, *The War Diaries*, 304 (*"more and more dogmatic"*).

327 *"It was a bluff":* OH, H. Alexander, Jan. 10–15, 1949, SM, CMH, Geog Files, II-5; F. H. Hinsley et al., *British Intelligence in the Second World War*, 185 (*No flinty-eyed assessment*).

327 *Moreover, the SHINGLE force was sized:* Molony V, 772; Frank James Price, *Troy H. Middleton: A Biography*, 169; corr, Troy H. Middleton to Hal C. Pattison, Sept. 8, 1964, NARA RG 319, OCMH, 2-3.7 CC3, Salerno to Cassino, box 255; Evelyn M. Cherpak, ed., *The Memoirs of Admiral H. Kent Hewitt*, 195.

327 *"Where can the enemy land?":* memo, S. Westphal, Dec. 8, 1943, VI Corps, G-2 periodic report No. 140, Feb. 1944, JPL, MHI, box 1; David Fraser, *Alanbrooke*, 398 (*Churchill continued to underestimate*).

327 *"imposed his will on the generals":* SSA, 328; W.G.F. Jackson, *Alexander of Tunis as Military Commander*, 258 (*"out of loyalty"*).

327 *"Operation SHINGLE is on!":* diary, MWC, Jan. 8, 1943, Citadel, box 65.

328 *"A unanimous agreement":* Kimball, ed., vol. 2, 657; Colville, 461 (*"garden path"*).

### *"Nothing Was Right Except the Courage"*

328 *On the chilly Sabbath morning:* Chester G. Starr, ed., *From Salerno to the Alps*, 77 (*sixteen thousand casualties*); StoC, 315; author visit, May 4, 2004; Margaret Bourke-White, *Purple Heart Valley*, 154, 176 (*"fell in gusts"*).

328 *Ahead lay a pastoral river plain:* "Engineer History, Fifth Army, Mediterranean Theater," n.d., MHI, 67, 70 (*seventy thousand aerial photos*); Molony V, 598; Martin Blumenson, *Bloody River*, 61.

329 *German "flooding program":* "Special Investigation and Interrogation Report: Operation Lightening [sic]," March 15, 1947, Military Intelligence Service, Austria, CMH, Geog Files, 370.2, 39.

329 *The highland glens above Cassino:* CtoA, 16; Frank Gervasi, "Battle at Cassino," *Collier's*, March 18, 1944, 20+; CtoA, 17; Alex Bowlby, *Countdown to Cassino*, 82; Albert Kesselring, "The Construction of Positions in the Italian Theater," Aug. 1948, FMS, #C-031, MHI, 4; Hans Bessell, "Construction of Strategic Field Fortifications in Italy," March 1947, FMS, #D-013, MHI, 3, 7–10 (*more concrete, mines, and barbed wire*).

329 *Clark now counted seven divisions:* StoA, 83–84 (*"momentum of our advance"*).

330 *In Operations Instructions No. 34:* ibid.; corr, MWC to John Meade, Sept. 22, 1955, SM, MHI, box 2; StoC, 314.

330 *Clark later denied paternity:* P. A. Crowl, "Command Decision: The Rapido River Crossing," lecture, Sept. 30, 1955, U.S. Army War College, SM, MHI, 1–2; StoC, 322; memo, "36th Division at the Rapido River, January 1944," n.d., Robert P. Patterson, WD, to U.S. Senate Committee on Military Affairs, CMH, 370.2 (*most direct route*).

330 *"As long as this condition existed":* corr, Don E. Carleton to Hal C. Pattison, Feb. 10, 1965, NARA RG 319, OCMH 2-3.7 CC3, Salerno to Cassino, box 256.

331 *The prospect of being cut to pieces:* StoC, 326; *Texas*, 295–96, 302 (*"I do not see how"*); diary, Jan. 16, 1944, FLW, HIA, box 1 (*"a tough job"*).

331 *"amiable mastiff":* Des Hickey and Gus Smith, *Operation Avalanche*, 54; "Statement by Major General Fred L. Walker, G.S.C.," Dec. 6, 1945, FLW, HIA, box 3 (*mustard burns*);

OH, Martin Blumenson, Apr. 13, 2004, author, Washington, D.C. (*excellent dancer*); notebook, n.d., FLW, HIA, box 6 (*jotted down unfamiliar words*); Lee Carraway Smith, *A River Swift and Deadly*, 4 ("*very good friends*"); OH, MWC, Rittgers (*give Walker command of the 36th*).

331 *Perhaps envious of his former protégé: Texas*, 207, 288–90 ("*Our wasteful policy*"); OH, MWC, Rittgers, 69–70 [redacted pages opened at author's request] (*Walker resented not receiving command*); Blumenson, *Bloody River*, 22 (*soldiers grumbled*).

332 *At fifty-six*: corr, FLW to Gov. Coke R. Stevenson, July 24, 1944, FLW, HIA, box 3; "Statement by Major General Fred L. Walker, G.S.C.," Dec. 6, 1945, FLW, HIA, box 3 (*Since the summer of 1942*); diary, Jan. 20, 1944, FLW, HIA, box 1 (*bad cold*).

332 "*I have mentioned the difficulties involved*": diary, Jan. 13, 16, 17, 1944, FLW, HIA, box 1; testimony, FLW, "The Rapido River Crossing," Committee on Military Affairs, U.S. House of Representatives, Feb. 20, 1946, CMH, 370.2, 26–30 (*proposed attacking up-river*); Smith, 22 ("*sounding so pessimistic*"); *Texas*, 296 ("*end in failure*"), 302 ("*We have to cross*").

332 "*sickly, whitish and weak*": Harold L. Bond, *Return to Cassino*, 27.

332 *Walker reviewed his attack plan: StoC*, 331; AAR, "Report of Operations, January 1944," 36th ID, MHI, 05-36 ("*fighting patrols*"); corr, FLW to Eric Sevareid, Feb. 26, 1946, FLW, HIA, box 3.

333 *Those were formidable*: memo, William A. Walker, "Report of Interview with Maj. Gen. Fred L. Walker," Feb. 4, 1946, MWC, Citadel, box 39, folder 9; testimony, R. J. Butchers, II Corps G-3, Jan. 24, 1944, IG investigation, CMH, 370.2 ("*very well organized*"); AAR, 141st Inf, Feb. 9, 1944, Aaron W. Wyatt, Jr., ASEQ, MHI (*Of seven patrol boats*); AAR, Thaddeu J. Session, "111th Engineer Combat Battalion, Operations in Italy, Jan. 1944," MHI (*four miles per hour*); "Synopsis of 36th Inf. Div. Activity," Jan. 24, 1944, II Corps, IG investigation, CMH, 370.2; Donato D'Epiro, *S. Angelo in Theodice*, 155 (*demolitionists had blown the bridge*); "Report on Reconnaissance of Rapido River, 16 Dec. 1943," Dec. 20, 1943, in "History of 81st Armored Reconnaissance Battalion," 1st AD, John F. Davis papers, USMA Arch, box 2 (*river had been dredged*); Smith, 24 ("*shoe-mouth deep*"), 25 ("*traumatic amputations*"); Clifford W. Dorman, "Too Soon for Heroes," ts, n.d., 19th Combat Engineers, author's possession, 73 (*hands and knees*); Alfred M. Beck et al., *The Corps of Engineers: The War Against Germany*, 191.

333 *Keyes listened intently*: OH, Robert W. Porter, Jr., June 30, 1950, NARA RG 319, OCMH, CA, box 005, 1 ("*unsound*"); OH, Robert W. Porter, Jr., 1981, John N. Sloan, SOOHP, MHI, 310 ("*Big Cassino*"), 324–31 ("*fishbowl*"), 323–24; OH, GK, Sept 22, 1955, Philip A. Crowl, SM, MHI, 1; OH, GK, Feb. 14, 1950, NARA RG 319, OCMH, CA, box 005: *StoC*, 326–27.

333 "*If the enemy withdraws forces now*": memo, GK to MWC, "Impending Operations," Dec. 28, 1943, II Corps IG, CMH, 370.2; memo, GK to MWC, Jan. 13, 1944, II Corps IG, CMH, 370.2 ("*effort of the 46th Division*"); Blumenson, *Bloody River*, 70 ("*gradualism*").

334 *Geoff Keyes knew his business*: Perhaps stopping Thorpe was relative; the West Point yearbook found his running in 1912 "the most wonderful and spectacular ever seen on our field." Army lost to the Carlisle Indian School, 27–6. Obit, *Assembly*, Sept. 1973, 121; *Howitzer*, 1913, 168.

334 *Son of a cavalryman*: Blumenson, *Bloody River*, 46–47; memo, A. C. Wedemeyer, Aug. 24, 1943, NARA RG 319, OCMH, 2-3.7 CC2, AFG file no. 319.1, box 247, appendix C ("*calm, deliberate, circumspect*"); Adleman and Walton, 89–90 ("*everything but a sense of humor*"); Chandler, vol. 3, 1465 ("*intensely human*").

334 "*God forbid*": GK, Jan. 16–18, 1943.

334 "*too cavalry*": Blumenson, *Bloody River*, 46–49; memo, William A. Walker, "Report of Interview" ("*visionary*").

335 *both men remained mute:* GK, "Statement Covering the Rapido River Operation, 20–22 Jan. 1944," Sept. 10, 1946, WD, in "The Rapido River Crossing," CMH, 370.2; testimony, R. J. Butchers, II Corps G-3, Jan. 24, 1944, IG investigation, CMH, 370.2.

335 *"We have done everything":* diary, Jan. 20, 1944, FLW, HIA, box 1.

335 *Sant'Angelo was a drab farm village:* author visits, Sept. 1995, May 2004, Nov. 2006; D'Epiro, 135–38, 151–56 (*"she-wolf"*).

335 *Three hundred impressed Italians:* Don Whitehead, "Beachhead Don," 78–80; "Investigation and Interrogation Report: Operation Lightening [*sic*]," 70 (*"strongest point"*); analysis, "Effect of Rapido Operation on German Plans and Dispositions," n.d., MWC, Citadel, box 39 (*"strongest single German division"*); Tenth Army journal cited in memo, Thomas North, "Rapido Operation Action," March 18, 1946, MWC, Citadel, box 39 (*"enemy has crept up"*).

335 *"The waiting is the worst part":* Matthew Parker, *Monte Cassino,* 92 (*"oil my tommy gun"*); Molony V, 609–11; Ralph S. Mavrogordato, "XIV Panzer Corps Defensive Operations Along the Garigliano, Gari, and Rapido Rivers, 17–31 January, 1944," Nov. 1955, NARA RG 319, E 145, R-78, 20; Robin Neillands, *Eighth Army,* 260–72 (*"Moving off in trucks"*); Field Marshal Lord Carver, *The Imperial War Museum Book of the War in Italy, 1943–1945,* 113 (*"blood wagons"*).

336 *They gained the far bank:* StoC, 320; John Ellis, *Cassino: The Hollow Victory,* 77 (*"mine marsh"*); Mavrogordato, "XIV Panzer Corps Defensive Operations," 20 (*storm the Liri Valley*).

336 *46th Division soldiers, drawn from Yorkshire:* Gregory Blaxland, *Alexander's Generals,* 33; David Scott Daniell, *The Royal Hampshire Regiment,* vol. 3, 153 (*"bleak, disturbing place"*).

336 *"Then nothing went right":* Daniell, 155, 157; "Engineer History, Fifth Army," 73; "Air Support of Fifth Army for Rapido River and Cassino Attacks," Apr. 7, 1944, HQ, Fifth Army, air support control, Robert J. Woods papers, "Report on Cassino Operations," MHI; Starr, ed., 88 (*Boats bucked and spun*); Blaxland, 38; StoC, 320.

336 *A few hours later the burly British:* Blaxland, 39; diary, FLW, Jan. 20, 1944, HIA, box 1.

336 *"Always the same story":* diary, GK, Jan. 20, 1943; *Calculated,* 269 (*"lack of strong aggressive leadership"*); "Engineer History, Fifth Army," 73; diary, MWC, Jan. 20, 1943, Citadel, box 65; Brian Harpur, *The Impossible Victory,* 121, 125 (*"Man of Destiny"*).

338 *"It is essential that I make the attack":* diary, MWC, Jan. 20, 1943, Citadel, box 65.

338 *Since the Salerno landings nineteen weeks earlier:* testimony, Andrew F. Price, XO, 141st Inf, "The Rapido River Crossing," U.S. House, 26–30 (*60 percent*); Smith, 44 (*three-quarters of the officers*); corr, John D. Goode to Robert L. Wagner, n.d., Texas MFM (*"no longer a team"*); Fred Walker, Jr., "Mission Impossible at Cassino," ts, 1986, MHI, 3, 8 (*units were understrength*); notebook, Will Lang, n.d., USMA Arch (*New bazooka teams*); corr, John E. Phillips to chief of staff, U.S. Army, July 8, 1946, CMH, Geog Files, 370.2 (*"physically, mentally, and morally"*).

338 *Several hundred replacements showed up:* OH, Paul D. Adams, 1975, Irving Monclova and Marlin Lang, SOOHP, MHI; Ray Wells, "Battalion Commander," *Fighting 36th Historical Quarterly,* spring 1992, part 2 (*"some would die"*); notebook, Will Lang, n.d., USMA Arch.

338 *"The mission should never":* Texas, 305–6; StoC, 332 (*extra bandoliers*); Smith, 36 (*"handed a cigar"*).

338 *At 7:30 P.M., sixteen artillery battalions:* narrative of events, and testimony, Andrew F. Price, XO, 141st Inf, 26–30; John E. Krebs, *To Rome and Beyond,* 48–49; Hamilton H. Howze, *A Cavalryman's Story,* 90–91; Brooks E. Kleber and Dale Birdsell, *The Chemical Warfare Service: Chemicals in Combat,* 443 (*smoke spiraled vertically*).

339 *The attack was to fall across a three-mile front:* corr, Phillips to chief of staff, July 8, 1946; Blumenson, *Bloody River,* 91.

339 *Along the rail tracks south of Trocchio:* AAR, Arthur J. Lazenby, 19th Engineer Regt, S-3, n.d., NARA RG 407, ENGR-19-03.0; Robert L. Wagner, *The Texas Army,* 103; Blumenson, *Bloody River,* 81; testimony, Leon F. Morand, II Corps asst. engineer, Jan. 24, 1944, IG investigation, CMH, 370.2 *(twenty rubber boats);* Herman M. Volheim, "The Operations of the 3rd Battalion, 143rd Infantry in the Attacks Across the Rapido River," 1949, IS *(Wooden catwalks);* Howze, 89 *(two hundred tanks waiting).*

340 *Hoisting the heavy boats:* "Operations on Rapido River," 141st Inf, Jan. 23, 1944, in AAR, "Report of Operations, January 1944," 36th ID *(rush of eastbound German shells);* "History of the 26th Infantry in the Present Struggle," ts, n.d., MRC FDM, 1991.25, box 445, 38; Flint Whitlock, *The Rock of Anzio,* 109 *("blood turn solid");* Franz Kurowski, *Battleground Italy, 1943–1945,* 78 *("Hitler's bandsaw");* testimony, John C. L. Adams, in IG investigation, NATOUSA, March 1, 1944, NARA RG 492, 333.5, box 1055 *("Riflemen tossed away");* Paul W. Pritchard, "Smoke Generator Operations in the Mediterranean and European Theaters of Operation," ts, 1985, U.S. Army Chemical School, 62 *(thousand smoke pots);* AAR, 68th Armored Field Artillery Bn, Feb. 1944, NARA RG 338, II Corps historical section, box 145 *("check all shells for mustard").*

340 *Little else went right:* "Operations on Rapido River," 141st Inf, Jan. 23, 1944; Wagner, 105; StoC, 333; Smith, 37, 41; testimony, R. J. Butchers, II Corps G-3, Jan 25, 1944, IG investigation, CMH, 370.2 *(Paddles, rifles, and human limbs);* AAR, 2nd Bn, 19th Engineer Regt, "Rapido River Crossing," Feb. 6, 1944, NARA RG 407, ENGR-19-03.0 *(switched to a brown cord);* AAR, 141st Inf Regt, Feb. 9, 1944, Aaron W. Wyatt, Jr., ASEQ, MHI *("hard when you're dying");* Frank Gervasi, *The Violent Decade,* 545 *("walked as men do in a cow pasture").*

340 *"a streetcar coming down sideways":* Smith, 42; Warner Wisian, "Reminiscence," ts, Nov. 1995, 141st Inf Regt, ASEQ, MHI *(dragged the cumbersome rubber boats).*

341 *Soldiers fell without ever firing a shot:* summary, IG investigation, NATOUSA, March 1, 1944, NARA RG 492, 333.5, box 1055; Smith, 38 *("Eight of us drowned"),* 41–42 *("octopus in a crooked sack");* corr, Phillips to chief of staff, July 8, 1946 *("I could hear paddles slapping").*

341 *helmets to scrape a few inches:* Warner Wisian, "Reminiscence"; "Report on Cassino Operations," June 5, 1944, HQ, Fifth Army, Robert J. Wood papers, MHI *(Thirty-one thousand artillery rounds);* corr, Goode to Wagner, n.d., Texas MFM *("tuning fork");* testimony, Leon F. Morand, Jan 24, 1944, IG investigation, CMH, 370.2 *(four MG-42s);* AAR, 2nd Bn, 19th Engineer Regt.

341 *"like a Judas goat":* corr, Goode to Wagner, n.d., Texas MFM; StoC, 335–36; AAR, "Operations on Rapido River," 141st Inf *("So many litter carriers");* Texas, 315–16 *("there were plenty").*

342 *Engineers stretched a net:* testimony, Andrew F. Price, 26–30.

342 *"I knew something was wrong":* Wagner, 92.

342 *Two crossing sites had been selected:* Volheim, "The Operations of the 3rd Battalion, 143rd Infantry"; AAR, "143rd Infantry," Jan. 1944, ASEQ, MHI; StoC, 337.

342 *lashing the buttocks, backs, and legs:* "Report on Cassino Operations," June 5, 1944, HQ, Fifth Army, Robert J. Wood papers, MHI, 7; AAR, "143rd Infantry," Jan. 1944, ASEQ, MHI *(Facing annihilation).*

342 *Five hundred yards downstream:* AAR, William H. Martin, "Narrative of Rapido Crossing," Jan. 27, 1944, 143rd Inf Regt, 36th ID, MHI, 05-36; StoC, 338; Volheim, "The Operations of the 3rd Battalion, 143rd Infantry" *("flashes seemed to turn the fog").*

342 *"I had to throw dirt at it":* testimony, Clarence D. Dalton, II Corps, Jan. 25, 1944, IG investigation, CMH, 370.2.

343 *"The attack last night was a failure":* diary, Jan. 21, 1943, FLW, HIA, box 1; Blumenson, *Bloody River,* 102.

343 *"bend every effort"*: StoC, 341; GK, "Statement Covering the Rapido River Operation" (*staff officers with a clipboard*).

343 *"Anybody can draw lines"*: diary, Jan. 21, 1944, FLW, HIA, box 1.

343 *An Ultra intercept two nights earlier:* Hinsley et al., 510–11; MEB, "Shifting of German Units Before and During Nettuno Landing," Jan. 1956, NARA RG 319, E 145, OCMH, R-75, 26; Blaxland, 38; Ralph Bennet, "Ultra and Some Command Decisions," in Walter Laquer, ed., *The Second World War: Essays in Military and Political History*, 223; StoC, 319 (*"a slender thread"*).

343 *"a dead man every ten yards"*: Smith, 60; Bill Hartung, ts, n.d., 143rd Inf, Texas MFM website, 36th ID Assoc, www.kwanah.com/36Division/pstoc.htm (*"what we were walking on"*).

344 *On the division left, the 143rd Infantry:* Volheim, "The Operations of the 3rd Battalion"; StoC, 341, 343 (*"couple of fingers shot off"*); Smith, 57 (*"my last old day"*).

344 *neglected to bring an air compressor:* Leonard B. Gallagher, II Corps engineer, "Memo C/S," Jan. 24, 1944, addendum, IG investigation, CMH, 370.2; Blumenson, *Bloody River*, 105–15 (*found no survivors*); AAR, 2nd Bn, 19th Engineer Regt (*"draw more of our troops over"*); StoC, 351 (*Some soldiers had balked*).

344 *"Fire wholeheartedly"*: Wagner, 112–14. Another account quotes Chapin's war cry as, "Fire foolhardily, men, fire foolhardily!" Smith, 53–54.

344 *Corraled by minefields and barbed wire:* The 141st Infantry bridgehead on January 22 was estimated as two hundred yards deep by six hundred yards wide. "Synopsis of 36th Inf. Div. Activity," Jan. 24, 1944, II Corps, IG investigation, CMH, 370.2; Wagner, 114 (*"May I shake hands?"*).

344 *GIs inched forward:* Russell J. Darkes, "Twenty-five Years in the Military," ts, n.d., Texas MFM, 28; affidavit, George G. Davis, 16th Engineer Bn, n.d., IG investigation, CMH, 370.2 (*"Get out of your holes"*); Robert Wallace, *The Italian Campaign*, 116–17 (*"pushed his body along"*).

345 *A private sobbed:* Ralph G. Martin, "Rapido Fight Shapes Up as One of Toughest Yet," Jan. 25, 1943, *Stars and Stripes*, 1; Gervasi, 544 (PIECES); Allan Palmer, "Casualty Survey, Cassino, Italy," *Wound Ballistics*, 536–37 (*"definitive treatment"*).

345 *Certainly the doctors were busy:* Charles M. Wiltse, *The Medical Department: Medical Service in the Mediterranean and Minor Theaters*, 244; Smith, 72, 74 (*"Patch up these holes"*).

345 *Three hundred German artillery rounds:* AAR, "Report of Operations, January 1944," 36th ID, chronology; GK, Jan. 22, 1944 (*"Something wrong"*); testimony, Leonard B. Gallagher, II Corps engineer, Jan. 24, 1944, and Wade M. Green, II Corps assistant engineer, Jan. 25, 1944, IG investigation, CMH, 370.2; AAR, 2nd Bn, 19th Engineer Regt (*"Talking or coughing drew fire"*); AAR, "Report of Operations, January 1944," 36th ID, chronology (*"no work being done"*).

345 *Smoke hardly helped:* Kleber and Birdsell, 444–45 (*complained about German smoke*); testimony, Henry H. Carden, XO, 143rd Inf, IG investigation, March 1, 1944, NATOUSA, NARA RG 492, 333.5, box 1055; testimony, Kenneth F. Zitzman, II Corps signal officer, Jan. 27, 1944, IG investigation, CMH, 370.2 (*only fifty yards*).

346 *"a pathetic inertia"*: Blumenson, *Bloody River*, 116; testimony, William B. Chase, II Corps asst. G-3, Jan. 25, 1944, IG investigation, CMH, 370.2 (*"The situation as I saw it"*); GK, "Statement Covering the Rapido River Operation"; *Texas*, 311–13 (*"groggy"*).

346 *But Clark in a phone call:* GK, Jan. 22, 1944; diary, FLW, Jan. 22, 1944, HIA, box 1 (*"not going to do it anyway"*); memo, William A. Walker, "Report of Interview" (*"might as well call it off"*).

346 *Clark "seemed inclined to find fault"*: GK, Jan. 23, 1944; diary, FLW, Jan. 22, 1944, HIA, box 1 (*"I have done everything possible"*); Krebs, 50 (*"Too many damned Germans"*).

346 *"Tell me what happened":* diary, GK, Jan. 23, 1944; diary, FLW, Jan. 23, 1944, HIA, box 7.

347 *As soon as Clark and Keyes drove off:* memo, W. H. Wilbur, Jan. 23, 1944, FLW, HIA, box 7; diary, FLW, Jan. 23, 1944, HIA, box 7.

347 *By midday on Sunday:* Clifford H. Peek, Jr., ed., *Five Years, Five Countries, Five Campaigns,* 39; AAR, "Report of Operations, January 1944," 36th ID, chronology; *StoC,* 346; Ray Wells, "Battalion Commander" (*deflected by the Parker pen*); Smith, 62–63 (*"I guess it's your leg"*).

347 *swam the river with one foot blown off:* Peek, ed., 39; Shelby Foote, *The Civil War,* vol. 2, 520 (*inured to supplication*); AAR, "Report of Operations, January 1944," 36th ID (*"American firing had ceased"*); Bruce L. Barger, *The Texas 36th Division,* 170–71 (*"I was never the same"*).

347 *Official medical records:* Wiltse, 244n.

347 *Some counts were a bit lower:* corr, Robert P. Patterson, WD, n.d., and corr, WD, Apr. 3, 1946, in "The Rapido River Crossing," U.S. House, 31; *StoC,* 346; memo, Thomas North to A. Gruenther, "Rapido Operation Action," March 18, 1946, and attached note to Gruenther, Apr. 5, 1944, MWC, Citadel, box 39; Wagner, 121n.

347 *Clark would accuse Walker:* OH, MWC, Rittgers, 71. Redacted pages opened at author's request.

347 *The Germans found 430 American bodies:* analysis, "Effect of Rapido Operation on German Plans and Dispositions," n.d., MWC, Citadel, box 39; diary, FLW, Jan. 23, 1944, HIA, box 7 (*"Freuen wir uns"*).

348 *"I had 184 men":* William L. Allen, *Anzio: Edge of Disaster,* 39; Wagner, 92; testimony, Andrew F. Price, 26–30 (*Two scarecrow battalions*); AAR, 2nd Bn, 19th Engineer Regt (*"bad tangled mess"*); Bowlby, 171 (*"crying halt"*).

348 *Clark soon summoned Walker:* Texas, 322–23,

348 *"No, you are doing all right":* memo, William A. Walker, "Report of Interview"; *Texas,* 322, 325 (*"I am marked for relief"*); OH, Adams, 1975, Monclova and Lang (*"no sins of commission"*).

348 *"a series of mishaps":* StoC, 350; *Calculated,* 282 (*"If I am to be accused"*).

349 *"Some blood had to be spilled":* StoC, 347–48; *Battle,* 181; Blumenson, *Bloody River,* 127 (*failed to enlighten Walker*).

349 *"From a military standpoint":* Wagner, 227; OH, Frido von Senger u. Etterlin, Sept. 22, 1955, Philip A. Crowl, SM, MHI, 2; MEB, "Shifting of German Units Before and During Nettuno Landing," 27; Mavrogordato, "XIV Panzer Corps Defensive Operations," 44.

349 *"The attack was insufficiently planned":* Charles W. Pence, "An Interview with Genfldm Albert Kesselring, Rapido River Crossing," May 6, 1946, ETHINT 71, Don E. Carleton papers, HIA, box 1; Wallace, 113 (*"this ain't the place"*); Lloyd M. Wells, *From Anzio to the Alps,* 50 (*"untainted by association"*).

349 *"edge of mutiny":* corr, Goode to Wagner, n.d., Texas MFM; C. L. Sulzberger, *A Long Row of Candles,* 231; AAR, "143rd Infantry," Jan. 1944, ASEQ, MHI (*"cannon fodder"*); Blumenson, *Bloody River,* 142 (*"faulty orders"*).

349 *That resolution would be revivied:* StoC, 351; "The Rapido River Crossing," U.S. House, Feb. 20 and March 18, 1946; Wagner, 224 (*"Walker's mental attitude"*).

350 *"Nothing was right except the courage":* Parker, 124.

350 *"den englischen Kommandeur":* diary, FLW, Jan. 23, 1944, box 7; Wagner, 123 (*towels and iodine*).

350 *They found a few survivors:* Bill Adler, ed., *World War II Letters;* Ray Wells, "Battalion Commander" (*half his face blown away*).

350 *For three hours they gathered the dead:* Texas, 318; notebook, Will Lang, n.d., USMA Arch (*German photographers*); Hal Boyle, quoted in Gervasi, 546 (*"blow that place all to hell"*).

350 *The short peace ended:* Bond, 49; AAR, "Report of Operations, January 1944," 36th ID; Smith, 107; Sulzberger, 223 (*ravenous dogs*).

### The Show Must Go On

351 *Much has happened through antiquity:* Virgil, *The Aeneid,* trans. Robert Fagles, 197; H. V. Morton, *A Traveller in Southern Italy,* 275–76 (*sixty trapdoors*); Norman Lewis, *Naples '44,* 154 (*lions here refused to eat*); http://www.geocities.com/lorensophia/bio.html.

351 *the staging for* SHINGLE *neared completion:* "Outline Plan, Operation SHINGLE," Fifth Army, Jan. 12, 1944, Robert J. Wood papers, MHI; S. W. Roskill, *White Ensign,* 333 (*four-hundred-ship armada*); AAR, "Mounting and Initial Phase of Operation SHINGLE," VI Corps, March 15, 1944, NARA RG 407, 206-3.0, box 3740 (*eighty-four LSTs*); Field-Marshal Lord Wilson, *Eight Years Overseas,* 193 (*meteorologists for days*); SSA, 334.

351 *A festive mood:* Fred Sheehan, *Anzio: Epic of Bravery,* 35; Wells, 51 (*Columns of jeeps*); SSA, 333 (*Italians vendors sang out*); Peter Verney, *Anzio 1944,* 29 (*Irish Guardsmen marched*); Leo G. Meyer, "Strategy and Logistical History: MTO," ts, n.d., CMH, 2-3.7 CC5, XXII-8; F. J. Lowry, "The Naval Side of the Anzio Invasion," *Proceedings,* Jan. 1954, 22+ (*portable organ*); diary, Robert M. Marsh, Jan. 21, 1944, 81st Armored Reconnaissance Bn, 1st AD, ASEQ, MHI.

352 *Bum boats swarmed:* Verney, 29; diary, William Russell Hinckley, Jan. 1944, author's possession (*"dagoes were fast"*); Hans Juergensen, *Beachheads and Mountains,* 27 ("*The show must go on*").

352 *Robert Capa arrived:* Robert Capa, *Slightly Out of Focus,* 120; Robert W. Black, *Rangers in World War II,* 136 (*6615th Ranger Force*).

352 *Boarding the* Princess Beatrix: AAR, "Report of Actions," 1st Ranger Bn, Jan. 22–Feb. 5, 1944, USMA, micro, MP63-8, roll 1; Anders Kjar Arnbal, *The Barrel-Land Dance Hall Rangers,* 217; Verney, 26 (*"love and nickel beer"*).

352 *"All that fanfare":* Edmund F. Ball, *Staff Officer with the Fifth Army,* 281–82.

353 *"no inclination to lighten burdens":* CM, 295; JPL, 305 (*turnover of lieutenants*); aide's diaries, Jan. 21, 1944, LKT Jr. papers, GCM Lib, box 18, folder 3 (*silver nitrate*).

353 *"I have many misgivings":* JPL, 322–23.

353 *The commander of VI Corps:* JPL, 141 (*iron-tipped cane*), 310 (*"I feel every year"*); Raleigh Trevelyan, *Rome '44,* 42 ("*Father Christmas*"); D.H.L. Fitzgerald, *History of the Irish Guards in the Second World War,* 201 (*"layers of overcoats"*).

353 *Born in West Virginia:* Benjamin S. Persons, *Relieved of Command,* 82; JPL, 2; OH, MWC, Rittgers, 66 (*privately preferred*).

353 *Lucas drove a jeep:* JPL, 145, 217 (*"unutterable swine"*); Wynford Vaughan-Thomas, *Anzio,* 30 (*"by the yard"*); Allen, 46; Carver, *Harding of Petherton,* 125; Ball, 316 (*"never seemed to want to hurt"*); Nicolson, 233 (*"no presence"*); John Nelson, "Always a Grenadier," ts, 1982, LHC, 38 (*"our spirits sank"*4); L. James Binder, *Lemnitzer,* 118–20 (*yellow fever*).

354 *"I think too often of my men":* JPL, 230, 295 (*"led to slaughter"*), 305 (*"*OVERLORD *would be unnecessary"*), 320, 322 ; Greenfield, ed., 254 (*"desperate attack"*); OH, JPL, May 24, 1948, SM, MHI; John S. D. Eisenhower, *They Fought at Anzio: A Study in Command* (forthcoming, University of Missouri Press, 2007), mss 178 (*last will and testament*).

354 *Could Alexander and others have:* Greenfield, ed., 256; weekly intelligence summary, No. 74, Jan. 24, 1944, AFHQ, CMH, Geog files, Italy, 370.2, 6 (*"very questionable"*); "Outline Plan, Operation SHINGLE," Jan. 12, 1943, Fifth Army, Robert J. Wood papers, MHI (*"lowering of morale"*); *Anzio Beachhead,* 6–7 (*no more than 31,000 Germans*); memo, E. Hughes to W. B. Smith, Feb. 1, 1944, Walter Bedell Smith papers, DDE Lib, box 7 (*"entertainment fund"*).

354 *Lucas beheld a different vision*: "Outline Plan, SHINGLE," Jan. 18, 1944, VI Corps, G-2, JPL papers, MHI, box 11; memo, Joseph L. Langevin, VI Corps G-2, to JPL, Jan. 4, 1944, JPL papers, MHI, box 12 (*"even under favorable conditions"*); JPL, 305 (*"Gallipoli"*).

354 *"John, there is no one"*: JPL, 305.

355 *Under Alexander's instructions to Clark*: Greenfield, ed., 251.

355 *"seize and secure a beachhead"*: "Outline Plan, Operation SHINGLE," Jan. 12, 1944, Fifth Army, NARA RG 331, AFHQ micro, R 97-I, box 270; Greenfield, ed., 251–53 (*Clark remained deliberately vague*); diary, MWC, Jan. 9, 1944, Citadel, box 65 (*"feature duster"*).

355 *In a private message*: JPL, 307.

355 *"Don't stick your neck out"*: JPL, 333; OH, JPL, May 24, 1948, SM, MHI (*"goddam Rome"*).

355 *The XII Air Support Command*: "Operation Plan SHINGLE," Jan. 8, 1944, XII Air Support Command, JPL papers, MHI, box 11; "Notes by Comd 1 (Br) Division," Jan. 2, 1944 (*"advance north towards fulfillment"*), and Jan. 20, 1944 (*"at last talking of plans"*) William R. C. Penney papers, LHC, Penney 8/2; Field Order no. 19, Jan. 15, 1944, VI Corps, NARA RG 319, OCMH, historical background files, American Forces in Action, Anzio, box 119; Nigel Hamilton, *Master of the Battlefield*, 441 (*"complete nonsense"*).

356 *The British failed to disembark*: AAR, "The First Division in Action," Apr. and July 1944, Philip L. E. Wood papers, LHC, Wood 2/2; Meyer, "Strategy and Logistical History: MTO," XXII-11 (*only eleven of thirty-seven*); J. W. Totten, "Anzio Artillery," ts, 1947, CGSC, Ft. L, CARL N-2253.6, 7; SSA, 332; JPL, 321 (*"I stood on the beach"*).

356 *"If this is to be a forlorn hope"*: diary, MWC, Jan. 19, 1944, Citadel, box 65 (*"overwhelming mismanagement"*); CM, 304 (*"I've got your report"*).

356 *land of omen and divination*: Livy, *The War with Hannibal*, trans. Aubrey de Sélincourt, 89, 94.

356 *ancient sailors' injunction*: Carver, *The Imperial War Museum Book of the War in Italy*, 119, 120 (*"more like a review"*); aide's diaries, Jan. 21, 1944, LKT Jr. papers, GCM Lib, box 18, folder 3 (*at 5:20 A.M.*); *Anzio Beachhead*, 14 (*Others snoozed*); Robert M. Hill and Elizabeth Craig, *In the Wake of War*, 55; diary, Hinckley, Jan. 1944 (*"Most talk is of home"*).

357 *"More training is certainly necessary"*: JPL, 319, 284–85 (*"Little Big Horn"*).

## CHAPTER 8: PERDITION

### *"Something's Happening"*

359 *Only the bakers were astir*: OH, Silvano Casaldi, director, Museum of the Allied Landings, Nettuno, May 7–8, 2004; e-mail, Silvano Casaldi to author, May 25, 2004; C.R.S. Harris, *Allied Administration of Italy, 1943–1945*, 160 (*coastal exclusion zone*); Francesco Rossi and Silvano Casaldi, *Those Days at Nettuno*, 39–41.

359 *Dusted with flour*: Rossi and Casaldi, 32–39, 44–50, 54–55; Frank M. Snowden, *The Conquest of Malaria: Italy, 1900–1962*, 186.

359 *"Keep still a moment"*: Rossi and Casaldi, 44–50.

360 *Three miles offshore*: aide's diaries, Jan. 22, 1944, LKT Jr., papers, GCM Lib, box 18, folder 3; Charles Moran, "The Anzio-Nettuno Landings, January 1944," n.d., SEM, NHC, box 49, 31; memo, Henry W. Noel, scout boat officer, "Report of marking of Ranger beach for SHINGLE," Jan. 23, 1944, SEM, NHC, box 47; *Anzio Beachhead*, 14; JPL, 325; AAR, "Beach Landing," May 30, 1944, PBS Branch, Military Intelligence Div, WD, NARA RG 334, NWC Lib, box 491 (*"a tremendous noise"*).

360 *Before the war*: Wynford Vaughan-Thomas, *Anzio*, 10–11; Frank Gervasi, *The Violent Decade*, 527–28; L. V. Bertarelli, *Southern Italy*, 246; William Shakespeare, *The Tragedy of Coriolanus*, act V, scene 6; Plutarch, *The Parallel Lives*, http://penelope.uchicago.edu/

Thayer/E/Roman/Texts/Plutarch/Lives/Coriolanus*.html; Raleigh Trevelyan, *Rome '44*, 41, 71; *SSA*, 335 (*Fortune*).

360 *Anchoring the VI Corps left flank:* AAR, "Mounting and Initial Phase of Operation SHINGLE," March 15, 1944, VI Corps, NARA RG 407, 206-3.0, box 3740, 4; *SSA*, 339 ("*No amount of shouting*"); AAR, A. G. Young, 3rd Beach Group, March 15, 1944, UK NA, CAB 106/393, 2 ("*waste of time*"); Vaughan-Thomas, 3 ("*half-plucked fowl*").

361 *twelve-foot lanes were cleared:* AAR, "Beach Landing," May 30, 1944, PBS Branch, WD, Military Intelligence Div, NARA RG 334, NWC Lib, box 491; John Lardner, "Anzio, February 10th," *The New Yorker Book of War Pieces*, 260–61 (*sleeping in a cowshed*); D.J.L. Fitzgerald, *History of the Irish Guards in the Second World War*, 216 ("*very gentlemanly*").

361 *Truscott's 3rd Division made land:* Unable to secure a license, the casino had never opened. Author visit, May 7, 2004; OH, Casaldi; William O. Darby and William H. Baumer, *Darby's Rangers: We Led the Way*, 147; Anders Kjar Arnbal, *The Barrel-Land Dance Hall Rangers*, 218 (*Christmas tree*); "Report on Enemy Demolitions at Anzio-Nettuno," March 1, 1944, AFHQ, G-2, CARL, N-6961 (*twenty tons of explosives*); Trevelyan, 43 (*Wehrmacht rustlers*).

361 "*could not believe my eyes*": JPL, 325; diary, MWC, Jan. 22, 1944, Citadel, box 65 ("*Paris-Bordeaux*"); *Calculated*, 288.

361 *Truscott made for shore:* aide's diaries, Jan. 22, 1944; *SSA*, 341; *StoC*, 359 (*blowing up bridges*).

362 *By sunrise at 7:30:* "The Mounting and Initial Phase of Operation SHINGLE," 4; Rossi and Casaldi, 101–3 (*Soldiers liberated six women*).

362 *DUKWs rolled through the streets:* film, "Liberation of Rome," Combat Report No. 1, 1944, NARA RG 111, CR001; Lardner, "Anzio, February 10th," 48; Milton Bracker, "When the Fight Means Kill or Be Killed," *NYT Magazine*, May 28, 1944, 10 ("*dusty, sweaty*"); Vaughan-Thomas, 91 ("*Move on, superman*"); Don Whitehead, "*Beachhead Don*," 100–103 ("*did not miss a man*").

362 *Success brought sightseers:* diary, MWC, Jan. 22, 1944, Citadel, box 65; S. W. Roskill, *The War at Sea, 1939–1945*, 305 (*Anzio's port*).

362 "*a chief umpire visiting*": David Erskin, *The Scots Guards, 1919–1955*, 201; Fitzgerald, 218 ("*I am very satsified*"); Nigel Nicolson, *Alex: The Life of Field Marshal Earl Alexander of Tunis*, 231 (*two men complimented Lucas*); Vaughan-Thomas, 51 ("*they concurred*").

362 *Left alone to command his battle:* The VI Corps command post formally moved ashore at two P.M. on January 23. "The Mounting and Initial Phase of Operation SHINGLE," 6; author visit, May 7, 1944; Rossi and Casaldi, 158 (*Sycamores ringed*); JPL, 337 (*brandy glass*). By another account, the half-empty glass contained wine. Rossi and Casaldi, 158.

362 *By midnight on D-day:* daily troop strength, Jan. 22, 1944, JPL papers, MHI, box 12; "The Mounting and Initial Phase of Operation SHINGLE," 5–6; *StoC*, 359 ("*very hard to believe*").

362 *White haze scarped the hills:* Bertarelli, 233; Trevelyan, 41 (*riding a white mule*), 54.

362 "*We knew the lights meant*": JPL, 340; Darby and Baumer, 149.

362 *Thirty-four miles from this window:* Molony V, 648; "Miscellaneous Intelligence," Jan. 10, 1944, VI Corps, JPL papers, MHI, box 11 (BOTANY); *StoC*, 385.

362 "*only sixteen miles from Rome*": Milton Bracker, "Harbor Captured," *NYT*, Jan. 23, 1944; "Censorship Takes Anzio," *Time*, Feb. 28, 1944, 46 ("*Alexander's brave troops*").

364 *The first alarm had come:* Molony V, 661; Vaughan-Thomas, 55 (*panicked officers*); "The Allied Landing at Nettuno-Anzio," German Naval Command war logs, Jan. 22, 1944, NARA RG 334, NWC Lib, ANSCOL, box 645 ("*a very bad time*").

364 "*There is not the slightest chance*": *StoC*, 319; A. G. Steiger, "The Italian Command, 4 Jan.–4 June 1944," July 1948, historical section, Canadian Army HQ, report #20, MHI, 6 ("*next four to six weeks*"); "The German Operation at Anzio," Apr. 1946, German Mili-

tary Document Section, Military Intelligence Div, WD, JPL papers, MHI, box 9, 10; Ralph Bennett, *Ultra and the Mediterranean Strategy*, 262.

364 *"huge wave about to break"*: Trevelyan, 50; Thomas R. Brooks, *The War North of Rome*, 27.

364 *Managing to steer the plane into a pond:* Kesselring was shot down five times during the war. Kenneth Macksey, *Kesselring: The Making of the Luftwaffe*, 191–92, 199.

364 *At six A.M. he told Berlin of the landings:* "The German Operation at Anzio," 11–14; B. H. Liddell Hart, *The Other Side of the Hill*, 372 (*prearranged march routes*); William L. Allen, *Anzio: Edge of Disaster*, 59 (*all or part of eleven divisions*); Albrecht Kesselring, *The Memoirs of Field-Marshal Kesselring*, 194 ("higgledy-piggledy jumble"); Hans-Wolfgang Schoch, "Deployment of Light Infantry Regiment 741 in the Anzio-Nettuno Beachhead," June 1947, FMS, #D-200, MHI, 2 (*Italians would toss flowers*).

365 *Allied air strategists had asserted:* Eduard Mark, *Aerial Interdiction in Three Wars*, 114, 131–32 (*Italian rail workers remained*); F. Specne, "Did Allied Air Interdiction Live Up to Expectations in the Italian Campaign, 1943–1944?" *Air Power Review*, RAF, vol. 8, no. 4 (winter 2005), 53+; Ralph S. Mavrogordato, "The Battle for the Anzio Beachhead," Apr. 1958, NARA RG 319, E 145, OCMH, R-124, 9 (*rerouted trains*); Allen, 67 (*within three days portions of eight divisions*).

365 *on "clear days it was possible":* Nigel Nicolson, *The Grenadier Guards in the War of 1939–1945*, vol. 2, 392; http://www.generals.dk/general/Mackensen/Eberhard_von_/Germany.html (*Mackensen*); Trevelyan, 89; Fred Sheehan, *Anzio: Epic of Bravery*, 136f.

366 *"insufficient for an attack":* "The German Operation at Anzio," 14.

366 *"Salerno complex":* Macksey, 201; directive, A. Hitler, Jan. 28, 1944, NARA RG 319, OCMH, CA, box 9 ("*holy hatred*").

366 *"Please answer the following":* msg, MWC to JPL, Jan. 24, 1943, JPL papers, MHI, box 12. The Army official history indicates that this query was on sent Jan. 23, but Lucas's papers show it was received Jan. 24 at 11:23 A.M.

366 *"must take some chances":* StoC, 386.

366 *"will attempt to contain our forces":* JPL to MWC, Jan. 24, 1943, JPL papers, MHI, box 12; JPL, 350–51 (*infantry fight*); Nicolson, *The Grenadier Guards*, 389–92 (*slept in pajamas*); Fitzgerald, 220 (*thin panes of ice*); George F. Howe, *The Battle History of the 1st Armored Division*, 282 (*Owls hooted*); Lawrence D. Collins, *The 56th Evac Hospital*, 200 ("All those hills").

366 *"fever-ridden corkcutters":* Fitzgerald, 223; Snowden, 146–47 (*a single night*).

367 *Mussolini had reclaimed:* Snowden, 155–61, 176 ("*rural warriors*"); Sheehan, 25 (*bright blue*).

367 *With Mussolini's apparent consent:* Siegfried Westphal, "The View of the Army Groups," 1947, MHI, FMS, #T-1a, chapter XI, 4–5; Col. Count von Klinckowstroem, "Italian Campaign," 1947, MHI, FMS, #T-1a, chapter X, 2–3 ("*what measures could be taken*"); Snowden, 187, 192 (*100,000 acres*), 193 ("*biological warfare*").

367 *"bog, bush, and water":* William Woodruff, *Vessel of Sadness*, 74; Trevelyan, 70 (*British patrols edged*); Fitzgerald, 225 (*Italian women clapped*); Lardner, "Anzio, February 10th," 48 ("*damned good people*"); Sheehan, 66; StoC, 387; Molony V, 669–70.

367 *"throat is worse today":* diary, Jan. 23, 1944, Don E. Carleton papers, HIA, box 1; *Anzio Beachhead*, 23.

368 *A Ranger lieutenant rummaging:* Martha Harris, ed., "The Harris Family in World War II," 45–47; Martin Gilbert, *Winston S. Churchill*, vol. 7, 662.

368 *Clark and Alexander came calling:* daily troop strength, Jan. 26, 1944, JPL papers, MHI, box 12; StoC, 387 (*finish seizing Campoleone*); JPL, 335 ("*splendid piece of work*"); OH, JPL, May 24, 1948, SM, MHI ("*really hurt the Germans*").

368 *H.M.S. Janus:* SSA, 344; http://uboat.net/allies/warships/ship/4450.html; Vaughan-Thomas, 60 ("*Roll Out the Barrel*").

368 *More than one hundred bombers:* SSA, 346–47; "Fifth Army Medical History," n.d., NARA RG 112, MTO surgeon general, box 6, 21–23 (*hospital ship* St. David); "Field Operations of the Medical Department in the MTOUSA," Nov. 10, 1945, NARA RG 407, E 427, 95-USF2-26-0 ("*I was being dragged*"); SSN, 346n.

369 *The strikes continued through the week:* corr, "Elwan" to Phil Lundeberg, Feb. 24, 1950, SEM papers, NHC, box 50 (*beachhead eavesdroppers*); SSA, 348–50 ("*terrific wall of flame*").

369 *Danger lurked below:* "Dictionary of American Fighting Ships," Department of the Navy, http://www.history.navy.mil/danfs/l17/lst-422.htm (LST-422); corr, William S. Hutchinson, Jr., CO, 83rd Chemical Bn, Oct. 13, 1944, to Charles S. Shadle, AFHQ, NARA RG 492, MTO, chemical warfare section, 200.6, box 1686; "Reports of Two LST-422 Survivors," *Muzzleblasts*, 83rd Chemical Mortar Battalion Veterans Association, Dec. 2004, http://www.4point2.org/muzzleblasts83/muzzleblasts-2004-dec.pdf, 5; Roskill, 307–8.

370 "*Using the boat hook*": "The Sinking of the *LST-422*," http://www.dvrbs.com/history-mil./LST-422.htm.

370 *mortar companies lost nearly three hundred men:* Brooks E. Kleber and Dale Birdsell, *The Chemical Warfare Service: Chemicals in Combat,* 446; "*LST-422,*" http://members.iinet.net.au/~gduncan/maritime-2b.html (*canvas bags*); George Rhoads, "WWII—The Story of Billy Rhoads," http://beoutrageous.com/IYP/billy%20rhoads.htm; http://www.abmc.gov/search/detailwwnew.php.

370 *One shell hit a fragrance shop:* Edmund F. Ball, *Staff Officer with the Fifth* Army, photo caption; Field Marshal Lord Carver, *The Imperial War Museum Book of the War in Italy, 1943–1945,* 125 ("*demented beings*").

370 "*We were the fish*": Howard D. Ashcraft, *As You Were,* 90.

370 "*I have not the slightest doubt*": John Slessor, *The Central Blue,* 562.

371 "*Apparently some of the higher levels*": JPL, 344.

371 *The excoriation of Old Luke:* Molony V, 687; Greenfield, ed., 262 ("*Having gained surprise*").

371 "*probably saved the forces at Anzio*": Michael Carver, *Harding of Petherton, Field-Marshal,* 125; Nicolson, *Alex,* 233 ("*within a week or fortnight*"); Allen, 117 ("*for every mile of advance*").

371 "*the actual course of events*": Molony V, 686; Field-Marshal Lord Wilson, *Eight Years Overseas,* 193 ("*irreparable disaster*"); Nicolson, *Alex,* 233 ("*absolutely full of inertia*"); Greenfield, ed., 264 ("*Had I been able to rush*").

## Through the Looking Glass

372 *On a brisk January day in 1752:* Nearby Cápua had been the largest, richest city in southern Italy before earning Rome's enmity by befriending Hannibal. H. V. Morton, *A Traveller in Southern Italy,* 267–68, 270 ("*beauty and gaiety*"). The slave revolt began in the Cápua amphitheater. Bertarelli, 258. Edward D. Churchill, *Surgeon to Soldiers,* 292; Walter L. Medding, "The Road to Rome," ts, n.d., 337th Engineer Regt, CEOH, box X-38, 55 (*hole-and-mirror contraption*); author visit, May 3, 2004; Karl Baedeker, *Southern Italy and Sicily,* 10; Charles J. Bové, "The Royal Palace of Caserta," n.d., Fifth Army, administrative files, USMA Arch.

373 *Captured on October 8:* "Engineer History, Fifth Army, Mediterranean Theater," n.d., MHI, 15; Carver, *The Imperial War Museum Book of the War in Italy,* 134 ("*muddling sort of maze*"); Churchill, *Surgeon to Soldiers,* 267; James Parton, "*Air Force Spoken Here,*" 387; Harold Macmillan, *War Diaries,* 365 ("*in disorder*"); Rupert Clarke, *With Alex at War,* 130 (*messed at the palace kennel*); "Trip Reports Concerning Use of ULTRA in the Mediterranean Theater, 1943–1944," n.d., NARA RG 457, E 9002, SRH-031, 73; Ronald Lewin, *Ultra Goes to War,* 325.

373 *Fifteen thousand soldiers:* Parton, 355, 386; Raymond H. Croll, memoir, ts, 1973, R. H. Croll papers, MHI, 215 (*"in and out of windows"*); corr, Graham Erdwurm to author, Sept. 5, 2003 (*"New England cotton mill"*); corr, Jon Clayton to family, Feb. 14, 1944, 7th Inf Regt, 3rd ID, ASEQ, MHI, 2 (*"midnight in a madhouse"*); John North, ed., *The Alexander Memoirs, 1940–1945,* 109 (*"whoever arrived first"*).

373 *The building had little heat:* Parton, 389 (*"shivering and scratching"*); Lavinia Holland-Hibbert Orde, "Better Late Than Never," ts, n.d., IWM, 96/34/1, 193; Medding, "The Road to Rome," X-38, 49–50, 53.

373 *The twelve hundred rooms:* Charles F. Marshall, *A Ramble Through My War,* 13; Medding, "The Road to Rome," X-38, 41, 55 (*soldiers' fingerprints*); corr, Clayton, Feb. 14, 1944 (*basketball court*); memoir, P. Royle, ts, 1972, IWM, 99/72/1, 116 (*venereal disease*); Lynn H. Nicholas, *The Rape of Europa,* 234; memo, H. M. Wilson, March 20, 1944; memo, J. L. Devers, March 20, 1944; corr, H. M. Wilson, March 28, 1944; corr, J. L. Devers, March 31, 1944, all in NARA RG 492, MTOUSA AG, 33.5-446, box 1431.

374 *An errant bomb had bent:* Churchill, *Surgeon to Soldiers,* 292 (*"stuffy, swank dining room"*); Bill Mauldin, *Up Front,* 139; Medding, "The Road to Rome," X-38, 48–49 (*palace porcelain*); letter, R.L.V. ffrench Blake to author, July 27, 2003 (*"if anyone dropped a plate"*).

374 *Officers in the palace bar:* Malcolm S. McLean, "Adventures in Occupied Areas," ts, 1975, MHI, 68; George Biddle, *Artist at War,* 223; Carver, *The Imperial War Museum Book of the War in Italy,* 138 (*"made less and less sense"*); Parton, 368 (*"big as cabbage leaves"*); David Hunt, *A Don at War,* 250–51 (*San Carlo Opera Company*); Marshall, 14; Medding, "The Road to Rome," X-38, 55.

374 *a "looking glass war":* Churchill, *Surgeon to Soldiers,* 292, 294; "History of the Aviation Engineers in the Mediterranean Theater of Operations," June 1946, historical section, AAF Engineer Command, CEOH, X-39; C. L. Sulzberger, *A Long Row of Candles,* 234; Nicolson, *The Grenadier Guards,* 368; JPL, 185 (*hungry soldiers soon emptied*); Medding, "The Road to Rome," X-38, 36–37, 59; Marshall, 13.

374 *engineers built a colony for generals:* Morton, 269; Bertarelli, 259; "History of the Aviation Engineers," X-39 (*"feeling of the men"*); Parton, 390.

375 *maintained twenty-two lofts:* AAR, 6681st Signal Pigeon Co, July 9, 1944, NARA RG 407, SGCO-6681-0.1, box 23228; Hunt, 250–51 (*"extremely noisy"*); Vaughan-Thomas, 201 (*"get in your bones"*).

375 *Clark rarely missed a chance:* diary, MWC, Jan. 28, 1944, Citadel, box 65; corr, Graham Erdwurm to author, Sept. 5, 2003 (*rope factories*); Medding, "The Road to Rome," X-38, 53; http://www.ibiblio.org/hyperwar/USN/ships/PT/PT-201.html; http://www.history.navy.mil/faqs/faq60-5.htm (*motor torpedo boats*); *Calculated,* 292; memo, HKH to Ernest J. King, June 6, 1944, "Report of the Engagement Between the USS *Sway* and PTs *201* and *206* on 28 January 1944," MWC, Citadel, box 3, folder 7 (*Neither boat crew took time*).

375 *Alexander had prodded Clark:* Martin Blumenson, *Mark Clark,* 187; Viscount Alexander of Tunis, "The Allied Armies in Italy," n.d., CMH, II-34 (*"Risks must be taken"*).

375 *"The left corner of Clark's mouth":* PP, 396; MWC to Renie, Jan. 18, 1944, personal corr, Citadel (*"by massaging my hair"*); diary, MWC, Jan. 23, 25, 28, 1944, Citadel, box 65.

376 *"The more stars a man gets":* Maurine Clark, *Captain's Bride, General's Lady,* 115; Blumenson, *Mark Clark,* 196–97 (*"You turn your lamb chops"*); MWC to Renie, Jan. 11, 1944, personal corr, Citadel (*"I am distressed"*).

376 *"an awfully good man":* Blumenson, *Mark Clark,* 196–97; Eisenhower diary, Nov. 23, 1943, HCB, DDE Lib, A-908 (*"victimized by his wife"*).

376 *"It causes me some embarrassment":* DDE to MWC, Nov. 22, 1943, DDE Lib, PP-pres, box 23. Released from restricted materials at author's request.

376 "*I do not want you to refer to me*": MWC to Renie, Nov. 27, Dec. 17, 1943, personal corr, Citadel.

377 *Clark's virtues as a commander:* OH, Jacob E. Smart, Nov. 1978, Arthur W. McCants and James C. Hasdorff, AFHRA 239.0512-1108 ("*broad-gauged*"); "Beyond the Bridgehead," *Time*, Oct. 4, 1943, 28+ ("*'ringside' visits*"); OH, Harry Lemley, 1974, Gerald F. Feeney, SOOHP, MHI, 2/32; Eric Sevareid, *Not So Wild a Dream*, 379 (*puzzled theatergoers*); Charles D'Orsa, "Trials and Tribulations of an Army G-4," ts, n.d., CARL, N-4906, 1 ("*I want my headquarters*").

377 "*The general was a difficult man*": Vernon A. Walters, *Silent Missions*, 93, 95; OH, Robert J. Wood, former asst. G-3, Fifth Army, March 4, 15, 1948, and "Memo for Mr. Matthews," March 22, 1948, SM, MHI ("*very impatient man*"); Sulzberger, 232 ("*rather Renaissance Florentine*").

377 "*entitled to take Rome*": Calculated, 289; Sulzberger, 231; Sevareid, 383.

378 *Since Salerno, battle casualties alone: Salerno*, 93–94; *From the Volturno to the Winter Line*, 114; *Fifth Army at the Winter Line*, 114; attributed to Joseph Stalin. Elizabeth Knowles, ed., *The Oxford Dictionary of Quotations*, 636 (*million deaths a statistic*); Chester G. Starr, ed., *From Salerno to the Alps*, 269 (*twenty thousand dead*).

378 "*Sometimes if I appear to be unreasonable*": Walters, 109.

378 "*what looked like a piece of driftwood*": Burtt Evans [*sic*] and Burgess W. Scott, "Nightmare Job at Anzio," March 3, 1944, in Steve Kluger, *Yank*, 159+.

378 *At 8:40 A.M., twelve miles south of Anzio:* memo, H. S. Strauss, CO, U.S.S. *Sway*, to CO, Task Force 81, Jan. 29, 1944, MWC papers, Citadel, box 3, folder 7.

378 *One minute after the initial challenge:* memo, S. M. Barnes, CO, Motor Torpedo Boat Squadron 15, to HKH, March 26, 1944, MWC, Citadel, box 3, folder 7; Gervasi, 533

379 "*What shall we do?*": Blumenson, *Mark Clark*, 175–77.

379 *Clark helped brace the helmsman:* memo, unsigned, to MWC, Jan. 28, 1944, MWC, corr, Oct. 1943–Jun 1944, box 3; Gervasi, 533; memo, Strauss, Jan. 29, 1944, ("*weight on the conscience*"); memo, HKH to King, June 6, 1944; diary, MWC, Jan. 28, 1944, Citadel, box 65 ("*as flagrant an error*").

379 "*a downward slant*": Calculated, 294; Rossi and Casaldi, 159; OH, Casaldi, May 7–8, 2004 (*into the wine cellars*); SSA, 356 ("*this white apartment house*").

379 *marooned all Navy pontoons ashore:* "Report on Port and Beach Operations at Anzio," 540th Engineer Combat Regt, Apr. 29, 1944, NARA RG 334, NWC Lib, ANSCOL, box 343; minutes, Anzio supply conference, Jan. 30, 1944, Naples, NARA RG 492, MTOUSA, transportation section, box 2697 (*civilian schooners*).

379 *As for the enemy:* Charles W. Crawford, III, "A Study of the Adequacy of the Intelligence Provided Maj. Gen. John P. Lucas," ts, June 1970, CARL, N-8224.494; "Historical Record, HQ, VI Corps, Mounting and Initial Phase of Operation SHINGLE," March 15, 1944, LKT Jr., GCM Lib, box 13, folder 2 ("*horse- and motorcycle-mounted*"); Sheehan, 71f (*estimated 72,000*); E. T. Williams and R. H. Humphreys, "Reports Received by U.S. War Department on Use of Ultra in the European Theater, WWII," Oct. 1945, NARA RG 457, E 9002, SRH-037, 9 ("*We deal not with the true*").

380 "*Our enemies did not react*": memo, "Morale of Troops," JPL to R.T. Frederick, Feb. 22, 1944, Robert T. Frederick papers, HIA, box 1.

380 *None of this surprised Clark:* Arthur F. Fournier, "Influence of Ultra Intelligence upon General Clark at Anzio," thesis, 1983, U.S. Army Command and General Staff College, Ft. L, 102–6; Mark, 129–30; Andrew Brookes, *Air War over Italy, 1943–1945*, 53 (*venereal disease hospital*); StoC, 388 ("*three full divisions*").

380 *Truscott today had drafted his order:* "Historical Record, HQ, VI Corps, Mounting and Initial Phase of Operation SHINGLE."

380 *short ride to the Villa Borghese:* SSA, 358.

380 "*His gloomy attitude*": JPL, 348–49; StoC, 390 ("*Will go all out*").

381 *On January 27 and 28 an obscure fighter unit: AAFinWWII*, 424.

381 *Blacks had fought in every American war:* Morris J. MacGregor, Jr., *Integration of the Armed Forces, 1940–1965*, 4; Hondon B. Hargrove, *Buffalo Soldiers in Italy*, 2; memo, Truman K. Gibson, Jr., office, secretary of war, to Ray E. Porter, Aug. 6, 1945, NARA RG 165, WD, special planning division, general corr, 291.2, box 32 (*four black Army regiments*); http://www.nps.gov/fols/Buffalo_Soldier/body_buffalo_soldier.html. Other accounts suggest the nickname derived from buffalo hides worn by the men to stay warm.

381 *"hopelessly inferior, lazy, slothful"*: Daniel K. Gibran, *The 92nd Infantry Division and the Italian Campaign in World War II*, 3; Krewasky A. Salter, *Combat Multipliers: African-American Soldiers in Four Wars*, 80 (*"a thousand years behind"*); "History of the Office of the Inspector General in World War II," 1946, CMH, 2-3.6 AA, 2–3, 12 (*Jim Crow laws*).

381 *When World War II began:* Ulysses Lee, *The Employment of Negro Troops*, 88, 416 (*633,000 soldiers*); "The Negro in the Navy," 1947, Bureau of Naval Personnel, "United States Naval Administration in WWII," 1 (*only six black sailors*), 14–15, 41 (*no black officers*); Salter, 82 (*"segregation will be maintained"*); Matt Schudel, "Frederick C. Branch Was 1st Black Officer in U.S. Marine Corps," Apr. 13, 2005, *WP*, B6.

382 *segregation "has proven satisfactory"*: memo, "War Department policy in regard to negroes," Oct. 16, 1940, WD, AG office, NARA RG 165, E 501, WD, special planning division, general corr, 291.2, box 32; "Attitudes of White Enlisted Men Toward Sharing Facilities with Negro Troops," July 30, 1942, SOS, research branch, NARA RG 165, E 501, WD, general corr, 291.2, box 32 (*"strong prejudice against sharing"*); Hargrove, 4 (*"not a sociological laboratory"*); memo, HQ, AGF, July 20, 1943, chief of staff journal, NARA RG 337 (*"93rd Division has three bands"*); Bernard C. Nalty, *Strength for the Fight*, 147 (*"fraught with danger"*).

382 *The 1940 Draft Act:* "African Americans in World War II," 1994, fact sheet, commemoration committee, 50th anniversary, WWII; David M. Kennedy, *Freedom from Fear*, 632–33 (*only 250 blacks*); Lee, 213 (*Mississippi congressional delegation*); Hargrove, 8; article, Deton J. Brooks, Jr., *Chicago Defender*, Nov. 6, 1943, in *Reporting World War II*, vol. 1, 662; Patrick K. O'Donnell, *Beyond Valor*, 108 (*German and Italian prisoner trustees*); *Time*, July 10, 1944, 65, in Bell I. Wiley, "The Training of Negro Troops," 1946, AGF, historical section, study no. 36, 13; "History of the Office of the Inspector General in World War II," 1946, CMH, 2-3.6 AA, 2–3, 12 (*"boy, darky"*); Alan M. Osur, "Separate and Unequal: Race Relations in the AAF During WWII," 7 (*"Double V"*), 32, 42, 45 (*"Heil, Hitler!"*).

382 *"lack of education and mechanical skill"*: Wiley, "The Training of Negro Troops," iii, 3 (*"too great a concentration of Negroes"*), 7; MacGregor, 24; memo, Gibson to Porter, Aug. 6, 1945 (*lowest two categories*).

383 *blacks were shunted into quartermaster companies:* Erna Risch and Chester L. Kieffer, *The Quartermaster Corps: Organization, Supply, and Services*, vol. 2, 168–69; Collins, 190; Lee, 406 (*only two in ten*); Hargrove, vii.

383 *the 92nd would endure trials:* Dale E. Wilson, "Recipe for Failure: Major General Edward M. Almond and Preparation of the U.S. 92nd Infantry Division for Combat in World War II," *Journal of Military History*, vol. 56, no. 3 (July 1992), 473; Gibran, 17, 21, 35–36 (*overbearing Virginian*); OH, Edward M. Almond, Nov. 16, 1953, Lee Nichols, NARA RG 319, OCMH, CA, box 005, 1–8 (*"The Negro doesn't care"*).

383 *Almond asserted that black officers lacked:* In a cover note, Lucian Truscott, then commander of Fifth Army, declared himself "in entire agreement." E. M. Almond, "Combat Effectiveness of Negro Officers and Enlisted Men," July 2, 1945, NARA RG 165, WD, special planning div, general corr, 291.2, box 34; Wiley, "The Training of Negro Troops," 8 (*"learn slowly"*).

383 *Such obstacles and more faced the 99th:* William Alexander Percy, "Jim Crow and Uncle Sam," *Journal of Military History,* vol. 67, no. 3 (July 2003), 773+; http://www.wpafb .af.mil/museum/history/prewwii/ta.htm; Benjamin O. Davis, Jr., *Benjamin O. Davis, Jr.: American,* 26–28, 75.

384 *A week before the invasion of Sicily:* Herman S. Wolk, "Pantelleria, 1943," *Air Force Magazine,* vol. 85, no. 6, June 2002; Charles E. Francis, *The Tuskegee Airmen,* 85; Stanley Sandler, *Segregated Skies,* 46 (*"proper reflexes"*); Percy, "Jim Crow and Uncle Sam," 773 (*"releasing a white squadron"*).

384 *Davis, who was promoted:* Lee, 450, 460; Francis, 75 (*"collection of born dive bombers"*); Richard G. Davis, *Carl A. Spaatz and the Air War in Europe,* 294 (*"fault of the whites"*); Percy, "Jim Crow and Uncle Sam," 773 (*225 missions*).

384 *Then came the morning of January 27:* Sandler, 56–57; Francis, 87 (*"I started firing"*).

385 *After refueling in Naples:* The official Army history claimed that thirteen German planes were destroyed. Davis and others claimed only twelve. Lee, 517; Davis, 104.

385 *"Negroes are doing their bit":* John C. McManus, *The Deadly Brotherhood,* 246.

## Jerryland

385 *On Saturday afternoon, January 29:* aide's diaries, Jan. 29, 1943; Francis A. Even, "The Tenth Engineers," ts, 1996, author's possession, 34; author visit, Borgo Montello formerly Conca, May 7, 2004; e-mail, S. Casaldi to author, June 28, 2004; Hugh A. Scott, *The Blue and White Devils,* 103.

385 *He still spoke in a raspy whisper:* diary, Jan. 24, 1944, Don E. Carleton papers, HIA, box 1; *CM,* 312; LKT Jr. to Sarah, Jan. 25, 1943, LKT Jr. papers, GCM Lib, box 1, folder 6.

386 *Two miles farther lay Highway 7 and Cisterna:* Acts, 28:15; Trevelyan, 74; Jeff R. Stewart, "The Ranger Force at the Battle of Cisterna," 2004, thesis, CGSC, Ft. L, 70 (*five major roads*); aide's diaries, Jan. 26, 1943; *CM,* 312.

386 *"Spirits are not particularly high":* G-2 periodic report No. 130, Feb. 5, 1944, VI Corps, JPL papers, MHI, box 1; attachment, G-2 periodic report No. 138, Feb. 13, 1944, VI Corps, JPL papers, MHI, box 1 (*"the air roars"*); "Estimate of the Situation," 3rd ID, G-2, Jan. 29, 1944, Robert W. Black papers, MHI, box 2, folder 10; Stewart, "The Ranger Force at the Battle of Cisterna," 64; Nicolson, *The Grenadier Guards in the War of 1939–1945,* 399–400 (*missed a turn*); Verney, 69–70; *CM,* 313; Allen, 70.

387 *Kesselring had planned a massive counterattack:* journal, Fourteenth Army, Jan. 29, 1944, "The German Operation at Anzio," Apr. 1946, German Military Document Section, Military Intelligence Div, WD, JPL papers, MHI, box 9; "Air Participation in Operation SHINGLE, Jan. 1–Feb. 15, 1944," Oct. 1945, CARL, N-11614, 10, appendices K and R (*foul weather obscured rail targets*); *Calculated,* 295 (*"not seriously considered"*); *CM,* 313 (*Thousands of grenadiers*); Anthony J. Abati, "Cisterna di Littoria: A Brave Yet Futile Effort," *Army History,* fall 1991, 13+; Lloyd Clark, *Anzio,* 136 (*exceeded 71,000*), 147; Molony V, 648 (*33 battalions*); note on Carraceto operations, William R. C. Penney, Jan. 29, 1944, LHC, 8/12.

387 *Darby's Rangers spent the afternoon:* Darby and Baumer, 157; Arnbal, 229 (*"solemn, tired, and quiet"*), 227 (*never carried personal letters*); OH, William P. Yarborough, 1975, J. R. Meese and H. P. Houser, SOOHP, MHI, 54 (*"cutthroats"*); Milton Lehman, "The Rangers Died Fighting at Dawn," mss, March 11, 1944, *Stars and Stripes,* "Combat Reports, 1st Ranger Battalion," USMA micro, MP63-8, roll 1 (*barbers stayed busy*); Martin Blumenson, *Anzio: The Gamble That Failed,* 97 (*"Mail arrived late Saturday"*); Hans Juergensen, *Beachheads and Mountains,* 24 (*like dry bones*).

388 *Darby had been busy since dawn:* AAR, "Account of Ranger Force During Period 28 January to 31 January 1944," HQ, Ranger Force, Feb. 2, 1944, "Combat Reports, 1st Ranger Battalion," USMA micro, MP63-8, roll 1 (*"avoiding contact"*); Michael J. King, *William*

*Orlando Darby,* 150–51; Jerome J. Haggerty, "A History of the Ranger Battalion in World War II," 1982, Ph.D. diss, Fordham University, MHI, 154; Darby and Baumer, 156 (*"Jerryland"*); Anthony J. Abati, "Cisterna di Littoria: A Brave Yet Futile Effort," *Army History,* fall 1991, 13+; Nicholas J. Grunzweig, "The Operations of the 1st Battalion, 7th Infantry, at Le Mole Creek Near Cisterna," 1949, IS.

388 *The size of the attack heartened him:* King, 150–51; James J. Altieri, *Darby's Rangers: An Illustrated Portrayal of the Original Rangers,* 74; Arnbal, 227; "The OSS Detachment at the Anzio Beachhead," NARA RG 226, E 99, OSS history office, box 39, 1, 4 (*only four enemy battalions*); "The Rangers," *Life,* July 2, 1944, 59+ (*"shaking with patriotism"*); Donald Downes, *The Scarlet Thread,* 150 (*"finest body of troops"*).

388 *Yet the expansion of the force:* Each Ranger battalion was about half the size of a regular infantry battalion, and was divided into six companies.

388 *Too many men still bunched up:* Michael J. King, "Rangers: Selected Combat Operations in World War II," June 1985, CSI, 31; Haggerty, "A History of the Ranger Battalion in World War II," 154; Thomas M. Johnson, "The Army's Fightingest Outfit Comes Home," Nov. 5, 1944, *St. Louis Post-Dispatch,* condensed in *Reader's Digest,* Dec. 1944, 51+ (*muffle a canteen*).

388 *Would Truscott's infantry quickly reinforce:* After the war, the 4th Ranger Battalion commander said Darby believed that the Cisterna attack was "too risky." OH, Roy Murray, May 21, 1948, SM, CMH, Geog Files, Italy 314.7.

388 *No Ranger reconnaissance*: David W. Hogan, Jr., *Raiders or Elite Infantry?,* 58, 60; Robert W. Black, *Rangers in World War II,* 150–51; Grunzweig, "The Operations of the 1st Battalion, 7th Infantry" (*hedgerows*); AAR, "Account of Ranger Force"; Ranger Force journal, Jan. 29, 1944, 1835 hrs, "Combat Reports, 1st Ranger Battalion," USMA micro, MP63-8, roll 1 (*"city may have considerable opposition"*).

389 *"Pistol Packin' Mama"*: James Altieri, *The Spearheaders,* 308–10; Darby and Baumer, 157–59; Oscar W. Koch, *G-2: Intelligence for Patton,* 40–43 (*sounds difficult for German-speakers*); Ranger Force journal, Jan. 30, 1944; Field Order no. 2 (*red Very flares*).

389 *"Morale of men excellent"*: AAR, 1st Ranger Bn, March 31, 1944, "Combat Reports, 1st Ranger Battalion," USMA micro, MP63-8, roll 1; Alvah H. Miller, "The Men of My Command," n.d., in "2004 Reunion Program Book," Fort Wayne, Ind., Aug. 2004, author's possession, 84.

389 *isolated farmhouse on the right side of the road:* Ranger Force journal, Jan. 29, 1944; King, 152; Altieri, *Darby's Rangers,* 75; StoC, 391.

389 *Barely half a mile up the Conca road:* AAR, 4th Ranger Bn, Feb. 15, 1944, and "Journal of Operations," 4th Ranger Bn, Jan. 22–31, 1944, Robert W. Black papers, MHI, box 4, folder 11; Altieri, *Darby's Rangers,* 75; OH, Roy Murray, May 21, 1948; "Personal Diary of Langan W. Swent," Jan. 30, 1944, Langan W. Swent papers, HIA, box 1 (*white pillar of flame*); Ranger Force journal, Jan. 30, 1944, 0433 hrs, "Combat Reports, 1st Ranger Battalion"; King, 154; Darby and Baumer, 159 (*"all was not well"*).

390 *"We could hear mortar and artillery"*: James P. O'Reilly, "A Tough Decision," 3rd Ranger Bn, in Altieri, *Darby's Rangers,* 80, 159–60 (*blown to pieces point-blank*).

390 *Dobson pressed ahead:* Lehman, "The Rangers Died Fighting at Dawn"; Darby and Baumer, 159; Carlo D'Este, *Fatal Decision,* 163; author visits, May 7, 2004, Nov. 30, 2006.

390 *A German sentry flopped:* Jack Dobson, "With the Rangers at Cisterna," Jan. 1945, told to Noland Norgaard, Associated Press, in Altieri, *Darby's Rangers,* 83; Black, 157; Stewart, "The Ranger Force at the Battle of Cisterna," 41; O'Donnell, 90 (*"I emptied my M-1"*); memo, "Capture of the First and Third Ranger Battalions," Charles M. Shunstrom to William O. Darby, July 10, 1944, "Combat Reports, 1st Ranger Battalion," USMA micro, MP63-8, roll 1.

391 *Dawn, that harsh betrayer:* Stewart, "The Ranger Force at the Battle of Cisterna," 42.

391 *"Then it opened up on us"*: Lehman, "The Rangers Died Fighting at Dawn"; Altieri, *Darby's Rangers,* 77; memo, "Capture of the First and Third Ranger Battalions," Shunstrom to Darby; D'Este, *Fatal Decision,* 165 (*Dobson shot a tank commander*).

391 *Step by step the Rangers retreated:* Stewart, "The Ranger Force at the Battle of Cisterna," 37; Micky T. Romine, "My Life in Combat, and as a POW," n.d., in "2004 Reunion Program Book," 89–89 (*"I have shot that man"*); Milton Lehman, "The Rangers Died Fighting at Dawn" (*"You could run about twenty yards"*).

392 *Rangers held in reserve:* memo, "Capture of the First and Third Ranger Battalions," Shunstrom to Darby; memo, "Operation at Sisterna" [*sic*], Charles M. Shunstrom, n.d., "Combat Reports, 1st Ranger Battalion," USMA micro, MP63-8, roll 1; Donald G. Taggart, *History of Third Infantry Division in World War II,* 119; Darby and Baumer, 167 (*"The tracers were flying"*); O'Donnell, 91 (*sprayed blood*); Black, 159, 164; AAR, 1st Ranger Bn, March 31, 1944.

392 *"Them bastards is giving up"*: O'Donnell, 91. Some eyewitnesses said the German armored vehicles were tanks. Testimony from James Robert Dew, May 24, 1945; Donald Richard Clark, Aug. 2, 1945; James D. Cooney, May 21, 1944, all in JAG case file, Cisterna shootings, War Crimes Office, NARA RG 153, box 536.

392 *"we shall shoot the prisoners"*: memo, "Capture of the First and Third Ranger Battalions," Shunstrom to Darby; King, 156–57; D'Este, 166.

392 *Darby for several hours had labored:* Taggart, 115; Ranger Force journal, Jan. 30, 1944, 0615 hrs (*"Murray is having a hell of a time"*); *Anzio Beachhead,* 30.

392 *News from Truscott's regiments:* Stewart, "The Ranger Force at the Battle of Cisterna," 61; Grunzweig, "The Operations of the 1st Battalion, 7th Infantry"; Joseph Edgar Martin, "Memoir of World War II," ts, 2003, author's possession; *Anzio Beachhead,* 31–32. Third Division soldiers earned four more Medals of Honor at Cisterna in the May 1944 breakout battle; thus, of thirty-one such decorations awarded the division's soldiers during World War II, more than one-quarter were for valorous acts in this one small Italian town. Nathan William White, *From Fedala to Berchtesgaden,* 82; D'Este, 174, 361.

393 *At seven A.M., the first radio dispatch:* King, 156–57; D'Este, 493n.

393 *"Some of the fellows are giving up"*: Darby and Baumer, 164.

393 *"Shoot if they come any closer"*: Taggart, 115.

393 *"They are coming into the building"*: Darby and Baumer, 164–65; King, "Rangers," 38–39 (*"So long, Colonel"*).

393 *"Use your head"*: Taggart, 115; Altieri, *The Spearheaders,* 312 (*"God bless all of you"*).

393 *"Ehalt, I leave everything"*: Black, 160.

393 *"My old sergeant major"*: Taggart, 115; King, 157; Altieri, *The Spearheaders,* 312; Darby and Baumer, 167 (*"couldn't stand the thought"*).

393 *"Situation is confused"*: aide's diaries, Jan. 30, 1944; Scott, 103–4 (*"tiny, darting figures"*).

394 *Confusion and cacophony persisted:* AAR, 1st Ranger Bn; AAR, 4th Ranger Bn, Feb. 15, 1944, and "Journal of Operations," 4th Ranger Bn, Jan. 22–31, 1944, Robert W. Black papers, MHI, box 4, folder 11; Altieri, *Darby's Rangers,* 76; Darby and Baumer, 159–60; diary, Jan. 30, 1944, Don E. Carleton papers, HIA, box 1 (*"Whole show is folded"*).

394 *"packing meat"*: Audie Murphy, *To Hell and Back,* 83, 107, 121; Juergensen, *Beachheads and Mountains,* 18, 23; Don Graham, *No Name on the Bullet,* 52–53 (*knocked Murphy senseless*).

394 *For a renewed push on Monday:* diary, Jan. 30–31, 1944, Don E. Carleton papers, HIA, box 1; aide's diaries, Jan. 30, 1944; *AAFinWWII,* vol. 3, 349; JJT, XII-9, 11, 15 (*"Not a man to let a weapon sit"*).

394 *"Toffey is rolling"*: Scott, 104; Taggart, 117; *Anzio Beachhead,* map no. 7; White, 84; Grunzweig, "The Operations of the 1st Battalion, 7th Infantry" (*"barely existed as a fighting*

*force"*); Darby and Baumer, 167; AAR, 4th Ranger Bn, Feb. 15, 1944, and "Journal of Operations," 4th Ranger Bn, Jan. 22–31, 1944; Murphy, 108.

395 *The division was spent: Anzio Beachhead*, 36, map no. 7; JJT, XII-16 ("*fearless leadership*").

395 *Darby drove to the bivouac:* Milton Lehman, "The Rangers Fought Ahead of Everybody," *Saturday Evening Post*, June 15, 1946, 50+; D'Este, 169.

395 *Captured Rangers shuffled:* film, "Liberation of Rome," 1944, combat report no. 1, NARA RG 111, CR001; O'Donnell, 96; Romine, "My Life in Combat, and as a POW," 88–89; memoir, Frank Mattivi, n.d., in "2004 Reunion Program Book," 88–89 ("*I am a prisoner*").

395 *The February 1 morning report:* morning report, 1st Ranger Bn, Feb. 1, 1944, Robert W. Black papers, MHI, box 2, folder 9; Hogan, 58; *Anzio Beachhead*, 30; Stewart, "The Ranger Force at the Battle of Cisterna," 57.

395 *An estimated 250 to 300:* Estimates of Rangers killed vary widely. While scholars such as Carlo D'Este put the number as high as three hundred, a report to the Ranger Battalions Association thirty years after the battle claimed, perhaps improbably, that only a dozen died. D'Este, 169; O'Donnell, 84; Black, 165. See also King, "Rangers," http://www-cgsc.army.mil/carl/resources/csi/King/King.asp#C.

395 *the 4th Battalion suffered:* Hogan, 58; memo, G. B. Devore, "Armored Replacements," March 18, 1944, AGF Board, AFHQ, DTL, Ft. B (*Anglo-American losses on January 30*); journal, Fourteenth Army, Jan. 31, 1944, 10 ("*enemy has suffered heavily*").

396 *The hunt for scapegoats:* diary, MWC, Jan. 30, 1944, Citadel, box 65; King, "Rangers," 31; OH, JPL, May 24, 1948, SM, MHI (*until Lucas pointed out*); Associated Press, March 8, 1944, cited in Marsha Henry Goff, "Reunion to Bring World War II Rangers to Lawrence," Lawrence [Kans.] *Journal-World*, May 19, 2006; Hogan, 58; Ivan Peterman, "Peterman Discloses Story of Lost Rangers at Anzio Beachhead," Apr. 15, 1944, *Philadelphia Inquirer*, 1; AAR, "Mounting and Initial Phase of Operation SHINGLE," March 15, 1944, VI Corps, NARA RG 407, 206-3.0, box 3740 ("*ascribed only to chance*").

396 *The beachhead on the VI Corps right:* Molony V, 676; diary, MWC, Feb. 4, 1944, Citadel, box 65 ("*consolidate your beachhead*").

396 *Lucas invited reporters to his upstairs suite:* Vaughan-Thomas, 90 ("*a mighty tough fighter*"); H. M. Wilson, "Report by the Supreme Allied Commander Mediterranean," 1946, part 1, 28 (*more than six thousand casualties*).

## CHAPTER 9: THE MURDER SPACE

*This World and the Next World at Strife*

398 *"indulged in his wild orgies":* Karl Baedeker, *Southern Italy*, 5; National Archeological Museum, Cassino; author visits, Sept. 1995, May 2004, Nov. 2006; *The Tiger Triumphs*, 50 ("*a preacher above his congregation*"); Tommaso Leccisotti, *Monte Cassino*, 13 ("*From here is the way*").

398 *Rounding the last bend:* David Hapgood and David Richardson, *Monte Cassino*, 238–39; Fred Majdalany, *Cassino: Portrait of a Battle*, 5; http://www.newadvent.org/cathen/02467b.htm ("*agreeable to the Lord*"); Leccisotti, 14–15, 19; "The Abbey of Montecassino," tourist brochure, n.d. ("*on a bright street*"); StoC, 401; Bradford A. Evans, *The Bombing of Monte Cassino*, 11–12; "Monte Cassino," *The Complete Poetical Works of Henry Wadsworth Longfellow*, http://www.worldwideschool.org/library/books/lit/poetry/TheCompletePoeticalWorksofHenryWadsworthLongfellow/chap21.html.

399 *The town below had first been bombed:* Leccisotti, 112; StoC, 399; Rudolf Böhmler, *Monte Cassino*, 105, 107–13 ("*To befoul the Abbey*"); Franz Kurowski, *The History of the Fallschirmpanzerkorps Hermann Göring*, 220 (*swag was breathtaking*); Hapgood and

Richardson, 35 (*silk-clad reliquaries*); Lynn H. Nicholas, *The Rape of Europa*, 244 (*fifteen crates went missing*).

399 *As the evacuation concluded:* StoC, 400–401; memo, "The bombing of Monte Cassino Abbey," W. M. Harris, Sept. 2, 1949, CMH, Geog Italy, 373.11 ("allein das Gebäude"); diary, WFST, Dec. 27, 1943, CMH, Geog Italy, 373.11 (*"best reserves must stand"*).

399 *"every rock-drilling machine":* Franz Kurowski, *Battleground Italy, 1943–1945*, 359; Leccisotti, 117; StoC, 400–401; diary, WFSt, Nov. 17, 1943 (*tobacco bonuses*); Böhmler, 163 (*German field hospitals*).

400 *The first stray shell:* Leccisotti, 118; Hapgood and Richardson, 7, 81, 100–101 ("*these terrible days*").

400 *Forty terrified women rushed:* memo, "Monte Cassino Abbey," HQ, Fifth Army, G-2, Feb. 28, 1944, in F. Jones, "The Bombing of Monte Cassino, 15 February 1944," Oct. 14, 1949, Cabinet Historical Section, UK PRO, CAB 106/699, appendix 3, 69; StoC, 401; Fred Majdalany, *Cassino: Portrait of a Battle*, 112–13 (*pounded on the oak door*); Leccisotti, 118 ("*Insane with fear*").

400 *The door swung open:* Leccisotti, 118; Herbert Bloch, "The Bombardment of Monte Cassino," 1973, CMH, Geog Italy, 373.11, 411.

400 *The failure of the frontal attack:* StoC, 367, 374; N. C. Phillips, *Official History of New Zealand in the Second World War: Italy*, vol. 1, 185 ("*dejected landscape*").

401 *The French nearly won through:* "Draft Report on FEC," n.d., SM, CMH, box 1.

401 *"Look for the fellow wearing":* "Special Report on Attitude of U.S. Troops Toward French," March 8, 1944, HQ, SOS, NATOUSA, NARA RG 492, 311.7, box 931; "Draft Report on FEC" (*bowing back the German line*); Gregory Blaxland, *Alexander's Generals*, 43 (*occupied Monte Belvedere*); Ralph S. Mavrogordato, "XIV Panzer Corps Defensive Operations Along the Garigliano, Gari, and Rapido Rivers," Nov. 1955, NARA RG 319, E 145, OCMH, R series, R-78, 57 (*escarpment so vital*).

401 *"It is ordinary men":* John Ellis, *Cassino: The Hollow Victory*, 65, 58 ("*tearing at his brains*"), 146–47 ("*That calmed them*"); Molony V, 627.

401 *Six German battalions:* Ian Gooderson, *Cassino 1944*, 65; operations report, 3rd Algerian Div, Feb. 16, 1944, in "French Action and Pertinent Orders, Rapido-Cassino," Fifth Army, HQ, Robert J. Wood papers, MHI ("*Hill 700 has been taken*"); Blaxland, 43 (*sip of water*); Douglas Porch, *The Path to Victory*, 533 ("*Haven't eaten or drunk*").

401 *"The human mechanism":* Ellis, 149; "Draft Report on FEC"; StoC, 372; Molony V, 629n (*a battalion each day*); Blaxland, 43 ("*could do no more*").

402 *Now the thankless task:* http://www.army.mil/CMH/topics/apam/100BnWW2.htm; 201 file, Charles W. Ryder papers, DDE Lib, box 2.

402 *the 34th attacked north of Cassino:* StoC, 371.

402 *The attack resumed farther north:* AAR, 2nd Bn, 168th Inf, CMH, Geog files, 370.2; StoC, 373, 377 ("*Cassino heights will be captured*"); OH, Andrew J. Goodpaster, Aug. 17, 2004, with author, Washington, D.C. (*S-mines popping*); AAR, "Attack on Cassino," G. B. Devore, Co C, 760th Tank Bn, attached to 756th Tank Bn, in report no. 140, AFG board, Apr. 3, 1944, CARL, N-7245-G (*followed the faint glow*); John L. Powers, "Crossing the Rapido," IJ, May 1945, 50+ (*six-inch ruts*); Kenneth Maitland Davies, *To the Last Man*, 122 (*phosphorus*); "Historical Narrative and Journal," G-3, 34th ID, Oct. 1943–May 1944, Charles W. Ryder papers, DDE Lib, box 4; GK, Feb. 1, 1944 ("*Believe we shall have Cassino*").

404 *Kesselring had shifted:* Chester G. Starr, ed., *From Salerno to the Alps*, 108; StoC, 374–75 ("*two boxers in the ring*"); Hapgood and Richardson, 75, 133–35; "The Background of the 135th Infantry," ts, n.d., Iowa GSM; Matthew Parker, *Monte Cassino*, 139 ("*every night the rumor*").

404 *In a two-acre field diced by German artillery:* James A. Luttrell, "The Operations of the 168th Infantry in the Rapido River Crossing," 1948, IS; Donald C. Landon, "The Operations of the 2nd Bn, 135th Inf in the Cassino Offensive," 1946, IS (*Six new lieutenants*);

Parker, 144 (*sulfa powder in salt shakers*); Belfrad H. Gray, Jr., "The Crossing of the Rapido River and Occupation of Positions Above Cassino by Company I, 168th Infantry," 1947, IS; Davies, 124–25; OH, Howard Kippenberger, Feb. 4 and 12, 1947, SM, MHI (*so hobbled by frozen feet*).

404 *three efforts were made to break through:* Majdalany, 85; *StoC*, 382–83; memoir, C. N. "Red" Morgan, 3rd Bn, 141st Inf, n.d., Texas MFM Web site, www.kwanah.com/36Division/pstoc.htm; Clifford H. Peek, Jr., ed., *Five Years, Five Countries, Five Campaigns*, 47 (*ricochet shell*).

404 *"within a bare 100 meters":* Molony V, 704; Porch (*attacked on too broad a front*); "34th Division Casualties, Cassino Operation," Feb. 15, 1944, MWC, corr, Citadel, box 3; censorship morale reports, Nov. 1943–June 1944, NARA RG 492, MTO AG, 311.7 (*"Personally I'm glad"*); GK, Feb. 10, 1944 (*"Full moon"*).

405 *"suspended by invisible wires":* Brian Harpur, *The Impossible Victory*, 57; Harold L. Bond, *Return to Cassino*, 82 (*smacked the roof*).

405 *Early on February 14:* "Historical Narrative and Journal," G-3, 34th ID; G. R. Stevens, *Fourth Indian Division*, 284; *StoC*, 374 (*seven hundred litter bearers*); Bond, 101–3 (*sawed logs*); William Shakespeare, *Henry IV, Part 2*, act 2, scene 2; B. Smith, "Waltonia," ts, 1981, IWM, 67/254/1 (*"Thank God their mothers"*); Robert Capa, *Slightly Out of Focus*, 116 (*white shoes*).

405 *an American detail delivered 150 corpses:* OH, Paul Adams, 1975, Irving Monclova and Marlin Lang, MHI, SOOHP; Nicholas M. Bozic, "36th Infantry Division, Salerno to Rome," ts, n.d., Texas MFM (*"bodies all over the hill"*); Hal Reese, IG, 36th ID, "Intermission at Cassino," n.d., Texas MFM (*"It is such a tragedy"*). Lt. Col. Reese was killed near Anzio three months later.

405 *Saddest of all:* G. L. Hanssen, *The Hanssens of Eastern Iowa*, 32–33, 39–44, 47.

406 *They had been at it so long:* Pyle, 127, 134–35.

406 *"They live and die so miserably":* James Tobin, *Ernie Pyle's War*, 132; OH, Harold Alexander, Jan. 10–15, 1949, SM, CMH, II-23; *StoC*, 383 (*"almost mutinous"*).

407 *Shit Corner:* memoir, P. Royle, ts, 1972, IWM, 99/72/1, 108; Thomas Drake Durrance, "Battle for the Abbey," ts, n.d., author's possession (*"Halt!"*); Paul Fussell, *Wartime*, 274–75 (*"Don't be scared"*).

407 *The lucky ones found shelter:* Nigel Nicolson, *Alex: The Life of Field Marshal Earl Alexander of Tunis*, 248; C. L. Sulzberger, *A Long Row of Candles*, 236 (*"steam"*); Martha Gellhorn, *The Face of War*, 131 (*"perfume and gasoline"*); Howard H. Peckham and Shirley A. Snyder, *Letters from Fighting Hoosiers*, vol. 2, 76 (*"We sit around quibbling"*); Warren P. Munsell, Jr., *The Story of a Regiment*, 40 (*Berlin Bitch*); Klaus H. Huebner, *A Combat Doctor's Diary*, 51 (*daily passwords*).

407 *The unlucky crouched in damp sangars:* memoir, Anthony "Butch" Buccieri, 133rd Inf Regt, written by John F. Sackheim, 2001, VHP; *StoC*, 380; C. Richard Eke, "A Game of Soldiers," IWM, 92/1/1, 91-92 (*wooden plows*); Blaxland, 55; Parker, 152 (*urinate, if necessary*); memoir, Henry E. Gardiner, ts, n.d., USMA Arch, 208; memo, N. P. Morrow to L. J. McNair, Jan. 28, 1944, AGF Board, NARA RG 407, E 427, NATOUSA (*99,000 sets*); "Operations in Italy, January 1944," 142nd Inf Regt, MHI, 603-142, 9 (*too thick for most GI boots*); Samuel David Spivey, *A Doughboy's Narrative*, 84 (*"a life of extremes"*).

407 *"the quartermaster must be running":* memoir, Gardiner, 214; June Wandrey, *Bedpan Commando*, 85 (*"Our meat is dead"*); Ivan Dmitri, *Flight to Everywhere*, 145 (*"no fresh milk"*); Maurice R. P. Bechard, "This Is an Account of What Was to Be," ts, n.d., 16th Armored Engineer Bn, 1st AD, ASEQ, MHI, 2 (*"fighting the whole fucking war"*); Neil McCallum, *Journey with a Pistol*, 142 (*"cold as a corpse"*).

408 *"disheveled, unshaven, unkempt":* J. B. Tomlinson, "Under the Banner of the Battleaxe," ts, n.d., IWM, 80/29/1, 105, 139,144; Parker, 207; C. T. Fram, "The Littlest Victory," ts, n.d., IWM 85/19/1, 72.

408 *"regular as a scythe-stroke"*: Lawrence Durrell, from *Sicilian Carousel,* in Alcie Leccese Powers, *Italy in Mind,* 82; Walter Bernstein, *Keep Your Head Down,* 149 (*"finger of God"*); StoC, 380 (*200,000 shells*); AAR, II Corps, Jan. 1944, NARA RG 407, E 427, 202-0.3, 15 (*240mm howitzer*); Peckham and Snyder, 68 (*"a lot of war bonds"*); Cyril Ray, *Algiers to Austria,* 119 (*"most heavily shelled pinpoint"*); Durrance, "Battle for the Abbey," 16 (*"pounding the soles of my feet"*); N. P. Morrow, "Field Artillery Technique and Procedure," Jan. 7, 1944, AGF observer report, file #56, NARA RG 337, box 52; N. P. Morrow, "Employment of Artillery in Italy," *FAJ,* Aug. 1944, 499+; "Lessons in Combat," 34th ID, Sept. 1944, Iowa GSM, 47 (*"murder space"*); "AFHQ Intelligence Notes No. 63," June 13, 1944, NARA RG 407, E 47, 95-AL1-2.18 (*"Wet earth"*).

409 *learned to relieve the overpressure:* Carl Rollyson, *Nothing Ever Happens to the Brave,* 193; Ray, 118; Spike Milligan, *Mussolini: His Part in My Downfall,* 255 (*"Digging and swearing"*); Alex Bowlby, *The Recollections of Rifleman Bowlby,* 26 (*"Keep your nut down"*).

409 *"Enlisted men expect everything"*: Douglas Allanbrook, *See Naples,* 180; Ben Shephard, *War of Nerves,* 237 (*"gutful men"*); "Lessons from the Italian Campaign," Apr. 14, 1944, 1st SSF, Robert D. Burhans papers, HIA, box 7 (*"Use good judgment"*).

409 *"Came across three dead G.I.s"*: Maurice R. P. Bechard, "This Is an Account of What Was to Be," ts, n.d., 16th Armored Engineer Bn, 1st AD, ASEQ, MHI, 2.

409 *Schubert's "Unfinished Symphony"*: Fussell, 183; John Muirhead, *Those Who Fall,* 101 (*"bright beads"*)

409 *"The initial crack"*: B. Smith, "Waltonia," ts, 1981, IWM, 67/254/1.

410 *"You could never lose it"*: memoir, P. Royle, t.s, 1972, IWM, 99/72/1, 106; Harpur, 65 (*"That brooding monastery"*).

410 *A new warlord arrived:* Paul Freyberg, *Bernard Freyberg, V.C.,* 458 (*"torch is now thrown"*).

410 *"I'm Freyberg"*: W. G. Stevens, *Freyberg, the Man,* 103, 35 (*"large all over"*); H. Essame, "A Controversial Campaign—Italy, 1943–45," *Army Quarterly and Defence Journal,* Jan. 1968, 219+ (*"shelling did everyone good"*); Stevens, *Freyberg, the Man,* 96 (*"lack of imagination"*); Freyberg, 112–13 (*"St. Sebastian"*), 186–87 (*"diastolic murmur"*); Peter Singleton-Gates, *General Lord Freyberg VC,* 8; obit, "Gen. Lord Freyberg, British Leader at Monte Cassino," *Washington Star,* July 5, 1963 (*"two wounds for every bullet"*); Michael Carver, ed., *The War Lords,* 583 (*india-rubber*); Lisa Chaney, *Hide-and-Seek With Angels: A Life of J. M. Barrie,* 316 (*"his lack of humour"*).

411 *lined it with flowering sage:* Freyberg, 51; Stevens, *Freyberg, the Man,* 56–57 (*"fine gloves"*), 60, 76 (*"your turn tomorrow"*).

411 *Even his admirers acknowledged:* Freyberg, 62–63 (*"wouldn't try to think"*), 118; "Operations of N.Z. Corps on the Fifth Army Front," part I, May 1944, HQ, AAI, UK NA, CAB 106/366, 4 (*a new creation*).

411 *"clean and spritely"*: E. D. Smith, *The Battles for Cassino,* 65; Phillips, 178–79; Majdalany, 102–3; B. Smith, "Waltonia," ts, 1981, IWM, 67/254/1 (*"crates of live chickens"*).

411 *At first Freyberg considered:* Molony V, 706–7; *Battle,* 193; Phillips, 222; Hapgood and Richardson, 151 (*"no brains"*); Howard Kippenberger, *Infantry Brigadier,* 356 (*"soviet of division commanders"*). Tuker considered Freyberg "brave as a lion" but "no planner of battles and a niggler in action." Raleigh Trevelyan, *Rome '44,* 133.

412 *"helpless lunacy"*: Bishenwar Prasad, ed., *Official History of the Indian Armed Forces in the Second World War, 1939–1945: The Campaign in Italy, 1943–1945,* 98 (*deemed Monte Cassino impregnable*), 105; F. Jones, "The Bombing of Monte Cassino, 23–25; "The Bombing of Cassino Abbey," 1965, monograph for official history, UK NA, CAB 101/229, 7.

412 *"No practicable means available"*: Singleton-Gates, 277.

412 *"Spadger still wants"*: GK, Feb. 11, 1944; diary, MWC, Feb. 4, 1944, Citadel, box 65 (*"bull in a china closet"*).

412 *"I would level the Vatican itself"*: censorship morale reports, Nov. 1943–June 1944, NARA RG 492, MTO AG, 311.7.

### The Bitchhead

412 *Sixty miles away:* beachhead census, D+10, JPL papers, MHI, box 12; Pyle, 173; Francesco Rossi and Silvano Casaldi, *Those Days at Nettuno,* frontispiece; Fred Sheehan, *Anzio: Epic of Bravery,* 102; *Anzio Beachhead,* 113 (*empty wine barrels*); Edmund F. Ball, *Staff Officer with the Fifth Army,* 294 (*sandstone seemed to telegraph*); "Engineer History, Fifth Army, Mediterranean Theater," n.d., MHI, 81 (*tunnel rumored to have been built by Nero*); Trevelyan, 152 (*"So back we go to World War I"*).

413 *"My cost of living"*: Flint Whitlock, *The Rock of Anzio,* 179.

413 *"We have found our religion"*: diary, William Russell Hinckley, Feb. 1944, author's possession; "Background Material, Historical Branch G-2," n.d., ASF, QM General, technical information branch, CMH, 000.75, 3 (*punctured all fifteen ovens*); Pyle, 168, 188; F. J. Lowry, "The Naval Side of the Anzio Invasion," *Proceedings,* Jan. 1954, 22+ (*skippers weighed anchor*); Justin F. Gleichauf, *Unsung Sailors: The Naval Armed Guard in World War II,* 293 (*"brighter than Yankee Stadium"*); Roberta Love Tayloe, *Combat Nurse,* 80 (*"Anzio, my Anzio"*).

413 *Hell's Half-Acre:* "Fifth Army Medical Service History," Feb. 1945, CMH, 19–20, 23 (*killed the VI Corps surgeon*); Charles M. Wiltse, *The Medical Department: Medical Service in the Mediterranean and Minor Theaters,* 275 (*a Luftwaffe bomber*); testimony, Paul Sauer, n.d., Fifth Army JAG, war crimes office, NARA RG 153, box 530 (*"I'm dying"*); Sheehan, 166 (*treated in the same hospital*).

414 *"God, help us"*: "Fifth Army Medical Service History," 24; Carlo D'Este, *Fatal Decision,* 2; journal, Fourteenth Army, Feb. 5, 1944, in "The German Operation at Anzio," German military document section, Military Intelligence Div, WD, MHI, JPL papers, box 9; corr, George H. Revelle, Jr., to wife, Feb. 5, 1944, author's possession (*"dog on an iceberg"*); George C. Harper, "The World War II Years," ts, 1999, 16th Armored Engineer Bn, 1st AD, MHI, ASEQ, 27 (*"outhouse"*); Pyle, 160; Malcolm Munthe, *Sweet Is War,* 182 (*"dining room table"*); David Cole, *Rough Road to Rome,* 199 (*"Morphine"*); Charles F. Marshall, *A Ramble Through My War,* 64 (*"too much iron"*).

414 *Deep holes grew deeper:* diary, Robert M. Marsh, Feb. 11, 1944, 81st Armored Reconnaissance Bn, 1st AD, MHI, ASEQ; Paul Dickson, *War Slang,* 113+; Ball, 295; William J. Sweet, Jr., "Operations of the 2nd Battalion, 504th Parachute Infantry Regiment, on the Anzio Beachhead," 1947, IS (*eliminate tree bursts*); Munthe, 182 (*"sons of the prophet"*); George Forty, *M4 Sherman,* 67 (*"can't get used to bein' scared"*); Paul W. Brown, *The Whorehouse of the World,* 392–93; T. Moffatt Burriss, *Strike and Hold,* 87 (*firing at the helmets*); Cole, 205 (*"shooting gallery"*).

415 *"Get moving"*: Tom Roe, *Anzio Beachhead,* 43, 53; John Lardner, "Anzio, February 10th," in *The New Yorker Book of War Pieces,* 262 (*"like sunburned skin"*); John Lardner, "The Show at Anzio," in John Stenbuck, ed., *Typewriter Battalion,* 117 (*"small, wet world"*); GK, March 25, 1944 (*Bitchhead*); Donald G. Taggart, ed., *History of the Third Infantry Division in World War II,* 125 (*"squirt of white tracer"*); Lloyd Clark, *Anzio,* 144 (*"I was alone"*); George Aris, *The Fifth British Division, 1939 to 1945,* 210–11, 239; Cole, 198 (*recalled his Virgil*).

415 *Yanks veered to the right:* Sweet, "Operations of the 2nd Battalion, 504th Parachute Infantry Regiment"; Trevelyan, 222 (*"Otto, Otto"*); Lloyd M. Wells, *From Anzio to the Alps,* 83 (*"Nerves became frayed"*); Pyle, 194.

415 *Grave diggers halted their poker game:* Allan Jaynes, "Mud, Misery and Messerschmitts," ts, 1990, 45th ID Mus; "The 30 Years of Army Experience of Thomas E. Hannum," ts, n.d., 91st Armored FA Bn, 1st AD, MHI, ASEQ, 74; Pyle, 194; Peter Verney, *Anzio 1944,* 86 (*"can never be as bad"*).

415 *disrupted Mackensen's timetable:* journal, Fourteenth Army, Feb. 3, 5, 12, 1944; AAR, 3 Inf Bde, Jan. 30–Feb 14, 1944, UK NA, CAB 106/850 (*exposed salient*).

416 *The attack fell heaviest:* Sheehan, 94; Wynford Vaughan-Thomas, *Anzio,* 96 (*"dirty, ragged wave"*), 101; Verney, 98 (*"Germans are at the door"*); D.J.L. Fitzgerald, *History of the Irish Guards in the Second World War,* 268, 275 (*"never saw so many people killed"*); Robley D. Evans et al., "American Armor at Anzio," 1949, AS, Ft. K, table; AAR, "Report on Action at Campoleone," 3 Inf Bde, Feb. 21, 1944, Philip L. E. Wood papers, LH, Wood 2/1 (*438 tubes*).

416 *"All the shells in hell":* Vaughan-Thomas, 106; StoC, 396; journal, Fourteenth Army, Feb. 4, 1944; *Anzio Beachhead,* 46.

416 *The attack resumed on Monday evening:* *Anzio Beachhead,* 55; Nigel Nicolson, *The Grenadier Guards in the War of 1939–1945,* vol. 2, 408 (*"Nothing heard of Number 1 company"*), 39 (*looking for breath plumes*); Verney, 137, 142 (*"hit in the arse"*); D'Este, 222 (*"eaten by pigs"*).

416 *Aided by a captured map:* journal, Fourteenth Army, Feb. 8, 1944; David Erskin, *The Scots Guards, 1919–1955,* 216–17, 221 (*"even more unpleasant"*).

417 *More unpleasant yet:* StoC, 396; *Anzio Beachhead,* 55; Vaughan-Thomas, 124; Erskin, 223 (*"Where is the sea?"*).

417 *On sleepless nights:* Trevelyan, 157; author visit, May 7, 2004 (*ramps for rolling barrels*); Rossi and Casaldi, 159; JPL, 367 (*hunched over plywood desks*); Marshall, 38, 41 (*maps with grease pencil markings*).

417 *"The old Hun is getting ready":* JPL, 360, 365 (*shrinking by nine thousand*); James Parton, "Air Force Spoken Here," 351 (*largest air command*); "Mediterranean Allied Air Forces in Operation SHINGLE, 1 Jan–18 March '44," 1945, CMH, 5-1 DA, 23–24 (*traveled from southern France*).

418 *"A terrible struggle all day":* JPL, 369; Rossi and Casaldi, 169 (*"hermaphrodites"*); msg, JPL to MWC, Feb. 9, 1944, 2040 hrs, JPL papers, MHI, box 12; Verney, 23; Molony V, 751 (*high-strung engineer*); OH, MWC, May 10–21, 1948, SM, MHI, 76 (*"good telephone operator"*); OH, JPL, May 24, 1948, SM, MHI (*"Well, I do"*).

418 *"Complete gaff, no decision":* diary, William R. C. Penney, Jan. 29, 1944, LH, 8/11, 8/14 (*"infuriating delay"*); D'Este, 221 (*"Corncob Charlie"*); Trevelyan, 157 (*"We'll lose the beachhead"*); Molony V, 738 (*"I trust you are satisfied"* and *"Clark might be the man to go"*); Martin Gilbert, *Winston S. Churchill,* vol. 7, *Road to Victory, 1941–1945,* 666; Winston S. Churchill, *Closing the Ring,* 488 (*"superiority in chauffeurs"*); Vaughan-Thomas, 111 (*"a great disappointment"*).

419 *As Mackensen tightened his grip:* *Anzio Beachhead,* 61; Verney, 128–29; Nicolson, *The Grenadier Guards,* 386; diary, William R. C. Penney, Jan. 29, 1944, LH, 8/19. (*"immediate corps plan"*); JPL, 370.

419 *He popped out of the command post:* CM, 329; Vaughan-Thomas, 127; diary, William R. C. Penney, Jan. 29, 1944, LH, 8/11, and msg, JPL to Penney, Feb. 11, 1944, 8/20 (*"reinforcements are on the way"*).

419 *A counterattack at dawn on Saturday:* Molony V, 736; Sheehan, 111; Whitlock, 171 (*"gray-coated infantry"*).

419 *General Alex had long been celebrated:* Sulzberger, 229–30 (*red hat drew fire*).

419 *"We wanted a breakthrough":* Vaughan-Thomas, 146 (*"Were any of you at Dunkirk?"*); Sheehan, 124 (*"German opposite us"*); Betsy Wade, ed., *Forward Positions: The War Correspondence of Homer Bigart,* 37 (*stories were censored*); "Censorship Takes Anzio," *Time,* Feb. 28, 1944, 46 (*"such rot"*); Phillip Knightley, *The First Casualty,* 330.

420 *"I tried to stop the tirade":* Vaughan-Thomas, 147 (La Traviata).

420 *Lucas was left alone:* JPL, 378–79 (*"I failed to chase the Hun"*).

420 *General Mackensen, the Hun himself:* journal, Fourteenth Army, Feb. 13, 1944 (*Lake Nemi*); author visit, Dec. 1, 2006; Fritz Meske, "The Anzio-Nettuno Bridgehead: A

German Account," *Die Wehrmacht,* March 8, 1944, in *MR,* June 1944 ("*not a flash of a gun*").

421 *the counterattack would fling six divisions: Anzio Beachhead,* 67; "German Version of the History of the Italian Campaign," CARL, N-16671.1-3, 90; *StoC,* 420; Vaughan-Thomas, 156.

421 *"concentrated, overwhelming, ruthless"*: Ralph S. Mavrogordato, "The Battle for the Anzio Beachhead," Apr. 1958, NARA RG 319, E 145, OCMH, R-series, R-124, 11,13; Vaughan-Thomas, 156; *StoC,* 419 (*delay their invasion*).

421 *mask the clank of approaching panzers:* journal, Fourteenth Army, Feb. 13 and 15, 1944; Eberhard von Mackensen, "Field Fortifications Around the Anzio-Nettuno Beachhead," 1950, MHI, FMS, #C-061, 7 (*streambeds ran perpendicular*); msg, Hermann Göring Div, Feb. 14, 1944, in VI Corps G-2 report no. 148, JPL papers, MHI, box 1 ("*for short errands*"); Sheehan, 124 ("*house lights*").

421 *"like the rolling of a drum"*: D'Este, 192; Henry Kaufman, *Vertrauensmann,* 20 (*Birds tumbled*); Whitlock, 185, 190 ("*coffee grinders*").

423 *They were not unexpected:* G-2 periodic report no. 141, Feb 16, 1944, JPL papers, MHI, box 1; G-2 weekly intelligence summary, no. 77, Feb. 12, 1944, AFHQ, NARA RG 407, E 427, 95-AL1-2.6; F.H. Hinsley et al., *British Intelligence in the Second World War,* 190–93; Ralph Bennett, *Ultra and the Mediterranean Strategy,* 267–68; James H. Cook, Jr., "The Operations of Company I, 179th Infantry, in the Vicinity of the Factory, Anzio Beachhead," 1949, IS (*few forward units had sufficient girded*); *StoC,* 420–21; Whitlock, 187 ("*I watched the dust*"); Fitzgerald, 335 ("*savage, brutish*"); "Defense of a Position by 2nd Battalion, 157th Infantry, 45th Division," n.d., AGF Board, NARA RG 407, 95-USF1-2.0, box 253; Ralph E. Niffenegger, "The Operations of the 3rd Platoon, Company G, 157th Infantry, Astride the Anzio–Albano Road," 1949, IS; Wells, 62–69; Vaughan-Thomas, 180 ("*a bastard of a place*").

423 *Forward companies of Royal Fusilier:* Sheehan, 119, 159–61; Burriss, 75 ("*flock of canaries*"); John Embry, "A Time to Honor," ts, n.d., 160th FA Bn, 45th ID Mus; Ball, 308 ("*Give us everything*").

423 *Grim as the day had been:* Molony V, 745; journal, Fourteenth Army, Feb. 16, 1944 ("*Enemy resistance*"); Sheehan, 159; N. P. Morrow, "Employment of Artillery in Italy," 499; *Anzio Beachhead,* 90.

424 *fourteen howling German battalions had driven: StoC,* 421; Cook, "The Operations of Company I, 179th Infantry" ("*verge of panic*").

424 *"179th lost 1,000 men"*: "Diary Notes of Gen. McLain," Feb. 18, 1944, MHI, OCMH WWII Europe interviews; Whitlock, 227; Munsell, 55 ("*tears rolled down*"); Wells, 57–58 ("*load my rifle*").

424 *Four hundred Allied gun tubes:* Roe, 62; Walter Karig, *Battle Report: The Atlantic War,* 284 ("*count the rivets*"); *AAFinWWII,* vol. 3, 356 ("*heaviest payload*").

425 *Jeeps careering to the rear:* Whitlock, *Anzio;* corr, John P. O'Malley to Yarborough, n.d., CJB, "Chrono. File: Sicily," box 48 ("*Don't leave the phone*"); R. Close-Brooks, "Anzio Beach-Head," ts, 1946, in James Scott Elliott papers, LH, 4 (*obliged to sit on the knees*).

425 *flinging the contents over the lip*: Robert A. Guenthner, "The Operations of Company F, 180th Infantry, Six Days Previous to and During the Major German Offensive," 1948, IS; Whitlock, 199 (*dull the glint*); Walter Fries, "29th Panzer Grenadier Division, February 1944," 1947, FMS, #D-141, MHI, 7–10; Edward A. Raymond, "The Caves of Anzio," *FAJ,* Dec. 1944, 851+; Starr, ed., 154; Whitlock, 224 ("*as small as you can*").

425 *"Men trickled back"*: Cook, "The Operations of Company I, 179th Infantry" ("*I guess you will relieve me*").

425 *He was right:* Molony V, 745 (*carving a bulge from the Allied line*); D'Este, 504n ("*not very attractive*").

426 *In the midst of the crisis:* diary, MWC, Feb. 16, 1944, Citadel, box 65; Mark M. Boatner III, *The Biographical Dictionary of World War II,* 399 (*"Iron Mike"*); OH, James M. Wilson, Jr., former Truscott aide, Apr. 23, 2004, with author, Washington, D.C.; JPL, 386.

426 *a Piper Grasshopper pilot spotted 2,500 Germans:* "Historical Record, Headquarters VI Corps, February 1944," Apr. 27, 1944, LKT Jr., papers, GCM Lib, box 13, folder 2; J. W. Totten, "Anzio Artillery," ts, 1946, CGSC, Ft. L, CARL, N-2253.6, 14; Fitzgerald, 346 (*"Bits of Kraut"*); William Seymour, *Yours to Reason Why,* 268–71 (*"struggling, field-gray figures"*); Embry, "A Time to Honor," 142 (*falling truck tailgates*); Nicolson, *The Grenadier Guards,* 412 (*32,000 rounds*); Wiley H. O'Mohundro, "From Mules to Missiles," ts, n.d., MHI, 55 (*"turned and ran"*); Verney, 174 (*"Light Brigade"*).

426 *At 9:30 P.M. a lull:* R. Close-Brooks, "Anzio Beach-Head," ts, 1946, in James Scott Elliott papers, LH, 4 (*Tanks lurched forward*); journal, Fourteenth Army, Feb. 17 and 18, 1944 (*"No decisive breakthrough"*).

427 *Lucas sensed his shifting fortunes:* Molony V, 748; Vaughan-Thomas, 171–74 (*cooks, drivers*); George F. Howe, *The Battle History of the 1st Armored Division,* 297; William L. Allen, *Anzio: Edge of Disaster,* 112–13.

427 *Harmon woke every morning:* E. N. Harmon, *Combat Commander,* 7, 12, 32; obit, *Assembly,* Dec. 1980, ENH; *Register of Graduates and Former Cadets,* 1989 ed., 314; OH, ONB, n.d., Kitty Buhler, MHI, 182 (*"poor man's George Patton"*); OH, Hamilton H. Howze, Apr. 1973, Robert T. Reed, SOOHP, MHI, 49 (*"hog on ice"*); *Texas,* 209 (*"stupidity of the high command"*); corr, E. N. Harmon to JPL, Feb. 12, 1944, ENH, box 1 (*"well-established plan"*); Jack F. Wilhm et al., "Armor in the Invasion of North Africa," 1950, AS, Ft. K (*"enemy has his troubles"*).

427 *"Give 'em hell!":* Whitlock, 235.

428 *Two hundred prisoners trotted:* Howe, 299; *Anzio Beachhead,* 86; Fries, "29th Panzer Grenadier Division, February 1944," 7–10; Vaughan-Thomas, 178 (*"made him worried"*).

428 *Mackensen's troops poked:* Molony V, 749; Fritz Wentzell, "The Italian Campaign from August 1943 to February 1945," Dec. 1945, CMH, Geog Files, Italy, 370.2, 43 (*"many hounds"*); journal, Fourteenth Army, Feb. 20, 1944 (*"evacuate the wounded"*); *Anzio Beachhead,* 91 (*mustered 673 men*).

428 *VI Corps casualties also exceeded five thousand:* StoC, 424; Whitlock, 248; Lawrence D. Collins, *The 56th Evac Hospital,* 169 (*nurses' summer fatigues*).

428 *"Message from Clark":* JPL, 393.

428 *"proved to be an old woman":* John Keegan, ed., *Churchill's Generals,* 120–21; msg, DDE to GCM, Feb. 16, 1944, SM, MHI, box 2.

429 *"done all he could":* OH, MWC, May 10–21, 1948, SM, MHI, 77; OH, Alexander, Jan. 10–15, 1949, II-18 (*"ambition was key"*); diary, MWC, Feb. 22, 26, 1944, MWC papers, Citadel, box 65 (*"old physically and mentally"*); John North, ed., *The Alexander Memoirs, 1940–1945,* 126 (*"That would be very bad"*); aide's diaries, Feb. 18, 1944, LKT Jr., Citadel, box 18, folder 3 (*"four or five days"*).

429 *At midmorning on February 22:* C. Webber, "Observers' Notes on the Italian Campaign," June 14, 1944, NARA RG 337, E 15A, AGF observer reports, #112, box 55, 4; OH, Theodore J. Conway, 1977, Robert F. Ensslin, SOOHP, MHI, III-10; OH, Harry O. Paxson, Nov. 1981, Herbert M. Hart, CEOH, 119–21; e-mail, Silvano Casaldi to author, Feb. 16, 2005; memo, R. W. Komer, "Report on Historical Observation in the Field," Feb. 24, 1944, in "Report on Activities of the Historical Section, Fifth Army," Nov. 1945, Chester G. Starr papers, HIA, box 1 (*"General Officers Only"*).

429 *"could no longer resist the pressure":* JPL, 394; *CM,* 328; OH, James M. Wilson, Jr., Apr. 23, 2004, with author, Washington, D.C.; diary, cover letter, JPL to son, Jan. 1, 1946, MHI.

429 *Despite persistent ailments:* aide's diaries, Feb. 11 and 14, 1944, LKT Jr., Citadel, box 18, folder 3; OH, Walter T. Kerwin, Jr., Nov. 1, 2004, with author, Washington, D.C.; *CM,* 325. Kerwin rose to four-star rank.

430 *"You can't relieve a corps commander"*: OH, JPL, May 24, 1948, SM, MHI; *CM*, 328; diary, MWC, Feb. 24, 1944, Citadel, box 65 (*"prefer to be second"*).

430 *The new corps commander returned:* diary, Don E. Carleton, Feb. 22, 1944, HIA, box 1; corr, LKT Jr., to Sarah, March 8, 1944, LKT Jr., papers, GCM Lib, box 1, folder 6.

430 *"cool, level, taciturn"*: OH, Theodore J. Conway, 1977, Robert F. Ensslin, SOOHP, MHI, III-10; diary, MWC, Feb. 22, 1944, MWC papers, Citadel, box 65 (*72,982 casualties*); MWC to Ann Clark, Feb. 27, 1944, personal corr, Citadel.

430 *"It is sheer nonsense"*: MWC to Renie, Feb. 27, 1944, personal corr, Citadel.

430 *Prodded by Hitler: Anzio Beachhead,* 99; corr, John W. O'Daniel to Hal C. Pattison, Sept. 3, 1964, NARA RG 319, OCMH, 2-3.7 CC3, box 256; Hugh A. Scott, *The Blue and White Devils,* 109.

430 *Truscott pinned a Bill Mauldin cartoon:* Vaughan-Thomas, 182.

431 *bloodiest month in the Mediterranean:* "Summary of Activities," June 1, 1944, NATOUSA, analysis and control division, CMH; Molony V, 750; memo, H. Alexander to MWC, Feb. 26, 1944, Robert T. Frederick papers, HIA, box 1 (*"He is quicker"*).

431 *"Without air support"*: Fritz Wentzell, "The Italian Campaign from August 1943 to February 1945," 20–23; Parton, 356 (*"flat on his back"*); Molony V, 747n; J. W. Totten, "Anzio Artillery," 10; Walter Kühn, "The Artillery at Anzio-Nettuno," March 1947, FMS, #D-158, CARL, N-17500.838.2, 11–15; memo, H. Alexander to MWC, Feb. 26, 1944, Robert T. Frederick papers, HIA, box 1; OH, Edward J. O'Neill, June 22, 1948, NARA RG 319, OCMH, CA, box 005 (*counterbattery fire in four minutes*); Arthur R. Harris, "The Bigger They Are the Harder They Fall," *FAJ,* May–June 1938, 229; Joseph M. Kolisch, POW interrogation report, Feb. 29, 1944, no. 405, HQ, Fifth Army, NARA RG 337, E 15A, AGF observer report no. 93, box 53; Andrew Brookes, *Air War over Italy, 1943–1945,* 60 (*three-quarters of all German battle casualties*).

431 *"the last year of the war"*: Walter von Unruh, "Inspection of the Italian Theater of War," 1947, FMS, #D-016, MHI, 34–35; Siegfried Westphal, "The Italian Campaign," chap. 13, NARA RG 319, OCMH, CA, box 9 (*"progressive exhaustion"*).

431 *"A turning point had been reached"*: Westphal, "The Italian Campaign"; A. G. Steiger, "The Italian Campaign, 4 Jan–4 June 1944," July 1948, report no. 20, Historical Section, Canadian Army HQ, MHI Lib, 17 (*"bowed down"*).

432 *German engineers trucked in:* Rossi and Casaldi, 192; Daniel Lang, "Letter from Rome," *New Yorker,* June 24, 1944, 52+; Roe, 73 (*"successor would soon"*); Fitzgerald, 321 (*"an old man now"*).

### *"Man Is Distinguished from the Beasts"*

432 *had gone missing at Anzio:* Captured on Feb. 7, 1944, Paul Freyberg escaped and eventually took refuge in Vatican City. Freyberg, 465, 470–71; Trevelyan, 146; *Mountain Inferno,* 743 (*"holding up all our lives"*).

432 *"consistent with military necessity"*: StoC, 397; "The Bombing of Cassino Abbey," CAB 101/229, 16 (*Eisenhower in turn warned*); memo, 15th Army Group to MWC, Jan 10, 1944, Fifth Army, AG file no. 105-32.7, SM, MHI (*"ecclesiastical centres"*); "Preservation of Works of Art in Italy," May 8, 1944, Henry C. Newton papers, MHI, box 4 (*"man is distinguished"*); Solly Zuckerman, *From Apes to Warlords,* 211 (*crew briefing packets*); Robert Wallace, *The Italian Campaign,* 120 (*"Venus Fixers"*).

433 *Bombs had damaged forty churches:* "The Damaged Neapolitan Churches," ts, n.d., and corr, Herbert L. Matthews, *NYT,* to DDE, Nov. 17, 1943, in monthly report, Allied Control Commission, subcommission for monuments, fine arts and archives, July 9, 1944, both in Henry C. Newton papers, MHI, box 4; "The Bombing of Cassino Abbey," CAB 101/229, 18 (*hit Castel Gandolfo*); Wallace, 120 (*"war in a museum"*).

433 *The unit ordered to capture:* Field Marshal Lord Carver, *The Imperial War Museum Book of the War in Italy, 1943–1945,* 144–45; "The Bombing of Cassino Abbey," CAB 101/229,

20 (*"Violation of Geneva Convention"*); "Monte Cassino Bombing," Dec. 1944, HQ, Fifth Army, CMH, Geog L Italy, 373.11 (*thirty machine guns*); StoC, 408 (*flash of field glasses*); John Ezard, "Error Led to Bombing of Monte Cassino," *Guardian* (U.K.), Apr. 4, 2000, 5 (*"Nazis Turn Monastery"*).

433 *flew in an observation plane:* OH, Ira Eaker, Feb. 1975, Hugh N. Ahmann, AFHRA, K239.0512-829, 444–47; Hapgood and Richardson, 185, 164 (*"I have Catholic gunners"*); North, ed., 120 (*"dead tooth"*); intel annex, HQ, Fifth Wing, Feb. 14, 1944, in Evans, *The Bombing of Monte Cassino.*

433 *Others passionately disagreed:* diary, MWC, Feb. 14, 1944, Citadel, box 65; GK, Feb. 2-5, 10, 12, 14, 1944; StoC, 405 (*two thousand refugees*); corr, MWC to GK, Feb. 4, 1944, NARA RG 200, "Personal-Official File," 130/76/1/4, box 3 (*"belligerent attitude"*).

434 *no better than "fifty–fifty":* Freyberg, 458; memo, A. Gruenther, "Monte Cassino Abbey Bombing," Feb. 12, 1944, MWC, Citadel, box 3, folder 5.

434 *"I now have five corps":* diary, MWC, Feb. 4, 1944, Citadel, box 65; memo, MWC, Feb. 13, 1944, Citadel, box 3, folder 5; StoC, 407; *Calculated*, 318 (*"If the Germans are not"*).

434 *"Bricks and mortar":* North, ed., 121, 130 (*"What are you doing"*); Hapgood and Richardson, 172 (*" 'they wouldn't let me use air' "*).

435 *"due to the political daintiness":* memo, MWC, Feb. 13, 1944, Citadel, box 3, folder 5 (*"unduly interfering"*).

435 *The attack would be launched quickly:* Molony V, 713; Phillips, 207 (*single token bomb*); Hapgood and Richardson, 191 (*lobbed two dozen shells*); Bloch, "The Bombardment of Monte Cassino," 403 (*"Amici italiani"*); StoC, 409.

435 *A pleasant morning sun:* Frido von Senger und Etterlin, *Neither Fear nor Hope*, 198–99, 208.

435 *For five months:* Corelli Barnett, ed., *Hitler's Generals*, 375–78; "Small World," CBS television segment, 1959, moderated by Edward R. Murrow; Hapgood and Richardson, 39 (*"more French than Prussian"*), 204; http://www.islandfarm.fsnet.co.uk/index.html (*killed at Cambrai*).

436 *In this war he had helped capture Cherbourg:* Senger, 5–6, 130, 163–67, 202; Boatner, 497–97; Frido von Senger und Etterlin, "War Diary of the Italian Campaign," 1953, FMS, #C-095b, MHI, 40–41, 78; StoC, 407.

436 *"The rotten thing is to keep fighting":* Hapgood and Richardson, 174.

436 *"annihilation was only a matter of time":* Senger, "War Diary of the Italian Campaign," 69. The British official history later accused Senger of exaggerating for effect. Molony V, 629n.

436 *"optimism is the elixir":* Senger, *Neither Fear nor Hope*, 227, 198–99 (*listening to evening concerts*); Hapgood and Richardson, 175; http://www.movies-and-more.ch/movies/1943/103327.php (Der Weisse Traum); Barnett, ed., 381 (*"Oh the loneliness"*).

437 *An officer in the 4th Indian Division:* Molony V, 713; Evans, 22 (*"gust upward"*); Homer R. Ankrum, *Dogfaces Who Smiled Through Tears*, 430 (*"smoke coming out of a man's ears"*).

437 *They were the first of 250 bombers:* AAFinWWII, vol. 3, 363; StoC, 411 (*hundreds of artillery rounds*); Durrance, "Battle for the Abbey," 10 (*"poplar trees"*).

437 *Soldiers on both sides of the hill:* Bloch, "The Bombardment of Monte Cassino," 407; Durrance, "Battle for the Abbey," 12–13 (*"Shovel it on"*); *Mountain Inferno*, 743 (*"hugging each other"*); Hapgood and Richardson, 213 (*"like all the other fools"*); Frank Gervasi, *The Violent Decade*, 560 (*"Beautiful precision"*).

437 *The leaflet barrage the previous evening:* StoC, 414; Böhmler, 166 (*confused attempts to contact*).

437 *Abbot Diamare planned to evacuate:* Majdalany, 128, 131–32 (*"beseech Christ"*); Leccisotti, 119–21; Hapgood and Richardson, 205, 209 (*stuffed their ears*).

438 *Thirteen hundred bombs:* Molony V, 713; Majdalany, 133–35; Böhmler, 169–70 (*"Parents abandoned"*); Leccisotti, 125 (*monks forced a passage*); Bloch, "The Bombardment of Monte Cassino," 406–7 (*"crazy with terror"*).

438 *No mortal would ever know how many died:* Hapgood and Richardson, 211; author visit, Monte Cassino abbey museum, Oct. 1, 1995; Molony V, 713.

438 *Alexander's headquarters asserted:* StoC, 411; "Monte Cassino Bombing," Dec. 1944, HQ, Fifth Army, CMH, Geog L Italy, 373.11 (*grenadiers searched the grounds*); Phillips, 218–19; Katriel Ben Arie, *Die Schlacht Bei Monte Cassino, 1944*, 201 (*field kitchen opened*).

438 *Not until dawn on Thursday:* Majdalany, 150, 152; Hapgood and Richardson, 218.

439 *The 4th Indian Division had expected:* "Operations of N.Z. Corps on the Fifth Army Front," 8–9; "The Bombing of Cassino Abbey," CAB 101/229, 14; Smith, 78; Stevens, *Fourth Indian Division*, 285 (*two dozen Indian troops were injured*); Majdalany, 142 (*"They told the monks"*).

439 *Freyberg's tactical incompetence:* "The Bombing of Cassino Abbey," 28; Carver, 143; Hapgood and Richardson, 153; corr, D.R.E.R. Bateman to F. Tuker, Feb. 18, 1959, IWM 72/117/1 (*"far out of his depth"*).

439 *Not until Tuesday night did the attack begin:* Majdalany, 144; Prasad, ed., 106–7; "Operations of N.Z. Corps on the Fifth Army Front," 9; Molony V, 714; Stevens, 287–90; *The Tiger Triumphs*, 47–48 (*trussed in tripwires*).

439 *But nine thousand Kiwi smoke shells:* OH, Kippenberger, Feb. 4 and 12, 1947; Phillips, 237; "Operations of N.Z. Corps on the Fifth Army Front," 15–16; Carver, 146–48 (*"A star shell went up"*); Prasad, ed., 111 (*Of two hundred mules*).

440 AVENGER *petered out:* Carver, 151; Senger, *Neither Fear nor Hope*, 206; Molony V, 713 (*"no military advantage"*); StoC, 417 (*"nothing beyond destruction"*).

440 *Military authorities pressured the OSS:* Jones, "The Bombing of Monte Cassino, 15 February 1944," 25–38; msg, Wilson to British chiefs of staff, in "Monte Cassino Bombing," Dec. 1944, HQ, Fifth Army, CMH, Geog L Italy, 373.11 (*"irrefutable evidence"*); John G. Norris, "Cassino Abbey Attack Order Laid to Briton," WP, Sept. 4, 1949, 1 (*no civilian bodies*); memo, psychological warfare, n.d. Wallace Carroll papers, LOC, box 1, folder 2, 12–15 (*campaign to blame Germany*).

440 *A German staff car picked him up:* Senger, "War Diary of the Italian Campaign," 83–84; "Monte Cassino Bombing," Dec. 1944, HQ, Fifth Army, CMH, Geog L Italy, 373.11 (*"Everything was done"*).

441 *Berlin overplayed its hand:* Hapgood and Richardson, 172, 224; Phillips, 220; Bloch, "The Bombardment of Monte Cassino," 386 (*"everlasting shame"*); J.F.C. Fuller, *The Second World War, 1939–1945*, 272; Brian Holden Reid, "The Italian Campaign, 1943–1945: A Reappraisal of Allied Generalship," *Journal of Strategic Studies*, March 1990, 128+ (*"imagination was petrified"*).

441 *"tomb of miscalculation":* Allanbrook, 175; Reid, "The Italian Campaign," 128 (*exhausted eight divisions*); Phillips, 241 (*"vistas of deadlock"*); msg, GCM to J. L. Devers, Feb. 18, 1944, "Eyes Only, General Devers, Incoming," NARA RG 492, MTOUSA, SGS, box 135.

441 *Public opinion in the United States:* George Gallup, "Public Would Bomb Religious Buildings," *NYT*, Apr. 19, 1944, 3.

441 *"Whenever I am offered a liqueur":* Texas, 330.

## CHAPTER 10: FOUR HORSEMEN

### *A Fairyland of Silver and Gold*

445 *"The bay was as blue":* Donald Downes, *The Scarlet Thread*, 166; Frank Gervasi, *The Violent Decade*, 562–63; Karl Baedeker, *Southern Italy and Sicily*, 27; Roger A. Freeman,

*The American Airman in Europe,* 36 (*"Chicken-a-shit"*); Norman Lewis, *Naples '44,* 93, 152, 187; obit, http://www.telegraph.co.uk/news/main.jhtml?xml=%2Fnews%2F2003%2F07%2F23%2Fdb2301.xml.

445 *"the most loathsome nest":* H. V. Morton, *A Traveller in Southern Italy,* 234, 273; Betsy Wade, ed., *Forward Positions: The War Correspondence of Homer Bigart,* 230; F. Majdalany, *The Monastery,* 52.

446 *Each afternoon, a hospital train:* Alton D. Brashear, *From Lee to Bari,* 175; Alan Moorehead, *Eclipse,* 69; Paul W. Pritchard, "Smoke Generator Operations in the Mediterranean and European Theaters of Operation," n.d., CMH, 4-7.1 FA 1, 49; Brooks E. Kleber and Dale Birdsell, *The Chemical Warfare Service: Chemicals in Combat,* 331; OH, Robert J. Wood, 1973–74, William E. Narus, SOOHP, MHI, 3–25 (*shine flashlights at the curb*); Margaret Bourke-White, *Purple Heart Valley,* 35; Lewis, 100 (*"thrust into their arms"*).

446 *"I&I":* Paul W. Brown, *The Whorehouse of the World,* 6; C. Richard Eke, "A Game of Soldiers," IWM, 92/1/1, 102 (*"passion wagons"*), 99 (*"Everywhere were G.I.s"*); Lloyd M. Wells, *From Anzio to the Alps,* 31; Masayo Umezawa Duus, *Unlikely Liberators,* 115; "History of the Peninsular Base Section," 1944, CMH, 8-4 HA 1 (*city jail*); Gervasi, 562; Joseph Edgar Martin, "Memoir of World War II," ts, 2003, author's possession, II-19; Brashear, 172 (*Red Cross auditorium*); memo, Office of the Special Service Office, Apr. 29, 1944, MWC, Citadel, box 3; Eugenia M. Kielar, *Thank You, Uncle Sam,* 80; Ralph G. Martin, *The G.I. War, 1941–1945,* 119 (*Bogart in the Hotel Parca*).

446 *So, too, was Pompeii:* Fred Howard, *Whistle While You Wait,* 120–21 (*House of the Two Bachelors*); corr, Jon Clayton to family, Feb. 14, 1944, ASEQ, 7th Inf Regt, 3rd ID, MHI (*"old Romans certainly knew"*); Lawrence D. Collins, *The 56th Evac Hospital,* 105 (*"evil-minded people"*).

447 *Soldiers also jammed the reopened San Carlo:* Walter L. Medding, "The Road to Rome," ts, n.d., CEOH, box X-38, 56; Richard S. Malone, *A Portrait of War, 1939–1943,* 204; Martin, 118 (*"That's good"*); John Guest, *Broken Images,* 164.

447 *New Neapolitan cabarets:* "Settled Front," *Time,* May 1, 1944, 27; Bourke-White, 101; Harold L. Bond, *Return to Cassino,* 135–36; Brashear, 171; memoir, Aidan Mark Sprot, ts, 1947, LH 109–10 and 117 (*aimed champagne corks*); Moorehead, 69 (*"nodule of lotus-eating"*); Eric Sevareid, *Not So Wild a Dream,* 419 (*straw hats*); Robert Capa, *Slightly Out of Focus,* 110; Collins, 131, 140; Paul A. Cundiff, *45th Infantry CP,* 164; diary, William Russell Hinckley, AAF, March 1944, author's possession.

447 *list the shades of the sea:* Guest, 166–67; Bourke-White, 102.

447 *"The people are terribly poor":* Kielar, 73; Robert W. Komer, "Civil Affairs and Military Government in the Mediterranean Theater," 1954, CMH, 2-3.7 AX, vi–26; "British Administrative History of the Italian Campaign," appendix, "distribution of civil supplies," 1946, NARA RG 94, E 427, 95-USF2-5.0; Bill Mauldin, *The Brass Ring,* 211 (*"wizened bundle"*); *Reporting World War II,* vol. 2, 39; Raleigh Trevelyan, *Rome '44,* 159 (*"snatched the bones"*).

448 *typhus raged unchecked:* "History of the Peninsular Base Section"; Brashear, 171; Edward D. Churchill, *Surgeon to Soldiers,* 295; Moorehead, 70 (*Carts hauled away the dead*); Albert E. Cowdrey, *Fighting for Life,* 122 (*killed three million*); *A Military Encyclopedia: Based on Operations in the Italian Campaign, 1943–1945,* HQ, 15th Army Group, n.d., CARL, N-11069-1, 518 (*90 percent of the civilian population*); Harry L. Coles and Albert K. Weinberg, *Civil Affairs: Soldiers Become Governors,* 325–26 (*"disordered throng"*); monthly report, AMG, public health and welfare dept, region 3, Dec. 1943, NARA RG 226, E 99, OSS history office, box 3.

448 *Army physicians had quarantined Naples:* minutes, "typhus committee," Jan. 7, 1944, Naples, NARA RG 331, AFHQ micro, R-235-D, job 78; Robert M. Hill and Elizabeth Craig Hill, *In the Wake of War,* 22; "Fifth Army Medical History," ts, n.d., NARA RG 112,

390/17/8/2-3, box 6, 100; "History of the Peninsular Base Section"; James Phinney Baxter III, *Scientists Against Time,* 368; "The ASF in World War II," ts, n.d., CMH, 3-1.1A AA, IV-3; Coles and Weinberg, 325–26; Malcolm S. McLean, "Adventures in Occupied Areas," ts, 1975, MHI, 71 (*"People queued up"*); James Stevens Simmons, "How Magic Is DDT?" *Saturday Evening Post,* Jan. 6, 1945, 18+. Later found to have grave environmental consequences, DDT was effectively banned in the United States in the early 1970s.

448 *"A victorious army found in Italy"*: "Operations of British, Indian and Dominion Forces in Italy," part V, n.d., UK NA, CAB 106/453, II-1; corr, Graham Erdwurm, former OSS officer, to author, Jan. 5, 2004 (*"army is all clapped-up"*); Peter Schrijvers, *The Crash of Ruin,* 181 (*world's largest bordello*); Spike Milligan, *Mussolini: His Part in My Downfall,* 157 (*"pox galore"*).

449 *With the average worker earning only sixty lire:* "Fifth Army Medical History," 71, 75 (*"60 percent of all women in Italy"*); Hill and Craig, 56; "History of the Peninsular Base Section"; "Observations at P.B.S.," ts, n.d., NARA RG 492, MTO, pm, gen'l corr, 290/54/26/2, box 2209 (*"finest pimp system"*); Brashear, 168–69 (*"DDT hairdos"* ); Bill Harr, *Combat Boots,* 52 (*hung a sign around his neck*); Charles M. Wiltse, *The Medical Department: Medical Service in the Mediterranean and Minor Theaters,* 258; Lewis, 112 (*"Madame Four-Dollars"*).

449 *The "perfunctory jogging"*: Don Graham, *No Name on the Bullet,* 74; "Logistical History of NATOUSA/MTOUSA," Nov. 1945, NARA RG 407, E, 427, 95-AL1-4, box 203, 299–300; "Fifth Army Medical History," 81–86; "Operations of British, Indian and Dominion Forces in Italy," part V, n.d., UK NA, CAB 106/453, II-1 (*"Italian strain of gonococci"*); Wiltse, 258; OH, Albert Kenner, May 27, 1948, FCP, MHI (*same black market price as morphine*); Eric Lax, *The Mold in Dr. Florey's Coat,* 227–28 (*"best military advantage"*).

449 *"Girls Who Take Boarders"*: Gervasi, 563; corr, G. Erdwurm to author, Jan. 5, 2004 (*"ablution centers"*); Brown, *The Whorehouse of the World,* 253, 290; "History of the Peninsular Base Section" (*15 percent*); "Fifth Army Medical Service History," 78 (*"whorespitals"*); Trevelyan, 295; "Observations at P.B.S."; Wiltse, 336; memo, N. P. Morrow, Feb. 26, 1944, VI Personnel Center, NARA RG 407, E 427, 95-USF1-2.0, AGF board reports (*tear gas grenades*).

450 *"The chaplains thought the whores"*: memoir, Edward R. Feagins, ts, n.d., 143rd Inf, Texas MFM, 30.

450 *"that huge and gassy thing"*: Phillip Knightley, *The First Casualty,* 320; "Beachheads and Mountains," MTO pamphlet, June 1945, Theodore J. Conway papers, MHI (*keep a single GI fighting*).

450 *"prodigy of organization"*: Eric Larrabee, *Commander in Chief,* 120; Bernard C. Nalty et al, *With Courage,* 137 (*86,000 planes*); Alan Gropman, ed., *The Big L,* 89–93; Henry F. Pringle, "Weapons Win Wars," ts, n.d., WD, CMH, 2-3.7 AB.B, 159; James A. Huston, *The Sinews of War,* 477 (*71 million rounds*).

450 *The nation's conversion from a commercial:* Richard Overy, *Why the Allies Won,* 195; *Logistics in World War II,* 95.

450 *In February 1944, the U.S. Army shipped:* Harold Larson, "Handling Army Cargo in the Second World War," ts, 1945, CMH, 4-13.1 AA 19, 5; OH, LeRoy Lutes, Nov. 12, 1974, Maclyn Burg, DDE Lib, OH-408, II-108 (*six million separate supply items*); Brehon B. Somervell, "Army Service Forces," Aug. 9, 1943, NARA RG 334, "Records of Interservice Agencies," NWC Library, ANSCOL, L-1-43, box 167; Lee B. Kennett, *G.I.: The American Soldier in World War II,* 96–97 (*three sheets per soldier*); Marvin A. Kreidberg and Merton G. Henry, *History of Military Mobilization in the United States Army, 1775–1945,* 674–75 (*Lend Lease program*); Overy, 254 (*"Second Fronts"*); OH, Frederick E. Morgan, n.d., FCP, MHI (*"American bounty"*).

451 *"one ship out of every five is stolen"*: corr, B. B. Somervell to DDE et al, March 23, 1945, and E. S. Hughes to B. B. Somervell, Apr. 26, 1943, NARA RG 336, ASF, historical program files, chief of transportation, 190/22/30/00, box 58; Lewis, 119 (*"derives from transactions"*); "Logistical History of NATOUSA/MTOUSA," 159, 176; memo, unsigned, to Walter A. Hardie, Dec. 28, 1944, NARA RG 492, MTO, pm, gen'l corr, 333, 290/54/26/2, box 2209 (*tapped fuel pipelines*); Gervasi, 566; Charles F. Marshall, *A Ramble Through My War*, 119 (*funeral hearses*); Hill and Hill, 17, 38 (*"Pork. Beef"*).

451 *A separate prison was built at the port:* memo, "Port of Naples," HQ, SOS, Sept. 11, 1944, NARA RG 492, MTO, pm, gen'l corr, 333, 290/54/26/2, box 2209; Schrijvers, 122 (*"whip the gold"*); Lewis, 134–35.

451 *"Total war" was largely a German concept:* http://www.britannica.com/eb/article-52981; Richard M. Leighton and Robert W. Coakley, *Global Logistics and Strategy: 1940–1943,* 14 (*Americans made it their own*); Overy, 198 (*fourfold in heavy guns*); Gropman, ed., 91 (*sevenfold in transport planes*), 54–55 (*tank production in 1943 alone*); John Ellis, *Brute Force*, xviii (*seventy thousand trucks*).

451 *Even though Kesselring's divisions:* Walter Warlimont, "The Drive on Rome," Sept. 1951, FMS, #C-097a, MHI, 11; "The German System of Supply in the Field," Feb. 1946, AFHQ, G-2, CARL, N-13305.1, 92, 85, 123 (*"severe pinch"*); Max Wehrig, "Duties and Operation of the Italian Section of the Chief of Wehrmacht Motor Transportation," 1947, FMS, #D-126, MHI, 23 (*three thousand different types*).

452 *Wehrmacht quartermasters reported:* "The German System of Supply in the Field," 86, 106, 135; Albert Kesselring et al., "German Version of the History of the Italian Campaign," n.d., CARL, N-16671.1-3, 227 (Shortages of trucks and dray horses); Hans Henrici, "The Use of Italian Industry in the Service of German Munitions Production," March 1947, FMS, #D-015, MHI, 1–2 (*scheme to produce German munitions*).

452 *Allied quartermasters had their own woes:* OH, Francis Oxx, PBS commander, May 21, 1948, NARA RG 319, OCMH, CA, box 005; msg, SOS NATOUSA to PEMBARK, Feb. 9, 1944, NARA RG 331, AFHQ micro, R-369-F, box 216; William G. Ashmore, "Supply Planning for Beachhead Operations," *Quartermaster Review*, Jan.–Feb. 1945, 18+ (*toll in water cans*); "Ordnance Activities in the Mediterranean Theater of Operations," Nov. 1942–June 1945, CMH, 5 (*ordnance requisitions, in sextuplicate*); Robert Wagner, *The Texas Army*, 195 (*"most hated folk in Italy"*); E. R. Keller, "Quartermasters—Battle Proved," *Quartermaster Review*, May–June 1944, 24+ (*4AA to 16EEE*).

452 *As the fifth year of carnage played out:* Leighton and Coakley, 14.

### The Weight of Metal

453 *Now overwatched by the gray stub:* Janusz Piekalkiewicz, *The Battle for Cassino*, 10.

453 *All approaches from the south:* Martha Gellhorn, *The Face of War*, 126–27; Christopher Buckley, *Road to Rome*, 308 (*"straight as a bar of steel"*); E. D. Smith, *The Battles for Cassino*, 99 (*"Time seems to have stopped"*).

453 *Not far from here, in 217 B.C.:* Livy, *The War with Hannibal*, 117–18; http://www.greek-texts.com/library/Plutarch/Fabius/eng/print/502.html.

453 *"master of his own destiny"*: Smith, 96; Field Marshal Lord Carver, *The Imperial War Museum Book of the War in Italy, 1943–1945,* 151; Bishenwar Prasad, ed., *Official History of the Indian Armed Forces in the Second World War, 1939–1945: The Campaign in Italy, 1943–1945,* 117; Andrew Brookes, *Air War over Italy,* 71 (*tail now wagged the dog*).

454 *"Anything that will divest me"*: diary, MWC, Feb. 28, 1944, Citadel, box 65. Until mid-February, when the responsibility had been shifted to others, Clark had also overseen the plans for landings in southern France, which eventually occurred in August 1944.

454 *Before that happy day arrived:* Battle, 209; Smith, 98 (*Minefields and inundations*); Prasad, ed., 119 (*"faith in the weight of metal"*).

454 *As the abbey had been pulverized:* Ian Gooderson, *Cassino 1944*, 93; *StoC*, 435 (*six to twelve hours*).

454 *The use of airpower to bludgeon:* msg, H. Arnold to I. Eaker and J. Devers, Feb. 24, 1943, NARA RG 492, MTOUSA, SGS, "Eyes Only, General Devers, Incoming," box 135; James Parton, "*Air Force Spoken Here*," 372 ("*lack of ingenuity*"); corr, H. Arnold to I. Eaker, n.d., NARA RG 319, OCMH, CA, box 6 ("*really make air history*").

455 *Lieutenant General Eaker yielded to no man:* OH, Ira C. Eaker, 1972, Joe B. Green, SOOHP, MHI; Mark M. Boatner III, *The Biographical Dictionary of World War II*, 145.

455 "*due to cratering and debris*": "Air Support of Fifth Army for Rapido River and Cassino Attacks," Apr. 7, 1944, HQ, Fifth Army, air support control, MHI, Robert J. Woods papers, "Report on Cassino Operations"; corr, I. Eaker to H. Arnold, March 6, 1944, NARA RG 319, OCMH, CA, box 6 ("*Do not set your heart*"); *StoC*, 434–35 ("*We shall go forward*").

455 *Yet in the absence of a plausible alternative:* *StoC*, 434–35; N. C. Phillips, *Official History of New Zealand in the Second World War*, vol. 1, 244 ("*deep sounding of its bell*").

457 *Freyberg insisted the bombing coincide:* Charles C. Bates and John F. Fuller, *America's Weather Warriors*, 78–80, 283n.

457 *Sickness or battle wounds claimed another Indian soldier:* Phillips, 252–53, 254–57, 261; Howard Kippenberger, *Infantry Brigadier*, 360 ("*undetected S-mine*"); Fred Majdalany, *Cassino: Portrait of a Battle*, 170.

457 *Never in his legendary career:* Phillips, 252–53.

457 *Unknown to Freyberg:* General Sir Sidney Chevalier Kirkman, article on 3rd and 4th Cassino, *Proceedings,* Royal Artillery Historical Society, Jan. 1969, 94+.

457 *The ground grew boggier:* Rudolf Böhmler, *Monte Cassino*, 208; Robert Geake, "Mule Pack Trains in Italy," *Cavalry Journal*, March–Apr. 1944, 74+; "Lessons from the Italian Campaign," March 10, 1944, NARA RG 407, E 427, NATOUSA, 95-USF1-04, box 250; Lewis A. Riggins, "Report on Italian Campaign," Dec. 31, 1943, DTL, Ft. B, 5 ("*mules are tranquil*"); "History of the Peninsular Base Section" (*packboards*).

458 "*engaged by a holocaust of fire*": Phillips, 258–59.

458 *At seven A.M. on Wednesday, March 15:* diary, MWC, March 15, 1944, Citadel, box 65; Bates and Fuller, 257 ("*frontal system over France*"); Prasad, ed., 127 ("*Bradman will be batting*").

458 *Operation* LUDLUM *had attracted an eager crowd:* Parton, 373; Harold Macmillan, *War Diaries,* 374 ("*calm, detached and attractive*"); Rupert Clarke, *With Alex at War,* photocopied letter ("*there are witches*").

458 *Before reaching Monte Trocchio:* *Calculated,* 330; diary, MWC, March 15, 1944, Citadel, box 65.

459 *Fifth Army comprised 438,782 soldiers:* memo, "JDB" to MWC, March 14, 1944, MWC, corr, Citadel, box 3; "Small World," CBS, 1959 ("*very depressed*"); diary, MWC, Feb. 27, 1944, Citadel, box 65 ("*whom the Lord loveth*"); MWC to Renie, March 5, 1944, MWC, personal corr, Citadel.

459 *If broad-gauged and resolute:* "Small World," CBS, 1959 ("*keen and abiding interest*"); GK, March 13, 1944; diary, MWC, March 1 ("*greatly annoyed*"), March 8 ("*difficult subordinate*"), March 11, 1944 ("*all dispatches sent personally*"), Citadel, box 65.

460 *A few days earlier, he had mailed Renie:* MWC to Renie, Feb. 10, 1944, in note from Renie Clark to GCM, Feb. 23, 1944, GCM papers, GCM Lib, corr, box 61; MWC to Renie, March 8, 1944, MWC, personal corr, Citadel.

460 "*Into the silence obtruded a drone*": J. B. Tomlinson, "Under the Banner of the Battleaxe," ts, n.d., IWM, 90/29/1, 126.

460 "*The object of the attack*": James Parton, "The Bombardment of Cassino, March 15, 1944, MAAF," Oct. 1944, CARL, N-6058; Brookes, 78; *StoC*, 410.

460 *"Sprout after sprout of black smoke"*: Parton, 373; Matthew Parker, *Monte Cassino*, 182 (*"Target cabbaged"*).

461 *"After a few minutes"*: Smith, 103; "The Bombardment of Cassino," Oct. 1, 1944, AFHRA, 622.310-4, 6–7, 24 (LENTIL, TROTSKY).

461 *"Stop those damn maniacs!"*: B. Smith, "Waltonia," ts, 1981, IWM 67/254/1; Paul Freyberg, *Bernard Freyberg, V.C.*, 466 (*"terrible one-sidedness"*); Phillip Knightley, *The First Casualty*, 326–30 (*"evidence of my own eyes"*).

461 *At 12:12 P.M.:* Parton, "The Bombardment of Cassino, March 15, 1944," CARL, N-6058; "The Bombardment of Cassino," AFHRA, 8 (*"flat as a stone city"*).

461 *Clark left his rooftop:* diary, MWC, March 15, 1944, Citadel, box 65; OH, H. Alexander, Jan. 10–15, 1949, SM, CMH, II-4 (*"could still be alive"*); speech, Ira C. Eaker, March 15, 1944, "Blue Network," transcript in MWC, corr, Citadel, box 3.

461 *He should have known better:* memo, office of the AA officer to chief of staff, HQ, Fifth Army, March 15, 1944, in "The Bombardment of Cassino," Oct. 1944, CARL, N-6058; msg, A.P. Juin to MWC, March 16, 1944, MWC, Citadel, box 3 (*killing fifteen French*); Clarke, photo caption (*Eighth Army command post*); Rowland Ryder, *Oliver Leese*, 160 (*"our American friends"*).

462 *Other bombs fell on the 4th Indian Division:* memo, "Summary of Reports of Bombing Behind Our Lines," HQ, MAAF, March 17, 1944, in "The Bombardment of Cassino," Oct. 1944, CARL, N-6058; "Draft Report on FEC," n.d., CMH, SM, box I; Brookes, 74. The tally given Clark on March 17 included 75 Allied dead and 250 wounded, but that number appears incomplete. StoC, 441n; Molony V, 785; "Report on Effect of Bombing and Shelling of Cassino, 15 March 1944," HQ, Fifth Army, Apr. 7, 1944, MHI, Robert J. Woods papers; Brookes, 74; "The Bombardment of Cassino," AFHRA, 29.

462 *In Venafro alone as many as 75 civilians:* "Report on Effect of Bombing and Shelling of Cassino, 15 March 1944"; bomb plot, HQ, MAAF, operations analysis section, Apr. 5, 1944, in Parton, "The Bombardment of Cassino" (*Of 2,366 bombs dropped*); "The Bombardment of Cassino," AFHRA, 7.

462 *Investigators found that flight leaders:* "Report of Investigation, Cassino Operation," HQ, USAAF, MTO, Apr. 12, 1944, in "The Bombardment of Cassino"; "The Bombardment of Cassino," AFHRA; Parton, 375; Molony V, 785.

462 *Freyberg's intelligence had assumed:* Parton, 373; interrogation report, Richard Heidrich, Nov. 13, 1946, Canadian Military HQ, MHI, SM, box 2; *The Tiger Triumphs*, 52 (*"ruthless and not overnice"*).

463 *Roughly half the paratroopers caught in Cassino:* Phillips, 345; StoC, 442 (*"scraps of paper"*), 443 (*eighty-nine of ninety-four tubes*); Böhmler, 210–11 (*"We could no longer see"*); Trevelyan, 199 (*"weep and rage"*); "The Bombardment of Cassino," AFHRA, 32 (*"Speak about women"*).

463 *The town was "blown asunder":* Molony V, 785; "The Bombardment of Cassino," 1944, MAAF, UK NA, AIR 8/1358, 11–12 (*"rendered comatose"*); memo, I. H. Crowne to L. Norstad, "Preliminary Memorandum on Cassino," May 23, 1944, HQ, MAAF, Lauris Norstad papers, DDE Lib, box 1 (*"two rows of houses remain intact"*); "Operations of N.Z. Corps on the Fifth Army Front," May 1944, HQ, AAI, part I, UK NA, CAB 106/366, 25; James Parton, "The Bombardment of Cassino" (*"Bombs falling three to four yards"*).

464 *"Cassino was so ideally situated":* interrogation report, Richard Heidrich; memo, Crowne to Norstad, "Preliminary Memorandum on Cassino."

464 *"The Germans would do well":* Böhmler, 213.

464 *Three hundred and fifty Allied tanks:* Phillips, 269–71, 298, 305, 336.

464 *The planned pace of one hundred yards' advance:* Molony V, 787; Phillips, 272 (*"like a flotilla"*); "Operations of N.Z. Corps," 28; Parton, "The Bombardment of Cassino."

464 *Teeming rain fell at dusk:* StoC, 443; "Operations of N.Z. Corps," 26; Majdalany, *Cassino*, 179.

465 *In the dying light, a single intrepid company:* John H. Green, "The Battles for Cassino," *AB,* No. 13, 1976, 1+; Phillips, 289, 347; "Report on Cassino Operations," June 5, 1944, HQ, Fifth Army, Robert J. Wood papers, MHI, 16; Smith, 116; "Operations of N.Z. Corps," 28 (*ruined radios and cut phone lines*).

465 *Several hundred feet above the town:* Dharm Pal, *The Campaign in Italy, 1943–1945,* 129; "Operations of N.Z. Corps," 27.

465 *This isolated, eight-acre lodgment:* Majdalany, *Cassino,* 201; Phillips, 349 ("*moral lien*").

465 *"The fire was so heavy":* Parker, 254; *The Tiger Triumphs,* 61–63 (*amputated limbs*); Majdalany, *Cassino,* 201 (*dead mule at the bottom*); Molony V, 794 (*mutinied rather than cross*); C. M. Emeis, "Report on Italian Campaign," June 15, 1944, NARA RG 337, AGF, observer reports, #111, box 55, 12; Prasad, ed., 131; Böhmler, 235 (*bags of blood*).

466 *Enough food and ammo fell:* Smith, 7, 126–27 ("*God help us all*").

466 *"Freyberg's handling":* diary, MWC, March 17, 1944, Citadel, box 65; Phillips, 299–301; Molony V, 793; Smith, 122.

466 *"I told Freyberg":* diary, MWC, March 17, 18, 23, 1944, Citadel, box 65; Phillips, 352 (*he intended to abandon the attack*).

466 *"Push on, you must go hard":* Majdalany, *Cassino,* 186; Smith, 125; Prasad, ed., 132.

467 *"Almost every building":* "Operations of N.Z. Corps," 31–32, 41–42; Molony V, 800 ("*unexpected encounters*"); Phillips, 323; *The Tiger Triumphs,* 59; Robert S. Rush, *The U.S. Infantryman in World War II,* 131 ("*Little Stalingrad*").

467 *Just before dawn, three hundred paratroopers:* Smith, 127; Majdalany, *Cassino,* 190–91; Stevens, 303 ("*smother of enemies*"); Parker, 237 (*through arrow loopholes*).

467 *An arcing signal flare: The Tiger Triumphs,* 56–57; Parker, 241 ("*We talked a bit*"); Prasad, ed., 135; Green, "The Battles for Cassino," 1+; Molony V, 797; Stevens, 305 (*fur-lined gloves*).

468 *Two thousand yards across the crest:* Green, "The Battles for Cassino," 1; AAR, "The Attack on Albenette House," n.d., Co. D, 760th Tank Bn, in "Report No. 140, Army Ground Forces Board, AFHQ-NATO," Apr. 3, 1944, CARL, N-7245-G ("*cause chaos*"); Prasad, ed., 137; Phillips, 311.

468 *Then the noose cinched:* Green, "The Battles for Cassino," 1+; "The Attack on Albenette House" ("*I hated to shoot the mules*"); Pal, 137.

468 *General von Senger on several occasions:* Frido von Senger und Etterlin, "War Diary of the Italian Campaign," 1953, FMS, #C-095b, MHI, 102–3; Frido von Senger und Etterlin, *Neither Fear nor Hope,* 226.

469 *Little reliable information:* Senger, *Neither Fear nor Hope,* 214–15; Smith, 119 ("*Things are not too splendid*"); Molony V, 791, 802; Böhmler, 233.

469 *Yet the failed Allied tank foray:* Böhmler, 233–35; Phillips, 304–5 (*22,000 smoke rounds*); Majdalany, *Cassino,* 188 ("*unpleasant wounds*"); Prasad, ed., 136 ("*screened nothing from nobody*").

469 *As for the town, Senger thought:* Senger, "War Diary of the Italian Campaign," 101; Senger, *Neither Fear nor Hope,* 216; Molony V, 793–94, 802–3.

469 *General Freyberg also prowled:* Stevens, 96; Phillips, 316 ("*Another lovely day*"); Freyberg, 467 (*his arithmetical scribbles*); Smith, 132 ("*both groggy*"); http://www.catholic-forum.com/saintS/saintb02.htm (*date St. Benedict died*); diary, MWC, March 21–22, 1944, Citadel, box 65 (*he rallied Alexander*); Winston S. Churchill, *Closing the Ring,* 509.

470 *"Unfortunately we are fighting":* Arthur Bryant, *Triumph in the West,* 127; "Report on Cassino Operations," 21; Majdalany, *Cassino,* 193 ("*Passchendaele*").

470 *Alexander concurred, as did Clark:* memo, A. Gruenther to I. Eaker, Apr. 5, 1944, in "The Bombardment of Cassino," CARL, N-6058; diary, MWC, March 23, 1944, Citadel, box 65.

470 *That calumny:* "Notes on Converation Between Commander 13 Corps and Lieut. Col. Nangle, commanding 1/9 Ghurka Rifles," ts, May 28, 1944, in diary, General Sir Sidney Chevalier Kirkman, Jan.–Sept. 1944, LHC; Trevelyan, 207 (*paper bag holding a*

*carrier pigeon*); Smith, 138 (*"spot of shooing"*); Kirkman, article on 3rd and 4th Cassino, 94+.

470 *At 8:15 P.M. on Friday, March 24:* "Operations of N.Z. Corps," 43–44; Molony V, 801n; Majdalany, *Cassino,* 204, 209 (*keg of rum*); Smith, 138 (*"Never will I forget"*).

471 *By late Saturday, a swastika flag:* Senger, "War Diary of the Italian Campaign," 93; Trevelyan, 208 (*"a heavy fall of snow"*).

471 *The New Zealand Corps disbanded at noon:* Prasad, ed., 142; Phillips, 341; Molony V, 803. During the last three weeks of March, the 1st Parachute and 15th Panzer Grenadier Divisions reported 1,800 casualties, but during the eleven-day battle for Cassino in March the German losses are estimated at roughly 1,200.

471 *"that valley of evil memory"*: Parton, 360; GK, March 24, 1944.

471 *"a persistent feeling that something, somewhere"*: StoC, 447; Molony V, 806; Smith, 141 (*"The strongest defences in Europe"*); Phillips, 344 (*"little of that tactical originality"*).

471 *Something had gone wrong:* Brian Holden Reid, "The Italian Campaign, 1943–1945: A Reappraisal of Allied Generalship," *Journal of Strategic Studies,* March 1990, 128+; OH, Andrew J. Goodpaster, Aug. 17, 2004, author (*"unsynchronized schemes"*); OH, Robert J. Wood, March 4 and 15, 1948, SM, MHI (*probing for soft spots*); "Report on Cassino Operations," June 5, 1944, HQ, Fifth Army, Robert J. Wood papers, MHI, 21 (*almost 600,000 artillery shells*); Phillips, 338 (*"a battle of the First World War"*).

472 *the strategy of "naked attrition"*: Molony V, 806n, 835, 852 (*"a crawling monster"*); Chester G. Starr, ed., *From Salerno to the Alps,* 120 (*six hundred tanks parked*); Phillips, 339 (*never could fling more than one-tenth*); J.F.C. Fuller, *The Second World War, 1939–1945,* 272; Reid, "The Italian Campaign, 1943–1945," 128+; Smith, 144 (*"military sins no less"*).

472 *"Bombardment alone never had"*: Calculated, 331; corr, E. N. Harmon to MWC, March 28, 1944, ENH, box 1.

472 *"A little later when snow goes off"*: Churchill, *Closing the Ring,* 509 (*"war weighs very heavy"*); Fuller, 274 (*"presiding deity"*).

472 *It weighed heavy on the far side:* Senger, *Neither Fear nor Hope,* 219.

### Dragonflies in the Sun

473 *"After you get whipped and humiliated"*: Parker, 69; Howard H. Peckham and Shirley A. Snyder, eds., *Letters from Fighting Hoosiers,* vol. 2, 71 (*"a callousness to death"*); corr, 324th Service Group, n.d., censorship morale reports, NARA RG 492, MTO, AG, 311.7 (*"We get quite a kick"*).

473 *"One goes on fighting, killing"*: Trevelyan, 1; Sevareid, 417; John Muirhead, *Those Who Fall,* 4, 122.

473 *"Watched an amputation last night"*: diary, John G. Wright, American Field Service driver, May 29, 1944, author's possession, 26; Schrijvers, 77 (*"possessed by a fury"*); e-mail, David Roberts to author, May 23, 2003 (*flatulent noises*); J. Glenn Gray, *The Warriors,* 139, 164 (*"help me to keep my humanity"*).

474 *A survey of infantry divisions:* Schrijvers, 77; John B. Romeiser, ed., *Combat Reporter,* 211 (*"The more you hate"*); Wagner, 64 (*"He has no right to do this"*); Collins, 97 (*wounded German prisoners*); Trevelyan, 149 (*"sure hate their guts"*).

474 *"There's no rules in this war"*: Quentin Reynolds, *The Curtain Rises,* 212; "Comment Sheets," censorship reports, NARA RG 492, MTO G-2, box 387 (*"Take No Prisoners"*).

474 *"three R's—ruthless, relentless, remorseless"*: diary, Norman Lee Baldwin, Dec. 13, 1943, HIA, N. L. Baldwin papers.

474 *"This is a war for keeps"*: Annette Tapert, ed., *Lines of Battle,* 124.

475 *Eager boys no longer scaled:* John Patrick Carroll-Abbing, *But for the Grace of God,* 63; Daniel Lang, "Letter from Rome," *New Yorker,* July 15, 1944 (*Allied flags flapped*); Jane Scrivener, *Inside Rome with the Germans,* 26 (*Jumpy German sentries*).

475 *"dragonflies in the sun"*: Scrivener, 60, 134–35 (*those queued up for water*); Robert Katz, *The Battle for Rome*, 205–19 (*a B-17 day*); Trevelyan, 229–30 (*Graffiti on city walls*); George F. Botjer, *Sideshow War*, 103 (*"Allies, don't worry"*).

475 *"Everything went"*: Scrivener, 36; Walter von Unruh, "Inspection of Italian Theater of War," 1947, FMS, #D-016, MHI, 17 (*"Do you want work?"*); Walter Warlimont, "OKW Activities—The Italian Theater, 1 Apr.–31 Dec. 1944," n.d., FMS, #C-099b, MHI, 13 (*Fifty thousand Italians*).

475 *The shadows soon deepened:* Michael Burleigh, *The Third Reich*, 741–42; Richard Lamb, *War in Italy, 1943–1945*, 41–42 (*arrest all Jews in the city*), 55; Botjer, 100 (*son of a Stuttgart chauffeur*); Trevelyan, 62, 117 (*"intolerant, cold, vengeful"*); Alessandro Portelli, *The Order Has Been Carried Out*, 85–86; Martin Gilbert, *The Second World War*, 467; Katz, 71–75; Dan Kurzman, *The Race for Rome*, 61; U.S. Holocaust Memorial Museum Web site, articles on Italy and Rome, http://www.ushmm.org/wlc/en/.

476 *Even for Romans not facing extermination:* C.R.S. Harris, *Allied Administration of Italy, 1943–1945*, 170; Trevelyan, 229 (*felling trees*); Robert H. Adleman and George Walton, *Rome Fell Today*, 81–82 (*neighborhoods went without power*); "Contributions of Italy Toward the Allied War Effort," Aug. 31, 1945, OSS, MHI Lib, 38n (*infant mortality spiked*); Kurt Mälzer, "The Problem of Rome During the Fighting Near Anzio-Nettuno," Jan. 1948, FMS, #D-314, MHI, 8 (*destruction of supply trucks*).

476 *Prices doubled:* Botjer, 92; Katz, 283, 276 (*shot them as they faced the Tiber*); Trevelyan, 229 (*ground chickpeas*).

476 *Blackshirts finding a film too tedious:* Botjer, 95; Scrivener, 148 (*five hundred eavesdroppers*), 152 (*priest condemned for subversion*); Trevelyan, 287; Portelli, 125.

476 *Soon half of Rome was said to be hiding:* Lang, "Letter from Rome"; Trevelyan, 97; Kurzman, 183 (*had their shoes removed*); Anthony Cave Brown, *The Last Hero*, 492 (*"They pulled out the hairs"*); Riccardo Luzzatto, *Unknown War in Italy*, 114 (*"Long live Italy"*).

477 *Allied planes flying from Brindisi:* "History of Special Operations (Air) in the Mediterranean Theater," n.d., U.K., NARA RG 94, E 427, 95-USF-2-0.3.0, 270/50/29-30/G-1, 5; Eugene Warner, "Morale Operations, Report for 16–30 April 1944," HQ 2677th HQ Co., OSS, MO branch, NARA RG 226, OSS history office, E 99, box 25, folder 1, 1–9 (*Intended to inspirit Italian insurgents*); OSS activities, March 1944, NATOUSA, NARA RG 226, E 99, OSS history office, box 122; Anthony Cave Brown, ed., *The Secret War Report of the OSS*, 222 (Das Neue Deutschland).

477 *In Rome, the OSS by March 1944:* "Italian Operations Centering on Rome," n.d., NARA RG 226, OSS history office, E, 99, box 41; Carl J. Friedrich, ed., *American Experiences in Military Government in World War II*, 133; Patrick K. O'Donnell, *Operatives, Spies, and Saboteurs*, 62 (*German order of battle*).

477 *No OSS spy in Rome was more flamboyant:* Katz, 49; http://muse.jhu.edu/cgi-bin/access.cgi?uri=/journals/annual_of_bernard_shaw_studies/v024/24.1carter.html (*George Bernard Shaw*); diary, Peter Tompkins, Jan. 1944, NARA RG 226, E 99, OSS history office, 190/6/10/7, box 47, 21, 42, 49 (*a Roman prince*); "Peter Tompkins, Author," obituary, *WP*, Feb. 1, 2007, B-6.

478 *Favoring a blue sharkskin suit:* Katz, 144; Peter Tompkins, "The OSS and Italian Partisans in World War II," *Studies in Intelligence*, spring 1998, http://www.cia.gov/csi/studies/spring98/OSS.html (*daily radio bulletins*); Brown, *The Last Hero*, 487–88, 495; "Italian Operations Centering on Rome."

478 *Still, it was part of the good fight:* diary, Tompkins, Feb.–March 1944, 55–58, 77, 61, 67, 70–71, 130; Brown, ed., 202; Brown, *The Last Hero*, 494.

478 *An estimated 25,000 Italian partisans:* "Contributions of Italy Toward the Allied War Effort," 26–27; "The Resistance Movement in German-Controlled Italy," CCS Joint Intel

Committee, March 8, 1944, weekly summary, #61, NARA RG 334, NWC Lib, box 326; Luzzatto, 80–82.

478 *"Singing at the top of our lungs"*: Katz, 204.

478 *From the Piazza del Popolo*: diary, Tompkins, 127–28; Portelli, 134.

479 *He was in fact a medical student*: Katz, 49–51, 57–62; Portelli, 161; author visits, May 10, 2004, Dec. 1, 2006.

479 *As the singing troops approached*: transcript, war crimes trial of Albert Kesselring, Feb.–Apr. 1947, Venice, NARA RG 492, MTO, AG HQ, 290/53/32/5-6, 000.5, boxes 816–18; Katz, 62, 72, 224.

479 *"blown down by a great wind"*: Trevelyan, 213; Portelli, 136–37, 139 (*"pulp with a coat"*); Katz, 68; diary, Tompkins, 127–28 (*at least one head*); Trevelyan, 213 (*firing wildly*).

479 *Lieutenant Colonel Kappler was enjoying*: Katz, 58–62; transcript, Kesselring trial (*thirty-two men dead*); Kurzman, 176 (*"Revenge!"*); Portelli, 142 (*water and salt*).

480 *Late that afternoon the German high command*: transcript, Kesselring trial.

480 *"I am giving you now a Führer order"*: ibid.; Kenneth Macksey, *Kesselring: The Making of the Luftwaffe*, 207; Lamb, 57.

480 *Kappler spent all night*: Katz, 101, 116–18; Lamb, 59 (*Kappler added fifteen more*); Trevelyan, 222; Portelli, 150, 175.

481 *"I feel the flowers growing"*: http://www.john-keats.com/biografie/chapter_viii.htm# last_days_and_death; Portelli, 7 (*tuberoses perfumed the air*); transcript, Kesseling trial (*Five sharp cracks*).

481 *Five by five by five they staggered*: Katz, 140–42; Portelli, 28.

481 *Relatives of the dead from the Bozen Regiment*: Botjer, 100.

481 *A brief public statement*: Katz, 273; Lamb, 61; "Under the German Yoke," ts, n.d., CEOH, X-39, 12–13, 16 (*"You will be avenged"*).

481 *"When Rome falls"*: memo, Wallace Carroll to "Bannes," Psychological Warfare Bureau, May 31, 1944, Wallace Carroll papers, LOC, box 1, folder 6.

482 *Not for three months*: diary, Tompkins, Jan. 19, 1944; statement, Brother Robert Pace, Oct. 1946, NARA RG 492, JAG war crimes branch, box 2046; Portelli, 191.

482 *some Roman families received a curt note*: Portelli, 188, and jacket art from archive of the Associazione Nazionale tra le Famiglie Italiane dei Martiri.

482 *"I dream of the hills"*: Trevelyan, 230.

## Chapter 11: A Kettle of Grief

### Dead Country

483 *Fifth Army meteorologists for months*: Charles C. Bates and John F. Fuller, *America's Weather Warriors*, 257, 282n; William Murray, "Naples: Variations on a Neapolitan Air," *NYT*, Nov. 19, 2000 (*one eye open*); Tom Gidwitz, "The Hero of Vesuvius," 2005, http://www.vesuvius.tomgidwitz.com/html/the_hero_of_vesuvius.html, chapter 7; "Activity of Vesuvius Between 1631 and 1944," http://vulcan.fis.uniroma3.it/vesuvio/1944eng_text .html; "Vesuvioinrete, il portale del vulcano Vesuvio," http://www.vesuvioinrete.it/e_sto-ria.htm; Moorehead, *Eclipse*, 69; memo on Vesuvius eruption, "Report of Mission," May 5, 1944, Fifth Army, MWC corr, Citadel, box 3 (*the smoke stopped*); Spike Milligan, *Where Have All the Bullets Gone?*, 20–21 (*more anxious*).

483 *The eruption began at 4:30 P.M.*: Susan Sontag, *The Volcano Lover*, in Alice Leccese Powers, *Italy in Mind*, 288–89; Walter L. Medding, "The Road to Rome," ts, n.d., CEOH, box X-38, 58; Alton D. Brashear, *From Lee to Bari*, 203–5; Eric Sevareid, *Not So Wild a Dream*, 367–69 (*"The risk of life"*); Norman Lewis, *Naples '44*, 104–6; *Texas*, 342 (*Peasants wept*).

484 *Just after nine P.M. on Tuesday*: Milligan, 20–21; memo on Vesuvius eruption, "Report of Mission" (*incandescent sheets*); "Activity of Vesuvius Between 1631 and 1944," http://vul-

can.fis.uniroma3.it/vesuvio/1944eng_text.html; Kenn C. Rust, *Twelfth Air Force Story*, 32; "Pliny the Younger's Observations," http://www.mcli.dist.maricopa.edu/tut/final/pliny.html ; Michael Howard, *Captain Professor*, 86.

484 *"Smoke of a thick oily character"*: Harold Macmillan, *War Diaries*, 397; David Erskin, *The Scots Guards, 1919–1955*, 229; Brashear, 207 (*snow showers*); Wynford Vaughan-Thomas, *Anzio*, 212–13 (*"this gesture of the gods"*); Lavinia Orde, "Better Late Than Never," ts, n.d., IWM, 96/34/1, 186; memoir, Aidan Mark Sprot, ts, 1947, LHC, 115.

484 *Twenty-six deaths were reported:* "Who's Afraid of Vesuvius?" *NYT*, Aug. 26, 2003; Brashear, 203–5; H. H. Dunham, "U.S. Army Transportation and the Italian Campaign," Sept. 1945, monograph #17, ASF, Chief of Transportation, NARA RG 336, 190/33/30/00, box 142, 199 (*Rail lines remained blocked*); Rust, 32; "History of the Aviation Engineers in the Mediterranean Theater of Operations," June 1946, AAF Engineer Command, CEOH, X-39 (*"enemy rocks"*).

484 *Ash mixed with rain:* W. H. Connerat, Jr., "Ordnance in the North Africa and Med Theater," ts, n.d., AFHQ, SM, MHI, box 2; corr, J. W. Crawford, Jr., Jan. 3, 2003, to author (*"Sweepers, start your brooms"*); Fred Howard, *Whistle While You Wait*, 165 (*"Never trust a volcano"*).

484 *The world had not ended:* Peter Verney, *Anzio 1944*, 156 (*"Anzio Worse Than Salerno"*); *Anzio Beachhead*, 105–6; Warren P. Munsell, Jr., *The Story of a Regiment*, 65.

485 *Wide-eyed they lined the rails:* Vaughan-Thomas, 191; memo, F. J. Lowry, "Guide to Merchant Vessels Unloading at Anzio," March 7, 1944, SEM, NHC, box 47 (*"The chances of being hit"*); "History of Ordnance Service in the Mediterranean Theater," ts, n.d., CMH, 8-4 JA, 85 (*fifty vehicles from an LST deck*); "Report on Port and Beach Operations at Anzio," Apr. 29, 1944, 540th Engineer Combat Regt, NARA RG 334, NWC Lib, box 343 (*three tons of cargo into a DUKW*); "The United States Eighth Fleet," ts, n.d., in "The Administrative History of the Eighth Fleet," #139, NHC, folder 2, 3 (*277 Luftwaffe raids*); Charles Moran, "The Anzio-Nettuno Landings, January 1944," ts, n.d., SEM, NHC, box 49, 56; memo, "Radio-Controlled Bombs Can Be Jammed," March 10, 1945, SEM, NHC, box 47, 5–7 (*Fritz-X bombs*).

485 *The toll could be seen in the hundred or so casualties:* Beachhead casualties in early spring 1944 averaged 107 per day. *Anzio Beachhead*, 105–6; "Evacuation of Casualties by L.S.T.," Apr. 1944, HQ, Combined Operations, GB COB X-22, NARA RG 334 NWC Lib, box 461.

485 *wounded men on litters:* Pyle, 196–97; Paul A. Cundiff, *45th Infantry CP*, 159 (*outscreamed the screaming shells*); OH, Russell W. Cloer, 7th Inf, May 26, 2006, with author (*"You came here to suffer"*).

485 *A British officer arriving in March:* David Cole, *Rough Road to Rome*, 191–92; Lloyd Clark, *Anzio*, 226 (*"a very moth eaten look"*); memoir, Henry E. Gardiner, ts, n.d., USMA Arch, 238.

485 *Most of the cargo hoisted:* "History of Ordnance Service in the Mediterranean Theater," 85, 88–91; "Engineer History, Fifth Army, Mediterranean Theater," n.d., MHI, 101; Charles D'Orsa, "Trials and Tribulations of an Army G-4," ts, n.d., Fifth Army, CARL, N-4906, 10. Further complicating Anzio logistics was the fact that most British and American weapons used incompatible ammunition. John A. Hixson, "Operation SHINGLE," *Military Review*, March 1989, 64+.

486 *That the cost was not greater:* Chester G. Starr, ed., *From Salerno to the Alps*, 173; Paul W. Pritchard, "Smoke Generator Operations in the Mediterranean and European Theaters of Operation," n.d., CMH, 4-7.1 FA 1; Walter A. Guild, "That Damned Smoke Again," *IJ*, Oct. 1944, 25+; Brooks E. Kleber and Dale Birdsell, *The Chemical Warfare Service: Chemicals in Combat*, 336–39.

486 *Six Allied divisions:* Milton Bracker, "Anzio, 20 Years After Battle, Evokes Memories," *NYT*, Jan. 22, 1964; Masayo Umezawa Duus, *Unlikely Liberators*, 131 (*"Dracula days"*);

OH, Michael S. Davison, 1976, Douglas H. Farmer and Dale K. Brudvig, SOOHP, MHI, 43 (*soldiers near the "dead country"*); Audie Murphy, *To Hell and Back,* 117 (*"We believe nothing"*); George F. Howe, *The Battle History of the 1st Armored Division,* 305; Vaughan-Thomas, 193; Robert Capa, *Slightly out of Focus,* 124; Bill Mauldin, *Up Front,* 193.

486 *The demand for sandbags:* Leo J. Meyer, "Strategy and Logistical History: MTO," ts, n.d., CMH, 2-3.7 CC5, XXII-26; Tom Roe, *Anzio Beachhead,* 82 (Mr. Lucky); Adrian Clements Gore, "This Was the Way It Was," Enid A. Gore, ed., 1987, IWM, 90/29/1, 23 (*"with one ear cocked"*); Munsell, 60, 63 (*"Men dreamed of steaks"*); Lawrence D. Collins, *The 56th Evac Hospital,* 192 (*"anziopectoris"*); Vaughan-Thomas, 191 (*"Anzonians"*).

486 *"The main thing you want"*: *Reporting World War II,* vol. 2, 56; Lee G. Miller, *The Story of Ernie Pyle,* 314; Don Whitehead, *"Beachhead Don,"* 106 (*"palsied old gentleman"*); James Tobin, *Ernie Pyle's War,* 152 (*"Instead of growing stronger"*).

487 *Those perturbations only intensified:* David Nichols, ed., *Ernie's War,* 238–42 (*"pressing your luck"*); Lee G. Miller, *An Ernie Pyle Album,* 96–97 (*"cut on my right cheek"*). Pyle returned to London, where he learned he had won a Pulitzer Prize for his reporting in 1943.

487 *Lucian Truscott had also pressed his luck:* OH, James M. Wilson, Jr., former LKT Jr. aide, Apr. 23, 2004, author, Washington, D.C.

487 *"I have almost become oblivious"*: corr, LKT Jr. to Sarah, March 8, 13, 26 and Apr. 18, 1944, LKT Jr., GCM Lib, box 1, folder 6.

487 *His throat still nagged him:* aide's diary, Apr. 1944, LKT Jr., GCM Lib, box 18, folder; diary, March 1, 2, 9, 12, 18, 19, 22, 30, 1944, VI Corps, Don E. Carleton papers, HIA, box 1; corr, LKT Jr. to Sarah, Apr. 16, 1944, LKT Jr., GCM Lib, box 1, folder 6 (*"lack of voice"*); diary fragment, Fred Walker, n.d., NARA RG 319, OCMH, CA, box 006; OH, Harry Lemley, 1974, Gerald F. Feeney, SOOHP, MHI, 2/44-51 (*remained energetic, buoyant*).

487 *"I can close my eyes and imagine"*: corr, LKT Jr. to Sarah, Apr. 19, 1944, LKT Jr., GCM Lib, box 1, folder 6; diary, Apr. 7, 9 (*slept eight hours straight*), 17, 1944, VI Corps, Don E. Carleton papers, HIA, box 1; Hugh A. Scott, *The Blue and White Devils,* 113 (*bathrobe and slippers*).

488 *But heartbreak was never further away:* Emajean Jordan Buechner, *Sparks,* 97–98.

488 *Truscott had ordered the beachhead evacuated:* C.R.S. Harris, *Allied Administration of Italy, 1943–1945,* 160; StoC, 451; Daniel J. Petruzzi, *My War Against the Land of My Ancestors,* 250; Francesco Rossi and Silvano Casaldi, *Those Days at Nettuno,* 201; corr, Ivar H. Aas to parents, March 24, 1944, provided author by Andrew Carroll; diary, Robert M. Marsh, March 9, 1944, 81st Armored Reconnaissance Bn, 1st AD, ASEQ, MHI (*cesarean delivery with an ax*).

488 *"This beachhead is the craziest place"*: corr, William J. Segan to Herman H. Segan, May 6, 1944, author's possession; Robert D. Burhans, *The First Special Service Force,* 194; Robert H. Adleman and George Walton, *The Devil's Brigade,* 177, 190; Carlo D'Este, *Fatal Decision,* 322 (*"I can't do a thing"*); Harold B. Simpson, *Audie Murphy, American Soldier,* 92; Dan Kurzman, *The Race for Rome,* 259–59; Duus, 130 (*watercress garnishes*).

488 *Troops played baseball:* Edmund F. Ball, *Staff Officer with the Fifth Army,* 327; Flint Whitlock, *The Rock of Anzio,* 260; William L. Allen, *Anzio: Edge of Disaster,* 130 (*waterskiers*); Ralph G. Martin, *The G.I. War, 1941–1945,* 141; Fred Sheehan, *Anzio: Epic of Bravery,* 174; Bill Harr, *Combat Boots,* 82–93.

489 *More than thirty Anzonian newspapers:* Edgar Clark, "Anzio Papers Headline Men Who Make the News," May 1, 1944, *Stars and Stripes,* draft, SM, MHI, box 2; John Lardner, "Anzio, February 10th," in *The New Yorker Book of War Pieces,* 263 (*"following rats"*); Verney, 227 (*beetle racing*); George Aris, *The Fifth British Division, 1939 to 1945,* 220, 225 (*Thousand of dollars were wagered*).

489 *Alcohol provided some consolation:* Charles F. Marshall, *A Ramble Through My War*, 73 (*"catacomb courage"*); Allen, 130; F. Eugene Liggett, "No, Not Yet: Military Memoirs," ts, n.d., 158th FA, ASEQ, MHI, 6 (*"Plastered in Paris"*); diary, Marsh, May 10, 1944 (*"The still blew up"*); *Stars and Stripes*, Apr. 25, 28, 1944, Italy edition, 1 (*first authorized beer*).

489 *Toffey's change-of-command party:* JJT, XII-27; Nathan William White, *From Fedala to Berchtesgaden*, 98.

490 *"There are days and other days":* JJT, XII-23, XIII-3, XIII-17 (*"Efficiency in general"*) XII-12 (*"seen about enough of Italy"*); White, 98 (*he had come full circle*).

490 *Only a few miles from the beetle races:* Vaughan-Thomas, 199, 202; Hans Paul Joachim Liebschner, "Iron Cross Roads," ts, 1999, IWM, 99/82/1, 82–83; corr, Albert Lewis Pyle to Carl Swickerath, Feb. 23, 1973, ALM, box 1 (*"Roosevelt is a Jew"*); Trevelyan, 208 (*trapped rats in empty sandbags*); R. W. Komer, "Report on Historical Observation from the Field," Feb. 24, 1944, Chester G. Starr papers, HIA, box 1.

490 *No field glasses could reveal:* "The German Operation at Anzio," Apr. 1946, Military Intelligence Division, WD, JPL papers, MHI, box 9, 75, 86–87, 99 (*"German divisions are battle weary"*); Walter Kühn, "The Artillery at Anzio-Nettuno," March 1947, FMS, D-158, CARL, N-17500.838.2, 11–13 (*"blast and gouge effect"*); Arthur Robert Moore, "Memoirs—World War II," ts, 1993, 1st AR, 1st AD, ASEQ, MHI, 5–6; Robley D. Evans et al., "American Armor at Anzio," ts, May 1949, CARL, N-490214, 80; Verney, 211 (*"Call the roll, Kesselring"*).

491 *A pair of seventy-foot barrels, named Robert and Leopold:* R. J. O'Rourke, *Anzio Annie*, 23, 43, 91–94, 141, 164; Francesco Rossi and Silvano Casaldi, *Those Days at Nettuno*, 177; Lida Mayo, *The Ordnance Department: On Beachhead and Battlefront*, 200; Marshall, 45.

491 *Yet it was the close fight:* White, 98; Donald E. MacDonald, *"My Buttons Are in the Way,"* s.p., 1952, HIA, 77n (*"saving it to use on Hitler"*); "Training Notes from the Sicilian Campaign," Oct. 25, 1943, AFHQ, G-3, CMH, Geog Sicily 353, 28 (*"pickers-off"*); OH, William P. Yarborough, 1975, J. R. Meese and H. P. Houser, SOOHP, MHI, 63 (*shield their eyes*).

491 *"The march up is something":* MacDonald, *"My Buttons Are in the Way,"* 26; Whitlock, 255 (*"skeletons in clothes"*); Joseph A. Springer, *Black Devil Brigade*, 145 (*Scouts sniffed the air*); David McClure, "How Audie Murphy Won His Medals," ts, Oct. 1969, and David McClure, "Audie Murphy," ts, Jan. 1958, both in ALM, box 1.

491 *More than four billion Allied leaflets:* "Psychological Warfare in the Mediterranean Theater," Aug. 1945, MTO; Margaret Bourke-White, *Purple Heart Valley*, 167 (*"Where is the hot water?"*); Burhans, 193 (*"Abe Levy" series*), 199; Roe, 85 (*"What goes on at home"*); William Woodruff, *Vessel of Sadness*, 139 (*"very cheeky"*).

492 *Enemies who could not be talked from their works:* Starr, ed., 171; Robert J. Williams, observer report, n.d., #93, NARA RG 337, E 15A, box 53; Springer, 165 (das dicke Ende kommt); AAR, 3rd ID, Apr. 14, 1944, DRL, Ft. B; William P. Yarborough, "House Party in Jerryland," *IJ*, July 1944, 8+ (*"House 5 and 6"*).

492 *In this "kettle of grief":* O'Rourke, 150; memoir, Gardiner, 243–44; "Engineer History, Fifth Army, Mediterranean Theater," n.d., CMH, 9-2.5 AB, 90 (*bomb on a combat engineer bivouac*); memoir, James R. Pritchard, ts, n.d., 68th Armored FA Bn, 1st AD, ASEQ, MHI, 35 (*pierced their Piper Grasshopper*); T. Moffatt Burriss, *Strike and Hold*, 78 (*"holding his face together"*); Adleman and Walton, 190 (*"got an extra foot"*).

492 *"Yesterday made 60 days":* censorship morale reports, Nov. 1943–June 1944, NARA RG 492, MTO AG, 311.7, box 931 (*"All the boys who never prayed"*); "Lessons from the Italian Campaign," March 15, 1945, HQ, MTO, CMH, Ital. 353, 72 (*"foxhole-itis"*); Collins, 190 (*S.I.W.*); OH, John A. Heintges, 1974, Jack A. Pellicci, SOOHP, MHI, 231 (*bottle of tranquilizers*); Albert E. Cowdrey, *Fighting for Life*, 150 (*Anzio Beachhead Psychiatric Society*); MacDonald, 43 (*"stumbling figure"*).

493 *"This war has become a very personal affair"*: censorship morale reports, Nov. 1943–June 1944; Michael Gonzalez, curator, 45th ID Mus, to author, March 25, 2005 (*German scalps*); letter, "Bob" to family in New Haven, Conn., Apr. 20, 1944, MCC, YU (*"Henry would shoot him again"*); Woodruff, 144 (*"struggle so hard"*); Liebschner, "Iron Cross Roads," 82 (*"simply refused to die"*); Martin, 127 (*"What's your name now"*).

493 *The days warmed, the seasons advanced:* memoir, Gardiner, 231; memoir, Pritchard, 35 (*camouflaging craters*); "Fifth Army Medical History," ts, n.d., NARA RG 112, MTO surgeon general, 390/17/8/2-3, box 6, 91–98; Meyer, "Stratgy and Logistical History: MTO," XXII-30.

493 *"We seem to be having phenomenal success"*: Collins, 167–69, 179; Edward D. Churchil, *Surgeon to Soldiers,* 279.

494 *The new season stirred the dull roots:* "Report of William Russell Criss," ts, n.d., 45th ID Mus, 317 (*"getting us fat"*); Marshall, 30 (*Axis Sally*).

494 *"Next to missing you all terribly"*: JJT, XIII-13; D'Este, 418 (*"where many of us ceased to be young"*).

### *"Put the Fear of God into Them"*

494 *High above the mud and the misery:* "Air Power in the Mediterranean," Feb. 1945, MAAF, historical section, MHI, 7, 10, 33 (*"non-operational"*); F. M. Sallagar, "Operation STRANGLE: A Case Study of Tactical Air Interdiction," Feb. 1972, RAND, R-851, 11 (*Barely five hundred German planes*); Edward B. Westermann, *Flak,* 234 (*4,300 German flak batteries*).

495 *a crewman flying from Italy listed in his* diary: Mina Curtiss, ed., *Letters Home,* 318; Albert F. Simpson, "Air Phase of the Italian Campaign to 1 January 1944," June 1946, AAFRH-115, CMH, 239, 255, 265, 365n; *AAFinWWII,* vol. 3, 55, 66 (*growing pains*); Kenn C. Rust, *Fifteenth Air Force Story,* 19 (*"disorganized mob"*).

495 *Losses in the fall of 1943:* Tami Davis Biddle, *Rhetoric and Reality in Air Warfare,* 224; Geoffrey Perret, *Winged Victory,* 265–69; "Target Priorities of the Eighth Air Force," May 15, 1945, HQ, Eighth AF, director of intel, Office of AF History, Bolling AFB, Md., 520.317A, 13; corr, Arthur T. Harris to Ira C. Eaker, Nov. 4, 1943, Eaker papers, Eighth AF corr, LOC, box 19 (*"small coal and steel towns"*); memo, H.H. Arnold, "Progress Made by the RAF and U.S. Eighth Air Force in the Combined Bomber Offensive," Nov. 7, 1943, NARA RG 243, section 3, envelope 194 (*bomb damage at Coventry*); Martin Gilbert, *Winston Churchill's War Leadership,* 44, 89 (*"ever learned to fly"*).

495 *As the war's fifth winter ended:* Westermann, 1 (*over a million civilians*); Biddle, 174, 205–7 (*long-range fighters*); *AAFinWWII,* vol. 3, 49; Richard G. Davis, *Carl A. Spaatz and the Air War in Europe,* 66; Leroy W. Newby, *Target Ploesti,* 38 (*"barroom brawlers"*); "Eighth Air Force Tactical Development," July 1945, Eighth AF, MHI (*"fear of God"*).

495 *offensive code-named* ARGUMENT: Glenn Infield, *Big Week,* 4, 44; *AAFinWWII,* vol. 3, 43 (*Allied losses were bitter*); James H. Doolittle, *I Could Never Be So Lucky Again,* 396 (*more Luftwaffe planes*); Davis, 322–26; John Ellis, *Brute Force,* 195, 204; Bernard C. Nalty et al., *With Courage,* 225, 228 (*less than a month*); e-mail, Conred C. Crane to author, March 2, 2007.

496 *"un-gear the German war economy"*: "The Effect of Allied Strategic Bombing on the Present Status of the War," Feb. 2, 1945, in "Air Power in the Mediterranean," 7, 10, 33; H. H. Arnold, *Global Mission,* 328; "An Analysis of the Weather Factor in This War," Apr. 1944, NARA RG 334, NWC Lib, AAF WIB A 4-44, box 27 (*average two tons of high explosives*); "Target Priorities of the Eighth Air Force," 21–23 (*German synthetic oil facilities*).

496 *Even so, the hard winter for airmen:* Davis, 358, 379; Charles R. Shrader, "Amicicide: The Problem of Friendly Fire in Modern War," Dec. 1982, CSI, 36 (*bombing Switzerland*).

496 *Losses remained dreadful:* Davis, 288; Ellis, *Brute Force* 220–21; Biddle, 204; Marvin A. Kreidberg and Merton G. Henry, *History of Military Mobilization in the United States Army, 1775–1945,* 647; Harry H. Crosby, *A Wing and a Prayer,* 95 (*"When a plane blew up"*).

497 *"When I fly a mission":* John Muirhead, *Those Who Fall,* 98; Stephen E. Ambrose, *The Wild Blue,* 169 (*"You must remember this"*); Nalty, 184 (*13,000 U.S. airmen*); Michael Burleigh, *The Third Reich,* 746 (*140,000 Allied crewmen*); censorship morale reports, Nov. 1943–June 1944, NARA RG 492, MTO AG, 311.7, box 931 (*"On my last four raids"*); Newby, 46 (*aluminum patches*); Howard, 51, 85 (*"the enlarged pupil"*).

497 *Propeller turbulence:* James S. Nanney, "Army Air Forces Medical Service in World War II," 1998, 9, 20–23; memo, "German Fighter Tactics Against Flying Fortresses," Dec. 8, 1943, HQ, Eighth AF, CARL, N-13354 (*"Sisters' Act"*); "Combat Informational Intelligence Series: Interview with Brig. Gen. H. S. Hansell," Aug. 9, 1943, RG 334, NWC Lib, box 14; Conrad C. Crane, *Bombs, Cities, and Civilians,* 54 (*"I didn't pray for myself"*).

497 *"variable one subject to local conditions":* "Air Power in the Mediterranean," 62. Air Force statistics indicated that casualty rates among airmen in the Mediterranean remained proportionally higher than those of the ground forces through the end of 1944. Simpson, "Air Phase of the Italian Campaign to 1 January 1944," 369. Many flying casualties in the Italy-based Twelfth Air Force were classified as "nervous disorders." James S. Nanney, "Army Air Forces Medical Service in World War II," 1998, 17.

497 *"Fly 'til I die":* Howard, 165.

497 *Among those affected by the ever spiraling quotas:* Michael C. Scoggins, "Joseph Heller's Combat Experiences in *Catch-22,*" *War, Literature & the Arts,* vol. 15, nos. 1 & 2 (2003), 213+; Joseph Heller, *Now and Then,* 181.

498 *Command of the Italian skies:* Sallagar, "Operation STRANGLE," 19 (*"German withdrawal"*).

498 *Extravagant claims for airpower's efficacy:* OH, Ira C. Eaker, Feb. 1975, Hugh N. Ahmann, AFHRA, K239.0512-829, 375–76; *Battle,* 14.

498 *Much of the thinking about how best:* Mark M. Boatner III, *The Biographical Dictionary of World War II,* 641; Vincent Orange, *Tedder,* 223; Solly Zuckerman, *From Apes to Warlords,* 185–95, 203, 209–10; Eduard Mark, *Aerial Interdiction in Three Wars,* 94; Molony VI, 35.

498 *"without critically weakening the enemy":* Andrew Brookes, *Air War over Italy, 1943–1945,* 80; *AAFinWWII,* vol. 3, 372–73 (*hard to cut*); Sallagar, "Operation STRANGLE," 26, 29; "Isolation of the Battlefield as Effected in the Italian Campaign," July 1944, HQ, AAF, CARL, N-9818, 7, 10–11; "Report on Operation STRANGLE, 19 March–11 May 1944," July 24, 1944, HQ, MATAF, AFHRA, 626.430, 3 (*"could have afforded to discard"*).

499 *Eaker and his apostles:* OH, Lauris Norstad, 1979, Hugh N. Ahmann, AFHRA, K239.0512-1116, 532; James Parton, *"Air Force Spoken Here,"* 381; H. M. Wilson, "Report by the Supreme Allied Commander," 1948, part II, 7.

499 STRANGLE *began badly:* Anthony Cave Brown, *The Last Hero,* 475–77; Patrick K. O'Donnell, *Operatives, Spies and Saboteurs,* 59–60; index, OSS operations, Italy, 1944, "Ginny," NARA RG 226, E 99, OSS history office, 190/6/7/6, box 40, 33; report, OSS activities, March 1944, NATOUSA, NARA RG 226, OSS history office, box 122 (*"Mission assumed lost"*).

499 *An Italian fisherman who spotted a dinghy:* Max Corvo, *The O.S.S. in Italy,* 155–62; affidavit, Capt. Clifford M. Bassett, M.D., and Capt. Robert J. Willoughby, M.D., May 24, 1945, forensic examination of "15 men dressed in American military uniforms on Punto Bianca," author's possession (*hands lashed with wire*); http://www.ess.uwe.ac.uk/WCC/dostler.htm; Brown, 480–81. General Dostler was tried at Caserta after the war and executed by firing squad.

499 *The bombing campaign proved more potent:* AAFinWWWII, vol. 3, 378–79 (*twenty-seven bridges*); 384; Sallagar, "Operation STRANGLE," 41n; memo, "How STRANGLE Worked on Four Targets," ts, n.d., Lauris Norstad papers, DDE Lib, box 18 (*hit at twenty-two points*).

500 *Stations, bridges, engine repair shops:* Sallagar, "Operation STRANGLE," 34, 38 (*tripled to seventy-five*), 46; "Analysis of Tactical Attacks on Bridges and Viaducts," n.d., HQ MAAF, CMH, Geog Italy, 370.2, 2; Klaus Stange, "Railroad Situation from January 1944," Apr. 1947, FMS, D-049, 8 (*shot up rail electrical conduits*); "Interdiction of Italian Railways," Apr. 15, 1944, HQ, MAAF, NARA RG 319, OCMH, CA, box 8 (*trains often halted in Florence*); Ernst Eggert, "Supply During Allied Offensive, May 1944," 1947, FMS, #D-128, MHI, 3–4 (*drums ran short*).

500 *Kesselring in early April:* Mark, 168; Albert Kesselring et al., "German Version of the History of the Italian Campaign," CARL, N-16671.1-3, 110 (*took nearly a week*); AAFin-WWII, vol. 3, 383; Walter von Unruh, "Inspection of Italian Theater of War," 1947, FMS, D-016, 18; Eggert, "Supply During Allied Offensive, May 1944," 8; Stange, "Railroad Situation from January 1944," 8–9 (*"difficulties seemed to pile up"*).

500 *With that maddening blend of dexterity:* Walter Warlimont, "OKW Activities—The Italian Theater, 1 Apr.–31 Dec. 1944," n.d., FMS, C-099b, 17–18; "Report on Operation STRANGLE, 19 March–11 May 1944," 3 (*For every boxcar destroyed*); Karl Theodor Koerner, "Rail Transportation Problems in Italy," Apr. 1947, FMS, D-010, MHI, 11 (*bridge spans across the Po*); Sallagar, "Operation STRANGLE," 54; Britt Bailey, "The German Situation in Italy," July 1951, NARA RG 319, E 145, OCMH, R-series mss, #R-50, 34; Mark, 178.

500 *"achieved nothing more than nuisance value":* StoC, 451; Kesselring et al., "German Version," 107–15; Molony VI, 42 (*grew sclerotic*); Parton, 384 (*"virtually without air support"*); "Air Power in the Mediterranean," 50 (*"not forced to withdraw"*).

### "You Are All Brave. You Are All Gentlemen"

501 *Spring crept up the Italian boot:* Harold L. Bond, *Return to Cassino*, 133; Farley Mowat, *The Regiment*, 184; Cyril Ray, *Algiers to Austria*, 122 (*flowers enameled the fields*); Walter Robson, *Letters from a Soldier*, 91; Klaus H. Huebner, *A Combat Doctor's Diary*, 59 (*whiff of charred villages*).

501 *Herders tended their white, sloe-eyed cattle:* Robson, 91; John Guest, *Broken Images*, 163, 172, 175; Medding, "The Road to Rome," 59 (*Children with big mallets*); "Report of William Russell Criss," ts, May 5, 1944, 45th ID Mus (*"I feel like a Dago"*); Margaret Bourke-White, "Over the Lines," in *Reporting World War II*, vol. 2, 753 (*like scattered coins*); corr, Russell Bodeen to Maxin Kohn, May 14, 1944, 141st Inf, 36th Div, ASEQ, MHI (*"field of blood red poppies"*).

501 *Only at Cassino did spring seem hesitant:* F. Majdalany, *The Monastery*, 48–49 (*"Golgotha"*); diary, John G. Wright, May 18, 1944, American Field Service, author's possession, 23–24 (*"down to bedrock"*); Jack Kros, *War in Italy*, chapter 6, 12 (*"Ghost Village"*); Diana F. Butler, ed., "Human Interest," UK NA, CAB 101/346, 1 (*crimped to a goat path*); Alex Bowlby, *The Recollections of Rifleman Bowlby*, 20.

502 *Yet in Cassino the living were also unseen:* Nigel Nicolson, *The Grenadier Guards in the War of 1939–1945*, vol. 2, 421–22 (*Fifteen hundred soldiers*); war diary, 1st Guards Bde, March–Apr. 1944, UK NA, WO 170/514, 4, 6–8 (*occupied a wide crescent*).

502 *Each evening Guardsmen porters:* George Aarons, "Cameraman in Cassino," May 21, 1944, *Yank*, 3+; C. T. Framp, "The Littlest Victory," ts, n.d., IWM, 85/19/1, 83 (*Most wore gym shoes*); Nicolson, 422–23 (*dead American nurse*); J. K. Windeatt, "Very Ordinary Soldier," ts, 1989, IWM, 90/20/1, 105 (*"smell marks"*); memoir, P. Royle, ts, 1972, IWM, 99/72/1, 109 (*"fairly serious stammer"*).

502 *"Good evening, Hans"*: Frank Beckett, *Prepare to Move*, 149; Nicolson, 421–24; Betsy Wade, ed., *Forward Positions: The War Correspondence of Homer Bigart*, 43–44; war diary, 1st Guards Bde, March–Apr. 1944, 8; Robson, 101–3.

502 *"There is no day"*: Fred Majdalany, *Cassino: Portrait of a Battle*, 198; Nicolson, 422 (*standing watch at their periscopes*); C. T. Framp, "The Littlest Victory," ts, n.d., IWM, 85/19/1, 84 ("*a dead world*"); memoir, P. Royle, ts, 1972, IWM, 99/72/1, 111 (*half-inch in their morning mugs*); Majdalany, *The Monastery*, 46 ("*deadly sameness*"), 24 ("*grotesque friezes*"); J. K. Windeatt, "Very Ordinary Soldier," ts, 1989, IWM, 90/20/1, 106 (*Ginger Rogers*).

503 *Life across the rubble*: Raleigh Trevelyan, *Rome '44*, 209 (*cologne*); Robert Mulcahy, "If You Die, You Die," *World War II*, vol. 21, no. 7; Robert Wagner, *The Texas Army*, 281 ("*the word 'catastrophe'*"); war diary, 1st Guards Bde, March–Apr. 1944, 7 (*swastika banners*); R. C. Taylor, "A Pocketfull of Time," ts, n.d., author's possession (*Death holding a pair of calipers*).

503 *"Everything is in the hands"*: "AFHQ Intelligence Notes No. 57," May 2, 1944, NARA RG 407, E 47, AFHQ, 95-AL1-2.18, box 164.

503 *"You are all brave"*: Michael Howard and John Sparrow, *The Coldstream Guards, 1920–1946*, 219.

503 *Shortly after seven A.M. on Monday, May 1:* MWC to Renie, Apr. 24, 1944, MWC, personal corr, Citadel.

504 *Mark Clark was a meticulous creature:* A. M. Gruenther to Maurine Clark, May 1, 1944, MWC, corr, box 3; signed lyrics, diary, MWC, Feb. 23, 1944, Citadel, box 65 ("Mile by mile").

504 *The trailer door swung open:* MWC to Renie, May 4, 1944, MWC, personal corr, Citadel; diary, MWC, May 1, 1944, Citadel, box 65; A.M. Gruenther to Maurine Clark, May 1, 1944, MWC, corr, box 3 ("*hard-boiled soldier*").

504 *"comes at a most inopportune moment"*: msg, MWC to J. L. Devers, Apr. 6, 1944, and GCM to J. L. Devers, Apr. 7, 1944, NARA RG 492, MTOUSA, SGS, "eyes only, General Devers, incoming," box 135; Maurine Clark, *Captain's Bride, General's Lady*, 115 ("*fluttery as a schoolgirl*"), 116–17; memo, GCM to MWC, Apr. 11, 1944, GCM papers, GCM Lib, corr, box 61 (*no hint of welcome*); "Momentous Days," ts, Apr. 1944, MWC, corr, Citadel, box 3.

504 *Mrs. Clark had been promoting:* Maurine Clark to GCM, Feb. 23, 1944, with MWC letter dated, Feb. 10, 1944, GCM papers, GCM Lib, corr, box 61.

505 *"You are aware"*: GCM to Maurine Clark, March 1, 1944, GCM papers, GCM Lib, corr, box 61.

505 *"I know it will be somewhat of a shock"*: MWC to mother, Apr. 17, 1944, GCM papers, GCM Lib, corr, box 61; diary, MWC, Apr 10, 1944, Citadel, box 65; http://www.greenbrier .com/site/other/about_history.aspx; Maurine Clark, 118 ("*sorry I took those guys prisoner*").

505 *Before returning to Italy:* http://www.bizjournals.com/washington/stories/2002/07/15/ focus10.html; Forrest C. Pogue, *George C. Marshall: Organizer of Victory*, 328; "Momentous Days" (*dozen powerful figures*); OH, MWC, May 10–21, 1948, SM, MHI, 53; press conference, MWC, May 9, 1944, Citadel, box 63, folder 3.

506 *the family cocker spaniel: Calculated*, 336–37; Maurine Clark, 119; MWC to Renie, May 4, 1944, MWC, personal corr, Citadel ("*seems like a dream*").

506 *Under Alexander's reorganization: Calculated*, 334n, 337; OH, Charles E. Saltzman, former deputy chief of staff, Fifth Army, March 26, 1948, NARA RG 319, OCMH, CA, box 005 (*Cool and remote*).

506 *"He treats his corps commanders"*: GK, May 4, 1944; OH, Edward J. O'Neill, VI Corps G-4, June 22, 1948, NARA RG 319, OCMH, CA, box 005 (*Truscott twice reminded him*); diary, MWC, Feb. 28, 1944, Citadel, box 65 ("*whining attitude*"); Martin Blumenson, *Mark*

*Clark,* 166 (*mathematics instructor*); L. James Binder, *Lemnitzer: A Soldier for His Time,* 129 (*Devers refused to deal directly*); OH, L. L. Lemnitzer, Jan. 16, 1948, SM, MHI ("*could not be together three minutes*"); OH, MWC, May 10–21, 1948, SM, MHI, 65 ("*too many bosses*"); OH, Jacob L. Devers, Aug. 12, 1958, FCP, GCM Lib, transcript, tape #68, 72–73 ("*God Almighty*").

506 "*acted in many high-handed ways*": diary, MWC, Feb. 19, 26 ("*in no way cooperating*"), 1944, Citadel, box 65; OH, L. L. Lemnitzer, Jan. 16, 1948, SM, MHI (*grew so insolent with Alexander*); D. Clayton James, *A Time for Giants,* 158–59 ("*vexatious attitude*"); Macmillan, 404–5 (*insurrection collapsed*).

507 "*Many happy returns*": MWC to Renie, May 4, 1944, MWC, personal corr, Citadel; Danchev, 527 ("*hoped to land a wildcat*"), 522, 534 ("*chariot of a lunatic*"); Martin Gilbert, *Churchill and America,* 292 ("*feeling of bitterness*").

507 "*Temperamental, very sensitive*": OH, Harold Alexander, Jan. 10–15, 1949, SM, CMH, geog files, II-8.

507 *Never frightened, perhaps, but often anxious: CM,* 353; *CtoA,* 23, 36; diary, MWC, Apr. 30, 1944, Citadel, box 65 John Ellis, *On the Front Lines,* 163 (*132 second lieutenants*); Robert R. Palmer et al., *The Procurement and Training of Ground Troops,* 185; "History of the Peninsular Base Section," 1944, CMH, 8-4 HA 1, vol. 2; "Investigation of the Replacement System," Nov. 6, 1943, NARA RG 492, MTO AG, 333.5-212; observer reports: Kenneth I. Hittle, "Report of Returned Overseas Observer," n.d., #83; M.S. Crallé, untitled, n.d., #90; George Artman, untitled, n.d., #94, all in NARA RG 337, E 15A, AGF, box 53; John Sloan Brown, *Draftee Division,* ix (*built mostly from draftees*); msg, MWC to GCM, May 17, 1944, MWC, Citadel, box 3 ("*age and physical reasons*"); corr, A. Gruenther to DDE, May 27, 1944, DDE Lib, PP-pres, corr, box 48.

508 *two British divisions still at Anzio:* diary, MWC, Feb. 27, Apr. 12 ("*Many British troops*"), 1944, Citadel, box 65; LKT Jr., "Notes on Future Operations," n.d., MWC, corr, box 3; *CM,* 352; Molony V, 421n; OH, LKT Jr., Apr. 3, 1958, SM, MHI.

508 "*Absenteeism and desertion*": note, William R.C. Penney, Apr. 21, 1944, LHC, Penney 8/33. More than three hundred British soldiers were executed for desertion or cowardice in World War I, but capital punishment for those crimes had been abolished in the 1930s. John Laffin, *Surgeons in the Field,* 281.

508 *On average, ten British soldiers:* "Operations of British, Indian and Dominion Forces in Italy," part V, n.d., UK NA, CAB 106/453, 1; Diana Butler, "The British Soldier in Italy, Sept. 1943–June 1944," ts, n.d., UK NA, CAB 101/224, 35, 43–44; Ben Shephard, *A War of Nerves,* 240 ("*slinkers*"); memo, Maj. Gen. John Yeldham Whitfield, CG, UK 6th Div, "Battle Absentees," Apr. 10, 1944, in James Scott Elliott papers, LHC ("*matter is hushed up*").

508 *The U.S. Army would convict 21,000 deserters:* "Military Executions," 1994, MHI, Ref Bib; memos, MWC to II Corps and VI Corps, March 13, 1944, and Dec. 4, 1943, NARA RG 338, II Corps JAG, 250.1, box 156; "Operations of British, Indian and Dominion Forces in Italy," 8; Morse P. Manson and Harry M. Grayson, "Why 2,776 American Soldiers in the Mediterranean Theater of Operation Were Absent Without Leave," *American Journal of Psychiatry,* July 1946, 50+.

508 "*I feel like my nervous system*": Stephen W. Ranson, "Military Medicolegal Problems in Field Psychiatry," *Bulletin of the U.S. Army Medical Department,* vol. 9, Nov. 1949, 181+; Michael D. Doubler, *Closing with the Enemy,* 242; Shephard, 217; memo, "Neuropsychiatric Treatment in the Combat Zone," June 12, 1943, circular letter no. 17, NARA RG 292, records of special staff, MTOUSA surgeon, box 2551; William C. Menninger, "Psychiatry in the War," June 1946, MHI, "professional papers," group 1; memo, "Psychiatric Services in the U.S. Army in NATOUSA," Dec. 31, 1943, NARA RG 292, records of special staff, MTOUSA surgeon, box 2551.

508 *All troops were at risk:* "Casualties, Wounded and Wounds, 1946–7," Army Field Forces, G-3, NARA RG 337, 704, 1942–1952, series 10, box 46, 11 (*70 percent of the casualties*); "Battle Casualties," *IJ*, Sept. 1949, 18+ ("whether *he will be hit*"); Palmer et al., 228. Ten combat days typically equaled seventeen calendar days in Army calculations. Bruce C. Clarke, "Study of AGF Battle Casualties," Sept. 1946, AGF HQ, NARA RG 537, E 16A, adm div subject file, 1942–1949, box 48.

509 *Treatment by "narcosynthesis":* "Fifth Army Medical Service History," Feb. 1945, CMH, 52; Brashear, 352–56 (*shock therapy*); Charles M. Wiltse, *The Medical Department: Medical Service in the Mediterranean and Minor Theaters,* 255; memo, Fifth Army surgeon, Oct. 2, 1944, NARA RG 292, records of special staff, MTOUSA surgeon, box 2551; Cowdrey, 148. Half of the Army's 2,400 psychiatrists were young physicians given a three-month crash course in psychiatry; most others had worked primarily with psychotics in state hospitals. Eli Ginberg, "Logistics of the Neuropsychiatric Problem of the Army," Feb. 1946, MHI, "professional papers," group 1.

509 *All of these issues impaired Fifth Army's:* OH, MWC, Nov. 17, 1959, FCP, GCM Lib, transcript of tape 37, 25.

509 *of dubious military value:* The U.S. Joint Chiefs in late March voiced doubt that "the capture of Rome is worth heavy engagement in Italy." Molony VI, 9.

509 *a rightful and prestigious prize:* OH, MWC, May 10–21, 1948, SM, MHI, 53; Kent Roberts Greenfield, ed., *Command Decisions,* 277, 280.

509 *But getting there quickly was paramount:* OH, Robert J. Wood, Fifth Army G-3 staff, March 4, 1948, NARA RG 319, OCMH, CA, box 005, 2–3; Greenfield, ed., 277, 280.

509 *"I know factually":* diary, MWC, May 5, 1944, Citadel, box 65.

## "On the Eve of Great Things"

509 *Alexander often quoted Lord Nelson's:* Viscount Alexander of Tunis, "The Allied Armies in Italy," n.d., CMH, II-41; http://www.wtj.com/archives/nelson/1805_10b.htm; Molony VI, 95, 97 (*equivalent of twenty-eight divisions*); Sidney T. Matthews, "The French Drive on Rome," *Revue Historique de l'Armée,* special issue, 1957, 123; *CtoA,* 40; Michael Carver, *Harding of Petherton, Field-Marshal,* 126; *Battle,* 203–5.

509 *"Between ourselves":* John Keegan, ed., *Churchill's Generals,* 121; H. E. Pulliam, "Operations in Italy," Sept. 1, 1944, AGF board, AFHQ, DTL, Ft. B, 2–3 ("*on an axis generally parallel*").

510 *Alexander's final order:* CtoA, 40; Nigel Nicolson, *Alex: The Life of Field Marshal Earl Alexander of Tunis,* 248; Carver, 134.

510 *"no invidious comparison":* minutes, conference, AFHQ chief of staff and French chief of staff, May 6, 1944, CMH, Geog files, Italy 337.

510 *Their commander, Lieutenant General Oliver W. H. Leese:* Gregory Blaxland, *Alexander's Generals,* 21–22; GK, Apr. 4, 1944 ("*ungainly bruiser*"); Rowland Ryder, *Oliver Leese,* ix (*horticultural succulents*), 152–53, 168; Douglas Porch, *The Path to Victory,* 513; Dominick Graham and Shelford Bidwell, *Tug of War,* 254.

510 *"having a baby":* Ryder, 163, 160 ("*I can work with Clark*"); OH, H. Alexander, Jan. 10–15, 1949, SM, CMH, II-8 ("*Not the pusher Clark was*"); Daniel G. Dancocks, *The D-Day Dodgers: The Canadians in Italy, 1943–1945,* 237 ("*like a whore in heat*").

510 *Leese's seven infantry and three armor divisions:* Molony V, 591n; Blaxland, 26 ("*ardour of a boy*"); Janusz Piekalkiewicz, *The Battle for Cassino,* 16, 102 (*fought both Germans and Russians*); Kurzman, 26; David Hapgood and David Richardson, *Monte Cassino,* 182–93.

511 *Anders's two divisions were understrength:* "Operations by 2nd Polish Corps Against the High Ground, Monte Cassino," ts, June 1944, possession of Roger Cirillo, 12; John Nelson, "Always a Grenadier," ts, 1982, LH, 44 ("*We never take prisoners*"); W. Anders, *An Army in Exile,* 170–73 ("*no men to spare*").

511 *"The eyes of suffering France"*: Michael Carver, ed., *The War Lords*, 604 (*"invading the mountains"*); *CtoA*, 24; Porch, 554 (*retraining his forces*).

511 *That meant scaling the Auruncis*: *CtoA*, 30; OH, Robert J. Wood, March 4 and 15, 1948, SM, MHI; OH, Lyman Lemnitzer, Jan. 16, 1948, SM, MHI.

511 *Wrapped in a greatcoat*: Frank Gervasi, *The Violent Decade*, 557; G. K. Tanham, "Battle-field Intelligence in World War II: A Case Study of the Fifth Army Front in Italy," Sept. 1956, Project RAND, RM-1792, CMH, iii–iv, 28 (*photo reconnaissance*); Diana F. Butler, "The French Expeditionary Corps in the Battle for Rome," n.d., UK NA, CAB 101/226, 3–5 (*persuaded first Keyes*); John Ellis, *Cassino: The Hollow Victory*, 47 (*"They like us a lot"*).

512 *Rather than employ the FEC*: Matthews, "The French Drive on Rome," 125–26; Butler, "The French Expeditionary Corps," 2–5.

512 *Clark's admiration for Juin*: memo, phone code names, March 5, 1944, Fifth Army, Robert J. Wood papers, MHI; Anthony Clayton, *Three Marshals of France*, 79 (*surrendered one of his four stars*); Carver, ed., 607 (*"Radiate confidence"*); *CtoA*, 35.

512 *Half a million players*: Clifford W. Dorman, "Too Soon for Heroes," ts, n.d., 19th Combat Engineers, author's possession, 78–79 (*"not to camouflage too well"*); Alexander, "The Allied Armies in Italy," III-9 (*twenty undetected French battalions*); Clayton, 83 (*soup-bowl helmets*); Butler, "The French Expeditionary Corps," 11 (*hand tools to minimize the noise*); Dharm Pal, *The Campaign in Italy, 1943–1945*, 158 (*scattered brushwood*).

512 *Canadian signalers in April*: Mark Zuehlke, *The Liri Valley*, 78; "Engineers in the Italian Campaign, 1943–1945," ts, n.d., UK, MHI, 88 (*spread garnished nets*); Harold E. Miller, "G-2 Report on Italian Campaign," June 15, 1944, NARA RG 337, AGF, observer report, #110, box 54, 10; Anthony Cave Brown, ed., *The Secret War Report of the OSS*, 217.

513 *Military traffic signs appeared*: Martha Gellhorn, "Cracking the Gothic Line," *Collier's*, Oct. 28, 1944, 24+; "Operations by 2nd Polish Corps Against the High Ground, Monte Cassino," 22–23 (*seven thousand mottled sniper suits*); "Engineer History, Fifth Army, Mediterranean Theater," MHI, 65 (*screens made of chicken wire*); Dancocks, 237.

513 *Scouts in canvas shoes*: Matthew Parker, *Monte Cassino*, 296; *The Tiger Triumphs*, 72; Neil Orpen, *Victory in Italy*, 28 (*South African troops lay low*).

513 *Every tree along Highway 6*: "History of Ordnance Service in the Mediterranean Theater," 77; Alfred M. Beck et al., *The Corps of Engineers: The War Against Germany*, 239, 250; AAR, 1621st Engineer Model Making Detachment, n.d., NARA RG 407, ENDT-1621-0.1, 270/62/12/1, box 19220 (*intricate terrain replicas*); Miller, "G-2 Report on Italian Campaign," 5 (*mixed ersatz inks*).

513 *Endless supply convoys crept forward*: William J. Diamond, "Water Is Life," *Military Engineer*, Aug. 1947, 330+; Orpen, 33 (*hoods wrapped in rubber pads*); "Fifth Army Medical History," 146 (*clop of hooves*); John Buchan, "Report on a Visit to the French Expeditionary Corps," Canadian Army, n.d., CMH, Geog files, Italy 337, 1 (*"No mules"*).

514 *"I think of you every day"*: corr, LKT Jr. to Sarah, May 3, 7, 14, 1944, LKT Jr. papers, GCM Lib, box 1, folder 6.

514 *More than one million tons of matériel*: OH, Francis Oxx, PBS CG, May 21, 1948, SM, MHI, box IIA1; "Engineer History, Fifth Army, Mediterranean Theater," CMH, 9-2.5 AB, 90; Allan L. Swaim, "The Operations of the Communications Platoon Headquarters Company, 15th Infantry Regiment, on Anzio Beachhead," 1947, IS, 16 (*jeep-drawn plow*); "10th Engineer Combat Battalion, Cisterna-Rome Operation," ts, n.d., CMH, Geog files, Italy, 314.7 (*stockade for five thousand prisoners*).

514 *Patrols reclaimed small swatches*: Earl M. Cooper, "The Operation of the 2nd Battalion, 180th Infantry at Anzio Beachhead," 1947, IS; msg, LKT Jr. to MWC, May 7, 1944, NARA RG 319, OCMH, CA, box 6 (*"one additional infantry division"*); *CtoA*, 117 (*trundled forward each night*); Moore, "Memoirs—World War II," 7–8 (*"It was crowded"*).

514 *In a letter to his old friend:* corr, ENH to L. J. McNair, May 8, 1944, ENH, MHI, box 1; corr, LKT Jr. to Sarah, May 11, 1944, LKT Jr. papers, GCM Lib, box 1, folder 6 (*"on the eve of great things"*).

514 *It was precisely this issue that General Alex:* Sidney T. Matthews, "Drive to Rome," ts, 1954, MHI, 26–27, 31; *CM,* 369.

515 *The quizzical tilt:* CtoA, 39 (*had eyed the stretch of Highway 6*); "Notes by General Alexander for Conference Held at HQ, AAI, on 2 April 1944," NARA RG 319, OCMH, CA, box 8 (*cut the highway at Valmontone*); Matthews, "Drive to Rome," 29 (*code-named* BUFFALO); memo, AFHQ, deputy chief of staff, March 21, 1944, NARA RG 331, AFHQ micro, R-225B (*might take a month*); "Notes on Conference," May 5, 1944, Fifth Army, MWC papers, Citadel, box 3 (*decisive battle of annihilation*); Pulliam, "Operations in Italy," 2–3 (*"thereby prevent the supply"*).

515 *"Gen. Alex arrived this morning":* msg, LKT Jr. to MWC, May 5, 1944, NARA RG 319, OCMH, CA, box 6.

515 *"Alex trying to run my army":* diary, MWC, May 5, 1944, Citadel, box 65.

516 *"The capture of Rome is the only important":* CM, 369, Matthews, "Drive to Rome," 31 (*detour onto other routes*).

516 *"I told him he had embarrassed me":* diary, MWC, May 8, 1944, Citadel, box 65.

516 *At four P.M. on Tuesday:* diary, MWC, May 9, 1944, Citadel, box 65; Clark press conference, May 9, 1944, MWC, Citadel, box 63, folder 3 (*"not quite up to strength"*); Matthews, "The French Drive on Rome," 122; Ralph Bennett, *Ultra and the Mediterranean Strategy,* 279–81; F. H. Hinsley et al., *British Intelligence in the Second World War,* 202.

516 *"Everybody throws everything they have":* "Notes on Conference," May 5, 1944; Clark press conference, May 9, 1944 (*"The more Boche we can hold"*).

517 *He made no mention of his quarrel:* In a postwar interview with the Army historian Sidney Matthews, Clark acknowledged that he "foresaw that the time might come when the shift in the axis would be desirable." OH, MWC, May 10–21, 1948, SM, MHI, 72.

517 *"The attack I would like to make":* Clark press conference, May 9, 1944.

517 *Albert Kesselring knew nothing:* Count von Klinckowstroem, "Italian Campaign," 1947, FMS, #T-1a, chap. 10, 5, 8; *Battle,* 227–28; Tanham, "Battlefield Intelligence in World War II," 33–35 (*nine of twenty-two Allied regimental command posts*); StoA, 211; Harold E. Miller, "G-2 Report on Italian Campaign," 7; Robin Kay, *Official History of New Zealand in the Second World War,* vol. 2, *Italy: From Cassino to Trieste,* 16.

517 *A Moroccan deserter several weeks earlier:* A. G. Steiger, "The Italian Campaign, 4 Jan.–4 June 1944," July 1948, Canadian Army HQ, historical section, report #20, 33; Kesselring et al, "German Version," 119 (*May 20 or later*); Bailey, "The German Situation in Italy," 114 (*did "not expect anything"*); Frido von Senger und Etterlin, "War Diary of the Italian Campaign," 1953, FMS, #C=095b, MHI, 114–16.

517 *If Kesselring was blind and misinformed:* Kesselring et al., "German Version," 117; *Battle,* 226; *CtoA,* 17–18, 111; Bailey, "The German Situation in Italy," 58 (*"make the enemy exhaust himself"*), 67; Molony VI, 71n; Porch, 549 (*82,000 held the southern front*).

518 *"To my great pleasure, everything is quiet":* Steiger, "The Italian Campaign," 39.

518 *"It was like a goodbye gift":* C. T. Framp, "The Littlest Victory," ts, n.d., IWM, 85/19/1, 102; Beckett, 150 (*conspicuously white animals*); Peter Schrijvers, *The Crash of Ruin,* 213, 216 (*guide to Italian cities*); Huebner, 61 (*"Blackjack for twenty dollars"*).

518 *"Who the hell would want to live here":* Fred Cederberg, *The Long Road Home,* 113; Majdalany, *Cassino: Portrait of a Battle,* 228 (*"a cause in its own right"*); Charles Connell, *Monte Cassino,* 179 (*"alive with rats"*); Trevelyan, 273.

519 *A dozen miles to the southwest:* Nicole Solignac O'Connor, "Mektoub: A Young Woman's War Journal," ts, 2002, author's possession, 124.

519 *On the gunline in the rear:* C. V. Clifton, "The 240mm Howitzer & the 8-inch Gun in a Mobile Situation," June 27, 1944, CARL, N-7276, 3; Mayo, 205; Constance M. Green et

al., *The Ordnance Department: Planning Munitions for War,* 362; N. P. Morrow, "Employment of Artillery in Italy," *FAJ,* Aug. 1944, 498+; "Lessons from the Italian Campaign," 91–94.

519 *"Busy days, nerve trying days"*: JJT, XIV-3-8.

519 *"If Alex is a military genius"*: GK, May 10, 1944; Nicolson, *Alex* (*"Our objective is the destruction"*); msg, W. Churchill to GCM, Apr. 16, 1944, NARA RG 165, E 422, OPD exec files, 390/38/2/4-5, box 18

519 *H-hour was fixed for eleven* P.M.: CtoA, 37; Orpen, 34; *The Princeton Class of 1942 During World War II,* 509 (*"I do not know where my son is"*); Alexander, "The Allied Armies in Italy," III-10 (*"strange, impressive silence"*); Michael Pearson, "Hard in the Attack: The Canadian Army in Sicily and Italy," Sept. 1996, Ph.D. diss, Carleton University, Ottawa, 332 (*"New boys with fear"*).

## CHAPTER 12: THE GREAT PRIZE
### *Shaking Stars from the Heavens*

521 *The BBC pips had not finished:* Matthew Parker, *Monte Cassino,* 309; Viscount Alexander of Tunis, "The Allied Armies in Italy," n.d., CMH, III-10 (*two thousand gun pits*); C. T. Framp, "The Littlest Victory," ts, n.d., IWM, 85/19/1, 102 (*"shake the very stars"*).

521 *Men peered from their trenches:* Diana F. Butler, ed., "Human Interest," n.d., UK NA, CAB 101/346, 3–4; Klaus H. Huebner, *A Combat Doctor's Diary,* 61–63, 73 (*"Rome, then home"*); Rowland Ryder, *Oliver Leese,* 165 (*Nightingales had sung*); David Scott Daniell, *The Royal Hampshire Regiment,* vol. 3, 167 (*"full of noises"*).

521 *Gunners draped wet rags:* Olgierd Terlecki, *Poles in the Italian Campaign, 1943–1945,* 73; Lida Mayo, *The Ordnance Department: On Beachhead and Battlefront,* 211 (*174,000 shells*); *Mountain Inferno,* 749 (*"bridge of iron"*); Martin Gilbert, *Winston S. Churchill,* vol. 7, 769 (*"Zip"*).

522 *At midnight on the Allied right:* E. D. Smith, *The Battles for Cassino,* 153, 162 (*"no Germans could possibly outlive"*); Fred Majdalany, *Cassino: Portrait of a Battle,* 231.

522 *"Soldiers! The moment for battle"*: W. Anders, *An Army in Exile,* 174; Raleigh Trevelyan, *Rome '44,* 269, 273 (*Troops surged up Snakeshead Ridge*); "Operations by 2nd Polish Corps Against the High Ground, Monte Cassino," June 1944, possession of Roger Cirillo, 26–31 (*Nine German battalions*).

522 *"Many of us had lost"*: Janusz Piekalkiewicz, *The Battle for Cassino,* 169, 172–73; Majdalany, *Cassino,* 246; Anders, 175–76 (*"small epics"*); CtoA, 44; Dan Kurzman, *The Race for Rome,* 235 (*"If they do not obey orders"*); "Operations by 2nd Polish Corps," 29 (*of twenty engineers"*); Robert Wallace, *The Italian Campaign,* 164 (*"how dreadful death can be"*).

522 *At dawn, the rising sun:* Charles Connell, *Monte Cassino,* 186 (*"sitting birds"*); memo, "Flamethrowers and Napalm," July 1944, HQ, 2nd Polish Corps, NARA RG 492, MTO chemical warfare section, 470.71, box 1756; Trevelyan, 271 (*"I was working on my knees"*).

523 *Yet even Polish valor could not win:* Terlecki, 75; *Battle,* 233; Piekalkiewicz, 171 (*"costly reconnaissance"*).

523 *"Let's pick some cornflowers"*: Ryder, 166.

523 *"What do we do now?"*: Kurzman, 215.

523 *Vehicles crept forward, hauling boats:* newsletter, 8th Indian Division, March–Nov. 1944, Dudley Russell papers, LH, 5; *The Tiger Triumphs,* 73 (*banged angle iron*).

523 *Fire they drew, but so did the rest:* Dharm Pal, *The Campaign in Italy, 1943–1945,* 160–61; Ryder, 166 (*"yellow London fog"*).

523 *Men stumped about in flame-stabbed confusion: The Tiger Triumphs,* 73; Pal, 161–62; Field Marshal Lord Carver, *The Imperial War Museum Book of the War in Italy, 1943–1945,* 184–85 (*"Oh, God, don't let me die"*).

524 *Twelve of sixteen Gurkha boats:* Pal, 162; Alexander, "The Allied Armies in Italy," III-11; David Scott Daniell, *History of the East Surrey Regiment,* vol. 4, 207.

524 *By midday, no battalion:* Gregory Blaxland, *Alexander's Generals,* 89; Robin Neillands, *Eighth Army,* 291 (*"an autocratic man"*); Molony VI, 99 (*"sough and whiffle"*); Parker, 314 (*"passed ever so slowly"*).

524 *Yet the enemy had missed:* Molony VI, 112; Kenneth Macksey, *Kesselring: The Making of the Luftwaffe,* 211; Blaxland, 95–96; *CtoA,* 55.

524 *Three bridges, dubbed Cardiff, Oxford, and Plymouth:* "Engineers in the Italian Campaign," ts, n.d., UK NA, CAB 106/575, 34–35; Pal, 165; *The Tiger Triumphs,* 74–75; newsletter, 8th Indian Division, March–Nov. 1944, Dudley Russell papers, LHC.

524 *Upstream between Sant'Angelo and Cassino town:* Daniell, *History of the East Surrey Regiment;* Beckett, 157–58 (*"Cries for help"*); Frank Mills, "Well Dressed at Cassino," n.d., author's possession, 3–4 (*glimpses of the abbey*).

525 *Gurkhas twice surged into Sant'Angelo:* Molony VI, 121; Pal, 165; *The Tiger Triumphs,* 75–76.

525 *Putrefying corpses were soaked in petrol:* memoir, P. Royle, 1972, IWM, 99/72/1, 122–23 (*"I had no regrets"*); Connell, 191 (*wounds dressed with paper*); Blaxland, 99 (*"This is real war"*).

525 *They pushed on:* C. N. Barclay, *History of the 16th/5th The Queen's Royal Lancers,* 125, 126n.

525 *"He was thrashing and fighting":* John Ellis, *On the Front Lines,* 331.

525 *Two secure bridgeheads merged: Battle,* 232–33; Molony VI, 80, 123; Trevelyan, 297 (*"Flames of Jerry guns"*).

525 *In four days Eighth Army would advance:* Trevelyan, 272; Molony VI, 128.

525 *"Mark Clark has laid 4–1":* Ryder, 170.

526 *Clark had troubles enough:* James C. Fry, *Combat Soldier,* 17, 33, 43; John J. Roche, "First Squad, First Platoon," 1983, 351st Inf, 88th ID, MHI, ASEQ, 6–7; Wyndham H. Bammer, "Operations of Company K, 339th Infantry, in the Attack on Hills 66 and 69," 1948, IS; Douglas Allanbrook, *See Naples,* 179 (*"who gets Rome?"*).

526 *Sheaves of fire from the entrenched 94th Division:* G. K. Tanham, "Battlefield Intelligence in World War II: A Case Study of the Fifth Army Front in Italy," Sept. 1956, Project RAND, RM-1792, CMH, 42; John J. Roche, "First Squad, First Platoon," 1983, 351st Inf, 88th ID, MHI, ASEQ, 6 (*"noise was all of a piece"*); John Sloan Brown, *Draftee Division,* 107 (*Red tracer vectors*); Eric Sevareid, *Not So Wild a Dream,* 390.

526 *"a serpentine column of steam":* Roche, "First Squad, First Platoon," 13; Sevareid, 388.

526 *Yet neither division moved far: CtoA,* 52, 54; Chester G. Starr, ed., *From Salerno to the Alps,* 201–2; http://www.wisc.edu/wisconsinpress/books/2387.htm; Sidney T. Matthews, "Writing Small Unit Actions with the Fifth Army in Italy," SM, MHI, box 2, 2 (*Frederick Schiller Faust*); Sevareid, 388 (*"stupefyingly dead"*); John E. Wallace, *The Blue Devil "Battle Mountain" Regiment in Italy,* 13–18; Alexander, "The Allied Armies in Italy," III-11.

527 *That left Juin's FEC:* Anthony Clayton, *Three Marshals of France,* 83–85; "Draft Report on FEC," SM, CMH, box 1; Starr, ed., 186–88.

527 *Plunging fire greeted them:* Diana F. Butler, "The French Expeditionary Corps in the Battle for Rome," Cabinet historical section, UK NA, CAB 101/226, 13; Claude R. Hinson, "755th Tank Battalion Supporting the 3rd Algerian Infantry Division of the French Expeditionary Corps During the Advance on Rome," 1948, IS (*singed hair and burning flesh*); George Bouille and Pierre Le Goyet, *Le Corps Expeditionnaire Française en Italie, 1943–1944,* n.d., MHI, trans. Antonio Ali Winston for author, 56–63 (*Counterattacking grenadiers*).

527 *By midmorning on Friday, May 12:* Douglas Porch, *The Path to Victory,* 556; Fred Majdalany, *Cassino,* 243; Butler, "The French Expeditionary Corps," 13; Starr, ed., 267n (*casualties approached sixteen hundred*); "Draft Report on FEC" (*"considerable alarm"*); Parker, 320 (*"dead take on a waxy look"*).

527 *Juin went forward shortly before noon:* Michael Carver, ed., *The War Lords,* 607; Butler, "The French Expeditionary Corps," 13 (*three wounded battalion commanders*); Sidney T. Matthews, "The French Drive on Rome," *Revue historique de l'armée,* special issue, 1957, 128 ("*the wrong foot*").

527 *Through much of the afternoon he scrambled:* Clayton, 83–85; John Buchan, "Report on a Visit to the French Expeditionary Corps," n.d., CMH, appendix A, 1 ("*It's gone wrong*"); "Draft Report on FEC"; *CtoA,* 61; Porch, 556 (*only reserve division*); Carver, ed., 607 ("*it will go*").

528 *It went, spectacularly:* Butler, "The French Expeditionary," 15; Porch, 556; Clayton, 83–85; Bouille and Le Goyet, 74–78 (*reported Monte Majo captured*); Heinrich von Vietinghoff, "71st Infantry Division in Italy," Sept. 1948, FMS, #C-025, MHI, 7–9, 22; Hans von Greiffenberg, "Field Fortifications in Central Italy," 1950, FMS, #C-071, MHI, 3–5, 16; *CtoA,* 61 ("*Accelerate the general withdrawal*").

528 *By Sunday the French had advanced:* Starr, ed., 188–89; Matthews, "The French Drive on Rome," 128–29; Molony VI, 139, 145 ("*En avant!*"), 140 ("*Most unpleasant*"); Bouille and Le Goyet, 78 (*worse than in Russia*); Parker, 341; *CtoA,* 62; Buchan, "Report on a Visit," appendix A, 1 ("*warfare to which we are accustomed*").

528 *The unpleasantries had only begun:* "Draft Report on FEC"; Starr, ed., 189–92.

528 "*Dark men, dark night*": Trevelyan, 271; Robert Capa, *Slightly Out of Focus,* photo, 113; Fry, 43 ("*troops of the last century*"); O'Connor, "*Mektoub,*" 119 ("*dozens of wristwatches*"); Hinson, "755th Tank Battalion," 10 (*One unit kept a tiger*); Joe Chmiel, "Invasion of Normandy," ts, n.d., in Matt Urban file, 60th Inf Regt, 9th ID, SOOHP, MHI ("*Smokie, smokie*").

529 *It was said that in Sicily:* Peter Schrijvers, *The Crash of Ruin,* 47; OH, Robert J. Wood, 1973, William E. Narus, SOOHP, MHI, 3–42; John Steinbeck, *Once There Was a War,* 168; Roberta Love Tayloe, *Combat Nurse,* 77, 79, 83 (*doctors assigned numbers*); Huebner, 81 ("*sing, chatter, and howl*"); Alan Williamson, "Adviser to French Colonial Troops," ts, n.d., Texas MFM, 4 ("*women, horses, and guns*").

529 *Up and up they climbed:* Starr, ed., 192–93; Butler, "The French Expeditionary Corps," 19 ("*sky was a changeless blue*").

529 *By four P.M. on May 15:* Starr, ed., 192–93; Molony VI, 149 ("*falling boulders*"); Butler, "The French Expeditionary Corps," 21; Buchan, "Report on a Visit," appendix F ("*grinning savages*").

530 *Men and beasts had exhausted themselves:* "Draft Report on FEC."

530 *On the French left:* Brown, 117, 120; *CtoA,* 65–68, 77; Starr, ed., 207 (*dust-churning flotilla*).

530 "*rushed off his feet*": Buchan, "Report on a Visit," 1; Matthews, "The French Drive on Rome," 128–29 (*nearly extinct 71st Division*); *CtoA,* 86 (*no more than one hundred riflemen*); Starr, ed., 210 (*terrorizing horses*); Macksey, 212 ("*One could cry*").

530 *All this buoyed the Allied high command:* diary, MWC, May 14, 1944, Citadel, box 65 ("*very pleased*"); Carver, ed., 607 ("*We've got them*").

530 *Only Clark remained somber:* diary, MWC, May 14, 1944, Citadel, box 65; *CtoA,* 77; Tanham, "Battlefield Intelligence in World War II," 53 (*compared with two miles*); *CtoA,* 71–73 ("*disciplinary action*"); Brown, 127 (*traffic snarls*).

531 "*I am disappointed*": diary, MWC, May 14, 1944, Citadel, box 65; GK, May 14, 1944 ("*Called me about 6 times*").

531 *Even as he lashed:* Starr, ed., 226; diary, MWC, May 15, 1944, Citadel, box 65 ("*effort of the Eighth Army*").

531 *That same Eighth Army:* Anders, 178; Terlecki, 83; Kurzman, 237; Ken Ford, *Cassino 1944,* 78–79; Molony VI, 130n ("*oddments*"); Rudolf Böhmler, *Monte Cassino,* 266 ("*Impossible to get wounded*").

531 *In danger of encirclement:* Albrecht Kesselring, *The Memoirs of Field-Marshal Kesselring,* 200–205; Jean-Yves Nasse, *Green Devils,* 113; Nigel Nicolson, *The Grenadier Guards in the War of 1939–1945,* vol. 2, 427; Butler, ed., "Human Interest," 4; war diary, 1st Guards Bde, May 18, 1944, UK NA, WO 170/514 (*"Cassino is lost"*).

532 *The struggle for the high ground:* "Operations by 2nd Polish Corps," 40; Anders, 179 (*six-man patrol*); John H. Green, "The Battles for Cassino," *AB,* no. 13, 1976, 1+ (*cracked church bell*); Piekalkiewicz, 181 (*Benedict's candlelit crypt*).

532 *Just before ten A.M. the lancers':* Anders, 178; Parker, 352-53; http://www.krakow-info.com/signal2.way; Trevelyan, 274.

532 *At 11:30 A.M. British signalers:* Butler, ed., "Human Interest," 4; Nicolson, 427–28; Ryder, 169; "Operations by 2nd Polish Corps," 41; Molony VI, 134; Smith, 172 (*"means a great deal"*).

532 *For the first time in five months:* war diary, 1st Guards Bde, May 18, 1944; Betsy Wade, ed., *Forward Positions: The War Correspondence of Homer Bigart,* 44–45; General Sir Sidney Chevalier Kirkman, "3rd and 4th Cassino," Royal Artillery Historical Society, *Proceedings,* vol. 11, no. 3, Jan. 1969, 94+.

532 *In the abbey itself, further investigation:* Trevelyan, 274; Tommaso Leccisotti, *Monte Cassino,* 132–33; E. T. DeWald, "Inspection Trip to Abbey of Monte Cassino, May 27, 1944," Henry C. Newton papers, MHI (*"a Mesopotamian tell"*).

533 *A solitary American fighter pilot:* Parker, 357; Walter Robson, *Letters from a Soldier,* 96–97.

533 *General von Senger, freshly bemedaled:* Frido von Senger und Etterlin, "War Diary of the Italian Campaign," 1953, FMS, #C-095b, MHI, 124; Vietinghoff, "71st Infantry Division in Italy," 31 (*found the Gustav Line ruptured*); Molony VI, 114, 143 (*"frightful"*); Frido von Senger und Etterlin, "The Drive on Rome," Sept. 1951, FMS, #C-097b, MHI, 11 (*"the corps had been breached"*); Neil Short, *German Defences in Italy in World War II,* 9n.

533 *"It was left to me":* Frido von Senger und Etterlin, *Neither Fear nor Hope,* 248.

533 *The task was formidable:* Albert Kesselring et al., "German Version of the History of the Italian Campaign," n.d., CARL, N-16671.1-3, 216; Walter Warlimont, "OKW Activities—The Italian Theater, 1 Apr.–31 Dec. 1944," n.d., FMS, #C-099b, MHI, 23 (*spotter planes*); F. M. Sallagar, "Operation STRANGLE: A Case Study of Tactical Air Interdiction," Feb. 1972, RAND, R-851, 68 (*"unremitting Allied fighter-bomber"*); II Corps G-2, May 19, 1944, NARA RG 319, OCMH, CA, box 6 (*horses had been killed*); memo, Joseph L. Langevin, VI Corps G-2, to LKT Jr., May 18, 1944, LKT Jr., GCM Lib, box 13, folder 4 (*59 German battalions*); John Ellis, *Brute Force,* 324 (*only 405 men fit to fight*).

534 *Italian supply-truck drivers:* journal, Fourteenth Army, May 19–22, 1944, "The German Operation at Anzio," Apr. 1946, WD, John Lucas papers, MHI, box 9, 104; Kesselring et al, "German Version," 127 (*barrages severed phone lines*); A. G. Steiger, "The Italian Campaign," July 1948, historical section, Canadian Army HQ, report no. 20, MHI, 59 (*"I demand a clear picture"*); F. W. Winterbotham, *The Ultra Secret,* 116.

534 *In truth, Kesselring had been outgeneraled:* W.G.F. Jackson, *Alexander of Tunis as Military Commander,* 285; Matthews, "The French Drive on Rome," 128–29; Sallagar, "Operation STRANGLE," 70–71 (*not until May 19*); Kesselring, *Memoirs,* 201–5; Senger, "The Drive on Rome," 11; Robin Kay, *Official History of New Zealand in the Second World War,* vol. 2, *From Cassino to Trieste,* 29; Walter Warlimont, *Inside Hitler's Headquarters, 1939–1945,* 416; Molony VI, 164.

534 *"offensive against the cultural center of Europe":* weekly air intelligence summary, #78, May 15, 1944, Fifth Army, G-3 journal, NARA RG 319, OCMH, CA, box 6; corr, May 18, 1944, in G-2 report, II Corps, June 3, 1944, Robert H. Adleman papers, HIA, box 13 (*"You have no idea"*).

534 *"like spontaneous fires exploding"*: Fred Cederberg, *The Long Road Home,* 121; Blaxland, 107 (*crammed along a six-mile front*); C. F. Comfort, *Artist at War,* 153 (*"a vaporous fantasy"*); Trevelyan, 297 (*"clear their own minefields"*).

535 *"the Shermans pitching like destroyers"*: Kay, 46; Robin Neillands, *Eighth Army,* 293; Carver, 317; Butler, ed., "Human Interest," 4–5 (*eighteen hours to travel thirteen miles*); Mark Zuehlke, *The Liri Valley,* 232 (*"nose to arse"*).

535 *If the Hitler Line lacked natural impediments:* Erich Rothe, "Tactical Mission, Trace and Organization of the 'Senger-Riegel,' " May 1947, FMS, #D-170, MHI, 3–6; Molony VI, 183; Mayo, 215; Short, 10, 18, 30–31, 50; John E. Krebs, *To Rome and Beyond,* 66 (*"only trace of the crew"*).

535 *"Head wounds are many"*: Huebner, 77.

535 *Sergeants doled out rum rations:* Cederberg, 121; Carver, 194 (*"I couldn't run a race"*); Butler, ed., "Human Interest," 3–5 (*"melancholy sight"*); Krebs, 77 (*shot through the heart*).

535 *On average a thousand German prisoners:* memo, "Advances Made by Fifth Army Corps [*sic*]," n.d., MWC papers, Citadel, box 3; "Interrogation Reports," May 1944, Combined Services Detailed Interrogation Center, NARA RG 407, E 47, AFHQ, 95-AL1-2.13, box 164 (*"weird and wonderful collection"*); Huebner, 76.

536 *As the second week of the Allied offensive:* CtoA, 94–97; author visits, May 6, 2004, Nov. 29, 2006; Blaxland, 119 (*eight hundred artillery shells*); Calculated, 323 (*bulldozers were needed*); Matthews, "The French Drive on Rome," 135 (*"bleeding to death"*); "Draft Report on FEC"; Butler, "The French Expeditionary Corps," 25–26.

536 *From west to east the Hitler Line:* CtoA, 156; weekly intel summary, "No. 91, week ending 22 May 1944," AFHQ G-2, NARA RG 407, E 427, 95-AL1-2.6 (*"The enemy has denuded"*).

*A Fifth Army Show*

536 *Mark Clark shifted his command post:* Calculated, 357; diary, MWC, May 22, 1944, Citadel, box 65; Sevareid, 393 (*"Sit down, gentlemen"*).

537 *For half an hour, unhurried and precise:* Robert H. Adleman and George Walton, *Rome Fell Today,* 188; Alexander, "The Allied Armies in Italy," III-16; Winston S. Churchill, *Closing the Ring,* 603; CM, 372.

537 *Under Operation* BUFFALO: diary, MWC, May 22, 1944, Citadel, box 65; Sevareid, 394; Adleman and Walton, 188.

537 *As the correspondents shuffled:* Sevareid, 394 (*"in personal command"*); msg, MWC to A. Gruenther, May 23, 1944, MWC papers, Citadel, box 63 (*"no restriction"*).

537 *If Clark had disclosed much:* Calculated, 350–51.

538 *A face-to-face meeting at Caserta:* msg, J. Harding to MWC, May 19, 1944, MWC papers, Citadel, box 63; Calculated, 351–53; diary, MWC, May 20, 1944, Citadel, box 65.

538 *Clark suspected double-dealing:* Texas, 370; diary, MWC, May 20 and 22, 1944, Citadel, box 65.

538 *"Hell, we shouldn't even be thinking"*: Adleman and Walton, 206–7; Calculated, 252–53 (*"more than deserved"*); msg, MWC to LKT Jr., May 21, 1944, 1705 hrs, LKT Jr. papers, GCM Lib, box 12, folder 11.

538 *"Regrouping would take place"*: diary, MWC, May 18, 1944, Citadel, box 65; Adleman and Walton, 206–7 (*"the great prize"*).

538 *"I'm just a dog-face soldier"*: Donald G. Taggart, ed., *History of the Third Infantry Division in World War II,* 149.

538 *Light rain had fallen:* CM, 371; Joseph A. Springer, *Black Devil Brigade,* 211 (*parachute cord*); John Shirley, *I Remember: Stories of a Combat Infantryman in World War II,* 4 (*after receiving no mail from home*); Sevareid, 395–96 (*"nothing ever new"*).

538 *Clark had snatched a few hours' rest:* MWC to Renie, May 26, 1944, MWC pers corr, Citadel; msg, MWC to A. Gruenther, May 23, 1944, MWC papers, Citadel, box 63; aide's diaries, May 23, 1944, LKT Jr., GCM Lib, box 18, folder 3; OH, Robert T. Frederick, Jan.

7, 1949, SM, MHI; *CM,* 371; *Calculated,* 357; Adleman and Walton, 188 (*Neither man said much*).

539 *"They can hear this in Rome":* Sevareid, 395; diary, Robert M. Marsh, May 23, 1944, 81st Armored Reconnaissance Bn, 1st AD, MHI, ASEQ (*like heat from a blacktop road*); *CtoA,* 120.

539 *Then, at 6:30, the riflemen spilled:* Frank M. Izenhour, "Breakout Anzio Beachhead," ts, 1946, CARL, N-2253.10; George F. Howe, *The Battle History of the 1st Armored Division,* 318; *CtoA,* 128; Shirley, 9 (*"I rolled him over"*).

541 *Farther east, Company K:* G-3 journal, 3rd ID, May 23, 1944, 0800 hrs, 1935 hrs, NARA RG 319, OCMH, CA, box 6 (*"It is going too slow"*); *CtoA,* 130, 133 (*"We have no such words"*).

541 *Just past noon, five more Sherman tanks:* msg, MWC to GCM, May 17, 1944, NARA RG 165, OPD, WD, top secret general corr, 312.4-319.1, box 16; Mayo, 210; OH, John A. Heintges, 1974, Jack A. Pellicci, SOOHP, MHI, 241; Shirley, 2–7.

541 *Yard by bloody yard:* Initial 3rd Division casualties for the day exceeded 1,600, but many of those were lost soldiers temporarily listed as missing. *CtoA,* 137; Taggart, ed., 164.

541 *Damaged boys outnumbered the litter bearers:* Nathan William White, *From Fedala to Berchtesgaden,* 113; Trevelyan, 284 (*"Must I be knocked off"*).

541 *Truscott's flanks found hard fighting:* *CtoA,* 120, 138; OH, Frederick, Jan. 7, 1949; William G. Sheldon, "Anzio to Rome, Battle, 1944, " ts, n.d., in Robert H. Adleman papers, HIA, box 7, 5–6; Robert D. Burhans, *The First Special Service Force,* 216–17; G-3 journal, VI Corps, May 23–24, NARA RG 319, OCMH, CA, box 6 (*"All hell has broken"*); Flint Whitlock, *The Rock of Anzio,* 288, 300 (*sidestepping skeletons*).

542 *By nightfall the 45th reported 458 casualties:* *CtoA,* 138; Van T. Barfoot, "The Operation of the 3rd Platoon, Company L, 157th Infantry, in the Battle of Anzio During the Push to Rome," 1948, IS. Sergeant Barfoot earned the Medal of Honor for his heroism on May 23.

542 *"The fellow in the bed next to me":* F. Eugene Liggett, "No, Not Yet: Military Memoirs," ts, n.d., 158th FA, 157th Inf, 45th ID, ASEQ, MHI, 7–8; Whitlock, 297 (*"always getting cold"*).

542 *"Whether or not we can get our tanks through":* corr, E. N. Harmon to David G. Barr, May 15, 1944, NARA RG 319, CA, box 6; OH, T. J. Conway, Fifth Army planner, June 27, 1950, NARA RG 319, OCMH, CA, box 5 (*hundred tanks in the first half hour*); OH, James S. Simmerman, CO, 2nd Bn, 13th Armored Regt, Apr. 24, 1950, SM, NARA RG 319, OCMH, CA, box 5 (*poorly marked American minefield*); "History of Ordnance Service in the Mediterranean Theater," n.d., CMH, 8-4 JA, 83; Howe, 324.

542 *On the left, however, Combat Command A:* *CtoA,* 121–23; AAR, "10th Engineer Combat Battalion, Cisterna-Rome Operation," ts, n.d., CMH, Geog Italy, 314.7; OH, Robert Linville, CO, 3rd Bn, 6th Armored Inf Regt, May 9, 1950, SM, NARA RG 319, OCMH, CA, box 5 (*tin cans filled with rocks*); Howe, 324.

542 *By one P.M. U.S. tanks had crossed:* AAR, "Salerno to Florence," Fifth Army Antiaircraft Artillery, 1945, MHI, 21–22.

542 *fear that a premature detonation:* OH, Linville, May 9, 1950; OH, ENH, Dec. 14, 1948; OH, Ben Crosby, XO, CCB, March 9, 1950, all in SM, NARA RG 319, OCMH, CA, box 5.

542 *The day had cost Harmon eighty-six tanks:* Anzio Beachhead, 119; OH, Lawrence R. Dewey, 1st AD chief of staff, July 20, 1948, SM, NARA RG 319, OCMH, CA, box 5; *StoA,* 267n.

543 *Yet across the front fifteen hundred enemy:* *CM,* 372–74; journal, Fourteenth Army, May 23, 1944, 107; *CtoA,* 140; Steiger, "The Italian Campaign," 74.

543 *"All attacks jumped off":* VI Corps G-3 journal file, May 23–24, 1944, NARA RG 319, OCMH, CA, box 6.

543 *Harmon's tanks looped behind Cisterna:* Howe, 325; Carmene J. DeFelice, "Carmene's Wartime Chronicle," ts, n.d., 12th AR, 1st AD, ASEQ, MHI; Audie Murphy, *To Hell and*

*Back,* 154 ("*shooting skeets*"); *CtoA,* 142–44; ADC journal, VI Corps, May 24, 1944, 1515 hrs, NARA RG 319, CA, box 6 ("*I could get into Valmontone*").

543 *Thursday morning was better yet:* Howe, 328; Wiley H. O'Mohundro, "From Mules to Missiles," ts, n.d., MHI, 57; "Lessons Learned in the Battle from the Garigliano to North of Rome," July 15, 1944, Fifth Army, training memo, #12, DTL, Ft. B, 10; Paul A. Cundiff, *45th Infantry CP,* 181 (*most destroyed town*); *CtoA,* 147, 155.

543 *Clark watched with pleasure:* Alfred M. Beck et al., *The Corps of Engineers: The War Against Germany,* 211; Sevareid, 400; *CtoA,* 220 (*filled the craters*).

544 "*The joining up of my two Fifth Army forces*": msg, MWC to A. Gruenther, May 25, 1944, MWC papers, Citadel, box 63.

544 "*you make damn sure that their communique*": diary, MWC, May 24, 1944, Citadel, box 65; Sevareid, 398.

544 "*Where in hell do you think you're going?*": "Beachhead Offensive," *Newsweek,* June 5, 1944, 23; Sevareid, 398.

544 *Three hours later Clark roared up:* diary, MWC, May 25, 1944, Citadel, box 65; Wynford Vaughan-Thomas, *Anzio,* 230; *Calculated,* 357; film, "Liberation of Rome," 1944, combat report no. 1, NARA RG 111, CR001 (*much backslapping*); msg, MWC, May 25, 1944, MWC papers, Citadel, box 63 ("*junction took place*").

545 "*It may have sounded dramatic*": MWC to Renie, May 26, 1944, personal corr, Citadel.

545 *Truscott drove toward his Conca command post:* CM, 375; *CtoA,* 153–54.

545 *The 1st Armored Division continued to bull:* Howe, 329; msg, MWC to A. Gruenther, May 26, 1944, MWC papers, Citadel, box 63 (*fratricidal air attacks*); diary, Robert M. Marsh, May 25, 26, 30, 1944.

545 *At the point of the VI Corps spear:* Bogardus S. Cairns, "The Breakout at Anzio," *MR,* Jan. 1949, 23+; *CtoA,* 168; OH, Hamilton H. Howze, June 16, 1949, SM, NARA RG 319, OCMH, CA, box 5 (*within a half mile*); Hamilton H. Howze, "The Rome Operation," ts, June 6, 1944, CMH, Geog files, Italy, 370.2, 3–7; OH, Hamilton H. Howze, Apr. 1973, Robert T. Reed, MHI, SOOHP, 38–40; corr, Don E. Carleton, former VI Corps chief of staff, to U.S. Army chief of military history, Jan. 12, 1960, NARA RG 319, OCMH, CA, box 4; *CM,* 375 ("*astride the German line*").

546 *That agreeable vision dissolved:* corr, LKT to U.S. Army chief of military history, Nov. 5, 1961, with witness statements from Don E. Carleton et al, NARA RG 319, OCMH, CA, box 4; *CM,* 375 ("*The boss wants you*").

546 *Truscott was dumbfounded:* Kent Roberts Greenfield, ed., *Command Decisions,* 276–78.

546 "*I discussed this with General Clark*": OH, James M. Wilson, Jr., LKT Jr. aide, Apr. 23, 2004, with author, Washington, D.C.

546 "*He's not at the beachhead*": corr, Carleton to chief of military history, Jan. 12, 1960, Don E. Carleton papers, HIA, box 1; *CM,* 375–76 ("*more complicated plan*").

546 *Then he fell silent: CtoA,* 165; corr, LKT to chief of military history, Nov. 5, 1961 ("*poor leadership*"); OH, LKT Jr., Apr. 3, 1958, SM, MHI; msg, GCM to J. Devers, May 26, 1944, NARA RG 492, MTOUSA, SGS, "eyes only, General Devers, incoming," box 135; corr, FLW to Harold L. Bond, Sept. 30, 1965, NARA RG 319, OCMH, CA, box 4; Sidney T. Matthews, "Drive to Rome," ts, 1954, MHI, 314 ("*we should do this thing*").

547 *Privately, however, the corps commander could not shake:* OH, Wilson, Apr. 23, 2004; aide's journal, VI Corps, May 25, 1944, NARA RG 319, OCMH, CA, box 6; OH, LKT Jr., Apr. 3, 1958; aide's diaries, May 25, 1944, LKT Jr., papers, GCM Lib, box 18, folder 3; Greenfield, ed., 281 ("*shooting the works*").

547 *Glum yet resigned:* A broken radio apprently prevented Mackensen's order from reaching Cisterna. Matthews, "Drive to Rome," 174, 188; Franz Kurowski, *Battleground Italy 1943–1945,* 226.

547 *After hours of street brawling around the Castle:* Vaughan-Thomas, *Anzo,* 225; OH, Jack M. Duncan and Ralph M. Flynn, 7th Inf Regt, Apr. 27, 1950, NARA RG 319, OCMH, CA,

box 5; White, 117 (*3rd Battalion of the 7th Infantry*). The Cisterna rubble "had the stillness of ancient ruins, but without their dignity." Sevareid, 402.

547 "*The fact that the enemy is withdrawing*": minutes, "Division Commanders' Meeting, 25 May 1944," VI Corps, NARA RG 319, OCMH, CA, box 8.

547 *None of his battle captains shared*: corr, Carleton to chief of military history, Jan. 12, 1960; OH, Wilson, Apr. 23, 2004; *CtoA*, 166; OH, LKT Jr., March 1, 1962, NARA RG 319, OCMH, CA, box 5 ("*I realize perfectly*").

547 "*I propose to begin this*": minutes, "Division Commanders' Meeting, 25 May 1944"; diary, MWC, May 26, 1944, Citadel, box 65 ("*the most direct route*"); OH, Wilson, Apr. 23, 2004 ("*These are the orders*").

548 "*This is ridiculous, for many roads*": diary, MWC, May 27, 1944, MWC papers, Citadel, box 65; OH, MWC, 1972–73, Forest S. Rittgers, Jr., MHI, 93–94.

548 *Senger subsequently confirmed*: Senger, *Neither Fear nor Hope*, 252. Tenth Army maps depcited four withdrawal routes besides Highway 6. Molony VI, 238; OH, LKT Jr., Apr. 3, 1958; *Battle*, 241.

548 *Clark also feared that German artillery*: Nigel Nicolson, *Alex: The Life of Field Marshal Earl Alexander of Tunis*, 252; OH, MWC, Rittgers, 93–94; Matthews, "Drive to Rome," 308–13 (*only the Göring reconnaissance battalion*); *CtoA*, 152, 157; R. J. O'Rourke, *Anzio Annie*, 177; Böhmler, 281.

548 *Two final points must be conceded*: OH, Robert W. Porter, Jr., 1981, John N. Sloan, SOOHP, MHI, 338.

549 "*scheming to get into Rome*": GK, May 28, 1944; Molony VI, 234 ("*thirst for glory*").

549 "*Not only did we intend*": *Calculated*, 352.

549 *The fixation . . . marred*: Matthews, "Drive to Rome," 312, 338, 200 ("*admirably situated to outflank*"); *CtoA*, 157 (*partial withdrawal of both armies*); Greenfield, ed., 276–79; Blaxland, 117; AAR, Wilhelm Schmalz, ts, n.d., NARA RG 319, OCMH, CA, box 9.

549 "*a terrible congestion of itineraries*": *Calculated*, 359; diary, MWC, May 27, 1944, Citadel, box 65 ("*no attack left in them*"); *Battle*, 231 ("*never appears to have accepted Alexander*"); Greenfield, ed., 280.

550 "*fire on the Eighth Army*": U.S. Army historian Sidney T. Matthews's detailed notes from interviews with Clark in May 1948 include this passage: "When Alexander told Clark he wanted the Eighth Army to take part in [Rome's] capture, he got pretty sore. He told Alex if he gave him such an order he would refuse to obey it and if Eighth Army tried to advance on Rome, Clark said he would have his troops fire on Eighth Army. Alex did not press the point to its conclusion." In interviews conducted by Matthews seven months later, Alexander denied ever telling Clark that he wanted Eighth Army to participate in the capture of Rome, and added that Clark "never told Alexander that if Alexander gave such an order he (Clark) would refuse to obey it." OH, MWC, May 10–21, 1948, SM, MHI, 60; OH, Harold Alexander, Jan. 10–15, 1949, SM, CMH, Geog files, III-13; Trevelyan, 303.

550 *Alexander had remained in the dark*: diary, MWC, May 26, 1944, Citadel, box 65; Matthews, "Drive to Rome," 319; msg, A. Gruenther to MWC, May 26, 1944, MWC papers, Citadel, box 63 ("*Gen. Alexander agreed*").

550 *Gruenther assured him*: Nicolson, *Alex*, 252 ("*pretty upset*"); L. James Binder, *Lemnitzer: A Soldier for His Time*, 122 ("*terribly disappointed*"); Jackson, *Alexander of Tunis as Military Commander*, 289 ("*should not 'urge'*"); *Battle*, 231 ("*prima donna*").

550 *The contretemps remained hidden*: Sevareid, 401; msg, GCM to J. Devers, May 26, 1944, NARA RG 492, MTOUSA, SGS, "eyes only, General Devers, incoming," box 135 ("*this hurts Clark*"); diary, MWC, May 27, 1944, MWC papers, Citadel, box 65 ("*I do not feel that his exploits*").

551 "*I never violated his orders*": Nicolson, *Alex*, 252; OH, Alexander, Jan. 10–15, 1949, III-7 (*Clark had assured him*).

551 *"power to command and readiness to obey"*: Livy, *The War with Hannibal*, 26; Churchill, *Closing the Ring*, 607 (*"Glory of this battle"*).

551 *"He is terrified"*: Ryder, 171–72; Carver, 207.

551 *Beneath brilliant vernal sunshine on May 26:* Hamilton H. Howze, *A Cavalryman's Story*, 109; Howze, "The Rome Operation," 10; *CtoA*, 169–70; OH, Howze, Reed, 43.

551 *The day soon darkened:* White, 118; *CtoA*, 168; Maurice R. P. Bechard, "This Is an Account of What Was to Be," ts, n.d., 16th Armored Eng Bn, 1st AD, MHI, ASEQ, 5; Howze, *A Cavalryman's Story*, 102; Howe, 331 (*"ruinous effect"*); OH, Bogardus S. Cairns, CO, 3rd Bn, 13th AR, Apr. 24, 1950, NARA RG 319, OCMH, CA, box 5; Howze, "The Rome Operation," 11.

552 *"All daytime movement"*: AAR, Schmalz; Franz Kurowski, *The History of the Fallschirmpanzerkorps Hermann Göring*, 244–45; Sallagar, "Operation STRANGLE," 72–74.

552 *Counterattacks against Howze's left flank:* OH, Howze, June 16, 1949; Howze, *A Cavalryman's Story*, 111 (*trucks heaped*), 129 (*"something to cling to"*); ADC journal, VI Corps, May 28, 1944, 1502 hrs.

552 *Reluctantly, Clark agreed to halt:* *CtoA*, 171; OH, MWC, May 10–21, 1948, 62; Matthews, "Drive to Rome," 370 (*traffic swept up and down*); Vaughan-Thomas, 226 (*"take your war"*).

552 *It was much too late:* Carver, 203 ("Unbek. Soldat"); Howe, 331–32; *CtoA*, 175; Matthews, "Drive to Rome," 354 (*"a little sticky"*).

552 *The I Parachute Corps improvised:* OH, ENH, Dec. 14, 1948, SM, and OH, Edwin A. Russell, G-3 of 1st AD, n.d., SM, both in NARA RG 319, OCMH, CA, box 5; Starr, ed., 247–49; Homer R. Ankrum, *Dogfaces Who Smiled Through Tears*, 501 (*"blood could be seen"*).

554 *Before dawn on Monday, May 29:* *CtoA*, 176; Starr, ed., 249; Lloyd Clark, *Anzio*, 306 ("An 88-mm round blew up the Sherman"); Howe, 333 (*sixty tanks*); Sheehan, 202.

554 *"The day's attack"*: Howze, *A Cavalryman's Story*, 111; Carver, 204 (*"grisly bric-a-brac"*); msg, J. Devers to GCM, May 31, 1944, and biographical sketch, Katherine Tupper Marshall papers, GCM Lib; msg, ENH to MWC, May 29, 1944, MWC, corr, Citadel, box 3; Eric Larrabee, *Commander in Chief*, 113.

554 *"halted at every point"*: *CtoA*, 180; intel summary, AFHQ G-2, May 29, 1945, no. 92, NARA RG 407, E 427, 95-AL1-2.6; Warlimont, "OKW Activities," 31–32.

554 *A reproachful Clark phoned Truscott:* Matthews, "Drive to Rome," 387; diary, MWC, May 30 and 31, 1944, Citadel, box 65; MWC to Renie, May 31, 1944, personal corr, Citadel.

555 *"The offensive has bogged"*: diary, Peter Tompkins, NARA RG 226, OSS history office, E 99, box 47, 260.

### The Cuckoo's Song

555 *It had bogged in the south, too:* G.W.L. Nicholson, *The Canadians in Italy, 1943–1945*, vol. 2, 425; Michael Person Cessford, "Hard in the Attack," Ph.D. diss, Carleton University, Ottawa, 357; Daniel G. Dancocks, *The D-Day Dodgers*, 253 (*"I just don't know"*); Zuehlke, 221 (*"Alouette"*), 322, 293.

555 *Eighth Army had long "lacked"*: Blaxland, 121; Molony VI, 290–91.

555 *"After months of static warfare"*: Molony VI, 241, 247, 285; Blaxland, 124; Cessford, "Hard in the Attack," 405–13.

556 *"Traffic criminals of every kind"*: Molony VI, 257, 291; Alex Bowlby, *The Recollections of Rifleman Bowlby*, 42 (*"I don't toil"*).

556 *The Sacco River valley beyond the Liri:* Neil Orpen, *Victory in Italy*, 44–47; Robson, 108 (*"You are welcome"*); Strome Galloway, *A Regiment at War*, 142–43 (*"rose and an egg"*).

556 *Canadian troops would enter Frosinone:* Molony VI, 276.

556 *"When we got to him"*: Dancocks, 253; Bowlby, 41 (*"six feet"*).

557 *On Leese's left, Juin and his FEC*: Richard Doherty, *A Noble Crusade*, 220; Molony VI, 168 (*"damned French"*), 253.

557 *Soon others damned them*: memo, Brunis M. Rogness, 17th FA, to MWC, May 29, 1944, NARA RG 338, Fifth Army HQ, general corr, 000.51, box 1.

557 *Another chaplain cited specifics:* memo, Raymond F. Copeland, 17th FA, to MWC, May 28, 1944; memo, Robert M. Douglass, 995th FA Bn, to MWC, June 2, 1944 (*"approximately 75 women"*); memos, Sam H. Long, 933rd FA Bn, to MWC, May 30 and June 1, 1944 (*"delegation of frenzied citizens"*); memo, C. C. Bank, 13th FA Bde, to MWC, May 31, 1944 (*all thirteen of his battalion commanders*), all in NARA RG 338, Fifth Army HQ, general corr, 000.51, box 1.

557 *Italian authorities tallied seven hundred:* Robert Katz, *The Battle for Rome*, 287; affidavit, May 25, 1944, in "Reports relative to acts of violence and use of force committed by Moroccan soldiers," May 25 1944, HQ, Italian 210th Infantry Division, Robert J. Wood papers, MHI (*"I was taken"*); Norman Lewis, *Naples '44*, 143.

558 *"At any hour of the day"*: corr, Giuseppe Cortese, 210th Italian Infantry Div, to MWC, May 25, 1944, NARA RG 338, Fifth Army HQ, general corr, 000.51, box 2.

558 *Vengeful Italians:* Lewis, 147; memo, Raymond F. Copeland, May 28, 1944 (*"a 'so-what' shrug"*); J. Glenn Gray, *The Warriors*, 67.

558 *General Juin was* not *laughing:* memo, A. Juin, "Ill Treatment of Civilian Population," May 24, 1944, Robert J. Wood papers, MHI; memos, A. Gruenther to MWC, May 27 and 29, 1944, MWC, corr, Citadel, box 3 (*Clark dispatched Gruenther*); memo, A. Juin, May 27, 1944, NARA RG 338, Fifth Army HQ, general corr, 000.51, box 1 (*"excited indignation"*); Edward L. Bimberg, *The Moroccan Goums*, 64; Kurzman, 251 (*hanged in village squares*).

558 *transport of Berber women:* Bimberg, 64; Kurzman, 228; Isobel Williams, "Law and Order in Allied Occupied Southern Italy, 1943–1945," Ph.D. diss, University of Wales, Swansea, 2005, and e-mail to author; letter, Ministerio della Difesa, "*statistica incidenti e crimini commessi dalle truppe alleate,*" Oct. 18, 1947, NARA RG 492, MTO, AG HQ records, 290/53/32/5-6, 000.5; Trevelyan, 277 (*"suffered more"*); Schrijvers, 47 (*"savages"*).

558 *Lucian Truscott was in pain:* Ernest F. Fischer, Jr., "A Classic Strategem on Monte Artemisio," draft, n.d., CMH, Geog files, 370.24, 5–6; aide's diaries, LKT Jr., May 30, 1944, GCM Lib, box 18, folder 3 (*cracked rib*); Matthews, "Drive to Rome," 375–78 (*"thing is cinch"*).

559 *The usual camp smells: Texas,* 421 (*hard-luck reputation*); OH, LKT Jr., Apr. 3, 1958, SM, MHI (*"crushing blow"*); Fisher, "A Classic Stratagem," 10.

559 *To the stocky officer at Truscott's elbow*: corr, FLW to Eric Sevareid, Feb. 26, 1946, FLW papers, HIA, box 3; *Texas*, 360–67 (*"can't always trust"*).

559 *"I am fed up"*: *Texas*, 335–36; GK, Apr. 25, 1944 (*"a new man"*).

560 *Now the new man was determined:* Kurzman, 317; Fisher, "A Classic Stratagem," 5–6; "ADC's Journal for Gen. Fred L. Walker," May 29, 1944, NARA RG 319, OCMH, CA, box 6 (*Piper Grasshopper*).

560 *"I didn't sleep much"*: *Texas*, 372–74; author visit, May 9, 2004.

560 *Truscott disagreed, brushing aside:* Matthews, "Drive to Rome," 365–66; Jack L. Scott, *Combat Engineer*, 70; Fisher, "A Classic Stratagem," 9 (*two-mile gap*).

560 *"You may have something"*: *Texas,* 375; Fisher, "A Classic Stratagem," 10–12; *CM,* 377; Matthews, "Drive to Rome," 381; Robert Wagner, *The Texas Army*, 171; *CtoA,* 186.

561 *"We are taking chances"*: diary, FLW, May 30, 1944, NARA RG 319, OCMH, CA, box 6.

561 *Albert Kesselring was alive:* Matthews, "Drive to Rome," 269; *CtoA,* 186; AAR, Schmalz; Kurowski, *Battleground Italy*, 224 (*The 362nd*); journal, Fourteenth Army, May 31, 1944, 118 (*thirty-three tanks*).

561 *"Douse that cigarette"*: memoir, Harvey Reves, ts, n.d., Texas MFM.

562 *"No news here"*: Wagner, 161; George Kerrigan, "The Velletri Road Block," ts, n.d., Texas MFM (*vowing to court-martial*); AAR, "Operations in Italy, May 1944," 142nd Inf Regt, NARA RG 319, OCMH, CA, box 6 (*"breathless anticipation"*).

562 *At eleven P.M., an hour late:* AAR, "Operations in Italy, May 1944," 142nd Inf Regt, ASEQ, MHI; Bruce L. Barger, *The Texas 36th Division,* 186 (*"expected to meet the enemy"*); Eric Sevareid, "On the Standards of the 36th Proudly Inscribe 'Velletri,'" *American Legion,* in *A Pictorial History of the 36th "Texas" Infantry Division* (*"corn popping"*); OH, George Lynch, 142nd Inf, Jan. 16, 1950, SM, MHI.

562 *The first gray wash:* AAR, "Operations in Italy, May 1944," 142nd Inf Regt, NARA RG 319, OCMH, CA, box 6; James M. Estepp, "I Left My Friend on Mt. Artemisio," ts, n.d., Texas MFM (*tiny figures in field gray*).

562 *Behind the column came the bulldozers:* Sevareid, 405; Fisher, "A Classic Stratagem," 5, 14–15; corr, FLW to Gov. Coke Stevenson, July 24, 1946, FLW papers, HIA, box 3; "Engineer History, Fifth Army, Mediterranean Theater," n.d., MHI, 128 (*two-man timber saws*); Barger, 189 (*"Up, up, up"*); Wagner, 171 (*"white tracing tape"*).

563 *Through the night:* Scott, 72; AAR, 143rd Inf Regt, vol. I, June 1944, NARA RG 319, OCMH, CA, box 6 (*"crows on a telephone line"*).

563 *Kesselring learned that the enemy:* Matthews, "Drive to Rome," 267–71, 274–75, 287, 298 (*mounted on bicycles*); CtoA, 185; journal, Fourteenth Army, May 31, 1944, 117.

563 *"cork out of a champagne bottle"*: Adleman and Walton, 17; OH, Paul D. Adams, 143rd Inf CO, 1975, Irving Monclova and Marlin Lang, SOOHP, MHI; corr, FLW to C. Stevenson, July 24, 1946; Michael B. Anderson, "Personal History," ts, n.d., Texas MFM (*"I measured him"*); OH, David W. Sisco, B Co., 142nd Inf, May 1950, NARA RG 319, OCMH, CA, box 5 (*filled with cognac*).

564 *"state of perturbation"*: Sevareid, "On the Standards of the 36th"; *Texas,* 377 (*"Most unbecoming"*).

564 *Through Thursday afternoon:* Fisher, "A Classic Stratagem," 15–17; memoir, Paul H. Duffey, 141st Inf, ts, n.d., Texas MFM (*"didn't bother me"*); CtoA, 200; dispatch, Wick Fowler, *Dallas Morning News,* n.d., in *A Pictorial History of the 36th "Texas" Infantry Division* (*"The town is yours"*).

564 *"torn wide open"*: AAR, Schmalz; Molony VI, 276; Wagner, 180 (*"Going fine"*).

### Expulsion of the Barbarians

564 *Cypress trees stood sentinel:* Harold L. Bond, *Return to Cassino,* 182; Sevareid, 408 (*dead man's boots*); Gray, 108; O'Rourke, 197 (*scratched their initials*).

564 *"Over each one of them"*: *Il Tempo,* June 1, 1984, from "The First Special Service Force: Participants in the Liberation of Rome," ts, n.d., MHI, 3; James O'Neill, "Welcome to Rome," *Yank,* June 18, 1944, 10+ (*"Is he hurt"*).

565 *Clark took nothing for granted:* CtoA, 188 (*"handsprings"*), 192 (*369,000 strong*); Starr, ed., 254; Howe, 337; msg, A. Gruenther to MWC, June 2, 1944, 2230 hrs, MWC, Citadel, box 63.

565 *"I'm disappointed in the 45th"*: G-2/G-3 journal, VI Corps, June 2, 1944, 1840 hrs, NARA RG 319, OCMH, CA, box 6.

565 *With casualties climbing:* Most of the damaged tanks were disabled by mines and soon repaired. Molony VI, 272, 277 (*"a combined attack"*); addendum, "Statistical Data on Italian Campaign," in corr, E. N. Harmon to GCM, July 15, 1944, GCM Lib, box 70; Matthews, "Drive to Rome," 411 (*"get into the act"*); "Clark's Mother Happy," NYT, June 5, 1944, 4 (*"frazzled out"*).

565 *"Rome is now in Allied hands"*: diary, MWC, June 2, 1944, Citadel, box 65; Churchill, *Closing the Ring,* 608; Neillands, 299 (*few Tommies could be found*); Patrick Howarth, *My God, Soldiers,* 165 (*Polish contingent*).

567 *"The attack today"*: diary, MWC, June 2, 1944, Citadel, box 65.

567 *Valmontone was found abandoned:* Molony VI, 276; journal, 3rd ID, June 2, 1944, 0730 hrs, NARA RG 319, OCMH, CA, box 8; *CtoA*, 202, 206; Schrijvers, 123 (*Italian barbers*).

567 *Palestrina, an ancient Etruscan town:* Karl Baedeker, *Central Italy and Rome,* 482–83; http://en.wikipedia.org/wiki/Palestrina.

567 *That would be his last dispatch:* JJT, XIV-14-16; OH, Russell W. Cloer, May 26, 2005, phone interview from Tampa; Russell W. Cloer, "A Short War Story," ts, 1998, 7th Inf Regt, 3rd ID MHI, ASEQ.

568 *"I am sending them home":* memo, MWC to A. Gruenther, June 7, 1944, MWC, Citadel, box 63.

568 *"Perhaps he was kept overseas":* JJT, XV-8-11, 14.

568 *Even before the American thrust:* Warlimont, "OKW Activities," 36.

568 *On June 2, he advised Berlin:* Ultra intercepted these dispatches. Ralph Bennett, *Ultra and the Mediterranean Strategy,* 285–86; Böhmler, 285 (*"huge snake"*).

568 *Vietinghoff himself was a casualty:* CtoA, 199; Blaxland, 131.

568 *Kesselring had earlier proposed:* CtoA, 203, 206; Molony VI, 235, 281 (*"Führer decision"*); Trevelyan, 305 (*Elefante*).

568 *The sound of gunfire:* John Patrick Carroll-Abbing, *But for the Grace of God,* 106; Jane Scrivener, *Inside Rome with the Germans,* 197, 187 (*"Brighter Berlin"*), 193; Lynn H. Nicholas, *The Rape of Europa,* 239 (*white peacocks*); Walter L. Medding, "The Road to Rome," ts, n.d., CEOH, box X-38, 76 (*pilfered the silverware*).

569 *"Germans streaming through":* diary, Tompkins, 272; Daniel Lang, "Letter from Rome," *New Yorker,* June 17, 1944, 65+ (*three and four abreast*); Scrivener, 195–96 (*"Wild-eyed, unshaven"*).

569 *And in the Gestapo cells:* Kurzman, 356–57.

569 *niggling suburban gunfights:* Molony VI, 281; Starr, ed, 263; Burhans, 242.

569 *"Looks as if the Boche":* journal, VI Corps, G-3, June 3, 1944, 1305 hrs, NARA RG 319, OCMH, CA, box 6; Howe, 339; Howze, 113.

570 *"No one is doing any work":* msg, A. Gruenther to MWC, June 3, 1944, 1615 hrs, MWC, Citadel, box 63; intel summary #333, II Corps, June 3, 1944, NARA RG 319, OCMH, CA, box 8 (*"a rout"*); msg, MWC to corps commanders, June 3, 1944, 1642 hrs, II Corps, G-3 journal, NARA RG 319, OCMH, CA, box 8 (*"destroy the enemy"*).

570 *Precisely who first crossed:* memos, MWC, "Initial Entry into Rome," Aug. 31 and Nov. 16, 1944, in "Reports on Capture of Rome," Chester G. Starr papers, HIA, box 1; dispatch, Seymour Korman, *Chicago Tribune,* June 9, 1944, Robert T. Frederick papers, HIA, box 1; *CtoA*, 212–16.

570 *Traffic jams and friendly fire:* OH, Cairns, Apr. 24, 1950; Howe, 344; Sevareid, 410; Richard Collier, *Fighting Words,* 157; diary, MWC, June 4, 1944, Citadel, box 65 (*Clark left Anzio*); Fred Sheehan, *Anzio: Epic of Bravery,* 210 (*"I'm holding off the artillery"*).

570 *As he walked with Frederick:* Clark later hung the perforated sign on his garden wall. *Calculated,* 363–64; Maurine Clark, *Captain's Bride, General's Lady,* 114.

571 *"one little gun stopping us":* OH, Cairns, Apr. 24, 1950; GK, June 4, 1944.

571 *By late Sunday the rear guards:* journal, VI Corps, G-3/G-2, June 4, 1944, 1215 hrs, NARA RG 319, OCMH, CA, box 6; Howe, 345–46 (*chocolate bars*); Adleman and Walton, 210 (*bombed that too*); John J. Roche, "First Squad, First Platoon," ts, 1983, 351st Inf Regt, 88th ID, ASEQ, MHI, 22 (*"too cluttered"*); Alton D. Brashear, *From Lee to Bari,* 238 (*S.P.Q.R.*).

571 *Howze at twilight led a tank company:* Howze, 117; *CtoA*, 218; Howze, "The Rome Operation," 19 (*"kissed me"*); AAR, 351st Inf Regt, June 1944, NARA RG 319, OCMH, CA, box 7 (*"Vino offered"*); Howe, 346; Roche, "First Squad, First Platoon," 22; David Hunt, *A Don at War,* 259; OH, Russell Cloer, 3rd ID, Sept. 11, 2001, ROHA (*summary execution*); Charles F. Marshall, *A Ramble Through My War,* 107 (*"won't be hard to be killed"*).

571 *Frederick set out for the Tiber:* Burhans, 244–45; *CtoA*, 218-19; dispatch, Korman, June 9, 1944; *Register of Graduates,* USMA, 1989 ed., 359; Adleman and Walton, 218.

572 *"a complete hysteria":* Howe, 346; Lang, "Letter from Rome," 65+ (*"Weekend!"*); Martin Blumenson, *Mark Clark,* 215–16; Sherman W. Pratt, *Autobahn to Berchtesgaden,* 403 (*"Welcome to the Liberators"*); Sheehan, 213; *Il Tempo,* June 4, 1984, from "The First Special Service Force," 3 (*"Brothers"*).

572 *Shortly before dawn, a column:* Medding, "The Road to Rome," 63–71; "History of the Fifth Army Counter Intelligence Corps Detachment," June 20, 1945, NARA RG 319, OCMH, CA, box 9; Marshall, 107–8, 113 (*Artie Shaw record*); "Attain by Surprise," ts, n.d., 30th Assault Unit, and "Inventory of Documents and Equipment Taken from the German Embassy Rome," June 8–23, 1943, 30th Assault Unit, LHC (*"revealed nothing"*).

572 *"Got across thirteen bridges":* G-2/G-3 journal, VI Corps, June 5, 1944, 0630 hrs.

572 *"Victory! Not for Mussolini":* Francesco Rossi and Silvano Casaldi, *Those Days at Nettuno,* 90.

572 *The Allied victory had cost:* Molony VI, 284. U.S. estimates of German casualties were somewhat lower; also, total Allied casualties in DIADEM were placed at 40,205. *CtoA,* 223.

573 *Columns of weary GIs shuffled:* Scrivener, 200; Sevareid, 412; Molony VI, 282 (*"Allies are in Rome"*).

573 *In classical Rome:* H. V. Morton, *A Traveller in Rome,* 60–64; John Julius Norwich, *The Middle Sea,* 33n; Brigitte Hintzen-Bohlen, *Art and Architecture: Rome and the Vatican City,* 39; Georgina Masson, *The Companion Guide to Rome,* 37, 44; Trevelyan, 319.

573 *At 7:30 Clark flew from Nettuno:* diary, MWC, June 5, 1944, Citadel, box 65; Adleman and Walton, 226 (*"the hell with that"*).

573 *Within minutes they were lost:* diary, MWC, June 5, 1944, Citadel, box 65; Kurzman, 421.

574 *"Well, gentlemen":* Sevareid, 414; Adleman and Walton, 226; *CM,* 379.

574 *Then it was off to a luncheon:* OH, Theodore J. Conway, 1977, Robert F. Ensslin, SOOHP, MHI, III-14; Vernon A. Walters, *Silent Missions,* 108; diary, MWC, June 5, 1944, Citadel, box 65 (*"the same thing"*).

574 *"We waded through crowds":* GK, June 5, 1944.

574 *"You have made the American people":* msg, FDR to MWC, June 6, 1944, MWC, Citadel, box 3; Harold Macmillan, *The Blast of War,* 415 (*"expulsion"*); Churchill, 611 (*"the great victory"*); Blaxland, 133–37 (*turning some British officers*); Warren F. Kimball, ed., *Churchill & Roosevelt: The Complete Correspondence,* vol. 3, 163.

575 *Across the capital the celebration:* Sheehan, 215; Huebner, 97 (*"beautiful girls"*); Collier, 157 (*"habit of twenty years"*); Adleman and Walton, 219; David Cole, *Rough Road to Rome,* 231 (*"had my hair cut"*).

575 *Exhausted soldiers wrapped:* diary, Tompkins, 272; Wallace, 178 (*"slept on the street"*); Murphy, 163.

575 *"Every block is interesting":* corr, George Revelle to Evelyn, June 14, 1944, author's possession; Sevareid, 415; Cundiff, 178 (*Priests offered tours*); Trevelyan, 322 (*"Hold it, Pope"*); editorial, "The Fall of Rome," *Life,* July 14, 1944, 38 (*"changing of the guard"*).

575 *"How do you like that?":* Walters, 97.

575 *"Boys, we're on the back page":* Collier, 157; Sevareid, 418.

576 *On June 6, Alexander:* Molony VI, 281; Blaxland, 139 (*"If only the country"*).

576 *Howitzers barked wheel to wheel:* Medding, "The Road to Rome," 65; memoir, Edward R. Feagins, 143rd Inf Regt, ts, n.d., Texas MFM, 45 (*"I often wondered"*).

576 *"C'mon, man, c'mon":* Stars and Stripes, June 5, Italy edition, 1; DeFelice, "Carmene's Wartime Chronicle" (*"Drove through Rome"*); G-3 journal, II Corps, June 5, 1944, 2015 hrs, NARA RG 319, OCMH, CA, box 8 (*"Beyond Rome"*).

576 *Olive-drab columns streamed:* Bond, 191; Medding, "The Road to Rome," 65; corr, FKW to H. L. Bond, Sept. 30, 1965; *Texas,* 387.

576 *Then up they climbed:* Morton, 79, 115, 352; http://en.wikipedia.org/wiki/Gianicolo; Bond, 199; Samuel Ball Platner, *A Topographical Dictionary of Ancient Rome*, 274, in http://penelope.uchicago.edu/Thayer/E/Gazetteer/Places/Europe/Italy/Lazio/Roma/ Rome/_Texts/PLATOP*/Janiculum.html.

## EPILOGUE

577 *More than three weeks passed:* JJT, XV-3; *Columbus* [Ohio] *Evening Dispatch*, June 26, 1944, 1, A8; *Columbus Dispatch*, June 3 and 8, 1944.

577 *The news from Rome: Columbus Sunday Dispatch*, June 4, 1944, 1, A5, B1, and June 11, B1; *Columbus Dispatch*, June 6, 1944, 1, A10, B1; *Columbus Evening Dispatch*, June 7, 1944, 1.

578 *The fatal telegram:* JJT, XV-6, 14; author visit, May 7, 2004; "Sicily-Rome American Cemetery and Memorial," American Battle Monuments Commission booklet, n.d., 3–18.

578 *Here, on Memorial Day in 1945:* Bob Fleisher, "Truscott Leads Memorial Day Rites," *Stars and Stripes* 2, no. 174, May 31, 1945, 1; Leda M. Silver, "Cartoonist for All Wars," *Retired Officer*, Oct. 1992, 42+; Bill Mauldin, *The Brass Ring*, 272.

578 *The fall of Rome proved:* Brooks, 29.

578 *"Morale is irresistibly high":* W.G.F. Jackson, *Alexander of Tunis as Military Commander*, 295; Thomas R. Brooks, *The War North of Rome*, 13 (*"advance is splendid"*).

579 *Kesselring had tried to persuade:* Albrecht Kesselring, *The Memoirs of Field-Marshal Kesselring*, 205; J. Duncan Love, "Artillery Usage in World War II," Apr. 1959, vol. II, Operations Research Office, Johns Hopkins University, 125 (*eight miles a day*); directive, A. Kesselring, June 13, 1944, NARA RG 492, MTO G-2, 319, box 354 (*"sadistic imaginativeness"*); Robert Wagner, *The Texas Army*, 202 (*"Damned shame"*).

579 *Alexander's blithe dismissal: Battle*, 255–57; OH, Charles de Gaulle, Jan. 14, 1947, FCP, MHI.

579 *"an overriding priority":* CtoA, 270; *Battle*, 247, 258; Chester G. Starr, ed., *From Salerno to the Alps*, 268 (*shrunk by more than half*); "Beachheads and Mountains," pamphlet, June 1945, MTO, Theodore J. Conway papers, MHI, box 2 (*peaked at 880,000*); Viscount Alexander of Tunis, "The Allied Armies in Italy," n.d., CMH, III-25 (*"disastrous"*); John North, ed., *The Alexander Memoirs, 1940–1945*, 41 (*"triumphant advance"*); *Calculated*, 369 (*"political mistakes"*).

580 *If their disappointment was understandable:* Molony VI, 274; *Battle*, 259; George F. Howe, "American Signal Intelligence in Northwest Africa and Western Europe," U.S. Cryptologic History, Series IV, vol. 1, NARA RG 57, SRH-391, 78 (*"neither strong nor quick"*); Eduard Mark, *Aerial Interdiction in Three Wars*, 208–9 (*"cloak of darkness"*); OH, Willis D. Crittenberger, July 19, 1947, NARA RG 319, OCMH, CA, box 5.

580 *The stress in Fifth Army:* OH, GK, Feb. 14, 1950, and Edward J. O'Neill, June 22, 1948, both in NARA RG 319, OCMH, CA, box 5; Robert H. Adleman and George Walton, *The Devil's Brigade*, 219 (*"infested with lice"*); CtoA, 236–37; memos, 1st AD G-4 to ENH, and 1st AD G-1 to ENH, both July 4, 1944, ENH papers, MHI, corr, box 1.

580 *If the past year had been:* Iris Origo, *War in Val D'Orcia*, xiii; Richard Lamb, *War in Italy, 1943–1945*, 64–66 (*ten Italian deaths*); "AFHQ History of Special Operations," July 1945, MTO, NARA RG 407, E 427, 95-Al1-3.0, box 173, 3 (*85,000 armed partisans*); obit, "Friedrich Engel: Nazi Officer Known as 'Butcher of Genoa,'" Associated Press, *Washington Post*, Feb. 14, 2006, B6.

580 *Alexander in late August: Battle*, 269, 287; B. H. Liddell Hart, *The Other Side of the Hill*, 344; Paul A. Cundiff, *45th Infantry CP*, 162 (*"wished that I were dead"*).

580 *"a vast holding operation":* CtoA, 235; H. Essame, "A Controversial Campaign—Italy, 1943–45," *Army Quarterly and Defence Journal*, Jan. 1968, 219+ (*twenty-nine nations*); Andrew Brookes, *Air War over Italy, 1943–1945*, 155 (*thousand cigarettes*).

581 *"Many men will never know"*: Annette Tapert, ed., *Lines of Battle,* 135; John Muirhead, *Those Who Fall,* 20.

581 *The 608-day campaign: Battle,* 317; Eugenio Corti, *The Last Soldiers of the King,* ix; *CtoA,* 545 *(equivalent to 40 percent)*; "Beachheads and Mountains" *(three-quarters of a million)*; "Tools of War," Dec. 1946, Peninsular Base Section, MHI; Starr, ed., 451–52; *Operations in Sicily and Italy,* USMA Dept. of Military Art and Engineering, 1947, 97. Another statistical summary lists as many as 29,560 American dead and missing in Italy. John Ellis, *World War II: A Statistical Survey,* 255. See also "U.S. Army Battle Casualties in Italy," n.d., CMH, Geog files, Italy, 704, which lists 30,050 U.S. dead, but without giving methodological detail.

581 *German casualties in Italy:* G. A. Shepperd, *The Italian Campaign, 1943–45,* 391; *CtoA,* 545; Corti, ix; Starr, ed., 451-52 *(212,000 prisoners)*; "Age Distribution of Dead in the German Ground Forces," OSS, Research and Analysis Branch, Apr. 3, 1945, NARA RG 334, NWC Lib, box 888.

581 *The Pontine Marshes:* "Richiesta di soccorsi per la popolazione di Anzio e Nettuno," Nov. 18, 1944, provided by Silvano Casaldi, curator, Museum of the Allied Landings, via Andrew Carroll; Donna Martha Budani, "Women, War, and Text: Orsognese Women's Experience in a Sector of the Italian Front in World War II," 1997, Ph.D. diss, American University, 24, 28 *(half million mines)*; "The Battle for San Pietro," *AB,* no. 18 (1977), 1+; Maurizio Zambardi, *War Memories,* trans. Monia Cozzolino, 72 *(disarm live shells)*.

581 *Sant'Angelo refugees:* Donato D'Epiro, *S. Angelo in Theodice,* 181–83.

582 *"The men that war does not kill"*: Vernon A. Walters, *Silent Missions,* 114; Lem Vannatta, "Summer of '43," 1988, Texas MFM *("scared for 23 months")*; J. Glenn Gray, *The Warriors,* 175 *("sooted")*; OH, Louis Bednar, Sept. 17, 2002, VHP *("smell of anything dead")*.

582 *"Any estimate of the value"*: Battle, 317; Jackson, 291 *("severely mauled")*; Walter Warlimont, *Inside Hitler's Headquarters, 1939–1945,* 416 *("sucked into the vortex")*; WSC, *Triumph and Tragedy,* 531 *("The principal task")*.

582 *"There is little doubt that Alexander"*: Douglas Porch, *The Path to Victory,* xii; Trumbull Higgins, "The Anglo-American Historians' War in the Mediterranean, 1942–1945," *Military Affairs,* Oct. 1970, 84+ *("never really knew")*.

582 *Others would be even harsher:* Porch, xi *("cul-de-sac")*; John Ellis, *Brute Force,* table 35 *(22 German divisions)*; Liddell Hart, 373; Higgins, "The Anglo-American Historians' War," 84; David M. Kennedy, *Freedom from Fear,* 596 *("war of attrition")*.

583 *"bound to their fixed plans"*: OH, Albert Kesselring, Sept. 18, 1945, R. H. Brock and O. J. Hale, SEM, NHC, box 47; A. Kesselring, "Concluding Remarks on the Mediterranean Campaign," 1948, FMS, #C-014, MHI, 25 *("tied down in Italy")*; Kesselring, *Memoirs,* 206 *("utterly failed")*.

583 *"to advance is to conquer"*: S.L.A. Marshall, *Men Against Fire,* 194; S. W. Roskill, *The War at Sea, 1939–1945,* 327 *(eleven German U-boats)*; Russell F. Weigley, *The American Way of War,* 356–57; Kent Roberts Greenfield, *American Strategy in World War II,* 114; "Air Power in the Mediterranean," Feb. 1945, MAAF, historical section, MHI, 11–12; Bernard C. Nalty et al., *With Courage,* 234; Porch, 668–69.

583 *"Events generate their own momentum"*: Martin Blumenson, "Sicily and Italy: Why and What For?," *MR,* Feb. 1966, 61; Richard M. Leighton, "Overlord Revisited: An Interpretation of the American Strategy in the European War, 1942–1944," *American Historical Review,* 919+ *(overwhelmed by the American hordes)*; SSA, 382.

584 *"Our war of attrition"*: William D. Hassett, *Off the Record with F.D.R.,* 192.

584 *Certainly lessons learned in Sicily:* A. Kesselring, "German Strategy During the Italian Campaign," FMS, #B-270, MHI, 37; Lida Mayo, *The Ordnance Department: On Beachhead and Battlefront,* 216–17.

584 *American soldiers could slug it out:* Peter R. Mansoor, *The GI Offensive in Europe,* 255; censorship morale reports, Nov. 1943–June 1944, MTO AG, NARA RG 492, 311.7, box 931 *("I really belong")*.

584 *On the day Rome fell:* "Strength of the Army," May 31, 1944, CMH; Eric Larrabee, *Commander in Chief*, 638.

584 *Of those eight million American soldiers:* "Summary of Activities," June 1, 1944, NATOUSA, analysis and control div., CMH; Edmund F. Ball, *Staff Officer with the Fifth Army*, 262 ("glad that I came").

585 *Kesselring continued to command:* Mark M. Boatner III, *The Biographical Dictionary of World War II*, 272–73.

585 *Some blew to other fronts:* 201 file, Charles W. Ryder papers, DDE Lib, box 2; "Notice of Award of Decoration," Oct. 23, 1944, FLW papers, HIA, box 3; *Texas*, 393 ("*will not be sorry*").

585 *Others were fated to remain:* "Small World," CBS, 1959 ("*never quite get over it*"); Peter Neville, *Mussolini*, 185–86; Benito Mussolini, *My Rise and Fall*, 322; Sergio Luzzatto, *The Body of Il Duce*, 46, 100–102, 117, 208–10.

585 *Alexander received:* Nigel Nicholson, *Alex: The Life of Field Marshal Earl Alexander of Tunis*, 238.

585 *"The limitations of his ability"*: Jackson, 295; Boatner, 6; http://www.gg.ca/gg/fgg/bios/01/alexander_e.asp.

585 *Geoffrey Keyes continued*: U.S. Third Army Web site, http://www.arcent.army.mil/history/com_bios/cg_gkeyes.asp.

585 *Bill Darby's life:* Michael J. King, "Rangers," June 1985, CSI, 41; Boatner, 117.

586 *"I tried to tell you"*: corr, LKT Jr. to Sarah, June 11 and 15, 1944, LKT Jr. papers, GCM Lib, box 1, folder 6; Boatner, 574.

586 *Clark also felt on edge:* MWC to Renie, June 8 and 11, July 4, 1944, MWC, personal corr, Citadel; Boatner, 98–99.

586 *"It is the most cruel and unfair"*: corr, MWC to Renie, March 13, 1946, "Rapido River Controversy, 1946," MWC, Citadel, box 39, folder 1; Sidney T. Matthews, "Writing Small Unit Actions with the Fifth Army in Italy," n.d., SM, MHI, box 2 (*commissioned an immense history*).

587 *"clairvoyant and energetic"*: Martin Blumenson, *Mark Clark*, 288; William L. Allen, *Anzio: Edge of Disaster*, 49 ("*had his limitations*").

587 *"tough old gut"*: Pyle, 201.

587 *"the dreamt land"*: Richard Wilbur, "A Baroque Wall-Fountain in the Villa Sciarra," in Alice Leccese Powers, *Italy in Mind*, 342.

587 *"the surge of a marching world"*: Pyle, 201–2.

587 *"misery, destruction, frustration"*: George Biddle, *Artist at War*, 240; Silver, "Cartoonist for All Wars," 42 ("*I stopped regarding the war*"); Glenn G. Clift, *A Letter from Salerno*, 10 ("*born deep inside us*"); Virgil, *The Aeneid*, trans. Robert Fagles, 145 (*circling stars*).

588 *"I watched a full moon"*: Gray, 34.

# SELECTED SOURCES

## BOOKS

Adleman, Robert H., and George Walton. *The Devil's Brigade*. Philadelphia: Chilton Books, 1966.

———. *Rome Fell Today*. New York: Bantam, 1970.

Agarossi, Elena. *A Nation Collapses: The Italian Surrender of September 1943*. New York: Cambridge University Press, 2000.

Adler, Bill, ed. *World War II Letters*. New York: St. Martin's Press, 2002.

*Aircraft of the World*. International Masters Publishers AB, 1997.

Allanbrook, Douglas. *See Naples*. Boston: Houghton Mifflin, 1995.

Allen, William L. *Anzio: Edge of Disaster*. New York: Elsevier-Dutton, 1978.

Altieri, James J. *Darby's Rangers: An Illustrated Portrayal of the Original Rangers*. Ranger Book Committee, 1977.

———. *The Spearheaders*. Indianapolis: Bobbs-Merrill, 1960.

Ambrose, Stephen E. *Eisenhower: Soldier, General of the Army, President-Elect, 1890–1952*. Vol. 1. New York: Simon & Schuster, 1983.

———. *The Wild Blue*. New York: Simon & Schuster, 2001.

Anders, W. *An Army in Exile*. Nashville: Battery Press, 1981.

Ankrum, Homer R. *Dogfaces Who Smiled Through Tears*. Lake Mills, Iowa: Graphic Publishing, 1987.

*Anzio Beachhead*. Washington, D.C.: Department of the Army, 1947.

Archald, Theresa. *G.I. Nightingale*. New York: W. W. Norton, 1945.

Ardery, Philip. *Bomber Pilot*. Lexington, Ky.: University Press of Kentucky, 1978.

Arie, Katriel Ben. *Die Schlacht bei Monte Cassino, 1944*. Freiburg, [West] Germany: Verlag Rombach, 1985.

Aris, George. *The Fifth British Division, 1939 to 1945*. London: Fifth Division Benevolent Fund, 1959.

Arnbal, Anders Kjar. *The Barrel-Land Dance Hall Rangers*. New York: Vantage Press, 1993.

Arnold, H. H. *Global Mission*. Blue Ridge Summit, Pa.: Tab Books, 1989.

Ashcraft, Howard D. *As You Were*. Parsons, W.Va.: McClain Printing, 1990.

Astor, Gerald. *Terrible Terry Allen*. New York: Presidio Press, 2003.

Atkinson, Rick. *An Army at Dawn*. New York: Henry Holt, 2002.

Ausland, John E. *The Last Kilometer*. Oslo, Norway: Land Productions, 1994.

Ayer, Fred, Jr. *Before the Colors Fade*. Dunwoody, Ga.: Norman S. Berg, 1971.

Badoglio, Pietro. *Italy in the Second World War*. Trans. Muriel Currey. Westport, Conn.: Greenwood, 1976.

Baedeker, Karl. *Central Italy and Rome*. Leipzig: Karl Baedeker, 1909.

———. *Southern Italy and Sicily*. Leipzig: Karl Baedeker, 1903.

Bailey, Leslie W. *Through Hell and High Water*. New York: Vantage, 1994.

Baldwin, Hanson. *Battles Lost and Won*. New York: Harper & Row, 1966.

Ball, Edmund F. *Staff Officer with the Fifth Army*. New York: Exposition Press, 1958.

Barclay, C. N. *History of the 16th/5th The Queen's Royal Lancers, 1926 to 1961*. Aldershot, U.K: Gale & Polden, 1963.

Baretta, Rosella. *Tabacco, tabaccari, e tabacchine nel Salento*. Trans. Robert Harp, for author. Brindisi, Italy: Schena, 1994.

Barger, Bruce L. *The Texas 36th Division*. Austin, Tex.: Eakin Press, 2002.

Barnett, Corelli, ed. *Hitler's Generals*. New York: Grove Weidenfeld, 1989.

Bartlett, Merrill L., ed. *Assault from the Sea*. Annapolis, Md.: Naval Institute Press, 1983.

Bates, Charles C., and John F. Fuller. *America's Weather Warriors*. College Station, Tex.: Texas A&M University Press, 1986.

Baumer, Robert W. *Before Taps Sounded*. S.P., 2000.

Baumgartner, John W., et al. *The 16th Infantry, 1798–1946*. 1946.

Baxter, James Phinney, III. *Scientists Against Time*. Boston: Atlantic Monthly Press, 1946.

Beale, Nick. *Air War Italy, 1944–1945*. Shrewsbury, U.K.: Airlife, 1996.

Beck, Alfred M., et al. *The Corps of Engineers: The War Against Germany*. Washington, D.C.: Center of Military History, 1985.

Beckett, Frank. *"Prepare to Move": With the 6th Armoured Division in Africa and Italy*. Grimsby, U.K.: S.P., 1994.

Beebe, Gilbert W., and Michael E. DeBakey. *Battle Casualties: Incidence, Mortality, and Logistic Consideration*. Springfield, Ill.: Charles C Thomas, 1952.

Beesly, Patrick. *Very Special Intelligence*. New York: Ballantine, 1977.

Behrens, C.B.A. *Merchant Shipping and the Demands of War*. London: Her Majesty's Stationery Office, 1955.

Belden, Jack. *Still Time to Die*. New York: Harper & Brothers Publishers, 1943.

Belvin, Betty McLain. *Ray McLain and the National Guard*. Manhattan, Kans.: Sunflower University Press, 1994.

Bennet, Ralph. *ULTRA and the Mediterranean Strategy*. New York: William Morrow, 1989.

Bennett, Donald V. *Honor Untarnished*. New York: Forge, 2003.

Bennett, Ralph. *Ultra and Mediterranean Strategy*. New York: William Morrow, 1989.

Berens, Robert J. *Citizen Soldier*. Ames, Iowa: Sigler, 1992.

Bergh, George S., and Reuben F. Erickson, eds. *A History of the Twenty-sixth General Hospital*. Minneapolis: Bureau of Engraving, 1946.

Berlin, Robert H. *U.S. Army World War II Corps Commanders*. Fort Leavenworth, Kans.: Combat Studies Institute, 1989.

Bernstein, Walter. *Keep Your Head Down*. New York: Viking, 1945.

Bertarelli, L. V. *Southern Italy*. Milan: Touring Club Italiano, 1925.

Biddle, George. *Artist at War*. New York: Viking, 1944.

———. *George Biddle's War Drawings*. New York: Hyperion, 1944.

Biddle, Tami Davis. *Rhetoric and Reality in Air Warfare*. Princeton, N.J.: Princeton University Press, 2002.

Biggs, Bradley. *Gavin*. Hamden, Conn.: Archon Books, 1980.

Bimberg, Edward L. *The Moroccan Goums*. Westport, Conn.: Greenwood Press, 1999.

Binder, L. James. *Lemnitzer: A Soldier for His Time*. Washington, D.C.: Brassey's, 1997.

Bishop, Leo V., et al., eds. *The Fighting Forty-fifth*. Baton Rouge, La.: Army and Navy Publishing, 1946.

Black, Robert W. *Rangers in World War II*. New York: Ballantine, 1992.

Blair, Clay. *Ridgway's Paratroopers*. Garden City, N.Y.: Dial Press, 1985.

Blaker, Gordon A. *Iron Knights: The United States 66th Armored Regiment, 1918–1945*. Shippensburg, Pa.: Burd Street Press, 1999.

Blaxland, Gregory. *Alexander's Generals*. London: William Kimber, 1979.

Blouet, Brian. *The Story of Malta*. Malta: Progress Press, 1993.

Blum, John Morton. *V Was for Victory*. New York: Harcourt Brace Jovanovich, 1976.
Blumenson, Martin. *Anzio: The Gamble That Failed*. Philadelphia: J. B. Lippincott, 1963.
————. *The Battle of the Generals*. New York: William Morrow, 1993.
————. *Bloody River*. Boston: Houghton Mifflin, 1970.
————. *Mark Clark*. New York: Congdon & Weed, 1984.
————. *Patton: The Man Behind the Legend, 1885–1945*. New York: William Morrow, 1985.
————. *The Patton Papers, 1940–1945*. New York: Da Capo, 1996.
————. *Salerno to Cassino*. United States Army in World War II. Washington, D.C.: United States Army, 1969.
————. *Sicily: Whose Victory?* New York: Ballantine, 1968.
Blythe, Ronald, ed. *Private Words*. New York: Viking, 1991.
Boatner, Mark M., III. *Biographical Dictionary of World War II*. Novato, Calif.: Presidio Press, 1990.
Böhmler, Rudolf. *Monte Cassino*. Trans. R. H. Stevens. London: Cassell, 1964.
Bolstad, Owen C. *Dear Folks: A Dog-Faced Infantryman in World War II*. S.p., 1993.
Bond, Harold L. *Return to Cassino*. London: J. M. Dent, 1964.
Booth, T. Michael, and Duncan Spencer. *Paratrooper: The Life of Gen. James M. Gavin*. New York: Simon & Schuster, 1994.
Bosworth, R.J.B. *Mussolini's Italy*. New York: Penguin, 2006.
Botjer, George F. *Sideshow War: The Italian Campaign, 1943–1945*. College Station, Tex.: Texas A&M University Press, 1996.
Bourke-White, Margaret. *Purple Heart Valley*. New York: Simon & Schuster, 1944.
Bowlby, Alex. *Countdown to Cassino*. New York: Sarpedon, 1995.
————. *The Recollections of Rifleman Bowlby*. London: Leo Cooper, 1969.
Bradford, Ernle. *Siege Malta, 1940–1943*. New York: William Morrow, 1986.
Bradley, Omar N. *A Soldier's Story*. New York: Henry Holt, 1951.
Bradley, Omar N., and Clay Blair. *A General's Life*. New York: Simon & Schuster, 1983.
Brashear, Alton D. *From Lee to Bari*. Richmond, Va.: Whittet & Shepperson, 1957.
Bredin, A.E.C. *Three Assault Landings*. Aldershot, U.K.: Gale & Polden, 1946.
Brendon, Piers. *Ike: His Life and Times*. New York: Harper & Row, 1986.
Brereton, Lewis H. *The Brereton Diaries*. New York: William Morrow, 1946.
Breuer, William B. *Agony at Anzio*. St. Louis: Zeus Publishers, 1985.
————. *Captain Cool! Paratrooper Legend*. St. Louis: Zeus Publishers, 1982.
————. *Drop Zone Sicily*. Novato, Calif.: Presidio Press, 1983.
Brinkley, David. *Washington Goes to War*. New York: Ballantine, 1989.
Brinkley, William. *The Ninety and Nine*. Garden City, N.Y.: Doubleday, 1966.
Brode, Patrick. *Casual Slaughters and Accidental Judgments*. Toronto: University of Toronto Press, 1997.
Brookes, Andrew. *Air War over Italy, 1943–1945*. Shepperton, Surrey, U.K.: Ian Allen, 2000.
Brooks, Stephen, ed. *Montgomery and the Eighth Army*. London: Bodley Head, 1991.
Brooks, Thomas R. *The War North of Rome, June 1944–May 1945*. New York: Sarpedon, 1996.
Brophy, Leo P., and George J. B. Fisher. *The Chemical Warfare Service: Organizing for War*. USAWWII. Washington, D.C.: U.S. Army 1989.
Brown, Anthony Cave. *Bodyguard of Lies*. New York: Harper & Row, 1975.
————. *The Last Hero: Wild Bill Donovan*. New York: Times Books, 1982.
————, ed. *The Secret War Report of the OSS*. New York: Berkley, 1976.
Brown, John Mason. *To All Hands*. New York: Whittlesey House, 1943.
Brown, John Sloan. *Draftee Division*. Novato, Calif.: Presidio Press, 1998.
Brown, Paul W. *The Whorehouse of the World*. Bloomington, Ind.: Authorhouse, 2004.
Browne, Anthony Montague. *Long Sunset*. London: Cassell, 1995.

Bryant, Arthur. *Triumph in the West.* Garden City, N.Y.: Doubleday, 1959.

———. *The Turn of the Tide.* London: Collins, 1957.

Buckley, Christopher. *Road to Rome.* London: Hodder & Stoughton, 1945.

Buechner, Emajean Jordan. *Sparks.* Metairie, La.: Thunderbird Press, 1991.

Buell, Thomas B. *Master of Sea Power: A Biography of Fleet Admiral Ernest J. King.* Boston: Little, Brown, 1980.

*Building the Navy's Bases in World War II.* Vol. 2. Washington, D.C.: Government Printing Office, 1947.

Bullock, Alan. *Hitler: A Study in Tyranny.* New York: Harper & Row, 1962.

Burhans, Robert D. *The First Special Service Force.* Nashville: Battery Press, 1978.

Burleigh, Michael. *The Third Reich.* New York: Hill and Wang, 2001.

Burriss, T. Moffatt. *Strike and Hold.* Washington: Brassey's, 2000.

Butcher, Harry C. *My Three Years with Eisenhower.* New York: Simon & Schuster, 1946.

*By Air to Battle.* London: His Majesty's Stationery Office, 1945.

Bykofsky, Joseph, and Harold Larson. *The Transportation Corps: Operations Overseas. USAWWII.* Washington, D.C.: U.S. Army, 2003.

Calvocoressi, Peter. *Top Secret Ultra.* New York: Pantheon, 1980.

Campbell, Rodney. *The Luciano Project.* New York: McGraw-Hill, 1977.

Cannon, Hardy D. *Box Seat over Hell.* S.p., 1985.

Capa, Robert. *Slightly Out of Focus.* New York: Modern Library, 1999.

Capelle, Russell B. *Casablanca to the Neckar: Recollections of the Grand Tour.* S.p., 1970.

Carroll-Abbing, John Patrick. *But for the Grace of God.* London: Secker & Warburg, 1966.

Carter, Ross S. *Those Devils in Baggy Pants.* New York: Signet, 1951.

Carver, Field Marshal Lord. *The Imperial War Museum Book of the War in Italy, 1943–1945.* London: Sidgwick & Jackson, 2001.

Carver, Michael. *Harding of Petherton, Field-Marshal.* London: Weidenfeld & Nicolson, 1978.

———. *Out of Step.* London: Hutchinson, 1989.

———, ed. *The War Lords: Military Commanders of the Twentieth Century.* Boston: Little, Brown, 1976.

Cederberg, Fred. *The Long Road Home.* Toronto: Stoddart, 1986.

Chalmers, W. S. *Full Cycle.* London: Hodder & Stoughton, 1959.

Chalou, George C., ed. *The Secrets War.* Washington, D.C.: NARA, 1992.

Champagne, Daniel R. *Dogface Soldiers.* Bennington, Vt.: Merriam Press, 2003.

Chandler, Alfred D., ed. *The Papers of Dwight David Eisenhower.* Vols. 2, 3. Baltimore: Johns Hopkins University Press, 1970.

Chaney, Lisa. *Hide-and-Seek with Angels: A Life of J. M. Barrie.* New York: St. Martin's Press, 2005.

Chatterton, George. *The Wings of Pegasus.* Nashville: Battery Press, 1982.

Cherpak, Evelyn M., ed. *The Memoirs of Admiral H. Kent Hewitt.* Newport, R.I.: Naval War College Press, 2004.

Churchill, Edward D. *Surgeon to Soldiers.* Philadelphia: J. B. Lippincott, 1972.

Churchill, Winston S. *Closing the Ring.* Boston: Houghton Mifflin, 1951.

———. *The Hinge of Fate.* Boston: Houghton Mifflin, 1950.

Clark, Lloyd. *Anzio: Italy and the Battle for Rome, 1944.* New York: Atlantic Monthly Press, 2006.

Clark, Mark W. *Calculated Risk.* New York: Harper & Brothers, 1950.

Clark, Maurine. *Captain's Bride, General's Lady.* New York: McGraw-Hill, 1956.

Clarke, Rupert. *With Alex at War.* London: Leo Cooper, 2000.

Clay, Steven E. *Blood and Sacrifice.* Chicago: Cantigny First Division Foundation, 2001.

Clayton, Aileen. *The Enemy Is Listening.* London: Hutchinson, 1980.

Clayton, Anthony. *Three Marshals of France*. London: Brassey's, 1992.

Clift, Glenn G. *A Letter from Salerno*. New York: New York Public Library, 1943.

Cline, Ray S. *Washington Command Post: The Operations Division. USAWWII.* Washington, D.C.: Department of the Army, 1951.

Coakley, Robert W., and Richard M. Leighton. *Global Logistics and Strategy, 1943–1945. USAWWII.* Washington, D.C.: Center of Military History, 1989.

Coates, John B., Jr., ed. *Orthopedic Surgery in the Mediterranean Theater of Operations. USAWWII.* Washington D.C.: Office of the Surgeon General, 1957.

Coates, Robert M. *South of Rome*. New York: William Sloane, 1965.

Codman, Charles R. *Drive*. Boston: Atlantic Monthly Press, 1957.

Coffey, Thomas M. *Hap*. New York: Viking, 1982.

Cole, David. *Rough Road to Rome*. London: William Kimber, 1983.

Coles, Harry L., and Albert K. Weinberg. *Civil Affairs: Soldiers Become Governors. USAWWII.* Washington, D.C.: Department of the Army, 1964.

Coll, Blanche D., et al. *The Corps of Engineers: Troops and Equipment. USAWWII.* Washington, D.C.: Chief of Military History, 1958.

Collier, Richard. *Fighting Words*. New York: St. Martin's Press, 1989.

Collins, Lawrence D. *The 56th Evac Hospital*. Denton, Tex.: University of North Texas Press, 1995.

Colville, John. *The Fringes of Power*. New York: W. W. Norton, 1985.

Colvin, Ian. *The Unknown Courier*. London: William Kimber, 1953.

Comfort, C. F. *Artist at War*. Toronto: Ryerson Press, 1956.

Connell, Charles. *Monte Cassino*. London: Elek Books, 1963.

Cooling, Benjamin Franklin, ed. *Case Studies in Close Air Support*. Washington, D.C.: Office of Air Force History, 1990.

Cooper, Duff. *Old Men Forget*. London: Rupert Hart-Davis, 1953.

Cooper, Matthew. *The German Army, 1933–1945*. Lanham, Md.: Scarborough House, 1990.

Coopers, Belton Y. *Death Traps*. Novato, Calif.: Presidio Press, 1998.

Corti, Eugenio. *The Last Soldiers of the King*. Trans. Manuela Arundel. Columbia, Mo.: University of Missouri Press, 2003.

Corvo, Max. *The O.S.S. in Italy, 1942–1945*. New York: Praeger, 1990.

Cowdrey, Albert E. *Fighting for Life*. New York: Free Press, 1994.

Crane, Conrad C. *Bombs, Cities, and Civilians*. Lawrence, Kans.: University Press of Kansas, 1993.

Craven, Wesley Frank, and James Lea Cate, eds. *The Army Air Forces in World War II*. Vol. 2, *Europe: TORCH to POINTBLANK, August 1942 to December 1943*. Chicago: University of Chicago Press, 1949.

———. *The Army Air Forces in World War II*. Vol. 3, *Europe: ARGUMENT to V-E Day*. Chicago: University of Chicago Press, 1951.

Crawford, Andy. *Mules Go to War*. Cincinnati: C. J. Krehbiel, 1979.

Cray, Ed. *General of the Army*. New York: Touchstone, 1990.

Crew, F.A.E. *The Army Medical Services*. Vol. 3. London: Her Majesty's Stationery Office, 1959.

Crosby, Harry H. *A Wing and a Prayer*. London: Robson, 1993.

Crosswell, D.K.R. *The Chief of Staff: The Military Career of General Walter Bedell Smith*. New York: Greenwood, 1991.

Cruickshank, Charles. *Deception in World War II*. New York: Oxford University Press, 1980.

Cundiff, Paul A. *45th Infantry CP*. Tampa, Fla.: S.p., 1987.

Cunningham, Viscount of Hyndhope. *A Sailor's Odyssey*. New York: E. P. Dutton, 1951.

Currier, Donald R. *50 Mission Crush.* Shippensburg, Pa.: Burd Street Press, 1992.

Curtis, Donald McB. *The Song of the Fighting First.* S.p., 1987.

Curtiss, Mina, ed. *Letters Home.* Boston: Little, Brown, 1944.

D'Epiro, Donato. *S. Angelo in Theodice.* S.p., 1994.

D'Este, Carlo. *Bitter Victory.* New York: E. P. Dutton, 1988.

———. *Eisenhower: A Soldier's Life.* New York: Henry Holt, 2002.

———. *Fatal Decision.* New York: HarperCollins, 1991.

———. *A Genius for War.* New York: Harper, 1996.

———. *World War II in the Mediterranean.* Chapel Hill, N.C.: Algonquin Books, 1990.

Danchev, Alex, and Daniel Todman, eds. *War Diaries, 1939–1945, Field Marshal Lord Alanbrooke.* Berkeley and Los Angeles: University of California Press, 2001.

Dancocks, Daniel G. *D-Day Dodgers: The Canadians in Italy, 1943–1945.* Toronto: McClelland and Stewart, 1991.

Daniell, David Scott. *History of the East Surrey Regiment.* London: Ernest Benn, 1957.

———. *The Royal Hampshire Regiment.* Vol. 3. Aldershot, U.K.: Gale & Polden, 1955.

Darby, William O., and William H. Baumer. *Darby's Rangers: We Led the Way.* San Rafael, Calif.: Presidio Press, 1980.

David, Saul. *Mutiny at Salerno.* London: Brassey's, 1995.

Davies, Kenneth Maitland. *To the Last Man.* St. Paul, Minn.: Ramsey County Historical Society, 1982.

Davis, Benjamin O., Jr. *Benjamin O. Davis, Jr.: American.* Washington, D.C.: Smithsonian Institution Press, 1991.

Davis, Kenneth S. *Dwight D. Eisenhower: Soldier of Democracy.* New York: Konecky, 1945.

———. *Experience of War.* Garden City, N.Y.: Doubleday, 1965.

———. *Soldier of Democracy.* Garden City, N.Y.: Doubleday, Doran & Co., 1945.

Davis, Melton S. *Who Defends Rome?* New York: Dial Press, 1972.

Davis, Richard G. *Carl A. Spaatz and the Air War in Europe.* Washington, D.C.: Center for Air Force History, 1993.

De Guingand, Francis. *Operation Victory.* New York: Scribners, 1947.

De Wiart, Adrian Carton. *Happy Odyssey.* London: Jonathan Cape, 1950.

Deakin, F. W. *The Brutal Friendship.* New York: Harper & Row, 1962.

Dickson, Paul. *War Slang.* New York: Pocket Books, 1994.

Dmitri, Ivan. *Flight to Everywhere.* New York: Whittlesey House, 1944.

Doherty, Richard. *A Noble Crusade.* Rockville Centre, N.Y.: Sarpedon, 1999.

Doolittle, James H., with Carroll V. Glines. *I Could Never Be So Lucky Again.* New York: Bantam, 1991.

Doubler, Michael D. *Closing with the Enemy.* Lawrence, Kans.: University of Kansas Press, 1994.

Douglas-Home, Charles. *Rommel.* New York: Saturday Review Press, 1973.

Downes, Donald. *The Scarlet Thread.* New York: British Book Centre, 1953.

Dugan, James, and Carroll Stewart. *Ploesti.* New York: Ballantine, 1973.

Duncan, William J. *RMS Queen Mary: Queen of the Queens.* Anderson, S.C.: Droke House, 1969.

Durnford-Slater, John. *Commando.* London: Greenhill Books, 2002.

Duus, Masayo Umezawa. *Unlikely Liberators.* Trans. Peter Duus. Honolulu: University of Hawaii Press, 1987.

Dwyer, John B. *Seaborne Deception: The History of U.S. Navy Beachjumpers.* New York: Praeger, 1992.

Eden, Anthony. *The Reckoning: The Memoirs of Anthony Eden, Earl of Avon.* Boston: Houghton Mifflin, 1965.

Edwards, Paul M., ed. *General Matthew B. Ridgway: An Annotated Bibliography.* Westport, Conn.: Greenwood Press, 1993.

Ehrman, John. *Grand Strategy.* Vol. 5, *August 1943–September 1944.* London: Her Majesty's Stationery Office, 1956.

Eisenhower, Dwight D. *At Ease: Stories I Tell to Friends.* Garden City, N.Y.: Doubleday, 1967.

———. *Crusade in Europe.* Baltimore: Johns Hopkins University Press, 1997.

———. *Letters to Mamie.* John S. D. Eisenhower, ed. Garden City, N.Y.: Doubleday, 1978.

Eisenhower, John S. D. *Allies: Pearl Harbor to D-Day.* Garden City, N.Y.: Doubleday, 1982.

———. *General Ike.* New York: Free Press, 2003.

———. *Strictly Personal.* Garden City, N.Y.: Doubleday, 1974.

Eke, C. Richard. *A Game of Soldiers.* Brighton, U.K.: S.p., 1997.

Ellis, John. *Brute Force: Allied Strategy and Tactics in the Second World War.* New York: Viking, 1990.

———. *Cassino: The Hollow Victory.* New York: McGraw-Hill, 1984.

———. *On the Front Lines.* London: John Wiley & Sons, 1991.

———. *World War II: A Statistical Survey.* New York: Facts on File, 1995.

Erskin, David. *The Scots Guards, 1991–1955.* London: William Clowes, 1956.

Essame, H. *Patton: A Study in Command.* New York: Scribners, 1974.

Eubank, Keith. *Summit at Teheran.* New York: William Morrow, 1985.

Evans, Bradford A. *The Bombing of Monte Cassino.* Montecassino, Italy: Pubblicazioni Cassinesi, 1988.

Farago, Ladislas. *Burn After Reading.* New York: Pinnacle, 1961.

———. *Patton: Ordeal and Triumph.* New York: Ivan Obolensky, 1964.

Farner, Frank, ed. *Thunderbird: 45th Infantry Division.* Tokyo: Toppan Printing, 1953.

Fergusson, Bernard. *The Watery Maze.* New York: Holt, Rinehart & Winston, 1961.

Fest, Joachim C. *Hitler.* Trans. Richard and Clara Winston. New York: Harcourt Brace, 1974.

ffrench Blake, R.L.V. *The 17th/21st Lancers.* London: Hamish Hamilton, 1968.

*Fifth Army at the Winter Line.* Washington, D.C.: Center of Military History, 1990.

Finke, Blythe Foote. *No Mission Too Difficult!* Chicago: Contemporary Books, 1995.

Fisher, Ernest F., Jr. *Cassino to the Alps. USAWWII.* Washington, D.C.: U.S. Army, 1977.

Fisher, George A. *The Story of the 180th Infantry Regiment.* San Angelo, Tex.: Newsfoto Publishing, 1947.

Fitzgerald, D.J.L. *History of the Irish Guards in the Second World War.* Aldershot, U.K.: Gale & Polden, 1949.

Flynn, George Q. *The Mess in Washington: Manpower Mobilization in World War II.* Westport, Conn.: Greenwood Press, 1979.

Ford, Ken. *Cassino 1944.* Botley, Oxford, U.K.: Osprey, 2004.

Foot, M.R.D., and J. M. Langley. *MI 9: Escape and Evasion, 1939–1945.* Boston: Little, Brown, 1980.

*Foreign Relations of the United States: The Conferences at Washington and Quebec, 1943.* Washington, D.C.: U.S. Government Printing Office, 1970.

Forty, George. *The Armies of George S. Patton.* London: Arms and Armour, 1996.

———. *M4 Sherman.* Poole, U.K.: Blandford Press, 1987.

Fowle, Barry W., ed. *Builders and Fighters: U.S. Army Engineers in World War II.* Fort Belvoir, Va.: U.S. Army Corps of Engineers, 1992.

Francis, Charles E. *The Tuskegee Airmen.* Boston: Branden Publishing, 1993.

Fraser, David. *Alanbrooke.* New York: Atheneum, 1982.

———. *Knight's Cross.* New York: HarperCollins, 1993.

Freeman, Roger A. *The American Airman in Europe.* Osceola, Wis.: Motorbooks International, 1991.

Freyberg, Paul. *Bernard Freyberg, V.C.* London: Hodder & Stoughton, 1991.

Friedrich, Carl J., ed. *American Experiences in Military Government in World War II.* New York: Rinehart & Co., 1948.

*From Pachino to Ortona: The Canadian Army at War*. Ottawa: King's Printer, 1947.
*From the Volturno to the Winter Line*. Washington, D.C.: Center of Military History, 1990.
Frost, John. *A Drop Too Many*. London: Buchan & Enright, 1982.
Fry, James C. *Combat Soldier*. Washington, D.C.: National Press, 1968.
Fuller, J.F.C. *The Second World War, 1939–1945*. London: Eyre & Spottiswoode, 1948.
Fussell, Paul. *Doing Battle: The Making of a Skeptic*. Boston: Back Bay, 1998.
———. *Wartime*. New York: Oxford University Press, 1989.
Galloway, Strome. *A Regiment at War*. S.p., 1979.
Garland, Albert N., and Howard McGaw Smyth. *Sicily and the Surrender of Italy*.
    *USAWWII*. Washington, D.C.: Center of Military History, 1993.
Gatchel, Theodore L. *At the Water's Edge*. Annapolis: Naval Institute Press, 1996.
Gavin, James M. *Airborne Warfare*. Washington, D.C.: Infantry Journal Press, 1947.
———. *On to Berlin*. New York: Viking, 1978.
Gellhorn, Martha. *The Face of War*. New York: Simon & Schuster, 1959.
Gervasi, Frank. *The Violent Decade*. New York: W. W. Norton, 1989.
Gibran, Daniel K. *The 92nd Infantry Division and the Italian Campaign in World War II*.
    Jefferson, N.C.: McFarland, 2001.
Gilbert, Martin. *Churchill and America*. New York: Free Press, 2005.
———. *The Second World War*. New York: Henry Holt, 1991.
———. *Winston Churchill's War Leadership*. New York: Vintage, 2004.
———. *Winston S. Churchill*. Vol. 7, *Road to Victory, 1941–1945*. Boston: Houghton Mifflin,
    1986.
Gleichauf, Justin F. *Unsung Sailors: The Naval Armed Guard in World War II*. Annapolis,
    Md.: Naval Institute Press, 1990.
Godson, Susan H. *Viking of Assault: Admiral John Lesslie Hall, Jr., and Amphibious
    Warfare*. Washington, D.C.: University Press of America, 1982.
Gooderson, Ian. *Cassino 1944*. London: Brassey's, 2003.
Goodwin, Doris Kearns. *No Ordinary Time*. New York: Touchstone, 1995.
Graham, Dominick, and Shelford Bidwell. *Tug of War: The Battle for Italy, 1943–1945*. New
    York: St. Martin's Press, 1986.
Graham, Don. *No Name on the Bullet*. New York: Viking, 1986.
Gray, J. Glenn. *The Warriors*. New York: Harcourt, Brace, 1959.
Green, Constance M., et al. *The Ordnance Department: Planning Munitions for War*.
    *USAWWII*. Washington, D.C.: Department of the Army, 1955.
Greene, Jack, and Alessandro Massignani. *The Naval War in the Mediterranean, 1940–1943*.
    London: Chatham, 2002.
Greenfield, Kent Roberts. *American Strategy in World War II: A Reconsideration*. Baltimore:
    Johns Hopkins University Press, 1963.
———, ed. *Command Decisions*. New York: Harcourt, Brace, 1959.
*The Grenadier Guards, 1939–1945*. Aldershot, U.K.: Gale & Polden, 1946.
Griffo, Pietro. *Gela*. Greenwich, Conn.: New York Graphic Society, n.d.
Gropman, Alan, ed. *The Big L: American Logistics in World War II*. Washington, D.C.:
    National Defense University Press, 1997.
Guest, John. *Broken Images*. London: Leo Cooper, 1970.
Gunther, John. *D Day*. New York: Harper & Brothers, 1944.
———. *Eisenhower: The Man and the Symbol*. New York: Harper & Brothers, 1951.
Hall, Fred W., Jr. *A Memoir of World War II*. S.p., 1997.
Hamilton, Nigel. *Master of the Battlefield: Monty's War Years, 1942–1944*. New York:
    McGraw-Hill, 1983.
Hammond, James W., Jr. *Poison Gas: The Myth Versus Reality*. Westport, Conn.:
    Greenwood Press, 1999.

Handel, Michael I., ed. *Strategic and Operational Deception in the Second World War.* London: Frank Cass, 1987.

Hanssen, G. L. *The Hanssens of Eastern Iowa.* Waldorf, Md.: R. A. Hanssen, 2000.

Hapgood, David, and David Richardson. *Monte Cassino.* New York: Congdon & Weed, 1984.

Harding, Stephen. *Gray Ghost: The R.M.S. Queen Mary at War.* Missoula, Mont.: Pictorial Histories Publishing, 1982.

———. *Great Liners at War.* Osceola, Wis.: Motorbooks International, 1997.

Hargrove, Hondon B. *Buffalo Soldiers in Italy.* Jefferson, N.C.: McFarland, 1985.

Harmon, E. N., with Milton MacKaye and William Ross MacKaye. *Combat Commander.* Englewood Cliffs, N.J.: Prentice-Hall, 1970.

Harpur, Brian. *The Impossible Victory.* New York: Hippocrene, 1981.

Harr, Bill. *Combat Boots.* New York: Exposition Press, 1952.

Harriman, W. Averell, and Elie Abel. *Special Envoy to Churchill and Stalin.* New York: Random House, 1975.

Harris, C.R.S. *Allied Administration of Italy, 1943–1945.* London: Her Majesty's Stationery Office, 1957.

Hart, Scott. *Washington at War, 1941–1945.* Englewood Cliffs, N.J.: Prentice-Hall, 1970.

Hassett, William D. *Off the Record with F.D.R.* New Brunswick, N.J.: Rutgers University Press, 1958.

Hastings, Donald W., et al. *Psychiatric Experiences of the Eighth Air Force.* New York: Josiah Macy, Jr., Foundation, 1944.

Hastings, Max. *Bomber Command.* New York: Dial, 1979.

Hatch, Alden. *General Ike.* Chicago: Consolidated Book Publishers, 1952.

Heathcote, T. A. *The British Field Marshals, 1763–1997.* London: Leo Cooper, 1999.

Heiber, Helmut, and David M. Glantz, eds. *Hitler and His Generals.* New York: Enigma Books, 2004.

Heller, Joseph. *Now and Then.* New York: Simon & Schuster, 1998.

Henius, Frank. *Italian Sentence Book for the Soldier.* Washington, D.C.: Infantry Journal, 1943.

Hickey, Des, and Gus Smith. *Operation Avalanche.* New York: McGraw-Hill, 1984.

Hickey, Michael. *Out of the Sky: A History of Airborne Warfare.* New York: Scribners, 1979.

Higgins, Trumbull. *Soft Underbelly.* New York: Macmillan, 1968.

Hill, Robert M., and Elizabeth Craig Hill. *In the Wake of War.* University, Ala.: University of Alabama Press, 1982.

Hinsley, F. H. *British Intelligence in the Second World War.* Vol. 2. New York: Cambridge University Press, 1981.

Hinsley, F. H., and C.A.G. Simkins. *British Intelligence in the Second World War.* Vol. 6, *Security and Counter-Intelligence.* New York: Cambridge University Press, 1990.

Hinsley, F. H., et al. *British Intelligence in the Second World War.* Vol. 3, part 1. London: Her Majesty's Stationery Office, 1984.

Hintzen-Bohlen, Brigitte. *Art and Architecture: Rome and the Vatican City.* New York: Barnes & Noble, 2005.

Hirshson, Stanley P. *General Patton: A Soldier's Life.* New York: HarperCollins, 2002.

*History 67th Armored Regiment.* Brunswick, Germany: Georg Westermann, 1945.

Hogan, David W., Jr. *Raiders or Elite Infantry?* Westport, Conn.: Greenwood Press, 1992.

Hope, Bob. *Don't Shoot, It's Only Me.* New York: G. P. Putnam's Sons, 1990.

———. *The Last Christmas Show.* New York: Doubleday, 1974.

Horrocks, Brian. *A Full Life.* London: Leo Cooper, 1974.

Hougen, John H. *The Story of the Famous 34th Infantry Division.* Nashville: Battery Press, 1949.

Houston, Donald E. *Hell on Wheels*. Novato, Calif.: Presidio Press, 1995.

Howard, Fred. *Whistle While You Wait*. New York: Duell, Sloan, & Pearce, 1945.

Howard, Michael. *Captain Professor: A Life in War and Peace*. New York: Continuum, 2006.

———. *Grand Strategy*. Vol. 4, *August 1942–September 1943*. London: Her Majesty's Stationery Office, 1972.

———. *The Mediterranean Strategy in the Second World War*. London: Greenhill Books, 1993.

———. *Strategic Deception in the Second World War*. New York: W. W. Norton, 1995.

Howard, Michael, and John Sparrow. *The Coldstream Guards, 1920–1946*. London: Oxford University Press, 1951.

Howarth, Patrick. *My God, Soldiers*. London: Hutchinson, 1989.

Howarth, Stephen, ed. *Men of War*. New York: St. Martin's Press, 1992.

Howarth, T.E.B., ed. *Monty at Close Quarters*. London: Leo Cooper, 1985.

Howe, George F. *The Battle History of the 1st Armored Division*. Washington, D.C.: Combat Forces Press, 1954.

Howze, Hamilton H. *A Cavalryman's Story*. Washington, D.C.: Smithsonian Institution Press, 1996.

Hoyt, Edwin P. *Backwater War*. Westport, Conn.: Praeger, 2002.

———. *The GI's War*. New York: Da Capo, 1988.

Huebner, Klaus H. *A Combat Doctor's Diary*. College Station, Tex.: Texas A&M University Press, 1987.

Hummer, John F. *An Infantryman's Journal*. Manassas, Va.: Ranger Associates, 1981.

Hunt, David. *A Don at War*. London: Frank Cass, 1990.

Huston, James A. *Out of the Blue*. Nashville: Battery Press, 1981.

———. *The Sinews of War: Army Logistics, 1775–1953*. Washington, D.C.: U.S. Army, 1966.

Hynes, Samuel. *The Soldiers' Tale: Bearing Witness to Modern War*. New York: Penguin, 1998.

Infield, Glenn B. *Big Week*. Washington, D.C.: Brassey's, 1993.

———. *Disaster at Bari*. New York: Macmillan, 1971.

Irving, David. *The Trail of the Fox*. New York: Thomas Congdon, 1977.

Ismay, Lord. *The Memoirs of General Lord Ismay*. New York: Viking, 1960.

*Italian Phrase Book*. Washington, D.C.: War Department, 1943.

Jackson, Carlton. *Allied Secret*. Norman, Okla.: Red River Books, 2001.

———. *Forgotten Tragedy: The Sinking of HMT Rohna*. Annapolis, Md.: Naval Institute Press, 1997.

Jackson, Robert. *Bomber!* New York: St. Martin's Press, 1980.

Jackson, W.G.F. *Alexander of Tunis as Military Commander*. London: B. T. Batsford, 1971.

———. *The Battle for Italy*. New York: Harper & Row, 1967.

James, D. Clayton, with Anne Sharp Wells. *A Time for Giants*. New York: Franklin Watts, 1987.

Jeffers, H. Paul. *In the Rough Rider's Shadow*. New York: Ballantine, 2002.

Jellison, Charles A. *Besieged: The World War II Ordeal of Malta, 1940–1942*. Hanover, N.H.: University Press of New England, 1984.

Jenkins, Roy. *Churchill*. New York: Farrar, Straus and Giroux, 2001.

Jensen, Marvin. *Strike Swiftly! The 70th Tank Battalion*. Novato, Calif.: Presidio Press, 1997.

Jewell, N.L.A. *Secret Mission Submarine*. Chicago: Ziff-Davis, 1944.

Johnson, Franklyn A. *One More Hill*. New York: Funk & Wagnalls, 1949.

Jones, Matthew. *Britain, the United States, and the Mediterranean War, 1942–1944*. New York: St. Martin's Press, 1996.

Joswick, Jerry J., and Lawrence A. Keating. *Combat Cameraman*. Philadelphia: Chilton, 1961.

Juergensen, Hans. *Beachheads and Mountains.* Tampa: Richard George Roland, 1998.

Kahn, David. *The Codebreakers.* New York: Macmillan, 1969.

Kaplan, Robert D. *Mediterranean Winter.* New York: Random House, 2004.

Karig, Walter. *Battle Report: The Atlantic War.* New York: Rinehart & Co., 1946.

Katz, Robert. *The Battle for Rome.* New York: Simon & Schuster, 2003.

———. *Massacre in Rome.* New York: Ballantine, 1973.

Kaufman, Henry. *Vertrauensmann.* New York: Rivercross, 1994.

Kay, Robin. *Official History of New Zealand in the Second World War: Italy.* Vol. 2, *From Cassino to Trieste.* Wellington, N.Z.: Department of Internal Affairs, 1967.

Keefer, Louis E. *Italian Prisoners of War in America.* New York: Praeger, 1992.

Keegan, John, ed. *Churchill's Generals.* New York: Grove Weidenfeld, 1991.

Kelly, Charles E. *One Man's War.* New York: Knopf, 1944.

Kelly, James E., ed. *The Wartime Letters of John and Vicki Kelly.* S.p., 2005.

Kennedy, David M. *Freedom from Fear.* New York: Oxford University Press, 1999.

Kennedy, John. *The Business of War.* London: Hutchinson, 1957.

Kennett, Lee B. *G.I.: The American Soldier in World War II.* New York: Scribners, 1987.

Kerwin, Paschal E. *Big Men of the Little Navy.* Paterson, N.J.: St. Anthony Guild Press, 1946.

Kesselring, Albrecht. *The Memoirs of Field-Marshal Kesselring.* London: Greenhill Books, 1997.

Kielar, Eugenia M. *Thank You, Uncle Sam.* Bryn Mawr, Pa.: Dorrance & Co., 1987.

Kimball, Warren F. *Churchill & Roosevelt: The Complete Correspondence.* Princeton, N.J.: Princeton University Press, 1987.

Kimmins, Anthony. *Half-time.* London: William Heinemann, 1947.

Kindsvatter, Peter S. *American Soldiers.* Lawrence, Kans.: University Press of Kansas, 2003.

King, Ernest J., and Walter Muir Whitehill. *Fleet Admiral King.* New York: W. W. Norton, 1952.

King, Michael J. *William Orlando Darby: A Military Biography.* Hamden, Conn.: Archon Books, 1981.

Kippenberger, Howard. *Infantry Brigadier.* London: Oxford University Press, 1949.

Kitching, George. *Mud and Green Fields.* St. Catharines, Ontario: Vanwell, 1993.

Kleber, Brooks E., and Dale Birdsell. *The Chemical Warfare Service: Chemicals in Combat.* USAWWII. Washington, D.C.: Center of Military History, 1990.

Kluger, Steve. *Yank.* New York: St. Martin's Press, 1991.

Knickerbocker, H. R., et al. *Danger Forward.* Washington, D.C.: Society of the First Division, 1947.

Knightley, Phillip. *The First Casualty.* New York: Harcourt Brace Jovanovich, 1975.

Koch, Oscar W., and Robert G. Hays. *G-2: Intelligence for Patton.* Philadelphia: Army Times Publishing, 1971.

Kogan, Norman. *Italy and the Allies.* Westport, Conn.: Greenwood Press, 1982.

Krebs, John E. *To Rome and Beyond.* S.p., 1981.

Kreidberg, Marvin A., and Merton G. Henry. *History of Military Mobilization in the United States Army, 1775–1945.* Washington, D.C.: Department of the Army, 1955.

Kros, Jack. *War in Italy: With the South Africans from Taranto to the Alps.* Johannesburg: Ashanti, 1992.

Kühn, Volkmar. *German Paratroopers in World War II.* Shepperton, U.K.: Ian Allen, 1978.

Kurowski, Franz. *Battleground Italy, 1943–1945.* Trans. Ian McMullen. Winnipeg: J. J. Fedorowicz, 2003.

———. *The History of the Fallschirmpanzerkorps Hermann Göring.* Winnipeg: J. J. Fedorowicz, 1995.

Kurzman, Dan. *The Race for Rome.* Garden City, N.Y.: Doubleday, 1975.

Laffin, John. *Surgeons in the Field.* London: J. M. Dent, 1970.

Lamb, Richard. *Montgomery in Europe, 1943–45.* New York: Franklin Watts, 1984.

———. *War in Italy, 1943–1945*. New York: St. Martin's Press, 1993.

Laqueur, Walter, ed. *The Second World War: Essays in Military and Political History*. London: Sage, 1982.

Larrabee, Eric. *Commander in Chief*. New York: Touchstone, 1987.

Lax, Eric. *The Mold in Dr. Florey's Coat*. New York: Henry Holt, 2004.

Le Goyet, P. *La Participation Française à la Campagne d'Italie*. Paris: Ministère des Armées, 1969.

Leahy, William D. *I Was There*. New York: Whittlesey House, 1950.

Leasor, James. *The Clock with Four Hands*. New York: Reynal & Co., 1959.

———. *War at the Top*. London: Michael Joseph, 1959.

Lebda, John F. *Million Miles to Go*. Victoria, B.C.: Trafford Publishing, 2001.

Leccisotti, Tommaso. *Monte Cassino*. Trans. Armand O. Citarella. Cassino, Italy: Abbey of Monte Cassino, 1987.

Lee, James Ward, et al., eds. *1941: Texas Goes to War*. Denton, Tex.: University of North Texas Press, 1991.

Lee, Ulysses. *The Employment of Negro Troops*. USAWWII. Washington, D.C.: Center of Military History, 2000.

Leighton, Richard M., and Robert W. Coakley. *Global Logistics and Strategy, 1940–1943*. Washington, D.C.: Center of Military History, 1995.

Lewin, Ronald. *Montgomery as Military Commander*. New York: Stein & Day, 1971.

———. *Rommel as Military Commander*. New York: Barnes & Noble, 1998.

———. *ULTRA Goes to War*. New York: Pocket Books, 1980.

Lewis, Norman. *In Sicily*. New York: St. Martin's Press, 2000.

———. *Naples '44*. New York: Pantheon, 1978.

Liddell Hart, B. H. *The Other Side of the Hill*. London: Cassell, 1951.

———, ed. *The Rommel Papers*. Trans. Paul Findlay. Pennington, N.J.: Collectors Reprints, 1995.

Linderman, Gerald F. *The World Within War*. New York: Free Press, 1997.

Linklater, Eric. *The Campaign in Italy*. London: His Majesty's Stationery Office, 1951.

Lloyd, Alan. *The Gliders*. Nashville: Battery Press, 1982.

Lochner, Louis P. *The Goebbels Diaries*. Garden City, N.Y.: Doubleday, 1948.

*Logistics in World War II*. Washington, D.C.: U.S. Army Center of Military History, 1993.

Longmate, Norman. *The G.I.'s: The Americans in Britain, 1942–1945*. New York: Scribners, 1975.

Luzzatto, Riccardo. *Unknown War in Italy*. London: New Europe, 1946.

Luzzatto, Sergio. *Body of Il Duce*. Trans. Frederika Randall. New York: Metropolitan Books, 2005.

Lyon, Peter. *Eisenhower: Portrait of the Hero*. Boston: Little, Brown, 1974.

MacDonald, Donald E. *"My Buttons Are in the Way."* S.p., 1992.

MacGregor, Morris J. *Integration of the Armed Forces, 1940–1965*. Washington, D.C.: U.S. Army, 1981.

Macksey, Kenneth. *Kesselring: The Making of the Luftwaffe*. New York: David McKay, 1978.

———. *Military Errors of World War II*. London: Cassell, 1999.

———. *Why the Germans Lose at War*. New York: Barnes & Noble, 1996.

Macmillan, Harold. *The Blast of War, 1939–1945*. New York: Harper & Row, 1967.

———. *War Diaries*. New York: St. Martin's Press, 1984.

Majdalany, Fred. *Cassino: Portrait of a Battle*. London: Cassell, 1999.

———. *The Monastery*. London: John Lane, 1945.

Major, Kevin. *Hold Fast!* Toronto: Clarke, Irwin & Co., 1978.

Malone, Dick. *Missing from the Record*. Toronto: Collins, 1946.

Malone, Richard S. *A Portrait of War, 1939–1943*. Toronto: Colllins, 1983.

Mansoor, Peter R. *The GI Offensive in Europe*. Lawrence, Kans.: University Press of Kansas, 1999.

Marchini, Ascanio. *Il Tabacco*. Trans. Robert Harp, for author. Rome: Atlantica Editrice, 1946.

Mark, Eduard. *Aerial Interdiction in Three Wars*. Washington, D.C.: Center for Air Force History, 1994.

Marks, Leo. *Between Silk and Cyanide*. New York: Free Press, 1998.

Marshall, Charles F. *A Ramble Through My War: Anzio and Other Joys*. Baton Rouge: Louisiana State University Press, 1998.

Marshall, Katherine Tupper. *Together*. New York: Tupper and Love, 1946.

Marshall, Malcolm, ed. *Proud Americans*. S.p., 1994.

Marshall, S.L.A. *Men Against Fire*. Alexandria, Va.: Byrrd Enterprises, 1961.

Martin, George E. *Blow, Bugle, Blow*. Bradenton, Fla.: Opuscula Press, 1986.

Martin, Ralph. *Boy from Nebraska: The Story of Ben Kuroki*. New York: Harper & Brothers, 1946.

Martin, Ralph G. *The G.I. War, 1941–1945*. Boston: Little, Brown, 1967.

Maslowski, Peter. *Armed with Cameras: The American Military Photographers of World War II*. New York: Free Press, 1993.

Mason, David. *Salerno: Foothold in Europe*. New York: Ballantine, 1972.

Mason, John T., Jr. *The Atlantic War Remembered*. Annapolis, Md.: U.S. Naval Institute, 1990.

Masson, Georgina. *The Companion Guide to Rome*. New York: Prentice Hall, 1986.

Masterman, J. C. *The Double-Cross System in the War of 1939 to 1945*. New Haven: Yale University Press, 1972.

Matloff, Maurice. *Strategic Planning for Coalition Warfare, 1943–1944. USAWWII*. Washington, D.C.: Center of Military History, 1994.

Matloff, Maurice, and Edwin M. Snell. *Strategic Planning for Coalition Warfare, 1941–1942. USAWWII*. Washington, D.C.: Office of the Chief of Military History, 1953.

Mauldin, Bill. *The Brass Ring*. New York: W. W. Norton, 1971.

———. *Up Front*. New York: Henry Holt, 1944.

Mayo, Lida. *The Ordnance Department: On Beachhead and Battlefront. USAWWII*. Washington, D.C.: U.S. Army, 1968.

McCallum, Neil. *Journey with a Pistol*. London: Gollancz, 1959.

McKeogh, Michael J., and Richard Lockridge. *Sgt. Mickey and General Ike*. New York: G. P. Putnam's Sons, 1946.

McManus, John C. *The Deadly Brotherhood*. Novato, Calif.: Presidio Press, 1998.

McMillan, Richard. *Twenty Angels over Rome*. London: Jarrolds, 1945.

Meachem, Jon. *Franklin and Winston*. New York: Random House, 2003.

Menen, Aubrey. *Four Days of Naples*. New York: Seaview, 1979.

Middleton, Drew. *Our Share of Night*. New York: Viking, 1946.

Miller, Donald L. *Masters of the Air*. New York: Simon & Schuster, 2006.

Miller, Lee G. *An Ernie Pyle Album*. New York: William Sloane, 1946.

———. *The Story of Ernie Pyle*. New York: Viking, 1950.

Miller, Merle. *Ike the Soldier*. New York: G. P. Putnam's Sons, 1987.

Milligan, Spike. *Mussolini: His Part in My Downfall*. London: Michael Joseph, 1978.

———. *Where Have All the Bullets Gone?* London: M&J Hobbs, 1985.

Mitchell, George C. *Matthew B. Ridgway: Soldier, Statesman, Scholar, Citizen*. Mechanicsburg, Pa.: Stackpole, 2002.

Mittelman, Joseph B. *Eight Stars to Victory*. Washington, D.C.: Ninth Infantry Division Association, 1948.

Molony, C.J.C. *The Mediterranean and Middle East*. Vol. 6, Part 1, *Victory in the Mediterranean. History of the Second World War*. London: Naval & Military Press, 2004.

Molony, C.J.C., et al. *The Mediterranean and Middle East*. Vol. 5, *The Campaign in Sicily and the Campaign in Italy. History of the Second World War*. London: Her Majesty's Stationery Office, 1973.

Montagu, Ewen. *Beyond Top Secret ULTRA*. New York: Coward-McCann, 1978.

———. *The Man Who Never Was*. New York: Bantam, 1969.

Montgomery, Viscount of Alamein. *El Alamein to the River Sangro*. London: Barrie & Jenkins, 1973.

Moorehead, Alan. *Eclipse*. New York: Harper & Row, 1968.

———. *Montgomery*. New York: Coward-McCann, 1946.

Moran, Lord. *Churchill: Taken from the Diaries of Lord Moran*. Boston: Houghton Mifflin, 1966.

Morgan, Kay Summersby. *Past Forgetting*. New York: Simon & Schuster, 1976.

Morison, Samuel Eliot. *History of United States Naval Operations in World War II*. Vol. 9, *Sicily-Salerno-Anzio, January 1943–June 1944*. Edison, N.J.: Castle Books, 2001.

———. *The Two-Ocean War*. New York: Galahad Books, 1997.

Morris, Eric. *Circles of Hell: The War in Italy, 1943–1945*. New York: Crown, 1993.

———. *Salerno: A Military Fiasco*. New York: Stein & Day, 1983.

Morton, H. V. *A Traveller in Rome*. London: Methuen, 1957.

———. *A Traveller in Southern Italy*. London: Methuen, 1969.

Mowat, Farley. *And No Birds Sang*. Boston: Little, Brown, 1979.

———. *The Regiment*. Toronto: McClelland & Stewart, 1981.

Muggeridge, Malcolm. *The Infernal Grove*. New York: William Morrow, 1974.

Muir, Malcolm, Jr., ed. *The Human Tradition in the World War II Era*. Wilmington, Del.: SR Books, 2001.

Muirhead, John. *Those Who Fall*. New York: Random House, 1986.

Munsell, Warren P., Jr. *The Story of a Regiment*. New York: S. p., 1946.

Munthe, Malcolm. *Sweet Is War*. London: Gerald Duckworth, 1954.

Murphy, Audie. *To Hell and Back*. New York: MJF Books, 1977.

Murphy, Robert. *Diplomat Among Warriors*. Garden City, N.Y.: Doubleday, 1964.

Mussolini, Benito. *My Rise and Fall*. New York: Da Capo Press, 1998.

Nalty, Bernard C. *Strength for the Fight*. New York: Free Press, 1986.

Nalty, Bernard C., et al. *With Courage: The U.S. Army Air Forces in World War II*. Washington, D.C.: Air Force History and Museums Program, 1994.

*Naples with Pompeii & the Amalfi Coast*. New York: DK Publishing, 2003.

Nasse, Jean-Yves. *Green Devils*. Paris: Histoire & Collections, 1997.

Neillands, Robin. *Eighth Army*. Woodstock, N.Y.: Overlook, 2004.

Nelson, Guy. *Thunderbird*. Oklahoma City, Okla.: 45th Div Association, 1970.

Neville, Peter. *Mussolini*. London: Routledge, 2004.

*The New Yorker Book of War Pieces*. New York: Schocken Books, 1998.

Nicholas, Lynn H. *The Rape of Europa*. New York: Vintage, 1995.

Nichols, David, ed. *Ernie's War*. New York: Touchstone, 1986.

Nicholson, G.W.L. *The Canadians in Italy, 1943–1945*. Vol. 2. Ottawa: Canadian Minister of National Defence, 1956.

Nicolson, Nigel. *Alex: The Life of Field Marshall Earl Alexander of Tunis*. New York: Atheneum, 1973.

———. *The Grenadier Guards in the War of 1939–1945*. Vol. 2. Aldershot, U.K.: Gale & Polden, 1949.

North, John, ed. *The Alexander Memoirs, 1940–1945*. New York: McGraw-Hill, 1962.

Norwich, John Julius. *The Middle Sea: A History of the Mediterranean*. New York: Doubleday, 2006.

O'Donnell, Patrick K. *Beyond Valor*. New York: Touchstone, 2001.

———. *Operatives, Spies, and Saboteurs*. New York: Free Press, 2004.

Orange, Vincent. *Coningham*. Washington, D.C.: Center for Air Force History, 1992.

———. *Tedder: Quietly in Command*. London: Frank Cass, 2004.

Origo, Iris. *War in Val D'Orcia*. Boston: David R. Godine, 1984.

O'Rourke, R. J. *Anzio Annie: She Was No Lady*. S.p., 1995.

Orpen, Neil. *Victory in Italy*. Cape Town, South Africa: Purnell, 1975.

Otway, T.B.H. *Airborne Forces*. London: Imperial War Museum, 1990.

Overy, Richard. *Why the Allies Won*. New York: W. W. Norton, 1997.

Pack, S.W.C. *Operation Husky*. New York: Hippocrene, 1977.

Packe, Michael. *First Airborne*. London: Secker & Warburg, 1948.

Pal, Dharm. *The Campaign in Italy, 1943–1945*. Calcutta: Combined Inter-services Historical Section, 1960.

Palmer, Bennett J. *The Hunter and the Hunted*. S.p., 2002.

Palmer, Robert R., et al. *The Procurement and Training of Ground Combat Troops. USAWWII*. Washington, D.C.: Center of Military History, 1991.

Pantanelli, Tonino. *Cassino Through the Ages*. Cassino, Italy: Tourist Board of Cassino, n.d.

Parker, Matthew. *Monte Cassino*. London: Headline, 2003.

Parkinson, Roger. *A Day's March Nearer Home*. New York: David McKay, 1974.

Parris, John A., Jr., and Ned Russell. *Springboard to Berlin*. New York: Thomas Y. Crowell, 1943.

Parton, James. *"Air Force Spoken Here": General Ira Eaker and the Command of the Air*. Bethesda, Md.: Adler & Adler, 1986.

Patton, George S. *War as I Knew It*. Boston: Houghton Mifflin, 1975.

Patton, Robert H. *The Pattons*. Washington, D.C.: Brassey's, 1994.

Pawle, Gerald. *The War and Colonel Warden*. New York: Knopf, 1963.

Pearl, Jack. *Blood-and-Guts Patton*. Derby, Conn.: Monarch Books, 1961.

Pearlman, Michael D. *To Make Democracy Safe for America*. Urbana: University of Illinois Press, 1984.

———. *Warmaking and American Democracy*. Lawrence, Kans.: University Press of Kansas, 1999.

Peckham, Howard H., and Shirley A. Snyder, eds. *Letters from Fighting Hoosiers*. Bloomington, Ind.: Indiana War History Commission, 1948.

Peek, H. Clifford, Jr., ed. *Five Years, Five Countries, Five Campaigns*. Munich, Germany: 141st Infantry Regiment Association, 1945.

Pellegrinelli, Marco. *La Battaglia di S. Pietro di John Huston*. Venafro, Italy: Edizioni Eva, 2001.

Peltier, Jean Gordon. *World War II Diary of Jean Gordon Peltier*. Groveland, Calif.: PerfectArt, 1998.

Perkins, Norris H. *North African Odyssey*. S.p., n.d.

Perret, Geoffrey. *There's a War to Be Won*. New York: Ballantine, 1991.

———. *Winged Victory*. New York: Random House, 1993.

Perry, Milton F., and Barbara W. Parke. *Patton and His Pistols*. Harrisburg, Pa.: Stackpole, 1957.

Persons, Benjamin S. *Relieved of Command*. Manhattan, Kans.: Sunflower University Press, 1997.

Pesce, Angelo. *Salerno 1943: Operation Avalanche*. Naples: Falcon Press, 1993.

Petruzzi, Daniel J. *My War Against the Land of My Ancestors*. Irving, Tex.: Fusion Press, 2000.

Philips, Henry Gerard. *The Making of a Professional: Manton S. Eddy, USA*. Westport, Conn.: Greenwood Press, 2000.

Philips, N. C. *Official History of New Zealand in the Second World War*. Vol. 1. Wellington, N.Z.: War History Branch, Department of Internal Affairs, 1957.

*A Pictorial History of the 36th Texas Infantry Division*. Austin, Tex.: 36th Division Association, 1946.

Piekalkiewicz, Janusz. *The Battle for Cassino*. Indianapolis: Bobbs-Merrill, 1980.

Pogue, Forrest C. *George C. Marshall: Organizer of Victory*. New York: Viking, 1973.

Pond, Hugh. *Salerno*. Boston: Little, Brown, 1961.

Pope, Dudley. *Flag 4: The Battle of Coastal Forces in the Mediterranean*. London: William Kimber, 1954.

Pöppel, Martin. *Heaven & Hell: The War Diary of a German Paratrooper*. Trans. Louise Willmot. Staplehurst, Kent, U.K.: Spellmount, 2000.

Porch, Douglas. *The Path to Victory*. New York: Farrar, Straus and Giroux, 2004.

Portelli, Alessandro. *The Order Has Been Carried Out*. New York: Palgrave Macmillan, 2003.

Potter, Neil, and Jack Frost. *The Queen Mary*. New York: John Day, 1961.

Powers, Alice Leccese. *Italy, in Mind*. New York: Vintage Books, 1997.

Prasad, Bishenwar, ed. *Official History of the Indian Armed Forces in the Second World War 1939–1945: The Campaign in Italy, 1943–45*. Delhi: Orient Longmans, 1960.

Pratt, Fletcher. *Eleven Generals: Studies in American Command*. New York: William Sloane, 1949.

Pratt, Sherman W. *Autobahn to Berchtesgaden*. Baltimore: Gateway Press, 1992.

Price, Frank James. *Troy H. Middleton: A Biography*. Baton Rouge: Louisiana State University Press, 1974.

*The Princeton Class of 1942 During World War II*. S.p., 2000.

Putkowski, Julian, and Julian Sykes. *Shot at Dawn*. London: Leo Cooper, 1992.

Pyle, Ernie. *Brave Men*. New York: Henry Holt, 1944.

Randle, Edwin Hubert. *Ernie Pyle Comes Ashore and Other Stories*. Clearwater, Fla.: Eldnar Press, 1972.

Ray, Cyril. *Algiers to Austria*. London: Eyre & Spottiswoode, 1952.

Reagen, Geoffrey. *Blue on Blue: A History of Friendly Fire*. New York: Avon Books, 1995.

Reilly, Michael F. *Reilly of the White House*. New York: Simon & Schuster, 1947.

Reit, Seymour. *Masquerade*. New York: Hawthorn, 1978.

Reminick, Gerald. *Nightmare in Bari*. Palo Alto, Calif.: Glencannon Press, 2001.

Renehan, Edward J., Jr. *The Lion's Pride*. New York: Oxford University Press, 1998.

*Reporting World War II*. Vols. 1 and 2. New York: Library of America, 1995.

Reynolds, Quentin. *By Quentin Reynolds*. New York: McGraw-Hill, 1963.

———. *The Curtain Rises*. New York: Random House, 1944.

Richardson, Charles. *Flashback*. London: William Kimber, 1985.

———. *From Churchill's Secret Circle to the BBC*. London: Brassey's, 1991.

———. *Send for Freddie*. London: William Kimber, 1987.

Ridgway, Matthew B. *Soldier: The Memoirs of Matthew B. Ridgway*. New York: Harper & Brothers, 1956.

Risch, Erna. *The Quartermaster Corps: Organization, Supply, and Services*. Vol. 1, *USAWWII*. Washington, D.C.: Department of the Army, 1953.

Risch, Erna, and Chester L. Kieffer. *The Quartermaster Corps: Organization, Supply, and Services*. Vol. 2, *USAWWII*. Washington, D.C.: Department of the Army, 1955.

Roach, Peter. *The 8.15 to War*. London: Leo Cooper, 1982.

Robinson, Don. *News of the 45th*. New York: Grosset & Dunlap, 1944.

Robson, Walter. *Letters from a Soldier*. London: Faber and Faber, 1960.

Roe, Tom. *Anzio Beachhead: Diary of a Signaller*. S.p., 1988.

Rollyson, Carl. *Nothing Ever Happens to the Brave*. New York: St. Martin's Press, 1990.

Romeiser, John B. *Combat Reporter: Don Whitehead's World War II Diary and Memoirs*. New York: Fordham University Press, 2006.

Roosevelt, Eleanor Butler. *Day Before Yesterday*. Garden City, N.Y.: Doubleday, 1959.

Roosevelt, Elliott. *As He Saw It*. New York: Duell, Sloan & Pearce, 1946.

Roskill, S. W. *The War at Sea, 1939–1945*. Vol. 3, Part I. London: Her Majesty's Stationery Office, 1960.

————. *White Ensign*. Annapolis, Md.: U.S. Naval Institute, 1960.

Ross, J. A. *Memoirs of an Army Surgeon*. Edinburgh: William Blackwood, 1948.

Rossi, Francesco, and Silvano Casaldi. *Those Days at Nettuno*. Nettuno, Italy: Edizioni Abete, 1989.

Roush, John H., ed. *World War II Reminiscences*. S.p., 1996.

Ruggero, Ed. *Combat Jump*. New York: HarperCollins, 2003.

Rush, Robert S. *The U.S. Infantryman in World War II*. Botley, Oxford, U.K.: Osprey, 2003.

Rust, Kenn C. *Fifteenth Air Force Story*. Terre Haute, Ind.: Sunshine House, 1976.

————. *Twelfth Air Force Story*. Temple City, Calif.: Historical Aviation, 1975.

Ryder, Rowland. *Oliver Leese*. London: Hamish Hamilton, 1987.

Salerno, Reynolds M. *Vital Crossroads*. Ithaca, N.Y.: Cornell University Press, 2002.

*Salerno: The American Operation from the Beaches to the Volturno*. Washington, D.C.: Center of Military History, 1990.

Salter, Fred H. *Recon Scout*. New York: Ballantine, 1994.

Salter, Krewasky A. *Combat Multipliers: African-American Soldiers in Four Wars*. Fort Leavenworth, Kans.: Combat Studies Institute Press, 2003.

Samwell, H. P. *An Infantry Officer with the Eighth Army*. Edinburgh: William Blackwood, 1945.

Sandler, Stanley. *Segregated Skies*. Washington, D.C.: Smithsonian Institution Press, 1992.

Saunders, Hilary St. George. *The Red Beret*. Nashville: Battery Press, 1985.

Schrijvers, Peter. *The Crash of Ruin*. New York: New York University Press, 1998.

Scott, Hugh A. *The Blue and White Devils*. Nashville: Battery Press, 1984.

Scott, Jack L. *Combat Engineer*. Baltimore: American Literary Press, 1999.

Scrivener, Jane. *Inside Rome with the Germans*. New York: Macmillan, 1945.

Seago, Edward. *With the Allied Armies in Italy*. London: Collins, 1945.

Seale, William. *The President's House*. Vol. 2. Washington, D.C.: White House Historical Association, 1986.

Semmes, Harry H. *Portrait of Patton*. New York: Appleton-Century-Crofts, 1955.

Sevareid, Eric. *Not So Wild a Dream*. New York: Atheneum, 1976.

Seymour, William. *Yours to Reason Why*. New York: St. Martin's Press, 1982.

Shaffer, Roger L. *Letters Home: A Soldier's Legacy*. Plano, Tex.: Republic of Texas Press, 1997.

Shama, H. Rex. *Pulse and Repulse*. Austin, Tex.: Eakin Press, 1995.

Shapiro, L.S.B. *They Left the Back Door Open*. Toronto: Ryerson, 1944.

Sheehan, Fred. *Anzio: Epic of Bravery*. Norman, Okla.: University of Oklahoma Press, 1964.

Sheffield, G. D., ed. *Leadership and Command*. London: Brassey's, 1997.

Shephard, Ben. *A War of Nerves*. Cambridge, Mass.: Harvard University Press, 2001.

Shepperd, G. A. *The Italian Campaign, 1943–1945*. New York: Praeger, 1968.

Sherwood, Robert. *Roosevelt and Hopkins: An Intimate History*. New York: Harper & Brothers, 1948.

Shirley, John. *I Remember: Stories of a Combat Infantryman in World War II*. Livermore, Calif.: Camino Press, 1993.

Short, Neil. *German Defences in Italy in World War II*. Botley, Oxford, U.K.: Osprey, 2006.

Showalter, Dennis. *Patton and Rommel*. New York: Berkley Caliber, 2005.

*The Sicilian Campaign*. Washington, D.C.: Department of the Navy, 1945.

Silvestri, Ennio. *The Long Road to Rome*. S.p., 1994.

Simpson, Harold B. *Audie Murphy, American Soldier*. Hillsboro, Tex.: Hill Junior College Press, 1975.

Simpson, Michael. *A Life of Admiral of the Fleet Andrew Cunningham*. London: Frank Cass, 2004.

Singleton-Gates, Peter. *General Lord Freyberg VC*. London: Michael Joseph, 1963.

Sixsmith, E.K.G. *Eisenhower as Military Commander*. New York: Da Capo Press, 1972.

Skorzeny, Otto. *Skorzeny's Secret Missions: War Memoirs of the Most Dangerous Man in Europe.* Trans. Jacques Le Clercq. New York: Dutton, 1950.

Slessor, John. *The Central Blue.* New York: Praeger, 1957.

Smith, Albert H., Jr. *The Sicily Campaign: Recollections of an Infantry Company Commander.* Blue Bell, Pa.: Society of the First Infantry Division, 2001.

Smith, Denis Mack. *Mussolini.* New York: Knopf, 1982.

Smith, E. D. *The Battles for Cassino.* New York: Scribners, 1975.

Smith, Lee Carraway. *A River Swift and Deadly.* Austin, Tex.: Eakin Press, 1989.

Snowden, Frank M. *The Conquest of Malaria: Italy, 1900–1962.* New Haven: Yale University Press, 2006.

Soffer, Jonathan M. *General Matthew B. Ridgway: From Progressivism to Reaganism, 1895–1993.* Westport, Conn.: Praeger, 1998.

Southern, George. *Poisonous Inferno.* Shrewsbury, U.K.: Airlife, 2002.

Spector, Ronald H. *At War at Sea.* New York: Viking, 2002.

Spiller, Roger J., ed. *Dictionary of American Military Biography.* Westport, Conn.: Greenwood Press, 1984.

Spivey, Samuel David. *A Doughboy's Narrative.* S.p., 1995.

Springer, Joseph A. *Black Devil Brigade.* New York: ibooks, 2001.

Staiger, Jörg. *Anzio-Nettuno.* Neckargemünd, [West] Germany: Kurt Vowinckel, 1962.

Stainforth, Peter. *Wings of the Wind.* London: Arms & Armour, 1982.

Starr, Chester G., ed. *From Salerno to the Alps.* Washington, D.C.: Infantry Journal Press, 1948.

*Statistical Review World War II.* Washington, D.C.: War Department, U.S. Army Service Forces, 1946.

Stegall, James R. *Grasshopper Pilot: Salerno to the Yalu.* Ravenhaus Press, 2002.

Steinbeck, John. *Once There Was a War.* New York: Viking, 1958.

Steinhof, Johannes. *Messerschmitts over Sicily.* Baltimore: Nautical and Aviation Publishing, 1987.

Stenbuck, Jack, ed. *Typewriter Battalion.* New York: William Morrow, 1995.

Stephen, Martin. *The Fighting Admirals: British Admirals of the Second World War.* Annapolis, Md.: Naval Institute Press, 1991.

Stern, Michael. *Into the Jaws of Death.* New York: Robert M. McBride, 1944.

Stevens, G. R. *Fourth Indian Division.* Toronto: McLaren and Son, n.d.

Stevens, W. G. *Freyberg, V.C., The Man, 1939–1945.* Wellington, N.Z.: Reed, 1965.

Stiles, Bert. *Serenade to the Big Red.* New York: W. W. Norton, 1947.

Stilwell, Joseph W., and Theodore H. White, ed. *The Stilwell Papers.* New York: William Sloane, 1948.

Stimson, Henry L., and McGeorge Bundy. *On Active Service in Peace and War.* New York: Harper, 1947.

Stoler, Mark A. *Allies and Adversaries.* Chapel Hill, N.C.: University of North Carolina Press, 2000.

———. *George C. Marshall: Soldier-Statesman of the American Century.* New York: Twayne, 1989.

Stradling, Harriet, ed. *Johnny.* Salt Lake City: Bookcraft, 1946.

Strong, Kenneth. *Intelligence at the Top.* Garden City, N.Y.: Doubleday, 1969.

Strutton, Bill, and Michael Pearson. *The Beachhead Spies.* New York: Ace Books, 1958.

Sulzberger, C. L. *A Long Row of Candles.* New York: Macmillan, 1969.

Summersby, Kay. *Eisenhower Was My Boss.* New York: Prentice-Hall, 1948.

Taggart, Donald G. *History of the Third Infantry Division in World War II.* Washington, D.C.: Infantry Journal Press, 1947.

Tapert, Annette, ed. *Lines of Battle.* New York: Times Books, 1987.

Tayloe, Roberta Love. *Combat Nurse.* Santa Barbara, Calif.: Fithian Press, 1988.

Taylor, John M. *General Maxwell Taylor: The Sword and the Pen*. New York: Doubleday, 1989.

Taylor, Maxwell D. *Swords and Plowshares*. New York: W. W. Norton, 1972.

Tedder, Lord. *With Prejudice*. Boston: Little, Brown, 1966.

Terlecki, Olgierd. *Poles in the Italian Campaign, 1943–1945*. Warsaw: Council for Protection of Monuments of Struggle and Martyrdom, 1972.

Thompson, W. H. *I Was Churchill's Shadow*. London: Christopher Johnson, 1951.

Thruelsen, Richard, and Elliot Arnold. *Mediterranean Sweep*. New York: Duell, Sloan & Pearce, 1944.

Thucydides. *History of the Peloponnesian War*. Trans. Rex Warner. London: Penguin, 1972.

Tickell, Jerrard. *Ascalon*. London: Hodder & Stoughton, 1964.

*The Tiger Triumphs*. London: H.M. Stationery Office, 1946.

Tobin, James. *Ernie Pyle's War*. Lawence, Kans.: University Press of Kansas, 1997.

Toland, John. *Adolf Hitler*. New York: Ballantine, 1981.

Tompkins, Peter. *Italy Betrayed*. New York: Simon & Schuster, 1966.

Towne, Allen N. *Doctor Danger Forward*. Jefferson, N.C.: McFarland, 2000.

Tregaskis, Richard. *Invasion Diary*. New York: Random House, 1944.

Trevelyan, Raleigh. *Rome '44*. New York: Viking, 1981.

Truscott, L. K., Jr. *Command Missions*. New York: E. P. Dutton, 1954.

Tully, Grace. *F.D.R., My Boss*. New York: Scribners, 1949.

Valentine, A. W. *We Landed in Sicily and Italy: A Story of the Devons*. Aldershot, U.K.: Gale & Polden, 1943.

Van Creveld, Martin. *Supplying War*. Cambridge: Cambridge University Press, 1977.

Vaughan-Thomas, Wynford. *Anzio*. New York: Holt, Rinehart & Winston, 1961.

Verney, Peter. *Anzio 1944: An Unexpected Fury*. London: B. T. Batsford, 1978.

Vian, Philip. *Action This Day*. London: Frederick Miller, 1960.

Vigneras, Marcel. *Rearming the French. USAWWII*. Washington, D.C.: Department of the Army, 1957.

Vining, Donald, ed. *American Diaries of World War II*. New York: Pepys Press, 1982.

Vokes, Chris. *Vokes: My Story*. Ottawa: Gallery Books, 1985.

Von Senger und Etterlin, Frido. *Neither Fear nor Hope*. Novato, Calif.: Presidio Press, 1989.

Voss, Frederick S. *Reporting the War*. Washington, D.C.: Smithsonian Press, 1994.

Wade, Betsy, ed. *Forward Positions: The War Correspondence of Homer Bigart*. Fayetteville, Ark.: University of Arkansas Press, 1992.

Wagner, Robert L. *The Texas Army*. Austin: S.p., 1972.

Walker, Fred L. *From Texas to Rome*. Dallas: Taylor Publishing, 1969.

Wallace, Robert. *The Italian Campaign*. Alexandria, Va.: Time-Life Books, 1978.

Walters, Vernon A. *Silent Missions*. Garden City, N.Y.: Doubleday, 1978.

Wandrey, June. *Bedpan Commando*. Elmore, Ohio: Elmore Publishing, 1989.

Warlimont, Walter. *Inside Hitler's Headquarters, 1939–1945*. Trans. R. H. Barry. Novato, Calif.: Presidio Press, 1964.

Warner, Phillip. *Horrocks: The General Who Led from the Front*. London: Hamish Hamilton, 1984.

Warren, John C. *Airborne Missions in the Mediterranean, 1942–1945*. USAF Historical Division, Air University, 1955.

Waugh, Evelyn. *The End of the Battle*. Boston: Back Bay Books, 2000.

Weckstein, Leon. *Through My Eyes*. Central Point, Ore.: Hellgate Press, 1999.

Wedemeyer, Albert C. *Wedemeyer Reports!* New York: Henry Holt, 1958.

Weigley, Russell F. *The American Way of War*. Bloomington: Indiana University Press, 1977.

Weinberg, Gerhard L. *A World at Arms*. Cambridge, U.K.: Cambridge University Press, 1995.

Welker, Robert H. *A Different Drummer*. Boston: Beacon Press, 1958.

Wellard, James. *The Man in a Helmet*. London: Eyre & Spottiswoode, 1947.

Wells, Lloyd M. *From Anzio to the Alps.* Columbia, Mo.: University of Missouri Press, 2004.

Westermann, Edward B. *Flak.* Lawrence, Kans.: University Press of Kansas, 2001.

Westmoreland, William C. *A Soldier Reports.* Garden City, N.Y.: Doubleday, 1976.

*What to Do Aboard a Transport.* Washington, D.C.: Science Service, 1943.

Wheeler, William Reginald, ed. *The Road to Victory: A History of Hampton Roads Port of Embarkation in World War II.* Vol. 1. Newport News, Va.: Yale University Press, 1946.

White, Nathan William. *From Fedala to Berchtesgaden.* 1974.

Whitehead, Don. *"Beachhead Don."* John B. Romeiser, ed. New York: Fordham University Press, 2004.

Whitehead, Ernest D. *World War II: An Ex-Sergeant Remembers.* Kearney, Neb.: Morris Publishing, 1996.

Whiting, Charles. *Bradley.* New York: Ballantine, 1971.

Whitlock, Flint. *The Rock of Anzio.* Boulder, Colo.: Westview, 1998.

Williams, David. *Liners in Battledress.* St. Catharines, Ontario: Vanwell Publishing, 1989.

Williams, Mary H., ed. *Chronology, 1941–1945. USAWWII.* Washington, D.C.: U.S. Army, 1960.

Wilson, Field-Marshall Lord. *Eight Years Overseas.* London: Hutchinson, 1950.

Wilt, Alan F. *War from the Top.* Bloomington: Indiana University Press, 1990.

Wiltse, Charles M. *The Medical Department: Medical Service in the Mediterranean and Minor Theaters. USAWWII.* Washington, D.C.: Center of Military History, 1987.

Winterbotham, F. W. *The Ultra Secret.* New York: Harper & Row, 1974.

Winton, John. *Cunningham.* London: John Murray, 1998.

Wiskemann, Elizabeth. *The Rome-Berlin Axis.* New York: Oxford University Press, 1949.

Woerpel, Don. *A Hostile Sky.* Marshall, Wis.: Andon Press, 1977.

Wood, Alan. *The Glider Soldiers.* Tunbridge Wells, U.K.: Spellmount, 1992.

Woodruff, William. *Vessel of Sadness.* Carbondale, Ill.: Southern Illinois University Press, 1978.

Young, Desmond. *Rommel, the Desert Fox.* New York: Harper & Row, 1950.

Zambardi, Maurizio. *Memorie di guerra.* Venafro, Italy: Edizioni Eva, n.d. Trans. Robert Harp, for author. Also trans. by Monia Cozzolino as *War Memories.* Venafro, Italy: www.edizionieva.com, 2006.

———. *San Pietro Infine.* Trans. Geny Di Palo. S.p., 1998.

Zuckerman, Solly. *From Apes to Warlords.* New York: Harper & Row, 1978.

Zuehlke, Mark. *The Gothic Line.* Vancouver: Douglas & McIntyre, 2003.

———. *The Liri Valley.* Toronto: Stoddart, 2001.

———. *Ortona.* Toronto: Stoddart, 1999.

## PERIODICALS

Aarons, George. "Cameraman in Cassino." *Yank* (May 21, 1944): 3+.

Abati, Anthony J. "Cisterna di Littoria: A Brave Yet Futile Effort." *Army History* (fall 1991): 13+.

Adams, Henry M. "Allied Military Government in Sicily 1943." *Military Affairs* (fall 1951): 157+.

"Allen and His Men." *Time* 42, no. 6 (Aug. 9, 1943): 30+.

Andrus, Clift. "Troina Addenda." *Field Artillery Journal* (March 1944): 163+.

" 'Anything, Anytime, Anywhere Bar Nothing': Remembering 'Paddy' Flint." *Journal of America's Military Past* 24, no. 1 (spring 1967): 52+.

Ardery, Philip P. "A Veteran of the August 1943 Ploesti Raid." *World War II* (July 2001): 85+.

Ashmore, William G. "Supply Planning for Beachhead Operations." *Quartermaster Review* (Jan.–Feb. 1945): 18+.

Banks, William D. "Target: Ploesti." *Harper's* 188, no. 1126 (March 1944): 299+.

"Battle Casualties." *Infantry Journal* (Sept. 1949): 18+.

"The Battle for San Pietro." *After the Battle*, no. 18 (1997): 1+.

"The Battle for Troina." *Life* (Aug. 30, 1943): 28+.

Baxter, W. C. "Goums Marocains." *Cavalry Journal* 53, no. 2 (March–Apr. 1944): 62+.

"Beachhead Offensive." *Newsweek* (June 5, 1944): 23.

Beard, Travis. "Turning the Tide at Salerno." *Naval History* 17, no. 5 (Oct. 2003): 34+.

Belden, Jack. "Battle of Sicily." *Time* 42, no. 4 (July 26, 1943): 27+.

Bess, Demaree. "Power Politics Succeeded in Italy." *Saturday Evening Post* (Oct. 30, 1943): 20+.

Biddle, George. "Report from the Italian Front." *Life* 16, no. 2 (Jan. 3, 1944): 13+.

Blumenson, Martin. "Sicily and Italy: Why and What For?" *Military Review* (Feb. 1966): 61+.

Cairns, Bogardus S. "The Breakout at Anzio." *Military Review* (Jan. 1949): 23+.

Capa, Robert. "The Surrender of Palermo." *Life* 15, no. 8 (Aug. 23, 1943): 25+.

"Censorship Takes Anzio." *Time* (Feb. 28, 1944): 46.

Clagett, John. "Admiral H. Kent Hewitt, U.S. Navy." *Naval College Review*. Two parts (summer and fall 1975): 60+, 72+.

Clark, Mark W. "Salerno." *After the Battle*, no. 95 (1997): 1+.

Cochran, Alexander S., Jr. "Low as We Could Go." *Military History* (Apr. 1985): 42+.

Collier, Cameron D. "Tiny Miracle: The Proximity Fuze." *Naval History* (July–Aug. 1999): 43+.

Connor, A. O. "On the Defense: Notes from the Anzio Beachhead." *Infantry Journal* (July 1944): 35+.

Couch, Joseph R. "Breaking the Gustav Line." *Field Artillery Journal* 34, no. 8 (Aug. 1944): 506+.

Crosswell, D.K.R. "The Chief of Staff." *Indiana Military History Journal* 13, no. 1 (Jan. 1988): 3+.

Cruse, Don. "Operation Torch 1942." *Aerograph, National Weather Service Newsletter* 22, no. 2 (May 1998).

Dahlen, Chester A. "Defense of a River Line." *Military Review* 29, no. 11 (Feb. 1950): 30+.

Darnell, Donald P. "Brigadier General Theodore Roosevelt, Jr." *World War II* (May 1998): 18+.

"Defender of Empire." *Time* (Feb. 28, 1944): 28+.

Denno, Bryce F. "Allen and Huebner: Contrast in Command." *Army* (June 1984): 62+.

———. "Eight-Ball Cannoneers." *Field Artillery Journal* (Jan.–Feb. 1983): 12+.

D'Este, Carlo. "The Slaps Heard Round the World." *MHQ: The Quarterly Journal of Military History* 8, no. 2 (winter 1996): 64+.

Deutschman, Paul E. "After the Battles." *Life* (June 19, 1944): 53+.

Diamond, William J. "Water Is Life." *Military Engineer* (Aug. 1947): 330+.

"Did Strategic Bombing Work?" *MHQ: The Quarterly Journal of Military History* 8, no. 3 (spring 1996): 29+.

Dixon, Thomas W. "Terry Allen." *Army* (April 1978): 57+.

D'Orsa, Charles S. "The Trials and Tribulations of an Army G-4." *Military Review* 25, no. 4 (July 1945): 23+.

Dzibuan, Stanley W. "When Engineers Fight as Infantry." *Army* (Sept. 1962): 68+.

Ellis, Lewis N. "Ploesti: A Pilot's Diary." *American Heritage* 34 (Oct.–Nov. 1983): 77+.

Essame, H. "A Controversial Campaign—Italy, 1943–45." *Army Quarterly and Defence Journal* (Jan. 1968): 219+.

"The Fall of Rome." *Life* (July 14, 1944): 38.

"FHQu Wolfsschanze." *After the Battle*, no. 19 (1977): 28+.

Fisher, Ernest F. "A Classic Stratagem on Monte Artemisio." *Military Review* (Feb. 1963): 79+.

Fitzpatrick, G.R.D. "Anzio and Its Lessons." *Military Review* (July 1951): 97+.

Fleisher, Bob. "Truscott Leads Memorial Day Rites." *Stars and Stripes* 2, no. 174 (May 31, 1945): 1.

Fuller, J.F.C. "The Why and Wherefore of the Italian Offensive." *Newsweek* (June 5, 1944): 22.

"G.I. Nightingale." *Time* (Feb. 28, 1944): 88.

Gavin, James M. "Airborne Plans and Operations in the Mediterranean Theater." *Infantry Journal* (Aug. 1946): 22+.

———. "Paratroops over Sicily." *Infantry Journal* (Nov. 1945): 25+.

Geake, Robert. "Mule Pack Trains in Italy." *Cavalry Journal* (March–Apr. 1944): 74+.

Gellhorn, Martha. "Cracking the Gothic Line." *Collier's* (Oct. 28, 1944): 24+.

"Geoffrey Keyes." *Assembly* (Sept. 1973): 121.

Gervasi, Frank. "Alexander the Modest." *Collier's* (Feb. 12, 1944): 13+.

———. "Battle at Cassino." *Collier's* (March 18, 1944): 20+.

Giangreco, D. M. "Spinning the Casualties: Media Strategies During the Roosevelt Administration." *Passport* 35, no. 3 (Dec. 2004): 22+.

Goldsmith, R.F.K. "The Development of Air Power in Joint Operations." *Army Quarterly and Defence Journal*, part 2 (Oct. 1967): 59+.

Gordon, John E. "The Strategic and Tactical Influence of Disease in World War II." *Military Review* 28, no. 12 (March 1949): 29+.

Gorlinski, Joseph S. "Naples: Case History in Invasion." *Military Engineer* 36 (Apr. 1944): 109+.

Green, John H. "The Battles for Cassino." *After the Battle*, no. 13 (1976): 1+.

Greene, Joseph I. "Operation CORKSCREW: Tough Decision." *Infantry Journal* 59, no. 5 (Nov. 1946): 20+.

Greenwood, John T. "The U.S. Army and Amphibious Warfare During World War II." *Army History* (summer 1993): 1+.

Guild, Walter A. "That Damned Smoke Again." *Infantry Journal* (Oct. 1944): 25+.

Hamburger, Philip. "Letter from Rome." *New Yorker* (July 7, 1944): 52+.

Hamilton. Maxwell. "Junior in Name Only." *The Retired Officer* (June 1981): 28+.

Hanson, Frederick R. "Combat Psychiatry." *Bulletin of the U.S. Army Medical Department* 9 (Nov. 1949).

Harmon, Ernest N. "From the Anzio Beachhead to Viterbo." *Military Review* (Nov. 1944): 38+.

Heiser, Joseph. "Prisoner of War." *T-Patcher News Letter* (winter 2003): 9+.

Heitmann, Jan. " 'Gomorrah'—The Hamburg Firestorm." *After the Battle* 70 (1990): 1+.

Hersey, John. "AMGOT at Work." *Life* 15, no. 8 (Aug. 23, 1943): 25.

———. "Nicosia Battle." *Time* (Aug. 9, 1943): 30+.

Hewitt, H. Kent. "The Allied Navies at Salerno." *United States Naval Institute Proceedings* 79, no. 9 (Sept. 1953): 958+.

———. "Naval Aspects of the Sicilian Campaign." *United States Naval Institute Proceedings* 79, no. 7 (July 1953): 705+.

Higgins, Trumbull. "The Anglo-American Historians' War in the Mediterranean, 1942–1945." *Military Affairs* 34, no. 3 (Oct. 1970): 84+.

Hixson, John A. "Operation SHINGLE: Combined Planning and Preparation." *Military Review* (March 1989): 64+.

Hood, Bruton F. "The Gran Sasso Raid." *Military Review* (Feb. 1959): 55+.

Hussa, Norman. "Action at Salerno." *Infantry Journal* 53, no. 6 (Dec. 1943): 25+.

Hutchinson, William S. "Use of the 4.2-inch Chemical Mortar in the Invasion of Sicily." *Military Review* (Nov. 1943): 13+.

"Italy Looks in Desperation for a Strong Man." *Life* 15, no. 6 (Aug. 9, 1943): 15+.

Jefford, C. G. "Fratricide: An Overview of Friendly Fire Incidents in the 20th Century." *Royal Air Force Historical Society Journal*, no. 34 (2005): 82+.

Kahn, E. J., Jr. "Education of an Army." *New Yorker* 20, no. 35 (Oct. 14, 1944): 21+, and no. 36 (Oct. 21, 1944): 34+.

———. "Something Rotten in the Fruit Salad." *Infantry Journal* (May 1946): 19+.

Keller, E. R. "Quartermasters—Battle-Proved." *Quartermaster Review* (May–June 1944): 24+.

Kent, George. "The Last Days of Dictator Benito Mussolini." *Reader's Digest* (Oct. 1944): 13+.

Kingseed, Cole C. "WWII's Airborne Commanders: 'The Stuff of Instant Legend.' " *Army* (July 1996): 31+.

Kohn, Richard H., ed. "The Scholarship on World War II." *Journal of Military History* 55, no. 3 (July 1991): 365+.

Krammer, Arnold P. "German Prisoners of War in the United States." *Military Affairs* 40, no. 2 (Apr. 1976): 67+.

Lang, Daniel. "Letter from Rome." *New Yorker* (June 17, 1944): 65+.

———. "Letter from Rome." *New Yorker* (June 24, 1944): 52+.

———. "Letter from Rome." *New Yorker* (July 15, 1944).

Lang, Will. "Doughboys' Beachhead." *Time* (Feb. 7, 1944): 22.

———. "Lucian King Truscott, Jr." *Life* (Oct. 2, 1944): 96+.

Lanning, Michael L. "Goodbye to Captain Waskow." *VFW Magazine* (May 1981): 19+.

Lardner, John. "Horrors of War in America." *Newsweek* (July 12, 1943): 12+.

Leighton, Richard M. "Overlord Revisited: An Interpretation of American Strategy in the European War, 1942–1944." *American Historical Review* 68, no. 4 (July 1963): 919+.

———. "Planning for Sicily." *United States Naval Institute Proceedings* (July 1962): 90+.

Lewis, Charles Lee. "The Byzantine Invasion of North Africa, Sicily, and Italy." *United States Naval Institute Proceedings* (Nov. 1943): 1435+.

Liebling, A. J. "Find 'Em, Fix 'Em, and Fight 'Em." *New Yorker* 19, no. 10 (Apr. 24, 1943): 21+, and no. 11 (May 1, 1943): 24+.

"Lieutenant Audie Murphy." *After the Battle*, no. 3 (1973): 28+.

Longmire, Carey. "The Beachhead-Happy Thunderbird." *Saturday Evening Post* (Nov. 30, 1946): 25+.

Lowry, F. J. "The Naval Side of the Anzio Invasion." *United States Naval Institute Proceedings* (Jan. 1954): 22+.

Lytton, Henry D. "Bombing Policy in the Rome and Pre–Normandy Invasion Aerial Campaigns." *Military Affairs* 47, no. 2 (Apr 1983): 53+.

MacLean, French L. "German General Officer Casualties in World War II: Lessons for Future War." *Military Review* 70, no. 4 (April 1990): 45+.

"Major Martin: The Story Continues." *After the Battle*, no. 64 (1989): 41+.

"Malta C.G." *After the Battle*, no. 10 (1975): 1+.

Manson, Morse P., and Harry M. Grayson. "Why 2,776 American Soldiers in the Mediterranean Theater of Operation Were Absent Without Leave." *American Journal of Psychiatry* (July 1946): 50+.

Margry, Karel. "The Invasion of Sicily." *After the Battle*, no. 77 (1992).

———. "Mustard Disaster at Bari." *After the Battle*, no. 79 (1993): 34+.

Matthews, Sidney T. "The French in the Drive on Rome." *Revue Historique de l'Armée.* Special issue, 1957.

McLain, Raymond S., Jr. "LTG Raymond S. McLain." *National Guard* (March 1987): 22+.

Melanephy, James P., and John G. Robinson. "*Savannah* at Salerno." *Surface Warfare* 6, no. 3 (March 1981): 2+.

Meske, Fritz. "The Anzio-Nettuno Bridgehead: A German Account." *Military Review* (June 1944).

———. "Die Wehrmacht." *Military Review* (June 1944).

Miles, Sherman. "Patton Preferred." *Atlantic Monthly* (Dec. 1947): 128+.

Miller, Merle. "Second Battle of Oran." *Yank* 3, no. 49 (25 May 1945): 2+.

Morgan, Roger. "The Man Who Almost Is." *After the Battle*, no. 54 (1986): 1+.

———. "The Second World War's Best Kept Secret Revealed." *After the Battle*, no. 94 (1996): 31+.

Morris, Ellen Birkett. "The Woman Behind the Man." *The Patton Saber* (fall 2002): 1.

Morris, W.H.H., Jr. "Salerno." *Military Review* 13, no. 12 (March 1944): 5+.

Morrow, N. P. "Employment of Artillery in Italy." *Field Artillery Journal* 34, no. 8 (Aug. 1944): 499+.

Mulcahy, Robert. "If You Die, You Die." *World War II* 21, no. 7 (Nov. 2006): 34.

Muller, F. M. "2nd Armored Division Combat Loading, Sicily." *Armored Cavalry Journal* (July–Aug. 1947): 2+.

Nalty, Bernard, and Truman Strobridge. "The Lucky Chase." *Sea Classics* (n.d.): 14+.

"News Published First Allied Paper in Sicily." *45th Division News* 5, no. 38 (July 10, 1945).

"1944." *Life* 16, no. 2 (Jan 3, 1944): 20.

O'Neill, James. "Welcome to Rome." *Yank* (June 18, 1944): 10+.

Owen, William V. "Transportation and Supply on Anzio." *Infantry Journal* (March 1946): 32.

Painton, Frederick C. "Dirty Work on the Road to Rome." *Saturday Evening Post* (Feb. 19, 1944).

Peracarro, Domenico. "The Italian Army in Africa, 1940–1943." *War & Society* 9, no. 2 (Oct. 1991): 103+.

Percy, William Alexander. "Jim Crow and Uncle Sam: The Tuskegee Flying Units and the U.S. Army Air Forces in Europe During World War II." *Journal of Military History* 67, no. 3 (July 2003): 773+.

Perry, George Sessions. "A Reporter at Large." *New Yorker* (July 24, 1943): 50+.

———. "A Reporter at Large." *New Yorker* (Aug. 14, 1943): 46+.

Peters, Walter. "Old Hands in the Business." *Yank* (May 28, 1944): 9+.

Pick, Charles F., Jr. "Torpedo on the Starboard Beam." *United States Naval Institute Proceedings* (Aug. 1970): 90+.

Polmar, Norman, and Thomas B. Allen. "The LST." *MHQ: The Quarterly Journal of Military History* 4, no. 4 (summer 1992): 68+.

Powers, John L. "Crossing the Rapido." *Infantry Journal* 56, no. 5 (May 1945): 50+.

Prickett, Jack Hamilton. "Invasion Points in Italy." *Quartermaster Review* (May–June 1944): 27+.

"The Rangers." *Life* (July 2, 1944): 59+.

Raymond, Edward A. "The Caves of Anzio." *Field Artillery Journal* (Dec. 1944): 851+.

———. "A Fight." *Field Artillery Journal* (March 1945): 156.

Reid, Brian Holden. "The Italian Campaign, 1943–1945: A Reappraisal of Allied Generalship." *Journal of Strategic Studies* 13, no. 1 (March 1990): 128+.

Reinartz, E. G. "Aviation Medicine in the Army." *Scientific Monthly* (Dec. 1944): 451+.

"The Rescue of Mussolini." *After the Battle*, no. 22 (1978): 12+.

Revelle, George H., Jr. "Under Fifth Army a Division G-4 Operates." *Military Review* 25, no. 3 (June 1945): 49+.

"Robert Tryon Frederick." *Assembly* (spring 1972): 106.

Rust, Kenn C., ed. "Out in the Blue: The War Diary of John R. 'Killer' Kane." *American Aviation Historical Society Journal* 28 (summer 1983), part 4: 126.

Sadkovich, James J. "Of Myths and Men: Rommel and the Italians in North Africa, 1940–1942." *International History Review* 13, no. 2 (May 1991): 284+.

Saunders, D. M. "The Bari Incident." *United States Naval Institute Proceedings* 93, no. 9 (Sept. 1967): 35+.

"Settled Front." *Time* (May 1, 1944): 27+.

Sevareid, Eric. "The Price We Pay in Italy." *Nation* (Dec. 9, 1944): 713+.

Shubert, Lyndon. "Eyewitness to the Raid on Ploesti." *Aviation History* (March 2000).

———. "Story of the *Vagabond King.*" *Eyewitness to War* (n.d.): 34+.

Silver, Leda M. "Cartoonist for All Wars." *Retired Officer Magazine* (Oct. 1992): 42+.

Simmons, James Stevens. "How Magic Is DDT?" *Saturday Evening Post* (Jan. 6, 1945): 18+.

Slim, Field Marshal Sir William. "Higher Command in War." *Military Review* (May 1990): 10+.

Smith, Mickey C., and Dennis Worthen. "Soldiers on the Production Line." *Pharmacy in History* 37 (1995): 183+.

Smyth, Howard McGaw. "The Armistice of Cassibile." *Military Review* 28, nos. 6 and 7 (Sept. and Oct. 1948).

———. "The Command of the Italian Armed Forces in World War II." *Military Affairs* 15, no. 1 (spring 1951): 38+.

"Soap Shrinkage." *Newsweek* (July 12, 1943): 57.

Spiller, Roger J. "The Price of Valor." *MHQ: The Quarterly Journal of Military History* (spring 1993): 100+.

"Stafford LeRoy Irwin." *Assembly* (July 1956).

Steckel, Francis C. "Morale Problems in Combat." *Army History* (summer 1994): 1+.

Stewart, Roy P. "Raymond S. McLain, America's Greatest Citizen Soldier." *Chronicles of Oklahoma* 59, no. 1 (spring 1981): 4+.

"The Taking of Rome." *Life* (June 26, 1944): 87.

Thomson, S. W. "Christmas in Ortona." *Canadian Military History* 2, no. 2 (autumn 1993): 24+.

Tice, Grady G. "POWs Never Forget War." *Commerce Journal* (March 4, 2001).

Turner, Thomas E. "Killer Kane." *Airman* (Aug. 1983): 38+.

Van Deusen, E. S. "Trucks That Go Down to the Sea." *Army Ordnance* 25 (Nov.–Dec. 1943): 555+.

Von Senger und Etterlin, Fridolin. "Die Abwehr der Achsenmächte auf Sizilien." *Allgemeine schweizerische Militär Zeitschrift* 116, no. 12 (Dec. 1950): 853+.

Wanke, Paul. "American Military Psychiatry and Its Role Among Ground Forces in World War II." *Journal of Military History* 63, no. 1 (Jan. 1999): 127+.

Weingartner, James J. "Massacre at Biscari: Patton and an American War Crime." *Historian* 52, no. 1 (Nov. 1989): 24+.

Welker, Robert H. "GI Jargon: Its Perils and Pitfalls." *Saturday Review of Literature* (Oct. 1944): 7+.

Wells, Ray. "Battalion Commander." *Fighting 36th Historical Quarterly* 12, no. 1 (spring 1992).

Wertenbaker, Charles Christian. "The Invasion Plan." *Life* (June 12, 1944): 95+.

———. "Omar Nelson Bradley." *Life* (June 5, 1944): 101+.

Wise, James E. "To Sicily with Alec Guinness." *Naval History* (June 2002): 37+.

Wittels, David G. "Are We Coddling Italian Prisoners?" *Saturday Evening Post* (March 3, 1945): 18+.

Worthen, Dennis B. "Pharmacists in World War II." *Journal of the American Pharmaceutical Association* 41, no. 3 (May–June 2001): 479+.

Yarborough, William P. "House Party in Jerryland." *Infantry Journal* 55, no. 1 (July 1944): 8+.

### NEWSPAPERS

"Army News Policy." *Army and Navy Register,* Apr. 8, 1944: 9.

Bracker, Milton. "Anzio, 20 Years After Battle, Evokes Memories." *New York Times,* Jan. 22, 1964.

———. "Railway Battles Fought in Italy." *New York Times,* Oct. 17, 1943.

———. "When the Fight Means Kill or Be Killed." *New York Times Magazine*, May 28, 1944: 10.

Clark, Edgar. "Beachhead Becomes More Anglo-American in Aspect." *Stars and Stripes*, April 21, 1944.

Coe, Donald. "Army Releases Patton Story After Denial." *Boston Traveler*, Nov. 23, 1943: 1

Cunningham, Andrew. "Operations in Connection with the Landing in the Gulf of Salerno on 9th September, 1943." *London Gazette*, Apr. 28, 1950: supplement.

Downs, Kenneth T. "Nothing Stopped the Timberwolves." *Saturday Evening Post*, Aug. 17, 1946: 20+.

Dunavan, Clair Panosian. "The Drug That Helped Win the War." *Los Angeles Times Book Review*, Apr. 11, 2004: R5.

Ezard, John. "Error Led to Bombing of Monte Cassino." *Guardian*, Apr. 4, 2000: 5.

Gallup, George. "Public Would Bomb Religious Buildings." *New York Times*, Apr. 19, 1944.

Gozzer, Tito Vittorio. "Towards Rome with the Allies." *Il Tempo*, May 29–June 4, 1984: 3.

Johnson, Thomas M. "The Army's Fightingest Outfit Comes Home." *St. Louis Post-Dispatch*, Nov. 5, 1944.

Kluckhohn, Frank L. " 'Attack, Attack Again' Is Alexander's Motto." *New York Times Magazine*, Aug. 8, 1943: 20+.

Levy, Claudia. "Pulitzer-Winning WWII Cartoonist Bill Mauldin Dies." *Washington Post*, Jan. 23, 2003: B6.

Matthews, Herbert L. "We Test a Plan for Governing Sicily." *New York Times Magazine*, Aug. 22, 1943: 3+.

Mecklin, John M. "Former Actor Sings Aria as He Fulfills Sicily War Mission." United Press, *New York World-Telegram*, Aug. 9, 1943.

Middleton, Drew. "The Battle Saga of a Tough Outfit." *New York Times*, Apr. 8, 1945: 8+.

Murray, William. "Naples: Variations on a Neapolitan Air." *New York Times*, Nov. 19, 2000.

"Navy Honors D.C. Officer, Weather Expert." *Washington Post*, Dec. 7, 1943: B9.

Norris, John G. "Cassino Abbey Attack Order Laid to Briton." *Washington Post*, Sept. 4, 1949, 1.

Peeples, Berneta. "Requiem." *Belton* (Tex.) *Journal*, Dec. 16, 1993.

"Peter Tompkins, author." Obituary. *Washington Post*, Feb. 1, 2007: B6.

Peterman, Ivan H. "Peterman Discloses Story of Lost Rangers at Anzio Beachhead." *Philadelphia Inquirer*, Apr. 15, 1944: 1.

———. "U.S.S. Savannah." *Philadelphia Inquirer*, series, Sept. 1943.

"Queen Mary." *New York Times*. Apr. 2004, Cunard Line advertising supplement: ZM1.

Reston, James B. "Churchill's Cigars." *New York Times Magazine*, Oct. 17, 1943: 37+.

Reynolds, Catharine. "Modern Comforts, Ancient Sites." *New York Times*, Sept. 3, 2000.

Saxson, Wolfgang. "N. A. Jewell Is Dead at 90." *New York Times*, Aug. 26, 2004: A13.

Schudel, Matt. "Frederick C. Branch Was 1st Black Officer in U.S. Marine Corps." *Washington Post*, Apr. 13, 2005: B6.

Sherwood, Seth. "In an Ancient Desert, a Modern Oasis Beckons." *New York Times*, Jan. 23, 2005.

Simeti, Mary Taylor. "Totally Immersed in Sicily." *New York Times*, March 2, 1997.

Sulzberger, C. L. "Life and Death of an American Bomber." *New York Times Magazine*, July 16, 1944: 5+.

Taylor, Henry J. "The Patton Story: He Slapped, He Raged, He Sobbed in Anger." *Cincinnati Post*, Feb. 28, 1947: 26.

Tutt, Bob. "Young Officer Was Father Figure." *Houston Chronicle*, Feb. 6, 1994: 28A.

"U.S. Study Pinpoints Near-Misses." *New York Times*, July 31, 2005: 8.

"Who's Afraid of Vesuvius?" *New York Times*, Aug. 26, 2003.

Wilson, P. W. "The Appian Road to Rome." *New York Times Magazine*, Oct. 17, 1943: 34.

Zielinski, Graeme. "Capt. Richard Steere, 92; Meteorologist for Patton." *Washington Post*, March 22, 2001: B6.

I also draw extensively on issues of the *Washington Post, Washington Evening Star,* and *New York Times* for May 1943, during the TRIDENT conference; and from issues of the *Columbus* (Ohio) *Dispatch* during June 1944.

## Papers, Letters, Collections, Personal Narratives, and Diaries

*The Citadel Archives and Museum, Charleston, S.C.:* Mark W. Clark Papers

*Dwight D. Eisenhower Presidential Library, Abilene, Kans.:* Harry C. Butcher Papers; Norman D. Cota Papers; Dwight D. Eisenhower Papers; Alfred M. Gruenther Papers; C. D. Jackson Papers; Thomas W. Mattingly Collection; Arthur S. Nevins Papers; Lauris Norstad Papers; George S. Patton file; Charles W. Ryder Papers; Walter Bedell Smith Papers; Barbara Wyden Papers

*45th Infantry Division Museum, Oklahoma City,* personal narratives: William Russell Criss; Harry W. Dobbyn; John Embry; George A. Fisher; Robert Barry Hutchins; Allen Jaynes; William H. Whitman; Kenneth D. Williamson

*Franklin D. Roosevelt Presidential Library, Hyde Park, N.Y.:* Anna Roosevelt Boettiger Papers; Stephen T. Early Papers; Harry L. Hopkins Papers; Verne Newton Collection; Franklin D. Roosevelt Papers; Henry A. Wallace diary, on microfilm

*George C. Marshall Foundation Research Library, Lexington, Va.:* George C. Marshall Papers; Katherine Tupper Marshall Papers; Frank McCarthy Collection; Lucian K. Truscott, Jr., Papers; Reginald Winn Collection

*Hoover Institution Archives, Stanford University, Palo Alto, Calif.:* Robert H. Adleman Papers; Norman Lee Baldwin Papers; Robert D. Burhans Papers; Don E. Carleton Papers; Ernest J. Dawley Papers; Robert T. Frederick Papers; George F. Hall Papers; John P. McKnight Papers; Walter J. Muller Papers; Robert D. Murphy Papers; Chester G. Starr Papers; Fred L. Walker Papers

*Imperial War Museum, London:* Gilbert Allnutt, "A Fusilier Remembers Italy"; D.R.E.R. Bateman Papers; A.A.C.W. Brown, "364 Days Service"; O. Carpenter, diary; Nev Coates, "From the London Blitz to the Champs Elysses"; R. H. Day, "We Landed at Nightfall"; C. R. Eke, "A Game of Soldiers"; C. T. Framp, "The Littlest Victory"; Charles Gairdner, diary; Adrian Clements Gore, "This Was the Way It Was"; I. G. Greenlees, "Memoirs of an Anglo-Italian"; Hans Paul Joachim Liebschner, "Iron Cross Roads"; Bernard L. Montgomery Papers; K. G. Oakley, "Sicily, 1943"; Lavinia Orde, "Better Late Than Never"; J. H. Parker-Jones, "My War"; J. E. Porter Papers; R. Priestly, "Volunteers"; G.B.B. Richey Papers; P. Royle, narrative; B. Smith, "Waltonia"; K. Shirley Smith diary; L. Stevenson, diary; H.A.J. Stiebel, "Over the Next Hill"; R. C. Taylor, "Seven Sunrays"; G. E. Thurbon, "Capture of Pantelleria"; J. B. Tomlinson, "Under the Banner of the Battleaxe"; J. K. Windeatt, "Very Ordinary Soldier"

*Library of Congress, Manuscript Division, Washington, D.C.:* Wallace Carroll Papers; H. Kent Hewitt Papers; Curtis LeMay Papers; George S. Patton Papers; Theodore Roosevelt, Jr., Papers; Carl A. Spaatz Papers

*Liddell Hart Centre for Military Archives, King's College, London:* William Ernest Victor Abraham, "Time Off for War"; Lord Alanbrooke Papers; C. W. Allfrey Collection; Ernest Henry Clarke, "Reminiscences"; R. Close-Brooks, "Anzio Beach-head"; James Scott Elliott Papers; H. M. Gale war diary; John Howson, memoir; B. H. Liddell Hart Collection; Sidney Chevalier Kirkman Papers; John Alec McKee Papers; John Nelson, "Always a Grenadier"; William R. C. Penney Papers; Digby Raeburn, "Some Recollections of a Scots Guardsman"; Dudley Russell Papers; Aidan Mark Sprot, memoir; Philip L. E. Wood Papers

*McCormick Research Center, First Division Museum, Cantigny, Ill.:* Clift Andrus, notes on *A Soldier's Story*; Joseph T. Dawson Collection; John P. Downing, "No Promotion"; Stanhope Brasfield Mason, "Reminiscences and Anecdotes of World War II"

*Miscellany:* Loyd J. Biss, materials on U.S.S. *Samuel Chase* provided to author; John M. Brooks, letter to author, Oct. 19, 2003; Paul W. Brown, letters to author, Oct. 4, 2003, and Jan. 19, 2004; Harold Burson, letter to author, Jan. 2, 2003; Robert E. Coffin, memoir, author's possession; Jerry Countess, memoir, author's possession; J. W. Crawford, Jr., letter to author, Jan. 29, 2003; Warren Davis, letter to author, March 3, 2004; Clifford W. Dorman, "Too Soon for Heroes," author's possession; Christopher Dunphie, letter to author, Jan. 29, 2004; Graham Erdwurm, letters to author, 2003–04; R.L.V. ffrench Blake, letter to author, July 27, 2003; G. L. Hanssen, *The Hanssens of Eastern Iowa,* author's possession; Donald V. Helgeson, letter to author, July 25 and Oct. 8, 2003; William Russell Hinckley, diary, author's possession; Fred Howard, letter to author, Oct. 2003; Geoffrey Keyes, diary, author's possession; James E. Lalley, letter to author, May 15, 2003; D. H. Leatham, letter to author, Jan. 30, 2003; Sanford H. Margalith, letter to author, Apr. 22, 2005; Joseph Edgar Martin, "Memoir of World War II," author's possession; Frank Mills, memoir, "Well Dressed at Cassino," author's possession; George Henry Revelle, Jr., letters, author's possession; Robert A. Riesman, letter to author, Sept. 10, 2002; David Roberts, e-mail to author, May 23, 2003; Heinz Seltmann, letter to author, June 9, 2005; R. C. Taylor, letter to author, Aug. 11, 2003; Joanne Speranza Walker, e-mail to author, Jan. 11, 2003; Aubrey L. Williams, letter to author, June 9, 2004

*National Archive, Rew, UK:* Harold R.L.G. Alexander Papers; Francis Tuker, letters to C.J.C. Molony; J.F.M. Whiteley, letters to John N. Kennedy

*Naval Historical Center, Washington, D.C.:* H. Kent Hewitt Papers; Samuel Eliot Morison Papers
  *Combat Narratives:* Mitchell Jamieson; John McFadzean; Curtis Shears

*Texas Military Forces Museum, Austin, personal narratives:* Edie Douglas Adkins; Michael B. Anderson; Nicholas M. Bozic; William D. Broderick; Richard M. Burrage; Russell J. Darkes; R. K. Doughty; James M. Estepp; Edward R. Feagins; Newton H. Fulbright; John D. Goode; Glendower O. Haedge; John Hartman; Harold G. Horning; LeRoy R. Houtson; Armand G. Jones; George Kerrigan; Wayne Kirby; Amil Kohutek; Herbert E. MacCombie; Julian "Dunie" Philips; Hal Reese; Lem Vannatta; Alan Williamson; Jack W. Wilson

*U.S. Army Military History Institute, Carlisle, Pa.:* Terry de la Mesa Allen Papers, Robert W. Black Papers; Clay and Joan Blair Collection; William S. Biddle Papers; Theodore J. Conway Papers; Raymond H. Croll Papers; Donald E. Currier Papers; Ralph P. Eaton Papers; James M. Gavin Papers; Chester B. Hansen Papers; Ernest N. Harmon Papers; Hamilton H. Howze Papers; David Irving Collection; Kenyon Joyce Papers; Walter T. Kerwin, Jr., Papers; John P. Lucas Papers; Sidney T. Matthews Papers; Malcolm S. McLean Papers; Frank J. McSherry Papers; Arthur S. Nevins Papers; Henry C. Newton Papers; Matthew B. Ridgway Papers; John E. Sloan Papers; Albert C. Wedemeyer Papers; Robert J. Wood Papers
  *Diaries and personal narratives contained in MHI Army Service Experiences Questionnaire:*
    *1st Armored Division* (Dexter F. Arnold; Maurice R. P. Bechard; Robert Bond; Mitchell E. Chafin; Carmene J. DeFelice; George C. Harper; Ralph H. Hempel; Robert J. Loe; James Bernard Mahon; Robert M. Marsh; John H. Mayo; Arthur Robert Moore; Gustav A. Mueller; Raymond Saidel; James Scott Stapel)
    *1st Infantry Division* (William T. Dillon; William E. Faust; Donald V. Helgeson; Harland W. Hendrick; Clarence B. Kling; George J. Koch; Jarvis Burns Moore; Quinton F. Reams; Kimball Richmond; Henry C. Rowland; Paul L. Skogsberg)
    *3rd Infantry Division* (Jon Clayton; Russell W. Cloer)
    *36th Infantry Division* (Russell Bodeen; Warner Wisian)

45th Infantry Division (Franci Accavallo; Ben C. Garbowski; Wayne M. Harris; Elmer W. Horton; Robert B. Hutchins; F. Eugene Liggett; Norman Maffei; Frederick T. McCue; Robert L. Moses; Louis G. Oberkramer; Richard Pisciotta; Frank E. Tinsch)

*U.S. Military Academy Special Collections, West Point, N.Y.:* Pietro Badoglio, letters; Bernard Shirley Carter, letters; Garrison H. Davidson Papers; John F. Davis Papers; Benjamin A. Dickson Papers; John Erbes Papers; Henry E. Gardiner Papers; Hobart Gay, diary; Will Lang, notebooks; Audie Leon Murphy Papers.

*Yale University Library, New Haven, Conn.:* Mina Curtiss Collection

## Author Interviews

Martin Blumenson; Harold Burson; Silvano Casaldi; Russell W. Cloer; J. W. Crawford; Arthur L. Funk; Andrew J. Goodpaster; Paul F. Gorman; Douglas Gould; Michael Howard; Walter Kerwin, Jr.; D. H. Leathem; Arthur Lehrman; Henry Gerard Phillips; Richard A. Williams; James M. Wilson, Jr.

*Interviewed by Antonio Ali Winston for author:* Homer Bishop; Lou Fiset; Richard Griffin; George Pickett

## Interview and Oral History Transcripts

*Columbia University, Oral History Research Office, N.Y.:* Mark W. Clark; Alfred Gruenther; H. Kent Hewitt; Arthur S. Nevins

*Dwight D. Eisenhower Presidential Library, Abilene, Kans.:* Charles L. Bolte; Dwight D. Eisenhower; LeRoy Lutes; Lauris Norstad

*Franklin D. Roosevelt Presidential Library, Hyde Park, N.Y.:* Ian Jacob

*George C. Marshall Library, Lexington, Va.:* Forrest C. Pogue interviews: Field Marshal Viscount Alanbrooke; Mark W. Clark; Jacob L. Devers

*Miscellany:* Hermann Balck, Battelle Columbus Laboratories, at U.S. Army War College

*National Archives, College Park, Md.:* OCMH interview, "Cassino to the Alps," RG 319: H. Adamson; Edward M. Almond; H. Chalstrom; T. J. Conway; Willis D. Crittenberger; Charles D'Orsa; Stephen T. Early; L. W. Gregory; Alfred M. Gruenther; Arden Higdon; Geoffrey Keyes; Larry K. Ladue; A. M. Lazar; William D. Leahy; Lyman L. Lemnitzer; Ray McLain; Phillip Norris; Edward J. O'Neill; Francis Oxx; Glenn T. Pillsbury; Robert W. Porter; Charles E. Saltzman; Ralph Tate; Lucian K. Truscott, Jr.; Arthur R. Wilson; Robert J. Wood
   "Interviews with Officers of 3rd ID": RG 319, OCMH, box 5

*National Folklife Center, Veterans' History Project, Library of Congress, Washington, D.C.:* Kenneth Apple; Louis Bednar; Jack Brown; Edward George Burns; Richard Dapprich; John Greuling; Boris Guleff; Irvin Hershberger; Roger Howland; Melvin H. McClain; Robert Richstatter

*Naval Historical Center, Washington, D.C.:* John F. Curtin; Charles William Harwood; H. Kent Hewitt; Samuel A. D. Hunter

*Rutgers Oral History Project, New Brunswick, N.J.:* Russell Cloer; Franklyn Johnson; Robert King; Maurice Meyers; Charles Mickett; George Mickett; Benjamin Roth; Russell Smalley

*U.S. Air Force Historical Research Agency, Maxwell AFB, Ala.:* Ira Eaker; Uzal G. Ent; Norman E. Fiske; G. P. Gibson; S. C. Godfrey; Malcolm Grow; H. S. Hansell; Leon W. Johnson; John R. Kane; Lauris Norstad; Jacob E. Smart

*U.S. Army Center of Military History, Fort McNair, Washington, D.C.:* Volturno River interviews, Geog files, Italy, 370.24: Theodore Bogart; C. E. Brokaw; Don Carleton; R. E. Clem; Francis Even; F. Q. Goodell; Robert O'Brien; Charles J. Parziale; Robert Petherick; J. C. Ruddell; H. G. Swacina; E. Thayer; R. C. Wilson; John F. Woods; R. T. Young

*U.S. Army Corps of Engineers Historical Division, Fort Belvoir, Va.:* Garrison H. Davidson; Herbert W. Ehrgott; Harry O. Paxson; Edwin L. Powell, Jr.; William Francis Powers

*U.S. Army Military History Institute, Carlisle, Pa.*

*Omar N. Bradley Papers:* Omar N. Bradley

*Sidney T. Matthews Papers:* Harold K. Alexander; C. M. Ankcorn; Mark C. Clark; Mark W. Clark; Bryce F. Denno; Dwight D. Eisenhower; William W. Eagles; Robert T. Frederick; Melvin J. Groves; H. Kent Hewitt; E. B. Howard; George F. Kennan; Howard Kippenberger; Lyman L. Lemnitzer; John P. Lucas; Effisio Marras; George C. Marshall; Stanhope B. Mason; Roy Murray; Lowell W. Rooks; John W. Scott; Walter Bedell Smith; Russell G. Spinney; Kenneth W. D. Strong; George A. Taylor; Lucian K. Truscott, Jr.; Frido von Senger u. Etterlin; Fred L. Walker; Henry Maitland Wilson; Robert J. Wood

*Forrest C. Pogue interviews:* Field Marshal Viscount Alanbrooke; Ray W. Barker; Arthur Coningham; Lord Cunningham of Hyndhope; Charles de Gaulle; James Gault; Hastings L. Ismay; Alphonse P. Juin; Albert Kenner; Alan G. Kirk; C. E. Lambe; J. H. Lee; R. A. McClure; Alan Moorehead; Frederick E. Morgan; Viscount Portal of Hungerford; Adolph Rosengarten, Jr.; Walter Bedell Smith

*OCMH WWII Europe Interviews:* Francis de Guingand; Walter Bedell Smith

*Senior Officer Oral History Program:* Paul D. Adams; Charles L. Bolte; Mark W. Clark; Robert E. Coffin; Theodore J. Conway; Michael S. Davison; Ira C. Eaker; William P. Ennis, Jr.; James M. Gavin; Hobart Gay; John A. Heintges; Robert A. Hewitt; Hamilton H. Howze; John E. Hull; Harry Lemley; Robert W. Porter, Jr.; Matthew B. Ridgway; Maxwell D. Taylor; Russell L. Vittrup; Robert J. Wood; William P. Yarborough

*U.S. Military Academy, West Point, N.Y.:* Matthew B. Ridgway

*U.S. Naval Institute, Annapolis, Md.:* Walter Ansel; Hanson Weightman Baldwin; George W. Bauernschmidt; Bernhard H. Bieri; Phil H. Bucklew; Joshua W. Cooper; George C. Dyer; Ralph K. James; Jackson K. Parker; U. S. Grant Sharp; Elliott B. Strauss; Edward K. Walker; Charles Wellborn, Jr.; F.E.M. Whiting

## Motion Pictures

National Archives

RG 111, Office of the Chief Signal Officer:

*The Battle of San Pietro,* Combat Report No. 2, 1945.

*The Big Change-Over,* Officer for Emergency Management, 208.211, 1942.

*How Strong Is the Enemy Today?* Film No. 2997, OSS, 1944.

*Liberation of Rome,* Combat Report No. 1, 1944.

*Salvage,* Office of War Information, 208.118, 1942.

RG 208:

"United News, No. 66," 1943.

"United News, No. 68," 1943.

*The Battle of San Pietro.* John Huston, director. 1945.

*Small World.* CBS, 1959, produced by Edward R. Murrow and Fred W. Friendly, #12A & #12B.

DVD on Mark W. Clark. The Citadel Archives and Museum.

## Miscellany

Bynell, H. D. "Logistical Operations in the Sicilian Campaign." Lecture, Army and Navy Staff College. March 14, 1944. NARA RG 334, NWC Lib.

Cochran, Alexander S. "Constructing a Military Coalition from Materials at Hand: The Case of Allied Force Headquarters." Paper, SMH conference, Apr. 16, 1999.

Conolly, Richard L. "The Landing at Salerno in World War II." Lecture, Naval Historical Foundation. May 14, 1957.

Crowl, P. A. "Command Decision: The Rapido River Crossing." Lecture. U.S. Army War College, Sept. 30, 1955. SM, MHI.

Darby, William O. "U.S. Rangers." Lecture, Army and Navy Staff College. Oct. 27, 1944. NARA RG 334, NWC Lib.

Eldredge, Walter J. "First Shot in Anger." Essay from http://www.4point2.org/firstshot.htm, visited Sept. 2, 2006.

"Enemy POW Camps in the USA in World War II." Fact sheet. Nov. 5, 2002. CMH.

Hewitt, H. K. "The Navy in the European Theater of Operations in World War II." Lecture, Naval War College. Jan. 4–7, 1947.

Johnston, Lewis E. "The Troop Carrier D-Day Flights." N.d. CD-ROM.

Kirk, Alan G. "Narrative by Rear Adm. Alan G. Kirk." Lecture, Pearl Harbor, Hawaii. Oct. 2, 1943. NHC.

Kupsky, Gregory, lecture on Axis POWs in Tennessee. May 21, 2004. SMH conference, Bethesda, Md.

Matloff, Maurice. "Mr. Roosevelt's Three Wars: FDR as War Leader." Harmon Memorial Lectures in Military History, no. 6, USAFA, 1964.

Menninger, William C. "Psychiatric Problems in War." Lecture. National War College, Washington, D.C., March 21, 1947.

Moran, Charles. "The Mediterranean Convoys." N.d. ONI, Combat Narrative #210. "WWII Histories and Historical Reports." NHC.

Pederson, Oscar. "Carrier Operations in Support of Amphibious Operations in the Mediterranean Theater." Lecture, Army and Navy Staff College. May 27, 1944. NARA RG 334, NWC Lib.

"The Price of Freedom." Exhibition, Smithsonian Institution, Museum of American History, Washington, D.C.

"The Rapido River Crossing." Hearings, Committee on Military Affairs, House of Representatives. Feb. 20 and March 18, 1946. Washington, D.C.: U.S. Government Printing Office, 1946.

Shrader, Charles R. "Amicicide: The Problem of Friendly Fire in Modern War." U.S. Army Combat Studies Institute, Dec. 1982.

Spaatz, Carl. Lecture, Army and Navy Staff College, Oct. 4, 1943, NWC Lib, RG 334.

Sullivan, W. A. Lecture to Society of Military Engineers. Cincinnati, Ohio. 1947.

"2004 [Ranger] Reunion Program Book." Aug. 25–30, 2004. Fort Wayne, Ind.

Weinberg, Gerhard L. "The Place of World War II in History." Lecture, U.S. Air Force Academy, 1995.

Wood, Robert J. "The Landing at Salerno." Lecture, Army and Navy Staff College. Dec. 28, 1944. NARA RG 319, OCMH, box 244.

A full list of manuscripts and other unpublished documents used in this book appears online at www.liberationtrilogy.com.

# ACKNOWLEDGMENTS

---

The second volume of the Liberation Trilogy is now complete, and once again I owe an inexpressible debt to many people without whom I would still be beating toward the Sicilian coast. The publication of volume one, *An Army at Dawn*, encouraged many veterans and their progeny, as well as others with an interest and expertise in World War II, to provide me with memoirs, oral histories, and sundry material about the Mediterranean campaigns, much of which appears in this volume for the first time. I would like to thank:

Blair Alexander, Consuelo Allen, John B. Babcock, John C. Beam, Homer Bishop, Loyd J. Bliss, Nathan Block, Martin Blumenson, William W. Bonning, John M. Brooks, Paul W. Brown, Charles F. Bryan, Jr., Harold Burson, W. W. Keen Butcher, Andrew Carroll, Russell W. Cloer, Robert E. Coffin, Mark H. Cohen, Barbara Moir Condos, Michael J. Corley, Jerry Countess, J. W. Crawford, John L. Creech, J. K. Cullen, Michael J. P. Cunneen, Jim Davies, Warren Davis, Carlo D'Este, Robert J. Dole, Clifford W. Dorman, Elizabeth Bradley Dorsey, Christopher Dunphie, Lawyn C. Edwards, John S. D. Eisenhower, Susan Eisenhower, Uzal W. Ent, Graham Erdwurm, Francis A. Even, James F. Fain, Alicia Ferrari, R.L.V. ffrench Blake, Lou Fiset, David G. Fivecoat, Frederic D. Floberg, James D. Ford, Arthur L. Funk, Libby Gill, George H. Goldstone, Andrew J. Goodpaster, Paul F. Gorman, Douglas Gould, Richard Griffin, Fred Groff III, Arthur T. Hadley, George L. Hanssen, Joseph Heiser, Donald V. Helgeson, Thomas A. Higbie, Al Hormel, Fred S. Howard, Michael Howard, Charles P. Jacobi, Hugh S. Jacobs, Julian R. Jacobs, Michael Jason, George Juskalian, Walter T. Kerwin, Jr., Geoffrey B. Keyes, J. Keith Killby, Charles E. Kirkpatrick, Sherry Klein, William A. Knowlton, Edward C. Koenig, Jr., Bernard J. La Plante, James E. Lalley, George L. Laurie, D. H. Leathem, Ralph Ledesma, Arthur Lehrman, Rod Liner, Roy Livengood, C. Vincent Lyness, Clement S. Mackowiak, Jack Maher, Howard R. Maier, Mark Mann, Sanford H. Margalith, Jack Marshall, Tom May, Meg McAleer, John C. McManus, Allan R. Millett, Derek R. Mills, Frank Mills, William W. Monning, Louis J. Murchio, Lovern "Jerry" Nauss, Eric J. Neuner, Mike Norris, Michael O'Connor, Dick

Oshlo, Robin K. Overcash, Adolph Panetta, Roy Paterson, Alan R. Perry, Henry Gerard Phillips, George Pickett, G. Kurt Piehler, Russell H. Raine, John Ray, Mark Reardon, Randy Revelle, Robert A. Riesman, David Roberts, John B. Romeiser, Theodore Roosevelt IV, Jack Russell, Frank Schultz, Michael H. Sebastian, Robert Segan, Heinz Seltmann, Nathan M. Shippee, Albert H. Smith, Arthur O. Spaulding, Frank J. Stech, Patti Stickle, James Stroud, Floride Hewitt Taylor, R. C. Taylor, Ray Thomas, John J. Toffey IV, Jason D. Umberger, Joanne Speranza Walker, George Watanabe, Aubrey L. Williams, Isobel Williams, Richard A. Williams, Randall J. Willis, James M. Wilson, Jr., Gary D. Winder, Harold R. Winton, Walter F. Winton, Jr., Dennis B. Worthen, John G. Wright, Eléonore M. Zimmermann, and Carolyn A. Zuttel.

Once again I gratefully acknowledge my debt to the hundreds of historians, memoirists, and others whose writings in the sixty years after the war will forever provide the foundation for all subsequent works of scholarship. I have again relied on the 114-volume *U.S. Army in World War II*, the official history known informally as the Green Series, as well as the official British *History of the Second World War*.

The ground speaks even when eyewitnesses no longer can, and I made several trips to the battle venues of volume two, beginning in the mid-1990s, when I served as Berlin bureau chief of *The Washington Post* and visited Salerno, Anzio, San Pietro, and Cassino for the first time. Other research forays included a visit to Sicily in September 1996 and extended trips to Italian battlefields in April 2004 and November 2006. For the last of these, I thank Gen. David D. McKiernan, commander of the U.S. Army in Europe, and two former chiefs of Army history, Maj. Gen. (ret.) William A. Stofft and Brig. Gen. (ret.) Harold Nelson.

The core of this narrative, like its predecessor, is drawn from primary, contemporaneous sources, which range from diaries, letters, and unpublished manuscripts to official records, after-action reports, and original maps. I am again deeply grateful for the professionalism and patience of several score historians and archivists in tracking down these thousands of documents. Any error of fact or judgment is mine alone.

At the National Archives in College Park, Maryland, I thank Richard Boylan, Timothy Mulligan, Larry McDonald, and, most particularly, Timothy K. Nenninger, the chief of modern military records and former president of the Society for Military History. Virtually every page of this book bears Tim's imprint, and I am deeply grateful for his expertise, humor, friendship, and willingness to read a portion of the manuscript.

The U.S. Army's Military History Institute, part of the Army Heritage and Education Center at Carlisle, Pennsylvania, is among the nation's finest archival repositories and *the* mother lode of Army history. For this volume, I visited MHI twenty-nine times, usually for two- or three-day stretches, and I am grateful for the hospitable professionalism of Col. Robert Dalessandro, the AHEC director, and to Conrad C. Crane, the MHI director, who read part of the manuscript. Thanks also to Richard J. Sommers, chief of patron services; Louise Arnold-Friend; Richard L. Baker; Steve Bye; Tom Hendrix; Gary Johnson; Shaun Kirkpatrick; Stanley Lanoue; Michael E. Lynch; Robert Mages; Mike Monahan; Mike Perry; Melinda Torres; and especially David A. Keough.

At the adjacent U.S. Army War College at Carlisle Barracks, where I held the Gen. Omar N. Bradley Chair of Strategic Leadership for the 2004–05 academic year, I thank the commandant, Maj. Gen. David H. Huntoon, Jr., and his faculty and staff, including the dean, Col. William T. Johnsen; Col. Charles D. Allen, director of leader development and my classroom copilot; and the library director, Bohdan I. Kohutiak. I am especially grateful to Tami Davis Biddle, the George C. Marshall Chair of Military Studies and a fine historian of airpower, who has been an exceptionally thoughtful and encouraging friend, and who read part of the manuscript.

Thanks also to Stephen P. Riley, executive director of the Army War College Foundation. The Omar Bradley chair is administered jointly with Dickinson College, and I appreciate the support of the president, William G. Durden, as well as Prof. Harry L. Pohlman and Col. (ret.) Jeffrey D. McCausland.

The U.S. Army Center of Military History at Fort McNair in Washington, D.C., again offered a rich vein of documents and expertise. Thanks to Brig. Gen. (ret.) John Sloan Brown, the former chief of military history, and his successor, Jeffrey J. Clarke, as well as to Richard Stewart, the chief historian; Col. Gary M. Bowman; Robert K. Wright, Jr.; Mary L. Haynes; and R. Cody Phillips.

At the Dwight D. Eisenhower Presidential Library in Abilene, Kansas, I am grateful to the director, Daniel D. Holt, for his help and hospitality, and to archivist David J. Haight. Similarly, at the Franklin D. Roosevelt Presidential Library in Hyde Park, New York, I thank the director, Cynthia M. Koch, and archivists Robert Parks, Alycia Vivona, Mark Renovitch, and especially Robert Clark, who also helped to have various Secret Service records declassified.

I had the good fortune to hold a media fellowship at the Hoover Institution on War, Revolution and Peace at Stanford University, for which I thank David Brady and Mandy MacCalla. Elena S. Danielson, the now-retired director of library and archives, and Carol A. Leadenham, assistant archivist for reference, were particularly gracious in opening the institution's extensive World War II holdings.

The ambitious Veterans History Project at the Library of Congress is a boon to historians; thanks to Eileen Simon, Sarah Rouse, W. Ralph Eubanks, and the able Eric Goldstein.

At the Citadel Archives and Museum in Charleston, South Carolina, the director, Jane McCrady Yates, was extraordinarily helpful in offering access to her vast collection of Mark W. Clark's papers, as well as to a biographical DVD, which she produced. My deep thanks also to Joanne D. Hartog, director of the library archives and special projects at the George C. Marshall Library at the Virginia Military Institute in Lexington, Virginia, which among other treasures holds the papers of Lucian K. Truscott, Jr.

Professor Mark A. Stoler of the University of Vermont, who has few peers as a scholar of twentieth-century diplomatic history, was kind enough to read and critique portions of the manuscript.

Once again I am grateful to the Robert R. McCormick Research Center at the First Division Museum in Cantigny, Illinois, for both archival excellence and professional assistance. I appreciate the help of John Votaw, the former executive director of the Cantigny First Division Foundation, and of his successor, Paul H. Herbert, as well as that of Andrew E. Woods and Eric Gillespie.

The Texas Military Forces Museum in Austin has a rich trove of material for the 36th Infantry Division. I appreciate assistance from John C. L. Scribner, the museum director and command historian, as well as Angie Rose, Bob Gates, and particularly archivist Brian Schenk.

Thanks to curator Michael E. Gonzalez and to Denise Neil-Binion at the 45th Infantry Division Museum in Oklahoma City. I also appreciate early assistance on the 34th Infantry Division from the Iowa Gold Star Museum at Fort Dodge, with thanks to director Jerry L. Gorden and to Richard A. Moss, secretary-treasurer of the 34th Infantry Division Association.

In the special collections department at the U.S. Military Academy library, thanks to Alan Aimone, Susan Lintelmann, Sheila H. Biles, Elaine McConnell, Deborah A. McKeon-Pogue, and Suzanne Christoff. Thanks also to the former West Point history department chairman, Brig. Gen. (ret.) Robert A. Doughty, and to his successor, Col. Lance A. Betros. Thanks also to the Combined Arms Research Library at Ft. Leavenworth, Kansas, including the director, Edwin B. Burgess, and Col. (ret.) Lawyn C. Edwards, former director of the Combat Studies Institute. Further thanks to Ericka L. Loze-Hudson, director of the Donovan Research Library at the Infantry School, Ft. Benning, Georgia, and to the acting command historian, David S. Stieghan. At the U.S. Army Corps of Engineers History Office at Ft. Belvoir, Virginia, thanks to historian Michael J. Brodhead.

I am again appreciative of encouragement and generous support from the Association of the United States Army, particularly from Gen. (ret.) Gordon R. Sullivan, the association president and former Army chief of staff; Lt. Gen. (ret.) Theodore G. Stroup, Jr.; and Lt. Gen. (ret.) Thomas G. Rhame. Lt. Col. (ret.) Roger Cirillo, Ph.D., the association director of operational and strategic studies, once again was exceptionally generous in sharing his vast expertise and amazing personal archive.

At the Air Force Historical Research Agency, at Maxwell Air Force Base, Alabama, I thank Charles F. O'Connell, Jr., the director, Toni Petito, Joseph D. Caver, and Robert E. Brown, Jr.

At the Naval Historical Center in Washington, D.C., thanks to Kathleen M. Lloyd and John Hodges in operational archives, and the Navy Department Library. At the Naval War College, in Newport, Rhode Island, I appreciate the help of Evelyn Cherpak, Barbara Donnelly, Shirley Fernandes, Alice Juda, and Jamie Radke. At the U.S. Naval Institute in Annapolis, Maryland, I thank Paul Stillwell, director of the history division, and Ann Hassinger, as well as Fred H. Rainbow, former editor in chief of *Proceedings*. At the U.S. Naval Academy, thanks to Mary A. DeCredico, former chair of the history department.

Thanks to Edward C. Tracy, executive director of the Tawani Foundation and former executive director of the Pritzker Military Library in Chicago, and to G. Kurt Piehler, director of the Center for the Study of War and Society at the University of Tennessee–Knoxville. I appreciate the support and encouragement of the National World War II Museum in New Orleans, including that of Gordon H. "Nick" Mueller, Sam Wegner, and Bill Detweiler.

I also thank Christine Weideman and Diane E. Kaplan at the Yale University Library's manuscripts and archives department; Lovetta Kramer, executive director of the RMS *Queen Mary* Foundation and Archive; Lorna Williams, library assistant in the special collections and archives at the University of Liverpool; Shaun Illingworth of the Rutgers University Oral History Archives; and the intrepid crew of *LST 325*, which berthed at Alexandria, Virginia, in May 2005, and is the only twenty-first-century survivor among eleven hundred LSTs built during World War II.

In the United Kingdom, I am grateful to the staff of the National Archive in Kew. At the Liddell Hart Centre for Military Archives at King's College in London, Kate O'Brien, Caroline Lam, and Patricia J. Methven, the director of archive services, were exceptionally helpful. Thanks also to the Department of Documents staff and trustees at the Imperial War Museum, particularly to Roderick Suddaby and Stephanie Clarke.

In Italy, thanks to Maurizio Zambardi and Lorenzo Picillo in San Pietro, and to Silvano Casaldi, director of the Museum of the Allied Landings in Nettuno. Antonio Ali Winston helped with both historical research and translations under an internship provided by the University of Chicago's Jeff Metcalf Fellows Program. Robert Harp very ably translated several Italian documents for me.

Master cartographer Gene Thorp once again displayed uncommon skill and forbearance in drawing the maps for this volume. My close friend and agent, Rafe Sagalyn, has been there from the beginning.

*The Washington Post*, my professional home for nearly a quarter century, is led by several extraordinary readers of history, notably chairman Donald E. Graham, publisher Bo Jones, executive editor Leonard Downie, Jr., and editorial page editor Fred Hiatt, who was generous enough to read the manuscript. I'm also grateful for the continued support and friendship of other *Post* colleagues, including Phil Bennett, Benjamin C. Bradlee, Rajiv Chandrasekaran, Stephen C. Fehr, Susan Glasser, David Hoffman, Robert G. Kaiser, Jeff Leen, Thomas E. Ricks, Margaret Shapiro, Steve Vogel, Tom Wilkinson, Bob Woodward, and fellow scribbler David Maraniss.

Thanks also to Tom Bowers, Michael Briggs, Tom Brokaw, Robert C. Callahan, Herman Chanowitz, Alexander S. Cochran, Edward M. Coffman, Steve Coll, Maj. Gen. (ret.) E. J. Delaune, Jr., Glenn Frankel, Maj. Gen. Benjamin C. Freakley, Arthur L. Funk, Paul Fussell, Arthur Hadley, Sir Max Hastings, Ken Hechler, David Kahn, Howard S. Koontz, Lewis Libby, James H. McCall, Col. H. R. McMaster, Lovern Nauss, Randy Norton, Gen. David H. Petraeus, Panthea Reid, Mark J. Reardon, David Roberts, Maj. Gen. (ret.) Robert H. Scales, Jr., Col. (ret.) Lewis "Bob" Sorley, Frank Stech, Layne A. Van Arsdale, David Von Drehle, Geoffrey D. W. Wawro, Gerhard L. Weinberg, James S. "Scott" Wheeler, and Maj. Gen. David Zabecki.

Grateful acknowledgment is made of permission to quote various materials: Stanford University, for the selected writings of Langan W. Swent; Viscount Montgomery of Alamein, for extracts from his father's writings; Geoffrey B. Keyes, for extracts from his father's diary; Jean Framp, for extracts from "The Littlest Victory" by Charles Framp; Jerry Countess, for extracts from his letters; John J. Toffey IV, for extracts from his manuscript, "A Game for the Young," and from his father's letters; John B. Romeiser, for extracts from the war diary of Don Whitehead; Paul W. Brown, for extracts from his memoir; the trustees of the Liddell Hart Centre for Military Archives, for extracts from the papers of W.E.V. Abraham, Lord Alanbrooke, C.W. Allfrey, J. S. Elliott, S. C. Kirkman, B. H. Liddell Hart, J. N. Nelson, W.R.C. Penney, Aidan Mark Sprot, and P.L.E. Wood; Joachim

Liebschner, for extracts from "Iron Cross Roads," which has recently been published by Athena Press; Gilbert Allnutt, for extracts from "A Fusilier Remembers Italy"; Mrs. J. K. Windeatt, for extracts from her late husband's "Very Ordinary Soldier"; Martin Smith, for extracts from *Waltonia*, the memoir of his father, Bert Smith; C. Richard Eke, for extracts from "A Game of Soldiers"; the copyright holder of K. G. Oakley's "Sicily, 1943"; John H. Clagett, for extracts from his unpublished biography of H. Kent Hewitt; and the Columbia University Oral History Research Office, for extracts from a 1961 interview of H. Kent Hewitt by John T. Mason.

In instances where current copyright holders could not be located, or where permissions arrived too late to be noted in this edition, I will gladly include acknowledgments in future editions.

I am once again in the debt of John Sterling, the president and publisher of Henry Holt and Company, whose contributions as my editor and friend for five books over the past two decades may be inferred from the dedication at the front of this volume. Thanks also at Holt to Maggie Richards, Kenn Russell, Richard Rhorer, Eileen Lawrence, Claire McKinney, Emily Montjoy Belford, Chuck Thompson, and the extraordinarily capable Jolanta Benal, who, as the copy editor on both volumes of the Liberation Trilogy, has improved every page.

My children, Rush and Sarah, helped enormously with document and photo research, bibliographical organization, and the inevitable technological rescues of their Luddite father. My wife, Jane, provided all the rest, as ever.

# INDEX

Entries in *italics* refer to maps. Military units are listed by nation in numerical order.

## ABOUT THE AUTHOR

RICK ATKINSON was a staff writer and senior editor at *The Washington Post* for more than twenty years. He is the best-selling author of *An Army at Dawn, The Long Gray Line, In the Company of Soldiers,* and *Crusade.* His many awards include Pulitzer Prizes for journalism and history. He lives in Washington, D.C.